ABA·LSAC
OFFICIAL GUIDE
TO ABA-APPROVED LAW SCHOOLS™

2012 EDITION

Produced by the Law School Admission Council and the American Bar Association Section of Legal Education and Admissions to the Bar

The Law School Admission Council (LSAC) is a nonprofit corporation that provides unique, state-of-the-art admission products and services to ease the admission process for law schools and their applicants worldwide. More than 200 law schools in the United States, Canada, and Australia are members of the Council and benefit from LSAC's services.

© 2011 by Law School Admission Council, Inc. and the American Bar Association

Library of Congress Catalog Number:

ISBN-13: 978-0-9821487-9-2

ISBN-10: 0-99821487-9-8

ISSN: 1534-3502

TABLE OF CONTENTS

The school-specific information contained in this edition of the *ABA-LSAC Official Guide to ABA-Approved Law Schools* was collected in 2010. Coverage dates vary within categories:

Bar Passage Data: First-time bar exam takers during the 2009 calendar year.
Employment/Placement: Class of 2009 graduates, as of February 2010.
Academic Attrition: Based on Fall 2009 enrollment.
GPA and LSAT Scores: Fall 2010 entering class.
JD degrees awarded: 2009–2010 academic year.
Tuition and Fees: 2010–2011 academic year.

INTRODUCTION

The *Official Guide to ABA-Approved Law Schools* is a joint effort of the Law School Admission Council (LSAC) and the American Bar Association Section of Legal Education and Admissions to the Bar (ABA).

The Law School Admission Council (LSAC) is a nonprofit corporation whose members are more than 200 law schools in the United States, Canada, and Australia. Headquartered in Newtown, PA, USA, the Council was founded in 1947 to facilitate the law school admission process. The Council has grown to provide unique state-of-the-art admission products and services for law schools and for approximately 85,000 law school applicants each year.

All law schools approved by the American Bar Association (ABA) are LSAC members. Canadian law schools recognized by a provincial or territorial law society or government agency are also members. Accredited law schools outside of the US and Canada are eligible for membership at the discretion of the LSAC Board of Trustees; Melbourne Law School, the University of Melbourne is the first LSAC-member law school outside of North America.

As the largest professional organization in the world, the American Bar Association is the national voice of the legal profession. The Council and the Accreditation Committee of the Section of Legal Education and Admissions to the Bar of the ABA are identified by the US Department of Education as the nationally recognized accrediting agency for professional schools of law. As of January 2011, a total of 200 institutions are approved by the American Bar Association.

The information contained in this book is collected separately by the ABA and LSAC from the ABA-approved law schools that are also members of the Law School Admission Council. One ABA-approved law school, the US Army Judge Advocate General's School, is a specialized law school that is not a member of the Law School Admission Council (see page 31). The two organizations agreed to combine this wealth of information to provide a comprehensive resource for data and descriptions about ABA-approved law schools.

Although no book or website can substitute for direct contact with admission professionals at the law schools, faculty, students, alumni, and prelaw advisors, this guide can inform the process of deciding whether, and where, to attend law school. This guide is designed to provide prospective law school applicants with basic information in a simple format that will facilitate comparisons among schools. In addition to statistics on all ABA-approved law schools, this book contains information intended to help individuals prepare for the rigors and costs associated with attending law school.

The ABA collects quantitative data as part of the accreditation process using questionnaires completed annually during the fall academic semester. Standard 509 of the *Standards and Rules of Procedure for Approval of Law Schools*, as adopted by the ABA House of Delegates in August 1996, states: "A law school shall publish basic consumer information. The information shall be published in a fair and accurate manner reflective of actual practice."

The data collected in the ABA annual questionnaire and published in this guide satisfy a law school's obligation to provide basic consumer information under Standard 509. The data are certified as fair and accurate by the dean of the law school.

The Law School Admission Council collects admission profile data and school descriptions each fall as a service to its member schools and to prospective law school applicants. The information provided by the law schools to LSAC in no way affects the ABA accreditation process and is not meant to satisfy a law school's publication requirements under Standard 509.

Neither LSAC nor ABA condones, approves, or sanctions use of the data contained in this book to rank law schools. Both organizations disapprove of any and all rankings. The deans of 178 law schools have published the following statement regarding rankings:

> The idea that all law schools can be measured by the same yardstick ignores the qualities that make you and law schools unique, and is unworthy of being an important influence on the choice you are about to make. As the deans of schools that range across the spectrum of several rating systems, we strongly urge you to minimize the influence of rankings on your own judgment. In choosing the best school for you, we urge you to get information about all the schools in which you might have some interest. ... Law schools may all have met the same standards of quality to become accredited, but they are quite different from each other. The unique characteristics of each law school will inform you why one school may be best for you and another school best for someone else. We want you to make the best choice for you.

The information contained in this edition of the *ABA-LSAC Official Guide to ABA-Approved Law Schools* was collected in fall 2010. Neither the ABA nor LSAC conducts an audit to verify the accuracy of the information submitted by the law schools. Some of the information, including ABA-accreditation status, may change. The LSAC website, LSAC.org, may contain updated information submitted by a law school. You should check the website of the ABA Section of Legal Education and Admissions to the Bar—americanbar.org/groups/legal_education—for updates regarding accreditation status, and the websites of the individual law schools for the most current information available.

CHAPTER 1: BEING A LAWYER

LAWYERS AND THEIR SKILLS

Law practice is so diverse that it is not possible to describe the so-called typical lawyer. Each lawyer works with different clients and different legal problems. Ordinarily, certain basic legal skills are required of all lawyers. They must know:

- how to analyze legal issues in light of the existing state of the law, the direction in which the law is headed, and relevant policy considerations;

- how to synthesize material in light of the fact that many issues are multifaceted and require the combination of diverse elements into a coherent whole;

- how to advocate the views of groups and individuals within the context of the legal system;

- how to give intelligent counsel on the law's requirements;

- how to write and speak clearly; and

- how to negotiate effectively.

Reading and Listening

Lawyers must be able to take in a great deal of information, often on topics about which they are unfamiliar. The ability to digest information from lengthy, dense texts is essential. Equally important is the ability to listen to clients and understand their unique issues and concerns.

Analyzing

Lawyers must be able to determine the fundamental elements of problems. They spend much time discerning the nature and significance of the many issues in a particular problem. In every issue, the lawyer must study the relationship between each element in order to arrive at an answer, result, or solution.

Synthesizing

Lawyers must have the ability to organize large amounts of material in a meaningful, focused, cogent manner. The complexities of many issues and the number of laws either directly or tangentially relevant make this kind of organization crucial.

Advocating

As an advocate, the lawyer's role is to represent his or her client's particular point of view and interests as vigorously as possible. The American judicial system assumes that equitable solutions will emerge from the clash of opposing interests. The success of this adversarial system of American law depends upon the talents and training of the lawyers who work as advocates within it, as speakers and as writers. Lawyers must be able to use their advocacy skills—both written and oral—to marshal evidence and present arguments as to why a particular outcome is desirable.

Counseling

Lawyers also spend a good deal of their time giving clients legal advice. Few ventures in the modern world can be undertaken without some understanding of the law. Through their knowledge of what the law involves, lawyers advise clients about partnerships, decisions, actions, and many other subjects. In many cases, the lawyer's role as a counselor serves as much to prevent litigation as to support it.

Writing and Speaking

Whether in the courtroom or the law office, lawyers must be effective communicators. If lawyers could not translate thoughts and opinions into clear and precise English, it would be difficult for the law to serve society. After all, the law is embodied in words, and many of the disputes that give birth to laws begin with language—its meaning, use, and interpretation. Litigation leads to written judicial opinions; congressional enactments are recorded as printed statutes; and even economic transactions must be expressed as formal, written contracts.

Negotiating

One of the lawyer's primary roles is reconciling divergent interests and opinions. When the parties to a proposed transaction disagree, the lawyer, acting as a facilitator, may be able to help them negotiate to a common ground. Although the client's interests are a lawyer's first priority, often those interests are served best after compromise and conciliation have paved the way to an equitable settlement. Because lawyers are trained to see the implications of alternative courses of action, they are often able to break an impasse.

A legal education is also excellent preparation for many other careers, because the course of study provides a framework for organizing knowledge and teaches an analytical approach to problems. Any or all of the skills described here are useful for those law school graduates who choose not to practice law, but to go into another field. Professions such as banking, insurance, real estate, public relations, human resources, government, education, and international trade are significant areas of employment for law school graduates. The fields of health care, media, and publishing have also attracted law school graduates to their ranks. Law school does not train you for any particular kind of law, but rather acts as a springboard into various professional opportunities. Among the skills learned in law school that are basic to a variety of nonlegal positions are ease in dealing with legal terminology and concepts, ability to analyze facts, and facility in persuading others.

FIELDS OF LAW

Lawyers are central figures in the life of a democratic country. They may deal with major courtroom cases or minor traffic disputes, complex corporate mergers or straightforward real estate transactions. Lawyers may work for giant industries, small businesses, government agencies, international organizations, public interest groups, legal aid offices, and universities—or they may work for themselves. They represent both the impoverished and the wealthy, the helpless and the powerful. Lawyers may work solo, in a small group, or in a large law firm.

About 74 percent of American lawyers are in private practice, most in small, one-person offices and some in large firms. Roughly 8 percent of the profession work for government agencies, 9 percent work for private industries and associations as salaried lawyers or as managers, 1 percent work for legal aid or as public defenders, 1 percent are in legal education, and 1 percent is in the judiciary. (About 5 percent are retired or inactive.) Many lawyers develop expertise in a particular field of law. Large law firms that provide a full range of legal services tend to employ more specialists. The solo practitioner, who must handle a variety of problems alone, may have greater opportunity to work in several areas. Of course, there are lawyers in large firms who maintain general practices, and lawyers in one-person offices who concentrate on a particular legal issue. Both specialized and general practice can be rewarding. One offers the satisfaction of mastering a particular legal discipline, and the other the challenge of exploring new fields. Following are brief descriptions of selected areas of specialization, though there are many areas of the law that can rightly fall into more than one category.

Civil Rights

Many lawyers entered law school wishing ultimately to work in the field of civil rights—the area of law that is concerned with the balance of governmental power and individual liberties. Although the number of full-time jobs in this field is relatively small, many lawyers whose principal practices are in other fields are able to work in this area by taking cases on a pro bono basis. Full-time civil rights attorneys often work for nonprofit, public interest law firms, or as part of a larger firm with a diverse practice.

Corporate and Securities Law

The corporate lawyer helps clients conduct their business affairs in a manner that is efficient and consistent with the law. The responsibilities of a corporate lawyer can range from preparing the initial articles of incorporation and bylaws for a new enterprise to handling a corporate reorganization under the provisions of federal bankruptcy law. Examples of other areas of corporate law practice include (but are not limited to) contract, intellectual property, legislative compliance, and liability matters.

Securities law is an extremely complex area that almost always requires the services of a specialist. Lawyers who acquire this specialty are involved with the formation, organization, and financing of corporations through securities such as stock, as well as mergers, acquisitions, and corporate takeovers.

Criminal Law

Criminal defense lawyers represent clients accused of crimes. Their public counterparts are the prosecutors and district attorneys who represent the interests of the state in the prosecution of those accused of crimes. Both types of criminal lawyers deal with fundamental issues of the law and personal liberty. They defend many of the basic rights considered crucial to the preservation of a free and just society.

Education Law

An education law attorney may provide advice, counsel, and representation to a school district or other educational agency in matters pertinent to education law, such as student residency, governance issues, the principal and teacher selection and retention process, student discipline, special-education law, tuition fraud, and in the development of educational policies. Other education law attorneys may represent parents with special-education or student-expulsion matters against a school district.

Employment and Labor Law

Employment and labor law addresses the legal rights of workers and their employers. Issues might include disputes regarding wages, hours, unlawful termination, child labor, workplace safety, workplace injury and disease, family and related leave, pension and benefit plans, the right to unionize, regulations of and negotiations with union employees, sexual harassment, government civil service systems, and discrimination based upon race, gender, age, and disabilities. Attorneys practicing employment and labor law might represent an individual employee, a group of employees, job applicants, a union, union employees, government workers, a large or small business or organization, a government agency, or interest groups.

Environmental and Natural Resources Law

Environmental law was born out of widespread public and professional concern about the fate of our natural resources. Lawyers in this field may tackle legal and regulatory issues relating to air and water quality, hazardous waste practice, natural gas transportation, oil and gas exploration and development, electric power licensing, water rights, toxic torts, public land use, marine resources, and energy trade regulation. They may work directly for governmental agencies that address environmental problems or represent corporations, public interest groups, and entities concerned about protecting the environment.

Family and Juvenile Law

Family, or domestic relations, law is concerned with relationships between individuals in the context of the family. Many lawyers who practice this kind of law are members of small law firms or are solo practitioners. They specialize in solving problems that arise among family members and in creating or dissolving personal relationships through such means as adoption or divorce.

Health Law

The practice of health law encompasses many different disciplines. Lawyers in this field can be in the private bar or at government agencies. Health lawyers can represent hospitals, physician groups, health maintenance organizations (HMOs), or individual doctors, among many others. Government health lawyers can investigate fraud, deal with Medicare policy and compliance, or oversee public health policy. Many health lawyers are engaged in the business of health care, spending significant time in mergers and acquisitions, tax law, employee benefits, and risk management issues. The impact of technology on health care has been great with health lawyers helping to guide their clients through intellectual property, biomedicine, and telemedicine issues. Other health lawyers specialize in bioethics and clinical ethics, representing universities and other research academic centers.

Immigration Law

US immigration law deals with legal issues and US policies relating to foreign nationals who come to the United States on a temporary or permanent basis, including the associated legal rights, duties, and obligations of aliens in the United States and the application processes and procedures involved with naturalization of foreign nationals who wish to become US citizens, as well as dealing with legal issues relating to people who are refugees, people who cross US borders by means of fraud or other illegal means, and those who traffic or otherwise illegally transport aliens into the United States. An immigration lawyer may assist clients with all aspects of immigration law, but many choose to specialize in subcategories of immigration law, due to the complexity of the law and the frequency of updates and changes. Specialization areas will include asylum/refugee law, business immigration law, and criminal and deportation defense. An attorney practicing in one of the above areas of immigration law may work for the government, a law firm, a community-based organization, or in-house for a company employing foreign nationals.

Intellectual Property Law

Intellectual property law is concerned with the protection of inventors' rights in their discoveries, authors' rights in their creations, and businesses' rights in their identifying marks. Often, an intellectual property lawyer will specialize in a particular area of the law. For example, for those attorneys with a technical background, patent law is a way to combine one's scientific and legal background into one practice. A copyright attorney counsels authors, composers, and artists on the scope of their rights in their creations and personal identities; negotiates contracts; and litigates to enforce these rights. In recent years, copyright law has also focused on technological advances, particularly developments in electronic publishing. Additionally, in today's global economy, intellectual property issues are at the forefront of international trade negotiations.

International Law

International law has grown significantly as a field of practice, reflecting the increasing interdependence of nations and economies. Immigration and refugee law also assumes increasing importance as more people move more frequently across national boundaries for business, tourism, or permanent resettlement. Public international law provides a limited range of job opportunities, particularly with national governments or international institutions or with public interest bodies. Private international law may offer more extensive employment opportunities, either through law firms or for corporations, banks, or telecommunications firms. Fluency in another language or familiarity with another culture can be a decided advantage for law school graduates who seek to practice in the international arena.

Real Estate Law

Real estate law generally involves anything dealing with real property (land). These laws are designed to determine who owns land and the buildings on it, who has a right to possess and use land or buildings, the sale and purchase of real property, landlord and tenant issues, the development of real property, and compliance with local, state, or national regulations affecting the use of real property. An attorney practicing real estate law may focus on contractual issues by drafting and reviewing contracts; some real estate attorneys may be more focused on litigation issues, such as determining the ownership of land in court, challenging or enforcing easements, seeking to allow the specific development of property, or trying to prevent or alter a planned development of real property. In addition, an attorney practicing real estate law may focus on a specific type of real estate law or a related area of law, such as oil and gas or natural resources law.

Sports and Entertainment Law

Sports law is divided between amateur and professional sports. At the amateur or university level, sports lawyers ensure that athletes and donors are in compliance with National Collegiate Athletic Association (NCAA) rules. They also work with colleges and universities that receive federal aid and are thus subject to Title IX of the Education Amendments of 1972, which prohibits discrimination on the basis of gender in athletic programs. At the professional level, sports lawyers address contract and antitrust issues. They may serve as agents to individual players or represent team owners. Entertainment law generally consists of legal issues affecting television, films, recordings, live performances, and other aspects of the entertainment industry. Entertainment law may involve employment law issues, such as contracts between actors and studios, labor law issues affecting trade unions, and intellectual property law, including the protection of creative works such as new songs and the collection of royalties. Entertainment lawyers may assist their clients in negotiating contracts for a record deal or for appearing in a movie, may ensure that their songwriting client obtains the correct amount of royalties for the songs he or she has written, or may go to court to litigate many issues involving the entertainment industry, including disputes over ideas for movies or songs.

Tax Law

In the past 50 years, the importance and complexity of federal, state, and local taxes have necessitated a specialty in this field of law. It is one area of the law where change is constant. The federal Internal Revenue Code and its associated regulations are now several thousand pages in length. New statutes, court decisions, and administrative rulings are issued frequently, and the tax lawyer must be alert to these changes. Economic planning usually includes attention to taxes, and the tax lawyer often assists clients in understanding and minimizing their tax liabilities.

A legal education is both challenging and rewarding. You will develop your analytical, synthesizing, creative, and logical thinking skills, and you will strengthen your reading and debating abilities. A legal education is necessary to become a lawyer in the United States, but it is also excellent preparation for many other careers, both because of the framework for organizing knowledge it provides and the analytical approach it brings to problems. Many teachers, businesspeople, and writers first obtained a legal education before pursuing careers other than law.

PREPARING FOR LAW SCHOOL

Statement on Prelaw Preparation
Prepared by the Pre-Law Committee of the ABA Section of Legal Education and Admissions to the Bar

No Single Path
There is no single path that will prepare you for a legal education. Students who are successful in law school, and who become accomplished professionals, come from many walks of life and educational backgrounds. Some law students enter law school directly from their undergraduate studies without having had any postbaccalaureate work experience. Others begin their legal education significantly later in life, and they bring to their law school education the insights and perspectives gained from their life experiences. Legal education welcomes and values diversity, and you will benefit from the exchange of ideas and different points of view that your colleagues will bring to the classroom.

Undergraduate Education
The ABA does not recommend any undergraduate majors or group of courses to prepare for a legal education. Students are admitted to law school from almost every academic discipline. You may choose to major in subjects that are considered to be traditional preparation for law school, such as history, English, philosophy, political science, economics, or business, or you may focus your undergraduate studies in areas as diverse as art, music, science, mathematics, computer science, engineering, nursing, or education. Whatever major you select, you are encouraged to pursue an area of study that interests and challenges you, while taking advantage of opportunities to develop your research and writing skills. Taking a broad range of difficult courses from demanding instructors is excellent preparation for legal education.

A sound legal education will build upon and further refine the skills, values, and knowledge that you already possess. The student who comes to law school lacking a broad range of basic skills and knowledge will face a difficult challenge.

Prelaw Advisor
Undergraduate institutions often assign a person to act as an advisor to current and former students who are interested in pursuing a legal education. That individual can help you with researching and identifying law schools to which you may want to apply. If you are still attending undergraduate school, your prelaw advisor can be helpful in selecting courses that can help you achieve your goal.

Core Skills and Values*
There are important skills and values, and significant bodies of knowledge that you can acquire prior to law school and that will provide a sound foundation for a legal education. These include analytic and problem-solving skills, critical reading abilities, writing skills, oral communication and listening abilities, general research skills, task organization and management skills, and the values of serving faithfully the interests of others while also promoting justice. If you wish to prepare adequately for a legal education, and for a career in law or for other professional services that involve the use of lawyering skills, you should seek educational, extracurricular, and life experiences that will assist you in developing those attributes. Some brief comments about each of the listed skills and values follow.

Analytic/Problem-Solving Skills
You should seek courses and other experiences that will engage you in critical thinking about important issues, challenge your beliefs, and improve your tolerance for uncertainty. Your legal education will demand that you structure and evaluate arguments for and against propositions that are susceptible to reasoned debate. Good legal education will teach you to "think like a lawyer," but the analytic and problem-solving skills required of lawyers are not fundamentally different from those employed by other professionals. Your law school experience will develop and refine those crucial skills, but you must enter law school with a reasonably well-developed set of analytic and problem-solving abilities.

Critical Reading Abilities
Preparation for legal education should include substantial experience at close reading and critical analysis of complex textual material, for much of what you will do as a law student and lawyer involves careful reading and comprehension of judicial opinions, statutes, documents, and other written materials. As with the other skills discussed in this Statement, you can develop your critical reading ability in a wide range of experiences, including the close reading of complex material in literature, political or economic theory, philosophy, or history. The particular nature of the materials examined is not crucial; what is important is that law school should not be the first time that you are rigorously engaged in the enterprise of carefully reading and understanding, and critically analyzing, complex written material of substantial length.

Writing Skills
As you seek to prepare for a legal education, you should develop a high degree of skill at written communication. Language is the most important tool of a lawyer, and lawyers must learn to express themselves clearly and concisely.

Legal education will provide you with good training in writing, and particularly in the specific techniques and forms of written expression that are common in the law. Fundamental writing skills, however, *must* be acquired and refined before you enter law school. You should seek rigorous and analytical writing opportunities, including preparing original pieces of substantial length and revising written work in response to constructive criticism.

Oral Communication and Listening Abilities
The ability to speak clearly and persuasively is another skill that is essential to your success in law school and the practice of law. You must also have excellent listening skills if you are to understand your clients and others with whom you will interact daily. As with writing skills, legal education provides excellent opportunities for refining oral communication skills, and particularly for practicing the forms and techniques of oral expression that are most common in the practice of law. Before coming to law school, however, you should seek to develop your basic speaking and listening skills by engaging

in debate, making formal presentations in class, or speaking before groups in school, the community, or the workplace.

General Research Skills
Although there are many research sources and techniques that are specific to the law, you do not have to have developed any familiarity with these specific skills or materials before entering law school. However, it would be to your advantage to come to law school having had the experience of undertaking a project that requires significant library research and the analysis of large amounts of information obtained from that research. The ability to use a personal computer is also necessary for law students, both for word processing and for computerized legal research.

Task Organization and Management Skills
To study and practice law, you are going to need to be able to organize large amounts of information, identify objectives, and create a structure for applying that information in an efficient way in order to achieve desired results. Many law school courses, for example, are graded primarily on the basis of one examination at the end of the course, and many projects in the practice of law require the compilation of large amounts of information from a wide variety of sources. You are going to need to be able to prepare and assimilate large amounts of information in an effective and efficient manner. Some of the requisite experience can be obtained through undertaking school projects that require substantial research and writing, or through the preparation of major reports for an employer, a school, or a civic organization.

The Values of Serving Others and Promoting Justice
Each member of the legal profession should be dedicated both to the objectives of serving others honestly, competently, and responsibly, and to the goals of improving fairness and the quality of justice in the legal system. If you are thinking of entering the legal profession, you should seek some significant experience, before coming to law school, in which you may devote substantial effort toward assisting others. Participation in public service projects or similar efforts at achieving objectives established for common purposes can be particularly helpful.

General Knowledge
In addition to the fundamental skills and values listed above, there are some basic areas of knowledge that are helpful to a legal education and to the development of a competent lawyer. Some of the types of knowledge that would maximize your ability to benefit from a legal education include:

- A **broad understanding of history**, including the various factors (social, political, economic, and cultural) that have influenced the development of our society in the United States.

- A **fundamental understanding of political thought** and of the contemporary American political system.

- Some **basic mathematical and financial skills**, such as an understanding of basic precalculus mathematics and an ability to analyze financial data.

- A **basic understanding of human behavior** and social interaction.

- An **understanding of diverse cultures** within and beyond the United States, of international institutions and issues, of world events, and of the increasing interdependence of the nations and communities within our world.

Conclusion
The skills, values, and knowledge discussed in this Statement may be acquired in a wide variety of ways. You may take undergraduate, graduate, or even high school courses that can assist you in acquiring much of this information. You may also gain much of this background through self-learning by reading, in the workplace, or through various other life experiences. Moreover, it is not essential that you come to law school having fully developed all of the skills, values, and knowledge suggested in this Statement. Some of that foundation can be acquired during the initial years of law school. However, if you begin law school having already acquired many of the skills, values, and knowledge listed in this Statement, you will have a significant advantage and will be well prepared to benefit fully from a challenging legal education.

*These core skill and value areas are drawn, in substantial part, from the Statement of Skills and Values contained in the 1992 Report of the American Bar Association Task Force on Law Schools and the Profession, *Legal Education and Professional Development—An Educational Continuum.*

OTHER RESOURCES

For a selected list of books, audiocassettes, and video programs pertaining to legal education and the legal profession, go to LSAC's website, LSAC.org. Search on "Resources for the Prelaw Candidate."

THE JURIS DOCTOR DEGREE

ABA-approved law schools generally require three years of full-time study to earn the Juris Doctor (JD) degree. Most schools with part-time programs require four years of part-time study to earn the JD degree. Most law schools share a common approach to training lawyers. However, they differ in the emphasis they give to certain subjects and teaching methods, such as opportunities for independent study, legal internships, participation in clinical programs, and involvement with governmental affairs.

Law school can be an intense, competitive environment. Students have little time for other interests, especially during the first year of law school. The ABA requires that no full-time student hold an outside job for more than 20 hours a week. Most schools encourage their students to become totally immersed in reading, discussing, and thinking about the law.

The First Year
The newness of the first year of law school is exciting for many and anxiety provoking for almost all. Professors expect you to be prepared in class, but in most courses, grades will be determined primarily from examinations administered at the end of the semester or, at some schools, the end of the year. The professor may give little feedback until the final examination.

The Case Method Approach
The "case method" is what first-year law students are likely to find least familiar. By focusing on the underlying principles that shape the law's approach to different situations, you will learn to distinguish among subtly different legal results and to identify the critical factors that determine a particular outcome. Once these distinctions are mastered, you should be able to apply this knowledge to new situations.

The case method involves the detailed examination of a number of related judicial opinions that describe an area of law. You will also learn to apply the same critical analysis to legislative materials and scholarly articles. The role of the law professor is to provoke and stimulate. For a particular case, he or she may ask questions designed to explore the facts presented, to determine the legal principles applied in reaching a decision, and to analyze the method of reasoning used. In this way, the professor encourages you to relate the case to others and to distinguish it from those with similar but inapplicable precedents. In order to encourage you to learn to defend your reasoning, the professor may adopt a position contrary to the holding of the case.

Because this process places much of the burden of learning on the student, classroom discussions can be exciting. They are also demanding. However uninformed, unprepared, or puzzled you may be, you will be expected to participate in these discussions.

The Ability to Think
The case method reflects the general belief that the primary purpose of law school is not to teach substantive law but to teach you to think like a lawyer. Teachers of law are less concerned about rules and technicalities than are their counterparts in many other disciplines. Although the memorization of specifics may be useful to you, the ability to be analytical and literate is considerably more important than the power of total recall. One reason for this approach to legal education is that in our common-law tradition, the law is constantly evolving and changing; thus, specific rules may quickly lose their relevance.

Law is more an art than a science. The reality lawyers seek in analyzing a case is not always well defined. Legal study, therefore, requires an attentive mind and a tolerance for ambiguity. Because many people believe incorrectly that the study of law involves the memorization of rules in books and principles dictated by learned professors, law schools often attract those people who especially value structure, authority, and order. The study of law does not involve this kind of certainty, however; complex legal questions do not have simple legal solutions.

The Curriculum
As a first-year law student, you will follow a designated course of study that may cover many of the following subjects:

- **Civil procedure**—the process of adjudication in the United States; that is, jurisdiction and standing to sue, motions and pleadings, pretrial procedure, the structure of a lawsuit, and appellate review of trial results.

- **Constitutional law**—the legislative powers of the federal and state governments, and questions of civil liberties and constitutional history, including detailed study of the Bill of Rights and constitutional freedoms.

- **Contracts**—the nature of enforceable promises and rules for determining appropriate remedies in case of nonperformance.

- **Criminal law and criminal procedure**—bases of criminal responsibility, the rules and policies for enforcing sanctions against individuals accused of committing offenses against the public order and well-being, and the rights guaranteed to those charged with criminal violations.

- **Legal method**—students' introduction to the organization of the American legal system and its processes.

- **Legal writing**—research and writing component of most first-year programs; requires students to research and write memoranda dealing with various legal problems.

- **Property law**—concepts, uses, and historical developments in the treatment of land, buildings, natural resources, and personal objects.

- **Torts**—private wrongs, such as acts of negligence, assault, and defamation, that violate obligations of the law.

In addition to attending classes, you may be required to participate in a moot court exercise in which you take responsibility for arguing a hypothetical court case.

After the first year, you will probably have the opportunity to select from a broad range of courses. Generally, you will take courses in administrative law, civil litigation, commercial law, corporations, evidence, family law, professional responsibility, taxation, and wills and trusts before completing your degree. These universal courses are basic to legal education. Every law school supplements this basic curriculum with additional courses, such as international law, environmental law, conflict of laws, labor law, criminal procedure, and jurisprudence.

Opportunities to Practice What Is Learned
Legal education is primarily academic, in that students devote most of their time to mastering general concepts and principles that shape the law. Most schools offer a variety of

professional skills courses as well. Through clinical programs, law schools offer students direct experience in legal practice. These programs allow second- and third-year students to render counseling, undertake legislative drafting, participate in court trials and appeals, and do other legal work for academic credit. Schools differ in the range and variety of practical education they offer, but the benefits of integrating this experience with theoretical study are well established.

Extracurricular Activities

Student organizations greatly supplement classroom learning. Typically, these organizations are dedicated to advancing the interests of particular groups of law students, such as black, women, or Hispanic students; or to promoting greater understanding of specific legal fields, such as environmental or international law; or to providing opportunities for involvement in professional, social, and sports activities.

A unique feature of American law schools is that law students manage and edit most of the legal profession's principal scholarly journals. Membership on the editorial staffs of these journals is considered a mark of academic distinction. Selection is ordinarily based on outstanding academic performance, writing ability, or both, as discussed on pages 18–19 of this book.

ADMISSION TO THE BAR

The Bar Examination*

In order to obtain a license to practice law, law school graduates must apply for bar admission through a state board of bar examiners. Most often this board is an agency of the highest state court in the jurisdiction, but occasionally the board is connected more closely to the state's bar association. The criteria for eligibility to take the bar examination or to otherwise qualify for bar admission are set by each state, not by the ABA or the Council of the Section of Legal Education and Admissions to the Bar.

Licensing involves a demonstration of worthiness in two distinct areas. The first is **competence**. For initial licensure, competence is ordinarily established by a showing that the applicant holds an acceptable educational credential (with some exceptions, a JD degree) from a law school that meets educational standards, and by achieving a passing score on the bar examination.

The most common testing configuration consists of a two-day bar examination, one day of which is devoted to the Multistate Bar Examination (MBE), a standardized 200-item test covering six areas (Constitutional Law, Contracts, Criminal Law, Evidence, Real Property, and Torts). The second day of testing is typically comprised of locally crafted essays from a broader range of subject matters. However, in a growing number of states, two nationally developed tests, the Multistate Essay Examination (MEE) and the Multistate Performance Test (MPT) may be used to round out the test.

In addition, almost all jurisdictions require that the applicant present an acceptable score on the Multistate Professional Responsibility Examination (MPRE), which is separately administered three times a year.

The second area of inquiry by bar examiners involves the **character and fitness** of applicants for a law license. In this regard, bar examiners seek background information concerning each applicant that is relevant to the appropriateness of granting a professional credential. Because law is a public profession, and because the degree of harm a lawyer, once licensed, can inflict is

substantial, decisions about who should be admitted to practice law are made carefully by bar examining boards.

Boards of bar examiners in most jurisdictions expect to hear from prospective candidates during the final year of law school. Bar examinations are administered at the end of February and July, with considerably more applicants taking the summer test because it falls after graduation from law school.

Some boards offer or require law student registration at an earlier point in law school. This preliminary processing, where available, permits the board to review character and fitness issues in advance.

As state-specific information is so important (and so variable) in the lawyer-licensing process, law students should contact the board of bar examiners in the jurisdictions in which they are most likely to practice law. Links to state boards are available through the National Conference of Bar Examiners website (ncbex.org).

*This section was written by Erica Moeser, President of the National Conference of Bar Examiners (NCBE).

General Information

Lawyers may practice only in the state or states where they are members of the bar in good standing. However, many states will admit a lawyer to its bar if the lawyer has been admitted to the bar of another state and has practiced law actively for a certain number of years. This is known as "admission by motion." Courts often grant temporary bar admission to out-of-state lawyers for the duration of a specific case.

Many states have student practice rules that, in conjunction with students' academic programs, admit advanced law students who are under the close supervision of an admitted lawyer. A few states require law students to register with the board of bar examiners before graduation or, in some cases, soon after they are enrolled in law school, if they intend to practice in those states. So, if you're planning to attend law school, you should check the bar admission requirements for those states in which you may wish to practice after graduation.

Federal courts set their own standards for admission. It is a common requirement for federal district court admission that the lawyer be admitted to the bar in the state in which the federal district is located or, for the applicant to have one valid state court admission.

Some state bar associations inquire about the law school admission records of those seeking admission to the bar. You should keep and maintain complete copies of all law school application records throughout the admission cycle and your law school career.

All states accept graduation from an ABA-approved law school as meeting the state's education requirement for eligibility to sit for the bar examination. A number of states have special rules that accept other forms of legal education as sufficient. A good source of information regarding bar admission requirements is the latest edition of the *NCBE/ABA's Comprehensive Guide to Bar Admission Requirements*, which is available online at americanbar.org/groups/legal_education. It should also be available in any law school library or can be ordered through the ABA Service Center at 1.800.285.2221. If you would like additional information relating to bar admissions about a specific state, please contact the appropriate authority in that state. Also, you may want to visit the websites for NCBE (ncbex.org), the ABA (americanbar.org/groups/legal_education), and LSAC (LSAC.org).

Distance Education

Educating a student for a Juris Doctor degree is a professional education of a most distinct variety. During a law school education, a student is expected to participate in a learning community to develop skills and knowledge that will advance the legal system, society, and the student's career. This law school experience involves interaction with faculty and fellow students outside the classroom as well as in class. Students also learn from each other by inquiry and challenge, review, and study groups.

ABA-approved law schools may not offer a JD degree program that is online or done through correspondence study. ABA-approved law schools may grant credit hours for distance education courses, but no more than 4-credit hours in any term, and no more than 12-credit hours toward the JD degree. Students should be aware that studying law by correspondence or other distance education programs would limit the ability to sit for the bar in many states.

Bar Associations

Bar associations are membership organizations designed to raise the standards of the legal profession and to encourage professionalism. Each state has its own bar association. In the majority of states, membership in the bar association is mandatory. There are also a variety of national, local, and special-interest bar associations. Many bar associations sponsor programs intended to broaden the availability of legal services and to familiarize the public with the legal profession. They also conduct extensive continuing legal education programs to help members update their skills and their knowledge of the law.

With nearly 400,000 members, the American Bar Association is the largest voluntary professional membership organization in the world. The ABA sponsors a number of programs dealing with legal education, law reform, judicial selection, and professional responsibility. The ABA also promulgates the "Model Rules of Professional Conduct" as an example to the states of the ethics standards that they should enact and enforce in regulating the practice of law in their jurisdiction.

Additionally, there are local and national chapters of bar associations for lawyers from minority groups. Among them are the National Bar Association (nationalbar.org), Hispanic National Bar Association (hnba.com), National Asian Pacific American Bar Association (napaba.org), and the National Native American Bar Association (www.nativeamericanbar.org). You may also find useful information at LSAC.org's Diversity in Law School section.

HOW LAW SCHOOLS DETERMINE WHOM TO ADMIT

Nationally, there are more applicants than spaces available in first-year classes. Schools rely heavily upon selection criteria that bear on expected performance in law school and can be applied objectively to all candidates. Law schools consider a variety of factors in admitting their students. The two factors that all candidates present—prior academic performance and the LSAT score—are fundamental to the admission process.

The most difficult admission decisions are those regarding candidates who are neither so well qualified nor so unsatisfactory as to present a clear-cut case for acceptance or denial. These applicants constitute the majority of the applicant pool at many law schools. However, if you assess your credentials accurately, your likelihood of admission to an ABA-accredited law school is strong.

Criteria That May Be Considered by Law School Admission Committees

- Undergraduate grade-point average

- LSAT score

- Undergraduate course of study

- Graduate work, if any

- College attended

- Improvement in grades and grade distribution

- College curricular and extracurricular activities

- Ethnic/racial background

- Individual character and personality

- Letters of recommendation

- Writing skills

- Personal statement or essay

- Work experience or other postundergraduate experiences

- Community activities

- Motivation to study and reasons for deciding to study law

- State of residency

- Obstacles that have been overcome

- Past accomplishments and leadership

- Conditional admission programs

- Anything else that stands out in an application

THE LAW SCHOOL ADMISSION TEST (LSAT)

The Law School Admission Test (LSAT) is a half-day, standardized test administered four times each year at designated testing centers throughout the world. All American Bar Association (ABA)-approved law schools, most Canadian law schools, and many other law schools require applicants (with a few very limited exceptions) to take the LSAT as part of the admission process.

The test consists of five 35-minute sections of multiple-choice questions. It provides a standard measure of acquired reading and verbal reasoning skills that law schools can use as one of several factors in assessing applicants. Four of the five sections contribute to the test taker's score. The unscored section, commonly referred to as the variable section, typically is used to pretest new test questions or to preequate new test forms. The placement of this section in the LSAT will vary. A 35-minute writing sample is administered at the end of the test. LSAC does not score the writing sample, but copies of the writing sample are sent to all law schools to which you apply.

The score scale for the LSAT is 120 to 180. Some schools place greater weight than others on the LSAT; most law schools do evaluate your full range of credentials.

What the Test Measures

The LSAT is designed to measure skills that are considered essential for success in law school: the reading and comprehension of complex texts with accuracy and insight; the organization and management of information and the ability to draw reasonable inferences from it; the ability to think critically; and the analysis and evaluation of the reasoning and arguments of others.

The three multiple-choice question types in the LSAT are:

Reading Comprehension Questions

These questions measure the ability to read, with understanding and insight, examples of lengthy and complex materials similar to those commonly encountered in law school. The Reading Comprehension section contains four sets of reading questions, each consisting of a selection of reading material, followed by five to eight questions that test reading and reasoning abilities.

Analytical Reasoning Questions

These questions measure the ability to understand a structure of relationships and to draw logical conclusions about that structure. You are asked to reason deductively from a set of statements and rules or principles that describe relationships among persons, things, or events. Analytical Reasoning questions reflect the kinds of complex analyses that a law student performs in the course of legal problem solving.

Logical Reasoning Questions

These questions assess the ability to analyze, critically evaluate, and complete arguments as they occur in ordinary language. Each Logical Reasoning question requires the test taker to read and comprehend a short passage, then answer a question about it. The questions are designed to assess a wide range of skills involved in thinking critically, with an emphasis on skills that are central to legal reasoning. These skills include drawing well-supported conclusions, reasoning by analogy, determining how additional evidence affects an argument, applying principles or rules, and identifying argument flaws.

Your Score as a Predictor of Law School Performance

The LSAT, like any admission test, is not a perfect predictor of law school performance. The predictive power of an admission test is limited by many factors, such as the complexity of the skills the test is designed to measure and the unmeasurable factors that can affect students' performances, such as motivation, physical and mental health, or work and family responsibilities. In spite of these factors, the LSAT compares very favorably with admission tests used in other graduate and professional fields of study. Additional information about scoring can be found on the LSAC website, LSAC.org.

Test Preparation

Most law school applicants familiarize themselves with test directions and question types, practice on sample tests, and study the information available on test-taking techniques and strategies. Although it is difficult to say when examinees are sufficiently prepared, very few people achieve their full potential without some preparation.

You should be so familiar with the instructions and question types that nothing you see on the test can delay or distract you from thinking about how to answer a question. At a minimum, you should review the descriptions of the question types on LSAC's website and simulate the day of the test by taking a practice test that includes a writing sample under actual time constraints. Taking a practice test under timed conditions helps you to estimate the amount of time you can afford to spend on each question in a section and to determine the question types for which you may need additional practice.

LSAC publishes a variety of materials to help you prepare for the LSAT. See the ad toward the back of this book, or visit LSAC's website—LSAC.org.

Academic Record

Undergraduate performance is generally an important indicator of how someone is likely to perform in law school. Hence, many law schools look closely at college grades when considering individual applications.

Course selection also can make a difference in admission evaluations. Applicants who have taken difficult or advanced courses in their undergraduate study often are evaluated in a more favorable light than students who have concentrated on easier or less advanced subjects.

Many law schools consider undergraduate-performance trends along with a student's numerical average. Thus, they may discount a slow start in a student's undergraduate career if he or she performs exceptionally well in the later school years. Similarly, admission committees may see an undergraduate's strong start followed by a mediocre finish as an indication of less potential to do well in law school. Candidates are advised to comment on irregular grade trends in their applications.

Grade Conversion Table

| LSAC Conversion | Grades as Reported on Transcripts | | | | |
4.0 Scale	A to F	1 to 5	100–0*	Four Passing Grades	Three Passing Grades
4.33	A+	1+	98–100	Highest Passing	Highest Passing
4.00	A	1	93–97	Grade (4.0)	Grade (4.0)
3.67	A–	1–	90–92		
3.50	AB				
3.33	B+	2+	87–89	Second Highest	Middle Passing
3.00	B	2	83–86	Passing Grade (3.0)	Grade (3.0)
2.67	B–	2–	80–82		
2.50	BC				
2.33	C+	3+	77–79	Third Highest	Lowest Passing
2.00	C	3	73–76	Passing Grade (2.0)	Grade (2.0)
1.67	C–	3–	70–72		
1.50	CD				
1.33	D+	4+	67–69	Lowest Passing	
1.00	D	4	63–66	Grade (1.0)	
0.67	D–	4–	60–62		
0.50	DE or DF				
0.00	E and F	5	Below 60	Failure (0.0)	Failure (0.0)

*In some instances, a school's numeric grading scale might be converted differently than shown here.

ADDITIONAL ADMISSION DECISION FACTORS

Law schools consider more than academic records and LSAT scores when evaluating applicants. Some of the most important factors are discussed below.

Letters of Recommendation and Evaluations

The most effective letters of recommendation and evaluations are those from professors who have known you well enough to write with candor, detail, and objectivity about your academic and personal achievements and potential. Letters that compare you to your academic peers are often considered the most useful. Work supervisors also can write in support of your application. Most law schools do not consider general, unreservedly praiseworthy letters helpful. Some schools do not require letters at all and may not read letters of recommendation if they receive them. In addition to or instead of letters of recommendation, many law schools are now also using an online tool that allows evaluators to rate a candidate's individual attributes in six categories: intellectual skill, personal qualities, integrity and honesty, communication, task management, and working with others.

Work Experience

Law schools want diverse, interesting classes, representative of a variety of backgrounds. A candidate who applies to law school several years after completing his or her undergraduate education, and who has demonstrated an ability to succeed in a nonacademic environment, is sometimes more motivated than one who continues his or her education without a break. In fact, only about one-third of law students enter directly from college.

Your Personal Essay

Each candidate to law school has something of interest to present. Maybe you've had some experience, some training, or some dream that sets you apart from others. Law schools want to recruit men and women who are qualified for reasons beyond grades and scores. The essay or personal statement in your application is the place to tell the committee about yourself.

In general, your evaluation of actual experiences and past accomplishments has more value to the committee than speculation about future accomplishments. Also, if you have overcome a serious obstacle in your life to get where you are today, by all means let the admission committee know about it. Any noteworthy personal experience or accomplishment may be an appropriate subject for your essay; however, be sure to do more than just state it. Describe your experience briefly but concretely, and why it had value to you, whether it is a job, your family, a significant accomplishment, or your upbringing. You are simultaneously trying to add information and create structure. Be brief, be factual, be comprehensive, and be organized. You are a storyteller here. You want a living person—you—to emerge. The statement is your opportunity to become vivid and alive to the reader, and it is an opportunity to demonstrate your ability to write and present a prose sample in a professional manner.

Graduate or Professional Study

Prior success or failure in other graduate or professional school work, including other law schools, may also be a factor in the admission committee's decision. In any case, you are required to report such work to any law school to which you apply.

Minority Applicants

Racial and ethnic diversity is essential to the study of law, and greatly benefits the law class, the law school, and the legal profession. All law schools actively seek students who are members of minority groups and strongly encourage minority applicants. (See chapter 6 for further details on minority recruitment and enrollment, and visit DiscoverLaw.org.)

International Applicants

Many students from other countries enroll at US law schools, most frequently in graduate programs (usually called LLM programs) that are designed to meet the needs of people who already hold a recognized law degree from another country but want to learn about the legal system of the United States.

Procedures and requirements for international applicants vary from school to school. You should contact the individual schools that interest you to learn about each school's particular requirements. Most schools will ask applicants for whom English is not their native language to take a standardized test such as the Test of English as a Foreign Language (TOEFL). Each school sets its own standard for required minimal scores on the tests.

Many schools require applicants educated outside the US, its territories, and Canada to use either LSAC's Credential Assembly Service or another evaluation service to authenticate and evaluate an applicant's grades and degrees for US admission committees. The applicant is responsible for the cost of this service, and some law schools will require the use of a specific service.

LSAC offers credential assembly services for the collection, authentication, evaluation, and distribution of all transcripts and TOEFL scores as appropriate for each law school to which the applicant applies. Detailed information about the services required by each law school is available at LSAC.org.

International students must also demonstrate the ability to pay for schooling in this country in order to apply for a student visa (F-1 form). You may be asked to complete a certification of finances form from the law school; if the school is satisfied that the student can pay, it will issue a form (I-20) to submit to the Immigration and Naturalization Service (INS) as part of your application for a student visa. Because of the time required to process entry visas, international applicants are encouraged to apply for admission as early in the process as possible.

International students may be eligible for institutional grants and loans, but are ineligible for federal loans, and (in most schools) are required to have a US cosigner for private loans. Contact the financial aid office at the schools to which you are applying for more details.

Interviews

In general, interviews are not a part of the law school admission process. You are encouraged to visit law schools to gather information, and often an appointment with admission personnel will be a part of the visit. The purpose of your conversation with the admission staff usually will be informational rather than evaluative and will not become a part of your admission file. An occasional school will grant an interview, and some may even request it, but, in general, you should not count on an interview as a means to state your case for admission; this is best done in the personal statement.

ASSESSING YOURSELF REALISTICALLY

When selecting law schools to which you will apply, the general philosophy is that you should have a threefold plan: dream a little, be realistic, and be safe. Most applicants have no trouble selecting dream schools—those that are almost, but not quite, beyond their grasp—or safe schools—those for which admission is virtually certain. A common strategic error made by applicants is failure to evaluate realistically their chances for admission to a particular law school. The admission data and law school admission profile grids in this book and online at LSAC.org are helpful sources, because the data are provided by the law schools directly to the ABA and LSAC.

Use the Admission Profile Grids in This Book

Check your qualifications against the admission profiles of the law schools that interest you. Most schools publish a grid that indicates the number of applicants with LSAT scores and GPAs like yours who were admitted in the most recent admission year. This gives you a general sense of your competitiveness at that school. These charts will help you determine which schools are your dream schools, your realistic schools, and your safe schools. If your profile meets or exceeds that of a school, it is likely that that school will be as interested in admitting you as you are in being admitted. Other statistics are contained in the school's ABA data, so that material should be read with care as well. A few words of caution: First, law schools consider many other factors beyond the LSAT score and GPA, as described in the previous section ("Additional Admission Decision Factors"), and the grids and data about these credentials only give you part of the story. Second, you should make your final decision about where you will apply only after obtaining additional information from each school. Third, the data in the grids are from a previous application year and may not reflect fluctuations in applicant volume that affect admission decisions.

Research Specific Law Schools That Interest You
Other sources of information include:

- **The school's admission office.** This is a good source for general information about the school and your chances for admission. Do not hesitate to request admission counseling. Be sure to obtain current catalogs and visit the websites for each law school you are considering.

- **Your college or university prelaw advisor.** LSAC provides the name of a prelaw advisor at your degree-granting institution. Your prelaw advisor can often provide you with reliable information about which law schools fit your personal profile. He or she may also be able to tell you which law schools have accepted students from your school in the past and provide you with an overview of the admitted students' credentials. This will help you to determine how law schools have treated applicants from your school in the recent past.

- **Law School Forums.** The Law School Forums, organized by the Law School Admission Council, are excellent opportunities to talk personally with law school representatives from around the country in one central, urban location—usually a hotel exhibit hall. Recent forums have been held in Atlanta, Boston, Chicago, Houston, Los Angeles, Miami, New York City, San Francisco Bay Area, Toronto, and Washington, DC. In 2010, 207 ABA-approved law schools participated in the forums, and about 9,900 people registered as attendees. Because traveling to a number of law schools can be expensive, many prospective law students find the forums to be the most productive means of gathering information and making school contacts. Forum admission is free; for dates and locations of 2011 Law School Forums, see the ad toward the back of this book, or visit LSAC's website—LSAC.org. Forum preregistration is also available on the LSAC website.

- **School representatives and alumni.** Take advantage of opportunities to talk with law school representatives and alumni. When you talk with alumni, remember that law schools sometimes change fairly quickly. Try to talk to a recent graduate or to one who is active in alumni affairs and therefore knowledgeable about the school as it is today.

- **School visits.** Law schools encourage you to visit. You can learn a great deal about a school from talks with students and faculty members. Many law schools have formal programs in which a currently enrolled student will take you on a tour of the campus and answer your questions. Firsthand experience can be quite valuable in assessing how you would fit into the school.

- **The Internet.** The websites of LSAC (LSAC.org) and the ABA (americanbar.org/groups/legal_education) provide links to the websites of ABA-approved law schools. The various avenues of online social networking are likely to provide many opportunities to link up, electronically at least, with students at law schools you are considering. Do keep in mind that a school may be a right (or wrong) fit for one person but not another. As is always true in online relationships, it's best to keep an open mind when it comes to comments from people you have never met in person. There is no substitution for seeing and experiencing a school for yourself.

Keep Your Options Open

Flexibility is a key word in the law school admission process. Keep your options open. Even during the early stages of the admission process, you should continually reevaluate your prospects and prepare alternative plans. For example, don't set your sights on only one law school and one plan of action. You could severely limit your potential and your chance to practice law.

WORKING WITH LSAC: REGISTERING FOR THE LSAT AND THE CREDENTIAL ASSEMBLY SERVICE (CAS)

The Law School Admission Council (LSAC) administers the LSAT and serves as a liaison for much of the communication between you and the law schools. The LSAC Credential Assembly Service centralizes and standardizes undergraduate academic records to simplify the law school admission process. This service also prepares a report for each law school to which you apply. The registration fee includes law school report preparation, letter of recommendation/evaluation and transcript processing, and access to electronic applications for all ABA-approved law schools.

Comprehensive information about the LSAT and the Credential Assembly Service can be found at the LSAC website, LSAC.org. The quickest and easiest way to register for both the LSAT and the Credential Assembly Service is online. If you need to obtain a paper registration form, call 215.968.1001.

Planning Ahead for Law School Deadlines

Most law schools have a variety of application requirements and deadlines that you must meet to be considered for admission. If you are applying to a number of schools, the various deadlines and requirements can be confusing. It probably will be helpful if you set up a detailed calendar that will remind you of when and what you must do to complete your applications.

In registering for the LSAT, be sure to give yourself enough time to select a convenient testing location and prepare for the test. You also should determine whether each law school in which you are interested will accept scores from the February LSAT administration, which is the last test date in each admission cycle.

Below is a chart listing all scheduled national test administrations, including alternate dates for Saturday Sabbath observers, along with corresponding deadlines and fees.

BASIC LSAT DATE AND DEADLINE INFORMATION (2011–2012)

All national test dates, both for regular test takers and test takers who are Saturday Sabbath observers, are listed below, along with corresponding regular registration deadlines. Dates shown represent receipt deadlines for mail, telephone, and online registration. The basic fee for the LSAT is $139 (published test centers only). Actual test dates for administrations **outside** the US, Canada, and the Caribbean, which are nondisclosed* tests, will vary. That information, as well as complete information regarding other LSAT options—such as deadlines and fees for late registrations and nonpublished test centers (domestic and foreign), test date and test center changes, and partial refunds—is available at LSAC.org.

National Test Dates

▪ **Regular**	Monday, June 6, 2011	Saturday, Oct. 1, 2011	Saturday, Dec. 3, 2011	Saturday, Feb. 11, 2012 Nondisclosed*
▪ **Saturday Sabbath Observers**		Tuesday, Oct. 4, 2011 Nondisclosed*	Monday, Dec. 5, 2011 Nondisclosed*	Monday, Feb. 13, 2012 Nondisclosed*
▪ **Score by E-mail**	June 29, 2011	Oct. 26, 2011	Jan. 6, 2012	March 7, 2012
▪ **Score Report mailed (approx.)**	July 7, 2011	Nov. 3, 2011	Jan. 14, 2012	March 11, 2012

Regular Registration Deadlines (online, mail, and telephone)

▪ **United States, Canada, and the Caribbean**	May 3, 2011	Aug. 30, 2011	Oct. 31, 2011	Jan. 10, 2012

*Persons who take a nondisclosed test receive only their scores. They do not receive their test questions, answer key, or individual responses.

THE CREDENTIAL ASSEMBLY SERVICE

The Credential Assembly Service collects the US and Canadian academic records of law school applicants and summarizes the undergraduate work according to a standard 4.0 system to simplify the admission process. Nearly all American Bar Association-approved law schools (and many non-ABA-approved schools) require that applicants use this service. Applicants who have studied for more than a year outside the US or Canada can use the Credential Assembly Service for transcript evaluation and authentication if required by the law schools to which they are applying.

The Credential Assembly Service prepares a report for each law school to which you apply. There is a registration fee for the service, as well as a fee for each law school report (go to LSAC.org for current fees). Your registration includes law school report preparation, letter of recommendation/evaluation and transcript processing, and access to electronic applications for all ABA-approved law schools.

The Credential Assembly Service creates your law school report by combining:

- scores and writing sample copies;

- an academic summary report;

- copies of all undergraduate, graduate, and law/professional school transcripts; and

- copies of letters of recommendation and evaluations, if applicable.

Canadian law schools receive an LSAT Law School Report containing scores and writing sample copies.

Fee Waivers

Fee waivers are available for the LSAT, the Credential Assembly Service (CAS), and *The Official LSAT SuperPrep*. For US citizens, US nationals, or permanent resident aliens of the United States with an Alien Registration Receipt Card (I-151 or I-551), fee waivers can be authorized by LSAC or ABA-approved law schools, which are listed on our website. Canadian citizens must submit their fee waiver request to a Canadian LSAC-member law school even if they plan to apply for admission to a US law school. Fee waivers cannot be granted by financial aid offices of undergraduate institutions, non-ABA-approved law schools, prelaw advisors, or any other individual or organization. Go to LSAC.org or any ABA-approved law school admission office for additional information about fee waivers.

THE ADMISSION PROCESS

Law school applicants can expect that the admission process will be competitive. Nationally, there are more applicants than spaces available in first-year classes; this means that, at some law schools, there will be considerable competition for seats. However, it is probably true that if you assess your credentials accurately, your likelihood of admission to an ABA-accredited law school is strong.

The Importance of Complete Files

Remember that law schools require complete files before making their decisions. A law school will consider your file complete when it has received your application, Credential Assembly Service (CAS) Law School Report (or LSAT Law School Report if the law school does not require the Credential Assembly Service), letters of recommendation or evaluations (if required), personal statement, any requirements unique to the particular school, and application fee.

Rolling Admission

Many law schools operate what is known as a rolling admission process: The school evaluates applications and informs candidates of admission decisions on a continuous basis over several months, usually beginning in late fall and extending to midsummer for wait-listed admissions.

Even if you have not yet taken the LSAT, it might be helpful to submit your application early so that your Credential Assembly Service file can be sent to law schools as soon as your test score is available. The earlier you apply, the more places the school is likely to have available. Most schools try to make comparable decisions throughout the admission season, even those that practice rolling admission. Still, it is disadvantageous to be one of the last applicants to complete a file. Furthermore, the more decisions you receive from law schools early in the process, the better able you will be to make your own decisions, such as whether to apply to more law schools or whether to accept a particular school's offer.

Applying to More Than One School

Last year, 53 percent of all applicants applied to five or fewer law schools. You should be sure to place your applications at schools representing a range of admission standards. Even if you have top qualifications, you should apply to a number of schools where you have an excellent chance of being admitted, based on your review of requirements and admissions standards. This is your insurance policy. If you apply to these schools in November, and are accepted to one or more in January or February, you may be disappointed but not panicked if you are later denied admission by your top choices. You should not anticipate that you are assured of acceptance at any particular law school; there are no guarantees. Each year, law schools must choose from among many qualified candidates to create a first-year school class.

The Preliminary Review of an Application

Applicants whose qualifications more than fulfill the school's admission standards are usually accepted by an admission committee during the first round of decisions. Candidates whose credentials fall below the school's standards are usually denied admission.

Many applications are not decided upon immediately. They are usually reviewed by a committee that bases its admission decision on many facets of each application (see "How Law Schools Determine Whom to Admit," page 9).

The length of time it takes the committee to review an application varies; consult the individual law schools to which you apply.

Waiting Lists

If you have strong qualifications, but you do not quite match the competition of those currently being admitted at a particular law school, you may be placed on a waiting list for possible admission at a later date. The law school will send you a letter notifying you of its final decision as early as April or as late as July.

Many schools rank students who are on the waiting list. Some law schools will tell you your rank. If a law school doesn't rank its waiting list, you might ask the admission office how many students have been placed on the waiting list.

Seat Deposits

Many law schools use seat deposits to help keep track of their new classes. For example, a typical fee might be $200, which is credited to your first-term tuition if you actually register at the school; if you don't register, the deposit may be forfeited or partially returned. A school may require a larger deposit around July 1, which is also credited to tuition. If you decline the offer of admission after you've paid your deposit, a portion of the money may be refunded, depending on the date you actually decline the offer. At some schools, you may not be refunded any of the deposit.

The official position of the Law School Admission Council is:

> Except under binding early decision plans, or for academic terms beginning in the spring or summer, no law school should require an enrollment commitment of any kind, to an offer of admission or scholarship prior to April 1. Admitted applicants who have submitted a timely financial aid application should not be required to commit to enroll by having to make a nonrefundable financial commitment until notified of financial aid awards that are within the control of the law school.

Multiple Deposit Notification

Each year, LSAC provides participating law schools with periodic reports detailing the number of applicants who have submitted seat deposits or commitments at other participating schools, along with identification of those other schools. Beginning May 15 each year, these reports also include the names and LSAC account numbers for all candidates who have deposits/commitments at multiple participating schools.

Ethical Conduct in Applying to Law School

The practice of law is an honorable, noble calling. Lawyers play an important role in society by serving both their clients' needs and the public good.

Your submission of an application for admission to law school is your first step in the process of becoming a lawyer. Now is the time, as you take this first, important step, to dedicate yourself to a personal standard for your conduct that consists of the highest levels of honesty and ethical behavior.

The legal profession requires its members to behave ethically in the practice of law at all times, in order to protect the interests of clients and the public. You must understand that those who aspire to join the legal profession will be held to the same high standards for truth, full disclosure, and accuracy that are applied to those who practice law. The legal profession has set standards for ethical conduct by lawyers. Similarly, law schools have set standards for ethical conduct by law school applicants through the Law School Admission Council (LSAC). These standards are known as the *LSAC Rules Governing Misconduct and Irregularities in the Admission Process*. Just as lawyers are required to study, understand, and comply with the ABA's ethical standards, law school applicants are expected to read, understand, and comply with LSAC's ethical standards.

If you fail to comply with LSAC's ethical standards, you may be barred from admission to law school. If you fail to disclose required information on your law school application, or if you engage in misconduct during the admission process that is discovered after you enroll in law school or start to practice law, you may face more serious sanctions. In appropriate cases, state and national bar authorities and other affected persons and institutions may also receive notification. Individual law schools and bar authorities determine what action, if any, they will take in response to a finding of misconduct or irregularity. Such action may include the closing of an admission file, revocation of an offer of admission, dismissal from law school through a school's internal disciplinary channels, or disbarment. Thus, a finding of misconduct or irregularity is a very serious matter.

Take the time, right now, to read LSAC's statement on misconduct and irregularities in the admission process presented below.

Misconduct and Irregularities in the Admission Process

The Law School Admission Council has established procedures for dealing with instances of possible candidate misconduct or irregularities on the LSAT or in the law school admission process. Misconduct or irregularity in the admission process is a serious offense with serious consequences. Intent is not an element of a finding of misconduct or irregularity. This means that an "honest mistake" is not a defense to a charge of misconduct or irregularity. Misconduct or irregularity is defined as the submission, as part of the law school admission process, including, but not limited to, regular, transfer, and visiting applications, of any information that is false, inconsistent, or misleading, or the omission of information that may result in a false or misleading conclusion, or the violation of any regulation governing the law school admission process, including any violation of LSAT test center regulations.

Examples of misconduct and irregularities include, but are not limited to:

- submission of false, inconsistent, or misleading statements or omission of information requested online or on forms as part of registering for the LSAT or using LSAC's Credential Assembly Services, or on individual law school application forms;

- submission of an altered or a nonauthentic transcript;

- submission of an application containing false, inconsistent, or misleading information;

- submission of an altered, nonauthentic, or unauthorized letter of recommendation;

- falsification of records;

- impersonation of another in taking the LSAT;

- switching of LSAT answer sheets with another;

- taking the LSAT for purposes other than applying to law school;

- copying on, or other forms of cheating on, the LSAT;

- obtaining advance access to test materials;

- theft of test materials;

- working on, marking, erasing, reading, or turning pages on sections of the LSAT during unauthorized times;

- bringing prohibited items into the test room;

- falsification of transcript information, school attendance, honors, awards, or employment;

- providing false, inconsistent, or misleading information in the admission and financial aid/scholarship application process; or

- attempt at any of the above.

A charge of misconduct or irregularity may be made prior to a candidate's admission to law school, after matriculation at a law school, or after admission to practice.

When alleged misconduct or irregularity brings into question the validity of the LSAC data about a candidate, the school may be notified of possible data error, and transmission of LSAT scores and academic summary reports will be withheld until the matter has been resolved by the Law School Admission Council's Misconduct and Irregularities in the Admission Process Subcommittee. The Council will investigate all instances of alleged misconduct or irregularities in the admission process in accordance with the *LSAC Rules Governing Misconduct and Irregularities in the Admission Process*. A subcommittee representative will determine whether misconduct or an irregularity has occurred. If the subcommittee representative determines that a preponderance of the evidence shows misconduct or irregularity, then a report of the determination is sent to all law schools to which the individual has applied, subsequently applies, or has matriculated. Notation that a misconduct or irregularity report is on file is also included on LSAT and LSAC Credential Assembly Service reports to law schools. Such reports are retained indefinitely. More information regarding misconduct and irregularity procedures may be obtained by writing to: LSAC, Misconduct and Irregularities in the Admission Process Subcommittee, 662 Penn Street, Newtown, PA 18940-1802, USA.

For some people, the choice of which law school to attend is an easy one. Applicants tend to select the schools they perceive to be the most prestigious or those that offer a program of particular interest or the greatest amount of financial support. Some need to stay in a particular area perhaps because of family or job obligations and will choose nearby schools with part-time programs.

However, the majority of applicants will have to weigh a variety of personal and academic factors to come up with a list of potential schools. Once you have a list, and more than one acceptance letter, you will have to choose a school. Applicants should consider carefully the offerings of each law school before making a decision. The quality of a law school is certainly a major consideration; however, estimations of quality are very subjective. You should consider the size, composition, and background of the student body as well as the location, size, and nature of the surrounding community. Remember that the law school is going to be your home for three years. Adjusting to law school and the general attitudes of a professional school is difficult enough without the additional hardship of culture shock. Don't choose a law school in a large city if you can't bear crowds, noise, and a fast pace. And, if you've lived your entire life in an urban environment, can you face the change you will experience in a small town? You also may want to ask yourself if you are already set in an unshakable lifestyle or if you are eager for a new environment.

Other significant factors are the particular strengths or interests of the faculty, the degree to which clinical experience or classroom learning is emphasized, the nature of any special programs offered, the number and type of student organizations, the range of library holdings, and whether a school is public or private. You may wish to consider a school with a strong minority recruitment, retention, and mentoring program, or one with an active student organization for students of your particular ethnic background.

At any rate, you should actually select more than one law school where you think you could succeed.

RANKING LAW SCHOOLS

Law Schools and Reputation
Many people will tell you to apply to the schools that take students in your GPA and LSAT ranges, and then enroll in the best one that accepts you. However, law school quality can be assessed in a number of ways.

There is a hierarchy of law schools based on reputation, job placement success, strength of faculty, and the prestige of the parent institution (if there is one). In fact, a study done at one university suggests that undergraduate students perceive schools not only in terms of a hierarchy but also in terms of hierarchical clusters. In other words, certain schools are grouped together in terms of equivalent quality and prestige. Also, there are books or magazine articles that assign law schools purported numerical quality rankings.

However, according to the ABA:

> No rating of law schools beyond the simple statement of their accreditation status is attempted or advocated by the official organizations in legal education. Qualities that make one kind of school good for one student may not be as important to another. The American Bar Association and its Section of Legal Education and Admissions to the Bar have issued disclaimers of any law school rating system. Prospective law students should

consider a variety of factors in making their choice among schools.[1]

Since there is no official ranking authority, you should be cautious in using such rankings. The factors that make up a law school's reputation—strength of curriculum, faculty, career services, ability of students, quality of library facilities, and the like—don't lend themselves to quantification. Even if the rankings were more or less accurate, the school's reputation is only one factor among many for you to consider.

What's in a Name?
While going to a "name" school may mean that you will have an easier time finding your first job, it doesn't necessarily mean that you will get a better legal education than if you go to a lesser-known law school. Some schools that were at their peaks years ago are still riding on the wave of that earlier reputation. Others have greatly improved their programs and have recruited talented faculty but have not yet made a name for themselves.

Once admitted, applicants should consider a variety of factors, such as the contacts you may acquire at a school in the area where you hope to practice, the size of the school, and cost. The substantive differences between schools should be your focus when making this important choice rather than the school's reputed ranking.

The Parent University
About 90 percent of ABA-approved law schools are part of a larger university, and there may be some advantages to attending a law school that is part of a university. Such law schools may have more options for joint-degree programs or for taking a nonlaw school course or two. They also may have more academic and social activities, campus theater groups, sports teams, and everything else that comes with university life. Perhaps most important, the university can act as a support system for the law school by providing a wealth of facilities, including student housing and support for career services.

National, Regional, and Local Schools
A national school will generally have an applicant population and a student body that draws almost indistinguishably from the nation as a whole and will have many international students as well. A regional school is likely to have a population that is primarily from the geographic region of its location, though many regional schools have students from all over the country; a number of regional schools draw heavily from a particular geographical area, yet graduates may find jobs all over the country. Generally speaking, a local school is drawing primarily on applicants who either come from or want to practice in the proximate area in which the school is located. Many local law schools have excellent reputations and compete with the national schools in faculty competence, in research-supporting activities, and in resources generally. Check the school's catalog or talk with the admission and placement staff to get a clear breakdown on where their students come from and where they are finding jobs.

[1] *ABA Standards and Rules of Procedure for Approval of Law Schools 2010–2011*, Council Statement 5, p. 145, American Bar Association, Chicago, IL, 2010.

EVALUATING LAW SCHOOLS

The best advice on how to select a law school is to choose the school that is best for you. The law schools invest substantial time and effort in evaluating prospective students, and applicants should evaluate law schools with equivalent care. The following are some features to keep in mind as you systematically evaluate law schools. (Costs and other financial criteria are not included below; they are discussed in chapter 9.)

Each listing in this book provides school-specific information in the following categories as well.

Enrollment/Student Body

The academic qualifications of the student body are important to consider. It's a good idea to select a law school where you will be challenged by your classmates. Use the applicant profile grids in this book to check the LSAT scores and GPAs for the previous year's entering class. Try to select a school where your averages will not be significantly different from those of your fellow law students. Because of the important role of student participation in law school classes, your legal education might not be as rewarding as it could be if you are not challenged by your classmates.

You might also inquire about the diversity of the student body. Are a majority of the students the same age, race, sex, and so on? Remember, differences among students will expose you to various points of view; this will be an important aspect of your law school education.

Find out how many students are in a typical class. Much of the learning in law school depends on the quality of class discussion. Small classes provide essential interaction; large classes (and the Socratic method) provide diversity, challenge, and a good mix of reactions, opinions, and criticism.

It is also important to find out the total number of students enrolled at the school. Not surprisingly, the larger law schools tend to offer a larger selection of courses. Of course, more doesn't always mean better, and no one student has time to take all the courses offered at a large school. However, if you think you want to sample a wide range of courses, you are apt to have more opportunity to do so at a law school with a large faculty.

Part of the law school learning experience takes place after class with fellow students and with members of the faculty. Check to see whether faculty and students are on campus for a substantial part of the day.

Larger schools may also offer more extracurricular programs, greater student services, and a larger library. However, faculties and administrators at smaller schools may be able to give students more attention, and students at smaller schools may experience greater camaraderie. The size of a school is a personal consideration. Some students thrive in large schools; others prefer a smaller student community. Ask yourself which kind of student you are.

Faculty

You will undoubtedly want to assess the faculties of the law schools you are considering. School catalogs and websites will give you some idea of the backgrounds of the full-time faculty—what specialties they have, what they have published, and their public service activities. If the catalog tells you only where degrees were earned, ask for more information. You may also want to check the latest edition of the Association of American Law Schools' *Directory of Law Teachers*, which is available at law school libraries. It may help you to know that some members of the faculty have interests similar to your own.

Is the faculty relatively diverse with respect to race, ethnic background, gender, degrees in other fields, and breadth of experience? A faculty with diverse backgrounds will have various points of view and experiences. This diversity will enrich your legal education, broaden your own point of view, and help prepare you for the variety of clients you will work with after law school.

How many full-time professors teach how many students—that is, what is the faculty-to-student ratio?

Although some of the most prestigious law schools are famous for their large sections in the introductory courses, they also provide smaller classes, clinics, simulations, and seminars in advanced subjects. According to the *ABA Standards and Rules of Procedure for Approval of Law Schools*, it is not favorable to have a full-time student-to-full-time faculty ratio of 30 to 1, or greater. Some schools may be especially attractive to some students because of their small faculty-to-student ratio.

Are some of the teachers recognized as authorities in their respective fields through their writings and professional activities? Law school catalogs and websites vary widely regarding information about faculty. Some merely list each faculty member's name along with schools attended and degrees earned. Others may provide details about publications, professional activities, and noteworthy achievements, particularly when an individual is an authority in his or her field.

Are there visiting professors, distinguished lecturers and visitors, symposiums, and the like at the schools you are considering? Law school lectureship programs are a good means of presenting the knowledge and views of academics outside of the particular law school you attend.

The Library and Other Physical Facilities

Chances are you will spend a good deal of time in the law library, so be sure to investigate the library and all that it has to offer. There are several factors to consider when assessing a law school library: the quality of the research resources, ease of access to both print and electronic resources, staff, facilities, and hours of operation. It is also good to determine if the library participates in regional or local networks for information retrieval and interlibrary loan.

Knowing that a library has a volume count of 250,000 or 2.5 million by itself does not provide good information about the quality of the library's collection, so it is vital to look at other factors. All ABA-approved law schools must maintain a library that has the research materials considered essential for the study of law; this includes both primary and secondary sources. Determine how many copies of these essential materials are available and if they are also available in an electronic format. Look to see if the library has any special collections or other important historical materials. If you plan to focus on a particular legal area, be sure to inquire about the library's resources on that topic. Find out all of the electronic resources to which the library subscribes (look beyond Westlaw and LexisNexis) and see if it is possible to access them remotely from off campus. If the law school is affiliated with a university, explore the print and electronic resources of the other campus libraries for possible cross-disciplinary research.

Reference librarians and other professional librarians serve a vital role in the law library. Consider how many professional librarians work in the library and what percentage of librarians have a law degree as well as a library and information science degree. Are there a sufficient number of reference librarians for the number of students and faculty being served? Do the reference librarians offer courses and workshops in legal research techniques, and—if so—how many or how often? Is the library staff helpful? Law schools with evening or part-time programs should make professional reference librarians available in the evenings and on weekends, so be sure to look at the reference desk hours. Also, determine if it is possible to contact the library staff via e-mail or real-time chat.

Since you will need to spend much of your time in the library, make sure its hours will accommodate whatever schedule you might have. While it is not necessary for a library to be open around the clock, it should be open before classes begin each day and remain open well into the night and weekends. Consider if there is a designated area in the library or law school to accommodate 24-hour study after the library closes.

Be sure the library has an adequate number of comfortable seats with at least enough carrels to accommodate a reasonable number of students at any given time. Either in the library or elsewhere in the law building, there should be suitable space for group study and other forms of collaborative work. Does the library have a variety of seating configurations so that students can find a comfortable spot to engage in intense study and research for long periods of time? In addition, consider if there is a food facility within the library, law school, or on campus that maintains generous hours throughout the day, evenings, and weekends.

Access to technology should be available not only in the library, but throughout the law school building and the university. Robust wireless connectivity is essential for efficient research and communication between students and professors, so ask about the quality of the wireless network. Although computer labs are no longer as vital to law students given the proliferation of laptops and netbooks, it may be helpful to determine if there is a computer lab in the library or elsewhere in the law school and whether there is a dedicated information technology department to handle law student technology needs. The information technology department should maintain extensive hours, similar to those of the law library, so that students may conveniently have their technology questions answered.

Curriculum

The range and quality of academic programs is one of the most important factors to consider when choosing a law school.

Almost all law schools follow the traditional first-year core curriculum of civil procedure, criminal law, contracts, legal research and writing, legal methods, torts, constitutional law, and property (see chapter 2). Do not assume that all law schools have programs that suit your personal needs and special interests. If you don't have any specific interests in mind—and many beginning students don't—try to make sure the school offers a wide range of electives so that you will have many options. A thorough grounding in basic legal theory will enable you to apply the principles learned to any area of law to which they pertain.

In fact, you shouldn't overemphasize your search for specialties; most law students are not specialists when they graduate, nor do they need to be. Generally speaking, new lawyers begin to find their specialties only in the second to fifth years of their careers. A well-rounded legal education is the best preparation for almost any career path you take. The schools' individual websites and the descriptions in this book will tell you a good deal about academic programs. You may also wish to ask school representatives questions such as: Does the school offer a variety of courses, or is it especially strong in certain areas; what sizes are the classes; are seminars and small-group classroom experiences available; and are there ample opportunities for developing writing, researching, and drafting skills?

Beyond the content of law school courses, other academic program considerations may be of interest to you as a prospective law student.

Special Programs and Academic Activities

Joint-Degree Programs
Joint-degree programs allow you to pursue law school and graduate degrees simultaneously. Almost every combination is available at some institutions; additionally, many law schools allow you to create your own joint-degree program, even if no such formal program is in place. Among the more popular degrees are the JD/MBA and the JD/MA in such areas as economics or political science. For details, check the individual school listings in this book or check the law school's recruitment materials.

Master of Laws (LLM) and Special-Degree Programs
Many law schools offer advanced degrees that allow students to take graduate-level law courses. The LLM degree is quite common and usually is tailored to individual interests. Some schools offer master of laws degrees with particular concentrations, such as a master of laws in taxation and master of comparative law. Students may enroll in LLM programs only after having received the JD degree.

A few schools also offer very specific, special-degree programs. Some of these specialties include a Doctorate in Civil Law, Doctor of Juridical Science, and Doctor of Jurisprudence and Social Policy. Schools also may offer certificate (or otherwise-designated) programs. Finding out what types of advanced degrees a law school offers may help you determine the emphases of the school. (See appendix B for a listing of post-JD programs.)

Part-Time and Evening Programs
Part-time programs may be offered either in the evening or the day. For the last five years, approximately 10 percent of first-year law students have enrolled in law school part time. The conventional wisdom is that if you are financially able to attend law school full time, you ought to do so.

Part-time programs generally take four years to complete instead of three years. While fewer than half of law schools offer part-time programs, if you have economic constraints that make attending a full-time program difficult, then a part-time program offers the opportunity to study law while you are working.

Clinical Programs
Many law schools offer students authentic experiences as lawyers by involving them with clients. The best clinical programs involve students in actual legal situations, simulations of such situations, or a combination of both, either at the school itself or in the community. Clinical programs at some schools offer a team-teaching approach; practical, professional skills are taught along with traditional classroom theory. In this manner, faculty can advise and work closely with students.

Moot Court Competitions
Schools that provide opportunities for students to rehearse trial and appellate advocacy in trial team and moot court competitions help them become adept at using interviewing, counseling, research, advocacy, and negotiation skills.

Student Journals
Most law schools have a law review—a journal of scholarly articles and commentaries on the law—and other student-edited scholarly journals. Writing for the journals of a school can be important to both your legal education and your career in law. Thus, evaluating the journals at a particular law school may be worthwhile when trying to choose the right school to attend.

Traditionally, student journal editors are chosen on the basis of academic standing, but writing ability, regardless of class rank, may also be a criterion. Today, a growing number of schools select journal editors by holding a competition in which students submit a previously assigned writing sample to the current editorial board. If you are on a journal, employers may assume you are either one of the brightest in your class, or an outstanding writer—or both.

If possible, check the journals of the schools you are considering. The character of the journal may be a reflection of the character of the institution that supports it.

Order of the Coif

Many law schools have a chapter of the Order of the Coif, a national honor society for outstanding students. Students are elected to Coif on the basis of scholarship and character. Check to see if the schools you are considering include such a chapter.

Academic Support Programs

Programs for students who need or who are expected to need assistance with legal analysis and writing are offered by most law schools. Students are invited to participate in these programs on the basis of either their entering credentials or their actual law school performance. This assistance may be offered in the summer prior to beginning law school, during the academic year, or both. The aim of academic support programs is to ensure that students have an equal opportunity to compete in law school. For further information about academic assistance programs, consult the admission office at the law school.

Student Organizations

You can also tell something about a law school's intellectual resources and its students by the number and range of student associations and organizations sponsored on campus. Many schools have chapters of the ABA Law Student Division; a student bar association; associations for minority groups, such as the Asian, Black, Hispanic, and Native American law student associations; and associations based on religious affiliations. Some, but not all, schools sponsor an environmental law society, a gay and lesbian law student society, a legal assistance society, a postconviction assistance project, a civil liberties group, a Federalist Society, a volunteer income-tax assistance program, a law student spouses' club, an international law society, a law and technology society, or a client-counseling society. Determine which associations are important to you and check individual law school catalogs to see which law schools offer what you need.

Career Services and Employment

One of the tests of a good law school is the effort the institution makes to help its students and graduates understand their career options and find satisfying employment. Planning a career in law requires students to integrate their legal education and personal goals in the context of the employment marketplace. Some students begin law school with a clear idea of how they expect to use their legal education (although they may change their minds along the way). Others are uncertain, or see a number of tempting possibilities. The career services office, faculty, and alumni of the school are valuable resources in the process of understanding and selecting among the many opportunities available to lawyers.

The first role of the career services office is to educate students about career opportunities in all sectors, including government and public service, law firms of all sizes and specialties, corporations, and so forth. To accomplish such a task, a law school may arrange panel presentations, meetings with practicing lawyers in different fields, and a library of career information materials. Career services professionals also collect and distribute vital information and resources; teach students job-search strategies, such as effective interviewing skills and employment research; and discuss students' individual interests, options, and presentation.

In performing all of these tasks, the career services office becomes a major marketing and outreach program for its law school and a valuable resource for both law students and graduates as they chart their career paths. One of the most visible career services provided by many law schools is the opportunity to interview with employers on campus for summer and full-time jobs. Ideally, the recruiters should represent a broad range of legal options (small and large firms, government agencies, public interest groups, corporate law departments) and sufficient geographic diversity to meet your needs. Be aware that the number of recruiters at the law school does not necessarily reflect the range of options open to students.

In most schools, only a small percentage of the class gets jobs through on-campus interviewing. Therefore, it is important to investigate the additional support provided by the career services staff and the experiences of the school's students and graduates in finding jobs.

Career services offices are concerned about all students, not just those at the top of the class rankings. Most spend a great deal of time and effort working with students individually and marketing the school to potential employers in order to increase students' options. Here are some questions you may want to ask about a school's career services:

- What programs does the school offer to introduce students to career options? Do they seem interesting, relevant, and timely?

- Are the career-counseling professionals accessible, respected, well-qualified, and supportive?

- Are the school's faculty and graduates involved in educating students about their career options?

- What types of employers, and how many, recruit on campus each year? What are the average number of interviews and offers per student? What percentage of students obtain jobs through the on-campus interviewing process?

- What positions have graduates taken in recent years? What jobs do students take during the summers? In what locales do students and graduates work? Are these employment profiles changing?

- What are the average or median salaries for the school's graduates?

- What percentage of students have accepted positions by graduation; within six months of graduation?

- Does the school offer career counseling and information for its graduates?

Pro Bono Programs

Many law schools have programs that offer students the opportunity to put their classroom instruction to work by offering services to the community at no charge. These programs often concentrate on helping indigent and marginalized populations. The programs vary in scope and style, but you should inquire at the law schools to which you are applying about their particular programs.

TRANSFERRING TO ANOTHER LAW SCHOOL

After starting law school, some law students seek to transfer to another law school. This occurs frequently enough to warrant advice and information. There are many reasons that law students seek to transfer, including financial reasons, job relocation of a spouse or partner, or to be closer to family. Occasionally law students will seek a transfer to another law school that they perceive as having a higher status or ranking.

There are several factors that should be taken into account when considering a decision to transfer to another law school and, frequently, a student contemplating transfer should obtain relevant information concerning the consequences of a transfer. First, many of the strongest and most sustaining relationships between lawyers occur during their first year of law school and these relationships last throughout the law student's career. Students often comment on the loss of community and close friendships they made in their first year when they transfer to another law school. Second, students transferring to another law school are often not eligible for scholarships at the new law school. This factor may be significant for students who are considering forgoing a scholarship award at their home law school when they transfer. Third, many law school law reviews, journals, and moot court programs do not permit transfer students to be considered for membership on the law review and moot court teams until after a year at the new law school. This may preclude transferring law students from being considered for law review at all or for selection for the editorial board of the law review, or for selection to a moot court team. Fourth, in many schools, course selection for the fall will already have been completed by the time the student's transfer application is accepted. As a result, there may be limited access to courses that are desired or perhaps needed as prerequisites for later advanced offerings. Fifth, many law schools do not include the transferring law student's grades earned at the prior law school in the class ranking, and some do not permit transfer students to be eligible for GPA-based graduation honors such as Order of the Coif.

The decision whether to transfer schools or remain at the law school of original matriculation is a difficult one. Some law students have no or little choice but to transfer law schools for personal or hardship reasons. Other law students considering a transfer do so to "game" the law school ranking phenomenon. This may be a dangerous gamble because of the negative aspects of law school transfers. Any law student considering transferring should gather as much information as possible concerning the ramifications of the transfer.

A CAREER IN LAW FOR MINORITY GROUP MEMBERS

Despite attempts to encourage the legal profession to reflect the population it serves, members of racial and ethnic groups remain underrepresented in the legal profession. Because lawyers must serve clients from diverse populations in a variety of settings, an increase in the number of lawyers from underrepresented minority groups is crucial. Individual clients, government agencies, and large private or public organizations are all better served by lawyers who offer diverse perspectives and experiences, including those of varied racial and ethnic backgrounds.

In addition, a law career can be a rewarding and fulfilling opportunity for men and women from minority groups. Legal training provides career flexibility in a world with global professional opportunities in business, government, education, and other areas.

Support for Diversity

Individual law schools and legal organizations are committed to continued progress toward alleviating the historic shortage of minority lawyers. For example, the Law School Admission Council has dedicated resources to numerous projects designed to increase the number of minority men and women who attend law schools. Both the American Bar Association Section of Legal Education and Admissions to the Bar (the official accrediting body for law schools) and the Association of American Law Schools (the professional organization of law teachers) require law schools to undertake efforts to ensure diverse faculties and students.

Early Preparation and DiscoverLaw.org

Begin preparation early—that is the best advice for people from racial and ethnic minority groups who are interested in pursuing careers in law. There are a number of programs designed to enhance the skills of minority students. Go to DiscoverLaw.org, a primary source of information for racially and ethnically diverse students who wish to explore career opportunities in law during their first and second year of undergraduate school, or even earlier. Discovering law when beginning to explore careers makes it easier to choose a path that will lead to a law degree. High school and first- and second-year undergraduates should visit DiscoverLaw.org for more information.

Admission to Law School

Admission to law school is competitive for all candidates, including minority group members. The key is to carefully select law schools based on solid research, to pay close attention to guidelines for submitting applications, and to apply early. Law schools often have different admission requirements, so it is important to do sufficient research on specific schools, and apply strategically. Read and reread the information in this book. Also, check school websites or catalogs.

Students may choose to seek advice from prelaw advisors, academic counselors, diversity program directors, and practicing attorneys. Carefully filter advice from others. Remember that every law school is different, and the primary source of information should be the admission office of the school to which the student is interested in applying.

Let the law schools you have selected know that you are interested. Often a school will have a specific outreach program targeted to minority students, designated diversity personnel for counseling, or a minority law student organization available to assist applicants. A personal visit is always recommended.

Don't be intimidated by the law school admission process. The schools evaluate every aspect of individual applications, including personal and educational background, undergraduate record, LSAT score, and letters of recommendation and evaluations. It may be advantageous to include information on racial or ethnic identity, especially if it has shaped personal experiences or demonstrated challenges overcome in educational background. Similarly, interesting life experiences and past employment experiences also add to the value of an application.

For information on the number and percentages of specific minority students and specific minority faculty at ABA-approved law schools, consult the individual school data pages and "Key Facts for Minority Law School Applicants" in this publication. Note: New aggregate categories for reporting racial/ethnicity data have been adopted in accordance with the final guidance issued by the US Department of Education in 2007 and required for implementation by 2011. For more information, see *Federal Register,* Volume 72 (October 19, 2007), "Final Guidance on Maintaining, Collecting, and Reporting Racial and Ethnic Data to the US Department of Education," pages 59266–59279 and The Race and Ethnicity Information Center of the Department of Education's Integrated Postsecondary Education Data System (nces.ed.gov/ipeds; on the home page of this site, go to IPEDS Resources. Scroll down and click on Race/Ethnicity Information Center).

Conditional Admission Programs

Law schools recognize that sometimes the numerical qualifiers and other admission credentials do not adequately assess all candidates for admission. Some law schools have developed conditional admission programs for this purpose. Conditional admission programs typically give students a chance to demonstrate their eligibility for admission to a particular school by taking one or two courses in the summer prior to the start of classes. Students who meet the required performance criteria are offered admission to that school. Guidelines for these programs vary, and candidates should contact the individual law school offering conditional programs to find out program requirements. A list of conditional admission programs can be found in the **Future JD Students** section of LSAC.org (on the **Diversity in Law School** menu).

Being in Law School

Once students are in law school, they will encounter a challenging but manageable academic program. Most law schools offer academic assistance programs to students who may need help during law school. Depending on the individual law school, these services may include additional assistance preparing for the bar examination. Very often a variety of services and programs are in place to ensure student success, including minority law student organizations.

Most students admitted to law school, including minority students, perform successfully in law school. They gain admission to the state bar of their choice. Most importantly, they are also able to make effective use of their law degrees, whether practicing law or following other career avenues.

For more information on opportunities in law for minority men and women, go to the **Future JD Students** section of LSAC.org, select **Racial/Ethnic Diversity** on the right-hand side of the page, and click on **Helpful Links**.

	Total # students (Full-time and Part-time)	All Hispanics		American Indian/Alaska Native		Asian		Black/African American		Native Hawaiian/Pacific Islander		2 or More Races		Nonresident Alien		Unknown		Total # and % Minority Students		Total Full-time Faculty, Fall	Total Full-time Faculty, Spring	Total # and % Full-time Minority Faculty, Fall		Total # and % Full-time Minority Faculty, Spring		Total # Part-time Minority Faculty, Fall	Total # Part-time Minority Faculty, Spring
	#	#	%	#	%	#	%	#	%	#	%	#	%	#	%	#	%	#	%	#	#	#	%	#	%	#	#
ALABAMA																											
Alabama	509	7	1.4	5	1.0	12	2.4	40	7.9	0	0.0	0	0.0	0	0.0	0	0.0	64	12.6	43	40	7	14.9	6	13.6	23	19
Faulkner	354	7	2.0	2	0.6	9	2.5	24	6.8	0	0.0	0	0.0	0	0.0	4	1.1	42	11.9	19	19	3	13.0	3	13.6	2	2
Samford	491	9	1.8	5	1.0	5	1.0	28	5.7	1	0.2	11	2.2	4	0.8	47	9.6	59	12.0	23	22	5	21.7	4	18.2	2	1
ARIZONA																											
Arizona	469	35	7.5	22	4.7	40	8.5	14	3.0	0	0.0	5	1.1	9	1.9	35	7.5	116	24.7	42	41	37	84.1	37	86.0	22	34
Arizona State	614	64	10.4	33	5.4	23	3.7	14	2.3	0	0.0	11	1.8	7	1.1	40	6.5	145	23.6	51	53	7	13.2	7	12.7	8	6
Phoenix	724	89	12.3	6	0.8	40	5.5	42	5.8	0	0.0	6	0.8	5	0.7	72	9.9	183	25.3	28	27	8	25.0	6	20.0	4	2
ARKANSAS																											
Arkansas	390	17	4.4	8	2.1	11	2.8	30	7.7	0	0.0	2	0.5	0	0.0	2	0.5	68	17.4	29	29	3	10.3	3	10.3	1	0
Arkansas-Little Rock	490	22	4.5	6	1.2	14	2.9	54	11.0	0	0.0	0	0.0	12	2.4	12	2.4	96	19.6	27	27	8	26.7	8	26.7	3	5
CALIFORNIA																											
California-Berkeley	916	113	12.3	16	1.7	153	16.7	44	4.8	19	2.1	0	0.0	37	4.0	125	13.6	345	37.7	69	75	15	16.7	13	13.8	3	5
California-Davis	589	48	8.1	1	0.2	133	22.6	9	1.5	1	0.2	18	3.1	15	2.5	72	12.2	210	35.7	42	47	17	39.5	17	36.2	3	1
California-Hastings	1,248	122	9.8	8	0.6	255	20.4	32	2.6	1	0.1	136	10.9	17	1.4	163	13.1	554	44.4	70	67	19	26.8	18	26.5	19	19
California-Los Angeles	999	91	9.1	18	1.8	160	16.0	44	4.4	1	0.1	20	2.0	19	1.9	201	20.1	334	33.4	73	76	11	12.8	13	14.8	2	1
California Western	919	107	11.6	6	0.7	114	12.4	25	2.7	2	0.2	17	1.8	6	0.7	65	7.1	271	29.5	44	39	7	15.6	7	17.5	4	4
Chapman	574	30	5.2	2	0.3	73	12.7	3	0.5	1	0.2	18	3.1	2	0.3	120	20.9	127	22.1	51	46	43	84.3	41	89.1	34	45
Golden Gate	732	48	6.6	6	0.8	126	17.2	16	2.2	8	1.1	6	0.8	12	1.6	94	12.8	210	28.7	39	32	10	23.8	8	22.9	8	9
La Verne	426	70	16.4	6	1.4	55	12.9	12	2.8	0	0.0	0	0.0	9	2.1	70	16.4	143	33.6	19	18	7	36.8	7	38.9	11	4
Loyola Marymount	1,289	158	12.3	4	0.3	225	17.5	50	3.9	2	0.2	68	5.3	15	1.2	89	6.9	507	39.3	66	65	12	18.2	11	16.7	29	41
Pacific, McGeorge	1,026	59	5.8	19	1.9	147	14.3	27	2.6	0	0.0	0	0.0	16	1.6	0	0.0	252	24.6	60	58	16	25.4	17	27.9	3	5
Pepperdine	667	37	5.5	1	0.1	53	7.9	25	3.7	0	0.0	17	2.5	0	0.0	150	22.5	133	19.9	34	34	5	14.3	4	11.4	4	3
San Diego	1,007	106	10.5	3	0.3	155	15.4	12	1.2	2	0.2	42	4.2	7	0.7	30	3.0	320	31.8	57	56	11	16.7	6	9.4	7	5
San Francisco	739	81	11.0	8	1.1	103	13.9	56	7.6	3	0.4	17	2.3	12	1.6	125	16.9	268	36.3	37	35	16	43.2	14	40.0	11	9
Santa Clara	983	83	8.4	9	0.9	251	25.5	27	2.7	9	0.9	25	2.5	28	2.8	0	0.0	404	41.1	63	57	15	23.1	13	22.4	8	11
Southern California	651	67	10.3	3	0.5	132	20.3	48	7.4	0	0.0	18	2.8	9	1.4	69	10.6	268	41.2	41	42	9	20.9	12	27.9	13	17
Southwestern	1,095	154	14.1	6	0.5	143	13.1	68	6.2	3	0.3	19	1.7	5	0.5	146	13.3	393	35.9	54	55	13	22.8	13	22.8	7	9
Stanford	571	58	10.2	9	1.6	56	9.8	58	10.2	0	0.0	17	3.0	10	1.8	46	8.1	198	34.7	62	63	16	23.5	16	23.2	3	10
Thomas Jefferson	966	117	12.1	7	0.7	8	0.8	57	5.9	111	11.5	0	0.0	9	0.9	0	0.0	300	31.1	38	39	11	26.2	9	22.5	3	3

Number and Percentage of Minority Students | Number and Percentage of Minority Faculty

School	Total # students (Full-time and Part-time)	All Hispanics #	%	American Indian/Alaska Native #	%	Asian #	%	Black/African American #	%	Native Hawaiian/Pacific Islander #	%	2 or More Races #	%	Nonresident Alien #	%	Unknown #	%	Total # and % Minority Students #	%	Total Full-time Faculty, Fall #	Total Full-time Faculty, Spring #	Total # and % Full-time Minority Faculty, Fall #	%	Total # and % Full-time Minority Faculty, Spring #	%	Total # Part-time Minority Faculty, Fall #	Total # Part-time Minority Faculty, Spring #
Western State	468	70	15.0	4	0.9	70	15.0	25	5.3	2	0.4	8	1.7	2	0.4	14	3.0	179	38.2	14	14	5	31.3	3	18.8	3	7
Whittier	642	79	12.3	5	0.8	103	16.0	20	3.1	0	0.0	0	0.0	2	0.3	146	22.7	207	32.2	31	28	14	45.2	15	53.6	6	4
COLORADO																											
Colorado	546	43	7.9	21	3.8	30	5.5	16	2.9	0	0.0	0	0.0	1	0.2	0	0.0	110	20.1	40	44	10	23.3	8	17.0	1	2
Denver	960	62	6.5	21	2.2	39	4.1	25	2.6	1	0.1	7	0.7	1	0.1	52	5.4	155	16.1	57	60	13	21.0	14	21.5	6	8
CONNECTICUT																											
Connecticut	620	53	8.5	3	0.5	46	7.4	31	5.0	0	0.0	0	0.0	8	1.3	52	8.4	133	21.5	44	43	6	11.5	6	12.2	7	9
Quinnipiac	467	17	3.6	2	0.4	22	4.7	11	2.4	0	0.0	2	0.4	11	2.4	29	6.2	54	11.6	26	25	2	6.3	2	6.5	1	1
Yale	629	46	7.3	1	0.2	83	13.2	41	6.5	0	0.0	17	2.7	32	5.1	16	2.5	188	29.9	69	65	8	10.5	9	12.2	9	5
DELAWARE																											
Widener	999	26	2.6	0	0.0	55	5.5	62	6.2	1	0.1	12	1.2	1	0.1	32	3.2	156	15.6	49	42	7	14.0	5	11.6	5	5
DISTRICT OF COLUMBIA																											
American	1,503	239	15.9	9	0.6	135	9.0	153	10.2	1	0.1	26	1.7	43	2.9	35	2.3	563	37.5	98	98	22	21.2	21	20.2	57	49
Catholic	858	28	3.3	1	0.1	82	9.6	39	4.5	3	0.3	6	0.7	34	4.0	205	23.9	159	18.5	53	53	7	12.5	7	12.7	4	5
District of Columbia	316	31	9.8	1	0.3	24	7.6	97	30.7	0	0.0	6	1.9	0	0.0	17	5.4	159	50.3	20	18	12	57.1	11	57.9	13	10
George Washington	1,709	100	5.9	7	0.4	160	9.4	94	5.5	4	0.2	0	0.0	39	2.3	216	12.6	365	21.4	96	80	23	21.7	15	16.9	11	22
Georgetown	1,960	91	4.6	4	0.2	142	7.2	150	7.7	3	0.2	44	2.2	47	2.4	250	12.8	434	22.1	125	122	23	17.8	16	12.7	6	12
Howard	473	22	4.7	2	0.4	17	3.6	377	79.7	3	0.6	0	0.0	11	2.3	9	1.9	421	89.0	21	21	23	88.5	25	92.6	30	26
FLORIDA																											
Ave Maria	468	54	11.5	1	0.2	12	2.6	19	4.1	1	0.2	11	2.4	4	0.9	6	1.3	98	20.9	19	20	6	23.1	4	16.7	0	3
Barry	717	70	9.8	3	0.4	31	4.3	27	3.8	7	1.0	0	0.0	9	1.3	105	14.6	138	19.2	33	25	9	27.3	6	24.0	4	6
Florida A&M	669	71	10.6	7	1.0	28	4.2	283	42.3	0	0.0	8	1.2	0	0.0	7	1.0	397	59.3	28	25	22	62.9	25	64.1	7	8
Florida Coastal	1,742	190	10.9	18	1.0	98	5.6	198	11.4	3	0.2	5	0.3	29	1.7	132	7.6	512	29.4	66	63	12	17.4	12	18.2	10	10
Florida	1,044	104	10.0	15	1.4	68	6.5	72	6.9	0	0.0	0	0.0	7	0.7	39	3.7	259	24.8	53	60	12	21.4	10	15.9	5	5
Florida International	588	233	39.6	3	0.5	23	3.9	54	9.2	0	0.0	20	3.4	2	0.3	9	1.5	333	56.6	31	28	17	53.1	16	53.3	17	19
Florida State	779	71	9.1	2	0.3	22	2.8	59	7.6	0	0.0	0	0.0	1	0.1	18	2.3	154	19.8	47	44	7	14.9	6	13.6	3	3
Miami	1,353	206	15.2	7	0.5	51	3.8	99	7.3	1	0.1	4	0.3	26	1.9	106	7.8	368	27.2	82	69	25	30.5	21	30.4	15	28
Nova Southeastern	1,100	212	19.3	7	0.6	43	3.9	64	5.8	11	1.0	0	0.0	17	1.5	108	9.8	337	30.6	51	52	15	25.0	16	26.2	9	9
St. Thomas	733	271	37.0	3	0.4	19	2.6	49	6.7	0	0.0	31	4.2	12	1.6	0	0.0	373	50.9	28	31	5	17.9	6	18.8	10	9

	Total # students (Full-time and Part-time)	All Hispanics		American Indian/ Alaska Native		Asian		Black/ African American		Native Hawaiian/ Pacific Islander		2 or More Races		Nonresident Alien		Unknown		Total # and % Minority Students		Total Full-time Faculty, Fall	Total Full-time Faculty, Spring	Total # and % Full-time Minority Faculty, Fall		Total # and % Full-time Minority Faculty, Spring		Total # Part-time Minority Faculty, Fall	Total # Part-time Minority Faculty, Spring
	#	#	%	#	%	#	%	#	%	#	%	#	%	#	%	#	%	#	%	#	#	#	%	#	%	#	#
Stetson	1,081	92	8.5	9	0.8	30	2.8	72	6.7	0	0.0	21	1.9	7	0.6	75	6.9	224	20.7	54	50	12	20.3	10	16.9	3	1
GEORGIA																											
Atlanta's John Marshall	630	31	4.9	9	1.4	11	1.7	128	20.3	28	4.4	0	0.0	1	0.2	19	3.0	207	32.9	29	28	8	22.9	6	20.7	2	3
Emory	792	75	9.5	6	0.8	88	11.1	55	6.9	0	0.0	16	2.0	19	2.4	60	7.6	240	30.3	57	59	4	6.9	5	8.3	1	1
Georgia	703	10	1.4	3	0.4	33	4.7	78	11.1	0	0.0	13	1.8	2	0.3	66	9.4	137	19.5	47	47	6	11.8	5	9.8	0	2
Georgia State	660	12	1.8	4	0.6	53	8.0	59	8.9	0	0.0	5	0.8	0	0.0	57	8.6	133	20.2	45	48	7	12.3	7	11.9	8	22
Mercer	439	12	2.7	6	1.4	21	4.8	42	9.6	1	0.2	0	0.0	0	0.0	36	8.2	82	18.7	27	29	3	11.1	3	10.3	2	2
HAWAI'I																											
Hawai'i	353	3	0.8	1	0.3	108	30.6	4	1.1	35	9.9	92	26.1	9	2.5	27	7.6	243	68.8	31	34	14	40.0	16	43.2	13	15
IDAHO																											
Idaho	349	24	6.9	8	2.3	7	2.0	5	1.4	0	0.0	13	3.7	2	0.6	23	6.6	57	16.3	17	18	2	9.5	2	8.3	0	0
ILLINOIS																											
Chicago	634	63	9.9	1	0.2	57	9.0	37	5.8	0	0.0	20	3.2	13	2.1	74	11.7	178	28.1	57	56	17	23.9	14	20.0	2	6
Chicago-Kent	970	66	6.8	0	0.0	60	6.2	41	4.2	20	2.1	35	3.6	26	2.7	99	10.2	222	22.9	65	62	8	12.1	7	11.1	6	11
DePaul	1,056	90	8.5	5	0.5	72	6.8	65	6.2	0	0.0	0	0.0	11	1.0	112	10.6	232	22.0	54	61	9	16.1	8	12.7	44	47
Illinois	640	41	6.4	6	0.9	61	9.5	45	7.0	0	0.0	5	0.8	27	4.2	47	7.3	158	24.7	41	40	10	20.4	9	18.8	6	8
John Marshall	1,442	116	8.0	6	0.4	89	6.2	120	8.3	0	0.0	44	3.1	10	0.7	43	3.0	375	26.0	68	65	11	14.7	11	15.3	13	8
Loyola-Chicago	851	49	5.8	1	0.1	36	4.2	60	7.1	0	0.0	15	1.8	10	1.2	31	3.6	161	18.9	50	48	9	15.0	6	10.7	10	7
Northern Illinois	332	24	7.2	1	0.3	14	4.2	24	7.2	1	0.3	5	1.5	0	0.0	22	6.6	69	20.8	15	14	8	42.1	6	33.3	1	1
Northwestern	817	61	7.5	7	0.9	153	18.7	67	8.2	0	0.0	22	2.7	56	6.9	0	0.0	310	37.9	79	80	11	11.1	13	13.1	17	20
Southern Illinois	382	6	1.6	5	1.3	12	3.1	10	2.6	1	0.3	0	0.0	0	0.0	24	6.3	34	8.9	26	24	4	14.8	3	12.5	0	0
INDIANA																											
Indiana-Bloomington	646	29	4.5	0	0.0	34	5.3	54	8.4	0	0.0	0	0.0	0	0.0	20	3.1	117	18.1	55	54	6	10.2	7	12.3	0	1
Indiana-Indianapolis	918	20	2.2	7	0.8	48	5.2	66	7.2	0	0.0	0	0.0	39	4.2	0	0.0	141	15.4	38	39	5	12.2	4	9.3	6	5
Notre Dame	564	62	11.0	7	1.2	45	8.0	29	5.1	1	0.2	14	2.5	8	1.4	34	6.0	158	28.0	45	40	8	17.4	6	14.6	10	13
Valparaiso	566	42	7.4	8	1.4	26	4.6	53	9.4	0	0.0	2	0.4	4	0.7	4	0.7	131	23.1	29	30	7	20.0	6	17.6	1	2
IOWA																											
Drake	463	13	2.8	1	0.2	6	1.3	27	5.8	0	0.0	0	0.0	0	0.0	66	14.3	47	10.2	27	27	3	10.7	4	13.8	2	2
Iowa	574	30	5.2	5	0.9	40	7.0	16	2.8	0	0.0	0	0.0	13	2.3	0	0.0	91	15.9	43	41	6	13.0	6	14.0	0	0
KANSAS																											

	Total # students (Full-time and Part-time)	All Hispanics		American Indian/ Alaska Native		Asian		Black/ African American		Native Hawaiian/ Pacific Islander		2 or More Races		Nonresident Alien		Unknown		Total # and % Minority Students		Total Full-time Faculty, Fall	Total Full-time Faculty, Spring	Total # and % Full-time Minority Faculty, Fall		Total # and % Full-time Minority Faculty, Spring		Total # Part-time Minority Faculty, Fall	Total # Part-time Minority Faculty, Spring
	#	#	%	#	%	#	%	#	%	#	%	#	%	#	%	#	%	#	%	#	#	#	%	#	%	#	#
Kansas	497	27	5.4	12	2.4	24	4.8	12	2.4	0	0.0	17	3.4	20	4.0	15	3.0	92	18.5	32	31	3	8.6	4	11.8	1	1
Washburn	454	16	3.5	10	2.2	11	2.4	16	3.5	0	0.0	0	0.0	7	1.5	11	2.4	53	11.7	29	29	6	19.4	4	13.3	0	0
KENTUCKY																											
Kentucky	419	6	1.4	3	0.7	6	1.4	39	9.3	2	0.5	0	0.0	0	0.0	3	0.7	56	13.4	25	19	3	12.0	2	10.0	9	10
Louisville-Brandeis	426	13	3.1	0	0.0	9	2.1	16	3.8	0	0.0	8	1.9	3	0.7	4	0.9	46	10.8	23	22	23	88.5	23	92.0	6	9
Northern Kentucky	614	11	1.8	2	0.3	12	2.0	27	4.4	0	0.0	2	0.3	0	0.0	37	6.0	54	8.8	28	27	4	14.3	4	14.3	1	1
LOUISIANA																											
Louisiana State	633	32	5.1	8	1.3	16	2.5	49	7.7	0	0.0	6	0.9	0	0.0	38	6.0	111	17.5	31	28	6	14.6	4	11.4	1	4
Loyola-New Orleans	834	75	9.0	7	0.8	34	4.1	121	14.5	1	0.1	0	0.0	5	0.6	47	5.6	238	28.5	41	37	12	24.0	12	25.0	2	3
Southern	721	51	7.1	2	0.3	5	0.7	411	57.0	0	0.0	1	0.1	0	0.0	4	0.6	470	65.2	34	34	22	62.9	22	62.9	13	12
Tulane	770	41	5.3	7	0.9	23	3.0	54	7.0	0	0.0	8	1.0	15	1.9	48	6.2	133	17.3	45	48	4	7.5	3	5.4	2	7
MAINE																											
Maine	278	10	3.6	4	1.4	2	0.7	6	2.2	6	2.2	0	0.0	3	1.1	0	0.0	28	10.1	14	16	0	0.0	0	0.0	0	0
MARYLAND																											
Baltimore	1,083	28	2.6	1	0.1	55	5.1	79	7.3	2	0.2	8	0.7	0	0.0	99	9.1	173	16.0	49	47	12	20.7	11	19.6	4	9
Maryland	967	81	8.4	3	0.3	90	9.3	103	10.7	1	0.1	16	1.7	8	0.8	22	2.3	294	30.4	62	65	13	20.6	15	22.7	5	3
MASSACHUSETTS																											
Boston College	797	52	6.5	3	0.4	91	11.4	31	3.9	0	0.0	10	1.3	14	1.8	74	9.3	187	23.5	50	51	10	19.6	11	20.8	2	1
Boston	822	67	8.2	3	0.4	82	10.0	42	5.1	2	0.2	13	1.6	22	2.7	67	8.2	209	25.4	65	53	9	13.4	9	15.8	9	12
Harvard	1,733	137	7.9	10	0.6	87	5.0	195	11.3	130	7.5	11	0.6	9	0.5	215	12.4	570	32.9	115	119	18	12.8	19	13.1	5	1
New England	1,132	26	2.3	0	0.0	49	4.3	16	1.4	0	0.0	22	1.9	7	0.6	192	17.0	113	10.0	38	37	33	82.5	33	89.2	4	4
Northeastern	629	61	9.7	8	1.3	60	9.5	76	12.1	0	0.0	0	0.0	1	0.2	102	16.2	205	32.6	36	35	9	25.0	8	22.9	10	4
Suffolk	1,681	65	3.9	4	0.2	126	7.5	44	2.6	0	0.0	21	1.2	39	2.3	52	3.1	260	15.5	76	67	12	15.0	13	18.3	4	5
Western New England	525	19	3.6	0	0.0	16	3.0	12	2.3	0	0.0	8	1.5	13	2.5	57	10.9	55	10.5	30	30	5	13.9	5	13.9	0	1
MICHIGAN																											
Detroit Mercy	727	25	3.4	4	0.6	21	2.9	89	12.2	0	0.0	0	0.0	148	20.4	0	0.0	139	19.1	36	37	5	11.9	6	14.0	1	4
Michigan	1,134	47	4.1	5	0.4	118	10.4	32	2.8	0	0.0	44	3.9	26	2.3	90	7.9	246	21.7	87	90	16	17.4	18	18.9	2	3
Michigan State	884	30	3.4	12	1.4	25	2.8	61	6.9	1	0.1	7	0.8	60	6.8	59	6.7	136	15.4	49	43	7	13.5	6	12.5	8	9
Thomas M. Cooley	3,931	219	5.6	19	0.5	202	5.1	521	13.3	10	0.3	81	2.1	213	5.4	109	2.8	1052	26.8	99	101	12	11.9	14	13.5	20	28

	Total # students (Full-time and Part-time) #	All Hispanics #	%	American Indian/Alaska Native #	%	Asian #	%	Black/African American #	%	Native Hawiian/Pacific Islander #	%	2 or More Races #	%	Nonresident Alien #	%	Unknown #	%	Total # and % Minority Students #	%	Total Full-time Faculty, Fall #	Total Full-time Faculty, Spring #	Total # and % Full-time Minority Faculty, Fall #	%	Total # and % Full-time Minority Faculty, Spring #	%	Total # Part-time Minority Faculty, Fall #	Total # Part-time Minority Faculty, Spring #
Wayne State	612	18	2.9	5	0.8	33	5.4	41	6.7	0	0.0	0	0.0	17	2.8	59	9.6	97	15.8	33	33	4	10.5	5	13.2	1	1
MINNESOTA																											
Hamline	652	25	3.8	5	0.8	41	6.3	22	3.4	1	0.2	2	0.3	2	0.3	36	5.5	96	14.7	33	33	3	8.8	5	15.2	3	4
Minnesota	752	29	3.9	7	0.9	56	7.4	24	3.2	2	0.3	16	2.1	19	2.5	40	5.3	134	17.8	55	59	4	6.9	5	7.9	63	75
St. Thomas-Minneapolis	475	9	1.9	2	0.4	29	6.1	15	3.2	1	0.2	1	0.2	0	0.0	46	9.7	57	12.0	26	19	6	20.7	5	21.7	6	7
William Mitchell	1,013	22	2.2	12	1.2	47	4.6	24	2.4	1	0.1	7	0.7	8	0.8	172	17.0	113	11.2	34	34	4	11.8	4	11.8	84	41
MISSISSIPPI																											
Mississippi	516	11	2.1	6	1.2	4	0.8	60	11.6	0	0.0	0	0.0	2	0.4	0	0.0	81	15.7	26	28	8	25.8	9	27.3	1	1
Mississippi College	547	5	0.9	1	0.2	5	0.9	50	9.1	0	0.0	0	0.0	0	0.0	13	2.4	61	11.2	26	25	4	15.4	4	16.0	6	1
MISSOURI																											
Missouri-Columbia	446	14	3.1	1	0.2	12	2.7	28	6.3	0	0.0	6	1.3	2	0.4	17	3.8	61	13.7	28	24	4	14.3	3	12.5	4	0
Missouri-Kansas City	483	19	3.9	3	0.6	14	2.9	25	5.2	0	0.0	0	0.0	8	1.7	41	8.5	61	12.6	29	30	4	11.8	4	11.4	4	0
St. Louis	938	30	3.2	4	0.4	35	3.7	47	5.0	0	0.0	18	1.9	7	0.7	19	2.0	134	14.3	52	47	7	10.8	6	10.0	7	15
Washington University	900	16	1.8	4	0.4	101	11.2	110	12.2	0	0.0	21	2.3	72	8.0	105	11.7	252	28.0	68	71	8	11.8	7	9.9	11	7
MONTANA																											
Montana	256	6	2.3	11	4.3	3	1.2	1	0.4	0	0.0	3	1.2	1	0.4	0	0.0	24	9.4	17	15	4	21.1	4	23.5	0	1
NEBRASKA																											
Creighton	471	14	3.0	1	0.2	20	4.2	13	2.8	0	0.0	1	0.2	0	0.0	2	0.4	49	10.4	20	20	3	13.0	3	13.0	1	1
Nebraska	414	7	1.7	4	1.0	9	2.2	10	2.4	0	0.0	0	0.0	2	0.5	0	0.0	30	7.2	25	25	2	7.7	1	3.8	0	0
NEVADA																											
Nevada	475	53	11.2	10	2.1	48	10.1	32	6.7	0	0.0	0	0.0	1	0.2	27	5.7	143	30.1	25	28	5	19.2	6	19.4	1	1
NEW HAMPSHIRE																											
New Hampshire	419	21	5.0	1	0.2	45	10.7	18	4.3	0	0.0	10	2.4	17	4.1	0	0.0	95	22.7	25	22	2	6.1	1	3.4	2	2
NEW JERSEY																											
Rutgers-Camden	789	43	5.4	4	0.5	67	8.5	42	5.3	1	0.1	0	0.0	6	0.8	0	0.0	157	19.9	51	53	6	11.1	6	10.7	1	6
Rutgers-Newark	839	85	10.1	3	0.4	104	12.4	132	15.7	0	0.0	6	0.7	11	1.3	0	0.0	330	39.3	38	32	12	30.0	11	34.4	0	1
Seton Hall	1,053	58	5.5	2	0.2	90	8.5	37	3.5	0	0.0	10	0.9	5	0.5	0	0.0	197	18.7	57	53	9	15.3	10	18.2	6	9
NEW MEXICO																											
New Mexico	351	100	28.5	26	7.4	3	0.9	15	4.3	5	1.4	1	0.3	1	0.3	30	8.5	150	42.7	23	23	10	35.7	10	38.5	13	8
NEW YORK																											

Number and Percentage of Minority Students

Number and Percentage of Minority Faculty

Number and Percentage of Minority Students | Number and Percentage of Minority Faculty

	Total # students (Full-time and Part-time)	All Hispanics #	All Hispanics %	American Indian/Alaska Native #	American Indian/Alaska Native %	Asian #	Asian %	Black/African American #	Black/African American %	Native Hawaiian/Pacific Islander #	Native Hawaiian/Pacific Islander %	2 or More Races #	2 or More Races %	Nonresident Alien #	Nonresident Alien %	Unknown #	Unknown %	Total # and % Minority Students #	Total # and % Minority Students %	Total Full-time Faculty, Fall #	Total Full-time Faculty, Spring #	Total # and % Full-time Minority Faculty, Fall #	Total # and % Full-time Minority Faculty, Fall %	Total # and % Full-time Minority Faculty, Spring #	Total # and % Full-time Minority Faculty, Spring %	Total # Part-time Minority Faculty, Fall #	Total # Part-time Minority Faculty, Spring #
Albany	720	28	3.9	4	0.6	31	4.3	15	2.1	0	0.0	6	0.8	11	1.5	104	14.4	84	11.7	44	46	11	23.9	10	21.3	6	7
Brooklyn	1,461	82	5.6	1	0.1	203	13.9	56	3.8	1	0.1	34	2.3	5	0.3	25	1.7	377	25.8	63	64	5	7.4	8	11.8	7	6
Buffalo	701	24	3.4	6	0.9	29	4.1	35	5.0	1	0.1	6	0.9	21	3.0	69	9.8	101	14.4	47	46	6	11.1	5	9.4	7	68
Cardozo	1,124	79	7.0	1	0.1	96	8.5	49	4.4	9	0.8	21	1.9	26	2.3	46	4.1	255	22.7	59	58	10	16.4	10	16.7	10	7
CUNY	440	64	14.5	1	0.2	48	10.9	41	9.3	1	0.2	11	2.5	7	1.6	2	0.5	166	37.7	31	33	18	50.0	15	40.5	2	3
Columbia	1,344	77	5.7	7	0.5	223	16.6	103	7.7	1	0.1	22	1.6	117	8.7	8	0.6	433	32.2	99	100	21	19.6	22	20.6	7	13
Cornell	615	72	11.7	10	1.6	87	14.1	40	6.5	0	0.0	9	1.5	46	7.5	0	0.0	218	35.4	50	45	9	17.6	7	15.2	5	0
Fordham	1,481	142	9.6	5	0.3	123	8.3	66	4.5	0	0.0	9	0.6	40	2.7	240	16.2	345	23.3	81	82	14	17.3	16	19.5	23	15
Hofstra	1,061	62	5.8	4	0.4	118	11.1	89	8.4	0	0.0	27	2.5	49	4.6	53	5.0	300	28.3	60	63	8	13.3	11	17.5	5	15
New York Law	1,923	224	11.6	10	0.5	63	3.3	139	7.2	1	0.1	30	1.6	0	0.0	230	12.0	467	24.3	65	58	9	12.7	7	10.9	11	10
New York	1,431	103	7.2	3	0.2	145	10.1	110	7.7	0	0.0	1	0.1	52	3.6	313	21.9	362	25.3	135	120	21	13.9	18	13.5	5	7
Pace	788	41	5.2	2	0.3	44	5.6	28	3.6	0	0.0	11	1.4	7	0.9	190	24.1	126	16.0	44	45	7	14.9	7	14.9	1	5
St. John's	940	88	9.4	0	0.0	39	4.1	53	5.6	10	1.1	41	4.4	12	1.3	104	11.1	231	24.6	47	44	8	16.0	9	18.8	4	7
Syracuse	638	28	4.4	1	0.2	63	9.9	19	3.0	1	0.2	16	2.5	15	2.4	81	12.7	128	20.1	45	41	11	18.3	11	19.0	1	3
Touro	828	60	7.2	0	0.0	59	7.1	76	9.2	2	0.2	0	0.0	13	1.6	42	5.1	197	23.8	38	36	4	9.5	3	7.7	5	8
NORTH CAROLINA																											
Campbell	450	15	3.3	0	0.0	9	2.0	15	3.3	0	0.0	0	0.0	1	0.2	0	0.0	39	8.7	23	23	3	13.0	4	16.7	1	2
Charlotte	812	37	4.6	13	1.6	16	2.0	103	12.7	0	0.0	0	0.0	0	0.0	28	3.4	169	20.8	34	25	11	31.4	9	34.6	29	29
Duke	681	54	7.9	2	0.3	60	8.8	45	6.6	0	0.0	4	0.6	14	2.1	53	7.8	165	24.2	59	54	11	.15.7	6	9.5	4	3
Elon	342	6	1.8	3	0.9	10	2.9	24	7.0	0	0.0	0	0.0	0	0.0	19	5.6	43	12.6	17	16	4	20.0	3	17.6	1	3
North Carolina	778	77	9.9	14	1.8	24	3.1	57	7.3	12	1.5	26	3.3	11	1.4	76	9.8	210	27.0	42	42	5	11.9	7	16.7	3	6
North Carolina Central	602	11	1.8	5	0.8	18	3.0	294	48.8	0	0.0	2	0.3	21	3.5	17	2.8	330	54.8	34	34	26	61.9	24	58.5	10	11
Wake Forest	487	21	4.3	6	1.2	14	2.9	32	6.6	0	0.0	8	1.6	0	0.0	35	7.2	81	16.6	44	42	9	18.8	8	16.7	0	2
NORTH DAKOTA																											
North Dakota	256	9	3.5	10	3.9	6	2.3	8	3.1	0	0.0	2	0.8	24	9.4	25	9.8	35	13.7	11	10	2	16.7	2	18.2	0	0
OHIO																											
Akron	506	19	3.8	2	0.4	18	3.6	31	6.1	0	0.0	0	0.0	0	0.0	43	8.5	70	13.8	28	25	3	9.1	3	10.3	1	2
Capital	656	11	1.7	0	0.0	13	2.0	47	7.2	0	0.0	4	0.6	8	1.2	30	4.6	75	11.4	30	27	4	11.4	3	10.3	3	5
Case Western	627	12	1.9	2	0.3	49	7.8	24	3.8	0	0.0	5	0.8	37	5.9	0	0.0	92	14.7	39	40	2	4.3	2	4.2	3	2

	Total # students (Full-time and Part-time) #	All Hispanics #	All Hispanics %	American Indian/Alaska Native #	American Indian/Alaska Native %	Asian #	Asian %	Black/African American #	Black/African American %	Native Hawaiian/Pacific Islander #	Native Hawaiian/Pacific Islander %	2 or More Races #	2 or More Races %	Nonresident Alien #	Nonresident Alien %	Unknown #	Unknown %	Total # and % Minority Students #	Total # and % Minority Students %	Total Full-time Faculty, Fall #	Total Full-time Faculty, Spring #	Total # and % Full-time Minority Faculty, Fall #	Total # and % Full-time Minority Faculty, Fall %	Total # and % Full-time Minority Faculty, Spring #	Total # and % Full-time Minority Faculty, Spring %	Total # Part-time Minority Faculty, Fall #	Total # Part-time Minority Faculty, Spring #
Cincinnati	408	11	2.7	0	0.0	18	4.4	25	6.1	1	0.2	7	1.7	3	0.7	0	0.0	62	15.2	28	31	6	20.7	5	15.6	1	1
Cleveland State	610	13	2.1	1	0.2	10	1.6	58	9.5	0	0.0	0	0.0	7	1.1	1	0.2	82	13.4	39	37	6	15.4	6	16.2	2	4
Dayton	524	11	2.1	1	0.2	11	2.1	33	6.3	1	0.2	5	1.0	6	1.1	0	0.0	62	11.8	25	23	4	14.8	5	20.0	2	2
Ohio Northern	313	3	1.0	2	0.6	4	1.3	23	7.3	0	0.0	0	0.0	9	2.9	16	5.1	32	10.2	22	21	4	18.2	5	23.8	0	0
Ohio State	693	36	5.2	5	0.7	43	6.2	48	6.9	1	0.1	8	1.2	16	2.3	44	6.3	141	20.3	33	40	5	11.9	9	18.4	1	3
Toledo	460	14	3.0	2	0.4	15	3.3	18	3.9	0	0.0	0	0.0	8	1.7	98	21.3	49	10.7	23	27	2	7.7	1	3.7	0	1
OKLAHOMA																											
Oklahoma	537	21	3.9	43	8.0	28	5.2	20	3.7	0	0.0	1	0.2	1	0.2	10	1.9	113	21.0	34	32	6	17.6	3	9.1	2	2
Oklahoma City	636	33	5.2	34	5.3	18	2.8	21	3.3	0	0.0	18	2.8	6	0.9	4	0.6	124	19.5	31	28	4	11.8	4	12.9	4	2
Tulsa	406	14	3.4	36	8.9	8	2.0	10	2.5	0	0.0	12	3.0	1	0.2	45	11.1	80	19.7	28	28	6	21.4	7	25.0	3	3
OREGON																											
Lewis & Clark	741	44	5.9	22	3.0	69	9.3	22	3.0	1	0.1	0	0.0	17	2.3	41	5.5	158	21.3	53	50	9	17.0	7	13.7	9	10
Oregon	526	16	3.0	7	1.3	39	7.4	15	2.9	1	0.2	12	2.3	9	1.7	24	4.6	90	17.1	29	27	9	25.7	5	16.1	1	3
Willamette	429	27	6.3	7	1.6	34	7.9	8	1.9	1	0.2	0	0.0	3	0.7	30	7.0	77	17.9	24	25	6	21.4	6	20.7	1	2
PENNSYLVANIA																											
Duquesne	688	9	1.3	2	0.3	8	1.2	20	2.9	0	0.0	0	0.0	0	0.0	0	0.0	39	5.7	25	25	4	15.4	4	15.4	3	3
Earle Mack, Drexel	440	23	5.2	2	0.5	23	5.2	32	7.3	0	0.0	0	0.0	3	0.7	24	5.5	80	18.2	24	21	8	29.6	9	34.6	5	6
Penn State	618	19	3.1	0	0.0	34	5.5	25	4.0	0	0.0	10	1.6	12	1.9	29	4.7	88	14.2	54	52	9	15.8	11	19.6	2	1
Pennsylvania	802	37	4.6	0	0.0	113	14.1	60	7.5	0	0.0	33	4.1	25	3.1	26	3.2	243	30.3	67	62	12	16.0	13	18.1	4	6
Pittsburgh	739	22	3.0	2	0.3	48	6.5	50	6.8	0	0.0	3	0.4	0	0.0	134	18.1	125	16.9	45	41	10	21.3	7	16.7	7	5
Temple	983	74	7.5	9	0.9	85	8.6	71	7.2	0	0.0	7	0.7	4	0.4	10	1.0	246	25.0	61	58	16	25.4	15	25.4	13	13
Villanova	765	65	8.5	7	0.9	57	7.5	17	2.2	0	0.0	0	0.0	4	0.5	13	1.7	146	19.1	38	34	4	8.2	3	6.7	5	6
Widener	453	17	3.8	1	0.2	20	4.4	12	2.6	0	0.0	6	1.3	1	0.2	8	1.8	56	12.4	24	22	5	20.0	4	16.7	0	0
PUERTO RICO																											
Inter American	866	866	100.0	0	0.0	0	0.0	0	0.0	0	0.0	0	0.0	0	0.0	0	0.0	866	100.0	23	21	24	100.0	22	100.0	44	47
Pontifical Catholic	834	833	99.9	0	0.0	0	0.0	0	0.0	0	0.0	0	0.0	0	0.0	0	0.0	833	99.9	17	16	21	100.0	20	100.0	25	27
Puerto Rico	737	0	0.0	0	0.0	0	0.0	0	0.0	0	0.0	0	0.0	193	26.2	544	73.8	0	0.0	24	24	27	96.4	25	89.3	58	57
RHODE ISLAND																											
Roger Williams	540	14	2.6	2	0.4	14	2.6	15	2.8	0	0.0	2	0.4	3	0.6	61	11.3	47	8.7	26	29	5	18.5	4	13.3	3	2
SOUTH CAROLINA																											

	Total # students (Full-time and Part-time)	All Hispanics		American Indian/ Alaska Native		Asian		Black/ African American		Native Hawaiian/ Pacific Islander		2 or More Races		Nonresident Alien		Unknown		Total # and % Minority Students		Total Full-time Faculty, Fall	Total Full-time Faculty, Spring	Total # and % Full-time Minority Faculty, Fall		Total # and % Full-time Minority Faculty, Spring		Total # Part-time Minority Faculty, Fall	Total # Part-time Minority Faculty, Spring
	#	#	%	#	%	#	%	#	%	#	%	#	%	#	%	#	%	#	%	#	#	#	%	#	%	#	#
Charleston	702	9	1.3	5	0.7	7	1.0	48	6.8	1	0.1	0	0.0	0	0.0	18	2.6	70	10.0	29	29	5	16.1	5	16.1	0	0
South Carolina	682	17	2.5	3	0.4	12	1.8	45	6.6	0	0.0	14	2.1	0	0.0	4	0.6	91	13.3	35	36	6	16.7	5	13.5	2	0
SOUTH DAKOTA																											
South Dakota	205	3	1.5	7	3.4	1	0.5	6	2.9	0	0.0	3	1.5	0	0.0	1	0.5	20	9.8	13	13	1	7.1	0	0.0	0	1
TENNESSEE																											
Memphis	432	8	1.9	4	0.9	8	1.9	35	8.1	0	0.0	0	0.0	0	0.0	14	3.2	55	12.7	18	20	18	100.0	20	95.2	9	5
Tennessee	482	26	5.4	2	0.4	25	5.2	56	11.6	0	0.0	13	2.7	3	0.6	4	0.8	122	25.3	27	25	3	10.0	2	7.7	0	0
Vanderbilt	586	28	4.8	6	1.0	24	4.1	54	9.2	0	0.0	0	0.0	21	3.6	40	6.8	112	19.1	36	34	8	22.2	9	26.5	2	2
TEXAS																											
Baylor	476	39	8.2	7	1.5	34	7.1	9	1.9	3	0.6	8	1.7	5	1.1	4	0.8	100	21.0	27	25	4	14.8	4	15.4	1	1
Houston	877	83	9.5	8	0.9	99	11.3	64	7.3	0	0.0	0	0.0	15	1.7	10	1.1	254	29.0	64	66	10	13.2	10	12.5	53	70
St. Mary's	828	214	25.8	7	0.8	25	3.0	31	3.7	0	0.0	6	0.7	0	0.0	0	0.0	283	34.2	28	31	8	22.2	8	21.1	6	8
SMU Dedman	887	78	8.8	17	1.9	64	7.2	47	5.3	0	0.0	4	0.5	3	0.3	59	6.7	210	23.7	41	41	10	21.7	11	24.4	13	9
South Texas	1,305	175	13.4	7	0.5	113	8.7	45	3.4	3	0.2	35	2.7	4	0.3	0	0.0	378	29.0	44	49	6	13.6	4	8.2	6	4
Texas	1,154	183	15.9	5	0.4	62	5.4	56	4.9	1	0.1	13	1.1	13	1.1	105	9.1	320	27.7	84	89	15	14.6	15	13.9	9	19
Texas Southern	571	159	27.8	3	0.5	41	7.2	254	44.5	0	0.0	2	0.4	10	1.8	0	0.0	459	80.4	30	34	23	76.7	27	77.1	11	22
Texas Tech	671	101	15.1	4	0.6	30	4.5	20	3.0	0	0.0	2	0.3	4	0.6	1	0.1	157	23.4	35	38	6	17.1	5	13.2	1	1
Texas Wesleyan	764	60	7.9	6	0.8	40	5.2	43	5.6	1	0.1	10	1.3	0	0.0	24	3.1	160	20.9	23	22	4	13.3	4	13.8	3	4
UTAH																											
Brigham Young	444	25	5.6	3	0.7	20	4.5	6	1.4	16	3.6	0	0.0	4	0.9	0	0.0	70	15.8	19	22	3	15.8	2	9.1	2	2
Utah	402	25	6.2	3	0.7	14	3.5	4	1.0	2	0.5	0	0.0	2	0.5	32	8.0	48	11.9	34	40	6	17.6	6	15.0	0	0
VERMONT																											
Vermont	607	14	2.3	2	0.3	18	3.0	14	2.3	0	0.0	10	1.6	5	0.8	65	10.7	58	9.6	34	35	8	14.5	6	11.5	1	1
VIRGINIA																											
Appalachian	313	9	2.9	2	0.6	7	2.2	7	2.2	0	0.0	12	3.8	1	0.3	14	4.5	37	11.8	16	18	2	12.5	3	16.7	0	0
George Mason	731	22	3.0	6	0.8	75	10.3	9	1.2	0	0.0	3	0.4	14	1.9	7	1.0	115	15.7	36	38	7	18.4	7	17.5	3	7
Liberty	313	12	3.8	1	0.3	13	4.2	16	5.1	0	0.0	17	5.4	3	1.0	1	0.3	59	18.8	18	17	6	31.6	5	27.8	1	7
Regent	428	16	3.7	12	2.8	24	5.6	23	5.4	0	0.0	0	0.0	3	0.7	16	3.7	75	17.5	21	21	5	20.0	4	16.7	2	0
Richmond	460	4	0.9	5	1.1	29	6.3	42	9.1	1	0.2	0	0.0	6	1.3	1	0.2	81	17.6	30	24	3	8.3	3	9.7	3	0

	Total # students (Full-time and Part-time)	All Hispanics		American Indian/Alaska Native		Asian		Black/African American		Native Hawaiian/Pacific Islander		2 or More Races		Nonresident Alien		Unknown		Total # and % Minority Students		Total Full-time Faculty, Fall	Total Full-time Faculty, Spring	Total # and % Full-time Minority Faculty, Fall		Total # and % Full-time Minority Faculty, Spring		Total # Part-time Minority Faculty, Fall	Total # Part-time Minority Faculty, Spring
	#	#	%	#	%	#	%	#	%	#	%	#	%	#	%	#	%	#	%	#	#	#	%	#	%	#	#
Virginia	1,106	56	5.1	9	0.8	102	9.2	68	6.1	0	0.0	19	1.7	11	1.0	146	13.2	254	23.0	78	77	9	11.4	8	10.3	5	12
Washington and Lee	407	13	3.2	1	0.2	17	4.2	26	6.4	1	0.2	9	2.2	8	2.0	21	5.2	67	16.5	35	35	3	8.6	6	16.7	0	1
William & Mary	628	11	1.8	2	0.3	22	3.5	81	12.9	1	0.2	5	0.8	3	0.5	92	14.6	122	19.4	39	34	7	17.9	5	14.7	4	3
WASHINGTON																											
Gonzaga	507	16	3.2	10	2.0	5	1.0	1	0.2	18	3.6	7	1.4	0	0.0	86	17.0	57	11.2	28	29	4	13.8	2	6.7	0	0
Seattle	1,011	60	5.9	10	1.0	95	9.4	32	3.2	17	1.7	37	3.7	9	0.9	36	3.6	251	24.8	65	60	16	24.2	15	24.6	3	9
Washington	550	27	4.9	15	2.7	67	12.2	11	2.0	0	0.0	6	1.1	16	2.9	58	10.5	126	22.9	50	44	13	24.1	12	25.0	2	11
WEST VIRGINIA																											
West Virginia	416	3	0.7	3	0.7	6	1.4	24	5.8	0	0.0	0	0.0	0	0.0	0	0.0	36	8.7	32	30	6	18.2	4	13.3	0	0
WISCONSIN																											
Marquette	758	45	5.9	6	0.8	25	3.3	37	4.9	0	0.0	0	0.0	2	0.3	2	0.3	113	14.9	33	35	5	12.8	5	12.2	3	5
Wisconsin	804	56	7.0	18	2.2	44	5.5	56	7.0	0	0.0	5	0.6	22	2.7	47	5.8	179	22.3	54	45	14	21.5	12	21.8	15	32
WYOMING																											
Wyoming	231	5	2.2	1	0.4	7	3.0	1	0.4	0	0.0	2	0.9	0	0.0	41	17.7	16	6.9	19	17	3	14.3	2	11.1	0	0

The Role of the ABA Section of Legal Education and Admissions to the Bar

Under Title 34, Chapter VI, §602 of the Code of Federal Regulations, the Council and the Accreditation Committee of the ABA Section of Legal Education and Admissions to the Bar are recognized by the United States Department of Education (DOE) as the accrediting agency for programs that lead to the JD degree. In this function, the Council and the Section are separate and independent from the ABA, as required by DOE regulations.

The Council of the Section promulgates the Standards and Rules of Procedure for Approval of Law Schools with which law schools must comply in order to be ABA-approved. The Standards establish requirements for providing a sound program of legal education. The law school approval process established by the Council is designed to provide a careful and comprehensive evaluation of a law school and its compliance with the Standards.

The Council is comprised of 21 voting members, no more than 10 of whom may be law school deans or faculty members. Other members of the Council include judges, practicing attorneys, one law student, and at least three public members. By tradition, the Chair rotates among a judge, an academic, and a practicing lawyer.

To assist in its accreditation function, the Council has created three Standing Committees, with a similar mix of membership. The Accreditation Committee (19 members) assists the Council in evaluating schools seeking provisional or full approval and monitoring approved schools. It meets five times per year, typically for two-and-a-half days at each meeting. The Standards Review Committee (14 members) assists in reviewing the Standards to assure that they are transparent and that they focus on matters that are central to quality legal education. The Council has established an extensive process to seek comment on current and proposed Standards. The Standards Review Committee meets four times a year, typically for a day-and-a-half. The Questionnaire Committee (10 members) assists in gathering and maintaining the vast information database concerning ABA-approved law schools and their programs. It meets three times each year for a one-day meeting.

The Council and the Accreditation Committee are assisted by the staff of the Office of the Consultant on Legal Education and Admissions to the Bar. As of September 1, 2006, Hulett H. ("Bucky") Askew is the Consultant on Legal Education.

The Standards for Approval of Law Schools, the associated Rules of Procedure, additional information about the accreditation process, and other information about legal education may be found on the website of the Section of Legal Education and Admissions to the Bar: americanbar.org/groups/legal_education.

ABA-Approved Schools

As of January 2011, a total of 200 institutions are approved by the Council: 199 confer the first degree in law (the JD degree); the other approved school is the US Army Judge Advocate General's School, which offers an officer's resident graduate course, a specialized program beyond the first degree in law. As of January 2011, five of the 200 approved law schools are provisionally approved: Charleston School of Law; Charlotte School of Law; Earle Mack School of Law at Drexel University; Elon University School of Law; and the University of La Verne College of Law.

With an increase in the number of approved law schools, total JD enrollment in approved schools has gone from approximately 98,042 students in 1972 to 147,525 in the fall of 2010. In that same period, enrollment of women increased from 11,878 to 69,009 and minority enrollment increased from 6,730 to 35,045.

The complete list of ABA-approved law schools can be viewed online at americanbar.org/groups/legal_education.

The Approval Process

Provisional Approval

A law school may not apply for provisional approval by the ABA until it has been in operation for one year. Schools considering applying for provisional approval are strongly encouraged to contact the Office of the Consultant as early as possible, and well before the year in which the school applies for provisional approval. The Consultant or other senior members of the Consultant's Office staff will meet with representatives of schools seeking provisional approval and provide them with extensive information about the Standards for Approval of Law Schools, the Rules of Procedure, and the accreditation process.

A school must apply for provisional approval after classes have begun in the fall term and before October 15, so that a full site evaluation can be properly scheduled for late in the fall or early in the spring term. The site evaluation process is described on page 32. The school is required to develop an extensive Self-Study, which describes the school in detail, contains a critical evaluation of the school's strengths and weaknesses, establishes goals for the school's future progress, and identifies the means of achieving those goals. The school also completes a Site Evaluation Questionnaire that provides much of the information that a site evaluation team needs to ascertain the basic facts concerning the school and its operation.

The fact-finding report of the initial site evaluation team is sent to the Accreditation Committee, which holds a hearing at which representatives of the school applying for provisional approval appear. After the hearing, the Accreditation Committee makes its recommendation concerning provisional approval to the Council.

A school that applies for provisional approval must establish that it "is in substantial compliance with each of the Standards" and must present "a reliable plan for bringing the school into full compliance with the Standards within three years after receiving provisional approval." The burden is on the school to establish that it fulfills these requirements. If the Accreditation Committee concludes that a school is in substantial compliance with the Standards and that the school has a reliable plan for coming into full compliance, the Committee will recommend that the Council grant provisional approval. If the Committee concludes that either the school is not in substantial compliance or does not have a reliable plan to come into full compliance in three years, it will recommend against provisional approval.

When a school seeks provisional approval, the final decision on the school's application is made by the Council. The Accreditation Committee's findings of fact are binding on the Council unless those findings are not supported by substantial evidence in the record, but the Accreditation Committee's conclusions and recommendations are not binding on the Council.

If the decision of the Council is to grant provisional approval, that decision is final and effective immediately upon notice to the school. If the decision of the Council is to deny provisional approval, the school has the right of appeal to an Appeals Panel appointed annually by the Council.

From an accreditation perspective, a school that is provisionally approved is entitled to all the rights of a fully approved law school. Similarly, from an ABA perspective, graduates of provisionally approved law schools are entitled to the same recognition that is accorded graduates of fully approved schools.

Obtaining Full Approval

Once a school has obtained provisional approval, it remains in provisional status for at least three years. Unless extraordinary circumstances justify an extension, a school may not remain in provisional status for more than five years. In order to be granted full approval, a school must demonstrate that it is in full compliance with each of the Standards; substantial compliance does not suffice. Again, the burden is upon the school to establish full compliance.

During a school's provisional status, the progress of the school is closely monitored. A visit to the school by a full site evaluation team is conducted in years two, four, and five after provisional approval, and a limited site evaluation by one or two site evaluators is conducted during years one and three. After each such site visit, a site evaluation report is submitted to the school and the Accreditation Committee. The Committee reviews the site report and the school's response and sends the school a letter summarizing its findings and indicating any areas where the Committee needs further information or where the school may be out of compliance with one or more Standards.

In the year in which a school is considered for full approval, the process is identical to that undertaken in connection with an application for provisional approval. Decisions on full approval are made only by the Council, by reviewing the findings, conclusions, and recommendations of the Accreditation Committee. If the decision of the Council is to grant full approval, that decision is final and effective immediately upon notice to the school. If the decision of the Council is to deny full approval, the school has the right of appeal to the Appeals Panel.

Oversight of Fully Approved Schools

Schools undergo a full site evaluation in the third year after full approval, and then a full sabbatical site evaluation every seven years.

Each law school is required to complete a comprehensive Annual Questionnaire, which inquires into facts relevant to continued compliance with accrediting Standards. The questionnaire elicits information and data regarding curriculum, faculty, facilities, fiscal and administrative capacity, technology resources, student profiles, bar passage rates, and student placement. Information obtained is reported to the Accreditation Committee on a fact sheet prepared by the Consultant's Office. For schools undergoing a sabbatical review, additional information is reported on a Site Evaluation Questionnaire and both questionnaires are reviewed by the site evaluation team and the Accreditation Committee.

The Accreditation Committee's actions upon review of a site report on a fully approved school are likely to take one of three forms. If the Committee concludes that the school fully complies with all the Standards, it writes the school with that conclusion and indicates that the school remains on the list of approved schools. In the remainder of the cases, the Committee will conclude either that the school does not appear to comply with one or more of the Standards, or that the Committee lacks sufficient information to determine whether or not the school complies. In either case, the Committee's action letter will indicate with specificity the Standard or Standards with which the school does not comply, or for which the Committee lacks sufficient information to determine compliance. The school will then be required, by a specific time, to indicate what steps it has taken to bring itself into compliance or to provide the information necessary to enable the Committee to determine compliance.

If facts indicating possible noncompliance are presented from any source, the Accreditation Committee may, in its discretion, send a special fact finder to ascertain facts for the Accreditation Committee's consideration on whether the school is in compliance. In addition, major changes in the program or organizational structure of the school may constitute grounds for a special site visit and action by the Accreditation Committee.

Once a finding of noncompliance is made, the school is required to appear at a show cause hearing and demonstrate that it complies with the Standards and that no remedial action is necessary. If the Accreditation Committee finds that the school is, in fact, out of compliance, then it gives the school no more than two years to come into compliance, absent a finding of good cause for extending that time period. If the school fails to come into compliance during that two-year period, the Accreditation Committee initiates action to remove the school from the list of approved law schools.

Site Evaluation Process

Site Evaluation Visits

When a site evaluation is required under the Rules of Procedure, the Office of the Consultant appoints a site evaluation team, typically of six or seven persons, to undertake a site evaluation of the school. The team chairperson is always an experienced site evaluator and frequently a present or former law school dean. The team usually consists of one or two academic law school faculty members, a law librarian, one faculty member with an expertise in professional skills instruction (clinic, simulation skills, or legal writing), one judge or practitioner, and, except on teams visiting a law school that is not affiliated with a university or college, one university administrator who is not a member of a law faculty.

The Site Team is responsible for submitting to the Accreditation Committee a report that addresses the factual information relevant to each of the Standards so that the Accreditation Committee can determine whether a school is in compliance with the Standards. The Section conducts annual workshops to train evaluators and chairs of site evaluation teams. Workshops are also conducted to prepare schools for site evaluation visits.

The site evaluation team carefully reviews the materials the school has provided and visits the school for a three-day period, often from Sunday afternoon through Wednesday morning, following the schedule as outlined in the Section's Conduct Memo (available on the Accreditation page of the Section website: americanbar.org/groups/legal_education). During that visit, the team meets with the dean and other leaders of the faculty and law school administration, and with the president and other university administrators (or, in the case of an independent law school, with the leadership of the board of trustees), and tries to have one member of the team meet individually with every member of the faculty. The team also visits as many classes as it can during its site evaluation in order to make judgments concerning the quality of instruction, holds an open meeting with students, and meets with student leaders. In addition, the team meets with alumni and members of the bar and judiciary who are familiar with the school.

At the end of the visit, the team meets with the dean and the president or, in the case of independent law schools, the board chair, to provide an oral report of the team's findings. Shortly after leaving the school, the team drafts and finalizes an extensive written site evaluation report. The report covers all aspects of the school's operation as outlined in the Format

Memo (available on the Accreditation page of the Section website: americanbar.org/groups/legal_education), including faculty and administration, the academic program, the student body and its success on the bar examination and in job placement, student services, library and information resources, financial resources, and physical facilities and technological capacities. The team's report should be candid in its evaluation of the school and its program and in reporting facts bearing on the school's compliance with the Standards.

The site report and any response by the school, as well as historical information and responses to the Questionnaires, are sent to the Accreditation Committee, and, where appropriate, to the Council to make compliance determinations.

Confidentiality

The Rules of Procedure for the Approval of Law Schools make clear that, in general, all matters relating to the accreditation of a law school are confidential.

Written by the ABA Standing Committee on Pro Bono and Public Service

When society confers the privilege to practice law on an individual, he or she accepts the responsibility to promote justice and to make justice equally accessible to all people. Thus, all lawyers should render some legal services without fee or expectation of fee for the good of the public (pro bono publico). Prospective students should be mindful of this responsibility when considering law as a career. The ABA Standards and Rules of Procedure for Approval of Law Schools require schools to provide substantial opportunities for students to participate in pro bono activities. Many schools offer a range of curricular and noncurricular pro bono opportunities and provide career-related public interest law resources, funding, and support. When choosing a law school, it is important to evaluate the law school's public interest and pro bono programs and curricula to find the law school that best matches the student's career-related goals and interests.

What Is Pro Bono?

The term "pro bono" comes from the Latin pro bono publico, which means "for the public good." The American Bar Association has described the parameters of pro bono for practicing lawyers in the *Model Rules of Professional Conduct*. Nearly every state has an ethical rule that calls upon lawyers to render pro bono services. For those states in which the *ABA Model Rules of Professional Conduct* have been adopted in whole or part, the pro bono responsibility is usually defined in *Rule 6.1*. *Model Rule 6.1*, the full text of which is located on page 35, states that lawyers should aspire to render—without fee—at least 50 hours of pro bono publico legal services per year, with an emphasis that these services be provided to people of limited means or nonprofit organizations that serve the poor. The rule recognizes that only lawyers have the special skills and knowledge needed to secure access to justice for low-income people, whose enormous unmet legal needs are well documented.

In the law school setting, pro bono generally refers to student provision of voluntary, law-related services to people of limited means or to community-based nonprofit organizations, for which the student does not receive academic credit or pay. Law students who do pro bono work accomplish more than satisfying much-needed legal needs. They also enhance their career development and make themselves more attractive to potential employers.

Pro Bono Opportunities in Law School

Some schools have formal pro bono programs, staffed by professionals who help match students with outside organizations that do pro bono work. Other schools provide administrative support for student groups engaged in pro bono work while others lack an organized school-wide program, but rely on student groups to form and run projects.

Typically, the opportunities cover a wide range of legal needs, such as family law, children's issues, consumer fraud, AIDS-related problems, housing, immigration, taxation, environmental law, criminal defense, elder law, and death penalty appeals. At least 36 law schools require students to engage in pro bono or public service as a condition of graduation. These schools may require a specific number of hours of pro bono legal service as a condition of graduation (e.g. 20–75 hours) or they may require a combination of pro bono legal service, clinical work, and community-based volunteer work. Law schools with voluntary rather than mandatory pro bono service policies encourage students to assist lawyers and legal aid organizations by offering incentives, such as awards at graduation or special notations on law school transcripts, or by making pro bono an important part of a school's culture.

Many law schools make financial assistance available to students participating in pro bono activities through summer and school-year fellowships or stipends. Some law schools offer loan repayment assistance through loan forgiveness, lower interest rates, or postponed payment of law school loans incurred by law graduates entering public interest employment. To be eligible for assistance, law students must earn income below a specified salary cap and usually must be employed by a nonprofit organization, a local, state or federal government, or a law-related public interest organization. A few schools offer postgraduate awards to law students who accept public interest positions upon graduation, and some outside fellowships are available.

Benefits of Pro Bono Programs in Law School

Pro bono programs help students develop professionalism and an understanding of a lawyer's responsibility to the community. Participation facilitates student involvement in the community and increases the availability of legal services to needy populations. Students benefit by being able to connect the legal theory learned in their classes with the practical legal issues faced by low-income individuals. They also gain valuable experience and legal skills that can enhance their career development and marketability.

Support for Pro Bono and Public Service in Law School

A number of organizations support pro bono and public service in law school, including the ABA Center for Pro Bono (www.americanbar.org/groups/probono_public_service.html), the Public Service Law Network Worldwide (www.pslawnet.org), Equal Justice Works (www.equaljusticeworks.org) the Association of American Law Schools (www.aals.org/probono/index.html), and the National Association for Law Placement (www.nalp.org/publicservice).

For a complete list of law school pro bono-related resources, see the ABA Center for Pro Bono website at www.americanbar.org/groups/probono_public_service.html.

ABA Model Rules of Professional Conduct *Rule 6.1*
Voluntary Pro Bono Publico Service

Every lawyer has a professional responsibility to provide legal services to those unable to pay. A lawyer should aspire to render at least (50) hours of pro bono publico legal services per year. In fulfilling this responsibility, the lawyer should:

(a) provide a substantial majority of the (50) hours of legal services without fee or expectation of fee to:

   (1) persons of limited means or

   (2) charitable, religious, civic, community, governmental, and educational organizations in matters which are designed primarily to address the needs of persons of limited means; and

(b) provide any additional services through:

   (1) delivery of legal services at no fee or substantially reduced fee to individuals, groups or organizations seeking to secure or protect civil rights, civil liberties or public rights, or charitable, religious, civic, community, governmental, and educational organizations in matters in furtherance of their organizational purposes, where the payment of standard legal fees would significantly deplete the organization's economic resources or would be otherwise inappropriate;

   (2) delivery of legal services at a substantially reduced fee to persons of limited means; or

   (3) participation in activities for improving the law, the legal system or the legal profession.

In addition, a lawyer should voluntarily contribute financial support to organizations that provide legal services to persons of limited means.

Legal education is an investment in your future and is, in most cases, a serious financial investment as well. As with any investment, it is important to consider the pros and cons of entering into such a large expenditure of effort, time, and money. Particularly in uncertain financial times, a realistic assessment of why you are seeking a legal education and how you will pay for it is critical.

It is not an exaggeration to say that the cost of a law school education could exceed $150,000. Tuition alone can range from a few thousand dollars to more than $50,000 a year, with housing, food, books, transportation, and personal expenses all adding to the total cost. Approximately 80 percent of law school students rely on education loans as their primary source of financial aid for law school. These loans must be paid back, and the more a student borrows, the longer the debt will have an impact on a student's life after graduation.

The single best source of information about financing a legal education is the financial aid office (or the website) of any LSAC-member law school. Visit LSAC.org for additional financial aid information and links to the law schools.

Financial Aid Options
Federal Direct Loans
The largest student loan programs are funded directly by the federal government. Federal student loans are generally offered at lower interest rates than commercial loans, and repayment of federal loans is usually postponed until after the end of your educational program. Some federal loans are awarded based on need; others are not. Loan types provided under the William D. Ford Federal Direct Loan Program include Direct Stafford Loans (for undergraduate and graduate students), Direct PLUS Loans for Graduate and Professional Degree Students (based on credit history), and Direct Consolidation Loans (to combine federal education loan debts into a single loan).

Before July 1, 2010, Stafford, Graduate PLUS, and Consolidation Loans were also made by private lenders under the Federal Family Education Loan (FFEL) Program. As a result of recent legislation, no further loans will be made under the FFEL Program. All new Stafford, Graduate PLUS, and Consolidation Loans come directly from the US Department of Education under the Direct Loan Program.

The Free Application for Student Aid (FAFSA) is a need-analysis tool used by the federal government and law schools for determining the combination of resources that will allow you to cover the cost of your legal education. The form is available online at fafsa.ed.gov. The US Department of Education's Federal Student Aid website —federalstudentaid.ed.gov—also provides a wealth of information about loans that are available from the federal government.

Private Loans
There are a number of private loan programs available for credit-worthy borrowers. The terms and conditions of private loan programs vary greatly. Pay careful attention to the explanations found in loan application brochures and consumer information. Lenders will analyze your credit report before approving a private loan. If you have a poor credit history, you may be denied a loan. If there is a mistake on your credit report—and there are often mistakes—you will want adequate time to correct the error. Obtain a copy of your free credit report from one of the major credit-reporting agencies by calling 1.877.322.8228 or go to annualcreditreport.com.

Some lenders make available postgraduate loans for bar-review study. Eligibility for these bar loans is based on the borrower's credit history and the lending institution's willingness to lend.

Debt Management
Dealing with a long-term financial obligation can be made easier through the implementation of sound debt management practices—before, during, and after law school.

Before entering law school, plan a financial strategy. Save as much money as possible to reduce the amount you will borrow. It is important to have a good credit history if you intend to borrow; Graduate PLUS and private loans are based on your credit history. If possible, pay off any outstanding consumer debt. Do not borrow any more than is absolutely necessary to pay for your expenses during law school, and minimize these expenses to the extent possible. In an unpredictable job market, it is not sensible to incur long-term debt for short-term luxuries.

The federal government (ed.gov) and many lenders have websites with loan repayment and budget calculators. Work closely with the financial aid advisor at the school you wish to attend to develop a realistic plan for covering your expenses while minimizing future debt.

Planning Ahead: Repayment of Your Loan
Your income after law school is an important factor in determining what constitutes manageable payments on your education loans. Although it may be difficult to predict what kind of job you will get (or want) after law school, or exactly what level of salary you will receive, it is important that you make some assessment of your goals for the purpose of sound debt management.

In addition to assessing expected income, you must also create a realistic picture of how much you can afford to pay back on a monthly basis while maintaining the lifestyle that you desire. (The money you borrow will be paid out of your future earnings and may have a significant effect on that lifestyle.) You may have to adjust your thinking about how quickly you can pay your loans back, or how much money you can afford to borrow, or just how extravagantly you expect to live in the years following your graduation from law school.

Your education loan debts represent a serious financial commitment that must be repaid. A default on any loan engenders serious consequences, including possible legal action against you by the lender or the government, or both.

Law school graduate debt of $100,000 amounts to almost $1,187 a month on a standard 10-year repayment plan. Most lenders offer graduated and income-sensitive repayment plans that lower monthly payment amounts but increase the number of years of repayment. Federal Direct Consolidation Loan allows students to repay their Federal Stafford, Federal Direct Loans, and Graduate PLUS loans on an extended repayment schedule, lasting up to 30 years. Stafford and Direct Loan lenders also offer income-based repayment options (IBR). This repayment allows borrowers to pay a small amount monthly toward their loans, depending on income and the loan amounts. There also may be forgiveness after 25 years, and federal loan forgiveness for government and nonprofit employees after 10 years. The federal government (ed.gov), and many lenders have websites with loan repayment and budget calculators.

Scholarships and Grants
A scholarship or grant is an award that does not have to be repaid. It may be given on the basis of need, or merit, or both. Most scholarships are offered by individual law schools or organizations. Among organizations that often offer

scholarships are local bar associations; fraternities, sororities, and other social clubs; religious or business organizations; and the US Department of Veterans Affairs (va.gov). The availability of scholarships and grants is limited, but worth researching. Law school admission and financial aid offices can provide information about the resources available. Be aware that many scholarships and grants are merit-based and may require a certain level of academic performance for continuation.

In addition, a number of companies offer tuition-reimbursement benefits to their employees and their employees' dependents.

Federal Work-Study

Federal work-study is a program that provides funding for students to work part time during the school year and full time during the summer months. Students sometimes work on campus in a variety of settings or in off-campus, nonprofit agencies. Additional information is available from any law school financial aid office. Not all schools participate in the federal work-study program.

Graduates Seeking Public Interest Careers

Students who seek to work in public service or the public interest sector of the profession face special challenges in financing their legal educations. Salaries for such jobs are comparatively low. Students graduating from law school with the average amount of indebtedness may find that the average entry-level public service or public interest salary ($43,000 for 2009 graduates) will not provide the resources needed to repay their law school loans and cover their basic living expenses.

Students can employ a number of strategies to make it easier (or possible) to pursue a career in the public service or public interest sectors. First, students can borrow less during law school (e.g., attend a lower-tuition institution; follow some of the debt management strategies mentioned in this chapter). Students may also take advantage of programs developed at some law schools to relieve the debt burden for those interested in public interest careers, including

fellowships, scholarships, and loan repayment assistance programs (LRAPs). LRAPs provide financial assistance to law school graduates working in the public interest sector, government, or other lower-paying legal fields. In most cases, this aid is given to graduates in the form of a forgivable loan to help repay their annual educational debt. Upon completion of the required service obligation, schools will forgive or cancel these loans for program participants. The number of law schools sponsoring LRAPs is limited. Most schools are unable to provide assistance to all applicants.

LRAPs are also administered by state bar foundations, public interest legal employers, and federal and state governments to assist law graduates in pursuing and remaining in public interest jobs. The federal government offers some options to assist graduates seeking legal careers in public service, including the new Income-Based Repayment (IBR) option for federal loan repayment and the Federal Loan Forgiveness Program. The IBR allows any federal education loan borrower the opportunity to make low monthly payments on their federal loans (including, but not limited to, those employed in public service positions), provided that income qualifications are met. The payments are equal to 15 percent of the difference between the borrower's earnings and 150 percent of the federal poverty level. The Federal Loan Forgiveness Program allows borrowers who work in government or nonprofits the opportunity to make payments under the IBR, then have their outstanding balances forgiven after 120 eligible payments. Please check with your school or directly with the Department of Education for details on these new programs.

For more information about loan repayment assistance programs or the income-based repayment program, visit www.americanbar.org/groups/legal_aid_indigent_defendants.html. or equaljusticeworks.org.

Note: All figures and calculations are based on current interest rates, loan terms, and fees, and are subject to change.

EMPLOYMENT PROSPECTS

Over the last two years, employment of recent law school graduates has been negatively affected by the national and regional economic situations. Prospective law students should make themselves aware of how this may affect their employment prospects after graduation.

Almost 93 percent of all 2009 graduates from ABA-accredited law schools reported employment status to their law school. Their overall employment rate was 88.3 percent of graduates for whom employment status was known, a rate that has decreased for two years in a row, from a 20-year high of 91.9 percent in 2007. This downward trend in the employment rate of recent law school graduates is the lowest rate since the last significant recession to affect the US legal economy in the mid-1990s.

Even in times of relative economic weakness, members of each graduating class acquire full- and part-time jobs with an array of public and private, legal and nonlegal organizations. Many, but not all, graduates obtain jobs as attorneys. One type of nonattorney job is a "JD-preferred" position, which may include jobs such as corporate contracts administrator, alternative dispute resolution specialist, government regulatory analyst, and FBI special agent or other law enforcement officers. Additional possibilities may include foreign service, jobs with legal publishers, and jobs in law school career services offices. There are other professional but nonlegal jobs that do not require a Juris Doctor and may or may not make specific use of legal skills and background.

Employment Status
Class of 2009† (as of February 15, 2010)

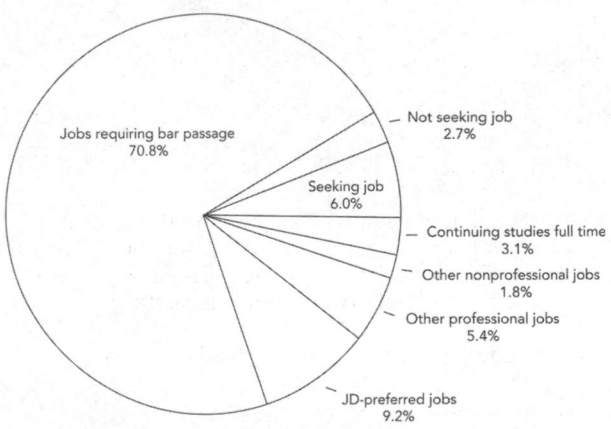

†Based on 40,833 graduates.
Note: A category of jobs for which type—e.g., bar passage required, or other—was not specified accounts for 1.14% of jobs but is not shown on the chart. Overall, almost 90% of jobs were reported as full time.

Future lawyers may have to devote considerable time and energy to secure a first job that they consider acceptable. Opportunities will vary from locality to locality and among legal disciplines; certain parts of the country are underrepresented by lawyers. Moreover, future demand for people with legal training is almost impossible to predict. Demand for legal services is substantially influenced by the state of the economy. Rising caseloads in the nation's courts and continuing federal and state regulations suggest that the

need for lawyers is growing. Whether this expanding need will match or fall short of the parallel growth in the number of practicing lawyers and law school graduates as they enter the profession is a question no one can answer with certainty.

TYPES OF EMPLOYMENT

Law graduates have in the past obtained legal, nonlegal, and full- and part-time jobs in the following general types of employment settings: private practice, public interest, government and the courts, business and industry, and academia.

Employer Types
Class of 2009† (as of February 15, 2010)

†Based on 36,046 jobs.
Note: The category for unknown employer type, representing 1.4% of jobs, is not shown.

Private practice includes all positions within a law firm, including solo practitioner, associate, law clerk, paralegal, and administrative or support staff.

Public interest includes positions funded by the Legal Services Corporation and others providing civil, legal, and indigent services. It also includes public defenders as well as positions with unions, nonprofit advocacy groups, and cause-related organizations.

Government jobs include all levels and branches of government, including prosecutor positions and positions with the military and all other agencies, such as the US Small Business Administration, state or local transit authorities, congressional committees, law enforcement, and social services.

Judicial clerkship is a one- or two-year appointment clerking for a judge on the federal, state, or local level. These jobs provide invaluable experience in the court system.

Business and industry jobs may include positions in accounting firms; insurance companies; banking and financial institutions; corporations, companies, and organizations of all sizes, such as private hospitals, retail establishments, and consulting and public relations firms; political campaigns; and trade associations.

Academic jobs might include work in admissions or administration in higher education or other academic settings.

Law-trained individuals also pursue a wide variety of nonlegal careers outside the practice of law itself. Lawyers also work in the media and public relations; as teachers at colleges, graduate schools, and law schools; and in politics and administration.

SALARY AS AN EMPLOYMENT FACTOR

Salary information was reported for 62 percent of those employed full time. The national median salary for the class of 2009 was $72,000, unchanged from that for the class of 2008. The median has more than doubled since 1985, when a national median was first compiled.

The highest paying jobs were the exception rather than the rule: Although salaries of more than $75,000 accounted for almost 48 percent of the salaries reported, salaries of $55,000 or less accounted for one-third of the salaries reported. Outside of private practice, most salaries were $75,000 or less, with medians ranging from just $43,000 for public interest jobs to $65,000 for jobs in business. It is evident that a $160,000 salary, or even a $145,000 salary, is not the norm but applies to a specific employment setting applicable to fewer than one in five employed graduates.

Differences in Salary Medians by Job and Employer Type

	Bar Passage Required	JD Preferred	Other Professional
All Types	$77,000	$52,000	$60,000
Academic	$47,000	$45,000	$49,200
Business	$65,000	$65,000	$70,000
Private Practice	$130,500	$41,600	$47,000
Government	$52,000	$52,000	$57,500
Public Interest	$42,855	$41,000	$46,250

Note: Figures reflect full-time jobs only.

PLANNING YOUR CAREER

The search for a full-time job is a process that is dictated not only by the effort and commitment of the candidate but also by the unique recruiting practices of various types of employers. For example, some law firms (typically large firms, which can predict their needs in advance) interview second-year law students on campus in the fall to participate in the firm's summer associate program. If a student's performance is acceptable and the hiring needs of the firm have remained consistent with the size of the summer class, the student may receive an offer for a full-time job following graduation. Students receiving such offers make a decision on whether to accept such an offer during the fall of their third year of law school. Some employers, especially government employers and small law firms, do a substantial portion of their hiring after graduation.

All students should take advantage of any programs and workshops offered by the career services office at their law school and should maintain contact with career services staff even after graduation. (See page 19 for more on the role of the career services office.)

A job-search strategy requires careful self-assessment in much the same way as a school-search strategy does. A legal career should meet the interests, abilities, capacities, and priorities of the individual lawyer. Career satisfaction is a result of doing what one likes to do, and being continually challenged by it. It is up to each job seeker to determine the best match of skills and specialties or types of practice.

RESOURCES FOR JOB SEEKERS

Here is a sample of the job-seeking and career books that are listed on LSAC's website (**Future JD Students/Search for the Right Law School/Essential Links**). Go to LSAC.org for the complete list, which includes books on law school and legal education, the legal profession, biographies, jurisprudence and legal issues, and financing law school.

Abrams, Lisa L. *The Official Guide to Legal Specialties: An Insider's Guide to Every Major Practice Area.* Washington, DC: NALP, 2000.

American Bar Association. *Dear Sisters, Dear Daughters: Strategies for Success from Multicultural Women Attorneys.* Chicago: ABA Publishing, 2009.

Bradley, Heather and **Miriam Bamberger Grogan.** *Judge for Yourself: Clarity, Choice, and Action in Your Legal Career.* Chicago: American Bar Association, produced in cooperation with the Minority Corporate Counsel Association, 2006.

Epstein, Phyllis Horn. *Women-at-Law: Lessons Learned Along the Pathways to Success.* Chicago: American Bar Association, 2004.

Fontaine, Valerie A. *The Right Moves: Job Search and Career Development Strategies for Lawyers.* Washington, DC: NALP, 2006.

Furi-Perry, Ursula. *Fifty Unique Legal Paths: How to Find the Right Job.* Chicago: American Bar Association, 2008.

Gerson, Donna. *Building Career Connections: Networking Tools for Law Students and New Lawyers.* Washington, DC: NALP, 2007.

____. *Choosing Small, Choosing Smart: Job Search Strategies for Lawyers in the Small Firm Market.* Rev. 2nd ed. Washington, DC: NALP, 2005.

Melcher, Michael F. *The Creative Lawyer: A Practical Guide to Authentic Professional Satisfaction.* Chicago: American Bar Association, 2007.

Munneke, Gary A., and **William D. Henslee.** *Nonlegal Careers for Lawyers.* 5th ed. Chicago: American Bar Association, 2006.

Munneke, Gary A., **William D. Henslee**, and **Ellen Wayne.** *The Legal Career Guide: From Law Student to Lawyer.* 5th ed. Chicago: American Bar Association, 2008.

You may also find useful information on the following sections of websites that are part of the American Bar Association, The Association for Legal Career Professionals (NALP), and the federal government, respectively.

www.americanbar.org/resources_for_lawyers.html

www.americanbar.org/lawstudent

www.nalpdirectory.com

http://nalp.org/recentgraduates

usajobs.opm.gov

www.bls.gov/opub/

Note: The charts, tables, and text in this chapter were adapted with permission from *Jobs & JD's: Employment and Salaries of New Law Graduates, Class of 2009*, published by The Association for Legal Career Professionals (NALP).

| | Career Placement | | | | | | | | | | | | | Bar Passage* | | |
| | Employment Status | | | | Type of Employment | | | | | | Location | | | | | |
	% Employment Status Known	% Employed	% Pursuing Graduate Degree	% Unemployed - Seeking, Not Seeking, or Studying for the Bar	% in Law Firms	% in Business & Industry	% in Government	% in Public Interest	% in Judicial Clerkships	% in Academia	% Employed in State	% Employed in Foreign Nations	# States Where Employed	State Where Most Take Exam	% Pass Rate for First-time Test Takers	% State's Overall Pass Rate for First-time Test Takers
Alabama																
Alabama	98.8	88.0	3.6	1.2	55.8	9.5	12.9	5.4	12.2	2.7	67.3	2.0	18	AL	96.19	86.51
Faulkner	100.0	86.1	0.0	13.9	43.5	17.7	27.4	1.6	8.1	0.0	82.3	0.0	9	AL	89.23	86.51
Samford	98.2	90.0	3.7	4.4	70.8	11.8	9.7	0.7	5.6	1.4	67.4	0.7	12	AL	92.38	86.51
Arizona																
Arizona	99.3	89.4	4.3	2.8	42.1	7.1	25.4	3.2	21.4	0.8	64.3	0.8	15	AZ	92.93	79.76
Arizona State	99.4	90.3	5.1	0.0	42.8	8.2	20.1	10.7	11.3	6.9	73.6	1.3	18	AZ	83.33	79.76
Phoenix	100.0	94.7	1.8	3.5	44.4	25.9	14.8	5.6	1.9	7.4	92.6	0.0	3	AZ	66.67	79.76
Arkansas																
Arkansas	98.4	85.0	9.2	5.8	52.9	12.7	18.6	4.9	5.9	2.9	64.7	0.0	15	AR	84.95	74.22
Arkansas-Little Rock	99.2	81.7	4.0	8.7	48.5	23.3	18.4	2.9	4.9	1.9	76.7	0.0	9	AR	64.08	74.22
California																
California-Berkeley	100.0	95.6	1.7	2.0	68.7	0.7	7.1	11.0	11.0	1.1	60.9	1.4	23	CA	91.63	73.19
California-Davis	99.5	96.3	2.6	0.0	56.3	4.9	10.9	6.6	4.9	6.0	76.0	0.0	10	CA	88.04	73.19
California-Hastings	97.8	86.5	2.0	6.1	59.4	9.1	11.6	6.2	4.8	8.8	87.8	0.3	18	CA	84.94	73.19
California-Los Angeles	99.2	93.9	1.4	1.7	68.4	4.7	5.9	6.8	9.1	5.0	82.6	0.9	15	CA	85.26	73.19
California Western	92.0	86.7	2.8	7.8	70.9	13.2	7.9	5.3	1.1	1.6	84.7	0.5	12	CA	76.06	73.19
Chapman	98.7	85.4	5.7	1.9	50.7	13.4	7.5	0.7	4.5	22.4	91.0	0.7	11	CA	77.63	73.19
Golden Gate	91.6	87.2	3.7	6.1	40.6	18.9	15.4	16.8	2.1	6.3	93.0	0.0	8	CA	64.16	73.19
La Verne	100.0	63.2	9.2	3.9	64.6	20.8	8.3	4.2	0.0	2.1	85.4	0.0	6	CA	29.69	73.19
Loyola Marymount	100.0	93.4	1.0	5.3	62.7	13.8	3.0	15.1	3.2	2.2	96.2	0.3	8	CA	82.93	73.19
Pacific, McGeorge	98.8	88.9	2.4	2.0	46.7	10.7	20.4	11.1	3.6	2.2	81.8	0.4	11	CA	77.41	73.19
Pepperdine	100.0	89.9	5.0	2.5	63.1	16.2	8.9	1.1	5.0	5.6	76.0	2.2	21	CA	80.00	73.19
San Diego	97.5	86.8	7.2	1.9	59.4	13.4	9.1	5.8	2.9	9.1	80.1	1.8	15	CA	75.76	73.19
San Francisco	96.4	93.1	0.0	3.7	31.8	15.9	4.5	2.3	1.1	10.8	48.9	0.0	8	CA	78.33	73.19
Santa Clara	98.5	85.9	0.8	4.3	42.7	15.5	9.1	5.9	3.2	3.2	59.1	0.5	8	CA	81.47	73.19
Southern California	98.1	95.1	1.0	2.0	78.5	5.6	5.1	3.1	4.1	3.1	86.2	0.5	9	CA	90.81	73.19
Southwestern	95.8	93.1	1.1	1.4	56.6	27.1	7.8	4.7	1.2	2.3	87.6	0.8	11	CA	61.23	73.19
Stanford	100.0	95.0	2.2	2.2	62.8	2.3	2.9	4.1	26.2	1.7	43.0	1.7	24	CA	93.27	73.19
Thomas Jefferson	85.9	84.7	4.2	11.1	58.1	21.9	8.7	6.9	1.2	1.2	83.1	2.5	18	CA	46.56	73.19
Western State	93.2	75.6	1.2	20.7	56.5	30.6	6.5	3.2	0.0	3.2	87.1	0.0	6	CA	47.67	73.19
Whittier	99.3	83.3	6.0	6.7	62.4	26.4	4.8	4.8	0.8	0.8	88.8	0.0	11	CA	62.28	73.19
Colorado																
Colorado	95.2	84.1	1.3	1.3	54.5	6.1	18.9	3.8	15.9	1.5	86.4	0.8	14	CO	92.91	85.67
Denver	97.2	86.8	3.8	8.5	39.9	14.5	26.7	11.5	3.4	0.7	77.0	0.3	21	CO	87.68	85.67
Connecticut																
Connecticut	95.7	89.9	2.0	6.0	48.6	19.6	10.6	2.2	12.3	6.7	59.8	1.7	16	CT	92.41	85.56
Quinnipiac	97.3	94.4	0.0	5.6	45.5	24.8	16.8	1.0	7.9	1.0	71.3	0.0	11	CT	89.66	85.56
Yale	100.0	96.5	2.5	0.5	40.4	3.1	11.9	13.5	30.6	0.5	4.7	4.1	27	NY	94.79	86.51
Delaware																
Widener	81.3	91.6	1.6	5.8	48.0	13.7	12.0	3.4	22.3	0.6	24.6	0.0	11	PA	85.85	85.69
District of Columbia																
American	99.1	82.2	5.2	7.6	42.6	13.9	16.9	12.3	10.4	3.6	45.4	1.6	29	NY	89.91	86.51
Catholic	99.2	88.6	3.4	5.5	37.1	22.9	20.0	1.4	12.4	4.3	51.9	0.0	19	MD	79.17	78.20
District of Columbia	92.8	67.2	6.2	23.4	34.9	18.6	18.6	18.6	7.0	2.3	48.8	0.0	8	MD	57.69	78.20

	Career Placement													Bar Passage*		
	Employment Status				Type of Employment						Location					
	% Employment Status Known	% Employed	% Pursuing Graduate Degree	% Unemployed - Seeking, Not Seeking, or Studying for the Bar	% in Law Firms	% in Business & Industry	% in Government	% in Public Interest	% in Judicial Clerkships	% in Academia	% Employed in State	% Employed in Foreign Nations	# States Where Employed	State Where Most Take Exam	% Pass Rate for First-time Test Takers	% State's Overall Pass Rate for First-time Test Takers
George Washington	99.5	97.3	0.7	1.4	60.7	8.0	12.8	4.3	6.3	5.9	52.3	0.9	26	NY	97.14	86.51
Georgetown	99.3	93.0	3.1	3.1	66.9	1.9	8.9	10.9	9.7	1.0	42.0	2.2	31	NY	93.49	86.51
Howard	91.7	90.1	0.8	5.8	47.7	9.2	19.3	5.5	13.8	0.9	48.6	0.9	19	MD	64.10	78.20
Florida																
Ave Maria	98.8	60.0	3.5	34.1	31.4	9.8	25.5	9.8	13.7	0.0	3.9	3.9	22	MI	80.00	86.87
Barry	92.7	69.5	2.4	23.8	52.6	18.4	14.9	5.3	3.5	4.4	75.4	0.0	15	FL	70.45	77.81
Florida A&M	84.4	63.1	4.3	29.8	43.8	12.4	25.8	4.5	1.1	4.5	93.3	0.0	5	FL	52.52	77.81
Florida Coastal	95.2	85.5	4.1	2.8	44.5	11.9	14.2	15.1	2.1	3.0	65.0	0.3	34	FL	78.77	77.81
Florida	99.8	87.0	10.1	0.5	50.9	8.9	19.5	6.2	5.1	9.2	74.3	0.3	19	FL	85.71	77.81
Florida International	99.2	91.5	4.3	0.0	54.2	16.8	13.1	0.0	3.7	12.1	86.0	0.0	11	FL	81.03	77.81
Florida State	98.9	91.9	2.7	0.0	50.6	11.3	23.8	8.4	2.5	3.3	76.2	1.3	18	FL	86.51	77.81
Miami	94.7	87.0	6.2	2.5	66.6	10.7	7.1	6.8	3.6	2.6	61.7	1.0	22	FL	80.77	77.81
Nova Southeastern	99.2	78.3	6.7	9.9	70.2	11.6	10.1	3.5	2.5	2.0	88.4	0.5	16	FL	83.87	77.81
St. Thomas	97.8	69.3	9.1	21.6	63.9	18.0	4.9	6.6	3.3	0.8	66.4	1.6	13	FL	73.61	77.81
Stetson	97.8	89.2	3.5	2.9	54.8	13.2	14.6	7.5	6.0	1.8	87.9	0.0	21	FL	81.05	77.81
Georgia																
Atlanta's John Marshall	100.0	90.5	0.0	3.2	48.2	29.8	14.0	4.4	3.5	0.0	85.1	0.9	9	GA	82.69	86.28
Emory	99.1	83.8	4.2	7.4	68.5	9.9	6.1	3.9	8.3	2.8	47.5	0.0	22	GA	91.82	86.28
Georgia	98.1	91.0	6.6	0.9	65.3	4.7	8.8	3.6	14.0	3.1	75.1	0.5	13	GA	94.48	86.28
Georgia State	98.9	90.7	3.8	1.6	62.7	19.9	9.6	2.4	2.4	3.0	92.8	1.2	10	GA	94.12	86.28
Mercer	100.0	77.4	5.7	15.1	55.3	13.0	18.7	5.7	5.7	1.6	78.0	0.8	10	GA	87.30	86.28
Hawai'i																
Hawai'i	95.5	90.5	8.3	1.2	36.8	11.8	11.8	3.9	32.9	2.6	88.2	1.3	6	HI	88.16	85.94
Idaho																
Idaho	97.9	80.4	10.9	6.5	44.6	10.8	10.8	1.4	27.0	1.4	60.8	0.0	12	ID	90.57	85.81
Illinois																
Chicago	100.0	99.0	0.5	0.5	79.9	3.4	2.5	3.4	9.3	1.5	32.4	2.0	23	IL	97.50	90.89
Chicago-Kent	96.9	90.3	3.6	4.0	64.5	15.1	10.8	3.6	2.0	4.0	84.5	0.4	20	IL	95.17	90.89
DePaul	99.1	85.8	2.2	6.6	50.0	26.1	12.1	4.4	1.5	4.4	77.6	0.4	19	IL	92.39	90.89
Illinois	100.0	85.9	7.8	0.5	66.7	11.5	4.8	6.7	6.7	3.6	61.2	1.2	24	IL	95.74	90.89
John Marshall	98.0	87.0	0.5	11.5	57.2	22.0	13.5	1.2	1.2	5.0	90.3	0.6	17	IL	85.11	90.89
Loyola-Chicago	97.4	91.6	4.7	2.3	52.9	19.0	16.8	5.1	4.4	1.8	80.7	0.7	18	IL	92.89	90.89
Northern Illinois	90.2	73.5	1.2	20.5	59.0	9.8	16.4	6.6	0.0	8.2	70.5	0.0	7	IL	79.73	90.89
Northwestern	99.2	95.7	1.9	0.0	76.5	5.7	1.6	2.8	9.3	3.2	39.7	2.0	23	IL	95.16	90.89
Southern Illinois	100.0	73.5	8.8	17.7	59.0	9.6	18.1	3.6	6.0	3.6	55.4	0.0	15	IL	90.54	90.89
Indiana																
Indiana-Bloomington	99.0	90.2	4.7	2.6	40.8	18.4	20.1	6.9	7.5	6.3	44.8	1.7	29	IN	95.83	82.74
Indiana-Indianapolis	98.9	92.1	2.3	5.3	48.2	14.7	22.9	2.0	2.0	3.7	80.8	0.0	19	IN	82.67	82.74
Notre Dame	100.0	93.4	2.0	1.0	52.4	9.2	11.4	7.6	15.1	3.8	9.7	0.0	29	IL	97.56	90.89
Valparaiso	100.0	70.9	1.2	17.6	42.7	21.4	18.8	7.7	2.6	4.3	32.5	0.0	23	IN	71.19	82.74
Iowa																
Drake	100.0	89.7	1.5	5.1	58.2	15.6	8.2	9.0	6.6	2.5	73.0	0.0	37	Iowa	96.39	93.17
Iowa	100.0	91.7	5.3	1.5	53.4	13.2	10.1	7.9	7.4	5.3	27.5	0.5	30	Iowa	94.34	93.17
Kansas																
Kansas	97.5	84.0	3.2	9.0	53.4	21.4	13.7	5.3	6.1	0.0	50.4	1.5	18	KS	75.00	86.23
Washburn	97.8	86.6	3.7	4.5	54.3	11.2	20.7	6.0	5.2	2.6	67.2	0.0	16	KS	84.09	86.23

| | Career Placement | | | | | | | | | | | | | Bar Passage* | | |
| | Employment Status | | | | Type of Employment | | | | | | Location | | | | | |
	% Employment Status Known	% Employed	% Pursuing Graduate Degree	% Unemployed - Seeking, Not Seeking, or Studying for the Bar	% in Law Firms	% in Business & Industry	% in Government	% in Public Interest	% in Judicial Clerkships	% in Academia	% Employed in State	% Employed in Foreign Nations	# States Where Employed	State Where Most Take Exam	% Pass Rate for First-time Test Takers	% State's Overall Pass Rate for First-time Test Takers
Kentucky																
Kentucky	99.3	94.0	3.0	0.7	52.4	7.9	8.7	9.5	17.5	2.4	80.2	0.0	15	KY	82.61	85.92
Louisville-Brandeis	98.2	95.5	3.6	0.9	57.5	14.2	11.3	7.5	7.5	1.9	79.2	0.9	14	KY	85.57	85.92
Northern Kentucky	97.0	91.5	0.0	6.2	42.0	26.9	14.3	6.7	5.0	5.0	57.1	0.0	9	KY	87.50	85.92
Louisiana																
Louisiana State	97.8	88.8	2.2	7.9	55.7	8.2	15.8	2.5	17.1	0.0	86.7	0.0	11	LA	89.24	73.73
Loyola-New Orleans	91.5	85.4	8.8	0.0	54.4	13.0	15.5	2.1	14.0	1.0	78.2	0.0	21	LA	70.17	73.73
Southern	100.0	91.9	1.6	6.5	43.9	13.2	23.7	3.5	14.0	1.8	80.7	0.9	10	LA	63.46	73.73
Tulane	95.3	92.2	2.4	3.7	55.8	16.4	7.5	9.7	8.0	2.2	42.5	2.2	24	LA	77.31	73.73
Maine																
Maine	100.0	78.5	6.5	14.0	45.2	24.7	12.3	8.2	6.8	2.7	69.9	0.0	10	ME	82.35	82.49
Maryland																
Baltimore	99.3	93.4	2.3	2.3	35.7	12.7	19.4	3.9	21.9	3.5	80.6	0.0	11	MD	81.85	78.20
Maryland	98.4	95.8	0.4	0.4	40.0	18.7	13.9	4.3	13.9	9.1	66.5	1.3	19	MD	85.08	78.20
Massachusetts																
Boston College	99.6	94.7	1.6	2.0	68.4	7.4	5.2	5.2	8.2	5.2	49.8	0.9	23	MA	95.17	89.77
Boston	99.6	94.8	2.6	2.2	62.6	5.9	3.9	1.2	8.7	17.3	49.6	2.4	24	MA	96.05	89.77
Harvard	100.0	97.5	0.9	1.1	66.7	4.0	2.7	5.4	20.6	0.5	11.6	2.7	38	NY	98.52	86.51
New England	94.9	78.8	4.7	15.2	46.2	29.1	14.5	1.3	6.8	1.7	63.7	0.4	22	MA	86.19	89.77
Northeastern	96.8	94.4	1.9	3.7	42.6	9.9	16.8	10.4	5.4	14.9	63.9	1.0	22	MA	95.09	89.77
Suffolk	96.7	83.0	1.7	14.2	50.1	20.0	13.8	2.6	4.7	4.4	78.2	0.3	22	MA	88.11	89.77
Western New England	93.4	77.1	5.3	15.9	48.9	19.8	16.0	3.1	9.9	2.3	31.3	0.8	20	MA	84.51	89.77
Michigan																
Detroit Mercy	100.0	75.4	1.4	16.6	65.4	19.5	6.3	1.9	3.8	3.1	61.0	15.1	12	MI	90.15	86.87
Michigan	99.5	96.8	1.7	0.5	72.5	2.8	2.5	8.1	13.6	0.3	11.6	2.0	37	NY	92.48	86.51
Michigan State	97.2	93.5	4.9	1.6	43.0	25.2	9.1	3.0	3.5	13.9	54.3	2.6	29	MI	94.74	86.87
Thomas M. Cooley	84.2	77.8	2.5	18.3	56.5	16.1	13.9	3.7	4.8	2.9	31.2	1.4	40	MI	88.32	86.87
Wayne State	100.0	83.1	2.7	8.7	68.4	14.5	8.6	2.0	1.3	5.3	92.8	0.0	9	MI	89.44	86.87
Minnesota																
Hamline	97.0	84.6	2.2	4.4	38.0	28.6	14.1	2.1	8.9	3.1	71.9	1.6	15	MN	88.83	89.58
Minnesota	100.0	94.1	2.4	1.2	47.1	12.1	10.4	11.7	11.2	0.4	50.8	1.7	27	MN	96.43	89.58
St. Thomas-Minneapolis	100.0	89.6	2.8	6.2	33.3	32.6	11.6	7.0	10.9	3.1	72.9	0.0	20	MN	90.91	89.58
William Mitchell	100.0	85.9	1.2	6.1	42.3	27.0	10.3	5.0	7.8	2.5	76.9	0.4	12	MN	85.39	89.58
Mississippi																
Mississippi	94.4	89.5	3.9	5.2	59.1	8.8	15.3	2.2	12.4	0.0	52.6	0.0	17	MS	90.57	85.21
Mississippi College	88.8	90.1	3.3	6.6	59.6	9.6	16.9	2.2	11.8	0.0	58.1	0.7	15	MS	77.57	85.21
Missouri																
Missouri-Columbia	95.4	78.5	4.9	6.9	63.7	7.1	15.9	1.8	9.7	0.9	77.0	0.9	11	MO	92.13	91.81
Missouri-Kansas City	100.0	91.3	2.0	4.7	53.3	21.2	12.4	3.6	9.5	0.0	72.3	0.0	10	MO	94.74	91.81
St. Louis	100.0	88.1	1.0	5.6	56.6	19.5	8.2	10.1	4.5	1.1	69.3	0.0	21	MO	95.77	91.81
Washington University	99.3	96.2	3.1	0.3	66.9	14.4	6.8	3.6	4.3	0.7	27.0	3.6	30	MO	96.47	91.81
Montana																
Montana	96.2	86.8	6.6	5.3	48.5	4.5	10.6	10.6	25.8	0.0	75.8	0.0	9	MT	94.03	88.64
Nebraska																
Creighton	97.9	86.7	3.5	8.4	49.2	21.8	9.7	8.1	8.9	2.4	50.8	0.0	22	Iowa	100.00	93.17
Nebraska	98.5	89.4	2.3	6.1	60.2	13.6	15.3	1.7	5.9	2.5	74.6	0.0	17	NE	92.31	87.93

	Career Placement										Location			Bar Passage*		
	Employment Status				Type of Employment						Location					
	% Employment Status Known	% Employed	% Pursuing Graduate Degree	% Unemployed - Seeking, Not Seeking, or Studying for the Bar	% in Law Firms	% in Business & Industry	% in Government	% in Public Interest	% in Judicial Clerkships	% in Academia	% Employed in State	% Employed in Foreign Nations	# States Where Employed	State Where Most Take Exam	% Pass Rate for First-time Test Takers	% State's Overall Pass Rate for First-time Test Takers
Nevada																
Nevada	100.0	94.3	0.7	0.7	60.6	4.5	4.5	7.6	20.5	2.3	86.4	0.8	8	NV	80.15	73.00
New Hampshire																
New Hampshire	92.0	81.9	3.9	12.6	59.6	17.3	5.8	7.7	4.8	4.8	20.2	1.0	24	NH	91.67	86.84
New Jersey																
Rutgers-Camden	98.7	85.2	3.4	9.3	40.1	14.9	2.5	1.5	35.6	4.0	64.9	0.0	13	NJ	80.00	83.64
Rutgers-Newark	99.2	91.3	0.8	7.5	42.7	16.8	6.8	0.9	31.8	0.9	65.0	0.5	10	NJ	81.45	83.64
Seton Hall	100.0	94.2	0.0	5.8	38.6	10.7	3.4	2.8	40.0	2.1	64.5	0.0	13	NJ	90.23	83.64
New Mexico																
New Mexico	100.0	92.0	1.8	2.7	48.1	3.8	20.2	13.5	8.7	2.9	83.7	1.9	12	NM	94.79	90.58
New York																
Albany	100.0	90.3	4.6	4.2	59.0	11.3	17.4	3.1	5.6	2.6	81.5	1.0	15	NY	82.89	86.51
Brooklyn	98.8	84.2	2.8	7.3	54.5	14.9	17.1	7.0	5.3	1.0	88.0	1.0	16	NY	87.97	86.51
Buffalo	97.6	90.1	5.8	1.6	58.9	14.6	11.0	6.4	4.1	3.7	80.8	0.5	18	NY	79.26	86.51
Cardozo	97.5	88.1	4.6	4.9	63.2	17.1	5.9	7.2	5.9	0.7	79.6	2.0	15	NY	89.52	86.51
CUNY	88.6	89.9	0.0	7.3	21.4	18.4	8.2	28.6	15.3	8.2	70.4	0.0	12	NY	80.39	86.51
Columbia	98.9	98.9	0.9	0.0	84.1	2.1	2.3	3.2	8.0	0.2	65.3	2.1	20	NY	96.06	86.51
Cornell	100.0	97.4	0.0	2.6	85.3	0.5	0.5	1.6	8.9	3.2	58.9	1.6	17	NY	93.65	86.51
Fordham	98.9	92.5	2.2	3.0	70.5	8.1	5.3	5.1	5.1	5.6	84.0	1.4	16	NY	89.84	86.51
Hofstra	96.7	94.3	3.1	2.0	52.4	17.6	13.0	3.3	2.1	4.5	84.5	0.0	19	NY	76.54	86.51
New York Law	93.8	88.3	4.6	5.8	44.5	23.1	8.0	15.7	3.3	3.0	75.5	1.4	12	NY	81.14	86.51
New York	100.0	97.0	1.9	0.4	71.6	2.2	4.2	10.3	10.7	1.1	63.7	2.2	27	NY	96.88	86.51
Pace	96.8	88.1	6.1	5.7	42.3	18.1	9.8	5.1	6.0	17.7	71.6	1.4	12	NY	84.26	86.51
St. John's	97.5	82.3	2.2	10.1	63.2	13.2	10.1	1.3	3.5	8.3	90.8	0.4	13	NY	91.34	86.51
Syracuse	93.5	86.7	7.4	3.0	44.3	20.5	14.2	8.0	10.2	2.8	50.6	1.1	25	NY	87.33	86.51
Touro	84.7	60.2	1.2	38.6	60.2	13.6	13.6	6.8	3.9	1.9	87.4	1.0	7	NY	75.79	86.51
North Carolina																
Campbell	100.0	89.7	2.1	7.2	70.1	8.0	14.9	1.1	2.3	0.0	81.6	0.0	5	NC	90.48	76.79
Charlotte	96.9	95.2	0.0	1.6	54.2	28.8	5.1	6.8	0.0	5.1	84.7	0.0	4	NC	67.31	76.79
Duke	100.0	95.4	2.3	0.0	70.3	5.7	2.4	4.3	16.7	0.5	11.5	1.4	28	NY	97.40	86.51
Elon	90.7	89.7	4.1	5.2	74.7	8.0	5.7	4.6	4.6	1.1	88.5	0.0	7	NC	82.65	76.79
North Carolina	97.8	92.8	1.8	2.3	55.3	10.7	9.2	14.1	9.2	1.5	65.5	0.0	22	NC	88.89	76.79
North Carolina Central	68.0	84.6	1.6	12.2	51.9	8.7	19.2	13.5	3.8	1.0	84.6	0.0	10	NC	80.54	76.79
Wake Forest	95.4	94.5	1.4	3.4	62.0	8.0	6.6	11.7	8.0	2.9	42.3	0.7	21	NC	92.41	76.79
North Dakota																
North Dakota	88.7	84.5	5.6	8.5	56.7	13.3	11.7	1.7	15.0	0.0	70.0	3.3	11	ND	86.00	86.76
Ohio																
Akron	95.1	88.3	0.0	8.0	44.6	23.1	25.6	1.7	1.7	2.5	78.5	0.0	16	OH	89.72	86.03
Capital	74.5	82.9	2.1	14.3	59.5	12.1	19.0	3.4	3.4	2.6	88.8	0.0	10	OH	88.02	86.03
Case Western	95.2	91.4	1.5	3.5	47.5	17.1	14.4	15.5	5.0	0.6	58.6	0.6	23	OH	82.42	86.03
Cincinnati	98.1	87.7	3.8	3.8	53.8	8.6	15.1	6.5	5.4	8.6	66.7	2.2	16	OH	89.19	86.03
Cleveland State	95.0	84.8	1.0	10.5	56.2	22.2	14.2	4.9	1.2	1.2	83.3	0.0	15	OH	82.63	86.03
Dayton	97.3	82.9	0.0	13.0	68.6	11.6	8.3	3.3	5.0	3.3	62.0	0.0	20	OH	80.23	86.03
Ohio Northern	87.5	92.9	1.2	4.8	50.0	12.8	11.5	5.1	7.7	3.8	51.3	0.0	14	OH	78.85	86.03
Ohio State	100.0	92.7	3.9	1.3	51.9	17.1	15.7	1.9	6.5	6.9	56.0	0.9	25	OH	93.53	86.03
Toledo	86.5	92.5	0.7	3.7	41.9	17.7	17.7	11.3	5.6	4.0	65.3	0.0	19	OH	87.80	86.03

School	% Employment Status Known	% Employed	% Pursuing Graduate Degree	% Unemployed - Seeking, Not Seeking, or Studying for the Bar	% in Law Firms	% in Business & Industry	% in Government	% in Public Interest	% in Judicial Clerkships	% in Academia	% Employed in State	% Employed in Foreign Nations	# States Where Employed	State Where Most Take Exam	% Pass Rate for First-time Test Takers	% State's Overall Pass Rate for First-time Test Takers
Oklahoma																
Oklahoma	100.0	90.3	1.8	4.2	58.4	16.8	16.8	2.7	2.0	3.4	72.5	0.7	13	OK	95.12	86.76
Oklahoma City	98.8	84.8	0.6	8.5	55.4	23.0	10.8	7.9	0.0	2.2	62.6	0.0	19	OK	83.17	86.76
Tulsa	99.4	95.7	1.8	0.6	63.7	9.6	14.6	3.2	1.3	6.4	69.4	0.0	21	OK	88.39	86.76
Oregon																
Lewis & Clark	98.3	89.6	4.3	1.7	47.8	12.1	15.5	13.0	5.8	5.8	75.4	1.9	17	OR	78.49	76.85
Oregon	93.9	87.6	5.9	6.5	46.3	6.0	14.9	14.2	15.7	3.0	63.4	2.2	13	OR	82.46	76.85
Willamette	99.2	92.2	2.3	0.8	48.7	13.4	15.1	5.9	7.6	9.2	73.1	0.0	11	OR	86.67	76.85
Pennsylvania																
Duquesne	88.8	87.4	2.7	9.8	56.2	16.2	10.6	1.2	11.2	1.9	67.5	0.0	16	PA	87.71	85.69
Earl Mack, Drexel	95.0	83.4	3.3	12.6	48.4	15.9	11.9	5.6	15.1	2.4	49.2	0.8	9	PA	89.84	85.69
Penn State	96.0	87.0	5.2	3.6	39.9	14.3	19.0	1.2	17.3	3.6	41.7	1.8	23	PA	88.78	85.69
Pennsylvania	100.0	97.7	1.6	0.8	73.8	4.0	4.0	2.4	15.1	0.8	16.3	1.6	24	NY	95.97	86.51
Pittsburgh	99.1	86.0	2.6	8.3	57.1	16.8	13.3	3.1	8.7	0.5	62.2	0.5	23	PA	91.91	85.69
Temple	99.6	87.7	3.5	7.4	47.0	12.4	10.4	7.6	15.3	6.0	67.9	0.4	18	PA	95.09	85.69
Villanova	99.1	86.7	3.4	9.9	55.0	16.8	8.4	5.4	9.4	1.0	57.9	0.0	20	PA	94.74	85.69
Widener	94.1	90.2	0.9	2.7	42.6	17.8	23.8	2.0	12.9	1.0	78.2	0.0	14	PA	93.07	85.69
Puerto Rico																
Inter American	96.3	85.7	4.8	9.5	30.6	44.4	16.1	1.1	2.2	5.6	92.2	0.0	0	PR	41.25	50.28
Pontifical Catholic	0.0	0.0	0.0	0.0	0.0	0.0	0.0	0.0	0.0	0.0	0.0	0.0	0	PR	36.43	50.28
Puerto Rico	16.6	76.7	6.7	16.7	43.5	26.1	8.7	0.0	13.0	8.7	91.3	0.0	0	PR	64.53	50.28
Rhode Island																
Roger Williams	85.5	81.8	9.4	7.5	47.7	15.4	10.8	6.9	14.6	2.3	40.0	0.8	19	RI	94.94	79.92
South Carolina																
Charleston	97.4	77.0	9.2	13.8	39.3	9.4	17.9	6.0	26.5	0.9	84.6	0.0	7	SC	77.46	78.19
South Carolina	94.7	88.8	3.4	7.3	52.9	8.7	15.0	3.4	18.4	1.5	75.7	0.5	15	SC	85.26	78.19
South Dakota																
South Dakota	100.0	84.9	4.1	8.2	45.2	12.9	4.8	8.1	22.6	1.6	72.6	0.0	11	SD	96.55	89.77
Tennessee																
Memphis	95.8	91.2	1.8	6.2	58.3	11.7	13.6	3.9	10.7	1.0	84.5	0.0	14	TN	88.18	82.44
Tennessee	98.6	92.8	2.9	3.6	62.5	6.2	14.8	1.6	12.5	2.3	80.5	0.0	13	TN	88.46	82.44
Vanderbilt	98.9	94.7	3.7	0.0	71.8	3.4	3.4	3.4	13.0	5.1	21.5	1.7	27	NY	97.30	86.51
Texas																
Baylor	97.7	89.8	2.4	5.5	70.2	6.1	14.9	0.9	6.1	1.8	81.6	0.0	15	TX	94.96	85.48
Houston	99.3	93.3	2.8	3.5	60.0	19.2	11.7	3.4	3.8	1.9	89.1	0.4	14	TX	91.25	85.48
St. Mary's	97.6	87.5	1.0	6.0	68.6	9.1	13.1	2.3	3.4	1.7	91.4	0.0	7	TX	83.60	85.48
SMU Dedman	100.0	89.3	4.6	2.6	67.5	19.3	6.9	1.5	4.0	0.7	93.4	0.0	16	TX	89.46	85.48
South Texas	89.9	88.5	1.8	5.0	61.5	19.4	12.4	0.7	3.3	2.3	94.3	0.0	10	TX	86.84	85.48
Texas	100.0	92.8	0.0	2.3	63.7	5.7	10.7	7.0	11.7	1.0	67.9	1.0	26	TX	93.19	85.48
Texas Southern	97.4	84.5	1.1	6.4	57.6	20.9	12.0	1.9	0.0	1.3	82.9	0.0	6	TX	67.90	85.48
Texas Tech	95.6	89.8	4.1	6.1	59.9	11.3	15.3	3.4	5.1	1.1	75.1	0.0	11	TX	93.37	85.48
Texas Wesleyan	86.8	85.3	2.8	11.3	58.3	25.8	8.6	2.0	2.0	2.6	83.4	0.0	9	TX	89.55	85.48
Utah																
Brigham Young	100.0	93.3	0.7	1.3	64.3	15.7	8.6	0.0	9.3	2.1	44.3	0.0	22	UT	90.12	88.94
Utah	100.0	92.5	3.8	2.3	62.6	7.3	17.9	3.3	7.3	1.6	79.7	0.0	16	UT	88.99	88.94

| | Career Placement | | | | | | | | | | | | | Bar Passage* | | |
| | Employment Status | | | | Type of Employment | | | | | | Location | | | | | |
	% Employment Status Known	% Employed	% Pursuing Graduate Degree	% Unemployed - Seeking, Not Seeking, or Studying for the Bar	% in Law Firms	% in Business & Industry	% in Government	% in Public Interest	% in Judicial Clerkships	% in Academia	% Employed in State	% Employed in Foreign Nations	# States Where Employed	State Where Most Take Exam	% Pass Rate for First-time Test Takers	% State's Overall Pass Rate for First-time Test Takers
Vermont																
Vermont	100.0	80.9	8.2	6.6	29.1	19.6	17.6	13.5	16.9	3.4	18.2	0.0	31	NY	56.25	86.51
Virginia																
Appalachian	85.3	57.6	5.1	37.4	63.2	1.8	14.0	5.3	14.0	0.0	29.8	1.8	12	VA	67.86	77.06
George Mason	99.6	96.5	0.0	0.4	42.5	21.3	14.5	1.4	10.0	10.4	48.9	0.9	18	VA	87.90	77.06
Liberty	96.4	79.2	1.9	18.9	42.9	19.0	23.8	4.8	4.8	4.8	38.1	0.0	13	VA	57.14	77.06
Regent	95.6	88.4	0.8	9.3	54.4	16.7	10.5	1.8	8.8	6.1	37.7	1.8	26	VA	75.93	77.06
Richmond	98.0	93.3	2.0	2.7	37.9	20.7	12.1	3.6	20.7	0.0	77.9	0.0	15	VA	82.68	77.06
Virginia	99.0	98.8	0.2	0.2	72.0	2.8	7.6	3.8	13.1	0.8	13.6	1.0	30	NY	95.69	86.51
Washington and Lee	98.6	87.5	5.1	5.9	58.0	10.9	7.6	1.7	19.3	0.8	31.9	0.8	26	VA	80.39	77.06
William & Mary	97.9	95.7	1.1	2.1	56.4	6.7	17.9	2.8	15.1	0.6	30.7	1.1	28	VA	88.24	77.06
Washington																
Gonzaga	98.9	86.2	5.5	3.9	54.5	21.8	10.3	5.1	6.4	1.9	46.2	0.6	25	WA	67.00	74.42
Seattle	100.0	87.2	4.2	5.6	46.6	23.5	14.3	7.8	5.4	2.4	86.7	1.0	15	WA	75.60	74.42
Washington	100.0	89.5	4.9	1.9	49.0	9.7	11.7	5.5	22.8	1.4	67.6	4.8	12	WA	87.50	74.42
West Virginia																
West Virginia	99.3	90.1	7.3	0.7	52.2	26.5	3.7	2.9	11.8	2.2	73.5	0.0	10	WV	81.25	81.16
Wisconsin																
Marquette	98.6	88.0	2.9	7.7	62.5	13.6	7.6	6.0	6.0	4.3	76.6	0.5	17	WI	100.00	90.80
Wisconsin	97.1	92.5	2.6	3.0	50.6	10.1	16.2	8.5	4.0	8.9	57.5	1.2	21	WI	100.00	90.80
Wyoming																
Wyoming	100.0	85.0	2.5	8.7	48.5	13.2	10.3	10.3	17.6	0.0	58.8	0.0	12	WY	91.67	79.34

*Bar Passage data for first-time bar exam takers in the 2009 calendar year.

(by region)

New England

Maine

1. **Portland—Population: 66,194**
   Maine—Enrollment: 278/0

Vermont

2. **South Royalton—Population: 694**
   Vermont—Enrollment: 607/0

New Hampshire

3. **Concord—Population: 42,695**
   New Hampshire—Enrollment: 419/0

Massachusetts

4. **Boston—Population: 617,594**
   Boston College—Enrollment: 796/0
   Boston University—Enrollment: 821/1
   Harvard (Cambridge, MA)—Enrollment: 1,733/0
   New England—Enrollment: 796/336
   Northeastern—Enrollment: 629/0
   Suffolk—Enrollment: 1,090/591

5. **Springfield—Population: 153,060**
   Western New England—Enrollment: 387/138

Connecticut

6. **Hamden—Population: 60,960**
   Quinnipiac—Enrollment: 340/127

7. **Hartford—Population: 124,775**
   Connecticut—Enrollment: 440/180

8. **New Haven—Population: 129,779**
   Yale—Enrollment: 629/0

Rhode Island

9. **Bristol—Population: 22,954**
   Roger Williams—Enrollment: 540/0

"Enrollment" represents the numbers of total full-time/total part-time students unless otherwise indicated.

Population information is derived from the US Bureau of the Census, Population Division, Washington, DC. Data are accurate as of the 2010 Census. City populations reflect the number of people residing in the city proper, not the metropolitan area, which would include outlying suburbs as well.

Northeast

New York

1. **Albany—Population: 97,856**
   Albany—Enrollment: 697/23
2. **Buffalo—Population: 261,310**
   Buffalo—Enrollment: 693/8
3. **Hempstead—Population: 53,891**
   Hofstra—Enrollment: 945/116
4. **Huntington—Population: 18,046**
   Touro—Enrollment: 601/227
5. **Ithaca—Population: 30,014**
   Cornell—Enrollment: 615/0
6. **New York City—Population: 8,175,133**
   Brooklyn—Enrollment: 1,293/168
   Cardozo, Yeshiva University—Enrollment: 1,025/99
   CUNY—Enrollment: 438/2
   Columbia—Enrollment: 1,343/1
   Fordham—Enrollment: 1,217/264
   New York Law School—Enrollment: 1,492/431
   New York University—Enrollment: 1,431/0
   St. John's (Jamaica, NY)—Enrollment: 764/176
7. **Syracuse—Population: 145,170**
   Syracuse—Enrollment: 635/3
8. **White Plains—Population: 56,853**
   Pace—Enrollment: 614/174

New Jersey

9. **Camden—Population: 77,344**
   Rutgers–Camden—Enrollment: 573/216
10. **Newark—Population: 277,140**
    Rutgers–Newark—Enrollment: 610/229
    Seton Hall—Enrollment: 704/349

Pennsylvania

11. **Carlisle—Population: 18,682**
    Penn State, Dickinson—Enrollment: 617/1
12. **Harrisburg—Population: 49,528**
    Widener—Enrollment: 350/103
13. **Philadelphia—Population: 1,526,006**
    Earl Mack, Drexel—Enrollment: 440/0
    Pennsylvania—Enrollment: 802/0
    Temple—Enrollment: 797/186
    Villanova (Villanova, PA)—Enrollment: 765/0
14. **Pittsburgh—Population: 305,704**
    Duquesne—Enrollment: 454/234
    Pittsburgh—Enrollment: 739/0

Midsouth

Kentucky

1. **Highland Heights—Population: 6,923**
   Northern Kentucky—Enrollment: 375/239
2. **Lexington—Population: 295,803**
   Kentucky—Enrollment: 419/0
3. **Louisville—Population: 597,337**
   Louisville's Brandeis—Enrollment: 379/47

West Virginia

4. **Morgantown—Population: 29,660**
   West Virginia—Enrollment: 410/6

Virginia

5. **Arlington—Population: 207,627**
   George Mason—Enrollment: 505/226
6. **Charlottesville—Population: 43,475**
   Virginia—Enrollment: 1,105/1
7. **Grundy—Population: 1,021**
   Appalachian—Enrollment: 313/0
8. **Lexington—Population: 7,042**
   Washington and Lee—Enrollment: 407/0
9. **Lynchburg—Population: 75,568**
   Liberty—Enrollment: 313/0
10. **Richmond—Population: 204,214**
    Richmond—Enrollment: 452/8
11. **Virginia Beach—Population: 437,994**
    Regent—Enrollment: 409/19
12. **Williamsburg—Population: 14,068**
    William & Mary—Enrollment: 628/0

Maryland

13. **Baltimore—Population: 620,961**
    Baltimore—Enrollment: 730/353
    Maryland—Enrollment: 734/233

District of Columbia

14. **Washington, DC—Population: 601,723**
    American—Enrollment: 1,243/260
    Catholic—Enrollment: 562/296
    District of Columbia—Enrollment: 256/60
    George Washington—Enrollment: 1,410/299
    Georgetown—Enrollment: 1,626/334
    Howard—Enrollment: 473/0

Delaware

15. **Wilmington—Population: 70,851**
    Widener—Enrollment: 647/352

Tennessee

16. **Knoxville—Population: 178,874**
    Tennessee—Enrollment: 482/0
17. **Memphis—Population: 646,889**
    Memphis—Enrollment: 408/24
18. **Nashville—Population: 601,222**
    Vanderbilt—Enrollment: 586/0

North Carolina

19. **Buies Creek—Population: 2,942**
    Campbell—Enrollment: 450/0
20. **Chapel Hill—Population: 57,233**
    North Carolina—Enrollment: 778/0
21. **Charlotte—Population: 731,424**
    Charlotte—Enrollment: 669/143
22. **Durham—Population: 228,330**
    Duke—Enrollment: 644/37
    North Carolina Central—Enrollment: 491/111
23. **Greensboro—Population: 269,666**
    Elon—Enrollment: 342/0
24. **Winston-Salem—Population: 229,617**
    Wake Forest—Enrollment: 487/0

Southeast

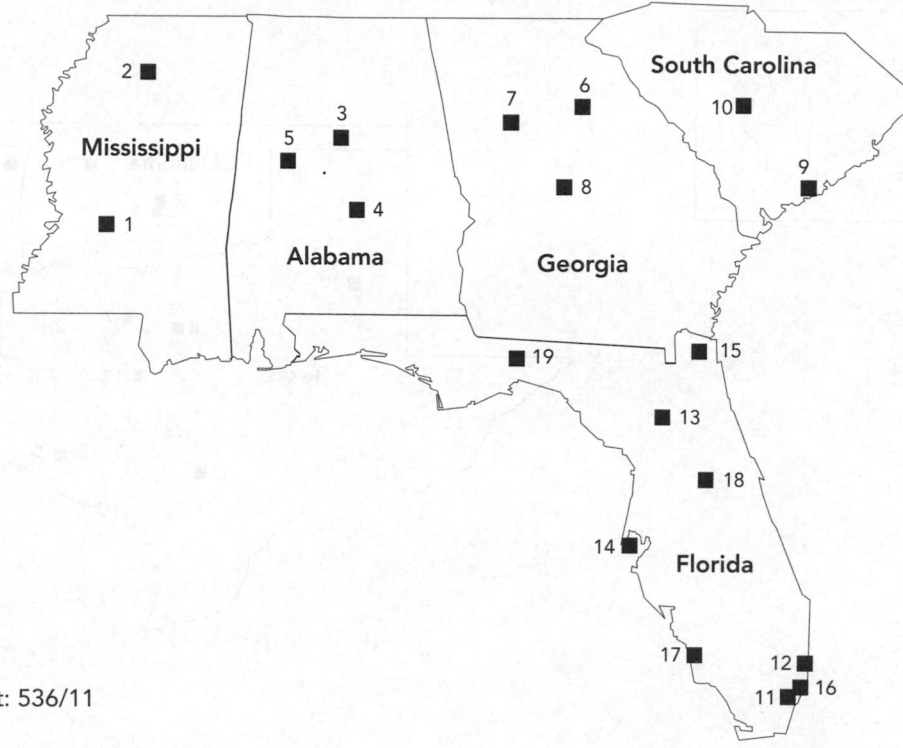

Mississippi
1. **Jackson—Population: 173,514**
   Mississippi College—Enrollment: 536/11
2. **Oxford—Population: 18,916**
   Mississippi—Enrollment: 516/0

Alabama
3. **Birmingham—Population: 212,237**
   Samford—Enrollment: 491/0
4. **Montgomery—Population: 205,764**
   Faulkner—Enrollment: 341/13
5. **Tuscaloosa—Population: 90,468**
   Alabama—Enrollment: 509/0

Georgia
6. **Athens—Population: 115,452**
   Georgia—Enrollment: 703/0
7. **Atlanta—Population: 420,003**
   Atlanta's John Marshall—Enrollment: 455/175
   Emory—Enrollment: 792/0
   Georgia State—Enrollment: 457/203
8. **Macon—Population: 91,351**
   Mercer—Enrollment: 439/0

South Carolina
9. **Charleston—Population: 120,083**
   Charleston—Enrollment: 520/182
10. **Columbia—Population: 129,272**
    South Carolina—Enrollment: 681/1

Florida
11. **Coral Gables—Population: 46,780**
    Miami—Enrollment: 1,334/19
12. **Ft. Lauderdale—Population: 165,521**
    Nova Southeastern—Enrollment: 894/206

13. **Gainesville—Population: 124,354**
    Florida—Enrollment: 1,044/0
14. **Gulfport—Population: 12,029**
    Stetson—Enrollment: 867/214
15. **Jacksonville—Population: 821,784**
    Florida Coastal—Enrollment: 1,683/59
16. **Miami—Population: 399,457**
    Florida International—Enrollment: 395/193
    St. Thomas—Enrollment: 733/0
17. **Naples—Population: 19,537**
    Ave Maria—Enrollment: 468/0
18. **Orlando—Population: 238,300**
    Barry—Enrollment: 553/164
    Florida A&M—Enrollment: 458/211
19. **Tallahassee—Population: 181,376**
    Florida State—Enrollment: 779/0

Puerto Rico
20. **Ponce—Population: 166,327**
    Pontifical Catholic—Enrollment: 535/299
21. **San Juan—Population: 395,326**
    Inter American—Enrollment: 474/392
    Puerto Rico—Enrollment: 545/192

South Central

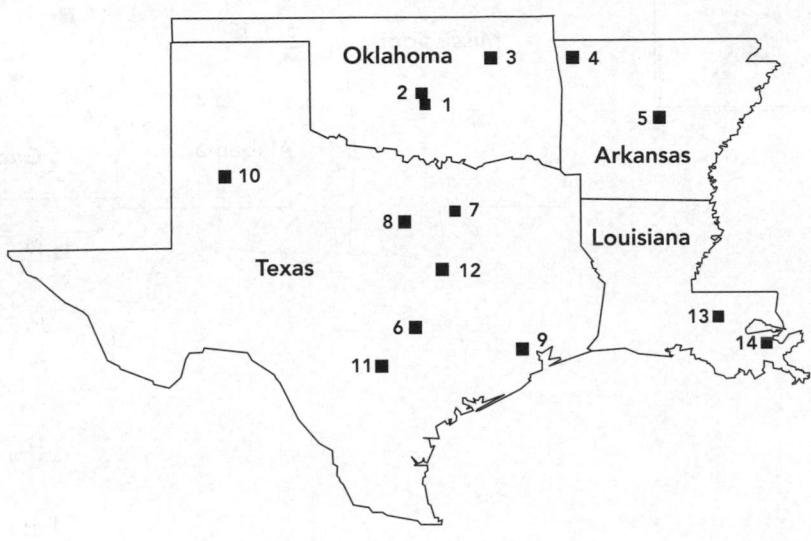

Oklahoma
1. **Norman—Population: 110,925**
   Oklahoma—Enrollment: 537/0
2. **Oklahoma City—Population: 579,999**
   Oklahoma City—Enrollment: 564/72
3. **Tulsa—Population: 391,906**
   Tulsa—Enrollment: 368/38

Arkansas
4. **Fayetteville—Population: 73,580**
   Arkansas–Fayetteville—Enrollment: 390/0
5. **Little Rock—Population: 193,524**
   Arkansas–Little Rock—Enrollment: 338/152

Texas
6. **Austin—Population: 790,390**
   Texas—Enrollment: 1,154/0
7. **Dallas—Population: 1,197,816**
   SMU Dedman—Enrollment: 549/338
8. **Fort Worth—Population: 741,206**
   Texas Wesleyan—Enrollment: 487/277
9. **Houston—Population: 2,099,451**
   Houston—Enrollment: 701/176
   South Texas—Enrollment: 1,009/296
   Texas Southern—Enrollment: 571/0

10. **Lubbock—Population: 229,573**
    Texas Tech—Enrollment: 671/0
11. **San Antonio—Population: 1,327,407**
    St. Mary's—Enrollment: 675/153
12. **Waco—Population: 124,805**
    Baylor—Enrollment: 466/10

Louisiana
13. **Baton Rouge—Population: 229,493**
    Louisiana State—Enrollment: 616/17
    Southern—Enrollment: 486/235
14. **New Orleans—Population: 343,829**
    Loyola–New Orleans—Enrollment: 681/153
    Tulane—Enrollment: 769/1

Mountain West

Idaho
1. **Moscow—Population: 23,800**
   Idaho—Enrollment: 349/0

Montana
2. **Missoula—Population: 66,788**
   Montana—Enrollment: 256/0

Wyoming
3. **Laramie—Population: 30,816**
   Wyoming—Enrollment: 231/0

Utah
4. **Provo—Population: 112,488**
   Brigham Young—Enrollment: 443/1
5. **Salt Lake City—Population: 186,440**
   Utah—Enrollment: 402/0

Colorado
6. **Boulder—Population: 97,385**
   Colorado—Enrollment: 546/0
7. **Denver—Population: 600,158**
   Denver—Enrollment: 768/192

Arizona
8. **Tempe—Population: 161,719**
   Arizona State—Enrollment: 614/0
9. **Tucson—Population: 520,116**
   Arizona—Enrollment: 469/0
10. **Phoenix—Population: 1,455,632**
    Phoenix—Enrollment: 514/210

New Mexico
11. **Albuquerque—Population: 545,852**
    New Mexico—Enrollment: 351/0

Far West

California

1. **Berkeley—Population: 112,580**
   California–Berkeley—Enrollment: 916/0
2. **Costa Mesa—Population: 109,960**
   Whittier—Enrollment: 475/167
3. **Davis—Population: 65,622**
   California–Davis—Enrollment: 589/0
4. **Fullerton—Population: 135,161**
   Western State—Enrollment: 318/150
5. **Los Angeles—Population: 3,792,621**
   California–Los Angeles—Enrollment: 999/0
   Loyola Marymount—Enrollment: 1,013/276
   Pepperdine—Enrollment: 667/0
   Southern California—Enrollment: 651/0
   Southwestern—Enrollment: 741/354
6. **Ontario—Population: 163,924**
   La Verne—Enrollment: 312/114
7. **Orange—Population: 136,416**
   Chapman—Enrollment: 546/28
8. **Sacramento—Population: 466,488**
   Pacific, McGeorge—Enrollment: 724/302

9. **San Diego—Population: 1,307,402**
   California Western—Enrollment: 786/133
   San Diego—Enrollment: 831/176
   Thomas Jefferson—Enrollment: 687/279
10. **San Francisco—Population: 805,235**
    California–Hastings—Enrollment: 1,247/1
    Golden Gate—Enrollment: 616/116
    San Francisco—Enrollment: 589/150
11. **Santa Clara—Population: 116,468**
    Santa Clara—Enrollment: 749/234
12. **Stanford—Population: 13,809**
    Stanford—Enrollment: 571/0

Hawai'i

13. **Honolulu—Population: 337,256**
    Hawai'i—Enrollment: 295/58

Nevada

14. **Las Vegas—Population: 583,756**
    Nevada–Las Vegas—Enrollment: 347/128

Northwest

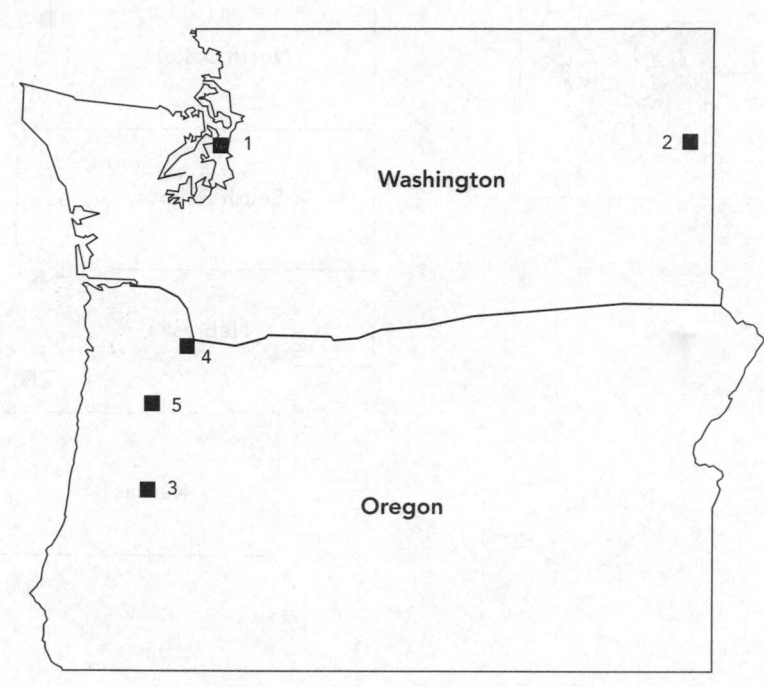

Washington

Oregon

Washington
1. **Seattle—Population: 608,660**
   Seattle—Enrollment: 808/203
   Washington—Enrollment: 550/0
2. **Spokane—Population: 208,916**
   Gonzaga—Enrollment: 503/4

Oregon
3. **Eugene—Population: 156,185**
   Oregon—Enrollment: 526/0
4. **Portland—Population: 583,776**
   Lewis & Clark—Enrollment: 529/212
5. **Salem—Population: 154,637**
   Willamette—Enrollment: 424/5

Midwest

North Dakota
1. **Grand Forks—Population: 52,838**
   North Dakota—Enrollment: 256/0

South Dakota
2. **Vermillion—Population: 10,571**
   South Dakota—Enrollment: 203/2

Nebraska
3. **Lincoln—Population: 258,379**
   Nebraska—Enrollment: 412/2
4. **Omaha—Population: 408,958**
   Creighton—Enrollment: 459/12

Iowa
5. **Des Moines—Population: 203,433**
   Drake—Enrollment: 451/12
6. **Iowa City—Population: 67,862**
   Iowa—Enrollment: 574/0

Kansas
7. **Lawrence—Population: 87,643**
   Kansas—Enrollment: 497/0
8. **Topeka—Population: 127,473**
   Washburn—Enrollment: 454/0

Missouri
9. **Columbia—Population: 108,500**
   Missouri–Columbia—Enrollment: 442/4
10. **Kansas City—Population: 459,787**
    Missouri–Kansas City—Enrollment: 459/24
11. **St. Louis—Population: 319,294**
    St. Louis—Enrollment: 800/138
    Washington University—Enrollment: 893/7

Great Lakes

Minnesota
1. **Minneapolis—Population: 382,578**
   Minnesota—Enrollment: 752/0
   St. Thomas—Enrollment: 475/0
2. **St. Paul—Population: 285,068**
   Hamline—Enrollment: 456/196
   William Mitchell—Enrollment: 667/346

Wisconsin
3. **Madison—Population: 233,209**
   Wisconsin—Enrollment: 755/49
4. **Milwaukee—Population: 594,833**
   Marquette—Enrollment: 585/173

Michigan
5. **Ann Arbor—Population: 113,934**
   Michigan—Enrollment: 1,134/0
6. **Detroit—Population: 713,777**
   Detroit Mercy—Enrollment: 572/155
   Wayne State—Enrollment: 482/130
7. **Lansing—Population: 114,297**
   Michigan State—Enrollment: 804/80
   Thomas M. Cooley—Enrollment: 691/3,240

Illinois
8. **Carbondale—Population: 25,902**
   Southern Illinois—Enrollment: 380/2
9. **Champaign—Population: 81,055**
   Illinois—Enrollment: 640/0
10. **Chicago—Population: 2,695,598**
    Chicago—Enrollment: 634/0
    Chicago-Kent—Enrollment: 785/185
    DePaul—Enrollment: 853/203
    John Marshall—Enrollment: 1,125/317
    Loyola–Chicago—Enrollment: 692/159
    Northwestern—Enrollment: 817/0
11. **DeKalb—Population: 43,862**
    Northern Illinois—Enrollment: 321/11

Indiana
12. **Bloomington—Population: 80,405**
    Indiana–Bloomington—Enrollment: 646/0
13. **Indianapolis—Population: 820,445**
    Indiana–Indianapolis—Enrollment: 595/323
14. **South Bend—Population: 101,168**
    Notre Dame—Enrollment: 564/0
15. **Valparaiso—Population: 31,730**
    Valparaiso—Enrollment: 531/35

Ohio
16. **Ada—Population: 5,952**
    Ohio Northern—Enrollment: 313/0
17. **Akron—Population: 199,110**
    Akron—Enrollment: 279/227
18. **Cincinnati—Population: 296,943**
    Cincinnati—Enrollment: 408/0
19. **Cleveland—Population: 396,815**
    Case Western Reserve—Enrollment: 624/3
    Cleveland State—Enrollment: 453/157
20. **Columbus—Population: 787,033**
    Capital—Enrollment: 486/170
    Ohio State—Enrollment: 693/0
21. **Dayton—Population: 141,527**
    Dayton—Enrollment: 524/0
22. **Toledo—Population: 287,208**
    Toledo—Enrollment: 365/95

ADMISSION DATA

	Application Fee ($)	Full-time									Part-time									Total							
		75% GPA	Median GPA	25% GPA	75% LSAT	Median LSAT	25% LSAT	# of Applicants	# of Offers	# of Matriculants	75% GPA	Median GPA	25% GPA	75% LSAT	Median LSAT	25% LSAT	# of Applicants	# of Offers	# of Matriculants	75% GPA	Median GPA	25% GPA	75% LSAT	Median LSAT	25% LSAT	Total # of Offers	Total # of Matriculants
Alabama																												
Alabama	40	3.92	3.80	3.50	167	165	159	2,384	543	161	0.00	0.00	0.00	0	0	0	0	0	0	3.92	3.80	3.41	167	165	159	543	161
Faulkner	50	3.42	3.12	2.80	154	150	148	913	480	145	0.00	0.00	0.00	0	0	0	0	0	0	3.42	3.12	2.80	154	150	148	480	145
Samford	50	3.55	3.32	3.06	158	155	153	1,678	561	166	0.00	0.00	0.00	0	0	0	0	0	0	3.55	3.32	3.06	158	155	153	561	166
Arizona																												
Arizona	65	3.71	3.50	3.33	164	162	161	2,035	668	157	0.00	0.00	0.00	0	0	0	0	0	0	3.71	3.50	3.33	164	162	161	668	157
Arizona State	60	3.75	3.57	3.34	164	161	158	2,457	590	191	0.00	0.00	0.00	0	0	0	0	0	0	3.75	3.57	3.34	164	161	158	590	191
Phoenix	50	3.37	3.02	2.69	153	149	148	2,350	1,682	290	3.47	3.11	2.75	153	150	146	342	193	102	3.37	3.04	2.70	153	150	148	1,875	392
Arkansas																												
Arkansas	0	3.80	3.55	3.29	160	157	153	1,514	402	138	0.00	0.00	0.00	0	0	0	0	0	0	3.80	3.55	3.29	160	157	153	402	138
Arkansas-Little Rock	0	3.65	3.32	3.00	157	154	151	1,524	365	103	3.43	3.11	2.96	156	152	151	161	48	54	3.59	3.27	2.98	157	154	151	413	157
California																												
California-Berkeley	75	3.87	3.79	3.64	170	167	162	8,297	852	286	0.00	0.00	0.00	0	0	0	0	0	0	3.87	3.79	3.64	170	167	162	852	286
California-Davis	75	3.80	3.69	3.53	165	163	160	4,020	943	196	0.00	0.00	0.00	0	0	0	0	0	0	3.80	3.69	3.53	165	163	160	943	196
California-Hastings	75	3.71	3.60	3.45	165	164	160	5,881	1,323	383	0.00	0.00	0.00	0	0	0	0	0	0	3.71	3.60	3.45	165	164	160	1,323	383
California-Los Angeles	75	3.87	3.77	3.56	170	168	165	8,748	1,436	308	0.00	0.00	0.00	0	0	0	0	0	0	3.87	3.77	3.56	170	168	165	1,436	308
California Western	55	3.48	3.23	2.99	157	154	151	2,628	1,228	355	3.66	3.34	2.94	157	155	151	203	67	27	3.49	3.24	2.99	157	154	151	1,295	382
Chapman	75	3.68	3.52	3.21	161	159	155	2,526	734	208	3.81	3.58	3.07	162	158	156	257	9	4	3.68	3.52	3.21	161	159	155	743	212
Golden Gate	60	3.40	3.12	2.84	156	154	151	2,276	1,326	268	3.24	2.99	2.67	155	153	151	378	126	52	3.38	3.10	2.82	156	154	151	1,452	320
La Verne	50	3.35	3.06	2.82	155	153	150	1,252	559	127	3.17	2.91	2.64	152	151	149	346	107	39	3.33	3.05	2.74	155	152	150	666	166
Loyola Marymount		3.72	3.57	3.33	163	161	159	5,303	1,485	340	3.61	3.38	3.09	161	159	155	2,566	104	63	3.70	3.56	3.31	163	161	158	1,589	403
Pacific, McGeorge	50	3.55	3.38	3.09	160	158	155	2,878	1,249	298	3.51	3.33	2.82	159	155	152	297	84	48	3.55	3.38	3.07	160	158	155	1,333	346
Pepperdine	60	3.75	3.62	3.31	165	163	159	3,422	965	222	0.00	0.00	0.00	0	0	0	0	0	0	3.75	3.62	3.31	165	163	159	965	222
San Diego	50	3.64	3.49	3.31	163	161	159	4,789	1,541	293	3.63	3.45	3.16	164	159	158	390	81	37	3.63	3.49	3.30	163	161	159	1,622	330
San Francisco	60	3.63	3.46	3.16	161	159	155	4,163	1,350	184	3.58	3.28	2.82	160	156	153	534	128	67	3.62	3.45	3.09	161	159	155	1,478	251
Santa Clara	75	3.55	3.35	3.14	162	160	158	4,511	1,846	238	3.47	3.24	2.94	161	159	157	448	235	76	3.53	3.32	3.08	162	160	158	2,081	314
Southern California	75	3.73	3.64	3.46	169	167	166	6,587	1,435	220	0.00	0.00	0.00	0	0	0	0	0	0	3.73	3.64	3.46	169	167	166	1,435	220
Southwestern	60	3.56	3.43	3.22	158	156	153	3,383	980	295	3.37	3.15	2.83	156	152	151	566	175	115	3.54	3.35	3.13	158	155	152	1,155	410
Stanford	100	3.94	3.88	3.74	173	170	167	4,248	379	180	0.00	0.00	0.00	0	0	0	0	0	0	3.94	3.88	3.74	173	170	167	379	180
Thomas Jefferson	50	3.25	3.01	2.73	154	151	149	2,776	1,375	318	3.20	2.92	2.70	152	149	147	421	229	104	3.24	3.00	2.71	153	151	149	1,604	422
Western State	50	3.35	3.10	2.84	152	150	148	1,588	925	174	3.40	3.17	2.80	153	150	148	450	206	68	3.36	3.12	2.83	153	150	148	1,131	242
Whittier	60	3.30	3.04	2.76	154	152	150	1,805	987	256	3.21	2.98	2.73	154	152	150	360	135	47	3.28	3.02	2.75	154	152	150	1,122	303
Colorado																												
Colorado	65	3.74	3.61	3.30	166	164	161	2,906	794	180	0.00	0.00	0.00	0	0	0	0	0	0	3.74	3.61	3.30	166	164	161	794	180
Denver	60	3.66	3.46	3.16	161	160	158	2,782	915	239	3.68	3.46	3.16	160	157	153	347	93	62	3.66	3.46	3.15	161	159	156	1,008	301
Connecticut																												
Connecticut	60	3.63	3.43	3.23	164	162	160	2,257	525	135	3.62	3.33	3.03	160	158	155	1,007	185	51	3.63	3.43	3.20	163	161	158	710	186
Quinnipiac	65	3.61	3.43	3.13	160	157	155	2,260	1,010	123	3.64	3.38	3.11	155	153	152	249	82	40	3.62	3.42	3.13	159	157	154	1,092	163
Yale	75	3.96	3.91	3.81	176	173	171	3,797	255	205	0.00	0.00	0.00	0	0	0	0	0	0	3.96	3.91	3.81	176	173	171	255	205
Delaware																												
Widener	60	3.45	3.19	2.86	154	153	151	1,869	1,096	259	3.48	3.16	2.88	152	150	148	487	245	130	3.47	3.18	2.86	154	152	150	1,341	389

	Application Fee ($)	Full-time									Part-time									Total							
		75% GPA	Median GPA	25% GPA	75% LSAT	Median LSAT	25% LSAT	# of Applicants	# of Offers	# of Matriculants	75% GPA	Median GPA	25% GPA	75% LSAT	Median LSAT	25% LSAT	# of Applicants	# of Offers	# of Matriculants	75% GPA	Median GPA	25% GPA	75% LSAT	Median LSAT	25% LSAT	Total # of Offers	Total # of Matriculants
District of Columbia																												
American	70	3.58	3.39	3.13	164	163	158	8,000	1,740	425	3.60	3.48	3.13	164	161	159	1,021	194	77	3.58	3.40	3.12	164	163	158	1,934	502
Catholic	65	3.56	3.34	3.12	161	159	157	2,680	964	197	3.44	3.24	2.98	159	157	155	692	172	77	3.53	3.32	3.08	161	159	156	1,136	274
District of Columbia	35	3.43	3.12	2.83	155	153	149	1,358	344	97	3.48	3.15	2.95	155	151	148	384	69	34	3.39	3.12	2.84	155	152	149	413	131
George Washington	80	3.88	3.79	3.42	168	167	162	8,197	1,991	489	3.84	3.51	3.18	167	162	160	1,048	100	34	3.87	3.79	3.39	168	167	162	2,091	523
Georgetown	85	3.78	3.65	3.41	172	171	169	11,524	2,442	469	3.79	3.70	3.39	170	167	164	2,393	198	122	3.78	3.67	3.45	172	170	168	2,640	591
Howard	60	3.50	3.20	3.00	156	154	151	1,836	430	156	0.00	0.00	0.00	0	0	0	0	0	0	3.50	3.20	3.00	156	154	151	430	156
Florida																												
Ave Maria	50	3.41	3.14	2.84	153	149	147	1,981	927	203	0.00	0.00	0.00	0	0	0	0	0	0	3.41	3.14	2.84	153	149	147	927	203
Barry	60	3.34	2.96	2.59	154	151	149	1,977	1,136	224	3.30	2.90	2.63	153	151	149	261	112	30	3.32	2.93	2.60	154	151	149	1,248	254
Florida A&M		3.28	3.00	2.69	150	147	144	1,561	514	230	3.40	3.11	2.73	151	147	145	292	103	58	3.30	3.03	2.71	150	147	144	617	288
Florida Coastal	0	3.42	3.15	2.86	152	149	146	6,021	4,174	782	3.26	3.03	2.65	151	146	145	294	102	26	3.42	3.14	2.86	152	149	146	4,276	808
Florida	30	3.84	3.67	3.44	164	162	160	3,357	817	310	0.00	0.00	0.00	0	0	0	0	0	0	3.84	3.67	3.44	164	162	160	817	310
Florida International	20	3.81	3.60	3.31	157	155	152	2,048	434	116	3.71	3.55	3.24	159	155	151	469	70	45	3.79	3.60	3.27	157	155	152	504	161
Florida State	30	3.70	3.52	3.30	164	162	161	3,621	803	199	0.00	0.00	0.00	0	0	0	0	0	0	3.70	3.52	3.30	164	162	161	803	199
Miami	60	3.60	3.40	3.16	160	158	156	4,909	2,311	489	0.00	0.00	0.00	0	0	0	0	0	0	3.60	3.40	3.16	160	158	156	2,311	489
Nova Southeastern	50	3.46	3.19	2.96	153	151	148	2,349	991	322	3.29	3.03	2.86	151	149	145	445	108	64	3.42	3.16	2.94	153	150	148	1,099	386
St. Thomas	60	3.37	3.01	2.72	153	150	148	2,165	1,094	275	0.00	0.00	0.00	0	0	0	0	0	0	3.37	3.01	2.72	153	150	148	1,094	275
Stetson	55	3.67	3.44	3.22	159	156	154	2,663	1,002	290	3.50	3.26	3.07	156	154	152	333	118	70	3.66	3.42	3.17	158	156	154	1,120	360
Georgia																												
Atlanta's John Marshall	50	3.29	2.95	2.60	153	150	148	1,623	713	209	3.31	3.02	2.62	152	150	148	346	122	56	3.30	2.97	2.61	153	150	148	835	265
Emory	70	3.69	3.54	3.34	167	166	166	4,583	1,245	293	0.00	0.00	0.00	0	0	0	0	0	0	3.69	3.54	3.34	167	166	166	1,245	293
Georgia	50	3.80	3.70	3.40	166	164	162	4,297	956	248	0.00	0.00	0.00	0	0	0	0	0	0	3.80	3.70	3.40	166	164	162	956	248
Georgia State	50	3.80	3.60	3.20	162	161	159	2,583	425	155	3.50	3.40	3.10	161	159	159	331	88	69	3.75	3.60	3.20	162	161	159	513	224
Mercer	50	3.62	3.41	3.03	158	156	153	1,915	609	166	0.00	0.00	0.00	0	0	0	0	0	0	3.62	3.41	3.03	158	156	153	609	166
Hawai'i																												
Hawai'i	60	3.75	3.45	3.23	159	157	154	1,093	203	86	3.62	3.40	3.05	156	154	151	337	47	27	3.72	3.45	3.19	159	156	153	250	113
Idaho																												
Idaho	50	3.54	3.30	2.96	157	154	151	862	378	130	0.00	0.00	0.00	0	0	0	0	0	0	3.54	3.30	2.96	157	154	151	378	130
Illinois																												
Chicago	75	3.87	3.78	3.59	172	171	168	5,579	849	205	0.00	0.00	0.00	0	0	0	0	0	0	3.87	3.78	3.59	172	171	168	849	205
Chicago-Kent	0	3.71	3.57	3.21	163	161	156	3,340	1,573	248	3.67	3.46	3.15	161	156	152	431	138	62	3.70	3.55	3.20	163	161	155	1,711	310
DePaul		3.63	3.45	3.09	162	160	158	5,109	2,094	257	3.68	3.55	3.44	157	154	152	661	216	55	3.64	3.48	3.13	161	160	156	2,310	312
Illinois	0	3.90	3.80	3.30	168	167	163	4,833	984	228	0.00	0.00	0.00	0	0	0	0	0	0	3.90	3.80	3.30	168	167	163	984	228
John Marshall		3.44	3.23	2.93	157	154	152	2,941	1,385	437	3.39	3.22	2.87	155	153	151	582	174	102	3.43	3.22	2.92	157	154	151	1,559	539
Loyola-Chicago	0	3.59	3.41	3.13	163	161	158	4,751	1,510	243	3.58	3.40	3.12	159	157	153	701	128	49	3.59	3.41	3.13	162	161	157	1,638	292
Northern Illinois	50	3.54	3.26	3.04	155	153	150	1,141	572	132	3.57	3.53	3.39	156	149	148	75	22	3	3.55	3.28	3.04	155	153	150	594	135
Northwestern	100	3.90	3.80	3.40	171	170	166	4,480	813	274	0.00	0.00	0.00	0	0	0	0	0	0	3.90	3.80	3.40	171	170	166	813	274
Southern Illinois		3.60	3.30	3.00	157	153	151	658	364	144	0.00	0.00	0.00	0	0	0	0	0	0	3.60	3.30	3.00	157	153	151	364	144
Indiana																												
Indiana-Bloomington	50	3.89	3.78	3.47	164	164	156	3,441	849	250	0.00	0.00	0.00	0	0	0	0	0	0	3.89	3.78	3.47	164	164	156	849	250
Indiana-Indianapolis	50	3.72	3.50	3.17	160	157	153	1,628	674	184	3.55	3.34	2.94	155	153	149	272	158	98	3.68	3.44	3.09	159	155	151	832	282
Notre Dame	65	3.73	3.57	3.39	168	167	162	4,022	661	172	0.00	0.00	0.00	0	0	0	0	0	0	3.73	3.57	3.39	168	167	162	661	172
Valparaiso	60	3.60	3.33	3.08	153	151	148	1,350	921	196	2.99	2.91	2.83	152	148	147	122	39	11	3.59	3.31	3.06	153	150	147	960	207

	Application Fee ($)	Full-time									Part-time									Total							
		75% GPA	Median GPA	25% GPA	75% LSAT	Median LSAT	25% LSAT	# of Applicants	# of Offers	# of Matriculants	75% GPA	Median GPA	25% GPA	75% LSAT	Median LSAT	25% LSAT	# of Applicants	# of Offers	# of Matriculants	75% GPA	Median GPA	25% GPA	75% LSAT	Median LSAT	25% LSAT	Total # of Offers	Total # of Matriculants
Iowa																												
Drake	50	3.71	3.41	3.07	158	156	153	1,129	553	155	0.00	0.00	0.00	0	0	0	2	0	0	3.71	3.41	3.07	158	156	153	553	155
Iowa	60	3.77	3.59	3.41	164	161	158	1,757	692	203	0.00	0.00	0.00	0	0	0	0	0	0	3.77	3.59	3.41	164	161	158	692	203
Kansas																												
Kansas	55	3.67	3.46	3.20	160	158	155	1,120	417	165	0.00	0.00	0.00	0	0	0	0	0	0	3.67	3.46	3.20	160	158	155	417	165
Washburn	40	3.55	3.22	2.91	158	155	153	1,102	435	169	0.00	0.00	0.00	0	0	0	0	0	0	3.55	3.22	2.91	158	155	153	435	169
Kentucky																												
Kentucky	50	3.76	3.55	3.19	162	160	157	1,191	433	135	0.00	0.00	0.00	0	0	0	0	0	0	3.76	3.55	3.19	162	160	157	433	135
Louisville-Brandeis	50	3.68	3.40	3.08	159	157	154	1,644	526	135	3.35	3.28	3.27	160	157	155	125	12	8	3.67	3.39	3.10	160	157	155	538	143
Northern Kentucky	40	3.57	3.32	3.05	157	155	153	959	451	137	3.72	3.20	2.95	156	153	150	186	99	62	3.63	3.28	3.05	157	155	152	550	199
Louisiana																												
Louisiana State	50	3.60	3.38	3.14	160	158	155	1,653	585	222	0.00	0.00	0.00	0	0	0	0	0	0	3.60	3.38	3.14	160	158	155	585	222
Loyola-New Orleans	40	3.61	3.38	3.13	157	154	151	1,745	765	200	3.44	3.22	2.95	154	151	149	168	95	46	3.59	3.34	3.09	157	153	150	860	246
Southern	25	3.14	2.86	2.61	148	145	143	1,077	397	229	3.04	2.77	2.45	148	144	142	253	123	91	3.08	2.69	2.56	148	145	143	520	320
Tulane	60	3.70	3.51	3.40	164	162	160	2,828	866	258	0.00	0.00	0.00	0	0	0	0	0	0	3.70	3.51	3.40	164	162	160	866	258
Maine																												
Maine	50	3.62	3.41	3.18	159	156	153	1,171	446	95	0.00	0.00	0.00	0	0	0	0	0	0	3.62	3.41	3.18	159	156	153	446	95
Maryland																												
Baltimore	60	3.67	3.48	2.97	158	156	153	1,930	810	233	3.47	3.10	2.81	154	151	149	513	234	130	3.63	3.31	2.90	157	155	151	1,044	363
Maryland	70	3.68	3.51	3.34	163	161	158	3,338	552	223	3.62	3.40	3.24	160	157	155	515	131	73	3.70	3.50	3.30	163	161	157	683	296
Massachusetts																												
Boston College	75	3.70	3.61	3.45	167	166	163	6,873	1,359	261	0.00	0.00	0.00	0	0	0	0	0	0	3.70	3.61	3.45	167	166	163	1,359	261
Boston	75	3.83	3.72	3.52	167	166	164	8,515	1,747	268	0.00	0.00	0.00	0	0	0	0	0	0	3.83	3.72	3.52	167	166	164	1,747	268
Harvard	85	3.96	3.89	3.78	176	173	171	7,574	833	561	0.00	0.00	0.00	0	0	0	0	0	0	3.96	3.89	3.78	176	173	171	833	561
New England	65	3.49	3.24	3.02	154	153	151	2,734	1,680	301	3.27	3.02	2.72	154	151	149	765	393	92	3.45	3.21	2.95	154	153	151	2,073	393
Northeastern	75	3.70	3.53	3.31	164	161	155	4,311	1,360	220	0.00	0.00	0.00	0	0	0	0	0	0	3.70	3.53	3.31	164	161	155	1,360	220
Suffolk	60	3.50	3.30	3.00	159	157	155	2,727	1,459	328	3.40	3.10	2.90	156	153	151	629	385	203	3.50	3.20	2.90	158	156	152	1,844	531
Western New England	50	3.55	3.19	2.90	155	153	151	1,317	699	133	3.38	3.07	2.86	155	153	150	244	90	35	3.52	3.15	2.89	155	153	151	789	168
Michigan																												
Detroit Mercy	50	3.44	3.20	2.96	155	151	147	1,543	662	201	3.30	3.04	2.80	150	146	144	226	122	56	3.40	3.17	2.93	154	150	146	784	257
Michigan	75	3.85	3.73	3.57	171	169	168	6,311	1,171	376	0.00	0.00	0.00	0	0	0	0	0	0	3.85	3.73	3.57	171	169	168	1,171	376
Michigan State	60	3.74	3.52	3.24	159	157	152	3,275	1,172	276	3.79	3.59	3.38	167	163	158	204	40	23	3.74	3.52	3.24	159	157	152	1,212	299
Thomas M. Cooley	0	3.29	2.99	2.62	154	150	146	4,211	3,553	260	3.36	3.00	2.61	149	145	143	711	548	1,323	3.35	2.99	2.61	151	146	144	4,101	1,583
Wayne State	50	3.62	3.41	3.19	159	156	153	1,219	552	173	3.62	3.08	2.91	156	155	151	116	44	24	3.62	3.40	3.13	159	156	153	596	197
Minnesota																												
Hamline	35	3.63	3.42	3.21	156	153	149	1,108	615	159	3.53	3.32	2.94	156	151	146	242	142	68	3.61	3.39	3.16	156	153	149	757	227
Minnesota	75	3.84	3.71	3.36	168	167	159	3,866	1,031	260	0.00	0.00	0.00	0	0	0	0	0	0	3.84	3.71	3.36	168	167	159	1,031	260
St. Thomas- Minneapolis		3.52	3.24	3.01	161	156	154	1,801	917	168	0.00	0.00	0.00	0	0	0	0	0	0	3.52	3.24	3.01	161	156	154	917	168
William Mitchell	50	3.60	3.40	3.17	159	156	153	1,298	673	274	3.53	3.20	2.90	158	153	149	150	129	83	3.59	3.37	3.14	159	156	152	802	357
Mississippi																												
Mississippi	40	3.69	3.51	3.26	158	156	151	1,602	532	199	0.00	0.00	0.00	0	0	0	0	0	0	3.69	3.51	3.26	158	156	151	532	199
Mississippi College	0	3.58	3.24	2.94	154	150	147	1,356	734	212	0.00	0.00	0.00	0	0	0	1	1	0	3.58	3.24	2.94	154	150	147	735	212

	Application Fee ($)	Full-time 75% GPA	Median GPA	25% GPA	75% LSAT	Median LSAT	25% LSAT	# of Applicants	# of Offers	# of Matriculants	Part-time 75% GPA	Median GPA	25% GPA	75% LSAT	Median LSAT	25% LSAT	# of Applicants	# of Offers	# of Matriculants	Total 75% GPA	Median GPA	25% GPA	75% LSAT	Median LSAT	25% LSAT	Total # of Offers	Total # of Matriculants
Missouri																											
Missouri-Columbia	55	3.76	3.43	3.06	161	159	157	1,024	393	148	0.00	0.00	0.00	0	0	0	0	0	0	3.76	3.43	3.06	161	159	157	393	148
Missouri-Kansas City	60	3.53	3.27	2.94	158	156	154	915	386	152	3.35	3.16	3.11	152	150	148	59	6	4	3.53	3.25	2.94	158	156	154	392	156
St. Louis	55	3.70	3.45	3.18	159	156	153	2,159	1,081	297	3.74	3.27	3.03	157	155	151	405	106	37	3.70	3.44	3.14	159	156	153	1,187	334
Washington University	70	3.80	3.70	3.30	168	167	162	4,386	948	276	0.00	0.00	0.00	0	0	0	0	0	0	3.80	3.70	3.30	168	167	162	948	276
Montana																											
Montana	60	3.75	3.42	3.14	158	155	153	527	197	85	0.00	0.00	0.00	0	0	0	0	0	0	3.75	3.42	3.14	158	155	153	197	85
Nebraska																											
Creighton	50	3.56	3.30	2.92	157	154	151	1,298	648	138	3.28	2.90	2.69	154	154	149	70	16	6	3.55	3.29	2.89	157	154	151	664	144
Nebraska	25	3.84	3.61	3.35	160	156	153	677	363	144	0.00	2.47	0.00	0	157	0	1	1	1	3.84	3.60	3.35	160	156	153	364	145
Nevada																											
Nevada	50	3.72	3.52	3.29	161	159	157	1,504	269	107	3.50	3.22	2.87	159	156	153	241	53	38	3.70	3.46	3.15	161	159	156	322	145
New Hampshire																											
New Hampshire	55	3.58	3.34	3.03	158	153	150	1,308	608	132	0.00	0.00	0.00	0	0	0	0	0	0	3.58	3.34	3.03	158	153	150	608	132
New Jersey																											
Rutgers-Camden	65	3.60	3.40	3.00	163	161	158	2,013	633	127	3.60	3.40	3.20	160	159	155	N/A	N/A	142	3.60	3.40	3.10	161	160	157	633	269
Rutgers-Newark	65	3.60	3.36	3.06	161	159	155	2,598	817	220	3.54	3.22	2.93	161	157	154	738	128	63	3.57	3.32	3.01	161	158	155	945	283
Seton Hall	65	3.69	3.51	3.26	162	160	158	3,179	1,580	249	3.54	3.30	3.00	156	153	150	854	269	109	3.65	3.43	3.17	161	159	155	1,849	358
New Mexico																											
New Mexico	50	3.60	3.40	3.10	159	156	153	1,147	242	116	0.00	0.00	0.00	0	0	0	0	0	0	3.60	3.40	3.10	159	156	153	242	116
New York																											
Albany	60	3.50	3.27	3.03	157	154	152	2,572	1,234	236	0.00	0.00	0.00	0	0	0	0	0	0	3.50	3.27	3.03	157	154	152	1,234	236
Brooklyn	0	3.67	3.47	3.27	165	163	162	5,053	1,447	417	3.58	3.34	3.10	163	161	160	931	158	69	3.66	3.45	3.24	165	163	162	1,605	486
Buffalo	75	3.69	3.48	3.17	160	158	155	1,894	714	219	0.00	0.00	0.00	0	0	0	0	0	0	3.69	3.48	3.17	160	158	155	714	219
Cardozo	75	3.74	3.62	3.47	166	164	161	5,091	1,217	279	3.72	3.55	3.24	161	160	158	843	184	103	3.74	3.60	3.42	166	163	160	1,401	382
CUNY	50	3.57	3.37	3.13	157	154	152	2,137	533	163	0.00	0.00	0.00	0	0	0	0	0	0	3.57	3.37	3.13	157	154	152	533	163
Columbia	80	3.82	3.72	3.61	175	172	170	9,012	1,187	404	0.00	0.00	0.00	0	0	0	0	0	0	3.82	3.72	3.61	175	172	170	1,187	404
Cornell	80	3.80	3.68	3.55	169	168	166	6,269	1,083	205	0.00	0.00	0.00	0	0	0	0	0	0	3.80	3.68	3.55	169	168	166	1,083	205
Fordham	70	3.77	3.62	3.38	168	166	163	7,469	1,789	398	3.71	3.52	3.26	166	164	160	1,414	144	79	3.76	3.60	3.36	168	166	163	1,933	477
Hofstra	0	3.69	3.58	3.17	160	158	156	4,851	1,922	355	3.61	3.57	3.01	159	157	151	583	63	10	3.69	3.58	3.17	160	158	156	1,985	365
New York Law	0	3.49	3.30	3.03	157	155	153	3,685	1,821	520	3.44	3.14	2.86	155	153	151	835	279	121	3.48	3.28	3.00	157	155	153	2,100	641
New York	75	3.86	3.71	3.57	175	172	169	8,461	1,771	476	0.00	0.00	0.00	0	0	0	0	0	0	3.86	3.71	3.57	175	172	169	1,771	476
Pace	65	3.58	3.40	3.13	156	154	152	2,639	1,065	265	3.52	3.34	3.01	156	153	149	443	102	34	3.57	3.40	3.12	156	154	152	1,167	299
St. John's	60	3.71	3.50	3.14	163	161	158	3,673	1,391	267	3.79	3.63	3.43	157	155	153	837	205	74	3.72	3.55	3.19	162	161	156	1,596	341
Syracuse	75	3.57	3.32	3.12	157	155	153	2,332	962	252	0.00	0.00	0.00	0	0	0	0	0	0	3.57	3.32	3.12	157	155	153	962	252
Touro	60	3.39	3.15	2.86	154	151	150	1,582	735	213	3.34	3.05	2.82	152	150	148	436	135	67	3.39	3.14	2.86	153	151	149	870	280
North Carolina																											
Campbell	50	3.59	3.37	3.12	158	156	154	1,469	486	162	0.00	0.00	0.00	0	0	0	0	0	0	3.59	3.37	3.12	158	156	154	486	162
Charlotte	50	3.35	3.06	2.75	152	150	148	3,328	2,065	390	3.22	2.88	2.63	152	149	148	419	189	78	3.34	3.04	2.73	152	149	148	2,254	468
Duke	70	3.90	3.80	3.68	171	170	168	7,905	1,044	238	0.00	0.00	0.00	0	0	0	0	0	0	3.90	3.80	3.68	171	170	168	1,044	238
Elon	50	3.40	3.10	2.80	159	155	153	885	361	132	0.00	0.00	0.00	0	0	0	0	0	0	3.40	3.10	2.80	159	155	153	361	132
North Carolina	70	3.73	3.51	3.34	165	163	159	3,044	546	254	0.00	0.00	0.00	0	0	0	0	0	0	3.73	3.51	3.34	165	163	159	546	254
North Carolina Central	40	3.54	3.19	2.87	149	145	142	2,097	360	172	3.63	3.43	3.18	156	148	145	868	101	34	3.55	3.26	2.91	150	146	143	461	206
Wake Forest	60	3.70	3.60	3.30	164	163	160	2,984	1,002	165	0.00	0.00	0.00	0	0	0	0	0	0	3.70	3.60	3.30	164	163	160	1,002	165

	Application Fee ($)	Full-time 75% GPA	Median GPA	25% GPA	75% LSAT	Median LSAT	25% LSAT	# of Applicants	# of Offers	# of Matriculants	Part-time 75% GPA	Median GPA	25% GPA	75% LSAT	Median LSAT	25% LSAT	# of Applicants	# of Offers	# of Matriculants	Total 75% GPA	Median GPA	25% GPA	75% LSAT	Median LSAT	25% LSAT	Total # of Offers	Total # of Matriculants
North Dakota																											
North Dakota	35	3.61	3.39	3.14	154	151	148	536	206	83	0.00	0.00	0.00	0	0	0	0	0	0	3.61	3.39	3.14	154	151	148	206	83
Ohio																											
Akron	0	3.69	3.46	3.29	158	157	155	1,700	622	105	3.51	3.19	3.05	154	152	151	303	160	72	3.61	3.37	3.10	158	155	152	782	177
Capital	40	3.53	3.33	3.05	155	153	150	1,081	623	187	3.52	3.12	2.87	155	151	148	186	87	59	3.52	3.29	3.00	155	153	150	710	246
Case Western	40	3.64	3.50	3.26	162	160	157	2,193	825	236	0.00	0.00	0.00	0	0	0	0	0	0	3.64	3.50	3.26	162	160	157	825	236
Cincinnati	35	3.80	3.56	3.36	162	161	157	1,823	775	144	0.00	0.00	0.00	0	0	0	0	0	0	3.80	3.56	3.36	162	161	157	775	144
Cleveland State	0	3.65	3.45	3.16	158	156	154	1,494	566	151	3.66	3.27	2.88	155	153	150	271	78	44	3.66	3.45	3.09	157	155	153	644	195
Dayton	50	3.41	3.11	2.81	154	152	150	2,147	1,186	207	0.00	0.00	0.00	0	0	0	0	0	0	3.41	3.11	2.81	154	152	150	1,186	207
Ohio Northern		3.70	3.49	2.94	156	154	149	1,291	484	120	0.00	0.00	0.00	0	0	0	0	0	0	3.70	3.49	2.94	156	154	149	484	120
Ohio State	60	3.82	3.66	3.45	164	163	160	2,703	962	230	0.00	0.00	0.00	0	0	0	0	0	0	3.82	3.66	3.45	164	163	160	962	230
Toledo	0	3.53	3.22	2.87	156	153	151	879	506	123	3.40	3.19	2.78	152	150	149	156	75	34	3.48	3.21	2.83	156	152	150	581	157
Oklahoma																											
Oklahoma	50	3.70	3.46	3.20	161	159	157	1,111	335	174	0.00	0.00	0.00	0	0	0	0	0	0	3.70	3.46	3.20	161	159	157	335	174
Oklahoma City	50	3.48	3.12	2.86	153	150	149	1,262	605	213	3.66	3.37	3.17	154	149	148	99	20	11	3.49	3.14	2.86	153	150	149	625	224
Tulsa	30	3.63	3.30	2.95	158	155	152	1,373	591	146	0.00	0.00	0.00	0	0	0	0	0	0	3.63	3.30	2.95	158	155	152	591	146
Oregon																											
Lewis & Clark	50	3.69	3.48	3.21	164	163	160	3,223	1,132	194	3.67	3.45	2.97	163	157	152	204	55	53	3.69	3.48	3.20	164	162	157	1,187	247
Oregon	50	3.66	3.43	3.18	161	159	157	2,285	902	177	0.00	0.00	0.00	0	0	0	0	0	0	3.66	3.43	3.18	161	159	157	902	177
Willamette	50	3.54	3.30	2.99	159	156	154	1,432	531	158	0.00	0.00	0.00	0	0	0	0	0	0	3.54	3.30	2.99	159	156	154	531	158
Pennsylvania																											
Duquesne	60	3.64	3.42	3.17	156	154	152	705	382	165	3.62	3.28	3.15	154	151	149	217	78	47	3.63	3.35	3.11	155	153	151	460	212
Earl Mack, Drexel	0	3.58	3.28	2.99	162	159	156	2,908	1,038	146	0.00	0.00	0.00	0	0	0	0	0	0	3.58	3.28	2.99	162	159	156	1,038	146
Penn State	60	3.80	3.60	3.40	161	159	157	5,326	1,551	228	0.00	0.00	0.00	0	0	0	0	0	0	3.80	3.60	3.40	161	159	157	1,551	228
Pennsylvania	80	3.90	3.85	3.54	171	170	166	6,003	866	250	0.00	0.00	0.00	0	0	0	0	0	0	3.90	3.85	3.54	171	170	166	866	250
Pittsburgh	55	3.63	3.38	3.07	161	160	158	2,756	954	259	0.00	0.00	0.00	0	0	0	0	0	0	3.63	3.38	3.07	161	160	158	954	259
Temple	60	3.64	3.47	3.24	164	162	160	4,279	1,696	271	3.54	3.28	3.03	161	159	157	403	117	55	3.63	3.44	3.20	164	161	159	1,813	326
Villanova	75	3.56	3.33	3.15	163	160	159	3,739	1,648	251	0.00	0.00	0.00	0	0	0	0	0	0	3.56	3.33	3.15	163	160	159	1,648	251
Widener	60	3.47	3.10	2.83	153	150	149	1,231	706	140	3.39	3.09	2.73	153	149	148	253	116	38	3.46	3.10	2.81	153	150	148	822	178
Puerto Rico																											
Inter American	63	3.60	3.39	3.16	142	139	136	561	295	477	3.52	3.19	2.90	141	137	134	348	169	392	3.57	3.32	3.09	142	139	135	464	869
Pontifical Catholic		3.62	3.30	3.00	137	134	127	393	228	190	3.50	3.12	2.89	136	133	131	186	114	99	3.58	3.30	2.97	138	135	132	342	289
Puerto Rico	20	3.83	3.59	3.34	145	143	141	243	162	147	3.75	3.56	3.15	149	146	143	188	59	50	3.80	3.59	3.34	150	146	142	221	197
Rhode Island																											
Roger Williams	60	3.50	3.30	3.00	154	151	149	1,501	949	198	0.00	0.00	0.00	0	0	0	0	0	0	3.50	3.30	3.00	154	151	149	949	198
South Carolina																											
Charleston	50	3.46	3.25	2.95	156	155	152	1,942	850	187	3.37	3.04	2.80	153	151	149	367	100	50	3.46	3.18	2.90	156	154	151	950	237
South Carolina	60	3.64	3.39	3.04	161	159	156	2,185	751	239	0.00	0.00	0.00	0	0	0	0	0	0	3.64	3.39	3.04	161	159	156	751	239
South Dakota																											
South Dakota	35	3.72	3.38	3.12	154	150	149	449	220	75	0.00	0.00	0.00	0	0	0	0	0	0	3.72	3.38	3.12	154	150	149	220	75
Tennessee																											
Memphis	25	3.56	3.31	3.06	158	156	154	964	301	148	3.09	2.91	2.67	152	149	145	0	12	10	3.56	3.29	3.03	157	155	153	313	158
Tennessee	15	3.81	3.60	3.38	162	160	156	1,508	410	169	0.00	0.00	0.00	0	0	0	0	0	0	3.81	3.60	3.38	162	160	156	410	169
Vanderbilt	50	3.82	3.72	3.50	170	169	165	4,885	1,100	193	0.00	0.00	0.00	0	0	0	0	0	0	3.82	3.72	3.50	170	169	165	1,100	193

	Application Fee ($)	Full-time									Part-time									Total							
		75% GPA	Median GPA	25% GPA	75% LSAT	Median LSAT	25% LSAT	# of Applicants	# of Offers	# of Matriculants	75% GPA	Median GPA	25% GPA	75% LSAT	Median LSAT	25% LSAT	# of Applicants	# of Offers	# of Matriculants	75% GPA	Median GPA	25% GPA	75% LSAT	Median LSAT	25% LSAT	Total # of Offers	Total # of Matriculants
Texas																											
Baylor	40	3.85	3.71	3.52	163	162	160	4,713	778	183	0.00	0.00	0.00	0	0	0	0	0	0	3.85	3.71	3.52	163	162	160	778	183
Houston	70	3.69	3.45	3.20	164	162	160	3,279	874	205	3.56	3.30	3.01	161	160	157	650	93	61	3.68	3.41	3.13	164	162	159	967	266
St. Mary's	55	3.40	3.07	2.72	156	154	151	1,718	768	255	3.21	2.87	2.48	154	151	149	247	80	46	3.36	3.03	2.68	156	153	151	848	301
SMU Dedman	75	3.86	3.75	3.38	166	164	157	2,327	566	177	3.71	3.50	3.00	163	160	159	765	163	77	3.82	3.67	3.29	165	163	156	729	254
South Texas	55	3.47	3.26	3.02	157	154	151	2,129	961	381	3.38	3.10	2.87	154	152	150	307	134	80	3.45	3.24	2.99	156	153	151	1,095	461
Texas	70	3.84	3.71	3.57	169	167	164	5,815	1,316	389	0.00	0.00	0.00	0	0	0	0	0	0	3.84	3.71	3.57	169	167	164	1,316	389
Texas Southern	55	3.33	3.01	2.74	149	148	145	2,228	667	212	0.00	0.00	0.00	0	0	0	0	0	0	3.33	3.01	2.74	149	148	145	667	212
Texas Tech	50	3.66	3.45	3.16	158	156	153	1,398	559	244	0.00	0.00	0.00	0	0	0	0	0	0	3.66	3.45	3.16	158	156	153	559	244
Texas Wesleyan	55	3.51	3.25	2.96	156	153	151	1,746	704	172	3.37	3.12	2.87	156	152	149	334	123	81	3.46	3.23	2.91	156	153	151	827	253
Utah																											
Brigham Young	50	3.86	3.75	3.45	167	164	161	772	219	150	0.00	0.00	0.00	0	0	0	0	0	0	3.86	3.75	3.45	167	164	161	219	150
Utah	60	3.82	3.63	3.46	164	161	157	1,365	394	122	0.00	0.00	0.00	0	0	0	0	0	0	3.82	3.63	3.46	164	161	157	394	122
Vermont																											
Vermont	60	3.55	3.35	3.13	159	156	153	1,056	628	212	0.00	0.00	0.00	0	0	0	0	0	0	3.55	3.35	3.13	159	156	153	628	212
Virginia																											
Appalachian	60	3.36	3.01	2.69	151	147	146	1,368	816	127	0.00	0.00	0.00	0	0	0	0	0	0	3.36	3.01	2.69	151	147	146	816	127
George Mason	35	3.82	3.68	3.30	165	164	159	4,697	1,232	234	3.82	3.73	3.10	164	164	157	1,835	127	69	3.82	3.72	3.27	165	164	158	1,359	303
Liberty	50	3.43	3.19	2.75	153	150	148	459	240	135	0.00	0.00	0.00	0	0	0	0	0	0	3.43	3.19	2.75	153	150	148	240	135
Regent	50	3.54	3.32	2.97	156	152	150	674	321	164	3.29	2.96	2.86	158	156	154	25	9	4	3.54	3.32	2.97	156	152	150	330	168
Richmond	35	3.63	3.47	3.16	163	162	159	2,105	558	146	0.00	0.00	0.00	0	0	0	0	0	0	3.63	3.47	3.16	163	162	159	558	146
Virginia	75	3.92	3.85	3.51	171	170	166	8,560	923	368	0.00	0.00	0.00	0	0	0	0	0	0	3.92	3.85	3.51	171	170	166	923	368
Washington and Lee	0	3.64	3.44	3.14	167	166	161	4,582	998	144	0.00	0.00	0.00	0	0	0	0	0	0	3.64	3.44	3.14	167	166	161	998	144
William & Mary	50	3.81	3.70	3.47	166	165	160	6,291	1,207	217	0.00	0.00	0.00	0	0	0	0	0	0	3.81	3.70	3.47	166	165	160	1,207	217
Washington																											
Gonzaga	50	3.57	3.36	3.11	157	155	154	1,924	762	183	0.00	0.00	0.00	0	0	0	0	0	0	3.57	3.36	3.11	157	155	154	762	183
Seattle	60	3.60	3.35	3.14	161	158	156	2,633	925	266	3.33	3.01	2.69	159	157	153	259	88	58	3.58	3.33	3.07	160	158	155	1,013	324
Washington	60	3.81	3.66	3.49	166	163	160	2,560	545	186	0.00	0.00	0.00	0	0	0	0	0	0	3.81	3.66	3.49	166	163	160	545	186
West Virginia																											
West Virginia	50	3.70	3.43	3.17	156	154	151	737	339	137	0.00	0.00	0.00	0	0	0	0	0	0	3.70	3.43	3.17	156	154	151	339	137
Wisconsin																											
Marquette	50	3.64	3.46	3.14	159	157	154	2,054	905	208	3.63	3.30	3.05	160	157	153	228	52	39	3.64	3.46	3.14	159	157	154	957	247
Wisconsin	56	3.76	3.63	3.29	164	163	158	2,829	599	246	0.00	0.00	0.00	0	0	0	0	0	0	3.76	3.63	3.29	164	163	158	599	246
Wyoming																											
Wyoming	50	3.71	3.43	3.23	157	154	151	624	217	82	0.00	0.00	0.00	0	0	0	0	0	0	3.71	3.43	3.23	157	154	151	217	82

Admission Fall 2010

| | Admission Fall 2010 | | | | | | | | | | | | | |
| | Student Body | | | | | Faculty | | | Tuition ($) | | | | Other | |
	# Full-time	# Part-time	% Men	% Women	% Minorities	# Full-time and Other	% Men	% Women	Student/Faculty Ratio	Resident, Full-time	Nonresident, Full-time	Resident, Part-time	Nonresident, Part-time	Official Guide Page #	Grid included ●
Alabama															
Alabama	509	0	57.6	42.4	12.6	47	63.8	36.2	10.1	15,760	28,070			76	●
Faulkner	341	13	59.9	40.1	11.9	23	73.9	26.1	14.4	31,020	31,020			284	●
Samford	491	0	56.2	43.8	12.0	23	73.9	26.1	17.9	33,155	33,155	19,695	19,695	652	●
Arizona															
Arizona	469	0	56.1	43.9	24.7	44	61.4	38.6	9.3	23,540	39,402			92	●
Arizona State	614	0	56.2	43.8	23.6	53	66.0	34.0	9.5	21,598	35,147			96	●
Phoenix	514	210	54.7	45.3	25.3	32	37.5	62.5	14.4	36,036	36,036	29,156	29,156	592	
Arkansas															
Arkansas	390	0	55.9	44.1	17.4	29	58.6	41.4	11.0	11,367	22,501			100	
Arkansas-Little Rock	338	152	54.1	45.9	19.6	30	43.3	56.7	13.0	11,456	23,451	8,010	16,007	104	●
California															
California-Berkeley	916	0	47.1	52.9	37.7	90	56.7	43.3	10.5	44,244	52,245			148	
California-Davis	589	0	50.8	49.2	35.7	43	48.8	51.2	11.3	41,763	50,595			152	●
California-Hastings	1,247	1	46.3	53.7	44.4	71	60.6	39.4	15.3	38,906	50,131			156	●
California-Los Angeles	999	0	52.5	47.5	33.4	86	64.0	36.0	11.2	40,616	50,639			160	●
California Western	786	133	46.4	53.6	29.5	45	68.9	31.1	17.9	40,780	40,780	28,660	28,660	164	●
Chapman	546	28	53.0	47.0	22.1	51	51.0	49.0	9.3	40,173	40,173	31,938	31,938	188	●
Golden Gate	616	116	45.6	54.4	28.7	42	50.0	50.0	14.9	38,375	38,375	29,485	29,485	332	●
La Verne	312	114	54.7	45.3	33.6	19	47.4	52.6	16.0	38,462	38,462	29,062	29,062	400	
Loyola Marymount	1,013	276	49.7	50.3	39.3	66	53.0	47.0	15.0	41,840	41,840	28,035	28,035	420	●
Pacific, McGeorge	724	302	51.8	48.2	24.6	63	63.5	36.5	12.7	39,989	39,989	26,603	26,603	576	●
Pepperdine	667	0	51.4	48.6	19.9	35	65.7	34.3	15.6	41,210	41,210			588	●
San Diego	831	176	52.4	47.6	31.8	66	68.2	31.8	13.6	41,414	41,414	29,904	29,904	656	●
San Francisco	589	150	45.9	54.1	36.3	37	54.1	45.9	15.3	38,800	38,800	27,745	27,745	660	●
Santa Clara	749	234	53.4	46.6	41.1	65	50.8	49.2	12.4	39,360	39,360	27,552	27,552	664	●
Southern California	651	0	52.1	47.9	41.2	43	58.1	41.9	12.8	48,434	48,434			692	●
Southwestern	741	354	48.2	51.8	35.9	57	57.9	42.1	14.3	39,110	39,110	23,546	23,546	704	●
Stanford	571	0	55.0	45.0	34.7	68	55.9	44.1	7.5	46,581	46,581			708	
Thomas Jefferson	687	279	58.8	41.2	31.1	42	42.9	57.1	17.6	19,350	19,350	13,500	13,500	752	
Western State	318	150	52.6	47.4	38.2	16	62.5	37.5	22.0	35,190	35,190	23,630	23,630	828	●
Whittier	475	167	49.7	50.3	32.2	31	41.9	58.1	16.5	37,975	37,975	25,325	25,325	832	●
Colorado															
Colorado	546	0	51.5	48.5	20.1	43	53.5	46.5	10.8	28,915	35,773			220	●
Denver	768	192	51.7	48.3	16.1	62	51.6	48.4	12.7	37,152	37,152	27,392	27,392	244	●
Connecticut															
Connecticut	440	180	56.0	44.0	21.5	52	53.8	46.2	10.6	21,508	44,398	15,024	31,044	228	●
Quinnipiac	340	127	52.0	48.0	11.6	32	62.5	37.5	13.0	42,740	42,740	30,180	30,180	608	●
Yale	629	0	50.7	49.3	29.9	76	76.3	23.7	7.7	50,750	50,750			862	●

| | Admission Fall 2010 | | | | | | | | | | | | | | |
| | Student Body | | | | | Faculty | | | | Tuition ($) | | | | Other | |
	# Full-time	# Part-time	% Men	% Women	% Minorities	# Full-time and Other	% Men	% Women	Student/Faculty Ratio	Resident, Full-time	Nonresident, Full-time	Resident, Part-time	Nonresident, Part-time	Official Guide Page #	Grid included
Delaware															
Widener	647	352	57.4	42.6	15.6	50	50.0	50.0	15.4	34,890	34,890	25,610	25,610	836	•
District of Columbia															
American	1,243	260	43.8	56.2	37.5	104	54.8	45.2	11.8	43,458	43,458	30,468	30,468	84	
Catholic	562	296	47.4	52.6	18.5	56	46.4	53.6	11.9	40,000	40,000	30,505	30,505	184	•
District of Columbia	256	60	42.4	57.6	50.3	21	52.4	47.6	12.6	9,480	18,330	6,630	12,630	256	
George Washington	1,410	299	54.5	45.5	21.4	106	54.7	44.3	14.8	43,999	43,999	34,034	34,034	316	•
Georgetown	1,626	334	52.9	47.1	22.1	129	66.7	33.3	12.3	45,105	45,105	39,120	39,120	320	
Howard	473	0	41.0	59.0	89.0	26	50.0	50.0	18.5	26,439	26,439			360	•
Florida															
Ave Maria	468	0	55.1	44.9	20.9	26	73.1	26.9	17.9	36,448	36,448			112	
Barry	553	164	52.6	47.4	19.2	33	60.6	39.4	18.6	32,650	32,650	24,640	24,640	120	•
Florida A&M	458	211	45.3	54.7	59.3	35	45.7	51.4	17.9	10,312	29,573	7,562	21,686	288	•
Florida Coastal	1,683	59	51.1	48.9	29.4	69	40.6	59.4	20.9	34,712	34,712	28,086	28,086	292	•
Florida	1,044	0	55.3	44.7	24.8	56	44.6	55.4	15.4	16,387	35,752			296	•
Florida International	395	193	48.8	51.2	56.6	32	50.0	50.0	14.7	15,520	30,224	10,786	20,894	300	
Florida State	779	0	60.5	39.5	19.8	47	55.3	44.7	14.3	16,371	35,934			304	•
Miami	1,334	19	57.6	42.4	27.2	82	51.2	48.8	14.6	38,024	38,024			452	•
Nova Southeastern	894	206	47.5	52.5	30.6	60	51.7	48.3	15.9	32,607	32,607	24,579	24,579	548	•
St. Thomas	733	0	53.2	46.8	50.9	28	46.4	53.6	19.7	33,082	33,082			648	•
Stetson	867	214	48.1	51.9	20.7	59	54.2	45.8	15.4	33,220	33,220	23,020	23,020	712	•
Georgia															
Atlanta's John Marshall	455	175	51.6	48.4	32.9	35	42.9	57.1	15.3	32,965		20,065		108	•
Emory	792	0	54.0	46.0	30.3	58	53.4	46.6	11.2	43,392	43,392			280	•
Georgia	703	0	54.8	45.2	19.5	51	58.8	41.2	12.2	15,814	33,620			324	•
Georgia State	457	203	53.2	46.8	20.2	57	50.9	49.1	10.6	13,310	34,334	11,382	26,186	328	•
Mercer	439	0	56.3	43.7	18.7	27	66.7	33.3	12.9	35,695	35,695			448	•
Hawai'i															
Hawai'i	295	58	41.9	58.1	68.8	35	45.7	54.3	8.0	16,421	30,485	13,761	25,481	348	•
Idaho															
Idaho	349	0	59.6	40.4	16.3	21	47.6	52.4	15.7	12,940	24,532			364	•
Illinois															
Chicago	634	0	55.7	44.3	28.1	71	66.2	33.8	9.1	46,185				200	
Chicago-Kent	785	185	54.9	45.1	22.9	66	66.7	33.3	11.7	40,050	40,050	29,300	29,300	204	•
DePaul	853	203	52.2	47.8	22.0	56	57.1	42.9	13.8	39,350	39,350	25,730	25,730	248	•
Illinois	640	0	58.8	41.3	24.7	49	53.1	46.9	12.8	36,420	43,420			368	
John Marshall	1,125	317	54.2	45.8	26.0	75	65.3	34.7	16.3	36,920	36,920	26,400	26,400	388	•
Loyola-Chicago	692	159	50.8	49.2	18.9	60	63.3	36.7	13.4	38,086	38,086	28,766	28,766	424	•
Northern Illinois	321	11	57.5	42.5	20.8	19	47.4	52.6	18.1	17,268	30,960			532	•
Northwestern	817	0	54.2	45.8	37.9	99	52.5	47.5	8.5	49,714				540	
Southern Illinois	380	2	62.0	38.0	8.9	27	48.1	51.9	12.2	14,746	33,097			696	•

	Student Body					Faculty				Tuition ($)				Other	
	# Full-time	# Part-time	% Men	% Women	% Minorities	# Full-time and Other	% Men	% Women	Student/Faculty Ratio	Resident, Full-time	Nonresident, Full-time	Resident, Part-time	Nonresident, Part-time	Official Guide Page #	Grid included •
Indiana															
Indiana-Bloomington	646	0	59.0	41.0	18.1	59	66.1	33.9	9.4	26,904	43,704			372	•
Indiana-Indianapolis	595	323	55.4	44.6	15.4	41	56.1	43.9	17.2	20,554	43,646	15,412	32,545	376	•
Notre Dame	564	0	58.3	41.7	28.0	46	71.7	28.3	10.3	40,805	40,805			544	
Valparaiso	531	35	56.5	43.5	23.1	35	74.3	25.7	15.6	36,800	36,800	22,980	22,980	776	
Iowa															
Drake	451	12	54.2	45.8	10.2	28	60.7	39.3	13.8	32,514	32,514			260	•
Iowa	574	0	55.2	44.8	15.9	46	63.0	37.0	11.3	24,154	42,922			384	
Kansas															
Kansas	497	0	60.8	39.2	18.5	35	57.1	42.9	12.9	15,561	27,038			392	•
Washburn	454	0	59.9	40.1	11.7	31	61.3	38.7	12.9	16,630	25,900			800	•
Kentucky															
Kentucky	419	0	58.0	42.0	13.4	25	72.0	28.0	15.5	16,982	29,424			396	•
Louisville-Brandeis	379	47	55.6	44.4	10.8	26	57.7	42.3	15.0	15,760	30,300	7,960	15,230	416	•
Northern Kentucky	375	239	56.5	43.5	8.8	28	67.9	32.1	15.8	15,124	32,882	10,492	33,208	536	•
Louisiana															
Louisiana State	616	17	58.6	41.4	17.5	41	68.3	31.7	17.0	16,148	30,228			412	•
Loyola-New Orleans	681	153	50.6	49.4	28.5	50	54.0	46.0	17.0	36,196	36,196	24,476	24,476	428	•
Southern	486	235	45.2	54.8	65.2	35	42.9	57.1	14.1	8,478	13,080	7,168	11,768	700	
Tulane	769	1	53.5	46.5	17.3	53	58.5	41.5	13.7	42,144	42,144			764	•
Maine															
Maine	278	0	53.2	46.8	10.1	16	62.5	37.5	15.0	21,994	32,824			432	•
Maryland															
Baltimore	730	353	50.2	49.8	16.0	58	53.4	46.6	16.0	25,224	37,368	18,830	26,394	116	•
Maryland	734	233	52.0	48.0	30.4	63	47.6	52.4	11.2	25,350	36,629	19,385	27,844	440	
Massachusetts															
Boston College	796	0	51.4	48.6	23.5	51	54.9	45.1	13.1	40,905	40,905			128	•
Boston	821	1	49.9	50.1	25.4	67	56.7	43.3	11.4	40,838				132	
Harvard	1,733	0	52.0	48.0	32.9	141	74.5	25.5	12.3	46,616				344	
New England	796	336	44.1	55.9	10.0	40	65.0	32.5	21.9	39,990	39,990	29,990	29,990	496	•
Northeastern	629	0	40.4	59.6	32.6	36	44.4	55.6	14.3	41,066				528	
Suffolk	1,090	591	53.0	47.0	15.5	80	60.0	40.0	17.0	41,120	41,120	30,914	30,914	716	•
Western New England	387	138	45.7	54.3	10.5	36	50.0	50.0	13.5	36,854	36,854	27,246	27,246	824	•
Michigan															
Detroit Mercy	572	155	52.4	47.6	19.1	42	52.4	47.6	15.3	34,010	34,010	27,224	27,224	252	•
Michigan	1,134	0	55.4	44.6	21.7	92	67.4	32.6	10.7	44,600	47,600			456	
Michigan State	804	80	57.0	43.0	15.4	52	50.0	50.0	15.6	34,045	34,045	28,220	28,220	460	•
Thomas M. Cooley	691	3240	51.2	48.8	26.8	101	58.4	41.6	22.4	30,644	30,644	19,714	19,714	748	
Wayne State	482	130	55.9	44.1	15.8	38	63.2	36.8	13.8	24,871	27,187	13,440	14,675	816	•
Minnesota															
Hamline	456	196	48.0	52.0	14.7	34	58.8	41.2	15.1	33,506	33,506	24,144	24,144	340	•
Minnesota	752	0	58.1	41.9	17.8	58	60.3	39.7	10.9	31,882	40,388			464	•

| | Admission Fall 2010 | | | | | | | | | | | | | | |
| | Student Body | | | | | Faculty | | | | Tuition ($) | | | | Other | |
	# Full-time	# Part-time	% Men	% Women	% Minorities	# Full-time and Other	% Men	% Women	Student/Faculty Ratio	Resident, Full-time	Nonresident, Full-time	Resident, Part-time	Nonresident, Part-time	Official Guide Page #	Grid included •
St. Thomas- Minneapolis	475	0	56.4	43.6	12.0	29	65.5	34.5	17.3	36,313				644	
William Mitchell	667	346	50.1	49.9	11.2	34	50.0	50.0	20.6	33,800	33,800	24,450	24,450	850	•
Mississippi															
Mississippi	516	0	55.6	44.4	15.7	31	71.0	29.0	15.2	10,275	22,470			468	•
Mississippi College	536	11	59.8	40.2	11.2	26	46.2	53.8	17.3	28,070				472	•
Missouri															
Missouri-Columbia	442	4	62.3	37.7	13.7	28	71.4	28.6	14.1	16,759	31,986			476	•
Missouri-Kansas City	459	24	60.9	39.1	12.6	34	58.8	41.2	13.3	15,550	29,500	8,542	15,982	480	•
St. Louis	800	138	53.4	46.6	14.3	65	44.6	55.4	14.8	35,475	35,475	25,815	25,815	636	•
Washington University	893	7	60.7	39.3	28.0	68	47.1	52.9	10.2	44,125				812	•
Montana															
Montana	256	0	57.0	43.0	9.4	19	47.4	52.6	13.1	11,062	26,186			484	•
Nebraska															
Creighton	459	12	59.2	40.8	10.4	23	73.9	26.1	19.5	31,386	31,386	18,292	18,292	236	•
Nebraska	412	2	63.0	37.0	7.2	26	73.1	26.9	13.3	13,337	28,649			488	
Nevada															
Nevada	347	128	56.0	44.0	30.1	26	38.5	61.5	13.4	20,838	34,238	13,606	22,228	492	
New Hampshire															
New Hampshire	419	0	58.0	42.0	22.7	33	54.5	45.5	14.9	37,000	37,000			500	
New Jersey															
Rutgers-Camden	573	216	60.1	39.9	19.9	54	61.1	38.9	11.6	22,382	33,173	18,816	27,853	624	•
Rutgers-Newark	610	229	55.2	44.8	39.3	40	55.0	45.0	17.8	24,977	35,897	16,274	23,554	628	•
Seton Hall	704	349	53.9	46.1	18.7	59	57.6	42.4	14.0	45,048	45,048	33,981	33,981	672	•
New Mexico															
New Mexico	351	0	47.0	53.0	42.7	28	39.3	60.7	12.4	13,660	30,604			504	•
New York															
Albany	697	23	55.8	44.2	11.7	46	45.7	54.3	13.3	40,120	40,120	30,128	30,128	80	
Brooklyn	1,293	168	52.4	47.6	25.8	68	50.0	50.0	18.3	46,635	46,635	35,065	35,065	140	
Buffalo	693	8	52.9	47.1	14.4	54	51.9	48.1	12.6	19,112	30,772			144	•
Cardozo	1,025	99	48.7	51.3	22.7	61	67.2	32.8	15.3	46,794	46,794	46,794	46,794	176	•
CUNY	438	2	36.4	63.6	37.7	36	33.3	66.7	10.9	11,952	18,732	425	750	212	•
Columbia	1,343	1	51.4	48.6	32.2	107	69.2	30.8	10.9	50,428	50,428			224	
Cornell	615	0	50.4	49.6	35.4	51	64.7	35.3	10.4	51,150	51,150			232	
Fordham	1,217	264	52.3	47.7	23.3	81	63.0	37.0	13.9	46,476	46,476	34,926	34,926	308	•
Hofstra	945	116	53.4	46.6	28.3	60	60.0	40.0	14.3	43,660	43,660	32,669	32,669	352	•
New York Law	1,492	431	48.9	51.1	24.3	71	66.2	33.8	23.1	46,460	46,460	35,700	35,700	508	•
New York	1,431	0	57.4	42.6	25.3	151	68.9	31.1	9.2	48,213				512	
Pace	614	174	43.5	56.5	16.0	47	63.8	36.2	13.2	39,794	39,794	29,858	29,858	572	•
St. John's	764	176	55.6	44.4	24.6	50	54.0	46.0	15.8	44,280	44,280	33,210	33,210	632	•
Syracuse	635	3	59.4	40.6	20.1	60	61.7	38.3	11.9	45,126	45,126			720	•
Touro	601	227	54.8	45.2	23.8	42	57.1	42.9	15.4	41,070	41,070	30,780	30,780	760	

	Student Body					Faculty				Tuition ($)				Other	
	# Full-time	# Part-time	% Men	% Women	% Minorities	# Full-time and Other	% Men	% Women	Student/Faculty Ratio	Resident, Full-time	Nonresident, Full-time	Resident, Part-time	Nonresident, Part-time	Official Guide Page #	Grid included •
North Carolina															
Campbell	450	0	48.4	51.6	8.7	23	73.9	26.1	15.5	32,280	32,280			168	•
Charlotte	669	143	48.4	51.6	20.8	35	40.0	60.0	17.5	34,990	34,990	28,292	28,292	196	
Duke	644	37	58.9	41.1	24.2	70	67.1	32.9	9.8	47,722	47,722			264	•
Elon	342	0	54.1	45.9	12.6	20	60.0	40.0	16.6	32,600	32,600			276	•
North Carolina	778	0	49.1	50.9	27.0	42	59.5	40.5	15.2	17,068	31,218			516	•
North Carolina Central	491	111	40.7	59.3	54.8	42	42.9	57.1	13.4	9,961	23,222	9,961	23,222	520	•
Wake Forest	487	0	59.1	40.9	16.6	48	56.3	43.8	9.5	37,230	37,230			796	
North Dakota															
North Dakota	256	0	54.7	45.3	13.7	12	75.0	25.0	19.6	10,163	22,323			524	•
Ohio															
Akron	279	227	56.3	43.7	13.8	33	54.5	45.5	13.1	21,451	33,408	17,462	27,028	72	•
Capital	486	170	55.6	44.4	11.4	35	62.9	37.1	16.7	32,074	32,074	21,014	21,014	172	•
Case Western	624	3	56.5	43.5	14.7	47	68.1	29.8	13.1	40,560	40,560			180	•
Cincinnati	408	0	57.8	42.2	15.2	29	44.8	55.2	11.2	20,946	36,526			208	•
Cleveland State	453	157	59.2	40.8	13.4	39	56.4	43.6	11.9	18,200	24,976	14,000	19,212	216	•
Dayton	524	0	61.5	38.5	11.8	27	51.9	48.1	17.2	33,674	33,674			240	•
Ohio Northern	313	0	62.9	37.1	10.2	22	63.6	36.4	11.8	31,264	31,264			552	•
Ohio State	693	0	57.4	42.6	20.3	42	59.5	40.5	15.5	24,468	39,418			556	•
Toledo	365	95	60.2	39.8	10.7	26	61.5	38.5	14.4	19,833	30,613	14,886	22,971	756	•
Oklahoma															
Oklahoma	537	0	55.3	44.7	21.0	34	67.6	32.4	14.0	18,105	28,034			560	•
Oklahoma City	564	72	58.6	41.4	19.5	34	58.8	41.2	16.6	33,925	33,925	22,640	22,640	564	•
Tulsa	368	38	61.1	38.9	19.7	28	57.1	42.9	11.5	30,320				768	•
Oregon															
Lewis & Clark	529	212	49.9	50.1	21.3	53	58.5	41.5	10.3	35,098	35,098	26,334	26,334	404	•
Oregon	526	0	55.5	44.5	17.1	35	48.6	51.4	15.7	24,031	29,953			568	•
Willamette	424	5	56.4	43.6	17.9	28	60.7	39.3	14.1	31,130	31,130			842	
Pennsylvania															
Duquesne	454	234	52.5	47.5	5.7	26	65.4	34.6	20.5	32,376	32,376	25,034	25,034	268	
Earl Mack, Drexel	440	0	55.5	44.5	18.2	27	48.1	51.9	15.7	34,450	34,450			272	•
Penn State	617	1	57.6	42.4	14.2	57	57.9	42.1	9.4	36,816	36,816			580	•
Pennsylvania	802	0	52.4	47.6	30.3	75	68.0	32.0	10.2	48,362	48,362			584	
Pittsburgh	739	0	57.1	42.9	16.9	47	57.4	42.6	13.8	26,550	34,176			596	•
Temple	797	186	56.7	43.3	25.0	63	60.3	39.7	12.6	18,206	31,220	14,692	25,108	724	
Villanova	765	0	57.3	42.7	19.1	49	53.1	46.9	16.4	36,690	36,690			788	
Widener	350	103	54.5	45.5	12.4	25	52.0	48.0	14.8	34,890	34,890	25,610	25,610	838	•
Puerto Rico															
Inter American	474	392	45.0	55.0	100.0	24	58.3	41.7	27.8	14,341	14,341	11,142	11,142	380	
Pontifical Catholic	535	299	52.4	47.6	99.9	21	71.4	28.6	33.2	14,126		10,766		600	
Puerto Rico	545	192	44.9	55.1	0.0	28	67.9	32.1	23.0	7,611	9,437	6,341	11,643	604	•

| | Admission Fall 2010 | | | | | | | | | | | | | | |
| | Student Body | | | | | Faculty | | | | Tuition ($) | | | | Other | |
	# Full-time	# Part-time	% Men	% Women	% Minorities	# Full-time and Other	% Men	% Women	Student/Faculty Ratio	Resident, Full-time	Nonresident, Full-time	Resident, Part-time	Nonresident, Part-time	Official Guide Page #	Grid included •
Rhode Island															
Roger Williams	540	0	50.2	49.8	8.7	27	51.9	48.1	16.4	38,010	38,010			620	•
South Carolina															
Charleston	520	182	55.3	44.7	10.0	31	48.4	51.6	17.4	35,606	35,606	28,608	28,608	192	•
South Carolina	681	1	59.2	40.8	13.3	36	58.3	41.7	15.9	20,236	40,494			680	•
South Dakota															
South Dakota	203	2	54.1	45.9	9.8	14	71.4	28.6	13.2	11,208	21,960	5,435	10,638	684	•
Tennessee															
Memphis	408	24	59.0	41.0	12.7	18	66.7	33.3	18.1	14,298	36,170	14,138	36,010	444	•
Tennessee	482	0	56.6	43.4	25.3	30	66.7	33.3	15.3	14,462	33,206			728	•
Vanderbilt	586	0	52.9	47.1	19.1	36	61.1	38.9	14.0	45,286	45,286			780	
Texas															
Baylor	466	10	49.8	50.2	21.0	27	77.8	22.2	14.8	40,904	40,904			124	•
Houston	701	176	57.5	42.5	29.0	76	68.4	31.6	10.4	26,731	36,903	18,953	25,735	356	•
St. Mary's	675	153	58.5	41.5	34.2	36	52.8	47.2	22.4	28,160	28,160	17,120	17,120	640	•
SMU Dedman	549	338	53.3	46.7	23.7	46	65.2	34.8	15.7	40,186	40,186	30,140	30,140	676	•
South Texas	1,009	296	53.3	46.7	29.0	44	63.6	36.4	21.0	26,340	26,340	17,760	17,760	688	•
Texas	1,154	0	53.6	46.4	27.7	103	59.2	40.8	10.9	28,669	44,638			732	•
Texas Southern	571	0	46.8	53.2	80.4	30	40.0	60.0	14.1	13,065	16,815			736	•
Texas Tech	671	0	58.9	41.1	23.4	35	62.9	37.1	14.9	17,351	25,751			740	•
Texas Wesleyan	487	277	50.4	49.6	20.9	30	63.3	36.7	24.8	27,440	27,440	19,690	19,690	744	•
Utah															
Brigham Young	443	1	64.9	35.1	15.8	19	68.4	31.6	18.1	10,280	20,560			136	•
Utah	402	0	57.2	42.8	11.9	34	67.6	32.4	8.9	18,231	36,209			772	•
Vermont															
Vermont	607	0	47.8	52.2	9.6	55	49.1	50.9	14.1	42,220	42,220			784	•
Virginia															
Appalachian	313	0	65.5	34.5	11.8	16	68.8	31.3	16.7	28,325	28,325			88	•
George Mason	505	226	59.2	40.8	15.7	38	81.6	18.4	14.0	22,222	36,278	18,290	29,836	312	•
Liberty	313	0	62.3	37.7	18.8	19	68.4	31.6	6.1	29,120				408	
Regent	409	19	52.8	47.2	17.5	25	68.0	32.0	16.1	31,410	31,410	24,235	24,235	612	•
Richmond	452	8	55.2	44.8	17.6	36	61.1	38.9	14.0	34,070	34,070			616	•
Virginia	1,105	1	55.2	44.8	23.0	79	75.9	24.1	11.9	42,500	47,500			792	
Washington and Lee	407	0	58.2	41.8	16.5	35	77.1	22.9	9.5	39,937				808	•
William & Mary	628	0	50.6	49.4	19.4	39	56.4	43.6	14.2	23,800	33,800			846	•
Washington															
Gonzaga	503	4	61.5	38.5	11.2	29	58.6	41.4	14.6	32,775	32,775			336	•
Seattle	808	203	49.2	50.8	24.8	66	57.6	42.4	12.3	37,330	37,330	31,098	31,098	668	•
Washington	550	0	51.1	48.9	22.9	54	51.9	48.1	9.7	24,339	37,299			804	•
West Virginia															
West Virginia	410	6	63.0	37.0	8.7	33	60.6	39.4	11.1	14,212	28,444			820	•

| | Admission Fall 2010 | | | | | | | | | | | | | | |
| | Student Body | | | | | Faculty | | | | Tuition ($) | | | | Other | |
	# Full-time	# Part-time	% Men	% Women	% Minorities	# Full-time and Other	% Men	% Women	Student/Faculty Ratio	Resident, Full-time	Nonresident, Full-time	Resident, Part-time	Nonresident, Part-time	Official Guide Page #	Grid included •
Wisconsin															
Marquette	585	173	56.9	43.1	14.9	39	51.3	48.7	16.7	36,300	36,300	21,750	21,750	436	•
Wisconsin	755	49	54.2	45.8	22.3	65	53.8	46.2	13.0	18,049	37,586	1,508	3,136	854	
Wyoming															
Wyoming	231	0	53.2	46.8	6.9	21	76.2	23.8	10.6	11,264	23,808			858	•

This chapter is designed to provide consumers with basic information in a simple format that will facilitate the consideration of ABA-approved law schools. Please note that applicants should not use this information as the sole source regarding application and admission. Rather, this book should supplement other avenues of evaluating respective schools, including making direct contact with admission officers, professors, students, alumni, or prelaw advisors.

The following section includes text and numerical data from 199 ABA-approved law schools that confer the first degree in law (the JD degree). The two pages of numerical data about each school were compiled from questionnaires completed during the fall 2010 academic semester and submitted by ABA-approved law schools to the ABA's Consultant on Legal Education as part of the accreditation process. The completed questionnaires provided to the Consultant's Office are certified by the dean of each law school. Each certification is submitted to the Consultant's Office as an assurance that the information provided accurately reflects prevailing conditions at the law school for which the certification is given. The Consultant's Office, however, does not directly audit the information submitted by the respective institutions on an annual basis.

The information contained in this book is only a small portion of what is collected in the questionnaire for accreditation purposes. Each page is divided into different segments as discussed below. In addition, many of the same data are displayed on the charts in chapters 10, 11, and 12 and in Appendix A to facilitate side-by-side comparisons.

In addition to the two pages of numerical data, each law school provides two pages of descriptive text to LSAC. LSAC edits these text pages for style and formatting, but does not verify the descriptive information provided by the schools. As part of this two-page spread, most schools provide applicant profile grids that illustrate admission prospects based on a combination of LSAT score and GPA. The data in these grids are based on 2009–2010 academic year admission decisions as reported by the schools to LSAC. The grids are intended to be indicative of the applicant profile of last year's entering law school classes; they should not be interpreted as predictors of the likelihood of admission for any applicant.

LSAC collects applicant profile data and school descriptions each fall as a service to its member schools and to prospective law school applicants. The information provided by the law schools to LSAC in no way affects the ABA accreditation process.

SCHOOL NAME

The law schools are arranged in alphabetical order by each institution's primary name. Please note that some schools are known by more than one name. Adjacent to the law school's name and contact information is the date that the school was granted ABA-approval. In some cases, that approval may be designated as provisional. A law school that has completed at least one full year of successful operation may apply for provisional approval. A law school is granted provisional approval when it establishes that it substantially complies with the Standards and Rules of Procedure for Approval of Law Schools and gives assurances that it will be in full compliance with all of the Standards within three years after receiving provisional approval. A designation of "Probation" means that the school is in substantial noncompliance with the Standards and is at risk of being removed from the list of approved law schools. It is the ABA's view that students at provisionally

approved law schools or those on probation and persons who graduate while a school is provisionally approved or on probation are entitled to the same recognition as students and graduates of fully approved law schools.

Multiple campuses: Some schools have multiple campuses. Contact the admission office of those schools for more information about curriculum offerings and application processes.

The Basics
The Basics section contains a variety of general information, sorted into the categories listed below.

Type of school: All ABA-approved law schools are either public or private. *Public* means that the school receives money from the state in which the school is located. *Private* indicates the school is not operated by the state.

Term: Indicates whether the school operates on a semester, quarter, or trimester system.

Application deadline: Not all schools have specific deadlines for admission applications. If the item was left blank in the questionnaire completed by the school, it generally means that the school considers applications on a continual basis until the class is filled.

Application fee: Fee charged by most law schools for processing an application for admission.

Financial aid deadline: Indicates the deadline for the school's financial aid form. (The school deadline may not be the same as federal and state deadlines.) If the item was left blank in the questionnaire completed by the school, it generally means that the school considers financial aid applications on a continuing basis.

Can first year start other than fall? Indicates whether the school has an entering class other than in the fall term.

Student-to-faculty ratio: Indicates the number of students relative to the number of instructors for the calendar year. The ratio is calculated by comparing faculty full-time equivalency (FTE) to FTE of JD enrollment. A general definition of faculty FTE is as follows: total full-time faculty plus additional instructional resources. Additional instructional resources include administrators who teach, as well as part-time faculty. Teaching administrators and part-time faculty are included in the faculty FTE at differing weighted factors ranging from .2 to .7. FTE of JD enrollment is calculated as follows: full-time JD enrollment plus two-thirds of part-time JD enrollment less enrollment in semester-abroad programs. For a detailed definition of the ABA's student-to-faculty ratio, please consult the ABA's Standards and Rules of Procedure for Approval of Law Schools at americanbar.org/groups/legal_education.

Student housing: Indicates the number of housing spaces available restricted to law students and number of graduate housing spaces for which law students are eligible.

Faculty and Administrators
This section of the two-page spread contains detailed information on the number, gender, and race of the teachers at the school for both semesters. It should be noted that some schools may have lower part-time numbers in the fall

semester because at their school most of the part-time instruction occurs in the spring semester. The five categories of faculty are mutually exclusive. Teachers on leave or sabbatical are not included in the full-time faculty count for the term they are on leave. The *Full-time* row indicates tenured or tenure-track faculty. *Other full-time* indicates nontenured professional skills instructors and nontenured legal writing instructors. *Deans, librarians, & others who teach* are law school administrators who teach at least halftime. Administrators who neither teach nor hold faculty rank are not included in these numbers. Administrators who teach are typically at the school and available to students during the entire year. For this reason, they are counted in fall and spring regardless of their teaching load. *Part-time* during the fall semester includes adjuncts, permanent part time, faculty from another unit, part-time professional skills, and emeritus part time. The *Total* row combines figures from the *Full-time* row through the *Part-time* row.

JD Enrollment and Ethnicity
This section represents the JD enrollment by ethnic category, gender, first-year student, and full-time/part-time status. Students are classified for purposes of enrollment statistics on the basis of whether they are carrying a full load in the division in which they are enrolled. Minority group enrollment is the total enrollment of students who classify themselves as Hispanic, but if not Hispanic, then Black or African American, American Indian or Alaska Native, Asian, Native Hawaiian or Other Pacific Islander, or Two or More Races. Although Puerto Rican law students enrolled in the three approved law schools in Puerto Rico are not classified as minority students in the Total Minority Enrollment chart in Appendix A, they are counted as minorities in all other areas. For more information, see *Federal Register*, Volume 72 (October 19, 2007) "Final Guidance on Maintaining, Collecting, and Reporting Racial and Ethnic Data to the US Department of Education," pp. 59266–59279; and The Race and Ethnicity Information Center of the Department of Education's Integrated Postsecondary Education Data System: nces.ed.gov/ipeds. Nonresident alien students (foreign nationals) and students whose ethnicity is unknown or unspecified are not included as minority students.

JD Degrees Awarded: This indicates the total number of JD degrees awarded during the 2009–2010 academic year.

Curriculum
All information in this category is based on the 12-month period beginning at the close of the prior academic year (e.g., June 2009 through May 2010). In courses where there was enrollment by both full-time and part-time students, schools were asked to classify each of those courses as full time or part time based on time of day and relative enrollment of full-time and part-time students. Some schools that have a part-time program experienced difficulty providing curriculum information that distinguished between full time and part time. In those cases, the part-time column contains zeros. A *small section* means a section of a substantive law course, which may include a legal writing component; small section does not mean a legal writing section standing alone. The *number of classroom course titles beyond first-year curriculum* refers only to classroom courses offered the previous year, not to clinical or field placement possibilities. If a title is offered in both the full-time program and part-time program, the school could count it once in each column. *Seminars* are defined as courses requiring a written work product and having an enrollment limited to no more than 25. A *simulation course* is one in which a substantial portion of the instruction is accomplished through the use of role-playing or drafting exercises (for example, trial advocacy, corporate planning and drafting, negotiations, and estate planning and drafting).

Faculty supervised clinical courses are those courses or placements with other agencies in which full-time faculty have primary professional responsibility for all cases on which students are working. *Field placements* refer to those cases in which someone other than full-time faculty has primary responsibility to the client; these placements are frequently called externships or internships. Schools were also asked not to double count a single course by classifying it both as full time and part time. *Number involved in law journals* and *Number involved in moot court or trial competitions* reflect those students beyond the first year who participated in those activities during the previous year regardless of whether they received credit.

Transfers
This section refers to the number of students who transferred in and transferred out of the law school in the 2009–2010 academic year.

Tuition and Fees

- *Full-time*: Represents the full-time tuition (plus annual fees) for the academic year for a typical first-year student.

- *Part-time*: Represents the part-time tuition (plus annual fees) for the academic year for a typical first-year student. Please note that some schools elected to report part-time tuition on a "per-credit-hour" basis.

- *Tuition Guarantee Program*: Indicates if the law school has a tuition policy that guarantees all entering students the same tuition rate throughout their enrollment.

Living Expenses
This represents the 2010–2011 academic year total living expenses (room, board, etc.) and book expenses for full-time, single, resident students *Living on campus*, *Living off campus*, and *Living at home*. Tuition and fee charges are not included. The figures are used in analyzing law student budgets for loan purposes. Many schools use the same budget amount for all three categories.

GPA and LSAT Scores
This section of the two-page spread contains statistics on the 2010 entering class. All persons in this particular category, regardless of whether they were admitted through any special admission program rather than through the normal admission process, were included. The admission year was calculated from October 1, 2009, through September 30, 2010. Schools that admit in the spring and/or summer were to include those students in the totals. Figures on matriculants include all students who attended at least one class during the first week of the term in which they were admitted. For a small number of schools, applications and admitted applicants are not identified by the school as full time or part time. Therefore, "N/A" appears under the full-time and part-time columns, and the total application and admission offers are entered under the total column.

Percentiles of GPA and LSAT: The GPA and LSAT scores represent the 75th percentile, 25th percentile, and the median scores of the entering class. For example, one quarter (25 percent) of the first-year class has credentials that are *below* the number given for the 25th percentile. Three quarters (75 percent) of the first-year class have credentials that are below the number given for the 75th percentile. One half (50 percent) of the first-year class has credentials that are *below* the number given for the median. For example, if a school reports a 25th percentile/median/75th percentile GPA— 3.01/3.25/3.47, then 25 percent of this first-year class had a GPA of *less than* 3.01, 50 percent of this class had a GPA of *less than* 3.25, and 75 percent of this class had a GPA of *less than* 3.47. The same principle holds for the 25th percentile/median/75th percentile LSAT score.

Grants and Scholarships (from prior year)
This indicates the number and percentage of students receiving internal grants or scholarships from law school or university sources. External grants such as state grants are not included. The percentages for full time and part time are based on the total number of full-time and part-time JD students, respectively. The total column percentage is based on total JD enrollment. Zeros are reported in those areas where a school did not provide data. The data represent information from the previous academic year.

Informational and Library Resources
This section of the two-page spread contains basic information about the law library. In addition, it contains brief information about the physical size of the school and the number of networked computers available.

- *Total amount spent on library materials:* Total expenditures for serial subscriptions (print, microforms, and nonprint), monographs (print, microforms, and nonprint), electronic resources purchased during the fiscal year, and electronic resources licensed for the fiscal year.

- *Study seating capacity inside the library:* Number of study seats available for library users.

- *Number of full-time equivalent professional librarians:* The number of full-time equivalent professional librarians who teach or hold faculty rank plus the number of full-time equivalent librarians who do not teach or hold faculty rank.

- *Hours per week library is open:* Number of hours per week that professional staff are on duty in the library.

- *Number of open, wired connections available to students:* Number of open, wired, network connections available to students or, if the library has a wireless network, the number of simultaneous users accommodated within.

- *Number of networked computers available for use by students:* Number of workstations in law school or library computer labs, plus workstations in the library for users that are not in computer labs.

- *Has wireless network:* Indicates the school has a wireless network.

- *Require computer:* Indicates whether the school requires students entering the law school to have a computer.

JD Attrition (from prior year)
Attrition percentages were based on fall 2009 enrollment. *Academic* attrition, for this purpose, refers to those students not continuing their legal studies between October 1, 2009, and October 1, 2010. *Other* attrition may include transfers and students who leave for other reasons.

Employment (nine months after graduation)
This section represents statistics on the employment status of the 2009 graduating class nine months after graduation. The employment percentages are based on the graduates whose employment status was "known." Hence, for the schools reporting a large percentage of graduates for whom the employment status is unknown, the percentage reported may not be a very accurate reflection of the actual percentage of the class as a whole. *Type of Employment* and *Geographic Location* percentages are based on the number of students employed.

Bar Passage Rates
This section refers to numbers and percentages of law school graduates who took the bar for the first time during calendar year 2009. The pass rates for each jurisdiction were obtained from the National Conference of Bar Examiners. In reporting their first-time bar passage rates, each school must account for at least 70 percent of its first-time takers in the year reported. For some schools, in order to reach this 70 percent threshold, they need to report data for only a single jurisdiction. Other schools may have to report pass rates for multiple jurisdictions in order to account for at least 70 percent of first-time takers in the reporting year. Note that pass rates can vary widely from jurisdiction to jurisdiction; similarly, pass rates among schools can also vary widely. In instances where a school's pass rate is 15 or more points below the states' pass rates, applicants are encouraged to contact the school and obtain data for their ultimate pass rates (i.e., pass rates of repeat takers). Note that Wisconsin permits graduates of the University of Wisconsin Law School and Marquette University Law School to exercise the "diploma privilege" and be admitted to the bar without taking the examination.

APPLICANT PROFILES

Applicant profiles are provided by some schools to give candidates information about the number of applicants and admitted applicants in each cell. For various reasons, the total number of applicants and admitted applicants does not equal the official totals that appear on the ABA data pages in this book.

The purpose of the applicant profiles is to provide information about the LSAT/GPA credentials of applicants and admitted applicants to the schools that provide the profiles. You will note that some schools provide alternatives to the grid format for their profile or no profile at all.

THE UNIVERSITY OF AKRON SCHOOL OF LAW

302 Buchtel Common
Akron, OH 44325-2901
Phone: 800.425.7668; Fax: 330.258.2343
E-mail: lawadmissions@uakron.edu; Website: www.uakron.edu/law

ABA
Approved
Since
1961

The Basics

Type of school	Public
Term	Semester
Application deadline	3/1
Application fee	$0
Financial aid deadline	5/1
Can first year start other than fall?	No
Student to faculty ratio	13.1 to 1
# of housing spaces available restricted to law students	
graduate housing for which law students are eligible	

Faculty and Administrators

	Total		Men		Women		Minorities	
	Spr	Fall	Spr	Fall	Spr	Fall	Spr	Fall
Full-time	25	28	16	17	9	11	2	3
Other full-time	4	5	1	1	3	4	1	0
Deans, librarians, & others who teach	5	5	3	3	2	2	0	0
Part-time	22	17	21	14	1	3	2	1
Total	56	55	41	35	15	20	5	4

Curriculum

	Full-Time	Part-Time
Typical first-year section size	63	50
Is there typically a "small section" of the first-year class, other than Legal Writing, taught by full-time faculty	Yes	Yes
If yes, typical size offered last year	31	27
# of classroom course titles beyond first-year curriculum	86	

# of upper division courses, excluding seminars, with an enrollment:		
	Under 25	76
	25–49	24
	50–74	5
	75–99	1
	100+	0

# of seminars	34	
# of seminar positions available	710	
# of seminar positions filled	160	148
# of positions available in simulation courses	904	
# of simulation positions filled	308	214
# of positions available in faculty supervised clinical courses	264	
# of faculty supervised clinical positions filled	42	21
# involved in field placements	27	9
# involved in law journals	51	22
# involved in moot court or trial competitions	17	5
# of credit hours required to graduate	88	

JD Enrollment and Ethnicity

	Men		Women		Full-Time		Part-Time		1st-Year		Total		JD Degs. Awd.
	#	%	#	%	#	%	#	%	#	%	#	%	
All Hispanics	7	2.5	12	5.4	13	4.7	6	2.6	6	3.0	19	3.8	1
Am. Ind./AK Nat.	0	0.0	2	0.9	1	0.4	1	0.4	1	0.5	2	0.4	1
Asian	8	2.8	10	4.5	11	3.9	7	3.1	8	4.0	18	3.6	6
Black/Af. Am.	17	6.0	14	6.3	10	3.6	21	9.3	5	2.5	31	6.1	3
Nat. HI/Pac. Isl.	0	0.0	0	0.0	0	0.0	0	0.0	0	0.0	0	0.0	0
2 or more races	0	0.0	0	0.0	0	0.0	0	0.0	0	0.0	0	0.0	0
Subtotal (minor.)	32	11.2	38	17.2	35	12.5	35	15.4	20	10.0	70	13.8	11
Nonres. Alien	0	0.0	0	0.0	0	0.0	0	0.0	0	0.0	0	0.0	0
White/Cauc.	224	78.6	169	76.5	220	78.9	173	76.2	163	81.1	393	77.7	112
Unknown	29	10.2	14	6.3	24	8.6	19	8.4	18	9.0	43	8.5	12
Total	285	56.3	221	43.7	279	55.1	227	44.9	201	39.7	506		135

Transfers

Transfers in	5
Transfers out	7

Tuition and Fees

	Resident	Nonresident
Full-time	$21,451	$33,408
Part-time	$17,462	$27,028
Tuition Guarantee Program	N	

Living Expenses

Estimated living expenses for singles

Living on campus	Living off campus	Living at home
$16,034	$16,034	$4,900

THE UNIVERSITY OF AKRON SCHOOL OF LAW

*ABA
Approved
Since
1961*

GPA and LSAT Scores

	Total	Full-Time	Part-Time
# of apps	2,003	1,700	303
# of offers	782	622	160
# of matrics	177	105	72
75% GPA	3.61	3.69	3.51
Median GPA	3.37	3.46	3.19
25% GPA	3.10	3.29	3.05
75% LSAT	158	158	154
Median LSAT	155	157	152
25% LSAT	152	155	151

Grants and Scholarships (from prior year)

	Total		Full-Time		Part-Time	
	#	%	#	%	#	%
Total # of students	517		279		238	
Total # receiving grants	241	46.6	170	60.9	71	29.8
Less than 1/2 tuition	90	17.4	51	18.3	39	16.4
Half to full tuition	63	12.2	45	16.1	18	7.6
Full tuition	80	15.5	66	23.7	14	5.9
More than full tuition	8	1.5	8	2.9	0	0.0
Median grant amount			$15,440		$5,702	

Informational and Library Resources

Total amount spent on library materials	$890,780
Study seating capacity inside the library	282
# of full-time equivalent professional librarians	4
Hours per week library is open	105
# of open, wired connections available to students	29
# of networked computers available for use by students	81
Has wireless network?	Y
Requires computer?	N

JD Attrition (from prior year)

	Academic	Other	Total	
	#	#	#	%
1st year	11	24	35	17.2
2nd year	7	2	9	6.6
3rd year	0	4	4	3.0
4th year	0	0	0	0.0

Employment (9 months after graduation)

	Total	Percentage
Employment status known	137	95.1
Employment status unknown	7	4.9
Employed	121	88.3
Pursuing graduate degrees	0	0.0
Unemployed (seeking, not seeking, or studying for the bar)	11	8.0
Type of Employment		
# employed in law firms	54	44.6
# employed in business and industry	28	23.1
# employed in government	31	25.6
# employed in public interest	2	1.7
# employed as judicial clerks	2	1.7
# employed in academia	3	2.5
Geographic Location		
# employed in state	95	78.5
# employed outside the US	0	0.0
# of states where employed		16

Bar Passage Rates

First-time takers	130	Reporting %	82.31
Average school %	89.72	Average state %	86.03
Average pass difference	3.69		

Jurisdiction	Takers	Passers	Pass %	State %	Diff %
Ohio	107	96	89.72	86.03	3.69

THE UNIVERSITY OF AKRON SCHOOL OF LAW

302 Buchtel Common
Akron, OH 44325-2901
Phone: 800.425.7668; Fax: 330.258.2343
E-mail: lawadmissions@uakron.edu; Website: www.uakron.edu/law

Introduction

Located in the heart of downtown Akron and just 45 minutes south of Cleveland, the University of Akron (UA) is one of the 50 largest universities in the country. UA is a comprehensive research and teaching university with degree programs ranging from the associate to the doctoral level. Founded in 1870, UA has celebrated nearly 140 years of academic excellence while forging ahead to meet the complex needs of today's students.

The Akron School of Law was founded in 1921 and merged with UA in 1959. More than 6,000 students have graduated from the law school. Akron Law alumni practice throughout the US and abroad.

More than 160 Akron Law alumni have been or currently are judges in 13 states and the District of Columbia, as well as in the federal court system.

Admission

In order to be considered for admission, the applicant must submit the application form and personal statement. The applicant must also take the LSAT and register for LSAC's Credential Assembly Service before the file may be sent to the Admissions Committee. An applicant may apply during his or her final year of undergraduate studies. The bachelor's degree coursework must be completed prior to law school matriculation. Decisions are made on a rolling basis as soon as the files are complete. The priority deadline is March 1, but applications are accepted throughout the spring and summer months. For more details on admission, please see our website at **www.uakron.edu/law**.

Students enrolled in an American Bar Association (ABA)–accredited law school may apply for transfer or transient status. A law student who has completed neither more nor less than one year (approximately 30 semester credit hours) and is in good academic standing may apply for transfer. A law student who has the dean's permission to visit for one or two semesters may apply for transient status. Consult **www.uakron.edu/law** for details.

Tuition/Fees and Financial Aid (Annual)

Admitted applicants are automatically considered for merit-based scholarships and may apply for need-based scholarships. Upper-division students may apply for merit-based and need-based scholarships. Students also have access to Stafford, Graduate PLUS, and alternative loans, as well as federal work-study funds (summer term only).

Flexible Scheduling

Akron Law offers a traditional full-time JD program, which law students may complete in two and one-half or three years. Akron Law also offers a flexible part-time program, which allows students to attend classes during daytime or evening hours. Part-time students may complete the JD program in as few as three and one-half years or as many as six years. A few upper-division classes are also offered at 7:30 AM to allow students to attend classes before work. Students

may transfer from full time to part time (or vice versa) as their needs dictate.

Physical Facilities

The law building includes a 1987 addition to the library and a 1993 addition to the original structure. The university's $200 million New Landscape for Learning campus improvement program includes a new Student Union, Student Recreation and Wellness Center, Student Affairs Building, academic buildings, and parking decks. Approximately 30 acres of new green space were added to the campus to create a more park-like setting. The law school is within one block of the Akron Municipal Court, the court of common pleas, and the Ninth District Court of Appeals. The federal court is a few blocks from campus. Although the law school is in the downtown Akron area, the campus is a green one bordered by grassy areas, decorative plantings, and fountains.

Intellectual Property Center

Patent, trademark, trade secret, copyright, licensing, and cyber law are among the many topics covered in the Intellectual Property (IP) Law program. Staffed by three full-time faculty, and supplemented by three full-time and additional part-time faculty with special expertise, Akron's IP program is one of the most extensive in the nation. Twenty-two IP courses are offered either every year or every other year, and more than six additional courses are planned.

In addition, Akron offers an LLM degree in Intellectual Property Law. This full-time or part-time graduate program provides law graduates with an opportunity to begin or continue a specialization in IP.

Curriculum/Special Programs

The first-year curriculum is traditional in content, using traditional and innovative interactive pedagogies. The upper-class curriculum is varied between basic courses and specialty courses, and also focuses on interactive learning pedagogies and development of crucial lawyering skills. All law students are eligible to participate in the programs offered and the services provided by the Academic Success Office. The director of academic success programs counsels students on study techniques, learning styles, time management, and other topics related to academic success. A comprehensive writing program designed to enhance students' skills in research, exposition, drafting, and argumentation is an integral part of the curriculum.

Specialized Studies: Business, Criminal, Intellectual Property, International, Litigation, Public, and Tax.

Joint Degrees: JD/Master in Business Administration, JD/Master in Taxation, JD/Master in Public Administration, and JD/Master in Applied Politics.

Certificate Programs: Intellectual Property and Litigation.

Study Abroad: Akron Law offers a five-week program in Geneva, Switzerland, in which law students may earn up to six hours of elective credit studying comparative law.

LLM Graduate Law Degree: Intellectual Property.

Competition Teams

Students have many opportunities to sharpen their litigation skills by participating in regional and national mock trial, moot court, and negotiation competitions. Our litigation teams have had almost unparalleled success in competitions throughout the United States and Europe. Each year, the National Institute of Trial Advocacy (NITA) ranks law school trial programs based on three-year averages of their performance in the three major national tournaments; Akron has been in the top 16 trial programs 17 times in the last 19 years. In 2007, Akron finished second in the NITA Tournament of Champions, third in the National Criminal Trial Competition, and first in the National Civil Trial Competition.

Legal Clinic

Students represent clients in court, at trial, and on appeal. A variety of opportunities for clinical training are offered. Programs offered include Appellate Review; Clinical Seminar; Criminal, Judicial, and Public External Placement clinics; Prisoner Legal Assistance Clinic; Street Law; New Business Legal Clinic; Civil Litigation Clinic; Trial Litigation Clinic; and pro bono opportunities.

Student Activities and Leadership

Our more than 20 law student organizations include the *Akron Law Review*, Black Law Students Association, Asian-Latino Law Students Association, Environmental Law Society, Intellectual Property and Technology Law Association, International Law Society, Law Association for Women, Akron Public Interest Law Society, Student Bar Association, and more. Elections for leadership positions are held each year for day and evening students.

Library and Technology

UA's campus is wireless, allowing for Internet and network access in any building on campus. The law library contains 287,000 volumes. Students have access to 47.6 million library items, 11 million unique titles that may be delivered through OhioLINK, 3.8 million library items through UA Libraries Catalog, and many full-text resources including 6,000 journals, more than 7.5 million articles, and 40,000 e-books. Law students also receive free access to LexisNexis and Westlaw.

Career Planning and Placement

The Career Planning and Placement Office (CPPO) director counsels law students on résumé writing, job searching, interviewing skills, and preparing for entrance into the legal profession. On-campus interviews, a minority clerkship program, an attorney-student mentor program, employment-related seminars, and career fairs are offered. Akron's extensive law alumni database enables the CPPO to assist students with networking opportunities nationwide. This office assists in the placement of students in law-related positions during summer sessions and upper-division years. Graduates receive placement assistance, on request, throughout their careers. Akron's reputation for excellence in legal education and a subsequent high bar passage rate facilitates competitive placements for students and graduates in all areas of practice.

Visiting Akron Law

Several programs are offered throughout the year for prospective and admitted students to interact with law students, alumni, faculty, and administration at the School of Law. In addition, guests are welcome to schedule an appointment to visit a class, take a tour, or meet with an admission representative. Prospective students may request additional information at **www.uakron.edu/law**. For those unable to visit Akron Law, our representatives can also be met on the recruitment road each fall. Consult our website for our national recruitment schedule.

APPLICANT PROFILE

The University of Akron School of Law

LSAT Score	GPA							
	3.75 +	3.51–3.74	3.25–3.50	3.00–3.24	2.75–2.99	2.50–2.74	Below 2.50	No GPA
160–180								
155–159								
150–154								
120–149								

■ Good Possibility   ☐ Possible   ▨ Slightly Possible

THE UNIVERSITY OF ALABAMA SCHOOL OF LAW

Box 870382
Tuscaloosa, AL 35487
Phone: 205.348.5440; Fax: 205.348.5439
E-mail: admissions@law.ua.edu; Website: www.law.ua.edu

ABA
Approved
Since
1926

The Basics

Type of school	Public
Term	Semester
Application deadline	
Application fee	$40
Financial aid deadline	
Can first year start other than fall?	No
Student to faculty ratio	10.1 to 1
# of housing spaces available restricted to law students	
graduate housing for which law students are eligible	

Faculty and Administrators

	Total		Men		Women		Minorities	
	Spr	Fall	Spr	Fall	Spr	Fall	Spr	Fall
Full-time	40	43	29	30	11	13	6	7
Other full-time	4	4	0	0	4	4	0	0
Deans, librarians, & others who teach	14	14	9	9	5	5	0	0
Part-time	31	37	26	32	5	5	19	23
Total	89	98	64	71	25	27	25	30

Curriculum

	Full-Time	Part-Time
Typical first-year section size	60	0
Is there typically a "small section" of the first-year class, other than Legal Writing, taught by full-time faculty	No	No
If yes, typical size offered last year		
# of classroom course titles beyond first-year curriculum	129	

# of upper division courses, excluding seminars, with an enrollment:	Under 25	87
	25–49	28
	50–74	6
	75–99	5
	100+	0

# of seminars	17	
# of seminar positions available	204	
# of seminar positions filled	180	0
# of positions available in simulation courses	406	
# of simulation positions filled	347	0
# of positions available in faculty supervised clinical courses	126	
# of faculty supervised clinical positions filled	124	0
# involved in field placements	90	0
# involved in law journals	160	0
# involved in moot court or trial competitions	92	0
# of credit hours required to graduate	90	

JD Enrollment and Ethnicity

	Men		Women		Full-Time		Part-Time		1st-Year		Total		JD Degs. Awd.
	#	%	#	%	#	%	#	%	#	%	#	%	
All Hispanics	4	1.4	3	1.4	7	1.4	0	0.0	2	1.2	7	1.4	3
Am. Ind./AK Nat.	3	1.0	2	0.9	5	1.0	0	0.0	3	1.8	5	1.0	2
Asian	7	2.4	5	2.3	12	2.4	0	0.0	4	2.5	12	2.4	5
Black/Af. Am.	13	4.4	27	12.5	40	7.9	0	0.0	14	8.6	40	7.9	16
Nat. HI/Pac. Isl.	0	0.0	0	0.0	0	0.0	0	0.0	0	0.0	0	0.0	0
2 or more races	0	0.0	0	0.0	0	0.0	0	0.0	0	0.0	0	0.0	0
Subtotal (minor.)	27	9.2	37	17.1	64	12.6	0	0.0	23	14.1	64	12.6	26
Nonres. Alien	0	0.0	0	0.0	0	0.0	0	0.0	0	0.0	0	0.0	0
White/Cauc.	266	90.8	179	82.9	445	87.4	0	0.0	140	85.9	445	87.4	148
Unknown	0	0.0	0	0.0	0	0.0	0	0.0	0	0.0	0	0.0	0
Total	293	57.6	216	42.4	509	100.0	0	0.0	163	32.0	509		174

Transfers

Transfers in	17
Transfers out	1

Tuition and Fees

	Resident	Nonresident
Full-time	$15,760	$28,070
Part-time		
Tuition Guarantee Program	N	

Living Expenses

Estimated living expenses for singles

Living on campus	Living off campus	Living at home
$16,467	$16,467	$16,467

ABA
Approved
Since
1926

GPA and LSAT Scores

	Total	Full-Time	Part-Time
# of apps	2,384	2,384	0
# of offers	543	543	0
# of matrics	161	161	0
75% GPA	3.92	3.92	0.00
Median GPA	3.80	3.80	0.00
25% GPA	3.41	3.50	0.00
75% LSAT	167	167	0
Median LSAT	165	165	0
25% LSAT	159	159	0

Grants and Scholarships (from prior year)

	Total		Full-Time		Part-Time	
	#	%	#	%	#	%
Total # of students	547		527		20	
Total # receiving grants	249	45.5	249	47.2	0	0.0
Less than 1/2 tuition	99	18.1	99	18.8	0	0.0
Half to full tuition	73	13.3	73	13.9	0	0.0
Full tuition	16	2.9	16	3.0	0	0.0
More than full tuition	61	11.2	61	11.6	0	0.0
Median grant amount			$12,500		$0	

Informational and Library Resources

Total amount spent on library materials	$1,268,183
Study seating capacity inside the library	506
# of full-time equivalent professional librarians	20
Hours per week library is open	100
# of open, wired connections available to students	73
# of networked computers available for use by students	81
Has wireless network?	Y
Requires computer?	N

JD Attrition (from prior year)

	Academic	Other	Total	
	#	#	#	%
1st year	2	11	13	7.0
2nd year	0	1	1	0.6
3rd year	0	0	0	0.0
4th year	0	0	0	0.0

Employment (9 months after graduation)

	Total	Percentage
Employment status known	167	98.8
Employment status unknown	2	1.2
Employed	147	88.0
Pursuing graduate degrees	6	3.6
Unemployed (seeking, not seeking, or studying for the bar)	2	1.2
Type of Employment		
# employed in law firms	82	55.8
# employed in business and industry	14	9.5
# employed in government	19	12.9
# employed in public interest	8	5.4
# employed as judicial clerks	18	12.2
# employed in academia	4	2.7
Geographic Location		
# employed in state	99	67.3
# employed in foreign countries	3	2.0
# of states where employed		18

Bar Passage Rates

First-time takers	149	Reporting %	78.52
Average school %	96.58	Average state %	86.49
Average pass difference	10.09		

Jurisdiction	Takers	Passers	Pass %	State %	Diff %
Alabama	105	101	96.19	86.51	9.68
Georgia	12	12	100.00	86.28	13.72

THE UNIVERSITY OF ALABAMA SCHOOL OF LAW

Box 870382
Tuscaloosa, AL 35487
Phone: 205.348.5440; Fax: 205.348.5439
E-mail: admissions@law.ua.edu; Website: www.law.ua.edu

Introduction

The University of Alabama School of Law, the only public law school in Alabama, offers students a nationally recognized, progressive legal education. The law school has served as the training ground for state and national leaders in the legal profession, business, and government. Law students are provided with an abundance of cultural, academic, and athletic opportunities through the university. The curriculum is traditional but diverse. The law school is student-centered; faculty and administration are accessible to students. Although the faculty's first priority is teaching, the professors are actively engaged in scholarly research and writing. Alabama is accredited by the ABA and the AALS.

Library and Physical Facilities

The law school building, which sits on 23 acres of the University of Alabama's campus in Tuscaloosa, was designed by Edward Durell Stone, the architect for the Museum of Modern Art in New York, the US Embassy in New Delhi, and the Kennedy Center for the Performing Arts. Construction on a new wing and renovations to the existing building were completed in 2006. The wing includes new classrooms, the clinical offices, a cafeteria, a career services suite, meeting rooms, and a 24-hour computer lab. The Bounds Law Library provides users with a substantial research collection, student study carrels, the Hugo Black Study, the Howell Heflin Conference Room, and the Payne Special Collections Room. The school is on a wireless network.

Special and Summer Programs

Clinical programs enable law students to gain valuable practical experience in interviewing clients, preparing cases, and participating in courtroom presentations. During the second and third years, students can choose to participate in the Elder Law, Domestic Violence, Civil, Community Development, Capital Defense, Mediation Law, or Criminal Defense clinics. Alabama guarantees every interested student the opportunity to participate in at least one clinic before graduating.

The externship program offers students practical experience while receiving credit. Externships are available during the summers and the second and third academic years. The law school's Public Interest Institute awards grants to encourage students to participate in the area of public interest and honors students who perform public interest work. The institute also has a full-time dean to assist students.

The joint JD/MBA program offers select students an opportunity to earn both an MBA and JD. Students may select from programs designed for them to earn both degrees within three or four years. The graduate program for international students provides international lawyers an opportunity to earn an LLM degree. The law school also offers a part-time LLM in Taxation program for JD degree holders.

The law school's two summer programs at the University of Fribourg in Fribourg, Switzerland, and the Australian National University in Canberra provide a unique international experience. Both programs include a course surveying the host country's national law and a comparative law doctrinal course. In addition, Alabama Law offers current students the opportunity to study abroad for a semester at Tel Aviv University in Israel and the National Law University of New Delhi in India.

Summer school is open to students who have completed the first year.

Admission

A student must obtain a bachelor's degree at an accredited institution before enrolling, but may apply during his or her senior year. Applicants must take the LSAT, preferably in June or October in the year preceding enrollment, and register for the Credential Assembly Service (CAS). Transcripts must show all schools attended. Application materials are available in the late summer each year and accepted in early fall. Applications are processed on a rolling basis. The two most significant factors for admission are the undergraduate GPA and LSAT score. However, the school believes that the law school experience is enriched by a diverse group of students. The Admissions Committee also considers other factors, such as honors, activities, unique work or service experience, difficulty of undergraduate courses, writing ability, trends in academic performance, leadership roles, travel experience, exceptional talents, career achievements, graduate school performance, and history of overcoming adversity. One letter of recommendation or LSAC evaluation is required. The law school recommends that letters be submitted to the Credential Assembly Service. A résumé is also required.

Student Activities

A broad range of student activities adds to the students' law school experience. Student organizations represent diverse interests. These include the Student Bar Association, Black Law Students Association, Public Interest Law Association, Civil Rights Law Students Association, Dorbin Association (women's group), Law Students for Choice, Gay-Straight Alliance, Environmental Law Society, International Law Society, Just Democracy, Labor and Employment Law Society, Law Democrats, Law Republicans, Business Law Society, Criminal Law Association, Defense Lawyers Association, Future Trial Lawyers Association, Christian Legal Society, Sports and Entertainment Law Society, and Latin American Law Association.

The School of Law also offers numerous writing opportunities. The *Alabama Law Review*, a nationally recognized law journal, is edited by students and devotes substantial space to national and state issues. The *Journal of the Legal Profession, Law and Psychology Review*, and *Alabama Civil Rights and Civil Liberties Law Review* are also student-edited law journals. Over 40 percent will graduate with journal experience.

Moot court and trial advocacy teams have enjoyed exceptional success over the years. The law school sponsors teams in several moot court, specialty, and trial advocacy competitions. The moot court and trial advocacy teams have won many team and individual awards in both regional and national competitions.

Expenses and Financial Aid

The majority of students enrolled in the School of Law finance their legal education through loans, savings, earnings, or family contributions. Applicants are considered automatically for first-year scholarships, which are typically based on factors such as GPA and LSAT performance. Scholarships sometimes are renewable during the second and third years—depending upon funding, the student's need, and whether the recipient maintains stated levels of academic achievement. Following acceptance by the law school, each admitted student who applies for federal aid through the Free Application for Federal Student Aid (FAFSA) receives a financial aid packet from the university's Financial Aid Office. Information on loans can be obtained by contacting Student Financial Aid, the University of Alabama, Box 870162, Tuscaloosa, AL 35487-0162; phone: 205.348.6756; website: www.financialaid.ua.edu. Applicants should complete the FAFSA form as soon after January 1 as possible, and may apply online at www.fafsa.ed.gov.

Career Services

The Career Services Office assists students in their efforts to find employment. The office provides individual career counseling, group presentations, speaker programs, and library and database resources. Seminars are presented on résumé writing, interviewing techniques, job-search techniques, judicial clerkships, and nontraditional legal jobs, to name a few. Extensive on-campus interviewing occurs. The law school also participates in job fairs in Atlanta, New York City, Chicago, and Washington, DC. The employment rate within nine months of graduation was 97.4 percent for the class of 2010 with approximately 40 percent practicing outside of Alabama. The national bar passage rate for the same class was 95 percent and the in-state bar passage rate was 95 percent.

Housing

The University of Alabama maintains residence halls and units for students; however, most law students live off campus. The cost of living in Tuscaloosa for a single law student ranges from approximately $500 to $1,100 per month. For information on university housing, students must contact the Office of Residential Life at the University of Alabama at housing@sa.ua.edu.

APPLICANT PROFILE

The University of Alabama School of Law
This grid includes only applicants who earned 120–180 LSAT scores under standard administrations.

LSAT Score	GPA								
	3.75 +	3.50–3.74	3.25–3.49	3.00–3.24	2.75–2.99	2.50–2.74	2.25–2.49	2.00–2.24	Below 2.00
175–180									
170–174									
165–169									
160–164									
155–159									
150–154									
145–149									
140–144									
135–139									
130–134									
125–129									
120–124									

■ Good Possibility   ☐ Possible   ▨ Unlikely

Reflects 99% of the total applicant pool; average LSAT data reported.

ALBANY LAW SCHOOL OF UNION UNIVERSITY

80 New Scotland Avenue
Albany, NY 12208-3494
Phone: 518.445.2326; Fax: 518.445.2369
E-mail: admissions@albanylaw.edu; Website: www.albanylaw.edu

The Basics

Type of school	Private
Term	Semester
Application deadline	3/1
Application fee	$60
Financial aid deadline	
Can first year start other than fall?	No
Student to faculty ratio	13.3 to 1
# of housing spaces available restricted to law students	
graduate housing for which law students are eligible	

Faculty and Administrators

	Total		Men		Women		Minorities	
	Spr	Fall	Spr	Fall	Spr	Fall	Spr	Fall
Full-time	46	44	21	21	25	23	9	10
Other full-time	1	2	0	0	1	2	1	1
Deans, librarians, & others who teach	6	6	4	3	2	3	1	2
Part-time	31	29	19	19	12	10	7	6
Total	84	81	44	43	40	38	18	19

Curriculum

	Full-Time	Part-Time
Typical first-year section size	68	0
Is there typically a "small section" of the first-year class, other than Legal Writing, taught by full-time faculty	No	No
If yes, typical size offered last year		
# of classroom course titles beyond first-year curriculum	133	

# of upper division courses, excluding seminars, with an enrollment:		
Under 25	76	
25–49	23	
50–74	14	
75–99	10	
100+	4	

# of seminars	42	
# of seminar positions available	924	
# of seminar positions filled	605	0
# of positions available in simulation courses	484	
# of simulation positions filled	335	0
# of positions available in faculty supervised clinical courses	112	
# of faculty supervised clinical positions filled	78	0
# involved in field placements	206	0
# involved in law journals	148	0
# involved in moot court or trial competitions	15	0
# of credit hours required to graduate	87	

JD Enrollment and Ethnicity

	Men		Women		Full-Time		Part-Time		1st-Year		Total		JD Degs. Awd.
	#	%	#	%	#	%	#	%	#	%	#	%	
All Hispanics	16	4.0	12	3.8	28	4.0	0	0.0	7	2.9	28	3.9	7
Am. Ind./AK Nat.	2	0.5	2	0.6	4	0.6	0	0.0	0	0.0	4	0.6	1
Asian	13	3.2	18	5.7	30	4.3	1	4.3	8	3.3	31	4.3	14
Black/Af. Am.	7	1.7	8	2.5	14	2.0	1	4.3	5	2.1	15	2.1	5
Nat. HI/Pac. Isl.	0	0.0	0	0.0	0	0.0	0	0.0	0	0.0	0	0.0	0
2 or more races	1	0.2	5	1.6	6	0.9	0	0.0	6	2.5	6	0.8	0
Subtotal (minor.)	39	9.7	45	14.2	82	11.8	2	8.7	26	10.7	84	11.7	27
Nonres. Alien	4	1.0	7	2.2	11	1.6	0	0.0	4	1.6	11	1.5	0
White/Cauc.	301	74.9	220	69.2	503	72.2	18	78.3	173	71.2	521	72.4	205
Unknown	58	14.4	46	14.5	101	14.5	3	13.0	40	16.5	104	14.4	12
Total	402	55.8	318	44.2	697	96.8	23	3.2	243	33.8	720		250

Transfers

Transfers in	8
Transfers out	11

Tuition and Fees

	Resident	Nonresident
Full-time	$40,120	$40,120
Part-time	$30,128	$30,128
Tuition Guarantee Program		N

Living Expenses

Estimated living expenses for singles

Living on campus	Living off campus	Living at home
N/A	$18,000	$9,100

ALBANY LAW SCHOOL OF UNION UNIVERSITY

ABA
Approved
Since
1930

GPA and LSAT Scores

	Total	Full-Time	Part-Time
# of apps	2,572	2,572	0
# of offers	1,234	1,234	0
# of matrics	236	236	0
75% GPA	3.50	3.50	0.00
Median GPA	3.27	3.27	0.00
25% GPA	3.03	3.03	0.00
75% LSAT	157	157	0
Median LSAT	154	154	0
25% LSAT	152	152	0

Grants and Scholarships (from prior year)

	Total		Full-Time		Part-Time	
	#	%	#	%	#	%
Total # of students	749		712		37	
Total # receiving grants	271	36.2	259	36.4	12	32.4
Less than 1/2 tuition	133	17.8	126	17.7	7	18.9
Half to full tuition	102	13.6	99	13.9	3	8.1
Full tuition	34	4.5	32	4.5	2	5.4
More than full tuition	2	0.3	2	0.3	0	0.0
Median grant amount			$20,000		$11,250	

Informational and Library Resources

Total amount spent on library materials	$1,776,608
Study seating capacity inside the library	432
# of full-time equivalent professional librarians	8
Hours per week library is open	104
# of open, wired connections available to students	1,142
# of networked computers available for use by students	95
Has wireless network?	Y
Requires computer?	N

JD Attrition (from prior year)

	Academic	Other	Total	
	#	#	#	%
1st year	7	0	7	2.7
2nd year	1	12	13	5.4
3rd year	0	0	0	0.0
4th year	0	0	0	0.0

Employment (9 months after graduation)

	Total	Percentage
Employment status known	216	100.0
Employment status unknown	0	0.0
Employed	195	90.3
Pursuing graduate degrees	10	4.6
Unemployed (seeking, not seeking, or studying for the bar)	9	4.2
Type of Employment		
# employed in law firms	115	59.0
# employed in business and industry	22	11.3
# employed in government	34	17.4
# employed in public interest	6	3.1
# employed as judicial clerks	11	5.6
# employed in academia	5	2.6
Geographic Location		
# employed in state	159	81.5
# employed outside the US	2	1.0
# of states where employed	15	

Bar Passage Rates

First-time takers	230	Reporting %	81.30
Average school %	82.89	Average state %	86.51
Average pass difference	−3.62		

Jurisdiction	Takers	Passers	Pass %	State %	Diff %
New York	187	155	82.89	86.51	−3.62

ALBANY LAW SCHOOL OF UNION UNIVERSITY

80 New Scotland Avenue
Albany; NY 12208-3494
Phone: 518.445.2326; Fax: 518.445.2369
E-mail: admissions@albanylaw.edu; Website: www.albanylaw.edu

Introduction

The only law school in the capital of New York State, Albany Law School is the oldest private, independent law school in North America. Our location, in the center of state government, provides unprecedented opportunities for internships, field placements, clinical experience, and career opportunities. Our world-class faculty is dedicated and accessible. Students have access to New York's highest court, federal courts, and the state legislature, as well as to a thriving tech-based economy. The employment rate for our graduates has been well above the national average for law schools for over 25 years.

The Academic Experience

From your first day at Albany Law School you will be challenged by a rigorous academic curriculum. You will get a firm foundation in fundamental areas of law, plus opportunities to shape your learning to fit your professional interests.

As a first-year student, you begin to acquire the skills that will become the foundation of your legal career. As part of our innovative Introduction to Lawyering course, you will represent a plaintiff or defendant in a simulated case where you conduct legal research, draft motions and memoranda, and participate in client interviews and negotiations. The class culminates with each student presenting an oral argument before some of the state's most notable attorneys.

As a second- and third-year student, you can focus your studies in one of 14 concentrations to complement coursework. Opportunities include 7 clinical projects and more than 150 field placement internships in the Albany region, many of them in state and federal government positions as well as in law firms and high-tech companies. Students also participate in real-world work through the Government Law Center, Clinic and Justice Center, and study-abroad programs. Some students pursue a joint-degree program with an area graduate school, earning a master's degree while working toward a Juris Doctor (JD) degree.

Real-Life Experience

Our groundbreaking legal centers and award-winning clinical programs provide the valuable hands-on experience that employers find desirable. You work alongside committed clinical faculty and practicing attorneys to assist low-income clients with real legal issues relating to health law, HIV/AIDS, disabilities, domestic violence, disputes with the Internal Revenue Service, issues relating to housing, and financial investments. You will also work with prosecutors, judges, and experienced attorneys through our field placement program.

Because of our unique location, you interact with the leaders in New York state government—countless Albany Law alumni—and visionaries building New York's high-technology base through the programs at the Government Law Center. In the Government Law Center you conduct research, contribute to publications, and participate in conferences and special projects that promote the study of the issues facing government, public policy, and public service.

Your Career

From your first week at school, our Career Center helps you develop a career plan and supports you throughout your job search. Professional career counselors help you define career goals, craft résumés and cover letters, prepare for interviews, and compare employment offers.

The Career Center is a state-of-the-art facility with multiple interview rooms set aside for professionals to conduct on-campus interviews. These rooms are equipped with all the amenities of a law office and are extremely popular with employers. Our job search software is exclusive to Albany Law students and alumni. Some 4,000 employers currently post jobs on the private system.

Job fairs, information sessions, workshops, and panel discussions on a variety of employment-related topics occur almost daily. The Career Center hosts more than 1,000 interviews each year and conducts off-campus interview programs in metropolitan areas, including New York City; Chicago; Washington, DC; and Boston, exclusively for Albany Law School students. Our alumni are avid supporters of these efforts and participate enthusiastically in center activities.

Our graduates find jobs in law firms, government agencies, public interest organizations, and business and industry throughout the country. About one-third of Albany Law School graduates work in the New York City metropolitan area, with large groups of alumni in Boston; Washington, DC; and business centers along the eastern seaboard as far south as Florida.

The employment rate for the class of 2009 was 90 percent—above the national average and consistently above national rates for over 25 years.

Our Community

The Albany Law School community of approximately 700 students, 55 full-time faculty, and 54 part-time faculty is intimate, respectful, and supportive. We welcome students and faculty with diverse backgrounds and talents, and provide an outstanding environment for the pursuit of scholarship, teaching, and public service.

The small size of our student body fosters an environment that encourages camaraderie and frequent contact between students and faculty. We are only a law school. Because we are independent, we are not attached to a larger university.

Nearly 12 percent of our students graduated five or more years before entering law school and had careers in other professions prior to beginning their legal studies. Nearly 50 percent of our students are women, over a third are from outside New York State, and 25 percent are members of a minority group.

Our Campus

Albany Law School's facilities honor our 159-year history, while supporting a twenty-first century legal education. The open design of the 53,000-square-foot Schaffer Law Library—a federal depository library—provides an inviting environment with seating for hundreds of students. Book and microfilm collections number more than half a million volumes, and the library supplements its collection with online databases and legal research systems, including

LexisNexis and Westlaw. The library also houses technological devices for the hearing and visually impaired.

The main building of Albany Law School is known as the 1928 Building, acknowledging its year of construction. The building has been recently renovated and houses contemporary lecture halls, seminar-style classrooms, two modern moot courtrooms, and smart classrooms with wireless Internet access and advanced audio, video, computing, and conferencing systems.

A 45,000-square-foot building built in 2000 houses the Albany Law School clinic, law centers, and administrative offices, as well as several classrooms, including a high-tech distance learning classroom. Our new bookstore and student center opened last year, along with a new state-of-the-art fitness center.

Student Life

You have dozens of opportunities to participate in student organizations and activities around specific academic, professional, social, cultural, or athletic interests.

Three student-edited journals, the *Albany Law Review*, the *Albany Law Journal of Science and Technology*, and the *Albany Government Law Review* offer cocurricular research and writing opportunities.

Our nationally recognized Moot Court Program enables you to develop skills in trial advocacy, appellate advocacy, client counseling, and negotiating while competing in both intramural and interscholastic competitions.

The Capital Region is home to 16 colleges and universities and boasts museums, galleries, restaurants, shops, theaters, nightclubs for every taste, venues that host professional sporting events, and performing arts centers that attract national acts. The Adirondack, Berkshire, and Catskill mountains offer skiing, camping, hiking, and water sports, as well as the Saratoga Race Course for thoroughbred and harness racing. Metropolitan centers in New York City, Boston, and Montreal are all within an easy drive and about 10 trains provide daily service to New York City. All major air carriers operate from the Albany International Airport and provide daily nonstop service to most eastern US cities, with connections worldwide.

Admission and Financial Aid

Albany Law School commits close to $5 million annually to scholarship assistance. Over 30 percent of first-year students receive awards that average $20,000 for each year of study. We offer grants based on academic merit, ranging from $5,000 to full-tuition scholarships.

When evaluating each individual application, the Admissions Committee takes a highly personalized, holistic approach, reviewing LSAT score, undergraduate grade-point average, strength of the undergraduate program, rigor of the undergraduate curriculum, and life experience. The committee seeks to enroll a student body that enriches the educational experience of all of its members. Albany Law School also seeks to provide future members of the bar who reflect the diversity and sensibilities of our society.

Approximately 90 percent of our students qualify for financial aid, via federal, state, and private loans, or for part-time employment to assist in meeting educational expenses.

We encourage you to visit Albany Law School—meet our faculty, speak with our students, and tour our beautiful facilities. We look forward to meeting you.

APPLICANT PROFILE

Albany Law School attracts talented, diverse students from a wide spectrum of backgrounds and experiences. Applicants come from the highest ranks of their prior graduate and undergraduate institutions. LSAT scores and prior academic performance are important in assisting our Admissions Committee in offering seats to applicants. Those indicators are, however, not the sole factors weighed when admission decisions are made. Interested applicants are encouraged to explore how their careers can be enhanced by an Albany Law School education. Contact the Admissions Office at 518.445.2326 to discuss your individual qualifications.

AMERICAN UNIVERSITY WASHINGTON COLLEGE OF LAW

4801 Massachusetts Avenue NW, Suite 507
Washington, DC 20016
Phone: 202.274.4101; Fax: 202.274.4107
E-mail: wcladmit@wcl.american.edu; Website: www.wcl.american.edu

ABA
Approved
Since
1940

The Basics

Type of school	Private
Term	Semester
Application deadline	3/1
Application fee	$70
Financial aid deadline	3/1
Can first year start other than fall?	No
Student to faculty ratio	11.8 to 1
# of housing spaces available restricted to law students	
graduate housing for which law students are eligible	25

Faculty and Administrators

	Total		Men		Women		Minorities	
	Spr	Fall	Spr	Fall	Spr	Fall	Spr	Fall
Full-time	98	98	55	57	43	41	20	21
Other full-time	6	6	0	0	6	6	1	1
Deans, librarians, & others who teach	11	12	4	4	7	8	2	2
Part-time	136	149	95	87	40	61	49	57
Total	251	265	154	148	96	116	72	81

Curriculum

	Full-Time	Part-Time
Typical first-year section size	77	95
Is there typically a "small section" of the first-year class, other than Legal Writing, taught by full-time faculty	Yes	No
If yes, typical size offered last year	45	

# of classroom course titles beyond first-year curriculum		301
# of upper division courses, excluding seminars, with an enrollment:	Under 25	192
	25–49	65
	50–74	41
	75–99	7
	100+	0

# of seminars		143
# of seminar positions available		2,188
# of seminar positions filled	1,162	583
# of positions available in simulation courses		1,203
# of simulation positions filled	530	365
# of positions available in faculty supervised clinical courses		224
# of faculty supervised clinical positions filled	210	14
# involved in field placements	290	7
# involved in law journals	366	8
# involved in moot court or trial competitions	81	3
# of credit hours required to graduate		86

JD Enrollment and Ethnicity

	Men		Women		Full-Time		Part-Time		1st-Year		Total		JD Degs. Awd.
	#	%	#	%	#	%	#	%	#	%	#	%	
All Hispanics	104	15.8	135	16.0	209	16.8	30	11.5	99	19.5	239	15.9	54
Am. Ind./AK Nat.	4	0.6	5	0.6	8	0.6	1	0.4	1	0.2	9	0.6	9
Asian	57	8.7	78	9.2	107	8.6	28	10.8	30	5.9	135	9.0	52
Black/Af. Am.	45	6.8	108	12.8	119	9.6	34	13.1	46	9.1	153	10.2	31
Nat. HI/Pac. Isl.	0	0.0	1	0.1	0	0.0	1	0.4	0	0.0	1	0.1	0
2 or more races	14	2.1	12	1.4	17	1.4	9	3.5	23	4.5	26	1.7	0
Subtotal (minor.)	224	34.0	339	40.1	460	37.0	103	39.6	199	39.3	563	37.5	154
Nonres. Alien	13	2.0	30	3.6	42	3.4	1	0.4	13	2.6	43	2.9	0
White/Cauc.	410	62.3	452	53.5	709	57.0	153	58.8	290	57.2	862	57.4	297
Unknown	11	1.7	24	2.8	32	2.6	3	1.2	5	1.0	35	2.3	5
Total	658	43.8	845	56.2	1243	82.7	260	17.3	507	33.7	1503		467

Transfers

Transfers in	43
Transfers out	39

Tuition and Fees

	Resident	Nonresident
Full-time	$43,458	$43,458
Part-time	$30,468	$30,468
Tuition Guarantee Program		N

Living Expenses

Estimated living expenses for singles

Living on campus	Living off campus	Living at home
$22,188	$22,188	$22,188

AMERICAN UNIVERSITY WASHINGTON COLLEGE OF LAW

ABA
Approved
Since
1940

GPA and LSAT Scores

	Total	Full-Time	Part-Time
# of apps	9,021	8,000	1,021
# of offers	1,934	1,740	194
# of matrics	502	425	77
75% GPA	3.58	3.58	3.60
Median GPA	3.40	3.39	3.48
25% GPA	3.12	3.13	3.13
75% LSAT	164	164	164
Median LSAT	163	163	161
25% LSAT	158	158	159

Grants and Scholarships (from prior year)

	Total		Full-Time		Part-Time	
	#	%	#	%	#	%
Total # of students	1,485		1,195		290	
Total # receiving grants	450	30.3	438	36.7	12	4.1
Less than 1/2 tuition	409	27.5	397	33.2	12	4.1
Half to full tuition	13	0.9	13	1.1	0	0.0
Full tuition	24	1.6	24	2.0	0	0.0
More than full tuition	4	0.3	4	0.3	0	0.0
Median grant amount			$11,000		$3,132	

Informational and Library Resources

Total amount spent on library materials	$2,105,214
Study seating capacity inside the library	596
# of full-time equivalent professional librarians	10
Hours per week library is open	119
# of open, wired connections available to students	2,160
# of networked computers available for use by students	166
Has wireless network?	Y
Requires computer?	N

JD Attrition (from prior year)

	Academic	Other	Total	
	#	#	#	%
1st year	0	41	41	8.5
2nd year	0	1	1	0.2
3rd year	0	0	0	0.0
4th year	0	0	0	0.0

Employment (9 months after graduation)

	Total	Percentage
Employment status known	445	99.1
Employment status unknown	4	0.9
Employed	366	82.2
Pursuing graduate degrees	23	5.2
Unemployed (seeking, not seeking, or studying for the bar)	34	7.6
Type of Employment		
# employed in law firms	156	42.6
# employed in business and industry	51	13.9
# employed in government	62	16.9
# employed in public interest	45	12.3
# employed as judicial clerks	38	10.4
# employed in academia	13	3.6
Geographic Location		
# employed in state	166	45.4
# employed outside the US	6	1.6
# of states where employed	29	

Bar Passage Rates

First-time takers	447	Reporting %	78.97
Average school %	84.14	Average state %	80.79
Average pass difference	3.35		

Jurisdiction	Takers	Passers	Pass %	State %	Diff %
New York	109	98	89.91	86.51	3.40
Maryland	106	85	80.19	78.20	1.99
Virginia	73	65	89.04	77.06	11.98
California	32	20	62.50	73.19	−10.69
Others (2)	33	29	87.88		

AMERICAN UNIVERSITY WASHINGTON COLLEGE OF LAW

4801 Massachusetts Avenue NW, Suite 507
Washington, DC 20016
Phone: 202.274.4101; Fax: 202.274.4107
E-mail: wcladmit@wcl.american.edu; Website: www.wcl.american.edu

Introduction

American University Washington College of Law (WCL) offers an opportunity for the study of law in the center of the nation's legal institutions. The law school is minutes from downtown Washington, yet offers the facilities and ambience of a campus environment in one of the city's most beautiful residential neighborhoods. Founded in 1896 by two women, the law school is national in character. WCL offers renowned programs in experiential learning (clinics and externships), international law, law and government, intellectual property, business, environmental law, health law, and gender. It is committed to the development of the intellectual abilities, professional values, and practical skills required to prepare lawyers to practice in an increasingly complex and transnational world.

Library and Physical Facilities

The John Sherman Myers and Alvina Reckman Myers Law Center houses the Pence Law Library, two courtrooms, classrooms, faculty offices, and administrative offices of the Washington College of Law. The two-story law library is the heart of the complex and seats over 600 students. The entire law school facility has wireless access, and most of the law library seating has wired access as well. The library has more than 600,000 volumes, access to multiple databases, and 14 group-study rooms in addition to individual study carrels and seating. There are a number of research stations and network printing is available to the community. The library collection includes European Community and US government depositories and the Baxter Collection in International Law. Students also have access to the university's library, the Library of Congress, specialized agency libraries, and other area law libraries to which the school is electronically linked. The law school also encompasses more than 12 program offices, several faculty offices, and conference rooms in two neighboring buildings.

Curriculum

The law school offers full- and part-time programs leading to the JD degree, which is awarded after satisfactory completion of 86 credit hours, 32 of which are prescribed. All degree candidates must also fulfill an upper-level writing requirement. While a modified version of the Socratic method is the dominant form of teaching in the first year, faculty increasingly employ such methodologies as role-playing, simulations, and small-group collaborative exercises. The goal is to develop the skills of critical analysis, provide perspectives on the law and lawyering, and deepen understanding of fundamental legal principles. In the Legal Rhetoric Program, basic legal research and writing skills are taught to groups of students by full-time faculty (23 students per section) and practicing attorneys (12 students per section). During the spring semester of the first year, students enroll in an elective first-year course in addition to their required courses. Examples of first-year elective courses are International Law, Introduction to Intellectual Property Law, and Introduction to Public Law. In the second and third years, students elect a course of study drawing from advanced courses, seminars, independent research, externships, and clinical programs. JD students take upper-level courses with LLM students, learning side by side with more than 180 practicing attorneys from around the world. Students are exposed to a variety of teaching approaches by the law school's distinguished full-time tenured and tenure-track faculty and adjunct professors.

Special Programs

While many of the advanced courses are taught in a traditional classroom setting, a variety of other innovative teaching modes are available to enhance research skills and provide professional training.

- **Clinical Program**—The Washington College of Law was one of the first law schools to develop modern clinical legal education. Typically, more than 200 second- and third-year students participate in one of the 10 law clinics each academic year—making the Clinical Program one of the largest in the nation. All ten clinics are open to third-year students and seven are open to second-year students. Full-time faculty and practitioners-in-residence work collaboratively to teach students about client-centered, ethical practices. The Clinical Program serves a diverse clientele including immigrants and refugees; victims/survivors of domestic violence; juveniles; criminal defendants; low-income taxpayers; individuals seeking help with family law, consumer, disability, and intellectual property issues; community groups; and nonprofit organizations. The 11 clinics include General Practice Clinic, Community and Economic Development Law Clinic, Criminal Justice Clinic, DC Law Students in Court Clinic, Disability Rights Law Clinic, Domestic Violence Law Clinic, Janet R. Spragens Federal Tax Clinic, Glushko-Samuelson Intellectual Property Law Clinic, Immigrant Justice Clinic, International Human Rights Law Clinic, and Women and the Law Clinic.
- **Dual-Degree Programs**—American University offers five domestic dual-degree programs for students seeking to enhance their law degree with additional graduate coursework. These programs are a JD/MA in International Affairs with the School of International Service; JD/MBA with the Kogod School of Business; and JD/MPA, JD/MPP, and JD/MS in Justice, Law, and Society programs with the School of Public Affairs. In addition to our domestic dual-degree programs, the law school offers four international dual-degree programs with law schools in Melbourne, Australia; Ottawa, Canada; Paris, France; and Madrid, Spain. These programs provide students more opportunities to practice law in the international arena.
- **Externship Program**—The program places upper-level students in many governmental, nonprofit, and public interest entities throughout the DC metropolitan area, the US, and abroad. More than 300 students participate in an externship each year.
- **Trial Advocacy Program**—The nationally recognized Stephen S. Weinstein Trial Advocacy Program prepares about 300 students each year to enter the legal community with solid trial litigation skills. The program emphasizes basic skills training, development of case theory and themes, analysis of strategies, and professional ethics.
- **Graduate Study**—Graduate study is available leading to either an LLM or SJD degree in International Legal Studies or Law and Government.

- **Summer Programs**—In addition to our summer session courses, the law school offers seven intensive summer institutes at our DC location in the areas of international arbitration, human rights, health law, intellectual property, law and government, and environmental law.
- **Study Abroad**—Students have the opportunity to study law for a semester in more than 18 different countries or through one of the law school's five summer abroad programs in Chile, Europe (London/Paris/Geneva), The Hague, Turkey, and Israel.

Admission

Applicants to the law school are admitted based on the strength of their entire academic and related record. The Committee on Admissions gives primary emphasis to the undergraduate record, LSAT scores, and major accomplishments and achievements, whether academic, work-related, or extracurricular. The committee considers the benefits from having racial, ethnic, cultural, economic, and geographic diversity among its students. Admission to the law school is highly selective and operates both a binding Early Decision Option and a modified rolling admission process, so early application is strongly encouraged.

Student Activities

The law school has four established journals and several publications edited and published by students. Journals include *Administrative Law Review*; *American University Law Review*; *American University International Law Review*; and

American University Journal of Gender, Social Policy, and the Law. Publications include *American Jurist*, *Business Law Brief* (will transition to a journal in 2011), *Criminal Law Brief*, *Health Law and Policy*, *Human Rights Brief*, the *Modern American*, and *Sustainable Development Law and Policy*. The Moot Court Honor Society sponsors appellate competitions for first-year and upper-level students and prepares students for a number of national and international interschool appellate competitions. The Mock Trial Honor Society sponsors a closing argument competition for first-year students and prepares student teams for national interschool mock trial competitions. There are more than 50 active student organizations, including the Asian-Pacific American Law Students Association, Black Law Students Association, Latino/a Law Students Association, South Asian Law Students Association, Lambda Law Society, International Trade Law Society, Intellectual Property Law Society, and Law and Government Society.

Career Services

Staffed by seven attorney counselors, the Office of Career and Professional Development provides individual career and professional development counseling to students and alumni on all aspects of the job search process, and sponsors dozens of educational and job-related programs throughout the year. The office coordinates both on- and off-campus recruitment for summer, academic year, and postgraduate positions, including regional interview programs in Atlanta, Boston, Chicago, New York, and the West Coast.

APPLICANT PROFILE

The Committee on Admissions considers a number of factors when evaluating a candidate for admission; therefore we elected not to include a grid based on undergraduate GPA and LSAT scores. Many applicants have similar scores, but each applicant has a unique background of academic, cultural, and professional experiences and achievements. The committee weighs all of these factors when determining a candidate's suitability for admission.

APPALACHIAN SCHOOL OF LAW

1169 Edgewater Drive, PO Box 2825
Grundy, VA 24614
Phone: 800.895.7411 (toll free) or 276.935.4349; Fax: 276.935.8496
E-mail: admissions@asl.edu; Website: www.asl.edu

The Basics

Type of school	Private
Term	Semester
Application deadline	7/1
Application fee	$60
Financial aid deadline	7/1
Can first year start other than fall?	No
Student to faculty ratio	16.7 to 1
# of housing spaces available restricted to law students	
graduate housing for which law students are eligible	

Faculty and Administrators

	Total		Men		Women		Minorities	
	Spr	Fall	Spr	Fall	Spr	Fall	Spr	Fall
Full-time	18	16	12	11	6	5	3	2
Other full-time	0	0	0	0	0	0	0	0
Deans, librarians, & others who teach	4	4	3	3	1	1	1	1
Part-time	0	1	0	1	0	0	0	0
Total	22	21	15	15	7	6	4	3

Curriculum

	Full-Time	Part-Time
Typical first-year section size	124	0
Is there typically a "small section" of the first-year class, other than Legal Writing, taught by full-time faculty	Yes	No
If yes, typical size offered last year	55	
# of classroom course titles beyond first-year curriculum	44	

# of upper division courses, excluding seminars, with an enrollment:		
	Under 25	18
	25–49	10
	50–74	3
	75–99	5
	100+	5

# of seminars	7	
# of seminar positions available	140	
# of seminar positions filled	74	0
# of positions available in simulation courses	392	
# of simulation positions filled	347	0
# of positions available in faculty supervised clinical courses	0	
# of faculty supervised clinical positions filled	0	0
# involved in field placements	112	0
# involved in law journals	48	0
# involved in moot court or trial competitions	35	0
# of credit hours required to graduate	90	

JD Enrollment and Ethnicity

	Men		Women		Full-Time		Part-Time		1st-Year		Total		JD Degs. Awd.
	#	%	#	%	#	%	#	%	#	%	#	%	
All Hispanics	3	1.5	6	5.6	9	2.9	0	0.0	7	5.7	9	2.9	4
Am. Ind./AK Nat.	0	0.0	2	1.9	2	0.6	0	0.0	1	0.8	2	0.6	0
Asian	5	2.4	2	1.9	7	2.2	0	0.0	4	3.3	7	2.2	3
Black/Af. Am.	1	0.5	6	5.6	7	2.2	0	0.0	1	0.8	7	2.2	8
Nat. HI/Pac. Isl.	0	0.0	0	0.0	0	0.0	0	0.0	0	0.0	0	0.0	0
2 or more races	6	2.9	6	5.6	12	3.8	0	0.0	5	4.1	12	3.8	0
Subtotal (minor.)	15	7.3	22	20.4	37	11.8	0	0.0	18	14.8	37	11.8	15
Nonres. Alien	1	0.5	0	0.0	1	0.3	0	0.0	0	0.0	1	0.3	0
White/Cauc.	179	87.3	82	75.9	261	83.4	0	0.0	103	84.4	261	83.4	78
Unknown	10	4.9	4	3.7	14	4.5	0	0.0	1	0.8	14	4.5	15
Total	205	65.5	108	34.5	313	100.0	0	0.0	122	39.0	313		108

Transfers

Transfers in	1
Transfers out	12

Tuition and Fees

	Resident	Nonresident
Full-time	$28,325	$28,325
Part-time		
Tuition Guarantee Program	Y	

Living Expenses

Estimated living expenses for singles

Living on campus	Living off campus	Living at home
N/A	$20,500	N/A

APPALACHIAN SCHOOL OF LAW

ABA
Approved
Since
2001

GPA and LSAT Scores

	Total	Full-Time	Part-Time
# of apps	1,368	1,368	0
# of offers	816	816	0
# of matrics	127	127	0
75% GPA	3.36	3.36	0.00
Median GPA	3.01	3.01	0.00
25% GPA	2.69	2.69	0.00
75% LSAT	151	151	0
Median LSAT	147	147	0
25% LSAT	146	146	0

Grants and Scholarships (from prior year)

	Total		Full-Time		Part-Time	
	#	%	#	%	#	%
Total # of students	334		334		0	
Total # receiving grants	68	20.4	68	20.4	0	0.0
Less than 1/2 tuition	7	2.1	7	2.1	0	0.0
Half to full tuition	33	9.9	33	9.9	0	0.0
Full tuition	28	8.4	28	8.4	0	0.0
More than full tuition	0	0.0	0	0.0	0	0.0
Median grant amount			$19,875		$0	

Informational and Library Resources

Total amount spent on library materials	$782,213
Study seating capacity inside the library	232
# of full-time equivalent professional librarians	4
Hours per week library is open	85
# of open, wired connections available to students	730
# of networked computers available for use by students	30
Has wireless network?	Y
Requires computer?	N

JD Attrition (from prior year)

	Academic	Other	Total	
	#	#	#	%
1st year	0	11	11	8.7
2nd year	18	13	31	26.1
3rd year	1	0	1	1.1
4th year	0	0	0	0.0

Employment (9 months after graduation)

	Total	Percentage
Employment status known	99	85.3
Employment status unknown	17	14.7
Employed	57	57.6
Pursuing graduate degrees	5	5.1
Unemployed (seeking, not seeking, or studying for the bar)	37	37.4
Type of Employment		
# employed in law firms	36	63.2
# employed in business and industry	1	1.8
# employed in government	8	14.0
# employed in public interest	3	5.3
# employed as judicial clerks	8	14.0
# employed in academia	0	0.0
Geographic Location		
# employed in state	17	29.8
# employed outside the US	1	1.8
# of states where employed	12	

Bar Passage Rates

First-time takers	109	Reporting %	104.59
Average school %	74.56	Average state %	80.83

Average pass difference −6.27

Jurisdiction	Takers	Passers	Pass %	State %	Diff %
Virginia	28	19	67.86	77.06	−9.20
Tennessee	22	20	90.91	82.44	8.47
North Carolina	19	11	57.89	76.79	−18.90
Kentucky	13	12	92.31	85.92	6.39
Others (12)	32	23	71.88		

APPALACHIAN SCHOOL OF LAW

1169 Edgewater Drive, PO Box 2825
Grundy, VA 24614
Phone: 800.895.7411 (toll free) or 276.935.4349; Fax: 276.935.8496
E-mail: admissions@asl.edu; Website: www.asl.edu

Introduction

Founded in 1994, the Appalachian School of Law produces civic-minded lawyers who go on to practice both in the Appalachian region and beyond. As a small, independent law school, ASL offers an intimate environment that is rare among institutions of higher learning. Located in the town of Grundy in southwestern Virginia, ASL provides a quiet setting for the study of law.

Curriculum

While providing a full, traditional legal curriculum, ASL emphasizes practical skills in an effort to help students succeed in real-world practice. Alternative dispute resolution and professional responsibility are infused throughout the curriculum. ASL also offers an Academic Success program to help students develop and refine the skills necessary to succeed in law school and pass the bar exam.

First-year students are introduced to basics such as civil procedure, contracts, property, and torts, as well as legal research, writing, and other essential skills. The program eases first-year students into the unique requirements of law studies, fosters collegiality and professionalism, and minimizes peer competition. Between their first and second years, students serve an externship with a judge, prosecutor, or legal services organization at sites across the nation.

Second-year students build their knowledge base in subjects such as constitutional law, evidence, secured transactions, business associations, dispute resolution, and more.

Third-year students take additional required courses, a seminar, capstone electives, and practicum courses that emphasize skill-based learning. Topics include negotiation, mediation, interviewing, law office practice, pretrial practice, and trial advocacy.

Community Service

ASL emphasizes community service in an effort to educate responsible civic leaders. Students complete 25 hours of service each semester in a project of their choosing. Although students are able to structure their service to meet their preferences and schedules, ASL assists students by scheduling one afternoon each week that they may devote to service projects. ASL-sponsored projects have included a conflict resolution program taught in public elementary schools; work with Buchanan Neighbors United, a group that provides housing repairs to improve substandard housing; a community recycling project; and a gender-bias study of the Virginia state court system.

Faculty

ASL's expanding faculty offers a depth of private and governmental practice experience as well as teaching experience. Faculty members have been former law clerks to federal and state court judges, government officials, and partners in small and large private law firms. The ASL faculty has published a variety of scholarly works in areas including constitutional law, legal ethics, and business and commercial matters. Small classes enable students to form meaningful relationships with faculty that further enrich their ASL experience.

Students and Student Organizations

ASL's active, enthusiastic student body hails from across the region and the country. The student body elects a Student Bar Association. Students may also participate in numerous student organizations, join the *Appalachian Journal of Law* and the *Appalachian Natural Resources Law Journal*, and compete on the award-winning moot court or trial advocacy teams. ASL has a family resource network for the spouses, partners, and families of law students. A speaker series brings a number of distinguished speakers to campus.

Facilities

ASL's historic classroom and office building was extensively renovated and won an award from the American Institute of Architects. The classroom building is constructed around a courtyard that serves as an informal gathering place. The renovated library provides a modern facility for research and studying. A third building houses student organizations and a coffee shop. The law school also occupies classroom and office space in the adjacent Booth Center for higher education. In 2010, ASL acquired a nearby building that will be renovated to provide classroom, clinic, and office space. Internet connections are available in most classrooms and the library. Wireless Internet access is also available.

Admission and Financial Aid

ASL accepts students who will benefit from a challenging curriculum in a caring environment. Admission decisions are not based on a single criterion; each item is considered in relation to the applicant's total qualifications. Besides undergraduate GPA and the LSAT, other considerations include an applicant's graduate work, character, work history, professional promise, personal commitment, recommendations, life experience, and other nonacademic achievements.

ASL offers a Pre-Admission Summer Opportunity (PASO) program for students who may have the potential to succeed as law students and lawyers, but whose skills and talents may not be reflected fully by their LSAT score and undergraduate performance. PASO provides participants an opportunity to experience law school coursework and allows faculty to evaluate the students' performances to assess their ability to succeed in law school. Participants who demonstrate potential to successfully complete ASL's three-year program are offered admission.

ASL offers both merit- and need-based scholarships. Merit-based scholarships are based on entering LSAT and GPA credentials; the application for admission serves as the application for a merit scholarship.

APPLICANT PROFILE

Appalachian School of Law

LSAT Score	GPA								
	3.75 +	3.50–3.74	3.25–3.49	3.00–3.24	2.75–2.99	2.50–2.74	2.25–2.49	2.00–2.24	Below 2.00
175–180	Very Likely	Very Likely	Very Likely	Very Likely	Very Likely	Very Likely	Very Likely	Possible	Unlikely
170–174	Very Likely	Very Likely	Very Likely	Very Likely	Very Likely	Very Likely	Very Likely	Possible	Unlikely
165–169	Very Likely	Very Likely	Very Likely	Very Likely	Very Likely	Very Likely	Very Likely	Possible	Unlikely
160–164	Very Likely	Very Likely	Very Likely	Very Likely	Very Likely	Very Likely	Very Likely	Possible	Unlikely
155–159	Very Likely	Very Likely	Very Likely	Very Likely	Very Likely	Very Likely	Very Likely	Possible	Unlikely
150–154	Very Likely	Very Likely	Very Likely	Very Likely	Very Likely	Very Likely	Possible	Unlikely	Unlikely
145–149	Possible	Possible	Possible	Possible	Possible	Possible	Unlikely	Unlikely	Unlikely
140–144	Unlikely	Unlikely	Unlikely	Unlikely	Unlikely	Unlikely	Unlikely	Unlikely	Unlikely
135–139	Unlikely	Unlikely	Unlikely	Unlikely	Unlikely	Unlikely	Unlikely	Unlikely	Unlikely
130–134	Unlikely	Unlikely	Unlikely	Unlikely	Unlikely	Unlikely	Unlikely	Unlikely	Unlikely
125–129	Unlikely	Unlikely	Unlikely	Unlikely	Unlikely	Unlikely	Unlikely	Unlikely	Unlikely

■ Very Likely   □ Possible   ▨ Unlikely

This grid represents data for 100 percent of the applicant pool for fall 2009 admission. It does not reflect the possibility of invitation to participate in the Pre-Admission Summer Opportunity program. This chart is to be used as a general guide only. Nonnumerical factors are strongly considered for all applicants.

THE UNIVERSITY OF ARIZONA JAMES E. ROGERS COLLEGE OF LAW

PO Box 210176, 1201 E. Speedway
Tucson, AZ 85721-0176
Phone: 520.621.7666; Fax: 520.626.3436
E-mail: eric.eden@law.arizona.edu; Website: www.law.arizona.edu

ABA
Approved
Since
1930

The Basics

Type of school	Public
Term	Semester
Application deadline	2/15
Application fee	$65
Financial aid deadline	3/1
Can first year start other than fall?	No
Student to faculty ratio	9.3 to 1
# of housing spaces available restricted to law students	
graduate housing for which law students are eligible	319

Faculty and Administrators

	Total		Men		Women		Minorities	
	Spr	Fall	Spr	Fall	Spr	Fall	Spr	Fall
Full-time	41	42	23	26	18	16	36	36
Other full-time	2	2	1	1	1	1	1	1
Deans, librarians, & others who teach	13	13	5	5	8	8	13	13
Part-time	48	35	33	21	15	14	34	22
Total	104	92	62	53	42	39	84	72

Curriculum

	Full-Time	Part-Time
Typical first-year section size	72	0
Is there typically a "small section" of the first-year class, other than Legal Writing, taught by full-time faculty	Yes	No
If yes, typical size offered last year	26	
# of classroom course titles beyond first-year curriculum	117	

# of upper division courses, excluding seminars, with an enrollment:		
Under 25	105	
25–49	23	
50–74	7	
75–99	2	
100+	1	

# of seminars	30	
# of seminar positions available	438	
# of seminar positions filled	352	0
# of positions available in simulation courses	304	
# of simulation positions filled	244	0
# of positions available in faculty supervised clinical courses	113	
# of faculty supervised clinical positions filled	104	0
# involved in field placements	115	0
# involved in law journals	99	0
# involved in moot court or trial competitions	27	0
# of credit hours required to graduate	88	

JD Enrollment and Ethnicity

	Men		Women		Full-Time		Part-Time		1st-Year		Total		JD Degs. Awd.
	#	%	#	%	#	%	#	%	#	%	#	%	
All Hispanics	16	6.1	19	9.2	35	7.5	0	0.0	10	6.4	35	7.5	17
Am. Ind./AK Nat.	8	3.0	14	6.8	22	4.7	0	0.0	3	1.9	22	4.7	10
Asian	19	7.2	21	10.2	40	8.5	0	0.0	14	9.0	40	8.5	15
Black/Af. Am.	7	2.7	7	3.4	14	3.0	0	0.0	4	2.6	14	3.0	6
Nat. Hl/Pac. Isl.	0	0.0	0	0.0	0	0.0	0	0.0	0	0.0	0	0.0	0
2 or more races	1	0.4	4	1.9	5	1.1	0	0.0	5	3.2	5	1.1	0
Subtotal (minor.)	51	19.4	65	31.6	116	24.7	0	0.0	36	23.1	116	24.7	48
Nonres. Alien	4	1.5	5	2.4	9	1.9	0	0.0	5	3.2	9	1.9	0
White/Cauc.	182	69.2	127	61.7	309	65.9	0	0.0	92	59.0	309	65.9	111
Unknown	26	9.9	9	4.4	35	7.5	0	0.0	23	14.7	35	7.5	0
Total	263	56.1	206	43.9	469	100.0	0	0.0	156	33.3	469		160

Transfers

Transfers in	3
Transfers out	5

Tuition and Fees

	Resident	Nonresident
Full-time	$23,540	$39,402
Part-time		
Tuition Guarantee Program		N

Living Expenses

Estimated living expenses for singles

Living on campus	Living off campus	Living at home
N/A	$21,571	$14,531

THE UNIVERSITY OF ARIZONA JAMES E. ROGERS COLLEGE OF LAW

ABA
Approved
Since
1930

GPA and LSAT Scores

	Total	Full-Time	Part-Time
# of apps	2,035	2,035	0
# of offers	668	668	0
# of matrics	157	157	0
75% GPA	3.71	3.71	0.00
Median GPA	3.50	3.50	0.00
25% GPA	3.33	3.33	0.00
75% LSAT	164	164	0
Median LSAT	162	162	0
25% LSAT	161	161	0

Grants and Scholarships (from prior year)

	Total		Full-Time		Part-Time	
	#	%	#	%	#	%
Total # of students	475		475		0	
Total # receiving grants	342	72.0	342	72.0	0	0.0
Less than 1/2 tuition	222	46.7	222	46.7	0	0.0
Half to full tuition	85	17.9	85	17.9	0	0.0
Full tuition	8	1.7	8	1.7	0	0.0
More than full tuition	27	5.7	27	5.7	0	0.0
Median grant amount			$10,000		$0	

Informational and Library Resources

Total amount spent on library materials	$1,015,221
Study seating capacity inside the library	379
# of full-time equivalent professional librarians	8
Hours per week library is open	99
# of open, wired connections available to students	0
# of networked computers available for use by students	32
Has wireless network?	Y
Requires computer?	N

JD Attrition (from prior year)

	Academic	Other	Total	
	#	#	#	%
1st year	0	2	2	1.3
2nd year	0	8	8	5.0
3rd year	0	2	2	1.2
4th year	0	0	0	0.0

Employment (9 months after graduation)

	Total	Percentage
Employment status known	141	99.3
Employment status unknown	1	0.7
Employed	126	89.4
Pursuing graduate degrees	6	4.3
Unemployed (seeking, not seeking, or studying for the bar)	4	2.8
Type of Employment		
# employed in law firms	53	42.1
# employed in business and industry	9	7.1
# employed in government	32	25.4
# employed in public interest	4	3.2
# employed as judicial clerks	27	21.4
# employed in academia	1	0.8
Geographic Location		
# employed in state	81	64.3
# employed outside the US	1	0.8
# of states where employed		15

Bar Passage Rates

First-time takers	139	Reporting %	71.22
Average school %	92.93	Average state %	79.76
Average pass difference	13.17		

Jurisdiction	Takers	Passers	Pass %	State %	Diff %
Arizona	99	92	92.93	79.76	13.17

THE UNIVERSITY OF ARIZONA JAMES E. ROGERS COLLEGE OF LAW

PO Box 210176, 1201 E. Speedway
Tucson, AZ 85721-0176
Phone: 520.621.7666; Fax: 520.626.3436
E-mail: eric.eden@law.arizona.edu; Website: www.law.arizona.edu

Introduction

Founded in 1915, the University of Arizona James E. Rogers College of Law is the oldest law school in Arizona and has a rich and distinguished history. The college is an integral part of the University of Arizona, one of the nation's leading research institutions and most spirited campuses. Arizona Law has a national reputation for providing its students with an exceptional education in a collegial and intellectually challenging atmosphere. The college is located in Tucson, a vibrant, environmentally unique, and culturally rich city of one million people that is home to an active legal and judicial community. The college is approved by the ABA, has been a member of the AALS since 1931, and has a chapter of the Order of the Coif.

The College

Five core values are the foundation of the college's culture: justice, professional integrity, educational excellence, public leadership, and community service. The environment of the college is further shaped by several key components. First, its size enables students and faculty to learn in a congenial atmosphere. Approximately 150 1L students join upperclass students, 36 full-time faculty, and many visiting scholars and lecturers in an intellectually stimulating community. Arizona Law offers a favorable student-faculty ratio (11:1) that enables full-time faculty to teach first-year classes in sections of 25 students. Second, the college has an outstanding, diverse faculty of gifted teachers and nationally recognized scholars. Third, the college offers 11 dual-degree programs in conjunction with world-class departments at the University of Arizona. Fourth, the college's generous financial aid program enables students to pursue a legal education without assuming an overwhelming debt burden. Fifth, the college attracts students of intelligence, energy, and commitment. The JD student body of 470 represents more than 160 undergraduate and graduate schools, many nationalities, diverse ethnic and cultural groups, and unique work, volunteer, and personal achievements. Finally, the college nurtures an ethic of public service and community involvement through volunteer activities for students, faculty, and staff organized by the College Community Service Board and various student organizations.

Library and Physical Facilities

In the fall of 2008, the Rogers College of Law opened a newly renovated state-of-the-art building and library—the Law Commons—designed to enhance student learning and engagement. The Rountree Hall clinical facility is adjacent to the Law Commons, and both are part of the 390-acre campus of the University of Arizona, located in central Tucson. The law library is one of the foremost legal research facilities in the Southwest. In addition to a strong Anglo-American collection, the library has nationally recognized collections in Mexican, Latin American, and water law. Students have access to the resources of the Arizona Health Sciences Library and university libraries, with collections exceeding 11 million volumes. The law library is a fully networked, technologically sophisticated facility that is constantly evolving to meet research needs.

Curriculum

Arizona Law has committed substantial faculty resources to the first-year curriculum and the development of research and writing skills. Each 1L meets in a section of 30 in one of the first-semester courses and shares all other classes with that group of students. Students enroll in a three-unit Legal Analysis, Writing, and Research class of 13 in the second semester. Students must also complete a special writing seminar during the second or third year.

After completing the first-year requirements, students have considerable flexibility in determining upper-division coursework. The college offers a rich variety of courses and provides opportunities to pursue a general curriculum or to focus studies in specialized areas of concentration, including Indigenous Peoples Law and Policy, Environmental Law, International Trade and Business, Criminal Law, Intellectual Property, Tax, Estates and Trusts, and Corporate Law.

In 2004, Arizona Law's nationally recognized Trial Advocacy Program won the Emil Gumpert Award from the American College of Trial Lawyers, awarded annually to the best trial advocacy program in the United States. The college also has numerous clinical opportunities that combine classroom instruction and field placements in child advocacy, domestic violence, immigration, indigenous peoples law, criminal defense and prosecution, and the judicial clerking program. The Arizona Supreme Court convenes annually at the college and hears arguments on cases under review. The college awards academic credit for congressional and executive agency internships in Washington, DC; a state legislative internship; an Arizona Governor's Office internship; a university attorney internship; and internship programs with several tribal governments.

The JD degree is normally completed in six semesters of full-time study; a total of 87 credits and a cumulative grade-point average of 2.0 are required to graduate.

Dual-Degree, LLM, and SJD Programs

The College of Law offers the following dual degrees: JD/PhD programs in Philosophy, Psychology, and Economics; JD/MA programs in American Indian Studies, Latin American Studies, Women's Studies, and Information Resources and Library Science; a JD/MBA; a JD/MPA; a JD/MS in Economics, Law, and Environment; and a JD/MMF in Management/Finance. Law students with a 2.75 GPA or better may take six units of coursework in another department and transfer that work to the College of Law for elective credit. The college offers two, one-year LLM programs in International Trade Law and in Indigenous Peoples Law and Policy, and a Doctor of Juridical Science (SJD) program.

Admission

Admission to the College of Law is very selective. All applications are reviewed in a holistic manner. In making decisions, all information submitted by applicants is considered, with significant focus on the strength of the candidate's undergraduate academic record, LSAT score, personal statement, résumé, and letters of recommendation. Additional factors include the nature and rigor of the undergraduate experience; graduate education; work and travel experience; unique talents, interests, or accomplishments; significant extracurricular activities; leadership, strength of character, and integrity; substantial community or public service; or other circumstances that have influenced the candidate's life or given him or her direction. The college fosters a dynamic learning community and welcomes students who bring diverse perspectives, ideas, and varied life experiences to the educational process. The deadline for applications is February 15. To complete a timely application, applicants must take the LSAT no later than February of the year of expected enrollment.

Tuition and Financial Aid

The tuition structure and generous financial aid program of the University of Arizona afford students the opportunity to pursue a legal education of outstanding quality with less debt burden than is typical of other fine law schools. Tuition and fees for JD students for the 2010–2011 year was $23,527 for Arizona residents and $39,389 for nonresidents. The College of Law awarded more than $3 million in merit- and need-based scholarships to JD students in 2010–2011.

Student Activities

The student body is self-governing through the Student Bar Association and there are more than 25 law student organizations that are an important part of institutional and student life. Students also participate in school governance by serving as voting members of student-faculty committees. The *Arizona Law Review*, the *Arizona Journal of International and Comparative Law*, and the *Arizona Journal of Environmental Law and Policy* are well-known student-operated and -edited scholarly journals on current legal problems. The students in the moot court and trial advocacy programs excel in national and state appellate advocacy competitions. College-sponsored community service projects are an important element in cultivating collaboration among students, faculty, and staff.

Career and Professional Development

Each 1L student is paired with an attorney mentor. Special programs on résumé, cover letter, and interviewing techniques are offered for 1Ls. Our on-campus Sonoran Desert Public Sector Career Fair, designed in particular for 1Ls, provides over 150 paid summer jobs, volunteer and for credit. Arizona Law students clerk nationally and throughout Arizona. In 2009, 92 percent of the 1L class had summer legal experience in 10 states and 9 foreign countries. The 2009 after-graduation employment rate was 94 percent, with 19.5 percent in judicial clerkships. Typically, one-third of our graduates practice in 15–20 states. Arizona Law graduates took the bar exam in 23 states in July 2009 with a 92 percent pass rate. Ninety-three percent of first-time takers passed the Arizona Bar, the highest of all law schools in Arizona and far exceeding the average pass rate of 84 percent. Average law firm salary was $104,535.

APPLICANT PROFILE

The University of Arizona James E. Rogers College of Law
This grid includes only applicants with 120–180 LSAT scores earned under standard administrations.

LSAT Score	3.75 +		3.50–3.74		3.25–3.49		3.00–3.24		2.75–2.99		2.50–2.74		2.25–2.49		2.00–2.24		Below 2.00		No GPA		Total	
	Apps	Adm	Apps	Adm	Apps	Adm	Apps	Adm	Apps	Adm	Apps	Adm	Apps	Adm	Apps	Adm	Apps	Adm	Apps	Adm	Apps	Adm
175–180	1	1	0	0	3	2	0	0	3	2	1	0	1	0	0	0	0	0	0	0	9	5
170–174	10	10	13	11	12	9	7	7	5	3	1	0	2	0	1	0	0	0	0	0	51	40
165–169	53	51	43	37	42	34	29	19	11	6	8	2	3	0	1	0	1	0	1	1	192	150
160–164	118	98	167	114	161	100	90	44	44	3	10	0	9	0	5	0	0	0	4	1	608	360
155–159	82	19	115	15	126	11	62	2	37	3	17	0	9	0	1	0	1	0	10	0	460	50
150–154	46	7	62	5	76	7	57	1	40	0	7	1	11	0	0	0	1	0	6	1	306	22
145–149	11	0	24	1	31	1	38	1	18	1	17	0	7	0	4	0	1	0	3	0	154	4
140–144	6	0	10	0	26	0	15	0	16	0	7	0	5	0	2	0	0	0	1	0	88	0
135–139	4	0	4	0	4	0	3	0	3	0	4	0	2	0	3	0	0	0	2	0	29	0
130–134	0	0	2	0	0	0	3	0	0	0	2	0	1	0	0	0	1	0	0	0	9	0
125–129	0	0	0	0	0	0	0	0	0	0	3	0	1	0	0	0	0	0	0	0	4	0
120–124	0	0	0	0	0	0	0	0	0	0	0	0	0	0	0	0	0	0	0	0	0	0
Total	331	186	440	183	481	164	304	74	177	18	77	3	51	0	17	0	5	0	27	3	1910	631

Apps = Number of Applicants
Adm = Number Admitted
Reflects 99% of the total applicant pool; highest LSAT data reported.

ARIZONA STATE UNIVERSITY—SANDRA DAY O'CONNOR COLLEGE OF LAW

Armstrong Hall, 1100 S. McAllister Avenue, PO Box 877906
Tempe, AZ 85287-7906
Phone: 480.965.1474; Fax: 480.727.7930
E-mail: law.admissions@asu.edu; Website: www.law.asu.edu

ABA
Approved
Since
1969

American Bar Association
Section of Legal Education
and Admissions to the Bar

The Basics

Type of school	Public
Term	Semester
Application deadline	11/1 2/1
Application fee	$60
Financial aid deadline	3/15
Can first year start other than fall?	No
Student to faculty ratio	9.5 to 1
# of housing spaces available restricted to law students	
graduate housing for which law students are eligible	

Faculty and Administrators

	Total		Men		Women		Minorities	
	Spr	Fall	Spr	Fall	Spr	Fall	Spr	Fall
Full-time	53	51	37	35	16	16	7	7
Other full-time	2	2	0	0	2	2	0	0
Deans, librarians, & others who teach	8	10	5	6	3	4	0	0
Part-time	41	36	29	27	12	9	6	8
Total	104	99	71	68	33	31	13	15

Curriculum

	Full-Time	Part-Time
Typical first-year section size	62	0
Is there typically a "small section" of the first-year class, other than Legal Writing, taught by full-time faculty	Yes	No
If yes, typical size offered last year	30	
# of classroom course titles beyond first-year curriculum	136	

# of upper division courses, excluding seminars, with an enrollment:		
	Under 25	92
	25–49	24
	50–74	6
	75–99	4
	100+	0

# of seminars	56	
# of seminar positions available	949	
# of seminar positions filled	811	0
# of positions available in simulation courses	220	
# of simulation positions filled	195	0
# of positions available in faculty supervised clinical courses	166	
# of faculty supervised clinical positions filled	147	0
# involved in field placements	248	0
# involved in law journals	86	0
# involved in moot court or trial competitions	250	0
# of credit hours required to graduate	89	

JD Enrollment and Ethnicity

	Men		Women		Full-Time		Part-Time		1st-Year		Total		JD Degs. Awd.
	#	%	#	%	#	%	#	%	#	%	#	%	
All Hispanics	31	9.0	33	12.3	64	10.4	0	0.0	25	13.1	64	10.4	20
Am. Ind./AK Nat.	17	4.9	16	5.9	33	5.4	0	0.0	7	3.7	33	5.4	10
Asian	9	2.6	14	5.2	23	3.7	0	0.0	7	3.7	23	3.7	6
Black/Af. Am.	9	2.6	5	1.9	14	2.3	0	0.0	6	3.1	14	2.3	4
Nat. HI/Pac. Isl.	0	0.0	0	0.0	0	0.0	0	0.0	0	0.0	0	0.0	0
2 or more races	7	2.0	4	1.5	11	1.8	0	0.0	9	4.7	11	1.8	0
Subtotal (minor.)	73	21.2	72	26.8	145	23.6	0	0.0	54	28.3	145	23.6	40
Nonres. Alien	3	0.9	4	1.5	7	1.1	0	0.0	2	1.0	7	1.1	0
White/Cauc.	239	69.3	183	68.0	422	68.7	0	0.0	126	66.0	422	68.7	120
Unknown	30	8.7	10	3.7	40	6.5	0	0.0	9	4.7	40	6.5	5
Total	345	56.2	269	43.8	614	100.0	0	0.0	191	31.1	614		167

Transfers

Transfers in	32
Transfers out	3

Tuition and Fees

	Resident	Nonresident
Full-time	$21,598	$35,147
Part-time		
Tuition Guarantee Program	N	

Living Expenses

Estimated living expenses for singles

Living on campus	Living off campus	Living at home
$20,044	$20,044	$20,044

ARIZONA STATE UNIVERSITY—SANDRA DAY O'CONNOR COLLEGE OF LAW

ABA Approved Since 1969

GPA and LSAT Scores

	Total	Full-Time	Part-Time
# of apps	2,457	2,457	0
# of offers	590	590	0
# of matrics	191	191	0
75% GPA	3.75	3.75	0.00
Median GPA	3.57	3.57	0.00
25% GPA	3.34	3.34	0.00
75% LSAT	164	164	0
Median LSAT	161	161	0
25% LSAT	158	158	0

Grants and Scholarships (from prior year)

	Total		Full-Time		Part-Time	
	#	%	#	%	#	%
Total # of students	576		576		0	
Total # receiving grants	280	48.6	280	48.6	0	0.0
Less than 1/2 tuition	175	30.4	175	30.4	0	0.0
Half to full tuition	50	8.7	50	8.7	0	0.0
Full tuition	27	4.7	27	4.7	0	0.0
More than full tuition	28	4.9	28	4.9	0	0.0
Median grant amount			$5,750		$0	

Informational and Library Resources

Total amount spent on library materials	$1,006,827
Study seating capacity inside the library	503
# of full-time equivalent professional librarians	6
Hours per week library is open	111
# of open, wired connections available to students	186
# of networked computers available for use by students	63
Has wireless network?	Y
Requires computer?	N

JD Attrition (from prior year)

	Academic	Other	Total	
	#	#	#	%
1st year	2	6	8	4.3
2nd year	0	8	8	4.0
3rd year	0	1	1	0.5
4th year	0	0	0	0.0

Employment (9 months after graduation)

	Total	Percentage
Employment status known	176	99.4
Employment status unknown	1	0.6
Employed	159	90.3
Pursuing graduate degrees	9	5.1
Unemployed (seeking, not seeking, or studying for the bar)	0	0.0
Type of Employment		
# employed in law firms	68	42.8
# employed in business and industry	13	8.2
# employed in government	32	20.1
# employed in public interest	17	10.7
# employed as judicial clerks	18	11.3
# employed in academia	11	6.9
Geographic Location		
# employed in state	117	73.6
# employed outside the US	2	1.3
# of states where employed	18	

Bar Passage Rates

First-time takers	182	Reporting %	79.12
Average school %	83.33	Average state %	79.76
Average pass difference	3.57		

Jurisdiction	Takers	Passers	Pass %	State %	Diff %
Arizona	144	120	83.33	79.76	3.57

ARIZONA STATE UNIVERSITY—SANDRA DAY O'CONNOR COLLEGE OF LAW

Armstrong Hall, 1100 S. McAllister Avenue, PO Box 877906
Tempe, AZ 85287-7906
Phone: 480.965.1474; Fax: 480.727.7930
E-mail: law.admissions@asu.edu; Website: www.law.asu.edu

Introduction

Founded in 1967, the Arizona State University—Sandra Day O'Connor College of Law combines the best traditions of American legal education with innovative programs supported by strong community partnerships. Our vision includes excellence in all we do, striving to have a meaningful impact on contemporary problems through teaching, research, and collaborative problem-solving. Students are attracted by the quality of the legal education, commitment to innovative teaching and scholarship, reasonable tuition, breadth and depth of the curriculum, numerous opportunities for experiential learning, and excellent student-to-faculty ratio. A busy calendar of conferences, seminars, and speakers enriches the student experience and fosters a strong sense of community. The college has an outstanding faculty, many opportunities for interdisciplinary learning, extensive pro bono opportunities, an exceptional legal writing program, and clinics of significant variety. Our students benefit greatly from the fact that Phoenix is the fifth largest city in the country and a state capital.

Admission

Every completed application receives full review and consideration by the Admissions Committee prior to a decision. Among the factors influencing the admission decision are undergraduate and previous graduate education, LSAT performance, quality and grading patterns of undergraduate institutions, demonstrated commitment to public service, work experience, leadership experience, extracurricular or community activities, history of overcoming economic or other disadvantages, personal experiences with discrimination, overcoming disability, geographic diversity, uniqueness of experience and background, maturity, ability to communicate, foreign language proficiency, honors and awards, service in the armed forces, publications, and exceptional personal talents.

Career Strategy and Professional Development Mentoring Center

Our graduates have proven success in the legal employment market and hold prominent positions and leadership roles throughout the international, national, and Arizona legal communities in business, politics, government, the judiciary, and private firms. A broad range of employers interview our students on campus, at regional interview programs sponsored by Career Services, and at job fairs. Through attorney-student mentor programs, speaker series and panels, networking events, career fairs, a large on-campus recruitment program, and individual career counseling, the Career Services professional staff serves students in all phases of their professional development and job search.

Curriculum

The College of Law offers one of the best student-to-faculty ratios in the country and a wide variety of courses. Because we have a large, nationally acclaimed faculty with high standards in both teaching and research, we have unusual depth in our course offerings. More than 70 percent of the classes in the second and third year have fewer than 20 students. As part of a premier research institution, the opportunities for interdisciplinary work are extensive. Concurrent degrees are offered with the MBA program, the PhD in Psychology, the PhD in Justice and Social Inquiry, and the MD with Mayo Medical School. Further, the college takes full advantage of its unique location in Phoenix by offering over 150 externships and countless opportunities to do pro bono work. Students also have wonderful opportunities to develop their legal writing skills because of our commitment to maintaining an excellent legal writing program.

Clinical Programs

The law school's Clinical Program offers students unparalleled opportunities to practice law in a variety of settings with people who have real legal problems. We offer eleven separate clinics—civil justice, criminal practice, family violence, healthcare entrepreneurship, immigration, Indian law, innovation advancement, mediation, patent litigation, post-conviction, and public defender—a greater variety of clinics than most law schools of any size. Under the supervision of faculty members who are experts in their subject matter, students manage real cases and represent clients in hearings and trials before courts and administrative agencies, assist in the commercialization and monetization of new technologies, and mediate cases pending in the judicial system. Because of our small student body, we are able to accommodate nearly every student who expresses an interest in the experiential learning offered through the Clinical Program.

Student Activities

To prepare proactive, socially conscious attorneys and leaders, we enhance the traditional classroom experience with many extracurricular and cocurricular activities. We have about 50 active student groups, from the ASU Bar Association and 30 professional affiliations to 20 pro bono groups. Plus, we grow and change with the interests of our students. On average, about 70 percent of our students participate in pro bono work of some kind, with about one third of the student body graduating with Pro Bono Distinction. Students are active in ASU student governance and in our communities with public service. Our students are competitive in moot court competitions, both regionally and internationally. Two traditional law journals, the *Arizona State Law Journal* and *Jurimetrics*, and two new online journals, the *Law Journal for Social Justice* and the *Sports and Entertainment Law Journal*, allow additional professional development opportunities for students.

Library and Physical Facilities

The College of Law is composed of Armstrong Hall and the John J. Ross-William C. Blakley Law Library and is set on the eastern edge of the university's beautiful, 700-acre Tempe campus. Armstrong Hall houses the legal clinic; the Center for Law, Science, and Innovation; the Indian Legal Program; the Center for Law and Global Affairs; the Diane Halle Center for Family Justice; the Program on Philosophy, Politics, and Law;

and the Cohen Student Center. The Ross-Blakley Law Library is a stunningly beautiful work of architecture with lots of windows to allow natural light in. Both Armstrong Hall and the Ross-Blakley Law Library are fully equipped with a wireless network.

Center for Law, Science, and Innovation

Founded in 1984, the Center for Law, Science, and Innovation is the oldest, largest, and most comprehensive law and science center in the country. Through the Center, students may receive a certificate in Law, Science, and Technology, specializing in environmental law, genomics and biotechnology law, health law, intellectual property law, or law and psychology. Every year, 10 students in each class are named Center Scholars. Center faculty and students edit and copublish, along with the American Bar Association, the prestigious, peer-refereed *Jurimetrics: The Journal of Law, Science, and Technology*, the oldest and most widely circulated journal in the field of law and science.

The Center for Law and Global Affairs

The Center for Law and Global Affairs supports and inspires research, education, and practice regarding new forms of transnational public-private governance that extend beyond the traditional paradigms of international law. The Center sponsors conferences, colloquia, courses, research, policy initiatives, and publications to study evolving forms of international law, to develop and apply new methodologies to better understand how the rule of law operates in diverse international contexts, to initiate and communicate new policy strategies, and to teach and train students and professionals to work more effectively in the new global regulatory environment. The Center creates an interdisciplinary community of scholars, practitioners, students, and community members interested in better understanding and affecting the relationship between law and an increasingly global world.

The Diane Halle Center for Family Justice

The Diane Halle Center for Family Justice, working with other ASU schools and with community partners, is pursuing direct representation and policy advocacy on core issues of domestic violence, juvenile justice, child abuse, family law, and human rights of children and families through multidisciplinary initiatives in education, advocacy, and scholarship. The Center was established with a $1 million grant from the Bruce T. Halle Family Foundation. The Center houses the Family Violence Legal Clinic.

Indian Legal Program

The Indian Legal Program enjoys a position of national preeminence. This preeminence is due to the large Native American student population, the Indian Law Certificate program, well-respected faculty, the Indian law curriculum, well-placed alumni, scholarly conferences, and the Indian Legal Clinic. An extraordinary faculty and long-term partnerships with tribal governments contribute to the strength and reputation of the College of Law in this critical area.

LLM Programs

The Master of Laws (LLM) program allows one year of post-JD study tailored to the scholarly and practice interests of participating students. Lawyers may pursue an LLM in Biotechnology and Genomics or an LLM in Tribal Policy, Law, and Government. They may choose to pursue an LLM focusing on US Law and Legal Institutions (for foreign lawyers who wish to learn about the US legal system), health law and policy, international law, or any of the other areas of strength in the law school's curriculum.

APPLICANT PROFILE

Arizona State University—Sandra Day O'Connor College of Law
This grid includes only applicants with 120–180 LSAT scores earned under standard administrations.

LSAT Score	3.75 +		3.50–3.74		3.25–3.49		3.00–3.24		2.75–2.99		2.50–2.74		2.25–2.49		2.00–2.24		Below 2.00		No GPA		Total	
	Apps	Adm	Apps	Adm	Apps	Adm	Apps	Adm	Apps	Adm	Apps	Adm	Apps	Adm	Apps	Adm	Apps	Adm	Apps	Adm	Apps	Adm
175–180	1	1	0	0	1	1	1	1	1	0	0	0	0	0	0	0	0	0	0	0	4	3
170–174	8	7	10	9	4	4	5	5	1	1	1	1	1	0	1	0	0	0	0	0	31	27
165–169	43	43	31	31	27	26	21	19	14	7	12	1	1	0	1	0	1	0	0	0	151	127
160–164	97	93	137	118	131	62	90	28	49	2	16	0	11	1	3	0	1	0	4	4	539	308
155–159	117	53	179	23	193	11	107	1	49	1	30	0	11	0	3	0	1	0	6	0	696	89
150–154	63	3	120	10	123	9	90	2	54	2	26	0	19	0	3	0	1	0	2	0	501	26
145–149	26	1	46	2	55	1	74	2	42	0	32	0	11	0	2	0	0	0	3	0	291	6
140–144	8	0	18	0	29	0	23	0	23	0	20	0	8	0	2	0	0	0	4	0	135	0
135–139	3	0	1	0	5	0	13	0	8	0	9	0	8	0	5	0	0	0	1	0	53	0
130–134	0	0	0	0	1	0	5	0	8	0	5	0	2	0	2	0	1	0	1	0	26	0
125–129	0	0	0	0	0	0	1	0	1	0	3	0	2	0	0	0	0	0	0	0	7	0
120–124	0	0	0	0	0	0	0	0	0	0	0	0	0	0	1	0	0	0	0	0	1	0
Total	366	201	543	193	569	114	430	58	250	13	154	2	74	1	23	0	5	0	21	4	2435	586

Apps = Number of Applicants
Adm = Number Admitted
Reflects 99% of the total applicant pool; highest LSAT data reported.

UNIVERSITY OF ARKANSAS SCHOOL OF LAW

Robert A. Leflar Law Center
Fayetteville, AR 72701
Phone: 479.575.3102; Fax: 479.575.3937
Website: http://law.uark.edu

The Basics

Type of school	Public
Term	Semester
Application deadline	4/1
Application fee	$0
Financial aid deadline	3/1
Can first year start other than fall?	No
Student to faculty ratio	11.0 to 1
# of housing spaces available restricted to law students	
graduate housing for which law students are eligible	

Faculty and Administrators

	Total		Men		Women		Minorities	
	Spr	Fall	Spr	Fall	Spr	Fall	Spr	Fall
Full-time	29	29	17	17	12	12	3	3
Other full-time	0	0	0	0	0	0	0	0
Deans, librarians, & others who teach	10	10	3	3	7	7	1	1
Part-time	23	21	17	15	6	6	0	1
Total	62	60	37	35	25	25	4	5

Curriculum

	Full-Time	Part-Time
Typical first-year section size	68	0
Is there typically a "small section" of the first-year class, other than Legal Writing, taught by full-time faculty	No	No
If yes, typical size offered last year		
# of classroom course titles beyond first-year curriculum	90	
# of upper division courses, excluding seminars, with an enrollment: Under 25	94	
25–49	20	
50–74	6	
75–99	3	
100+	0	
# of seminars	10	
# of seminar positions available	150	
# of seminar positions filled	120	0
# of positions available in simulation courses	220	
# of simulation positions filled	205	0
# of positions available in faculty supervised clinical courses	142	
# of faculty supervised clinical positions filled	122	0
# involved in field placements	80	0
# involved in law journals	74	0
# involved in moot court or trial competitions	44	0
# of credit hours required to graduate	90	

JD Enrollment and Ethnicity

	Men		Women		Full-Time		Part-Time		1st-Year		Total		JD Degs. Awd.
	#	%	#	%	#	%	#	%	#	%	#	%	
All Hispanics	9	4.1	8	4.7	17	4.4	0	0.0	8	5.9	17	4.4	3
Am. Ind./AK Nat.	3	1.4	5	2.9	8	2.1	0	0.0	2	1.5	8	2.1	5
Asian	8	3.7	3	1.7	11	2.8	0	0.0	3	2.2	11	2.8	4
Black/Af. Am.	13	6.0	17	9.9	30	7.7	0	0.0	9	6.6	30	7.7	18
Nat. HI/Pac. Isl.	0	0.0	0	0.0	0	0.0	0	0.0	0	0.0	0	0.0	0
2 or more races	1	0.5	1	0.6	2	0.5	0	0.0	2	1.5	2	0.5	0
Subtotal (minor.)	34	15.6	34	19.8	68	17.4	0	0.0	24	17.6	68	17.4	30
Nonres. Alien	0	0.0	0	0.0	0	0.0	0	0.0	0	0.0	0	0.0	0
White/Cauc.	182	83.5	138	80.2	320	82.1	0	0.0	111	81.6	320	82.1	107
Unknown	2	0.9	0	0.0	2	0.5	0	0.0	1	0.7	2	0.5	0
Total	218	55.9	172	44.1	390	100.0	0	0.0	136	34.9	390		137

Transfers

Transfers in	5
Transfers out	1

Tuition and Fees

	Resident	Nonresident
Full-time	$11,367	$22,501
Part-time		
Tuition Guarantee Program	N	

Living Expenses

Estimated living expenses for singles

Living on campus	Living off campus	Living at home
$16,138	$16,138	$16,138

UNIVERSITY OF ARKANSAS SCHOOL OF LAW

ABA
Approved
Since
1928

GPA and LSAT Scores

	Total	Full-Time	Part-Time
# of apps	1,514	1,514	0
# of offers	402	402	0
# of matrics	138	138	0
75% GPA	3.80	3.80	0.00
Median GPA	3.55	3.55	0.00
25% GPA	3.29	3.29	0.00
75% LSAT	160	160	0
Median LSAT	157	157	0
25% LSAT	153	153	0

Grants and Scholarships (from prior year)

	Total		Full-Time		Part-Time	
	#	%	#	%	#	%
Total # of students	398		398		0	
Total # receiving grants	139	34.9	139	34.9	0	0.0
Less than 1/2 tuition	84	21.1	84	21.1	0	0.0
Half to full tuition	47	11.8	47	11.8	0	0.0
Full tuition	0	0.0	0	0.0	0	0.0
More than full tuition	8	2.0	8	2.0	0	0.0
Median grant amount			$6,000		$0	

Informational and Library Resources

Total amount spent on library materials	$892,656
Study seating capacity inside the library	412
# of full-time equivalent professional librarians	6
Hours per week library is open	98
# of open, wired connections available to students	73
# of networked computers available for use by students	46
Has wireless network?	Y
Requires computer?	N

JD Attrition (from prior year)

	Academic	Other	Total	
	#	#	#	%
1st year	0	10	10	7.2
2nd year	0	0	0	0.0
3rd year	1	1	2	1.4
4th year	0	0	0	0.0

Employment (9 months after graduation)

	Total	Percentage
Employment status known	120	98.4
Employment status unknown	2	1.6
Employed	102	85.0
Pursuing graduate degrees	11	9.2
Unemployed (seeking, not seeking, or studying for the bar)	7	5.8
Type of Employment		
# employed in law firms	54	52.9
# employed in business and industry	13	12.7
# employed in government	19	18.6
# employed in public interest	5	4.9
# employed as judicial clerks	6	5.9
# employed in academia	3	2.9
Geographic Location		
# employed in state	66	64.7
# employed outside the US	0	0.0
# of states where employed		15

Bar Passage Rates

First-time takers	118	Reporting %	78.81
Average school %	84.95	Average state %	74.22

Average pass difference 10.73

Jurisdiction	Takers	Passers	Pass %	State %	Diff %
Arkansas	93	79	84.95	74.22	10.73

UNIVERSITY OF ARKANSAS SCHOOL OF LAW

Robert A. Leflar Law Center
Fayetteville, AR 72701
Phone: 479.575.3102; Fax: 479.575.3937
Website: http://law.uark.edu

Introduction

The University of Arkansas School of Law is located on the main university campus at Fayetteville, a city of approximately 67,000 in Northwest Arkansas. The School of Law, established in 1924, has continuously sought to provide high-quality legal education in a university community. In 1926 the School of Law was approved by the ABA and in 1927 became a member of the AALS.

Enrollment/Student Body

Although approximately 75 to 80 percent of the students are Arkansas residents, others are from every part of the United States. Since the school has no undergraduate course prerequisites, the academic backgrounds and nonacademic experiences of the students are varied.

Library and Physical Facilities

The law library has over 314,000 volumes and volume equivalents. Students are trained in the techniques of computer-assisted legal research as well as in traditional research methods. The law library is a federal and state depository for government documents.

Curriculum

The primary function of the University of Arkansas School of Law is to prepare lawyers who will render the highest quality of professional service to their clients, who are interested in and capable of furthering legal process and reform, and who are prepared to fill the vital role of the lawyer as a community leader. The school offers a full-time, three-year program leading to the JD degree. The degree is conferred upon satisfactory completion of 90 semester hours, including 42 hours of required courses. The first-year curriculum is required. A broad selection of elective second- and third-year courses is available. Students who have completed the first year of law school may earn up to 12 semester hours of credit in summer school, and graduation can be accelerated by one semester of summer coursework.

The School of Law offers a joint JD/MBA program with the College of Business Administration. If a student is accepted into both programs, a maximum of six hours of approved upper-level elective law courses may be used as duplicative credit toward the MBA degree, and a maximum of six hours of approved graduate courses in business administration may be used as duplicative credit toward the JD degree.

The Department of Political Science in the Graduate School and the School of Law cooperate in offering a dual-degree program that allows a student to pursue the MPA and the JD degrees concurrently. Students must be admitted to the MPA program, the School of Law, and the dual-degree program.

The School of Law and the Department of Political Science provide a dual JD/MA degree in International Law and Politics. This program's students must be admitted both to the School of Law and the Graduate School's Department of Political Science. The Graduate Program in Agriculture Law provides opportunities for advanced study, creative research, and specialized professional training in this rapidly developing area of law. The program is designed to prepare a small number of carefully selected attorneys as specialists in the legal problems of agriculture production, distribution, and marketing.

Applicants for admission as candidates for the Master of Laws (LLM) in Agricultural Law must have earned a JD or LLB degree from a fully accredited law school in the United States. Graduates from a law school in another country may be admitted upon the approval of the Agricultural Law Program Committee.

Admission

First-year students are admitted in the fall and only for full-time study. Prior to enrolling in the School of Law, applicants must have completed all requirements for an undergraduate degree from an accredited four-year college. Admission is based on the applicant's LSAT score and undergraduate GPA. In a small percentage of cases, additional criteria such as age; gender; cultural, ethnic, and racial background; geographic origin; socioeconomic background and status; undergraduate major; graduate studies; career objectives; nonacademic work; and other life experiences are considered by a faculty admission committee. Preference is given to Arkansas residents. For the current status of this preference, contact the school. A nonrefundable tuition deposit is required of all admitted candidates.

The law school's application deadline is April 1 of the year in which admission is sought. Applicants must take the LSAT no later than February. Applications completed after April 1 will be considered only on a space-available basis.

Housing

Housing for single students is available in campus dormitories. For more information about housing, please contact the Housing Office, University of Arkansas, Fayetteville, AR 72701; Phone: 479.575.3951. Information is also available at http://housing.uark.edu. A variety of private off-campus housing options are available in Fayetteville and surrounding communities, within easy commuting distance of the law school. For more information, please visit http://offcampushousing.uark.edu/.

Student Activities

The *Arkansas Law Review* is a legal periodical published quarterly by the students of the School of Law in cooperation with the Arkansas Bar Association. Candidates for the *Law Review* are selected on the basis of scholarship and writing ability. The *Journal of Food Law and Policy* is a legal periodical published twice a year by students of the School of Law. Candidates for the journal are selected from the second- and third-year law classes by the editorial board on the basis of scholarship and writing ability.

Students in their second and third years are encouraged to compete in an intramural moot court competition, and Arkansas students participate in national moot court competitions. The University of Arkansas School of Law also participates in the ABA Law Student Division Client Counseling Competition. The law school operates a legal aid clinic providing counseling and representation for university students and indigent persons seeking legal assistance. An Arkansas Supreme Court Rule permits senior law students, upon certification and under supervision, to appear in court on a no-fee basis.

The Student Bar Association sponsors a variety of academic and social activities. All students are also eligible for membership in the Law Student Division of the Arkansas Bar Association. Three of the largest national legal fraternities, Delta Theta Phi, Phi Alpha Delta, and Phi Delta Phi, maintain active chapters at the school. The Women's Law Student Association was organized to provide an opportunity for women to discuss and work with common professional interests and problems. Members of the Arkansas Chapter of the Black Law Students Association work as a collective body to inform black students of the availability and advantages of a legal education, to promote the academic success of black law students at Arkansas, and to increase the awareness and commitment of the legal profession to the black community. Other organizations include the Christian Legal Society, Lambda, the Federalist Society, the Asian Pacific American Law Student Association, and Equal Justice Works.

Expenses and Financial Aid

Students are expected to make sufficient financial arrangements for the first year of study without the necessity of seeking employment. All law students are required to be full-time students. All financial aid in the form of Perkins Loans (formerly NDSL), higher education loans, and work-study grants is processed by the University of Arkansas Office of Student Financial Aid, University of Arkansas, Fayetteville, AR 72701. Merit scholarships are awarded to some entering students. Applications for a limited number of other scholarships are distributed following fall registration in August.

Career Planning and Placement

The law school maintains an Office of Career Planning and Placement with a full-time, highly qualified director and staff to assist and advise students and graduates. Services offered by the office include on-campus interviews for permanent and summer employment; individual career counseling sessions; workshops and handbooks regarding résumé preparation, interviewing skills and techniques, and job searches; panels of lawyers who present programs on a variety of topics; a job bulletin; and a comprehensive placement library. The office also maintains employment and bar passage statistics.

Applicant Profile Not Available

UNIVERSITY OF ARKANSAS AT LITTLE ROCK, WILLIAM H. BOWEN SCHOOL OF LAW

1201 McMath Avenue
Little Rock, AR 72202-5142
Phone: 501.324.9903; Fax: 501.324.9909
E-mail: lawadm@ualr.edu; Website: www.law.ualr.edu

The Basics

Type of school	Public
Term	Semester
Application deadline	4/14
Application fee	$0
Financial aid deadline	3/1
Can first year start other than fall?	No
Student to faculty ratio	13.0 to 1
# of housing spaces available restricted to law students	
graduate housing for which law students are eligible	

Faculty and Administrators

	Total		Men		Women		Minorities	
	Spr	Fall	Spr	Fall	Spr	Fall	Spr	Fall
Full-time	27	27	14	13	13	14	8	8
Other full-time	3	3	1	0	2	3	0	0
Deans, librarians, & others who teach	13	13	2	2	11	11	6	6
Part-time	45	36	29	23	16	13	5	3
Total	88	79	46	38	42	41	19	17

Curriculum

	Full-Time	Part-Time
Typical first-year section size	99	60
Is there typically a "small section" of the first-year class, other than Legal Writing, taught by full-time faculty	No	No
If yes, typical size offered last year		

# of classroom course titles beyond first-year curriculum		126
# of upper division courses, excluding seminars, with an enrollment:	Under 25	106
	25–49	29
	50–74	10
	75–99	17
	100+	0

# of seminars		22
# of seminar positions available		352
# of seminar positions filled	138	189
# of positions available in simulation courses		375
# of simulation positions filled	233	126
# of positions available in faculty supervised clinical courses		56
# of faculty supervised clinical positions filled	41	15
# involved in field placements	45	7
# involved in law journals	52	8
# involved in moot court or trial competitions	18	4
# of credit hours required to graduate		90

JD Enrollment and Ethnicity

	Men		Women		Full-Time		Part-Time		1st-Year		Total		JD Degs. Awd.
	#	%	#	%	#	%	#	%	#	%	#	%	
All Hispanics	15	5.7	7	3.1	14	4.1	8	5.3	7	4.4	22	4.5	5
Am. Ind./AK Nat.	2	0.8	4	1.8	6	1.8	0	0.0	4	2.5	6	1.2	2
Asian	9	3.4	5	2.2	12	3.6	2	1.3	8	5.1	14	2.9	5
Black/Af. Am.	17	6.4	37	16.4	36	10.7	18	11.8	17	10.8	54	11.0	13
Nat. HI/Pac. Isl.	0	0.0	0	0.0	0	0.0	0	0.0	0	0.0	0	0.0	0
2 or more races	0	0.0	0	0.0	0	0.0	0	0.0	0	0.0	0	0.0	0
Subtotal (minor.)	43	16.2	53	23.6	68	20.1	28	18.4	36	22.8	96	19.6	25
Nonres. Alien	6	2.3	6	2.7	8	2.4	4	2.6	4	2.5	12	2.4	0
White/Cauc.	209	78.9	161	71.6	254	75.1	116	76.3	113	71.5	370	75.5	91
Unknown	7	2.6	5	2.2	8	2.4	4	2.6	5	3.2	12	2.4	6
Total	265	54.1	225	45.9	338	69.0	152	31.0	158	32.2	490		122

Transfers

Transfers in	4
Transfers out	4

Tuition and Fees

	Resident	Nonresident
Full-time	$11,456	$23,451
Part-time	$8,010	$16,007
Tuition Guarantee Program	N	

Living Expenses

Estimated living expenses for singles

Living on campus	Living off campus	Living at home
$15,040	$15,040	$15,040

UNIVERSITY OF ARKANSAS AT LITTLE ROCK, WILLIAM H. BOWEN SCHOOL OF LAW

ABA
Approved
Since
1969

GPA and LSAT Scores

	Total	Full-Time	Part-Time
# of apps	1,514	1,524	161
# of offers	413	365	48
# of matrics	157	103	54
75% GPA	3.59	3.65	3.43
Median GPA	3.27	3.32	3.11
25% GPA	2.98	3.00	2.96
75% LSAT	157	157	156
Median LSAT	154	154	152
25% LSAT	151	151	151

Grants and Scholarships (from prior year)

	Total		Full-Time		Part-Time	
	#	%	#	%	#	%
Total # of students	471		316		155	
Total # receiving grants	206	43.7	162	51.3	44	28.4
Less than 1/2 tuition	127	27.0	94	29.7	33	21.3
Half to full tuition	60	12.7	54	17.1	6	3.9
Full tuition	19	4.0	14	4.4	5	3.2
More than full tuition	0	0.0	0	0.0	0	0.0
Median grant amount			$4,113		$1,500	

Informational and Library Resources

Total amount spent on library materials	$916,811
Study seating capacity inside the library	396
# of full-time equivalent professional librarians	11
Hours per week library is open	100
# of open, wired connections available to students	1
# of networked computers available for use by students	67
Has wireless network?	Y
Requires computer?	N

JD Attrition (from prior year)

	Academic	Other	Total	
	#	#	#	%
1st year	2	10	12	7.3
2nd year	5	9	14	8.5
3rd year	0	1	1	0.9
4th year	0	0	0	0.0

Employment (9 months after graduation)

	Total	Percentage
Employment status known	126	99.2
Employment status unknown	1	0.8
Employed	103	81.7
Pursuing graduate degrees	5	4.0
Unemployed (seeking, not seeking, or studying for the bar)	11	8.7
Type of Employment		
# employed in law firms	50	48.5
# employed in business and industry	24	23.3
# employed in government	19	18.4
# employed in public interest	3	2.9
# employed as judicial clerks	5	4.9
# employed in academia	2	1.9
Geographic Location		
# employed in state	79	76.7
# employed outside the US	0	0.0
# of states where employed	9	

Bar Passage Rates

First-time takers	129	Reporting %	79.84
Average school %	64.08	Average state %	74.22

Average pass difference −10.14

Jurisdiction	Takers	Passers	Pass %	State %	Diff %
Arkansas	103	66	64.08	74.22	−10.14

UNIVERSITY OF ARKANSAS AT LITTLE ROCK, WILLIAM H. BOWEN SCHOOL OF LAW

1201 McMath Avenue
Little Rock, AR 72202-5142
Phone: 501.324.9903; Fax: 501.324.9909
E-mail: lawadm@ualr.edu; Website: www.law.ualr.edu

About the UALR Bowen School of Law

The William H. Bowen School of Law is located in the heart of Little Rock, within a five-minute drive of state and federal courts as well as some of Arkansas's largest law firms and corporations. Established in 1975, the law school is fully accredited by the ABA and is a member of the AALS. In addition to being the seat of state government, Little Rock is Arkansas's legal, business, and financial center. The city's vibrant legal community affords students and alumni many professional opportunities.

Admission

Bowen seeks to enroll approximately 150 students each year. The law school takes a holistic approach to admission, as the Admissions Committee assesses a wide array of applicant factors. The law school values inclusion and is committed to enrolling students of diverse ethnicities and backgrounds. The application deadline is April 15, though candidates are strongly encouraged to apply by January 15. First-year students are admitted for the fall semester only.

Bowen hosts prospective students throughout the year. In addition to attending scheduled events, prospective students may contact the Admissions Office for individual tours, class visits, and meetings with faculty members and current students.

Juris Doctor Curriculum

The Juris Doctor (JD) curriculum seeks to provide students with strong foundations in the traditional areas of law, while providing a diverse selection of electives. To receive the JD, students must complete 90 credit hours with a cumulative GPA of 2.0 (on a 4.0 scale) or better. Courses are prescribed during the first year of full-time study (or the first two years of part-time study). After that, most of the curriculum is elective, allowing students to explore their interests in many areas. Course descriptions and further information about the Bowen curriculum can be found at www.law.ualr.edu/academics/curriculum.asp.

Concurrent Degrees

Bowen allows students to pursue law degrees while concurrently pursuing master's degrees in business administration (JD/MBA), public administration (JD/MPA), public health (JD/MPH), or public service (JD/MPS). A concurrent degree in law and medicine is also offered (JD/MD). In order to be eligible for one of the concurrent-degree programs, students must be offered admission into both the law school and the school offering the other desired degree.

Enrollment Divisions

Bowen offers both full-time and part-time divisions. Full-time study generally takes three years to complete. Part-time study is generally completed in four years. In both divisions, study may be accelerated by attending summer school.

The environment for full-time students is one of a traditional "academy," where students spend significant portions of their days on campus engaging in various curricular and extracurricular activities.

Bowen is one of the few law schools in the country that is statutorily mandated to offer a part-time division. The division attracts many successful professionals, including state legislators and business executives.

Faculty

The faculty is made up of an outstanding group of scholars, practitioners, and teachers. Full-time professors teach virtually all required courses in both the full-time and part-time divisions. Experienced adjunct professors teach upper-level courses in their areas of specialty. The quality and accessibility of professors are often cited by Bowen students as "favorite things" about the school.

Academic Support

Bowen provides a comprehensive academic support program. This support begins prior to the first class during the week-long orientation program. Once classes begin, the principles taught in orientation are reinforced through a series of relevant workshops and seminars. The assistant dean for academic support also provides advising services to all students, helping them develop study plans, choose courses, and prepare for exams. Finally, Bowen helps ease the transition from law student to lawyer by offering an in-house bar exam prep course.

Clinical Programs

Bowen has three legal clinics that help students bridge the gap between theory learned in the classroom and practice. Through their clinic work, students practice law under the supervision of a faculty member, while at the same time helping to fill unmet legal needs in the community.

Litigation Clinic: Students represent clients involved in many types of cases within the broad areas of juvenile delinquency and family law. Qualified students receive special licenses to practice law in Arkansas.

Mediation Clinic: Students gain valuable experience in the rapidly expanding area of alternative dispute resolution. After extensive training, clinic students act as mediators in disputes relating to child abuse and neglect, juvenile delinquency, custody and visitation, special education, and small claims.

Tax Clinic: Students represent taxpayers involved in disputes with the IRS. Clinic students gain litigation and negotiation experience while acquiring significant knowledge of tax law.

Externships

The Public Service Externship provides students with another opportunity to gain hands-on experience and make significant professional contacts. Externships consist of field placements in government agencies, nonprofit legal services organizations, judiciary offices, and the Arkansas

Legislature. Externship students earn academic credit for their participation.

Facilities and Library

Bowen is housed in a historic building originally constructed in the 1930s to house the state's medical school. The spacious facility contains over 150,000 square feet and is compliant with the Americans with Disabilities Act.

The six-story structure has modern classrooms and courtrooms. A renovation was completed recently to install smart technology in the classrooms and courtrooms and wireless Internet throughout the building. The Lecture Capture system allows professors to record lectures (video and audio) and make them available to students via the web.

Wrapped around a four-story atrium, the library seats over 300 and houses two computer labs. The library is open seven days a week, and librarians are available on weekdays and Saturdays.

Cost and Financial Aid

With full-time resident tuition around $11,000, Bowen is an exceptional value. In addition, most nonresident students at Bowen earn scholarships that lower their tuition to no more than the resident rate. The law school participates in the Federal Stafford Loan Program, the Federal Graduate PLUS Loan Program, and the Federal Work-Study Program, as well as major private loan programs.

Scholarships

The Bowen School of Law automatically considers all admitted applicants for three scholarships.

Bowen scholarships cover full tuition and fees for up to 90 credit hours. Recipients have exceptional academic credentials, strong LSAT scores, and demonstrated leadership qualities.

Merit scholarships are awarded in amounts up to $21,000. These scholarships are awarded based on an array of factors, including academic achievement, LSAT scores, diversity, and quality of application materials. Personal statements are critical to the selection of merit scholarship recipients.

Nonresident scholarships are awarded in an amount that equals the out-of-state fees required to attend Bowen. All nonresident students are eligible for these scholarships.

Bowen Fellowship Program

Applicants who submit all required materials by January 1 and meet the criteria listed below may be considered for a Bowen Fellowship. Bowen Fellows receive a scholarship of up to full tuition and are given first choice of faculty research assistantships. In addition to the earlier application deadline, Bowen Fellowship applicants must have

- an LSAT score of 159 or higher;
- an undergraduate GPA of 3.3 or higher; and
- a sincere desire to attend Bowen full time.

Student Life

The relatively small student body at Bowen lends itself to a supportive and engaging community. On the curricular side, the *UALR Law Review* and the Moot Court Board are highly sought-after activities. Extracurricular organizations include the ABA, ACLU, Arkansas Bar Association, Arkansas Association of Women Lawyers, Asian Pacific American Law Students Association, Black Law Students Association, Lambda, Christian Legal Society, Hispanic Law Students Association, International Law Society, Part-Time Students Association, Student Animal Defense Fund, and Student Bar Association.

APPLICANT PROFILE

University of Arkansas at Little Rock, William H. Bowen School of Law
This grid includes only applicants who earned 120–180 LSAT scores under standard administrations.

LSAT Score	3.75 +		3.50–3.74		3.25–3.49		3.00–3.24		2.75–2.99		2.50–2.74		2.25–2.49		2.00–2.24		Below 2.00		No GPA		Total	
	Apps	Adm	Apps	Adm	Apps	Adm	Apps	Adm	Apps	Adm	Apps	Adm	Apps	Adm	Apps	Adm	Apps	Adm	Apps	Adm	Apps	Adm
175–180	0	0	0	0	0	0	0	0	0	0	0	0	0	0	0	0	0	0	0	0	0	0
170–174	0	0	0	0	1	0	1	1	0	0	0	0	0	0	0	0	0	0	0	0	2	1
165–169	5	4	1	1	2	2	1	1	3	2	3	1	0	0	1	1	1	0	0	0	17	12
160–164	14	12	5	5	8	5	12	8	16	10	3	0	5	2	2	1	2	0	3	3	70	46
155–159	23	17	27	20	35	20	36	24	36	17	37	20	22	9	7	2	1	0	7	3	231	132
150–154	41	26	63	39	79	33	85	26	67	18	34	5	20	4	9	1	3	0	7	3	408	155
145–149	33	15	45	10	84	12	86	11	73	9	49	1	32	2	16	0	5	0	9	2	432	62
140–144	15	1	17	1	40	1	52	0	59	0	44	0	31	0	13	0	0	0	15	0	286	3
135–139	2	0	9	0	14	0	16	0	27	0	23	0	13	0	8	0	3	0	7	0	122	0
130–134	1	0	2	0	4	0	11	0	6	0	20	0	5	0	5	0	4	0	3	0	61	0
125–129	1	0	1	0	2	0	1	0	4	0	3	0	2	0	3	0	1	0	2	0	20	0
120–124	0	0	0	0	0	0	0	0	0	0	0	0	1	0	0	0	1	0	0	0	2	0
Total	135	75	170	76	269	73	301	71	291	56	216	27	131	17	64	5	21	0	53	11	1651	411

Apps = Number of Applicants
Adm = Number Admitted
Reflects 99% of the total applicant pool; highest LSAT data reported.

ATLANTA'S JOHN MARSHALL LAW SCHOOL

1422 W. Peachtree Street NW
Atlanta, GA 30309
Phone: 404.872.3593; Fax: 404.873.3802
E-mail: admissions@johnmarshall.edu; Website: www.johnmarshall.edu

ABA
Approved
Since
2005

AMERICAN BAR ASSOCIATION
Section of Legal Education
and Admissions to the Bar

The Basics

Type of school	Private
Term	Semester
Application deadline	8/1
Application fee	$50
Financial aid deadline	7/1
Can first year start other than fall?	No
Student to faculty ratio	15.3 to 1
# of housing spaces available restricted to law students	
graduate housing for which law students are eligible	

Faculty and Administrators

	Total		Men		Women		Minorities	
	Spr	Fall	Spr	Fall	Spr	Fall	Spr	Fall
Full-time	28	29	9	11	19	18	6	6
Other full-time	1	6	1	4	0	2	0	2
Deans, librarians, & others who teach	5	5	3	3	2	2	2	2
Part-time	19	17	13	11	6	6	3	2
Total	53	57	26	29	27	28	11	12

Curriculum

	Full-Time	Part-Time
Typical first-year section size	49	45
Is there typically a "small section" of the first-year class, other than Legal Writing, taught by full-time faculty	No	No
If yes, typical size offered last year		

# of classroom course titles beyond first-year curriculum		51
# of upper division courses, excluding seminars, with an enrollment:	Under 25	95
	25–49	36
	50–74	6
	75–99	0
	100+	0
# of seminars		4
# of seminar positions available		103
# of seminar positions filled	32	31
# of positions available in simulation courses		332
# of simulation positions filled	250	82
# of positions available in faculty supervised clinical courses		0
# of faculty supervised clinical positions filled	0	0
# involved in field placements	82	17
# involved in law journals	23	12
# involved in moot court or trial competitions	24	5
# of credit hours required to graduate		88

JD Enrollment and Ethnicity

	Men		Women		Full-Time		Part-Time		1st-Year		Total		JD Degs. Awd.
	#	%	#	%	#	%	#	%	#	%	#	%	
All Hispanics	16	4.9	15	4.9	18	4.0	13	7.4	21	7.8	31	4.9	6
Am. Ind./AK Nat.	3	0.9	6	2.0	8	1.8	1	0.6	6	2.2	9	1.4	1
Asian	9	2.8	2	0.7	7	1.5	4	2.3	3	1.1	11	1.7	5
Black/Af. Am.	44	13.5	84	27.5	81	17.8	47	26.9	55	20.4	128	20.3	30
Nat. HI/Pac. Isl.	17	5.2	11	3.6	25	5.5	3	1.7	24	8.9	28	4.4	0
2 or more races	0	0.0	0	0.0	0	0.0	0	0.0	0	0.0	0	0.0	0
Subtotal (minor.)	89	27.4	118	38.7	139	30.5	68	38.9	109	40.4	207	32.9	42
Nonres. Alien	1	0.3	0	0.0	1	0.2	0	0.0	0	0.0	1	0.2	0
White/Cauc.	228	70.2	175	57.4	302	66.4	101	57.7	158	58.5	403	64.0	115
Unknown	7	2.2	12	3.9	13	2.9	6	3.4	3	1.1	19	3.0	9
Total	325	51.6	305	48.4	455	72.2	175	27.8	270	42.9	630		166

Transfers

Transfers in	10
Transfers out	14

Tuition and Fees

	Resident	Nonresident
Full-time	$32,965	
Part-time	$20,065	
Tuition Guarantee Program		N

Living Expenses

Estimated living expenses for singles

Living on campus	Living off campus	Living at home
N/A	$21,000	N/A

ABA Approved Since 2005

GPA and LSAT Scores

	Total	Full-Time	Part-Time
# of apps	1,969	1,623	346
# of offers	835	713	122
# of matrics	265	209	56
75% GPA	3.30	3.29	3.31
Median GPA	2.97	2.95	3.02
25% GPA	2.61	2.60	2.62
75% LSAT	153	153	152
Median LSAT	150	150	150
25% LSAT	148	148	148

Grants and Scholarships (from prior year)

	Total		Full-Time		Part-Time	
	#	%	#	%	#	%
Total # of students	555		371		184	
Total # receiving grants	18	3.2	11	3.0	7	3.8
Less than 1/2 tuition	0	0.0	0	0.0	0	0.0
Half to full tuition	0	0.0	0	0.0	0	0.0
Full tuition	18	3.2	11	3.0	7	3.8
More than full tuition	0	0.0	0	0.0	0	0.0
Median grant amount			$0		$0	

Informational and Library Resources

Total amount spent on library materials	$644,378
Study seating capacity inside the library	212
# of full-time equivalent professional librarians	6
Hours per week library is open	86
# of open, wired connections available to students	181
# of networked computers available for use by students	26
Has wireless network?	Y
Requires computer?	N

JD Attrition (from prior year)

	Academic	Other	Total	
	#	#	#	%
1st year	2	6	8	3.4
2nd year	2	14	16	10.9
3rd year	0	0	0	0.0
4th year	0	0	0	0.0

Employment (9 months after graduation)

	Total	Percentage
Employment status known	126	100.0
Employment status unknown	0	0.0
Employed	114	90.5
Pursuing graduate degrees	0	0.0
Unemployed (seeking, not seeking, or studying for the bar)	4	3.2
Type of Employment		
# employed in law firms	55	48.2
# employed in business and industry	34	29.8
# employed in government	16	14.0
# employed in public interest	5	4.4
# employed as judicial clerks	4	3.5
# employed in academia	0	0.0
Geographic Location		
# employed in state	97	85.1
# employed outside the US	1	0.9
# of states where employed	9	

Bar Passage Rates

First-time takers	122	Reporting %	85.25
Average school %	82.69	Average state %	86.28

Average pass difference −3.59

Jurisdiction	Takers	Passers	Pass %	State %	Diff %
Georgia	104	86	82.69	86.28	−3.59

ATLANTA'S JOHN MARSHALL LAW SCHOOL

1422 W. Peachtree Street NW
Atlanta, GA 30309
Phone: 404.872.3593; Fax: 404.873.3802
E-mail: admissions@johnmarshall.edu; Website: www.johnmarshall.edu

The Dean's Introduction

Atlanta's John Marshall Law School has been educating lawyers and leaders in Georgia since 1933 and now attracts students from around the country. We provide a rigorous, high-quality program of legal education that produces competent and ethical lawyers who are dedicated to helping people, especially in underserved communities. We intentionally instill in our students a sense of obligation to the community and to the legal profession—an obligation to pursue justice, rather than mere personal gain, and to improve society, rather than to solely advance personal ambition. Whether our graduates remain in law practice, become judges, enter politics, or succeed in business, these rich values stay with them.

The Mission

The mission of the Law School is to prepare highly competent and professional lawyers who possess a strong social conscience, continually demonstrate high ethical standards, and are committed to the improvement of the legal system and society. The school is dedicated to providing a quality educational opportunity to nontraditional or adult learners, and to other significantly underserved segments of the community. We emphasize the highest standards of ethical and professional conduct. As Supreme Court Justice Thurgood Marshall once said, "There's only one kind of reputation a young lawyer gets in a hurry." Graduates of this law school are trained to do the right thing.

Atlanta Living

The Law School campus is centrally located in midtown Atlanta, the social, cultural, and economic hub of the South. It is in close proximity to Atlanta's largest law firms, as well as government offices, state and federal courts, and nonprofit legal organizations. Atlanta also boasts an extensive array of arts, music, sports, and recreational events, making it an exciting place to live.

Facilities, Library, and Modern Technology

The Law School is housed in a modern, nine-story building located on one of the major streets in Atlanta. Additional classroom and faculty offices are housed in an adjoining building connected by a two-story pedestrian bridge. A new conference center, including a 400-seat auditorium, will allow for a constant flow of student programs and symposia.

The Law School has made the inclusion of new technologies throughout the school a priority. All students and faculty enjoy direct and unlimited access to wireless Internet, massive online legal databases, as well as new state-of-the-art technology in multiple classrooms that allows for interactive learning experiences. Students can take both midterm and final exams on their laptops and download them to the school's network.

Our library spreads over three floors, contains over 200,000 total volumes and equivalents, and provides students and faculty with access to all legal materials necessary to learn the skill of legal research.

Dedicated Faculty

The John Marshall faculty make the difference in the student experience and are committed to students' success throughout their legal education and beyond. The faculty are dedicated to providing an intellectually rigorous academic program while instilling the highest sense of professional, ethical, and moral responsibilities that are required of members of the legal profession. All of our faculty members have extensive practical experience in their respective fields of expertise, bringing real-world experience into the classroom. Our low student-to-faculty ratio is one of the best among American law schools. All first-year and required courses are taught in small classes, and professors are easily accessible to their students outside of class. Our small class sizes and low student-to-faculty ratio create a supportive environment where students can enjoy learning and express their views.

Commitment to Diversity

Because John Marshall's educational environment focuses on an interactive learning process, a diverse student body is essential to providing a broad range of perspectives in the classroom and the Law School community. The fall 2010 entering class of 265 students was made up of 46 percent women and 38 percent minorities. The student body is not only ethnically diverse, but it is varied in life experience and professional backgrounds. In the 2010 entering class, the median age of full-time students was 25, and the median age of part-time students was 30.

The Legal Program

John Marshall's rigorous program of study is designed toward the development of intellectual, analytical, and lawyering skills. From the first-year curriculum, with its predetermined set of core courses, through the third year, with courses that emphasize practical skill development, the degree program is designed to promote analytical reasoning, precision in both oral and written communication, and problem-solving skills. Upper-class students can pursue their areas of interest through a broad variety of elective courses.

Full-Time and Part-Time Law Study. John Marshall remains dedicated to providing access to legal education to both traditional and nontraditional students by offering both full-time and part-time law programs. Individuals who are unable to devote themselves to the study of law full time may attend either the part-time evening or part-time day program.

The **Honors Program in Criminal Justice** is a unique, innovative curriculum for students planning to be prosecutors, public defenders, or criminal defense lawyers. The Honors Program immerses the student in the criminal justice field from the first day of law school, integrates skills classes with criminal law, and introduces students to the leading prosecutors and defense lawyers in this country. Graduates of this JD program will earn a truly valuable credential.

The **Legal Skills and Professionalism Program** takes a holistic approach to preparing students for success during and after law school. Beginning with writing, the program teaches legal skills and professionalism. The same tools that students use to draft documents in their writing classes are employed to solve legal problems in Negotiations, Mediation, Trial Advocacy, Client Interviewing and Counseling, and other skills courses. In addition, a professionalism component is built into every course in the program, preparing students to confront and resolve real-world professionalism issues as they learn to solve legal problems and meet client goals. The Law School faculty come with diverse law practice backgrounds, including criminal defense and prosecution, administrative law, domestic relations practice, and corporate/transactional work.

Academic Support. Tools for academic growth and professional success are not only fostered through interactive classroom teaching, but also through individual advisement and group workshops. The director of academic achievement meets individually with students and also plans lectures and special programs to assist in the development of students' legal writing, studying, and exam skills, including the bar exam.

Pro Bono and Externship Programs. The director of pro bono and externships encourages students to be involved in pro bono work, both legal and nonlegal. The director also supervises students in externships throughout Atlanta, including externships for academic credit. Externship placements include the ACLU, Atlanta City Council, Atlanta Legal Aid Society, Department of Homeland Security, district attorney and public defender offices throughout the city, the Georgia Recording Artist Association, the Landlord/Tenant Mediation Project, the Georgia Innocence Project, the Georgia Court of Appeals, and the Southern Center for Human Rights, among others. In 2007, John Marshall established the Micronesian Externship Program, which places students in judicial chambers and government law offices in Guam, the Commonwealth of the Northern Marianas, the Federated States of Micronesia, and the Republic of Palau.

Career Development

The Office of Career Development offers individualized, professional advice to students about their personal career goals and tailors strategies to assist students in reaching those goals. In addition to providing résumé and interview workshops to facilitate job searches, John Marshall also participates in the Georgia Law School Consortium to plan job fairs and other state-wide recruiting efforts, such as judicial clerkships; placement with prosecutors, public interest agencies, and public defenders; and minority recruiting. As a member of the National Association of Law Placement, John Marshall allows its students the opportunity to attend regional hiring consortia that attract private and government recruiters throughout the Southeast.

Admission

The Admissions Committee is committed to finding a well-rounded and diverse group of students. In addition to the candidate's academic record and standardized test results, the Admissions Committee will examine with particular care those factors that indicate a high probability for success in law study. Such factors include life experiences, personal or family hardships overcome, demonstrated personal and professional achievements, ability to overcome life's obstacles, the capacity for rigorous intellectual study, the self-discipline demanded by the profession, and a commitment to be of service to the profession and society as a whole.

Law School Visits

The Office of Admissions makes numerous college visits and holds open houses throughout the year to provide prospective students with information and guidance about the law school admission process. Please visit our website for additional information regarding the dates and times of events. We also invite you to contact us for a personalized tour, to sit in on a class, or to meet personally with an admission professional.

APPLICANT PROFILE

Atlanta's John Marshall Law School
This grid includes only applicants who earned 120–180 LSAT scores under standard administrations.

LSAT Score	GPA								
	3.75 +	3.50–3.74	3.25–3.49	3.00–3.24	2.75–2.99	2.50–2.74	2.25–2.49	2.00–2.24	Below 2.00
155–180	Likely	Likely	Likely	Likely	Likely	Likely	Likely	Possible	Unlikely
150–154	Likely	Likely	Likely	Likely	Likely	Possible	Possible	Possible	Unlikely
145–149	Possible	Possible	Possible	Possible	Possible	Possible	Unlikely	Unlikely	Unlikely
120–144	Unlikely	Unlikely	Unlikely	Unlikely	Unlikely	Unlikely	Unlikely	Unlikely	Unlikely

■ Likely　　▨ Possible　　□ Unlikely

AVE MARIA SCHOOL OF LAW

1025 Commons Circle
Naples, FL 34119-1376
Phone: 239.687.5300; Fax: 239.352.2890
E-mail: info@avemarialaw.edu; Website: www.avemarialaw.edu

The Basics

Type of school	Private
Term	Semester
Application deadline	7/1
Application fee	$50
Financial aid deadline	6/1
Can first year start other than fall?	No
Student to faculty ratio	17.9 to 1
# of housing spaces available restricted to law students	113
graduate housing for which law students are eligible	

Faculty and Administrators

	Total		Men		Women		Minorities	
	Spr	Fall	Spr	Fall	Spr	Fall	Spr	Fall
Full-time	20	19	15	14	5	5	3	5
Other full-time	4	7	2	5	2	2	1	1
Deans, librarians, & others who teach	6	6	5	5	1	1	1	1
Part-time	14	9	11	8	3	1	3	0
Total	44	41	33	32	11	9	8	7

Curriculum

	Full-Time	Part-Time
Typical first-year section size	105	0
Is there typically a "small section" of the first-year class, other than Legal Writing, taught by full-time faculty	No	No
If yes, typical size offered last year		
# of classroom course titles beyond first-year curriculum	81	
# of upper division courses, excluding seminars, with an enrollment: Under 25	55	
25–49	12	
50–74	9	
75–99	0	
100+	0	
# of seminars	22	
# of seminar positions available	348	
# of seminar positions filled	166	0
# of positions available in simulation courses	128	
# of simulation positions filled	95	0
# of positions available in faculty supervised clinical courses	49	
# of faculty supervised clinical positions filled	28	0
# involved in field placements	26	0
# involved in law journals	27	0
# involved in moot court or trial competitions	26	0
# of credit hours required to graduate	90	

JD Enrollment and Ethnicity

	Men		Women		Full-Time		Part-Time		1st-Year		Total		JD Degs. Awd.
	#	%	#	%	#	%	#	%	#	%	#	%	
All Hispanics	24	9.3	30	14.3	54	11.5	0	0.0	27	13.4	54	11.5	6
Am. Ind./AK Nat.	0	0.0	1	0.5	1	0.2	0	0.0	1	0.5	1	0.2	0
Asian	7	2.7	5	2.4	12	2.6	0	0.0	3	1.5	12	2.6	6
Black/Af. Am.	5	1.9	14	6.7	19	4.1	0	0.0	13	6.5	19	4.1	1
Nat. HI/Pac. Isl.	1	0.4	0	0.0	1	0.2	0	0.0	0	0.0	1	0.2	0
2 or more races	3	1.2	8	3.8	11	2.4	0	0.0	1	0.5	11	2.4	0
Subtotal (minor.)	40	15.5	58	27.6	98	20.9	0	0.0	45	22.4	98	20.9	13
Nonres. Alien	3	1.2	1	0.5	4	0.9	0	0.0	0	0.0	4	0.9	0
White/Cauc.	211	81.8	149	71.0	360	76.9	0	0.0	150	74.6	360	76.9	67
Unknown	4	1.6	2	1.0	6	1.3	0	0.0	6	3.0	6	1.3	0
Total	258	55.1	210	44.9	468	100.0	0	0.0	201	42.9	468		84

Transfers

Transfers in	1
Transfers out	20

Tuition and Fees

	Resident	Nonresident
Full-time	$36,448	$36,448
Part-time		
Tuition Guarantee Program		N

Living Expenses

Estimated living expenses for singles

Living on campus	Living off campus	Living at home
$20,999	$20,999	$20,999

AVE MARIA SCHOOL OF LAW

ABA
Approved
Since
2002

GPA and LSAT Scores

	Total	Full-Time	Part-Time
# of apps	1,981	1,981	0
# of offers	927	927	0
# of matrics	203	203	0
75% GPA	3.41	3.41	0.00
Median GPA	3.14	3.14	0.00
25% GPA	2.84	2.84	0.00
75% LSAT	153	153	0
Median LSAT	149	149	0
25% LSAT	147	147	0

Grants and Scholarships (from prior year)

	Total		Full-Time		Part-Time	
	#	%	#	%	#	%
Total # of students	375		375		0	
Total # receiving grants	216	57.6	216	57.6	0	0.0
Less than 1/2 tuition	133	35.5	133	35.5	0	0.0
Half to full tuition	48	12.8	48	12.8	0	0.0
Full tuition	35	9.3	35	9.3	0	0.0
More than full tuition	0	0.0	0	0.0	0	0.0
Median grant amount			$15,000		$0	

Informational and Library Resources

Total amount spent on library materials	$594,882
Study seating capacity inside the library	103
# of full-time equivalent professional librarians	4
Hours per week library is open	108
# of open, wired connections available to students	20
# of networked computers available for use by students	29
Has wireless network?	Y
Requires computer?	N

JD Attrition (from prior year)

	Academic	Other	Total	
	#	#	#	%
1st year	0	31	31	14.9
2nd year	0	2	2	2.2
3rd year	0	0	0	0.0
4th year	0	0	0	0.0

Employment (9 months after graduation)

	Total	Percentage
Employment status known	85	98.8
Employment status unknown	1	1.2
Employed	51	60.0
Pursuing graduate degrees	3	3.5
Unemployed (seeking, not seeking, or studying for the bar)	29	34.1
Type of Employment		
# employed in law firms	16	31.4
# employed in business and industry	5	9.8
# employed in government	13	25.5
# employed in public interest	5	9.8
# employed as judicial clerks	7	13.7
# employed in academia	0	0.0
Geographic Location		
# employed in state	2	3.9
# employed outside the US	2	3.9
# of states where employed	22	

Bar Passage Rates

First-time takers	79	Reporting %	75.95
Average school %	69.98	Average state %	83.55

Average pass difference −13.57

Jurisdiction	Takers	Passers	Pass %	State %	Diff %
Michigan	20	16	80.00	86.87	−6.87
Florida	10	5	50.00	77.81	−27.81
Texas	8	6	75.00	85.48	−10.48
New York	5	2	40.00	86.51	−46.51
Others (6)	17	13	76.47		

AVE MARIA SCHOOL OF LAW

1025 Commons Circle
Naples, FL 34119-1376
Phone: 239.687.5300; Fax: 239.352.2890
E-mail: info@avemarialaw.edu; Website: www.avemarialaw.edu

Introduction

Ave Maria School of Law offers students a distinctive legal education that focuses on professional excellence, the moral foundations of the law, and the harmony of faith and reason. As a national Catholic law school, Ave Maria is committed to producing highly competent graduates who are able to reflect critically on the law, the principles that undergird it, and their role within the legal system.

With a student-to-faculty ratio of approximately 20 to 1, Ave Maria students benefit from ready access to experienced faculty members who prepare students to practice at the highest level and to succeed on bar exams throughout the country. The quality of Ave Maria's academic program is recognized by judges throughout the nation who have hired graduates as judicial clerks—with 57 clerkships secured by members of the 2003–2009 graduating classes, most of these federal clerkships.

In the summer of 2009, Ave Maria School of Law relocated to southwest Florida, just seven miles inland of the Gulf of Mexico. The new location will enhance the school's ability to fulfill its distinctive mission as a Catholic law school dedicated to professional excellence. In the new location, students have found employment and externship opportunities with courts and law firms in nearby Naples and Fort Myers, while the law school's clinical programs have found new opportunities as well. With no other law school located in this rapidly developing region, which is expected to double its population in the next two decades, the School of Law has been both a catalyst and a beneficiary of the area's dynamic growth.

Ave Maria School of Law encourages applications from students of all faiths who seek a distinctive legal education enriched by the Catholic intellectual tradition.

Curriculum

Ave Maria School of Law awards the Juris Doctor degree after three years (90 credits) of full-time residential study. The required curriculum of 60 credits ensures that all students develop those skills that are fundamental to the effective practice of law—analysis, reasoning, problem solving, research, writing, oral advocacy, and others. Through elective courses, students have the opportunity to focus on specific subject areas of interest, such as commercial law, employment law, international law, and intellectual property law. A central tenet of the educational philosophy at Ave Maria is that law and morality are inherently intertwined.

Faculty

At the core of the Ave Maria School of Law education is the faculty who teach and mentor students. Faculty members bring to the classroom their experience as attorneys in private practice, as judicial clerks, and as teachers and administrators at other law schools. In hiring faculty, the law school administration has sought individuals who would be able to translate the mission of the School of Law in the classroom, in their scholarship, and in their service. Ave Maria faculty members actively contribute to the profession through their legal research, writing, and involvement in professional and civic organizations. Our faculty includes 34 full-time professors. Select upper-level courses are taught by adjunct faculty members drawn from area law firms, corporations, and the judiciary.

Enrollment/Student Body

While many of Ave Maria's students come to the School of Law directly from their undergraduate institutions, others have earned postgraduate degrees and have work experience in fields including business, medicine, engineering, the military, and education. More than 170 different undergraduate colleges are represented at the School of Law, including Brigham Young University, Christendom College, College of William and Mary, Dartmouth College, Franciscan University, University of Notre Dame, Providence College, the University of Florida, and many other fine schools.

Career Services/Placement

Ave Maria School of Law graduates accept employment with an array of employers in all regions of the country, including national and regional law firms such as Akin Gump, Sidley Austin, Butzel Long, Reed Smith, Roetzel and Andress, Skadden Arps, and Holland and Hart. Graduates have also been successful in obtaining employment with state and federal governmental agencies, including the US Departments of Justice, Homeland Security, and Defense, as well as multiple prosecutors' offices nationwide.

The Career Services Office uses a proactive and individualized approach to assist students during each stage of the career-search process—counseling, strategizing, résumé and cover letter preparation, interviewing, and consideration of employment offers. The full-time staff of three, two of whom are attorneys, is dedicated to expanding employment opportunities for students through the cultivation of relationships with legal employers throughout the region and the nation.

Library/Physical Facilities

The Ave Maria Law School Library is housed in an environment that is both welcoming and conducive to research and study. Materials are available in all formats; the collection is particularly strong in digital resources. Apart from a fine compilation of US and international primary and secondary legal materials, the Ave Maria Law Library's collection emphasizes the areas of canon law, bioethics and biotechnology, natural law, and related philosophy, history, political science, and economics titles. Seating in the library includes a variety of carrel, table, group study, and soft seating. Leisure reading in the form of magazines and daily newspapers is provided.

Admission

Ave Maria School of Law enrolls talented individuals from diverse backgrounds who seek a rigorous and distinctive legal education. To this end, Ave Maria evaluates applicants from a whole-person perspective and considers many factors, including work experience, activities, background, obstacles overcome, accomplishments, undergraduate and graduate school records, Law School Admission Test (LSAT) scores, letters of reference, and the applicant's personal statement. Ave Maria recognizes that a diverse student body, drawn from throughout the United States and internationally, enriches the educational experience.

Student Activities

By providing opportunities for interaction among students, faculty, and the legal community, Ave Maria School of Law ensures a vibrant professional atmosphere and a constructive law school experience. A five-day orientation program, a Distinguished Speaker Series, conferences, and the Board of Visitors Mentor Program, together with a challenging and comprehensive curriculum, provide Ave Maria students with an exceptional law school experience. A multitude of student organizations offers students the opportunity to pursue their specific areas of interest and augment their law school education.

APPLICANT PROFILE

Housing

Ave Maria School of Law's campus in Naples, Florida, offers on-site housing as well as close-by apartments, condominiums, and single-family homes. The law school provides assistance to students during their search for housing and, if applicable, roommates.

Expenses/Financial Aid

Ave Maria School of Law offers a generous scholarship program that annually provides scholarships ranging from $5,000 up to full tuition to approximately 60 percent of the entering class. Additionally, the School of Law annually awards scholarships ranging from $5,000 to $10,000 to entering students who have a record of service and leadership in select areas. Tuition for members of the fall 2010 entering class is $35,948.

Ave Maria School of Law has chosen not to provide an admission profile grid. This reflects our commitment to consider every applicant from a whole-person perspective. Every component of the application is carefully reviewed,

and, while qualifications as measured by LSAT and GPA are important, equal consideration is also given to the applicant's background, letters of recommendation, and personal statement.

UNIVERSITY OF BALTIMORE SCHOOL OF LAW

1420 North Charles Street
Baltimore, MD 21201
Phone: 410.837.4459; Fax: 410.837.4188
E-mail: lwadmiss@ubalt.edu; Website: http://law.ubalt.edu

ABA Approved Since 1972

The Basics

Type of school	Public
Term	Semester
Application deadline	7/15
Application fee	$60
Financial aid deadline	3/1
Can first year start other than fall?	No
Student to faculty ratio	16.0 to 1
# of housing spaces available restricted to law students	
graduate housing for which law students are eligible	

Faculty and Administrators

	Total		Men		Women		Minorities	
	Spr	Fall	Spr	Fall	Spr	Fall	Spr	Fall
Full-time	47	49	26	26	21	23	8	10
Other full-time	9	9	5	5	4	4	3	2
Deans, librarians, & others who teach	6	6	3	3	3	3	0	0
Part-time	76	65	49	46	26	18	9	4
Total	138	129	83	80	54	48	20	16

Curriculum

		Full-Time	Part-Time
Typical first-year section size		54	41
Is there typically a "small section" of the first-year class, other than Legal Writing, taught by full-time faculty		No	No
If yes, typical size offered last year			
# of classroom course titles beyond first-year curriculum		147	
# of upper division courses, excluding seminars, with an enrollment:	Under 25	175	
	25–49	33	
	50–74	16	
	75–99	10	
	100+	0	
# of seminars		37	
# of seminar positions available		726	
# of seminar positions filled		362	106
# of positions available in simulation courses		972	
# of simulation positions filled		547	203
# of positions available in faculty supervised clinical courses		180	
# of faculty supervised clinical positions filled	119	20
# involved in field placements	105	11
# involved in law journals	362	44
# involved in moot court or trial competitions	101	6
# of credit hours required to graduate		87	

JD Enrollment and Ethnicity

	Men		Women		Full-Time		Part-Time		1st-Year		Total		JD Degs. Awd.
	#	%	#	%	#	%	#	%	#	%	#	%	
All Hispanics	14	2.6	14	2.6	17	2.3	11	3.1	11	2.6	28	2.6	5
Am. Ind./AK Nat.	0	0.0	1	0.2	0	0.0	1	0.3	1	0.2	1	0.1	1
Asian	27	5.0	28	5.2	44	6.0	11	3.1	21	5.0	55	5.1	19
Black/Af. Am.	23	4.2	56	10.4	32	4.4	47	13.3	39	9.3	79	7.3	19
Nat. HI/Pac. Isl.	1	0.2	1	0.2	0	0.0	2	0.6	0	0.0	2	0.2	0
2 or more races	5	0.9	3	0.6	6	0.8	2	0.6	7	1.7	8	0.7	0
Subtotal (minor.)	70	12.9	103	19.1	99	13.6	74	21.0	79	18.9	173	16.0	45
Nonres. Alien	0	0.0	0	0.0	0	0.0	0	0.0	0	0.0	0	0.0	0
White/Cauc.	416	76.5	395	73.3	568	77.8	243	68.8	312	74.6	811	74.9	241
Unknown	58	10.7	41	7.6	63	8.6	36	10.2	22	5.3	99	9.1	42
Total	544	50.2	539	49.8	730	67.4	353	32.6	418	38.6	1083		328

Transfers

Transfers in	11
Transfers out	25

Tuition and Fees

	Resident	Nonresident
Full-time	$25,224	$37,368
Part-time	$18,830	$26,394
Tuition Guarantee Program	N	

Living Expenses

Estimated living expenses for singles

Living on campus	Living off campus	Living at home
N/A	$21,800	$8,200

UNIVERSITY OF BALTIMORE SCHOOL OF LAW

ABA
Approved
Since
1972

GPA and LSAT Scores

	Total	Full-Time	Part-Time
# of apps	2,443	1,930	513
# of offers	1,044	810	234
# of matrics	363	233	130
75% GPA	3.63	3.67	3.47
Median GPA	3.31	3.48	3.10
25% GPA	2.90	2.97	2.81
75% LSAT	157	158	154
Median LSAT	155	156	151
25% LSAT	151	153	149

Grants and Scholarships (from prior year)

	Total		Full-Time		Part-Time	
	#	%	#	%	#	%
Total # of students	1,103		672		431	
Total # receiving grants	193	17.5	149	22.2	44	10.2
Less than 1/2 tuition	88	8.0	51	7.6	37	8.6
Half to full tuition	105	9.5	98	14.6	7	1.6
Full tuition	0	0.0	0	0.0	0	0.0
More than full tuition	0	0.0	0	0.0	0	0.0
Median grant amount			$22,136		$3,909	

Informational and Library Resources

Total amount spent on library materials	$753,027
Study seating capacity inside the library	317
# of full-time equivalent professional librarians	12
Hours per week library is open	94
# of open, wired connections available to students	29
# of networked computers available for use by students	36
Has wireless network?	Y
Requires computer?	N

JD Attrition (from prior year)

	Academic	Other	Total	
	#	#	#	%
1st year	10	29	39	9.2
2nd year	1	4	5	1.7
3rd year	1	0	1	0.3
4th year	0	0	0	0.0

Employment (9 months after graduation)

	Total	Percentage
Employment status known	303	99.3
Employment status unknown	2	0.7
Employed	283	93.4
Pursuing graduate degrees	7	2.3
Unemployed (seeking, not seeking, or studying for the bar)	7	2.3
Type of Employment		
# employed in law firms	101	35.7
# employed in business and industry	36	12.7
# employed in government	55	19.4
# employed in public interest	11	3.9
# employed as judicial clerks	62	21.9
# employed in academia	10	3.5
Geographic Location		
# employed in state	228	80.6
# employed outside the US	0	0.0
# of states where employed		11

Bar Passage Rates

First-time takers	311	Reporting %	83.28
Average school %	81.85	Average state %	78.20
Average pass difference	3.65		

Jurisdiction	Takers	Passers	Pass %	State %	Diff %
Maryland	259	212	81.85	78.20	3.65

UNIVERSITY OF BALTIMORE SCHOOL OF LAW

1420 North Charles Street
Baltimore, MD 21201
Phone: 410.837.4459; Fax: 410.837.4188
E-mail: lwadmiss@ubalt.edu; Website: http://law.ubalt.edu

Introduction

Founded in 1925, the University of Baltimore is one of 13 institutions in the University System of Maryland. Although UB is the sixth largest public law school in the country with approximately 1,000 JD students, the school prides itself on excellent classroom teaching, small law school sections, and personalized service.

The School of Law remains committed to its traditional values of community involvement, public interest, access, and diversity. Regardless of a graduate's area of practice, the school believes that all of its students should be exposed to the traditional obligation of lawyers to serve the poor and the common good. Finally, the school values a diverse faculty, staff, and student body as an essential part of its pedagogical mission. The School of Law is accredited by the ABA and AALS.

Admission

The School of Law has established an admission policy designed to obtain a diverse and well-qualified student body. In evaluating applicant files, the Admission Committee considers not only the cumulative undergraduate grade-point average and the LSAT score, but also nontraditional factors that may be relevant in determining an applicant's ability to succeed in law school. Applicants are encouraged to discuss fully in a personal statement any such factors they wish the committee to consider in evaluating their application.

Enrollment/Student Body

The School of Law provides three options for pursuing a law degree: a full-time day program, a part-time evening program, and a part-time day program. Approximately a third of the student body is part time, making the part-time division one of the largest in the nation. Over 88 percent of the classes are composed of 50 students or less. The School of Law typically offers between 60 and 65 classes a semester.

Curriculum

The School of Law provides a rich curriculum in both day and evening divisions, offering a wide variety of specialized courses in addition to a solid core curriculum. Our legal skills offerings are especially strong as the School of Law is one of the national leaders in "narrowing the gap" between legal education and the legal profession. Our skills programs begin with the first-year courses in legal analysis, research, and writing and culminate with one of the best legal clinics in the nation. Upper-level courses offer students a range of in-depth concentrations that provide students with a sophisticated understanding of a particular area of law.

Library

The library's permanent collection contains approximately 354,000 books and bound volume equivalents. The collection includes the published reports of federal and state courts, statutes, administrative materials, and secondary materials such as treatises, legal encyclopedias, digests, citators, form books, looseleaf services, and law reviews. The library staff believes that technology should not be considered separate from the study and practice of law: professional reference librarians are available to students seven days a week to show students how to use the computer-assisted legal systems, as well as how to access the library's many web-based resources. The library's two computer labs are open to law students during library hours and, along with the wireless network, provide access to word processing, LexisNexis, Westlaw, the Internet, online catalogs, and other resources.

Joint Degrees

The School of Law offers six joint degrees: JD with MBA, MPA, MS in Criminal Justice, MS in Negotiations and Conflict Management, LLM in Taxation, and the PhD in Policy Science.

Special Programs

Areas of Concentration—The School of Law has an innovative curriculum that allows students the opportunity to develop an in-depth knowledge in a particular area of the law. Students may take courses in one of nine areas of concentration: business law, criminal practice, estate planning, family law, intellectual property, international and comparative law, litigation and advocacy, public and governmental service, and real estate practice.

Centers—Students may also gain specialized knowledge in particular areas of the law through participation in the activities of the Law School's centers, including the **Center for Families, Children, and the Courts**, which focuses on the development and implementation of family court planning and reform initiatives throughout the country. The **Center for International and Comparative Law** promotes the study and understanding of international and comparative law and the political and economic institutions that support the international legal order. The center places special emphasis on environmental law, human rights, intellectual property, and international business transactions. The **Center on Applied Feminism** serves as a bridge between feminist legal theory and the law. The center examines how feminist theory can benefit legal practitioners in representing clients, shape legal doctrine, and play a role in policy debates and implementation. The **Stephen L. Snyder Center for Litigation Skills** supports and enhances the acclaimed litigation skills training of the School of Law through a variety of programs and activities, including lectures by prominent lawyers and judges, special conferences, and litigation research. The **Center for Sport and the Law** was established in 2009 with the support of the Baltimore Orioles professional baseball franchise and the Baltimore Ravens professional football franchise to foster academic leadership, community engagement, and student excellence in the theoretical and practical aspects of amateur and professional sports law.

Law Review and Other Periodicals give students an opportunity to hone their skills in research, analysis, and writing. The *University of Baltimore Law Review* offers an in-depth analysis of issues of current concern to practitioners and judges alike. The *Law Forum* specializes in articles that trace developing trends in the law.

Clinical, Advocacy, and Internship Programs—Professional development is fostered through clinics in which students represent individuals and organizations in litigation and transactional matters. Clinics include the **Appellate Practice Clinic**, which enables students to brief and argue a case in the Maryland Court of Special Appeals; the **Civil Advocacy Clinic**, which focuses on such issues as consumer protection, public benefits cases, and landlord-tenant disputes; the **Community Development Clinic**, which represents nonprofit community organizations in a variety of housing, economic, social, and cultural development areas; the **Criminal Practice Clinic**, in which students handle misdemeanor and felony matters in the district and circuit courts; the **Disability Law Clinic**, which provides representation to patients in involuntary commitment hearings; the **Family Law Clinic**, where students represent low-income clients seeking child custody, support, divorce, and protection from domestic violence; the **Family Mediation Clinic**, which permits students to co-mediate family law disputes and engage in projects designed to improve the practice of family mediation; the **Immigrant Rights Clinic**, which enables students to represent low-income immigrants in Immigration Court and in the District Court of Maryland, as well as work with immigrant advocates to develop programs that increase access to justice for immigrant communities; the **Innocence Project Clinic**, which provides students with the opportunity to review records, interview clients and witnesses, conduct legal research, devise investigative strategies, draft pleadings, and argue motions in cases involving claims of wrongful conviction; and the **Tax Clinic**, which enables students to represent low-income clients before the Internal Revenue Service and the US Tax Court. **Internship Programs** give students experience clerking for academic credit in the public and private sector, including positions in the executive, legislative, and judicial branches of state and local governments.

Financial Aid

The university's Financial Aid Office administers federal, state, and institutional loan programs. First-year and transfer applicants are advised to apply for financial aid well in advance of the March 1 deadline. Students are automatically considered for merit-based scholarships. The School of Law awarded more than $1.3 million in scholarships to students matriculating in 2010.

Career Services

The professional staff of the Law Career Development Office (LCDO) works individually and collectively to establish effective, dynamic relationships with law students and graduates seeking to articulate, develop, and achieve their career goals. By forging cooperative relationships with a host of employers, regionally and nationally, in the public and private sectors, the LCDO and the School of Law have demonstrated significant success in meeting the needs of our law students and alumni who are competing in a challenging and evolving market. Through a host of services, including individual counseling, career workshops, mock interviews, on-campus and off-campus recruitment programs, internship and externship programs, as well as a detailed and extensive library of resources, the LCDO seeks to provide each and every law student and graduate with job search strategies and the tools to succeed in their professional careers. In addition, through the innovative EXPLOR Program, the LCDO offers first-year students opportunities to gain substantive legal experience their first summer and establish a solid foundation for future success.

APPLICANT PROFILE

University of Baltimore School of Law
This grid includes only applicants who earned 120–180 LSAT scores under standard administrations.

LSAT Score	GPA								
	3.75 +	3.50–3.74	3.25–3.49	3.00–3.24	2.75–2.99	2.50–2.74	2.25–2.49	2.00–2.24	Below 2.00
175–180	Good Possibility	Good Possibility	Good Possibility	Good Possibility	Good Possibility	Good Possibility	Possible	Unlikely	Unlikely
170–174	Good Possibility	Good Possibility	Good Possibility	Good Possibility	Good Possibility	Good Possibility	Possible	Unlikely	Unlikely
165–169	Good Possibility	Good Possibility	Good Possibility	Good Possibility	Good Possibility	Good Possibility	Possible	Unlikely	Unlikely
160–164	Good Possibility	Good Possibility	Good Possibility	Good Possibility	Good Possibility	Good Possibility	Possible	Unlikely	Unlikely
155–159	Good Possibility	Good Possibility	Good Possibility	Good Possibility	Possible	Possible	Possible	Unlikely	Unlikely
150–154	Good Possibility	Good Possibility	Possible	Possible	Possible	Possible	Unlikely	Unlikely	Unlikely
145–149	Possible	Possible	Possible	Unlikely	Unlikely	Unlikely	Unlikely	Unlikely	Unlikely
140–144	Unlikely	Unlikely	Unlikely	Unlikely	Unlikely	Unlikely	Unlikely	Unlikely	Unlikely
Below 140	Unlikely	Unlikely	Unlikely	Unlikely	Unlikely	Unlikely	Unlikely	Unlikely	Unlikely

■ Good Possibility   ▨ Possible   □ Unlikely

BARRY UNIVERSITY DWAYNE O. ANDREAS SCHOOL OF LAW

6441 East Colonial Drive
Orlando, FL 32807
Phone: 321.206.5600
E-mail: krupert@mail.barry.edu; Website: www.barry.edu/law

The Basics

Type of school	Private
Term	Semester
Application deadline	5/1
Application fee	$60
Financial aid deadline	4/15
Can first year start other than fall?	No
Student to faculty ratio	18.6 to 1
# of housing spaces available restricted to law students	
graduate housing for which law students are eligible	

Faculty and Administrators

	Total		Men		Women		Minorities	
	Spr	Fall	Spr	Fall	Spr	Fall	Spr	Fall
Full-time	25	33	14	20	11	13	6	9
Other full-time	0	0	0	0	0	0	0	0
Deans, librarians, & others who teach	9	5	4	2	5	3	2	1
Part-time	45	25	34	23	11	2	6	4
Total	79	63	52	45	27	18	14	14

Curriculum

	Full-Time	Part-Time
Typical first-year section size	65	55
Is there typically a "small section" of the first-year class, other than Legal Writing, taught by full-time faculty	No	No
If yes, typical size offered last year		

# of classroom course titles beyond first-year curriculum		217	
# of upper division courses, excluding seminars, with an enrollment:	Under 25	129	
	25–49	31	
	50–74	17	
	75–99	10	
	100+	2	
# of seminars		26	
# of seminar positions available		520	
# of seminar positions filled		279	117
# of positions available in simulation courses		755	
# of simulation positions filled		415	214
# of positions available in faculty supervised clinical courses		48	
# of faculty supervised clinical positions filled		23	9
# involved in field placements		34	41
# involved in law journals		48	12
# involved in moot court or trial competitions		44	16
# of credit hours required to graduate		90	

JD Enrollment and Ethnicity

	Men		Women		Full-Time		Part-Time		1st-Year		Total		JD Degs. Awd.
	#	%	#	%	#	%	#	%	#	%	#	%	
All Hispanics	32	8.5	38	11.2	55	9.9	15	9.1	34	13.0	70	9.8	27
Am. Ind./AK Nat.	1	0.3	2	0.6	3	0.5	0	0.0	3	1.1	3	0.4	0
Asian	11	2.9	20	5.9	26	4.7	5	3.0	15	5.7	31	4.3	3
Black/Af. Am.	11	2.9	16	4.7	21	3.8	6	3.7	17	6.5	27	3.8	19
Nat. HI/Pac. Isl.	0	0.0	7	2.1	7	1.3	0	0.0	7	2.7	7	1.0	0
2 or more races	0	0.0	0	0.0	0	0.0	0	0.0	0	0.0	0	0.0	0
Subtotal (minor.)	55	14.6	83	24.4	112	20.3	26	15.9	76	29.1	138	19.2	53
Nonres. Alien	5	1.3	4	1.2	9	1.6	0	0.0	7	2.7	9	1.3	3
White/Cauc.	253	67.1	212	62.4	353	63.8	112	68.3	158	60.5	465	64.9	162
Unknown	64	17.0	41	12.1	79	14.3	26	15.9	20	7.7	105	14.6	28
Total	377	52.6	340	47.4	553	77.1	164	22.9	261	36.4	717		246

Transfers

Transfers in	2
Transfers out	26

Tuition and Fees

	Resident	Nonresident
Full-time	$32,650	$32,650
Part-time	$24,640	$24,640
Tuition Guarantee Program	N	

Living Expenses

Estimated living expenses for singles

Living on campus	Living off campus	Living at home
N/A	$24,150	$24,150

BARRY UNIVERSITY DWAYNE O. ANDREAS SCHOOL OF LAW

*ABA
Approved
Since
2002*

GPA and LSAT Scores

	Total	Full-Time	Part-Time
# of apps	2,238	1,977	261
# of offers	1,248	1,136	112
# of matrics	254	224	30
75% GPA	3.32	3.34	3.30
Median GPA	2.93	2.96	2.90
25% GPA	2.60	2.59	2.63
75% LSAT	154	154	153
Median LSAT	151	151	151
25% LSAT	149	149	149

Grants and Scholarships (from prior year)

	Total		Full-Time		Part-Time	
	#	%	#	%	#	%
Total # of students	771		609		162	
Total # receiving grants	543	70.4	447	73.4	96	59.3
Less than 1/2 tuition	468	60.7	390	64.0	78	48.1
Half to full tuition	75	9.7	57	9.4	18	11.1
Full tuition	0	0.0	0	0.0	0	0.0
More than full tuition	0	0.0	0	0.0	0	0.0
Median grant amount			$8,000		$6,000	

Informational and Library Resources

Total amount spent on library materials	$920,397
Study seating capacity inside the library	346
# of full-time equivalent professional librarians	8
Hours per week library is open	106
# of open, wired connections available to students	0
# of networked computers available for use by students	55
Has wireless network?	Y
Requires computer?	N

JD Attrition (from prior year)

	Academic	Other	Total	
	#	#	#	%
1st year	22	26	48	18.7
2nd year	1	6	7	2.8
3rd year	1	2	3	1.2
4th year	0	1	1	6.7

Employment (9 months after graduation)

	Total	Percentage
Employment status known	164	92.7
Employment status unknown	13	7.3
Employed	114	69.5
Pursuing graduate degrees	4	2.4
Unemployed (seeking, not seeking, or studying for the bar)	39	23.8
Type of Employment		
# employed in law firms	60	52.6
# employed in business and industry	21	18.4
# employed in government	17	14.9
# employed in public interest	6	5.3
# employed as judicial clerks	4	3.5
# employed in academia	5	4.4
Geographic Location		
# employed in state	86	75.4
# employed outside the US	0	0.0
# of states where employed		15

Bar Passage Rates

First-time takers	164	Reporting %	80.49
Average school %	70.45	Average state %	77.81
Average pass difference	−7.36		

Jurisdiction	Takers	Passers	Pass %	State %	Diff %
Florida	132	93	70.45	77.81	−7.36

BARRY UNIVERSITY DWAYNE O. ANDREAS SCHOOL OF LAW

6441 East Colonial Drive
Orlando, FL 32807
Phone: 321.206.5600
E-mail: krupert@mail.barry.edu; Website: www.barry.edu/law

A Growing Presence in Higher Education

Founded in early 1993, the University of Orlando School of Law admitted its first class in 1995. In March of 1999, the School of Law became a part of Barry University, a Catholic international university located in Miami Shores, Florida. The affiliation is an extremely positive one, since both administrations have the same focus—to offer quality academics grounded in a strong ethical foundation with the goal of preparing qualified, competent practicing attorneys.

The School of Law is situated on a charming 20-acre campus in East Orlando, about 15 minutes from downtown. The School of Law facilities include a two-story, 20,000-square-foot Law Center building; a 9,000-square-foot Administration and Moot Court building; a 9,000-square-foot classroom and faculty office building; and a 36,000-square-foot law library.

The Barry Law mission guides everything the law school does, from awarding and maintaining scholarships to arranging mentors, to providing career service, academic success guidance, and bar prep programs. The School of Law is proud of the quality education provided, with an emphasis on social justice and a spiritual dimension, all within a caring environment. Candidates who choose to study at Barry Law will enjoy the benefits of a mission-centered university where students get the attention they need to succeed.

The Perfect Venue for Your Legal Education

Central Florida is one of the fastest growing areas in the country. A host of attractions bring millions of visitors to central Florida each year. Just an hour away are the Kennedy Space Center and the beaches of the Atlantic.

Orlando is a major commercial center; many national corporations have headquarters in the city. The area is fast becoming a television and motion picture production center.

Central Florida provides a wealth of first-hand exposure to the practice of corporate and entertainment law, as well as juvenile and criminal law. The Advisory Board is composed of many prominent central Florida attorneys, judges, government officials, and others in the community. Their community affiliations enhance the networking and career opportunities available to Barry's students.

Central Florida enjoys a year-round subtropical climate and offers a wide range of cultural and recreational activities. Accommodations in the immediate area include fully furnished or unfurnished apartments as well as a wide range of single-family dwellings. Orlando has a large number of hotels and executive lodges that offer reduced rates on a weekly or monthly basis.

Orlando is the ideal venue to pursue your legal education.

Mission and Goals of the School of Law

Barry University School of Law seeks to offer a quality legal education in a caring environment that will enable its graduates to apply the skills and knowledge they have acquired to their own personal development, and to the good of society, through the competent and ethical practice of law. The School of Law seeks to provide a learning environment that challenges students to accept intellectual, personal, ethical, spiritual, and social responsibilities. The school commits itself to assuring a religious dimension in an atmosphere of religious freedom and to providing community service.

An Overview

The School of Law teaches students to become responsible lawyers, trained to assume an active role in the legal community. Students are trained to act in strict accord with the highest ethical standards and to exercise their professional skills competently, with sensitivity to the needs and concerns of their clients.

The School of Law offers a three-year daytime program structured for full-time students. The School of Law also offers a four-year extended studies program in the evening to accommodate working adults or anyone who is unable to pursue full-time study.

Students at the School of Law have many opportunities to experience the "law-in-action" concept, both in the classroom and through practical application. The law school offers a collegial student/professor relationship indicative of legal education at its best.

Through the in-house Children and Families Clinic, Barry students gain solid practical experience working on actual cases involving disadvantaged children in need of legal services. The School of Law also offers an Immigration Clinic and the Earth Justice Clinic, focusing on environmental law. Additionally, Barry Law offers a wealth of externship opportunities that allow students to further develop their skills as emerging attorneys while working in various venues. Externship placement currently includes opportunities in the following areas: civil government, civil poverty, judicial, mediation, public defender, and state attorney.

Juris Doctor

The School of Law offers the Juris Doctor (JD) degree. All students in the program must complete 90 semester hours of study in areas that are essential to the understanding and practice of law. Students in the fall entering class must complete required courses in subjects that provide a common core of understanding in the law. Students may choose from a wide variety of electives to meet the remaining requirements necessary for graduation.

Scholarship Program

The School of Law proudly offers a merit-based scholarship program. Generally, between 80 and 90 percent of the entering class receives a Barry Law scholarship between $1,000 and $23,000. Admitted candidates are automatically considered for scholarships and do not need to complete any additional forms. If a scholarship is offered to a candidate, notice will be sent with the acceptance letter.

Scholarships are offered for three years for full-time students and four years for part-time students. The law GPA required to maintain an institutional scholarship ranges from 2.6 to 3.0. The majority of enrolled students are able to meet the fair and reasonable renewal requirements; for those who do not meet the law GPA, the scholarship can be prorated in some situations and then adjusted to initial levels once the requisite law GPA is achieved. Contact the financial aid office for more questions in this regard.

Barry Law also offers a Scholarship Bonus Program to second- and third-year students. Students who rank in the top 10 percent and hold at least a 3.2 grade-point average after the first and second year of law school are offered a 75 percent scholarship. What great motivation to rank in the top 10 percent, among other obvious reasons!

Program Objective

The School of Law combines traditional and innovative teaching methods to provide a dynamic, professional program. The JD curriculum is designed to develop students' analytical ability, communication skills, and understanding of the codes of professional responsibility and ethics that are central to the practice of law. The faculty utilizes a variety of teaching methods, including simulations and role-playing.

Seminars and advanced courses in the second and third year of study provide close interaction with faculty.

Barry Law emphasizes research and writing proficiency from the first day of class. Armed with a strong foundation in research and writing, Barry Law students gain an advantage in the legal marketplace.

Graduation Requirements

To be eligible to receive the degree of JD, a student must (1) complete 90 academic credits of instruction with a cumulative grade-point average of 2.0 or above, (2) earn a cumulative grade-point average of 1.8 for all required courses and a passing grade in each of the required courses, (3) successfully complete the writing requirement, (4) complete a minimum of 60 out of 90 academic credits in residence at Barry University School of Law, (5) successfully complete the pro bono requirement, (6) satisfy all financial obligations to Barry University, and (7) be approved by the faculty for graduation.

APPLICANT PROFILE

Barry University Dwayne O. Andreas School of Law

LSAT Score	GPA								
	3.75 +	3.50–3.74	3.25–3.49	3.00–3.24	2.75–2.99	2.50–2.74	2.25–2.49	2.00–2.24	Below 2.00
175–180	■	■	■	■	■	■	■	■	□
170–174	■	■	■	■	■	■	■	■	□
165–169	■	■	■	■	■	■	■	■	□
160–164	■	■	■	■	■	■	■	▨	□
155–159	■	■	■	■	■	■	▨	□	□
150–154	■	■	■	■	■	▨	▨	□	□
145–149	▨	▨	▨	▨	▨	▨	□	□	□
140–144	□	□	□	□	□	□	□	□	□
Below 140	□	□	□	□	□	□	□	□	□

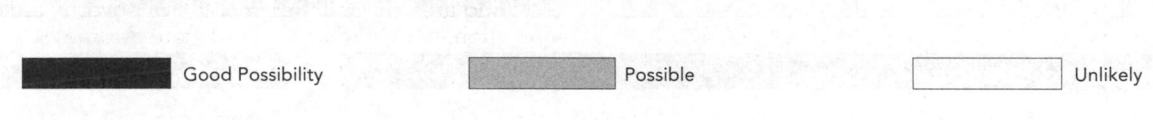

■ Good Possibility   ▨ Possible   □ Unlikely

BAYLOR UNIVERSITY SCHOOL OF LAW

1114 South University Parks Drive, One Bear Place #97288
Waco, TX 76798-7288
Phone: 254.710.2529; Fax: 254.710.2316
E-mail: BaylorLaw@baylor.edu; Website: www.baylor.edu/law

The Basics

Type of school	Private		
Term	Quarter		
Application deadline	11/1	2/1	3/1
Application fee	$40		
Financial aid deadline	2/1		
Can first year start other than fall?	Yes		
Student to faculty ratio	14.8 to 1		
# of housing spaces available restricted to law students graduate housing for which law students are eligible	48		

Faculty and Administrators

	Total		Men		Women		Minorities	
	Spr	Fall	Spr	Fall	Spr	Fall	Spr	Fall
Full-time	25	27	20	21	5	6	4	4
Other full-time	1	0	1	0	0	0	0	0
Deans, librarians, & others who teach	6	5	3	2	3	3	0	0
Part-time	22	18	18	14	4	4	1	1
Total	54	50	42	37	12	13	5	5

Curriculum

	Full-Time	Part-Time
Typical first-year section size	56	0
Is there typically a "small section" of the first-year class, other than Legal Writing, taught by full-time faculty	Yes	No
If yes, typical size offered last year	45	
# of classroom course titles beyond first–year curriculum	90	
# of upper division courses, excluding seminars, with an enrollment: Under 25	84	
25–49	37	
50–74	11	
75-99	12	
100+	0	
# of seminars	5	
# of seminar positions available	106	
# of seminar positions filled	106	0
# of positions available in simulation courses	1,078	
# of simulation positions filled	1,078	0
# of positions available in faculty supervised clinical courses	32	
# of faculty supervised clinical positions filled	32	0
# involved in field placements	128	0
# involved in law journals	86	0
# involved in moot court or trial competitions	68	0
# of credit hours required to graduate	126	

JD Enrollment and Ethnicity

	Men		Women		Full-Time		Part-Time		1st-Year		Total		JD Degs. Awd.
	#	%	#	%	#	%	#	%	#	%	#	%	
All Hispanics	21	8.9	18	7.5	37	7.9	2	20.0	9	4.9	39	8.2	5
Am. Ind./AK Nat.	1	0.4	6	2.5	7	1.5	0	0.0	2	1.1	7	1.5	0
Asian	15	6.3	19	7.9	33	7.1	1	10.0	4	2.2	34	7.1	5
Black/Af. Am.	4	1.7	5	2.1	9	1.9	0	0.0	3	1.6	9	1.9	2
Nat. HI/Pac. Isl.	0	0.0	3	1.3	3	0.6	0	0.0	0	0.0	3	0.6	0
2 or more races	2	0.8	6	2.5	8	1.7	0	0.0	1	0.5	8	1.7	0
Subtotal (minor.)	43	18.1	57	23.8	97	20.8	3	30.0	19	10.4	100	21.0	16
Nonres. Alien	2	0.8	3	1.3	5	1.1	0	0.0	0	0.0	5	1.1	0
White/Cauc.	189	79.7	178	74.5	360	77.3	7	70.0	162	88.5	367	77.1	146
Unknown	3	1.3	1	0.4	4	0.9	0	0.0	2	1.1	4	0.8	0
Total	237	49.8	239	50.2	466	97.9	10	2.1	183	38.4	476		162

Transfers

Transfers in	0
Transfers out	1

Tuition and Fees

	Resident	Nonresident
Full-time	$40,904	$40,904
Part-time		
Tuition Guarantee Program	N	

Living Expenses

Estimated living expenses for singles

Living on campus	Living off campus	Living at home
$17,737	$16,821	$10,608

ABA
Approved
Since
1931

GPA and LSAT Scores

	Fall	Spring	Summer	Total
# of apps	3,122	1,076	515	4,713
# of offers	526	159	93	778
# of matrics	105	50	28	183
75% GPA	3.87	3.81	3.84	3.85
Median GPA	3.73	3.65	3.75	3.71
25% GPA	3.60	3.35	3.16	3.52
75% LSAT	164	161	162	163
Median LSAT	162	159	160	162
25% LSAT	162	156	157	160

Grants and Scholarships (from prior year)

	Total		Full-Time		Part-Time	
	#	%	#	%	#	%
Total # of students	465		465		0	
Total # receiving grants	396	85.2	396	85.2	0	0.0
Less than 1/2 tuition	238	51.2	238	51.2	0	0.0
Half to full tuition	80	17.2	80	17.2	0	0.0
Full tuition	59	12.7	59	12.7	0	0.0
More than full tuition	19	4.1	19	4.1	0	0.0
Median grant amount			$5,754		$0	

Informational and Library Resources

Total amount spent on library materials	$1,289,721
Study seating capacity inside the library	279
# of full-time equivalent professional librarians	6
Hours per week library is open	108
# of open, wired connections available to students	783
# of networked computers available for use by students	44
Has wireless network?	Y
Requires computer?	N

JD Attrition (from prior year)

	Academic	Other	Total	
	#	#	#	%
1st year	1	16	17	8.9
2nd year	2	0	2	1.3
3rd year	0	0	0	0.0
4th year	0	0	0	0.0

Employment (9 months after graduation)

	Total	Percentage
Employment status known	127	97.7
Employment status unknown	3	2.3
Employed	114	89.8
Pursuing graduate degrees	3	2.4
Unemployed (seeking, not seeking, or studying for the bar)	7	5.5
Type of Employment		
# employed in law firms	80	70.2
# employed in business and industry	7	6.1
# employed in government	17	14.9
# employed in public interest	1	0.9
# employed as judicial clerks	7	6.1
# employed in academia	2	1.8
Geographic Location		
# employed in state	93	81.6
# employed outside the US	0	0.0
# of states where employed		15

Bar Passage Rates

First-time takers	124	Reporting %		95.97
Average school %	94.96	Average state %		85.48
Average pass difference	9.48			

Jurisdiction	Takers	Passers	Pass %	State %	Diff %
Texas	119	113	94.96	85.48	9.48

BAYLOR UNIVERSITY SCHOOL OF LAW

1114 South University Parks Drive, One Bear Place #97288
Waco, TX 76798-7288
Phone: 254.710.2529; Fax: 254.710.2316
E-mail: BaylorLaw@baylor.edu; Website: www.baylor.edu/law

Introduction

Baylor University School of Law is a private, ABA-approved law school and is a member of the Association of American Law Schools. Formally organized in 1857, Baylor law school is the oldest law school in Texas and is located on the campus of Baylor University in Waco, Texas. Waco is located in central Texas, has a total area population of over 220,000, and offers a diverse and rich array of cultural and recreational opportunities, as well as very moderate living costs.

Baylor law school stands at the forefront of practice-oriented law schools nationally. Baylor is clear about its mission—to equip students upon graduation to practice law effectively and ethically. Students are trained and mentored in all facets of law, including theoretical analysis, practical application, legal writing, advocacy, professional responsibility, and negotiation and counseling skills.

Enrollment/Diversity

Baylor law school is small by choice, with entering classes of approximately 50 students in the spring, 30 in the summer, and 80 in the fall. Baylor law school has a target student population of 420. We keep our program small because we are interested in producing quality, not quantity.

Baylor law school is deeply committed to enrolling classes that are rich in diversity. Indeed, diversity is an important element of our educational mission. The total minority enrollment in the law school for the fall 2010 term was 21.9 percent. While the Law School Admission Test (LSAT) score and undergraduate grade-point average are strong indicators for academic ability, Baylor is committed to considering carefully all factors of every applicant's application file, including socioeconomic disadvantage, bilingual language skills, work experience, community involvement, leadership roles, and communication skills. These factors enable us to enroll classes that are well qualified and especially distinctive.

Faculty

Baylor law school is committed to providing its students with a classroom and courtroom experience that will prepare them fully for the practice. Faculty members, committed to the equally important missions of teaching and scholarship, hold degrees from law schools and universities throughout the nation and include former law clerks for various appellate courts throughout the nation.

Faculty members are experts in their areas and have substantial practical experience. They produce a significant amount of legal scholarship, which results in their demand as speakers at legal institutes and civic functions. One of the distinctive features of the faculty is that professors maintain unrestricted hours for student consultation. Every professor is available for lending advice and guidance in all academic, professional, and other matters of concern to students.

Facilities and Technology

The home of Baylor law school, the award-winning Sheila and Walter Umphrey Law Center, was dedicated in 2002. At every stage of the design of the Law Center, the most important goal was to put teaching first. The building houses every facility a modern law school requires: classrooms that are unsurpassed as teaching facilities; an advocacy suite, including state-of-the-art courtrooms that provide the optimum environment for advocacy training—Baylor's centerpiece of excellence; a large, two-story appellate advocacy courtroom/classroom; a library with comfortable study and seating space in several impressive reading rooms; a student lounge and patio overlooking the Brazos River; and faculty offices that support faculty mentoring, which is the hallmark of our program.

Technology permeates the Law Center, including data and electric ports at virtually every seat in the building, along with a concurrent wireless network. Classrooms are equipped with cutting-edge technology, including audio, video, and Internet access. The automatic cameras in the courtrooms can be aimed at a desired location in the room through use of joystick controllers mounted in the console tabletops. The law school uses a sophisticated course-management system that allows the faculty to post assignments, syllabi, and course announcements, and provides discussion boards.

Trial Advocacy Program

Procedure is the tool of the trial lawyer, and the bedrock of Baylor law school's nationally ranked advocacy program is Practice Court—an ultra-intensive study of civil procedure. In addition to the science of procedure, students will learn the art of trial advocacy in a rigorous and tough six-month program of skills training during the third year of law school. Students try lawsuits from beginning to end. This course prepares students to be competent, responsible, and ethical lawyers.

Baylor law school has a long record of successfully competing at the national and regional levels in both moot court and mock trial interscholastic competitions. In fact, because of its standing as one of the top advocacy programs in the nation, Baylor law school is consistently invited to the prestigious Tournament of Champions. Baylor law school is also proud to host its own elite invitational trial advocacy competition, the National Top Gun Mock Trial Competition, which includes the top student advocates from other nationally recognized programs.

Curriculum and Special Programs

The required curriculum is structured to provide a logical progression for legal study from fundamental legal doctrine in first-year courses to increasingly more sophisticated and complex second- and third-year courses. The challenging curriculum, along with providing students the opportunity to perform specialized lawyering tasks under the direct supervision of accomplished lawyers, also prepares them for the rigors of any type of modern legal practice. Additionally, students have the opportunity to complete a more concentrated course of study and training in seven areas of interest: general civil litigation, business litigation, business transactions, criminal practice, estate planning, administrative practice, and intellectual property. There are also three joint degrees: JD/MBA, JD/MTax, and JD/MPPA.

Baylor law school views the legal profession as a service endeavor. As such, Baylor law school was honored to receive the 2010 Commitment to Service Award from the Texas

Access to Justice Commitment in recognition of the school's commitment to service.

Scholarships and Financial Aid

Baylor law school has an extraordinarily generous scholarship program. Scholarships are awarded to entering students based primarily on undergraduate GPA and LSAT scores. These scholarships are automatically awarded to students who qualify. Scholarship awards generally range from one-half to full tuition. The law school also participates in nationally recognized financial aid programs. Texas residents are eligible for the Texas Tuition Equalization Grant.

Admission

Baylor law school has three entering classes—spring (February), summer (May), and fall (August)—with completely separate application processes. Each class has far more applications than seats available; however, admission to the spring or summer classes is slightly less competitive than admission to the fall class.

The admissions process considers each application in its entirety and considers many factors beyond test scores and undergraduate GPA. Such factors include employment experience, demonstrated leadership potential, cocurricular and extracurricular activities, ethnicity, academic performance trends, undergraduate major, caliber of undergraduate school, life experience, circumstances of particular disadvantage, and any other relevant information submitted by the applicant. Any factors the applicant would like the Admission Committee to take into consideration should be addressed in a personal statement.

Student Life

Students will find a stimulating variety of enjoyable student activities and organizations that will enhance their legal education. Students can compete interscholastically on Baylor law school's nationally recognized mock trial and moot court teams. Students can hone their writing and legal scholarship abilities by being a member of the *Baylor Law Review*, which is a legal periodical published quarterly by the students under the supervision of faculty. Baylor law school also offers a wide array of "special interest" student organizations focused on particular areas of law.

Career Services and Bar Passage

The Career Development Office is committed year-round to providing students with the support and resources they need in pursuing their chosen career paths. Shortly after graduation, approximately 93 percent of our 2010 graduates seeking employment were employed or enrolled in graduate-degree programs. Baylor law school graduates find positions throughout the nation in private practice in large and small firms, government agencies, judicial clerkships, public interest organizations, and public and private corporations.

The Career Development Office provides extensive one-on-one training on job-search techniques, interview skills, job strategies, and résumé- and cover letter-writing techniques. The office coordinates an on-campus interview program and posts job listings from employers around the country. The office also hosts regular seminars to foster professional development for students.

Our record of success on the Texas bar exam is unsurpassed by any other Texas law school. In July 2010, 94.64 percent of Baylor graduates passed the Texas bar exam the first time. The overall state pass rate was 86.37 percent. Baylor law school has had the highest pass rate 14 times since 2001. Graduates taking other state bar exams have been exceptionally successful as well.

APPLICANT PROFILE

Baylor University School of Law
This grid includes only fall 2010 applicants who earned 120–180 LSAT scores under standard administrations.

LSAT Score	3.75 +		3.50–3.74		3.25–3.49		3.00–3.24		2.75–2.99		2.50–2.74		2.25–2.49		2.00–2.24		Below 2.00		No GPA		Total	
	Apps	Adm	Apps	Adm	Apps	Adm	Apps	Adm	Apps	Adm	Apps	Adm	Apps	Adm	Apps	Adm	Apps	Adm	Apps	Adm	Apps	Adm
175–180	0	0	1	1	0	0	0	0	0	0	0	0	0	0	0	0	0	0	0	0	1	1
170–174	17	15	10	10	13	9	9	0	2	0	1	0	3	0	0	0	0	0	1	1	56	35
165–169	65	64	53	53	50	32	41	1	20	0	15	0	9	1	3	0	1	0	3	1	260	152
160–164	184	128	210	130	186	74	105	4	60	1	42	0	17	0	9	0	0	0	6	1	819	338
155–159	156	0	215	0	190	0	166	0	76	0	55	0	28	0	9	0	1	0	8	0	904	0
150–154	77	0	111	0	113	0	126	0	65	0	31	0	23	0	7	0	1	0	7	0	561	0
145–149	24	0	35	0	55	0	61	0	50	0	25	0	18	0	11	0	3	0	3	0	285	0
140–144	8	0	16	0	18	0	28	0	21	0	18	0	11	0	6	0	0	0	1	0	127	0
135–139	3	0	2	0	6	0	12	0	4	0	11	0	8	0	2	0	1	0	3	0	52	0
130–134	0	0	2	0	1	0	4	0	3	0	7	0	2	0	1	0	2	0	1	0	23	0
125–129	0	0	0	0	0	0	0	0	1	0	0	0	1	0	1	0	0	0	0	0	3	0
120–124	0	0	0	0	0	0	0	0	0	0	1	0	0	0	0	0	0	0	0	0	1	0
Total	534	207	655	194	632	115	552	5	302	1	206	0	120	1	49	0	9	0	33	3	3092	526

Apps = Number of Applicants
Adm = Number Admitted
Reflects 99% of the total fall 2010 applicant pool; highest LSAT data reported.

BOSTON COLLEGE LAW SCHOOL

Office of Admissions, 885 Centre Street
Newton, MA 02459
Phone: 617.552.4351; Fax: 617.552.2917
E-mail: bclawadm@bc.edu; Website: www.bc.edu/law

ABA
Approved
Since
1932

The Basics

Type of school	Private
Term	Semester
Application deadline	3/1
Application fee	$75
Financial aid deadline	3/15
Can first year start other than fall?	No
Student to faculty ratio	13.1 to 1
# of housing spaces available restricted to law students	
graduate housing for which law students are eligible	32

Faculty and Administrators

	Total		Men		Women		Minorities	
	Spr	Fall	Spr	Fall	Spr	Fall	Spr	Fall
Full-time	51	50	30	28	21	22	11	10
Other full-time	2	1	0	0	2	1	0	0
Deans, librarians, & others who teach	12	12	3	3	9	9	1	1
Part-time	39	37	26	29	12	7	1	2
Total	104	100	59	60	44	39	13	13

Curriculum

	Full-Time	Part-Time
Typical first-year section size	88	0
Is there typically a "small section" of the first-year class, other than Legal Writing, taught by full-time faculty	Yes	No
If yes, typical size offered last year	30	
# of classroom course titles beyond first-year curriculum	153	
# of upper division courses, excluding seminars, with an enrollment: Under 25	34	
25–49	20	
50–74	17	
75–99	11	
100+	4	
# of seminars	61	
# of seminar positions available	904	
# of seminar positions filled	719	0
# of positions available in simulation courses	894	
# of simulation positions filled	679	0
# of positions available in faculty supervised clinical courses	119	
# of faculty supervised clinical positions filled	104	0
# involved in field placements	92	0
# involved in law journals	174	0
# involved in moot court or trial competitions	46	0
# of credit hours required to graduate	85	

JD Enrollment and Ethnicity

	Men		Women		Full-Time		Part-Time		1st-Year		Total		JD Degs. Awd.
	#	%	#	%	#	%	#	%	#	%	#	%	
All Hispanics	30	7.3	22	5.7	52	6.5	0	0.0	18	6.9	52	6.5	18
Am. Ind./AK Nat.	1	0.2	2	0.5	3	0.4	0	0.0	0	0.0	3	0.4	3
Asian	35	8.5	56	14.5	91	11.4	0	0.0	21	8.0	91	11.4	20
Black/Af. Am.	11	2.7	20	5.2	31	3.9	0	0.0	12	4.6	31	3.9	10
Nat. HI/Pac. Isl.	0	0.0	0	0.0	0	0.0	0	0.0	0	0.0	0	0.0	0
2 or more races	4	1.0	6	1.6	10	1.3	0	0.0	9	3.4	10	1.3	0
Subtotal (minor.)	81	19.8	106	27.4	187	23.5	0	0.0	60	23.0	187	23.5	51
Nonres. Alien	6	1.5	8	2.1	14	1.8	0	0.0	6	2.3	14	1.8	0
White/Cauc.	280	68.3	242	62.5	521	65.5	0	100.0	157	60.2	522	65.5	188
Unknown	43	10.5	31	8.0	74	9.3	0	0.0	38	14.6	74	9.3	16
Total	410	51.4	387	48.6	796	99.9	0	0.1	261	32.7	797		260

Transfers

Transfers in	7
Transfers out	6

Tuition and Fees

	Resident	Nonresident
Full-time	$40,905	$40,905
Part-time		
Tuition Guarantee Program	N	

Living Expenses

Estimated living expenses for singles

Living on campus	Living off campus	Living at home
N/A	$18,690	N/A

BOSTON COLLEGE LAW SCHOOL

ABA
Approved
Since
1932

GPA and LSAT Scores

	Total	Full-Time	Part-Time
# of apps	6,873	6,873	0
# of offers	1,359	1,359	0
# of matrics	261	261	0
75% GPA	3.70	3.70	0.00
Median GPA	3.61	3.61	0.00
25% GPA	3.45	3.45	0.00
75% LSAT	167	167	0
Median LSAT	166	166	0
25% LSAT	163	163	0

Grants and Scholarships (from prior year)

	Total		Full-Time		Part-Time	
	#	%	#	%	#	%
Total # of students	814		812		0	
Total # receiving grants	424	52.1	424	52.2	0	0.0
Less than 1/2 tuition	232	28.5	232	28.6	0	0.0
Half to full tuition	188	23.1	188	23.2	0	0.0
Full tuition	3	0.4	3	0.4	0	0.0
More than full tuition	1	0.1	1	0.1	0	0.0
Median grant amount		$15,000			$0	

Informational and Library Resources

Total amount spent on library materials	$1,521,518
Study seating capacity inside the library	673
# of full-time equivalent professional librarians	10
Hours per week library is open	105
# of open, wired connections available to students	1,014
# of networked computers available for use by students	143
Has wireless network?	Y
Requires computer?	N

JD Attrition (from prior year)

	Academic	Other	Total	
	#	#	#	%
1st year	1	9	10	3.8
2nd year	0	1	1	0.3
3rd year	0	0	0	0.0
4th year	0	0	0	0.0

Employment (9 months after graduation)

	Total	Percentage
Employment status known	244	99.6
Employment status unknown	1	0.4
Employed	231	94.7
Pursuing graduate degrees	4	1.6
Unemployed (seeking, not seeking, or studying for the bar)	5	2.0
Type of Employment		
# employed in law firms	158	68.4
# employed in business and industry	17	7.4
# employed in government	12	5.2
# employed in public interest	12	5.2
# employed as judicial clerks	19	8.2
# employed in academia	12	5.2
Geographic Location		
# employed in state	115	49.8
# employed outside the US	2	0.9
# of states where employed		23

Bar Passage Rates

First-time takers	242	Reporting %	92.56
Average school %	95.54	Average state %	88.62
Average pass difference	6.92		

Jurisdiction	Takers	Passers	Pass %	State %	Diff %
Massachusetts	145	138	95.17	89.77	5.40
New York	79	76	96.20	86.51	9.69

BOSTON COLLEGE LAW SCHOOL

Office of Admissions, 885 Centre Street
Newton, MA 02459
Phone: 617.552.4351; Fax: 617.552.2917
E-mail: bclawadm@bc.edu; Website: www.bc.edu/law

Introduction

Since its founding in 1929, Boston College Law School has earned a national reputation for educational excellence and the highest standards of professionalism while fostering a unique spirit of community among its students, faculty, and staff. The diverse curriculum is designed to help students develop the skills and knowledge needed to adapt successfully to changes in society and the legal profession. Boston College Law School is located on an attractive 40-acre campus in Newton, Massachusetts, just minutes from downtown Boston. It is fully accredited and has a chapter of the Order of the Coif, the prestigious national law school honorary society.

Library and Physical Facilities

Stretched over 40 acres of rolling hills and gently sloping lawns, the BC Law campus is an intriguing mix of old-style elegance and new-world innovation—a testament to the power of technology, engineering, and design. Students can connect to the network anywhere. Data ports are available from every library carrel, as well as every classroom seat in the East Wing; wireless technology is also available anywhere in the library and in every classroom. The library encourages individual or group study, with its desk and lounge areas, computer centers, audiovisual resource rooms, and private study rooms. Each computer center is fully equipped for searching LexisNexis and Westlaw databases; legal periodical literature; official publications of Massachusetts, the United States, and the United Nations; and other legal indices. With its soaring atrium entry and light-filled spaces, the East Wing includes classrooms and faculty offices, administrative offices for a Career Services Center and a Career Resources Library, two conference rooms, and the John J. and Mary Daly Curtin Public Interest Center (a suite of offices for student groups working on public service projects). The East Wing's brick exterior complements the law library and the Stuart House administration building, as well as the Barat House alumni and development building. The three buildings form an attractive interior courtyard for outdoor use by the law school community.

All academic, administrative, library, and service facilities are accessible to physically challenged persons.

Curriculum

The faculty of Boston College Law School strongly believes in the importance of a general legal education designed to enable graduates to adapt to the changing demands of law practice. Areas of particular focus include international law, constitutional law, business law, dispute resolution, immigration law, environmental law, criminal law, family law, tax law, intellectual property law, and clinical programs.

In the first year, all students take traditional courses, including Civil Procedure, Constitutional Law, Contracts, Property Law, Criminal Law, and Torts. In addition, an intensive, two-semester Legal Reasoning, Research, and Writing course is required. In the spring semester, students are allowed to take one three-credit elective. More than 100 courses offered in the second and third years are elective.

Externships

The **Semester in Practice** program offers individually designed placement with judges, government agencies, public interest organizations, and law firms in the greater Boston area. The **International Human Rights** semester in practice offers a unique opportunity to work at an international human rights organization such as the International Criminal Court, the Special Tribunal for Cambodia, the Inter-American Court of Human Rights, the Jesuit Refugee Service, and internationally-oriented NGOs in the US. The course is designed to provide students with real-world experience and critical insight into international legal institutions, and to prepare them for international legal practice, with special emphasis on human rights. The **Attorney General Program** provides an intensive full-year clinical experience in the Government Bureau of the Massachusetts Office of the Attorney General. The **Judicial Process** course includes placement with a specific superior court justice. The **London Program** has both academic and experiential components. The program provides students with a critical insight into comparative legal institutions with special emphasis on international regulatory process, whether in environmental or securities regulation, antitrust, intellectual property, or human rights.

Clinical Programs

The Law School is committed to making clinical experiences available to all students who desire them. At the **Boston College Legal Assistance Bureau** (LAB), students assume responsibility for representation of indigent clients through the **Civil Litigation**, **Housing**, **Women and the Law,** and **Community Enterprise** clinics.

Students in the **Criminal Justice Clinic** prosecute or defend criminal cases in state court. The **Judge and Community Courts** class examines the interaction between the local court and the community it serves. In **Juvenile Rights Advocacy**, students advocate for troubled youth and work toward juvenile justice policy reform. In the **Immigration Law Clinic**, students advise clients and work on administrative and appellate litigation under the supervision of practicing attorneys.

Extracurricular and Cocurricular Activities

Selected students may participate in the following writing programs: *Boston College Law Review, Boston College Environmental Affairs Law Review, Boston College International and Comparative Law Review, Boston College Third World Law Journal,* and the *Uniform Commercial Code Reporter-Digest.*

Boston College Law School supports over a dozen different competitions, including negotiation, client counseling, moot court, and mock trial. In addition, selected students may compete in national moot court competitions. These competitions allow students to enhance negotiation, counseling, and oral advocacy skills. Over the years, Boston College has performed extremely well in regional and national competitions, which are judged by faculty, state and federal judges, and practicing attorneys.

Admission

The Law School has no minimum cutoff either for GPA or LSAT. Academic achievement and LSAT scores are extremely significant, but work and professional experience, college extracurricular activities, the quality of recommendations, and the personal statement also play an important role in decision making.

In evaluating the undergraduate record, class rank as well as courses taken are considered. If the LSAT has been taken more than once, all scores are considered in the review process. Boston College Law School strongly encourages applications from qualified minority, disabled, or other students who have been socially, economically, or culturally disadvantaged. Each applicant is evaluated in an effort to ensure that all relevant credentials are favorably considered. The Law School has been very successful both in admitting minority and special students and in retaining them to graduation.

Expenses and Financial Aid

The Financial Aid Office administers the Law School's scholarship and grant programs, federal and private loan programs, and the Federal Work-Study Program. Scholarship funds are awarded on the basis of both need and merit. Approximately 83 percent of the students currently enrolled are awarded financial aid and 50 percent of these students receive scholarship and grant assistance as part of their financial aid awards. Each year, three entering students are awarded full-tuition Public Service Scholarships because of their demonstrated commitment to public interest law. The Law School also offers a Loan Repayment Assistance Program for graduates who pursue careers in legal services, government, and not-for-profit corporations.

Housing

The Office of Residential Life offers a limited number of leased residences to full-time Boston College graduate students. Residences are located in the Brighton area within a one-mile radius of our campus. In addition, the Boston College Off-Campus Housing Office provides information about neighborhoods, lists of local rental agencies, maps of local areas, and public transportation information. The office also maintains housing listings that include house rentals and renting rooms in private homes and apartments. In addition, a graduate housing fair is held in June to assist students in their housing search. For more information, please visit the Office of Residential Life website at www.bc.edu/offices/reslife/.

Career Services

The Office of Career Services is dedicated to helping students make the transition from law student to employed professional. The range of opportunities for graduates spans virtually the entire spectrum of legal practice. Each year more than 1,000 prospective employers solicit applications from Boston College law students. During the 2009–2010 recruitment season, approximately 270 law firms, government agencies, corporations, and public interest organizations from 25 states interviewed Boston College students as part of on- and off-campus recruiting programs and an additional 150 employers requested résumé collections. More than 12,000 alumni are presently practicing in 50 states and 19 foreign countries.

APPLICANT PROFILE

Boston College Law School
This grid includes only applicants who earned 120–180 LSAT scores under standard administrations.

LSAT Score	GPA															
	3.75 +		3.50–3.74		3.25–3.49		3.00–3.24		2.75–2.99		Below 2.75		No GPA		Total	
	Apps	Adm	Apps	Adm	Apps	Adm	Apps	Adm	Apps	Adm	Apps	Adm	Apps	Adm	Apps	Adm
175–180	13	9	15	11	16	8	8	3	6	0	2	0	0	0	60	31
170–174	89	76	112	79	114	55	52	12	28	1	14	0	3	0	412	223
165–169	365	269	568	345	377	141	178	27	55	4	36	0	33	10	1612	796
160–164	602	121	854	102	601	29	267	10	90	1	48	0	53	1	2515	264
150–159	338	24	494	19	423	9	277	6	115	0	82	0	51	0	1780	58
140–149	39	0	75	0	84	0	87	0	59	0	59	0	15	0	418	0
Below 140	4	0	4	0	15	0	16	0	13	0	27	0	8	0	87	0
Total	1450	499	2122	556	1630	242	885	58	366	6	268	0	163	11	6884	1372

Apps = Number of Applicants
Adm = Number Admitted
Reflects 99% of the total applicant pool; highest LSAT data reported.

BOSTON UNIVERSITY SCHOOL OF LAW

765 Commonwealth Avenue
Boston, MA 02215
Phone: 617.353.3100
E-mail: bulawadm@bu.edu; Website: www.bu.edu/law

The Basics

Type of school	Private
Term	Semester
Application deadline	3/1
Application fee	$75
Financial aid deadline	3/1
Can first year start other than fall?	No
Student to faculty ratio	11.4 to 1
# of housing spaces available restricted to law students	
graduate housing for which law students are eligible	810

Faculty and Administrators

	Total		Men		Women		Minorities	
	Spr	Fall	Spr	Fall	Spr	Fall	Spr	Fall
Full-time	53	65	31	36	22	29	7	9
Other full-time	4	2	4	2	0	0	2	0
Deans, librarians, & others who teach	8	8	4	4	4	4	0	0
Part-time	87	79	58	58	29	21	12	9
Total	152	154	97	100	55	54	21	18

Curriculum

	Full-Time	Part-Time
Typical first-year section size	90	0

	Yes	No
Is there typically a "small section" of the first-year class, other than Legal Writing, taught by full-time faculty	Yes	No
If yes, typical size offered last year	45	

# of classroom course titles beyond first-year curriculum		196
# of upper division courses, excluding seminars, with an enrollment:	Under 25	94
	25–49	56
	50–74	8
	75–99	7
	100+	5
# of seminars		82
# of seminar positions available		1,494
# of seminar positions filled	1,251	0
# of positions available in simulation courses		481
# of simulation positions filled	438	0
# of positions available in faculty supervised clinical courses		189
# of faculty supervised clinical positions filled	140	0
# involved in field placements	71	0
# involved in law journals	323	0
# involved in moot court or trial competitions	40	0
# of credit hours required to graduate		84

JD Enrollment and Ethnicity

	Men		Women		Full-Time		Part-Time		1st-Year		Total		JD Degs. Awd.
	#	%	#	%	#	%	#	%	#	%	#	%	
All Hispanics	35	8.5	32	7.8	67	8.2	0	0.0	26	9.7	67	8.2	8
Am. Ind./AK Nat.	0	0.0	3	0.7	3	0.4	0	0.0	3	1.1	3	0.4	0
Asian	27	6.6	55	13.3	82	10.0	0	0.0	31	11.6	82	10.0	29
Black/Af. Am.	15	3.7	27	6.6	42	5.1	0	0.0	11	4.1	42	5.1	9
Nat. HI/Pac. Isl.	1	0.2	1	0.2	2	0.2	0	0.0	0	0.0	2	0.2	0
2 or more races	9	2.2	4	1.0	13	1.6	0	0.0	4	1.5	13	1.6	0
Subtotal (minor.)	87	21.2	122	29.6	209	25.5	0	0.0	75	28.0	209	25.4	46
Nonres. Alien	8	2.0	14	3.4	22	2.7	0	0.0	5	1.9	22	2.7	0
White/Cauc.	288	70.2	236	57.3	523	63.7	1	100.0	161	60.1	524	63.7	190
Unknown	27	6.6	40	9.7	67	8.2	0	0.0	27	10.1	67	8.2	21
Total	410	49.9	412	50.1	821	99.9	1	0.1	268	32.6	822		270

Transfers

Transfers in	16
Transfers out	15

Tuition and Fees

	Resident	Nonresident
Full-time	$40,838	
Part-time		
Tuition Guarantee Program	N	

Living Expenses

Estimated living expenses for singles

Living on campus	Living off campus	Living at home
$17,618	$17,618	$12,730

BOSTON UNIVERSITY SCHOOL OF LAW

ABA Approved Since 1925

GPA and LSAT Scores

	Total	Full-Time	Part-Time
# of apps	8,515	8,515	0
# of offers	1,747	1,747	0
# of matrics	268	268	0
75% GPA	3.83	3.83	0.00
Median GPA	3.72	3.72	0.00
25% GPA	3.52	3.52	0.00
75% LSAT	167	167	0
Median LSAT	166	166	0
25% LSAT	164	164	0

Grants and Scholarships (from prior year)

	Total		Full-Time		Part-Time	
	#	%	#	%	#	%
Total # of students	830		827		3	
Total # receiving grants	534	64.3	534	64.6	0	0.0
Less than 1/2 tuition	297	35.8	297	35.9	0	0.0
Half to full tuition	217	26.1	217	26.2	0	0.0
Full tuition	0	0.0	0	0.0	0	0.0
More than full tuition	20	2.4	20	2.4	0	0.0
Median grant amount			$15,000		$0	

Informational and Library Resources

Total amount spent on library materials	$1,758,253
Study seating capacity inside the library	600
# of full-time equivalent professional librarians	11
Hours per week library is open	102
# of open, wired connections available to students	22
# of networked computers available for use by students	94
Has wireless network?	Y
Requires computer?	N

JD Attrition (from prior year)

	Academic	Other	Total	
	#	#	#	%
1st year	0	18	18	6.6
2nd year	0	5	5	1.8
3rd year	1	0	1	0.4
4th year	0	0	0	0.0

Employment (9 months after graduation)

	Total	Percentage
Employment status known	268	99.6
Employment status unknown	1	0.4
Employed	254	94.8
Pursuing graduate degrees	7	2.6
Unemployed (seeking, not seeking, or studying for the bar)	6	2.2
Type of Employment		
# employed in law firms	159	62.6
# employed in business and industry	15	5.9
# employed in government	10	3.9
# employed in public interest	3	1.2
# employed as judicial clerks	22	8.7
# employed in academia	44	17.3
Geographic Location		
# employed in state	126	49.6
# employed outside the US	6	2.4
# of states where employed	24	

Bar Passage Rates

First-time takers	265	Reporting %	92.08
Average school %	96.31	Average state %	88.54
Average pass difference	7.77		

Jurisdiction	Takers	Passers	Pass %	State %	Diff %
Massachusetts	152	146	96.05	89.77	6.28
New York	92	89	96.74	86.51	10.23

BOSTON UNIVERSITY SCHOOL OF LAW

765 Commonwealth Avenue
Boston, MA 02215
Phone: 617.353.3100
E-mail: bulawadm@bu.edu; Website: www.bu.edu/law

Introduction

Boston University School of Law offers one of the finest legal educations in the nation, attracting students from all over the country and abroad. A pioneer in American legal education, the school was founded in 1872 on the principles that legal education should be open to all men and women of ability without regard to background or beliefs, and that it should balance theory and analysis with practical training. Today, the school's innovative curriculum combines theoretical courses, clinical training, and specialized offerings—including concentrations, dual degrees, and semesters abroad. The full-time faculty of distinguished scholars and teachers ranks among the most productive of the nation's law schools and is known for its superb teaching. The students represent a range of educational backgrounds, ethnicities, races, age groups, and employment histories.

The city of Boston is a great place to study law and launch a career. BU Law's location presents students with enormous opportunities. They can gain invaluable experience through the myriad job and internship opportunities that flow from Boston's status as a major business, financial, and legal center. Boston is home to many high-tech and start-up companies, as well as leading institutions in health care, finance, and many other fields. In addition, Boston is a major government center. It is both the state capital and the home of numerous federal institutions such as the Federal Reserve Bank of Boston, making the city a laboratory for clinics, pro bono volunteering, and externships.

Faculty

At BU Law, our faculty members make the difference—to our students, as teachers; to the law, as scholars; and to the local and global community, as advocates. Our students routinely cite the faculty's excellence in teaching as one of the chief virtues of the school. BU Law faculty members come from a range of backgrounds, and include six US Supreme Court clerks and representatives of such diverse intellectual movements as law and economics and feminist legal theory. Fourteen faculty members have doctoral degrees in various disciplines and dozens have extensive experience shaping public policy and representing clients. They have authored texts in key fields, such as securitization, labor and employment, federal courts, contracts, copyright, and administrative law, among others. Impassioned advocates who frequently lend their expertise to pro bono causes—locally, nationally, and internationally—BU Law faculty members take pride in sharing these experiences inside and outside of the classroom.

Curriculum

BU Law offers one of the widest ranges of academic opportunities available at any American law school. At BU Law, students can explore virtually any area of law from among the school's 150 classes and seminars. They can concentrate and focus their studies, if they choose, in any of five important fields—international law, health law, intellectual property law, business organizations and finance law, or litigation and dispute resolution—and thus, design a

curriculum around courses that prepare them for exciting work in specific areas of interest.

Dual-Degree Programs

Students can pursue any of 11 dual-degree programs, combining law study with graduate coursework in a program that leads to a JD and a master's degree. Those dual degrees include a JD/MA in International Relations, JD/MS in Mass Communications, JD/MBA, JD/MBA in Health Sector Management, JD/MA in Preservation Studies, JD/MA in Philosophy, and JD/MPH in Public Health. Students interested in tax or banking can earn a combined JD/Master of Laws (LLM) degree in these fields on an accelerated basis. BU Law recently launched two three-year, international dual-degree programs leading to a JD from Boston University simultaneously with an LLM in European Law from the Université Panthéon-Assas (Paris II), or an LLM in Asian Legal Studies from the National University of Singapore.

Study Abroad

Students at BU Law can immerse themselves in a foreign legal culture for a semester, studying international and comparative law in one of BU Law's 13 semester-long, study-abroad programs. Programs offered in 2010–2011 include Oxford University (United Kingdom); Université Jean Moulin Lyon III (France); Universidad Pontificia Comillas de Madrid (Spain); Leiden University (the Netherlands); Bucerius Law School, Hamburg (Germany); Université Panthéon-Assas, Paris II (France); University of Florence (Italy); University of Hong Kong (China); Tsinghua University (China); University of Buenos Aires (Argentina); Tel Aviv University (Israel); National University of Singapore (Singapore); and the Graduate Institute of International and Development Studies, Geneva (Switzerland).

Clinical Programs

For hands-on practical training, BU Law has long been recognized for having some of the finest clinical offerings in the country. Students can gain valuable experience through the Criminal Litigation Program (Prosecution, Adult and Juvenile Defense); the Civil Litigation Program (Housing, Employment, Family, and Disability Clinic; the Asylum and Human Rights Clinic; and the Employment Rights Clinic); the Semester in Practice Program (in Washington, DC; Atlanta, Georgia; or Geneva, Switzerland); the Community Courts Program (in which students spend one day per week in a community-based court); the Legal Externship Program (placements in judges' chambers, law firms, government agencies, and public interest organizations); and the Health Law Externship Program. BU Law's Legislative Clinic includes the Africa i-Parliaments Clinic, American Legislative Practice, and the Legislative Policy and Drafting Clinic.

Public Interest Programs

BU Law has a long tradition of training public service leaders. The BU Law Career Development and Public Service Office (CDO) runs an in-house Pro Bono program and helps provide pathways to public interest employment. While still in school, students have participated in—and sometimes created!—any number of pro bono projects. Every year, they also join Spring Break Pro Bono Trips to such locations as New Orleans, Louisiana, to address post-Hurricane Katrina legal issues; Harlingen, Texas, to assist with the South Texas Pro Bono Asylum Representation Project; Detroit, Michigan, to provide legal services to the country's poorest urban residents; Montpelier, Vermont, to provide assistance in the Public Defender's Office; and Phnom Penh, Cambodia, to work with an NGO dedicated to fighting human trafficking. The Public Interest Project (PIP) provides grants through fundraising efforts to support students working in summer public interest jobs.

Student Life

Students are encouraged to engage in student organizations, extracurricular activities, and community service. BU Law supports six nationally recognized law journals run by students. The Dean hosts lunches and town hall meetings with students to provide updates and solicit feedback. The school frequently organizes brown bag lunches for students with faculty speakers. The Student Government Association (SGA) and the more than 30 active student organizations work on projects initiated by students. The Live Well, Learn Well program helps law students find ways to maintain healthy lifestyles consistent with their busy lives. The Academic Enhancement Program features workshops on issues such as work/family balance; law school exam-taking strategies; and time and stress management. A comprehensive Diversity Month program includes speakers and panel discussions on legal and social issues related to diversity, as well as social events celebrating cultural differences.

Career Development

The BU Law Career Development and Public Service Office (CDO) is committed to helping each law student see all the possibilities that a BU Law degree affords them. The CDO offers a comprehensive program of services to students and alumni including personal advising, instructional workshops and events, and print and online resources. Students benefit from the expertise of a diverse range of attorney career advisers and participate in numerous workshops to hone job search skills and learn strategies for choosing a career that fits the student's interests and talents. Alumni assist students in the Mock Interview Program, the First-Year Mentoring Program, and participate in panel discussions, receptions, and individual advising sessions. BU Law offers an extensive on- and off-campus recruiting program. Hundreds of employers from every practice type and setting recruit BU Law students. Our graduates pursue careers throughout the US and around the world in large, mid-size, and small law firms; federal, state, and local government; nonprofit organizations; business; and academia. In 2009, 97 percent of graduates were employed within nine months of graduation, and BU Law remains committed to preparing all of its graduates with the substantive knowledge, practical legal skills, networking opportunities, and job search strategies to meet today's challenges in the legal employment market.

Financial Aid

Boston University School of Law is committed to making a legal education affordable. Through scholarship awards as well as federal and private loans, the School of Law provides funding for over 80 percent of its enrolled JD students. BU Law assists approximately 65 percent of JD students with scholarship aid awarded on the basis of academic merit and financial need. With the exception of our merit-only scholarships, students need to apply for scholarship aid and should follow the complete instructions that are available on our website. BU Law offers support during and after law school to students pursuing a career in public interest law. Our Public Interest Scholars Program provides substantial financial support to a select group of students who have been engaged in public interest work prior to law school, and who plan to pursue a career in public service. In addition, alumni pursuing public interest careers are eligible to participate in our Loan Repayment Assistance Program.

APPLICANT PROFILE

Each year Boston University School of Law enrolls a class of students characterized by extraordinary academic achievements and diverse life experiences. LSAT scores and undergraduate GPAs are important components of an application, but numbers alone never determine an admissions decision. The Admissions Committee carefully evaluates each applicant's essays, transcripts, letters of recommendation, and any other information that helps us to understand the applicant's potential. BU Law's founding commitment to diversity, starting in 1872, continues to inform our admissions decisions today. We encourage each applicant to share with us how they might contribute to BU Law's vibrant learning community. The Admissions Committee is not looking for any one quality or set of experiences but seeks to enroll a class that represents the widest range of human experience and aspiration.

BRIGHAM YOUNG UNIVERSITY—J. REUBEN CLARK LAW SCHOOL

340 JRCB
Provo, UT 84602-8000
Phone: 801.422.4277; Fax: 801.422.0389
E-mail: admissions@law.byu.edu; Website: www.law.byu.edu

ABA
Approved
Since
1974

The Basics

Type of school	Private
Term	Semester
Application deadline	3/1
Application fee	$50
Financial aid deadline	5/1
Can first year start other than fall?	No
Student to faculty ratio	18.1 to 1
# of housing spaces available restricted to law students	
graduate housing for which law students are eligible	

Faculty and Administrators

	Total		Men		Women		Minorities	
	Spr	Fall	Spr	Fall	Spr	Fall	Spr	Fall
Full-time	22	19	16	13	6	6	2	3
Other full-time	0	0	0	0	0	0	0	0
Deans, librarians, & others who teach	18	18	14	14	4	4	1	1
Part-time	32	43	21	32	11	11	2	2
Total	72	80	51	59	21	21	5	6

Curriculum

	Full-Time	Part-Time
Typical first-year section size	75	0
Is there typically a "small section" of the first-year class, other than Legal Writing, taught by full-time faculty	Yes	No
If yes, typical size offered last year	50	
# of classroom course titles beyond first–year curriculum		124
# of upper division courses, excluding seminars, with an enrollment: Under 25		50
25–49		23
50–74		8
75-99		1
100+		4
# of seminars		28
# of seminar positions available		567
# of seminar positions filled	344	0
# of positions available in simulation courses		769
# of simulation positions filled	603	0
# of positions available in faculty supervised clinical courses		12
# of faculty supervised clinical positions filled	10	0
# involved in field placements	252	0
# involved in law journals	192	0
# involved in moot court or trial competitions	115	0
# of credit hours required to graduate		90

JD Enrollment and Ethnicity

	Men		Women		Full-Time		Part-Time		1st-Year		Total		JD Degs. Awd.
	#	%	#	%	#	%	#	%	#	%	#	%	
All Hispanics	17	5.9	8	5.1	25	5.6	0	0.0	10	6.7	25	5.6	8
Am. Ind./AK Nat.	2	0.7	1	0.6	3	0.7	0	0.0	0	0.0	3	0.7	2
Asian	11	3.8	9	5.8	20	4.5	0	0.0	3	2.0	20	4.5	3
Black/Af. Am.	3	1.0	3	1.9	6	1.4	0	0.0	2	1.3	6	1.4	3
Nat. HI/Pac. Isl.	12	4.2	4	2.6	16	3.6	0	0.0	8	5.4	16	3.6	0
2 or more races	0	0.0	0	0.0	0	0.0	0	0.0	0	0.0	0	0.0	0
Subtotal (minor.)	45	15.6	25	16.0	70	15.8	0	0.0	23	15.4	70	15.8	21
Nonres. Alien	0	0.0	4	2.6	4	0.9	0	0.0	1	0.7	4	0.9	0
White/Cauc.	243	84.4	127	81.4	369	83.3	1	100.0	125	83.9	370	83.3	115
Unknown	0	0.0	0	0.0	0	0.0	0	0.0	0	0.0	0	0.0	8
Total	288	64.9	156	35.1	443	99.8	1	0.2	149	33.6	444		145

Transfers

Transfers in	2
Transfers out	2

Tuition and Fees

	Resident	Nonresident
Full-time	$10,280	$20,560
Part-time		
Tuition Guarantee Program	N	

Living Expenses

Estimated living expenses for singles

Living on campus	Living off campus	Living at home
$12,600	$12,600	$5,450

BRIGHAM YOUNG UNIVERSITY—J. REUBEN CLARK LAW SCHOOL

*ABA
Approved
Since
1974*

GPA and LSAT Scores

	Total	Full-Time	Part-Time
# of apps	772	772	0
# of offers	219	219	0
# of matrics	150	150	0
75% GPA	3.86	3.86	0.00
Median GPA	3.75	3.75	0.00
25% GPA	3.45	3.45	0.00
75% LSAT	167	167	0
Median LSAT	164	164	0
25% LSAT	161	161	0

Grants and Scholarships (from prior year)

	Total		Full-Time		Part-Time	
	#	%	#	%	#	%
Total # of students	447		447		0	
Total # receiving grants	136	30.4	136	30.4	0	0.0
Less than 1/2 tuition	51	11.4	51	11.4	0	0.0
Half to full tuition	42	9.4	42	9.4	0	0.0
Full tuition	40	8.9	40	8.9	0	0.0
More than full tuition	3	0.7	3	0.7	0	0.0
Median grant amount			$4,990		$0	

Informational and Library Resources

Total amount spent on library materials	$1,091,047
Study seating capacity inside the library	906
# of full-time equivalent professional librarians	11
Hours per week library is open	105
# of open, wired connections available to students	533
# of networked computers available for use by students	28
Has wireless network?	Y
Requires computer?	Y

JD Attrition (from prior year)

	Academic	Other	Total	
	#	#	#	%
1st year	0	0	0	0.0
2nd year	1	3	4	2.6
3rd year	0	2	2	1.3
4th year	0	0	0	0.0

Employment (9 months after graduation)

	Total	Percentage
Employment status known	150	100.0
Employment status unknown	0	0.0
Employed	140	93.3
Pursuing graduate degrees	1	0.7
Unemployed (seeking, not seeking, or studying for the bar)	2	1.3
Type of Employment		
# employed in law firms	90	64.3
# employed in business and industry	22	15.7
# employed in government	12	8.6
# employed in public interest	0	0.0
# employed as judicial clerks	13	9.3
# employed in academia	3	2.1
Geographic Location		
# employed in state	62	44.3
# employed outside the US	0	0.0
# of states where employed		22

Bar Passage Rates

First-time takers	145	Reporting %	80.00
Average school %	88.79	Average state %	84.18
Average pass difference	4.61		

Jurisdiction	Takers	Passers	Pass %	State %	Diff %
Utah	81	73	90.12	88.94	1.18
California	35	30	85.71	73.19	12.52

The information on these pages was provided by the law school.

BRIGHAM YOUNG UNIVERSITY—J. REUBEN CLARK LAW SCHOOL

340 JRCB
Provo, UT 84602-8000
Phone: 801.422.4277; Fax: 801.422.0389
E-mail: admissions@law.byu.edu; Website: www.law.byu.edu

Introduction

Since its founding just over 30 years ago, the J. Reuben Clark Law School at Brigham Young University has been distinguished by the strength of its program and the accomplishments of its graduates. The Law School has produced 13 United States Supreme Court clerkships and has an enviable placement record throughout the country in all branches of the legal profession. The Law School's relatively small entering class size of 150 lends itself to individualized instruction, while the university, with its 30,000 students, provides all the athletic, cultural, and social opportunities that a student may expect from a larger school. The Law School is fully accredited by the American Bar Association, is a member of the Association of American Law Schools, and has a chapter of the Order of the Coif.

Library and Physical Facilities

The Howard W. Hunter Law Library is one of the most technologically advanced law libraries in the world. It houses 475 individual study carrels with full Internet and LAN computer connectivity (hardwired and wireless). Thus, each student in his or her private study space has access to electronic resources that include Westlaw, LexisNexis, and the growing Hunter Law Library Electronic Reserve, which contains archives of past examinations. In convenient locations, printers, copy machines, and scanners are available for students on all library floors. The law library also contains 18 group-study rooms (4 of which are family-support rooms to assist parents who need to view closed-circuit broadcasts of classes) and spacious casual seating in open areas. Office and research space, along with a conference room for the Law School's four scholarly journals, two advocacy groups, and the Student Bar Association, are also conveniently located in the library. Specialized rooms are dedicated to video viewing, interactive video, microforms, and television hookups. The Rex E. Lee Reading Room and the fourth floor Quiet Reading Room provide ample space for special seminars and receptions. The library houses a collection of over 500,000 volumes or volume equivalents. Via interlibrary loan, students have access to many more titles found in the catalogs and collections of over 9,100 other worldwide institutions that, like Hunter Library, subscribe to the Online Computer Library Center.

Faculty and Curriculum

The combination of the small entering class size and our internationally renowned faculty creates unique opportunities for learning. Together, our faculty seek to meet the challenge of making a difference worldwide as they engage in joint research, publishing, and advocacy. The objective of the Law School's curriculum is to maximize the students' mastery of legal reasoning and legal methods while teaching a core of the basic substantive rules of the law. Approximately 150 courses and seminars are offered each year by a faculty of 26 full-time members and over 70 adjunct faculty members. In addition, the Law School provides opportunities for students to develop practical skills through international and US externships with private law firms, corporations, and

agencies, as well as public defenders, legal services, city and county attorneys, judges, attorneys general, and guardians ad litem. Students receive one credit for every 50 hours of work.

The Rex E. Lee Advocacy Program

In addition to knowing the law, lawyers must synthesize complex information, analyze and formulate strategy, predict outcomes, and present information persuasively. The Rex E. Lee Advocacy Program administers a two-semester required course for first-year law students in the essential skills of legal writing, research, analysis, and oral advocacy. Students receive individualized attention during one-on-one conferences with instructors and teaching assistants and in small classes. In the Advocacy Program, students learn and practice the critical skills that bring success in both law school and the profession.

International Center for Law and Religion Studies

The BYU International Center for Law and Religion Studies promotes freedom of religion by studying and disseminating information on the laws, principles, and institutions affecting the interaction of state and religion throughout the world. The center works with scholars, government leaders, nongovernment groups, and religious organizations from a variety of countries and faith traditions, playing an important role in promoting religious liberty and the accompanying relationships between governments and religious organizations.

The Externship Program

The Law School offers an academic externship program as a capstone experience to students following their first year of law school. This program allows students to work with judges, law firms, corporations, public interest groups, and government organizations throughout the world. During the summer of 2010, 236 students externed with over 200 employers, earning an average of four units of law school credit. Forty-seven of those placements were international, with externships in 30 different countries.

The Academic Success Program

The Academic Success Program (ASP) is designed to help students adjust to and meet the rigorous demands of a legal education. The ASP offers legal skills workshops with personal feedback, weekly tutorial sessions in each first-year course, individual tutoring, and one-on-one legal writing instruction to all students upon request and by dean's referral.

Cocurricular Programs

The objective of the cocurricular program at the Law School is to make a law review-quality experience available to larger numbers of students. Comparable standards of excellence in research, writing, and editing are offered in six programs: the *Brigham Young University Law Review*, the Board of Advocates Moot Court, Trial Advocacy, the *BYU Journal of Public Law*, the *Brigham Young University Education and Law Journal*, and *International Law and Management Review*.

Career Services

The Career Services Office (CSO) is available to all students and graduates seeking employment. The CSO offers two legal career-planning courses featuring skills training and presentations by practicing attorneys who participate as guest lecturers. The office also publishes a *Professional Development Handbook*, *Job Hunt Book*, *Public Service Handbook*, and *Judicial Clerkship Handbook* and maintains a webpage with links for both students and employers. About 98 percent of the graduates who are seeking work accept employment within nine months after graduation, and graduates are placed in all 50 states and a number of foreign countries. The CSO brings firms to campus every year for on-campus interviews and has interviewing events and job fairs in DC, New York, Southern California, and Nevada.

APPLICANT PROFILE

Brigham Young University—J. Reuben Clark Law School
This grid includes only applicants who earned 120–180 LSAT scores under standard administrations.

LSAT Score	3.75 +		3.50–3.74		3.25–3.49		3.00–3.24		2.75–2.99		2.50–2.74		2.25–2.49		2.00–2.24		Below 2.00		No GPA		Total	
	Apps	Adm	Apps	Adm	Apps	Adm	Apps	Adm	Apps	Adm	Apps	Adm	Apps	Adm	Apps	Adm	Apps	Adm	Apps	Adm	Apps	Adm
175–180	2	2	1	0	2	2	0	0	1	0	0	0	0	0	0	0	0	0	0	0	6	4
170–174	16	14	7	6	4	3	2	1	1	1	1	0	0	0	0	0	0	0	0	0	31	25
165–169	45	37	23	21	25	18	10	7	3	2	1	0	1	0	3	1	0	0	1	1	112	87
160–164	69	54	52	10	44	9	26	3	9	0	3	1	1	0	1	0	1	0	2	2	208	79
155–159	35	9	49	4	33	2	20	1	10	0	4	1	2	0	2	0	0	0	3	0	158	17
150–154	19	1	31	1	30	2	17	0	20	0	2	1	3	1	0	0	0	0	2	0	124	6
145–149	9	2	13	0	15	1	16	0	10	0	11	0	1	0	0	0	1	0	6	0	82	3
140–144	3	1	0	0	4	0	13	1	7	1	5	0	4	0	0	0	0	0	4	0	40	3
135–139	1	0	1	0	0	0	0	0	1	0	3	0	0	0	0	0	0	0	1	0	7	0
130–134	0	0	0	0	1	0	1	0	1	0	2	0	0	0	1	0	0	0	0	0	6	0
125–129	0	0	0	0	0	0	0	0	1	0	0	0	0	0	1	0	0	0	0	0	2	0
120–124	0	0	0	0	0	0	0	0	0	0	0	0	0	0	0	0	0	0	0	0	0	0
Total	199	120	177	42	158	37	105	13	64	4	32	3	12	1	8	1	2	0	19	3	776	224

Apps = Number of Applicants
Adm = Number Admitted
Reflects 99% of the total applicant pool; highest LSAT data reported.

BROOKLYN LAW SCHOOL

250 Joralemon Street
Brooklyn, NY 11201-9846
Phone: 718.780.7906; Fax: 718.780.0395
E-mail: admitq@brooklaw.edu; Website: www.brooklaw.edu

*ABA
Approved
Since
1937*

The Basics

Type of school	Private
Term	Semester
Application deadline	
Application fee	$0
Financial aid deadline	
Can first year start other than fall?	No
Student to faculty ratio	18.3 to 1
# of housing spaces available restricted to law students	558
graduate housing for which law students are eligible	

Faculty and Administrators

	Total		Men		Women		Minorities	
	Spr	Fall	Spr	Fall	Spr	Fall	Spr	Fall
Full-time	64	63	32	32	32	31	6	4
Other full-time	4	5	3	2	1	3	2	1
Deans, librarians, & others who teach	8	8	3	3	5	5	1	1
Part-time	93	86	63	61	30	25	6	7
Total	169	162	101	98	68	64	15	13

Curriculum

	Full-Time	Part-Time
Typical first-year section size	45	31
Is there typically a "small section" of the first-year class, other than Legal Writing, taught by full-time faculty	Yes	No
If yes, typical size offered last year	40	
# of classroom course titles beyond first-year curriculum	194	

# of upper division courses, excluding seminars, with an enrollment:		
	Under 25	132
	25–49	50
	50–74	20
	75–99	17
	100+	11

# of seminars	83	
# of seminar positions available	1,209	
# of seminar positions filled	1,026	39
# of positions available in simulation courses	1,224	
# of simulation positions filled	990	75
# of positions available in faculty supervised clinical courses	335	
# of faculty supervised clinical positions filled	321	6
# involved in field placements	713	16
# involved in law journals	271	13
# involved in moot court or trial competitions	114	11
# of credit hours required to graduate	86	

JD Enrollment and Ethnicity

	Men		Women		Full-Time		Part-Time		1st-Year		Total		JD Degs. Awd.
	#	%	#	%	#	%	#	%	#	%	#	%	
All Hispanics	35	4.6	47	6.8	76	5.9	6	3.6	25	5.2	82	5.6	23
Am. Ind./AK Nat.	1	0.1	0	0.0	1	0.1	0	0.0	0	0.0	1	0.1	1
Asian	81	10.6	122	17.6	179	13.8	24	14.3	62	12.8	203	13.9	67
Black/Af. Am.	22	2.9	34	4.9	44	3.4	12	7.1	20	4.1	56	3.8	30
Nat. HI/Pac. Isl.	1	0.1	0	0.0	1	0.1	0	0.0	1	0.2	1	0.1	0
2 or more races	15	2.0	19	2.7	32	2.5	2	1.2	10	2.1	34	2.3	0
Subtotal (minor.)	155	20.2	222	31.9	333	25.8	44	26.2	118	24.4	377	25.8	121
Nonres. Alien	2	0.3	3	0.4	5	0.4	0	0.0	1	0.2	5	0.3	0
White/Cauc.	593	77.4	461	66.3	933	72.2	121	72.0	348	71.9	1054	72.1	329
Unknown	16	2.1	9	1.3	22	1.7	3	1.8	17	3.5	25	1.7	9
Total	766	52.4	695	47.6	1293	88.5	168	11.5	484	33.1	1461		463

Transfers

Transfers in	32
Transfers out	24

Tuition and Fees

	Resident	Nonresident
Full-time	$46,635	$46,635
Part-time	$35,065	$35,065
Tuition Guarantee Program		N

Living Expenses

Estimated living expenses for singles

Living on campus	Living off campus	Living at home
$23,250	$23,250	$8,980

ABA
Approved
Since
1937

GPA and LSAT Scores

	Total	Full-Time	Part-Time
# of apps	5,984	5,053	931
# of offers	1,605	1,447	158
# of matrics	486	417	69
75% GPA	3.66	3.67	3.58
Median GPA	3.45	3.47	3.34
25% GPA	3.24	3.27	3.10
75% LSAT	165	165	163
Median LSAT	163	163	161
25% LSAT	162	162	160

Grants and Scholarships (from prior year)

	Total		Full-Time		Part-Time	
	#	%	#	%	#	%
Total # of students	1,458		1,278		180	
Total # receiving grants	1065	73.0	1004	78.6	61	33.9
Less than 1/2 tuition	559	38.3	525	41.1	34	18.9
Half to full tuition	392	26.9	371	29.0	21	11.7
Full tuition	3	0.2	3	0.2	0	0.0
More than full tuition	111	7.6	105	8.2	6	3.3
Median grant amount			$20,600		$16,125	

Informational and Library Resources

Total amount spent on library materials	$1,265,357
Study seating capacity inside the library	665
# of full-time equivalent professional librarians	10
Hours per week library is open	108
# of open, wired connections available to students	1,984
# of networked computers available for use by students	142
Has wireless network?	Y
Requires computer?	N

JD Attrition (from prior year)

	Academic	Other	Total	
	#	#	#	%
1st year	2	29	31	6.3
2nd year	1	1	2	0.4
3rd year	0	0	0	0.0
4th year	0	0	0	0.0

Employment (9 months after graduation)

	Total	Percentage
Employment status known	493	98.8
Employment status unknown	6	1.2
Employed	415	84.2
Pursuing graduate degrees	14	2.8
Unemployed (seeking, not seeking, or studying for the bar)	36	7.3
Type of Employment		
# employed in law firms	226	54.5
# employed in business and industry	62	14.9
# employed in government	71	17.1
# employed in public interest	29	7.0
# employed as judicial clerks	22	5.3
# employed in academia	4	1.0
Geographic Location		
# employed in state	365	88.0
# employed outside the US	4	1.0
# of states where employed	16	

Bar Passage Rates

First-time takers	481	Reporting %	98.54
Average school %	87.97	Average state %	86.51
Average pass difference	1.46		

Jurisdiction	Takers	Passers	Pass %	State %	Diff %
New York	474	417	87.97	86.51	1.46

BROOKLYN LAW SCHOOL

250 Joralemon Street
Brooklyn, NY 11201-9846
Phone: 718.780.7906; Fax: 718.780.0395
E-mail: admitq@brooklaw.edu; Website: www.brooklaw.edu

The Law Campus

Situated at the junction of the Brooklyn Heights Historic District, the Brooklyn Civic Center, and downtown Brooklyn, our school boasts a location unrivaled for its legal, cultural, and historical character. Students share their environs with federal and state judges, government officials, and lawyers in private practice, many of them alumni. Within a few-block radius are the US District Court; US Bankruptcy Court; US Attorney's Office; the New York State Supreme Court, Appellate Division; Family Court; the Brooklyn District Attorney; the Kings County Surrogate's Court; the New York City Civil and Criminal Courts; the Legal Aid Society; and numerous law firms. These are our laboratories, a backdrop for learning few schools can replicate.

Renaissance Brooklyn

Multibillion-dollar construction projects have recast Brooklyn as the new center of New York City's energy. Overlooking New York Harbor and lower Manhattan lies Brooklyn's most charming neighborhood, Brooklyn Heights, where you will find much of our campus. The first New York City neighborhood to be designated as a historic district, many Heights original townhouses, brownstone mansions, carriage houses, churches, and public buildings survive, recalling old-world urban elegance. Many of our students and faculty live here in residence halls or in private apartments and homes located on graceful, tree-lined streets. Nearby neighborhoods—Carroll Gardens, Cobble Hill, Park Slope, Williamsburg, and DUMBO (Down Under the Manhattan Bridge Overpass)—also offer trendy, affordable housing and a profusion of bistros, boutiques, galleries, and clubs, all contributing to Brooklyn's growing reputation as the hippest part of New York City.

Manhattan at Our Doorstep

Minutes away is the financial, legal, business, and cultural crossroads of the world: Manhattan. Proximity to Wall Street gives students easy access to school-year externships and summer jobs with major law firms and financial institutions. Students enjoy a great campus in a dynamic urban environment, softened by a small-neighborhood feel. This is New York City on a human scale—Manhattan without the hassle.

Building for Your Future

In recent years, BLS has undertaken $136 million in capital improvements to serve its needs well into the twenty-first century. Ten residences—including our largest, the 21-story high-rise, Feil Hall—allow us to **guarantee housing** to all first-year students, engendering a strong sense of campus community. The library offers more than 589,000 multiformat volumes, periodicals, and databases accessible on and off campus. As one of the largest and most modern in the city, the 78,000-square-foot facility boasts 27 group-study rooms, seating for nearly 700, and five PC/Mac labs hosting nearly 100 workstations. We offer over 2,400 other student-accessible network connections throughout our academic and residential buildings as well as over 2,000 Wi-Fi connections.

Our Faculty: Diverse, Brilliant, and User-Friendly

Our 72 full-time faculty members, joined by nearly 140 adjuncts (including many distinguished judges, practitioners, and corporate counsel), comprise one of the largest faculties in New York. They are extraordinarily talented and, above all, superb teachers. Shaping public policy and making law in the community at large, they are also prolific authors. They are recognized nationally and globally for their scholarship in such areas as Capital Defender and Criminal Law, Commercial and Bankruptcy Law, Corporate and Securities Law, Evidence, Family Law, Gender Discrimination, Human Rights, Information Privacy and Internet Law, Intellectual Property, International Business Law, Tax, and Torts. BLS offers a congenial community. Its learning environment, while rigorous and challenging, remains supportive and nurturing. Faculty members are accessible to students in a way that few faculties are. There is a strong correlation between the priority we assign to teaching and mentoring and student success on the bar examination. Our 2010 graduates who took the New York State Bar Examination for the first time had a 90 percent passing rate, well ahead of the 78 percent statewide rate for first-time takers.

Our Alumni: Accomplished and Accessible

One of our great strengths is the size, stature, and loyalty of our more than 18,500 graduates in 49 states and Washington, DC; 3 US territories; and 32 foreign countries—among the largest alumni families of any law school.

Our Students: The Best and the Brightest

The 2010 entering class included students from 35 states and Washington, DC, and 2 foreign countries. Nearly two-thirds of the class are graduates of many of the nation's most prestigious colleges and universities. Sixty-eight percent completed undergraduate work at least one year before enrolling here. Nearly 61 percent had LSAT scores of 163 or higher. Minorities represented approximately 25 percent of the class; 46 percent of the students were women.

The Career Center

Our Career Center is staffed by seven attorney-counselors and two attorneys dedicated to job development/employer relations in the public and private sectors. Job listings are readily available to students and graduates via the Internet. An average of 96 percent of students in the 2005–2009 graduating classes were employed nine months after graduation, placing us among the top law schools nationwide. For current salary information, visit the School's website to review the Statistics and Profile section at www.brooklaw.edu/Admissions/statisticsandprofile/admissionstatistics.aspx.

First-Year Program of Study

Day students take one core course in a seminar section of about 40 students, allowing for significant individualized skills training. Our goal is to help students cultivate the ability to think clearly, analyze problems thoroughly and carefully, and recognize that no legal issue exists in a social, philosophical, economic, or political vacuum. Students participate in a Legal Writing Program structured to fully develop their writing abilities. An Academic Success Program, combining an early-start summer course with a series of support workshops, helps students reach their potential. This contributes to our exceptionally high retention rate between the first and second year.

Upperclass Program of Study: The Art and Craft of Lawyering

Our **upperclass curriculum** bridges the gap between law school and law practice, making law school something students enjoy, not merely endure. Students create individualized programs, choosing from approximately 240 electives in 19 concentrations and areas of interest. Five **Certificate Programs** (in Business, Criminal, Intellectual Property, International, and Real Estate Law) recognize a student's depth of study and proficiency in these practice areas. Nearly 60 percent of all students and 75 percent of full-time students participate in one or more of our **24 clinics**, including nearly 330 enrolled this year in one of our in-house clinics and over 700 students participating in externships in legal departments and judicial chambers, experiencing the law in real time. Simulation courses enrolled nearly 1,100 students this past year.

Beyond the Core Curriculum

Consistently recognized as among the country's top law schools in supporting public interest law, Brooklyn's **Edward V. Sparer Public Interest Law Fellowship Program** has placed over 450 students in a wide array of summer internships at leading public interest organizations nationwide and abroad. **Public Service Grants** award up to $5,000 per student to support public service employment. The **Dennis J. Block Center for the Study of International Business Law**, and its Fellowship Program, provide a rewarding educational experience for those pursuing careers in that field. An **International Human Rights Fellowship Program** awards up to four $5,000 stipends for summer internships allowing students to work with prestigious human rights organizations overseas. **Global Justice Fellowships** are funded by the student-run International Law Society. We sponsor four student-edited journals: the *Brooklyn Law Review*, the *Journal of Law and Policy*, the *Brooklyn Journal of International Law*, and the *Brooklyn Journal of Corporate, Financial, and Commercial Law*. **Zaretsky Bankruptcy and Commercial Law Fellowships** are awarded to students based on demonstrated academic achievement and commitment to those areas of law. Over the past decade, our **Moot Court** teams have garnered 20 national championships and 39 other first prizes. Our **Center for the Study of Law, Language, and Cognition** explores how developments in the cognitive sciences—including neuroscience, psychology, and linguistics—have dramatic implications for the theory and practice of law. Our **Center for Health, Science and Public Policy** engages students in the legal issues and public policy concerns confronting health care organizations. **Joint-degree** options allow students to simultaneously earn master's degrees in business administration, city and regional planning, urban planning, political science, or library and information science. Finally, we offer **exchange programs** in Argentina, England, Germany, Hong Kong, and Ireland and summer **study-abroad programs** in China and Italy.

APPLICANT PROFILE

Admission to Brooklyn Law School is based on an appraisal of each applicant's character and fitness, commitment to legal education, academic achievement, aptitude for successful law study, life experience, and other pertinent indications of professional promise. BLS does not offer an LSAT/GPA admission profile; numbers alone cannot provide a comprehensive assessment of a candidate's potential for law school success. While matrices may be helpful, too often they discourage those with profiles slightly below published numerical benchmarks who may still be competitive for admission. Moreover, such profiles reduce the selection process to a two-dimensional matrix which fails to portray accurately our admission practices. To be sure, candidates with high test scores and commensurate grades are more likely to gain admission than those with lower grades and scores. Nevertheless, no combination of grades and scores guarantees admission. Nonquantifiable factors also significantly influence our decisions. A partial list includes quality of schools attended, strength of the program of study, grade trends, content of faculty recommendations, cogency of the candidate's writing, campus leadership, significant service to the community, nature and quality of any work experience or foreign study/travel, awards and honors, and military service. We have a century-long tradition of offering opportunities to members of underrepresented groups. For more, see www.brooklaw.edu.

UNIVERSITY AT BUFFALO LAW SCHOOL, THE STATE UNIVERSITY OF NEW YORK (SUNY)

309 John Lord O'Brian Hall
Buffalo, NY 14260
Phone: 716.645.2907; Fax: 716.645.6676
E-mail: law-admissions@buffalo.edu; Website: www.law.buffalo.edu

ABA
Approved
Since
1936

The Basics

Type of school	Public
Term	Semester
Application deadline	3/1
Application fee	$75
Financial aid deadline	3/1
Can first year start other than fall?	No
Student to faculty ratio	12.6 to 1
# of housing spaces available restricted to law students	124
graduate housing for which law students are eligible	674

Faculty and Administrators

	Total		Men		Women		Minorities	
	Spr	Fall	Spr	Fall	Spr	Fall	Spr	Fall
Full-time	46	47	23	25	23	22	5	6
Other full-time	7	7	3	3	4	4	0	0
Deans, librarians, & others who teach	11	12	5	5	5	6	1	1
Part-time	84	44	54	34	30	9	68	37
Total	148	110	85	67	62	41	74	44

Curriculum

	Full-Time	Part-Time
Typical first-year section size	70	0
Is there typically a "small section" of the first-year class, other than Legal Writing, taught by full-time faculty	No	No
If yes, typical size offered last year		
# of classroom course titles beyond first-year curriculum	218	

# of upper division courses, excluding seminars, with an enrollment:		
Under 25	154	
25–49	47	
50–74	22	
75–99	4	
100+	0	

# of seminars	45	
# of seminar positions available	443	
# of seminar positions filled	307	0
# of positions available in simulation courses	1,019	
# of simulation positions filled	782	0
# of positions available in faculty supervised clinical courses	117	
# of faculty supervised clinical positions filled	72	0
# involved in field placements	97	0
# involved in law journals	348	0
# involved in moot court or trial competitions	82	0
# of credit hours required to graduate	90	

JD Enrollment and Ethnicity

	Men		Women		Full-Time		Part-Time		1st-Year		Total		JD Degs. Awd.
	#	%	#	%	#	%	#	%	#	%	#	%	
All Hispanics	12	3.2	12	3.6	24	3.5	0	0.0	5	2.3	24	3.4	10
Am. Ind./AK Nat.	1	0.3	5	1.5	6	0.9	0	0.0	3	1.4	6	0.9	1
Asian	13	3.5	16	4.8	28	4.0	1	12.5	8	3.7	29	4.1	9
Black/Af. Am.	11	3.0	24	7.3	34	4.9	1	12.5	8	3.7	35	5.0	8
Nat. HI/Pac. Isl.	1	0.3	0	0.0	1	0.1	0	0.0	1	0.5	1	0.1	0
2 or more races	5	1.3	1	0.3	6	0.9	0	0.0	5	2.3	6	0.9	1
Subtotal (minor.)	43	11.6	58	17.6	99	14.3	2	25.0	30	13.8	101	14.4	29
Nonres. Alien	11	3.0	10	3.0	21	3.0	0	0.0	4	1.8	21	3.0	10
White/Cauc.	272	73.3	238	72.1	505	72.9	5	62.5	164	75.6	510	72.8	215
Unknown	45	12.1	24	7.3	68	9.8	1	12.5	19	8.8	69	9.8	14
Total	371	52.9	330	47.1	693	98.9	8	1.1	217	31.0	701		268

Transfers

Transfers in	28
Transfers out	12

Tuition and Fees

	Resident	Nonresident
Full-time	$19,112	$30,772
Part-time		
Tuition Guarantee Program	N	

Living Expenses

Estimated living expenses for singles

Living on campus	Living off campus	Living at home
$19,555	$19,555	$19,555

UNIVERSITY AT BUFFALO LAW SCHOOL, THE STATE UNIVERSITY OF NEW YORK (SUNY)

ABA
Approved
Since
1936

GPA and LSAT Scores

	Total	Full-Time	Part-Time
# of apps	1,894	1,894	0
# of offers	714	714	0
# of matrics	219	219	0
75% GPA	3.69	3.69	0.00
Median GPA	3.48	3.48	0.00
25% GPA	3.17	3.17	0.00
75% LSAT	160	160	0
Median LSAT	158	158	0
25% LSAT	155	155	0

Grants and Scholarships (from prior year)

	Total		Full-Time		Part-Time	
	#	%	#	%	#	%
Total # of students	726		718		8	
Total # receiving grants	456	62.8	456	63.5	0	0.0
Less than 1/2 tuition	422	58.1	422	58.8	0	0.0
Half to full tuition	0	0.0	0	0.0	0	0.0
Full tuition	30	4.1	30	4.2	0	0.0
More than full tuition	4	0.6	4	0.6	0	0.0
Median grant amount			$550		$0	

Informational and Library Resources

Total amount spent on library materials	$1,324,449
Study seating capacity inside the library	590
# of full-time equivalent professional librarians	12
Hours per week library is open	103
# of open, wired connections available to students	11
# of networked computers available for use by students	43
Has wireless network?	Y
Requires computer?	N

JD Attrition (from prior year)

	Academic	Other	Total	
	#	#	#	%
1st year	0	7	7	3.4
2nd year	1	16	17	6.8
3rd year	0	0	0	0.0
4th year	0	0	0	0.0

Employment (9 months after graduation)

	Total	Percentage
Employment status known	243	97.6
Employment status unknown	6	2.4
Employed	219	90.1
Pursuing graduate degrees	14	5.8
Unemployed (seeking, not seeking, or studying for the bar)	4	1.6
Type of Employment		
# employed in law firms	129	58.9
# employed in business and industry	32	14.6
# employed in government	24	11.0
# employed in public interest	14	6.4
# employed as judicial clerks	9	4.1
# employed in academia	8	3.7
Geographic Location		
# employed in state	177	80.8
# employed outside the US	1	0.5
# of states where employed	18	

Bar Passage Rates

First-time takers	239	Reporting %	90.79
Average school %	79.26	Average state %	86.51

Average pass difference −7.25

Jurisdiction	Takers	Passers	Pass %	State %	Diff %
New York	217	172	79.26	86.51	−7.25

UNIVERSITY AT BUFFALO LAW SCHOOL, THE STATE UNIVERSITY OF NEW YORK (SUNY)

309 John Lord O'Brian Hall
Buffalo, NY 14260
Phone: 716.645.2907; Fax: 716.645.6676
E-mail: law-admissions@buffalo.edu; Website: www.law.buffalo.edu

New York State's Law School

The University at Buffalo Law School is the only law school in the State University of New York (SUNY) system. Since 1887, our law school has prepared lawyers to practice in New York City; Washington, DC; and other major cities across the country and around the world. The University at Buffalo campus provides its 30,000 students access to vast resources in world-class undergraduate and graduate fields of study that include medicine, engineering, pharmaceutical sciences, and business management. Each year, we graduate over 200 well-educated and diverse lawyers who are ready to practice law in fields such as corporate law, tax law, public service, criminal law, and intellectual property.

Located in Amherst, New York—a suburb of Buffalo—the Law School has a small-school feel with all the advantages of a large university, including access to other professional and graduate departments, Division I sports, a fine arts center, a concert hall, and numerous other academic, social, and cultural opportunities. The greater Buffalo area offers a wide variety of social and cultural activities such as downhill skiing, water sports, professional sports, a world-class symphony orchestra, professional theaters, nightlife, and access to Canada, all within minutes of the Law School. You can live comfortably, not to mention affordably, in Buffalo, the second largest city in New York.

Library and Physical Facilities

The Law School is housed in John Lord O'Brian Hall, a seven-story building including a state-of-the-art courtroom that provides students with an opportunity to watch judges and lawyers in action. The library is the core of the Law School, occupying six of the seven floors, including a law-student-only reading room with space for 84 students.

Like the Law School, the law library is committed to providing students with exceptional research and writing instructors. This enables first-year law students to gain one-on-one instruction in various research methods.

In January 2011, the Law School unveiled a newly renovated student lounge and classrooms. The Law School has also added state-of-the-art technology to enhance faculty teaching and student learning.

Curriculum

The Law School provides a flexible curriculum that affords students a broad range of curricular options, practical coursework, and special programs. Our curriculum emphasizes the study of law as well as the practical application of law to prepare our students to practice their profession upon graduation. The Law School offers a large number of interdisciplinary courses and programs in a variety of concentrations that include Family Law, Finance Transactions, Tax Law, Environmental Law, Civil Litigation, Criminal Law, Health Law, International Law, and an Intellectual Property Concentration and Technology Transfer Certification.

Instruction is offered in two semesters from early September to May, including a January bridge term and a summer session from mid-May to mid-July. Six full-time semesters or five full-time semesters plus two summer sessions are required for graduation.

Beyond the first year, students are required to complete 60 semester credit hours, including at least one seminar. The upper-division program is wholly elective.

The Law School also offers the LLM degree in Criminal Law and a general LLM for international and domestic students. For international students, there are special courses designed to introduce them to American law and to prepare them for the New York State bar exam. All students benefit from our small-group personalized approach that allows them to design their own curriculum.

Dual-Degree Programs—The State University of New York at Buffalo is New York State's largest campus in its university system. The campus includes nationally recognized schools of Pharmacy and Pharmaceutical Sciences, Medicine and Biomedical Sciences, and Engineering and Applied Sciences. Access to these and many other graduate and professional schools within the campus offer unparalleled access to dual-degree programs, which permit students to earn credit toward a master's or PhD degree jointly with the JD. In recent years, the most active dual-degree programs have been with management, political science, philosophy, public health, legal information management and analysis, social work, sociology, and economics.

Legal Skills

The University at Buffalo Law School's Legal Skills initiative is the cornerstone of the school's curriculum. The initiative focuses on developing and producing practice-ready lawyers who are able to meet the challenges of the legal profession. A key component of the initiative is the Legal Analysis, Writing, and Research (LAWR) program. The three semesters of required LAWR coursework allow every student to receive the necessary training in these skills broken into manageable segments.

Another integral part of the Legal Skills Initiative is the Trial Technique Program, which includes our Buffalo-Niagara Trial Tournament, Trial Teams, and Trial Technique classes. Each year, UB Law hosts the Buffalo-Niagara Trial Tournament that draws over 125 students from over 30 law schools around the nation. In recent years UB Law's Trial Team has won more awards than any other school at the American Bar Association regional competition. Our Trial Technique classes culminate each semester with a mock trial in a downtown Buffalo courtroom.

Special Programs

Clinical Programs—Skills training in the clinical program is coordinated with substantive law courses to give students a theoretical understanding of practical issues. Students serve clients and conduct research and fieldwork in areas such as economic development, affordable housing, mediation, family violence, elder law, and environmental and development law.

New York City Program in Finance and Law—Provides University at Buffalo law students with an introduction to New York City's financial markets and a gateway to its highly competitive financial-sector job market. Each year, approximately 25 students are selected to participate in this unique program, which is located in New York City.

Externships

Each semester over 50 law school students are placed in supervised externships and another 20 or more students are placed in judicial clerkships. Externships and judicial clerkships provide law students with unique legal and public service experience as they work in a variety of government and nonprofit organizations, and get credit for doing so. Students learn how to work with a client and address the client's specific needs and goals—something that's difficult to teach in a classroom.

Our students help judges, attorneys, and legislators with pressing legal questions that arise in ongoing cases, in the development of public policy or legislation, and in response to citizen inquiries or problems.

Law School Culture and Student Activities

University at Buffalo Law School students experience a relaxed, friendly, and collaborative atmosphere. There are ample extracurricular activities. The Student Bar Association, an elected representative body, oversees all law school student organizations. Our Moot Court Board sponsors mock appellate practice competitions, the *Opinion* is the student newspaper, the *Buffalo Law Review* is a professional journal edited by students, and there are specialty journals in environmental law, affordable housing and community development law, intellectual property, criminal law, human rights law, and social policy concerning women.

Admission

Each year the University at Buffalo Law School enrolls just over 200 first-year students. All first-year students start in the fall semester. Transfer and visiting students can start in either the fall or spring semesters. Our application priority deadline is March 1. LSAT and LSAC Credential Assembly Service are required.

Although we have a limited number of seats for each incoming class, we do consider qualitative factors in addition to the traditional quantitative factors (GPA and LSAT). These factors include, but are not limited to, academic achievement, personal statements, character traits, writing ability, recommendations, and work experience. If an application reveals that the applicant has been educationally, socially, economically, or otherwise disadvantaged, the Admissions Committee will review the application for signs of achievement that should lead to success in law school.

Expenses and Financial Aid

UB is able to offer state-subsidized tuition to New York residents and a reasonable out-of-state tuition charge. In-state tuition—$17,450; out-of-state tuition—$29,110; estimated additional expenses—$22,000. (Tuition and living expenses are subject to change without notice.)

This results in overall educational expenses that are less than half the cost of many law schools. Dean's tuition waivers and scholarships are available to students demonstrating high academic achievement, and state aid is offered on a need basis to qualified students. Additional alumni-sponsored scholarships are offered to second- and third-year students.

Career Services

The ultimate goal of nearly every law student is establishing their career upon graduation. Ninety-six percent of the University at Buffalo Law School graduates find positions or enter advanced degree programs within months of their graduation. Our Career Services Office (CSO) provides job search and résumé services for third-year and LLM students, and helps first- and second-year students conduct their summer job searches. As products of New York State's Law School, many UB Law graduates find employment in New York City and Buffalo; however, a number of our graduates find positions in other regions of the country.

For more information about career services, contact the office: telephone, 716.645.2056; fax, 716.645.7336; e-mail, law-careers@buffalo.edu.

APPLICANT PROFILE

University at Buffalo Law School, The State University of New York (SUNY)
This grid includes only applicants who earned 120–180 LSAT scores under standard administrations.

LSAT Score	GPA 3.75 +		3.50–3.74		3.25–3.49		3.00–3.24		2.75–2.99		2.50–2.74		2.25–2.49		2.00–2.24		Below 2.00		No GPA		Total	
	Apps	Adm	Apps	Adm	Apps	Adm	Apps	Adm	Apps	Adm	Apps	Adm	Apps	Adm	Apps	Adm	Apps	Adm	Apps	Adm	Apps	Adm
175–180	0	0	0	0	0	0	1	1	0	0	0	0	0	0	0	0	0	0	0	0	1	1
170–174	3	3	6	5	5	5	1	1	2	0	0	0	0	0	0	0	0	0	0	0	17	14
165–169	13	12	11	11	12	12	11	10	7	6	6	3	5	1	4	1	0	0	0	0	69	56
160–164	42	42	60	59	59	58	36	35	26	22	16	7	6	3	1	0	0	0	1	0	247	226
155–159	65	58	121	99	120	65	93	46	61	31	23	3	12	1	8	1	0	0	1	0	504	304
150–154	94	49	104	39	97	8	110	9	55	4	27	2	12	0	5	0	3	0	3	0	510	111
145–149	34	3	42	6	51	2	66	0	46	1	26	1	16	0	4	0	2	0	1	0	288	13
140–144	14	0	18	0	32	0	32	0	21	0	15	0	11	0	5	0	1	0	0	0	149	0
135–139	3	0	7	0	14	0	9	0	11	0	13	0	5	0	5	0	1	0	0	0	68	0
130–134	1	0	3	0	3	0	4	0	3	0	1	0	4	0	0	0	1	0	0	0	20	0
125–129	0	0	0	0	0	0	0	0	2	0	2	0	2	0	0	0	1	0	0	0	7	0
120–124	0	0	0	0	0	0	0	0	0	0	0	0	0	0	0	0	0	0	0	0	0	0
No LSAT	0	0	0	0	0	0	0	0	0	0	0	0	0	0	0	0	0	0	14	0	14	0
Total	269	167	372	219	393	150	363	102	234	64	129	16	73	5	32	2	9	0	20	0	1894	725

Apps = Number of Applicants   Adm = Number Admitted   Reflects 99% of the total applicant pool; highest LSAT data reported.

UNIVERSITY OF CALIFORNIA, BERKELEY, SCHOOL OF LAW

2850 Telegraph Avenue, Suite 500
Berkeley, CA 94705-7220
Phone: 510.642.2274; Fax: 510.643.6222
E-mail: admissions@law.berkeley.edu; Website: www.law.berkeley.edu

The Basics

Type of school	Public
Term	Semester
Application deadline	2/1
Application fee	$75
Financial aid deadline	3/2
Can first year start other than fall?	No
Student to faculty ratio	10.5 to 1
# of housing spaces available restricted to law students	
graduate housing for which law students are eligible	1,300

Faculty and Administrators

	Total		Men		Women		Minorities	
	Spr	Fall	Spr	Fall	Spr	Fall	Spr	Fall
Full-time	75	69	50	44	25	25	12	14
Other full-time	19	21	6	7	13	14	1	1
Deans, librarians, & others who teach	13	13	5	5	8	8	1	1
Part-time	77	50	43	34	34	16	5	3
Total	184	153	104	90	80	63	19	19

Curriculum

	Full-Time	Part-Time
Typical first-year section size	97	0
Is there typically a "small section" of the first-year class, other than Legal Writing, taught by full-time faculty	Yes	No
If yes, typical size offered last year	27	
# of classroom course titles beyond first-year curriculum	222	

# of upper division courses, excluding seminars, with an enrollment:		
Under 25	93	
25–49	54	
50–74	12	
75–99	9	
100+	6	

# of seminars	96	
# of seminar positions available	2,605	
# of seminar positions filled	1,299	0
# of positions available in simulation courses	1,863	
# of simulation positions filled	1,014	0
# of positions available in faculty supervised clinical courses	483	
# of faculty supervised clinical positions filled	309	0
# involved in field placements	133	0
# involved in law journals	351	0
# involved in moot court or trial competitions	64	0
# of credit hours required to graduate	85	

JD Enrollment and Ethnicity

	Men #	Men %	Women #	Women %	Full-Time #	Full-Time %	Part-Time #	Part-Time %	1st-Year #	1st-Year %	Total #	Total %	JD Degs. Awd.
All Hispanics	54	12.5	59	12.2	113	12.3	0	0.0	52	18.4	113	12.3	29
Am. Ind./AK Nat.	5	1.2	11	2.3	16	1.7	0	0.0	8	2.8	16	1.7	7
Asian	70	16.2	83	17.1	153	16.7	0	0.0	59	20.8	153	16.7	39
Black/Af. Am.	18	4.2	26	5.4	44	4.8	0	0.0	13	4.6	44	4.8	12
Nat. HI/Pac. Isl.	8	1.9	11	2.3	19	2.1	0	0.0	10	3.5	19	2.1	0
2 or more races	0	0.0	0	0.0	0	0.0	0	0.0	0	0.0	0	0.0	0
Subtotal (minor.)	155	36.0	190	39.2	345	37.7	0	0.0	142	50.2	345	37.7	93
Nonres. Alien	19	4.4	18	3.7	37	4.0	0	0.0	12	4.2	37	4.0	0
White/Cauc.	204	47.3	205	42.3	409	44.7	0	0.0	110	38.9	409	44.7	136
Unknown	53	12.3	72	14.8	125	13.6	0	0.0	19	6.7	125	13.6	54
Total	431	47.1	485	52.9	916	100.0	0	0.0	283	30.9	916		294

Transfers

Transfers in	46
Transfers out	2

Tuition and Fees

	Resident	Nonresident
Full-time	$44,244	$52,245
Part-time		
Tuition Guarantee Program	N	

Living Expenses

Estimated living expenses for singles

Living on campus	Living off campus	Living at home
$21,721	$21,721	$21,721

UNIVERSITY OF CALIFORNIA, BERKELEY, SCHOOL OF LAW

ABA
Approved
Since
1923

GPA and LSAT Scores

	Total	Full-Time	Part-Time
# of apps	8,297	8,297	0
# of offers	852	852	0
# of matrics	286	286	0
75% GPA	3.87	3.87	0.00
Median GPA	3.79	3.79	0.00
25% GPA	3.64	3.64	0.00
75% LSAT	170	170	0
Median LSAT	167	167	0
25% LSAT	162	162	0

Grants and Scholarships (from prior year)

	Total		Full-Time		Part-Time	
	#	%	#	%	#	%
Total # of students	892		892		0	
Total # receiving grants	571	64.0	571	64.0	0	0.0
Less than 1/2 tuition	311	34.9	311	34.9	0	0.0
Half to full tuition	231	25.9	231	25.9	0	0.0
Full tuition	6	0.7	6	0.7	0	0.0
More than full tuition	23	2.6	23	2.6	0	0.0
Median grant amount			$16,369		$0	

Informational and Library Resources

Total amount spent on library materials	$2,856,887
Study seating capacity inside the library	307
# of full-time equivalent professional librarians	15
Hours per week library is open	100
# of open, wired connections available to students	207
# of networked computers available for use by students	87
Has wireless network?	Y
Requires computer?	N

JD Attrition (from prior year)

	Academic	Other	Total	
	#	#	#	%
1st year	0	2	2	0.7
2nd year	0	3	3	1.0
3rd year	0	1	1	0.3
4th year	0	0	0	0.0

Employment (9 months after graduation)

	Total	Percentage
Employment status known	294	100.0
Employment status unknown	0	0.0
Employed	281	95.6
Pursuing graduate degrees	5	1.7
Unemployed (seeking, not seeking, or studying for the bar)	6	2.0
Type of Employment		
# employed in law firms	193	68.7
# employed in business and industry	2	0.7
# employed in government	20	7.1
# employed in public interest	31	11.0
# employed as judicial clerks	31	11.0
# employed in academia	3	1.1
Geographic Location		
# employed in state	171	60.9
# employed outside the US	4	1.4
# of states where employed		23

Bar Passage Rates

First-time takers	258	Reporting %	83.33
Average school %	91.63	Average state %	73.19

Average pass difference 18.44

Jurisdiction	Takers	Passers	Pass %	State %	Diff %
California	215	197	91.63	73.19	18.44

UNIVERSITY OF CALIFORNIA, BERKELEY, SCHOOL OF LAW

2850 Telegraph Avenue, Suite 500
Berkeley, CA 94705-7220
Phone: 510.642.2274; Fax: 510.643.6222
E-mail: admissions@law.berkeley.edu; Website: www.law.berkeley.edu

Introduction

Learning at Berkeley Law means joining a stimulating intellectual community that is part of a tradition of academic excellence, professional leadership, and public service. Berkeley's location in the San Francisco Bay Area, with influences from Silicon Valley and the Pacific Rim, provides an unparalleled opportunity to study at one of the world's leading institutions of legal education and research. Its academic program includes specialized study in business, law, and economics; environmental law; law and technology; international and comparative legal studies; and social justice and public interest. The curriculum is complemented by research centers and clinical programs that provide real client work. Berkeley Law offers a broad three-year curriculum leading to the JD degree and postgraduate programs leading to LLM and JSD degrees. The interdisciplinary Jurisprudence and Social Policy (JSP) program leads to MA and PhD degrees. The school is a member of AALS and is ABA approved.

Location

UC Berkeley occupies a beautiful 1,232-acre campus bordered by wooded rolling hills. Berkeley is known for its intellectual, social, and political engagement. With its multinational population, rich diversity of arts, and sense of political adventure, Berkeley reflects and affects the rest of the country. Yet, it is an intimate city of friendly neighborhoods, renowned restaurants, coffeehouses, bookstores, parks, and open spaces. Across the bay lies San Francisco, home to internationally recognized museums, the opera, ballet, symphony, and restaurants. The mild climate makes outdoor activities possible year-round.

Students

Berkeley Law seeks a student body with a broad set of interests, life experiences, and perspectives. The intellectual excellence, varied skill sets, and backgrounds of the students are among its great strengths. Students received undergraduate degrees from more than 100 universities, about half at schools outside California.

Faculty

Berkeley's faculty members are internationally recognized experts in fields ranging from law and technology, to youth violence and juvenile justice, to environmental law. They include recipients of Fulbright and Guggenheim fellowships and a MacArthur "genius" grant, as well as authors of casebooks used worldwide. Lecturers are drawn from prominent law firms and institutions.

Library and Physical Facilities

The law library is one of the finest law collections in the world. Its extensive holdings include the Robbins Religious and Civil Law Collection of titles in ecclesiastical, civil, comparative, and international law, and extensive collections of foreign, comparative, human rights, and environmental law. The law library is also a depository for United States, United Nations, and European Union documents and is linked to the university system's holdings of more than seven million volumes.

The law library provides online databases, three computer labs with Internet access, four spacious reading rooms, and a photocopying service. Multimedia capabilities are available. Wireless access is available throughout the law school complex and much of the Berkeley campus.

The school is composed of four adjoining buildings with classrooms, seminar rooms, auditoriums, the law library, lounges, reception rooms, a café, dining and study areas, and offices.

Housing

The campus Housing Office offers apartments, rental listings, residence halls, and student family apartments. One of the residence halls, Manville Hall, is a studio apartment complex reserved for law students. International House accommodates students from the United States and abroad.

Admission

Requirements: bachelor's degree, LSAT, and registration with LSAC's Credential Assembly Service; application fee: $75; deadline: February 1 (early application strongly preferred).

Applicants' LSAT scores and undergraduate grade-point averages (GPAs) are important criteria for evaluating academic ability. Applicants may use the mean LSAT percentile and undergraduate GPAs of the previous year's admitted applicant pool as a guide for assessing their chances of admission. Because Berkeley Law takes other factors into account in making admission decisions, higher or lower scores and grades neither ensure nor preclude admission.

Student Activities

Students edit and publish 12 legal periodicals: *Asian American Law Journal*; *Berkeley Business Law Journal*; *Berkeley Journal of African American Law and Policy*; *Berkeley Journal of Criminal Law*; *Berkeley Journal of Employment and Labor Law*; *Berkeley Journal of Gender, Law and Justice*; *Berkeley Journal of International Law*; *Berkeley La Raza Law Journal*; *Berkeley Journal of Middle Eastern and Islamic Law*; *Berkeley Technology Law Journal*; *California Law Review*; and *Ecology Law Quarterly*.

More than 50 student groups focus on a variety of interests, including animal law, disability law, sports and entertainment law, and workers' rights.

JD Curriculum

Berkeley Law's broad and innovative curriculum is one of the most dynamic among law schools. Opportunities for study in specific areas of the law connect students to our renowned faculty members. The first-year curriculum includes Civil Procedure, Contracts, Criminal Law, Legal Research and Writing, Property, Torts, Written and Oral Advocacy, and two elective courses. The flexible second- and third-year curriculums offer a variety of legal topics and course styles, including seminars, individual and group research projects, clinical work, and judicial externships. Students may work on clinical projects providing direct legal services to clients or work with lawyers on large cases or legal matters. The Center for Clinical Education, Berkeley Law's in-house clinical facility, offers the Death Penalty Clinic; the International Human Rights Law Clinic; and the Samuelson Law, Technology, and Public Policy Clinic. The East Bay Community Law Center is the community-based component of the program. Other clinical opportunities include the Domestic Violence Practicum and field placements.

Centers and Institutes

Berkeley Law's centers and institutes act as incubators for cutting-edge legal research, where students collaborate with leading scholars and practitioners working on complex issues. Projects are often centered on specific cases or legislation, and can have broad influence on law and policy in such areas as business, philosophy, public policy, sociology, and technology. The centers also sponsor conferences, roundtables, and other presentations on pertinent issues. They push the frontiers of legal scholarship and make Berkeley one of the most exciting places in the world to study law. They include:

- Berkeley Center for Law, Business, and the Economy
- Berkeley Center for Law and Technology
- Center for Law, Energy, and the Environment
- Center for the Study of Law and Society
- Chief Justice Earl Warren Institute on Law and Social Policy
- Human Rights Center
- Institute for Legal Research
- Miller Institute for Global Challenges and Law
- Kadish Center for Morality, Law, and Public Affairs

- Robert D. Burch Center for Tax Policy and Public Finance
- Thelton E. Henderson Center for Social Justice

Financial Aid

Requirements: FAFSA need analysis form; Need Access Application; the deadline for priority consideration is March 2.

The law school seeks to provide need-based financial aid sufficient to permit any admitted student to attend. A majority of the students receive some form of financial aid.

The financial aid awarded by UC Berkeley's Financial Aid Office is need-based and includes mostly federal student loans. The financial aid awarded by Berkeley Law includes federal student loans and other campus-based awards such as work study. Additionally, the law school administers a variety of grants and scholarships based on financial need and/or need and academic merit.

Career Development

The Office of Career Development is a resource for students, alumni, and prospective employers. It operates one of the largest on-campus recruitment programs in the country, provides opportunities for legal employment, and maintains an online job database of positions available throughout the nation. The staff conducts career counseling, résumé workshops, and programs on traditional and nontraditional law careers in the private and public sectors.

Applicant Profile Not Available

UNIVERSITY OF CALIFORNIA, DAVIS SCHOOL OF LAW (KING HALL)

Admission Office, 400 Mrak Hall Drive
Davis, CA 95616-5201
Phone: 530.752.6477
E-mail: admissions@law.ucdavis.edu; Website: www.law.ucdavis.edu

*ABA
Approved
Since
1968*

The Basics

Type of school	Public
Term	Semester
Application deadline	2/1
Application fee	$75
Financial aid deadline	3/2
Can first year start other than fall?	No
Student to faculty ratio	11.3 to 1
# of housing spaces available restricted to law students	
graduate housing for which law students are eligible	844

Faculty and Administrators

	Total		Men		Women		Minorities	
	Spr	Fall	Spr	Fall	Spr	Fall	Spr	Fall
Full-time	47	42	26	21	21	21	17	16
Other full-time	0	1	0	0	0	1	0	1
Deans, librarians, & others who teach	10	9	2	2	8	7	4	4
Part-time	16	18	11	13	5	5	1	3
Total	73	70	39	36	34	34	22	24

Curriculum

	Full-Time	Part-Time
Typical first-year section size	72	0
Is there typically a "small section" of the first-year class, other than Legal Writing, taught by full-time faculty	Yes	No
If yes, typical size offered last year	36	
# of classroom course titles beyond first-year curriculum		92
# of upper division courses, excluding seminars, with an enrollment: Under 25		41
25–49		30
50–74		6
75–99		5
100+		8
# of seminars		17
# of seminar positions available		298
# of seminar positions filled	217	0
# of positions available in simulation courses	502	
# of simulation positions filled	431	0
# of positions available in faculty supervised clinical courses	129	
# of faculty supervised clinical positions filled	125	0
# involved in field placements	129	0
# involved in law journals	255	0
# involved in moot court or trial competitions	165	0
# of credit hours required to graduate		88

JD Enrollment and Ethnicity

	Men		Women		Full-Time		Part-Time		1st-Year		Total		JD Degs. Awd.
	#	%	#	%	#	%	#	%	#	%	#	%	
All Hispanics	20	6.7	28	9.7	48	8.1	0	0.0	22	11.5	48	8.1	19
Am. Ind./AK Nat.	1	0.3	0	0.0	1	0.2	0	0.0	0	0.0	1	0.2	1
Asian	63	21.1	70	24.1	133	22.6	0	0.0	34	17.7	133	22.6	51
Black/Af. Am.	6	2.0	3	1.0	9	1.5	0	0.0	3	1.6	9	1.5	4
Nat. HI/Pac. Isl.	0	0.0	1	0.3	1	0.2	0	0.0	0	0.0	1	0.2	0
2 or more races	10	3.3	8	2.8	18	3.1	0	0.0	18	9.4	18	3.1	0
Subtotal (minor.)	100	33.4	110	37.9	210	35.7	0	0.0	77	40.1	210	35.7	77
Nonres. Alien	6	2.0	9	3.1	15	2.5	0	0.0	2	1.0	15	2.5	0
White/Cauc.	155	51.8	137	47.2	292	49.6	0	0.0	98	51.0	292	49.6	82
Unknown	38	12.7	34	11.7	72	12.2	0	0.0	15	7.8	72	12.2	34
Total	299	50.8	290	49.2	589	100.0	0	0.0	192	32.6	589		195

Transfers

Transfers in	11
Transfers out	13

Tuition and Fees

	Resident	Nonresident
Full-time	$41,763	$50,595
Part-time		
Tuition Guarantee Program	N	

Living Expenses

Estimated living expenses for singles

Living on campus	Living off campus	Living at home
N/A	$16,700	N/A

UNIVERSITY OF CALIFORNIA, DAVIS SCHOOL OF LAW (KING HALL)

ABA Approved Since 1968

GPA and LSAT Scores

	Total	Full-Time	Part-Time
# of apps	4,020	4,020	0
# of offers	943	943	0
# of matrics	196	196	0
75% GPA	3.80	3.80	0.00
Median GPA	3.69	3.69	0.00
25% GPA	3.53	3.53	0.00
75% LSAT	165	165	0
Median LSAT	163	163	0
25% LSAT	160	160	0

Grants and Scholarships (from prior year)

	Total		Full-Time		Part-Time	
	#	%	#	%	#	%
Total # of students	606		606		0	
Total # receiving grants	495	81.7	495	81.7	0	0.0
Less than 1/2 tuition	342	56.4	342	56.4	0	0.0
Half to full tuition	148	24.4	148	24.4	0	0.0
Full tuition	0	0.0	0	0.0	0	0.0
More than full tuition	5	0.8	5	0.8	0	0.0
Median grant amount			$12,579		$0	

Informational and Library Resources

Total amount spent on library materials	$961,722
Study seating capacity inside the library	311
# of full-time equivalent professional librarians	8
Hours per week library is open	67
# of open, wired connections available to students	0
# of networked computers available for use by students	84
Has wireless network?	Y
Requires computer?	N

JD Attrition (from prior year)

	Academic	Other	Total	
	#	#	#	%
1st year	0	17	17	7.9
2nd year	1	1	2	1.0
3rd year	0	0	0	0.0
4th year	0	0	0	0.0

Employment (9 months after graduation)

	Total	Percentage
Employment status known	190	99.5
Employment status unknown	1	0.5
Employed	183	96.3
Pursuing graduate degrees	5	2.6
Unemployed (seeking, not seeking, or studying for the bar)	0	0.0
Type of Employment		
# employed in law firms	103	56.3
# employed in business and industry	9	4.9
# employed in government	20	10.9
# employed in public interest	12	6.6
# employed as judicial clerks	9	4.9
# employed in academia	11	6.0
Geographic Location		
# employed in state	139	76.0
# employed outside the US	0	0.0
# of states where employed	10	

Bar Passage Rates

First-time takers	195	Reporting %	94.36
Average school %	88.04	Average state %	73.19
Average pass difference	14.85		

Jurisdiction	Takers	Passers	Pass %	State %	Diff %
California	184	162	88.04	73.19	14.85

UNIVERSITY OF CALIFORNIA, DAVIS SCHOOL OF LAW (KING HALL)

Admission Office, 400 Mrak Hall Drive
Davis, CA 95616-5201
Phone: 530.752.6477
E-mail: admissions@law.ucdavis.edu; Website: www.law.ucdavis.edu

Introduction

The School of Law at the University of California, Davis, is a national center of legal learning characterized by the scholarly excellence and ambition of its faculty and student body, as well as an abiding commitment to being a diverse community serving the welfare of its constituents and the world around it. It is fully accredited by the American Bar Association and is a member of the Association of American Law Schools. The school is housed in a newly expanded state-of-the-art building, King Hall, named for Dr. Martin Luther King Jr. in honor of his efforts to bring social and political justice to disadvantaged peoples.

The Davis campus, a major research university consistently among the country's top 20 in research funding, is a little over an hour from San Francisco, and 15 minutes from Sacramento, within easy reach of major recreational areas such as Napa, Carmel, and Lake Tahoe. The campus occupies 3,600 acres within the bike-friendly and charming college town of Davis.

The law school's idyllic surroundings and close proximity to the Bay Area and the state capital create abundant opportunities for a well-rounded educational and professional experience. The campus offers a full range of excellent graduate and professional programs.

Library and Physical Facilities

Faculty offices, classrooms, and the Mabie Law Library are housed in King Hall, which has just undergone a major expansion and renovation that makes it one of the most beautiful and functional facilities in the country. It has two moot courtrooms, a pretrial-skills laboratory, a large computer lab, study carrels, student journal offices, lounges, an infant care co-op, and offices for student organizations, all easily accessible to disabled students. Each law student has 24-hour access to the building.

Study carrels are assigned to first-year students, and librarians assist students with legal research needs. Students enjoy access to numerous legal print and online resources via the library and California Digital Library.

Classrooms have the latest in audiovisual and multimedia technology. Wireless Internet access is available throughout the law school.

Curriculum

The School of Law offers a three-year, full-time program in law leading to the Juris Doctor degree, and a postgraduate program leading to an LLM. At King Hall, a faculty with a national reputation for cutting-edge scholarship and devoted teaching is combined with an outstanding and diverse student body. The faculty includes worldwide leaders in many fields, including Constitutional Law; Intellectual Property; Environmental Law; Civil Rights; Critical Race Theory; Trusts, Wills, and Estates; Property; Contracts; Corporate Law and Securities; Evidence; Criminal Law and Procedure; Civil Procedure; Complex Litigation; Latinos and the Law; and Immigration Law and Policy. Each first-year section typically has about 65 students, and each student is taught at least one of the required first-year courses in a small group of

30–35 students. A distinctive feature of the school is a weeklong introductory course that precedes the formal first-year curriculum. Upper-division courses may be selected within broad areas of concentration such as criminal justice, business and taxation, civil litigation, estate planning and taxation, labor and employment law, environmental law, human rights and social justice law, immigration law, intellectual property, international law, and constitutional and other public law. Students may also combine JD studies with another graduate or professional program such as an MBA.

Special Programs

The school is known for its superb clinical programs in which students work under the supervision of practicing lawyers in many different substantive areas. Students also participate in externships in trial and appellate courts as well as in federal, state, and local government offices and nonprofit organizations throughout California and in Washington, DC.

The law school has four in-house clinics: Immigration, Civil Rights, Prison Law, and Family Protection. The Immigration Law Clinic, in which students work with one of the best immigration faculties in the United States, allows students to assist immigrants facing deportation.

Students participating in the Civil Rights Clinic appear in federal court in constitutional litigation, representing people who might otherwise have no counsel.

The Family Protection Clinic represents many low-income people who are not native English speakers and who need family law and domestic violence assistance.

First-year students perform an oral argument as a part of the required legal research and writing program, and can later participate, if they choose, in the formal Moot Court Program, which emphasizes appellate advocacy. Skills courses cover the major elements of both litigation and nonlitigation practice. These include pretrial skills (interviewing, counseling, and document drafting); negotiation, mediation, and alternative dispute resolution; business planning; and trial practice. The school has enjoyed excellent success in state, national, and international competitions in moot court and negotiations.

Students in the Public Interest Law Program receive a certificate based on required coursework, practical experience, and community service. This program culminates each year in a public service graduation ceremony, at which a graduating student is presented with the Martin Luther King Jr. Community Service Award. Students in the Environmental Law Program receive a certificate for completion of an environmental curriculum. King Hall students can also participate in a Pro Bono Program designed to both help address the unmet legal service needs of disadvantaged persons and nonprofit organizations and impress upon students the professional responsibility of lawyers to perform public service.

Admission

While the admission process is highly selective, it is by no means mechanical. The Admission Committee seeks excellent students of diverse backgrounds and interests. Each application is carefully reviewed with consideration given to many factors, including undergraduate grades and trends, LSAT scores, economic and other disadvantages, advanced studies, work experience, extracurricular and community activities, maturity, and commitment to the study of law. Residency is not a factor in the admission process. Open houses and information sessions for prospective applicants occur throughout the year. Guided tours can be arranged.

Student Life

King Hall is unusual among the nation's leading law schools for its wonderful sense of community. The student body is small compared to that of most schools, which lessens competition among a highly qualified student cohort. Students work extraordinarily well with each other, faculty, administrators, and staff. Faculty and administrators have an open-door policy for students. Cooperation and collegiality are the hallmarks of intellectual life at King Hall, and alumni look back fondly on their law school years.

An academic support program, including a bar preparation component during the third year, is available to all students. Students run five journals: the *UC Davis Law Review* and specialized journals in international law, environmental law, juvenile justice law, and business law.

Students sit on the student/faculty Educational Policy, Faculty Appointments, and Admission Committees. There are about 30 active student organizations encompassing a wide variety of interests. The La Raza Law Students Association's Lorenzo Patiño banquet honoring an alumnus and the King Hall Legal Foundation auction to raise funds for public interest are two of many student-sponsored events that highlight each academic year. The extremely positive attitude of King Hall students was noted and commented upon in our most recent ABA inspection report.

Expenses and Financial Aid

The School of Law Financial Aid office is available for the exclusive use of law students who desire counseling and advice. All financial aid services, from entrance through graduation, are administered at the law school. The school participates in all nationally recognized aid programs, such as Federal Perkins Loans and Federal Work-Study, and participates as well in the Federal Direct Loan Program. Over 63 percent of King Hall students receive need-based grants as part of their financial aid awards. Each year, two entering students are selected to receive the prestigious Martin Luther King Jr. Scholarships based on demonstrated commitment to public interest. University student loan and grant funds are available for child care. FAFSA and Need Access forms are required for aid consideration.

Housing

A wide variety of reasonably priced housing is available in the local community. The university maintains on-campus apartments for students and student families.

Career Services

The Career Services office successfully and enthusiastically assists students in securing rewarding summer and post-JD positions. Approximately 100 employers visit the campus to interview students, and many others advertise using the school's online database. Career Services presents speakers and training workshops geared to student needs and to the hiring cycles of various segments of the legal and law-related job markets. Students also have access to many professional opportunities through job fairs, online nationwide listings, and other sources. Almost all students are employed at graduation.

APPLICANT PROFILE

University of California, Davis School of Law (King Hall)
This grid includes only applicants who earned 120–180 LSAT scores under standard administrations.

LSAT Score	GPA																			
	3.75 +		3.50–3.74		3.25–3.49		3.00–3.24		2.75–2.99		2.50–2.74		2.25–2.49		2.00–2.24		Below 2.00		No GPA		Total	
	Apps	Adm	Apps	Adm	Apps	Adm	Apps	Adm	Apps	Adm	Apps	Adm	Apps	Adm	Apps	Adm	Apps	Adm	Apps	Adm	Apps	Adm
175–180	4	4	3	3	6	5	6	3	3	1	1	0	0	0	0	0	0	0	0	0	23	16
170–174	28	27	40	37	30	24	24	12	11	2	6	0	2	0	1	1	1	0	3	1	146	104
165–169	103	96	153	132	136	84	85	22	51	4	23	0	3	0	2	0	3	0	9	5	568	343
160–164	242	185	419	147	375	23	208	9	81	3	44	1	10	0	3	0	1	0	27	5	1410	373
155–159	177	48	255	22	212	3	123	0	73	1	26	0	17	0	3	0	0	0	21	1	907	75
150–154	73	13	132	9	119	2	112	0	45	0	25	0	12	0	5	0	2	0	14	0	539	24
145–149	24	1	47	0	55	0	51	0	43	0	18	0	6	0	3	0	0	0	6	0	253	1
140–144	3	0	14	0	23	0	20	0	21	0	17	0	5	0	2	0	0	0	1	0	106	0
135–139	0	0	2	0	6	0	13	0	12	0	7	0	5	0	5	0	0	0	1	0	51	0
130–134	0	0	0	0	2	0	1	0	1	0	2	0	0	0	0	0	0	0	0	0	6	0
125–129	0	0	1	0	0	0	0	0	1	0	0	0	1	0	0	0	0	0	0	0	3	0
120–124	0	0	0	0	0	0	0	0	0	0	0	0	0	0	0	0	0	0	0	0	0	0
Total	654	374	1066	350	964	141	643	46	342	11	169	1	61	0	24	1	7	0	82	12	4012	936

Apps = Number of Applicants
Adm = Number Admitted
Reflects 99% of the total applicant pool; highest LSAT data reported.

UNIVERSITY OF CALIFORNIA, HASTINGS COLLEGE OF THE LAW

200 McAllister Street
San Francisco, CA 94102
Phone: 415.565.4623; Fax: 415.581.8946
E-mail: admiss@uchastings.edu; Website: www.uchastings.edu

The Basics

Type of school	Public
Term	Semester
Application deadline	3/1
Application fee	$75
Financial aid deadline	3/1
Can first year start other than fall?	No
Student to faculty ratio	15.3 to 1
# of housing spaces available restricted to law students	280
graduate housing for which law students are eligible	280

Faculty and Administrators

	Total		Men		Women		Minorities	
	Spr	Fall	Spr	Fall	Spr	Fall	Spr	Fall
Full-time	67	70	42	43	25	27	17	18
Other full-time	1	1	0	0	1	1	1	1
Deans, librarians, & others who teach	5	5	1	1	4	4	2	2
Part-time	126	103	82	61	44	41	19	19
Total	199	179	125	105	74	73	39	40

Curriculum

	Full-Time	Part-Time
Typical first-year section size	80	0
Is there typically a "small section" of the first-year class, other than Legal Writing, taught by full-time faculty	No	No
If yes, typical size offered last year		
# of classroom course titles beyond first-year curriculum	177	
# of upper division courses, excluding seminars, with an enrollment: Under 25	144	
25–49	46	
50–74	18	
75–99	20	
100+	2	
# of seminars	70	
# of seminar positions available	1,401	
# of seminar positions filled	983	0
# of positions available in simulation courses	1,652	
# of simulation positions filled	1,271	0
# of positions available in faculty supervised clinical courses	233	
# of faculty supervised clinical positions filled	193	0
# involved in field placements	179	0
# involved in law journals	461	0
# involved in moot court or trial competitions	125	0
# of credit hours required to graduate	86	

JD Enrollment and Ethnicity

	Men		Women		Full-Time		Part-Time		1st-Year		Total		JD Degs. Awd.
	#	%	#	%	#	%	#	%	#	%	#	%	
All Hispanics	59	10.2	63	9.4	122	9.8	0	0.0	47	12.2	122	9.8	32
Am. Ind./AK Nat.	6	1.0	2	0.3	8	0.6	0	0.0	0	0.0	8	0.6	3
Asian	98	17.0	157	23.4	255	20.4	0	0.0	89	23.1	255	20.4	98
Black/Af. Am.	11	1.9	21	3.1	32	2.6	0	0.0	11	2.9	32	2.6	14
Nat. HI/Pac. Isl.	0	0.0	1	0.1	1	0.1	0	0.0	1	0.3	1	0.1	0
2 or more races	121	20.9	15	2.2	136	10.9	0	0.0	20	5.2	136	10.9	0
Subtotal (minor.)	295	51.0	259	38.7	554	44.4	0	0.0	168	43.6	554	44.4	147
Nonres. Alien	3	0.5	14	2.1	17	1.4	0	0.0	2	0.5	17	1.4	0
White/Cauc.	202	34.9	312	46.6	514	41.2	0	0.0	188	48.8	514	41.2	188
Unknown	78	13.5	85	12.7	162	13.0	1	100.0	27	7.0	163	13.1	77
Total	578	46.3	670	53.7	1247	99.9	1	0.1	385	30.8	1248		421

Transfers

Transfers in	22
Transfers out	23

Tuition and Fees

	Resident	Nonresident
Full-time	$38,906	$50,131
Part-time		
Tuition Guarantee Program	N	

Living Expenses

Estimated living expenses for singles

Living on campus	Living off campus	Living at home
$19,930	$19,930	$19,930

UNIVERSITY OF CALIFORNIA, HASTINGS COLLEGE OF THE LAW

ABA
Approved
Since
1939

GPA and LSAT Scores

	Total	Full-Time	Part-Time
# of apps	5,881	5,881	0
# of offers	1,323	1,323	0
# of matrics	383	383	0
75% GPA	3.71	3.71	0.00
Median GPA	3.60	3.60	0.00
25% GPA	3.45	3.45	0.00
75% LSAT	165	165	0
Median LSAT	164	164	0
25% LSAT	160	160	0

Grants and Scholarships (from prior year)

	Total		Full-Time		Part-Time	
	#	%	#	%	#	%
Total # of students	1,299		1,292		7	
Total # receiving grants	992	76.4	992	76.8	0	0.0
Less than 1/2 tuition	982	75.6	982	76.0	0	0.0
Half to full tuition	10	0.8	10	0.8	0	0.0
Full tuition	0	0.0	0	0.0	0	0.0
More than full tuition	0	0.0	0	0.0	0	0.0
Median grant amount			$7,900		$0	

Informational and Library Resources

Total amount spent on library materials	$1,540,729
Study seating capacity inside the library	796
# of full-time equivalent professional librarians	10
Hours per week library is open	102
# of open, wired connections available to students	481
# of networked computers available for use by students	146
Has wireless network?	Y
Requires computer?	N

JD Attrition (from prior year)

	Academic	Other	Total	
	#	#	#	%
1st year	2	10	12	2.6
2nd year	1	25	26	6.2
3rd year	0	0	0	0.0
4th year	0	0	0	0.0

Employment (9 months after graduation)

	Total	Percentage
Employment status known	407	97.8
Employment status unknown	9	2.2
Employed	352	86.5
Pursuing graduate degrees	8	2.0
Unemployed (seeking, not seeking, or studying for the bar)	25	6.1
Type of Employment		
# employed in law firms	209	59.4
# employed in business and industry	32	9.1
# employed in government	41	11.6
# employed in public interest	22	6.2
# employed as judicial clerks	17	4.8
# employed in academia	31	8.8
Geographic Location		
# employed in state	309	87.8
# employed outside the US	1	0.3
# of states where employed	18	

Bar Passage Rates

First-time takers	417	Reporting %	92.33
Average school %	84.94	Average state %	73.19
Average pass difference	11.75		

Jurisdiction	Takers	Passers	Pass %	State %	Diff %
California	385	327	84.94	73.19	11.75

UNIVERSITY OF CALIFORNIA, HASTINGS COLLEGE OF THE LAW

200 McAllister Street
San Francisco, CA 94102
Phone: 415.565.4623; Fax: 415.581.8946
E-mail: admiss@uchastings.edu; Website: www.uchastings.edu

Introduction

UC Hastings College of the Law offers a superb legal education in San Francisco, one of the world's great cities. Hastings was the first public law school in California, founded in 1878 as the law department of the University of California. The faculty at Hastings is composed of exceptional teachers who are also nationally known scholars. They are accessible to students and encourage a collaborative learning environment. Hastings has produced more judges than any other law school in the state, and its graduates can be found practicing law throughout California and the nation, in every kind of setting. Hastings graduates also have a significant presence in business and government.

The law school is situated in the heart of the city, near City Hall, state and federal courts, the arts district, the financial district, and the downtown shopping area. This central location provides access for students to pursue internships and externships with judges, city and state agencies, and nearby nonprofit research and advocacy groups. The location also provides unparalleled opportunities for recreation: theater, music, restaurants, professional and amateur sports, and a world-class transportation system.

Library, Technology, and Housing

Hastings is an urban campus with three buildings, all having wireless Internet access. The classroom building was renovated in 2000, and renovation of the library/administration building was completed in the fall of 2007. The new library is designed to be both comfortable and functional, with small-group study rooms, both open areas and individual carrels, and access to traditional and online research tools. McAllister Tower is a splendid, remodeled art deco building with 250 apartments, many with stunning views of the city. The building also features a comfortable lounge and a gym, including a basketball court often frequented by local attorneys and judges as well as Hastings students.

Curriculum

The UC Hastings curriculum offers a broad spectrum of basic and specialized courses. The law school's curricular strengths mirror the strengths of San Francisco. Students can focus on international human rights and business law, public interest law, intellectual property law, business and tax law, or litigation and its alternatives. San Francisco is a global city that draws on experts from Silicon Valley and the greater Bay Area to enrich course offerings.

Special Programs

- **Concentrations**: Students may earn a certificate of concentration in any of the following areas: Civil Litigation, Criminal Law, Law and Health Sciences, Intellectual Property, International Law, Social Justice Lawyering, or Tax Law.
- **Clinics and Judicial Externships**: Hastings provides an exciting and diverse array of opportunities for students to gain practical experience. Under clinical faculty supervision, students represent real clients in in-house and out-placement clinics specializing in community development, environmental law, labor and employment, housing and disability rights, law reform, international human rights, immigrants' rights, and legislation. In these clinics, students learn a variety of lawyering techniques, including counseling and planning, litigation, alternative dispute resolution, and legislation. Simulation courses teach trial and appellate advocacy, negotiation, mediation, contract drafting, problem solving, and professional ethics. More than 100 students a year spend a semester serving as externs in the state and federal courts, including the Supreme Court of California.
- **International Programs**: Hastings offers an exceptionally strong curriculum focusing on international human rights, as well as international business and trade law. In addition, students may participate in the work of the Center for Gender and Refugee Studies, the Immigrants' Rights Clinic, and the Hastings-to-Haiti Partnership. Hastings also offers a dozen study-abroad programs in Argentina, Australia, China, Denmark, England, France, Germany, Hungary, Italy, and the Netherlands and supports students who wish to study abroad in other locations.
- **Joint-Degree Programs**: Hastings students may participate in a joint-degree program with any accredited graduate program. Hastings students have simultaneously earned degrees in public policy, public health, and business administration, among others.
- **Legal Education Opportunity Program (LEOP)**: LEOP recognizes that the traditional academic criteria used to determine admission might not be the best indicators of academic potential for students from nontraditional backgrounds. LEOP admits students who have had to overcome significant obstacles and assists them to excel academically.
- **Centers and Institutes**: Students have opportunities to work in the law school's highly acclaimed research and advocacy centers: the Center for Gender and Refugee Studies, the Center for Negotiation and Dispute Resolution, the Center for State and Local Government Law, the Center for WorkLife Law, and the Public Law Research Institute.
- **LLM Program**: Graduates of non-US law schools may earn a master of laws degree in US Legal Studies.

Cocurricular and Student Activities

The strength and diversity of the Hastings student body are reflected in more than 60 student organizations that sponsor intellectual, social, and political events. Hastings publishes nine student-edited law reviews. The *Hastings Law Journal* is a general-interest publication. In addition, eight specialty law reviews focus on a variety of issues, including business law, constitutional law, communication and entertainment law, international and comparative law, environmental law, science and technology, and the law relating to race or gender. Students may also join the college's award-winning moot court, negotiation, client counseling, and trial practice teams, which compete in state, national, and international competitions. Students also engage in a variety of legal and nonlegal community service activities in and around the Hastings neighborhood.

Financial Aid

The majority of UC Hastings students receive need-based and merit-based financial assistance from college-administered sources. Scholarships and grants recognize and encourage the achievement, service, and professional promise of students. Students who pursue qualifying public interest and government sector employment may receive loan repayment assistance after graduation through the Public Interest Career Assistance Program (PICAP).

Career Services

UC Hastings offers one of the most comprehensive law career services offices in the West. The office assists students and alumni in clarifying their goals, acquiring job search strategies, and honing interviewing techniques. It provides access to full-time, part-time, and summer job listings. Every year, more than 200 employers visit the campus to interview students for both summer associate positions and permanent postgraduation employment. Several hundred additional employers from throughout the nation participate in the recruit-by-mail program.

APPLICANT PROFILE

University of California, Hastings College of the Law
This grid includes only applicants who earned 120–180 LSAT scores under standard administrations.

LSAT Score	GPA																					
	3.75 +		3.50–3.74		3.25–3.49		3.00–3.24		2.75–2.99		2.50–2.74		2.25–2.49		2.00–2.24		Below 2.00		No GPA		Total	
	Apps	Adm	Apps	Adm	Apps	Adm	Apps	Adm	Apps	Adm	Apps	Adm	Apps	Adm	Apps	Adm	Apps	Adm	Apps	Adm	Apps	Adm
175–180	16	16	7	7	16	7	11	4	4	0	3	0	0	0	0	0	0	0	1	1	58	35
170–174	39	31	77	58	47	26	39	10	20	2	10	0	5	0	2	0	2	0	3	1	244	128
165–169	174	129	242	192	233	125	137	45	63	1	32	0	9	0	3	0	1	0	20	11	914	503
160–164	336	189	594	231	507	75	289	13	93	4	49	0	20	1	8	0	0	0	37	6	1933	519
155–159	189	19	360	33	311	10	192	6	114	1	49	0	23	1	5	0	0	0	29	0	1272	70
150–154	91	8	198	24	179	4	152	4	91	1	44	0	25	0	7	0	1	0	23	0	811	41
145–149	36	5	58	9	83	1	96	1	65	0	37	0	17	0	7	0	0	0	12	0	411	16
140–144	8	1	20	4	37	0	45	0	29	0	29	0	14	0	2	0	0	0	6	0	190	5
135–139	4	0	4	0	8	0	14	0	13	0	14	0	9	0	4	0	3	0	2	0	75	0
130–134	0	0	1	0	2	0	0	0	2	0	4	0	1	0	2	0	1	0	1	0	14	0
125–129	0	0	1	0	0	0	0	0	1	0	2	0	1	0	1	0	0	0	0	0	6	0
120–124	0	0	0	0	0	0	0	0	0	0	0	0	0	0	0	0	0	0	0	0	0	0
Total	893	398	1562	558	1423	248	975	83	495	9	273	0	124	2	41	0	8	0	134	19	5928	1317

Apps = Number of Applicants
Adm = Number Admitted
Reflects 99% of the total applicant pool; highest LSAT data reported.

UNIVERSITY OF CALIFORNIA AT LOS ANGELES (UCLA) SCHOOL OF LAW

Law Admissions Office, 71 Dodd Hall, Box 951445
Los Angeles, CA 90095-1445
Phone: 310.825.2080
E-mail: admissions@law.ucla.edu; Website: www.law.ucla.edu

ABA
Approved
Since
1950

The Basics

Type of school	Public
Term	Semester
Application deadline	2/1
Application fee	$75
Financial aid deadline	3/2
Can first year start other than fall?	No
Student to faculty ratio	11.2 to 1
# of housing spaces available restricted to law students	
graduate housing for which law students are eligible	141

Faculty and Administrators

	Total		Men		Women		Minorities	
	Spr	Fall	Spr	Fall	Spr	Fall	Spr	Fall
Full-time	76	73	53	48	23	25	12	10
Other full-time	12	13	4	7	8	6	1	1
Deans, librarians, & others who teach	9	10	7	5	2	5	2	1
Part-time	35	18	24	15	11	3	1	2
Total	132	114	88	75	44	39	16	14

Curriculum

	Full-Time	Part-Time
Typical first-year section size	80	0
Is there typically a "small section" of the first-year class, other than Legal Writing, taught by full-time faculty	Yes	No
If yes, typical size offered last year	40	
# of classroom course titles beyond first-year curriculum	200	

# of upper division courses, excluding seminars, with an enrollment:		
Under 25	82	
25–49	24	
50–74	17	
75–99	13	
100+	7	

# of seminars	69	
# of seminar positions available	1,084	
# of seminar positions filled	923	0
# of positions available in simulation courses	213	
# of simulation positions filled	207	0
# of positions available in faculty supervised clinical courses	168	
# of faculty supervised clinical positions filled	141	0
# involved in field placements	62	0
# involved in law journals	586	0
# involved in moot court or trial competitions	16	0
# of credit hours required to graduate	87	

JD Enrollment and Ethnicity

	Men		Women		Full-Time		Part-Time		1st-Year		Total		JD Degs. Awd.
	#	%	#	%	#	%	#	%	#	%	#	%	
All Hispanics	41	7.8	50	10.5	91	9.1	0	0.0	29	9.4	91	9.1	28
Am. Ind./AK Nat.	9	1.7	9	1.9	18	1.8	0	0.0	6	1.9	18	1.8	1
Asian	79	15.1	81	17.1	160	16.0	0	0.0	47	15.2	160	16.0	70
Black/Af. Am.	18	3.4	26	5.5	44	4.4	0	0.0	11	3.6	44	4.4	13
Nat. HI/Pac. Isl.	0	0.0	1	0.2	1	0.1	0	0.0	1	0.3	1	0.1	0
2 or more races	11	2.1	9	1.9	20	2.0	0	0.0	20	6.5	20	2.0	0
Subtotal (minor.)	158	30.2	176	37.1	334	33.4	0	0.0	114	36.9	334	33.4	112
Nonres. Alien	10	1.9	9	1.9	19	1.9	0	0.0	3	1.0	19	1.9	0
White/Cauc.	249	47.5	196	41.3	445	44.5	0	0.0	140	45.3	445	44.5	150
Unknown	107	20.4	94	19.8	201	20.1	0	0.0	52	16.8	201	20.1	80
Total	524	52.5	475	47.5	999	100.0	0	0.0	309	30.9	999		346

Transfers

Transfers in	34
Transfers out	7

Tuition and Fees

	Resident	Nonresident
Full-time	$40,616	$50,639
Part-time		
Tuition Guarantee Program	N	

Living Expenses

Estimated living expenses for singles

Living on campus	Living off campus	Living at home
N/A	$21,438	$12,957

UNIVERSITY OF CALIFORNIA AT LOS ANGELES (UCLA) SCHOOL OF LAW

ABA
Approved
Since
1950

GPA and LSAT Scores

	Total	Full-Time	Part-Time
# of apps	8,748	8,748	0
# of offers	1,436	1,436	0
# of matrics	308	308	0
75% GPA	3.87	3.87	0.00
Median GPA	3.77	3.77	0.00
25% GPA	3.56	3.56	0.00
75% LSAT	170	170	0
Median LSAT	168	168	0
25% LSAT	165	165	0

Grants and Scholarships (from prior year)

	Total #	Total %	Full-Time #	Full-Time %	Part-Time #	Part-Time %
Total # of students	1,011		1,011		0	
Total # receiving grants	682	67.5	682	67.5	0	0.0
Less than 1/2 tuition	522	51.6	522	51.6	0	0.0
Half to full tuition	126	12.5	126	12.5	0	0.0
Full tuition	1	0.1	1	0.1	0	0.0
More than full tuition	33	3.3	33	3.3	0	0.0
Median grant amount			$10,670		$0	

Informational and Library Resources

Total amount spent on library materials	$2,055,000
Study seating capacity inside the library	774
# of full-time equivalent professional librarians	14
Hours per week library is open	121
# of open, wired connections available to students	1,820
# of networked computers available for use by students	637
Has wireless network?	Y
Requires computer?	N

JD Attrition (from prior year)

	Academic #	Other #	Total #	Total %
1st year	0	17	17	5.3
2nd year	0	7	7	2.1
3rd year	1	2	3	0.9
4th year	0	0	0	0.0

Employment (9 months after graduation)

	Total	Percentage
Employment status known	361	99.2
Employment status unknown	3	0.8
Employed	339	93.9
Pursuing graduate degrees	5	1.4
Unemployed (seeking, not seeking, or studying for the bar)	6	1.7
Type of Employment		
# employed in law firms	232	68.4
# employed in business and industry	16	4.7
# employed in government	20	5.9
# employed in public interest	23	6.8
# employed as judicial clerks	31	9.1
# employed in academia	17	5.0
Geographic Location		
# employed in state	280	82.6
# employed outside the US	3	0.9
# of states where employed	15	

Bar Passage Rates

First-time takers	352	Reporting %	88.64
Average school %	85.26	Average state %	73.19
Average pass difference	12.07		

Jurisdiction	Takers	Passers	Pass %	State %	Diff %
California	312	266	85.26	73.19	12.07

UNIVERSITY OF CALIFORNIA AT LOS ANGELES (UCLA) SCHOOL OF LAW

Law Admissions Office, 71 Dodd Hall, Box 951445
Los Angeles, CA 90095-1445
Phone: 310.825.2080
E-mail: admissions@law.ucla.edu; Website: www.law.ucla.edu

Introduction

Located in the heart of Southern California, and nestled in a beautiful and safe residential neighborhood, UCLA School of Law is less than seven miles from the Pacific Ocean, and is housed on the UCLA campus. The law school has established a world-class learning environment that brings together talented, prolific legal scholars and enthusiastic, exceptional students. UCLA Law acquired and maintains its strong standing by creating pioneering academic programs, cultivating top legal scholars, and educating students who go on to be leaders in our society.

Los Angeles, with its rich social and cultural scene, offers unparalleled access to numerous recreational opportunities and activities, such as sporting events, theaters, museums, and live performances. UCLA Law is close enough to the thriving metropolis of Los Angeles for students to partake in the vibrant social and cultural scene, yet secluded enough for students to focus on their legal studies. The incredible weather, the international reach of the city, and the intellectually stimulating environment all contribute to a student's law school experience.

Curriculum

The law school offers a three-year, full-time course of study leading to a Juris Doctor degree. Evening, summer, or part-time programs are not offered. UCLA differs from many other institutions in that it invests major resources in its first-year Lawyering Skills program. This program combines the beginning of skills training, such as client interviewing and counseling, with traditional legal research and writing. As a requirement for graduation, each student must complete a course in Professional Responsibility and a Substantial Analytic Writing (SAW) project during the second or third year of law school. The law school also provides students with a small, intimate learning environment that includes three small classes for the first year and upper-level courses that typically meet off campus (including at faculty members' homes).

Faculty

The UCLA School of Law faculty is a treasured asset. Faculty members are leaders in their respective fields and are the mainstay of UCLA Law's high-quality legal education programs. They are some of the finest teachers in the academy, expanding the frontiers of interdisciplinary legal scholarship. Each year, the UCLA Law faculty demonstrates the caliber of its intellectual abilities by publishing groundbreaking scholarship in leading academic journals and law reviews, and the work is widely cited.

Special Programs

Academic Specializations: UCLA School of Law is unique in that it offers students an opportunity to specialize in five specific areas of the law: Business Law and Policy, Critical Race Studies, Entertainment and Media Law and Policy, Law and Philosophy, and the David J. Epstein Program in Public Interest Law and Policy.

Centers: UCLA School of Law has always emphasized progressive research on relevant topics. We have consistently generated groundbreaking scholarship by providing our faculty access to the tools and resources they need to conduct thoughtful, interdisciplinary research. Centers include:

- Center for Law and Economics
- Emmett Center on Climate Change and the Environment
- Empirical Legal Scholars Program
- Empirical Research Group
- Globalization and Labor Standards
- Native Nations Law and Policy Center
- Negotiation and Conflict Resolution Program
- Program on Understanding Law, Science, and Evidence (PULSE)
- Richard S. Ziman Center for Real Estate
- UCLA-RAND Center of Law and Public Policy
- Williams Institute on Sexual Orientation Law and Public Policy

Study-Abroad and Externship Programs: Law students may spend one semester abroad through student exchange agreements with universities in Argentina, France, Israel, Japan, Norway, Spain, and Switzerland. Some students also obtain approval for an individualized study-abroad program. UCLA Law has an extensive national and international student externship program. The law school has developed a core group of judicial and agency externships which include externships with federal judges, government agencies, public interest law firms, and nonprofit organizations. In addition, the UCDC Program is a uniquely collaborative full-time externship program in Washington, DC. Both full-time and part-time externships are available. Students can also propose new agency externships tailored to their academic goals.

Clinical Law Program: Since pioneering clinical legal education in the early 1970s, UCLA Law's Clinical Law Program has blazed a path of innovation and excellence. Typically, there are more than 30 clinical offerings each year with more than 300 clinical spots available for students. Some examples include the Civil Rights Litigation Clinic, Criminal Defense Clinic, Environmental Law Clinic, Immigration Clinic, International Justice Clinic, Mediation Clinic, Sports and the Law Clinic, and Supreme Court Clinic.

Joint Degrees

A number of students find it advantageous to pursue formal training in another field of study concurrently with their legal training. Typically, such concurrent-degree programs lead, after four years of study, to the simultaneous award of a Juris Doctor and an advanced degree from another school or department. Formal joint-degree programs are offered in the following areas: JD/MA (Afro-American Studies), JD/MA (American Indian Studies), JD/MBA (Anderson School of Management), JD/PhD (Philosophy), JD/MPH (Public Health), JD/MPP (Public Policy), JD/MSW (Social Welfare), and JD/MA (Urban Planning).

Student Life and Student Activities

A collegial environment at UCLA Law affords students many opportunities for participation and leadership in numerous student organizations and student-edited journals. UCLA School of Law has 13 student journals managed and edited by students on a wide range of topics.

Diverse student interests are represented in approximately 40 student organizations. The Moot Court Honors Program is open to all second- and third-year students and offers a large and effective program of mock appellate advocacy. The program also hosts a first-year competition, as well as the prestigious Roscoe Pound competition.

Housing

There are many housing options open to UCLA Law students, and the law school hosts a web-based service to help students with their roommate search. There are both university-owned and privately-owned apartments from which to choose.

Admission and Financial Aid

All applicants must have a baccalaureate degree from an accredited university or college of approved standing and must take the LSAT no later than the February administration. Students are admitted for the fall semester only. Admission is based primarily on proven outstanding academic and intellectual ability measured largely by the LSAT and the quality of undergraduate education as determined by not only the GPA, but also by such factors as the breadth, depth, and rigor of the undergraduate educational program. The Admissions Committee may also consider whether economic, physical, or other hardships and challenges have been overcome. Distinctive programmatic contributions, community or public service, letters of recommendation, work experience, career achievement, language ability, and career goals (with particular attention paid to the likelihood of the applicant representing underrepresented communities) are also factors taken into consideration.

Both need- and merit-based aid are available. All admitted students are automatically considered for merit scholarships. To apply for need-based aid, the FAFSA (www.fafsa.ed.gov) and the Need Access application (www.needaccess.org) should be filed no later than March 2. Applicants admitted to the law school as nonresident students (for tuition purposes) are eligible to be considered for resident classification if certain eligibility requirements are met. Most nonresident law students are able to achieve residency status during the second year of law school.

Career Services

The Office of Career Services provides students and alumni with professional career services and acts as a liaison between students and employers. Each first-year student is assigned to a counselor who will assist him/her through all the phases of career preparation, from the first-year summer job to postgraduate employment. The office is also dedicated to advising and assisting students interested in pursuing postgraduate judicial clerkships—highly sought-after positions secured by more than 9 percent of the class of 2009.

The office coordinates on-campus interviews and off-campus career fairs with approximately 350 interviewers from law firms, corporations, government agencies, and public interest organizations visiting the school annually. The office also hosts numerous panels, programs, and events, including an annual Small/Mid-Sized Law Firm Reception, an annual Government Reception and Information Fair, and an Alumni Mentor Program.

UCLA Law graduates are in high demand among employers from all major sectors of the country, with California, New York, and Washington, DC, representing the largest employment markets for our students.

Students and graduates seeking to pursue public interest employment can take advantage of the opportunities offered by our Office of Public Interest Programs. There is a loan repayment assistance program to increase the ability of JD graduates to pursue public service legal careers.

APPLICANT PROFILE

University of California at Los Angeles (UCLA) School of Law
This grid includes only applicants who earned 120–180 LSAT scores under standard administrations.

LSAT Score	3.75 +		3.50–3.74		3.25–3.49		3.00–3.24		2.75–2.99		2.50–2.74		2.25–2.49		2.00–2.24		Below 2.00		No GPA		Total	
	Apps	Adm	Apps	Adm	Apps	Adm	Apps	Adm	Apps	Adm	Apps	Adm	Apps	Adm	Apps	Adm	Apps	Adm	Apps	Adm	Apps	Adm
175–180	120	74	89	33	63	16	30	2	10	2	2	0	0	0	0	0	1	0	5	1	320	128
170–174	477	303	474	202	273	55	113	9	34	1	8	0	6	0	1	0	1	0	19	2	1406	572
165–169	934	443	795	131	452	25	190	4	68	1	24	1	11	0	3	0	3	0	35	2	2515	607
160–164	553	59	684	15	446	16	208	3	63	0	39	1	16	0	4	0	1	0	51	1	2065	95
155–159	208	14	305	10	228	5	136	2	71	0	34	0	15	0	4	0	0	0	28	1	1029	32
150–154	89	5	151	6	163	1	131	0	64	0	31	0	22	0	5	0	1	0	24	0	681	12
145–149	27	0	63	0	82	0	77	0	63	0	34	0	12	0	7	0	0	0	11	0	376	0
140–144	6	0	22	0	30	0	45	0	34	0	26	0	13	0	7	0	1	0	11	0	195	0
135–139	2	0	9	0	11	0	11	0	18	0	15	0	5	0	12	0	1	0	5	0	89	0
130–134	0	0	1	0	5	0	4	0	9	0	4	0	4	0	1	0	1	0	2	0	31	0
125–129	0	0	1	0	0	0	1	0	1	0	2	0	0	0	0	0	0	0	0	0	5	0
120–124	0	0	0	0	0	0	0	0	0	0	0	0	0	0	1	0	0	0	1	0	2	0
Total	2416	898	2594	397	1753	118	946	20	435	4	219	2	104	0	45	0	10	0	192	7	8714	1446

Apps = Number of Applicants
Adm = Number Admitted
Reflects 99% of the total applicant pool; highest LSAT data reported.

CALIFORNIA WESTERN SCHOOL OF LAW

225 Cedar Street
San Diego, CA 92101
Phone: 800.255.4252, ext. 1401 or 619.525.1401
E-mail: admissions@cwsl.edu; Website: www.CaliforniaWestern.edu

ABA
Approved
Since
1962

The Basics

Type of school	Private
Term	Semester
Application deadline	4/1 11/1
Application fee	$55
Financial aid deadline	4/1 10/14
Can first year start other than fall?	Yes
Student to faculty ratio	17.9 to 1
# of housing spaces available restricted to law students	
graduate housing for which law students are eligible	

Faculty and Administrators

	Total		Men		Women		Minorities	
	Spr	Fall	Spr	Fall	Spr	Fall	Spr	Fall
Full-time	39	44	24	30	15	14	6	6
Other full-time	1	1	1	1	0	0	1	1
Deans, librarians, & others who teach	12	13	4	5	8	8	2	3
Part-time	40	37	26	21	14	16	4	4
Total	92	95	55	57	37	38	13	14

Curriculum

	Full-Time	Part-Time
Typical first-year section size	77	0
Is there typically a "small section" of the first-year class, other than Legal Writing, taught by full-time faculty	No	No
If yes, typical size offered last year		
# of classroom course titles beyond first-year curriculum	119	

# of upper division courses, excluding seminars, with an enrollment:		
	Under 25	131
	25–49	30
	50–74	13
	75–99	18
	100+	6

# of seminars	35	
# of seminar positions available	858	
# of seminar positions filled	486	68
# of positions available in simulation courses	1,830	
# of simulation positions filled	1,183	133
# of positions available in faculty supervised clinical courses	71	
# of faculty supervised clinical positions filled	62	5
# involved in field placements	156	14
# involved in law journals	63	8
# involved in moot court or trial competitions	33	1
# of credit hours required to graduate	89	

JD Enrollment and Ethnicity

	Men		Women		Full-Time		Part-Time		1st-Year		Total		JD Degs. Awd.
	#	%	#	%	#	%	#	%	#	%	#	%	
All Hispanics	45	10.6	62	12.6	92	11.7	15	11.3	41	12.5	107	11.6	20
Am. Ind./AK Nat.	3	0.7	3	0.6	5	0.6	1	0.8	1	0.3	6	0.7	3
Asian	43	10.1	71	14.4	99	12.6	15	11.3	43	13.1	114	12.4	30
Black/Af. Am.	9	2.1	16	3.2	19	2.4	6	4.5	4	1.2	25	2.7	7
Nat. HI/Pac. Isl.	1	0.2	1	0.2	2	0.3	0	0.0	1	0.3	2	0.2	0
2 or more races	5	1.2	12	2.4	16	2.0	1	0.8	6	1.8	17	1.8	0
Subtotal (minor.)	106	24.9	165	33.5	233	29.6	38	28.6	96	29.3	271	29.5	66
Nonres. Alien	2	0.5	4	0.8	6	0.8	0	0.0	1	0.3	6	0.7	0
White/Cauc.	281	66.0	296	60.0	499	63.5	78	58.6	219	66.8	577	62.8	169
Unknown	37	8.7	28	5.7	48	6.1	17	12.8	12	3.7	65	7.1	23
Total	426	46.4	493	53.6	786	85.5	133	14.5	328	35.7	919		263

Transfers

Transfers in	1
Transfers out	11

Tuition and Fees

	Resident	Nonresident
Full-time	$40,780	$40,780
Part-time	$28,660	$28,660
Tuition Guarantee Program		N

Living Expenses

Estimated living expenses for singles

Living on campus	Living off campus	Living at home
N/A	$23,050	$14,970

CALIFORNIA WESTERN SCHOOL OF LAW

ABA
Approved
Since
1962

GPA and LSAT Scores

	Total	Full-Time	Part-Time
# of apps	2,816	2,628	203
# of offers	1,295	1,228	67
# of matrics	382	355	27
75% GPA	3.49	3.48	3.66
Median GPA	3.24	3.23	3.34
25% GPA	2.99	2.99	2.94
75% LSAT	157	157	157
Median LSAT	154	154	155
25% LSAT	151	151	151

Grants and Scholarships (from prior year)

	Total		Full-Time		Part-Time	
	#	%	#	%	#	%
Total # of students	892		791		101	
Total # receiving grants	383	42.9	355	44.9	28	27.7
Less than 1/2 tuition	198	22.2	185	23.4	13	12.9
Half to full tuition	111	12.4	102	12.9	9	8.9
Full tuition	9	1.0	8	1.0	1	1.0
More than full tuition	65	7.3	60	7.6	5	5.0
Median grant amount			$19,200		$13,500	

Informational and Library Resources

Total amount spent on library materials	$1,249,602
Study seating capacity inside the library	437
# of full-time equivalent professional librarians	10
Hours per week library is open	110
# of open, wired connections available to students	540
# of networked computers available for use by students	87
Has wireless network?	Y
Requires computer?	N

JD Attrition (from prior year)

	Academic	Other	Total	
	#	#	#	%
1st year	41	18	59	18.8
2nd year	0	3	3	1.0
3rd year	0	2	2	0.7
4th year	0	0	0	0.0

Employment (9 months after graduation)

	Total	Percentage
Employment status known	218	92.0
Employment status unknown	19	8.0
Employed	189	86.7
Pursuing graduate degrees	6	2.8
Unemployed (seeking, not seeking, or studying for the bar)	17	7.8
Type of Employment		
# employed in law firms	134	70.9
# employed in business and industry	25	13.2
# employed in government	15	7.9
# employed in public interest	10	5.3
# employed as judicial clerks	2	1.1
# employed in academia	3	1.6
Geographic Location		
# employed in state	160	84.7
# employed outside the US	1	0.5
# of states where employed	12	

Bar Passage Rates

First-time takers	231	Reporting %	100.00
Average school %	77.93	Average state %	73.67
Average pass difference	4.26		

Jurisdiction	Takers	Passers	Pass %	State %	Diff %
California	213	162	76.06	73.19	2.87
Nevada	7	7	100.00	73.00	27.00
New York	4	4	100.00	86.51	13.49
Arizona	3	3	100.00	79.76	20.24
Others (2)	4	4	100.00		

CALIFORNIA WESTERN SCHOOL OF LAW

225 Cedar Street
San Diego, CA 92101
Phone: 800.255.4252, ext. 1401 or 619.525.1401
E-mail: admissions@cwsl.edu; Website: www.CaliforniaWestern.edu

Introduction

California Western School of Law is the independent San Diego law school that educates lawyers as creative problem solvers and principled advocates—lawyers who frame the practice of law as a helping, collaborative profession. The law school's centers and institutes offer students many opportunities to explore the full scope of the law in real-life situations. California Western, accredited by the ABA (1962) and AALS (1967), emphasizes both theory and practice—rigorous academics and renowned real-world clinical programs—and invites students to explore the wide expanse of the law while preparing for practice.

Library and Physical Facilities

The award winning, four-story, 50,000-square-foot law library was dedicated in 2000 by US Supreme Court Justice Anthony Kennedy. The library holds more than 333,000 volumes, approximately 3,905 serial subscriptions, microforms currently equivalent to 154,000 volumes, audio- and videotapes, computer software, and interactive videos. The library also offers an excellent computer lab. The law library is wired with high-speed digital lines for fast network communications. There are 250 data ports for laptop computers in the building.

   Renovations to the historic classroom building at California Western have provided several large lecture halls, office space for 30 on-campus student organizations, an 1,840-square-foot student lounge, individual study rooms, and a computer lab. Students enjoy additional access to the student network and Internet via campus-wide wireless technology.

Curriculum

The California Western curriculum offers a broad and diverse selection of courses. The law school provides a rigorous, traditional legal education with an emphasis on developing problem-solving, communication, writing, and analytical skills. Areas of concentration are also offered in eight fields of study: business law; international law; labor and employment law; child, family, and elder law; criminal law; creative problem solving; intellectual property, telecommunications, and technology-regulations law; and health law and policy. Numerous academic programs, including clinical placements and skills-based learning, supplement the course curriculum.

   In addition to the traditional three-year curriculum, California Western offers a trimester academic calendar that allows students to study law year-round to complete their legal education in two years. California Western also offers a part-time day program.

Interdisciplinary Programs

California Western offers several dual-degree programs, allowing students to study two disciplines concurrently. The dual-degree program with the University of California, San Diego, offers degrees in political science (JD/PhD) and history (JD/PhD). California Western and the University of California, San Diego, also offer a joint degree in health law studies (MAS). In addition, California Western offers a dual-degree program with San Diego State University in both business (JD/MBA) and social work (JD/MSW).

University of California San Diego Affiliation

California Western and the University of California San Diego have an Agreement of Association that provides broad interdisciplinary opportunities for the faculty and students of both institutions. These opportunities include joint academic degrees, joint research efforts, a vibrant speaker series, sharing of facilities, and community outreach programs.

Study-Abroad Programs

Students have the opportunity to study in academic programs throughout the world, including in Chile, England, Ireland, Malta, and the Czech Republic. Additionally, semester-abroad opportunities are available at Victoria University of Wellington in New Zealand, the University of Aarhus in Denmark, the University of Paris X-Nanterre in France, and at Leiden University School of Law in the Netherlands. Students may also choose to do an academic internship with the International Criminal Process Clinic at The Hague, the Netherlands.

Special Programs

The Center for Creative Problem Solving investigates collaborative approaches to communication, conflict resolution, and problem solving. The Center develops curriculum, research, and projects to educate students and lawyers on methods for preventing problems and creatively solving those problems that already exist. It also houses *Proyecto ACCESO*, a Latin American center for training lawyers, judges, law students, government officials, and community leaders in the skills of oral advocacy, problem solving, and other forms of conflict resolution.

   Through the California Innocence Project, law students work alongside practicing criminal defense lawyers to seek the release of wrongfully convicted prisoners. Law students assist in the investigation, write briefs, and advocate for the release of clients.

   The Institute of Health Law Studies is a health law center that focuses on "improving health care today for all our tomorrows." It performs research, participates in advocacy activities, engages in community service, and provides education to advance its mission.

   The law school offers the LLM in Trial Advocacy specializing in Federal Criminal Law. International lawyers who are interested in studying comparative law or the US legal system may pursue the Master of Laws in Comparative Law (LLM) and the Master of Comparative Law (MCL).

Clinical Internship Program

California Western's Clinical Internship Program provides opportunities for students to gain practical lawyering experience in law offices, corporations, government agencies, and courts. Nearly 70 percent of California Western students participate in this popular program. Students have the opportunity to intern in almost any area of law. Out-of-town internships are available for students interested in developing these skills outside of

San Diego. Our students have worked in many countries, including Argentina, Brazil, Chile, China, England, the Philippines, Poland, Singapore, Spain, Sweden, and Switzerland. Students have arranged internships at the United Nations, the Asian Development Bank, the International Criminal Tribunal for Rwanda, Paramount Studios, the Federal Communications Commission, and the US Department of State.

Student Activities

The *Law Review* and the *International Law Journal* publish articles by academic scholars and practitioners as well as by California Western students. Students edit and manage these publications under supervision from faculty advisors and a professional staff.

The Moot Court Honors Board allows students interested in trial and appellate advocacy skills to practice and compete against other students. Under the supervision and guidance of faculty coaches, students also participate in advocacy competitions around the country. California Western advocacy teams are nationally recognized, and our students have won many regional and national awards in these competitions.

California Western has a vibrant student government. Nearly 30 student organizations reflect a broad range of interests and diversity.

Career Services

Career Services offers individualized, professional advice to students about their personal career goals and tailors strategies to assist students in reaching those goals. The department coordinates the on-campus recruitment program, career development programming, practice-area panel discussions, national alumni mentor network, Pro Bono Honors and Public Service Programs, and access to technological resources for career development. Prospective employers and alumni regularly visit the campus to meet with interested students.

Alumni

California Western's nearly 8,000 alumni work in large firms, domestic and foreign governments, large corporations, private practice, the judiciary, and academia. The law school's Alumni Admissions Recruiter program matches alumni with prospective students in the areas in which they reside. The Admissions Office can provide prospective students with a list of alumni in their area who are available to talk with them about employment opportunities and career advice.

Diversity

California Western's belief is that a richly diversified student body enhances the academic and interpersonal experiences of the law school. Half of the student body is female and approximately one-third is of an ethnic minority. California Western does not discriminate on the basis of race, color, creed, religion, sex, national origin, disability, sexual orientation, or veteran status.

Admission

Admission decisions are made on a rolling basis. Applicants are admitted based on an evaluation of the LSAT score, undergraduate academic record, personal statement, letters of recommendation, and other criteria, including work experience, campus and community activities, life/personal experiences, and evidence of leadership promise. Students are admitted to California Western to begin in August and January. Bachelor's degree and registration with LSAC's Credential Assembly Service are required. Application deadlines: fall—April 1; spring—November 1.

Financial Aid and Scholarships

More than 85 percent of California Western's students receive some form of financial assistance to fund their legal education. Need-based financial aid includes loans and work study. Numerous scholarships are awarded based on academic criteria and LSAT scores. Scholarships include the prestigious Kennedy Scholarship, the Robert J. Grey Jr. Scholarship, and the Trustees' Scholarship which, among other benefits, provide full tuition for three years. Other merit-based full and partial scholarships are awarded to incoming students, including diversity, career transition, and creative problem-solving scholarships. Academic achievement scholarships are available to continuing students. Scholarships are awarded by the Admissions Office after reviewing student admission applications.

APPLICANT PROFILE

California Western School of Law
This grid includes only applicants who earned 120–180 LSAT scores under standard administrations.

LSAT Score	3.75 +		3.50–3.74		3.25–3.49		3.00–3.24		2.75–2.99		2.50–2.74		Below 2.50		No GPA		Total	
	Apps	Adm	Apps	Adm	Apps	Adm	Apps	Adm	Apps	Adm	Apps	Adm	Apps	Adm	Apps	Adm	Apps	Adm
170–180	1	1	1	1	0	0	2	2	0	0	2	2	1	1	0	0	7	7
165–169	1	1	4	4	2	1	3	2	3	3	4	4	3	3	0	0	20	18
160–164	10	9	26	23	36	35	38	33	28	28	11	9	20	14	3	2	172	153
155–159	48	46	61	57	93	92	114	106	84	64	56	33	48	15	7	6	511	419
150–154	39	39	128	112	188	143	233	122	148	53	95	17	63	1	12	6	906	493
145–149	28	19	77	28	129	28	151	13	113	3	62	4	57	1	10	3	627	99
140–144	8	0	24	0	39	0	58	0	52	0	45	0	32	0	9	0	267	0
Below 140	2	0	4	0	8	0	17	0	23	0	13	0	21	0	2	0	90	0
Total	137	115	325	225	495	299	616	278	451	151	288	69	245	35	43	17	2600	1189

Apps = Number of Applicants   Adm = Number Admitted   Reflects 99% of the total applicant pool; highest LSAT data reported.

Miscellaneous applicants with no LSAT (i.e., MCL/LLM program) and nonstandard administration not in grid.

CAMPBELL UNIVERSITY, NORMAN ADRIAN WIGGINS SCHOOL OF LAW

225 Hillsborough Street
Raleigh, NC 27603
Phone: 919.865.5988; Fax: 919.865.5992
E-mail: admissions@law.campbell.edu; Website: www.law.campbell.edu

ABA
Approved
Since
1979

Section of Legal Education
and Admissions to the Bar

The Basics

Type of school	Private
Term	Semester
Application deadline	4/1
Application fee	$50
Financial aid deadline	3/1
Can first year start other than fall?	No
Student to faculty ratio	15.5 to 1
# of housing spaces available restricted to law students	
graduate housing for which law students are eligible	

Faculty and Administrators

	Total		Men		Women		Minorities	
	Spr	Fall	Spr	Fall	Spr	Fall	Spr	Fall
Full-time	23	23	17	17	6	6	4	3
Other full-time	1	0	0	0	1	0	0	0
Deans, librarians, & others who teach	5	5	2	2	3	3	3	3
Part-time	28	21	21	17	7	4	2	1
Total	57	49	40	36	17	13	9	7

Curriculum

	Full-Time	Part-Time
Typical first-year section size	40	0
Is there typically a "small section" of the first-year class, other than Legal Writing, taught by full-time faculty	Yes	No
If yes, typical size offered last year	40	
# of classroom course titles beyond first-year curriculum		113

# of upper division courses, excluding seminars, with an enrollment:		
	Under 25	39
	25–49	19
	50–74	14
	75–99	4
	100+	0

# of seminars		41
# of seminar positions available		738
# of seminar positions filled	475	0
# of positions available in simulation courses	290	
# of simulation positions filled	266	0
# of positions available in faculty supervised clinical courses		44
# of faculty supervised clinical positions filled	44	0
# involved in field placements	107	0
# involved in law journals	57	0
# involved in moot court or trial competitions	160	0
# of credit hours required to graduate		90

JD Enrollment and Ethnicity

	Men		Women		Full-Time		Part-Time		1st-Year		Total		JD Degs. Awd.
	#	%	#	%	#	%	#	%	#	%	#	%	
All Hispanics	4	1.8	11	4.7	15	3.3	0	0.0	1	0.6	15	3.3	3
Am. Ind./AK Nat.	0	0.0	0	0.0	0	0.0	0	0.0	0	0.0	0	0.0	1
Asian	3	1.4	6	2.6	9	2.0	0	0.0	4	2.4	9	2.0	3
Black/Af. Am.	4	1.8	11	4.7	15	3.3	0	0.0	7	4.3	15	3.3	6
Nat. HI/Pac. Isl.	0	0.0	0	0.0	0	0.0	0	0.0	0	0.0	0	0.0	0
2 or more races	0	0.0	0	0.0	0	0.0	0	0.0	0	0.0	0	0.0	0
Subtotal (minor.)	11	5.0	28	12.1	39	8.7	0	0.0	12	7.3	39	8.7	13
Nonres. Alien	1	0.5	0	0.0	1	0.2	0	0.0	0	0.0	1	0.2	0
White/Cauc.	206	94.5	204	87.9	410	91.1	0	0.0	152	92.7	410	91.1	93
Unknown	0	0.0	0	0.0	0	0.0	0	0.0	0	0.0	0	0.0	0
Total	218	48.4	232	51.6	450	100.0	0	0.0	164	36.4	450		106

Transfers

Transfers in	1
Transfers out	2

Tuition and Fees

	Resident	Nonresident
Full-time	$32,280	$32,280
Part-time		
Tuition Guarantee Program		N

Living Expenses

Estimated living expenses for singles

Living on campus	Living off campus	Living at home
N/A	$26,650	$26,650

CAMPBELL UNIVERSITY, NORMAN ADRIAN WIGGINS SCHOOL OF LAW

ABA
Approved
Since
1979

GPA and LSAT Scores

	Total	Full-Time	Part-Time
# of apps	1,469	1,469	0
# of offers	486	486	0
# of matrics	162	162	0
75% GPA	3.59	3.59	0.00
Median GPA	3.37	3.37	0.00
25% GPA	3.12	3.12	0.00
75% LSAT	158	158	0
Median LSAT	156	156	0
25% LSAT	154	154	0

Grants and Scholarships (from prior year)

	Total		Full-Time		Part-Time	
	#	%	#	%	#	%
Total # of students	405		405		0	
Total # receiving grants	136	33.6	136	33.6	0	0.0
Less than 1/2 tuition	113	27.9	113	27.9	0	0.0
Half to full tuition	18	4.4	18	4.4	0	0.0
Full tuition	5	1.2	5	1.2	0	0.0
More than full tuition	0	0.0	0	0.0	0	0.0
Median grant amount			$10,325		$0	

Informational and Library Resources

Total amount spent on library materials	$1,027,959
Study seating capacity inside the library	266
# of full-time equivalent professional librarians	5
Hours per week library is open	108
# of open, wired connections available to students	0
# of networked computers available for use by students	26
Has wireless network?	Y
Requires computer?	N

JD Attrition (from prior year)

	Academic	Other	Total	
	#	#	#	%
1st year	3	8	11	6.9
2nd year	0	0	0	0.0
3rd year	0	1	1	0.9
4th year	0	0	0	0.0

Employment (9 months after graduation)

	Total	Percentage
Employment status known	97	100.0
Employment status unknown	0	0.0
Employed	87	89.7
Pursuing graduate degrees	2	2.1
Unemployed (seeking, not seeking, or studying for the bar)	7	7.2
Type of Employment		
# employed in law firms	61	70.1
# employed in business and industry	7	8.0
# employed in government	13	14.9
# employed in public interest	1	1.1
# employed as judicial clerks	2	2.3
# employed in academia	0	0.0
Geographic Location		
# employed in state	71	81.6
# employed outside the US	0	0.0
# of states where employed		5

Bar Passage Rates

First-time takers	97	Reporting %	89.69
Average school %	90.81	Average state %	76.80
Average pass difference	14.01		

Jurisdiction	Takers	Passers	Pass %	State %	Diff %
North Carolina	84	76	90.48	76.79	13.69
Virginia	3	3	100.00	77.06	22.94

CAMPBELL UNIVERSITY, NORMAN ADRIAN WIGGINS SCHOOL OF LAW

225 Hillsborough Street
Raleigh, NC 27603
Phone: 919.865.5988; Fax: 919.865.5992
E-mail: admissions@law.campbell.edu; Website: www.law.campbell.edu

Introduction

The Norman Adrian Wiggins School of Law at Campbell University is a highly demanding, purposely small, and intensely personal community of faculty and students. Campbell Law's aim, guided by transcendent values, is to develop lawyers who possess moral conviction, social compassion, and professional competence; who view the law as a calling to serve others and to create a more just society.

Campbell Law School is a private law school that is fully accredited by the American Bar Association, boasting more than three decades of excellence in legal education. Located within walking distance of the North Carolina state legislature; federal and state courts; federal, state, and local government agencies; and the region's top law firms, corporations, and nonprofits, Campbell Law provides a living legal laboratory to its students.

Campbell Law School encourages students to examine the relationship between spiritual and legal issues, to explore the theological foundations for law, to think differently about justice and the legal system, and to consider how they can help achieve a more just and merciful society. While embracing an intellectual perspective rooted in Christian tradition, Campbell Law School is committed to free and open discussion of ideas. Students are under no obligation to embrace any particular way of thinking.

For the past 21 years, Campbell Law's record of success on the North Carolina bar exam is unsurpassed by any other North Carolina law school.

Ranked No. 1 by *Forbes* as the "Best Place for Business and Careers" in 2008 and 2009, Raleigh offers a rich cultural history in a progressive setting. Raleigh is located just a few hours from legendary beaches in one direction and the scenic Blue Ridge Mountains in the other.

Enrollment

Campbell Law School is one of the smallest ABA-accredited private law schools in the country. With a limited first-year enrollment, students enjoy the many advantages of a law school that remains purposely small. Our community of students and faculty is intensely personal—students build a network of relationships that supports them during their legal studies and extends far beyond graduation.

Currently, our student body is comprised of 410 students from 24 different states, holding degrees from 109 colleges and universities, with 57 different majors represented. Campbell Law School is committed to enrolling a diverse student body and has an overall minority enrollment of 10 percent.

Faculty

Campbell Law School's faculty is a community of scholars who make teaching their priority. They are readily accessible and serve students as mentors, coaches, and professional role models. All faculty have open-door office policies and are available to consult regularly with students on an individual basis. Our professors are deeply committed to the search for knowledge through meaningful legal scholarship, but never at the expense of their devotion to the academic success and professional development of each student.

Facilities and Technology

Campbell Law School is located in the heart of downtown Raleigh. Each of the Law School's classrooms and courtrooms have video cameras to record lectures that most professors post via Blackboard for student review and use. In addition, the entire Law School is wireless, including student access to printers.

Curriculum

Campbell Law School holds students to the highest standards of thinking, speaking, and writing logically. To accomplish this goal, the course of instruction is exceptionally rigorous.

In a national survey, Campbell Law School's Trial Advocacy Program has been called one of the most rigorous in the nation. Every second-year student is required to plan and participate in a mock trial. Because of this, our graduates are exceptionally well prepared to advocate for their clients, whether in the boardroom or the courtroom.

Campbell Law School offers a joint Juris Doctor/Master of Business Administration degree, and has pioneered a joint Juris Doctor/Master of Trust and Wealth Management degree, which is the only program of its kind in the country. Both of these programs can be completed within three years.

Special Programs

The Juvenile Justice Project is a collaboration between Campbell Law School and the North Carolina Governor's Crime Commission. Students are trained in the application of mediation and other alternative dispute-resolution processes and have the opportunity to assist in the mediation of juvenile law disputes.

Prisoner Assistance and Legal Services (PALS) provides our students an opportunity to serve older prisoners by addressing the unique problems of aging in prison.

Externship programs provide students with a meaningful education experience in a public service environment. Students receive up to two hours of academic credit for uncompensated, substantive legal work through externship placements.

The Senior Law Clinic serves the legal needs of low-income senior citizens in the greater Raleigh region.

Student Publications and Organizations

One of the primary motivations for keeping enrollment limited at Campbell Law School is to offer all students outstanding opportunities to gain valuable experiences in activities and organizations.

Campbell Law Review is a student publication of scholarly writings on current legal topics. It is a valued research tool for judges, attorneys, legislatures, educators, and students. Writers and editors for the *Campbell Law Review* are students who demonstrate the highest degree of academic excellence. Participation is by invitation only.

Campbell Law Observer is a monthly student publication that features reports on recent state and federal court opinions, scholarly articles on current legal topics, and subjects of general interest to members of the legal community.

Campbell Law School is also the official international headquarters for the Delta Theta Phi Law Fraternity, one of the leading professional law fraternities in the world.

Admission

Campbell Law School's Admissions Committee takes seriously its responsibility for admitting qualified applicants. Campbell Law believes each applicant we accept has the potential to succeed in our program and pursue a legal education and professional career consistent with Campbell Law School's vision and tradition of excellence. The Admissions Committee bases its selection on the applicant's academic credentials, including LSAT score, undergraduate grade-point average (UGPA), level of writing skills, breadth of studies, and other criteria including, but not limited to, the work, life, and leadership experience, depth of particular interest, and any other aspect of an applicant's background suggesting suitability for the study and practice of law.

Summer Performance-Based Admission Program

Select students who are not offered regular admission in the fall class may be invited to participate in the Summer Performance-Based Admission Program (PBAP). Between 35 and 50 applicants are admitted to this program and attend a seven-week session each summer. Admission to the fall class is offered to those students who perform satisfactorily in both courses. Historically, 25–33 percent of the PBAP class gain admission to the fall class.

Expenses and Financial Aid

Campbell Law School recognizes the high cost of a quality education. Every effort is made to ensure that no qualified applicant is denied the opportunity to study law for financial reasons. Assistance may be provided in the form of institutional scholarships, endowed scholarships, loans, and work-study programs. Approximately 35 percent of students receive scholarship assistance. Approximately 95 percent of students receive financial aid.

In and Around Raleigh

The Raleigh area offers students many housing options in a mix of urban, suburban, and rural areas. The Raleigh community combines the charm of small town roots with easy access to urban amenities. The region offers housing for every taste and budget.

The city offers a variety of museums, performance centers, and other cultural scenes. The area also offers a full schedule of collegiate and professional spectator sports including Atlantic Coast Conference (ACC) basketball and football, and is home to the Carolina Hurricanes (NHL).

Career Services

The Career and Professional Development Center helps students chart a course toward securing summer and permanent employment from their first semester at Campbell Law School.

Employers of Campbell Law School graduates include small and large firms, courts, all branches of the military, judges, government agencies and offices, public service organizations, and corporations. Our 2009 graduates enjoyed an employment rate that exceeded 92 percent within nine months of graduation.

While 80 percent of Campbell Law graduates remain in North Carolina to practice law, 20 percent choose to practice across the nation and around the world. Currently, Campbell Law alumni live and practice in 40 states and six countries.

APPLICANT PROFILE

Campbell University, Norman Adrian Wiggins School of Law
This grid includes only applicants who earned 120–180 LSAT scores under standard administrations.

LSAT Score	GPA 3.75 +		3.50–3.74		3.25–3.49		3.00–3.24		2.75–2.99		2.50–2.74		2.25–2.49		2.00–2.24		Below 2.00		No GPA		Total	
	Apps	Adm	Apps	Adm	Apps	Adm	Apps	Adm	Apps	Adm	Apps	Adm	Apps	Adm	Apps	Adm	Apps	Adm	Apps	Adm	Apps	Adm
175–180	0	0	0	0	0	0	0	0	1	1	0	0	0	0	0	0	0	0	0	0	1	1
170–174	4	4	0	0	0	0	2	1	1	0	0	0	0	0	0	0	0	0	0	0	7	5
165–169	7	7	2	2	9	8	9	8	7	5	2	1	0	0	1	0	1	0	1	1	39	32
160–164	11	9	31	28	45	40	21	20	19	12	13	5	8	0	2	0	1	0	1	0	152	114
155–159	38	34	60	51	83	73	54	41	40	13	23	3	13	1	3	0	1	0	3	2	318	218
150–154	47	24	76	29	105	27	103	14	58	6	31	2	15	0	8	1	1	0	2	0	446	103
145–149	16	3	31	3	56	0	62	1	42	0	33	0	12	0	4	0	1	0	3	0	260	7
140–144	9	0	14	0	25	0	27	0	21	0	20	0	8	0	4	0	1	0	4	0	133	0
135–139	2	0	4	0	6	0	8	0	5	0	10	0	6	0	6	0	1	0	0	0	48	0
130–134	0	0	1	0	5	0	6	0	1	0	2	0	3	0	4	0	1	0	2	0	25	0
125–129	0	0	0	0	0	0	0	0	1	0	0	0	0	0	2	0	0	0	0	0	3	0
120–124	0	0	0	0	0	0	0	0	0	0	0	0	0	0	0	0	0	0	0	0	0	0
Total	134	81	219	113	334	148	292	85	196	37	134	11	65	1	34	1	8	0	16	3	1432	480

Apps = Number of Applicants
Adm = Number Admitted
Reflects 100% of the total applicant pool; highest LSAT data reported.

CAPITAL UNIVERSITY LAW SCHOOL

303 E. Broad Street
Columbus, OH 43215-3200
Phone: 614.236.6310; Fax: 614.236.6972
E-mail: admissions@law.capital.edu; Website: www.law.capital.edu

ABA
Approved
Since
1950

The Basics

Type of school	Private
Term	Semester
Application deadline	5/1
Application fee	$40
Financial aid deadline	4/1
Can first year start other than fall?	No
Student to faculty ratio	16.7 to 1
# of housing spaces available restricted to law students	
graduate housing for which law students are eligible	

Faculty and Administrators

	Total		Men		Women		Minorities	
	Spr	Fall	Spr	Fall	Spr	Fall	Spr	Fall
Full-time	27	30	18	21	9	9	3	4
Other full-time	2	5	1	1	1	4	0	0
Deans, librarians, & others who teach	8	7	3	3	5	4	1	1
Part-time	30	26	24	21	6	5	5	3
Total	67	68	46	46	21	22	9	8

Curriculum

	Full-Time	Part-Time
Typical first-year section size	92	56
Is there typically a "small section" of the first-year class, other than Legal Writing, taught by full-time faculty	Yes	No
If yes, typical size offered last year	46	
# of classroom course titles beyond first-year curriculum	181	

# of upper division courses, excluding seminars, with an enrollment:	Under 25	121
	25–49	27
	50–74	16
	75–99	9
	100+	0

	Full-Time	Part-Time
# of seminars	9	
# of seminar positions available	141	
# of seminar positions filled	88	30
# of positions available in simulation courses	1,246	
# of simulation positions filled	450	119
# of positions available in faculty supervised clinical courses	81	
# of faculty supervised clinical positions filled	53	9
# involved in field placements	157	16
# involved in law journals	64	7
# involved in moot court or trial competitions	27	4
# of credit hours required to graduate	89	

JD Enrollment and Ethnicity

	Men		Women		Full-Time		Part-Time		1st-Year		Total		JD Degs. Awd.
	#	%	#	%	#	%	#	%	#	%	#	%	
All Hispanics	3	0.8	8	2.7	7	1.4	4	2.4	8	3.3	11	1.7	1
Am. Ind./AK Nat.	0	0.0	0	0.0	0	0.0	0	0.0	0	0.0	0	0.0	0
Asian	6	1.6	7	2.4	3	0.6	10	5.9	6	2.5	13	2.0	6
Black/Af. Am.	17	4.7	30	10.3	29	6.0	18	10.6	15	6.2	47	7.2	11
Nat. HI/Pac. Isl.	0	0.0	0	0.0	0	0.0	0	0.0	0	0.0	0	0.0	0
2 or more races	3	0.8	1	0.3	4	0.8	0	0.0	4	1.7	4	0.6	0
Subtotal (minor.)	29	7.9	46	15.8	43	8.8	32	18.8	33	13.7	75	11.4	18
Nonres. Alien	0	0.0	8	2.7	8	1.6	0	0.0	0	0.0	8	1.2	0
White/Cauc.	315	86.3	228	78.4	417	85.8	126	74.1	208	86.3	543	82.8	134
Unknown	21	5.8	9	3.1	18	3.7	12	7.1	0	0.0	30	4.6	23
Total	365	55.6	291	44.4	486	74.1	170	25.9	241	36.7	656		175

Transfers

Transfers in	3
Transfers out	10

Tuition and Fees

	Resident	Nonresident
Full-time	$32,074	$32,074
Part-time	$21,014	$21,014
Tuition Guarantee Program	N	

Living Expenses

Estimated living expenses for singles

Living on campus	Living off campus	Living at home
$13,785	$13,785	$13,785

CAPITAL UNIVERSITY LAW SCHOOL

ABA
Approved
Since
1950

GPA and LSAT Scores

	Total	Full-Time	Part-Time
# of apps	1,267	1,081	186
# of offers	710	623	87
# of matrics	246	187	59
75% GPA	3.52	3.53	3.52
Median GPA	3.29	3.33	3.12
25% GPA	3.00	3.05	2.87
75% LSAT	155	155	155
Median LSAT	153	153	151
25% LSAT	150	150	148

Grants and Scholarships (from prior year)

	Total		Full-Time		Part-Time	
	#	%	#	%	#	%
Total # of students	648		461		187	
Total # receiving grants	319	49.2	262	56.8	57	30.5
Less than 1/2 tuition	249	38.4	205	44.5	44	23.5
Half to full tuition	70	10.8	57	12.4	13	7.0
Full tuition	0	0.0	0	0.0	0	0.0
More than full tuition	0	0.0	0	0.0	0	0.0
Median grant amount			$10,000		$6,000	

Informational and Library Resources

Total amount spent on library materials	$1,159,874
Study seating capacity inside the library	460
# of full-time equivalent professional librarians	5.95
Hours per week library is open	92
# of open, wired connections available to students	113
# of networked computers available for use by students	35
Has wireless network?	Y
Requires computer?	N

JD Attrition (from prior year)

	Academic	Other	Total	
	#	#	#	%
1st year	21	21	42	17.0
2nd year	2	5	7	3.7
3rd year	0	1	1	0.6
4th year	0	0	0	0.0

Employment (9 months after graduation)

	Total	Percentage
Employment status known	140	74.5
Employment status unknown	48	25.5
Employed	116	82.9
Pursuing graduate degrees	3	2.1
Unemployed (seeking, not seeking, or studying for the bar)	20	14.3
Type of Employment		
# employed in law firms	69	59.5
# employed in business and industry	14	12.1
# employed in government	22	19.0
# employed in public interest	4	3.4
# employed as judicial clerks	4	3.4
# employed in academia	3	2.6
Geographic Location		
# employed in state	103	88.8
# employed outside the US	0	0.0
# of states where employed		10

Bar Passage Rates

First-time takers	183	Reporting %	91.26
Average school %	88.02	Average state %	86.03
Average pass difference	1.99		

Jurisdiction	Takers	Passers	Pass %	State %	Diff %
Ohio	167	147	88.02	86.03	1.99

CAPITAL UNIVERSITY LAW SCHOOL

303 E. Broad Street
Columbus, OH 43215-3200
Phone: 614.236.6310; Fax: 614.236.6972
E-mail: admissions@law.capital.edu; Website: www.law.capital.edu

Introduction

Capital University Law School, located in downtown Columbus, is at the epicenter of Ohio's legal, business, and government community. Our location provides students with an ideal environment to study law and a wealth of opportunities to gain practical legal experience, meet future employers, and establish a network of contacts within the legal arena. The Law School is within walking distance of the Ohio Supreme Court, the Ohio Court of Appeals, the Ohio Attorney General's Office, the state legislature, major law firms, numerous state agencies, and Fortune 500 corporations.

Innovation and leadership are intrinsic traits of our heritage. For more than a century, Capital Law School has produced some of the finest judges, partners, and associates of respected law firms; officials at all levels of government; business professionals; and influential community leaders. We invite you to closely examine all of the factors that distinguish this law school:

- Outstanding faculty
- Superior bar passage and employment rates
- Innovative curriculum
- Extensive and diverse externship opportunities
- Remarkable alumni
- High-value tuition (Capital Law voted a "Best Value Law School" by the *National Jurist* magazine. (www.nxtbook.com/nxtbooks/cypress/nationaljurist0909/#/30)

Curriculum

Capital University Law School is committed to providing our full- and part-time students a first-rate education. The Law School's comprehensive curriculum balances theoretical knowledge and practical applications of the law. Courses are both intellectually challenging and cutting edge, equipping our students with essential lawyering skills necessary for effective, creative, and ethical legal counseling and advocacy. By graduation, our alumni have made the transition from law student to legal practitioner—prepared to meet the challenges and demands of the evolving practice of law.

Teaching is a core value at Capital University Law School. Capital Law students describe the faculty as knowledgeable, accessible, collegial, cooperative, and true mentors. Outside of the classroom, our faculty are accomplished scholars who distinguish themselves through their research, scholarship, and authorship of books and journal publications. In a recent study, Capital Law School's faculty is noted for scholarly productivity.

To learn more about Capital Law's rich curriculum and distinguished faculty, visit www.law.capital.edu.

Multicultural Affairs

Capital University Law School takes pride in its history of providing a legal education for groups who historically have been excluded from or underrepresented in law schools. Capital University Law School is committed to supporting and embracing diversity in all of its forms. The Law School actively recruits students of all races and sexual orientations.

Students come to Capital with diverse educational, cultural, social, and professional backgrounds. Capital University Law School embraces and values the varied perspectives our students bring to the school.

Capital has many programs and benefits that support students of color. The presence of minority faculty, a director of multicultural affairs, availability of financial aid, academic as well as nonacademic support, and participation in the Columbus Bar Association Minority Clerkship Program are some of the things available to our students. In addition to the services at the Law School, Columbus also presents a diverse and supportive community in which our law students can live, learn, play, and explore.

Special Programs

Diversity of opportunity is a trademark of Capital University Law School. Capital Law students have the unique opportunity to create their own academic path and pursue their personal passions through our specialized and innovative academic programs.

Concentrations

The Law School's concentration certificates allow students to focus their electives in specific areas of the law by combining theoretical and practical classroom experience with faculty expertise. Capital offers concentrations in eight specialty areas:

- Children and Family Law
- Civil Litigation
- Criminal Litigation
- Dispute Resolution
- Environmental Law
- Governmental Affairs
- Labor and Employment Law
- Small Business Entities and Publicly Held Companies

Joint-Degree Programs

The Law School's joint-degree programs allow students to advance their education without delaying their career plans. These accelerated programs enable students to complete two degrees with a substantial reduction in total credit hours and in less time than it would take to obtain them separately. Capital offers a Juris Doctor with any of the following degrees:

- Master of Business Administration
- Master of Sports Administration
- Master of Science in Nursing
- Master of Theology
- Master of Laws in Business
- Master of Laws in Business and Taxation
- Master of Laws in Taxation

Centers and Legal Clinics

Our commitment to immersing you in the real-world environment of law is best exemplified by our diverse externship program, along with our centers and legal clinics. Students enrich their academic environment by working closely with clinical attorneys and experiencing the challenges and rewards of practicing law and giving back to the community-at-large. The Law School's centers and clinics include:

- The Center for Dispute Resolution
- The National Center for Adoption Law and Policy
- The General Litigation Clinic

- The Mediation Clinic
- The Family Advocacy Clinic
- The Small Business Clinic

Admission

Capital University Law School seeks to attract a diverse pool of applicants who are motivated, committed, and possess the requisite skills and abilities to study law. Admission to the Law School is based on a thorough review of each individual's application file in its entirety. Rarely does any single factor, either LSAT score or undergraduate grade-point average, determine a candidate's status.

The Law School's Admission Committee thoughtfully and thoroughly evaluates the competitiveness and difficulty of each candidate's undergraduate and graduate coursework, personal statement, letters of recommendation, employment history, writing ability, leadership experience, extracurricular activities, general background, and any additional information the candidate feels is important to the admission decision. All of these factors, along with the LSAT score and grade-point average, are weighed during the admission process.

Student Activities

Capital Law School offers many organizations and activities to help you round out your education. Extra- and cocurricular activities range from more than 20 student groups and at least 10 competition teams to the *Capital University Law Review*. Clubs are educational, professional, and social while encouraging the legal community's collaboration and engagement. Student organizations at Capital University Law School offer many opportunities for leadership development, networking, and interaction with professionals in various specialties.

The Law School supports associations for students with common values and backgrounds, as well as groups focused on specific areas of law such as sports and entertainment, environmental issues, and intellectual property. The *Capital University Law Review* provides the legal community scholarly analysis of contemporary legal issues. Students may expand their writing and editing skills through membership on the *Law Review*. Those wishing to hone their skills and test them in competition will want to investigate Capital's highly successful moot court teams. Students may participate in national competitions, such as the Philip C. Jessup International Law and the Frederick Douglass Moot Court competitions. Teams also are selected in the areas of environmental law, sports law, labor law, and tax.

Professional Development

The Capital Law School Office of Professional Development provides individual career counseling for students and alumni and a wide variety of career-related programs, including Continuing Legal Education Programs for alumni. The office provides an online job posting board, coordinates employer recruiting programs, and maintains an extensive library of books and other relevant resources. It also houses the Law School's Public Interest Center and administers the Pro Bono Recognition Program.

Capital Law School graduates pursue a variety of legal and nonlegal employment opportunities. For the class of 2009, 87.6 percent of those graduates seeking employment were employed within nine months of graduation. Private practice is the largest of these areas, with approximately 59 percent of the graduating class entering this field. Many Capital graduates enter public service (26 percent), which includes government, public interest, and judicial clerkship positions, while others find employment in corporations and academia.

APPLICANT PROFILE

Capital University Law School

LSAT Score	GPA								
	3.75 +	3.50–3.74	3.25–3.49	3.00–3.24	2.75–2.99	2.50–2.74	2.25–2.49	2.00–2.24	Below 2.00
175–180									
170–174									
165–169									
160–164									
155–159									
150–154									
145–149									
140–144									
135–139									
130–134									
125–129									
120–124									

■ Very Likely   □ Possible   ▨ Unlikely

BENJAMIN N. CARDOZO SCHOOL OF LAW, YESHIVA UNIVERSITY

55 Fifth Avenue
New York, NY 10003
Phone: 212.790.0274; Fax: 212.790.0482
E-mail: lawinfo@yu.edu; Website: www.cardozo.yu.edu

ABA
Approved
Since
1978

The Basics

Type of school	Private
Term	Semester
Application deadline	4/1
Application fee	$75
Financial aid deadline	4/1
Can first year start other than fall?	Yes
Student to faculty ratio	15.3 to 1
# of housing spaces available restricted to law students	120
graduate housing for which law students are eligible	

Faculty and Administrators

	Total		Men		Women		Minorities	
	Spr	Fall	Spr	Fall	Spr	Fall	Spr	Fall
Full-time	58	59	35	40	23	19	10	10
Other full-time	2	2	1	1	1	1	0	0
Deans, librarians, & others who teach	5	6	3	4	2	2	1	2
Part-time	90	92	62	61	28	31	7	10
Total	155	159	101	106	54	53	18	22

Curriculum

	Full-Time	Part-Time
Typical first-year section size	50	50
Is there typically a "small section" of the first-year class, other than Legal Writing, taught by full-time faculty	No	No
If yes, typical size offered last year		

# of classroom course titles beyond first-year curriculum		153
# of upper division courses, excluding seminars, with an enrollment:	Under 25	49
	25–49	38
	50–74	23
	75–99	11
	100+	16

# of seminars		63
# of seminar positions available		1,304
# of seminar positions filled	923	0
# of positions available in simulation courses		754
# of simulation positions filled	590	0
# of positions available in faculty supervised clinical courses		168
# of faculty supervised clinical positions filled	155	0
# involved in field placements	266	0
# involved in law journals	357	0
# involved in moot court or trial competitions	64	0
# of credit hours required to graduate		84

JD Enrollment and Ethnicity

	Men		Women		Full-Time		Part-Time		1st-Year		Total		JD Degs. Awd.
	#	%	#	%	#	%	#	%	#	%	#	%	
All Hispanics	30	5.5	49	8.5	72	7.0	7	7.1	27	7.8	79	7.0	28
Am. Ind./AK Nat.	0	0.0	1	0.2	1	0.1	0	0.0	0	0.0	1	0.1	1
Asian	32	5.9	64	11.1	85	8.3	11	11.1	31	8.9	96	8.5	34
Black/Af. Am.	20	3.7	29	5.0	44	4.3	5	5.1	20	5.7	49	4.4	11
Nat. HI/Pac. Isl.	3	0.5	6	1.0	9	0.9	0	0.0	0	0.0	9	0.8	0
2 or more races	9	1.6	12	2.1	21	2.0	0	0.0	0	0.0	21	1.9	0
Subtotal (minor.)	94	17.2	161	27.9	232	22.6	23	23.2	78	22.4	255	22.7	83
Nonres. Alien	6	1.1	20	3.5	25	2.4	1	1.0	7	2.0	26	2.3	0
White/Cauc.	422	77.1	375	65.0	731	71.3	66	66.7	236	67.8	797	70.9	281
Unknown	25	4.6	21	3.6	37	3.6	9	9.1	27	7.8	46	4.1	8
Total	547	48.7	577	51.3	1025	91.2	99	8.8	348	31.0	1124		383

Transfers

Transfers in	39
Transfers out	5

Tuition and Fees

	Resident	Nonresident
Full-time	$46,794	$46,794
Part-time	$46,794	$46,794
Tuition Guarantee Program		N

Living Expenses

Estimated living expenses for singles

Living on campus	Living off campus	Living at home
$24,459	$24,459	N/A

BENJAMIN N. CARDOZO SCHOOL OF LAW, YESHIVA UNIVERSITY

*ABA
Approved
Since
1978*

GPA and LSAT Scores

	Total	Full-Time	Part-Time
# of apps	5,518	5,091	843
# of offers	1,401	1,217	184
# of matrics	382	279	103
75% GPA	3.74	3.74	3.72
Median GPA	3.60	3.62	3.55
25% GPA	3.42	3.47	3.24
75% LSAT	166	166	161
Median LSAT	163	164	160
25% LSAT	160	161	158

Grants and Scholarships (from prior year)

	Total		Full-Time		Part-Time	
	#	%	#	%	#	%
Total # of students	1,121		1,020		101	
Total # receiving grants	627	55.9	608	59.6	19	18.8
Less than 1/2 tuition	338	30.2	322	31.6	16	15.8
Half to full tuition	182	16.2	180	17.6	2	2.0
Full tuition	104	9.3	103	10.1	1	1.0
More than full tuition	3	0.3	3	0.3	0	0.0
Median grant amount			$21,000		$6,000	

Informational and Library Resources

Total amount spent on library materials	$1,676,351
Study seating capacity inside the library	446
# of full-time equivalent professional librarians	8
Hours per week library is open	88
# of open, wired connections available to students	30
# of networked computers available for use by students	188
Has wireless network?	Y
Requires computer?	N

JD Attrition (from prior year)

	Academic	Other	Total	
	#	#	#	%
1st year	1	17	18	5.2
2nd year	0	4	4	1.0
3rd year	0	1	1	0.3
4th year	0	0	0	0.0

Employment (9 months after graduation)

	Total	Percentage
Employment status known	345	97.5
Employment status unknown	9	2.5
Employed	304	88.1
Pursuing graduate degrees	16	4.6
Unemployed (seeking, not seeking, or studying for the bar)	17	4.9
Type of Employment		
# employed in law firms	192	63.2
# employed in business and industry	52	17.1
# employed in government	18	5.9
# employed in public interest	22	7.2
# employed as judicial clerks	18	5.9
# employed in academia	2	0.7
Geographic Location		
# employed in state	242	79.6
# employed outside the US	6	2.0
# of states where employed	15	

Bar Passage Rates

First-time takers	361	Reporting %	92.52
Average school %	89.52	Average state %	86.51
Average pass difference	3.01		

Jurisdiction	Takers	Passers	Pass %	State %	Diff %
New York	334	299	89.52	86.51	3.01

BENJAMIN N. CARDOZO SCHOOL OF LAW, YESHIVA UNIVERSITY

55 Fifth Avenue
New York, NY 10003
Phone: 212.790.0274; Fax: 212.790.0482
E-mail: lawinfo@yu.edu; Website: www.cardozo.yu.edu

Introduction

Cardozo Law offers students a stimulating intellectual educational experience, rooted in the values of ethics, public service, and scholarship. Known for providing high intellectual standards and pioneering hands-on experiences, Cardozo Law also provides students with a deep understanding of how law relates to other expressions of the human spirit, including philosophy, economics, politics, history, art, and literature. Cardozo offers superb programs in intellectual property law, criminal law, alternative dispute resolution, international and human rights law, public interest law, and legal theory. A highly energetic and supportive faculty engages students from 43 countries and all regions of the United States. Extensive clinical and externship opportunities draw on the resources available in New York City, and programs, centers, and clinics, such as the Innocence Project and the Heyman Center for Corporate Governance, are well known for innovation and leadership. Unique hands-on clinical opportunities are offered, including the Holocaust Claims Restitution Clinic, the Indie Film Clinic, and the Kathryn O. Greenberg Immigration Justice Clinic. These clinics train students in connecting theory with practical application of the law. A Cardozo legal education emphasizes the pursuit of intellectual excellence while providing a wealth of lawyering opportunities.

Faculty

Professors at Cardozo are accessible and engaged in all aspects of students' professional development. They are committed to making the classroom experience vital and engaging, as well as to pursuing serious scholarship, with more than half holding advanced degrees, such as PhDs, in addition to their law degrees. Cultivating an atmosphere of intellectual dialogue and curiosity, faculty members work closely with students on conferences that attract world-class guest speakers in all legal specialties. Cardozo Law professors have extensive connections within the New York City legal community and elsewhere. Many who teach here are prolific writers. They are frequently cited among academics worldwide and write publications that serve as required reading in law schools throughout the nation. Cardozo's clinical faculty is known for its innovative leadership. From the renowned Innocence Project to the pioneering Indie Film Clinic, our faculty members help students to develop hands-on skills in courtrooms, negotiations, transactional law experience, public policy advocacy, and mediation practice. Cardozo faculty members see it as their job to prepare students to be ready to practice law as leaders in a new age, and to hold fast to the core values of justice, equality, and ethics.

A Campus in New York City

Cardozo is located in a vibrant neighborhood in Greenwich Village, just blocks from Union Square. It is easily accessible to all points in New York City, including the courts, Wall Street, Midtown, and the art and music centers on the East and West Sides of Manhattan. The law school's state-of-the-art facility includes a moot courtroom, additional library space, a center for student life, student and faculty offices, and fully wired classrooms and seminar rooms.

The Cardozo residence hall is located on a residential, tree-lined street just one block south of the main building. Studio, one-bedroom, and two-bedroom apartments—all of which are air-conditioned, fully furnished, and equipped with kitchens—are available for incoming students.

Students/Student Activities

The student body at Cardozo is a diverse and impressive group. A typical entering class includes graduates from more than 135 colleges, and from 35 states and 9 foreign countries. Roughly 24 percent of the class are members of minority groups and 45 percent have been out of college between one and four years. Approximately 7 percent hold at least one graduate degree.

More than half of the second- and third-year students participate on one of six student-edited journals or in the Moot Court Honor Society. Scholarly journals include the *Cardozo Law Review, Cardozo Arts and Entertainment Law Journal, Cardozo Journal of International and Comparative Law, Cardozo Journal of Law and Gender, Cardozo Journal of Conflict Resolution,* and *Cardozo Public Law, Policy, and Ethics Journal.*

Career Services

Cardozo students benefit from a large network of working alumni and a career services office staffed by six professional counselors, all of whom have JD degrees. Students are offered individual assistance with interviewing techniques, résumé writing, and job-search strategies, as well as workshops and opportunities for learning about a variety of legal careers from attorneys in the field.

Ninety-three percent of those reporting from the class of 2009 were employed within several months of graduation. Approximately 60 percent of these graduates went into private practice at a median starting salary of $160,000. Nearly 20 percent of the class entered the public sector in a broad range of positions, including jobs in judges' chambers, governmental agencies, and public interest organizations.

Clinical Opportunities/Special Programs

Cardozo has a commitment to a particular style of education that seeks to blend theory and practice—to expose students to the abstractions, intellectual and ethical conundrums, and overarching theories of the American legal system, as well as to the concrete skills and values they need to be first-rate attorneys. A wealth of clinical programs combines professional work experience with academic supervision, yielding students uniquely qualified to apply what they have studied. Nearly 400 students each year take advantage of one of these opportunities to represent real clients (under the supervision of expert attorneys), gaining invaluable skills while performing important community service representing the poor, the elderly, and the indigent.

In the **Innocence Project**, students represent prisoners whose innocence may be proved through DNA testing; in the **Prosecutor Practicum**, students work in the Manhattan District Attorney's Office; the **Bet Tzedek Legal Services Clinic** provides legal assistance to the elderly and disabled; the **Mediation Clinic** provides training and certification in alternative dispute resolution; the **Human Rights and Genocide Clinic** provides students with the opportunity to design and implement creative solutions to improve the lives of victims of human rights abuses throughout the world; Cardozo's simulation-based **Intensive Trial Advocacy Program** sharpens students' trial skills; and students in the **Criminal Defense Clinic** represent defendants in Manhattan Criminal Court. Other clinics include the **Family Court Clinic**, **Tax Clinic**, **Criminal Appeals Clinic**, **Divorce Mediation Clinic**, **Housing Rights Clinic**, **Immigration Justice Clinic**, **Indie Film Clinic**, **Labor and Employment Law Clinic**, and **Securities Arbitration Clinic**.

Externships offer students the opportunity to work in a legal position, thereby developing important skills and gaining significant real-world experience. Through externships and internships, students can obtain credit for substantive legal work under the direct supervision of an attorney or judge at the work site. The **Intellectual Property Law Program** combines a specialized curriculum with related externships in this burgeoning area of practice; the **Alexander Judicial Fellows Program** places outstanding third-year students in clerkships with prominent federal judges; the **Entertainment Law Experience** enables students to complete legal internships during the school year or the summer with entertainment law employers; the **Heyman/ACCA In-House Counsel Internship** introduces second- and third-year students to the practice of law in a corporate law department; in the **Holocaust Claims Restitution Practicum**, students pursue claims made by Holocaust survivors and their heirs; the **Immigration Law Externship** places students in law offices and agencies handling immigration matters; and the **Corporation Counsel's Appellate Externship** places students in the Appeals Division of the New York City Law Department (Corporation Counsel).

Cardozo's Center for Public Service Law emphasizes the school's commitment to serving the greater public good and helping students find meaningful ways to engage in public service. In the summer of 2010, more than 240 first- and second-year students received summer funding to allow them to work either domestically or abroad in the public sector at legal services providers, public interest organizations, government agencies, district attorneys' offices, the US Attorney's Office, and federal and state judicial chambers. The Public Service Scholars Program awards scholarships to students who demonstrate a deep commitment to public service through their application for admission. The

Post-Graduate Public Service Fellowship provides new graduates with funding to work in the public sector prior to entering full-time employment. The Laurie M. Tisch Loan Repayment Assistance Program (LRAP) benefits graduates who choose to pursue careers in public interest/public service law by assisting with some of the burden of large educational debts. Intellectual life at Cardozo extends beyond the classroom. The school sponsors numerous conferences, panels, and symposia that provoke dialogue and critical thought on wide-ranging topics in constitutional law, communications law and policy, human rights, corporate governance, and legal ethics.

Curriculum

Cardozo offers a rich curriculum that has been especially recognized for its offerings in intellectual property law (students may receive both the JD and master of laws [LLM] degrees in seven semesters), alternative dispute resolution (students may receive both the JD and master of laws [LLM] degrees in seven semesters), criminal law, corporate law, and international law. Upper-level courses are elective except for a course in professional responsibility, completion of advanced legal research, an upper-level writing requirement, and fulfillment of minimal distribution requirements.

Cardozo offers LLM degrees in dispute resolution and advocacy, intellectual property law, comparative legal thought, and general studies. A joint-degree program between Cardozo and the Wurzweiler School of Social Work allows students to earn both the JD and MSW degrees in four years of study.

Admission/Alternative Entry/Financial Aid

Students may enter Cardozo in the fall, in January, or in May. Those entering in January complete six semesters of law school in two-and-a-half years. Those entering in May complete the first-year curriculum in three part-time semesters, while the second and third years are completed on a full-time basis (students will graduate in three years). These alternative entry programs can be particularly appealing to midyear graduates and returning students.

Both need- and merit-based scholarships are available. Approximately 82 percent of the students receive some financial aid. Instructions on applying for aid can be found at www.cardozo.yu.edu/studentfinance.

APPLICANT PROFILE

Benjamin N. Cardozo School of Law, Yeshiva University
This grid includes only applicants who earned 120–180 LSAT scores under standard administrations.

LSAT Score	GPA																
	3.75 +		3.50–3.74		3.25–3.49		3.00–3.24		2.75–2.99		2.50–2.74		Below 2.50		No GPA		Total	
	Apps	Adm	Apps	Adm	Apps	Adm	Apps	Adm	Apps	Adm	Apps	Adm	Apps	Adm	Apps	Adm	Apps	Adm
170–180	83	47	66	38	75	42	34	7	16	1	6	0	6	1	2	0	288	136
165–169	193	143	250	191	197	94	124	28	56	7	31	3	14	0	25	6	890	472
160–164	325	164	458	195	394	61	211	25	102	4	43	0	31	0	35	5	1599	454
155–159	136	33	241	48	267	35	160	18	93	8	39	1	36	0	29	3	1001	146
150–154	61	6	126	12	136	8	126	5	71	1	30	1	28	0	10	0	588	33
Below 150	26	0	70	0	83	0	98	0	85	0	54	0	48	0	22	0	486	0
Total	824	393	1211	484	1152	240	753	83	423	21	203	5	163	1	123	14	4852	1241

Apps = Number of Applicants
Adm = Number Admitted
Reflects 99% of the total applicant pool; highest LSAT data reported.

CASE WESTERN RESERVE UNIVERSITY SCHOOL OF LAW

11075 East Boulevard
Cleveland, OH 44106
Phone: 216.368.3600, 800.756.0036; Fax: 216.368.0185
E-mail: lawadmissions@case.edu, lawmoney@case.edu; Website: http://law.case.edu

ABA Approved Since 1923

The Basics

Type of school	Private
Term	Semester
Application deadline	11/30 2/1 4/1
Application fee	$40
Financial aid deadline	5/1
Can first year start other than fall?	No
Student to faculty ratio	13.1 to 1
# of housing spaces available restricted to law students	
graduate housing for which law students are eligible	

Faculty and Administrators

	Total		Men		Women		Minorities	
	Spr	Fall	Spr	Fall	Spr	Fall	Spr	Fall
Full-time	40	39	25	26	15	13	2	1
Other full-time	8	8	5	6	2	1	0	1
Deans, librarians, & others who teach	3	3	1	1	2	2	0	0
Part-time	57	36	37	23	20	13	2	5
Total	108	86	68	56	39	29	4	7

Curriculum

	Full-Time	Part-Time
Typical first-year section size	80	0
Is there typically a "small section" of the first-year class, other than Legal Writing, taught by full-time faculty	No	No
If yes, typical size offered last year		
# of classroom course titles beyond first-year curriculum	149	
# of upper division courses, excluding seminars, with an enrollment: Under 25	131	
25–49	47	
50–74	12	
75–99	5	
100+	2	
# of seminars	21	
# of seminar positions available	178	
# of seminar positions filled	148	0
# of positions available in simulation courses	286	
# of simulation positions filled	244	0
# of positions available in faculty supervised clinical courses	64	
# of faculty supervised clinical positions filled	63	0
# involved in field placements	76	0
# involved in law journals	124	0
# involved in moot court or trial competitions	40	0
# of credit hours required to graduate	88	

JD Enrollment and Ethnicity

	Men		Women		Full-Time		Part-Time		1st-Year		Total		JD Degs. Awd.
	#	%	#	%	#	%	#	%	#	%	#	%	
All Hispanics	8	2.3	4	1.5	12	1.9	0	0.0	7	2.9	12	1.9	4
Am. Ind./AK Nat.	1	0.3	1	0.4	2	0.3	0	0.0	1	0.4	2	0.3	1
Asian	22	6.2	27	9.9	48	7.7	1	33.3	20	8.4	49	7.8	15
Black/Af. Am.	10	2.8	14	5.1	24	3.8	0	0.0	12	5.0	24	3.8	6
Nat. HI/Pac. Isl.	0	0.0	0	0.0	0	0.0	0	0.0	0	0.0	0	0.0	0
2 or more races	1	0.3	4	1.5	5	0.8	0	0.0	1	0.4	5	0.8	0
Subtotal (minor.)	42	11.9	50	18.3	91	14.6	1	33.3	41	17.2	92	14.7	27
Nonres. Alien	17	4.8	20	7.3	37	5.9	0	0.0	21	8.8	37	5.9	0
White/Cauc.	295	83.3	203	74.4	496	79.5	2	66.7	177	74.1	498	79.4	160
Unknown	0	0.0	0	0.0	0	0.0	0	0.0	0	0.0	0	0.0	29
Total	354	56.5	273	43.5	624	99.5	3	0.5	239	38.1	627		223

Transfers

Transfers in	12
Transfers out	29

Tuition and Fees

	Resident	Nonresident
Full-time	$40,560	$40,560

Part-time	
Tuition Guarantee Program	N

Living Expenses

Estimated living expenses for singles

Living on campus	Living off campus	Living at home
$18,105	$18,105	$18,105

CASE WESTERN RESERVE UNIVERSITY SCHOOL OF LAW

ABA Approved Since 1923

GPA and LSAT Scores

	Total	Full-Time	Part-Time
# of apps	2,193	2,193	0
# of offers	825	825	0
# of matrics	236	236	0
75% GPA	3.64	3.64	0.00
Median GPA	3.50	3.50	0.00
25% GPA	3.26	3.26	0.00
75% LSAT	162	162	0
Median LSAT	160	160	0
25% LSAT	157	157	0

Grants and Scholarships (from prior year)

	Total #	Total %	Full-Time #	Full-Time %	Part-Time #	Part-Time %
Total # of students	640		618		22	
Total # receiving grants	358	55.9	358	57.9	0	0.0
Less than 1/2 tuition	307	48.0	307	49.7	0	0.0
Half to full tuition	45	7.0	45	7.3	0	0.0
Full tuition	6	0.9	6	1.0	0	0.0
More than full tuition	0	0.0	0	0.0	0	0.0
Median grant amount			$9,000		$0	

Informational and Library Resources

Total amount spent on library materials	$1,294,116
Study seating capacity inside the library	344
# of full-time equivalent professional librarians	11
Hours per week library is open	104
# of open, wired connections available to students	100
# of networked computers available for use by students	94
Has wireless network?	Y
Requires computer?	N

JD Attrition (from prior year)

	Academic #	Other #	Total #	Total %
1st year	2	34	36	17.1
2nd year	5	1	6	2.8
3rd year	0	0	0	0.0
4th year	0	0	0	0.0

Employment (9 months after graduation)

	Total	Percentage
Employment status known	198	95.2
Employment status unknown	10	4.8
Employed	181	91.4
Pursuing graduate degrees	3	1.5
Unemployed (seeking, not seeking, or studying for the bar)	7	3.5
Type of Employment		
# employed in law firms	86	47.5
# employed in business and industry	31	17.1
# employed in government	26	14.4
# employed in public interest	28	15.5
# employed as judicial clerks	9	5.0
# employed in academia	1	0.6
Geographic Location		
# employed in state	106	58.6
# employed outside the US	1	0.6
# of states where employed	23	

Bar Passage Rates

First-time takers	191	Reporting %	76.96
Average school %	77.54	Average state %	85.17

Average pass difference –7.63

Jurisdiction	Takers	Passers	Pass %	State %	Diff %
Ohio	91	75	82.42	86.03	–3.61
New York	20	14	70.00	86.51	–16.51
California	15	7	46.67	73.19	–26.52
Illinois	12	10	83.33	90.89	–7.56
Pennsylvania	9	8	88.89	85.69	3.20

The information on these pages was provided by the law school.

CASE WESTERN RESERVE UNIVERSITY SCHOOL OF LAW

11075 East Boulevard
Cleveland, OH 44106
Phone: 216.368.3600, 800.756.0036; Fax: 216.368.0185
E-mail: lawadmissions@case.edu, lawmoney@case.edu; Website: http://law.case.edu

Welcome

Case Western Reserve University School of Law has responded to the growing complexities of the ever-changing legal, social, and economic environments by implementing major curricular reforms. The result is an innovative program that provides our students with an enhanced classical legal education, an extensive array of hands-on learning opportunities for in-depth study in key fields, extensive coursework in emerging and leading-edge areas of the law (over 140 upper-level courses, more than half of which have fewer than 25 students), an understanding of the context in which legal matters and disputes take place, knowledge of other disciplines that can be used to solve legal problems, and unique methods of instruction.

The Curriculum and Concentrations

Shape the Law; Serve the World: We serve as our students' partners and counselors to guide them to become lawyers who help clients achieve their strategic goals, take leadership roles in their communities, and address key societal issues. The centerpiece of our curriculum is the four-semester CaseArc program, which coordinates experientially based instruction in fundamental lawyering skills with traditional classroom methods for teaching legal analysis.

Capstone Service Opportunities: We offer a capstone service opportunity for our students. Our six labs, four clinics, and eleven externship programs offer students the opportunity not only to study the law in practice, but also to contribute to its development. Just a few examples: submit a memorandum for prosecutors in one of several international criminal tribunals through our **International War Crimes Research Lab**; do research on consumer protection and anticompetitive practice issues in our **Federal Trade Commission Externship**; assist US attorneys in prosecuting civil and criminal matters through our **US Attorney Externships**; gain in-house experience through our **General Counsel** or **Hospital Law Externships**; conduct research and write memos for death penalty cases in our **Death Penalty Labs**; or conduct an examination of a medical expert in a Social Security disability claim in the **Health Law Clinic**.

Optional Concentration Program: Our Concentration Program offers in-depth learning in an area of interest and of value to employers seeking increased contributions from new lawyers. Options: Law and Technology, Law and the Arts, Criminal Law, Business Organizations, Litigation, Health Law, International Law, Individual Rights and Social Reform, and Public and Regulatory Institutions.

Dual-Degree Programs: Management, Bioethics, Social Work, Biochemistry, Medicine, Nonprofit Management, Public Health, Legal History, and Political Science.

Academic Centers

The Academic Centers provide rich opportunities that stimulate learning, networking, and career development, and include first-year electives, special seminars and symposia, clinical opportunities, internships, and work-abroad opportunities.
- Center for Business Law and Regulation
- Center for the Interdisciplinary Study of Conflict and Dispute Resolution
- Center for Law, Technology, and the Arts
- Center for Professional Ethics
- Center for Social Justice
- Frederick K. Cox International Law Center
- Law-Medicine Center
- Milton A. Kramer Law Clinic Center

Work and Study Abroad

Our students have far-ranging opportunities to work abroad and to receive generous stipends that support their international internships. Each year, we fund approximately 30 international law-related summer internships and postgraduate fellowships for work abroad or in the United States with an international organization, a governmental agency, or nonprofit agency. Just a sampling of recent placements:
- Commonwealth Human Rights Initiative, New Delhi, India
- Human Rights Watch, New York, NY
- International Criminal Tribunal for Rwanda, Arusha, Tanzania
- International Trade Centre, Geneva, Switzerland
- Microsoft Corporation, Beijing, China
- Pennsylvania Immigration Resource Center, York, PA
- Special Tribunal for Lebanon, The Netherlands
- United Nations Development Programme, New York, NY
- US Department of Justice Immigration Court, Miami, FL
- US Department of Justice, Executive Office for Immigration Review, Cleveland, OH

The law school also offers a number of stipends for summer internships in environmental and health law, as well as for public interest and social justice internships.

Commitment to Career Success

The Career Services Office (CSO) has implemented an ambitious program that delivers to our students real job opportunities with leading employers coast to coast. Our aggressive approach to employer development and outreach has resulted in great job success for our graduates: a 93 percent employment rate for our class of 2009 (national average: 91.3 percent); a median salary of $75,000 for our class of 2009 (national median: $72,000); and 54 percent of our students employed through a CSO-sponsored program (national figure: 41 percent). More than 315 employers participate in our fall recruitment programs, which include on-campus interviews as well as interview programs in New York, Chicago, Los Angeles, Boston, and Washington, DC.

The University and Cleveland

Case Western Reserve University stands among the nation's foremost independent research institutions. It is 17th among private universities in federal research and development awards and has an endowment of well over $1 billion. The law school is located on the university's campus in the heart of University Circle—a collection of nearly 40 cultural, medical, educational, religious, and social service institutions in a park-like setting on over 500 acres of land.

Cleveland is a world corporate center for leading national and multinational companies that specialize in transportation, insurance, retail, commercial banking, and finance. It is the headquarters for several of the nation's largest law firms and home to a number of foreign consulates. It is also a city of medicine with dozens of Cleveland hospitals and medical centers, including University Hospitals of Cleveland, the Cleveland Clinic, MetroHealth Medical Center, and other facilities with international reputations for outstanding patient care and contributions to medical research.

Unique neighborhoods are within walking distance of campus and offer students and young professionals modern and safe places to live, shop, dine, network, and socialize. Housing is also very affordable. A recent student survey indicated that the average per person monthly rent for a single was $700, $450 for shared accommodations, and $900 for family accommodations.

Student Activities and Leadership

There are more than 30 student organizations reflecting the wide range of our students' interests, including the Black Law Students Association, Asian Pacific American Law Students Association, Federalist Society, National Lawyers Guild, Lambda Law Students Association, and Student Animal Legal Defense Fund. Our students contribute to the community through organizations such as Cultivating Connections, Street Law, and Big Buddies, in cooperation with Big Brothers/Big Sisters. Our student organizations not only allow students the opportunity to explore legal interests with peers, but also provide a valuable proving ground for leadership skill development. Our student organization leaders have also taken leadership roles in their groups' national and regional organizations, and have the opportunity to represent Case Western at national and regional conferences. Our scholarly journals are the *Case Western Reserve Law Review*; the *Journal of International Law*; *Health Matrix: Journal of Law-Medicine*; and the *Journal of Law, Technology, and the*

Internet. There is also ample opportunity for participation in moot court and mock trial competitions.

Admission and Financial Aid

The Admission Process—Our admission process is selective. Each applicant receives full-file review. The Early Decision program application deadline is November 15; applicants are notified by December 15. The regular admission process begins in December and concludes by May 15, at which time a summer waiting list is established. The application fee is waived for candidates who apply electronically.

Financial Aid and Scholarships—Each year, we offer Academic Scholarships ranging from $5,000 to full tuition; Leadership Grants, awarded to students with unique backgrounds whose records demonstrate leadership qualities and who will enrich the diversity of the student body; interest area scholarships; and up to two Law-Medicine Fellowships, which provide a combination of scholarship aid and summer research fellowship.

Loan Repayment Assistance Program—We provide financial assistance for selected graduates who use their legal training to provide services that are in the public interest.

Visiting Case Western Reserve University School of Law

We offer many opportunities for prospective students to visit the law school. Just check our website to watch our video, check the schedule for the annual Open House, or schedule an individual visit (or all three of the above).

APPLICANT PROFILE

Case Western Reserve University School of Law
This grid includes only applicants who earned 120–180 LSAT scores.

LSAT Score	GPA						
	3.75 +	3.50–3.74	3.25–3.49	3.00–3.24	2.75–2.99	2.50–2.74	Below 2.50
165–180							
163–164							
161–162							
159–160							
157–158							
154–156							
150–153							
Below 150							

■ Good Possibility   ▨ Possibility   □ Slight Possibility

THE CATHOLIC UNIVERSITY OF AMERICA, COLUMBUS SCHOOL OF LAW

Cardinal Station
Washington, DC 20064
Phone: 202.319.5151; Fax: 202.319.6285
E-mail: admissions@law.edu; Website: www.law.edu

ABA
Approved
Since
1925

AMERICAN BAR ASSOCIATION
Section of Legal Education
and Admissions to the Bar

The Basics

Type of school	Private
Term	Semester
Application deadline	3/11
Application fee	$65
Financial aid deadline	7/1
Can first year start other than fall?	No
Student to faculty ratio	11.9 to 1
# of housing spaces available restricted to law students graduate housing for which law students are eligible	5

Faculty and Administrators

	Total		Men		Women		Minorities	
	Spr	Fall	Spr	Fall	Spr	Fall	Spr	Fall
Full-time	53	53	27	25	26	28	6	6
Other full-time	2	3	1	1	1	2	1	1
Deans, librarians, & others who teach	3	3	2	2	1	1	1	1
Part-time	66	46	47	32	18	13	5	4
Total	124	105	77	60	46	44	13	12

Curriculum

	Full-Time	Part-Time
Typical first-year section size	70	40
Is there typically a "small section" of the first-year class, other than Legal Writing, taught by full-time faculty	Yes	Yes
If yes, typical size offered last year	35	28
# of classroom course titles beyond first-year curriculum	137	
# of upper division courses, excluding seminars, with an enrollment: Under 25	127	
25–49	39	
50–74	13	
75–99	5	
100+	1	
# of seminars	50	
# of seminar positions available	808	
# of seminar positions filled	345	193
# of positions available in simulation courses	272	
# of simulation positions filled	157	49
# of positions available in faculty supervised clinical courses	152	
# of faculty supervised clinical positions filled	91	30
# involved in field placements	202	15
# involved in law journals	197	36
# involved in moot court or trial competitions	40	7
# of credit hours required to graduate	84	

JD Enrollment and Ethnicity

	Men		Women		Full-Time		Part-Time		1st-Year		Total		JD Degs. Awd.
	#	%	#	%	#	%	#	%	#	%	#	%	
All Hispanics	15	3.7	13	2.9	18	3.2	10	3.4	12	4.4	28	3.3	12
Am. Ind./AK Nat.	1	0.2	0	0.0	0	0.0	1	0.3	0	0.0	1	0.1	2
Asian	29	7.1	53	11.8	51	9.1	31	10.5	17	6.2	82	9.6	19
Black/Af. Am.	14	3.4	25	5.5	16	2.8	23	7.8	14	5.1	39	4.5	18
Nat. HI/Pac. Isl.	3	0.7	0	0.0	1	0.2	2	0.7	0	0.0	3	0.3	0
2 or more races	4	1.0	2	0.4	2	0.4	4	1.4	1	0.4	6	0.7	0
Subtotal (minor.)	66	16.2	93	20.6	88	15.7	71	24.0	44	16.1	159	18.5	54
Nonres. Alien	15	3.7	19	4.2	21	3.7	13	4.4	10	3.6	34	4.0	0
White/Cauc.	226	55.5	234	51.9	313	55.7	147	49.7	153	55.8	460	53.6	187
Unknown	100	24.6	105	23.3	140	24.9	65	22.0	67	24.5	205	23.9	43
Total	407	47.4	451	52.6	562	65.5	296	34.5	274	31.9	858		284

Transfers

Transfers in	3
Transfers out	23

Tuition and Fees

	Resident	Nonresident
Full-time	$40,000	$40,000
Part-time	$30,505	$30,505
Tuition Guarantee Program	N	

Living Expenses

Estimated living expenses for singles

Living on campus	Living off campus	Living at home
$26,050	$26,050	$26,050

THE CATHOLIC UNIVERSITY OF AMERICA, COLUMBUS SCHOOL OF LAW

ABA Approved Since 1925

GPA and LSAT Scores

	Total	Full-Time	Part-Time
# of apps	3,372	2,680	692
# of offers	1,136	964	172
# of matrics	274	197	77
75% GPA	3.53	3.56	3.44
Median GPA	3.32	3.34	3.24
25% GPA	3.08	3.12	2.98
75% LSAT	161	161	159
Median LSAT	159	159	157
25% LSAT	156	157	155

Grants and Scholarships (from prior year)

	Total		Full-Time		Part-Time	
	#	%	#	%	#	%
Total # of students	890		574		316	
Total # receiving grants	328	36.9	242	42.2	86	27.2
Less than 1/2 tuition	309	34.7	224	39.0	85	26.9
Half to full tuition	17	1.9	16	2.8	1	0.3
Full tuition	1	0.1	1	0.2	0	0.0
More than full tuition	1	0.1	1	0.2	0	0.0
Median grant amount			$10,000		$6,500	

Informational and Library Resources

Total amount spent on library materials	$1,524,298
Study seating capacity inside the library	502
# of full-time equivalent professional librarians	11
Hours per week library is open	115
# of open, wired connections available to students	243
# of networked computers available for use by students	107
Has wireless network?	Y
Requires computer?	N

JD Attrition (from prior year)

	Academic	Other	Total	
	#	#	#	%
1st year	1	25	26	9.9
2nd year	0	2	2	0.7
3rd year	0	0	0	0.0
4th year	0	0	0	0.0

Employment (9 months after graduation)

	Total	Percentage
Employment status known	237	99.2
Employment status unknown	2	0.8
Employed	210	88.6
Pursuing graduate degrees	8	3.4
Unemployed (seeking, not seeking, or studying for the bar)	13	5.5
Type of Employment		
# employed in law firms	78	37.1
# employed in business and industry	48	22.9
# employed in government	42	20.0
# employed in public interest	3	1.4
# employed as judicial clerks	26	12.4
# employed in academia	9	4.3
Geographic Location		
# employed in state	109	51.9
# employed outside the US	0	0.0
# of states where employed		19

Bar Passage Rates

First-time takers	247	Reporting %	75.30
Average school %	77.42	Average state %	79.27
Average pass difference	−1.85		

Jurisdiction	Takers	Passers	Pass %	State %	Diff %
Maryland	96	76	79.17	78.20	0.97
Virginia	58	43	74.14	77.06	−2.92
New York	32	25	78.13	86.51	−8.38

THE CATHOLIC UNIVERSITY OF AMERICA, COLUMBUS SCHOOL OF LAW

Cardinal Station
Washington, DC 20064
Phone: 202.319.5151; Fax: 202.319.6285
E-mail: admissions@law.edu; Website: www.law.edu

Introduction

Founded in 1897, the Catholic University of America, Columbus School of Law is located on the 193-acre campus of the university. Students and faculty have easy access to nearly limitless legal resources: the Supreme Court, Congress, the United States and District of Columbia courts, and other federal, executive, and administrative agencies and branches of government. For a campus so close to a center of world power, it is peaceful, pleasant, and scenic, offering a sense of neighborhood and community. Classes are small and personal.

The law school is proud of its vibrant intellectual tradition and extends it to exploring new intersections of issues of law and morality. Students are trained and encouraged to use their hearts and minds, in concert with their skills, to practice effectively in the complex world of the twenty-first century. The school welcomes students of all religious, racial, and ethnic backgrounds to a program that is renowned for its consistently high number of graduates entering public and community service. The Columbus School of Law has been a member of the AALS since 1921 and was approved by the ABA in 1925.

Enrollment/Student Body

Total enrollment is typically more than 900 students. Law students come from nearly every state and a dozen foreign countries. More than 30 percent of the school's enrollment is part time, making its evening program one of the most flexible and accommodating available anywhere. First-year classes typically have 32 to 70 students. Upper-class courses range from 10 to 70 students. Faculty members keep posted office hours and are accessible for informal sessions, making for a more personalized education.

Faculty

The 64-member full-time faculty bring a wealth of experience and expertise to the classroom. The majority have practiced in the private sector. Adjunct faculty members are primarily active legal practitioners and complement the "real-world" flavor of course offerings. Classroom instruction is supplemented by many distinguished guest speakers, such as federal appellate judges, justices of the US Supreme Court, and leading academicians and theologians from around the world.

Library and Physical Facilities

The Library of Congress and specialized law collections throughout the city complement the law school's legal collections of over 425,000 volumes and numerous research databases. The law school facility, completed in 1994, houses all components of the law school. Law students have full access to other campus facilities, including a 40-acre athletic complex.

Curriculum

The prescribed first-year curriculum and method of teaching are designed to develop the analytical skills that characterize the able lawyer and to give the student familiarity with the major substantive areas of law. It is also designed as an introduction to jurisprudence and the Catholic intellectual tradition as it relates to the larger questions of social justice. While lawyers traditionally have been heavily involved with the commercial interests of private or corporate clients, law is becoming increasingly responsive to problems that affect the public interest. The CUA law school curriculum is designed to provide students with the basic knowledge to become effective lawyers in a changing legal environment.

Special Programs

CUA Law's institutes and special programs offer certification of a student's developed expertise in his or her chosen legal specialty. Each program provides invaluable externship opportunities, offering for-credit placements that are available nowhere else but in Washington, DC.

The Institute for Communications Law Studies offers unique specialized training in communications law, ranging from First Amendment law to FCC practices and procedures. Students are trained to think critically about the broader impact that mass media has upon society and human behavior.

The Comparative and International Law Institute provides superb background training to students who intend to specialize in international law. The institute offers a six-week summer-abroad program at the Jagiellonian University in Cracow, Poland.

The Law and Public Policy Program is designed for students who desire to make a difference through legislative change. The program combines classroom study in legislative and administrative processes with externships in government agencies and advocacy organizations that affect national public policy.

The Securities Law Program integrates a broad concentration of securities and corporate law courses with a required externship program. Adjunct instructors and program faculty bring vast knowledge to the classroom, as many have practiced with the Securities and Exchange Commission (SEC), the National Association of Securities Dealers (NASD), and private firms.

The Interdisciplinary Program on Law and Religion was created to provide a forum for study, research, and public discussion of the questions that arise from the nexus of law and religion. These include many of society's most challenging issues, such as bioethics, international human rights, and marriage law.

The Program of Studies in Jurisprudence exists to promote inquiry into the role of law in relation to culture and culture's orientation to the human good. The scope of its inquiry is both theoretical and practical. In its theoretical aspect, the program aims to contribute to the academic fields of jurisprudence, the philosophy of law, and Christian political and social ethics. In its practical dimension, it seeks to foster the renewal and transformation of culture, under contemporary circumstances, through law and law reform.

Clinical Programs

Columbus Community Legal Services recently observed its 40th year of assisting the underserved population of the nation's capital. The law school offers eight clinical programs, including five that emphasize client representation, case planning, and trial and administrative advocacy. Nine simulation courses are also offered that closely approximate real-life lawyering through simulated courtroom, mediation, and arbitration exercises. The two other clinical offerings are the SEC Observer Program and the Legal Externship Program.

Admission

While considerable weight is given to an applicant's grade-point average and LSAT score, admission decisions are also influenced by such factors as leadership potential, class rank, substantial involvement in volunteer community service activities, potential for contributing to diversity, and relevant work experience. Close attention is also paid to a candidate's personal statement and reasons for wanting to study at CUA.

Student Activities

The Catholic University Law Review, the Journal of Contemporary Health Law and Policy, and CommLaw Conspectus: Journal of Communications Law and Policy are scholarly law journals staffed and published by outstanding students. The Moot Court Board, in addition to facilitating at least eight intraschool competitions each year, also hosts two major contests at CUA: the National Telecommunications Competition and the Sutherland Cup. There are over 40 voluntary student organizations at the Columbus School of Law, encompassing a broad range of professional interests, ethnic and racial affiliations, political and religious perspectives, and recreational activities.

Financial Aid

Following the offer of admission, all prospective students are automatically evaluated for merit-based scholarships. Approximately 25–30 percent of each year's entering class has been awarded a scholarship. Given the significant financial investment of a law degree, the Office of Financial Aid is committed to providing all students with timely information and guidance.

Career Services

The Office of Career and Professional Development actively supports students and graduates in their search for employment by providing counseling as well as workshops, panel discussions, and access to a national alumni network. A comprehensive on-campus interviewing program is conducted annually. The school's small size makes it possible for all students to secure guidance with individualized career strategy and planning.

Housing

The Washington, DC, metropolitan area boasts many off-campus housing opportunities for prospective law students. Each summer, the Office of Admissions assists incoming students with the housing search by coordinating a roommate name exchange, a housing workshop, and an online housing forum. Graduate housing is available on campus. The law school is convenient to public transportation, including Washington's Metrorail system.

APPLICANT PROFILE

The Catholic University of America, Columbus School of Law
This grid includes only applicants who earned 120–180 LSAT scores under standard administrations.

LSAT Score	3.75 +		3.50–3.74		3.25–3.49		3.00–3.24		2.75–2.99		2.50–2.74		Below 2.50		No GPA		Total	
	Apps	Adm	Apps	Adm	Apps	Adm	Apps	Adm	Apps	Adm	Apps	Adm	Apps	Adm	Apps	Adm	Apps	Adm
170–180	3	3	4	4	2	2	5	4	2	1	0	0	3	2	0	0	19	16
165–169	21	19	27	26	29	27	21	20	12	11	10	7	4	2	1	1	125	113
160–164	86	82	144	132	166	152	105	88	54	42	27	16	24	9	6	5	612	526
155–159	98	65	200	119	278	119	187	53	117	24	67	6	39	2	13	5	999	393
150–154	63	13	157	15	217	18	189	20	104	6	52	1	47	1	15	1	844	75
145–149	24	1	54	1	81	3	98	7	83	2	32	0	28	1	11	0	411	15
140–144	6	0	20	0	29	0	42	0	43	0	26	0	20	0	8	0	194	0
Below 140	3	0	8	0	15	0	15	0	17	0	14	0	19	0	3	0	94	0
Total	304	183	614	297	817	321	662	192	432	86	228	30	184	17	57	12	3298	1138

Apps = Number of Applicants
Adm = Number Admitted
Reflects 99% of the total applicant pool; highest LSAT data reported.

CHAPMAN UNIVERSITY SCHOOL OF LAW

One University Drive
Orange, CA 92866
Phone: 877.CHAPLAW or 714.628.2500; Fax: 714.628.2501
E-mail: lawadm@chapman.edu; Website: www.chapman.edu/law

ABA
Approved
Since
1998

Section of Legal Education
and Admissions to the Bar

The Basics

Type of school	Private		
Term	Semester		
Application deadline	4/15	4/15	4/15
Application fee	$75		
Financial aid deadline	3/2		
Can first year start other than fall?	No		
Student to faculty ratio	9.3 to 1		
# of housing spaces available restricted to law students			
graduate housing for which law students are eligible			20

Faculty and Administrators

	Total		Men		Women		Minorities	
	Spr	Fall	Spr	Fall	Spr	Fall	Spr	Fall
Full-time	46	51	25	26	21	25	41	43
Other full-time	0	0	0	0	0	0	0	0
Deans, librarians, & others who teach	7	5	4	3	3	2	5	2
Part-time	48	36	36	31	12	5	45	34
Total	101	92	65	60	36	32	91	79

Curriculum

	Full-Time	Part-Time
Typical first-year section size	65	65
Is there typically a "small section" of the first-year class, other than Legal Writing, taught by full-time faculty	Yes	No
If yes, typical size offered last year	40	

# of classroom course titles beyond first-year curriculum		167
# of upper division courses, excluding seminars, with an enrollment:	Under 25	110
	25–49	26
	50–74	14
	75–99	0
	100+	0
# of seminars		17
# of seminar positions available		311
# of seminar positions filled	144	12
# of positions available in simulation courses		536
# of simulation positions filled	342	11
# of positions available in faculty supervised clinical courses		240
# of faculty supervised clinical positions filled	127	7
# involved in field placements	179	5
# involved in law journals	195	0
# involved in moot court or trial competitions	66	1
# of credit hours required to graduate		88

JD Enrollment and Ethnicity

	Men		Women		Full-Time		Part-Time		1st-Year		Total		JD Degs. Awd.
	#	%	#	%	#	%	#	%	#	%	#	%	
All Hispanics	15	4.9	15	5.6	28	5.1	2	7.1	9	4.3	30	5.2	9
Am. Ind./AK Nat.	1	0.3	1	0.4	2	0.4	0	0.0	0	0.0	2	0.3	1
Asian	34	11.2	39	14.4	68	12.5	5	17.9	25	12.0	73	12.7	27
Black/Af. Am.	1	0.3	2	0.7	3	0.5	0	0.0	1	0.5	3	0.5	5
Nat. HI/Pac. Isl.	1	0.3	0	0.0	1	0.2	0	0.0	1	0.5	1	0.2	0
2 or more races	4	1.3	14	5.2	18	3.3	0	0.0	18	8.7	18	3.1	0
Subtotal (minor.)	56	18.4	71	26.3	120	22.0	7	25.0	54	26.0	127	22.1	46
Nonres. Alien	2	0.7	0	0.0	2	0.4	0	0.0	1	0.5	2	0.3	0
White/Cauc.	188	61.8	137	50.7	311	57.0	14	50.0	124	59.6	325	56.6	93
Unknown	58	19.1	62	23.0	113	20.7	7	25.0	29	13.9	120	20.9	30
Total	304	53.0	270	47.0	546	95.1	28	4.9	208	36.2	574		171

Transfers

Transfers in	12
Transfers out	3

Tuition and Fees

	Resident	Nonresident
Full-time	$40,173	$40,173
Part-time	$31,938	$31,938
Tuition Guarantee Program		N

Living Expenses

Estimated living expenses for singles

Living on campus	Living off campus	Living at home
$30,139	$30,139	$18,349

CHAPMAN UNIVERSITY SCHOOL OF LAW

ABA
Approved
Since
1998

GPA and LSAT Scores

	Total	Full-Time	Part-Time
# of apps	2,783	2,526	257
# of offers	743	734	9
# of matrics	212	208	4
75% GPA	3.68	3.68	3.81
Median GPA	3.52	3.52	3.58
25% GPA	3.21	3.21	3.07
75% LSAT	161	161	162
Median LSAT	159	159	158
25% LSAT	155	155	156

Grants and Scholarships (from prior year)

	Total		Full-Time		Part-Time	
	#	%	#	%	#	%
Total # of students	547		510		37	
Total # receiving grants	192	35.1	190	37.3	2	5.4
Less than 1/2 tuition	85	15.5	84	16.5	1	2.7
Half to full tuition	30	5.5	30	5.9	0	0.0
Full tuition	49	9.0	48	9.4	1	2.7
More than full tuition	28	5.1	28	5.5	0	0.0
Median grant amount			$34,156		$0	

Informational and Library Resources

Total amount spent on library materials	$1,109,628
Study seating capacity inside the library	286
# of full-time equivalent professional librarians	8
Hours per week library is open	106
# of open, wired connections available to students	587
# of networked computers available for use by students	69
Has wireless network?	Y
Requires computer?	N

JD Attrition (from prior year)

	Academic	Other	Total	
	#	#	#	%
1st year	6	8	14	7.7
2nd year	0	0	0	0.0
3rd year	0	0	0	0.0
4th year	0	0	0	0.0

Employment (9 months after graduation)

	Total	Percentage
Employment status known	157	98.7
Employment status unknown	2	1.3
Employed	134	85.4
Pursuing graduate degrees	9	5.7
Unemployed (seeking, not seeking, or studying for the bar)	3	1.9
Type of Employment		
# employed in law firms	68	50.7
# employed in business and industry	18	13.4
# employed in government	10	7.5
# employed in public interest	1	0.7
# employed as judicial clerks	6	4.5
# employed in academia	30	22.4
Geographic Location		
# employed in state	122	91.0
# employed outside the US	1	0.7
# of states where employed	11	

Bar Passage Rates

First-time takers	159	Reporting %	95.60
Average school %	77.63	Average state %	73.19
Average pass difference	4.44		

Jurisdiction	Takers	Passers	Pass %	State %	Diff %
California	152	118	77.63	73.19	4.44

CHAPMAN UNIVERSITY SCHOOL OF LAW

One University Drive
Orange, CA 92866
Phone: 877.CHAPLAW or 714.628.2500; Fax: 714.628.2501
E-mail: lawadm@chapman.edu; Website: www.chapman.edu/law

Introduction

Chapman University School of Law is located in the historic Old Towne district of Orange, California. We are part of the university that is 144 years old. The law school, established in 1995, received full approval by the ABA in 2002 and AALS accreditation in January 2006.

The law school has gained a national reputation for its high-quality faculty, students, and facilities. The law school has focus areas in entertainment law, international law, taxation, environmental/real estate/land use, and advocacy and dispute resolution; joint JD/MBA degrees and joint JD/MFA degrees in film producing; and LLM degrees in taxation and prosecutorial science. We also offer clinical opportunities in the areas of family violence, immigration law, elder law, constitutional law, and appellate practice. Our students have obtained rewarding externship and internship opportunities. The law school's successes have been aided by its location in vibrant and dynamic Orange County.

Affiliation with a well-established university allows for cross-disciplinary engagement, joint degrees, and a lively and engaging intellectual environment beyond the classroom. Chapman University offers an impressive selection of artistic and cultural opportunities for its students.

Enrollment/Student Body

Chapman Law has committed itself to building a small, talented, and diverse student body. Total student enrollment in 2009–2010 was approximately 575 law students.

The 2009 entering class consisted of 181 law students. The students were divided into three first-year sections. The Legal Research and Writing course has a maximum of 20 students in each of nine sections. Currently, about 10 percent of the entering class comes from outside California; that number is expected to increase over the next few years as Chapman's reputation reaches a more national audience. The minority enrollment is 23 percent.

Competition for seats is keen. Approximately 31 percent of applicants in the 2009 applicant pool were admitted.

Faculty

Chapman has assembled an impressive law faculty (including four former US Supreme Court clerks) who are excellent teachers, accomplished scholars, and outstanding mentors. Chapman Law's environment is conducive to learning. Students have access to the faculty and frequent opportunities to engage them in both formal and informal settings. Our student-to-faculty ratio is 10.1 to 1.

Library and Physical Facilities

The beautiful Donald P. Kennedy Hall opened in 1999 with state-of-the-art learning facilities in its classrooms, law library, and trial and appellate courtrooms.

Library holdings now exceed 348,000 volumes and volume equivalents. The collection is fully accessible to students both in hard copy and through the computer network.

Library carrels and desktops are generous in number, and many are wired for Internet access. Several group study rooms are available for student use and extended research.

Two state-of-the-art courtrooms provide computers, cameras, and electronic blackboards for trial advocacy exercises, competitions, and formal hearings by visiting courts.

Special Programs/Clinics/Externships

The law school offers the JD/MBA and JD/MFA programs, affording students the opportunity to earn the equivalent of two accredited professional degrees in four years instead of the typical five. Chapman's George L. Argyros School of Business and Economics is AACSB accredited. Our Dodge College of Film and Media Arts is housed in a state-of-the-art building with the latest digital technology.

About 10 percent of the students choose to focus their electives in one of five certificate areas: entertainment law, international law, tax law, environmental/real estate/land use, or advocacy and dispute resolution. The Tax-Law Emphasis Program affords students the opportunity to represent claimants against the IRS in the US Tax Court Clinic. The Center for Land Resources allows students to network with practicing professionals. In the Externship Program, students receive placements in the offices of appellate judges, trial judges, district attorneys, and public defenders, where they gain hands-on experience and academic credit.

Clinic offerings include family violence/immigration law, elder law, entertainment, constitutional litigation, mediation, tax law, and appellate practice. Nearly all clinics allow students additional opportunities to represent actual clients in an array of legal settings.

The law school's Academic Achievement Program assists students in the mastery of the skills necessary to become successful law students and productive attorneys. The program includes individualized counseling and instruction, as well as group workshops and peer tutoring.

Admission

The School of Law seeks to admit stellar students who are passionately interested in a legal education that will challenge them to grow intellectually, ethically, and professionally. The law school seeks a diverse student body that will make a meaningful contribution to the legal profession. Many variables enter into the decision-making process. The applicant's entire file is considered, and each application is individually reviewed. The Admission Committee reviews the traditional numbers—your academic record and LSAT—but also considers additional indicators of potential success in law school. Such indicators include the nature and rigor of the undergraduate discipline, an upward trend in academic performance, coursework, writing ability, employment history, graduate-level courses taken and degrees earned, scholarly achievement, community and volunteer service, research projects, demonstrated leadership ability, fluency in foreign languages, personal background (including a history of overcoming adversity), and unusual contributions or other maturing experiences.

Electronic applications are required. Two letters of recommendation are required; these should be submitted directly to LSAC. A personal statement and résumé are also required, and they should be submitted with your application. Applying early is encouraged as the entering class is filled on a rolling basis, and scholarship funds (merit and need) may be exhausted early in the admission cycle. Please follow the application instructions closely. Transfer and visitor applicants should visit our website.

There is a priority consideration deadline of April 1, 2012, for merit-based scholarships. The application deadline for the fall 2012 entering class is April 15, 2012.

Student Curricular and Cocurricular Activities

The law school offers many activities that enrich the academic program and provide important training in leadership. Three journals offer valuable experience in research, writing, and editing. The Student Bar Association administers a full range of programs. Other organizations include, but are not limited to, the Minority Law Students Association, the Asian Pacific American Law Students Association, the Public Interest Law Foundation, the Federalist Society, and the student-run Honor Council.

Externships allow students to earn academic credit while working in a variety of government agencies, judges' chambers, and public interest organizations, developing the practical skills and confidence they will need after graduation.

Chapman offers a range of advocacy experiences, including participation in mock trial, moot court, client counseling, international law, and negotiation competitions. Chapman teams have won regional competitions and have performed competitively in national and international tournaments. The Moot Court Board and the Mock Trial Board administer their programs and provide excellent practical training.

Scholarships and Financial Aid

Chapman Law offers a generous merit- and need-based scholarship program. For the 2010 entering class, more than 56 percent of new students received scholarships. After the first year, law students are eligible to renew their merit scholarships provided they maintain a GPA of 3.0 or above in their classes after the first-year grades are posted. For 2010, over $5.5 million in scholarship funds were distributed among a student body of approximately 550. This included merit- and need-based scholarships.

Chapman also offers a full range of loan programs to complement students' financial needs, including Stafford loans, Graduate PLUS loans, Perkins loans, and private loans. All students receiving scholarship funds and/or loans should plan to file the FAFSA. International students are eligible for merit scholarships.

Career Services

Chapman Law provides students and alumni with comprehensive career services and resources that aid them in selecting their career direction and in reaching their goals. The office is composed of a director, two assistant directors, and a recruitment coordinator. The Career Services Office facilitates interviews for our students with legal employers during our On-Campus Interview and Résumé Collection Program in both the fall and spring. The office also provides students the opportunity to meet with prominent members of the legal community through frequent panels, a highly successful Attorney Mentor Program, and an extensive Mock Interview Program. In keeping with the Chapman mission of personalized education, the counselors meet with individual students to review résumés and cover letters; to aid in self-assessment and goal orientation; to discuss specific opportunities unique to the student's needs; and to provide training, support, and feedback in all aspects of exploring career options.

APPLICANT PROFILE

Chapman University School of Law
This grid includes only applicants who earned 120–180 LSAT scores under standard administrations.

LSAT Score	GPA																				
	3.75 +		3.50–3.74		3.25–3.49		3.00–3.24		2.75–2.99		2.50–2.74		2.25–2.49		2.00–2.24		Below 2.00		No GPA		Total	
	Apps	Adm	Apps	Adm	Apps	Adm	Apps	Adm	Apps	Adm	Apps	Adm	Apps	Adm	Apps	Adm	Apps	Adm	Apps	Adm	Apps	Adm
175–180	1	1	0	0	1	1	0	0	0	0	0	0	0	0	0	0	0	0	0	0	2	2
170–174	0	0	4	4	1	1	2	2	1	1	2	2	0	0	1	0	0	0	0	0	11	10
165–169	12	12	6	6	20	19	17	15	14	11	8	3	7	1	1	0	1	0	0	0	86	67
160–164	37	36	60	60	63	59	68	64	34	20	29	6	16	1	4	0	0	0	2	2	313	248
155–159	55	54	122	119	172	74	147	39	97	14	56	1	31	1	6	0	1	0	7	6	694	308
150–154	37	23	144	65	196	8	190	6	139	0	75	0	39	1	6	0	2	0	8	0	836	103
145–149	17	0	60	1	108	1	135	3	96	0	41	0	26	0	15	0	2	0	8	0	508	5
140–144	6	0	21	0	30	0	46	0	46	0	39	0	22	0	4	0	0	0	6	0	220	0
135–139	2	0	1	0	7	0	10	0	14	0	7	0	8	0	6	0	2	0	4	0	61	0
130–134	0	0	0	0	3	0	6	0	6	0	5	0	2	0	5	0	1	0	1	0	29	0
125–129	0	0	0	0	0	0	0	0	0	0	2	0	0	0	1	0	0	0	0	0	3	0
120–124	0	0	0	0	0	0	0	0	0	0	0	0	0	0	0	0	0	0	0	0	0	0
Total	167	126	418	255	601	163	621	129	447	46	264	12	151	4	49	0	9	0	36	8	2763	743

Apps = Number of Applicants
Adm = Number Admitted
Reflects 99% of the total applicant pool; highest LSAT data reported.

CHARLESTON SCHOOL OF LAW

81 Mary Street, PO Box 535
Charleston, SC 29402
Phone: 843.377.2143; Fax: 843.329.0491
E-mail: info@charlestonlaw.edu; Website: www.charlestonlaw.edu

Provisional ABA Approved Since 2006

The Basics

Type of school	Private
Term	Semester
Application deadline	3/1 4/1
Application fee	$50
Financial aid deadline	4/1
Can first year start other than fall?	No
Student to faculty ratio	17.4 to 1
# of housing spaces available restricted to law students	
graduate housing for which law students are eligible	

Faculty and Administrators

	Total		Men		Women		Minorities	
	Spr	Fall	Spr	Fall	Spr	Fall	Spr	Fall
Full-time	29	29	14	14	15	15	4	4
Other full-time	2	2	1	1	1	1	1	1
Deans, librarians, & others who teach	12	12	6	6	6	6	1	1
Part-time	28	35	17	22	11	13	0	0
Total	71	78	38	43	33	35	6	6

Curriculum

	Full-Time	Part-Time
Typical first-year section size	63	50
Is there typically a "small section" of the first-year class, other than Legal Writing, taught by full-time faculty	No	No
If yes, typical size offered last year		

# of classroom course titles beyond first-year curriculum		109
# of upper division courses, excluding seminars, with an enrollment:	Under 25	98
	25–49	20
	50–74	20
	75–99	6
	100+	0

# of seminars		27
# of seminar positions available		556
# of seminar positions filled	269	99
# of positions available in simulation courses		660
# of simulation positions filled	302	122
# of positions available in faculty supervised clinical courses		0
# of faculty supervised clinical positions filled	0	0
# involved in field placements	84	24
# involved in law journals	97	18
# involved in moot court or trial competitions	31	7
# of credit hours required to graduate		88

JD Enrollment and Ethnicity

	Men		Women		Full-Time		Part-Time		1st-Year		Total		JD Degs. Awd.
	#	%	#	%	#	%	#	%	#	%	#	%	
All Hispanics	5	1.3	4	1.3	7	1.3	2	1.1	3	1.3	9	1.3	0
Am. Ind./AK Nat.	1	0.3	4	1.3	3	0.6	2	1.1	4	1.7	5	0.7	0
Asian	5	1.3	2	0.6	5	1.0	2	1.1	3	1.3	7	1.0	1
Black/Af. Am.	19	4.9	29	9.2	31	6.0	17	9.3	16	6.8	48	6.8	8
Nat. HI/Pac. Isl.	0	0.0	1	0.3	1	0.2	0	0.0	1	0.4	1	0.1	0
2 or more races	0	0.0	0	0.0	0	0.0	0	0.0	0	0.0	0	0.0	0
Subtotal (minor.)	30	7.7	40	12.7	47	9.0	23	12.6	27	11.4	70	10.0	9
Nonres. Alien	0	0.0	0	0.0	0	0.0	0	0.0	0	0.0	0	0.0	0
White/Cauc.	346	89.2	268	85.4	459	88.3	155	85.2	198	83.5	614	87.5	172
Unknown	12	3.1	6	1.9	14	2.7	4	2.2	12	5.1	18	2.6	3
Total	388	55.3	314	44.7	520	74.1	182	25.9	237	33.8	702		184

Transfers

Transfers in	5
Transfers out	4

Tuition and Fees

	Resident	Nonresident
Full-time	$35,606	$35,606
Part-time	$28,608	$28,608
Tuition Guarantee Program	N	

Living Expenses

Estimated living expenses for singles

Living on campus	Living off campus	Living at home
N/A	$19,250	$19,250

CHARLESTON SCHOOL OF LAW

ABA
Approved
Since
2006

GPA and LSAT Scores

	Total	Full-Time	Part-Time
# of apps	2,156	1,942	367
# of offers	950	850	100
# of matrics	237	187	50
75% GPA	3.46	3.46	3.37
Median GPA	3.18	3.25	3.04
25% GPA	2.90	2.95	2.80
75% LSAT	156	156	153
Median LSAT	154	155	151
25% LSAT	151	152	149

Grants and Scholarships (from prior year)

	Total		Full-Time		Part-Time	
	#	%	#	%	#	%
Total # of students	659		459		200	
Total # receiving grants	236	35.8	219	47.7	17	8.5
Less than 1/2 tuition	232	35.2	215	46.8	17	8.5
Half to full tuition	3	0.5	3	0.7	0	0.0
Full tuition	1	0.2	1	0.2	0	0.0
More than full tuition	0	0.0	0	0.0	0	0.0
Median grant amount			$7,500		$5,000	

Informational and Library Resources

Total amount spent on library materials	$832,672
Study seating capacity inside the library	405
# of full-time equivalent professional librarians	5
Hours per week library is open	104
# of open, wired connections available to students	0
# of networked computers available for use by students	6
Has wireless network?	Y
Requires computer?	Y

JD Attrition (from prior year)

	Academic	Other	Total	
	#	#	#	%
1st year	4	12	16	6.7
2nd year	5	2	7	3.5
3rd year	0	3	3	1.6
4th year	0	1	1	2.6

Employment (9 months after graduation)

	Total	Percentage
Employment status known	152	97.4
Employment status unknown	4	2.6
Employed	117	77.0
Pursuing graduate degrees	14	9.2
Unemployed (seeking, not seeking, or studying for the bar)	21	13.8
Type of Employment		
# employed in law firms	46	39.3
# employed in business and industry	11	9.4
# employed in government	21	17.9
# employed in public interest	7	6.0
# employed as judicial clerks	31	26.5
# employed in academia	1	0.9
Geographic Location		
# employed in state	99	84.6
# employed outside the US	0	0.0
# of states where employed	7	

Bar Passage Rates

First-time takers	199	Reporting %	86.93
Average school %	77.46	Average state %	78.19

Average pass difference −0.73

Jurisdiction	Takers	Passers	Pass %	State %	Diff %
South Carolina	173	134	77.46	78.19	−0.73

CHARLESTON SCHOOL OF LAW

The information on these pages was provided by the law school.

81 Mary Street, PO Box 535
Charleston, SC 29402
Phone: 843.377.2143; Fax: 843.329.0491
E-mail: info@charlestonlaw.edu; Website: www.charlestonlaw.edu

Introduction

The Charleston School of Law (CSOL) offers students the unique opportunity to study the time-honored practice of law amid the beauty and grace of one of the South's oldest and most prestigious cities, Charleston, South Carolina. Founded in 2003, CSOL is a freestanding school. The School of Law received provisional approval from the ABA in December 2006, and graduates are qualified to seek admission to the bar in all 50 states and the District of Columbia.

Located in beautiful downtown Charleston, South Carolina, the school is conveniently situated near the historic "four corners of the law" as well as the thriving legal community and the federal and county courthouses. The open intellectual environment at CSOL complements the progressive nature of the city of Charleston. With its diverse economy, rich cultural heritage, thriving tourist industry, and natural amenities, the city—home to one of the nation's busiest ports—is a hub of activity. Charleston is attractive, fun, and consistently named one of the best places in the country to live, work, and learn. The city is home to other institutions of higher education, including the Medical University of South Carolina, the Citadel, and the College of Charleston. The 580,000-person metropolitan area is served by a strong program of cultural activities. Spoleto Festival USA, an internationally renowned arts festival of opera, dance, music, and theater, draws more than 85,000 people to the city each summer. Visitors and residents delight in Charleston's nationally recognized restaurants, vibrant nightlife, walks along the historic Battery, tours of historic homes, boating, sailing, golf, and beachcombing on nearby Sullivan's Island, Isle of Palms, Folly Beach, or Kiawah Island.

Library

The Sol Blatt Jr. Law Library, located in a historic 1857 railroad building, offers the feel of Charleston while housing a wireless network that provides access to an ever-growing digital collection. In just six years, the library has built a digital and print collection that includes over 600,000 titles.

Students have access to the full text of primary and secondary sources of American law twenty-four hours a day, seven days a week from anywhere in the world via the Internet. In addition to the traditional legal databases of Westlaw and Lexis, students also have electronic access to the full text of materials from BNA, CCH, CIAO, HeinOnline, LLMC, LexisNexis Congressional, LexisNexis State Capital, Matthew Bender, RIA Checkpoint, and Supreme Court Records and Briefs. To cost effectively train to be twenty-first century lawyers, students learn to integrate print and electronic research in a study space that manages to combine the historical charm of Charleston with the functionality of twenty-first century access to digital information.

Expenses and Financial Aid

Tuition for the 2010–2011 academic year was as follows: full time—$35,606; part time—$28,608; estimated living expenses—$14,000. The school offers both need-based and academic merit-based scholarships. Applicants wanting to be considered for merit scholarships must have a complete file on or before February 1. Merit-based scholarship decisions are made in early March. Need-based scholarship applications must be postmarked no later than May 15. Applicants should be eligible for federal student loans and are encouraged to complete the FAFSA no later than April 15.

Admission

CSOL requires applicants to have earned a bachelor's degree from an accredited institution prior to enrolling in the school. CSOL offers both a full- and part-time program of study leading to the Juris Doctor degree. Beginning students are accepted for the fall semester only. All applicants are required to take the LSAT and register with LSAC's Credential Assembly Service. Applicants should submit a completed application, a personal statement, and two letters of recommendation, plus pay a $50 application fee. A résumé may also be submitted. Applicants who are accepted will be required to submit a dean's certification form from all colleges or universities attended for 12 or more credit hours. Applications for the full-time program must be submitted on or before March 1; the deadline for those applying to the part-time program is April 1.

Consideration is given to many factors; however, the two most important factors in reviewing an application are the cumulative undergraduate GPA and the LSAT. If an applicant has multiple LSAT scores, the highest score will be considered. A score is valid for three years. Other factors taken into consideration are graduate work, military or significant work experience, letters of recommendation, the personal statement, and community service.

Curriculum

Students at CSOL study law as a profession with an emphasis on excellence in the classroom. The low faculty-to-student ratio is a testament to the student-centered focus. Small class size promotes individual inquiry in a collegial learning atmosphere. The goals of CSOL include teaching the practice of law as a profession with the chief aim of providing public service, and instituting and coordinating legal outreach programs for the South Carolina and American Bars; local, state, and federal governments; and the general population.

Courses in torts, property, contracts, civil procedure, and legal writing and research comprise the first-year curriculum. Required upper-level courses include business associations, commercial law, constitutional law, criminal law, criminal procedure, domestic relations, equity, evidence, insurance, trusts and estates, and professional responsibility, as well as an advanced writing requirement and a skills course.

All students are required to perform a minimum of 30 hours of public service prior to graduation and to participate in a professionalism program during each of the three years of law school.

Special Programs

The school offers a dynamic externship program that provides students the opportunity to gain practical work experience in legal business environments while earning course credit. Students have the opportunity to work under the direct supervision of members of the judiciary and attorneys in private practice, as well as in the public sector or in public interest jobs.

In 2010, more than 110 organizations, including county public defenders' offices, state agencies, state and federal courts, and nonprofit agencies in South Carolina and beyond, offered more than 120 externship opportunities to students.

Courses in admiralty and maritime law are available to students enrolled in the school. The Charleston Maritime Law Institute was founded by students and publishes the *Maritime Law Bulletin* (MALABU).

Housing

The school does not offer on-campus housing. Charleston offers many options for off-campus living. Whether a student opts to live in the downtown historic district, at one of the nearby beaches, or in one of the many convenient neighborhoods and communities, carriage houses, apartments, or rental houses are available. The office of admission works with incoming and continuing students to find housing in the Charleston area.

Student Activities

Students have the opportunity to work on the publication of two law reviews. A student board publishes the *Charleston Law Review* on a quarterly basis. Students may also work with federal magistrate judges to publish the printed edition of the *Federal Courts Law Review*.

Moot court opportunities are also available to students enrolled in the school. In the school's first-ever national competition in 2006, the National Constitutional Law Moot Court Competition, a team of students from CSOL won the grand prize.

The school has more than 30 student organizations, including, but not limited to, the Student Bar Association, the Black Law Student Association, the International Law Society, the Environmental Law Society, the Real Estate Society, the Student Trial Lawyers Association, and Women in Law.

Career Services

The Career Services Office provides a wide range of career development services for CSOL students and creates opportunities to connect students with employers in an efficient and supportive manner. The office serves as a liaison between students and legal employers. The staff provides individual career counseling, programming on career-related issues, and individualized résumé-writing assistance. They also coordinate the on-campus interview program and résumé-forwarding service, as well as the school's participation in national and regional career fairs. In addition, the staff is responsible for the maintenance of a dynamic database of employers and an online career resource center.

The office is available to assist students in finding part-time employment while enrolled in law school, as well as summer employment and full-time permanent employment upon graduation. The Charleston area provides myriad opportunities for part-time employment while students are enrolled in their second and third years of law school.

CSOL prepares students for careers in all areas of legal practice. Regardless of a student's path after graduation, CSOL strives to instill in students the value of public service. All students must complete 30 hours of pro bono legal service under the supervision of an attorney licensed in South Carolina before they graduate. The Career Services Office develops and supports pro bono opportunities in the legal community and provides guidance to students in their selection of pro bono work.

APPLICANT PROFILE

Charleston School of Law

LSAT Score	GPA								
	3.75 +	3.50–3.74	3.25–3.49	3.00–3.24	2.75–2.99	2.50–2.74	2.25–2.49	2.00–2.24	Below 2.00
175–180									
170–174									
165–169									
160–164									
155–159									
150–154									
145–149									
140–144									
135–139									
130–134									
125–129									
120–124									

Good Possibility   Possible   Unlikely

CHARLOTTE SCHOOL OF LAW

2145 Suttle Avenue
Charlotte, NC 28208
Phone: 704.971.8500; Fax: 704.971.8599
E-mail: admissions@charlottelaw.edu; Website: www.charlottelaw.edu

Provisional ABA Approved Since 2008

The Basics

Type of school	Private
Term	Semester
Application deadline	1/10 8/10
Application fee	$50
Financial aid deadline	
Can first year start other than fall?	Yes
Student to faculty ratio	17.5 to 1
# of housing spaces available restricted to law students	
graduate housing for which law students are eligible	

Faculty and Administrators

	Total		Men		Women		Minorities	
	Spr	Fall	Spr	Fall	Spr	Fall	Spr	Fall
Full-time	25	34	11	13	14	21	9	11
Other full-time	1	1	1	1	0	0	0	0
Deans, librarians, & others who teach	8	8	2	2	6	6	2	3
Part-time	29	29	16	15	13	14	29	29
Total	63	72	30	31	33	41	40	43

JD Enrollment and Ethnicity

	Men		Women		Full-Time		Part-Time		1st-Year		Total		JD Degs. Awd.
	#	%	#	%	#	%	#	%	#	%	#	%	
All Hispanics	13	3.3	24	5.7	30	4.5	7	4.9	19	3.9	37	4.6	5
Am. Ind./AK Nat.	8	2.0	5	1.2	10	1.5	3	2.1	9	1.8	13	1.6	0
Asian	11	2.8	5	1.2	13	1.9	3	2.1	12	2.4	16	2.0	1
Black/Af. Am.	29	7.4	74	17.7	76	11.4	27	18.9	77	15.7	103	12.7	4
Nat. HI/Pac. Isl.	0	0.0	0	0.0	0	0.0	0	0.0	0	0.0	0	0.0	0
2 or more races	0	0.0	0	0.0	0	0.0	0	0.0	0	0.0	0	0.0	0
Subtotal (minor.)	61	15.5	108	25.8	129	19.3	40	28.0	117	23.8	169	20.8	10
Nonres. Alien	0	0.0	0	0.0	0	0.0	0	0.0	0	0.0	0	0.0	0
White/Cauc.	317	80.7	298	71.1	519	77.6	96	67.1	352	71.5	615	75.7	71
Unknown	15	3.8	13	3.1	21	3.1	7	4.9	21	4.3	28	3.4	0
Total	393	48.4	419	51.6	669	82.4	143	17.6	492	60.6	812		81

Curriculum

	Full-Time	Part-Time
Typical first-year section size	75	55
Is there typically a "small section" of the first-year class, other than Legal Writing, taught by full-time faculty	No	No
If yes, typical size offered last year		
# of classroom course titles beyond first-year curriculum	70	
# of upper division courses, excluding seminars, with an enrollment: Under 25	54	
25–49	21	
50–74	3	
75–99	6	
100+	2	
# of seminars	12	
# of seminar positions available	240	
# of seminar positions filled	101	26
# of positions available in simulation courses	60	
# of simulation positions filled	41	9
# of positions available in faculty supervised clinical courses	118	
# of faculty supervised clinical positions filled	61	13
# involved in field placements	26	5
# involved in law journals	42	17
# involved in moot court or trial competitions	15	4
# of credit hours required to graduate	90	

Transfers

Transfers in	4
Transfers out	18

Tuition and Fees

	Resident	Nonresident
Full-time	$34,990	$34,990
Part-time	$28,292	$28,292
Tuition Guarantee Program		N

Living Expenses

Estimated living expenses for singles

Living on campus	Living off campus	Living at home
N/A	$22,020	$22,020

CHARLOTTE SCHOOL OF LAW

ABA
Approved
Since
2008

GPA and LSAT Scores

	Total	Full-Time	Part-Time
# of apps	3,747	3,328	419
# of offers	2,254	2,065	189
# of matrics	468	390	78
75% GPA	3.34	3.35	3.22
Median GPA	3.04	3.06	2.88
25% GPA	2.73	2.75	2.63
75% LSAT	152	152	152
Median LSAT	149	150	149
25% LSAT	148	148	148

Grants and Scholarships (from prior year)

	Total		Full-Time		Part-Time	
	#	%	#	%	#	%
Total # of students	481		380		101	
Total # receiving grants	282	58.6	241	63.4	41	40.6
Less than 1/2 tuition	265	55.1	225	59.2	40	39.6
Half to full tuition	16	3.3	15	3.9	1	1.0
Full tuition	1	0.2	1	0.3	0	0.0
More than full tuition	0	0.0	0	0.0	0	0.0
Median grant amount			$6,000		$5,500	

Informational and Library Resources

Total amount spent on library materials	$805,546
Study seating capacity inside the library	9,639
# of full-time equivalent professional librarians	8
Hours per week library is open	105
# of open, wired connections available to students	0
# of networked computers available for use by students	56
Has wireless network?	Y
Requires computer?	Y

JD Attrition (from prior year)

	Academic	Other	Total	
	#	#	#	%
1st year	21	29	50	18.1
2nd year	2	6	8	7.0
3rd year	0	2	2	2.7
4th year	0	0	0	0.0

Employment (9 months after graduation)

	Total	Percentage
Employment status known	62	96.9
Employment status unknown	2	3.1
Employed	59	95.2
Pursuing graduate degrees	0	0.0
Unemployed (seeking, not seeking, or studying for the bar)	1	1.6
Type of Employment		
# employed in law firms	32	54.2
# employed in business and industry	17	28.8
# employed in government	3	5.1
# employed in public interest	4	6.8
# employed as judicial clerks	0	0.0
# employed in academia	3	5.1
Geographic Location		
# employed in state	50	84.7
# employed outside the US	0	0.0
# of states where employed	4	

Bar Passage Rates

First-time takers	59	Reporting %	93.22
Average school %	69.09	Average state %	76.86
Average pass difference	−7.77		

Jurisdiction	Takers	Passers	Pass %	State %	Diff %
North Carolina	52	35	67.31	76.79	−9.48
South Carolina	3	3	100.00	78.19	21.81

CHARLOTTE SCHOOL OF LAW

2145 Suttle Avenue
Charlotte, NC 28208
Phone: 704.971.8500; Fax: 704.971.8599
E-mail: admissions@charlottelaw.edu; Website: www.charlottelaw.edu

Introduction

Welcome to Charlotte School of Law! The law is one of the oldest, most noble, and rewarding of all callings. It is also a profession that is undergoing rapid change as the Internet, knowledge management, internationalization, and other forces converge to challenge and redefine what we mean by legal practice. We are also seeing an expansion of the group to whom we provide legal services, and greatly amplify uses to which one may apply a legal education.

At Charlotte Law we have an educational model that is designed to meet the needs of a twenty-first-century lawyer. This includes a focus on you, the student. Our goal is to provide an intense engagement with faculty and staff, a personalized experience, and a rigorous yet innovative program of study that will maximize your chances of law school success, passage on the bar exam, and career opportunities.

Charlotte Law will also make you "practice-ready" by providing a program of comprehensive professional development that includes not only legal theory, but also exposure to legal practice and the inculcation of important personal, generic, and legal skills required of a rapidly changing legal profession.

Charlotte Law focuses on servant leadership. Tomorrow's lawyers cannot work in isolation, but must be engaged in, and contribute to, their communities. Such involvement will provide you with a lifelong career that is both professionally and personally rewarding, and represents the highest form of professional education.

An important part of the Charlotte Law "magic" has to do with our location in Charlotte, North Carolina. Charlotte is a dynamic, rapidly growing, international city which offers a rich array of family, educational, sports/recreational, cultural, and other opportunities. Our pleasant weather and close proximity to the sea and mountains provide a wonderful venue in which to study and pursue a career afterward. Indeed, North and South Carolina have one of the lowest proportions of lawyers in the United States and collectively is one of the fastest growing regions in the country.

Finally, knowing that seeing is believing, we invite you to visit Charlotte Law to see and feel the difference. When you do, we are confident that you will find in Team Charlotte one of the most exciting, vibrant, and enriching learning communities, dedicated to helping you achieve your full potential both personally and professionally.

Mission

Our entire academic mission is structured around three core concepts that we strongly believe make the Charlotte Law experience a unique and powerful one. These three ideals drive decision making as well as our academic approach; together they form a keen vision for the school.

- Practical preparation is critical. A rigorous curriculum has been created to ensure that our students are equipped with practical skills that will allow them to thrive in a professional setting. Students are taught not only the traditions and theory of law, but also how to apply this learning through critical thinking and analytical skill sets.

We address what using a law degree in real life can mean to an individual both personally and professionally.

- Our students are our focus. Our faculty is driven by a desire to motivate and energize the student community in every aspect of the Charlotte School of Law experience. Professors are accessible mentors who take an active role in the development of students and help them to embrace their legal education and capitalize on the opportunities within the school's and community's network of resources. Student success is of the utmost importance to everyone at the institution, on every level.

- It is essential to reflect our community. The Charlotte School of Law believes strongly that tomorrow's leaders must reflect and interact effectively with an eclectic collective of people and cultures. Consequently, our inclusive environment fosters a demanding, yet supportive, educational setting for a richly diverse community.

Faculty and Administration

The Charlotte School of Law faculty and administration have come together from various backgrounds and achievements to design a practice-ready curriculum and a supportive environment where students are inspired to learn, prepared to serve, and qualified to lead with excellence. Our faculty includes outstanding legal scholars, former trial attorneys, corporate leaders, and government officials who interact with students on a daily basis. Every member of our team is deeply committed to making sure our students have the skills to bridge each area of legal practice and are better equipped for professional life no matter what path they choose for themselves upon graduation. Our student-to-faculty ratio is 17 to 1.

Program Options

The need for legal literacy has become a reality of complex contemporary business and government. A law degree adds value to almost any career one can imagine, and an increasing number of professionals are finding in the JD degree an experience that equips them well with the analytical, writing, counseling, and advocacy skills that are invaluable, no matter what one's calling.

Charlotte School of Law offers a full-time day program and a part-time program. In order to accommodate the varied needs of our students, the part-time program can be completed during the day or in the evening. Charlotte School of Law is one of few law schools to offer a spring program that starts in January. Both programs require the completion of 90 credit hours for graduation.

Admission

The Charlotte School of Law attracts applicants from not only North and South Carolina, but also from all over the United States. The process to gain admission is competitive; however, those who have scored well on the Law School Admission Test (LSAT) and have a good undergraduate grade-point average (in addition to other indicators of success) are good candidates to study law in our student-centered program.

Charlotte Law offers a full-time program (completed in three years) and a flexible part-time program (completed in four years, summers included). Applications are accepted and reviewed throughout the academic year for entrance into either our fall or spring class. We do not have an application deadline; however, in order to have the best chance of being selected to join the Charlotte Law family, you are encouraged to get your application in early and to complete the application process early (have all required materials on file). Early applicants with competitive numbers have the **best** chance of receiving a merit-based scholarship award.

The Charlotte Law admission office staff will attempt to notify an applicant if a required item is missing from the application file. However, the applicant remains ultimately responsible for ensuring that the application file is completed in a timely fashion. Applicants are strongly encouraged to retain copies of all application information submitted.

File Review Process: Fall semester applications are reviewed after October 1 of each year. The file review process continues until the class-size goal is met.

January semester applications are reviewed after September 1 of each year. The file review process continues until the class-size goal is met.

Deferred Admission: Charlotte School of Law does not defer admission from one year to the following year. However, an applicant may be granted a deferral within the same academic year, that is, from fall matriculation to spring matriculation. Otherwise, applicants who are offered admission but do not enroll must reapply.

Transfer/Visiting Students: Applications to transfer to Charlotte School of Law or to attend as a visiting student are evaluated by the Admissions Committee and the Academic Dean on a case-by-case basis. **Transfer or visiting status is granted only to applicants who are currently in law school.** If such an applicant is accepted, further details, instructions, and forms will be sent to the accepted applicant. Contact the admission office with questions: 704.971.8542 or admissions@charlottelaw.edu.

Financial Aid

The cost to attend law school may make your dream seem out of reach. Before you move to plan B, stop and think about the cost associated with anything worth doing. Law school is an investment in you and an investment in your future.

To offset the cost of tuition, Charlotte Law offers various merit-based scholarship awards to applicants who qualify. We also have a performance-based scholarship program for continuing students.

Contact our financial aid office today to discuss your financing options before you decide to give up on your dream: 704.971.8543 or financialaid@charlottelaw.edu.

APPLICANT PROFILE

Charlotte School of Law has elected not to publish an admission profile based on LSAT score and UGPA. While both numerical indicators are very important in understanding an applicant's potential for success in law school, those two factors are not the only ones taken into consideration.

Charlotte Law currently uses no form of indexing system in reaching its admission decisions. Each completed application file is thoroughly reviewed in its entirety by a team of faculty and admission professionals.

THE UNIVERSITY OF CHICAGO LAW SCHOOL

Admissions Office, 1111 E. 60th Street
Chicago, IL 60637
Phone: 773.702.9494; Fax: 773.834.0942
E-mail: admissions@law.uchicago.edu; Website: www.law.uchicago.edu

ABA
Approved
Since
1923

The Basics

Type of school	Private
Term	Quarter
Application deadline	2/1
Application fee	$75
Financial aid deadline	2/1
Can first year start other than fall?	No
Student to faculty ratio	9.1 to 1
# of housing spaces available restricted to law students	
graduate housing for which law students are eligible	659

Faculty and Administrators

	Total		Men		Women		Minorities	
	Spr	Fall	Spr	Fall	Spr	Fall	Spr	Fall
Full-time	56	57	36	36	20	21	10	14
Other full-time	14	14	12	11	2	3	4	3
Deans, librarians, & others who teach	4	4	2	2	2	2	0	0
Part-time	70	25	60	19	10	6	6	2
Total	144	100	110	68	34	32	20	19

Curriculum

		Full-Time	Part-Time
Typical first-year section size		96	0
Is there typically a "small section" of the first-year class, other than Legal Writing, taught by full-time faculty		No	No
If yes, typical size offered last year			
# of classroom course titles beyond first-year curriculum		195	
# of upper division courses, excluding seminars, with an enrollment:	Under 25	29	
	25–49	27	
	50–74	18	
	75–99	6	
	100+	7	
# of seminars		122	
# of seminar positions available		2,443	
# of seminar positions filled		1,580	0
# of positions available in simulation courses		105	
# of simulation positions filled		101	0
# of positions available in faculty supervised clinical courses		120	
# of faculty supervised clinical positions filled		120	0
# involved in field placements		0	0
# involved in law journals		122	0
# involved in moot court or trial competitions		8	0
# of credit hours required to graduate		105	

JD Enrollment and Ethnicity

	Men		Women		Full-Time		Part-Time		1st-Year		Total		JD Degs. Awd.
	#	%	#	%	#	%	#	%	#	%	#	%	
All Hispanics	34	9.6	29	10.3	63	9.9	0	0.0	22	10.7	63	9.9	15
Am. Ind./AK Nat.	0	0.0	1	0.4	1	0.2	0	0.0	1	0.5	1	0.2	0
Asian	23	6.5	34	12.1	57	9.0	0	0.0	17	8.3	57	9.0	25
Black/Af. Am.	16	4.5	21	7.5	37	5.8	0	0.0	18	8.7	37	5.8	14
Nat. HI/Pac. Isl.	0	0.0	0	0.0	0	0.0	0	0.0	0	0.0	0	0.0	0
2 or more races	12	3.4	8	2.8	20	3.2	0	0.0	7	3.4	20	3.2	0
Subtotal (minor.)	85	24.1	93	33.1	178	28.1	0	0.0	65	31.6	178	28.1	60
Nonres. Alien	7	2.0	6	2.1	13	2.1	0	0.0	3	1.5	13	2.1	0
White/Cauc.	213	60.3	156	55.5	369	58.2	0	0.0	116	56.3	369	58.2	104
Unknown	48	13.6	26	9.3	74	11.7	0	0.0	22	10.7	74	11.7	30
Total	353	55.7	281	44.3	634	100.0	0	0.0	206	32.5	634		199

Transfers

Transfers in	27
Transfers out	6

Tuition and Fees

	Resident	Nonresident
Full-time	$46,185	
Part-time		
Tuition Guarantee Program	N	

Living Expenses

Estimated living expenses for singles

Living on campus	Living off campus	Living at home
$21,060	$21,060	$21,060

THE UNIVERSITY OF CHICAGO LAW SCHOOL

ABA
Approved
Since
1923

GPA and LSAT Scores

	Total	Full-Time	Part-Time
# of apps	5,579	5,579	0
# of offers	849	849	0
# of matrics	205	205	0
75% GPA	3.87	3.87	0.00
Median GPA	3.78	3.78	0.00
25% GPA	3.59	3.59	0.00
75% LSAT	172	172	0
Median LSAT	171	171	0
25% LSAT	168	168	0

Grants and Scholarships (from prior year)

	Total		Full-Time		Part-Time	
	#	%	#	%	#	%
Total # of students	590		590		0	
Total # receiving grants	294	49.8	294	49.8	0	0.0
Less than 1/2 tuition	266	45.1	266	45.1	0	0.0
Half to full tuition	26	4.4	26	4.4	0	0.0
Full tuition	2	0.3	2	0.3	0	0.0
More than full tuition	0	0.0	0	0.0	0	0.0
Median grant amount			$10,800		$0	

Informational and Library Resources

Total amount spent on library materials	$2,110,570
Study seating capacity inside the library	483
# of full-time equivalent professional librarians	10
Hours per week library is open	82
# of open, wired connections available to students	1,115
# of networked computers available for use by students	26
Has wireless network?	Y
Requires computer?	Y

JD Attrition (from prior year)

	Academic	Other	Total	
	#	#	#	%
1st year	0	0	0	0.0
2nd year	0	7	7	3.5
3rd year	0	0	0	0.0
4th year	0	0	0	0.0

Employment (9 months after graduation)

	Total	Percentage
Employment status known	206	100.0
Employment status unknown	0	0.0
Employed	204	99.0
Pursuing graduate degrees	1	0.5
Unemployed (seeking, not seeking, or studying for the bar)	1	0.5
Type of Employment		
# employed in law firms	163	79.9
# employed in business and industry	7	3.4
# employed in government	5	2.5
# employed in public interest	7	3.4
# employed as judicial clerks	19	9.3
# employed in academia	3	1.5
Geographic Location		
# employed in state	66	32.4
# employed outside the US	4	2.0
# of states where employed		23

Bar Passage Rates

First-time takers	206	Reporting %	79.61
Average school %	91.46	Average state %	85.97
Average pass difference	5.49		

Jurisdiction	Takers	Passers	Pass %	State %	Diff %
Illinois	80	78	97.50	90.89	6.61
New York	51	46	90.20	86.51	3.69
California	33	26	78.79	73.19	5.60

THE UNIVERSITY OF CHICAGO LAW SCHOOL

Admissions Office, 1111 E. 60th Street
Chicago, IL 60637
Phone: 773.702.9494; Fax: 773.834.0942
E-mail: admissions@law.uchicago.edu; Website: www.law.uchicago.edu

Introduction

Chicago graduates lead and innovate in government, public interest, academia, and business, as well as law. For this reason, Chicago aims not to certify lawyers, but to train well-rounded, critical, and socially conscious thinkers and doers. Three cornerstones provide the foundation for Chicago's educational mission: the marketplace of ideas, participatory learning, and interdisciplinary inquiry.

Enrollment/Student Body

Our students' chief passions are ideas. They have shown this passion through their academic success, and they exhibit signs of great professional promise. Over 5,500 applicants seek approximately 190 seats in each incoming class. Chicago students come from more than 100 undergraduate institutions with degrees in nearly every discipline, and one in ten have graduate degrees. Many of our students have also had interesting and successful careers before law school.

Faculty

What distinguishes Chicago faculty is their devotion to both teaching and scholarship. This might seem a contradiction at first, but at Chicago, teaching and scholarship complement each other. Chicago professors blaze trails in legal thought, and their revolutionary ideas infuse classroom discussion with immediacy and excitement. Our professors write the books, draft the statutes, and decide the cases that students read at law schools across America. During the 2010–2011 academic year, our faculty will teach more than 170 courses and seminars at the Law School.

Curriculum

As a first-year student, you will take a core sequence covering five principal areas of the law: contracts, torts, property, criminal law, and civil procedure; a required interdisciplinary course called Elements of the Law; an elective; and a year-long course on research and writing. This curriculum familiarizes you with the basic principles of Anglo-American law, cultivates legal reasoning, develops writing ability, and introduces students to interdisciplinary approaches to the law.

In the second and third years, you can choose courses from the full range of Chicago's more than 170 classes. Generally, classes are small; more than 60 percent have fewer than 25 students in them. Additionally, in an average year, about one-third of the second- and third-year students take classes in other divisions of the university. We do not ask our students to choose a concentration but rather let them put together a personalized education based on their individual interests.

Special Programs

The Law School encourages interdisciplinary work. All students may take 12 hours of coursework anywhere in the university. Students may also apply for three formal joint-degree programs either at the same time they apply to the Law School or in their first year. They may also work with Law School and university staff to arrange concurrent degrees.

Formal joint-degree programs are with the Booth School of Business (MBA, PhD), the Harris School of Public Policy (MPP), and the Committee on International Relations (MA).

The Law School is home to a wide variety of research programs. These programs provide excellent outlets for both the theoretical and empirical work of both faculty and students. In addition, these programs host conferences, publish working papers, and support journals. Centers currently at the Law School include the Center for Civil Justice, the Center for Comparative Constitutionalism, the Center for Studies in Criminal Justice, the John M. Olin Program in Law and Economics, and the Center for Law, Philosophy, and Human Values.

The Law School is committed to making big contributions to topics of national interest—health care, animal rights, and immigration policy just to name a few. The Chicago Policy Initiatives encourage faculty members and students to work together, think hard about important social problems, and propose solutions. Current projects include the Chicago Policy Initiative on Animal Law, Chicago Foster Care Project, and Climate Change Online.

Clinical Opportunities

Housed in the Arthur Kane Center, our clinics involve more than 120 students each year in representing clients with real-world problems. The Mandel Legal Aid Clinic handles matters involving appellate advocacy, criminal and juvenile justice, employment discrimination, civil rights, housing, immigration, mental health, and federal criminal law. The Institute for Justice Clinic on Entrepreneurship assists aspiring entry-level entrepreneurs from low- and moderate-income neighborhoods. We also have the Immigrant Children's Advocacy Project, which provides a unique opportunity for our students to draw on immigration law, international law, family, and children's rights law. Recently added is the Exoneration Project, which provides representation to clients who are asserting their actual innocence in state and federal court. The Law School also partners with outside agencies to provide additional clinical opportunities to our students.

Student Activities

About 40 percent of upper-class students serve on one of the three student-edited journals, which include the *University of Chicago Law Review*, the *University of Chicago Legal Forum*, and the *Chicago Journal of International Law*. The Hinton Moot Court Board conducts a program in appellate advocacy for upper-class students, and first-year students participate in a moot court as part of the Bigelow Legal Research and Writing Program. More than 50 student organizations provide opportunities for the exploration of legal specialties, affiliation with like-minded students, or networking within identity groups.

Career Services

Our career services office assists students with permanent and summer employment. Seven professional career advisors counsel students in one-on-one planning sessions. Programs on types of practices and nontraditional careers are organized throughout the year for students. The office focuses on individualized counseling and coaching based on each student's career and life goals. The top five destinations our graduates choose for employment are Chicago, Los Angeles, New York, San Francisco, and Washington, DC.

Location

Hyde Park provides Chicago students with the best of all possible worlds—a campus with a college-town atmosphere just a few miles from the downtown area of a vibrant city. Hyde Park is a dynamic community with parks, museums, and multiple bookstores. The Law School is located at the southern end of campus, facing an expansive "front lawn" known as the Midway Plaisance. Surrounding the Law School is a tree-lined, diverse residential neighborhood, a sandy Lake Michigan beach, and two sprawling parks. The campus itself is a Gothic masterpiece where limestone buildings built around tree-shaded quadrangles sport gargoyles, ivy, and turrets. The Law School's modern building promotes interaction among faculty and students, while the recently remodeled library and classroom wing enhance the learning experience.

Housing

A graduate residence hall, located two blocks from the Law School, is available to law students. Most rooms are singles with private baths. In addition, the university has plenty of single- and married-student neighborhood housing available. Many students choose to rent housing from private landlords. Housing in Chicago is very affordable compared to most major cities. Buses run frequently throughout the surrounding neighborhood, providing transportation to and from residences and the Law School. Public transportation is easily accessible to other neighborhoods in Chicago.

Admission

Each year we seek to create a community from among the best and brightest law school applicants. We want students who are intellectually curious, lively, and collegial in their academic approach. We want students who will take their legal education seriously, but not take themselves too seriously. And because we are preparing students to enter a multifaceted profession, we want multidimensional students with a wide range of talents, backgrounds, experiences, and accomplishments. We do not use indices, formulas, or cutoffs.

Financial Aid

Your Chicago legal education is an investment in your future. Because many students will not have sufficient personal resources to make this investment, Chicago provides generous financial aid. Twenty students in the Class of 2014 will receive Rubenstein Scholarships, covering full tuition for all three years. Approximately 50 percent of Chicago Law students receive scholarships. The Law School also provides funding for students who work in public interest positions during their summers. After graduation, the Law School provides financial assistance to graduates who enter careers in public interest legal work through our generous Hormel Public Interest Program. Graduates earning $72,000 or less in a government, nonprofit, or public interest job can receive benefits.

APPLICANT PROFILE

We seek to create a community from among the best, the brightest, and the most interesting law school applicants. We do not believe that the LSAT and GPA alone provide us with sufficient information to evaluate an applicant's likely contributions to our community; therefore, we do not use any formulas, indices, or numerical cutoffs. We do not provide an applicant profile here because it would be based solely on the LSAT and GPA.

CHICAGO-KENT COLLEGE OF LAW, ILLINOIS INSTITUTE OF TECHNOLOGY

Office of Admissions, 565 West Adams Street
Chicago, IL 60661
Phone: 312.906.5020; Fax: 312.906.5274
E-mail: admissions@kentlaw.edu; Website: www.kentlaw.edu

ABA
Approved
Since
1936

The Basics

Type of school	Private
Term	Semester
Application deadline	3/1
Application fee	$0
Financial aid deadline	4/1
Can first year start other than fall?	Yes
Student to faculty ratio	11.7 to 1
# of housing spaces available restricted to law students	
graduate housing for which law students are eligible	5

Faculty and Administrators

	Total		Men		Women		Minorities	
	Spr	Fall	Spr	Fall	Spr	Fall	Spr	Fall
Full-time	62	65	38	43	24	22	7	8
Other full-time	1	1	1	1	0	0	0	0
Deans, librarians, & others who teach	4	4	2	2	2	2	1	1
Part-time	92	94	69	72	23	22	11	6
Total	159	164	110	118	49	46	19	15

Curriculum

	Full-Time	Part-Time
Typical first-year section size	56	37
Is there typically a "small section" of the first-year class, other than Legal Writing, taught by full-time faculty	No	No
If yes, typical size offered last year		
# of classroom course titles beyond first-year curriculum	146	

# of upper division courses, excluding seminars, with an enrollment:	Under 25	202
	25–49	60
	50–74	21
	75–99	4
	100+	3

# of seminars	42	
# of seminar positions available	560	
# of seminar positions filled	276	63
# of positions available in simulation courses	581	
# of simulation positions filled	255	226
# of positions available in faculty supervised clinical courses	241	
# of faculty supervised clinical positions filled	216	21
# involved in field placements	206	17
# involved in law journals	56	9
# involved in moot court or trial competitions	74	3
# of credit hours required to graduate	87	

JD Enrollment and Ethnicity

	Men #	Men %	Women #	Women %	Full-Time #	Full-Time %	Part-Time #	Part-Time %	1st-Year #	1st-Year %	Total #	Total %	JD Degs. Awd.
All Hispanics	33	6.2	33	7.6	48	6.1	18	9.7	31	10.0	66	6.8	8
Am. Ind./AK Nat.	0	0.0	0	0.0	0	0.0	0	0.0	0	0.0	0	0.0	0
Asian	25	4.7	35	8.0	42	5.4	18	9.7	26	8.4	60	6.2	20
Black/Af. Am.	18	3.4	23	5.3	28	3.6	13	7.0	15	4.8	41	4.2	17
Nat. HI/Pac. Isl.	9	1.7	11	2.5	15	1.9	5	2.7	0	0.0	20	2.1	0
2 or more races	16	3.0	19	4.3	32	4.1	3	1.6	13	4.2	35	3.6	0
Subtotal (minor.)	101	18.9	121	27.7	165	21.0	57	30.8	85	27.3	222	22.9	55
Nonres. Alien	14	2.6	12	2.7	23	2.9	3	1.6	9	2.9	26	2.7	0
White/Cauc.	354	66.4	269	61.6	516	65.7	107	57.8	168	54.0	623	64.2	183
Unknown	64	12.0	35	8.0	81	10.3	18	9.7	49	15.8	99	10.2	26
Total	533	54.9	437	45.1	785	80.9	185	19.1	311	32.1	970		267

Transfers

Transfers in	22
Transfers out	9

Tuition and Fees

	Resident	Nonresident
Full-time	$40,050	$40,050
Part-time	$29,300	$29,300
Tuition Guarantee Program	N	

Living Expenses

Estimated living expenses for singles

Living on campus	Living off campus	Living at home
$22,044	$22,044	$22,044

CHICAGO-KENT COLLEGE OF LAW, ILLINOIS INSTITUTE OF TECHNOLOGY

ABA
Approved
Since
1936

GPA and LSAT Scores

	Total	Full-Time	Part-Time
# of apps	3,771	3,340	431
# of offers	1,711	1,573	138
# of matrics	310	248	62
75% GPA	3.70	3.71	3.67
Median GPA	3.55	3.57	3.46
25% GPA	3.20	3.21	3.15
75% LSAT	163	163	161
Median LSAT	161	161	156
25% LSAT	155	156	152

Grants and Scholarships (from prior year)

	Total		Full-Time		Part-Time	
	#	%	#	%	#	%
Total # of students	948		769		179	
Total # receiving grants	549	57.9	470	61.1	79	44.1
Less than 1/2 tuition	284	30.0	223	29.0	61	34.1
Half to full tuition	192	20.3	178	23.1	14	7.8
Full tuition	55	5.8	51	6.6	4	2.2
More than full tuition	18	1.9	18	2.3	0	0.0
Median grant amount			$20,000		$6,115	

Informational and Library Resources

Total amount spent on library materials	$658,352
Study seating capacity inside the library	460
# of full-time equivalent professional librarians	12
Hours per week library is open	96
# of open, wired connections available to students	1,770
# of networked computers available for use by students	32
Has wireless network?	Y
Requires computer?	Y

JD Attrition (from prior year)

	Academic	Other	Total	
	#	#	#	%
1st year	8	24	32	10.5
2nd year	3	4	7	2.1
3rd year	0	0	0	0.0
4th year	0	0	0	0.0

Employment (9 months after graduation)

	Total	Percentage
Employment status known	278	96.9
Employment status unknown	9	3.1
Employed	251	90.3
Pursuing graduate degrees	10	3.6
Unemployed (seeking, not seeking, or studying for the bar)	11	4.0
Type of Employment		
# employed in law firms	162	64.5
# employed in business and industry	38	15.1
# employed in government	27	10.8
# employed in public interest	9	3.6
# employed as judicial clerks	5	2.0
# employed in academia	10	4.0
Geographic Location		
# employed in state	212	84.5
# employed outside the US	1	0.4
# of states where employed		20

Bar Passage Rates

First-time takers	271	Reporting %	99.26
Average school %	95.17	Average state %	90.89
Average pass difference	4.28		

Jurisdiction	Takers	Passers	Pass %	State %	Diff %
Illinois	269	256	95.17	90.89	4.28

CHICAGO-KENT COLLEGE OF LAW, ILLINOIS INSTITUTE OF TECHNOLOGY

Office of Admissions, 565 West Adams Street
Chicago, IL 60661
Phone: 312.906.5020; Fax: 312.906.5274
E-mail: admissions@kentlaw.edu; Website: www.kentlaw.edu

Introduction

Chicago-Kent College of Law, Illinois Institute of Technology, is a national leader in legal education, recognized for the strength of its faculty and for its innovative approaches to traditional legal education. The second oldest law school in Illinois, Chicago-Kent was founded in 1888 by two judges who believed that legal education should be available to working men and women. The law school's first female student graduated in 1891, and the first African American woman admitted to the bar in Illinois (and the second admitted to practice law in the United States) was a graduate of the class of 1894. Today, Chicago-Kent students come from 38 states and 15 countries. Forty-five percent of the students are women, and 21 percent are students of color. The law school is also proud to count among its students and graduates the 2007 and 2008 National Trial Competition champions, the 2008 and 2009 National Moot Court Competition champions, and the winners of the 2010 National Institute for Trial Advocacy Tournament of Champions.

Drawing on its distinctive affiliation with Illinois Institute of Technology, Chicago-Kent is at the vanguard of exploring new frontiers in the law raised by biotechnology, cyberspace, environmental regulation, intellectual property, international business transactions and trade, and much more. Chicago-Kent is located in downtown Chicago, the heart of the city's commercial and legal communities. The law school is accredited by the American Bar Association and is a member of the Association of American Law Schools and the Order of the Coif.

Faculty

The foundation for academic excellence at Chicago-Kent is derived from its faculty, who engage in broad-ranging legal scholarship and research. As advisors frequently approached for their expertise, faculty members help shape policy and thinking on a variety of issues, and make it a point to involve students in their particular areas of influence.

Library and Facilities

Chicago-Kent's modern, ten-story building features a three-story atrium, five-level library, technologically advanced courtroom, auditorium, computer labs, student lounges, and cafeteria. Chicago-Kent's library is one of the largest law school libraries in the country. The collection includes the Library of International Relations and a wealth of material on environmental and energy law, intellectual property law, international trade law, and labor law.

The law school houses a robust computer network infrastructure. The wireless network is accessible throughout the building and supports the latest protocols. In addition, there are over 1,900 wired network connections located in key areas, including the library, individual seats in the majority of classrooms, and student lounge areas.

Affordable housing is available in nearby urban and suburban neighborhoods. Furnished apartments are available for Chicago-Kent students at Tailor Lofts, a new loft-style development located within walking distance of the law school in student-friendly Greektown. Dormitory housing is available on the university's main campus, approximately five miles south of the law school. A free shuttle runs between the two campuses. The law school is close to all public transportation downtown.

Curriculum

Both full-time and part-time programs are available. Full-time students usually complete the JD degree in three years. Part-time students usually finish in four years. Students may apply to transfer between divisions after completing the first year. First-year class sizes typically range from 30 to 90 students.

Degrees available include JD, JD/MBA, JD/MPA, JD/MPH, JD/LLM in Taxation, JD/LLM in Financial Services Law, JD/LLM in Family Law, JD/MS in Finance, JD/MS in Environmental Management and Sustainability, LLM in Taxation, LLM in Financial Services Law, LLM in Family Law, LLM in International Intellectual Property Law, and LLM in International and Comparative Law.

Practical Skills Training

Legal Research and Writing—Chicago-Kent's acclaimed legal research and writing program is one of the most comprehensive in the nation. The three-year, five-course curriculum teaches students to research, analyze, and communicate effectively about a wide range of legal problems.

Clinical Education—The Law Offices of Chicago-Kent, one of the largest in-house clinical education programs in the country, offers 10 in-house clinical practice areas and a broad range of externships with government agencies, not-for-profit organizations, and federal and state court judges.

Trial Advocacy—The law school offers a two-semester sequence in trial advocacy and an intensive course taught by veteran judges and experienced practitioners.

Certificate Programs

Criminal Litigation—The program emphasizes both theory and practical skills development to provide comprehensive and balanced preparation for a career in criminal prosecution or defense.

Environmental and Energy Law—The program's interdisciplinary approach to the problems of environmental regulation and natural resources allocation prepares students for practice through a series of courses in law, economic and public policy analysis, and the scientific aspects of environmental problems.

Intellectual Property Law—The program focuses on issues relating to patent, trademark, copyright, trade secrets, and unfair competition, both in the United States and abroad.

International and Comparative Law—The program encompasses study in international business and trade, international and comparative law, and international human rights.

Labor and Employment Law—The program provides students with theoretical and practical training in the law governing the workplace.

Litigation and Alternative Dispute Resolution—The program stresses the connection between legal doctrine, skills and values, and the art of lawyering. It is designed to educate students to become reflective practitioners with a lawyering identity that incorporates high standards of competence, ethics, and social responsibility.

Public Interest Law—The program provides students with a background in public interest law and policy, in addition to individualized curriculum and career planning. The law school also supports a number of public interest resources and activities, including the Center for Access to Justice and Technology, which aims to make justice more accessible to the public through the use of the Internet.

Institutes and Centers

Chicago-Kent is home to eight institutes and centers with missions that range from conducting scholarly and practical research on legal and social issues to providing topical programming to developing public interest services. Through these initiatives, many of which involve cross-disciplinary projects, students learn to appreciate and adapt to major social and global influences that can change the legal profession and its practice. These institutes and centers include
- Center for Access to Justice and Technology
- Center for Open Government
- Global Law and Policy Initiative
- IIT Center for Diabetes Research and Policy
- Institute for Law and the Humanities
- Institute for Law and the Workplace
- Institute for Science, Law, and Technology
- Jury Center

Admission

Admission is highly selective. Each application is individually reviewed and decisions are based on a range of factors, including quantitative and qualitative criteria. Although the GPA and LSAT are important criteria, consideration also is given to nonnumerical factors such as the nature and rigor of the undergraduate curriculum, writing ability, graduate work and professional experience, extracurricular activities, diversity, and the personal statement. The admission requirements for the full- and part-time divisions are the same. The law school is committed to attracting and retaining students from a variety of racial, ethnic, economic, geographic, and educational backgrounds.

Student Activities

Student editors and staff, in association with a faculty editor, publish the *Chicago-Kent Law Review* in symposium format. Moot Court and Trial Advocacy teams successfully compete in local, regional, and national competitions each year, providing numerous opportunities to develop litigation expertise. Diverse student interests are represented in a wide variety of social, political, and professional student groups.

Scholarship Support

Substantial scholarship assistance is offered to entering and continuing students based on factors that include merit, financial need, and contribution to the law school community. The Honors Scholars Program provides renewable scholarships of full tuition and living expenses, research assistantships, and special seminars to a select group of students who demonstrate exceptional academic and leadership ability.

Career Services

The Office of Career Services, with six full-time staff, offers individual counseling on résumé writing, interview techniques, and job-search strategies and sponsors both on- and off-campus interview programs. Typically, more than 90 percent of graduates who seek employment find professional positions within nine months of graduation.

APPLICANT PROFILE

Chicago-Kent College of Law, Illinois Institute of Technology
This grid includes only applicants who earned 120–180 LSAT scores under standard administrations.

LSAT Score	GPA																		
	3.75 +		3.50–3.74		3.25–3.49		3.00–3.24		2.75–2.99		2.50–2.74		2.25–2.49		2.00–2.24		Below 2.00		No GPA
	Apps	Adm	Apps	Adm	Apps	Adm	Apps	Adm	Apps	Adm	Apps	Adm	Apps	Adm	Apps	Adm	Apps	Adm	Apps	Adm	Apps	Adm
170–180	24	16	25	17	16	15	9	9	7	5	7	6	1	1	2	2	1	0	1	1	93	72
165–169	76	63	82	68	71	68	53	50	43	38	29	28	12	11	2	1	1	0	6	4	375	331
160–164	130	126	213	195	218	173	168	131	66	54	40	25	17	11	8	1	0	0	20	13	880	729
155–159	162	135	259	151	226	38	163	19	117	13	51	3	32	1	10	1	1	0	27	4	1048	365
150–154	84	63	155	69	203	24	158	19	94	3	49	1	29	0	11	1	4	0	22	4	809	184
Below 150	26	5	54	6	108	1	131	1	102	1	80	0	47	0	19	0	9	0	38	1	614	15
Total	502	408	788	506	842	319	682	229	429	114	256	63	138	24	52	6	16	0	114	27	3819	1696

Apps = Number of Applicants
Adm = Number Admitted
Reflects 99% of the total applicant pool; highest LSAT data reported.

This grid represents admission data for applicants to both the full- and part-time programs. The information in this grid is to be used only as an approximate gauge of the likelihood of admission and not as a guarantee. Individual accomplishments and other nonnumerical factors are also of importance to the Admissions Committee.

UNIVERSITY OF CINCINNATI COLLEGE OF LAW

PO Box 210040, Office of Admission and Financial Aid
Cincinnati, OH 45221-0040
Phone: 513.556.0078; Fax: 513.556.2391
E-mail: admissions@law.uc.edu; Website: www.law.uc.edu

ABA
Approved
Since
1923

AMERICAN BAR ASSOCIATION
Section of Legal Education
and Admissions to the Bar

The Basics

Type of school	Public
Term	Semester
Application deadline	12/1 3/1
Application fee	$35
Financial aid deadline	3/1
Can first year start other than fall?	No
Student to faculty ratio	11.2 to 1
# of housing spaces available restricted to law students	
graduate housing for which law students are eligible	408

Faculty and Administrators

	Total		Men		Women		Minorities	
	Spr	Fall	Spr	Fall	Spr	Fall	Spr	Fall
Full-time	31	28	15	13	16	15	5	6
Other full-time	1	1	0	0	1	1	0	0
Deans, librarians, & others who teach	6	6	4	4	2	2	0	0
Part-time	40	28	28	19	12	9	1	1
Total	78	63	47	36	31	27	6	7

Curriculum

	Full-Time	Part-Time
Typical first-year section size	72	0
Is there typically a "small section" of the first-year class, other than Legal Writing, taught by full-time faculty	Yes	No
If yes, typical size offered last year	23	
# of classroom course titles beyond first-year curriculum	110	
# of upper division courses, excluding seminars, with an enrollment: Under 25	71	
25–49	23	
50–74	6	
75–99	3	
100+	0	
# of seminars	20	
# of seminar positions available	305	
# of seminar positions filled	225	0
# of positions available in simulation courses	366	
# of simulation positions filled	302	0
# of positions available in faculty supervised clinical courses	52	
# of faculty supervised clinical positions filled	52	0
# involved in field placements	143	0
# involved in law journals	132	0
# involved in moot court or trial competitions	80	0
# of credit hours required to graduate	90	

JD Enrollment and Ethnicity

	Men		Women		Full-Time		Part-Time		1st-Year		Total		JD Degs. Awd.
	#	%	#	%	#	%	#	%	#	%	#	%	
All Hispanics	5	2.1	6	3.5	11	2.7	0	0.0	4	2.8	11	2.7	0
Am. Ind./AK Nat.	0	0.0	0	0.0	0	0.0	0	0.0	0	0.0	0	0.0	0
Asian	10	4.2	8	4.7	18	4.4	0	0.0	6	4.2	18	4.4	5
Black/Af. Am.	8	3.4	17	9.9	25	6.1	0	0.0	9	6.3	25	6.1	8
Nat. HI/Pac. Isl.	0	0.0	1	0.6	1	0.2	0	0.0	1	0.7	1	0.2	0
2 or more races	2	0.8	5	2.9	7	1.7	0	0.0	7	4.9	7	1.7	0
Subtotal (minor.)	25	10.6	37	21.5	62	15.2	0	0.0	27	18.8	62	15.2	17
Nonres. Alien	0	0.0	3	1.7	3	0.7	0	0.0	2	1.4	3	0.7	0
White/Cauc.	211	89.4	132	76.7	343	84.1	0	0.0	115	79.9	343	84.1	112
Unknown	0	0.0	0	0.0	0	0.0	0	0.0	0	0.0	0	0.0	0
Total	236	57.8	172	42.2	408	100.0	0	0.0	144	35.3	408		129

Transfers

Transfers in	9
Transfers out	1

Tuition and Fees

	Resident	Nonresident
Full-time	$20,946	$36,526
Part-time		
Tuition Guarantee Program	N	

Living Expenses

Estimated living expenses for singles

Living on campus	Living off campus	Living at home
$16,596	$16,596	$16,596

UNIVERSITY OF CINCINNATI COLLEGE OF LAW

ABA
Approved
Since
1923

GPA and LSAT Scores

	Total	Full-Time	Part-Time
# of apps	1,823	1,823	0
# of offers	775	775	0
# of matrics	144	144	0
75% GPA	3.80	3.80	0.00
Median GPA	3.56	3.56	0.00
25% GPA	3.36	3.36	0.00
75% LSAT	162	162	0
Median LSAT	161	161	0
25% LSAT	157	157	0

Grants and Scholarships (from prior year)

	Total		Full-Time		Part-Time	
	#	%	#	%	#	%
Total # of students	391		391		0	
Total # receiving grants	275	70.3	275	70.3	0	0.0
Less than 1/2 tuition	181	46.3	181	46.3	0	0.0
Half to full tuition	89	22.8	89	22.8	0	0.0
Full tuition	4	1.0	4	1.0	0	0.0
More than full tuition	1	0.3	1	0.3	0	0.0
Median grant amount			$6,500		$0	

Informational and Library Resources

Total amount spent on library materials	$1,000,303
Study seating capacity inside the library	334
# of full-time equivalent professional librarians	8
Hours per week library is open	93
# of open, wired connections available to students	6
# of networked computers available for use by students	61
Has wireless network?	Y
Requires computer?	N

JD Attrition (from prior year)

	Academic	Other	Total	
	#	#	#	%
1st year	0	5	5	3.6
2nd year	0	0	0	0.0
3rd year	0	0	0	0.0
4th year	0	0	0	0.0

Employment (9 months after graduation)

	Total	Percentage
Employment status known	106	98.1
Employment status unknown	2	1.9
Employed	93	87.7
Pursuing graduate degrees	4	3.8
Unemployed (seeking, not seeking, or studying for the bar)	4	3.8
Type of Employment		
# employed in law firms	50	53.8
# employed in business and industry	8	8.6
# employed in government	14	15.1
# employed in public interest	6	6.5
# employed as judicial clerks	5	5.4
# employed in academia	8	8.6
Geographic Location		
# employed in state	62	66.7
# employed outside the US	2	2.2
# of states where employed	16	

Bar Passage Rates

First-time takers	103	Reporting %	82.52
Average school %	90.59	Average state %	86.36
Average pass difference	4.23		

Jurisdiction	Takers	Passers	Pass %	State %	Diff %
Ohio	74	66	89.19	86.03	3.16
New York	6	6	100.00	86.51	13.49
Illinois	5	5	100.00	90.89	9.11

UNIVERSITY OF CINCINNATI COLLEGE OF LAW

PO Box 210040, Office of Admission and Financial Aid
Cincinnati, OH 45221-0040
Phone: 513.556.0078; Fax: 513.556.2391
E-mail: admissions@law.uc.edu; Website: www.law.uc.edu

Introduction

The College of Law has a rich heritage and proud traditions. Throughout its 178-year history, graduates have been leaders of the bench and bar, served in senior governmental positions, been active in the public service community, and succeeded in business, academia, and countless other fields. As the premier small, urban, public law school in America, the college is focused on being nationally recognized for its excellence, relevance, and impact. The size of the school allows for small classes and a high degree of personal interaction with faculty and other students. The law school is located on UC's recently renovated main campus in Clifton, approximately 10 minutes north of the city's central business district. This provides easy access to state, county, and federal courts, including the US Court of Appeals for the Sixth Circuit. A charter member of the AALS, UC was one of the first law schools to have a chapter of the Order of the Coif and to be approved by the ABA.

Student Body

The 414 students in the College of Law, approximately 135 per class, come from an amazingly wide variety of backgrounds, experiences, and perspectives. The student body is also talented academically, as the 75th/25th LSAT and UGPA percentiles for fall 2010 are 162/157 and 3.80/3.38. The College of Law is committed to enrolling a diverse class, as 17 percent of our students are from minority backgrounds, about 40 percent are female, and 39 percent enroll from states other than Ohio. The average age of the entering class is 25; however, 18 percent of the class is 27 or older.

Faculty

The college employs a full-time faculty of 32 who pride themselves on their teaching, scholarship, and accessibility to students. As the core of the academic program, faculty members bring areas of expertise into the classroom that add depth, perspective, and professionalism to the law students' studies. The student-to-faculty ratio of 10:1 provides ample opportunities for individual discussions with faculty or in-depth research in areas of interest.

Library and Physical Facilities

The Robert S. Marx Law Library has a seasoned staff that is able to assist students with research and technical questions. Two computer labs and a wireless network throughout the law building enable students to maximize online research capabilities, and our skilled IT staff members are readily available to assist law students. The law library, which can seat the entire law student body at one time, manages collections carefully to support faculty and student research and the college curriculum.

Curriculum

First-year students are divided into six individual sections, creating an unusual advantage of very small first-year sections (typically no larger than 25). The small-section modules allow for further inquiry beyond the typical first-year curriculum. First-year students take three courses in small sections during the academic year with opportunities to study with all members of their class over the entire year. The upper level is well balanced between theory and skills-related courses. Institutes and research centers exist in the areas of international human rights, criminal law (Ohio Innocence Project–OIP), corporate law, law and psychiatry, the center for practice, and a newly established Race, Gender, and Social Justice research center. In addition, the college offers joint programs with women's studies, business, political science, community planning, and social work. In addition to OIP, the law school also offers clinical opportunities via the Appellate Law Clinic (Sixth Circuit Court of Appeals), the Indigent Defense Clinic, and the Domestic Violence and Civil Protection Order Clinic (DVCP) housed downtown at the Cincinnati Legal Aid offices. In January 2010, the College of Law announced the opening of the Entrepreneurship and Community Development Clinic (ECDC), which focuses on small businesses.

Special Programs

The College of Law recognizes that a lawyer needs both a firm grasp on subject matter and expertise in professional skills. The college, therefore, has developed an extensive legal research and writing program that not only encompasses first-year courses, but upper-level courses as well. The Center for Professional Development provides students with extern experiences, which are opportunities to work with practicing attorneys and public clinics. The Rosenthal Institute for Justice has been endowed to ensure that popular programs like the Ohio Innocence Project are available to students now and in the future. Each institute and research center offers a fellowship program, research opportunities, and in-depth study in their respective areas. The college was the first to offer a joint degree in law and women's studies, and has the oldest endowed international human rights program at an American law school, the Urban Morgan Institute for Human Rights.

Admission Standards

Admission to the college is based upon a selective review of each applicant's file by the Admissions Committee. Although the Admissions Committee relies on the grade-point average and LSAT score to determine the applicant's academic potential, other nonquantitative factors believed to be relevant to success in law school are considered; that is, the quality of the applicant's education, participation in community service, employment experience, graduate work, and letters of recommendation. The educational philosophy of the college reflects a belief that a quality legal education is enhanced through having a heterogeneous student body. The committee, therefore, also considers race, cultural background, unusual personal circumstances, and age. Admission decisions are made on a rolling basis. The College of Law has also instituted a binding Early Decision Program. Students interested in applying through the Early Decision Program must have a completed application on file by

December 1. The college is committed to enrolling a diverse and engaging class each year.

Student Activities

The College of Law offers numerous opportunities for students to sharpen their legal writing, advocacy, and leadership skills. The *University of Cincinnati Law Review* was founded in 1927 and was the first law review published by an Ohio law school. The Urban Morgan Institute for Human Rights edits the *Human Rights Quarterly*, the leading international human rights journal in the world. The *Immigration and Nationality Law Review* is an annual publication of papers on the subjects of immigration and citizenship. The *Freedom Center Journal*, a collaboration between the law school and the National Underground Railroad Freedom Center, offers opportunities to publish scholarly works about cutting-edge issues of today, informed by the legacy of historic struggles for freedom. The College of Law also offers a well-respected Moot Court Program with teams participating in many national competitions. The college hosts the Rendigs National Products Liability Moot Court Competition each spring.

Expenses and Financial Aid

For the 2010–2011 academic year, resident and nonresident tuition and fees are $20,946 and $36,526, respectively. The Graduate Metro Rate (for those residing in approved northern Kentucky counties) is $21,186. Nonresidents can reclassify as state residents by becoming independent and self-sustaining for their first year in law school. Cincinnati is a cosmopolitan yet affordable Midwestern city with living expenses estimated at $16,596 for the nine-month academic year. Cincinnati was recently ranked the fifth least expensive city in the nation in which to live. Scholarships are awarded to approximately 65 percent of the student body in order to attract an academically talented and diverse student body. The FAFSA should be filed by March 1 as a priority deadline in order to qualify for student loan packages by spring. A large percentage of second- and third-year students work with law firms, companies, and agencies in the Greater Cincinnati area to offset living expenses or student loan debt.

Placement

Since 2001, Ohio has been one of the top 10 states for entry level legal employment, and our graduates obtain a number of positions in the State of Ohio. Additionally, our 2009 graduates took positions in 16 other states, the District of Columbia, and two foreign countries. Annually, about half of our graduates enter private practice and one-third of those graduates work in offices of two to ten attorneys. The class of 2009 was no exception.

In addition to those working in private practice, our 2009 graduates accepted positions with public interest organizations (6 percent), government offices (10 percent), as well as in business (9 percent) and academia (9 percent). Notably, members of the class of 2009 were selected as finalists in the Presidential Management Fellowship Program, served as Equal Justice Works Fellows, and obtained clerkships (5 percent) among the nation's highest courts.

APPLICANT PROFILE

University of Cincinnati College of Law
This grid includes only applicants who earned 120–180 LSAT scores under standard administrations.

LSAT Score	3.75 +		3.50–3.74		3.25–3.49		3.00–3.24		2.75–2.99		2.50–2.74		2.25–2.49		2.00–2.24		Below 2.00		No GPA		Total	
	Apps	Adm	Apps	Adm	Apps	Adm	Apps	Adm	Apps	Adm	Apps	Adm	Apps	Adm	Apps	Adm	Apps	Adm	Apps	Adm	Apps	Adm
175–180	1	1	1	1	0	0	0	0	0	0	0	0	0	0	0	0	0	0	0	0	2	2
170–174	10	10	8	8	6	6	5	5	2	1	5	3	3	0	0	0	0	0	0	0	39	33
165–169	29	28	39	38	30	30	36	28	17	5	13	1	5	2	1	0	1	0	1	1	172	133
160–164	140	128	160	147	142	104	114	59	57	9	30	3	12	1	4	0	0	0	8	6	667	457
155–159	87	66	115	26	96	10	75	4	34	1	20	0	6	0	3	0	0	0	11	1	447	108
150–154	52	12	66	10	53	7	42	2	25	1	9	0	8	0	1	0	2	0	3	0	261	32
145–149	20	5	23	2	29	1	23	0	15	0	13	0	3	0	4	0	0	0	6	0	136	8
140–144	0	0	6	0	8	0	16	0	11	0	6	0	2	0	1	0	0	0	0	0	50	0
135–139	1	0	2	0	2	0	4	0	3	0	4	0	3	0	2	0	0	0	4	0	25	0
130–134	0	0	0	0	3	0	3	0	1	0	2	0	1	0	1	0	1	0	0	0	12	0
125–129	0	0	0	0	0	0	2	0	0	0	0	0	1	0	1	0	0	0	1	0	5	0
120–124	0	0	0	0	0	0	0	0	0	0	0	0	0	0	0	0	0	0	1	0	1	0
Total	340	250	420	232	369	158	320	98	165	17	102	7	44	3	18	0	4	0	35	8	1817	773

Apps = Number of Applicants
Adm = Number Admitted
Reflects 100% of the total applicant pool; highest LSAT data reported.

CITY UNIVERSITY OF NEW YORK SCHOOL OF LAW

65-21 Main Street
Flushing, NY 11367
Phone: 718.340.4210; Fax: 718.340.4435
E-mail: admissions@mail.law.cuny.edu; Website: www.law.cuny.edu

ABA
Approved
Since
1985

AMERICAN BAR ASSOCIATION
Section of Legal Education
and Admissions to the Bar

The Basics

Type of school	Public
Term	Semester
Application deadline	3/15
Application fee	$50
Financial aid deadline	5/2
Can first year start other than fall?	No
Student to faculty ratio	10.9 to 1
# of housing spaces available restricted to law students	
graduate housing for which law students are eligible	

Faculty and Administrators

	Total		Men		Women		Minorities	
	Spr	Fall	Spr	Fall	Spr	Fall	Spr	Fall
Full-time	33	31	15	11	18	20	13	14
Other full-time	4	5	1	1	3	4	2	4
Deans, librarians, & others who teach	13	15	4	4	9	11	5	7
Part-time	13	9	7	3	6	6	3	2
Total	63	60	27	19	36	41	23	27

Curriculum

	Full-Time	Part-Time
Typical first-year section size	80	0
Is there typically a "small section" of the first-year class, other than Legal Writing, taught by full-time faculty	Yes	No
If yes, typical size offered last year	20	

# of classroom course titles beyond first-year curriculum		44
# of upper division courses, excluding seminars, with an enrollment:	Under 25	42
	25–49	14
	50–74	3
	75–99	1
	100+	3
# of seminars		24
# of seminar positions available		600
# of seminar positions filled	547	0
# of positions available in simulation courses		695
# of simulation positions filled	651	0
# of positions available in faculty supervised clinical courses		254
# of faculty supervised clinical positions filled	189	0
# involved in field placements	42	0
# involved in law journals	45	0
# involved in moot court or trial competitions	47	0
# of credit hours required to graduate		91

JD Enrollment and Ethnicity

	Men #	Men %	Women #	Women %	Full-Time #	Full-Time %	Part-Time #	Part-Time %	1st-Year #	1st-Year %	Total #	Total %	JD Degs. Awd.
All Hispanics	23	14.4	41	14.6	64	14.6	0	0.0	26	15.7	64	14.5	15
Am. Ind./AK Nat.	1	0.6	0	0.0	1	0.2	0	0.0	1	0.6	1	0.2	0
Asian	18	11.3	30	10.7	46	10.5	2	100.0	17	10.2	48	10.9	17
Black/Af. Am.	18	11.3	23	8.2	41	9.4	0	0.0	17	10.2	41	9.3	9
Nat. HI/Pac. Isl.	0	0.0	1	0.4	1	0.2	0	0.0	1	0.6	1	0.2	0
2 or more races	4	2.5	7	2.5	11	2.5	0	0.0	5	3.0	11	2.5	0
Subtotal (minor.)	64	40.0	102	36.4	164	37.4	2	100.0	67	40.4	166	37.7	43
Nonres. Alien	2	1.3	5	1.8	7	1.6	0	0.0	4	2.4	7	1.6	0
White/Cauc.	93	58.1	172	61.4	265	60.5	0	0.0	95	57.2	265	60.2	79
Unknown	1	0.6	1	0.4	2	0.5	0	0.0	0	0.0	2	0.5	1
Total	160	36.4	280	63.6	438	99.5	2	0.5	166	37.7	440		126

Transfers

Transfers in	1
Transfers out	3

Tuition and Fees

	Resident	Nonresident
Full-time	$11,952	$18,732
Part-time	$425	$750
Tuition Guarantee Program		N

Living Expenses

Estimated living expenses for singles

Living on campus	Living off campus	Living at home
N/A	$15,743	$6,072

CITY UNIVERSITY OF NEW YORK SCHOOL OF LAW

ABA
Approved
Since
1985

GPA and LSAT Scores

	Total	Full-Time	Part-Time
# of apps	2,137	2,137	0
# of offers	533	533	0
# of matrics	163	163	0
75% GPA	3.57	3.57	0.00
Median GPA	3.37	3.37	0.00
25% GPA	3.13	3.13	0.00
75% LSAT	157	157	0
Median LSAT	154	154	0
25% LSAT	152	152	0

Grants and Scholarships (from prior year)

	Total		Full-Time		Part-Time	
	#	%	#	%	#	%
Total # of students	406		406		0	
Total # receiving grants	118	29.1	118	29.1	0	0.0
Less than 1/2 tuition	75	18.5	75	18.5	0	0.0
Half to full tuition	0	0.0	0	0.0	0	0.0
Full tuition	43	10.6	43	10.6	0	0.0
More than full tuition	0	0.0	0	0.0	0	0.0
Median grant amount			$646		$0	

Informational and Library Resources

Total amount spent on library materials	$587,121
Study seating capacity inside the library	223
# of full-time equivalent professional librarians	9
Hours per week library is open	61
# of open, wired connections available to students	62
# of networked computers available for use by students	113
Has wireless network?	Y
Requires computer?	N

JD Attrition (from prior year)

	Academic	Other	Total	
	#	#	#	%
1st year	7	3	10	6.1
2nd year	0	4	4	3.5
3rd year	0	1	1	0.8
4th year	0	0	0	0.0

Employment (9 months after graduation)

	Total	Percentage
Employment status known	109	88.6
Employment status unknown	14	11.4
Employed	98	89.9
Pursuing graduate degrees	0	0.0
Unemployed (seeking, not seeking, or studying for the bar)	8	7.3
Type of Employment		
# employed in law firms	21	21.4
# employed in business and industry	18	18.4
# employed in government	8	8.2
# employed in public interest	28	28.6
# employed as judicial clerks	15	15.3
# employed in academia	8	8.2
Geographic Location		
# employed in state	69	70.4
# employed outside the US	0	0.0
# of states where employed	12	

Bar Passage Rates

First-time takers	118	Reporting %	86.44
Average school %	80.39	Average state %	86.51
Average pass difference	−6.12		

Jurisdiction	Takers	Passers	Pass %	State %	Diff %
New York	102	82	80.39	86.51	−6.12

CITY UNIVERSITY OF NEW YORK SCHOOL OF LAW

65-21 Main Street
Flushing, NY 11367
Phone: 718.340.4210; Fax: 718.340.4435
E-mail: admissions@mail.law.cuny.edu; Website: www.law.cuny.edu

Mission

Following its motto of "Law in the Service of Human Needs," the mission of the City University of New York (CUNY) School of Law is to train excellent public interest lawyers through a curriculum that integrates doctrine, legal theory, clinical education, and professional responsibility.

Academic Program

CUNY Law's unique and integrated curriculum has made it a national leader in progressive legal education heralded by the Carnegie Foundation for the Advancement of Teaching. The curriculum engages students in a thoughtful combination of rigorous coursework in traditional substantive areas and a lawyering program that teaches the skills recognized by the American Bar Association as necessary for competent practice (problem solving, legal analysis and reasoning, legal research, factual investigation, and communication—including legal writing and oral argument, counseling, negotiation, litigation and alternative dispute resolution procedures, organization and management of legal work, and recognition and resolution of ethical dilemmas). All first-year students take a required two-semester Lawyering Seminar where they focus on the fundamental skills of legal analysis and legal writing and engage in simulations requiring a wide range of lawyering tasks. They draft documents, interview and counsel clients, engage in negotiations, and make arguments before trial and appellate courts. Faculty guidance, supervision, and feedback permeate the process. In the second year, each student elects a four-credit Lawyering Seminar focused on developing more advanced lawyering skills in a subject matter area of his or her choice, including trial practice, mediation, labor, and appellate advocacy. Twenty-two CUNY law students were offered Revson Fellowships in the summer of 2010. Excellent and comprehensive academic support is provided by the Irene Diamond Professional Skills Center.

Clinical Programs

Clinical Programs include Community Economic Development, Criminal Defense, Elder Law, Equality, Health Law, Immigrant and Refugee Rights, International Women's Human Rights, and Mediation. Following Lawyering Seminars in the first two years, all students have opportunities to participate in 12- to 16-credit clinical courses in their third year. Students engage in individual representation of clients and work on projects in collaboration with community groups, organizers, and international organizations to address issues of social justice. Recent work includes legal victories in low-wage labor campaigns, amicus briefs to international tribunals, community education projects throughout New York, and interdisciplinary representation of clients who have suffered trauma from torture and domestic abuse.

Diversity

The diversity of New York City is reflected in our dynamic student body and faculty. Women constitute 64 percent of the student body; minorities, 36 percent. Faculty percentages are similar: 62 percent are women and 47 percent are people of color. The concern for diversity is also threaded through the curriculum; for example, a required course for all first-year students is Liberty, Equality, and Due Process, which examines issues of racial and gender equality and sexual orientation in the context of legal and historical analysis.

Student Life

Despite the relatively small size of the law school, numerous student organizations thrive on campus. Students also have a major role in the law school's governance, recognizing and preparing them for their future as professionals and community leaders. One exemplary student program is the Mississippi Project that, since 1992, has sent a delegation of law students to Mississippi over midyear break to work with lawyers in civil rights organizations across the state. CUNY students work and learn together in an exceptionally collaborative, noncompetitive atmosphere and interact on a first-name basis with the faculty. The student experience is further enriched by New York City's cultural offerings and by the exceptional resources of the third-largest university system in the country, CUNY.

Faculty

Most of this diverse faculty have themselves been public interest practitioners, with experience in a wide area of issues, including employment discrimination, immigration, racial justice, environmental law, women's rights, labor, and international law. They have worked in China, Haiti, South Africa, Mongolia, Costa Rica, the Middle East, Russia, Papua New Guinea, Australia, Central America, the Philippines, and many other countries. Their prestigious awards include Fulbright, Ford, MacArthur, Revson, Rockefeller, and National Endowment for the Humanities fellowships. Their scholarship reflects their interest in, among other areas, international human rights and access to justice for underserved communities.

Career Opportunities

CUNY law graduates are employed in the full range of public interest jobs—legal services and public defender organizations, government agencies, international human rights organizations, not-for-profits, and the judiciary. Approximately 85–90 percent of alumni/ae secure positions within nine months of graduation. Historically, 60–65 percent of graduates enter the public interest/public service profession each year, while 25–30 percent are employed at private firms from large to small and solo community-based practices. CUNY law graduates are consistently awarded judicial clerkships and prestigious public interest postgraduate fellowships that include the Equal Justice Works, Skadden, Echoing Green, Yale Public Interest Initiative grants, and the Georgetown University Law Center fellowships, as well as the Fulbright. Although the vast majority are employed in the mid-Atlantic states, CUNY graduates can be found throughout the United States and abroad where they are engaged in international human rights work.

Child Care

The law school offers an on-site Children's Center, which provides high-quality, reasonably priced day care for infants and toddlers of students, faculty, and staff. The Center provides an age-appropriate curriculum based on the National Association for the Education of Young Children (NAEYC) standards. The Center enables parents to pursue their education and further their career while fulfilling their responsibility to their children.

Special Opportunities

The law school offers a number of unique programs and initiatives that enrich the experience of students and provide continuing support for graduates. The Community Legal Resource Network of alumni provides resources and supports graduates working in solo or small-firm practices in underserved communities. The LaunchPad for Justice, through a special practice order in conjunction with the New York State Courts, provides an opportunity for recent grads to argue in court on behalf of individuals facing housing legal issues, while waiting for admission to the NY State Bar. CUNY Law's nationally ranked clinical program provides students with direct legal representation to underserved communities. Finally, the law school is part of a rich university, the City University of New York, and law students may take some interdisciplinary graduate courses with the approval of the Academic Dean.

Nontraditional Students

The law school's student profile includes many individuals returning to school after careers, and many who possess advanced degrees. The average age of the student body is 27; some students enter directly from undergraduate school while others are older, making the law school a comfortable environment.

Affordable Tuition

CUNY offers an excellent legal education at substantially less than half the cost of most private law schools.

APPLICANT PROFILE

City University of New York School of Law
This grid includes only applicants who earned 120–180 LSAT scores under standard administrations.

LSAT Score	3.75 +		3.50–3.74		3.25–3.49		3.00–3.24		2.75–2.99		2.50–2.74		2.25–2.49		2.00–2.24		Below 2.00		No GPA		Total	
	Apps	Adm	Apps	Adm	Apps	Adm	Apps	Adm	Apps	Adm	Apps	Adm	Apps	Adm	Apps	Adm	Apps	Adm	Apps	Adm	Apps	Adm
175–180	1	1	0	0	0	0	0	0	1	0	0	0	0	0	0	0	0	0	0	0	2	1
170–174	0	0	6	5	2	2	0	0	1	1	2	1	0	0	1	0	0	0	0	0	12	9
165–169	4	4	10	8	11	9	10	8	8	2	2	0	1	0	1	0	0	0	0	0	47	31
160–164	31	27	32	26	36	28	28	15	24	6	11	3	7	1	2	0	0	0	3	2	174	108
155–159	36	25	69	51	71	38	75	32	41	16	30	7	27	2	8	1	4	0	12	6	373	178
150–154	46	25	119	43	126	53	167	42	79	15	46	2	25	2	11	0	5	1	16	1	640	184
145–149	36	4	69	5	103	5	137	3	89	1	64	0	32	0	15	0	2	0	22	1	569	19
140–144	14	0	37	0	47	0	55	0	65	0	28	0	25	0	6	0	3	0	16	0	296	0
135–139	3	0	3	0	7	0	17	0	17	0	9	0	5	0	2	0	0	0	4	0	67	0
130–134	0	0	1	0	3	0	3	0	4	0	9	0	5	0	1	0	0	0	2	0	28	0
125–129	0	0	0	0	1	0	1	0	3	0	1	0	1	0	0	0	1	0	0	0	8	0
120–124	0	0	0	0	0	0	0	0	0	0	0	0	0	0	0	0	0	0	0	0	0	0
Total	171	86	346	138	407	135	493	100	332	41	202	13	128	5	47	1	15	1	75	10	2216	530

Apps = Number of Applicants
Adm = Number Admitted
Reflects 99% of the total applicant pool; highest LSAT data reported.

CLEVELAND STATE UNIVERSITY—CLEVELAND-MARSHALL COLLEGE OF LAW

Office of Admission, 1801 Euclid Avenue, LB 138
Cleveland, OH 44115-2214
Phone: 216.687.2304, toll-free 866.687.2304; Fax: 216.687.6881
E-mail: admissions@law.csuohio.edu; Website: www.law.csuohio.edu

ABA
Approved
Since
1957

The Basics

Type of school	Public
Term	Semester
Application deadline	5/1
Application fee	$0
Financial aid deadline	5/1
Can first year start other than fall?	No
Student to faculty ratio	11.9 to 1
# of housing spaces available restricted to law students	
graduate housing for which law students are eligible	25

Faculty and Administrators

	Total		Men		Women		Minorities	
	Spr	Fall	Spr	Fall	Spr	Fall	Spr	Fall
Full-time	37	39	20	22	17	17	6	6
Other full-time	0	0	0	0	0	0	0	0
Deans, librarians, & others who teach	6	6	2	1	4	5	1	0
Part-time	33	33	25	26	8	7	4	2
Total	76	78	47	49	29	29	11	8

Curriculum

	Full-Time	Part-Time
Typical first-year section size	56	36
Is there typically a "small section" of the first-year class, other than Legal Writing, taught by full-time faculty	No	No
If yes, typical size offered last year		
# of classroom course titles beyond first-year curriculum	85	
# of upper division courses, excluding seminars, with an enrollment: Under 25	93	
25–49	35	
50–74	12	
75–99	0	
100+	0	
# of seminars	17	
# of seminar positions available	255	
# of seminar positions filled	166	63
# of positions available in simulation courses	251	
# of simulation positions filled	107	144
# of positions available in faculty supervised clinical courses	90	
# of faculty supervised clinical positions filled	65	16
# involved in field placements	67	10
# involved in law journals	80	12
# involved in moot court or trial competitions	26	5
# of credit hours required to graduate	90	

JD Enrollment and Ethnicity

	Men #	Men %	Women #	Women %	Full-Time #	Full-Time %	Part-Time #	Part-Time %	1st-Year #	1st-Year %	Total #	Total %	JD Degs. Awd.
All Hispanics	8	2.2	5	2.0	9	2.0	4	2.5	6	3.1	13	2.1	7
Am. Ind./AK Nat.	1	0.3	0	0.0	1	0.2	0	0.0	1	0.5	1	0.2	1
Asian	4	1.1	6	2.4	6	1.3	4	2.5	2	1.0	10	1.6	7
Black/Af. Am.	25	6.9	33	13.3	33	7.3	25	15.9	19	9.8	58	9.5	9
Nat. HI/Pac. Isl.	0	0.0	0	0.0	0	0.0	0	0.0	0	0.0	0	0.0	0
2 or more races	0	0.0	0	0.0	0	0.0	0	0.0	0	0.0	0	0.0	0
Subtotal (minor.)	38	10.5	44	17.7	49	10.8	33	21.0	28	14.4	82	13.4	24
Nonres. Alien	3	0.8	4	1.6	6	1.3	1	0.6	2	1.0	7	1.1	0
White/Cauc.	319	88.4	201	80.7	398	87.9	122	77.7	163	84.0	520	85.2	148
Unknown	1	0.3	0	0.0	0	0.0	1	0.6	0	0.0	1	0.2	3
Total	361	59.2	249	40.8	453	74.3	157	25.7	193	31.8	610		179

Transfers

Transfers in	4
Transfers out	9

Tuition and Fees

	Resident	Nonresident
Full-time	$18,200	$24,976
Part-time	$14,000	$19,212
Tuition Guarantee Program	N	

Living Expenses

Estimated living expenses for singles

Living on campus	Living off campus	Living at home
$18,800	$18,800	$18,800

CLEVELAND STATE UNIVERSITY—CLEVELAND-MARSHALL COLLEGE OF LAW

*ABA
Approved
Since
1957*

GPA and LSAT Scores

	Total	Full-Time	Part-Time
# of apps	1,765	1,494	271
# of offers	644	566	78
# of matrics	195	151	44
75% GPA	3.66	3.65	3.66
Median GPA	3.45	3.45	3.27
25% GPA	3.09	3.16	2.88
75% LSAT	157	158	155
Median LSAT	155	156	153
25% LSAT	153	154	150

Grants and Scholarships (from prior year)

	Total		Full-Time		Part-Time	
	#	%	#	%	#	%
Total # of students	639		482		157	
Total # receiving grants	203	31.8	177	36.7	26	16.6
Less than 1/2 tuition	96	15.0	85	17.6	11	7.0
Half to full tuition	42	6.6	36	7.5	6	3.8
Full tuition	65	10.2	56	11.6	9	5.7
More than full tuition	0	0.0	0	0.0	0	0.0
Median grant amount			$8,238		$4,119	

Informational and Library Resources

Total amount spent on library materials	$958,813
Study seating capacity inside the library	493
# of full-time equivalent professional librarians	8
Hours per week library is open	95
# of open, wired connections available to students	183
# of networked computers available for use by students	121
Has wireless network?	Y
Requires computer?	N

JD Attrition (from prior year)

	Academic	Other	Total	
	#	#	#	%
1st year	10	22	32	15.9
2nd year	0	0	0	0.0
3rd year	0	0	0	0.0
4th year	0	0	0	0.0

Employment (9 months after graduation)

	Total	Percentage
Employment status known	191	95.0
Employment status unknown	10	5.0
Employed	162	84.8
Pursuing graduate degrees	2	1.0
Unemployed (seeking, not seeking, or studying for the bar)	20	10.5
Type of Employment		
# employed in law firms	91	56.2
# employed in business and industry	36	22.2
# employed in government	23	14.2
# employed in public interest	8	4.9
# employed as judicial clerks	2	1.2
# employed in academia	2	1.2
Geographic Location		
# employed in state	135	83.3
# employed outside the US	0	0.0
# of states where employed		15

Bar Passage Rates

First-time takers	180	Reporting %	95.56
Average school %	83.14	Average state %	86.17

Average pass difference –3.03

Jurisdiction	Takers	Passers	Pass %	State %	Diff %
Ohio	167	138	82.63	86.03	–3.40
Illinois	5	5	100.00	90.89	9.11

CLEVELAND STATE UNIVERSITY—CLEVELAND-MARSHALL COLLEGE OF LAW

Office of Admission, 1801 Euclid Avenue, LB 138
Cleveland, OH 44115-2214
Phone: 216.687.2304, toll-free 866.687.2304; Fax: 216.687.6881
E-mail: admissions@law.csuohio.edu; Website: www.law.csuohio.edu

Introduction

Since 1897, C|M|LAW has provided an excellent legal education to a strong and diverse student body. Our law school has a proud heritage: it was the first law school in Ohio to admit women; it was one of the first law schools in Ohio to admit students of color; and our graduates have served for decades in prominent positions in law firms, the judiciary, government, and business. Today, our graduates are practicing law with distinction around the world. C|M|LAW offers a distinctive legal education that is flexible and affordable with full- and part-time (day and evening) options and reasonable tuition that allows our students to graduate in a position of greater financial strength. In 2010, C|M|LAW was the recipient of the Law School Admission Council's first Diversity Matters Award in recognition of our commitment to diversity in the law school and the legal profession.

Location

C|M|LAW is located on the western-end of Cleveland State University's modern, urban campus in downtown Cleveland. In 2011, C|M|LAW opened its state-of-the-art, technology-enhanced trial courtroom providing simulation-based learning and mock trial opportunities for law students and legal professionals. Designed to look and function exactly like a federal courtroom, this facility enables C|M|LAW students to prepare to be outstanding trial lawyers. Students at C|M|LAW enjoy all that the city has to offer, including the Cleveland Museum of Art, the world-renowned Cleveland Orchestra, Botanical Gardens, Playhouse Square, the House of Blues, and professional sports teams. On North Coast Harbor sit the Great Lakes Science Center, and the Rock and Roll Hall of Fame and Museum. The law school is in close proximity to the federal, state, and county courthouses. Cleveland is also the headquarters for many large corporations and law firms.

The Curriculum

The C|M|LAW curriculum blends traditional legal theory with lawyering skills development. Though C|M|LAW students prepare for careers in all areas of legal practice, the law school offers concentrations in Business Law, Civil Litigation and Dispute Resolution, Criminal Law, Employment and Labor Law, and International and Comparative Law. The Center for Health Law and Policy provides focused study in the areas of health law regulation, health law policy and ethics, and health law business and litigation. Clinical programs offer students academic credit for serving clients in the areas of law and public policy, employment law, urban development, fair housing, environmental law, and community health advocacy. Externship programs include the Judicial Externship Program in which students work with state, appellate, and federal court judges; the Public Interest Externship Program designed to offer experiences in office settings such as the county prosecutor and public defender, the bankruptcy trustee, the Office of Immigration and Customs Enforcement, and the US Attorney (civil and criminal); and the Independent Externship Program where students may propose a placement in a public service office.

Joint-Degree Programs and Graduate Program

Five joint-degree programs are offered: the JD/MPA (Master of Public Administration); the JD/MUPDD (Master of Urban Planning, Design, and Development); the JD/MBA (Master of Business Administration); the JD/MAES (Master of Arts in Environmental Studies); and the JD/MSES (Master of Science in Environmental Science). The law school also offers a graduate LLM degree.

Pro Bono Program

The Pro Bono Program at C|M|LAW offers a variety of community service opportunities. Popular placements include teaching practical law in public high schools, assisting with the legal needs of women recently released from incarceration, or addressing the concerns of the poor by delivering legal assistance in cooperation with local attorneys and community agencies.

Admission

While admission to C|M|LAW is competitive, it need not be intimidating. The admission committee reviews all applications with care and sensitivity, taking into consideration academic performance, LSAT scores, work and life experience, and readiness for the rigors of legal education. We are committed to enrolling academically talented and diverse students. In doing so, we recognize and embrace that academic talent and diversity can be identified in many interesting and exciting ways. Undergraduate grades and LSAT results are the most significant factors in our admission decision; however, an applicant's personal statement, letters of recommendation, and overall strength of the file are factors also strongly considered in the admission process. Criteria for admission are identical for full- and part-time applicants.

The Legal Career Opportunities Program

The Legal Career Opportunities Program (LCOP), our alternate admission program, invites applications from individuals who demonstrate the ability to succeed in law school but have encountered life circumstances or other adversities that have affected their traditional academic indicators, such as LSAT scores and/or undergraduate grades. In most cases, applicants to the LCOP program have academic indicators that are a bit lower than those of regularly admitted applicants; however, LCOP applicants demonstrate through their career and professional accomplishments, personal statements, letters of recommendation, graduate work, and/or significantly improved academic performance over a period of time, their likelihood for success in law school. LCOP is not a provisional program. Being admitted through the program is acceptance to the law school. Students admitted through LCOP are required to enroll in a course during the summer prior to the beginning of their first year.

Scholarships, Financial Aid, and Loan Repayment Assistance

Applicants are considered for scholarships at the time of admission. Our financial aid program utilizes merit-based scholarships and federal loan programs. C|M|LAW has a loan repayment assistance program (LRAP) to help support students choosing to work in public service jobs upon graduation.

Library and Technology

The C|M|LAW library is one of the 15 largest academic law libraries in the country. The law library is a superior research and learning facility where our students prepare for legal practice in the twenty-first century with access to electronic research services, a computer lab, group study rooms, and a research instruction room. The library even includes a Professional and Study Skills room dedicated to helping students study smarter and succeed in law school. Our students study in a four-story, light-filled space that includes over 200 carrels with built-in power and wireless access for laptop computers. Cutting-edge technology is used in classrooms, our moot courtroom, and our new electronic trial courtroom. Our wireless network allows use of laptops anywhere at the law school. The technology staff assists students with installing software, providing laptops for examinations, and even helping students pick the right computer for law school. C|M|LAW has been recognized for our use and support of technology by the American Association of Law Libraries and *National Jurist* magazine.

Career Services

From day one, we help you build your future. Employers have confidence in the education our students receive and value C|M|LAW graduates. When it's time for you to begin your job search, we will be ready to help you, be it in Northeast Ohio or any region across the country. Our professional staff are members of the bar and have experience and relationships within the legal community, providing them with valuable resources in the job search process. Individual counseling is at the core of our services, but counseling is only one of the many resources we make available to you. At C|M|LAW, numerous opportunities exist for you to gain practical experience (law clerk and research assistant positions, externships, clinics) and participate in programs that give you exposure to potential employers in large and small law firms, government, public interest organizations, and in-house settings. We have alumni in all 50 states, working as attorneys, judges, in-house counsel, professors and university administrators, government employees, human resource professionals, and the list goes on. Your possibilities are endless and our generous network of alumni and law school friends continue to open doors through the generations of our graduates.

Housing and Student Life

C|M|LAW students, faculty, staff, and alumni work hard to provide all students the necessary academic and professional support to learn law and live justice. C|M|LAW offers the Academic Excellence Program (academic support), the Ohio Bar Examination Strategies and Tactics course, first year peer advising, a long-standing alumni mentoring program, over 30 student organizations, and award-winning Moot Court and Trial teams. The University is a dynamic, growing, engaged, and urban campus that has built a new student center, new education building, created on-campus restaurants, expanded parking facilities, and created new green spaces, just in the last two years. C|M|LAW students live in convenient and affordable housing in downtown Cleveland and surrounding suburbs. The University offers on-campus housing and meal plans. The Office of Admission maintains a roommate referral list and is available to assist students in locating off-campus housing. In addition, tuition includes free public transportation and a brand-new transit center, located two blocks from C|M|LAW, was completed in late 2010.

APPLICANT PROFILE

Cleveland State University—Cleveland-Marshall College of Law
This grid includes only applicants who earned 120–180 LSAT scores under standard administrations.

LSAT Score	GPA																
	3.75 +		3.50–3.74		3.25–3.49		3.00–3.24		2.75–2.99		2.50–2.74		Below 2.50		No GPA		Total	
	Apps	Adm	Apps	Adm	Apps	Adm	Apps	Adm	Apps	Adm	Apps	Adm	Apps	Adm	Apps	Adm	Apps	Adm
170–180	2	2	1	1	0	0	2	2	0	0	0	0	0	0	0	0	5	5
165–169	9	9	4	4	6	6	4	4	1	1	1	1	3	3	0	0	28	28
160–164	14	14	34	34	20	20	24	22	14	13	6	5	12	2	0	0	124	110
155–159	45	45	49	47	52	51	47	43	46	39	24	18	23	5	11	6	297	254
150–154	48	31	72	41	105	50	111	44	71	17	39	9	46	6	9	2	501	200
145–149	20	4	54	5	80	5	89	7	60	5	45	0	46	0	18	0	412	26
140–144	10	0	31	1	49	1	45	1	45	1	44	0	39	0	15	1	278	5
Below 140	3	0	8	1	15	0	33	0	23	0	26	0	40	0	15	0	163	1
Total	151	105	253	134	327	133	355	123	260	76	185	33	209	16	68	9	1808	629

Apps = Number of Applicants
Adm = Number Admitted
Reflects 99% of the total applicant pool; highest LSAT data reported.

UNIVERSITY OF COLORADO LAW SCHOOL

Office of Admissions, UCB 403, Wolf Law Building
Boulder, CO 80309-0403
Phone: 303.492.7203; Fax: 303.492.2542
E-mail: lawadmin@colorado.edu; Website: www.colorado.edu/law

ABA Approved Since 1923

The Basics

Type of school	Public
Term	Semester
Application deadline	11/15 3/15
Application fee	$65
Financial aid deadline	4/1
Can first year start other than fall?	No
Student to faculty ratio	10.8 to 1
# of housing spaces available restricted to law students	
graduate housing for which law students are eligible	575

Faculty and Administrators

	Total		Men		Women		Minorities	
	Spr	Fall	Spr	Fall	Spr	Fall	Spr	Fall
Full-time	44	40	25	21	19	19	8	10
Other full-time	3	3	2	2	1	1	0	0
Deans, librarians, & others who teach	6	4	4	3	2	1	2	1
Part-time	18	19	11	16	6	3	2	1
Total	71	66	42	42	28	24	12	12

Curriculum

	Full-Time	Part-Time
Typical first-year section size	83	0
Is there typically a "small section" of the first-year class, other than Legal Writing, taught by full-time faculty	Yes	No
If yes, typical size offered last year	35	
# of classroom course titles beyond first-year curriculum	106	

# of upper division courses, excluding seminars, with an enrollment:		
	Under 25	85
	25–49	32
	50–74	13
	75–99	5
	100+	0

# of seminars	17	
# of seminar positions available	228	
# of seminar positions filled	185	0
# of positions available in simulation courses	363	
# of simulation positions filled	292	0
# of positions available in faculty supervised clinical courses	130	
# of faculty supervised clinical positions filled	108	0
# involved in field placements	199	0
# involved in law journals	143	0
# involved in moot court or trial competitions	62	0
# of credit hours required to graduate	89	

JD Enrollment and Ethnicity

	Men		Women		Full-Time		Part-Time		1st-Year		Total		JD Degs. Awd.
	#	%	#	%	#	%	#	%	#	%	#	%	
All Hispanics	21	7.5	22	8.3	43	7.9	0	0.0	16	8.9	43	7.9	13
Am. Ind./AK Nat.	12	4.3	9	3.4	21	3.8	0	0.0	9	5.0	21	3.8	4
Asian	10	3.6	20	7.5	30	5.5	0	0.0	9	5.0	30	5.5	18
Black/Af. Am.	9	3.2	7	2.6	16	2.9	0	0.0	6	3.3	16	2.9	4
Nat. HI/Pac. Isl.	0	0.0	0	0.0	0	0.0	0	0.0	0	0.0	0	0.0	0
2 or more races	0	0.0	0	0.0	0	0.0	0	0.0	0	0.0	0	0.0	0
Subtotal (minor.)	52	18.5	58	21.9	110	20.1	0	0.0	40	22.2	110	20.1	39
Nonres. Alien	0	0.0	1	0.4	1	0.2	0	0.0	0	0.0	1	0.2	0
White/Cauc.	229	81.5	206	77.7	435	79.7	0	0.0	140	77.8	435	79.7	142
Unknown	0	0.0	0	0.0	0	0.0	0	0.0	0	0.0	0	0.0	0
Total	281	51.5	265	48.5	546	100.0	0	0.0	180	33.0	546		183

Transfers

Transfers in	13
Transfers out	1

Tuition and Fees

	Resident	Nonresident
Full-time	$28,915	$35,773
Part-time		
Tuition Guarantee Program	N	

Living Expenses

Estimated living expenses for singles

Living on campus	Living off campus	Living at home
$17,236	$14,919	$10,602

UNIVERSITY OF COLORADO LAW SCHOOL

*ABA
Approved
Since
1923*

GPA and LSAT Scores

	Total	Full-Time	Part-Time
# of apps	2,906	2,906	0
# of offers	794	794	0
# of matrics	180	180	0
75% GPA	3.74	3.74	0.00
Median GPA	3.61	3.61	0.00
25% GPA	3.30	3.30	0.00
75% LSAT	166	166	0
Median LSAT	164	164	0
25% LSAT	161	161	0

Grants and Scholarships (from prior year)

	Total #	Total %	Full-Time #	Full-Time %	Part-Time #	Part-Time %
Total # of students	547		547		0	
Total # receiving grants	270	49.4	270	49.4	0	0.0
Less than 1/2 tuition	145	26.5	145	26.5	0	0.0
Half to full tuition	66	12.1	66	12.1	0	0.0
Full tuition	4	0.7	4	0.7	0	0.0
More than full tuition	55	10.1	55	10.1	0	0.0
Median grant amount			$9,432		$0	

Informational and Library Resources

Total amount spent on library materials	$1,408,813
Study seating capacity inside the library	444
# of full-time equivalent professional librarians	8
Hours per week library is open	104
# of open, wired connections available to students	81
# of networked computers available for use by students	78
Has wireless network?	Y
Requires computer?	N

JD Attrition (from prior year)

	Academic #	Other #	Total #	Total %
1st year	0	2	2	1.2
2nd year	0	5	5	2.7
3rd year	0	1	1	0.5
4th year	0	0	0	0.0

Employment (9 months after graduation)

	Total	Percentage
Employment status known	157	95.2
Employment status unknown	8	4.8
Employed	132	84.1
Pursuing graduate degrees	2	1.3
Unemployed (seeking, not seeking, or studying for the bar)	2	1.3
Type of Employment		
# employed in law firms	72	54.5
# employed in business and industry	8	6.1
# employed in government	25	18.9
# employed in public interest	5	3.8
# employed as judicial clerks	21	15.9
# employed in academia	2	1.5
Geographic Location		
# employed in state	114	86.4
# employed outside the US	1	0.8
# of states where employed		14

Bar Passage Rates

First-time takers	166	Reporting %	84.94
Average school %	92.91	Average state %	85.67
Average pass difference	7.24		

Jurisdiction	Takers	Passers	Pass %	State %	Diff %
Colorado	141	131	92.91	85.67	7.24

UNIVERSITY OF COLORADO LAW SCHOOL

Office of Admissions, UCB 403, Wolf Law Building
Boulder, CO 80309-0403
Phone: 303.492.7203; Fax: 303.492.2542
E-mail: lawadmin@colorado.edu; Website: www.colorado.edu/law

Introduction

Colorado Law, established in 1892, is located on the Boulder campus of the University of Colorado and lies at the foot of the Rocky Mountains. High admission standards, a relatively small student body, and a favorable faculty-to-student ratio assure a stimulating and challenging academic environment that encourages class participation and interaction with faculty. The school is a charter member of the AALS and is ABA approved.

Faculty

Faculty members have a demonstrated record of excellence in teaching, research, and public service. They include some of the nation's leading scholars; particular strengths evidenced by faculty publications are constitutional law, natural resources and environmental law, Indian law, energy, business, dispute resolution, and telecommunications law.

Physical Facilities and Library

The law school is housed in the 180,000-square-foot Wolf Law Building, located on the edge of the CU Boulder campus. The Wolf Law Building features state-of-the-art classrooms, two high-tech courtrooms, and the largest resource collection and most technologically advanced law library in the 12-state Rocky Mountain region. The Wolf Law Building is the first LEED Gold-certified public law school building in the country under the standards of the US Green Building Council's certification program.

The William A. Wise Law Library, the largest law library in the state, serves the students, staff, and faculty of Colorado Law, as well as the bench and bar. The library holds over 500,000 volumes and provides access to thousands of electronic journals and databases. Law students also have access to the resources of other university and college libraries in Colorado through a statewide delivery system. Students can connect laptops to the school's wireless network or use one of the 65 computers available in the library to perform online legal research.

Special Programs

Clinics—In the **Criminal Defense Clinic**, students learn basic criminal practice skills and represent clients in actual cases, from beginning to end, in municipal and county courts in Boulder County.

In the **Civil Practice Clinic**, students represent low-income clients in a variety of civil law settings, including family court and in front of administrative law judges. Students take the lead in all hearings and trials.

The **Appellate Advocacy Clinic** alternates annually between cases from the public defender's office and from the attorney general's office. Each student, under direct supervision of an instructor, is responsible for completing an appellate brief and attending the oral argument in the Colorado Supreme Court or the Colorado Court of Appeals.

In the **Juvenile Law Clinic**, students represent children and youth who are abused, neglected, or accused of a crime, addressing all of the legal needs of the child client. They also represent school districts as the petitioner in truancy matters.

In the **Family Law Clinic**, students provide legal services to low-income Coloradans who need help with family law matters such as divorces, issues related to parenting time, and child support.

The **American Indian Law Clinic** provides students with faculty-supervised experience giving legal assistance in matters including tribal sovereignty, child welfare, preservation of tribal identity, employment discrimination, public benefits, preservation of Native lands, and more.

In the **Entrepreneurial Law Clinic**, students work with local entrepreneurs, providing transactional legal services for the formation and development of small businesses.

The **Technology Law and Policy Clinic** gives students the opportunity to advocate in the public interest concerning technology issues before regulatory entities, courts, legislatures, and standard-setting bodies.

The **Natural Resources Litigation Clinic** involves students in representing public interest clients in environmental cases related to federal public lands, wildlife, and other issues. The Natural Resources Law Center has three major areas of activity: research and publication, legal education, and the distinguished visitors and fellows program.

Research Centers—The Byron R. White Center for the Study of American Constitutional Law furthers the study, teaching, and publication of constitutional law. The White Center hosts the annual Ira C. Rothgerber Constitutional Law Conference on contemporary constitutional issues and supports research in constitutional law.

The Silicon Flatirons Center for Law, Technology, and Entrepreneurship's mission is to create an environment for analyzing the dynamic changes in the telecommunications marketplace and regulatory environment.

The Center for Energy and Environmental Security is an interdisciplinary research and policy center. It is designed to facilitate progress toward a global, sustainable energy future through the innovative use of laws, policies, quality information, and technology solutions.

Curriculum

In addition to strong and varied course offerings, students can earn a certificate in tax, American Indian law, intellectual property and technology law, juvenile and family law, or environmental law.

The first-year curriculum is required of all students. During the second and third years, students may emphasize such areas of the law as natural resources, environmental law, criminal law, business, constitutional law, tax, public interest, American Indian law, litigation, intellectual property law, and jurisprudence. Established joint-degree programs are the JD/MBA, JD/MD, JD/MPA, JD/MST, JD/MURP, and a JD/MS or PhD in Environmental Science.

Students can broaden their international perspectives and understanding of law and law practice by participating in the JD/LLB dual-degree program with the University of Alberta Faculty of Law. This dual-degree program enhances the ability of both law schools to prepare lawyers to practice in a global community.

The University of Colorado Law School has a partnership with the University of San Diego (USD) School of Law to give our students access to an extensive Summer Law Study

Abroad program. They offer courses in seven locations: Barcelona, Dublin, Florence, London, Oxford, Paris, and Moscow/St. Petersburg (Russia).

Students also have the opportunity to attend Bucerius Law School in Germany and Bar Ilan University in Israel through international exchange programs offered during the academic year. These programs are independent of the partnership with USD.

Colorado Law School offers Master of Laws (LLM) degrees in three areas of study in which the strength of our faculty, curriculum, and programs are recognized nationally and internationally. The areas of study are entrepreneurial law, information technology and intellectual property, and natural resources law.

Admission

Admission to Colorado Law is competitive. At a minimum, a bachelor's degree from an institution that is accredited by an agency recognized by the US Department of Education is required. The LSAT and registration with LSAC's Credential Assembly Service is required. Offers of admission are influenced heavily by GPA and LSAT score, but they are considered in the context of the entire application. Substantial weight is accorded to special qualities such as leadership, character, diversity, and commitment to service. The school seeks to increase the ethnic, cultural, and other diversity of its student body. The binding Early Decision application deadline is November 15; the regular application deadline is March 15. The earliest admission letters go out in December, and the class is filled on a rolling basis. Admission is sometimes possible from a waiting list. Colorado Law accepts a small number of transfer students for the fall semester. Law Students may seek visiting status in the fall or spring semester. Transfer and visitor admission criteria include law school performance.

Financial Aid

Scholarships for incoming students are based on merit. Nonresident students qualify for lower resident tuition rates by maintaining domicile in Colorado for 12 consecutive months. Students may not be employed during their first year, but limited outside employment is compatible with second- and third-year schedules. Current students may apply for additional scholarships and awards for their second and third years. Students applying for financial aid should file the FAFSA as soon as possible after January 1 and before the priority deadline of April 1.

Student Activities

Over 35 student organizations invite participation in projects, programs, and social activities. The *University of Colorado Law Review*, *Journal on Telecommunications and High Technology Law*, and *Colorado Journal of International Environmental Law and Policy* are scholarly journals edited entirely by students. Students also participate in a number of moot court competitions and have won regional, national, and international recognition in these events.

Housing

For information about the university's family housing, call 303.492.6384. Most students live in apartments and houses in the surrounding community.

Career Development

Colorado Law students find satisfying careers after law school with the assistance of an energetic and dedicated staff in the Office of Career Development. The professional counselors advise students and alumni on decisions about career direction, professionalism, legal employers, and alternatives to traditional legal careers. Specifically, the office directly assists students in finding internships, externships, clerkships, and other job opportunities during and after law school. The office solicits employers nationwide to interview on campus and to hire students through off-campus programs. The office helped develop the Colorado Pledge to Diversity 1L Summer Clerkship Program.

APPLICANT PROFILE

University of Colorado Law School
This grid includes only applicants who earned 120–180 LSAT scores under standard administrations.

LSAT Score	3.75 +		3.50–3.74		3.25–3.49		3.00–3.24		2.75–2.99		2.50–2.74		2.25–2.49		2.00–2.24		Below 2.00		No GPA		Total	
	Apps	Adm	Apps	Adm	Apps	Adm	Apps	Adm	Apps	Adm	Apps	Adm	Apps	Adm	Apps	Adm	Apps	Adm	Apps	Adm	Apps	Adm
175–180	3	2	3	3	1	1	3	1	1	1	0	0	0	0	1	1	0	0	1	1	13	10
170–174	21	19	22	20	32	21	13	10	8	6	2	0	0	0	1	0	0	0	0	0	99	76
165–169	84	74	99	81	82	58	52	29	29	6	14	2	7	2	0	0	1	0	5	2	373	254
160–164	188	129	294	134	230	67	129	20	52	4	20	2	9	1	4	0	1	0	5	1	932	358
155–159	142	29	186	17	172	7	122	7	46	1	24	0	6	0	1	0	1	0	6	0	706	61
150–154	56	6	85	1	110	6	93	3	41	0	26	0	17	0	4	0	2	0	4	1	438	17
145–149	13	3	29	0	45	1	48	0	26	0	21	0	5	0	4	0	1	0	3	0	195	4
140–144	3	0	13	0	11	0	20	0	16	0	13	0	12	0	1	0	0	0	2	0	91	0
135–139	1	0	2	0	0	0	3	0	8	0	5	0	3	0	5	0	0	0	1	0	28	0
130–134	0	0	0	0	0	0	0	0	4	0	3	0	0	0	0	0	0	0	1	0	8	0
125–129	0	0	0	0	0	0	0	0	0	0	0	0	0	0	1	0	0	0	1	0	2	0
120–124	0	0	0	0	0	0	0	0	0	0	0	0	0	0	1	0	0	0	0	0	1	0
Total	511	262	733	256	683	161	483	70	231	18	128	4	59	3	23	1	6	0	29	5	2886	780

Apps = Number of Applicants   Adm = Number Admitted   Reflects 99% of the total applicant pool; highest LSAT data reported.

COLUMBIA UNIVERSITY SCHOOL OF LAW

435 West 116th Street
New York, NY 10027
Phone: 212.854.2670; Fax: 212.854.1109
E-mail: admissions@law.columbia.edu; Website: www.law.columbia.edu/admissions

The Basics

Type of school	Private
Term	Semester
Application deadline	11/15 2/15
Application fee	$80
Financial aid deadline	3/1
Can first year start other than fall?	No
Student to faculty ratio	10.9 to 1
# of housing spaces available restricted to law students	489
graduate housing for which law students are eligible	631

Faculty and Administrators

	Total		Men		Women		Minorities	
	Spr	Fall	Spr	Fall	Spr	Fall	Spr	Fall
Full-time	100	99	70	67	30	32	19	18
Other full-time	7	8	6	7	1	1	3	3
Deans, librarians, & others who teach	17	17	5	6	12	11	3	3
Part-time	124	95	90	68	34	27	13	7
Total	248	219	171	148	77	71	38	31

Curriculum

	Full-Time	Part-Time
Typical first-year section size	105	0
Is there typically a "small section" of the first-year class, other than Legal Writing, taught by full-time faculty	Yes	No
If yes, typical size offered last year	36	

# of classroom course titles beyond first-year curriculum		222
# of upper division courses, excluding seminars, with an enrollment:	Under 25	79
	25–49	45
	50–74	29
	75–99	8
	100+	18

# of seminars		124
# of seminar positions available		2,421
# of seminar positions filled	1,939	0
# of positions available in simulation courses		447
# of simulation positions filled	440	0
# of positions available in faculty supervised clinical courses		158
# of faculty supervised clinical positions filled	158	0
# involved in field placements	139	0
# involved in law journals	679	0
# involved in moot court or trial competitions	57	0
# of credit hours required to graduate		83

JD Enrollment and Ethnicity

	Men		Women		Full-Time		Part-Time		1st-Year		Total		JD Degs. Awd.
	#	%	#	%	#	%	#	%	#	%	#	%	
All Hispanics	36	5.2	41	6.3	77	5.7	0	0.0	30	7.5	77	5.7	29
Am. Ind./AK Nat.	3	0.4	4	0.6	7	0.5	0	0.0	4	1.0	7	0.5	0
Asian	99	14.3	124	19.0	223	16.6	0	0.0	75	18.7	223	16.6	57
Black/Af. Am.	29	4.2	74	11.3	103	7.7	0	0.0	36	9.0	103	7.7	32
Nat. HI/Pac. Isl.	0	0.0	1	0.2	1	0.1	0	0.0	0	0.0	1	0.1	0
2 or more races	7	1.0	15	2.3	22	1.6	0	0.0	1	0.2	22	1.6	0
Subtotal (minor.)	174	25.2	259	39.7	433	32.2	0	0.0	146	36.3	433	32.2	130
Nonres. Alien	51	7.4	66	10.1	117	8.7	0	0.0	31	7.7	117	8.7	0
White/Cauc.	460	66.6	326	49.9	785	58.5	1	100.0	225	56.0	786	58.5	264
Unknown	6	0.9	2	0.3	8	0.6	0	0.0	0	0.0	8	0.6	1
Total	691	51.4	653	48.6	1343	99.9	1	0.1	402	29.9	1344		430

Transfers

Transfers in	78
Transfers out	2

Tuition and Fees

	Resident	Nonresident
Full-time	$50,428	$50,428
Part-time		
Tuition Guarantee Program	N	

Living Expenses

Estimated living expenses for singles

Living on campus	Living off campus	Living at home
$21,700	$21,700	$5,800

Official ABA Data

COLUMBIA UNIVERSITY SCHOOL OF LAW

ABA
Approved
Since
1923

GPA and LSAT Scores

	Total	Full-Time	Part-Time
# of apps	9,012	9,012	0
# of offers	1,187	1,187	0
# of matrics	404	404	0
75% GPA	3.82	3.82	0.00
Median GPA	3.72	3.72	0.00
25% GPA	3.61	3.61	0.00
75% LSAT	175	175	0
Median LSAT	172	172	0
25% LSAT	170	170	0

Grants and Scholarships (from prior year)

	Total		Full-Time		Part-Time	
	#	%	#	%	#	%
Total # of students	1,310		1,309		1	
Total # receiving grants	643	49.1	643	49.1	0	0.0
Less than 1/2 tuition	457	34.9	457	34.9	0	0.0
Half to full tuition	141	10.8	141	10.8	0	0.0
Full tuition	36	2.7	36	2.8	0	0.0
More than full tuition	9	0.7	9	0.7	0	0.0
Median grant amount			$15,000		$0	

Informational and Library Resources

Total amount spent on library materials	$2,661,456
Study seating capacity inside the library	369
# of full-time equivalent professional librarians	17
Hours per week library is open	104
# of open, wired connections available to students	3,028
# of networked computers available for use by students	135
Has wireless network?	Y
Requires computer?	N

JD Attrition (from prior year)

	Academic #	Other #	Total #	Total %
1st year	0	0	0	0.0
2nd year	0	2	2	0.4
3rd year	0	0	0	0.0
4th year	0	0	0	0.0

Employment (9 months after graduation)

	Total	Percentage
Employment status known	440	98.9
Employment status unknown	5	1.1
Employed	435	98.9
Pursuing graduate degrees	4	0.9
Unemployed (seeking, not seeking, or studying for the bar)	0	0.0
Type of Employment		
# employed in law firms	366	84.1
# employed in business and industry	9	2.1
# employed in government	10	2.3
# employed in public interest	14	3.2
# employed as judicial clerks	35	8.0
# employed in academia	1	0.2
Geographic Location		
# employed in state	284	65.3
# employed outside the US	9	2.1
# of states where employed	20	

Bar Passage Rates

First-time takers	435	Reporting %	75.86
Average school %	96.06	Average state %	86.51
Average pass difference	9.55		

Jurisdiction	Takers	Passers	Pass %	State %	Diff %
New York	330	317	96.06	86.51	9.55

COLUMBIA UNIVERSITY SCHOOL OF LAW

435 West 116th Street
New York, NY 10027
Phone: 212.854.2670; Fax: 212.854.1109
E-mail: admissions@law.columbia.edu; Website: www.law.columbia.edu/admissions

Introduction

Columbia Law School is distinguished, perhaps uniquely among leading US law schools, as an international center of legal education that stimulates its students to consider the full dimensions of the possibility of the law—as an intellectual pursuit, as a career, and as an instrument of human progress. The character of academic and social life at Columbia is fiercely democratic, dynamic, creative, and innovative. The Law School is especially committed to educating students of differing perspectives, from diverse backgrounds, and with varied life experiences.

Professional prospects for Columbia Law School graduates are quite extraordinary. Our graduates proceed to productive careers in every conceivable arena of practice, business, and advocacy. While Columbia-trained attorneys are especially well-regarded for their work in corporate law and finance, an unusually high number also serve as state and federal judges, prosecutors, civil rights and human rights advocates, legal scholars, public defenders, entrepreneurs, business executives, elected government officials, and national and international leaders. Many alumni contribute significantly to the shaping of US culture at large. Currently, our graduates serve in leadership roles across the fields of government, art, music, film, publishing, science, professional athletics, philanthropy, and higher education.

With an exceptionally talented student body and faculty and a strong tradition of encouraging students with specialized interests to develop those interests in depth, Columbia Law School provides a legal education that gives our students a singular capacity for imagination, originality, and high responsibility in their professional lives.

JD Student Body Profile

Columbia continues to place among the handful of the most highly selective JD programs in our nation—as evaluated by the principal criteria used to measure admission selectivity (application volume, acceptance rates, LSAT scores, and academic performance). Indeed, in recent years, the demand for a Columbia legal education has never been greater, and the academic credentials of our entering classes are stronger than ever. Columbia's JD student body is further distinguished by standing as one of the most culturally diverse among America's leading law schools. Men and women choosing to study law at Columbia hail from the small towns, farms, and suburbs of the West, Midwest, and South; the industrial corridors and ivy halls of the Northeast; the inner cities of every major US metropolis; and the international centers of Europe, Asia, Africa, and Latin America.

Each entering class reflects the broad range of economic, ethnic, and cultural backgrounds found in the United States. And from around the world, we welcome students who will enrich learning at Columbia and thereafter advance the developing legal cultures of their homelands.

With one of the largest percentages of international students in its JD program of any leading law school; with one of the very highest percentages of students of color; with its students hailing from 48 states, roughly 43 foreign countries, and more than 200 different colleges and universities; and with 15 percent of its JD students having earned at least one graduate or professional degree before studying law, Columbia's student body abounds with a diversity of life experiences, cultural backgrounds, and intellectual perspectives.

The Law School Campus

Columbia Law School's main building, Jerome Greene Hall, has undergone significant expansion and improvements devoted primarily to our students, including library renovations and the creation of a student commons that includes a student lounge and café. New seminar rooms and state-of-the-art multimedia classrooms have also been designed to provide students with full Internet and other legal research access. Across the street from Greene Hall is William C. Warren Hall, home to the Columbia Law Review, Morningside Heights Legal Services (a law school clinic serving our community), and the Center for Public Interest Law.

William and June Warren Hall includes amphitheater-style classrooms equipped with modern teaching resources, a center for the law school's international programs, and conference facilities. It is also home to the offices of Admissions, Financial Aid, Registration Services, Student Services, Graduate Legal Studies, and International Programs.

The expansion of the law school's facilities have greatly enhanced the quality of life and learning at Columbia. Students have a superb learning environment that is conducive to community building and social and intellectual engagement, and reflects the changing nature of legal education in the twenty-first century.

Library Resources and Research Facilities

Columbia's library is one of the largest and most comprehensive law collections in the world. It is especially rich in US law and legal history, international law, comparative law, Roman law, and the legal literature of the major European countries, China, and Japan. Access to the Internet and electronic documents provide additional resources, with materials from Germany, South Africa, and a wide range of international organizations. In addition, the many libraries of the university, containing more than seven million volumes, are available to law students.

The law library's online catalog provides complete access to the library's collection, acts as an index to the major legal serials, and provides access to the online catalogs of other major law school libraries. Columbia provides its law students with some of the most sophisticated technologies of any law school in the nation.

Curriculum

The foundation of the JD program consists of Legal Methods (an intensive three-week introductory course), Legal Practice Workshop (a two-semester course that provides training in legal research, writing, and analysis), Contracts, Torts, Constitutional Law, Civil Procedure, Property, Criminal Law, Foundation Year Moot Court, and one elective focusing on the law's engagement with public policy, the intellectual and historical foundations of the rule of law, or the law's transnational and comparative expression. Recent elective offerings have included Art of Legal Persuasion; Critical Legal Thought; Foundations of the Regulatory State; Law and Contemporary Society; Law and Economics; Law and Social Science; Lawyering Across Multiple Legal Orders; Legislation; Principles of Intellectual Property; Regulation: Decentralization and Globalization; the Regulatory and Administrative State; the Rule of Law: Perspectives and Philosophy; and Terror and Consent.

Columbia has a special commitment to clinical education, which places the student in the role of a lawyer doing a lawyer's actual work under intensive faculty supervision. Some examples of clinical opportunities are Lawyering in the Digital Age, Nonprofit Organizations/Small Business, Child Advocacy, Mediation, Environmental Law, Human Rights, and a clinic in Sexuality and Gender Law, the first clinic of its type in the nation. Unique to Columbia is a summer program which places more than 150 students in civil and human rights internships in law firms and organizations throughout this country and around the world. Especially distinguished are Columbia's offerings in international, foreign, and comparative law; constitutional law and theory; corporate and securities law; intellectual property; critical race theory; human rights; and public interest law.

Research Centers and Special Programs

Research centers and special programs include the Kernochan Center for Law, Media, and the Arts; Julius Silver Program in Law, Science, and Technology; Center for Climate Change Law; Center for Law and Philosophy; Center for Law and Economic Studies; Center for the Study of Law and Culture; Center for Public Interest Law; Program on Careers in Law and Teaching; Human Rights Institute; Parker School of Foreign and Comparative Law; Center for Chinese Legal Studies; Center for Japanese Legal Studies; Center for Korean Legal Studies; European Legal Studies Center; Center for Contract and Economic Organization; Center on Corporate Governance; Center on Crime, Community, and the Law; Center on Global Legal Problems; Center for Institutional and Social Change; Vale Columbia Center on Sustainable International Investment; Social Justice Initiatives; and the Charles Evans Gerber Transactional Studies Program.

Admission

All first-year students enter in mid-August. Candidates applying for regular admission should apply after September 1 of the year preceding their desired matriculation, but before February 15, the application deadline. Early Decision candidates must complete their applications by November 15 and are notified in December. All other applications are generally reviewed in the order in which they are completed, and decisions are made and sent out on a rolling basis.

Applicant Profile Not Available

UNIVERSITY OF CONNECTICUT SCHOOL OF LAW

45 Elizabeth Street
Hartford, CT 06105
Phone: 860.570.5100; Fax: 860.570.5153
E-mail: admissions@law.uconn.edu; Website: www.law.uconn.edu

ABA
Approved
Since
1933

The Basics

Type of school	Public
Term	Semester
Application deadline	3/15
Application fee	$60
Financial aid deadline	3/15
Can first year start other than fall?	No
Student to faculty ratio	10.6 to 1
# of housing spaces available restricted to law students	
graduate housing for which law students are eligible	

Faculty and Administrators

	Total		Men		Women		Minorities	
	Spr	Fall	Spr	Fall	Spr	Fall	Spr	Fall
Full-time	43	44	28	26	15	18	6	6
Other full-time	6	8	2	2	4	6	0	0
Deans, librarians, & others who teach	8	8	2	2	6	6	1	2
Part-time	71	54	56	43	15	11	9	7
Total	128	114	88	73	40	41	16	15

Curriculum

	Full-Time	Part-Time
Typical first-year section size	61	60
Is there typically a "small section" of the first-year class, other than Legal Writing, taught by full-time faculty	Yes	Yes
If yes, typical size offered last year	31	30

# of classroom course titles beyond first-year curriculum		161
# of upper division courses, excluding seminars, with an enrollment:	Under 25	100
	25–49	26
	50–74	11
	75–99	0
	100+	0
# of seminars		66
# of seminar positions available		1,238
# of seminar positions filled	755	210
# of positions available in simulation courses		940
# of simulation positions filled	447	195
# of positions available in faculty supervised clinical courses		260
# of faculty supervised clinical positions filled	231	12
# involved in field placements	122	72
# involved in law journals	171	21
# involved in moot court or trial competitions	49	1
# of credit hours required to graduate		86

JD Enrollment and Ethnicity

	Men		Women		Full-Time		Part-Time		1st-Year		Total		JD Degs. Awd.
	#	%	#	%	#	%	#	%	#	%	#	%	
All Hispanics	24	6.9	29	10.6	35	8.0	18	10.0	19	10.2	53	8.5	7
Am. Ind./AK Nat.	2	0.6	1	0.4	1	0.2	2	1.1	1	0.5	3	0.5	1
Asian	19	5.5	27	9.9	37	8.4	9	5.0	12	6.5	46	7.4	17
Black/Af. Am.	17	4.9	14	5.1	23	5.2	8	4.4	6	3.2	31	5.0	13
Nat. HI/Pac. Isl.	0	0.0	0	0.0	0	0.0	0	0.0	0	0.0	0	0.0	0
2 or more races	0	0.0	0	0.0	0	0.0	0	0.0	0	0.0	0	0.0	0
Subtotal (minor.)	62	17.9	71	26.0	96	21.8	37	20.6	38	20.4	133	21.5	38
Nonres. Alien	3	0.9	5	1.8	7	1.6	1	0.6	5	2.7	8	1.3	0
White/Cauc.	253	72.9	174	63.7	298	67.7	129	71.7	128	68.8	427	68.9	150
Unknown	29	8.4	23	8.4	39	8.9	13	7.2	15	8.1	52	8.4	21
Total	347	56.0	273	44.0	440	71.0	180	29.0	186	30.0	620		212

Transfers

Transfers in	20
Transfers out	3

Tuition and Fees

	Resident	Nonresident
Full-time	$21,508	$44,398
Part-time	$15,024	$31,044
Tuition Guarantee Program		N

Living Expenses

Estimated living expenses for singles

Living on campus	Living off campus	Living at home
N/A	$18,740	$9,490

ABA
Approved
Since
1933

GPA and LSAT Scores

	Total	Full-Time	Part-Time
# of apps	2,376	2,257	1,007
# of offers	710	525	185
# of matrics	186	135	51
75% GPA	3.63	3.63	3.62
Median GPA	3.43	3.43	3.33
25% GPA	3.20	3.23	3.03
75% LSAT	163	164	160
Median LSAT	161	162	158
25% LSAT	158	160	155

Grants and Scholarships (from prior year)

	Total		Full-Time		Part-Time	
	#	%	#	%	#	%
Total # of students	641		450		191	
Total # receiving grants	374	58.3	321	71.3	53	27.7
Less than 1/2 tuition	133	20.7	106	23.6	27	14.1
Half to full tuition	214	33.4	188	41.8	26	13.6
Full tuition	12	1.9	12	2.7	0	0.0
More than full tuition	15	2.3	15	3.3	0	0.0
Median grant amount			$10,000		$7,000	

Informational and Library Resources

Total amount spent on library materials	$1,408,939
Study seating capacity inside the library	919
# of full-time equivalent professional librarians	8
Hours per week library is open	89
# of open, wired connections available to students	778
# of networked computers available for use by students	137
Has wireless network?	Y
Requires computer?	N

JD Attrition (from prior year)

	Academic	Other	Total	
	#	#	#	%
1st year	0	11	11	6.0
2nd year	0	9	9	4.4
3rd year	0	0	0	0.0
4th year	0	0	0	0.0

Employment (9 months after graduation)

	Total	Percentage
Employment status known	199	95.7
Employment status unknown	9	4.3
Employed	179	89.9
Pursuing graduate degrees	4	2.0
Unemployed (seeking, not seeking, or studying for the bar)	12	6.0
Type of Employment		
# employed in law firms	87	48.6
# employed in business and industry	35	19.6
# employed in government	19	10.6
# employed in public interest	4	2.2
# employed as judicial clerks	22	12.3
# employed in academia	12	6.7
Geographic Location		
# employed in state	107	59.8
# employed outside the US	3	1.7
# of states where employed	16	

Bar Passage Rates

First-time takers	224	Reporting %	96.43
Average school %	88.88	Average state %	85.88
Average pass difference	3.00		

Jurisdiction	Takers	Passers	Pass %	State %	Diff %
Connecticut	145	134	92.41	85.56	6.85
New York	71	58	81.69	86.51	−4.82

UNIVERSITY OF CONNECTICUT SCHOOL OF LAW

45 Elizabeth Street
Hartford, CT 06105
Phone: 860.570.5100; Fax: 860.570.5153
E-mail: admissions@law.uconn.edu; Website: www.law.uconn.edu

Introduction

As a result of several decades of sustained intellectual and foundational growth, the University of Connecticut School of Law has emerged as one of the leading public law schools in the United States. Because of Connecticut's extraordinary ratio of full-time students to full-time faculty, 75 percent of the advanced courses have 25 or fewer students. An outstanding and accessible faculty; an intensive first-year skills program; a rich and varied curriculum, including more than a dozen legal clinics; four student-edited journals; student organizations active across the spectrum of legal and social concerns; a regular flow of visiting lecturers; and a committed body of graduates throughout the country, combine to make the University of Connecticut a law school of exceptional strength.

Library and Physical Facilities

The campus, listed on the National Register of Historic Places, is arguably the most beautiful in the United States. The library, completed in 1996, is one of the largest legal research and technology centers in the world, with more than 500,000 volumes housed in the 120,000-square-foot facility.

With its immediate neighbors—the Hartford Seminary, the University of Hartford, the Connecticut Historical Society, and the Connecticut Attorney General's Office—the school is part of an academic enclave in a turn-of-the-century residential neighborhood.

Dual-Degree Programs

The law school offers several interdisciplinary programs: JD/LLM in Insurance Law, JD/Master of Business Administration, JD/Master of Public Administration, JD/Master of Public Health, and JD/Master of Social Work.

International Study Programs

The economic and political realities of globalization place new demands on the graduates of the law school. International law occupies an increasingly prominent place in the curriculum, reinforced by the student-edited *Connecticut Journal of International Law*. The law school has formal and informal study-abroad programs with universities in Aix-en-Provence, Berlin, Dublin, Exeter, Haifa, Leiden, London, Mannheim, San Juan, Siena, and Tilburg. These relationships bring a wealth of international visitors to the school. Legal scholars have visited and lectured from Argentina, Bosnia, China, the Czech Republic, France, Germany, Great Britain, Hungary, Israel, Japan, Korea, the Netherlands, Poland, Russia, South Africa, Taiwan, and Ukraine.

The LLM in United States Legal Studies for graduates of foreign law schools provides further opportunity for our students to learn from and study with peers trained in different legal systems.

Student Activities

Selected students may participate in one of four student-edited journals: the *Connecticut Law Review*, the *Connecticut Journal of International Law*, the *Connecticut Insurance Law Journal*, and the *Connecticut Public Interest Law Journal*.

The Connecticut Moot Court Board and the Mock Trial Association provide students with the opportunity to practice oral advocacy in intramural and interscholastic competitions. Participants have placed extremely well in regional, national, and international competitions.

The Student Bar Association is the representative student government of the school. It manages an annual budget consisting of funds derived from the student activities fee and university tuition to support the various student organizations and to generally enhance the quality of student life. Under the governance of the Student Bar, a large number of student-run organizations, reflecting the diversity of our students, have active chapters on campus.

Special Programs

Connecticut was a pioneer in clinical legal education, and our clinics continue to be a distinguishing strength of the school. If you are interested in the way law intersects with other disciplines or with such varied topics as human rights, intellectual property, or health care, you will find courses and specialists to meet your needs. Offerings in environmental law are supplemented by a semester exchange program with Vermont Law School.

The **Center for Children's Advocacy, Inc.**, a nonprofit corporation affiliated with the law school, works on behalf of the legal rights of underprivileged children. The **Connecticut Urban Legal Initiative, Inc.**, another nonprofit corporation housed at the law school, identifies neighborhood problems that typify urban blight and devises strategies to address them. The **Insurance Law Center** offers a specialized insurance curriculum with its LLM program, innovative research initiatives on the role of insurance in law and society, conferences and workshops, and the student-edited *Connecticut Insurance Law Journal*.

The **Intellectual Property Certificate Program** exposes participants to a broad curriculum of courses, from classes on patent, trademark, and copyright law to specialized seminars, including those in art law, cyberlaw, and European Union IP law. In addition, our Intellectual Property and Entrepreneurship clinic was selected by the US PTO to participate in a special clinical program. The **Tax Studies Certificate Program** affords an opportunity to participate in a supervised writing project, externship, or clinic in the area of tax law. Participants in the certificate program may begin their tax studies in Federal Income Tax in their first year and continue the study of taxation in a variety of courses during the last four semesters of law school. A **Human Rights Certificate Program** offers students the opportunity to work with world-renowned experts at the law school and the College of Liberal Arts and Sciences in a demanding and varied interdisciplinary study of global affairs and social justice. The law school has also created a **Law and Public Policy Certificate Program**, a flexible program in which students may enroll in a diverse collection of courses with faculty at the law school and within the University of Connecticut's Department of Public Policy.

The **Semester in Washington, DC**, places selected students in selected federal agencies, legislative offices, or nonprofit groups for one semester of service.

Career Planning

Connecticut operates a comprehensive career planning office for the benefit of students and alumni. The school offers a geographically diverse on-campus interviewing program, extensive individual and group counseling, a resource library, job listings, employment information sessions, and newsletters.

The school holds three off-campus interview programs each fall in Washington, DC; Boston; and New York City, and schedules on-campus interviews throughout the year. In addition, the school participates in several off-site job fairs.

Within six months of graduation, 89.9 percent of the Class of 2009 were employed, including 12.3 percent in judicial clerkships.

Character and Fitness

In accordance with Section 504(a) of the American Bar Association's Standards for Approval of Law Schools, applicants to the Law School should understand that there are character, fitness, and other qualifications for admission to the bar. Applicants are therefore encouraged, prior to matriculation, to determine what those requirements are in the states in which the applicant intends to practice. Additional information is available at the website of the National Conference of Bar Examiners. Please also review the Admission to the Bar section of the University of Connecticut School of Law Student Handbook.

Services for Students With Disabilities

The director of student services, Dr. Jane Thierfeld Brown, works with students with disabilities in the development and implementation of reasonable accommodations to allow access to the school's physical facilities as well as its educational and extracurricular programs.

Students with disabilities who are considering applying or who have been admitted to the School of Law are invited to tour the campus. Students may contact the dean's office for discussion of accommodations.

APPLICANT PROFILE

University of Connecticut School of Law
This grid includes only full-time applicants with LSAT scores earned under standard administrations.

LSAT Score	3.75 +		3.50–3.74		3.25–3.49		3.00–3.24		2.75–2.99		2.50–2.74		2.25–2.49		2.00–2.24		Below 2.00		No GPA		Total	
	Apps	Adm	Apps	Adm	Apps	Adm	Apps	Adm	Apps	Adm	Apps	Adm	Apps	Adm	Apps	Adm	Apps	Adm	Apps	Adm	Apps	Adm
175–180	1	1	1	1	1	1	0	0	1	0	0	0	0	0	0	0	0	0	0	0	4	3
170–174	7	4	12	9	11	6	6	1	3	1	4	0	0	0	1	0	0	0	0	0	44	21
165–169	33	24	49	42	41	28	41	14	20	6	10	2	3	0	2	0	2	0	5	1	206	117
160–164	93	71	164	116	176	86	105	29	48	7	18	4	13	2	6	0	1	0	5	3	629	318
155–159	93	16	176	31	175	22	115	9	50	6	22	0	12	0	4	0	1	0	14	0	662	84
150–154	41	10	98	15	128	8	87	11	58	2	19	2	10	0	5	0	2	0	7	1	455	49
145–149	16	1	34	1	50	3	46	1	26	0	22	1	8	0	3	0	2	0	8	2	215	9
140–144	11	0	17	1	22	1	21	1	18	0	16	0	10	0	4	0	1	0	3	0	123	3
135–139	3	0	0	0	7	0	14	0	8	0	5	0	4	0	3	0	1	0	0	0	45	0
130–134	0	0	1	0	1	0	0	0	3	0	2	0	2	0	0	0	1	0	0	0	10	0
125–129	0	0	0	0	0	0	0	0	1	0	1	0	0	0	0	0	0	0	0	0	2	0
120–124	0	0	0	0	0	0	0	0	0	0	0	0	0	0	1	0	0	0	0	0	1	0
Total	298	127	552	216	612	155	435	66	236	22	119	9	62	2	29	0	11	0	42	7	2396	604

Apps = Number of Applicants
Adm = Number Admitted
Reflects 99% of total applicant pool; highest LSAT data reported.

CORNELL LAW SCHOOL

Myron Taylor Hall
Ithaca, NY 14853-4901
Phone: 607.255.5141
E-mail: lawadmit@lawschool.cornell.edu; Website: www.lawschool.cornell.edu

ABA Approved Since 1923

The Basics

Type of school	Private
Term	Semester
Application deadline	2/1
Application fee	$80
Financial aid deadline	3/15
Can first year start other than fall?	No
Student to faculty ratio	10.4 to 1
# of housing spaces available restricted to law students	48
graduate housing for which law students are eligible	150

Faculty and Administrators

	Total		Men		Women		Minorities	
	Spr	Fall	Spr	Fall	Spr	Fall	Spr	Fall
Full-time	45	50	31	33	14	17	7	9
Other full-time	1	1	0	0	1	1	0	0
Deans, librarians, & others who teach	10	11	4	5	6	6	1	1
Part-time	19	30	17	22	2	8	0	5
Total	75	92	52	60	23	32	8	15

JD Enrollment and Ethnicity

	Men #	%	Women #	%	Full-Time #	%	Part-Time #	%	1st-Year #	%	Total #	%	JD Degs. Awd.
All Hispanics	35	11.3	37	12.1	72	11.7	0	0.0	28	13.7	72	11.7	9
Am. Ind./AK Nat.	7	2.3	3	1.0	10	1.6	0	0.0	2	1.0	10	1.6	2
Asian	29	9.4	58	19.0	87	14.1	0	0.0	29	14.1	87	14.1	22
Black/Af. Am.	16	5.2	24	7.9	40	6.5	0	0.0	11	5.4	40	6.5	10
Nat. HI/Pac. Isl.	0	0.0	0	0.0	0	0.0	0	0.0	0	0.0	0	0.0	0
2 or more races	1	0.3	8	2.6	9	1.5	0	0.0	9	4.4	9	1.5	0
Subtotal (minor.)	88	28.4	130	42.6	218	35.4	0	0.0	79	38.5	218	35.4	43
Nonres. Alien	17	5.5	29	9.5	46	7.5	0	0.0	8	3.9	46	7.5	0
White/Cauc.	205	66.1	146	47.9	351	57.1	0	0.0	118	57.6	351	57.1	141
Unknown	0	0.0	0	0.0	0	0.0	0	0.0	0	0.0	0	0.0	0
Total	310	50.4	305	49.6	615	100.0	0	0.0	205	33.3	615		192

Curriculum

	Full-Time	Part-Time
Typical first-year section size	102	0
Is there typically a "small section" of the first-year class, other than Legal Writing, taught by full-time faculty	Yes	No
If yes, typical size offered last year	34	
# of classroom course titles beyond first-year curriculum	139	

# of upper division courses, excluding seminars, with an enrollment:	Under 25	50
	25–49	24
	50–74	8
	75–99	5
	100+	6

# of seminars	45	
# of seminar positions available	709	
# of seminar positions filled	584	0
# of positions available in simulation courses	198	
# of simulation positions filled	153	0
# of positions available in faculty supervised clinical courses	172	
# of faculty supervised clinical positions filled	165	0
# involved in field placements	60	0
# involved in law journals	312	0
# involved in moot court or trial competitions	177	0
# of credit hours required to graduate	84	

Transfers

Transfers in	0
Transfers out	15

Tuition and Fees

	Resident	Nonresident
Full-time	$51,150	$51,150
Part-time		
Tuition Guarantee Program		N

Living Expenses

Estimated living expenses for singles

Living on campus	Living off campus	Living at home
$18,600	$18,600	$18,600

ABA Approved Since 1923

GPA and LSAT Scores

	Total	Full-Time	Part-Time
# of apps	6,269	6,269	0
# of offers	1,083	1,083	0
# of matrics	205	205	0
75% GPA	3.80	3.80	0.00
Median GPA	3.68	3.68	0.00
25% GPA	3.55	3.55	0.00
75% LSAT	169	169	0
Median LSAT	168	168	0
25% LSAT	166	166	0

Grants and Scholarships (from prior year)

	Total #	Total %	Full-Time #	Full-Time %	Part-Time #	Part-Time %
Total # of students	622		622		0	
Total # receiving grants	241	38.7	241	38.7	0	0.0
Less than 1/2 tuition	178	28.6	178	28.6	0	0.0
Half to full tuition	63	10.1	63	10.1	0	0.0
Full tuition	0	0.0	0	0.0	0	0.0
More than full tuition	0	0.0	0	0.0	0	0.0
Median grant amount			$18,000		$0	

Informational and Library Resources

Total amount spent on library materials	$1,551,161
Study seating capacity inside the library	422
# of full-time equivalent professional librarians	8
Hours per week library is open	132
# of open, wired connections available to students	32
# of networked computers available for use by students	63
Has wireless network?	Y
Requires computer?	N

JD Attrition (from prior year)

	Academic #	Other #	Total #	Total %
1st year	0	16	16	7.8
2nd year	0	0	0	0.0
3rd year	0	0	0	0.0
4th year	0	0	0	0.0

Employment (9 months after graduation)

	Total	Percentage
Employment status known	195	100.0
Employment status unknown	0	0.0
Employed	190	97.4
Pursuing graduate degrees	0	0.0
Unemployed (seeking, not seeking, or studying for the bar)	5	2.6
Type of Employment		
# employed in law firms	162	85.3
# employed in business and industry	1	0.5
# employed in government	1	0.5
# employed in public interest	3	1.6
# employed as judicial clerks	17	8.9
# employed in academia	6	3.2
Geographic Location		
# employed in state	112	58.9
# employed outside the US	3	1.6
# of states where employed	17	

Bar Passage Rates

First-time takers	187	Reporting %	79.14
Average school %	90.54	Average state %	84.53
Average pass difference	6.01		

Jurisdiction	Takers	Passers	Pass %	State %	Diff %
New York	126	118	93.65	86.51	7.14
California	22	16	72.73	73.19	–0.46

CORNELL LAW SCHOOL

Myron Taylor Hall
Ithaca, NY 14853-4901
Phone: 607.255.5141
E-mail: lawadmit@lawschool.cornell.edu; Website: www.lawschool.cornell.edu

Lawyers in the Best Sense

When Cornell University's founding president, Andrew Dickson White, began to lay plans for a law department at Cornell University, he wrote that he wanted to educate "not swarms of hastily prepared pettifoggers, but a fair number of well-trained, large-minded, morally based *lawyers in the best sense . . .*" He hoped graduates of the school would become "a blessing to the country, at the bar, on the bench, and in various public bodies." More than a century since President White's vision, this ideal still holds true. A small, top-tier law school located in beautiful surroundings, Cornell draws on, and contributes to, the resources of a great university, consistently producing well-rounded lawyers and accomplished practitioners cut from a different cloth. Cornell is a national center of learning located in Ithaca, New York, the heart of the Finger Lakes region of New York State. The law school's small classes, broad curriculum, and distinguished faculty, combined with the advantages of being part of one of the world's leading research universities, make it ideal for those who value both depth and breadth in their legal studies. Students find Ithaca to be a safe and nonstressful, yet culturally rich, environment in which to pursue legal studies.

Enrollment/Student Body

Sixty percent of Cornell's entering students have taken one or more years between completion of their undergraduate degree and enrollment in law school. Selective admission standards, combined with an emphasis on applicants' unique records and achievements, ensure that the student body is made up of people with wide-ranging interests, skills, concerns, and backgrounds.

Library, Physical Facilities, and Computing

The law school is located in the renovated and expanded Myron Taylor Hall, at the heart of the scenic 740-acre Cornell University campus. Hughes Hall, the law school dormitory, is adjacent to the main law school building and contains single rooms for about 45 students and a dining facility.

Cornell is one of the nation's leaders in the development and support of electronic legal research. It combines outstanding collections with professional expertise and access to worldwide electronic information sources for Anglo-American, as well as foreign and international law. Students have access to the full array of Internet services. The law school's multiple-node network, wireless network, and computer terminals are available to students for word processing, legal research, statistical analysis, and database management. Students also have access to the many satellite computer clusters and mainframe facilities located on the university campus.

Faculty

Cornell's faculty are known not only as prolific scholars but also as great teachers. Tenured and tenure-track faculty teach and produce scholarship in their area of law; clinical faculty run client-focused and simulation courses centered around legal aid and several specialty clinics; and a large number of visitors, associated faculty from other university divisions, and adjunct faculty teach at the school each year. Many of the latter group are legal scholars and professors from other countries who teach in the law school's significant international program.

Curriculum/Clinical Studies

Cornell offers a national law curriculum leading to the JD degree. First-year students take a group of required courses and an intensive lawyering course stressing a variety of legal research, writing, and advocacy techniques. After the first year, students may choose from a wide range of elective courses, including many seminars and problem courses.

The Cornell Legal Aid Clinic, offering legal services to individuals financially unable to employ an attorney, provides students with the chance to engage in the supervised practice of law under the direction of experienced attorneys. Clinical faculty also conduct a variety of other specialized clinics and skills courses within the regular curriculum. Students can select from a bevy of clinical courses, such as the Public Interest Clinic (three different levels); the Immigration Appellate Law and Advocacy Clinic; Capital Punishment: Post Conviction Litigation Clinic; Criminal Defense Trial Clinic; Indigent Representation; International Human Rights Clinic; Labor Law Clinic; Prosecution Trial Clinic; Regulation Room; Securities Law Clinic; Water Law Clinic; and US Attorney's Office Clinic.

Joint Degrees

Being part of a world-renowned university, and the interdisciplinary environment it provides, is of great benefit. Cornell Law School and Cornell University offer many opportunities for combined-degree programs, including both three- and four-year programs for the JD/MBA (Business degree from the Johnson School of Graduate Management); JD/MPA (Public Affairs degree from the Cornell Institute of Public Affairs); JD/MILR (Labor Relations degree from the School of Industrial and Labor Relations); JD/MRP (Regional Planning degree from the College of Architecture, Art, and Planning); and a JD/MA or PhD in a variety of fields (Master's or PhD degree from the Graduate School). Law students can also take as many as 12 credits outside of the law school for law school credit.

International Legal Studies

The Berger International Legal Studies Program is one of the country's oldest and most distinguished programs in international legal education. The Clarke Program in East Asian Law and Culture brings an exciting interdisciplinary and humanistic focus to the study of law in East Asia. Cornell's comprehensive program features a unique JD specialization opportunity; a three-year JD/LLM degree in International and Comparative Law; a four-year JD/Master en Droit (French law degree) program; a three-year JD/MLLP (German law degree) program; a three-year JD/Master in Global Business Law; a Paris summer institute with the Sorbonne Law School at the Université Paris 1 (Panthéon-Sorbonne); a comprehensive speaker series; Mori, Hamada, and Matsumoto (Tokyo law firm) Faculty Exchange; Conseil d'Etat Clerkship (French Supreme Court Clerkship); a founding member of the Turin

Interuniversity Centre; a large number of visiting foreign professors and scholars; a weekly luncheon discussion series; international moot court competitions; law clinics; internships; and a leading journal of international and comparative law edited by students. Students have the option to spend one semester abroad at a partner law school (we have agreements with 15 partner schools in 11 different countries), or to design an individual "term away" at a foreign law facility with which Cornell is not partnered.

In addition, the Clarke Initiative for Law and Development in the Middle East sponsors seminars, colloquia, and lectures and supports student and faculty exchanges with institutions in the region.

Programs and Projects

Cornell Law School is the home for several unique programs and projects of interest to students. These programs and projects include the following: Avon Global Center for Women and Justice (improve access to justice in an effort to eliminate violence against women and girls); Death Penalty Project (clinics and symposia related to capital punishment); e-Rulemaking Initiative (technology and practice of e-rulemaking); Clarke Scholars Program (visiting scholars); ILR-Law School Program on Conflict Resolution (raising the standards of arbitration, mediation and other methods of alternative dispute resolution); Institute for Social Sciences; Journal of Empirical Legal Studies (only legal journal dedicated exclusively to empirical legal scholarship); Lay Participation in Law International Research Collaborative (transnational collaborative team dedicated to research on lay participation in court systems); Legal Information Institute (world's leading investigator of new ways to perform electronic legal research); Clarke Business Law Institute (classes, more faculty, seminars, conferences, and other programming); BR Legal (represent start-up companies); and Empirical Studies Project (empirical study of court cases).

Student Activities

Student-edited law journals include the Cornell Law Review (published continuously since 1916), the Cornell International Law Journal (established in 1967), and the Cornell Journal of Law and Public Policy. Student organizations and activities include American Constitution Society, Asian Pacific American Law Students Association, Black Law Students Association, Briggs Society of International Law, Business Law Society, Christian Legal Society, Cornell Advocates for Human Rights, Cornell Animal Legal Defense Fund, Cornell Sports and Entertainment Law Consortium, Cornell Law Student Association, Cornell Law United, Cornell Law Democrats, Cornell Law Republicans, Environmental Law Society, Federalist Society, J. Reuben Clark Law Society, Jewish Law Student Association, LAMBDA, Latino American Law Students Association, Law Students for Reproductive Justice, MS JD Board, Moot Court Board, National Lawyers Guild, Native American Law Students Association, Phi Alpha Delta, Phi Delta Phi, Public Interest Law Union, South Asian Law Students Association, Students for Marriage Equality, Transfer Network Association, and the Women's Law Coalition.

Expenses and Financial Aid

Cornell offers an institutional-based financial aid program. About 50 percent of students receive scholarship aid (awards averaging more than $14,500 per year), with a higher percentage receiving government-backed loans.

Our Public Interest Low Income Protection Plan, one of the most generous of such programs, assists those choosing qualifying public interest law jobs through the use of a moderated loan repayment plan and loan forgiveness.

Career Services

Cornell's students continue to be among the most recruited in the country. Every fall, hundreds of employers from across the country recruit Cornell students on campus and at job fairs in Boston, Los Angeles, New York, and Washington, DC. A professionally staffed Career Services Office provides employment counseling to students and serves as a liaison to legal employers. In addition, Cornell has two full-time professional staff members (Assistant Dean and Director for Public Service) dedicated to public interest job opportunities and counseling.

APPLICANT PROFILE

Admission to Cornell Law is very competitive. Members of the most recent entering class had an aggregate 3.70 undergraduate grade-point average and median LSAT scores that placed them in the 97th percentile nationwide (168). But Cornell Law does not evaluate candidates by the numbers alone. The admission committee carefully considers such nonquantifiable factors as extracurricular and community activities, life experience and work background, and recommendations. Cornell Law subscribes to the university's 130-year tradition of affirmative action, and members of traditionally underrepresented minority groups are encouraged to mention their status where they think it is relevant. The decision to offer admission ultimately rests on whether the committee is convinced that the applicant will be an energetic, productive, and successful member of the Cornell Law community and eventually, the legal profession.

CREIGHTON UNIVERSITY SCHOOL OF LAW

2500 California Plaza
Omaha, NE 68178
Phone: 402.280.2586; Fax: 402.280.3161
E-mail: lawadmit@creighton.edu; Website: www.creighton.edu/law

ABA
Approved
Since
1924

The Basics

Type of school	Private
Term	Semester
Application deadline	5/1
Application fee	$50
Financial aid deadline	7/1
Can first year start other than fall?	No
Student to faculty ratio	19.5 to 1
# of housing spaces available restricted to law students	
graduate housing for which law students are eligible	

Faculty and Administrators

	Total		Men		Women		Minorities	
	Spr	Fall	Spr	Fall	Spr	Fall	Spr	Fall
Full-time	20	20	15	15	5	5	2	2
Other full-time	3	3	2	2	1	1	1	1
Deans, librarians, & others who teach	12	12	8	8	4	4	1	1
Part-time	21	21	15	11	6	10	1	1
Total	56	56	40	36	16	20	5	5

Curriculum

	Full-Time	Part-Time
Typical first-year section size	87	0
Is there typically a "small section" of the first-year class, other than Legal Writing, taught by full-time faculty	No	No
If yes, typical size offered last year		
# of classroom course titles beyond first-year curriculum	82	
# of upper division courses, excluding seminars, with an enrollment: Under 25	76	
25–49	28	
50–74	9	
75–99	4	
100+	0	
# of seminars	13	
# of seminar positions available	250	
# of seminar positions filled	210	0
# of positions available in simulation courses	545	
# of simulation positions filled	498	0
# of positions available in faculty supervised clinical courses	32	
# of faculty supervised clinical positions filled	22	0
# involved in field placements	56	0
# involved in law journals	38	0
# involved in moot court or trial competitions	54	0
# of credit hours required to graduate	94	

JD Enrollment and Ethnicity

	Men		Women		Full-Time		Part-Time		1st-Year		Total		JD Degs. Awd.
	#	%	#	%	#	%	#	%	#	%	#	%	
All Hispanics	9	3.2	5	2.6	14	3.1	0	0.0	7	4.7	14	3.0	5
Am. Ind./AK Nat.	0	0.0	1	0.5	1	0.2	0	0.0	0	0.0	1	0.2	0
Asian	11	3.9	9	4.7	20	4.4	0	0.0	5	3.4	20	4.2	5
Black/Af. Am.	7	2.5	6	3.1	11	2.4	2	16.7	5	3.4	13	2.8	1
Nat. HI/Pac. Isl.	0	0.0	0	0.0	0	0.0	0	0.0	0	0.0	0	0.0	0
2 or more races	0	0.0	1	0.5	1	0.2	0	0.0	1	0.7	1	0.2	0
Subtotal (minor.)	27	9.7	22	11.5	47	10.2	2	16.7	18	12.1	49	10.4	11
Nonres. Alien	0	0.0	0	0.0	0	0.0	0	0.0	0	0.0	0	0.0	0
White/Cauc.	251	90.0	169	88.0	410	89.3	10	83.3	131	87.9	420	89.2	128
Unknown	1	0.4	1	0.5	2	0.4	0	0.0	0	0.0	2	0.4	1
Total	279	59.2	192	40.8	459	97.5	12	2.5	149	31.6	471		140

Transfers

Transfers in	3
Transfers out	6

Tuition and Fees

	Resident	Nonresident
Full-time	$31,386	$31,386
Part-time	$18,292	$18,292
Tuition Guarantee Program	N	

Living Expenses

Estimated living expenses for singles

Living on campus	Living off campus	Living at home
$15,880	$15,880	$6,880

CREIGHTON UNIVERSITY SCHOOL OF LAW

ABA
Approved
Since
1924

GPA and LSAT Scores

	Total	Full-Time	Part-Time
# of apps	1,368	1,298	70
# of offers	664	648	16
# of matrics	144	138	6
75% GPA	3.55	3.56	3.28
Median GPA	3.29	3.30	2.90
25% GPA	2.89	2.92	2.69
75% LSAT	157	157	154
Median LSAT	154	154	154
25% LSAT	151	151	149

Grants and Scholarships (from prior year)

	Total		Full-Time		Part-Time	
	#	%	#	%	#	%
Total # of students	484		471		13	
Total # receiving grants	227	46.9	227	48.2	0	0.0
Less than 1/2 tuition	169	34.9	169	35.9	0	0.0
Half to full tuition	41	8.5	41	8.7	0	0.0
Full tuition	15	3.1	15	3.2	0	0.0
More than full tuition	2	0.4	2	0.4	0	0.0
Median grant amount			$8,000		$0	

Informational and Library Resources

Total amount spent on library materials	$1,481,241
Study seating capacity inside the library	371
# of full-time equivalent professional librarians	6
Hours per week library is open	106
# of open, wired connections available to students	176
# of networked computers available for use by students	44
Has wireless network?	Y
Requires computer?	N

JD Attrition (from prior year)

	Academic	Other	Total	
	#	#	#	%
1st year	5	11	16	8.7
2nd year	0	1	1	0.6
3rd year	0	0	0	0.0
4th year	0	0	0	0.0

Employment (9 months after graduation)

	Total	Percentage
Employment status known	143	97.9
Employment status unknown	3	2.1
Employed	124	86.7
Pursuing graduate degrees	5	3.5
Unemployed (seeking, not seeking, or studying for the bar)	12	8.4
Type of Employment		
# employed in law firms	61	49.2
# employed in business and industry	27	21.8
# employed in government	12	9.7
# employed in public interest	10	8.1
# employed as judicial clerks	11	8.9
# employed in academia	3	2.4
Geographic Location		
# employed in state	63	50.8
# employed outside the US	0	0.0
# of states where employed	22	

Bar Passage Rates

First-time takers	139		Reporting %	100.00
Average school %	91.38		Average state %	88.40
Average pass difference	2.98			

Jurisdiction	Takers	Passers	Pass %	State %	Diff %
Iowa	43	43	100.00	93.17	6.83
Nebraska	32	28	87.50	87.93	–0.43
Colorado	13	13	100.00	85.67	14.33
Utah	9	9	100.00	88.94	11.06
Others (17)	42	34	80.95		

CREIGHTON UNIVERSITY SCHOOL OF LAW

2500 California Plaza
Omaha, NE 68178
Phone: 402.280.2586; Fax: 402.280.3161
E-mail: lawadmit@creighton.edu; Website: www.creighton.edu/law

The School of Law

The School of Law, established in 1904, has been a member of the Association of American Law Schools (AALS) since 1907 and was approved by the American Bar Association (ABA) in 1924. Alumni from the law school are practicing in all 50 states and in several foreign countries. The law school's current enrollment is 472. Students come from 39 states, 3 foreign countries, and 165 undergraduate institutions.

Introduction

Creighton University, a privately endowed and supported Jesuit university, was founded in 1878. Creighton is the most diverse educational institution of its size in the nation. In addition to the School of Law, Creighton has a School of Medicine, School of Dentistry, School of Pharmacy and Health Professions, School of Nursing, College of Business Administration, College of Arts and Sciences, and a Graduate School, making it the center of professional education in the Midwest. The university is located just blocks from downtown Omaha, a metropolitan area with a population of approximately 800,000. Known as the River City, Omaha is the heart of the Midlands and the largest metroplex between Chicago and Denver.

Faculty

The faculty is composed of 27 full-time professors and a group of part-time specialists chosen from the bench and bar. Creighton's full-time faculty members have earned reputations as outstanding classroom teachers. In addition, faculty scholarship brings to the classroom insights gained through the publication of leading texts and thought-provoking articles. A distinguished adjunct faculty of judges and practicing attorneys teach courses in specialty areas. Faculty offices surround the Law School Commons, making them easily accessible to students. Faculty members maintain an open-door policy that encourages students to drop in to discuss the latest case, current events, or the newest restaurant in town.

Library and Physical Facilities

The School of Law is entirely contained in the Ahmanson Law Center. The attractive Klutznick Law Library/McGrath North Mullin and Kratz Legal Research Center encompasses 45,480 assignable square feet and is located on both levels of the Law Center. Wireless network coverage is campus-wide. Many tables and carrels are also wired with both power and data connections. A variety of comfortable individual, group study, reading room, and computer-use seating options are available in a pleasant, service-oriented setting. In addition to other legal information specialists, the Law Library employs four lawyer-librarians (JD/MLS librarians) who each deliver reference service and teach. The Law Library provides access to one of the finest legal collections in the region. It houses a large, carefully selected array of print and electronic Anglo-American, comparative, and international law resources. Other features of the library include three computer labs, two reading rooms, and an inspiring rare book collection comprised primarily of British legal texts and treatises from the sixteenth to the nineteenth centuries.

Areas of Concentration

Students may earn a certificate indicating that they focused their studies in a particular area of concentration. Areas of concentration are (a) Business Law, (b) Criminal Law and Procedure, (c) International and Comparative Law, and (d) Litigation. The curriculum prepares students for the practice of law in any state.

Combined-Degree Programs

Creighton's School of Law, College of Business Administration, and Graduate School offer a JD/MBA, a JD/MS in Information Technology Management, a JD/MS in Negotiation and Dispute Resolution, a JD/MA in International Relations, and a JD/MS in Government Organization and Leadership.

Clinics and Internships

The Milton R. Abrahams Legal Clinic provides third-year students with the opportunity to learn the lawyering process in a way that is not provided in most law school courses. Clinic students represent low-income clients on a variety of civil matters that vary in complexity. Students conduct interviews, prepare pleadings, conduct legal research and writing, and appear in court for hearings and trials. Clinic students are certified to practice law under the supervision of clinic faculty and licensed attorneys.

The Community Economic Development (CED) Law Clinic provides third-year students with an opportunity to work on a broad range of transactional and business law issues affecting community development. Students in the CED Clinic represent a client base of small business owners and nonprofit and community-based organizations that serve low-income communities across the state of Nebraska and Western Iowa. Students will get valuable hands-on experience while helping entrepreneurs create and maintain jobs.

Students may also participate in a broad variety of internships with city, county, and federal legal offices in the Omaha area.

Werner Institute for Negotiation and Dispute Resolution

The Werner Institute, the most richly endowed program of its kind in the country, is an emerging national leader in the field of conflict resolution with an interdisciplinary curriculum leading to graduate certificates and master's degrees in the field. The institute places a strong emphasis on a systems approach to conflict resolution and focuses on the preparation of leaders in the field with specialized applications in areas of greatest need, such as conflict within and among organizations, businesses, health care, and communities.

Student Activities

The Student Bar Association (SBA) is the student government of the law school. The purpose of the organization is to make law students aware of the obligations and opportunities existing for lawyers through SBA activities, promote a consciousness of professional responsibility, and provide a forum for student activities. The *Creighton Law Review*, edited and managed by students, is a scholarly legal journal that is circulated nationally and internationally. The school has over 20 different active student organizations.

Financial Aid and Scholarships

Creighton University School of Law offers two types of financial aid: merit-based scholarships and federal government loans. Students seeking financial aid and scholarships must complete the Free Application for Federal Student Aid (FAFSA). Creighton University participates in the US Department of Education's Direct Loan Program. All first-year scholarships have merit requirements, including, but not limited to, LSAT score and undergraduate grade-point average. Admitted applicants with an LSAT score and undergraduate grade-point average above Creighton's medians for the previous year will receive strong consideration for scholarship assistance. Applicants who qualify for a scholarship will be notified at the time of acceptance.

Frances M. Ryan Diversity Scholarship Program

The School of Law actively recruits minority students and has a substantial diversity scholarship program. Applicants who wish to be considered for a Ryan Diversity Scholarship must make note of it on their admission application.

Career Development Office

The Career Development Office provides a full array of services to Creighton Law students, including individual career counseling, a law alumni network stretching from coast to coast, on-campus and off-campus interview programs, alumni networking events in a variety of cities nationwide, and a dynamic website that allows students to explore career opportunities throughout the world. Nine months after graduation, nearly 92 percent of the class of 2009 were employed or enrolled in a full-time degree program. Graduates from the class of 2009 are working in the areas of business, government, private practice, and public interest, and as judicial clerks, in 23 states and the District of Columbia.

APPLICANT PROFILE

Creighton University School of Law
This grid includes only applicants who earned 120–180 LSAT scores under standard administrations.

LSAT Score	3.75 +		3.50–3.74		3.25–3.49		3.00–3.24		2.75–2.99		2.50–2.74		2.25–2.49		2.00–2.24		Below 2.00		No GPA		Total	
	Apps	Adm	Apps	Adm	Apps	Adm	Apps	Adm	Apps	Adm	Apps	Adm	Apps	Adm	Apps	Adm	Apps	Adm	Apps	Adm	Apps	Adm
175–180	0	0	0	0	0	0	0	0	0	0	0	0	0	0	0	0	0	0	0	0	0	0
170–174	3	2	2	2	1	1	0	0	0	0	0	0	0	0	0	0	0	0	0	0	6	5
165–169	8	8	4	3	6	6	0	0	4	4	1	1	2	2	1	1	1	1	1	1	28	27
160–164	35	35	28	28	25	25	23	22	8	8	6	6	6	5	5	3	1	1	3	2	140	135
155–159	44	43	51	49	60	59	42	39	30	26	23	16	15	9	3	3	2	1	3	3	273	248
150–154	52	44	72	59	118	66	69	30	63	14	30	9	14	4	5	0	1	0	5	1	429	227
145–149	24	7	51	4	70	3	54	2	48	3	31	0	19	0	8	0	1	0	4	0	310	19
140–144	8	0	13	0	20	0	33	0	19	0	20	0	8	0	1	0	1	0	4	0	127	0
135–139	4	0	2	0	5	0	4	0	6	0	7	0	7	0	4	0	1	0	3	0	43	0
130–134	0	0	0	0	1	0	3	0	4	0	5	0	1	0	1	0	1	0	2	0	18	0
125–129	0	0	0	0	0	0	0	0	1	0	1	0	0	0	1	0	0	0	0	0	3	0
120–124	0	0	0	0	0	0	0	0	0	0	0	0	0	0	0	0	0	0	0	0	0	0
Total	178	139	223	145	306	160	228	93	183	55	124	32	72	20	29	7	9	3	25	7	1377	661

Apps = Number of Applicants
Adm = Number Admitted
Reflects 99% of the total applicant pool; highest LSAT data reported.

UNIVERSITY OF DAYTON SCHOOL OF LAW

300 College Park, 112 Keller Hall
Dayton, OH 45469-2760
Phone: 937.229.3555; Fax: 937.229.4194
E-mail: lawinfo@notes.udayton.edu; Website: http://law.udayton.edu

ABA
Approved
Since
1975

The Basics

Type of school	Private
Term	Semester
Application deadline	3/1 5/1
Application fee	$50
Financial aid deadline	3/1 5/1
Can first year start other than fall?	Yes
Student to faculty ratio	17.2 to 1
# of housing spaces available	
restricted to law students	24
graduate housing for which law students are eligible	52

Faculty and Administrators

	Total		Men		Women		Minorities	
	Spr	Fall	Spr	Fall	Spr	Fall	Spr	Fall
Full-time	23	25	14	14	9	11	5	4
Other full-time	2	2	0	0	2	2	0	0
Deans, librarians, & others who teach	8	8	3	3	5	5	2	2
Part-time	29	22	24	15	5	7	2	2
Total	62	57	41	32	21	25	9	8

Curriculum

	Full-Time	Part-Time
Typical first-year section size	90	0
Is there typically a "small section" of the first-year class, other than Legal Writing, taught by full-time faculty	No	No
If yes, typical size offered last year		
# of classroom course titles beyond first-year curriculum	74	

# of upper division courses, excluding seminars, with an enrollment:		
	Under 25	79
	25–49	16
	50–74	7
	75–99	8
	100+	2

# of seminars	11	
# of seminar positions available	220	
# of seminar positions filled	129	0
# of positions available in simulation courses	436	
# of simulation positions filled	330	0
# of positions available in faculty supervised clinical courses	21	
# of faculty supervised clinical positions filled	21	0
# involved in field placements	141	0
# involved in law journals	42	0
# involved in moot court or trial competitions	17	0
# of credit hours required to graduate	90	

JD Enrollment and Ethnicity

	Men		Women		Full-Time		Part-Time		1st-Year		Total		JD Degs. Awd.
	#	%	#	%	#	%	#	%	#	%	#	%	
All Hispanics	6	1.9	5	2.5	11	2.1	0	0.0	3	1.5	11	2.1	8
Am. Ind./AK Nat.	0	0.0	1	0.5	1	0.2	0	0.0	0	0.0	1	0.2	1
Asian	4	1.2	7	3.5	11	2.1	0	0.0	5	2.5	11	2.1	4
Black/Af. Am.	18	5.6	15	7.4	33	6.3	0	0.0	9	4.4	33	6.3	11
Nat. HI/Pac. Isl.	1	0.3	0	0.0	1	0.2	0	0.0	0	0.0	1	0.2	0
2 or more races	3	0.9	2	1.0	5	1.0	0	0.0	4	2.0	5	1.0	0
Subtotal (minor.)	32	9.9	30	14.9	62	11.8	0	0.0	21	10.3	62	11.8	24
Nonres. Alien	3	0.9	3	1.5	6	1.1	0	0.0	1	0.5	6	1.1	1
White/Cauc.	287	89.1	169	83.7	456	87.0	0	0.0	181	89.2	456	87.0	118
Unknown	0	0.0	0	0.0	0	0.0	0	0.0	0	0.0	0	0.0	0
Total	322	61.5	202	38.5	524	100.0	0	0.0	203	38.7	524		143

Transfers

Transfers in	3
Transfers out	24

Tuition and Fees

	Resident	Nonresident
Full-time	$33,674	$33,674
Part-time		
Tuition Guarantee Program	N	

Living Expenses

Estimated living expenses for singles

Living on campus	Living off campus	Living at home
$15,500	$15,500	$15,500

UNIVERSITY OF DAYTON SCHOOL OF LAW

*ABA
Approved
Since
1975*

GPA and LSAT Scores

	Total	Full-Time	Part-Time
# of apps	2,147	2,147	0
# of offers	1,186	1,186	0
# of matrics	207	207	0
75% GPA	3.41	3.41	0.00
Median GPA	3.11	3.11	0.00
25% GPA	2.81	2.81	0.00
75% LSAT	154	154	0
Median LSAT	152	152	0
25% LSAT	150	150	0

Grants and Scholarships (from prior year)

	Total		Full-Time		Part-Time	
	#	%	#	%	#	%
Total # of students	500		500		0	
Total # receiving grants	272	54.4	272	54.4	0	0.0
Less than 1/2 tuition	255	51.0	255	51.0	0	0.0
Half to full tuition	17	3.4	17	3.4	0	0.0
Full tuition	0	0.0	0	0.0	0	0.0
More than full tuition	0	0.0	0	0.0	0	0.0
Median grant amount			$8,500		$0	

Informational and Library Resources

Total amount spent on library materials	$805,993
Study seating capacity inside the library	489
# of full-time equivalent professional librarians	4
Hours per week library is open	102
# of open, wired connections available to students	0
# of networked computers available for use by students	31
Has wireless network?	Y
Requires computer?	N

JD Attrition (from prior year)

	Academic	Other	Total	
	#	#	#	%
1st year	10	27	37	18.1
2nd year	4	1	5	3.4
3rd year	0	0	0	0.0
4th year	0	0	0	0.0

Employment (9 months after graduation)

	Total	Percentage
Employment status known	146	97.3
Employment status unknown	4	2.7
Employed	121	82.9
Pursuing graduate degrees	0	0.0
Unemployed (seeking, not seeking, or studying for the bar)	19	13.0
Type of Employment		
# employed in law firms	83	68.6
# employed in business and industry	14	11.6
# employed in government	10	8.3
# employed in public interest	4	3.3
# employed as judicial clerks	6	5.0
# employed in academia	4	3.3
Geographic Location		
# employed in state	75	62.0
# employed outside the US	0	0.0
# of states where employed	20	

Bar Passage Rates

First-time takers	151	Reporting %	71.52
Average school %	80.56	Average state %	86.10
Average pass difference	-5.54		

Jurisdiction	Takers	Passers	Pass %	State %	Diff %
Ohio	86	69	80.23	86.03	-5.80
Indiana	8	8	100.00	82.74	17.26
Illinois	7	5	71.43	90.89	-19.46
Kentucky	7	5	71.43	85.92	-14.49

UNIVERSITY OF DAYTON SCHOOL OF LAW

300 College Park, 112 Keller Hall
Dayton, OH 45469-2760
Phone: 937.229.3555; Fax: 937.229.4194
E-mail: lawinfo@notes.udayton.edu; Website: http://law.udayton.edu

Introduction and Mission

The mission of the School of Law is to enroll a diverse group of intellectually curious, self-disciplined, and well-motivated men and women, and to educate them in the substantive and procedural principles of public and private law. We seek to graduate highly qualified attorneys who will uphold the highest professional standards and recognize that service to others is the chief measure of professional competence.

We are a full-time JD program, providing a distinguished tradition of concern for the individual student in a supportive and professional environment. Our curriculum gives students a foundation in traditional courses but also helps them develop their skills with innovative programs such as our legal skills courses and curricular concentrations. Our diverse student body of 450 promotes ample opportunity for one-on-one interaction with faculty, staff, and fellow students, creating an atmosphere of collegiality and active involvement in a myriad of law school organizations. We also have LLM and MSL programs in Intellectual Property and Technology. The University of Dayton School of Law is accredited by the ABA and is a member of the AALS.

Keller Hall and the University of Dayton

Joseph E. Keller Hall is a 122,500-square-foot complex featuring a dramatic atrium, a variety of classroom space, and a spacious law library with technology integrated throughout the building. Ready access is provided via our wireless network from virtually any location in the law building. Every seat in the 325,000-volume **Zimmerman Law Library** has access to a power outlet. The school's wireless network is also accessible from every seat in the library. The library also contains a computer training center where students learn to conduct online and computer-based research. Group study rooms allow students to meet in groups of up to 20.

Founded in 1850, the **University of Dayton** enrolls more than 10,000 undergraduate and graduate students in a campus setting. Located minutes from the city's center, the campus contains a fitness center and provides student services, on-campus housing, child care, meal plans, and banking. On-campus housing is available for half of the entering law students within three blocks of the law school.

The Dayton Community

With a population of approximately 850,000, the Dayton Metro Area offers the many amenities of larger urban areas while retaining its scenic, lush, and green open spaces. As the birthplace of the Wright Brothers, the city offers a variety of flight-related museums and events, as well as a variety of other cultural and recreational activities. Housing is varied and affordable, as are shopping, restaurants, and entertainment districts. Many state and local parks are available for biking, swimming, hiking, and boating. If students want to explore beyond Dayton, they can reach Cincinnati or Columbus in a 50–75 minute drive, or the quaint towns of Yellow Springs, Waynesville, or Lebanon within a 30-minute drive from campus.

Curriculum and Programs

Summer or Fall Start—Entering students may choose between a May or an August start to begin their full load of first-year courses.

Two-, Two-and-a-half, or Three-Year Law Degree—Students may complete their studies in either five semesters (accelerated) or six semesters (traditional). The summer-start combined with the five-semester accelerated study option allows a student to earn a JD in two calendar years.

Curriculum—Dayton Law offers a traditional education that blends theory and practice with a focus on attaining essential lawyering and problem-solving skills. The emphasis on acquiring legal skills through real-world practical experience, capstone and clinic courses, and a required externship prepares students for a successful legal career. Students may choose from various curricular concentrations focused on particular areas of the law, and are awarded a certificate in their chosen area upon graduation and successful completion of required concentration courses.

Externships—An externship is a semester-long legal apprenticeship in a legal setting, such as a governmental agency, law firm, corporation, court, or legal aid office. An externship provides students the opportunity to practice their craft, to observe highly respected attorneys and judges at work, and to network with the legal community.

Capstone Courses—Upper-level capstone courses are designed as a synthesis and completion of previously studied material. In these courses, students demonstrate their ability to apply to real and simulated legal problems the substantive knowledge and practical skills acquired during their education.

Graduate Programs

Master of Laws (LLM) in Intellectual Property and Technology Law—This program is for students who already possess a JD and desire to further their legal expertise in the area of intellectual property.

Master of Study of Law (MSL) in Intellectual Property and Technology Law—This program is for students who do not possess a JD but desire to gain an in-depth understanding of intellectual property.

Faculty

With backgrounds that span a spectrum of legal endeavors, many of our faculty members are known nationally for their expertise and scholarship. As prominent scholars and leaders, our professors transfer their expertise to students both inside and outside of the classroom. Students consistently praise our faculty, not only for their outstanding teaching skills, but also for their constant involvement in, concern for, and support of students' lives.

Student Life

Collegiality, support, and a positive atmosphere distinguish our student body, which benefits from the diversity of classmates in race, age, gender, and background. Students may participate in organizations that help develop writing, research, and oral advocacy skills; those that speak to their mutual professional interests; or those that provide support of a student's personal and biographical background and interests. Our Student Bar Association is made up of officers and representatives from each class who oversee all student organizations and is the voice of student governance at the law school.

Career Services and Bar Passage

Our Career Services Office Assistant Dean and his staff are committed to providing comprehensive career planning and placement services to assist students with identifying and securing positions commensurate with each individual's interests and career goals. Over half of our students are employed in private practice and about one-third find positions in business, industry, the government, or the military. Our graduates are employed in most states and several countries. They take an active interest in the life of the law school, participating in panel discussions, mentor programs, and alumni events, as well as contributing their time and resources to various scholarship and fundraising activities.

Our graduates have been consistently successful in bar passage and attribute this success to our curriculum as well as to our excellent **Road to Bar Passage Program**. This program involves students from their first year of law school right through to the exam. A series of workshops informs students about bar examinations and how to prepare for them.

Admission

The Admissions Committee looks for a well-rounded and diverse group of students. Undergraduate GPA and LSAT score are highly considered, but commitment, motivation, leadership, and a breadth and depth of experiences are also a large part of the applicant review. Decisions are made on a rolling basis, beginning November 1 and continuing through late spring.

Financial Aid

Approximately half of the entering class receive scholarships. The majority of our scholarships are merit based, with the goal of diversifying the class also taken into consideration. Renewal of merit scholarships is dependent upon academic performance at the end of the preceding two semesters.

Federal Direct loans up to $20,500 are also available to our students. Alternative loans may also be used to cover the cost of a legal education, should scholarships and federal loans not do so. Federal and alternative loans are available pending a student's citizenship status and credit rating.

Prospective Students

Prospective students are encouraged to contact the Office of Admissions to schedule informational visits or obtain assistance with questions or concerns. Office hours are 8:30 AM to 4:30 PM, Monday through Friday.

APPLICANT PROFILE

University of Dayton School of Law
This grid includes only applicants who earned 120–180 LSAT scores under standard administrations.

LSAT Score	3.75 +		3.50–3.74		3.25–3.49		3.00–3.24		2.75–2.99		2.50–2.74		2.25–2.49		2.00–2.24		Below 2.00		No GPA		Total	
	Apps	Adm	Apps	Adm	Apps	Adm	Apps	Adm	Apps	Adm	Apps	Adm	Apps	Adm	Apps	Adm	Apps	Adm	Apps	Adm	Apps	Adm
175–180	0	0	0	0	0	0	0	0	0	0	0	0	0	0	0	0	0	0	0	0	0	0
170–174	0	0	1	1	0	0	1	1	0	0	0	0	1	1	0	0	0	0	0	0	3	3
165–169	3	3	1	1	3	2	4	4	0	0	0	0	3	1	0	0	1	0	0	0	15	11
160–164	15	15	23	23	27	26	24	23	10	10	9	9	6	5	2	2	0	0	1	1	117	114
155–159	43	42	42	39	58	55	55	52	51	47	31	25	22	16	2	2	1	0	0	0	305	278
150–154	60	58	91	84	110	104	119	112	119	107	64	57	31	20	11	4	3	0	5	0	613	546
145–149	41	11	77	25	135	34	132	32	113	22	69	6	22	3	12	1	3	0	8	0	612	134
140–144	8	0	22	2	38	1	48	1	41	0	24	0	8	0	3	0	0	0	3	0	195	4
135–139	2	0	4	0	11	0	10	0	15	0	7	0	5	0	4	0	1	0	3	0	62	0
130–134	1	0	0	0	2	0	5	0	4	0	2	0	0	0	2	0	1	0	2	0	19	0
125–129	0	0	0	0	0	0	1	0	0	0	1	0	1	0	1	0	0	0	0	0	4	0
120–124	0	0	0	0	0	0	0	0	0	0	0	0	0	0	0	0	0	0	1	0	1	0
Total	173	129	261	175	384	222	399	225	353	186	207	97	99	46	37	9	10	0	23	1	1946	1090

Apps = Number of Applicants
Adm = Number Admitted
Reflects 99% of the total applicant pool; highest LSAT data reported.

UNIVERSITY OF DENVER STURM COLLEGE OF LAW

2255 E. Evans Avenue, Suite 115
Denver, CO 80208
Phone: 303.871.6135; Fax: 303.871.6992
E-mail: admissions@law.du.edu; Website: www.law.du.edu

The Basics

Type of school	Private
Term	Semester
Application deadline	
Application fee	$60
Financial aid deadline	3/1
Can first year start other than fall?	No
Student to faculty ratio	12.7 to 1
# of housing spaces available restricted to law students	
graduate housing for which law students are eligible	21

Faculty and Administrators

	Total		Men		Women		Minorities	
	Spr	Fall	Spr	Fall	Spr	Fall	Spr	Fall
Full-time	60	57	32	29	28	28	14	13
Other full-time	5	5	3	3	2	2	0	0
Deans, librarians, & others who teach	12	12	7	7	5	5	3	3
Part-time	51	56	40	43	10	12	8	6
Total	128	130	82	82	45	47	25	22

Curriculum

	Full-Time	Part-Time
Typical first-year section size	80	65
Is there typically a "small section" of the first-year class, other than Legal Writing, taught by full-time faculty	Yes	Yes
If yes, typical size offered last year	40	40
# of classroom course titles beyond first-year curriculum	207	
# of upper division courses, excluding seminars, with an enrollment: Under 25	240	
25–49	48	
50–74	25	
75–99	7	
100+	2	
# of seminars	20	
# of seminar positions available	370	
# of seminar positions filled	326	44
# of positions available in simulation courses	272	
# of simulation positions filled	231	41
# of positions available in faculty supervised clinical courses	106	
# of faculty supervised clinical positions filled	99	7
# involved in field placements	324	28
# involved in law journals	163	17
# involved in moot court or trial competitions	44	2
# of credit hours required to graduate	90	

JD Enrollment and Ethnicity

	Men #	Men %	Women #	Women %	Full-Time #	Full-Time %	Part-Time #	Part-Time %	1st-Year #	1st-Year %	Total #	Total %	JD Degs. Awd.
All Hispanics	25	5.0	37	8.0	49	6.4	13	6.8	11	3.7	62	6.5	21
Am. Ind./AK Nat.	12	2.4	9	1.9	16	2.1	5	2.6	8	2.7	21	2.2	5
Asian	15	3.0	24	5.2	32	4.2	7	3.6	8	2.7	39	4.1	17
Black/Af. Am.	10	2.0	15	3.2	15	2.0	10	5.2	10	3.4	25	2.6	10
Nat. HI/Pac. Isl.	0	0.0	1	0.2	1	0.1	0	0.0	0	0.0	1	0.1	0
2 or more races	2	0.4	5	1.1	5	0.7	2	1.0	2	0.7	7	0.7	0
Subtotal (minor.)	64	12.9	91	19.6	118	15.4	37	19.3	39	13.1	155	16.1	56
Nonres. Alien	1	0.2	0	0.0	1	0.1	0	0.0	0	0.0	1	0.1	0
White/Cauc.	401	80.8	351	75.6	607	79.0	145	75.5	234	78.8	752	78.3	269
Unknown	30	6.0	22	4.7	42	5.5	10	5.2	24	8.1	52	5.4	25
Total	496	51.7	464	48.3	768	80.0	192	20.0	297	30.9	960		350

Transfers

Transfers in	26
Transfers out	9

Tuition and Fees

	Resident	Nonresident
Full-time	$37,152	$37,152
Part-time	$27,392	$27,392
Tuition Guarantee Program	N	

Living Expenses

Estimated living expenses for singles

Living on campus	Living off campus	Living at home
$16,707	$16,707	$16,707

UNIVERSITY OF DENVER STURM COLLEGE OF LAW

ABA
Approved
Since
1923

GPA and LSAT Scores

	Total	Full-Time	Part-Time
# of apps	3,129	2,782	347
# of offers	1,008	915	93
# of matrics	301	239	62
75% GPA	3.66	3.66	3.68
Median GPA	3.46	3.46	3.46
25% GPA	3.15	3.16	3.16
75% LSAT	161	161	160
Median LSAT	159	160	157
25% LSAT	156	158	153

Grants and Scholarships (from prior year)

	Total		Full-Time		Part-Time	
	#	%	#	%	#	%
Total # of students	1,018		786		232	
Total # receiving grants	304	29.9	271	34.5	33	14.2
Less than 1/2 tuition	159	15.6	139	17.7	20	8.6
Half to full tuition	99	9.7	88	11.2	11	4.7
Full tuition	45	4.4	43	5.5	2	0.9
More than full tuition	1	0.1	1	0.1	0	0.0
Median grant amount			$17,600		$10,000	

Informational and Library Resources

Total amount spent on library materials	$1,387,798
Study seating capacity inside the library	329
# of full-time equivalent professional librarians	4
Hours per week library is open	108
# of open, wired connections available to students	1,535
# of networked computers available for use by students	28
Has wireless network?	Y
Requires computer?	Y

JD Attrition (from prior year)

	Academic	Other	Total	
	#	#	#	%
1st year	8	16	24	8.1
2nd year	2	4	6	1.6
3rd year	0	0	0	0.0
4th year	0	0	0	0.0

Employment (9 months after graduation)

	Total	Percentage
Employment status known	341	97.2
Employment status unknown	10	2.8
Employed	296	86.8
Pursuing graduate degrees	13	3.8
Unemployed (seeking, not seeking, or studying for the bar)	29	8.5
Type of Employment		
# employed in law firms	118	39.9
# employed in business and industry	43	14.5
# employed in government	79	26.7
# employed in public interest	34	11.5
# employed as judicial clerks	10	3.4
# employed in academia	2	0.7
Geographic Location		
# employed in state	228	77.0
# employed outside the US	1	0.3
# of states where employed	21	

Bar Passage Rates

First-time takers	317	Reporting %	89.59
Average school %	87.68	Average state %	85.67
Average pass difference	2.01		

Jurisdiction	Takers	Passers	Pass %	State %	Diff %
Colorado	284	249	87.68	85.67	2.01

UNIVERSITY OF DENVER STURM COLLEGE OF LAW

2255 E. Evans Avenue, Suite 115
Denver, CO 80208
Phone: 303.871.6135; Fax: 303.871.6992
E-mail: admissions@law.du.edu; Website: www.law.du.edu

Introduction

The University of Denver Sturm College of Law opened its doors in 1892 and has been breaking ground in legal education ever since. Our faculty pride themselves in training students for successful careers as legal practitioners by offering a variety of challenging and exciting courses in addition to experiential learning opportunities through our Student Law Office, externships with law firms, and clerkships with judges. Our new building, with over 181,000 square feet spanning four stories, is the first law building to be awarded the Gold Leadership in Energy and Environmental Design (LEED) certification by the US Green Building Council. Downtown Denver—where the state legislature, courthouses, regional federal agencies, state agencies, and law firms are found—is 10 minutes away by Light Rail, and the Rocky Mountains are just a short drive to the west.

Curriculum/Special Programs

Denver Law provides a solid foundation of core classes on which to build your career in law. In addition, we offer a wide range of specialized classes that permit our faculty to bring their scholarship into the classroom.

Lawyering Process Course—The first year curriculum includes an innovative Lawyering Process course, which provides first-year students an introduction to the law and the legal system, and teaches students how to research legal questions and write about them in several formats.

Environmental and Natural Resources Law—Drawing upon its location in one of the nation's natural resource and energy capitals, Denver Law offers a rich program in environmental and natural resources law. Extensive course offerings are supplemented with abundant opportunities for externships at local natural resource companies, environmental advocacy and protection groups, and government enforcement agencies. Students may also participate in our Environmental Law Clinic, student organizations, the *Water Law Review*, writing competitions, and natural resources moot court competitions.

International Legal Studies—The International Legal Studies program is designed for students interested in international comparative law, international organizations, or transnational business. Students in the program may work on the *Denver Journal of International Law and Policy* as staff members and editors. The International Law Society and Ved Nanda Center for International Law sponsor a rich schedule of outside speakers and an annual conference focused on a current issue in international law.

Business Law—As one of the nation's biggest tourism magnets, Denver provides a practical backdrop for students interested in business and commercial law. In addition to foundation courses and specialized seminars, corporate internships and highly prized one-semester assignments with large local corporations are available for interested students to pursue.

Lawyering in Spanish—This program celebrates the globalization of Spanish culture by providing an opportunity to learn the specialized vocabulary and counseling techniques required to represent Spanish-speaking clients in the United States and abroad.

Clinics—In 1904 Denver Law launched the first Student Law Office (SLO) in the United States. The SLO offers the following clinics: Civil Litigation, Civil Rights, Community Law, Criminal Representation, Environmental, and Mediation/Arbitration. Students represent indigent clients at all levels of the dispute resolution process. If the case reaches the litigation phase, the student handles all aspects of pretrial, trial preparation, and the trial itself under faculty supervision.

Student Activities

Trial Advocacy—The Advocacy Department at Denver Law provides its students with the highest quality preparation for success in their professional careers by providing education and simulation in the four areas of advocacy—Client Advocacy, Pre-Trial Advocacy, Trial Advocacy, and Appellate Advocacy. The department achieves this through innovative professional skills courses, simulated courtroom situations, and competitive tournaments. The department's three national trial teams and eight moot court teams consistently garner awards and recognition at both regional and nationally-ranked tournaments, and the school's Moot Court Board produces six competitions per academic year.

Journals—Five scholarly journals are edited at Denver Law, allowing students to participate in research in varied fields. Academic credit is awarded for work on the *Denver University Law Review*, *Denver Journal of International Law and Policy*, *Sports and Entertainment Law Journal*, *Transportation Law Journal*, and the *University of Denver Water Law Review*.

Student Organizations—A wide range of student organizations contribute to the vibrant environment of the Sturm College of Law. Among those groups are the Animal Legal Defense Fund, Asian Pacific American Law Students' Association, Black Law Students' Association, Business Law Society, Christian Legal Society, Federalist Society, International Law Society, Intellectual Property Law Society, Natural Resources and Environmental Law Society, Jewish Law Students Association, Latino Law Students Association, Native American Law Students Association, Phi Alpha Delta, Public Interest Law Group, and Sports and Entertainment Law Society.

Admission

All applications should be submitted online and reach the Sturm College of Law between September and February to receive maximum consideration for admission for the following August. Students may only begin law study in the fall semester. Applicants must take the LSAT and register with LSAC's Credential Assembly Service. LSAT scores and records of academic performance are individually evaluated in the admission process. The applicant's personal statement, résumé, and letters of recommendation are thoroughly reviewed as well as work experience, significant personal accomplishments, leadership roles, a commitment to community service, and other activities that show initiative, growth, and maturity.

Expenses and Financial Aid

All admitted students are considered for scholarships. No additional application is required, except for the Chancellor Scholarship. Scholarships offered to entering first-year students may be renewed each year based on satisfactory academic performance.

The Chancellor Scholar program is offered to students with a demonstrated history of excellence in scholarship and public service. The program awards full-tuition scholarships to a limited number of qualified students committed to public interest issues. The scholarships are available to entering first-year day-division and evening-division students.

Additional one-year scholarships may be offered to continuing students based on law school performance. Students may also apply for federal loans, up to the cost of attendance.

Career Services

The Career Development Center (CDC) assists students and alumni in the formulation of career plans and connects potential employers with qualified applicants. Their services include educating students and alumni in developing necessary skills to locate and obtain satisfying and meaningful employment, connecting students and alumni to the world of work, and facilitating employers' connections with students and alumni.

Housing

On-campus graduate housing is available at the University of Denver. However, the majority of law students choose to live off campus.

APPLICANT PROFILE

University of Denver Sturm College of Law
This grid includes only applicants who earned 120–180 LSAT scores under standard administrations.

LSAT Score	GPA																				
	3.75 +		3.50–3.74		3.25–3.49		3.00–3.24		2.75–2.99		2.50–2.74		2.25–2.49		2.00–2.24		Below 2.00		No GPA		Total	
	Apps	Adm	Apps	Adm	Apps	Adm	Apps	Adm	Apps	Adm	Apps	Adm	Apps	Adm	Apps	Adm	Apps	Adm	Apps	Adm	Apps	Adm
175–180	0	0	0	0	0	0	1	1	0	0	0	0	0	0	1	1	0	0	0	0	2	2
170–174	6	5	3	3	9	8	3	3	6	5	0	0	1	1	1	0	0	0	1	1	30	26
165–169	30	25	28	18	21	16	23	18	12	7	10	4	7	0	1	1	2	0	2	1	136	90
160–164	84	75	134	115	136	113	103	94	60	40	34	14	20	1	11	0	1	0	8	2	591	454
155–159	134	83	224	125	283	75	226	42	116	13	72	2	30	0	13	0	3	0	11	1	1112	341
150–154	76	31	123	28	190	13	165	10	87	2	49	0	24	0	9	0	3	0	12	0	738	84
145–149	27	1	39	3	81	1	112	1	59	1	36	0	25	0	7	0	1	0	14	1	401	8
140–144	8	0	7	0	19	0	21	0	23	0	12	0	13	0	2	0	1	0	2	0	108	0
135–139	1	0	3	0	1	0	1	0	12	0	3	0	5	0	0	0	0	0	2	0	28	0
130–134	0	0	0	0	1	0	0	0	2	0	6	0	0	0	1	0	0	0	1	0	11	0
125–129	0	0	0	0	0	0	0	0	0	0	1	0	0	0	1	0	0	0	1	0	3	0
120–124	0	0	0	0	0	0	0	0	0	0	1	0	0	0	1	0	0	0	0	0	2	0
Total	366	220	561	292	741	226	655	169	377	68	224	20	125	2	48	2	11	0	54	6	3162	1005

Apps = Number of Applicants
Adm = Number Admitted
Reflects 99% of the total applicant pool; highest LSAT data reported.

DEPAUL UNIVERSITY COLLEGE OF LAW

25 East Jackson Boulevard
Chicago, IL 60604-2219
Phone: 312.362.6831 or 800.428.7453; Fax: 312.362.5280
E-mail: lawinfo@depaul.edu; Website: www.law.depaul.edu

ABA
Approved
Since
1925

The Basics

Type of school	Private
Term	Semester
Application deadline	3/1
Application fee	
Financial aid deadline	4/1
Can first year start other than fall?	No
Student to faculty ratio	13.8 to 1
# of housing spaces available restricted to law students	
graduate housing for which law students are eligible	254

Faculty and Administrators

	Total		Men		Women		Minorities	
	Spr	Fall	Spr	Fall	Spr	Fall	Spr	Fall
Full-time	61	54	35	30	26	24	8	9
Other full-time	2	2	2	2	0	0	0	0
Deans, librarians, & others who teach	3	3	2	2	1	1	1	1
Part-time	69	65	46	40	23	25	47	44
Total	135	124	85	74	50	50	56	54

Curriculum

	Full-Time	Part-Time
Typical first-year section size	101	97
Is there typically a "small section" of the first-year class, other than Legal Writing, taught by full-time faculty	No	No
If yes, typical size offered last year		
# of classroom course titles beyond first-year curriculum	157	

# of upper division courses, excluding seminars, with an enrollment:		
	Under 25	164
	25–49	31
	50–74	14
	75–99	12
	100+	3

# of seminars	17	
# of seminar positions available	340	
# of seminar positions filled	122	30
# of positions available in simulation courses	458	
# of simulation positions filled	54	356
# of positions available in faculty supervised clinical courses	210	
# of faculty supervised clinical positions filled	150	0
# involved in field placements	153	0
# involved in law journals	83	0
# involved in moot court or trial competitions	44	0
# of credit hours required to graduate	86	

JD Enrollment and Ethnicity

	Men		Women		Full-Time		Part-Time		1st-Year		Total		JD Degs. Awd.
	#	%	#	%	#	%	#	%	#	%	#	%	
All Hispanics	30	5.4	60	11.9	68	8.0	22	10.8	20	6.4	90	8.5	38
Am. Ind./AK Nat.	3	0.5	2	0.4	3	0.4	2	1.0	2	0.6	5	0.5	0
Asian	28	5.1	44	8.7	54	6.3	18	8.9	28	9.0	72	6.8	16
Black/Af. Am.	20	3.6	45	8.9	50	5.9	15	7.4	20	6.4	65	6.2	27
Nat. HI/Pac. Isl.	0	0.0	0	0.0	0	0.0	0	0.0	0	0.0	0	0.0	0
2 or more races	0	0.0	0	0.0	0	0.0	0	0.0	0	0.0	0	0.0	0
Subtotal (minor.)	81	14.7	151	29.9	175	20.5	57	28.1	70	22.4	232	22.0	81
Nonres. Alien	3	0.5	8	1.6	11	1.3	0	0.0	2	0.6	11	1.0	0
White/Cauc.	396	71.9	305	60.4	574	67.3	127	62.6	221	70.8	701	66.4	205
Unknown	71	12.9	41	8.1	93	10.9	19	9.4	19	6.1	112	10.6	31
Total	551	52.2	505	47.8	853	80.8	203	19.2	312	29.5	1056		323

Transfers

Transfers in	18
Transfers out	12

Tuition and Fees

	Resident	Nonresident
Full-time	$39,350	$39,350
Part-time	$25,730	$25,730
Tuition Guarantee Program	Y	

Living Expenses

Estimated living expenses for singles

Living on campus	Living off campus	Living at home
$23,045	$23,045	$23,045

ABA Approved Since 1925

GPA and LSAT Scores

	Total	Full-Time	Part-Time
# of apps	5,770	5,109	661
# of offers	2,310	2,094	216
# of matrics	312	257	55
75% GPA	3.64	3.63	3.68
Median GPA	3.48	3.45	3.55
25% GPA	3.13	3.09	3.44
75% LSAT	161	162	157
Median LSAT	160	160	154
25% LSAT	156	158	152

Grants and Scholarships (from prior year)

	Total		Full-Time		Part-Time	
	#	%	#	%	#	%
Total # of students	1,027		772		255	
Total # receiving grants	615	59.9	502	65.0	113	44.3
Less than 1/2 tuition	443	43.1	341	44.2	102	40.0
Half to full tuition	161	15.7	159	20.6	2	0.8
Full tuition	1	0.1	1	0.1	0	0.0
More than full tuition	10	1.0	1	0.1	9	3.5
Median grant amount			$15,000		$4,000	

Informational and Library Resources

Total amount spent on library materials	$1,229,636
Study seating capacity inside the library	510
# of full-time equivalent professional librarians	8
Hours per week library is open	94
# of open, wired connections available to students	20
# of networked computers available for use by students	210
Has wireless network?	Y
Requires computer?	N

JD Attrition (from prior year)

	Academic	Other	Total	
	#	#	#	%
1st year	13	20	33	9.1
2nd year	0	1	1	0.3
3rd year	1	0	1	0.4
4th year	1	0	1	4.5

Employment (9 months after graduation)

	Total	Percentage
Employment status known	317	99.1
Employment status unknown	3	0.9
Employed	272	85.8
Pursuing graduate degrees	7	2.2
Unemployed (seeking, not seeking, or studying for the bar)	21	6.6
Type of Employment		
# employed in law firms	136	50.0
# employed in business and industry	71	26.1
# employed in government	33	12.1
# employed in public interest	12	4.4
# employed as judicial clerks	4	1.5
# employed in academia	12	4.4
Geographic Location		
# employed in state	211	77.6
# employed outside the US	1	0.4
# of states where employed	19	

Bar Passage Rates

First-time takers	320	Reporting %	86.25
Average school %	92.39	Average state %	90.89
Average pass difference	1.50		

Jurisdiction	Takers	Passers	Pass %	State %	Diff %
Illinois	276	255	92.39	90.89	1.50

DEPAUL UNIVERSITY COLLEGE OF LAW

25 East Jackson Boulevard
Chicago, IL 60604-2219
Phone: 312.362.6831 or 800.428.7453; Fax: 312.362.5280
E-mail: lawinfo@depaul.edu; Website: www.law.depaul.edu

Introduction

DePaul University is the largest private university in Illinois and enjoys the advantages of its vibrant urban setting. Its strong reputation for academic excellence is distinguished by its dedicated faculty, unrivaled professional skills training, and its genuine sense of community.

Located in the heart of Chicago's business and legal communities, the College of Law affords extensive contact with Chicago's legal community. It is within walking distance of the state and federal courts, government offices, and many law firms. DePaul law alumni include the mayor of Chicago, numerous state and federal judges, and managing partners of Chicago law firms. The college offers full-time, part-time, and summer programs. DePaul is fully accredited by the ABA, and is a member of AALS and the Order of the Coif.

Students

Founded in 1898 by Vincentian Fathers as a school for children of immigrants, DePaul University students represent a rich diversity in age, ethnicity, education, and career experiences. Because of the broad diversity of backgrounds and experiences of its law students, there is a connectedness within the institution that creates a genuine sense of community. Forty-three percent of students in the entering class of 2010 were women, while 23 percent were minorities. More than half of the students in the 2010 entering full-time class were from out of state. The average age of both full-time and part-time students is 24. More than 120 colleges and universities were represented in the entering class.

Faculty

DePaul faculty members, including many who have earned advanced degrees, are recognized scholars who represent a variety of professional backgrounds and interests. Consistent with the university's Vincentian mission of service to the community, faculty members work tirelessly in service to the legal profession and to the community, and they have achieved national recognition in teaching, research, scholarly activities, and professional service. The faculty is extremely accessible, approachable, and deeply committed to its students.

Library, Research Centers, and Institutes

The three-story law library offers extensive resources for study and research. Its staff includes 7 professional librarians and 12 full-time support staff.

The College of Law also maintains 15 research centers and institutes:

- Health Law Institute
- International Aviation Law Institute
- International Human Rights Law Institute
- International Weapons Control Center
- Asian Legal Studies Institute
- Schiller, DuCanto, and Fleck Family Law Center
- Center for Intellectual Property Law and Information Technology
- Center for Justice in Capital Cases
- Center for Animal Law
- Center for Public Interest Law
- Center for Dispute Resolution
- Center for Law and Science
- Center for Art, Museum, and Cultural Heritage Law
- Center for Jewish Law and Judaic Studies
- Center for Church-State Studies

Special Programs

Academic Support Program: DePaul is committed to ensuring that all students have the tools they need to attain academic success. Toward that end, DePaul has one of the premier academic support programs in the nation.

Legal Clinic: Students gain valuable hands-on experience in ten clinical concentrations: Advanced Immigrant Detainee, Asylum/Immigration, Civil Rights Law, Criminal Appeals, Death Penalty, Family Law, Misdemeanor, Poverty Law, Special Education Advocacy, and Technology/Intellectual Property.

Field Placement Program: Providing students with academic credit through supervised field work, externships are offered by federal and state judges, various municipal agencies, and a number of nonprofit and for-profit organizations.

Mediation Program: Students learn essential client counseling skills by working with mediators on cases referred by the County Domestic Relations Courts.

Skills Competitions: As a leader in the field of professional skills, DePaul has enjoyed considerable success in skills competitions. DePaul student teams regularly place among the top in both regional and national moot court competitions.

Certificate Programs: DePaul offers 11 comprehensive certificate programs, including Business Law, Child and Family Law, Criminal Law, Health Law, International and Comparative Law, Public Interest Law, Taxation, and four in Intellectual Property Law (General, Arts and Museum, Information Technology, and Patents).

Asian Legal Studies Institute: Students receive academic credit for summer courses taken at Beijing Foreign Studies University in China. Students focus on legal principles and planning related to international transactions in the Asia-Pacific region. Lectures are presented by professors from DePaul and major Chinese law schools.

Chiapas Human Rights Practicum: Conducted entirely in Spanish, the practicum places student workers in human rights offices in the state of Chiapas, Mexico, where basic human rights violations are an everyday reality.

European Legal Studies Program: This program offers students the option to study in Madrid, Spain, or Prague, the Czech Republic. The programs include a number of tours of legal, business, and political institutions in each country.

Human Rights Law in the Americas: Located in San José, Costa Rica, this program introduces students to the basic principles of international law with an overview of the inter-American human rights system.

Legal Dimensions of Doing Business in Latin America: Taking place in Buenos Aires, Argentina, students study the legal principles and practices that shape business law in Latin America.

University College Dublin (UCD) Student Exchange Program: DePaul and UCD have a student exchange program in which second-year students undertake legal studies abroad during their spring semester.

Joint-Degree and Master of Laws (LLM) Programs: DePaul offers five joint-degree and four master of laws programs:

- JD/MBA in coordination with DePaul's nationally recognized Kellstadt Graduate School of Business.
- JD/MS in Public Service Management promotes effective management of government and nonprofit organizations.
- JD/MA in International Studies offers concentrations in International Political Economy and Global Culture and complements DePaul's strong international law offerings.
- JD/MA and JD/MS in Computer Science explore the intersections of law, computer science, telecommunications, and information systems.
- DePaul's master of laws (LLM) programs include Health Law, Intellectual Property Law, International Law, and Taxation.

Special First-Year Legal Writing Sections: Students may apply for a seat in one of three special sections of Legal Analysis, Research, and Communication, focusing on child and family law, intellectual property law, and public interest law.

Housing

Located in Chicago's Loop just two blocks south of the law school, the University Center of Chicago (UCC) is a recently developed residence hall offering furnished apartments and suites. Amenities include a rooftop garden, multimedia rooms, a fitness center, food court, laundry facilities, shops on the lower level, 24-hour security, and keycard access to the building and elevators.

Admission

DePaul adheres to a policy of nondiscrimination and encourages applications from traditionally underrepresented groups. Admission decisions are based on a variety of factors, and each file is reviewed thoroughly. Undergraduate GPA and LSAT scores are significant admission criteria. For the 2010–2011 academic year, 5,136 candidates applied for admission to the full-time program, while 668 applied to the part-time program. Admitted students are automatically considered for available merit-based scholarships.

Career Services

Alumni, faculty, and students contribute to an active and aggressive career services network. The teaching and publishing reputations of the faculty, as well as the largest alumni bench and bar network in the Chicago area, complement three full-time DePaul law career services officers.

APPLICANT PROFILE

DePaul University College of Law
This grid includes only applicants who earned 120–180 LSAT scores under standard administrations.

LSAT Score	3.75 +		3.50–3.74		3.25–3.49		3.00–3.24		2.75–2.99		2.50–2.74		2.25–2.49		2.00–2.24		Below 2.00		No GPA		Total	
	Apps	Adm	Apps	Adm	Apps	Adm	Apps	Adm	Apps	Adm	Apps	Adm	Apps	Adm	Apps	Adm	Apps	Adm	Apps	Adm	Apps	Adm
175–180	2	2	2	2	7	6	0	0	0	0	1	1	0	0	0	0	0	0	1	1	13	12
170–174	11	11	17	16	15	12	7	7	8	8	7	3	3	2	2	0	0	0	0	0	70	59
165–169	61	56	71	66	61	57	58	51	46	37	23	16	18	11	2	0	1	0	3	2	344	296
160–164	214	192	343	322	338	302	235	210	129	113	75	56	35	20	16	8	0	0	17	13	1402	1236
155–159	209	154	356	247	377	74	302	9	176	6	88	0	39	0	15	0	1	0	21	8	1584	498
150–154	114	43	236	67	342	29	279	7	181	2	78	1	49	0	17	0	4	0	13	1	1313	150
145–149	31	9	85	20	140	12	145	1	110	0	60	1	35	0	19	0	5	0	10	1	640	44
120–144	16	0	38	0	55	1	75	0	75	0	60	0	46	0	15	0	5	0	11	0	396	1
Total	658	467	1148	740	1335	493	1101	285	725	166	392	78	225	33	86	8	16	0	76	26	5762	2296

Apps = Number of Applicants
Adm = Number Admitted
Reflects 99% of the total applicant pool; highest LSAT data reported.

UNIVERSITY OF DETROIT MERCY SCHOOL OF LAW

Admissions Office, 651 East Jefferson Avenue
Detroit, MI 48226
Phone: 313.596.0264
E-mail: udmlawao@udmercy.edu; Website: www.law.udmercy.edu

ABA
Approved
Since
1933

AMERICAN BAR ASSOCIATION
Section of Legal Education
and Admissions to the Bar

The Basics

Type of school	Private
Term	Semester
Application deadline	4/15
Application fee	$50
Financial aid deadline	4/1
Can first year start other than fall?	No
Student to faculty ratio	15.3 to 1
# of housing spaces available restricted to law students	
graduate housing for which law students are eligible	

Faculty and Administrators

	Total		Men		Women		Minorities	
	Spr	Fall	Spr	Fall	Spr	Fall	Spr	Fall
Full-time	37	36	18	17	19	19	6	5
Other full-time	6	6	5	5	1	1	0	0
Deans, librarians, & others who teach	16	16	8	8	8	8	1	1
Part-time	33	29	20	22	13	7	4	1
Total	92	87	51	52	41	35	11	7

Curriculum

	Full-Time	Part-Time
Typical first-year section size	63	34
Is there typically a "small section" of the first-year class, other than Legal Writing, taught by full-time faculty	No	No
If yes, typical size offered last year		
# of classroom course titles beyond first-year curriculum	119	
# of upper division courses, excluding seminars, with an enrollment: Under 25	120	
25–49	39	
50–74	7	
75–99	0	
100+	0	
# of seminars	13	
# of seminar positions available	208	
# of seminar positions filled	110	28
# of positions available in simulation courses	851	
# of simulation positions filled	572	100
# of positions available in faculty supervised clinical courses	209	
# of faculty supervised clinical positions filled	99	31
# involved in field placements	115	7
# involved in law journals	49	8
# involved in moot court or trial competitions	59	5
# of credit hours required to graduate	90	

JD Enrollment and Ethnicity

	Men #	Men %	Women #	Women %	Full-Time #	Full-Time %	Part-Time #	Part-Time %	1st-Year #	1st-Year %	Total #	Total %	JD Degs. Awd.
All Hispanics	7	1.8	18	5.2	19	3.3	6	3.9	11	4.0	25	3.4	2
Am. Ind./AK Nat.	1	0.3	3	0.9	4	0.7	0	0.0	2	0.7	4	0.6	0
Asian	12	3.1	9	2.6	17	3.0	4	2.6	8	2.9	21	2.9	10
Black/Af. Am.	39	10.2	50	14.5	49	8.6	40	25.8	44	16.1	89	12.2	24
Nat. HI/Pac. Isl.	0	0.0	0	0.0	0	0.0	0	0.0	0	0.0	0	0.0	0
2 or more races	0	0.0	0	0.0	0	0.0	0	0.0	0	0.0	0	0.0	0
Subtotal (minor.)	59	15.5	80	23.1	89	15.6	50	32.3	65	23.8	139	19.1	36
Nonres. Alien	78	20.5	70	20.2	144	25.2	4	2.6	69	25.3	148	20.4	44
White/Cauc.	244	64.0	196	56.6	339	59.3	101	65.2	139	50.9	440	60.5	121
Unknown	0	0.0	0	0.0	0	0.0	0	0.0	0	0.0	0	0.0	0
Total	381	52.4	346	47.6	572	78.7	155	21.3	273	37.6	727		201

Transfers

Transfers in	1
Transfers out	41

Tuition and Fees

	Resident	Nonresident
Full-time	$34,010	$34,010
Part-time	$27,224	$27,224
Tuition Guarantee Program	N	

Living Expenses

Estimated living expenses for singles

Living on campus	Living off campus	Living at home
N/A	$21,334	$13,795

ABA Approved Since 1933

GPA and LSAT Scores

	Total	Full-Time	Part-Time
# of apps	1,769	1,543	226
# of offers	784	662	122
# of matrics	257	201	56
75% GPA	3.40	3.44	3.30
Median GPA	3.17	3.20	3.04
25% GPA	2.93	2.96	2.80
75% LSAT	154	155	150
Median LSAT	150	151	146
25% LSAT	146	147	144

Grants and Scholarships (from prior year)

	Total		Full-Time		Part-Time	
	#	%	#	%	#	%
Total # of students	730		586		144	
Total # receiving grants	189	25.9	159	27.1	30	20.8
Less than 1/2 tuition	174	23.8	147	25.1	27	18.8
Half to full tuition	15	2.1	12	2.0	3	2.1
Full tuition	0	0.0	0	0.0	0	0.0
More than full tuition	0	0.0	0	0.0	0	0.0
Median grant amount			$5,000		$2,250	

Informational and Library Resources

Total amount spent on library materials	$1,233,270
Study seating capacity inside the library	265
# of full-time equivalent professional librarians	6
Hours per week library is open	92
# of open, wired connections available to students	0
# of networked computers available for use by students	33
Has wireless network?	Y
Requires computer?	N

JD Attrition (from prior year)

	Academic	Other	Total	
	#	#	#	%
1st year	15	49	64	22.8
2nd year	1	4	5	2.5
3rd year	0	0	0	0.0
4th year	0	0	0	0.0

Employment (9 months after graduation)

	Total	Percentage
Employment status known	211	100.0
Employment status unknown	0	0.0
Employed	159	75.4
Pursuing graduate degrees	3	1.4
Unemployed (seeking, not seeking, or studying for the bar)	35	16.6
Type of Employment		
# employed in law firms	104	65.4
# employed in business and industry	31	19.5
# employed in government	10	6.3
# employed in public interest	3	1.9
# employed as judicial clerks	6	3.8
# employed in academia	5	3.1
Geographic Location		
# employed in state	97	61.0
# employed outside the US	24	15.1
# of states where employed	12	

Bar Passage Rates

First-time takers	204	Reporting %	76.96
Average school %	85.34	Average state %	86.82

Average pass difference –1.48

Jurisdiction	Takers	Passers	Pass %	State %	Diff %
Michigan	132	119	90.15	86.87	3.28
New York	25	15	60.00	86.51	–26.51

UNIVERSITY OF DETROIT MERCY SCHOOL OF LAW

Admissions Office, 651 East Jefferson Avenue
Detroit, MI 48226
Phone: 313.596.0264
E-mail: udmlawao@udmercy.edu; Website: www.law.udmercy.edu

Introduction

Founded in 1912, the University of Detroit Mercy (UDM) School of Law is a private law school in downtown Detroit sponsored by the Society of Jesus (Jesuits) and the Sisters of Mercy of the Americas. Located opposite the General Motors headquarters in the Renaissance Center, the School of Law is within walking distance of federal and state courts, downtown law firms, and Detroit's municipal center. Windsor, Ontario, Canada, is a five-minute drive by tunnel or bridge across the Detroit River. Metropolitan Detroit not only offers renowned cultural institutions like the Detroit Institute of Art and the Detroit Opera House, but also provides a distinctive setting for the study of contemporary legal issues such as energy and the environment, immigration, global transactions, and complex corporate transactions.

The School of Law offers a comprehensive legal education through day and evening programs that incorporate a broad array of required and elective courses to prepare practice-ready graduates. The school is approved by the ABA and is a member of the AALS.

Law School Campus

The UDM Law campus includes newly renovated classrooms and common areas with wireless access, administrative and student services offices, a bookstore, a cafeteria, and student organization offices, all located within the law school complex. The school's Kresge Law Library contains comfortable individual and group study, reading, and computer areas. The library houses more than 340,000 volumes and serves as a federal depository.

Curriculum

UDM Law offers a three-year, full-time program and day and evening part-time programs leading to the JD degree. Required courses include Analytical Tools, Contracts, Property, Torts, Civil Procedure, Applied Legal Theory and Analysis, Criminal Law, Constitutional Law, Evidence, Professional Responsibility, Taxation, two Law Firm Program courses, an international or comparative law elective, a clinic, and a seminar.

UDM Law's first-year Analytical Tools course not only introduces students to statutory analysis and interpretation, but requires them to solve legal problems that cut across torts, contracts, property, and civil procedure. Applied Legal Theory and Analysis immerses first-year students in the fundamental lawyering skills of communication, research, legal analysis and reasoning, and problem-solving. In its Law Firm Program courses, third-year students receive work assignments, feedback, and professional skills development as if they were first-year lawyers in law firms, government agencies, and other legal settings. Law Firm Program courses focus on a substantive area of the law or a type of practice. The School's 2010–2011 Law Firm Program included more than 20 courses in areas such as Bankruptcy, Environmental Law, Floor Financing, Health Law, Immigration Law, International Arbitration, Software Licensing, and Toxic Torts.

UDM Law's legal education program offers several clinical opportunities: Appellate Advocacy Clinic through the State Appellate Defender Office; Asylum Law Clinic; Consumer Defense Clinic; Criminal Trial Clinic; Immigration Law Clinic; Mediation Training and the Mediation Clinic; Mortgage Foreclosure Clinic; Urban Law Clinic; the Veterans Law Clinic, a veteran's clinic for appeals; and a wide array of externships. UDM's Mobile Law Offices have taken the clinic's immigration, veterans, and other services beyond the campus and into the community.

Special Programs

- **JD/LED**—The University of Detroit Mercy School of Law (UDM) and the Instituto Tecnológico y de Estudios Superiores de Monterrey (ITESM), Mexico's leading private law school, have partnered to offer the Degree of the Americas program, a multiple-degree program that allows students bilingual in Spanish and English to earn law degrees in three countries: the United States, Mexico, and Canada. Students enrolled in this program can earn two (JD/LED) or three (JD/LLB/LED) degrees in significantly less time than would be required for each degree pursued independently. UDM School of Law is the only US ABA-approved law school to provide students bilingual in Spanish and English an opportunity to take so many courses in Mexican law. As part of this program, UDM offers 14 courses in Mexican law taught in Spanish by professors from ITESM. All UDM students may take these courses as electives and have them count toward their degree.

- **Joint JD/MBA**—The School of Law and the College of Business Administration collaborate to offer an integrated degree program leading to the JD and MBA degrees. Students enrolled in the joint-degree program can earn both degrees in significantly less time than would be required for degrees pursued independently. Students are first admitted to and attend law school. At the end of the first year of law school, students apply to the joint-degree program.

- **Dual Canadian and American JD**—The School of Law and the University of Windsor Faculty of Law offer a unique Dual JD program designed to educate students to understand the legal doctrines and cultures of the United States and Canada. Students complete 60 credits at UDM and 44 credits at Windsor. Most required courses taken at both law schools cover US and Canadian law relevant to the subject areas. The program enables the successful student to obtain an American Bar Association-approved Juris Doctor (JD) from the University of Detroit Mercy and Canadian JD from Windsor.

- **Intellectual Property Law Institute**—Through a consortium with other law schools, the School of Law offers a wide variety of courses in intellectual property such as Copyright Law, Patent Law, Computer Law, Entertainment Law, and others.

- **French Scholar Program**—The School of Law participates in a professional exchange program with the University of Clermont-Ferrand. French scholars visiting the law school each spring teach a comparative law course in English while UDM scholars teach at Clermont-Ferrand.

- **Special Summer Program (SSP)**—The School of Law offers this program for applicants who do not meet the minimum standards for admission, but who show potential for the study of law. This seven-week program, beginning in late May, requires students to demonstrate ability in the study of substantive law and in legal writing and research in order to gain admission as a regular student in the fall semester.

Student Organizations and Activities

The School of Law's students edit and publish the *Law Review*, a quarterly publication of scholarly articles.

A student **Moot Court Board of Advocacy** administers the School of Law's Keenan and Professional Responsibility competitions; participates in state, regional, and national competitions in first amendment law, ethics, and other areas; and helps to administer the G. Mennen Williams mandatory moot court competition for first-year students. Moot court members at UDM annually participate in several distinctive national competitions, including the Niagra Cup, the McGee National Civil Rights competition, and Immigration Law (best brief). In 2009, UDM Law's Moot Court team won the first national invitational moot court competition.

The **Student Bar Association (SBA)**, affiliated with the Law Student Division of the American Bar Association, plays a significant role in student affairs. As the student government of the school, the SBA authorizes other student organizations, including the Black Law Student Alliance, the Environmental Law Society, Phi Alpha Delta, St. Thomas More Society, the Women's Law Caucus, the Arab and Chaldean Law Student Society, the Sports and Entertainment Law Society, and many others. Students also regularly publish a student newsletter, *In Brief*.

In 2006, UDM School of Law received the Judy M. Weightman Memorial Public Interest Award from the American Bar Association (ABA) Student Law Division.

This award recognizes outstanding community service projects, public interest programming, and strong commitment to helping others in need. UDM's Student Bar Association nominated UDM for this award.

Career Services

The school's Career Services Office provides students with a wide range of opportunities through which they may explore career paths in law. The office sponsors a Preparing to Practice series for upper-class students that introduces them to a variety of practice areas and issues. The Career Services staff provide career counseling services, including résumé and cover letter review. The office administers the school's annual on-campus interview programs, maintains a job information hotline and newsletter, sponsors a mock interview program for first-year students, and hosts special events to acquaint students with practitioners.

Admission

The School of Law encourages applicants to submit an application for admission by April 15. The Admission Committee considers all elements of an application, including undergraduate grade-point average, Law School Admission Test scores, writing skills, leadership and maturity as evidenced by work and service experiences, graduate work, letters of recommendation, and the personal statement. The committee reviews applications as they become complete on a continuous basis and communicates decisions as early as possible. An applicant may accept an offer of admission by submitting the required nonrefundable deposits, which are credited toward tuition. The University of Detroit Mercy and the School of Law adhere to nondiscrimination policies.

APPLICANT PROFILE

University of Detroit Mercy School of Law
This grid includes only applicants who earned 120–180 LSAT scores under standard administrations.

LSAT Score	3.75 +		3.50–3.74		3.25–3.49		3.00–3.24		2.75–2.99		2.50–2.74		2.25–2.49		2.00–2.24		Below 2.00		No GPA		Total	
	Apps	Adm	Apps	Adm	Apps	Adm	Apps	Adm	Apps	Adm	Apps	Adm	Apps	Adm	Apps	Adm	Apps	Adm	Apps	Adm	Apps	Adm
175–180	0	0	1	0	0	0	0	0	0	0	0	0	0	0	0	0	0	0	1	1	2	1
170–174	1	1	2	2	0	0	1	1	0	0	0	0	0	0	0	0	0	0	0	0	4	4
165–169	1	1	4	3	3	3	3	3	1	1	3	3	1	1	0	0	1	0	6	6	23	21
160–164	3	3	9	8	12	11	4	4	4	3	2	2	2	2	1	1	0	0	36	31	73	65
155–159	13	12	19	17	32	31	33	26	23	14	14	12	5	1	2	1	0	0	71	49	212	163
150–154	14	13	39	36	56	48	53	45	36	25	27	22	15	5	5	0	3	2	73	14	321	210
145–149	13	10	33	29	65	55	64	45	72	51	42	18	28	7	10	2	4	0	53	4	384	221
140–144	10	8	18	15	52	23	59	23	71	8	40	2	35	1	14	0	2	0	24	3	325	83
135–139	5	0	3	0	17	0	17	0	28	0	20	0	17	0	6	0	5	0	19	0	137	0
130–134	1	0	3	0	2	0	4	0	10	0	10	0	6	0	4	0	4	0	5	0	49	0
125–129	0	0	1	0	0	0	4	0	1	0	3	0	0	0	1	0	3	0	0	0	13	0
120–124	0	0	0	0	0	0	0	0	0	0	0	0	0	0	1	0	0	0	1	0	2	0
Total	61	48	132	110	239	171	242	147	246	102	161	59	109	17	44	4	22	2	289	108	1545	768

Apps = Number of Applicants
Adm = Number Admitted
Reflects 99% of the total applicant pool; highest LSAT data reported.

UNIVERSITY OF THE DISTRICT OF COLUMBIA—DAVID A. CLARKE SCHOOL OF LAW

4200 Connecticut Avenue NW
Washington, DC 20008
Phone: 202.274.7341; Fax: 202.274.5583
E-mail: lawadmission@udc.edu; Website: www.law.udc.edu

ABA
Approved
Since
1991

The Basics

Type of school	Public	
Term	Semester	
Application deadline	3/15	
Application fee	$35	
Financial aid deadline	3/1	3/31
Can first year start other than fall?	No	
Student to faculty ratio	12.6 to 1	
# of housing spaces available restricted to law students		
graduate housing for which law students are eligible		

Faculty and Administrators

	Total		Men		Women		Minorities	
	Spr	Fall	Spr	Fall	Spr	Fall	Spr	Fall
Full-time	18	20	10	11	8	9	10	11
Other full-time	1	1	0	0	1	1	1	1
Deans, librarians, & others who teach	3	3	1	1	2	2	1	1
Part-time	17	20	9	9	8	11	10	13
Total	39	44	20	21	19	23	22	26

Curriculum

	Full-Time	Part-Time
Typical first-year section size	95	60
Is there typically a "small section" of the first-year class, other than Legal Writing, taught by full-time faculty	Yes	No
If yes, typical size offered last year	45	
# of classroom course titles beyond first-year curriculum	43	

# of upper division courses, excluding seminars, with an enrollment:	Under 25	32
	25–49	15
	50–74	3
	75–99	2
	100+	0

# of seminars	8	
# of seminar positions available	96	
# of seminar positions filled	93	0
# of positions available in simulation courses	145	
# of simulation positions filled	126	0
# of positions available in faculty supervised clinical courses	169	
# of faculty supervised clinical positions filled	169	0
# involved in field placements	27	0
# involved in law journals	42	0
# involved in moot court or trial competitions	3	0
# of credit hours required to graduate	90	

JD Enrollment and Ethnicity

	Men		Women		Full-Time		Part-Time		1st-Year		Total		JD Degs. Awd.
	#	%	#	%	#	%	#	%	#	%	#	%	
All Hispanics	16	11.9	15	8.2	30	11.7	1	1.7	7	5.6	31	9.8	9
Am. Ind./AK Nat.	0	0.0	1	0.5	1	0.4	0	0.0	1	0.8	1	0.3	1
Asian	6	4.5	18	9.9	20	7.8	4	6.7	10	7.9	24	7.6	5
Black/Af. Am.	39	29.1	58	31.9	73	28.5	24	40.0	39	31.0	97	30.7	26
Nat. HI/Pac. Isl.	0	0.0	0	0.0	0	0.0	0	0.0	0	0.0	0	0.0	0
2 or more races	3	2.2	3	1.6	4	1.6	2	3.3	5	4.0	6	1.9	0
Subtotal (minor.)	64	47.8	95	52.2	128	50.0	31	51.7	62	49.2	159	50.3	41
Nonres. Alien	0	0.0	0	0.0	0	0.0	0	0.0	0	0.0	0	0.0	0
White/Cauc.	62	46.3	78	42.9	114	44.5	26	43.3	54	42.9	140	44.3	37
Unknown	8	6.0	9	4.9	14	5.5	3	5.0	10	7.9	17	5.4	2
Total	134	42.4	182	57.6	256	81.0	60	19.0	126	39.9	316		81

Transfers

Transfers in	6
Transfers out	9

Tuition and Fees

	Resident	Nonresident
Full-time	$9,480	$18,330
Part-time	$6,630	$12,630
Tuition Guarantee Program		N

Living Expenses

Estimated living expenses for singles

Living on campus	Living off campus	Living at home
N/A	$31,734	$16,434

UNIVERSITY OF THE DISTRICT OF COLUMBIA—DAVID A. CLARKE SCHOOL OF LAW

ABA
Approved
Since
1991

GPA and LSAT Scores

	Total	Full-Time	Part-Time
# of apps	1,742	1,358	384
# of offers	413	344	69
# of matrics	131	97	34
75% GPA	3.39	3.43	3.48
Median GPA	3.12	3.12	3.15
25% GPA	2.84	2.83	2.95
75% LSAT	155	155	155
Median LSAT	152	153	151
25% LSAT	149	149	148

Grants and Scholarships (from prior year)

	Total #	Total %	Full-Time #	Full-Time %	Part-Time #	Part-Time %
Total # of students	293		266		27	
Total # receiving grants	156	53.2	142	53.4	14	51.9
Less than 1/2 tuition	92	31.4	85	32.0	7	25.9
Half to full tuition	19	6.5	16	6.0	3	11.1
Full tuition	45	15.4	41	15.4	4	14.8
More than full tuition	0	0.0	0	0.0	0	0.0
Median grant amount			$4,500		$4,000	

Informational and Library Resources

Total amount spent on library materials	$765,248
Study seating capacity inside the library	230
# of full-time equivalent professional librarians	8
Hours per week library is open	102
# of open, wired connections available to students	14
# of networked computers available for use by students	20
Has wireless network?	Y
Requires computer?	Y

JD Attrition (from prior year)

	Academic #	Other #	Total #	Total %
1st year	3	8	11	9.0
2nd year	0	4	4	4.8
3rd year	0	0	0	0.0
4th year	0	0	0	0.0

Employment (9 months after graduation)

	Total	Percentage
Employment status known	64	92.8
Employment status unknown	5	7.2
Employed	43	67.2
Pursuing graduate degrees	4	6.2
Unemployed (seeking, not seeking, or studying for the bar)	15	23.4
Type of Employment		
# employed in law firms	15	34.9
# employed in business and industry	8	18.6
# employed in government	8	18.6
# employed in public interest	8	18.6
# employed as judicial clerks	3	7.0
# employed in academia	1	2.3
Geographic Location		
# employed in state	21	48.8
# employed outside the US	0	0.0
# of states where employed	8	

Bar Passage Rates

First-time takers	69	Reporting %	100.00
Average school %	60.88	Average state %	76.88

Average pass difference −16.00

Jurisdiction	Takers	Passers	Pass %	State %	Diff %
Maryland	26	15	57.69	78.20	−20.51
District of Columbia	15	10	66.67	68.17	−1.50
Virginia	11	5	45.45	77.06	−31.61
California	4	2	50.00	73.19	−23.19
Others (9)	13	10	76.92		

The information on these pages was provided by the law school.

UNIVERSITY OF THE DISTRICT OF COLUMBIA—DAVID A. CLARKE SCHOOL OF LAW

4200 Connecticut Avenue NW
Washington, DC 20008
Phone: 202.274.7341; Fax: 202.274.5583
E-mail: lawadmission@udc.edu; Website: www.law.udc.edu

Introduction

In 1986, the District of Columbia Council authorized the establishment of the District of Columbia School of Law. The council created a dual mission for the School of Law and charged its Board of Governors with a mandate to recruit and enroll, to the degree feasible, students from ethnic, racial, or other population groups that in the past had been underrepresented among persons admitted to the bar. It also charged the board with representing the legal needs of low-income persons, particularly those who reside in the District of Columbia.

The DC School of Law, the only publicly funded law school in Washington, DC, merged with the University of the District of Columbia (UDC) in 1996 and became the University of the District of Columbia School of Law. In April 1998, the UDC School of Law was named the UDC David A. Clarke School of Law (UDC-DCSL). The law school operates full-time day and part-time evening programs leading to the JD degree as well as an LLM program.

Library and Physical Facilities

The School of Law is located on the University of the District of Columbia's Van Ness campus in the upper northwest section of Washington, DC, a neighborhood known for its harmonious blend of residences, businesses, embassies, and the Rock Creek Park.

The law library is a teaching-, research-, and practice-oriented library. It contains more than 257,000 volumes and volume equivalents. The law library expands its collection on an ongoing basis, with an emphasis on reference and scholarly materials that support legal education and the clinical programs. The library's online catalog is available at http://catalog.law.udc.edu/search.

The Charles N. and Hilda H. M. Mason Law Library is a beautiful and modern facility that provides the traditional and high-tech resources required for today's study of the law. In addition, the Internet and law library resources are accessible via the law library's wireless LAN throughout the law library and the School of Law.

The university and law school campus are conveniently located on the Metro's Red Line at the UDC/Van Ness subway stop.

Curriculum

Consistent with UDC School of Law's mission, the basic program is designed to provide a well-rounded theoretical and practical legal education that will enable students to be effective and ethical advocates, and to represent the legal needs of low-income residents through the school's legal clinics.

Full-time and part-time first-year students participate in Orientation, which introduces them to the study of law and to the School of Law community. During Orientation, students take Law and Justice, a course which introduces legal, political, social, and philosophical aspects of poverty and inequality in American society. They also take Lawyering Process I. Students participate in the Dean's Reception and in other events planned by the Dean of Students and student organizations.

In the first year, students must complete 40 hours of community service and take a prescribed program consisting of required courses and one elective course. After the first year, students must also take courses in Evidence, Constitutional Law I and II, Professional Responsibility, and Moot Court. Each UDC-DCSL student is required to produce significant pieces of writing each of the three years of study. The School of Law offers summer courses and clinics, including an internship program; it does not allow early graduation.

While the emphasis of the school is on public interest law, the overall curriculum—clinic and classroom—provides the skills necessary to pursue any field of law.

Clinical Program

Students are required to complete two, seven-credit clinics during their second and third years. The clinics offered in the 2010–2011 academic year were Housing and Consumer, HIV/AIDS, Juvenile and Special Education, Legislation, Government Accountability Project, Community Development and Small Business, Low-Income Taxpayer, and the new Immigration Law Clinic (fall 2010).

Academic Support and Summer Program

UDC-DCSL considers academic support to be an integral part of its course of study. Students in academic difficulty at the end of their first semester may apply to the enhanced program, which may involve adjusting course loads, taking a legal reasoning course, counseling, and group and individual tutoring. In addition, faculty members hold extra review sessions during the semester in required courses and provide sample examination questions with model answers.

The School of Law offers the Mason Enhancement Program for Academic Success, a four-week conditional-admission summer program, to selected entering students.

Internship Program

Students in the second and third year may elect to do a four- or ten-credit internship, where they may work in federal or local government agencies; judicial, legislative, or congressional offices; or in public interest legal organizations. Students are required to attend a weekly internship seminar at the school. The School of Law emphasizes the importance of supervision, educational merit, and public service in each internship. Students may also participate in the Summer Public Interest Fellowship Program.

Admission

Admission is based upon academic and nonacademic achievements and professional promise. UDC-DCSL considers the applicant's LSAT score and grades in tandem with other criteria that it believes may provide a more accurate measure of a candidate's determination, commitment, and potential for success in the study of law. The Admission Committee also considers other submitted application materials, such as the personal statement and essays, recommendations, community service, and employment experience. Applicants are encouraged to contact the Admission Office or to visit www.law.udc.edu for information about visiting the School of Law, sitting in on a class, and attending one of the Law Day-Open House programs or Information Sessions.

Financial Assistance and Scholarships

The financial aid policy provides students with financial assistance to support full-time and part-time study. This is usually accomplished through a combination of scholarships, grants, and loans. These include merit- and need-based scholarships, the Federal Stafford and GradPLUS loan programs, and federal and other work-study employment. About 63 percent of UDC-DCSL students receive scholarship assistance, and 96 percent receive some form of financial aid. Detailed information about financial aid application policies and procedures is available on the School of Law's website.

Student Activities

The first issue of the annual *District of Columbia Law Review* was published in 1992. Active student organizations include the Student Bar Association, Black Law Students Association, International Law Students Association, Voces Juridicas, OutLaw, Women's Law Society, Sports and Entertainment Student Lawyers Association, Christian Law Society, Phi Alpha Delta, Innocence Project, and the National Lawyers Guild.

Career Services

The Career Services Office provides employment information, individual career counseling, and résumé assistance to the School of Law's student body and graduates. The office maintains listings of permanent job openings, fellowships, summer clerkships, and part-time opportunities. The office also coordinates potential internship sites and invites employers to conduct on-campus interviews. The office provides resources for career planning, counseling sessions to assist students in developing their career goals, résumé workshops, and other relevant seminars.

APPLICANT PROFILE

The David A. Clarke School of Law prides itself on its admission philosophy, comprehensive and competitive admission process, and student diversity. While the applicant profile grids can be helpful to students, they may also discourage some students whose numerical profiles are slightly below the school's LSAT and GPA medians, but whose life experiences, for example, may be compelling. Numbers do not always provide an accurate picture of an applicant's potential for law study or motivation to succeed. The School of Law, therefore, does not provide an applicant profile grid, but rather a brief description of its student body. The student body is a diverse and accomplished group. The age range of students is 20 to 62 years. The average age is 28 years. People of color comprise about half of the student body, and women comprise more than half of the students. More than 33 states and over 115 undergraduate schools are represented in the student body. About 125 students are admitted each year. Smaller class sizes provide students with an ideal student-to-faculty ratio and a rich theoretical and practical learning environment. The LSAT mean for the fall 2010 entering class was 153, and the 25th and 75th LSAT percentiles were 149 and 155, respectively. The GPA mean was 3.10. The student body represents strong competency and contribution potential for the study of law.

DRAKE UNIVERSITY LAW SCHOOL

2507 University Avenue
Des Moines, IA 50311-4505
Phone: 800.44.DRAKE, ext. 2782 or 515.271.2782; Fax: 515.271.1990
E-mail: lawadmit@drake.edu; Website: www.law.drake.edu

ABA
Approved
Since
1923

The Basics

Type of school	Private
Term	Semester
Application deadline	4/1
Application fee	$50
Financial aid deadline	3/1
Can first year start other than fall?	Yes
Student to faculty ratio	13.8 to 1
# of housing spaces available restricted to law students	
graduate housing for which law students are eligible	82

Faculty and Administrators

	Total		Men		Women		Minorities	
	Spr	Fall	Spr	Fall	Spr	Fall	Spr	Fall
Full-time	27	27	17	16	10	11	3	3
Other full-time	2	1	2	1	0	0	1	0
Deans, librarians, & others who teach	10	10	5	5	5	5	0	0
Part-time	18	19	11	13	7	6	2	2
Total	57	57	35	35	22	22	6	5

Curriculum

	Full-Time	Part-Time
Typical first-year section size	75	0
Is there typically a "small section" of the first-year class, other than Legal Writing, taught by full-time faculty	No	No
If yes, typical size offered last year		
# of classroom course titles beyond first-year curriculum		99

# of upper division courses, excluding seminars, with an enrollment:	Under 25	84
	25–49	30
	50–74	5
	75–99	6
	100+	0

# of seminars		18
# of seminar positions available		340
# of seminar positions filled	231	0
# of positions available in simulation courses		520
# of simulation positions filled	294	0
# of positions available in faculty supervised clinical courses		120
# of faculty supervised clinical positions filled	113	0
# involved in field placements	132	0
# involved in law journals	81	0
# involved in moot court or trial competitions	51	0
# of credit hours required to graduate		90

JD Enrollment and Ethnicity

	Men		Women		Full-Time		Part-Time		1st-Year		Total		JD Degs. Awd.
	#	%	#	%	#	%	#	%	#	%	#	%	
All Hispanics	8	3.2	5	2.4	13	2.9	0	0.0	5	3.1	13	2.8	4
Am. Ind./AK Nat.	1	0.4	0	0.0	1	0.2	0	0.0	0	0.0	1	0.2	0
Asian	3	1.2	3	1.4	6	1.3	0	0.0	2	1.2	6	1.3	5
Black/Af. Am.	12	4.8	15	7.1	27	6.0	0	0.0	7	4.3	27	5.8	8
Nat. HI/Pac. Isl.	0	0.0	0	0.0	0	0.0	0	0.0	0	0.0	0	0.0	0
2 or more races	0	0.0	0	0.0	0	0.0	0	0.0	0	0.0	0	0.0	0
Subtotal (minor.)	24	9.6	23	10.8	47	10.4	0	0.0	14	8.7	47	10.2	18
Nonres. Alien	0	0.0	0	0.0	0	0.0	0	0.0	0	0.0	0	0.0	0
White/Cauc.	185	73.7	165	77.8	338	74.9	12	100.0	130	80.7	350	75.6	123
Unknown	42	16.7	24	11.3	66	14.6	0	0.0	17	10.6	66	14.3	1
Total	251	54.2	212	45.8	451	97.4	12	2.6	161	34.8	463		142

Transfers

Transfers in	7
Transfers out	0

Tuition and Fees

	Resident	Nonresident
Full-time	$32,514	$32,514
Part-time		
Tuition Guarantee Program		N

Living Expenses

Estimated living expenses for singles

Living on campus	Living off campus	Living at home
N/A	$17,560	$5,230

*ABA
Approved
Since
1923*

GPA and LSAT Scores

	Total	Full-Time	Part-Time
# of apps	1,131	1,129	2
# of offers	553	553	0
# of matrics	155	155	0
75% GPA	3.71	3.71	0.00
Median GPA	3.41	3.41	0.00
25% GPA	3.07	3.07	0.00
75% LSAT	158	158	0
Median LSAT	156	156	0
25% LSAT	153	153	0

Grants and Scholarships (from prior year)

	Total		Full-Time		Part-Time	
	#	%	#	%	#	%
Total # of students	467		451		16	
Total # receiving grants	276	59.1	276	61.2	0	0.0
Less than 1/2 tuition	144	30.8	144	31.9	0	0.0
Half to full tuition	99	21.2	99	22.0	0	0.0
Full tuition	19	4.1	19	4.2	0	0.0
More than full tuition	14	3.0	14	3.1	0	0.0
Median grant amount			$15,000		$0	

Informational and Library Resources

Total amount spent on library materials	$963,326
Study seating capacity inside the library	705
# of full-time equivalent professional librarians	6
Hours per week library is open	109
# of open, wired connections available to students	192
# of networked computers available for use by students	123
Has wireless network?	Y
Requires computer?	N

JD Attrition (from prior year)

	Academic	Other	Total	
	#	#	#	%
1st year	2	0	2	1.2
2nd year	0	0	0	0.0
3rd year	0	0	0	0.0
4th year	0	0	0	0.0

Employment (9 months after graduation)

	Total	Percentage
Employment status known	136	100.0
Employment status unknown	0	0.0
Employed	122	89.7
Pursuing graduate degrees	2	1.5
Unemployed (seeking, not seeking, or studying for the bar)	7	5.1
Type of Employment		
# employed in law firms	71	58.2
# employed in business and industry	19	15.6
# employed in government	10	8.2
# employed in public interest	11	9.0
# employed as judicial clerks	8	6.6
# employed in academia	3	2.5
Geographic Location		
# employed in state	89	73.0
# employed outside the US	0	0.0
# of states where employed	37	

Bar Passage Rates

First-time takers	121	Reporting %	76.86
Average school %	95.71	Average state %	92.92
Average pass difference	2.79		

Jurisdiction	Takers	Passers	Pass %	State %	Diff %
Iowa	83	80	96.39	93.17	3.22
Illinois	10	9	90.00	90.89	−0.89

DRAKE UNIVERSITY LAW SCHOOL

2507 University Avenue
Des Moines, IA 50311-4505
Phone: 800.44.DRAKE, ext. 2782 or 515.271.2782; Fax: 515.271.1990
E-mail: lawadmit@drake.edu; Website: www.law.drake.edu

Introduction

Drake University Law School can trace its history back to 1865, making it one of the nation's 25 oldest law schools. Accredited by the ABA, the Law School provides a personal education with a low (13:1) student-to-faculty ratio. Our commitment to an education that balances theory and practice has earned the Law School a reputation for training proven practitioners.

Drake Law School is the only law school in Iowa's capital city. The close relationship between Drake Law School and the greater Des Moines area legal community provides students the opportunity to get hands-on experience with the executive, judicial, and legislative branches of state government; the federal courts; federal and state administrative agencies; and a wide array of law firms and businesses.

Legal Clinic

The Drake Legal Clinic, housed in the beautiful Neal and Bea Smith Law Center, is one of the best training facilities in the country. The center operates much like a real law firm providing incomparable hands-on experience to students who participate. This state-of-the-art facility includes a technologically enhanced courtroom, office space for students, a library, and seminar rooms.

First-Year Trial Practicum

The only program of its kind in the country, the Trial Practicum adds an important experiential learning dimension to the first-year curriculum. During the spring semester, students observe an actual state court trial—from jury selection to verdict—in the courtroom of the Neal and Bea Smith Law Center. Breakout discussion groups and posttrial debriefings of the attorneys, judges, and jurors poignantly illustrate how law on the books becomes law in action.

Centers of Excellence and Certificate Programs

Agricultural Law Center—Our internationally recognized agricultural law program addresses the important issues in American and international law and policy regarding food production. Students conduct research, publish an agricultural law journal, and write articles on a wide range of topics. The center frequently hosts international agricultural law scholars who teach courses on international issues and topics such as farmland preservation, legal issues in biotechnology, and tax planning for agricultural businesses. The center also offers a series of one-week courses for students and attorneys in the Summer Agricultural Law Institute. The center offers a **Food and Agricultural Law Certificate** program, the first of its kind at an American law school.

Constitutional Law Center—Drake is one of only four schools selected to receive a congressional endowment for the establishment of a Constitutional Law Resource Center. The center sponsors a lecture series and annual symposia featuring nationally recognized constitutional scholars. The nationally renowned Dwight D. Opperman Lecture in

Constitutional Law has been delivered by 10 current and former justices of the United States Supreme Court. The center also offers a **Constitutional Law and Civil Rights Certificate** program and conducts the Summer Institute in Constitutional Law, a program designed for first-year students interested in getting their law school careers off to an early start. Students beginning in the Summer Institute who elect to take additional summer courses may accelerate their studies and graduate in December of their third year.

Intellectual Property Law Center—Our dynamic center offers an innovative curriculum, providing students with a solid foundation in both the theoretical and practical aspects of intellectual property law. The center features an annual summer institute that brings together judges, policymakers, industry leaders, attorneys, academics, and students to explore cutting-edge issues at the intersection of intellectual property, biotechnology, and agricultural sciences. In addition, the center serves as an international research hub, fostering partnerships with leading research institutions from around the world. Every year, the center sponsors groundbreaking symposia and distinguished lectures, hosts eminent speakers and internationally recognized experts, publishes books and an occasional paper series, and develops international research and outreach programs.

Center for Legislative Practice—Drake is one of only a few schools in the country that offers a **Legislative Practice Certificate**. Classroom study and a wide range of internships expose students to the underpinnings of legislative and rule-making processes. Students who complete the program are uniquely prepared to work for administrative or government agencies, to research and draft legislation, to represent businesses and organizations with government interests, or to work in a variety of other public policy making positions. Drake's close proximity to the state capital and other state and federal offices, trade associations, union headquarters, and public interest group agencies provides students with numerous opportunities to learn firsthand how these institutions operate.

The **Middleton Center for Children's Rights** pursues a broad agenda, advancing children's rights through the legal process, training, public information, and public policy formation. Drake Law students learn the interdisciplinary process essential to addressing the complex issues involved in child welfare and children's rights.

The **Health Law Certificate** program is for students interested in preparing for professional success and personal satisfaction through leadership and service in the health care and health law communities.

The **International and Comparative Law and Human Rights Certificate** program combines coursework in Drake's international and comparative law and related course offerings with a required study-abroad experience.

Litigation and Dispute Resolution Certification—Drake Law School has achieved a well-deserved reputation for its education and training of future litigators, mediators, negotiators, and judges. Our alumni are well represented among the nation's leading trial and appellate lawyers and on both the federal and state courts. The Litigation and Dispute Resolution Certificate program capitalizes on the school's traditional strengths in advocacy and dispute resolution.

Summer in France

Add an international element to your legal education by participating in our summer program at the University of Nantes Law School in France. Classes in comparative and international law and on-site visits to European legal institutions allow you to absorb and experience another country's legal system and be better prepared to practice law in a global society.

Joint-Degree Programs

Students may combine their Juris Doctor degree with the Master of Business Administration, Master of Public Administration, or Doctor of Pharmacy degree from Drake University. Students may also combine the JD degree with a Master of Arts in Political Science or Master of Science in Agricultural Economics (in cooperation with Iowa State University); a Master of Social Work (in cooperation with the University of Iowa); a Master of Health Care Administration; or a Master of Public Health (in cooperation with Des Moines University).

Student Activities

Drake Law students participate in many student organizations and cocurricular activities. Drake students publish two journals, the *Drake Law Review* and the *Journal of Agricultural Law*. *Drake Law Review* was named among the nation's 30 most-cited legal periodicals by the courts from 1997 to 2008. Drake moot court teams consistently win regional competitions and finish strongly in national competitions. The award-winning Student Bar Association and honorary societies provide students with leadership,

public service, and learning opportunities. Drake students have also formed more than 30 organizations around their special interests, including Drake Law Women, Black Law Students Association, Asian Pacific Law Student Association, Hispanic Law Student Association, International Law Society, Christian Legal Society, Environmental Law Society, Federalist Society, American Constitution Society, National Lawyers Guild, Intellectual Property Law Society, Agricultural Law Society, Alternative Dispute Resolution Society, and an organization for students with alternative sexual orientation.

Networking

Drake Law School alumni practice in 49 states and several foreign countries. The Career Development Office has a comprehensive, national alumni network set up to assist students with their career plans no matter where they want to go. Attorneys who participate in the alumni career network help students learn about the job market in their state and help ensure a smooth transition for students from law school to practice. Many area alumni also participate in our Partner's Program, which pairs first-year law students with practicing attorneys.

Career Development

The Career Development Office offers career planning and counseling services, assistance with résumés and cover letter preparation, salary and geographical employment statistics, nationwide job postings, and state bar examination information. The office also arranges interviews—both on and off campus—and exchanges job listings with 90 other law schools around the country.

APPLICANT PROFILE

Drake University Law School
This grid includes only applicants who earned 120–180 LSAT scores under standard administrations.

LSAT Score	3.75 +		3.50–3.74		3.25–3.49		3.00–3.24		2.75–2.99		2.50–2.74		2.25–2.49		2.00–2.24		Below 2.00		No GPA		Total	
	Apps	Adm	Apps	Adm	Apps	Adm	Apps	Adm	Apps	Adm	Apps	Adm	Apps	Adm	Apps	Adm	Apps	Adm	Apps	Adm	Apps	Adm
175–180	1	1	0	0	0	0	1	1	1	1	0	0	0	0	0	0	0	0	0	0	3	3
170–174	2	2	1	1	0	0	1	1	1	1	0	0	0	0	0	0	0	0	0	0	5	5
165–169	7	6	9	9	6	6	1	1	0	0	1	1	2	2	1	1	1	0	1	1	29	27
160–164	32	31	16	16	20	20	15	15	10	10	3	3	5	5	3	2	0	0	0	0	104	102
155–159	42	41	60	55	59	57	54	50	23	22	13	8	19	10	6	2	2	0	0	0	278	245
150–154	40	29	62	40	78	43	74	27	50	8	32	6	12	0	4	1	2	0	2	0	356	154
145–149	18	5	28	3	44	2	46	5	39	1	26	0	12	0	7	0	0	0	4	0	224	16
140–144	7	0	13	0	11	0	22	0	13	0	6	0	4	0	1	0	1	0	3	0	81	0
135–139	0	0	3	0	0	0	3	0	5	0	11	0	5	0	2	0	0	0	0	0	29	0
130–134	1	0	0	0	2	0	4	0	2	0	1	0	0	0	1	0	0	0	1	0	12	0
125–129	0	0	0	0	0	0	0	0	2	0	0	0	1	0	2	0	0	0	0	0	5	0
120–124	0	0	0	0	0	0	0	0	0	0	0	0	0	0	0	0	0	0	0	0	0	0
Total	150	115	192	124	220	128	221	100	146	43	93	18	60	17	27	6	6	0	11	1	1126	552

Apps = Number of Applicants
Adm = Number Admitted
Reflects 99% of the total applicant pool; highest LSAT data reported.

DUKE UNIVERSITY SCHOOL OF LAW

Science Drive & Towerview Road, Box 90393
Durham, NC 27708-0393
Phone: 919.613.7020; Fax: 919.613.7257
E-mail: admissions@law.duke.edu; Website: http://admissions.law.duke.edu

ABA
Approved
Since
1931

The Basics

Type of school	Private
Term	Semester
Application deadline	2/15
Application fee	$70
Financial aid deadline	3/15
Can first year start other than fall?	Yes
Student to faculty ratio	9.8 to 1
# of housing spaces available restricted to law students	
graduate housing for which law students are eligible	

Faculty and Administrators

	Total		Men		Women		Minorities	
	Spr	Fall	Spr	Fall	Spr	Fall	Spr	Fall
Full-time	54	59	41	42	13	17	5	9
Other full-time	9	11	4	5	5	6	1	2
Deans, librarians, & others who teach	11	11	5	5	6	6	0	0
Part-time	58	35	39	20	19	15	7	4
Total	132	116	89	72	43	44	13	15

Curriculum

		Full-Time	Part-Time
Typical first-year section size		72	0
Is there typically a "small section" of the first-year class, other than Legal Writing, taught by full-time faculty		Yes	No
If yes, typical size offered last year		35	
# of classroom course titles beyond first-year curriculum		195	
# of upper division courses, excluding seminars, with an enrollment:	Under 25	69	
	25–49	30	
	50–74	8	
	75–99	6	
	100+	3	
# of seminars		84	
# of seminar positions available		1,162	
# of seminar positions filled		955	0
# of positions available in simulation courses		375	
# of simulation positions filled		347	0
# of positions available in faculty supervised clinical courses		138	
# of faculty supervised clinical positions filled		131	0
# involved in field placements		86	0
# involved in law journals		306	0
# involved in moot court or trial competitions		122	0
# of credit hours required to graduate		84	

JD Enrollment and Ethnicity

	Men		Women		Full-Time		Part-Time		1st-Year		Total		JD Degs. Awd.
	#	%	#	%	#	%	#	%	#	%	#	%	
All Hispanics	27	6.7	27	9.6	50	7.8	4	10.8	21	8.7	54	7.9	12
Am. Ind./AK Nat.	2	0.5	0	0.0	2	0.3	0	0.0	0	0.0	2	0.3	0
Asian	35	8.7	25	8.9	60	9.3	0	0.0	28	11.6	60	8.8	14
Black/Af. Am.	21	5.2	24	8.6	43	6.7	2	5.4	8	3.3	45	6.6	17
Nat. HI/Pac. Isl.	0	0.0	0	0.0	0	0.0	0	0.0	0	0.0	0	0.0	0
2 or more races	2	0.5	2	0.7	4	0.6	0	0.0	3	1.2	4	0.6	0
Subtotal (minor.)	87	21.7	78	27.9	159	24.7	6	16.2	60	24.8	165	24.2	46
Nonres. Alien	6	1.5	8	2.9	14	2.2	0	0.0	4	1.7	14	2.1	0
White/Cauc.	275	68.6	174	62.1	420	65.2	29	78.4	175	72.3	449	65.9	142
Unknown	33	8.2	20	7.1	51	7.9	2	5.4	2	0.8	53	7.8	26
Total	401	58.9	280	41.1	644	94.6	37	5.4	241	35.4	681		216

Transfers

Transfers in	5
Transfers out	8

Tuition and Fees

	Resident	Nonresident
Full-time	$47,722	$47,722
Part-time		
Tuition Guarantee Program	N	

Living Expenses

Estimated living expenses for singles

Living on campus	Living off campus	Living at home
$17,190	$17,190	$17,190

DUKE UNIVERSITY SCHOOL OF LAW

ABA
Approved
Since
1931

GPA and LSAT Scores

	Total	Full-Time	Part-Time
# of apps	7,905	7,905	0
# of offers	1,044	1,044	0
# of matrics	238	238	0
75% GPA	3.90	3.90	0.00
Median GPA	3.80	3.80	0.00
25% GPA	3.68	3.68	0.00
75% LSAT	171	171	0
Median LSAT	170	170	0
25% LSAT	168	168	0

Grants and Scholarships (from prior year)

	Total #	Total %	Full-Time #	Full-Time %	Part-Time #	Part-Time %
Total # of students	661		626		35	
Total # receiving grants	495	74.9	495	79.1	0	0.0
Less than 1/2 tuition	440	66.6	440	70.3	0	0.0
Half to full tuition	41	6.2	41	6.5	0	0.0
Full tuition	13	2.0	13	2.1	0	0.0
More than full tuition	1	0.2	1	0.2	0	0.0
Median grant amount			$16,000		$0	

Informational and Library Resources

Total amount spent on library materials	$1,713,771
Study seating capacity inside the library	585
# of full-time equivalent professional librarians	11
Hours per week library is open	168
# of open, wired connections available to students	894
# of networked computers available for use by students	100
Has wireless network?	Y
Requires computer?	N

JD Attrition (from prior year)

	Academic #	Other #	Total #	Total %
1st year	0	8	8	3.5
2nd year	0	0	0	0.0
3rd year	0	0	0	0.0
4th year	0	0	0	0.0

Employment (9 months after graduation)

	Total	Percentage
Employment status known	219	100.0
Employment status unknown	0	0.0
Employed	209	95.4
Pursuing graduate degrees	5	2.3
Unemployed (seeking, not seeking, or studying for the bar)	0	0.0
Type of Employment		
# employed in law firms	147	70.3
# employed in business and industry	12	5.7
# employed in government	5	2.4
# employed in public interest	9	4.3
# employed as judicial clerks	35	16.7
# employed in academia	1	0.5
Geographic Location		
# employed in state	24	11.5
# employed outside the US	3	1.4
# of states where employed	28	

Bar Passage Rates

First-time takers	190	Reporting %	100.00
Average school %	94.20	Average state %	81.82
Average pass difference	12.38		

Jurisdiction	Takers	Passers	Pass %	State %	Diff %
New York	77	75	97.40	86.51	10.89
California	35	30	85.71	73.19	12.52
North Carolina	33	29	87.88	76.79	11.09
Virginia	10	10	100.00	77.06	22.94
Others (7)	35	35	100.00		

DUKE UNIVERSITY SCHOOL OF LAW

Science Drive & Towerview Road, Box 90393
Durham, NC 27708-0393
Phone: 919.613.7020; Fax: 919.613.7257
E-mail: admissions@law.duke.edu; Website: http://admissions.law.duke.edu

Introduction

Duke Law School is one of the nation's leading law schools, known for its emphasis on leadership, ethics, scholarly research, and programs that serve the profession and the community. Students come to Duke Law from every state and, as alumni, work in top law firms and companies around the country and world.

One of the reasons students choose Duke Law is its collaborative environment, where growth is encouraged not only through rigorous scholarship, but also through cooperation and support. Because the school is small, students enjoy uniquely close interactions with faculty and fellow students. Duke Law's faculty members are among the nation's most respected experts in fields ranging from constitutional law and national security to intellectual property and international business. In addition, professors are deeply dedicated to teaching and are accessible and responsive to students. Their open-door policy encourages students to ask questions, continue discussions, and seek advice on specialized interests. Faculty-student interaction extends beyond the classroom to committee work, research, pro bono opportunities, career counseling, and mentoring. Ultimately, students experience a supportive environment where the focus is on training and developing the whole person in an atmosphere that values different perspectives, backgrounds, and orientations.

Enrollment/Student Body

Duke Law admits a select group of students with diverse backgrounds who have in common a record of academic excellence. In 2010, JD students came to Duke from 40 states and 8 foreign countries. These students represented 116 different undergraduate institutions and had a wealth of different experiences. Approximately 34 percent of the students entering Duke Law in 2010 came directly from college, while the other 66 percent entered law school after gaining experience for a year or more in another profession or graduate school.

Faculty

Central to Duke Law's success is its faculty. Well respected in the legal field, Duke Law professors are known for groundbreaking legal scholarship that impacts public policy and the legal profession. A large number of faculty are also practitioners in both the public and private sectors in the United States and abroad. Their backgrounds are as varied as they are distinguished: they are former Fulbright Scholars, Rhodes Scholars, and Marshall Scholars. A number of faculty members have served as Supreme Court clerks, and one was the chief judge for the US Court of Military Appeals. Faculty members hold joint appointments in departments throughout the university and have obtained PhDs in a wide variety of disciplines. Several visiting professors from abroad teach at Duke Law each year, and many full-time faculty members have extensive international connections.

Dual Degrees

Duke Law faculty believe that society is best served by lawyers with diverse education and training. The law school jointly sponsors numerous academic and professional programs in conjunction with other schools or departments at Duke University. In addition, students may pursue a three-year JD/DESS (Diplôme d'études supérieures spécialisées) in global business law in partnership with Université Paris I and Sciences Po in Paris.

The law school and the graduate school jointly sponsor programs of study in law and several other disciplines, including (at the master's level) Art History, Biomedical Engineering, Classical Studies, Cultural Anthropology, East Asian Studies, Economics, Electrical and Computer Engineering, English, Environmental Science and Policy, History, Humanities, International Development Policy, Literature, Mechanical Engineering, Philosophy, Political Science, Psychology, Religion, Romance Studies, and Sociology. The only additional time necessary to obtain both degrees is the summer prior to the first year of school. At the doctoral level, dual programs in Philosophy and Political Science are available.

The law school offers dual-professional degrees with the Fuqua School of Business, the Divinity School, the Nicholas School of the Environment, the School of Medicine, and the Sanford School of Public Policy. A special option is available to complete the JD/MBA in seven semesters.

Duke Law students may also earn graduate certificates in Slavic, Eurasian, and East European Legal Studies; Health Care Policy; Health System Management; or Women's Studies.

Special Programs

- **JD/LLM in International and Comparative Law**—Duke Law has pioneered a unique joint-degree program that makes it possible for students to earn a JD and a Master of Laws in International and Comparative Law concurrently in three years. The only additional time needed is the summer prior to the first year of law school and the first half of the following summer, during which students attend one of Duke's Institutes in Transnational Law, either in Switzerland or Hong Kong.
- **International Study Abroad and Externships**—Duke Law has arrangements with 21 top foreign universities, which give all interested Duke students an opportunity to study abroad. Duke Law also offers international externship opportunities at public sector institutions that engage in international work. Duke has preapproved externships, but students are also encouraged to submit their own proposals.
- **Legal Clinics**—Duke Law School's clinical program has grown exponentially and houses a variety of clinics that offer a wide range of hands-on opportunities. A newly constructed clinical office suite brings a number of the programs together, allowing them to function as a public interest law firm. Clinical opportunities include: AIDS Legal Project, Animal Law Clinic, Appellate Litigation Clinic, Children's Law Clinic, Community Enterprise Clinic,

Environmental Law and Policy Clinic, Guantanamo Defense Clinic, and Wrongful Convictions Clinic.
- **Centers**—Interdisciplinary collaboration at Duke is fostered by a number of centers and programs, including the Arts Project; Center for Criminal Justice and Professional Responsibility; Center for Genome Ethics, Law, and Policy; Center for the Study of the Public Domain; Center on Law, Ethics, and National Security; Global Capital Markets Center; Nicholas Institute for Environmental Policy Solutions; and Program in Public Law. The school also is establishing two new centers: the Center for Sports and the Law and the Center on Race and Politics.
- **Duke in DC**—Duke Law offers students with an interest in public policy at the federal level the opportunity to spend a semester in Washington, DC. They will pursue an externship that may include positions on Capitol Hill, on the personal staff of house members and senators, with congressional committees, with NGOs and lobbying groups, and in the executive branch.

Admission and Financial Aid

Admission to Duke Law School is highly competitive. In addition to the academic criteria, other factors may help to distinguish some applicants. These include capacity for leadership, dedication to community service, excellence in a particular field, motivation, graduate study, work experience, extracurricular activities, and character.

Duke Law tries to achieve broad diversity in terms of general background, geography, and undergraduate institutions represented. Students are chosen not only for their potential for academic success, but also because of qualities that will enhance the overall character of the class.

Admitted applicants are eligible for consideration for merit- and need-based scholarship awards. A select group of outstanding entering students are chosen each year as Mordecai Scholars and receive a full-tuition scholarship. Mordecai Scholars possess a record of extraordinary

leadership and scholarly achievement prior to law school, and the personal qualities that are likely to result in community involvement and leadership.

Cocurricular Activities

Scholarship in the classroom is reinforced through a variety of opportunities for hands-on leadership training and professional experience. Through pro bono work, legal clinics, public interest projects, moot court, and opportunities for scholarly writing and editing on eight different legal journals, Duke prepares students for the real-world practice of law.

Professional Development

The award-winning Duke Blueprint provides structure to students' legal education and professional development by challenging them to engage intellectually, embody integrity, build relationships, serve the community, and become effective leaders.

Duke Law graduates find employment in all sectors of the legal profession and in all parts of the United States and the world. Many begin their careers in law firms. Top law firms from across the country interview on campus each year, and the number of interviews available and offers made far exceeds the number of students interviewing. Others pursue judicial clerkships—15 percent of the graduating class of 2009—or work for government agencies or business enterprises. Historically, nearly 100 percent of each class finds employment and average salaries are among the highest in the country.

Duke places special emphasis on support for students interested in a career in public service. Staff from both the Career Center and the Office of Pro Bono and Public Interest help students find opportunities both during and after law school. The law school provides financial support for these goals with grants to subsidize summer employment and a Loan Repayment Assistance Program for graduates who enter a life of public service.

APPLICANT PROFILE

Duke University School of Law
This grid includes only applicants who earned 120–180 LSAT scores under standard administrations.

LSAT Score	GPA															
	3.75 +		3.50–3.74		3.25–3.49		3.00–3.24		2.75–2.99		2.50–2.74		Below 2.50		No GPA		Total	
	Apps	Adm	Apps	Adm	Apps	Adm	Apps	Adm	Apps	Adm	Apps	Adm	Apps	Adm	Apps	Adm	Apps	Adm
170–180	993	455	785	302	290	14	106	0	35	0	12	0	5	0	31	1	2257	772
165–169	1182	189	727	18	296	5	128	0	33	0	12	0	12	0	38	0	2428	212
160–164	970	29	453	19	282	3	135	1	35	0	14	0	10	0	31	1	1930	53
155–159	154	4	160	3	166	1	85	0	24	0	10	0	9	0	22	0	630	8
150–154	56	1	73	0	59	0	61	0	32	0	19	0	11	0	12	0	323	1
145–149	20	0	22	0	35	0	38	0	17	0	10	0	13	0	9	0	164	0
140–144	8	0	12	0	19	0	20	0	16	0	7	0	10	0	7	0	99	0
Below 140	2	0	6	0	8	0	8	0	7	0	9	0	8	0	5	0	53	0
Total	3385	678	2238	342	1155	23	581	1	199	0	93	0	78	0	155	2	7884	1046

Apps = Number of Applicants
Adm = Number Admitted
Reflects 99% of the total applicant pool; highest LSAT data reported.

DUQUESNE UNIVERSITY SCHOOL OF LAW

201 Edward J. Hanley Hall, 900 Locust Street
Pittsburgh, PA 15282-0700
Phone: 412.396.6296; Fax: 412.396.1073
E-mail: campion@duq.edu; Website: www.duq.edu/law

ABA
Approved
Since
1960

The Basics

Type of school	Private	
Term	Semester	
Application deadline	4/1	5/1
Application fee	$60	
Financial aid deadline	5/31	
Can first year start other than fall?	No	
Student to faculty ratio	20.5 to 1	
# of housing spaces available		
restricted to law students		
graduate housing for which law students are eligible		

Faculty and Administrators

	Total		Men		Women		Minorities	
	Spr	Fall	Spr	Fall	Spr	Fall	Spr	Fall
Full-time	25	25	18	17	7	8	4	4
Other full-time	1	1	0	0	1	1	0	0
Deans, librarians, & others who teach	8	8	4	4	4	4	2	2
Part-time	45	36	30	25	15	11	3	3
Total	79	70	52	46	27	24	9	9

Curriculum

	Full-Time	Part-Time
Typical first-year section size	83	64
Is there typically a "small section" of the first-year class, other than Legal Writing, taught by full-time faculty	Yes	No
If yes, typical size offered last year	50	
# of classroom course titles beyond first-year curriculum	88	

# of upper division courses, excluding seminars, with an enrollment:	Under 25	31
	25–49	23
	50–74	39
	75–99	12
	100+	0

# of seminars	20	
# of seminar positions available	251	
# of seminar positions filled	128	35
# of positions available in simulation courses	247	
# of simulation positions filled	41	175
# of positions available in faculty supervised clinical courses	98	
# of faculty supervised clinical positions filled	51	19
# involved in field placements	40	17
# involved in law journals	24	14
# involved in moot court or trial competitions	64	8
# of credit hours required to graduate	86	

JD Enrollment and Ethnicity

	Men		Women		Full-Time		Part-Time		1st-Year		Total		JD Degs. Awd.
	#	%	#	%	#	%	#	%	#	%	#	%	
All Hispanics	4	1.1	5	1.5	7	1.5	2	0.9	2	0.9	9	1.3	1
Am. Ind./AK Nat.	1	0.3	1	0.3	1	0.2	1	0.4	1	0.5	2	0.3	1
Asian	6	1.7	2	0.6	6	1.3	2	0.9	2	0.9	8	1.2	0
Black/Af. Am.	8	2.2	12	3.7	14	3.1	6	2.6	9	4.2	20	2.9	9
Nat. HI/Pac. Isl.	0	0.0	0	0.0	0	0.0	0	0.0	0	0.0	0	0.0	0
2 or more races	0	0.0	0	0.0	0	0.0	0	0.0	0	0.0	0	0.0	0
Subtotal (minor.)	19	5.3	20	6.1	28	6.2	11	4.7	14	6.5	39	5.7	12
Nonres. Alien	0	0.0	0	0.0	0	0.0	0	0.0	0	0.0	0	0.0	0
White/Cauc.	342	94.7	307	93.9	426	93.8	223	95.3	203	94.4	649	94.3	192
Unknown	0	0.0	0	0.0	0	0.0	0	0.0	0	0.0	0	0.0	0
Total	361	52.5	327	47.5	454	66.0	234	34.0	217	31.3	688		204

Transfers

Transfers in	0
Transfers out	0

Tuition and Fees

	Resident	Nonresident
Full-time	$32,376	$32,376
Part-time	$25,034	$25,034
Tuition Guarantee Program		N

Living Expenses

Estimated living expenses for singles

Living on campus	Living off campus	Living at home
$12,304	$12,304	$3,650

ABA
*Approved
Since
1960*

GPA and LSAT Scores

	Total	Full-Time	Part-Time
# of apps	930	705	217
# of offers	460	382	78
# of matrics	212	165	47
75% GPA	3.63	3.64	3.62
Median GPA	3.35	3.42	3.28
25% GPA	3.11	3.17	3.15
75% LSAT	155	156	154
Median LSAT	153	154	151
25% LSAT	151	152	149

Grants and Scholarships (from prior year)

	Total		Full-Time		Part-Time	
	#	%	#	%	#	%
Total # of students	704		446		258	
Total # receiving grants	212	30.1	160	35.9	52	20.2
Less than 1/2 tuition	129	18.3	90	20.2	39	15.1
Half to full tuition	26	3.7	19	4.3	7	2.7
Full tuition	48	6.8	43	9.6	5	1.9
More than full tuition	9	1.3	8	1.8	1	0.4
Median grant amount			$11,000		$3,941	

Informational and Library Resources

Total amount spent on library materials	$821,529
Study seating capacity inside the library	411
# of full-time equivalent professional librarians	8
Hours per week library is open	102
# of open, wired connections available to students	25
# of networked computers available for use by students	74
Has wireless network?	Y
Requires computer?	N

JD Attrition (from prior year)

	Academic	Other	Total	
	#	#	#	%
1st year	6	0	6	2.6
2nd year	1	0	1	0.5
3rd year	0	0	0	0.0
4th year	0	0	0	0.0

Employment (9 months after graduation)

	Total	Percentage
Employment status known	183	88.8
Employment status unknown	23	11.2
Employed	160	87.4
Pursuing graduate degrees	5	2.7
Unemployed (seeking, not seeking, or studying for the bar)	18	9.8
Type of Employment		
# employed in law firms	90	56.2
# employed in business and industry	26	16.2
# employed in government	17	10.6
# employed in public interest	2	1.2
# employed as judicial clerks	18	11.2
# employed in academia	3	1.9
Geographic Location		
# employed in state	108	67.5
# employed outside the US	0	0.0
# of states where employed	16	

Bar Passage Rates

First-time takers	206	Reporting %	86.89
Average school %	87.71	Average state %	85.69
Average pass difference	2.02		

Jurisdiction	Takers	Passers	Pass %	State %	Diff %
Pennsylvania	179	157	87.71	85.69	2.02

DUQUESNE UNIVERSITY SCHOOL OF LAW

201 Edward J. Hanley Hall, 900 Locust Street
Pittsburgh, PA 15282-0700
Phone: 412.396.6296; Fax: 412.396.1073
E-mail: campion@duq.edu; Website: www.duq.edu/law

Introduction

The Duquesne University School of Law is a Catholic law school that has been in existence since 1911 and is the only multiple-division law school in western Pennsylvania. Admission requirements, instruction, and the nature and scope of the work required of students are identical for both the full-time day division and the part-time evening and part-time day divisions. The School of Law is approved by the ABA and is a member of the AALS.

Situated on the attractive 43-acre Duquesne University campus, the law school is within walking distance to the vibrant Pittsburgh downtown legal, corporate, and government communities.

Recognized as one of the best cities in which to practice law and a center for corporate and legal headquarters, Pittsburgh is a leading metropolis for high technology ventures and a thriving arts and cultural community, with major-league sports entertainment.

Library and Physical Facilities

Duquesne's proximity to the Pittsburgh region's legal center makes the law school library a major source for legal research and information services. The Duquesne law library has assumed management responsibility of the Allegheny County Law Library, resulting in one of the largest collections of legal materials in Pennsylvania.

The law school recently completed a $12 million renovation and expansion, adding 33,000 square feet to Hanley Hall. The four new floors of space include a state-of-the-art moot courtroom (giving us three), three new technology-aided classrooms with ports and power sources at every seat, an upgraded lounge area with a cafeteria, new faculty and administrative offices, student locker areas, a conference room, and a wireless computer lab.

Curriculum

The course of study offered at the School of Law is sufficiently broad to prepare students for practice in all states. Three years are required for completion of the course of study in the day division, four years in the evening division and the part-time day division. Eighty-six credits are required for graduation.

While emphasis is placed upon skills such as legal research and writing and trial advocacy, the required courses are sufficiently broad to provide all students with the requisite skills to become competent lawyers in any field of practice. A wide selection of elective courses, seminars, and student in-house and internal clinics allows students to focus on specialized legal fields and explore the contemporary problems of law and society.

Admission

Bachelor's degree required. Application deadlines: day, April 1; evening, May 1; part-time day, June 1; rolling admission. LSAT and registration with LSAC's Credential Assembly Service (CAS) required.

All candidates for admission must take the LSAT, register for the Credential Assembly Service (CAS), and be graduates of an accredited college or university before enrolling in the law school. Personal interviews are not granted, but applicants are encouraged to schedule an appointment to visit the school for an information session or a tour of the facilities.

The admission process is selective. Most applicants apply well in advance of the deadlines. Students are admitted only for the fall semester.

In evaluating applications, the complete academic record is reviewed with consideration given to the competitiveness of the undergraduate institution, the college major, rank in class, and the overall academic performance. The LSAT is considered an important factor. Graduate study, extracurricular activities, and recommendations also contribute to the committee's assessment. Work experience is considered when an applicant has been employed full time for a significant length of time.

Joint-Degree Programs

The School of Law offers the following joint-degree programs: JD/MBA, JD/MS-Environmental Science and Management, JD/MA-Healthcare Ethics, and JD/MDiv.

Clinical Opportunities

The School of Law operates five in-house live client clinics.

The **Economic and Community Development Law Clinic** is a unique, nationally recognized clinic. Students represent nonprofit organizations that provide a vast array of greatly needed services to the community. Through the **Civil and Family Justice Law Clinic**, students represent indigent individuals who would not otherwise find assistance through the civil justice system. The **Criminal Advocacy Clinic** is operated in cooperation with the Allegheny County District Attorney's and Public Defender's offices. Through the **Federal Low Income Tax Practicum**, students learn litigation skills as they represent clients in appeals conferences, settlement negotiations, and before the US Tax Court. The **Securities Arbitration Practicum**, created with the support of the Securities and Exchange Commission, is designed to enable law students to represent small investors through the NASD Dispute Resolution process.

International Programs

The law school has established a summer program and faculty exchange with the Chinese University of Political Science and Law (CUPL). Located in Beijing, CUPL, with official ties to China's Ministry of Justice, is the most prestigious center for legal study in all of China. Duquesne has an outstanding ABA-approved summer program of study on Comparative Law and the European Union at the American College, Dublin. The Duquesne law school has recently established an ABA-approved program for law students in Vatican City, focusing on subjects relating to Canon Law and Roman Law. Duquesne is the only law school offering a program for law students within Vatican City.

Student Activities

The Student Bar Association maintains a liaison between students and faculty and sponsors social and professional activities for the student body.

Membership in the *Duquesne Law Review* is based on the demonstrated academic ability of the student as well as his or her interest in becoming active in this publication. *Juris*, the law school news magazine, is an ABA award-winning publication containing articles of current interest to the entire legal community. Students also publish the *Duquesne Business Law Journal*.

Financial Aid

Duquesne consistently strives to ensure that the outstanding private legal education provided by the law school is within the reach of all qualified students. Merit scholarships are awarded to outstanding day-division applicants, grants-in-aid are awarded primarily on the basis of need, and state and federal government-sponsored loans are available.

Housing

Law students have access to an array of housing options throughout the neighborhoods of Pittsburgh and the surrounding communities. The Office of Commuter Affairs will assist law students in their search for housing by providing a list of available locations. For further information, please write to the Office of Commuter Affairs, Duquesne University, Pittsburgh, PA 15282, or call 412.396.6660.

Career Services

The Career Services Office staff offers assistance to students and alumni who are interested in obtaining full-time, part-time, and summer employment. The office offers a fall and spring on-campus interview program in which law firms, government agencies, corporations, and accounting firms conduct individual interviews.

The School of Law is a member of the National Association for Law Placement, the National Association for Public Interest Law Publication Network, and the Allegheny County Bar Association Minority Job Fair.

Graduates have consistently been placed at a rate at or above 90 percent within six months of graduation. The law school has nearly 5,000 alumni throughout the United States and in several foreign countries.

APPLICANT PROFILE

The law school recognizes the different strengths presented by our day division, evening division, and part-time day students and acknowledges that the diversity in the groups cannot be accurately or completely represented in a single grid of average undergraduate GPA and LSAT scores. Graduate degrees, personal and professional accomplishments, and extensive employment experience predominate in the evening, part-time, and day divisions.

These factors are considered crucial to an individual assessment of admissibility. Applications are reviewed individually, and factors such as leadership experience, community service, and other nonacademic experiences are considered. Applicants should contact the Admissions Office for specific information on the current year's class; phone: 412.396.6296. Applicants are encouraged to visit the law school.

EARLE MACK SCHOOL OF LAW, DREXEL UNIVERSITY

3320 Market Street, Suite 100
Philadelphia, PA 19104
Phone: 215.895.1529
E-mail: LawAdmissions@drexel.edu; Website: www.earlemacklaw.drexel.edu/admissions

Provisional | ABA Approved Since 2008

The Basics

Type of school	Private
Term	Semester
Application deadline	8/1
Application fee	$0
Financial aid deadline	5/1
Can first year start other than fall?	No
Student to faculty ratio	15.7 to 1
# of housing spaces available restricted to law students	
graduate housing for which law students are eligible	356

Faculty and Administrators

	Total		Men		Women		Minorities	
	Spr	Fall	Spr	Fall	Spr	Fall	Spr	Fall
Full-time	21	24	11	13	10	11	7	7
Other full-time	5	3	0	0	5	3	2	1
Deans, librarians, & others who teach	8	7	4	4	4	3	2	2
Part-time	52	31	31	17	21	14	6	5
Total	86	65	46	34	40	31	17	15

Curriculum

	Full-Time	Part-Time
Typical first-year section size	77	0
Is there typically a "small section" of the first-year class, other than Legal Writing, taught by full-time faculty	No	No
If yes, typical size offered last year		
# of classroom course titles beyond first-year curriculum	104	

# of upper division courses, excluding seminars, with an enrollment:		
	Under 25	92
	25–49	26
	50–74	8
	75–99	1
	100+	0

# of seminars	12	
# of seminar positions available	200	
# of seminar positions filled	158	0
# of positions available in simulation courses	430	
# of simulation positions filled	325	0
# of positions available in faculty supervised clinical courses	8	
# of faculty supervised clinical positions filled	8	0
# involved in field placements	222	0
# involved in law journals	50	0
# involved in moot court or trial competitions	39	0
# of credit hours required to graduate	85	

JD Enrollment and Ethnicity

	Men		Women		Full-Time		Part-Time		1st-Year		Total		JD Degs. Awd.
	#	%	#	%	#	%	#	%	#	%	#	%	
All Hispanics	14	5.7	9	4.6	23	5.2	0	0.0	4	2.7	23	5.2	4
Am. Ind./AK Nat.	2	0.8	0	0.0	2	0.5	0	0.0	0	0.0	2	0.5	0
Asian	12	4.9	11	5.6	23	5.2	0	0.0	9	6.0	23	5.2	5
Black/Af. Am.	15	6.1	17	8.7	32	7.3	0	0.0	18	12.1	32	7.3	11
Nat. HI/Pac. Isl.	0	0.0	0	0.0	0	0.0	0	0.0	0	0.0	0	0.0	0
2 or more races	0	0.0	0	0.0	0	0.0	0	0.0	0	0.0	0	0.0	0
Subtotal (minor.)	43	17.6	37	18.9	80	18.2	0	0.0	31	20.8	80	18.2	20
Nonres. Alien	3	1.2	0	0.0	3	0.7	0	0.0	0	0.0	3	0.7	0
White/Cauc.	182	74.6	151	77.0	333	75.7	0	0.0	110	73.8	333	75.7	87
Unknown	16	6.6	8	4.1	24	5.5	0	0.0	8	5.4	24	5.5	2
Total	244	55.5	196	44.5	440	100.0	0	0.0	149	33.9	440		112

Transfers

Transfers in	9
Transfers out	1

Tuition and Fees

	Resident	Nonresident
Full-time	$34,450	$34,450
Part-time		
Tuition Guarantee Program		N

Living Expenses

Estimated living expenses for singles

Living on campus	Living off campus	Living at home
$21,488	$21,311	$21,076

EARLE MACK SCHOOL OF LAW, DREXEL UNIVERSITY

*ABA
Approved
Since
2008*

GPA and LSAT Scores

	Total	Full-Time	Part-Time
# of apps	2,908	2,908	0
# of offers	1,038	1,038	0
# of matrics	146	146	0
75% GPA	3.58	3.58	0.00
Median GPA	3.28	3.28	0.00
25% GPA	2.99	2.99	0.00
75% LSAT	162	162	0
Median LSAT	159	159	0
25% LSAT	156	156	0

Grants and Scholarships (from prior year)

	Total		Full-Time		Part-Time	
	#	%	#	%	#	%
Total # of students	410		410		0	
Total # receiving grants	358	87.3	358	87.3	0	0.0
Less than 1/2 tuition	159	38.8	159	38.8	0	0.0
Half to full tuition	175	42.7	175	42.7	0	0.0
Full tuition	0	0.0	0	0.0	0	0.0
More than full tuition	24	5.9	24	5.9	0	0.0
Median grant amount			$20,267		$0	

Informational and Library Resources

Total amount spent on library materials	$1,024,314
Study seating capacity inside the library	327
# of full-time equivalent professional librarians	8
Hours per week library is open	93
# of open, wired connections available to students	731
# of networked computers available for use by students	16
Has wireless network?	Y
Requires computer?	Y

JD Attrition (from prior year)

	Academic	Other	Total	
	#	#	#	%
1st year	1	2	3	1.9
2nd year	2	2	4	2.9
3rd year	0	0	0	0.0
4th year	0	0	0	0.0

Employment (9 months after graduation)

	Total	Percentage
Employment status known	151	95.0
Employment status unknown	8	5.0
Employed	126	83.4
Pursuing graduate degrees	5	3.3
Unemployed (seeking, not seeking, or studying for the bar)	19	12.6
Type of Employment		
# employed in law firms	61	48.4
# employed in business and industry	20	15.9
# employed in government	15	11.9
# employed in public interest	7	5.6
# employed as judicial clerks	19	15.1
# employed in academia	3	2.4
Geographic Location		
# employed in state	62	49.2
# employed outside the US	1	0.8
# of states where employed		9

Bar Passage Rates

First-time takers	151	Reporting %	84.77
Average school %	89.84	Average state %	85.69
Average pass difference	4.15		

Jurisdiction	Takers	Passers	Pass %	State %	Diff %
Pennsylvania	128	115	89.84	85.69	4.15

EARLE MACK SCHOOL OF LAW, DREXEL UNIVERSITY

3320 Market Street, Suite 100
Philadelphia, PA 19104
Phone: 215.895.1529
E-mail: LawAdmissions@drexel.edu; Website: www.earlemacklaw.drexel.edu/admissions

Introduction

Drexel University has long believed in the value of experiential education and promoted learning opportunities for students outside of the classroom. This deeply rooted educational philosophy led the Earle Mack School of Law at Drexel University to develop imaginative approaches to legal education that produce outstanding lawyers who share a commitment to serving the public good.

Our approach integrates theory and practice so that students master both legal principles and the real-world skills needed to apply them. By adapting Drexel University's signature emphasis on hands-on learning to the law school setting, we are forging connections between legal educators, practitioners, and the public we aim to serve, thereby fostering a new civic professionalism.

We give students a multitude of opportunities for hands-on learning. The Co-op Program allows opportunities to gain experience in a variety of legal settings. The Clinical Program allows students to represent clients in criminal and civil matters though our in-house Appellate Litigation Clinic and Field Clinics with three of Philadelphia's premiere public interest organizations. Our top-notch Trial Advocacy Program prepares students to argue before trial and appellate courts. Our Pro Bono program provides yet another avenue for gaining practical experience.

The law school has demonstrated its strong support for the Co-op Program in many ways: by allotting a significant number of credits for the program, by hiring faculty with extensive practice experience to teach the classroom component and to work closely with the supervising attorneys in the field, and by maintaining a low faculty-to-student ratio. Well over 100 co-op partners and other supervising attorneys have joined us to help realize this new vision of professional legal education for the twenty-first century.

Location

Located in the University City neighborhood just adjacent to downtown Philadelphia, the law school is mere blocks from the heart of one of the nation's largest and most dynamic legal communities. University City is so named because of the 40,000 students from Drexel University and the University of Pennsylvania who combine to create an exciting, vibrant community. Thanks to our location, affordable student housing is located a short walk or trolley ride away, and students are able to meet after class at many of the nearby restaurants, trendy shops, and bars.

Faculty and Curriculum

Our faculty of nationally recognized scholars and experienced practitioners share a commitment to innovative teaching and the integration of theory and practice.

Professors at the Earle Mack School of Law have distinguished backgrounds in scholarship and legal practice. The faculty includes pioneers who helped establish disciplines like health law and who are engaged in path-breaking approaches to legal education.

In the first year, we offer strong introductory classes that emphasize professionalism. The first-year curriculum also features a rigorous introduction to legal methods, which starts during orientation. First-year students also receive an introduction to the skills of interviewing, negotiation, and counseling, and gain critical legal writing and oral advocacy skills.

Upper-level students choose from elective courses in areas as diverse as e-commerce law, criminal law, employment law, family law, international law, animal rights, bioethics, sports law, and securities law. Courses from Trial Advocacy to Transactional Lawyering feature simulations that allow students to put their skills to practice while they're still in class.

For students seeking an in-depth introduction to a single area of practice, the law school offers three concentrations in the fields of intellectual property, health law, and business and entrepreneurship law. In partnership with Drexel University's respected Psychology Department, we offer a joint JD-PhD in psychology; with Drexel's LeBow College of Business, we offer a joint JD-MBA; with the School of Public Health, a joint JD-MPH; and with the College of Arts and Sciences, a joint JD-MSPP.

With varied concentration options, an intensive emphasis on skills, and professors who bring practice into the classroom, the curriculum prepares students to enter professional practice with confidence and savvy.

Admission

When considering applicants, the Earle Mack School of Law does not employ cutoffs or numerical formulas. Rather, we look at an applicant's entire application and take into consideration both objective factors like the LSAT and GPA, as well as subjective factors like leadership skills, work experience, and commitment to service.

We utilize rolling admissions, which means it is never too late to apply. Nevertheless, we encourage students to apply as early in the year as possible, since scholarship and admission decisions are weighted favorably towards early applicants.

Co-op Program

Our Co-op Program provides a unique opportunity for law students to synthesize the legal theory learned in the classroom with the critical knowledge and professional skills learned in the field under the close supervision of experienced practitioners. Our commitment to integrating the Co-op Program into the curriculum and the singular focus students give to their placements distinguish it from experiential programs offered by other law schools.

The Co-op Program is a semester-long field placement during the second or third year of study that allows a student to work in a law firm, corporation, judicial office, public interest organization, or government agency. Each placement is chosen for the quality experience that it can provide law students as part of their overall academic experience. Students learn the law relevant to the practice area and the skills needed to succeed there. They also get acquainted with the host institution and the industries to which it belongs while building professional networks with the practitioners who work there.

Clinical Program

Students gain firsthand experience representing clients while earning academic credit through our year-long Clinical Program.

The Civil Litigation Field Clinic, which operates in tandem with the AIDS Law Project of Pennsylvania, allows students to represent clients in Landlord-Tenant Court, in guardianship cases, and in administrative-law hearings to determine eligibility for disability benefits.

The Criminal Litigation Field Clinic, which operates in partnership with the Defender Association of Philadelphia, allows students to represent clients in preliminary hearings on felonies and to argue legal motions and try misdemeanor cases in Philadelphia's municipal court.

The Public Health and Environmental Law Field Clinic, developed in concert with the Public Interest Law Center of Philadelphia, enables students to help community leaders and neighborhood organizations explore and pursue legal strategies to address environmental and public health concerns.

Our in-house Appellate Litigation Clinic offers students the unique opportunity to practice law before state and federal appellate courts. Students provide valuable legal services to needy individuals who otherwise would not be able obtain representation to appeal matters involving constitutional law, criminal law, immigration law, and the rights of the indigent and the incarcerated.

Trial Advocacy Program

The law school's innovative Trial Advocacy Program trains students in the essential practical skills of litigation.

In Pretrial Advocacy, students learn how to interview a client, plan pretrial investigation, identify and retain experts, and draft pleadings and motions. During the trial preparation phase, students also learn how to develop the cornerstone of any successful litigation strategy: a theory of the case. They also learn deposition strategies and techniques, as well as other discovery techniques.

In Trial Advocacy, experienced trial lawyers and judges teach effective trial techniques by providing live demonstrations relating to jury selection, opening and closing statements, and direct- and cross-examination of lay and expert witnesses. Students also learn how computer technology is used to create and introduce state-of-the-art trial exhibits that will enhance the presentation of evidence at trial. Trial Advocacy ends with a capstone experience in which each student litigates a mock trial in a real courtroom before real judges and veteran attorneys.

Pro Bono Service

Providing pro bono service to individuals or groups traditionally underserved by the private bar is the goal of our mandatory 50-hour Pro Bono Service Requirement. Students will make an immediate impact in the world by helping those most in need. In addition, the program strives to educate students about their ethical responsibility to provide assistance and improve access to legal services throughout their legal careers. Finally, the program highlights public service opportunities that students may want to pursue as a career path.

Working with supervising attorneys, students develop their legal skills and gain practical, hands-on experience in a real legal setting. The Pro Bono Service Requirement is a vital part of our curriculum that demonstrates the commitment of faculty and administrators to developing our students' professionalism.

APPLICANT PROFILE

Earle Mack School of Law, Drexel University

LSAT Score	GPA								
	3.75 +	3.50–3.74	3.25–3.49	3.00–3.24	2.75–2.99	2.50–2.74	2.25–2.49	2.00–2.24	Below 2.00
175–180									
170–174									
165–169									
160–164									
155–159									
150–154									
145–149									
140–144									
120–139									

Good Possibility   Possible   Unlikely

ELON UNIVERSITY SCHOOL OF LAW

201 North Greene Street
Greensboro, NC 27401
Phone: 336.279.9200; Fax: 336.279.8199
E-mail: law@elon.edu; Website: www.law.elon.edu

Provisional ABA Approved Since 2008

The Basics

Type of school	Private
Term	Semester
Application deadline	10/1 6/30
Application fee	$50
Financial aid deadline	
Can first year start other than fall?	No
Student to faculty ratio	16.6 to 1
# of housing spaces available restricted to law students	
graduate housing for which law students are eligible	

Faculty and Administrators

	Total		Men		Women		Minorities	
	Spr	Fall	Spr	Fall	Spr	Fall	Spr	Fall
Full-time	16	17	11	11	5	6	3	4
Other full-time	1	3	0	1	1	2	0	0
Deans, librarians, & others who teach	6	6	3	3	3	3	2	2
Part-time	26	12	19	10	7	2	3	1
Total	49	38	33	25	16	13	8	7

Curriculum

	Full-Time	Part-Time
Typical first-year section size	30	0
Is there typically a "small section" of the first-year class, other than Legal Writing, taught by full-time faculty	Yes	No
If yes, typical size offered last year	30	
# of classroom course titles beyond first-year curriculum	63	
# of upper division courses, excluding seminars, with an enrollment: Under 25	21	
25–49	18	
50–74	6	
75–99	3	
100+	0	
# of seminars	9	
# of seminar positions available	167	
# of seminar positions filled	115	0
# of positions available in simulation courses	254	
# of simulation positions filled	193	0
# of positions available in faculty supervised clinical courses	52	
# of faculty supervised clinical positions filled	49	0
# involved in field placements	37	0
# involved in law journals	22	0
# involved in moot court or trial competitions	25	0
# of credit hours required to graduate	90	

JD Enrollment and Ethnicity

	Men		Women		Full-Time		Part-Time		1st-Year		Total		JD Degs. Awd.
	#	%	#	%	#	%	#	%	#	%	#	%	
All Hispanics	4	2.2	2	1.3	6	1.8	0	0.0	2	1.5	6	1.8	0
Am. Ind./AK Nat.	0	0.0	3	1.9	3	0.9	0	0.0	2	1.5	3	0.9	0
Asian	8	4.3	2	1.3	10	2.9	0	0.0	3	2.3	10	2.9	2
Black/Af. Am.	6	3.2	18	11.5	24	7.0	0	0.0	11	8.4	24	7.0	3
Nat. HI/Pac. Isl.	0	0.0	0	0.0	0	0.0	0	0.0	0	0.0	0	0.0	0
2 or more races	0	0.0	0	0.0	0	0.0	0	0.0	0	0.0	0	0.0	0
Subtotal (minor.)	18	9.7	25	15.9	43	12.6	0	0.0	18	13.7	43	12.6	5
Nonres. Alien	0	0.0	0	0.0	0	0.0	0	0.0	0	0.0	0	0.0	0
White/Cauc.	154	83.2	126	80.3	280	81.9	0	0.0	103	78.6	280	81.9	90
Unknown	13	7.0	6	3.8	19	5.6	0	0.0	10	7.6	19	5.6	2
Total	185	54.1	157	45.9	342	100.0	0	0.0	131	38.3	342		97

Transfers

| Transfers in | 2 |
| Transfers out | 4 |

Tuition and Fees

	Resident	Nonresident
Full-time	$32,600	$32,600
Part-time		
Tuition Guarantee Program	N	

Living Expenses

Estimated living expenses for singles

Living on campus	Living off campus	Living at home
N/A	$22,200	N/A

ELON UNIVERSITY SCHOOL OF LAW

ABA Approved Since 2008

GPA and LSAT Scores

	Total	Full-Time	Part-Time
# of apps	885	885	0
# of offers	361	361	0
# of matrics	132	132	0
75% GPA	3.40	3.40	0.00
Median GPA	3.10	3.10	0.00
25% GPA	2.80	2.80	0.00
75% LSAT	159	159	0
Median LSAT	155	155	0
25% LSAT	153	153	0

Grants and Scholarships (from prior year)

	Total		Full-Time		Part-Time	
	#	%	#	%	#	%
Total # of students	315		315		0	
Total # receiving grants	259	82.2	259	82.2	0	0.0
Less than 1/2 tuition	214	67.9	214	67.9	0	0.0
Half to full tuition	33	10.5	33	10.5	0	0.0
Full tuition	12	3.8	12	3.8	0	0.0
More than full tuition	0	0.0	0	0.0	0	0.0
Median grant amount			$7,500		$0	

Informational and Library Resources

Total amount spent on library materials	$706,992
Study seating capacity inside the library	333
# of full-time equivalent professional librarians	6
Hours per week library is open	102
# of open, wired connections available to students	102
# of networked computers available for use by students	32
Has wireless network?	Y
Requires computer?	N

JD Attrition (from prior year)

	Academic	Other	Total	
	#	#	#	%
1st year	5	5	10	8.3
2nd year	0	0	0	0.0
3rd year	0	0	0	0.0
4th year	0	0	0	0.0

Employment (9 months after graduation)

	Total	Percentage
Employment status known	97	90.7
Employment status unknown	10	9.3
Employed	87	89.7
Pursuing graduate degrees	4	4.1
Unemployed (seeking, not seeking, or studying for the bar)	5	5.2
Type of Employment		
# employed in law firms	65	74.7
# employed in business and industry	7	8.0
# employed in government	5	5.7
# employed in public interest	4	4.6
# employed as judicial clerks	4	4.6
# employed in academia	1	1.1
Geographic Location		
# employed in state	77	88.5
# employed outside the US	0	0.0
# of states where employed	7	

Bar Passage Rates

First-time takers	105	Reporting %	93.33
Average school %	82.65	Average state %	76.79
Average pass difference	5.86		

Jurisdiction	Takers	Passers	Pass %	State %	Diff %
North Carolina	98	81	82.65	76.79	5.86

ELON UNIVERSITY SCHOOL OF LAW

201 North Greene Street
Greensboro, NC 27401
Phone: 336.279.9200; Fax: 336.279.8199
E-mail: law@elon.edu; Website: www.law.elon.edu

Introduction

Elon University School of Law was established in 2006 at a dedication ceremony led by retired US Supreme Court Justice Sandra Day O'Connor. Excellence in the law through engaged learning and leadership development forms the center of the school's mission and purpose. The program of legal education at Elon Law prepares students to be not only successful lawyers who excel at the highest levels of the profession, but also global citizens who lead in solving challenges facing their communities, nation, and world.

Location

Elon University School of Law is located in downtown Greensboro, North Carolina, the third largest city in North Carolina, with a regional population of about 1.5 million. The law school is located at the center of the area's legal community, including major law firms, government offices, and district and federal courts. The downtown area also provides a rich cultural environment, with restaurants, music venues, museums and theaters, a new minor league baseball stadium, and recreational facilities. All law students are provided free memberships to a new YMCA just a few blocks from the law school.

Advisory Board

The law school's advisory board includes prominent judges, attorneys, and business leaders who advise the university in shaping the vision for the school and its future development. The board is chaired by David Gergen, who held positions in the administrations of Presidents Nixon, Ford, Reagan, and Clinton. The board also includes two former North Carolina governors, three former North Carolina Supreme Court chief justices, a former president of the American Bar Association, and a former US ambassador.

Curriculum

The law school operates on a three-term model, with fall and spring semesters of 13 weeks and a winter term offering courses and practical experiences in leadership and the law. While at Elon, students take a wide array of required courses and electives, and each student selects at least one of four concentrations in their second year: Business, Litigation, Public Interest, and General Practice.

Leadership Emphasis

Over the course of the three-year program, Elon Law incorporates the best of leadership education through courses, community activities, and capstone experiences. Elon lawyers will begin their careers as knowledgeable, self-aware, skillful, and innovative professionals. Elon Law prepares its graduates to be not only successful lawyers who can excel at the highest levels of the profession, but also leading contributors to the well-being of the region, nation, and world. In addition to a rigorous core curriculum that allows students to develop extensive legal knowledge, taught by a faculty with a passion for innovative teaching, the school also provides students with in-depth skills training, teamwork experiences, opportunities for direct client engagement, and an innovative Preceptor Program through which experienced lawyers from a broad range of practice settings mentor law students. The Joseph M. Bryan Distinguished Leadership Lecture Series brings accomplished leaders from a variety of disciplines to Elon to share their experiences and perspectives.

Preceptor Program

More than 50 volunteer attorneys serve annually as preceptors to Elon's first-year law students. As professional advisors, they observe and provide feedback to students about their classroom performances and invite students to accompany them to observe trials, initial client interviews, depositions, and/or mediations. Through these experiences, students are mentored and guided in their professional development and entry to the legal profession.

Clinics

Two clinical programs at Elon Law put legal theory into practice, providing students with essential lawyering skills through casework management, research, writing, client interaction, and courtroom advocacy, while also helping individuals in need. Current clinical offerings include the Juvenile Justice Intervention and Mediation Clinic and a Wills Clinic. The Legal Aid Housing and Domestic Relations field placement program and externships in governmental, judicial, and public interest law offices provide students with additional opportunities to gain practical legal experience.

Engaged Learning and CELL

In addition to offering students extensive field-based experiences with practicing attorneys, judges, and business leaders, Elon law professors employ various methods of instruction, including Socratic, group presentations, projects, and problem method, actively engaging students in their studies. To facilitate the faculty's development as excellent teachers and their ability to tap students' potential for learning, the law school has established the Center for Engaged Learning in the Law (CELL).

Law Library

The depth and breadth of the Elon Law library collection compares favorably with other law schools and is considerably larger than typical academic law libraries at their earliest stage of development. Students may access a wide variety of digital and online databases from both on- and off-campus locations. The collection is designed specifically to support the four practice-area concentrations with additional emphasis in the areas of leadership and professional ethics. The library, like the rest of the law school building, is served by a wireless network with full, high-speed Internet access.

Facilities

The School of Law is located in the four-floor, 84,000-square-foot H. Michael Weaver Building, specially designed to support Elon's engaged approach to legal education. Elon Law is one of only a few schools in the nation to house a working court. The North Carolina Business Court uses the school's high-tech courtroom, and the court's offices are also located within the building, giving students the opportunity to observe and interact with judges and attorneys. The law school's facilities also include a clinical law center, tiered classrooms with extensive multimedia capabilities, a spacious and comfortable library, full wireless network access, and a coffee bar and welcoming common area for students.

Career Services

The Career Services Office provides professional development workshops and networking opportunities for students and alumni, coordinates on-campus interview sessions and résumé requests for employers, builds relationships with prospective employers of students and alumni, and schedules job fair participation nationwide. Ninety-five percent of the class of 2009 has secured legal employment, and students at Elon Law continue to have significant success in securing employment after graduation and in internship placements with judges, law firms, and other legal employers across the nation.

Admission

Each year, the law school seeks to enroll a talented and diverse class of approximately 130 students. The law school offers two decision cycles: early decision and regular decision. Early-decision applicants agree that, if offered admission, they will enroll at Elon Law. Early-decision candidates receive decisions by December 31. Regular-decision applications are accepted throughout the admission cycle and decisions on these applications are made on a rolling basis throughout this period, with most decisions made by the middle of April. Prospective students are encouraged to visit the school to speak with an admission professional, tour the law school with a student ambassador, and visit a class.

Financial Planning

Financial aid is available to law students in the form of scholarships and loans. Scholarships are awarded on the basis of academic merit and financial need. Merit scholarships are awarded based on applicants' potential for outstanding contributions to the law school, the legal profession, and society. Admitted applicants are automatically considered for merit-based scholarships. Need-based scholarships are based on the FAFSA information. Many law students participate in federal loan programs such as subsidized Federal Stafford Loans, unsubsidized Federal Stafford Loans, and GradPlus Loans.

Student Activities

A rich variety of student activities, organizations, and leadership opportunities make extracurricular life at Elon an excellent complement to classroom learning. Student activities at Elon Law cover a wide spectrum of academic interest areas, identity groups, political affiliations, sports, moot court activities, and service organizations.

In addition to the *Elon Law Review*, Moot Court Program, and Student Bar Association, there are over 20 active student organizations, including the Black Law Students Association, Federalist Society, Latin American Law Students Association, and Women's Law Association. The Moot Court Program is student run and coordinates intramural and national competitions, as well as participates in regional, national, and international competitions. The Student Bar Association, along with the student organizations, sponsor a range of professional, service, athletic, and social events.

APPLICANT PROFILE

Elon University School of Law

LSAT Score	GPA								
	3.75 +	3.50–3.74	3.25–3.49	3.00–3.24	2.75–2.99	2.50–2.74	2.25–2.49	2.00–2.24	Below 2.00
175–180									
170–174									
165–169									
160–164									
155–159									
150–154									
145–149									
140–144									
135–139									
130–134									
125–129									
120–124									

■ Good Possibility   □ Possible   ▨ Unlikely

EMORY UNIVERSITY SCHOOL OF LAW

Gambrell Hall, 1301 Clifton Road
Atlanta, GA 30322-2770
Phone: 404.727.6802; Fax: 404.727.2477
E-mail: lawinfo@law.emory.edu; Website: www.law.emory.edu

ABA
Approved
Since
1923

The Basics

Type of school	Private
Term	Semester
Application deadline	3/1
Application fee	$70
Financial aid deadline	3/1 5/1
Can first year start other than fall?	No
Student to faculty ratio	11.2 to 1
# of housing spaces available restricted to law students	
graduate housing for which law students are eligible	826

Faculty and Administrators

	Total		Men		Women		Minorities	
	Spr	Fall	Spr	Fall	Spr	Fall	Spr	Fall
Full-time	59	57	32	31	27	26	5	4
Other full-time	1	1	0	0	1	1	0	0
Deans, librarians, & others who teach	5	5	4	4	1	1	2	2
Part-time	36	36	28	31	8	5	1	1
Total	101	99	64	66	37	33	8	7

Curriculum

	Full-Time	Part-Time
Typical first-year section size	84	0
Is there typically a "small section" of the first-year class, other than Legal Writing, taught by full-time faculty	Yes	No
If yes, typical size offered last year	42	
# of classroom course titles beyond first-year curriculum	113	

# of upper division courses, excluding seminars, with an enrollment:		
Under 25	98	
25–49	28	
50–74	16	
75–99	5	
100+	3	

# of seminars	33	
# of seminar positions available	345	
# of seminar positions filled	245	0
# of positions available in simulation courses	1,058	
# of simulation positions filled	952	0
# of positions available in faculty supervised clinical courses	80	
# of faculty supervised clinical positions filled	77	0
# involved in field placements	240	0
# involved in law journals	172	0
# involved in moot court or trial competitions	100	0
# of credit hours required to graduate	90	

JD Enrollment and Ethnicity

	Men		Women		Full-Time		Part-Time		1st-Year		Total		JD Degs. Awd.
	#	%	#	%	#	%	#	%	#	%	#	%	
All Hispanics	40	9.3	35	9.6	75	9.5	0	0.0	22	7.5	75	9.5	30
Am. Ind./AK Nat.	2	0.5	4	1.1	6	0.8	0	0.0	0	0.0	6	0.8	2
Asian	44	10.3	44	12.1	88	11.1	0	0.0	39	13.3	88	11.1	28
Black/Af. Am.	16	3.7	39	10.7	55	6.9	0	0.0	15	5.1	55	6.9	28
Nat. HI/Pac. Isl.	0	0.0	0	0.0	0	0.0	0	0.0	0	0.0	0	0.0	0
2 or more races	6	1.4	10	2.7	16	2.0	0	0.0	15	5.1	16	2.0	0
Subtotal (minor.)	108	25.2	132	36.3	240	30.3	0	0.0	91	31.0	240	30.3	88
Nonres. Alien	10	2.3	9	2.5	19	2.4	0	0.0	8	2.7	19	2.4	0
White/Cauc.	275	64.3	198	54.4	473	59.7	0	0.0	179	60.9	473	59.7	137
Unknown	35	8.2	25	6.9	60	7.6	0	0.0	16	5.4	60	7.6	22
Total	428	54.0	364	46.0	792	100.0	0	0.0	294	37.1	792		255

Transfers

Transfers in	32
Transfers out	8

Tuition and Fees

	Resident	Nonresident
Full-time	$43,392	$43,392
Part-time		
Tuition Guarantee Program		N

Living Expenses

Estimated living expenses for singles

Living on campus	Living off campus	Living at home
$25,410	$25,410	$25,410

EMORY UNIVERSITY SCHOOL OF LAW

ABA
Approved
Since
1923

GPA and LSAT Scores

	Total	Full-Time	Part-Time
# of apps	4,583	4,583	0
# of offers	1,245	1,245	0
# of matrics	293	293	0
75% GPA	3.69	3.69	0.00
Median GPA	3.54	3.54	0.00
25% GPA	3.34	3.34	0.00
75% LSAT	167	167	0
Median LSAT	166	166	0
25% LSAT	166	166	0

Grants and Scholarships (from prior year)

	Total		Full-Time		Part-Time	
	#	%	#	%	#	%
Total # of students	715		715		0	
Total # receiving grants	527	73.7	527	73.7	0	0.0
Less than 1/2 tuition	282	39.4	282	39.4	0	0.0
Half to full tuition	227	31.7	227	31.7	0	0.0
Full tuition	2	0.3	2	0.3	0	0.0
More than full tuition	16	2.2	16	2.2	0	0.0
Median grant amount			$20,000		$0	

Informational and Library Resources

Total amount spent on library materials	$1,197,782
Study seating capacity inside the library	516
# of full-time equivalent professional librarians	8
Hours per week library is open	86
# of open, wired connections available to students	64
# of networked computers available for use by students	72
Has wireless network?	Y
Requires computer?	N

JD Attrition (from prior year)

	Academic	Other	Total	
	#	#	#	%
1st year	0	1	1	0.4
2nd year	0	11	11	4.8
3rd year	0	0	0	0.0
4th year	0	0	0	0.0

Employment (9 months after graduation)

	Total	Percentage
Employment status known	216	99.1
Employment status unknown	2	0.9
Employed	181	83.8
Pursuing graduate degrees	9	4.2
Unemployed (seeking, not seeking, or studying for the bar)	16	7.4
Type of Employment		
# employed in law firms	124	68.5
# employed in business and industry	18	9.9
# employed in government	11	6.1
# employed in public interest	7	3.9
# employed as judicial clerks	15	8.3
# employed in academia	5	2.8
Geographic Location		
# employed in state	86	47.5
# employed outside the US	0	0.0
# of states where employed	22	

Bar Passage Rates

First-time takers	155	Reporting %	70.97
Average school %	91.82	Average state %	86.28
Average pass difference	5.54		

Jurisdiction	Takers	Passers	Pass %	State %	Diff %
Georgia	110	101	91.82	86.28	5.54

EMORY UNIVERSITY SCHOOL OF LAW

Gambrell Hall, 1301 Clifton Road
Atlanta, GA 30322-2770
Phone: 404.727.6802; Fax: 404.727.2477
E-mail: lawinfo@law.emory.edu; Website: www.law.emory.edu

Introduction

Emory's location in Atlanta, a national business and legal center, gives law students the opportunity to take advanced classes from, and work with, some of the leading judges and lawyers in the United States. Atlanta also is one of America's most beautiful and culturally diverse cities.

The law school also benefits from being located on the campus of Emory University, which was founded in 1836. Emory University School of Law is accredited by the American Bar Association, is a member of the Association of American Law Schools, and has a chapter of the Order of the Coif.

Curriculum

The basic program of study involves three years of full-time study leading to the JD degree. The fall semester runs from late August to mid-December; the spring semester begins in early January and ends in mid-May.

The program of courses for the first year is generally prescribed, though beginning with the spring 2011 semester, first-year students may choose one elective. The program of courses for the second and third years primarily is elective. Students can sample a broad spectrum of courses or concentrate on a particular area of law.

All first-year courses and the basic second- and third-year courses are taught by full-time faculty members. A distinguished group of judges and practicing attorneys offer specialized courses.

Library and Physical Facilities

Emory School of Law is located in Gambrell Hall, part of Emory's 630-acre campus in Druid Hills, six miles southeast of downtown Atlanta.

Gambrell Hall contains classrooms, faculty offices, administrative offices, student-organization offices, and a 325-seat auditorium. The school provides wireless Internet access throughout its facilities. Gambrell Hall also houses a state-of-the-art courtroom with computer connections for judge, counsel, and jury; a document camera; a DVD player; videoconferencing; and a four-camera operation with feeds to remote locations.

The Hugh F. MacMillan Law Library sits adjacent to Gambrell Hall and is designed for easy student access. Students are trained on LexisNexis and Westlaw terminals and learn both the techniques of computer-assisted legal research and traditional research methods. Students also may use the library's computer labs that offer Apple and PC computers.

Special Programs

Emory Law combines a practical and disciplined approach toward the study of law with a commitment to providing students experiential learning opportunities that engage them in the many roles the law plays in our society. Our students engage the law through learning opportunities that create graduates who are ready to apply their knowledge to make an impact in real and significant ways, as lawyers and as citizens of the world. We teach the practice of law through

our outstanding programs in trial techniques, intellectual property, child advocacy, and environmental law, as well as through expanded emphasis on transactional skills. Our centers of excellence in law and religion, world law, feminism and legal theory, and transactional law are interdisciplinary, integrative, and international in approach.

Emory's Trial Techniques Program affords our students exposure to the challenges of conducting direct and cross-examination, developing a case theory and approach, and conducting opening and closing arguments. More than half of the students participate in Emory's field placement program, where students may earn academic credit clerking for a federal judge, researching intellectual property issues for major corporations such as the Coca-Cola Company, and representing clients on behalf of Atlanta Legal Aid.

Emory Law's Center for Transactional Law and Practice is at the forefront of educating students and professionals on topics related to business transactions. Students participate through Emory's Transactional Law Certificate Program, while the center offers a number of workshops and seminars designed specifically for practicing attorneys. The center also regularly hosts a conference for educators in the area of teaching transactional skills.

Students also may gain practical experience in intellectual property and corporate/commercial law by participating in TI:GER (Technological Innovation: Generating Economic Results), a program of technology and business law cosponsored by Emory's School of Law and Economics Department and Georgia Institute of Technology's Dupree School of Management. Students may participate in one of Emory's own clinics: the Barton Child Law and Policy Clinic, working to promote and protect the well-being of neglected and abused children; the Barton Juvenile Defender Clinic, representing children charged with delinquent acts; the Turner Environmental Law Clinic, offering a practical clinical education to the aspiring environmental attorney; or the International Humanitarian Law Clinic, focusing on upholding the rule of law on behalf of detainees and on educating and training officials in war-torn countries on humanitarian law.

Emory offers a comprehensive international law program and is home to the World Law Institute. Emory Law capitalizes on the presence of other strong campus programs by combining coursework and programs to create unique and synergistic programs of study. The law school offers joint-degree programs with Emory's Goizueta School of Business, Candler School of Theology, School of Public Health, and the Graduate School of Arts and Sciences.

Admission

The law school accepts beginning students for the fall term only. Prior to enrollment, a student must have earned a bachelor's degree from an approved institution. Applications for admission must be received by Emory no later than March 1. Early applications are encouraged. Many factors are considered in making admission decisions. Of particular importance are academic accomplishments and LSAT scores. Extracurricular activities, work experience, level of quality and difficulty of undergraduate courses, performance in graduate school, and letters of recommendation are also considered. We encourage applications from members of underrepresented groups, and such applicants should provide the Dean of Admission with specific information about their background or accomplishments that would be of particular interest. Applicants are encouraged to visit the law school. Upon acceptance, applicants are required to submit a nonrefundable $750 tuition deposit to reserve a space in the entering class.

Student Activities

A wide variety of organizations and activities are available to students. There are three law reviews at Emory—*Emory Law Journal, Emory Bankruptcy Developments Journal,* and *Emory International Law Review*—and more than 30 percent of the second- and third-year students are involved in law review research, writing, and editing.

Students also participate in moot court and mock trial. Each first-year student prepares a brief and presents an oral argument. In addition, many second- and third-year students compete in intramural and national moot court competitions.

There are approximately 40 student organizations reflecting a broad range of special interest and social groups as well as a very active Student Bar Association.

Career Services

A full-time career services office assists students in obtaining permanent, summer, and part-time employment. It arranges interviews with employers from many parts of the country and maintains extensive files on a wide variety of professional opportunities across the United States. Many Emory graduates join private law firms after graduation. Others work as judicial clerks, enter government service, or work for banks, corporations, or legal aid agencies.

The majority of Emory's students stay in the Southeast. Approximately 25 percent work in the Northeast and Mid-Atlantic. Smaller percentages work in the Midwest, Southwest, and West.

The career services office provides extensive training on résumé writing, interview skills, and job-search techniques, as well as numerous opportunities to network with attorneys in a variety of practice areas and settings.

APPLICANT PROFILE

Emory University School of Law

LSAT Score	GPA								
	3.75 +	3.50–3.74	3.25–3.49	3.00–3.24	2.75–2.99	2.50–2.74	2.25–2.49	2.00–2.24	Below 2.00
175–180									
170–174									
165–169									
160–164									
155–159									
150–154									
145–149									
140–144									
135–139									
130–134									
125–129									
120–124									

■ Good Possibility   □ Possible   ▨ Unlikely

Note: This graph reflects admission decisions as of 6/1/09 and is to be used as a general guide to determining chances for admittance. It does not reflect actual decisions but should serve as a guideline.

Average LSAT data reported.

FAULKNER UNIVERSITY, THOMAS GOODE JONES SCHOOL OF LAW

5345 Atlanta Highway
Montgomery, AL 36109
Phone: 334.386.7210
E-mail: law@faulkner.edu; Website: www.faulkner.edu/law

ABA
Approved
Since
2006

The Basics

Type of school	Private
Term	Semester
Application deadline	6/15
Application fee	$50
Financial aid deadline	7/1
Can first year start other than fall?	No
Student to faculty ratio	14.4 to 1
# of housing spaces available restricted to law students	
graduate housing for which law students are eligible	

Faculty and Administrators

	Total		Men		Women		Minorities	
	Spr	Fall	Spr	Fall	Spr	Fall	Spr	Fall
Full-time	19	19	14	15	5	4	3	3
Other full-time	3	4	1	2	2	2	0	0
Deans, librarians, & others who teach	10	10	5	5	5	5	0	0
Part-time	6	5	3	2	3	3	2	2
Total	38	38	23	24	15	14	5	5

Curriculum

	Full-Time	Part-Time
Typical first-year section size	75	0
Is there typically a "small section" of the first-year class, other than Legal Writing, taught by full-time faculty	No	No
If yes, typical size offered last year		
# of classroom course titles beyond first-year curriculum	41	

# of upper division courses, excluding seminars, with an enrollment:		
	Under 25	42
	25–49	19
	50–74	3
	75–99	0
	100+	0

	Full-Time	Part-Time
# of seminars	8	
# of seminar positions available	96	
# of seminar positions filled	70	8
# of positions available in simulation courses	206	
# of simulation positions filled	152	22
# of positions available in faculty supervised clinical courses	95	
# of faculty supervised clinical positions filled	78	1
# involved in field placements	53	2
# involved in law journals	39	5
# involved in moot court or trial competitions	59	1
# of credit hours required to graduate	90	

JD Enrollment and Ethnicity

	Men #	Men %	Women #	Women %	Full-Time #	Full-Time %	Part-Time #	Part-Time %	1st-Year #	1st-Year %	Total #	Total %	JD Degs. Awd.
All Hispanics	3	1.4	4	2.8	7	2.1	0	0.0	4	2.7	7	2.0	1
Am. Ind./AK Nat.	2	0.9	0	0.0	2	0.6	0	0.0	1	0.7	2	0.6	3
Asian	4	1.9	5	3.5	8	2.3	1	7.7	6	4.1	9	2.5	0
Black/Af. Am.	13	6.1	11	7.7	24	7.0	0	0.0	5	3.4	24	6.8	5
Nat. HI/Pac. Isl.	0	0.0	0	0.0	0	0.0	0	0.0	0	0.0	0	0.0	0
2 or more races	0	0.0	0	0.0	0	0.0	0	0.0	0	0.0	0	0.0	0
Subtotal (minor.)	22	10.4	20	14.1	41	12.0	1	7.7	16	11.0	42	11.9	9
Nonres. Alien	0	0.0	0	0.0	0	0.0	0	0.0	0	0.0	0	0.0	0
White/Cauc.	189	89.2	119	83.8	296	86.8	12	92.3	126	86.3	308	87.0	76
Unknown	1	0.5	3	2.1	4	1.2	0	0.0	4	2.7	4	1.1	0
Total	212	59.9	142	40.1	341	96.3	13	3.7	146	41.2	354		85

Transfers

Transfers in	1
Transfers out	10

Tuition and Fees

	Resident	Nonresident
Full-time	$31,020	$31,020
Part-time		
Tuition Guarantee Program	N	

Living Expenses

Estimated living expenses for singles

Living on campus	Living off campus	Living at home
N/A	$22,400	N/A

FAULKNER UNIVERSITY, THOMAS GOODE JONES SCHOOL OF LAW

ABA
Approved
Since
2006

GPA and LSAT Scores

	Total	Full-Time	Part-Time
# of apps	913	913	0
# of offers	480	480	0
# of matrics	145	145	0
75% GPA	3.42	3.42	0.00
Median GPA	3.12	3.12	0.00
25% GPA	2.80	2.80	0.00
75% LSAT	154	154	0
Median LSAT	150	150	0
25% LSAT	148	148	0

Grants and Scholarships (from prior year)

	Total		Full-Time		Part-Time	
	#	%	#	%	#	%
Total # of students	341		323		18	
Total # receiving grants	110	32.3	110	34.1	0	0.0
Less than 1/2 tuition	43	12.6	43	13.3	0	0.0
Half to full tuition	51	15.0	51	15.8	0	0.0
Full tuition	16	4.7	16	5.0	0	0.0
More than full tuition	0	0.0	0	0.0	0	0.0
Median grant amount			$15,500		$0	

Informational and Library Resources

Total amount spent on library materials	$639,563
Study seating capacity inside the library	213
# of full-time equivalent professional librarians	5
Hours per week library is open	98
# of open, wired connections available to students	205
# of networked computers available for use by students	40
Has wireless network?	Y
Requires computer?	N

JD Attrition (from prior year)

	Academic	Other	Total	
	#	#	#	%
1st year	18	31	49	32.7
2nd year	1	2	3	3.4
3rd year	0	0	0	0.0
4th year	0	0	0	0.0

Employment (9 months after graduation)

	Total	Percentage
Employment status known	72	100.0
Employment status unknown	0	0.0
Employed	62	86.1
Pursuing graduate degrees	0	0.0
Unemployed (seeking, not seeking, or studying for the bar)	10	13.9
Type of Employment		
# employed in law firms	27	43.5
# employed in business and industry	11	17.7
# employed in government	17	27.4
# employed in public interest	1	1.6
# employed as judicial clerks	5	8.1
# employed in academia	0	0.0
Geographic Location		
# employed in state	51	82.3
# employed outside the US	0	0.0
# of states where employed	9	

Bar Passage Rates

First-time takers	75	Reporting %	89.33
Average school %	89.56	Average state %	86.39
Average pass difference	3.17		

Jurisdiction	Takers	Passers	Pass %	State %	Diff %
Alabama	65	58	89.23	86.51	2.72
Tennessee	2	2	100.00	82.44	17.56

FAULKNER UNIVERSITY, THOMAS GOODE JONES SCHOOL OF LAW

5345 Atlanta Highway
Montgomery, AL 36109
Phone: 334.386.7210
E-mail: law@faulkner.edu; Website: www.faulkner.edu/law

Introduction

Faulkner University's Thomas Goode Jones School of Law has a long and rich tradition of educating students for the practice of law in Alabama. The school was founded in 1928 by Circuit Judge Walter B. Jones and named in honor of his father, a former soldier, lawyer, and governor. In 1901, at the urging of Booker T. Washington, Thomas Goode Jones was appointed by President Theodore Roosevelt to be United States District Judge for the Northern and Middle Districts of Alabama. He authored the Alabama Code of Ethics, a document that was the first state code of ethics and the model for the American Bar Association's 1908 Canons of Professional Ethics.

The School of Law is committed to the education of outstanding lawyers. In keeping with its distinctive Christian mission, the school embraces academic excellence and emphasizes a strong commitment to integrity within a caring Christian environment that sustains and nurtures faith. Students are encouraged to dedicate their lives to the service of others.

The School of Law became part of Faulkner University in 1983. Since its inception, the school has produced over 2,000 alumni who have become practicing attorneys, judges, and other contributors to the legal profession. The American Bar Association granted provisional approval of the School of Law in June 2006.

Montgomery and the River Region

The School of Law is located in the capital of Alabama. Montgomery is widely known as the birthplace of the Confederacy and the civil rights movement. It is regarded as one of the nation's most historically significant cities. One can visit the First White House of the Confederacy and the steps of the state capitol building where Jefferson Davis was sworn in as president of the Confederate States of America. On these same steps, Dr. Martin Luther King Jr. completed the freedom march from Selma to Montgomery. Here Dr. King asked for equality for all people, regardless of race. Other historic sites include the Dexter Avenue King Memorial Baptist Church, the Civil Rights Memorial designed by Maya Lin, and the Rosa L. Parks Library and Museum.

Along with its rich history, Montgomery is known for its contribution to the arts. Its most notable contribution is the Wynton M. Blount Cultural Park, which includes the Montgomery Museum of Fine Arts, the internationally acclaimed Alabama Shakespeare Festival, and the beautiful Shakespeare Gardens.

Montgomery offers a small-town atmosphere with big-city amenities that add to the quality of life enjoyed by all who reside in the capital city. It is also an excellent place to study law with the Supreme Court of Alabama, the Alabama legislature, and over 200 law firms and other organizations that employ lawyers within a short driving distance of campus.

Library and Physical Facilities

The George H. Jones Jr. Law Library supports the School of Law's curriculum and the legal research requirements of its students and faculty. It provides access to legal and academic materials offered by the latest technology. Computers on both floors of the library enable free access to the Internet, word processing packages, and legal databases. A spacious computer lab facilitates computer-assisted legal instruction and research. Data ports are available throughout the library, and every study room and study carrel is electronically wired and ready for laptop computers.

The School of Law is housed in a beautiful, neo-Federal-style building that accommodates the George H. Jones Jr. Law Library, the Judge Walter B. Jones Moot Court Room, and the Institute for Dispute Resolution. It includes state-of-the-art research and lecture facilities with seven classrooms and two large conference rooms. All classrooms are outfitted for laptop computers and wireless Internet is available throughout the building and library. Students have access to the student lounge for congregation and conference rooms for student organization meetings.

Institute for Dispute Resolution

The Alternative Dispute Resolution (ADR) Program enables law students to integrate their knowledge of conflict management principles and dispute resolution processes with professional skills. This program allows students to receive training normally available only through on-the-job experience after graduation.

Students can earn a certificate in ADR, which is not a supplemental degree but an opportunity for Juris Doctor candidates to enrich their skills training while still in law school. The certificate in ADR requires completion of the following courses: Arbitration, Dispute Resolution Processes, Interviewing/Counseling and Negotiation, Mediation Clinic, and an elective skills course. All of the certificate courses contain both an academic component and a skills component.

Clinical Opportunities and Externships

The School of Law operates three clinical programs: the Mediation Clinic, the Family Violence Clinic, and the Elder Law Clinic. The Mediation Clinic allows students to mediate cases set for trial at Montgomery County District Court. The Family Violence Clinic provides pro bono services for clients unable to pay for representation and works in conjunction with the Legal Services Corporation of Alabama and the Family Sunshine Center. Students with limited-practice authority cards interview clients, provide advice, prepare pleadings, and represent clients in court proceedings. Students without limited-practice authority cards assist in case preparation and research. The School of Law and Legal Services Corporation of Alabama are the recipients of the Family Sunshine Center's President's Special Service Award in recognition of outstanding service and support through the Family Violence Clinic.

The School of Law established the Elder Law Clinic after receiving a grant from the federal government through the Commerce, Justice, and Science spending bill. This clinic provides pro bono services in matters of estate planning, Medicare, nursing home issues, Social Security, long-term care insurance, and disability planning to name a few.

The School of Law's Externship Program affords students the opportunity to supplement their classroom experience by working in a variety of legal settings. Externships include a classroom component that covers topics relating to the legal system, judicial process, and professionalism. Students develop their lawyering skills and gain real-world experience in the legal community, as they work side by side with judges and practicing attorneys, under the supervision of the director of clinical programs and externships.

Public Interest Program

As part of a Christian university, the School of Law seeks not only to provide legal knowledge and practical skills necessary to produce competent and ethical members of the legal community, but also to instill in students an attitude of service. This commitment to serve those who otherwise could not afford such assistance complements the legal profession's rich tradition of service.

The Public Interest Program provides opportunities for students to begin their career of service while utilizing the practical skills obtained in their legal education. This program is voluntary and provides students with opportunities to work for nonprofit organizations, government agencies, and private attorneys or firms conducting pro bono legal work. Students are challenged to perform at least 50 hours of voluntary service during their law school career. Students providing public interest service qualify for recognition, including notation of service on transcripts, a certificate of accomplishment, special recognition in the graduation program, and eligibility for the Public Interest Service Award.

Student Organizations

The Student Bar Association (SBA) serves the student body and every student is a member. The SBA fosters relationships with members of the legal community and sponsors social

functions and fundraising events. Other student organizations at the law school include American Association for Justice, American Constitution Society, Animal Law Society, Black Law Students Association, Board of Advocates, Christian Legal Society, Federalist Society, Honor Court, Jones Law Republicans, Phi Alpha Delta, and Women Students Association.

The *Faulkner Law Review* is a scholarly legal journal published by student editors and members. Members write comments and notes on legal developments and landmark cases. They also select and edit articles submitted for publication by lawyers, judges, professors, and other scholars. Membership is considered an honor and provides students an opportunity to hone their research and writing skills.

Scholarships, Tuition, and Fees

The School of Law offers merit-based scholarships to qualified entering students. Admitted applicants are automatically under scholarship consideration. Awards range from 10 percent tuition forgiveness to 100 percent tuition forgiveness. Scholarships are also available to upper-level students who perform well academically in law school.

Please consult the law school's website for current tuition rates. Students pay a Student Activities Fee of $350, which is charged only once at the outset of a student's law school career and an Emergency Notification Fee of $10, which is charged per semester.

APPLICANT PROFILE

Faulkner University, Thomas Goode Jones School of Law

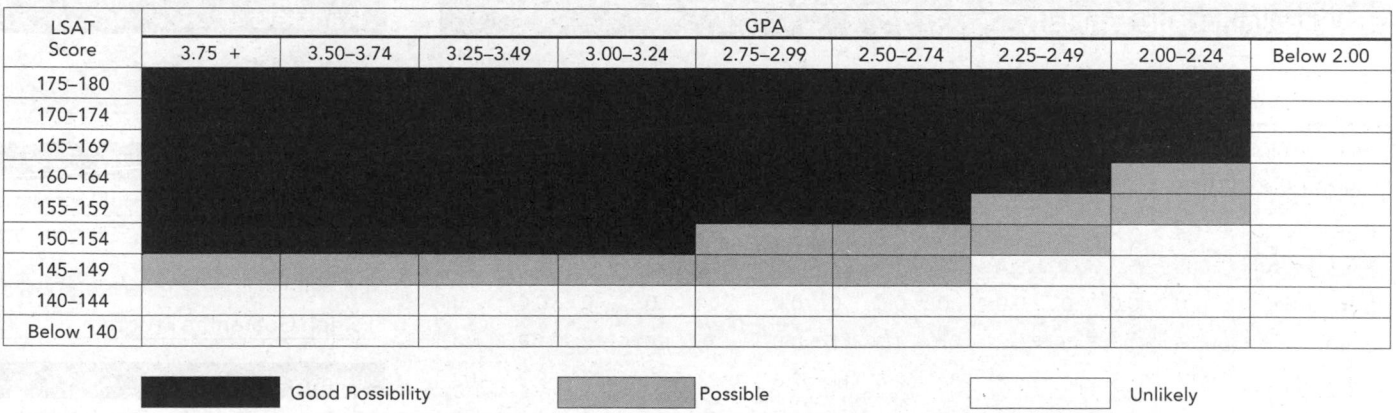

LSAT Score	GPA								
	3.75 +	3.50–3.74	3.25–3.49	3.00–3.24	2.75–2.99	2.50–2.74	2.25–2.49	2.00–2.24	Below 2.00
175–180									
170–174									
165–169									
160–164									
155–159									
150–154									
145–149									
140–144									
Below 140									

■ Good Possibility   ▨ Possible   ☐ Unlikely

FLORIDA A&M UNIVERSITY COLLEGE OF LAW

201 Beggs Avenue
Orlando, FL 32801
Phone: 407.254.3268; Fax: 407.254.3213
E-mail: famulaw.admissions@famu.edu; Website: www.law.famu.edu

ABA
Approved
Since
2004

The Basics

Type of school	Public
Term	Semester
Application deadline	5/31
Application fee	
Financial aid deadline	3/1
Can first year start other than fall?	No
Student to faculty ratio	17.9 to 1
# of housing spaces available restricted to law students	
graduate housing for which law students are eligible	

Faculty and Administrators

	Total		Men		Women		Minorities	
	Spr	Fall	Spr	Fall	Spr	Fall	Spr	Fall
Full-time	25	28	12	12	13	16	17	19
Other full-time	14	7	8	4	5	2	8	3
Deans, librarians, & others who teach	11	11	4	4	7	7	9	9
Part-time	11	12	7	8	4	4	8	7
Total	61	58	31	28	29	29	42	38

Curriculum

		Full-Time	Part-Time
Typical first-year section size		60	60
Is there typically a "small section" of the first-year class, other than Legal Writing, taught by full-time faculty		No	No
If yes, typical size offered last year			
# of classroom course titles beyond first-year curriculum		122	
# of upper division courses, excluding seminars, with an enrollment:	Under 25	87	
	25–49	25	
	50–74	14	
	75–99	0	
	100+	0	
# of seminars		16	
# of seminar positions available		320	
# of seminar positions filled		151	59
# of positions available in simulation courses		370	
# of simulation positions filled		221	55
# of positions available in faculty supervised clinical courses		168	
# of faculty supervised clinical positions filled		88	32
# involved in field placements		20	0
# involved in law journals		41	6
# involved in moot court or trial competitions		28	1
# of credit hours required to graduate		90	

JD Enrollment and Ethnicity

	Men		Women		Full-Time		Part-Time		1st-Year		Total		JD Degs. Awd.
	#	%	#	%	#	%	#	%	#	%	#	%	
All Hispanics	28	9.2	43	11.7	40	8.7	31	14.7	12	4.2	71	10.6	26
Am. Ind./AK Nat.	5	1.7	2	0.5	2	0.4	5	2.4	3	1.0	7	1.0	1
Asian	12	4.0	16	4.4	20	4.4	8	3.8	12	4.2	28	4.2	2
Black/Af. Am.	106	35.0	177	48.4	217	47.4	66	31.3	131	45.5	283	42.3	73
Nat. HI/Pac. Isl.	0	0.0	0	0.0	0	0.0	0	0.0	0	0.0	0	0.0	0
2 or more races	5	1.7	3	0.8	7	1.5	1	0.5	4	1.4	8	1.2	0
Subtotal (minor.)	156	51.5	241	65.8	286	62.4	111	52.6	162	56.3	397	59.3	102
Nonres. Alien	0	0.0	0	0.0	0	0.0	0	0.0	0	0.0	0	0.0	0
White/Cauc.	142	46.9	123	33.6	167	36.5	98	46.4	124	43.1	265	39.6	42
Unknown	5	1.7	2	0.5	5	1.1	2	0.9	2	0.7	7	1.0	1
Total	303	45.3	366	54.7	458	68.5	211	31.5	288	43.0	669		145

Transfers

Transfers in	2
Transfers out	11

Tuition and Fees

	Resident	Nonresident
Full-time	$10,312	$29,573
Part-time	$7,562	$21,686
Tuition Guarantee Program	N	

Living Expenses

Estimated living expenses for singles

Living on campus	Living off campus	Living at home
N/A	$22,615	$10,630

FLORIDA A&M UNIVERSITY COLLEGE OF LAW

ABA
Approved
Since
2004

GPA and LSAT Scores

	Total	Full-Time	Part-Time
# of apps	1,853	1,561	292
# of offers	617	514	103
# of matrics	288	230	58
75% GPA	3.30	3.28	3.40
Median GPA	3.03	3.00	3.11
25% GPA	2.71	2.69	2.73
75% LSAT	150	150	151
Median LSAT	147	147	147
25% LSAT	144	144	145

Grants and Scholarships (from prior year)

	Total #	Total %	Full-Time #	Full-Time %	Part-Time #	Part-Time %
Total # of students	613		385		228	
Total # receiving grants	61	10.0	46	11.9	15	6.6
Less than 1/2 tuition	29	4.7	23	6.0	6	2.6
Half to full tuition	17	2.8	16	4.2	1	0.4
Full tuition	15	2.4	7	1.8	8	3.5
More than full tuition	0	0.0	0	0.0	0	0.0
Median grant amount			$5,000		$5,000	

Informational and Library Resources

Total amount spent on library materials	$729,029
Study seating capacity inside the library	416
# of full-time equivalent professional librarians	4
Hours per week library is open	100
# of open, wired connections available to students	6
# of networked computers available for use by students	50
Has wireless network?	Y
Requires computer?	N

JD Attrition (from prior year)

	Academic #	Other #	Total #	Total %
1st year	32	24	56	24.0
2nd year	11	4	15	8.2
3rd year	1	0	1	0.6
4th year	0	0	0	0.0

Employment (9 months after graduation)

	Total	Percentage
Employment status known	141	84.4
Employment status unknown	26	15.6
Employed	89	63.1
Pursuing graduate degrees	6	4.3
Unemployed (seeking, not seeking, or studying for the bar)	42	29.8
Type of Employment		
# employed in law firms	39	43.8
# employed in business and industry	11	12.4
# employed in government	23	25.8
# employed in public interest	4	4.5
# employed as judicial clerks	1	1.1
# employed in academia	4	4.5
Geographic Location		
# employed in state	83	93.3
# employed outside the US	0	0.0
# of states where employed	5	

Bar Passage Rates

First-time takers	154	Reporting %	90.26
Average school %	52.52	Average state %	77.81

Average pass difference −25.29

Jurisdiction	Takers	Passers	Pass %	State %	Diff %
Florida	139	73	52.52	77.81	−25.29

FLORIDA A&M UNIVERSITY COLLEGE OF LAW

201 Beggs Avenue
Orlando, FL 32801
Phone: 407.254.3268; Fax: 407.254.3213
E-mail: famulaw.admissions@famu.edu; Website: www.law.famu.edu

A Unique History

The College of Law is proud to be a part of Florida A&M
University (FAMU), the largest single-campus historically black
university in the United States in terms of enrollment and in
terms of the number of baccalaureate degrees granted.
Founded in 1887, FAMU is a comprehensive, public,
coeducational, and fully accredited land-grant university
offering a broad range of instruction, research, and service
programs at the undergraduate, graduate, and professional
levels. Located on the highest of seven hills in the capital city of
Tallahassee, FAMU is the third oldest of the nine institutions in
Florida's State University System. The College of Law's rich
tradition of excellence dates back to its original founding in
1949. Between 1949 and 1968, the College of Law graduated
57 students. In 2002, the FAMU College of Law reopened in
downtown Orlando, Florida, as the only public law school in
Central Florida. In 2006, the College of Law moved into its
brand-new permanent building at 201 Beggs Avenue. The
College of Law offers a quality legal education at an affordable
price in state-of-the-art facilities and has been nationally
recognized for its diverse student body and its clinical
programs. The College of Law received full accreditation from
the American Bar Association in July 2009.

The College of Law is located in Orlando, considered to be
one of the most beautiful and dynamic cities in Florida. A
racially and culturally diverse community, Orlando is
considered not only one of the fastest growing metropolitan
areas in Florida, but also one of the fastest major employment
markets in the nation. Orlando offers affordable housing, great
weather year-round, and easy access to cultural and
recreational activities such as Disney World, Universal Studios,
and various professional athletic teams. Located in the heart of
downtown, the College of Law is within walking distance of
government buildings, courthouses, and a wide variety of
cultural, educational, and recreational opportunities.

An Active and Multicultural Student Body

Since opening in the fall of 2002, FAMU College of Law has
admitted eight entering classes and has a current student
enrollment exceeding 600 students. The College of Law has
consistently received national recognition as one of the most
diverse law schools in the nation, making for a classroom
experience unduplicated elsewhere. The College of Law is
committed to helping its students further develop their talents,
professional skills, and goals. To that end, we offer cocurricular
and extracurricular activities, including our award-winning
competition teams. These cocurricular and extracurricular
programs enhance not only the study of the law, but students'
leadership and professional abilities and oral and written
communication skills. FAMU College of Law students are very
active within the law school and in the Central Florida
community. As students at a recently reestablished law school,
they have taken on the challenge of establishing organizations
that will serve current and future students for years to come. The
FAMU College of Law Student Bar Association supports and
governs all student activities and organizations at the College of
Law. Since 2002, students have founded the Jesse J. McCrary
Jr. Chapter of the National Black Law Students Association;
the Association of Trial Lawyers of America; the Women's Law

Caucus; the Entertainment, Arts, and Sports Law Society; the
Hispanic Law Students; the Federalist Society; Phi Alpha
Delta; and many other student organizations.

Programs of Study

The FAMU College of Law offers both a full-time day
program and a part-time evening program of study. Full-time
day program students must successfully complete six
semesters or three academic years in order to fulfill their
degree requirements. Enrollment in the day program
represents a commitment to the full-time study of law.
Part-time evening program students must successfully
complete their degree requirements in four years consisting
of eight semesters and three summers. Part-time evening
classes typically meet Monday through Thursday beginning at
6:00 PM. The part-time evening program is designed for
students who are unable to attend school on a full-time basis
and want to earn a law degree while working full time.
Courses in both programs demand the same standards of
performance by students and are taught by full-time faculty
members who are assisted by adjunct faculty.

Curriculum

The law school offers a rigorous traditional curriculum of
required and elective courses that are complemented by
extensive skills training that includes an intensive three-year
writing program and a strong clinical program. The College of
Law's curriculum is designed to provide students with both
the intellectual and practical skills necessary to meet the
demands of the modern practice of law by combining
theoretical coursework with clinical and practical experiences.
Through the use of elective courses and leading practitioners
as adjunct faculty, students are introduced to emerging
trends and developments in the law.

The Center for International Law and Justice

The Center for International Law and Justice was created to
cultivate student interest in human rights and freedom,
providing students with a substantive background in
international law and foreign affairs as well as the application
of policy in the developing world—specifically, Africa, Asia,
the Caribbean, and Latin America. Beginning in the first year
of study, students may opt into the international law track.
The center offers a new certificate of study in **International
Human Rights Law and Global Justice Studies**. In addition,
the center annually awards an International Human Rights
Fellowship, which provides scholarship and summer internship
support to a student with a track record of public service and
a keen interest or experience in international human rights
law and international affairs.

A Commitment to Public Service

At the core of the College of Law mission is a commitment to
public service. As such, all students are required to engage in
public service by participating in and satisfactorily completing
one of several available clinical offerings or by completing at
least 20 hours in a pro bono experience. The College of Law was

recently ranked seventh in the nation for providing clinical opportunities by *National Jurist* magazine. The Clinical Program educates students in the practical art of lawyering, while providing quality legal representation to underserved individuals and organizations. Additionally, the Clinical Program helps students explore career potential by exposing them to a broad spectrum of legal opportunities. Via a combination of in-house clinics and externships, the Clinical Program includes the following practice areas: Guardian Ad Litem, Community Economic Development, Housing, Homelessness and Legal Advocacy, Criminal Defense, Criminal Prosecution, Death Penalty, and Volunteer Income Tax Assistance.

Amazing Affordability

Tuition rates at FAMU College of Law are consistently the most affordable among Florida law schools, and nationally, FAMU Law tuition rates offer a tremendous value. For the 2010–2011 academic year, tuition for Florida residents was $343.74 per credit hour, and tuition for non-Florida residents was $985.77 per credit hour. Approximately 90 percent of law students are receiving some form of financial aid, including federal loans and merit-based scholarships. Merit-based scholarships are awarded to a select number of entering full-time and part-time students who have excelled academically and who possess other outstanding qualifications for the study of law. All admitted students are automatically considered for these awards, which vary from $1,000 to full-tuition.

The Admission Process

Admission to the College of Law has become increasingly competitive. Accordingly, applicants are strongly encouraged to apply early in the process to maximize chances for admission. The law school seeks diligent, hardworking students with a broad array of talents and experiences who demonstrate both an exceptional aptitude for the study of law and a strong history of, or commitment to, public service. Selection for admission is based on a thorough evaluation of all factors in an applicant's file. While an applicant's academic record and LSAT performance are weighted heavily in the evaluation process, the Admissions Committee considers other factors, including writing ability, as evidenced by the LSAT writing sample and the personal statement; community and public service; academic honors and awards; work experience; leadership ability; extracurricular activities; letters of recommendation; and character and motivation.

Applicant Profile

While an applicant's undergraduate record and LSAT score are important, they are not the sole determinants for admission to law school. There are no combinations of grades or scores that assure admission or denial. An applicant's transcripts are analyzed for breadth and depth of coursework, trends in grades, and rank. The competitiveness of an applicant's school and major are taken into consideration as are special activities, honors, and awards received by the applicant. Other aspects of the application significantly influence the decision, such as work experience and evidence of a commitment to, or interest in, public service. In making its decision, the faculty Admissions Committee aims to enroll an entering class of students with the strongest combination of qualifications and the greatest potential to contribute to FAMU College of Law and to the legal profession.

APPLICANT PROFILE

Florida A&M University College of Law
This grid includes only applicants who earned 120–180 LSAT scores under standard administrations.

LSAT Score	GPA																				
	3.75 +		3.50–3.74		3.25–3.49		3.00–3.24		2.75–2.99		2.50–2.74		2.25–2.49		2.00–2.24		Below 2.00		No GPA		Total	
	Apps	Adm	Apps	Adm	Apps	Adm	Apps	Adm	Apps	Adm	Apps	Adm	Apps	Adm	Apps	Adm	Apps	Adm	Apps	Adm	Apps	Adm
175–180	0	0	0	0	0	0	0	0	0	0	0	0	0	0	0	0	0	0	0	0	0	0
170–174	0	0	0	0	0	0	0	0	0	0	0	0	0	0	0	0	0	0	0	0	0	0
165–169	2	1	1	1	0	0	0	0	0	0	0	0	2	2	0	0	0	0	0	0	5	4
160–164	3	3	3	2	7	6	3	2	1	1	2	0	3	3	0	0	0	0	1	0	23	17
155–159	6	3	9	7	18	12	15	11	12	8	15	10	4	3	2	1	1	1	2	1	84	57
150–154	6	5	26	20	30	21	46	35	46	29	33	19	23	9	15	4	5	2	1	1	231	145
145–149	27	15	51	35	70	45	106	52	98	48	86	34	39	16	25	4	4	0	15	5	521	254
140–144	19	7	44	14	84	24	122	33	125	24	98	20	56	5	23	1	9	0	16	0	596	128
135–139	6	0	13	0	27	0	47	0	47	1	50	0	30	0	19	0	6	0	10	0	255	1
130–134	3	0	3	0	8	0	17	0	12	0	18	0	9	0	13	0	1	0	8	0	92	0
125–129	0	0	1	0	2	0	1	0	4	0	2	0	3	0	2	0	1	0	1	0	17	0
120–124	0	0	0	0	0	0	1	0	1	0	1	0	0	0	0	0	0	0	1	0	4	0
Total	72	34	151	79	246	108	358	133	346	111	305	83	169	38	99	10	27	3	55	7	1828	606

Apps = Number of Applicants
Adm = Number Admitted
Reflects 99% of the total applicant pool; highest LSAT data reported.

FLORIDA COASTAL SCHOOL OF LAW

8787 Baypine Road
Jacksonville, FL 32256
Phone: 904.680.7710, Toll-free: 877.210.2591; Fax: 904.680.7692
E-mail: admissions@fcsl.edu; Website: www.fcsl.edu

ABA
Approved
Since
2002

The Basics

Type of school	Private
Term	Semester
Application deadline	8/1
Application fee	$0
Financial aid deadline	
Can first year start other than fall?	Yes
Student to faculty ratio	20.9 to 1
# of housing spaces available restricted to law students	
graduate housing for which law students are eligible	

Faculty and Administrators

	Total		Men		Women		Minorities	
	Spr	Fall	Spr	Fall	Spr	Fall	Spr	Fall
Full-time	63	66	29	28	34	38	12	12
Other full-time	3	3	1	0	2	3	0	0
Deans, librarians, & others who teach	10	11	2	3	8	8	2	2
Part-time	46	52	34	37	12	15	3	10
Total	122	132	66	68	56	64	17	24

Curriculum

	Full-Time	Part-Time
Typical first-year section size	78	0
Is there typically a "small section" of the first-year class, other than Legal Writing, taught by full-time faculty	No	No
If yes, typical size offered last year		

# of classroom course titles beyond first-year curriculum	121	
# of upper division courses, excluding seminars, with an enrollment: Under 25	153	
25–49	63	
50–74	69	
75–99	3	
100+	1	
# of seminars	19	
# of seminar positions available	376	
# of seminar positions filled	298	0
# of positions available in simulation courses	2,183	
# of simulation positions filled	1,885	0
# of positions available in faculty supervised clinical courses	178	
# of faculty supervised clinical positions filled	161	0
# involved in field placements	293	0
# involved in law journals	54	0
# involved in moot court or trial competitions	126	0
# of credit hours required to graduate	90	

JD Enrollment and Ethnicity

	Men		Women		Full-Time		Part-Time		1st-Year		Total		JD Degs. Awd.
	#	%	#	%	#	%	#	%	#	%	#	%	
All Hispanics	98	11.0	92	10.8	182	10.8	8	13.6	86	11.0	190	10.9	30
Am. Ind./AK Nat.	11	1.2	7	0.8	17	1.0	1	1.7	11	1.4	18	1.0	9
Asian	44	4.9	54	6.3	95	5.6	3	5.1	50	6.4	98	5.6	27
Black/Af. Am.	52	5.8	146	17.1	192	11.4	6	10.2	101	12.9	198	11.4	34
Nat. HI/Pac. Isl.	2	0.2	1	0.1	3	0.2	0	0.0	3	0.4	3	0.2	0
2 or more races	2	0.2	3	0.4	5	0.3	0	0.0	2	0.3	5	0.3	0
Subtotal (minor.)	209	23.5	303	35.6	494	29.4	18	30.5	253	32.3	512	29.4	101
Nonres. Alien	14	1.6	15	1.8	29	1.7	0	0.0	16	2.0	29	1.7	0
White/Cauc.	585	65.7	484	56.8	1034	61.4	35	59.3	455	58.0	1069	61.4	265
Unknown	82	9.2	50	5.9	126	7.5	6	10.2	60	7.7	132	7.6	64
Total	890	51.1	852	48.9	1683	96.6	59	3.4	784	45.0	1742		433

Transfers

Transfers in	2
Transfers out	91

Tuition and Fees

	Resident	Nonresident
Full-time	$34,712	$34,712
Part-time	$28,086	$28,086
Tuition Guarantee Program		N

Living Expenses

Estimated living expenses for singles

Living on campus	Living off campus	Living at home
N/A	$20,110	$20,110

FLORIDA COASTAL SCHOOL OF LAW

ABA
Approved
Since
2002

GPA and LSAT Scores

	Total	Full-Time	Part-Time
# of apps	6,315	6,021	294
# of offers	4,276	4,174	102
# of matrics	808	782	26
75% GPA	3.42	3.42	3.26
Median GPA	3.14	3.15	3.03
25% GPA	2.86	2.86	2.65
75% LSAT	152	152	151
Median LSAT	149	149	146
25% LSAT	146	146	145

Grants and Scholarships (from prior year)

	Total #	Total %	Full-Time #	Full-Time %	Part-Time #	Part-Time %
Total # of students	1,605		1,539		66	
Total # receiving grants	640	39.9	602	39.1	38	57.6
Less than 1/2 tuition	603	37.6	573	37.2	30	45.5
Half to full tuition	37	2.3	29	1.9	8	12.1
Full tuition	0	0.0	0	0.0	0	0.0
More than full tuition	0	0.0	0	0.0	0	0.0
Median grant amount			$7,000		$10,000	

Informational and Library Resources

Total amount spent on library materials	$1,216,781
Study seating capacity inside the library	516
# of full-time equivalent professional librarians	15
Hours per week library is open	105
# of open, wired connections available to students	3,780
# of networked computers available for use by students	126
Has wireless network?	Y
Requires computer?	N

JD Attrition (from prior year)

	Academic #	Other #	Total #	Total %
1st year	57	85	142	21.4
2nd year	12	21	33	6.8
3rd year	0	0	0	0.0
4th year	0	0	0	0.0

Employment (9 months after graduation)

	Total	Percentage
Employment status known	394	95.2
Employment status unknown	20	4.8
Employed	337	85.5
Pursuing graduate degrees	16	4.1
Unemployed (seeking, not seeking, or studying for the bar)	11	2.8
Type of Employment		
# employed in law firms	150	44.5
# employed in business and industry	40	11.9
# employed in government	48	14.2
# employed in public interest	51	15.1
# employed as judicial clerks	7	2.1
# employed in academia	10	3.0
Geographic Location		
# employed in state	219	65.0
# employed outside the US	1	0.3
# of states where employed		34

Bar Passage Rates

First-time takers	412	Reporting %	70.87
Average school %	78.77	Average state %	77.81
Average pass difference	0.96		

Jurisdiction	Takers	Passers	Pass %	State %	Diff %
Florida	292	230	78.77	77.81	0.96

FLORIDA COASTAL SCHOOL OF LAW

8787 Baypine Road
Jacksonville, FL 32256
Phone: 904.680.7710, Toll-free: 877.210.2591; Fax: 904.680.7692
E-mail: admissions@fcsl.edu; Website: www.fcsl.edu

Introduction

Fully accredited by the ABA, Florida Coastal School of Law offers the finest legal education, coupling traditional approaches with student/faculty partnerships and practical, real-world perspectives. Led by exceptional internationally accomplished faculty, Coastal Law creates an innovative educational experience that produces first-rate lawyers with uncompromised ethics and professional responsibility, as well as sharp legal skills.

Our Students

Coastal Law students represent more than 320 undergraduate colleges and universities from nearly every state in the United States, as well as Puerto Rico, the Virgin Islands, Canada, Germany, and China. While enrolled, students work closely with faculty members who not only share their legal expertise, but also their experiences, perspectives, and expansive networks. We believe our supportive learning environment makes a difference in students' educational experiences and personal growth, ultimately giving them an edge in professional preparation.

Our Faculty

Coastal Law's full-time faculty members represent approximately 50 ABA-accredited law schools from across the country including Harvard University, George Washington University, Duke University, Georgetown University, Columbia University, New York University, and the University of Florida. Together, they boast international legal and academic accomplishments, from authoring dozens of case books and articles to counseling the Iraqi Constitutional Commission and advising the United Nations' war crimes tribunal in The Hague. Further, as former judges, government officials, general and in-house counsel, corporate executives, and attorneys practicing in law firms, they offer realistic legal perspectives.

Our City

Coastal Law is located in Jacksonville, a metropolitan center of more than one million people, including one of the youngest populations in Florida. Boasting 68 miles of ocean coastline, 300 miles of riverfront, and one of the largest park systems in the country, it offers an outstanding array of outdoor activities of all types. In addition, the city is dotted with unique neighborhoods, exceptional arts, entertainment, culture, and a variety of professional sports, including the NFL, PGA Tour, LPGA, ATP Tennis, and baseball. Jacksonville provides the idyllic setting for a legal education during warm winters and beach-filled summers.

Our Facilities

Meticulously designed by one of the top firms of its kind worldwide, to reflect both our traditional and realistic approaches to legal education, Florida Coastal School of Law's lake-front campus boasts 220,000 square feet of state-of-the-art learning technologies. From our interactive trial and appellate courtrooms, to our computer labs, podcasting capabilities, and wireless technology, the tools at Coastal Law make us one of the most sophisticated legal facilities nationwide.

Curriculum and Certificate Programs

Among the many advantages that set Coastal Law apart from our comparator schools is the curriculum, which allows our students to align career choices with specialized areas of expertise. Successful completion of a certificate program not only represents significant learning, but can also exhibit to potential employers a student's dedication to the corresponding practice area. Coastal Law offers five certificate programs: **Sports Law**, **Family Law**, **International and Comparative Law**, **Environmental Law**, and **Advanced Legal Research**, **Writing**, and **Drafting**.

Live Client Clinics

Under the supervision of full-time faculty members, Coastal Law students can gain experience representing indigent clients, and play a part in each phase of legal representation including the initial client interview, case planning and development, drafting letters and pleadings, discovery and negotiation, and even representing their clinic clients in court and administrative hearings. Clinical programs include: the **Family Law Clinic**, the **Consumer Law Clinic**, the **Immigrant Rights Clinic**, the **Disability and Benefits Clinic**, and the **Housing Rights Clinic**.

Joint-Degree Programs

The Davis College of Business at Jacksonville University, a first-tier program, and Florida Coastal School of Law have created a joint-degree program through which qualified students may pursue a Juris Doctor (JD) and a master's degree in business administration (MBA) from both schools simultaneously. Graduates with a joint JD/MBA degree can develop the skills needed to pursue careers in the business and legal professions, especially where those areas overlap, such as investment and commercial banking, management consulting, government regulation, and business policy analysis. In addition to concurrently participating in the academic and social life of both schools, students will be able to obtain both diplomas in four years, as compared to the five years required to earn both degrees when pursued separately.

Bar Preparation and Success

Coastal Law graduates taking the bar exam in Florida and in other states often excel. To ensure our graduates are well prepared for the exam, we work with students to identify personal learning styles and customize time management skills. Coastal Law students also have open access to our academic success counselors and to bar preparation classes and study groups. Coastal provides every student with the resources required to succeed academically, on the bar exam, and as they transition into practice.

Career Services

Coastal Law's Career Services Department (CSD) is committed to empowering students and alumni to pursue the careers of their choice. From individual counseling, résumé critiques, and job-search strategies to attorney panels and on-campus interviewing programs, the CSD offers comprehensive services and resources that can guide students along individual career paths. In addition, the CSD offers our alumni assistance in making changes in practice, career direction, or geographic area.

Closing Invitation From the Dean

The basic curriculum and the traditional three-year time period required for legal education have remained very constant for more than a century. However, it is more important than ever that a law school take maximum advantage of this limited time to prepare its graduates to enter the profession well equipped. At Florida Coastal School of Law, the study of law blends acquiring a comprehensive knowledge of the law with developing the critical thinking and practical skills essential to its practice. Ensuring the careful balance of each of these components is an integral part of the educational process we deliver. To determine whether Florida Coastal School of Law is right for you, feel free to contact any member of our law school community and ask about their experiences here. We also welcome visitors and encourage campus tours.

APPLICANT PROFILE

Florida Coastal School of Law
This grid includes only applicants who earned 120–180 LSAT scores under standard administrations.

LSAT Score	GPA																			
	3.75 +		3.50–3.74		3.25–3.49		3.00–3.24		2.75–2.99		2.50–2.74		2.25–2.49		2.00–2.24		Below 2.00		No GPA		Total	
	Apps	Adm	Apps	Adm	Apps	Adm	Apps	Adm	Apps	Adm	Apps	Adm	Apps	Adm	Apps	Adm	Apps	Adm	Apps	Adm	Apps	Adm
175–180	0	0	0	0	0	0	0	0	0	0	0	0	0	0	0	0	0	0	0	0	0	0
170–174	0	0	0	0	0	0	0	0	0	0	1	1	0	0	0	0	0	0	0	0	1	1
165–169	1	1	2	2	1	1	1	1	2	2	1	1	1	1	0	0	0	0	0	0	9	9
160–164	8	8	13	13	17	17	23	22	11	10	12	11	3	2	3	2	0	0	1	1	91	86
155–159	84	83	158	157	165	159	167	163	106	98	104	96	31	24	9	6	4	0	6	1	834	787
150–154	139	132	272	257	346	326	387	366	302	273	227	200	69	31	24	4	6	0	4	2	1776	1591
145–149	111	106	225	203	373	313	423	328	248	175	182	92	82	3	33	0	6	0	16	4	1699	1224
140–144	36	23	81	41	139	47	176	29	177	23	145	21	66	0	29	1	3	0	11	2	863	187
135–139	7	0	17	1	34	0	63	2	53	3	44	1	30	0	14	0	3	0	8	0	273	7
130–134	1	0	2	0	6	0	11	0	8	0	15	0	10	0	6	0	3	0	3	0	65	0
125–129	1	0	0	0	2	0	0	0	2	0	2	0	2	0	0	0	1	0	0	0	10	0
120–124	0	0	0	0	0	0	0	0	0	0	0	0	0	0	0	0	0	0	1	0	1	0
Total	388	353	770	674	1083	863	1251	911	909	584	733	423	294	61	118	13	26	0	50	10	5622	3892

Apps = Number of Applicants
Adm = Number Admitted
Reflects 99% of the total applicant pool; highest LSAT data reported.

UNIVERSITY OF FLORIDA, FREDRIC G. LEVIN COLLEGE OF LAW

141 Bruton-Geer Hall, PO Box 117622
Gainesville, FL 32611-7622
Phone: 352.273.0890, Toll-free: 877.429.1297; Fax: 352.392.4087
E-mail: admissions@law.ufl.edu; Website: www.law.ufl.edu

ABA
Approved
Since
1925

The Basics

Type of school	Public
Term	Semester
Application deadline	3/15
Application fee	$30
Financial aid deadline	4/7
Can first year start other than fall?	No
Student to faculty ratio	15.4 to 1
# of housing spaces available restricted to law students	
graduate housing for which law students are eligible	

Faculty and Administrators

	Total		Men		Women		Minorities	
	Spr	Fall	Spr	Fall	Spr	Fall	Spr	Fall
Full-time	60	53	27	24	33	29	9	11
Other full-time	3	3	1	1	2	2	1	1
Deans, librarians, & others who teach	16	17	10	10	6	7	2	2
Part-time	39	36	28	25	10	10	5	5
Total	118	109	66	60	51	48	17	19

Curriculum

	Full-Time	Part-Time
Typical first-year section size	105	0
Is there typically a "small section" of the first-year class, other than Legal Writing, taught by full-time faculty	Yes	No
If yes, typical size offered last year	50	
# of classroom course titles beyond first-year curriculum	174	

# of upper division courses, excluding seminars, with an enrollment:		
Under 25	88	
25–49	52	
50–74	28	
75–99	10	
100+	11	

# of seminars	38	
# of seminar positions available	594	
# of seminar positions filled	464	0
# of positions available in simulation courses	532	
# of simulation positions filled	488	0
# of positions available in faculty supervised clinical courses	138	
# of faculty supervised clinical positions filled	101	0
# involved in field placements	295	0
# involved in law journals	351	0
# involved in moot court or trial competitions	96	0
# of credit hours required to graduate	88	

JD Enrollment and Ethnicity

	Men		Women		Full-Time		Part-Time		1st-Year		Total		JD Degs. Awd.
	#	%	#	%	#	%	#	%	#	%	#	%	
All Hispanics	53	9.2	51	10.9	104	10.0	0	0.0	35	11.3	104	10.0	43
Am. Ind./AK Nat.	6	1.0	9	1.9	15	1.4	0	0.0	6	1.9	15	1.4	1
Asian	35	6.1	33	7.1	68	6.5	0	0.0	15	4.8	68	6.5	20
Black/Af. Am.	27	4.7	45	9.6	72	6.9	0	0.0	25	8.1	72	6.9	19
Nat. HI/Pac. Isl.	0	0.0	0	0.0	0	0.0	0	0.0	0	0.0	0	0.0	0
2 or more races	0	0.0	0	0.0	0	0.0	0	0.0	0	0.0	0	0.0	0
Subtotal (minor.)	121	21.0	138	29.6	259	24.8	0	0.0	81	26.1	259	24.8	83
Nonres. Alien	5	0.9	2	0.4	7	0.7	0	0.0	0	0.0	7	0.7	0
White/Cauc.	422	73.1	317	67.9	739	70.8	0	0.0	224	72.3	739	70.8	280
Unknown	29	5.0	10	2.1	39	3.7	0	0.0	5	1.6	39	3.7	18
Total	577	55.3	467	44.7	1044	100.0	0	0.0	310	29.7	1044		384

Transfers

Transfers in	37
Transfers out	13

Tuition and Fees

	Resident	Nonresident
Full-time	$16,387	$35,752
Part-time		
Tuition Guarantee Program	N	

Living Expenses

Estimated living expenses for singles

Living on campus	Living off campus	Living at home
$13,800	$14,930	$6,550

UNIVERSITY OF FLORIDA, FREDRIC G. LEVIN COLLEGE OF LAW

*ABA
Approved
Since
1925*

GPA and LSAT Scores

	Total	Full-Time	Part-Time
# of apps	3,357	3,357	0
# of offers	817	817	0
# of matrics	310	310	0
75% GPA	3.84	3.84	0.00
Median GPA	3.67	3.67	0.00
25% GPA	3.44	3.44	0.00
75% LSAT	164	164	0
Median LSAT	162	162	0
25% LSAT	160	160	0

Grants and Scholarships (from prior year)

	Total #	Total %	Full-Time #	Full-Time %	Part-Time #	Part-Time %
Total # of students	1,106		1,106		0	
Total # receiving grants	420	38.0	420	38.0	0	0.0
Less than 1/2 tuition	345	31.2	345	31.2	0	0.0
Half to full tuition	60	5.4	60	5.4	0	0.0
Full tuition	9	0.8	9	0.8	0	0.0
More than full tuition	6	0.5	6	0.5	0	0.0
Median grant amount			$2,800		$0	

Informational and Library Resources

Total amount spent on library materials	$1,281,541
Study seating capacity inside the library	765
# of full-time equivalent professional librarians	7
Hours per week library is open	98
# of open, wired connections available to students	0
# of networked computers available for use by students	46
Has wireless network?	Y
Requires computer?	Y

JD Attrition (from prior year)

	Academic #	Other #	Total #	Total %
1st year	0	10	10	3.3
2nd year	0	14	14	3.5
3rd year	0	2	2	0.5
4th year	0	0	0	0.0

Employment (9 months after graduation)

	Total	Percentage
Employment status known	424	99.8
Employment status unknown	1	0.2
Employed	369	87.0
Pursuing graduate degrees	43	10.1
Unemployed (seeking, not seeking, or studying for the bar)	2	0.5
Type of Employment		
# employed in law firms	188	50.9
# employed in business and industry	33	8.9
# employed in government	72	19.5
# employed in public interest	23	6.2
# employed as judicial clerks	19	5.1
# employed in academia	34	9.2
Geographic Location		
# employed in state	274	74.3
# employed outside the US	1	0.3
# of states where employed	19	

Bar Passage Rates

First-time takers	362	Reporting %	88.95
Average school %	85.71	Average state %	77.81
Average pass difference	7.90		

Jurisdiction	Takers	Passers	Pass %	State %	Diff %
Florida	322	276	85.71	77.81	7.90

UNIVERSITY OF FLORIDA, FREDRIC G. LEVIN COLLEGE OF LAW

141 Bruton-Geer Hall, PO Box 117622
Gainesville, FL 32611-7622
Phone: 352.273.0890, Toll-free: 877.429.1297; Fax: 352.392.4087
E-mail: admissions@law.ufl.edu; Website: www.law.ufl.edu

Introduction

The University of Florida Levin College of Law is one of the nation's most comprehensive and widely respected law schools. It was founded in 1909, has been a member of the Association of American Law Schools since 1920, and was approved by the American Bar Association in 1925. It boasts an impressive list of distinguished visitors to campus, including five Supreme Court justices in the last five years. Its beautiful campus features expansive, state-of-the-art facilities thanks to efforts such as a $25 million expansion and renovation project completed in 2005 and a trial advocacy center completed in November 2009.

The college's faculty are highly accomplished scholars, educators, and practitioners whose broad knowledge base and strong teaching skills are highly praised in student evaluations. Many are authors of treatises, casebooks, or major books used by law schools and practitioners throughout the nation, as well as hundreds of articles in law reviews and specialty journals.

The law school is known for graduating state and national legal, political, business, government, and educational leaders, and for nurturing a strong alumni network, the UF Law "Gator Nation." UF Law graduates include five ABA presidents—including 2010–11 President Stephen Zack—numerous federal and state judges, partners in major national and international law firms, members of Congress and the cabinet, governors, and state legislators. Alumni support has built the endowment into one of the largest in the country for public law schools. This, combined with the state's financial assistance, allows the college to remain affordable while its academic quality rivals many of the best-known private colleges.

The University of Florida is one of the nation's largest and most comprehensive universities, is a member of the prestigious Association of American Universities, and is recognized as one of the nation's leading research universities by the Carnegie Commission on Higher Education. The campus occupies 2,000 acres, mostly within the city of Gainesville's 131,000-population area in North Central Florida. The area is consistently ranked among the best places to live in America, with extensive educational, cultural, and recreational offerings.

Programs and Curriculum

The Levin College of Law offers students both strong fundamentals and a diverse range of specializations and interdisciplinary options. The activities and scholarship of its unusually large faculty allow for numerous interesting programs and curricular concentrations. More than 70 courses and 15–20 seminars are offered each semester. Students can earn a certificate in Environmental and Land Use Law, Estates and Trusts Practice, Family Law, Intellectual Property Law, or International and Comparative Law. The Levin College of Law also offers one of the most extensive joint-degree programs of any US law school, including popular joint degrees in Business, Public Health/Medicine, Education, and Engineering, among many other areas. Students can gain hands-on experience in litigation, negotiation, mediation, client relations, and government service at the highest levels

through a broad array of courses, study-abroad opportunities, externships, pro bono work, and clinical programs. The first-year curriculum is required, as is a second-year drafting course. JD candidates must produce—under close faculty supervision—a major, written, finished product that shows evidence of original systematic scholarship based on individual research. Students often satisfy this requirement through a "senior paper" produced while enrolled in a seminar.

The richness and diversity of the school's faculty, student body, and course offerings are strengthened by the presence of its top ranked Graduate Tax Program—leading to an LLM in Taxation, LLM in International Taxation, or SJD in Taxation. The school also offers an LLM in Environmental and Land Use Law, as well as an LLM in Comparative Law for foreign lawyers. In addition, UF is a major hub for international legal programs and has decades of experience and relationships in Latin America and Europe. The college's innovative centers and institutes include the Center for Governmental Responsibility, Center on Children and Families, Center for the Study of Race and Race Relations, Camp Center for Estate and Elder Law Planning, and Institute for Dispute Resolution.

Student/Extracurricular Activities

More than 65 active extracurricular organizations at the law school help students develop valuable skills and professional contacts as well as make a positive difference in the community. Students can earn credits and polish their legal skills through cocurricular organizations such as the *Florida Law Review, Florida Journal of International Law, University of Florida Journal of Law and Public Policy, Journal of Technology Law and Policy,* and trophy-winning US and international moot court and trial teams.

Library and Facilities

Following completion in 2005 of a major expansion and renovation project, the Lawton Chiles Legal Information Center is now one of the largest academic law libraries in the Southeast and among the top 20 in the nation in terms of space. The expanded library offers comfortable study areas, reading rooms, computer training labs, multimedia workstations, and reference rooms for use by students and faculty. Two new three-story education buildings feature spacious, state-of-the-art classrooms equipped to offer the latest in teaching technology, including desktop outlets for laptop use, wireless Internet access, and "smart podia."

The most recent addition to the law school is a sophisticated, high-tech, two-and-a-half story advocacy center with a fully functional trial and appellate courtroom, audience gallery, and bench for seven judges, completed in November 2009.

Career Development

Professional counselors in the college's Center for Career Development offer a wide variety of services and programs to help students plan a self-directed career search and develop marketing skills that will serve them for many years to come.

Staff members help students develop legal credentials; capitalize on their diverse strengths and experiences; explore legal and nontraditional career paths; and find summer internships, externships, and clerkships, as well as permanent postgraduation employment. They also help link students with alumni, practitioners, and the community, and host large on-campus recruiting events that bring numerous employers to campus each year. Other resources include workshops and seminars on practical career skills, individual career and job-search counseling, on- and off-campus networking events, and a web-based job bank with downloadable handouts, samples, and forms.

Admission

Through its admissions process, the Levin College of Law seeks to admit and enroll students who will excel academically, attain the highest standards of professional excellence and integrity, and bring vision, creativity and commitment to the legal profession. The LSAT, LSAC Credential Assembly Service, admissions statement, and résumé are required. Recommendation letters are not required, but up to four will be accepted. A bachelor's degree from an accredited college or university is required prior to enrollment.

The admissions staff and the faculty admissions committee base their decisions on the applicant's academic credentials, including LSAT score, UGPA, level of writing skills, and breadth of studies, as well as on other information including, but not limited to, the applicant's work and other life experience, leadership experience, depth of particular interest, and any other aspect of an applicant's background suggesting suitability for the study and practice of law.

Students may transfer in August, January, or May from ABA-approved law schools, but only applicants who have completed the required first-year, full-time curriculum before enrolling at UF and who are in the upper one-third of their class will be considered. A transfer certification form from the dean is required and no more than 29 semester hours will be transferred.

The law school seeks to enroll approximately 300 (full-time only) students each fall. The college places great importance on obtaining a diverse class and actively recruits minority students. To arrange an appointment or a tour of the law school, contact the Admissions Office.

Expenses and Financial Aid

The 2010–2011 tuition is $16,386.60 for Florida residents and $35,751.30 for nonresidents. Additional expenses total approximately $15,080 for books, supplies, computer (required), clothing, room, food, transportation, student orientation fee (entering students only), and personal/insurance.

Merit-based and merit/need-based scholarships and grants, and short- and long-term loans (FAFSA required) are available to qualified students. Merit awards are based on information collected in the application for admission. To be considered for merit/need-based scholarships and need-based grants, admitted students must submit a FAFSA and a UF Law Financial Aid Application for need-based scholarships and grants.

Housing

Housing is available for single students in dormitories and for families in university apartments. Plentiful off-campus housing is available. New and current UF law students may access the UF College of Law Roommate Referral System online.

APPLICANT PROFILE

University of Florida, Fredric G. Levin College of Law
This grid includes only applicants who earned 120–180 LSAT scores under standard administrations.

LSAT Score	GPA 3.75 +		3.50–3.74		3.25–3.49		3.00–3.24		2.75–2.99		2.50–2.74		2.25–2.49		2.00–2.24		Below 2.00		No GPA		Total	
	Apps	Adm	Apps	Adm	Apps	Adm	Apps	Adm	Apps	Adm	Apps	Adm	Apps	Adm	Apps	Adm	Apps	Adm	Apps	Adm	Apps	Adm
175–180	1	1	3	3	2	2	3	3	2	1	0	0	0	0	0	0	0	0	0	0	11	10
170–174	16	16	15	12	14	13	8	6	4	1	2	1	2	0	0	0	0	0	0	0	61	49
165–169	70	64	76	66	59	51	49	28	27	3	15	2	6	1	2	0	0	0	3	0	307	215
160–164	175	151	249	155	241	79	114	19	61	5	23	1	10	0	4	0	0	0	16	8	893	418
155–159	207	73	274	13	229	9	147	2	82	4	33	0	15	0	3	1	0	0	29	1	1019	103
150–154	107	8	153	5	154	4	132	4	71	0	23	1	20	0	3	0	1	0	17	0	681	22
145–149	35	0	51	1	79	0	90	0	39	0	24	0	11	0	5	0	1	0	8	0	343	1
140–144	17	0	27	1	29	0	23	0	24	0	14	0	12	0	2	0	0	0	4	0	152	1
135–139	0	0	3	0	4	0	5	0	9	0	10	0	4	0	8	0	0	0	2	0	45	0
130–134	0	0	1	0	2	0	4	0	3	0	2	0	3	0	0	0	0	0	0	0	15	0
125–129	0	0	0	0	0	0	0	0	1	0	1	0	0	0	1	0	0	0	0	0	3	0
120–124	0	0	0	0	0	0	0	0	0	0	0	0	0	0	0	0	0	0	0	0	0	0
Total	628	313	852	256	813	158	575	62	323	14	147	5	83	1	28	1	2	0	79	9	3530	819

Apps = Number of Applicants
Adm = Number Admitted
Reflects 99% of the total applicant pool; highest LSAT data reported.

FLORIDA INTERNATIONAL UNIVERSITY COLLEGE OF LAW

RDB 1055
Miami, FL 33186
Phone: 305.348.8006; Fax: 305.348.2965
E-mail: lawadmit@fiu.edu; Website: http://law.fiu.edu/

The Basics

Type of school	Public
Term	Semester
Application deadline	5/1
Application fee	$20
Financial aid deadline	3/1
Can first year start other than fall?	No
Student to faculty ratio	14.7 to 1
# of housing spaces available restricted to law students	
graduate housing for which law students are eligible	43

Faculty and Administrators

	Total		Men		Women		Minorities	
	Spr	Fall	Spr	Fall	Spr	Fall	Spr	Fall
Full-time	28	31	15	16	13	15	14	16
Other full-time	2	1	0	0	2	1	2	1
Deans, librarians, & others who teach	6	5	4	4	2	1	4	3
Part-time	20	19	12	12	7	4	19	17
Total	56	56	31	32	24	21	39	37

JD Enrollment and Ethnicity

	Men		Women		Full-Time		Part-Time		1st-Year		Total		JD Degs. Awd.
	#	%	#	%	#	%	#	%	#	%	#	%	
All Hispanics	103	35.9	130	43.2	155	39.2	78	40.4	68	41.0	233	39.6	68
Am. Ind./AK Nat.	1	0.3	2	0.7	0	0.0	3	1.6	1	0.6	3	0.5	0
Asian	7	2.4	16	5.3	17	4.3	6	3.1	9	5.4	23	3.9	2
Black/Af. Am.	24	8.4	30	10.0	30	7.6	24	12.4	19	11.4	54	9.2	9
Nat. HI/Pac. Isl.	0	0.0	0	0.0	0	0.0	0	0.0	0	0.0	0	0.0	0
2 or more races	10	3.5	10	3.3	12	3.0	8	4.1	2	1.2	20	3.4	0
Subtotal (minor.)	145	50.5	188	62.5	214	54.2	119	61.7	99	59.6	333	56.6	84
Nonres. Alien	0	0.0	2	0.7	1	0.3	1	0.5	1	0.6	2	0.3	2
White/Cauc.	139	48.4	105	34.9	174	44.1	70	36.3	65	39.2	244	41.5	57
Unknown	3	1.0	6	2.0	6	1.5	3	1.6	1	0.6	9	1.5	8
Total	287	48.8	301	51.2	395	67.2	193	32.8	166	28.2	588		151

Curriculum

	Full-Time	Part-Time
Typical first-year section size	58	49
Is there typically a "small section" of the first-year class, other than Legal Writing, taught by full-time faculty	No	No
If yes, typical size offered last year		

# of classroom course titles beyond first-year curriculum		72
# of upper division courses, excluding seminars, with an enrollment:	Under 25	122
	25–49	35
	50–74	14
	75–99	6
	100+	0

# of seminars		12
# of seminar positions available		206
# of seminar positions filled	130	47
# of positions available in simulation courses		155
# of simulation positions filled	97	23
# of positions available in faculty supervised clinical courses		78
# of faculty supervised clinical positions filled	64	6
# involved in field placements	41	12
# involved in law journals	34	2
# involved in moot court or trial competitions	30	8
# of credit hours required to graduate		90

Transfers

Transfers in	1
Transfers out	10

Tuition and Fees

	Resident	Nonresident
Full-time	$15,520	$30,224
Part-time	$10,786	$20,894
Tuition Guarantee Program		N

Living Expenses

Estimated living expenses for singles

Living on campus	Living off campus	Living at home
$18,678	$24,016	$12,156

FLORIDA INTERNATIONAL UNIVERSITY COLLEGE OF LAW

ABA
Approved
Since
2004

GPA and LSAT Scores

	Total	Full-Time	Part-Time
# of apps	2,516	2,048	469
# of offers	504	434	70
# of matrics	161	116	45
75% GPA	3.79	3.81	3.71
Median GPA	3.60	3.60	3.55
25% GPA	3.27	3.31	3.24
75% LSAT	157	157	159
Median LSAT	155	155	155
25% LSAT	152	152	151

Grants and Scholarships (from prior year)

	Total		Full-Time		Part-Time	
	#	%	#	%	#	%
Total # of students	623		294		329	
Total # receiving grants	180	28.9	144	49.0	36	10.9
Less than 1/2 tuition	125	20.1	124	42.2	1	0.3
Half to full tuition	50	8.0	17	5.8	33	10.0
Full tuition	0	0.0	0	0.0	0	0.0
More than full tuition	5	0.8	3	1.0	2	0.6
Median grant amount			$5,000		$5,000	

Informational and Library Resources

Total amount spent on library materials	$822,378
Study seating capacity inside the library	322
# of full-time equivalent professional librarians	8
Hours per week library is open	95
# of open, wired connections available to students	35
# of networked computers available for use by students	54
Has wireless network?	Y
Requires computer?	N

JD Attrition (from prior year)

	Academic	Other	Total	
	#	#	#	%
1st year	23	12	35	14.8
2nd year	2	2	4	2.1
3rd year	0	0	0	0.0
4th year	0	0	0	0.0

Employment (9 months after graduation)

	Total	Percentage
Employment status known	117	99.2
Employment status unknown	1	0.8
Employed	107	91.5
Pursuing graduate degrees	5	4.3
Unemployed (seeking, not seeking, or studying for the bar)	0	0.0
Type of Employment		
# employed in law firms	58	54.2
# employed in business and industry	18	16.8
# employed in government	14	13.1
# employed in public interest	0	0.0
# employed as judicial clerks	4	3.7
# employed in academia	13	12.1
Geographic Location		
# employed in state	92	86.0
# employed outside the US	0	0.0
# of states where employed	11	

Bar Passage Rates

First-time takers	121	Reporting %	100.00
Average school %	81.82	Average state %	78.11
Average pass difference	3.71		

Jurisdiction	Takers	Passers	Pass %	State %	Diff %
Florida	116	94	81.03	77.81	3.22
Illinois	2	2	100.00	90.89	9.11
California	1	1	100.00	73.19	26.81
Minnesota	1	1	100.00	89.58	10.42
Tennessee	1	1	100.00	82.44	17.56

FLORIDA INTERNATIONAL UNIVERSITY COLLEGE OF LAW

RDB 1055
Miami, FL 33186
Phone: 305.348.8006; Fax: 305.348.2965
E-mail: lawadmit@fiu.edu; Website: http://law.fiu.edu/

Introduction

The Florida International University College of Law was established by an act of the Florida legislature in June 2000. Its first class was admitted in the fall of 2002 and received approval by the ABA in 2004.

Florida International University is a public research university which enrolls over 40,000 students, most on its beautiful University Park campus, where the College of Law is located. This campus is the site of the new state-of-the-art law building designed by nationally and internationally renowned architect Robert A. M. Stern. The campus enjoys nearby access to South Florida's beaches, Everglades National Park, and the Florida Keys.

The College of Law reflects the diverse character and the international perspective of the city of Miami. The curriculum incorporates important developments in the globalization of both public and private law. The academic program takes a pervasive approach to both international and comparative law, incorporating their perspectives into all domestic law classes.

Curriculum and Special Programs

The FIU College of Law's academic program, while devoted to all the traditional components of an excellent American legal education, also emphasizes international and comparative law. To this end, the required curriculum includes a three-hour, first-year course titled Introduction to International and Comparative Law. Further, all domestic law courses include an international or comparative law dimension. This pervasive approach to international and comparative law encourages students to analyze legal systemic, political, economic, social, and other cultural differences that may contribute to different legal treatment of comparable problems in different countries. The College of Law also offers a foreign summer program in Sevilla, Spain.

As Miami's premier public research university, FIU offers a broad range of high quality, graduate-level degree programs. Law students interested in interdisciplinary study may take advantage of several joint-degree programs, including the following: JD/Master of Business Administration, JD/Master of International Business, JD/Master of Latin American and Caribbean Studies, JD/Master of Public Administration, JD/MS in Psychology, JD/Master of Social Work, JD/MS in Criminal Justice, and JD/Master of Science in Environmental Sciences.

In addition to a strong doctrinal program, the College of Law's Clinical Program advances the law school's goals of educating lawyers for the ethical and effective practice of law and of promoting community service through the representation of real clients. Presently, there are eight clinics available—the Carlos A. Costa Immigration and Human Rights Clinic; the Community Development Clinic; the Investor Advocacy Clinic; the Consumer Bankruptcy Clinic; the Education Advocacy Clinic; the Environmental Clinic; the Health, Ethics, Law and Policy Clinic; and the Immigrant Children's Justice Clinic—as well as externships in Criminal/Civil Law and the Florida Judiciary. The curriculum also emphasizes instruction in the legal skills and values of the profession. The Legal Skills and Values Program combines demanding traditional instruction in legal research and writing with an introduction to other lawyering skills, like interviewing and counseling, and issues of professionalism.

Moreover, as a public, urban law school, the College of Law is committed to serving the community of which it is a part by educating future lawyers who will understand the value—to the community and to themselves personally—of helping those in need. In recognition of this important mission, students must satisfy a community service requirement.

Admission

The FIU College of Law offers both a full-time day and part-time evening program. The review of applications is done on a rolling basis. An LSAC Credential Assembly Service report, three letters of recommendation, and a personal statement are required.

While a prospective student's academic record and LSAT performance are weighted heavily in the evaluative process, the Admissions Committee considers other factors, including leadership ability, commitment to public service, command of global issues, work history, military service, any history of criminality or academic misconduct, and evidence of obstacles that an applicant may have overcome (for example, English is not the applicant's native language, discrimination, economic or family hardship, and severe medical conditions, etc.). The Admissions Committee encourages each applicant to answer all questions with candor, detail, and, where appropriate, to give specific examples of relevant background experiences.

Transfer students from other ABA-approved law schools may apply if they are in good standing at their current institutions. Visit our website at http://law.fiu.edu/ for additional information.

Financial Aid

The primary financial aid resources available to students are loans and need- or merit-based scholarships. Students must apply for financial aid (FAFSA) to be considered for any type of loan or need-based scholarship. No separate application is needed for merit-based scholarships. Eligible students will be considered based on the information provided in their admission application. Financial aid is granted on an annual basis, and awards are subject to student eligibility and availability of funds. Tuition is comparable to other Florida state-supported law schools at $473 per credit for Florida residents and $932 per credit for nonresidents. An additional $24,776 (approximate) can be expected to cover room and board, books, transportation, and personal expenses. Please call 305.348.8006 for further information.

Library

The Law Library supports the law school curriculum, the research needs of its students and faculty, and the public's interest in access to critical legal materials. It contains approximately 220,000 volumes in book and microform format. The Law Library provides law students with a full range of electronic legal information resources, including Westlaw, LexisNexis, HeinOnline, BNA, CCH, and other web-based databases. When performing background, factual, and/or interdisciplinary research, law students draw upon the Green Library on FIU's Maidique campus, which offers access to more than 1.5 million volumes and extensive electronic resources. The Law Library is staffed by five full-time and two part-time professional librarians, two of whom have law degrees. In addition to a comprehensive collection of core US materials, the library has an extensive collection of international, comparative, and foreign law materials, with a particular focus on Latin America and the Caribbean, international trade, and the workings of international tribunals and multilateral institutions.

Career Development Office

The Career Development Office (CDO) provides a multitude of expert services and professional resources to assist students and alumni in finding employment and launching careers in the legal profession. The CDO continues to cultivate outstanding relationships with many leading employers, in Florida and nationwide, including a host of public service employers, federal agencies, and the Courts.

Professional and personal satisfaction is critical to any successful legal or law related career. The CDO dedicates its considerable energies and resources to assisting students with developing individualized short- and long-term career strategies that allow students to successfully navigate through a broad spectrum of career options. The CDO serves as a resource for students and informational bridge between students and employers based in the South Florida community, regionally and throughout the nation.

CDO Services include the following:

- Personalized career counseling
- Application material review
- Skills workshops and programming
- Panel discussions on career choices in the private, public, government, and alternative sectors
- Professional development programs
- Interview programs
- Career Resource Library
- Job Postings—FIU Law Symplicity Job Bank

The CDO is committed to providing students with the tools necessary to pursue a wide range of career opportunities and to make informed career-related decisions.

Student Activities

Success in law school involves more than just intellectual curiosity and a sense of purpose. It involves the refining of time management skills, handling stress proactively, and forging relationships with faculty and peers. It also involves making the best possible use of available services and opportunities. Students bring a wealth of distinctive educational and professional experiences to the College of Law. However, they all share a common interest and goal: service to the law school, the local community, and the profession. Together with the support of the faculty and the administration, students have created a number of organizations and cocurricular activities reflective of this commitment. In its brief but productive history, the College of Law has established a thriving clinical and externship program, award-winning moot court and trial advocacy programs competing locally and nationally against teams throughout the country, and 23 student organizations, including the Student Bar Association.

APPLICANT PROFILE

The Florida International University College of Law Admissions Committee seeks to enroll a diverse group of students who have demonstrated academic and personal achievement. While a prospective student's academic record and LSAT performance are weighted heavily in the evaluative process, the Admissions Committee considers other factors, including leadership ability, commitment to public service, command of global issues, work history, military service, any history of criminality or academic misconduct, and evidence of obstacles that an applicant may have overcome (for example, English is not the applicant's native language, discrimination, economic or family hardship, severe medical condition, disability, etc.).

THE FLORIDA STATE UNIVERSITY COLLEGE OF LAW

425 West Jefferson Street
Tallahassee, FL 32306-1601
Phone: 850.644.3787; Fax: 850.644.7284
E-mail: admissions@law.fsu.edu; Website: www.law.fsu.edu

ABA
Approved
Since
1968

The Basics

Type of school	Public
Term	Semester
Application deadline	5/1
Application fee	$30
Financial aid deadline	3/1
Can first year start other than fall?	No
Student to faculty ratio	14.3 to 1
# of housing spaces available restricted to law students	
graduate housing for which law students are eligible	1,000

Faculty and Administrators

	Total		Men		Women		Minorities	
	Spr	Fall	Spr	Fall	Spr	Fall	Spr	Fall
Full-time	44	47	25	26	19	21	6	7
Other full-time	0	0	0	0	0	0	0	0
Deans, librarians, & others who teach	15	14	3	3	12	11	4	3
Part-time	28	30	22	22	6	8	3	3
Total	87	91	50	51	37	40	13	13

Curriculum

	Full-Time	Part-Time
Typical first-year section size	82	0
Is there typically a "small section" of the first-year class, other than Legal Writing, taught by full-time faculty	No	No
If yes, typical size offered last year		
# of classroom course titles beyond first-year curriculum	115	
# of upper division courses, excluding seminars, with an enrollment: Under 25	79	
25–49	26	
50–74	24	
75–99	6	
100+	3	
# of seminars	28	
# of seminar positions available	727	
# of seminar positions filled	463	0
# of positions available in simulation courses	924	
# of simulation positions filled	641	0
# of positions available in faculty supervised clinical courses	49	
# of faculty supervised clinical positions filled	49	0
# involved in field placements	147	0
# involved in law journals	148	0
# involved in moot court or trial competitions	89	0
# of credit hours required to graduate	88	

JD Enrollment and Ethnicity

	Men		Women		Full-Time		Part-Time		1st-Year		Total		JD Degs. Awd.
	#	%	#	%	#	%	#	%	#	%	#	%	
All Hispanics	40	8.5	31	10.1	71	9.1	0	0.0	22	11.0	71	9.1	12
Am. Ind./AK Nat.	1	0.2	1	0.3	2	0.3	0	0.0	0	0.0	2	0.3	1
Asian	12	2.5	10	3.2	22	2.8	0	0.0	3	1.5	22	2.8	4
Black/Af. Am.	21	4.5	38	12.3	59	7.6	0	0.0	14	7.0	59	7.6	22
Nat. HI/Pac. Isl.	0	0.0	0	0.0	0	0.0	0	0.0	0	0.0	0	0.0	0
2 or more races	0	0.0	0	0.0	0	0.0	0	0.0	0	0.0	0	0.0	0
Subtotal (minor.)	74	15.7	80	26.0	154	19.8	0	0.0	39	19.5	154	19.8	39
Nonres. Alien	0	0.0	1	0.3	1	0.1	0	0.0	1	0.5	1	0.1	1
White/Cauc.	388	82.4	218	70.8	606	77.8	0	0.0	153	76.5	606	77.8	202
Unknown	9	1.9	9	2.9	18	2.3	0	0.0	7	3.5	18	2.3	3
Total	471	60.5	308	39.5	779	100.0	0	0.0	200	25.7	779		245

Transfers

Transfers in	74
Transfers out	7

Tuition and Fees

	Resident	Nonresident
Full-time	$16,371	$35,934
Part-time		
Tuition Guarantee Program	N	

Living Expenses

Estimated living expenses for singles

Living on campus	Living off campus	Living at home
$17,875	$17,875	$17,875

THE FLORIDA STATE UNIVERSITY COLLEGE OF LAW

*ABA
Approved
Since
1968*

GPA and LSAT Scores

	Total	Full-Time	Part-Time
# of apps	3,621	3,621	0
# of offers	803	803	0
# of matrics	199	199	0
75% GPA	3.70	3.70	0.00
Median GPA	3.52	3.52	0.00
25% GPA	3.30	3.30	0.00
75% LSAT	164	164	0
Median LSAT	162	162	0
25% LSAT	161	161	0

Grants and Scholarships (from prior year)

	Total		Full-Time		Part-Time	
	#	%	#	%	#	%
Total # of students	763		763		0	
Total # receiving grants	282	37.0	282	37.0	0	0.0
Less than 1/2 tuition	212	27.8	212	27.8	0	0.0
Half to full tuition	51	6.7	51	6.7	0	0.0
Full tuition	8	1.0	8	1.0	0	0.0
More than full tuition	11	1.4	11	1.4	0	0.0
Median grant amount			$2,000		$0	

Informational and Library Resources

Total amount spent on library materials	$874,223
Study seating capacity inside the library	422
# of full-time equivalent professional librarians	10
Hours per week library is open	168
# of open, wired connections available to students	0
# of networked computers available for use by students	42
Has wireless network?	Y
Requires computer?	Y

JD Attrition (from prior year)

	Academic	Other	Total	
	#	#	#	%
1st year	3	12	15	6.1
2nd year	1	1	2	0.7
3rd year	0	0	0	0.0
4th year	0	0	0	0.0

Employment (9 months after graduation)

	Total	Percentage
Employment status known	260	98.9
Employment status unknown	3	1.1
Employed	239	91.9
Pursuing graduate degrees	7	2.7
Unemployed (seeking, not seeking, or studying for the bar)	0	0.0
Type of Employment		
# employed in law firms	121	50.6
# employed in business and industry	27	11.3
# employed in government	57	23.8
# employed in public interest	20	8.4
# employed as judicial clerks	6	2.5
# employed in academia	8	3.3
Geographic Location		
# employed in state	182	76.2
# employed outside the US	3	1.3
# of states where employed		18

Bar Passage Rates

First-time takers	247	Reporting %	87.04
Average school %	86.51	Average state %	77.81
Average pass difference	8.70		

Jurisdiction	Takers	Passers	Pass %	State %	Diff %
Florida	215	186	86.51	77.81	8.70

THE FLORIDA STATE UNIVERSITY COLLEGE OF LAW

425 West Jefferson Street
Tallahassee, FL 32306-1601
Phone: 850.644.3787; Fax: 850.644.7284
E-mail: admissions@law.fsu.edu; Website: www.law.fsu.edu

Introduction

Florida State University College of Law is recognized as one of the nation's top-tier law schools in terms of academic reputation. The school encourages close working relationships among students and faculty of the sort that characterize the best liberal arts colleges. Cutting-edge faculty members make it a priority to be available to students outside and inside the classroom.

Our attentive faculty greatly values the insights of other disciplines that can be brought to bear upon the study of law. It is important to the faculty to integrate into the study of law insights from such diverse disciplines as history, philosophy, psychology, sociology, economics, and finance.

Florida State offers law students a wealth of legal employment opportunities. Located in Tallahassee, a city with more than 500 law firms and numerous government agencies, Florida State University College of Law is just steps away from the state Capitol, the Florida Supreme Court, and the United States District Court for the Northern District of Florida.

The fall 2010 entering class at the Florida State University College of Law had an average LSAT score of 162, with a 164 at the 75th percentile and a 161 at the 25th percentile (the highest LSAT scores in the state of Florida).

Enrollment/Student Body

Florida State University College of Law receives 18 applications for every seat in its entering class. Accepting students from a wide variety of backgrounds enriches the law school experience. Currently, the talented and diverse student body represents 32 states, 16 countries, and 164 colleges and universities. *Hispanic Business* magazine (2010) recognizes us as one of the nation's "Top Ten Law Schools for Hispanics."

Curriculum

Florida State University College of Law's three-year curriculum is deep and diverse. It begins with traditional courses and expands to include the latest in theoretical and interdisciplinary analyses. The first-year curriculum is rigorous, traditional, and prescribed. It provides a foundation in history, doctrine, process, and analysis that students need to fully appreciate more specialized elective courses offered in the second and third years of law school.

The law school has four cocurricular academic organizations, including two student-edited journals, and trial and appellate advocacy teams. The journals include the *Florida State University Law Review* and the *Journal of Land Use and Environmental Law*, and all have been rated high on "impact factor" by Washington and Lee University. The law school's advocacy teams are regionally and nationally competitive. In 2010, for example, the school's moot court team won first place in four national competitions.

Special Programs

Florida State University College of Law has especially strong programs in environmental law, international law, and business, with certificate programs in environmental law and international law. The law school's program in environmental law is recognized as one of the best in the country. The law school also has one of the best criminal law programs in the region and the litigation program is extremely textured.

Building on its highly ranked environmental law program, Florida State University College of Law offers an LLM in Environmental Law and Policy. The law school's newest degree offering gives JD holders the opportunity to concentrate in, or enhance their knowledge of, environmental law, land use law, natural resources law, and energy law.

The law school also offers an LLM in American Law for foreign lawyers, which provides foreign graduate students trained in law the opportunity to develop an understanding of the American legal system and the role of law in the United States.

Florida State University College of Law offers eight joint-degree programs in cooperation with other colleges, schools, and departments at Florida State. The joint degrees bring together law with business, economics, information studies, international affairs, public administration, social work, child and family sciences, and urban and regional planning.

Florida State University College of Law has one of the most extensive externship programs in the United States. The clinical externship program places students in more than 80 offices throughout Florida and elsewhere. Students may even select international externships in locations around the world including with the International Bar Association in London, The Hague, and the Supreme Court of Botswana.

The law school's Public Interest Law Center provides on-campus clinical legal training for second- and third-year students. Students are certified by the Florida Supreme Court to practice law as interns and, under the supervision of licensed attorneys, are responsible for all facets of cases to which they are assigned.

Florida State University College of Law also sponsors a summer program at Oxford University in England. As the oldest ongoing summer program in Oxford sponsored by a US law school, it provides students with a unique opportunity to study comparative law and the history of the common law and its institutions in their original setting.

Library and Physical Facilities

The physical facilities of Florida State University College of Law consist of B.K. Roberts Hall, the connected Research Center, and the Village Green, which is comprised of four restored houses. All of the law school's classrooms are either new or recently remodeled. Classrooms are equipped with technology podiums that allow professors to present multimedia lectures. A strong wireless infrastructure allows students to utilize the Internet during class.

Florida State University College of Law students have 24/7 access to the research center. The distinctive feature of the research center is that its faculty proactively trains students and other faculty members to produce highly sophisticated, cost-effective legal research. For example, we offer specialized courses in efficient research relating to environmental law, economics, business and tax law, and international law. The law school's research center was also significantly remodeled in 2007. Highlights include an improved student seating area for studying and cosmetic improvements in the lobby and circulation desk area.

Florida State University College of Law is acquiring, as an addition, a 50,000-square-foot modern courthouse directly across the street from its present facilities. Among other things, this acquisition will give the College of Law one of the nation's finest facilities for trial and appellate advocacy. It will also house the Public Interest Law Center's Children's Advocacy and Family Law Clinics.

Student Activities

Students have the opportunity to participate in many extracurricular organizations. More than 30 student and service organizations allow students to become leaders at the law school and active participants in the legal community. Some of the active student organizations include the American Constitution Society; Real Estate and Trust Law Society; Public Interest Law Students Association; Women's Law Symposium; Black Law Students Association; Christian Legal Society; Entertainment, Art, and Sports Law Society; Federalist Society; International Law Students Association; Dispute Resolution Society; Environmental Law Society; Lawtinos; and OUTLaw. Both Phi Delta Phi and Phi Alpha Delta legal honoraries maintain a chapter on campus. In addition, Florida State University College of Law was granted a chapter of the Order of the Coif in 1979. The Student Bar Association received the 2010 Public Interest National Achievement Award from the Law Student Division of the American Bar Association. In both 2008 and 2009, the Law Student Division selected Florida State as the "SBA of the Year." This group serves an active student government role and coordinates many law school-sponsored social activities, community projects, and programs.

Career Services and Bar Exam

The law school provides assistance to law students, graduates, and legal employers through its Placement Office. Our successful and enthusiastic alumni remain very engaged in our law school. Florida State University College of Law students have access to a list of more than 600 alumni who have volunteered to serve them as Placement Mentors. Students are encouraged to take advantage of the law school's on- and off-campus interviewing programs and individual career counseling services. A variety of seminars and workshops on career options, résumé writing, and interviewing skills are also available.

Ninety-eight percent of the graduating class of 2009 was placed within nine months of graduation. Graduates work in 49 states and in major markets including Atlanta, Chicago, New York, Los Angeles, and Washington, DC. Graduates are prominent in all Florida cities and have placed first in the state in six of the last ten administrations of the Florida Bar Exam. Graduates who take the exam in jurisdictions outside of Florida do equally well.

APPLICANT PROFILE

The Florida State University College of Law Fall 2010 Decisions
This grid includes only applicants who earned 120–180 LSAT scores under standard administrations.

LSAT Score	GPA 3.75 +		3.50–3.74		3.25–3.49		3.00–3.24		2.75–2.99		2.50–2.74		2.25–2.49		2.00–2.24		Below 2.00		No GPA		Total	
	Apps	Adm	Apps	Adm	Apps	Adm	Apps	Adm	Apps	Adm	Apps	Adm	Apps	Adm	Apps	Adm	Apps	Adm	Apps	Adm	Apps	Adm
175–180	0	0	1	1	1	1	2	2	1	1	0	0	0	0	0	0	0	0	0	0	5	5
170–174	7	6	9	9	5	5	5	5	3	2	1	1	1	0	0	0	0	0	1	1	32	29
165–169	32	32	35	35	33	31	38	35	23	20	14	4	10	2	2	0	0	0	1	0	188	159
160–164	133	129	178	167	184	137	130	70	60	17	33	3	16	0	4	0	0	0	6	3	744	526
155–159	193	37	277	21	269	7	171	7	91	3	41	0	23	0	4	0	1	0	16	0	1086	75
150–154	131	3	173	6	193	0	160	0	75	0	42	0	20	0	6	0	1	0	14	0	815	9
145–149	36	0	73	0	91	0	104	0	50	0	44	0	21	0	5	0	0	0	4	0	428	0
140–144	15	0	23	0	43	0	42	0	36	0	22	0	16	0	3	0	1	0	1	0	202	0
135–139	3	0	6	0	10	0	13	0	14	0	12	0	7	0	7	0	1	0	3	0	76	0
130–134	0	0	0	0	1	0	5	0	8	0	3	0	5	0	1	0	1	0	1	0	25	0
125–129	2	0	1	0	0	0	0	0	1	0	0	0	2	0	1	0	2	0	0	0	9	0
120–124	0	0	0	0	0	0	0	0	0	0	0	0	0	0	1	0	0	0	0	0	1	0
Total	552	207	776	239	830	181	670	119	362	43	212	8	121	2	34	0	7	0	47	4	3611	803

Apps = Number of Applicants
Adm = Number Admitted
Reflects highest reported LSAT score for each applicant.

FORDHAM UNIVERSITY SCHOOL OF LAW

140 West 62nd Street
New York, NY 10023
Phone: 212.636.6810; Fax: 212.636.7984
E-mail: lawadmissions@law.fordham.edu; Website: http://law.fordham.edu

ABA
Approved
Since
1936

AMERICAN BAR ASSOCIATION
Section of Legal Education
and Admissions to the Bar

The Basics

Type of school	Private
Term	Semester
Application deadline	3/1
Application fee	$70
Financial aid deadline	4/1
Can first year start other than fall?	No
Student to faculty ratio	13.9 to 1
# of housing spaces available restricted to law students	130
graduate housing for which law students are eligible	69

Faculty and Administrators

	Total		Men		Women		Minorities	
	Spr	Fall	Spr	Fall	Spr	Fall	Spr	Fall
Full-time	82	81	52	51	30	30	16	14
Other full-time	0	0	0	0	0	0	0	0
Deans, librarians, & others who teach	19	19	6	6	13	13	3	3
Part-time	164	141	107	82	57	59	15	23
Total	265	241	165	139	100	102	34	40

Curriculum

	Full-Time	Part-Time
Typical first-year section size	80	80
Is there typically a "small section" of the first-year class, other than Legal Writing, taught by full-time faculty	Yes	Yes
If yes, typical size offered last year	40	40
# of classroom course titles beyond first-year curriculum	232	

# of upper division courses, excluding seminars, with an enrollment:		
	Under 25	65
	25–49	56
	50–74	23
	75–99	14
	100+	10

# of seminars	203	
# of seminar positions available	3,383	
# of seminar positions filled	1,728	947
# of positions available in simulation courses	1,667	
# of simulation positions filled	975	430
# of positions available in faculty supervised clinical courses	419	
# of faculty supervised clinical positions filled	273	14
# involved in field placements	279	76
# involved in law journals	368	33
# involved in moot court or trial competitions	196	6
# of credit hours required to graduate	83	

JD Enrollment and Ethnicity

	Men		Women		Full-Time		Part-Time		1st-Year		Total		JD Degs. Awd.
	#	%	#	%	#	%	#	%	#	%	#	%	
All Hispanics	78	10.1	64	9.1	128	10.5	14	5.3	49	10.3	142	9.6	49
Am. Ind./AK Nat.	2	0.3	3	0.4	5	0.4	0	0.0	3	0.6	5	0.3	2
Asian	53	6.8	70	9.9	94	7.7	29	11.0	52	10.9	123	8.3	35
Black/Af. Am.	30	3.9	36	5.1	51	4.2	15	5.7	21	4.4	66	4.5	40
Nat. Hl/Pac. Isl.	0	0.0	0	0.0	0	0.0	0	0.0	0	0.0	0	0.0	0
2 or more races	3	0.4	6	0.8	7	0.6	2	0.8	1	0.2	9	0.6	0
Subtotal (minor.)	166	21.4	179	25.3	285	23.4	60	22.7	126	26.4	345	23.3	126
Nonres. Alien	16	2.1	24	3.4	31	2.5	9	3.4	8	1.7	40	2.7	0
White/Cauc.	469	60.6	387	54.7	716	58.8	140	53.0	298	62.5	856	57.8	251
Unknown	123	15.9	117	16.5	185	15.2	55	20.8	45	9.4	240	16.2	99
Total	774	52.3	707	47.7	1217	82.2	264	17.8	477	32.2	1481		491

Transfers

Transfers in	24
Transfers out	14

Tuition and Fees

	Resident	Nonresident
Full-time	$46,476	$46,476
Part-time	$34,926	$34,926
Tuition Guarantee Program		N

Living Expenses

Estimated living expenses for singles

Living on campus	Living off campus	Living at home
$25,092	$25,092	$25,092

FORDHAM UNIVERSITY SCHOOL OF LAW

ABA
Approved
Since
1936

GPA and LSAT Scores

	Total	Full-Time	Part-Time
# of apps	8,883	7,469	1,414
# of offers	1,933	1,789	144
# of matrics	477	398	79
75% GPA	3.76	3.77	3.71
Median GPA	3.60	3.62	3.52
25% GPA	3.36	3.38	3.26
75% LSAT	168	168	166
Median LSAT	166	166	164
25% LSAT	163	163	160

Grants and Scholarships (from prior year)

	Total		Full-Time		Part-Time	
	#	%	#	%	#	%
Total # of students	1,469		1,160		309	
Total # receiving grants	531	36.1	480	41.4	51	16.5
Less than 1/2 tuition	414	28.2	378	32.6	36	11.7
Half to full tuition	112	7.6	97	8.4	15	4.9
Full tuition	5	0.3	5	0.4	0	0.0
More than full tuition	0	0.0	0	0.0	0	0.0
Median grant amount			$10,000		$9,900	

Informational and Library Resources

Total amount spent on library materials	$1,758,041
Study seating capacity inside the library	442
# of full-time equivalent professional librarians	14
Hours per week library is open	119
# of open, wired connections available to students	601
# of networked computers available for use by students	223
Has wireless network?	Y
Requires computer?	N

JD Attrition (from prior year)

	Academic	Other	Total	
	#	#	#	%
1st year	0	3	3	0.6
2nd year	0	15	15	3.2
3rd year	2	0	2	0.4
4th year	0	0	0	0.0

Employment (9 months after graduation)

	Total	Percentage
Employment status known	465	98.9
Employment status unknown	5	1.1
Employed	430	92.5
Pursuing graduate degrees	10	2.2
Unemployed (seeking, not seeking, or studying for the bar)	14	3.0
Type of Employment		
# employed in law firms	303	70.5
# employed in business and industry	35	8.1
# employed in government	23	5.3
# employed in public interest	22	5.1
# employed as judicial clerks	22	5.1
# employed in academia	24	5.6
Geographic Location		
# employed in state	361	84.0
# employed outside the US	6	1.4
# of states where employed	16	

Bar Passage Rates

First-time takers	433	Reporting %	100.00
Average school %	89.84	Average state %	86.51
Average pass difference	3.33		

Jurisdiction	Takers	Passers	Pass %	State %	Diff %
New York	433	389	89.84	86.51	3.33

FORDHAM UNIVERSITY SCHOOL OF LAW

140 West 62nd Street
New York, NY 10023
Phone: 212.636.6810; Fax: 212.636.7984
E-mail: lawadmissions@law.fordham.edu; Website: http://law.fordham.edu

Introduction

Fordham Law has been dedicated to preparing great lawyers and great leaders for over a century. The school is proud of its unique approach to a complete legal education that places strong focus on academic excellence, the craft of lawyering, and unwavering focus on ethics and the obligation of public service. The commitment to these values, combined with the school's New York City location, provides Fordham Law graduates an unparalleled opportunity to pursue a broad spectrum of career choices. Today, Fordham is seventh among schools placing the greatest number of attorneys in the nation's top 25 law firms. Beyond that, the school's signature public service and human rights programs educate lawyers who work to create significant change in the world. A faculty distinguished by its commitment both to teaching and to scholarship creates an atmosphere in which students feel appreciated and valued as they prepare to become part of the next generation of leaders.

Fordham lawyers practice in 49 states, in the District of Columbia, and in 73 nations around the world. Among our 18,000 living alumni are partners and associates of leading law firms, CEOs of major corporations, academics, and individuals engaged in public service. Fordham's campus is a mere two blocks from Central Park, adjacent to Lincoln Center for the Performing Arts, and steps away from the Columbus Circle subway hub. This central Manhattan location provides convenient access to all New York City has to offer, enabling students to begin their careers at the center of the world's legal, financial, and cultural capital. Fordham puts a strong focus on the importance of experiential education and our location puts students close to a broad range of professional opportunities at some of the largest law firms in the world, the busiest federal and state courts, the US Attorney General's Offices, the United Nations, a myriad of state and federal agencies, and Wall Street.

Curriculum

Fordham's faculty of scholar-teachers recognize the importance of welcoming students, being accessible, and encouraging them. The large faculty enables Fordham to offer a remarkable depth of courses that reinforce its traditional strengths in contracts, commercial law, corporate law, evidence, and international law, as well as enhance its significant scholarship in the fields of constitutional law and jurisprudence, international human rights, legal ethics, legal history, intellectual property, and clinical legal education.

Fordham also promotes the art and science of legal analysis and the cultivation of a vigorous ongoing dialogue between students and professor through the following nationally renowned academic centers:

Brendan Moore Advocacy Center fosters the teaching and study of lawyers as advocates, with special emphasis on client representation at the trial level.

Center for Corporate, Securities, and Financial Law serves as the focal point for the school's business law programs and includes roundtable discussions with business leaders, corporate law practitioners, and state and federal regulators.

The Leitner Center for International Law and Justice contributes to the promotion of social justice by encouraging knowledge of, and respect for, international law and human rights standards. The center oversees an annual fact-finding mission, providing law students the opportunity to participate in human rights work overseas.

Louis Stein Center for Law and Ethics promotes the integration of ethical perspectives in legal practice, legal institutions, and the development of the law generally. The center also oversees the Stein Scholars Program, a program for students who demonstrate commitment to public service and who undertake specialized academic work in legal ethics.

The Feerick Center for Social Justice and Dispute Resolution brings together the major stakeholders responsible for solving our most difficult urban social issues. Uniquely combining the insights of a think tank, the urgency inherent in a mission to achieve social justice, the balance required of a mediation center, and the educational mission of a law school, the center works with all parties to frame concrete and achievable solutions to the endemic problems plaguing the urban poor. The center also houses a clinic, providing hands-on social justice experience to students each year.

The Center on Law and Information Policy (CLIP) will make significant contributions to the development of law and policy for the information economy and teach the next generation of leaders. CLIP focuses on five key areas of technology law and policy, regulation of information innovation and knowledge creation, privacy and security, technology and governance, and the protection of intellectual property and information.

Cocurricular Activities

There are six student-edited law journals at Fordham, as well as two intramural moot court competitions.

The school also participates in interschool competitions, fielding award-winning appellate moot court teams, trial advocacy teams, and alternative dispute resolution teams.

Worldwide Significance

Long before "globalism" was mainstream, Fordham was devoting resources to programs that, today, are internationally known, including:

- the nation's preeminent Center on European Union Law;
- the school's Stein Center for Law and Ethics;
- an International Antitrust Law and Policy Conference, now in its 38th year;
- an annual International Intellectual Property Law Conference, now in its 19th year;
- the Leitner Center for International Law and Justice;
- a Belfast/Dublin summer program, which offers two weeks of study in each city with a special emphasis on international alternative dispute resolution;
- a summer program in Seoul, Korea, at Sungkyunkwan University College of Law (SKKU) offers courses in international and comparative law as well as internships at local law firms, companies, and governmental offices;
- a Ghana summer law program, building on our long and successful history of partnership with Ghanaian legal institutions, offers students the opportunity to study

Ghanaian and international law, as well as internships in Ghana;

- semester study-abroad programs offered in Italy, the Netherlands, Germany, Spain, Mexico, Canada, Korea, and the People's Republic of China; and
- five graduate degree programs—the LLM in International Business and Trade Law; the LLM in Banking, Corporate, and Finance Law; the LLM in Intellectual Property and Information Technology Law; the LLM in International Law and Justice; and the LLM in US and Comparative Law—that have created a network of Fordham alumni in more than 80 countries.

Experiential Programs

Fordham's clinical program encourages students to integrate legal analysis with lawyering theory and skills by assuming lawyering roles or performing lawyering functions in problem-solving settings. Fordham Law's clinical program—one of the largest in the nation—engages more than 300 students in live-client clinics and simulation courses in 15 practice areas, including an innovative interdisciplinary Child and Family Litigation Clinic, where students are placed on teams supervised by law, social work, and psychology faculty. Fordham also offers one of the widest ranges of externship placements in American legal education—more than 250 opportunities at nonprofit and nongovernmental organizations and in state and federal courts.

Career Services and Placement

Fordham's career services office assists students and alumni in planning their careers. For the past several years, between 97 and 100 percent of our graduates obtained employment within nine months of graduation. The program features:

- an on-campus interview program that brings more than 250 potential employers to campus to conduct more than 6,000 individual student interviews;
- a searchable, proprietary, online database of job listings; and
- individualized student counseling, mock videotaped interviews with optional critiques, seminars on interviewing skills and networking, and assistance with résumé preparation, including 24-hour turnaround time for edits.

Public Service

Fordham believes that the development of a lifelong commitment to public service is an integral part of a legal education. Last year, Fordham law students volunteered almost 135,000 hours of public service. More than half of the graduating class devoted 50 or more hours of their time through the school's nationally recognized Public Interest Resource Center (PIRC). The PIRC's 23 student-run organizations address issues concerning the environment, housing for the poor, domestic violence, unemployment, police brutality, the death penalty, immigration, and community service. Fordham also has a Loan Repayment Assistance Program (LRAP) to assist those who pursue public service careers. Today, Fordham continues to set the standard for law schools nationwide by assisting and inspiring those students who, regardless of their ultimate career choice, are committed to the spirit of pro bono publico—work for the public good.

Living at Lincoln Center

Approximately 80 spaces are set aside for entering students in McMahon Hall, the university's Lincoln Center residence. Students live in two- or three-bedroom apartments, each of which contains private bedrooms, a living room, full kitchen, and bath. Preference is given to those students who live beyond a commutable distance from the law school. Inquiries regarding housing should be directed to the law school Office of Admissions.

Applicant Profile

Fordham's Admissions Committee—comprised of full-time faculty members and administrators—evaluates each complete application received. While the best available evidence suggests that LSAT scores and undergraduate GPAs should be accorded significant weight in evaluating most applicants, the Admissions Committee believes that securing the most interesting, diverse, and exciting class involves the evaluation of other qualitative factors as well. The combination of academic excellence and experiences is considered in evaluating applicants' potential contributions to their success at Fordham and beyond.

APPLICANT PROFILE

Fordham University School of Law
This grid includes only applicants who earned 120–180 LSAT scores under standard administrations.

LSAT Score	GPA													
	3.75 +		3.50–3.74		3.25–3.49		3.00–3.24		Below 3.00		No GPA		Totals	
	Apps	Adm	Apps	Adm	Apps	Adm	Apps	Adm	Apps	Adm	Apps	Adm	Apps	Adm
170–180	129	120	192	170	160	112	79	28	61	7	7	4	628	441
165–169	409	369	579	407	400	183	224	49	149	6	43	9	1804	1023
160–164	600	144	879	114	720	58	364	17	231	8	70	4	2864	345
155–159	263	20	434	31	423	30	273	15	228	2	42	0	1663	98
120–154	168	7	353	5	399	4	378	2	524	5	105	0	1927	23
Total	1569	660	2437	727	2102	387	1318	111	1193	28	267	17	8886	1930

Apps = Number of Applicants   Adm = Number Admitted   Reflects 100% of the total applicant pool; highest LSAT data reported.

GEORGE MASON UNIVERSITY SCHOOL OF LAW

3301 Fairfax Drive MS 1G3
Arlington, VA 22201
Phone: 703.993.8010; Fax: 703.993.8088
E-mail: lawadmit@gmu.edu; Website: www.law.gmu.edu

The Basics

Type of school	Public
Term	Semester
Application deadline	4/1
Application fee	$35
Financial aid deadline	3/1
Can first year start other than fall?	No
Student to faculty ratio	14.0 to 1
# of housing spaces available	
restricted to law students	
graduate housing for which law students are eligible	

Faculty and Administrators

	Total		Men		Women		Minorities	
	Spr	Fall	Spr	Fall	Spr	Fall	Spr	Fall
Full-time	38	36	31	31	7	5	6	6
Other full-time	2	2	0	0	2	2	1	1
Deans, librarians, & others who teach	2	3	2	3	0	0	0	0
Part-time	98	71	69	55	29	16	7	3
Total	140	112	102	89	38	23	14	10

Curriculum

	Full-Time	Part-Time
Typical first-year section size	63	56
Is there typically a "small section" of the first-year class, other than Legal Writing, taught by full-time faculty	No	No
If yes, typical size offered last year		
# of classroom course titles beyond first-year curriculum	156	

# of upper division courses, excluding seminars, with an enrollment:		
	Under 25	159
	25–49	37
	50–74	8
	75–99	1
	100+	0

# of seminars	35	
# of seminar positions available	525	
# of seminar positions filled	243	251
# of positions available in simulation courses	276	
# of simulation positions filled	198	74
# of positions available in faculty supervised clinical courses	122	
# of faculty supervised clinical positions filled	86	27
# involved in field placements	81	14
# involved in law journals	143	24
# involved in moot court or trial competitions	36	18
# of credit hours required to graduate	89	

JD Enrollment and Ethnicity

	Men		Women		Full-Time		Part-Time		1st-Year		Total		JD Degs. Awd.
	#	%	#	%	#	%	#	%	#	%	#	%	
All Hispanics	14	3.2	8	2.7	19	3.8	3	1.3	10	3.4	22	3.0	14
Am. Ind./AK Nat.	4	0.9	2	0.7	3	0.6	3	1.3	3	1.0	6	0.8	1
Asian	39	9.0	36	12.1	45	8.9	30	13.3	27	9.1	75	10.3	24
Black/Af. Am.	1	0.2	8	2.7	3	0.6	6	2.7	4	1.3	9	1.2	11
Nat. HI/Pac. Isl.	0	0.0	0	0.0	0	0.0	0	0.0	0	0.0	0	0.0	0
2 or more races	2	0.5	1	0.3	1	0.2	2	0.9	1	0.3	3	0.4	0
Subtotal (minor.)	60	13.9	55	18.5	71	14.1	44	19.5	45	15.2	115	15.7	51
Nonres. Alien	9	2.1	5	1.7	11	2.2	3	1.3	8	2.7	14	1.9	0
White/Cauc.	361	83.4	234	78.5	416	82.4	179	79.2	237	79.8	595	81.4	166
Unknown	3	0.7	4	1.3	7	1.4	0	0.0	7	2.4	7	1.0	4
Total	433	59.2	298	40.8	505	69.1	226	30.9	297	40.6	731		222

Transfers

Transfers in	0
Transfers out	10

Tuition and Fees

	Resident	Nonresident
Full-time	$22,222	$36,278
Part-time	$18,290	$29,836
Tuition Guarantee Program		N

Living Expenses

Estimated living expenses for singles

Living on campus	Living off campus	Living at home
$15,490	$23,210	$10,500

GEORGE MASON UNIVERSITY SCHOOL OF LAW

*ABA
Approved
Since
1980*

GPA and LSAT Scores

	Total	Full-Time	Part-Time
# of apps	5,227	4,697	1,835
# of offers	1,359	1,232	127
# of matrics	303	234	69
75% GPA	3.82	3.82	3.82
Median GPA	3.72	3.68	3.73
25% GPA	3.27	3.30	3.10
75% LSAT	165	165	164
Median LSAT	164	164	164
25% LSAT	158	159	157

Grants and Scholarships (from prior year)

	Total		Full-Time		Part-Time	
	#	%	#	%	#	%
Total # of students	697		480		217	
Total # receiving grants	85	12.2	67	14.0	18	8.3
Less than 1/2 tuition	68	9.8	61	12.7	7	3.2
Half to full tuition	13	1.9	3	0.6	10	4.6
Full tuition	0	0.0	0	0.0	0	0.0
More than full tuition	4	0.6	3	0.6	1	0.5
Median grant amount			$8,000		$8,000	

Informational and Library Resources

Total amount spent on library materials	$1,071,640
Study seating capacity inside the library	369
# of full-time equivalent professional librarians	6
Hours per week library is open	98
# of open, wired connections available to students	888
# of networked computers available for use by students	42
Has wireless network?	Y
Requires computer?	N

JD Attrition (from prior year)

	Academic	Other	Total	
	#	#	#	%
1st year	3	21	24	9.7
2nd year	0	3	3	1.8
3rd year	2	1	3	1.4
4th year	0	0	0	0.0

Employment (9 months after graduation)

	Total	Percentage
Employment status known	229	99.6
Employment status unknown	1	0.4
Employed	221	96.5
Pursuing graduate degrees	0	0.0
Unemployed (seeking, not seeking, or studying for the bar)	1	0.4
Type of Employment		
# employed in law firms	94	42.5
# employed in business and industry	47	21.3
# employed in government	32	14.5
# employed in public interest	3	1.4
# employed as judicial clerks	22	10.0
# employed in academia	23	10.4
Geographic Location		
# employed in state	108	48.9
# employed outside the US	2	0.9
# of states where employed	18	

Bar Passage Rates

First-time takers	226	Reporting %	78.32
Average school %	88.14	Average state %	77.19
Average pass difference	10.95		

Jurisdiction	Takers	Passers	Pass %	State %	Diff %
Virginia	157	138	87.90	77.06	10.84
Maryland	20	18	90.00	78.20	11.80

GEORGE MASON UNIVERSITY SCHOOL OF LAW

3301 Fairfax Drive MS 1G3
Arlington, VA 22201
Phone: 703.993.8010; Fax: 703.993.8088
E-mail: lawadmit@gmu.edu; Website: www.law.gmu.edu

Introduction

George Mason University School of Law sits on the doorstep of the nation's capital. One of Virginia's public law schools, it was established by authority of the Virginia General Assembly in 1979. By virtue of its unparalleled location, George Mason is able to offer its students numerous opportunities for practical experiences during their law school career.

Library and Physical Facilities

In 1999, the law school relocated to a state-of-the-art facility, Hazel Hall, equipped with electrical and data connections at every classroom and library seat, and two ultramodern moot courtrooms. The opening of a large plaza and new building in January 2011 expanded the facilities available to law students.

The school is a member of the library network of the Consortium for Continuing Higher Education in Northern Virginia, affording access to general university and public library collections.

Enrollment/Student Body

George Mason University is an equal opportunity/affirmative action institution.

Curriculum

George Mason University School of Law offers both full- and part-time divisions. The full-time division operates during the day and takes three years to complete. Students who elect the part-time division study at night during the first year and generally take four years to complete the requirements for the Juris Doctor degree.

George Mason offers an interdisciplinary approach to legal study. A grounding in economics and basic mathematical and financial skills is important to a sophisticated legal education and to the development of a competent attorney. To ensure that George Mason graduates have this grounding, all students take a first-year course in Economic Foundations.

George Mason law students complete a three-year legal writing program, which emphasizes the use of technology and continual practice of skills in the development of actual transactions and cases.

The curriculum begins with exposure to the courses fundamental to a well-rounded legal education. Students at George Mason may also elect to enroll in one of our specialty programs, thus demonstrating depth as well as breadth in their training. All specialties are offered in both the full-time and part-time divisions.

George Mason has a number of programs offering students practical experience: Immigration Law, Public Interest Law, Domestic Relations, Law and Mental Illness, Regulatory Law, Patent Law, the Clinic for Legal Assistance to Service Members, and the Legal Clinic. As a leader in technology and law, George Mason is the headquarters for the National Center for Technology and Law, which brings together academics, high-tech industry leaders, and policymakers to debate and formulate national policy to keep pace with technological advances. George Mason is also home to the Center for Infrastructure Protection (CIP), a program that fully integrates the disciplines of law, policy, and technology for enhancing the security of cyber networks and economic processes supporting the nation's critical infrastructure.

Special Programs

- **Homeland and National Security Law**—enables students interested in specializing in this field to present potential employers (both in government and in the private sector) with a credential that reflects a solid foundation in homeland and national security law.
- **Corporate and Securities Law**—prepares students to work in a variety of fields related to corporate law and financial markets. By developing a thorough understanding of both law and underlying theory, students are prepared to deal with rapidly changing business and legal environments.
- **Regulatory Law**—prepares students for practice in, and before, the numerous agencies that regulate business and other activities. Students are taught economics, the economic analysis of law, administrative law, legislation, lobbying, and negotiation, as well as several substantive areas of regulatory law.
- **International Business**—prepares students for practice in the rapidly changing global business community and provides them with a well-rounded legal education emphasizing analytical and writing skills.
- **Litigation Law**—provides an academic program for students interested in litigation and other dispute resolution processes. This is not a clinical training program. The track courses focus on the processes of dispute resolution and lawyers' roles from an analytical perspective.
- **Intellectual Property Law**—is designed for students having a degree in engineering or one of the physical or biological sciences who intend to practice within the field of intellectual property.
- **Technology Law Program**—combines coursework in the fields of technology law, intellectual property law, and business law. The program prepares students for work in law firms that serve high-technology clients, as in-house counsel for Internet start-up companies, and as attorneys for state and federal regulatory agencies with jurisdiction over technology industries.
- **LLM Programs**—for students wishing to pursue specialized study beyond the JD, George Mason offers two LLM programs: (1) the **LLM in Law and Economics**, and (2) the **LLM in Intellectual Property Law**. Detailed information about these programs is available at www.law.gmu.edu/academics/llm.html.
- Additionally, George Mason offers programs in Criminal Law, Legal and Economic Theory, Personal Law, and Tax Law.

Admission

Two of the primary factors considered in the admission process are performance on the LSAT and undergraduate grade-point average. Other factors that are considered include difficulty of undergraduate major, undergraduate institution attended, possession of advanced degrees, writing ability, recommendations, extracurricular activities, employment experience, demonstrated commitment to public and community service, leadership skills and experience, history of overcoming personal or professional challenges, and other academic, personal, and professional achievements.

Student Activities

George Mason University provides many services to enhance the law school experience and enable students to take full advantage of the university's educational and personal enrichment opportunities.

Student activities include the *George Mason Law Review*; *Civil Rights Law Journal*; the *Journal of Law, Economics, and Policy*; the *Journal of International Commercial Law*; a prestigious moot court program; an active trial advocacy program; a newspaper; and numerous law-related organizations. Students have an unparalleled opportunity to gain experience in such varied settings as the Office of the US Attorney for both the District of Columbia and the Eastern District of Virginia, as well as federal courts and agencies, local governments, and private firms. Information about Mason's various student organizations can be found at http://law.gmu.org.

Diversity Student Services, Academic Support Services, Disability Support Services, and the Office of Veterans Services provide specialized assistance, as does the Counseling Center, where a staff of professionals help students to reach personal, social, and academic goals.

Expenses and Financial Aid

George Mason University participates in the Direct Lending Program. There is no deadline for applying for financial aid, but applicants should complete the FAFSA as soon as possible in order to assure the timely award of aid.

In addition to loans available through the Direct Lending Program, George Mason students are eligible for a number of merit-based fellowships.

Career Services

The Office of Career, Academic, and Alumni Services aids students and alumni in finding permanent, part-time, and summer jobs, as well as school year externships and internships, by serving as a clearinghouse for information on available positions. It also advises on résumé and interview preparation and coordinates on-campus interviews. More than 150 firms, businesses, and government agencies recruit on campus each year. Graduates find employment in the legal profession throughout the country.

APPLICANT PROFILE

George Mason University School of Law
This grid includes only applicants who earned 120–180 LSAT scores under standard administrations.

LSAT Score	3.75 +		3.50–3.74		3.25–3.49		3.00–3.24		2.75–2.99		2.50–2.74		2.25–2.49		2.00–2.24		Below 2.00		No GPA		Total	
	Apps	Adm	Apps	Adm	Apps	Adm	Apps	Adm	Apps	Adm	Apps	Adm	Apps	Adm	Apps	Adm	Apps	Adm	Apps	Adm	Apps	Adm
175–180	3	0	3	0	4	2	1	0	3	1	1	0	0	0	0	0	0	0	0	0	15	3
170–174	13	4	24	10	23	11	23	12	7	3	9	2	5	2	3	0	0	0	0	0	107	44
165–169	95	78	166	138	152	120	108	85	54	33	37	22	11	3	3	2	0	0	14	9	640	490
160–164	299	268	433	143	395	74	246	54	92	12	50	9	28	3	8	2	1	0	39	7	1591	572
155–159	226	167	311	27	273	4	204	2	125	3	62	1	32	0	9	0	2	0	22	1	1266	205
150–154	105	16	146	5	178	0	161	0	89	0	55	0	30	0	13	0	3	0	25	0	805	21
145–149	31	1	63	0	75	0	104	0	80	0	51	0	28	0	14	0	2	0	13	0	461	1
140–144	6	0	23	0	41	0	47	0	55	0	41	0	17	0	5	0	3	0	9	0	247	0
135–139	3	0	14	0	13	0	24	0	22	0	17	0	9	0	10	0	3	0	9	0	124	0
130–134	0	0	1	0	3	0	7	0	9	0	11	0	5	0	3	0	1	0	3	0	43	0
125–129	1	0	0	0	0	0	1	0	3	0	2	0	1	0	3	0	1	0	0	0	12	0
120–124	0	0	0	0	0	0	0	0	0	0	1	0	0	0	0	0	0	0	0	0	1	0
Total	782	534	1184	323	1157	211	926	153	539	52	337	34	166	8	71	4	16	0	134	17	5312	1336

Apps = Number of Applicants
Adm = Number Admitted
Reflects 99% of the total applicant pool; highest LSAT data reported.

THE GEORGE WASHINGTON UNIVERSITY LAW SCHOOL

2000 H Street NW
Washington, DC 20052
Phone: 202.994.7230; Fax: 202.994.3597
E-mail: jdadmit@law.gwu.edu; Website: www.law.gwu.edu

ABA
Approved
Since
1923

The Basics

Type of school	Private
Term	Semester
Application deadline	12/15 3/31
Application fee	$80
Financial aid deadline	1/1 6/1
Can first year start other than fall?	No
Student to faculty ratio	14.8 to 1
# of housing spaces available restricted to law students	538
graduate housing for which law students are eligible	390

Faculty and Administrators

	Total		Men		Women		Minorities	
	Spr	Fall	Spr	Fall	Spr	Fall	Spr	Fall
Full-time	80	96	53	56	26	39	13	21
Other full-time	9	10	1	2	8	8	2	2
Deans, librarians, & others who teach	18	17	9	8	9	9	3	3
Part-time	205	156	150	115	55	41	22	11
Total	312	279	213	181	98	97	40	37

Curriculum

		Full-Time	Part-Time
Typical first-year section size		96	57
Is there typically a "small section" of the first-year class, other than Legal Writing, taught by full-time faculty		Yes	No
If yes, typical size offered last year		38	
# of classroom course titles beyond first-year curriculum		229	
# of upper division courses, excluding seminars, with an enrollment:	Under 25	357	
	25–49	99	
	50–74	47	
	75–99	14	
	100+	12	
# of seminars		51	
# of seminar positions available		846	
# of seminar positions filled		397	168
# of positions available in simulation courses		1,386	
# of simulation positions filled		410	810
# of positions available in faculty supervised clinical courses		169	
# of faculty supervised clinical positions filled		144	25
# involved in field placements		381	81
# involved in law journals		247	15
# involved in moot court or trial competitions		307	47
# of credit hours required to graduate		84	

JD Enrollment and Ethnicity

	Men		Women		Full-Time		Part-Time		1st-Year		Total		JD Degs. Awd.
	#	%	#	%	#	%	#	%	#	%	#	%	
All Hispanics	51	5.5	49	6.3	91	6.5	9	3.0	44	8.1	100	5.9	45
Am. Ind./AK Nat.	2	0.2	5	0.6	6	0.4	1	0.3	0	0.0	7	0.4	5
Asian	80	8.6	80	10.3	120	8.5	40	13.4	48	8.8	160	9.4	42
Black/Af. Am.	41	4.4	53	6.8	66	4.7	28	9.4	33	6.1	94	5.5	30
Nat. HI/Pac. Isl.	1	0.1	3	0.4	3	0.2	1	0.3	3	0.6	4	0.2	0
2 or more races	0	0.0	0	0.0	0	0.0	0	0.0	0	0.0	0	0.0	0
Subtotal (minor.)	175	18.8	190	24.5	286	20.3	79	26.4	128	23.5	365	21.4	122
Nonres. Alien	18	1.9	21	2.7	37	2.6	2	0.7	14	2.6	39	2.3	10
White/Cauc.	625	67.1	464	59.7	913	64.8	176	58.9	361	66.2	1089	63.7	306
Unknown	114	12.2	102	13.1	174	12.3	42	14.0	41	7.5	216	12.6	68
Total	932	54.5	777	45.5	1410	82.5	299	17.5	545	31.9	1709		506

Transfers

Transfers in	97
Transfers out	16

Tuition and Fees

	Resident	Nonresident
Full-time	$43,999	$43,999
Part-time	$34,034	$34,034
Tuition Guarantee Program		Y

Living Expenses

Estimated living expenses for singles

Living on campus	Living off campus	Living at home
$26,450	$26,450	$26,450

THE GEORGE WASHINGTON UNIVERSITY LAW SCHOOL

ABA Approved Since 1923

GPA and LSAT Scores

	Total	Full-Time	Part-Time
# of apps	9,245	8,197	1,048
# of offers	2,091	1,991	100
# of matrics	523	489	34
75% GPA	3.87	3.88	3.84
Median GPA	3.79	3.79	3.51
25% GPA	3.39	3.42	3.18
75% LSAT	168	168	167
Median LSAT	167	167	162
25% LSAT	162	162	160

Grants and Scholarships (from prior year)

	Total		Full-Time		Part-Time	
	#	%	#	%	#	%
Total # of students	1,632		1,328		304	
Total # receiving grants	793	48.6	770	58.0	23	7.6
Less than 1/2 tuition	477	29.2	455	34.3	22	7.2
Half to full tuition	91	5.6	91	6.9	0	0.0
Full tuition	124	7.6	124	9.3	0	0.0
More than full tuition	101	6.2	100	7.5	1	0.3
Median grant amount			$15,000		$7,500	

Informational and Library Resources

Total amount spent on library materials	$2,989,149
Study seating capacity inside the library	637
# of full-time equivalent professional librarians	22
Hours per week library is open	110
# of open, wired connections available to students	54
# of networked computers available for use by students	71
Has wireless network?	Y
Requires computer?	Y

JD Attrition (from prior year)

	Academic	Other	Total	
	#	#	#	%
1st year	1	22	23	4.4
2nd year	0	3	3	0.6
3rd year	0	2	2	0.4
4th year	0	0	0	0.0

Employment (9 months after graduation)

	Total	Percentage
Employment status known	554	99.5
Employment status unknown	3	0.5
Employed	539	97.3
Pursuing graduate degrees	4	0.7
Unemployed (seeking, not seeking, or studying for the bar)	8	1.4
Type of Employment		
# employed in law firms	327	60.7
# employed in business and industry	43	8.0
# employed in government	69	12.8
# employed in public interest	23	4.3
# employed as judicial clerks	34	6.3
# employed in academia	32	5.9
Geographic Location		
# employed in state	282	52.3
# employed outside the US	5	0.9
# of states where employed		26

Bar Passage Rates

First-time takers	531	Reporting %	100.00
Average school %	93.98	Average state %	80.82
Average pass difference	13.16		

Jurisdiction	Takers	Passers	Pass %	State %	Diff %
New York	140	136	97.14	86.51	10.63
Virginia	116	103	88.79	77.06	11.73
Maryland	82	74	90.24	78.20	12.04
California	61	56	91.80	73.19	18.61
Others (28)	132	130	98.48		

THE GEORGE WASHINGTON UNIVERSITY LAW SCHOOL

2000 H Street NW
Washington, DC 20052
Phone: 202.994.7230; Fax: 202.994.3597
E-mail: jdadmit@law.gwu.edu; Website: www.law.gwu.edu

Introduction

Established in 1865, the George Washington University Law School is the oldest law school in the District of Columbia. Its history of academic excellence, significant contributions to legal scholarship, and outstanding record of service to the community have earned GW a position of local, national, and international prominence. Its talented student body is one of the most diverse of any national law school, and its students graduate to become leaders in all areas of practice. While GW has long been recognized as a leader in fields including constitutional law, intellectual property law, international law, environmental law, public interest law, government procurement, and clinical education, all of the law school's academic programs reflect the demands of a changing profession and the global nature of society and the law.

Facilities and Library

The law school complex extends along two sides of the University Yard, the largest open space on GW's urban campus. Its attractive and comfortable classrooms and three moot courtrooms incorporate technology to support a broad range of teaching methods. "Smart podiums" provide access to the Internet and local network, and support videoconferencing. Cameras and microphones allow faculty to teach online in streaming video or record classes for later viewing or listening. Power outlets for notebook computers are provided at each student station in most classrooms. The entire facility is wireless.

More than 600,000 volumes are at the core of the Jacob Burns Law Library's research collection. In addition, the library offers a variety of legal and law-related databases and automated indexes to enhance research capabilities. A staff of 40 full-time and numerous part-time employees administer and maintain the library during its liberal hours of operation and offer information, instruction, and other research support services.

Law students also have full access to the many amenities of the GW campus, including the Lerner Health and Wellness Center, a state-of-the-art complex featuring a wide range of fitness facilities and classes.

Curriculum

One of the law school's greatest strengths is the richness and diversity of its curriculum. With more than 250 elective courses and seminars, students have an opportunity to sample a broad array of areas of the law and to tailor their programs to their interests and career aspirations. In addition to traditionally taught classes, the curriculum includes a number of simulation courses that teach skills such as drafting, trial and appellate advocacy, negotiations, mediation, and over a dozen different clinical programs in which students learn skills while working directly with clients.

To teach this extensive curriculum, a dynamic and accessible full-time faculty is joined by distinguished members of the bar and bench who teach some of the more specialized courses on an adjunct basis. Excellence in teaching is highly prized at GW, a fact that is readily apparent from scores and comments on semester course evaluations.

Clinical Programs and Public Interest

GW's long-standing commitment to public service has culminated in a wide variety of opportunities for students to serve the community while gaining important practical experience. A nationally recognized clinical program gives students the opportunity to work with real clients—many of whom might otherwise be without representation—while at the same time honing their skills. Clinical programs include civil litigation, consumer mediation, domestic violence advocacy, federal and criminal appeal, environmental law, health rights law, immigration, international human rights, older prisoners, public justice advocacy, small business/community development, and vaccine injury.

A student-faculty public interest committee publicizes and encourages student participation in volunteer legal activities, provides career development programs, and administers the Pro Bono Program, which extends special commendation to students who engage in a certain number of pro bono hours while attending the law school. The law school makes public service a more feasible option for its students by providing special forms of financial assistance in the form of summer subsidies, fellowships for third-year students, and loan reimbursement assistance for recent graduates of the law school.

The law school takes full advantage of its location in the nation's capital through its extensive externship program, which lets students work on a broad range of issues in government agencies, nonprofit organizations, and courts.

Joint-Degree and Study-Abroad Programs

Joint degrees are offered in the areas of business, public administration, public health, public policy, international affairs, history, and women's studies.

Summer study-abroad opportunities include the GW-Oxford Program in International Human Rights Law, the GW-Munich Intellectual Property Law Program, the GW-Augsburg (Germany) Student Exchange Program, and two new exchange programs in Groningen in the Netherlands and in Milan, Italy. GW is also a member of the North American Consortium on Legal Education (NACLE), which allows students to study at member Canadian and Mexican law schools.

Student Activities

Membership is available on seven publications—the *George Washington Law Review*, the *George Washington International Law Review*, the *Journal of Energy and Environmental Law*, the *Public Contract Law Journal* (cosponsored by the ABA section), the *Federal Circuit Bar Journal*, the *American Intellectual Property Law Quarterly Journal* (published by AIPLA and housed at GW), and the *International Law in Domestic Courts Journal*. Three skills boards—the Moot Court Board, Mock Trial Board, and Alternative Dispute Resolution Board—provide opportunities for participation in inter- and intrascholastic competitions. In addition, approximately 45 student groups are active at the law school, sponsoring social, educational, career, and public interest related programs. Each year, the Enrichment

Program hosts a series of distinguished speakers. Recent guests have included Supreme Court justices, legal scholars, popular authors, and leaders from government and public interest organizations.

Career Development

The Career Development Office provides effective career advising services to students and alumni, enabling them to engage in a meaningful job search, to compete as professionals in the employment market, and to make well-informed choices leading to long-term career satisfaction. The CDO offers a broad range of services, including individual counseling, group seminars, substantive legal practice area programs, interviewing programs, job and internship fairs, online job postings, handouts, a career resource library, an alumni career advisor network, a biweekly newsletter, and a comprehensive website.

Financial Assistance

The Law Financial Aid Office counsels and assists applicants and current students in applying for various sources of financial aid: federal and commercial loans at negotiated, competitive terms; need-based tuition grants; and outside scholarships. All applicants are considered for merit-based aid, including general merit awards, as well as public interest, environmental, and Teach for America merit scholarships. An estimated 85 percent of GW law students receive some sort of financial aid.

The law school's Loan Reimbursement Assistance Program (LRAP) is designed to alleviate the financial burdens of GW law graduates who pursue public interest employment. The LRAP assists qualified graduates by providing "forgivable" loans to those whose annual income—after taking into consideration their annual law school loan payments—falls below a certain target income.

APPLICANT PROFILE

The George Washington University Law School
This grid includes only applicants who earned 120–180 LSAT scores under standard administrations.

LSAT Score	3.75 +		3.50–3.74		3.25–3.49		3.00–3.24		2.75–2.99		2.50–2.74		2.25–2.49		2.00–2.24		Below 2.00		No GPA		Total	
	Apps	Adm	Apps	Adm	Apps	Adm	Apps	Adm	Apps	Adm	Apps	Adm	Apps	Adm	Apps	Adm	Apps	Adm	Apps	Adm	Apps	Adm
175–180	18	16	26	23	28	17	13	10	4	3	4	2	0	0	0	0	1	0	3	2	97	73
170–174	144	131	185	143	145	90	81	39	35	11	14	1	8	0	2	0	1	0	9	4	624	419
165–169	593	482	721	294	483	158	259	62	105	12	54	6	11	3	6	1	0	0	50	14	2282	1032
160–164	733	363	1002	15	724	13	359	9	135	5	61	3	28	0	6	0	1	0	72	8	3121	416
155–159	285	57	384	10	344	12	221	6	106	1	50	2	21	0	6	0	1	0	41	0	1459	88
150–154	113	7	182	3	187	1	170	1	91	0	44	0	25	0	8	0	2	0	30	0	852	12
145–149	31	0	67	0	76	0	71	0	60	0	35	0	18	0	7	0	3	0	18	0	386	0
140–144	11	0	26	0	37	0	34	0	38	0	29	0	15	0	6	0	3	0	7	0	206	0
135–139	3	0	7	0	16	0	16	0	15	0	15	0	5	0	7	0	3	0	2	0	89	0
130–134	0	0	2	0	5	0	3	0	5	0	8	0	1	0	3	0	3	0	3	0	33	0
125–129	1	0	1	0	1	0	1	0	1	0	2	0	3	0	1	0	1	0	2	0	14	0
120–124	0	0	0	0	0	0	0	0	0	0	1	0	0	0	0	0	0	0	0	0	1	0
Total	1932	1056	2603	488	2046	291	1228	127	595	32	317	14	135	3	52	1	19	0	237	28	9164	2040

Apps = Number of Applicants
Adm = Number Admitted
Reflects 99% of the total applicant pool; highest LSAT data reported.

GEORGETOWN UNIVERSITY LAW CENTER

600 New Jersey Avenue, NW, Room 589
Washington, DC 20001
Phone: 202.662.9010; Fax: 202.662.9439
E-mail: admis@law.georgetown.edu; Website: www.law.georgetown.edu

ABA Approved Since 1924

The Basics

Type of school	Private
Term	Semester
Application deadline	3/1
Application fee	$85
Financial aid deadline	3/1
Can first year start other than fall?	No
Student to faculty ratio	12.3 to 1
# of housing spaces available restricted to law students	291
graduate housing for which law students are eligible	

Faculty and Administrators

	Total		Men		Women		Minorities	
	Spr	Fall	Spr	Fall	Spr	Fall	Spr	Fall
Full-time	122	125	80	84	42	41	15	22
Other full-time	4	4	2	2	2	2	1	1
Deans, librarians, & others who teach	25	22	7	7	18	15	5	5
Part-time	159	132	121	107	38	25	12	6
Total	310	283	210	200	100	83	33	34

Curriculum

	Full-Time	Part-Time
Typical first-year section size	119	124
Is there typically a "small section" of the first-year class, other than Legal Writing, taught by full-time faculty	Yes	Yes
If yes, typical size offered last year	28	32
# of classroom course titles beyond first-year curriculum	434	

# of upper division courses, excluding seminars, with an enrollment:		
Under 25	183	
25–49	76	
50–74	29	
75–99	13	
100+	12	

# of seminars	302	
# of seminar positions available	4,586	
# of seminar positions filled	2,224	1,023
# of positions available in simulation courses	1,890	
# of simulation positions filled	991	454
# of positions available in faculty supervised clinical courses	257	
# of faculty supervised clinical positions filled	247	10
# involved in field placements	192	0
# involved in law journals	690	45
# involved in moot court or trial competitions	154	8
# of credit hours required to graduate	85	

JD Enrollment and Ethnicity

	Men		Women		Full-Time		Part-Time		1st-Year		Total		JD Degs. Awd.
	#	%	#	%	#	%	#	%	#	%	#	%	
All Hispanics	49	4.7	42	4.5	73	4.5	18	5.4	22	3.7	91	4.6	29
Am. Ind./AK Nat.	3	0.3	1	0.1	4	0.2	0	0.0	3	0.5	4	0.2	0
Asian	59	5.7	83	9.0	112	6.9	30	9.0	19	3.2	142	7.2	59
Black/Af. Am.	48	4.6	102	11.0	130	8.0	20	6.0	50	8.5	150	7.7	50
Nat. HI/Pac. Isl.	2	0.2	1	0.1	3	0.2	0	0.0	0	0.0	3	0.2	0
2 or more races	15	1.4	29	3.1	36	2.2	8	2.4	7	1.2	44	2.2	0
Subtotal (minor.)	176	17.0	258	27.9	358	22.0	76	22.8	101	17.2	434	22.1	153
Nonres. Alien	31	3.0	16	1.7	47	2.9	0	0.0	10	1.7	47	2.4	0
White/Cauc.	695	67.1	534	57.8	1021	62.8	208	62.3	315	53.6	1229	62.7	420
Unknown	134	12.9	116	12.6	200	12.3	50	15.0	162	27.6	250	12.8	60
Total	1036	52.9	924	47.1	1626	83.0	334	17.0	588	30.0	1960		647

Transfers

Transfers in	61
Transfers out	13

Tuition and Fees

	Resident	Nonresident
Full-time	$45,105	$45,105
Part-time	$39,120	$39,120
Tuition Guarantee Program	N	

Living Expenses

Estimated living expenses for singles

Living on campus	Living off campus	Living at home
$22,895	$22,895	$16,710

*ABA
Approved
Since
1924*

GPA and LSAT Scores

	Total	Full-Time	Part-Time
# of apps	12,405	11,524	2,393
# of offers	2,640	2,442	198
# of matrics	591	469	122
75% GPA	3.78	3.78	3.79
Median GPA	3.67	3.65	3.70
25% GPA	3.45	3.41	3.39
75% LSAT	172	172	170
Median LSAT	170	171	167
25% LSAT	168	169	164

Grants and Scholarships (from prior year)

	Total		Full-Time		Part-Time	
	#	%	#	%	#	%
Total # of students	1,982		1,628		354	
Total # receiving grants	637	32.1	629	38.6	8	2.3
Less than 1/2 tuition	414	20.9	406	24.9	8	2.3
Half to full tuition	219	11.0	219	13.5	0	0.0
Full tuition	4	0.2	4	0.2	0	0.0
More than full tuition	0	0.0	0	0.0	0	0.0
Median grant amount			$16,300		$4,000	

Informational and Library Resources

Total amount spent on library materials	$2,968,222
Study seating capacity inside the library	878
# of full-time equivalent professional librarians	27
Hours per week library is open	107
# of open, wired connections available to students	840
# of networked computers available for use by students	218
Has wireless network?	Y
Requires computer?	Y

JD Attrition (from prior year)

	Academic	Other	Total	
	#	#	#	%
1st year	0	25	25	4.2
2nd year	0	2	2	0.3
3rd year	0	0	0	0.0
4th year	0	0	0	0.0

Employment (9 months after graduation)

	Total	Percentage
Employment status known	673	99.3
Employment status unknown	5	0.7
Employed	626	93.0
Pursuing graduate degrees	21	3.1
Unemployed (seeking, not seeking, or studying for the bar)	21	3.1
Type of Employment		
# employed in law firms	419	66.9
# employed in business and industry	12	1.9
# employed in government	56	8.9
# employed in public interest	68	10.9
# employed as judicial clerks	61	9.7
# employed in academia	6	1.0
Geographic Location		
# employed in state	263	42.0
# employed outside the US	14	2.2
# of states where employed	31	

Bar Passage Rates

First-time takers	674	Reporting %	77.15
Average school %	90.96	Average state %	81.41
Average pass difference	9.55		

Jurisdiction	Takers	Passers	Pass %	State %	Diff %
New York	261	244	93.49	86.51	6.98
Maryland	107	102	95.33	78.20	17.13
California	84	69	82.14	73.19	8.95
Virginia	68	58	85.29	77.06	8.23

GEORGETOWN UNIVERSITY LAW CENTER

600 New Jersey Avenue, NW, Room 589
Washington, DC 20001
Phone: 202.662.9010; Fax: 202.662.9439
E-mail: admis@law.georgetown.edu; Website: www.law.georgetown.edu

Introduction

Georgetown Law, founded in 1870, is a dynamic and diverse intellectual community in which to study law. Not only does its curriculum include a staggering number of courses and seminars, but its distinguished full-time faculty is one of the nation's largest and is augmented by the experience and perspective of outstanding members of the bench and bar. The goal is education in its fullest sense—not only mastery of law, but a sense of the philosophical, political, and ethical dimensions of law. Preeminent in the fields of constitutional, international, and tax law, as well as clinical legal education, Georgetown Law's faculty is also known for its expertise in civil rights, corporate law, environmental law, family law, feminist jurisprudence, health law, human rights, immigration and refugee law, intellectual property law, legal history, and securities law. The Supreme Court, the Congress of the United States, and the Library of Congress are within walking distance of the campus, forming a unique environment for creative legal thought and learning.

The Law Center Campus

Georgetown Law's campus is the culmination of a longtime goal to create a campus that will nurture students in mind, body, and spirit. McDonough Hall, with its lecture halls, seminar rooms, faculty offices, bookstore, student dining area, and lounges, is the academic center of the campus.

The Hotung building brings all the major components of Georgetown Law's international programs under one roof and includes the John Wolff International and Comparative Law Library. The Sport and Fitness Center features a four-lane lap pool, basketball and racquetball courts, and a café and lounge with wireless network connectivity.

The Law Center's Edward Bennett Williams Law Library houses the fourth largest academic law library collection in the nation. The library also provides students with access to web-based services providing the most advanced research support available.

The campus features a vibrant residential program, with housing for approximately 300 students in the Gewirz Student Center. The building offers a variety of apartment styles with one, two, and three bedrooms with full kitchens and baths in each suite. Apartments designed for students with disabilities are also available. Resident Fellows offer programming to the 1L residents throughout the academic year ranging from fireside chats with faculty members, to talent shows, to informal seminars on course outlining and exam-taking.

Curriculum

Georgetown Law offers full-time and part-time programs leading to the JD degree. Entry to both programs is in the fall. First-year students in the full-time program choose either the A or B curriculum. Curriculum A is the traditional first-year curriculum, which parallels those at all other major law schools, and includes one elective course in the spring semester. Curriculum B includes courses that emphasize the sources of law in history, philosophy, political theory, and economics. It also seeks to reflect the increasingly public nature of contemporary law. Rather than an elective,

Curriculum B students take a fall seminar in legal theory. Full-time students are required to be in residence for six semesters; part-time students must be in residence for eight semesters or its equivalent.

The curriculum includes an innovative program for first-year students titled "Week One: Law in a Global Context." Involving an intensive week of study of complex problems of international and transnational law, the purpose is to deepen students' understanding of how legal problems increasingly transcend national boundaries and involve more than one legal system. The skills-based format of Week One also introduces students to Georgetown Law's extensive experiential curriculum, where students may choose from problem-solving, simulation, externship and other experiential learning courses, up to and including our nationally and internationally recognized clinics.

Georgetown Law offers a large and wide-ranging upper-level curriculum. Of the more than 350 courses offered to upper-class students, more than 150 have enrollments under 25 students. The only upper-class course requirements are a course in professional responsibility and a seminar or approved supervised research project meeting the upper-class legal writing requirement.

Joint Degrees

Georgetown Law offers 15 joint-degree programs: JD/Master of Public Policy; JD/Master of Science in Foreign Service; JD/Master of Arts in Arab Studies; JD/Master of Arts in German and European Studies; JD/Master of Arts in Latin American Studies; JD/Master of Arts in Russian and East European Studies; JD/Master of Arts in Security Studies; JD/Master of Business Administration; JD/Master of Public Health (with Johns Hopkins School of Public Health); JD/Master of Arts or Doctorate in Philosophy; JD/Doctorate in Government; JD/LLM in Taxation; JD/LLM in Securities and Financial Regulation; JD/LLM in International Business and Economic Law; and the JD/LLM in National Security Law.

Transnational, International, and Comparative Law Programs

Georgetown Law has many highly regarded programs dealing with different aspects of cross-border law.

Students have the unique opportunity to study for a semester in London at the Center for Transnational Legal studies, a Georgetown-led partnership of over 20 leading schools from five continents. Distinguished faculty, drawn from around the world, teach a transnational curriculum to a global student body in a context where there is no host school, majority nationality, or domestic legal system.

The Global Law Scholars Program, which combines language skills with directed legal training, provides an opportunity for a limited number of full-time JD students to prepare for a law practice involving more than one legal system.

Georgetown Law also offers a summer law program in London with distinguished professors from Europe and the US, as well as the opportunity to study abroad for a semester at prestigious institutions in Europe, Asia, India, Israel, Latin America, and Australia.

The Law Center's International Summer Internship Program offers opportunities to work abroad in law firms, corporations, and government organizations. Georgetown Law's Institute of International Economic Law awards a certificate in World Trade Organization studies to students who fulfill special course requirements.

Clinical Programs and Public Interest Law

Georgetown Law, a pioneer in clinical legal education, offers an unmatched clinical program. Our 14 clinics offer approximately 300 students per year an opportunity to enroll in clinics where (1) they represent clients in court or in administrative hearings, or (2) they work in a nontrial context in federal and local agencies, schools, and other institutions.

Georgetown Law's unparalleled public interest offerings include a Loan Repayment Assistance Program, a stand-alone public interest career office, guaranteed summer funding for public interest and government internships, a comprehensive student pro bono program, an extensive and diverse public interest curriculum, and public interest scholarships and a public interest fellowship program. The Office of Public Interest and Community Service (OPICS) houses a public interest resource library, provides specialist career advising on government and nonprofit internships and employment, oversees student and student group volunteer activities, and serves as the student liaison to the faculty and administration.

Admission

Georgetown Law evaluates candidates on two scales: academic or objective criteria and personal criteria. Academic information includes undergraduate and graduate records and LSAT scores. Personal factors include extracurricular activities, recommendations, work experience, and diversity of background. Georgetown Law does not use numerical cutoffs. Early application is encouraged since Georgetown Law employs a rolling admission process.

Student Activities

Cocurricular life at the Law Center centers around the more than 75 law student organizations which support students' personal, social, spiritual, political, and professional interests. The largest of these organizations, the student-led Barristers' Council, fields dozens of teams in appellate advocacy, mock trial, and alternative dispute resolution divisions, and competes successfully in national and international competitions. Students also share in the governance of the Law Center through the Student Bar Association and more than a dozen student/faculty committees, and supplement their academic pursuits by editing and publishing 11 scholarly journals and the *Law Weekly*, the award-winning school newspaper.

Financial Aid

Georgetown Law offers need-based, three-year financial aid grants to approximately one-third of the entering full-time class. Federal and commercial loans, along with on- and off-campus work-study opportunities, are also available. Approximately 90 percent of Georgetown Law's JD students obtain financial aid.

Acknowledged as one of the nation's top programs by Equal Justice Works, Georgetown Law's Loan Repayment Assistance Program assists JD graduates in pursuing careers in public service.

Career Services

The Office of Career Services (OCS) offers a wide range of career counseling and related programming. First-year students work closely with advisors who counsel them individually throughout law school. The fall recruiting program is one of the largest in the country, and OCS sponsors a robust judicial clerkship application process.

APPLICANT PROFILE

Since the Georgetown Law Admissions Committee takes into consideration a number of factors in evaluating whether a candidate would be suitable for admission, we cannot provide an applicant profile based solely on GPA and LSAT scores. In making such determinations, the Committee focuses on various aspects of a candidate's background and experience that, in combination with a candidate's academic record and LSAT score, give insight into a candidate's suitability for admission.

UNIVERSITY OF GEORGIA SCHOOL OF LAW

Harold Hirsch Hall, 225 Herty Drive
Athens, GA 30602-6012
Phone: 706.542.7060; Fax: 706.542.5556
E-mail: ugajd@uga.edu; Website: www.law.uga.edu

ABA
Approved
Since
1930

The Basics

Type of school	Public
Term	Semester
Application deadline	3/1
Application fee	$50
Financial aid deadline	3/1
Can first year start other than fall?	No
Student to faculty ratio	12.2 to 1
# of housing spaces available restricted to law students	
graduate housing for which law students are eligible	732

Faculty and Administrators

	Total		Men		Women		Minorities	
	Spr	Fall	Spr	Fall	Spr	Fall	Spr	Fall
Full-time	47	47	31	29	16	18	5	6
Other full-time	4	4	0	1	4	3	0	0
Deans, librarians, & others who teach	6	6	3	3	3	3	0	0
Part-time	25	13	20	12	5	1	2	0
Total	82	70	54	45	28	25	7	6

Curriculum

	Full-Time	Part-Time
Typical first-year section size	78	0
Is there typically a "small section" of the first-year class, other than Legal Writing, taught by full-time faculty	No	No
If yes, typical size offered last year		

# of classroom course titles beyond first-year curriculum			139
# of upper division courses, excluding seminars, with an enrollment:	Under 25		125
	25–49		43
	50–74		14
	75–99		6
	100+		0
# of seminars			29
# of seminar positions available			522
# of seminar positions filled	509		0
# of positions available in simulation courses			396
# of simulation positions filled	362		0
# of positions available in faculty supervised clinical courses			483
# of faculty supervised clinical positions filled	460		0
# involved in field placements	135		0
# involved in law journals	199		0
# involved in moot court or trial competitions	370		0
# of credit hours required to graduate			88

JD Enrollment and Ethnicity

	Men		Women		Full-Time		Part-Time		1st-Year		Total		JD Degs. Awd.
	#	%	#	%	#	%	#	%	#	%	#	%	
All Hispanics	5	1.3	5	1.6	10	1.4	0	0.0	3	1.2	10	1.4	2
Am. Ind./AK Nat.	1	0.3	2	0.6	3	0.4	0	0.0	2	0.8	3	0.4	0
Asian	17	4.4	16	5.0	33	4.7	0	0.0	13	5.2	33	4.7	9
Black/Af. Am.	24	6.2	54	17.0	78	11.1	0	0.0	28	11.2	78	11.1	25
Nat. HI/Pac. Isl.	0	0.0	0	0.0	0	0.0	0	0.0	0	0.0	0	0.0	0
2 or more races	6	1.6	7	2.2	13	1.8	0	0.0	1	0.4	13	1.8	0
Subtotal (minor.)	53	13.8	84	26.4	137	19.5	0	0.0	47	18.9	137	19.5	40
Nonres. Alien	2	0.5	0	0.0	2	0.3	0	0.0	0	0.0	2	0.3	0
White/Cauc.	294	76.4	204	64.2	498	70.8	0	0.0	182	73.1	498	70.8	140
Unknown	36	9.4	30	9.4	66	9.4	0	0.0	12	4.8	66	9.4	32
Total	385	54.8	318	45.2	703	100.0	0	0.0	241	35.4	703		212

Transfers

Transfers in	5
Transfers out	1

Tuition and Fees

	Resident	Nonresident
Full-time	$15,814	$33,620
Part-time		
Tuition Guarantee Program		N

Living Expenses

Estimated living expenses for singles

Living on campus	Living off campus	Living at home
$12,710	$16,018	$10,150

ABA
Approved
Since
1930

GPA and LSAT Scores

	Total	Full-Time	Part-Time
# of apps	4,297	4,297	0
# of offers	956	956	0
# of matrics	248	248	0
75% GPA	3.80	3.80	0.00
Median GPA	3.70	3.70	0.00
25% GPA	3.40	3.40	0.00
75% LSAT	166	166	0
Median LSAT	164	164	0
25% LSAT	162	162	0

Grants and Scholarships (from prior year)

	Total		Full-Time		Part-Time	
	#	%	#	%	#	%
Total # of students	694		694		0	
Total # receiving grants	372	53.6	372	53.6	0	0.0
Less than 1/2 tuition	152	21.9	152	21.9	0	0.0
Half to full tuition	213	30.7	213	30.7	0	0.0
Full tuition	6	0.9	6	0.9	0	0.0
More than full tuition	1	0.1	1	0.1	0	0.0
Median grant amount			$7,500		$0	

Informational and Library Resources

Total amount spent on library materials	$1,127,254
Study seating capacity inside the library	455
# of full-time equivalent professional librarians	9
Hours per week library is open	121
# of open, wired connections available to students	0
# of networked computers available for use by students	31
Has wireless network?	Y
Requires computer?	N

JD Attrition (from prior year)

	Academic	Other	Total	
	#	#	#	%
1st year	2	7	9	3.7
2nd year	0	0	0	0.0
3rd year	1	0	1	0.5
4th year	0	0	0	0.0

Employment (9 months after graduation)

	Total	Percentage
Employment status known	212	98.1
Employment status unknown	4	1.9
Employed	193	91.0
Pursuing graduate degrees	14	6.6
Unemployed (seeking, not seeking, or studying for the bar)	2	0.9
Type of Employment		
# employed in law firms	126	65.3
# employed in business and industry	9	4.7
# employed in government	17	8.8
# employed in public interest	7	3.6
# employed as judicial clerks	27	14.0
# employed in academia	6	3.1
Geographic Location		
# employed in state	145	75.1
# employed outside the US	1	0.5
# of states where employed	13	

Bar Passage Rates

First-time takers	201	Reporting %	100.00
Average school %	95.05	Average state %	85.78
Average pass difference	9.27		

Jurisdiction	Takers	Passers	Pass %	State %	Diff %
Georgia	181	171	94.48	86.28	8.20
New York	10	10	100.00	86.51	13.49
North Carolina	6	6	100.00	76.79	23.21
California	1	1	100.00	73.19	26.81
Others (3)	3	3	100.00		

UNIVERSITY OF GEORGIA SCHOOL OF LAW

Harold Hirsch Hall, 225 Herty Drive
Athens, GA 30602-6012
Phone: 706.542.7060; Fax: 706.542.5556
E-mail: ugajd@uga.edu; Website: www.law.uga.edu

Introduction

The University of Georgia School of Law (Georgia Law), founded in 1859, is on the campus of the University of Georgia in Athens, Georgia. The university provides an excellent setting for the study of law with superb libraries and outstanding academic, cultural, recreational, and social opportunities. Athens, a town of 100,000, is the commercial and legal center for northeast Georgia and is approximately one hour from downtown Atlanta. Athens also features a cultural richness ranging from local restaurants and quirky shops to the latest in the alternative music scene.

The School of Law is approved by the ABA, is a member of the AALS, and has a chapter of the Order of the Coif.

The Student Body

The law school student body shares a strong sense of community, and the school prides itself on the collegiality among students, faculty, and staff. The entering class usually numbers in the low 200s, and the entire student body, including LLM students, averages 650 students. The law school is also a vital part of the university community, which supports a cosmopolitan mix of over 33,000 undergraduate, graduate, and professional students. Many law students take advantage of these assets by taking courses in other schools and colleges of the university and by participating in the intellectual and social life of the campus.

Curriculum

The law curriculum is rich and diverse. The first year of study consists of required core courses; after its completion, students may choose from a wealth of classes, seminars, and clinical programs to suit their interests.

Clinical program opportunities, both criminal and civil, abound. Clinical education expands upon the classroom knowledge by providing essential experiential learning. Students interested in criminal law can participate in the Prosecutorial Clinic, the Criminal Defense Clinic, or the Capital Assistance Project. Students interested in environmental law, family law, public interest law, and any of a number of other areas of study will find that the Civil Externship Clinic, Family Violence Clinic, Land Use Clinic, Mediation Practicum, Public Interest Practicum, Environmental Law Practicum, Special Education Practicum, and Appellate Litigation Clinic add to their understanding and preparedness.

Faculty

While some law schools choose to emphasize either scholarship or teaching, the University of Georgia seeks a balance of the two, firmly believing that classroom teaching is enhanced by scholarly expertise. The college town setting fosters student-faculty interaction by increasing faculty availability and promoting a conducive atmosphere for dialogue.

The faculty includes authors of some of our country's leading legal scholarship, recipients of the university's highest honors for teaching excellence, Fulbright Scholars, and former law clerks for the US Supreme Court and appellate courts. Most bring practical experience to the classroom as well; they have been trial and corporate attorneys, and many continue to accept pro bono cases or serve as consultants.

Faculty expertise is expanded by the addition of outstanding adjuncts, attorneys from the region's most powerful firms, international attorneys, government leaders, and prominent practitioners. In addition, the law school's Dean Rusk Center—International, Comparative, and Graduate Legal Studies annually is host to several international scholars who may teach mini-courses in their areas of interest. Recent courses include international human rights, dispute settlement in the World Trade Organization, and EC competition law.

Educational Enrichment Programs

University of Georgia law students have several opportunities to expand their educational horizons. First, joint programs with other schools and colleges in the university enable students to complete two degrees in less time than it would take to pursue them separately. Existing joint programs include JD/MBA (business administration), JD/MPA (public administration), JD/MHP (historic preservation), JD/MSW (social work), and JD/MEd in Sports Studies.

Students may also take graduate coursework in other schools and colleges of the university and have it count as elective credit toward the 88 semester hours required for graduation. For example, students interested in tax law might take courses in the school of accounting, and students interested in public policy might take courses in the School of Public and International Affairs. Finally, those who are not interested in the joint-degree programs, but want more coursework than can be satisfied by elective credit, may pursue other advanced degrees at the same time they are fulfilling the requirements for the law degree.

Study Abroad

Nothing helps one to better understand the culture of another country than actually studying and living in a foreign land. At Georgia Law, this concept is fully embraced. Several opportunities for legal study and work experience in other parts of the world are provided on an annual basis. They include:

Georgia Law at Oxford—This exciting 15-week program runs from January through April and is one of the few semester-long study-abroad programs offered by an American law school. Selected second- and third-year law students take four courses and receive 12 semester hours of credit.

Global Internship Program—Established in 2001, this initiative provides students with six to ten weeks of study or work experience in one of more than 25 countries spanning the world. Each participant receives funding from the law school to help offset travel and living costs.

Georgia Law Summer Program in Brussels and Geneva—Hosted by two highly prestigious European institutions of higher learning: L'Institut d'Études Européennes, Facultés universitaires Saint-Louis (IEE) in Brussels and the Graduate Institute of International and Development Studies (Graduate Institute) in Geneva, this three week course is designed to provide an introduction to the legal system of the European Union, with an emphasis on EU business law, as well as a concentrated study of international trade law practice under the WTO.

Georgia Law Summer Program in China—Partnering with Tsinghua University in Beijing and Fudan University in Shanghai, this three-week study-abroad program in China's two largest cities offers an introduction to the Chinese legal system with an emphasis on commercial and trade law. There is the potential for Georgia Law students to remain in the country at the end of the program for a four- to six-week internship in one of several law firms. Georgia Law students received partial tuition scholarships in the summer of 2010.

Equal Justice Foundation Fellowships—These awards provide grants to law students who engage in public interest legal work in positions that otherwise would not be funded. Recently, EJF fellowship recipients have used their funds to gain international experience and aid foreign causes.

Library and Physical Facilities

The law library's vast collection makes it among the largest in legal education. While it has extensive holdings in international law, it focuses on being a functional library serving the needs of students. The university's main library is adjacent to the law school and is one of the largest research libraries in the nation.

The law school is headquartered in Hirsch Hall on the northern edge of the campus, the most scenic and historic section of the university. Dean Rusk Hall, adjacent to Hirsch Hall, provides additional classroom and office space. The majority of clinical settings are just a short walk away in the downtown area.

Career Services

The law school offers a fully staffed career services office that assists law students and graduates. Placement rates are among the highest in the nation, and a very high percentage of students work as summer associates around the country prior to beginning the second and third years of study. The career services website is a comprehensive source of information.

Alumni practice in 47 states and over 50 countries. Employers from all 50 states and 25 countries have utilized the Legal Career Services Office to target Georgia Law students for summer and full-time employment.

Advocacy Programs

Georgia Law's accomplished Moot Court and Mock Trial programs focus on developing critical oral and written advocacy skills. Team members learn how to write persuasively and how to make convincing oral presentations that will withstand intense scrutiny by the court. Through this incredible practical learning experience, Georgia Law students become powerful advocates.

Georgia Law's Moot Court and Mock Trial programs have won several national titles, regional crowns, and state trophies.

Student Publications

Students at Georgia Law publish three highly regarded legal journals: the *Georgia Law Review*, the *Georgia Journal of International and Comparative Law*, and the *Journal of Intellectual Property Law*, a nationally recognized IP specialty journal. The journals, which are frequently cited by federal and state courts, textbooks, treatises, and other law reviews, follow the customary format, with articles from leading scholars and practitioners comprising the bulk of the content and another section consisting of student notes.

APPLICANT PROFILE

University of Georgia School of Law
This grid includes only applicants who earned 120–180 LSAT scores under standard administrations.

LSAT Score	3.75 +		3.50–3.74		3.25–3.49		3.00–3.24		2.75–2.99		2.50–2.74		2.25–2.49		2.00–2.24		Below 2.00		No GPA		Total	
	Apps	Adm	Apps	Adm	Apps	Adm	Apps	Adm	Apps	Adm	Apps	Adm	Apps	Adm	Apps	Adm	Apps	Adm	Apps	Adm	Apps	Adm
170–180	47	44	46	40	51	37	22	11	12	4	6	1	3	0	0	0	1	0	0	0	188	137
165–169	140	122	185	142	139	108	97	59	45	10	34	4	11	0	4	0	0	0	7	5	662	450
160–164	304	111	459	103	405	55	240	32	108	2	55	1	19	0	14	0	0	0	23	3	1627	307
155–159	134	13	174	6	175	8	101	3	66	0	25	0	4	0	3	0	0	0	11	0	693	30
150–154	71	16	96	6	118	4	93	1	62	0	27	0	14	0	6	0	2	0	10	0	499	27
145–149	25	3	35	3	74	0	68	0	39	0	32	0	11	0	8	0	2	0	6	0	300	6
140–144	13	3	11	0	29	0	29	0	22	0	13	0	9	0	4	0	0	0	7	0	137	3
Below 140	7	0	9	0	9	0	7	0	15	0	19	0	12	0	3	0	3	0	6	0	90	0
Total	741	312	1015	300	1000	212	657	106	369	16	211	6	83	0	42	0	8	0	70	8	4196	960

Apps = Number of Applicants
Adm = Number Admitted
Reflects 99% of the total applicant pool; highest LSAT data reported.

GEORGIA STATE UNIVERSITY COLLEGE OF LAW

PO Box 4037
Atlanta, GA 30302-4037
Phone: 404.413.9000; Fax: 404.413.9225
E-mail: admissions@law.gsu.edu; Website: http://law.gsu.edu

The Basics

Type of school	Public
Term	Semester
Application deadline	3/15
Application fee	$50
Financial aid deadline	4/1
Can first year start other than fall?	No
Student to faculty ratio	10.6 to 1
# of housing spaces available restricted to law students	
graduate housing for which law students are eligible	650

Faculty and Administrators

	Total Spr	Total Fall	Men Spr	Men Fall	Women Spr	Women Fall	Minorities Spr	Minorities Fall
Full-time	48	45	29	26	19	19	6	6
Other full-time	11	12	2	3	9	9	1	1
Deans, librarians, & others who teach	13	13	7	7	6	6	4	4
Part-time	44	12	27	8	17	4	22	8
Total	116	82	65	44	51	38	33	19

Curriculum

	Full-Time	Part-Time
Typical first-year section size	70	70
Is there typically a "small section" of the first-year class, other than Legal Writing, taught by full-time faculty	No	No
If yes, typical size offered last year		
# of classroom course titles beyond first-year curriculum	114	
# of upper division courses, excluding seminars, with an enrollment: Under 25	96	
25–49	33	
50–74	18	
75–99	0	
100+	0	
# of seminars	27	
# of seminar positions available	405	
# of seminar positions filled	144	70
# of positions available in simulation courses	216	
# of simulation positions filled	147	62
# of positions available in faculty supervised clinical courses	135	
# of faculty supervised clinical positions filled	99	26
# involved in field placements	94	22
# involved in law journals	52	23
# involved in moot court or trial competitions	55	23
# of credit hours required to graduate	90	

JD Enrollment and Ethnicity

	Men #	Men %	Women #	Women %	Full-Time #	Full-Time %	Part-Time #	Part-Time %	1st-Year #	1st-Year %	Total #	Total %	JD Degs. Awd.
All Hispanics	6	1.7	6	1.9	7	1.5	5	2.5	3	1.3	12	1.8	7
Am. Ind./AK Nat.	3	0.9	1	0.3	4	0.9	0	0.0	3	1.3	4	0.6	2
Asian	25	7.1	28	9.1	41	9.0	12	5.9	22	9.8	53	8.0	12
Black/Af. Am.	22	6.3	37	12.0	37	8.1	22	10.8	24	10.7	59	8.9	22
Nat. Hi/Pac. Isl.	0	0.0	0	0.0	0	0.0	0	0.0	0	0.0	0	0.0	0
2 or more races	3	0.9	2	0.6	4	0.9	1	0.5	0	0.0	5	0.8	0
Subtotal (minor.)	59	16.8	74	23.9	93	20.4	40	19.7	52	23.2	133	20.2	47
Nonres. Alien	0	0.0	0	0.0	0	0.0	0	0.0	0	0.0	0	0.0	0
White/Cauc.	258	73.5	212	68.6	325	71.1	145	71.4	148	66.1	470	71.2	134
Unknown	34	9.7	23	7.4	39	8.5	18	8.9	21	9.4	57	8.6	18
Total	351	53.2	309	46.8	457	69.2	203	30.8	224	33.9	660		199

Transfers

Transfers in	5
Transfers out	2

Tuition and Fees

	Resident	Nonresident
Full-time	$13,310	$34,334
Part-time	$11,382	$26,186
Tuition Guarantee Program	N	

Living Expenses

Estimated living expenses for singles

Living on campus	Living off campus	Living at home
$15,226	$14,515	$7,810

GEORGIA STATE UNIVERSITY COLLEGE OF LAW

ABA
Approved
Since
1984

GPA and LSAT Scores

	Total	Full-Time	Part-Time
# of apps	2,914	2,583	331
# of offers	513	425	88
# of matrics	224	155	69
75% GPA	3.75	3.80	3.50
Median GPA	3.60	3.60	3.40
25% GPA	3.20	3.20	3.10
75% LSAT	162	162	161
Median LSAT	161	161	159
25% LSAT	159	159	159

Grants and Scholarships (from prior year)

	Total		Full-Time		Part-Time	
	#	%	#	%	#	%
Total # of students	673		480		193	
Total # receiving grants	148	22.0	104	21.7	44	22.8
Less than 1/2 tuition	50	7.4	30	6.3	20	10.4
Half to full tuition	26	3.9	12	2.5	14	7.3
Full tuition	72	10.7	62	12.9	10	5.2
More than full tuition	0	0.0	0	0.0	0	0.0
Median grant amount			$2,500		$2,000	

Informational and Library Resources

Total amount spent on library materials	$1,134,551
Study seating capacity inside the library	335
# of full-time equivalent professional librarians	13
Hours per week library is open	103
# of open, wired connections available to students	926
# of networked computers available for use by students	141
Has wireless network?	Y
Requires computer?	N

JD Attrition (from prior year)

	Academic	Other	Total	
	#	#	#	%
1st year	7	7	14	6.6
2nd year	2	0	2	1.0
3rd year	0	0	0	0.0
4th year	0	0	0	0.0

Employment (9 months after graduation)

	Total	Percentage
Employment status known	183	98.9
Employment status unknown	2	1.1
Employed	166	90.7
Pursuing graduate degrees	7	3.8
Unemployed (seeking, not seeking, or studying for the bar)	3	1.6
Type of Employment		
# employed in law firms	104	62.7
# employed in business and industry	33	19.9
# employed in government	16	9.6
# employed in public interest	4	2.4
# employed as judicial clerks	4	2.4
# employed in academia	5	3.0
Geographic Location		
# employed in state	154	92.8
# employed outside the US	2	1.2
# of states where employed	10	

Bar Passage Rates

First-time takers	189	Reporting %	89.95
Average school %	94.12	Average state %	86.28
Average pass difference	7.84		

Jurisdiction	Takers	Passers	Pass %	State %	Diff %
Georgia	170	160	94.12	86.28	7.84

GEORGIA STATE UNIVERSITY COLLEGE OF LAW

PO Box 4037
Atlanta, GA 30302-4037
Phone: 404.413.9000; Fax: 404.413.9225
E-mail: admissions@law.gsu.edu; Website: http://law.gsu.edu

Introduction

Georgia State University College of Law is located in downtown Atlanta, the center for legal, financial, and governmental activities in the Southeast. This location provides easy access to federal, state, and local courts and agencies; the state capital and legislature; corporations; major law firms in the metropolitan area; and the library and other facilities of Georgia State University.

The College of Law began operation in 1982. The College of Law is accredited by the ABA and is a member of the AALS.

Library and Physical Facilities

The College of Law library is designed and equipped to meet the demanding research needs of today's students, faculty members, staff, and members of the legal community. With a collection of more than 163,404 hard-copy volumes and more than 191,256 microform-equivalent volumes, the library provides research materials in American, British, Canadian, and international law. Students find a host of computer applications available in the law library computer lab, which is staffed by computer consultants. The college dedicates state-of-the-art computer equipment for training purposes only in our computer training room. The classrooms and study carrels accommodate laptop computers.

The College of Law is one of the leading law schools in the Southeast. Located on a 39-acre campus in the heart of downtown Atlanta, the building houses a moot courtroom equipped with state-of-the-art video technology and provides activities directed toward trial and appellate advocacy. Students have access to many other campus facilities, including the athletic complex, which offers a variety of individual fitness opportunities and team sports.

Curriculum

The college offers students the opportunity to study full or part time and provides a traditional yet innovative curriculum. It offers extensive coverage of the foundational areas of the law to first-year students while providing an array of elective opportunities in public and private law. Opportunities range from the study of legal philosophy and jurisprudence to vital skills training through courses in litigation, counseling, negotiation, legal drafting, and alternative dispute resolution.

The growth of technology in our lives is reflected in courses in Intellectual Property and Computers and the Law; in our innovative course, Law and the Internet; and in the increasing use of computer programs and online discussion groups. Opportunities exist for in-depth study in international and comparative law, environmental law, health law, tax law, employment law, commercial law, and bankruptcy.

Admission

The College of Law actively seeks to enroll a student body with diversity in educational, cultural, and racial backgrounds that will enrich the educational experience of the entire group.

Applicants are encouraged to visit. Please make arrangements through the Office of Admissions to tour the campus; talk with students, faculty, and admissions staff; or attend a class.

Special Programs

Joint-Degree Programs—Seven joint JD and master's degree programs are available with Georgia State University's J. Mack Robinson College of Business, the Andrew Young School of Policy Studies, the Department of Philosophy in the College of Arts and Sciences, and the College of Architecture at the Georgia Institute of Technology.

International Programs—Students have the opportunity to participate in two summer-abroad programs. These are the Transnational Comparative Dispute Resolution Program in Europe and the Summer Legal and Policy Study Program in comparative and international law in Brazil. ·

Clinics—The Low-Income Taxpayer Clinic and the Health Law Partnership (HeLP) Clinic provide a live-client component to the college's Lawyer Skills Externship Development Program. Both clinics give students hands-on, real-life experience in client representation and handling cases. Work in the Tax Clinic teaches case management, evidence gathering, document preparation, interviewing, counseling, and effective negotiation. The Health Law Partnership Clinic offers a community service clinic that provides students with opportunities to work on cases related to children's health and welfare, including clinics on site at three Atlanta-area children's hospitals where low-income children and their families are eligible for these services aimed at eliminating socioeconomic barriers to optimum health.

Externships—Externships are designed to tie theoretical knowledge to a practical base of experience in the profession. Externships involve actual participation in rendering legal services. Students interested in the externship program should contact the Lawyer Skills Development Externship Office.

Trial Advocacy—The College of Law offers students an extensive variety of opportunities in the area of trial advocacy. Our litigation workshop, offered each spring semester, provides second-year students with an intensive skills training experience. Working in small seminar groups, students are asked to conduct drafting and simulation exercises on all phases of the pretrial and trial process, including a full jury trial. In addition to the workshop, the college offers several advanced litigation courses in which students can further enhance their advocacy skills in civil and criminal areas.

Moot Court—Each year, students compete in several of the most challenging and prestigious moot court competitions throughout the country. The Moot Court Program has achieved substantial renown and success in its 28-year history. The National Moot Court Competition, sponsored by the Association of the Bar of the City of New York, is the oldest and most recognized national competition, and the College of Law became the first law school in Georgia to place first in that competition. Teams from the college have since won numerous other competitions.

Centers—The College of Law has two centers: the Center for Law, Health, and Society and the Center for the

Comparative Study of Metropolitan Growth. The Center for Law, Health, and Society promotes the integration of health law and ethics into (1) health policy and research, (2) the health sciences, (3) the provision of health services, and (4) the interdisciplinary education of law students. The Center for the Comparative Study of Metropolitan Growth produces research, teaching, and academic exchange on the range of issues relating to metropolitan growth.

Student Activities

The *Georgia State University Law Review* is published four times a year by students who have demonstrated outstanding writing and academic skills.

The college also boasts a nationally renowned student mock trial program in which our students compete annually in numerous mock trial competitions held at locations throughout the country. Our student teams have amassed an incredible record of success at the national, regional, and state levels. The College of Law has won four national championships, competed in five national finals, and won eight regional and several state championships.

The College of Law regards student organizations as an important part of a legal education experience and encourages participation in our wide variety of organizations, some traditionally found in law schools, some less common. The college recognizes 30 organizations, most of which are affiliated with national professional associations. We are proud of the accomplishments of these groups.

Career Services

The Career Services Office offers a broad range of services. Students may begin using the office in November of the first year of law school and may continue utilizing career planning services throughout their careers. Specific programs geared toward minority students are the Atlanta Bar Association Minority Clerkship Program and the Southeastern Minority Job Fair. Typically, over 93 percent of each graduating class accepts employment within six months of graduation.

APPLICANT PROFILE

Georgia State University College of Law
This grid includes only applicants who earned 120–180 LSAT scores under standard administrations.

LSAT Score	3.75 +		3.50–3.74		3.25–3.49		3.00–3.24		2.75–2.99		2.50–2.74		Below 2.50		No GPA		Total	
	Apps	Adm	Apps	Adm	Apps	Adm	Apps	Adm	Apps	Adm	Apps	Adm	Apps	Adm	Apps	Adm	Apps	Adm
170–180	3	3	6	5	5	2	4	4	2	1	1	0	0	0	0	0	21	15
165–169	12	10	28	21	21	15	21	14	8	3	11	3	2	0	1	1	104	67
160–164	68	54	111	81	119	72	94	49	37	7	23	2	22	3	6	5	480	273
155–159	82	32	137	45	185	51	138	30	87	10	41	3	31	0	11	3	712	174
150–154	64	6	118	12	136	7	150	7	80	0	42	0	34	0	7	1	631	33
145–149	29	0	44	0	87	0	109	0	69	0	58	0	49	0	7	0	452	0
140–144	12	0	16	0	51	0	60	0	46	0	38	0	42	0	6	0	271	0
Below 140	7	0	13	0	25	0	38	0	40	0	44	0	49	0	7	0	223	0
Total	277	105	473	164	629	147	614	104	369	21	258	8	229	3	45	10	2894	562

Apps = Number of Applicants
Adm = Number Admitted
Reflects 99% of the total applicant pool; highest LSAT data reported.

GOLDEN GATE UNIVERSITY SCHOOL OF LAW

536 Mission Street, Office of Admissions
San Francisco, CA 94105-2968
Phone: 415.442.6630 or 800.GGU.4YOU; Fax: 415.442.6631
E-mail: lawadmit@ggu.edu; Website: www.ggu.edu/law

ABA
Approved
Since
1956

AMERICAN BAR ASSOCIATION
Section of Legal Education
and Admissions to the Bar

The Basics

Type of school	Private
Term	Semester
Application deadline	4/1
Application fee	$60
Financial aid deadline	
Can first year start other than fall?	No
Student to faculty ratio	14.9 to 1
# of housing spaces available restricted to law students	
graduate housing for which law students are eligible	

Faculty and Administrators

	Total		Men		Women		Minorities	
	Spr	Fall	Spr	Fall	Spr	Fall	Spr	Fall
Full-time	32	39	18	21	14	18	8	10
Other full-time	3	3	0	0	3	3	0	0
Deans, librarians, & others who teach	8	8	2	2	6	6	0	0
Part-time	72	71	37	37	35	34	9	8
Total	115	121	57	60	58	61	17	18

Curriculum

	Full-Time	Part-Time
Typical first-year section size	70	45
Is there typically a "small section" of the first-year class, other than Legal Writing, taught by full-time faculty	No	No
If yes, typical size offered last year		

# of classroom course titles beyond first-year curriculum		162

# of upper division courses, excluding seminars, with an enrollment:	Under 25	189
	25–49	48
	50–74	3
	75–99	4
	100+	0

# of seminars		42
# of seminar positions available		391
# of seminar positions filled	306	35
# of positions available in simulation courses		393
# of simulation positions filled	346	36
# of positions available in faculty supervised clinical courses		78
# of faculty supervised clinical positions filled	30	3
# involved in field placements	171	18
# involved in law journals	86	6
# involved in moot court or trial competitions	79	6
# of credit hours required to graduate		88

JD Enrollment and Ethnicity

	Men		Women		Full-Time		Part-Time		1st-Year		Total		JD Degs. Awd.
	#	%	#	%	#	%	#	%	#	%	#	%	
All Hispanics	28	8.4	20	5.0	39	6.3	9	7.8	23	7.2	48	6.6	16
Am. Ind./AK Nat.	4	1.2	2	0.5	5	0.8	1	0.9	3	0.9	6	0.8	1
Asian	45	13.5	81	20.4	107	17.4	19	16.4	57	17.9	126	17.2	35
Black/Af. Am.	8	2.4	8	2.0	12	1.9	4	3.4	7	2.2	16	2.2	3
Nat. HI/Pac. Isl.	6	1.8	2	0.5	4	0.6	4	3.4	0	0.0	8	1.1	0
2 or more races	3	0.9	3	0.8	6	1.0	0	0.0	5	1.6	6	0.8	0
Subtotal (minor.)	94	28.1	116	29.1	173	28.1	37	31.9	95	29.8	210	28.7	55
Nonres. Alien	2	0.6	10	2.5	12	1.9	0	0.0	4	1.3	12	1.6	0
White/Cauc.	202	60.5	214	53.8	348	56.5	68	58.6	184	57.7	416	56.8	93
Unknown	36	10.8	58	14.6	83	13.5	11	9.5	36	11.3	94	12.8	25
Total	334	45.6	398	54.4	616	84.2	116	15.8	319	43.6	732		175

Transfers

Transfers in	2
Transfers out	23

Tuition and Fees

	Resident	Nonresident
Full-time	$38,375	$38,375
Part-time	$29,485	$29,485
Tuition Guarantee Program		N

Living Expenses

Estimated living expenses for singles

Living on campus	Living off campus	Living at home
N/A	$23,515	N/A

GOLDEN GATE UNIVERSITY SCHOOL OF LAW

ABA
Approved
Since
1956

GPA and LSAT Scores

	Total	Full-Time	Part-Time
# of apps	2,654	2,276	378
# of offers	1,452	1,326	126
# of matrics	320	268	52
75% GPA	3.38	3.40	3.24
Median GPA	3.10	3.12	2.99
25% GPA	2.82	2.84	2.67
75% LSAT	156	156	155
Median LSAT	154	154	153
25% LSAT	151	151	151

Grants and Scholarships (from prior year)

	Total #	Total %	Full-Time #	Full-Time %	Part-Time #	Part-Time %
Total # of students	637		529		108	
Total # receiving grants	234	36.7	200	37.8	34	31.5
Less than 1/2 tuition	179	28.1	152	28.7	27	25.0
Half to full tuition	47	7.4	43	8.1	4	3.7
Full tuition	8	1.3	5	0.9	3	2.8
More than full tuition	0	0.0	0	0.0	0	0.0
Median grant amount			$10,875		$5,000	

Informational and Library Resources

Total amount spent on library materials	$1,243,574
Study seating capacity inside the library	460
# of full-time equivalent professional librarians	7
Hours per week library is open	95
# of open, wired connections available to students	572
# of networked computers available for use by students	130
Has wireless network?	Y
Requires computer?	N

JD Attrition (from prior year)

	Academic #	Other #	Total #	Total %
1st year	25	26	51	20.6
2nd year	3	2	5	2.6
3rd year	1	2	3	1.6
4th year	0	0	0	0.0

Employment (9 months after graduation)

	Total	Percentage
Employment status known	164	91.6
Employment status unknown	15	8.4
Employed	143	87.2
Pursuing graduate degrees	6	3.7
Unemployed (seeking, not seeking, or studying for the bar)	10	6.1
Type of Employment		
# employed in law firms	58	40.6
# employed in business and industry	27	18.9
# employed in government	22	15.4
# employed in public interest	24	16.8
# employed as judicial clerks	3	2.1
# employed in academia	9	6.3
Geographic Location		
# employed in state	133	93.0
# employed outside the US	0	0.0
# of states where employed	8	

Bar Passage Rates

First-time takers	176	Reporting %	98.30
Average school %	64.16	Average state %	73.19
Average pass difference	−9.03		

Jurisdiction	Takers	Passers	Pass %	State %	Diff %
California	173	111	64.16	73.19	−9.03

GOLDEN GATE UNIVERSITY SCHOOL OF LAW

536 Mission Street, Office of Admissions
San Francisco, CA 94105-2968
Phone: 415.442.6630 or 800.GGU.4YOU; Fax: 415.442.6631
E-mail: lawadmit@ggu.edu; Website: www.ggu.edu/law

Introduction

Founded in 1901, Golden Gate University School of Law is located in the heart of San Francisco's legal and financial district. The law school is noted for integrating legal theory and practical skills training. Golden Gate has a distinguished faculty who share a strong commitment to both excellence in teaching and accessibility to students. The law school is a fully ABA-accredited program and is a member in good standing of the AALS.

Program Options

The law school offers both a full-time day and a part-time evening program. The full-time program involves three years of study and the part-time program involves four years of study. Golden Gate Law also offers an enhanced JD program under the Honors Lawyering Program and offers two formal joint-degree programs.

Honors Lawyering Program

The Honors Lawyering Program (HLP) takes a unique approach to legal education, integrating the theory, skills, and values learned in the classroom with actual work in the legal community—a modern version of the traditional apprenticeship. HLP students attend a regular first-year curriculum, participate in an intensive skills-focused summer session, and work at a full-time fall apprenticeship. In the spring, students return to full-time classes with a new appreciation for the application of law to practice. During their third year, students complete a second apprenticeship and have the option to enroll in additional, practice-based courses. HLP courses meet in small sections that integrate lawyering skills training with the substantive law curriculum. By the third week, students begin representing real clients under the guidance and supervision of the professors, who are themselves practicing attorneys. Students may apprentice in private law firms, companies, courts, government agencies, and public interest organizations.

Public Interest Law

At Golden Gate Law, the law curriculum and programs integrate public interest law and service to the community. Students may earn a public interest law certificate of specialization by completing 14 credits of approved elective courses, a 150-hour public interest practicum, and 25 hours of work for a campus or community organization. Students with prior commitment to public and community service may be selected to participate in the Public Interest Law Scholars Program (PISP), which provides students with scholarships and a summer employment stipend.

Joint Degrees and Certificates of Specialization

Students may earn the following joint degrees: JD/MBA and JD/PhD in Clinical Psychology.

Golden Gate also offers JD students the opportunity to earn specialization certificates in Business Law, Criminal Law, Environmental Law, Intellectual Property Law, International Law, Labor and Employment Law, Litigation, Public Interest Law, Real Estate Law, and Taxation. Requirements for the areas of specialization vary, but students generally complete coursework and clinical practice to earn a certificate.

Clinical Programs

Golden Gate University has one of the most extensive clinical programs in the country, offering students opportunities to earn academic credit while working closely with practicing attorneys.

The law school has three on-site clinics. In the Women's Employment Rights Clinic, students represent low-income women with employment-related problems. Through the Environmental Law and Justice Clinic, students assist Northern California communities in protecting their environmental interests and reducing their exposure to toxins. Our Pro Bono Tax Clinic provides assistance to low-income individuals in tax disputes before the California Board of Equalization.

In field placement externships, students work under the supervision of faculty, judges, and attorneys in government agencies, law offices, and judges' chambers. These include Capital Post-Conviction Defense, Criminal Litigation, Consumer Rights, Environmental Law, Family Law, Homeless Advocacy, Judicial Externship Program, Real Estate Law, and Youth Law.

Summer Programs

Students in our study-abroad program take courses covering a number of international topics currently of interest in the legal world. The curriculum combines introductory courses on the host country's legal systems and comparative law courses. Students also benefit from learning under the guidance of faculty from Golden Gate University School of Law, from faculty and practitioners at other ABA-accredited law schools, and from faculty and practitioners in the host country. Golden Gate Law currently offers a summer-abroad program in Paris, France.

Graduate Programs

Golden Gate University School of Law offers five LLM programs: Environmental Law, Intellectual Property Law, International Legal Studies, Taxation, and US Legal Studies. It also offers an SJD program in International Legal Studies.

Law Library

The Law Library houses the largest law collection in the San Francisco financial district—more than 350,000 volumes. Its holdings include a comprehensive series of case law reporters, statutes, digests, encyclopedias, periodicals, and treatises dealing with American law; a strong tax collection; a microforms collection; and a growing body of work in environmental law, law and literature, and international law. International law holdings target selected Pacific Rim countries and English, Canadian, and other Commonwealth materials. Students in the Law Library have access to the Internet and a variety of Internet-based legal databases.

Career Services and Placement

The Law Career Services (LCS) office helps students prepare for a successful legal career by providing many services throughout law school and beyond. LCS helps students research the legal market, develop contacts, and build skills through jobs and internships. For first-year students, LCS provides an online *Job Search Guide* and workshops on writing résumés and cover letters. For upper-division students, LCS offers print and online job listings; talks by graduates about their career experiences; individual and small-group career counseling; job-search skills workshops, panels, and events highlighting the career paths of Golden Gate alumni and other attorneys; special recruitment programs; and more. Many of these services continue after graduation.

Law Reviews, Journals, and Student Organizations

Golden Gate Law publishes the *Golden Gate University Law Review*, the *Environmental Law Journal*, and the *Annual Survey of International and Comparative Law*. The *Law Review* and journals provide students with the opportunity to showcase their research, writing, and editing skills. The law school also has more than 25 student organizations ranging from groups representing minority students to groups focusing on specific areas of law. An active student government represents the law school student body on important issues facing individuals, student organizations, and the law school. Through these groups, students have many opportunities to participate in programs and attend lectures hosted by a variety of organizations and journals. These opportunities enrich the law school learning experience, and students are strongly encouraged to participate at all levels.

Admission and Scholarships

Golden Gate University School of Law awards scholarships to both entering and continuing students. All students are reviewed for scholarships as part of the admission process.

Golden Gate Law also offers a Public Interest Scholars Program (PISP) Scholarship and an Environmental Law Scholarship. These scholarships are awarded in the amount of $5,000 per year, on a three- or four-year basis. Both the PISP Scholarship and the Environmental Law Scholarship require a separate statement of interest and a list of prior commitment/activities from the student to be considered.

APPLICANT PROFILE

Golden Gate University School of Law
This grid includes only applicants who earned 120–180 LSAT scores under standard administrations.

LSAT Score	3.75 +		3.50–3.74		3.25–3.49		3.00–3.24		2.75–2.99		2.50–2.74		2.25–2.49		2.00–2.24		Below 2.00		No GPA		Total	
	Apps	Adm	Apps	Adm	Apps	Adm	Apps	Adm	Apps	Adm	Apps	Adm	Apps	Adm	Apps	Adm	Apps	Adm	Apps	Adm	Apps	Adm
175–180	0	0	0	0	0	0	0	0	0	0	0	0	0	0	0	0	0	0	0	0	0	0
170–174	3	3	2	2	0	0	3	3	0	0	0	0	0	0	0	0	0	0	0	0	8	8
165–169	5	5	3	3	7	7	9	6	4	4	4	4	2	1	0	0	1	1	1	1	36	32
160–164	20	18	42	40	42	39	50	46	26	23	18	15	7	5	6	4	3	1	4	3	218	194
155–159	48	46	98	92	119	110	122	106	105	84	62	49	39	25	15	9	4	2	11	5	623	528
150–154	51	44	138	101	171	131	214	153	152	81	86	39	44	14	22	9	2	0	14	6	894	578
145–149	21	11	41	15	108	22	130	20	129	19	58	5	31	3	14	1	2	0	9	0	543	96
140–144	8	2	20	2	38	1	49	4	39	0	48	1	26	0	3	0	2	0	8	0	241	10
135–139	4	1	5	1	13	0	16	1	17	0	15	0	17	0	8	0	3	0	4	0	102	3
130–134	0	0	0	0	1	0	2	0	2	0	6	0	1	0	7	0	0	0	1	0	20	0
125–129	0	0	1	0	0	0	1	0	0	0	3	0	1	0	0	0	0	0	0	0	6	0
120–124	0	0	0	0	0	0	0	0	0	0	0	0	0	0	0	0	0	0	0	0	0	0
Total	160	130	350	256	499	310	596	339	474	211	300	113	168	48	75	23	17	4	52	15	2691	1449

Apps = Number of Applicants
Adm = Number Admitted
Reflects 99% of the total applicant pool; highest LSAT data reported.

GONZAGA UNIVERSITY SCHOOL OF LAW

PO Box 3528
Spokane, WA 99220-3528
Phone: 800.793.1710 or 509.313.5532; Fax: 509.313.3697
E-mail: admissions@lawschool.gonzaga.edu; Website: www.law.gonzaga.edu

ABA
Approved
Since
1951

The Basics

Type of school	Private
Term	Semester
Application deadline	2/1 4/15
Application fee	$50
Financial aid deadline	2/1
Can first year start other than fall?	Yes
Student to faculty ratio	14.6 to 1
# of housing spaces available restricted to law students	
graduate housing for which law students are eligible	507

Faculty and Administrators

	Total		Men		Women		Minorities	
	Spr	Fall	Spr	Fall	Spr	Fall	Spr	Fall
Full-time	29	28	15	17	14	11	2	4
Other full-time	1	1	0	0	1	1	0	0
Deans, librarians, & others who teach	5	5	3	3	2	2	1	1
Part-time	36	31	26	23	10	8	0	0
Total	71	65	44	43	27	22	3	5

JD Enrollment and Ethnicity

	Men		Women		Full-Time		Part-Time		1st-Year		Total		JD Degs. Awd.
	#	%	#	%	#	%	#	%	#	%	#	%	
All Hispanics	11	3.5	5	2.6	16	3.2	0	0.0	8	4.5	16	3.2	2
Am. Ind./AK Nat.	7	2.2	3	1.5	10	2.0	0	0.0	3	1.7	10	2.0	0
Asian	3	1.0	2	1.0	5	1.0	0	0.0	0	0.0	5	1.0	6
Black/Af. Am.	0	0.0	1	0.5	1	0.2	0	0.0	0	0.0	1	0.2	1
Nat. HI/Pac. Isl.	10	3.2	8	4.1	18	3.6	0	0.0	7	3.9	18	3.6	0
2 or more races	3	1.0	4	2.1	7	1.4	0	0.0	2	1.1	7	1.4	0
Subtotal (minor.)	34	10.9	23	11.8	57	11.3	0	0.0	20	11.2	57	11.2	9
Nonres. Alien	0	0.0	0	0.0	0	0.0	0	0.0	0	0.0	0	0.0	0
White/Cauc.	230	73.7	134	68.7	361	71.8	3	75.0	120	67.0	364	71.8	169
Unknown	48	15.4	38	19.5	85	16.9	1	25.0	39	21.8	86	17.0	3
Total	312	61.5	195	38.5	503	99.2	4	0.8	179	35.3	507		181

Curriculum

	Full-Time	Part-Time
Typical first-year section size	90	0
Is there typically a "small section" of the first-year class, other than Legal Writing, taught by full-time faculty	Yes	No
If yes, typical size offered last year	45	
# of classroom course titles beyond first-year curriculum		98
# of upper division courses, excluding seminars, with an enrollment: Under 25		68
25–49		27
50–74		16
75–99		1
100+		0
# of seminars		1
# of seminar positions available		19
# of seminar positions filled	19	0
# of positions available in simulation courses		342
# of simulation positions filled	342	0
# of positions available in faculty supervised clinical courses		165
# of faculty supervised clinical positions filled	165	0
# involved in field placements	150	0
# involved in law journals	69	0
# involved in moot court or trial competitions	32	0
# of credit hours required to graduate		90

Transfers

Transfers in	3
Transfers out	16

Tuition and Fees

	Resident	Nonresident
Full-time	$32,775	$32,775
Part-time		
Tuition Guarantee Program		N

Living Expenses

Estimated living expenses for singles

Living on campus	Living off campus	Living at home
$14,365	$14,365	$14,365

ABA Approved Since 1951

GPA and LSAT Scores

	Total	Full-Time	Part-Time
# of apps	1,924	1,924	0
# of offers	762	762	0
# of matrics	183	183	0
75% GPA	3.57	3.57	0.00
Median GPA	3.36	3.36	0.00
25% GPA	3.11	3.11	0.00
75% LSAT	157	157	0
Median LSAT	155	155	0
25% LSAT	154	154	0

Grants and Scholarships (from prior year)

	Total #	Total %	Full-Time #	Full-Time %	Part-Time #	Part-Time %
Total # of students	526		516		10	
Total # receiving grants	385	73.2	385	74.6	0	0.0
Less than 1/2 tuition	337	64.1	337	65.3	0	0.0
Half to full tuition	29	5.5	29	5.6	0	0.0
Full tuition	19	3.6	19	3.7	0	0.0
More than full tuition	0	0.0	0	0.0	0	0.0
Median grant amount			$12,000		$0	

Informational and Library Resources

Total amount spent on library materials	$882,080
Study seating capacity inside the library	507
# of full-time equivalent professional librarians	5
Hours per week library is open	110
# of open, wired connections available to students	140
# of networked computers available for use by students	83
Has wireless network?	Y
Requires computer?	N

JD Attrition (from prior year)

	Academic #	Other #	Total #	Total %
1st year	5	20	25	13.4
2nd year	0	0	0	0.0
3rd year	0	0	0	0.0
4th year	0	0	0	0.0

Employment (9 months after graduation)

	Total	Percentage
Employment status known	181	98.9
Employment status unknown	2	1.1
Employed	156	86.2
Pursuing graduate degrees	10	5.5
Unemployed (seeking, not seeking, or studying for the bar)	7	3.9
Type of Employment		
# employed in law firms	85	54.5
# employed in business and industry	34	21.8
# employed in government	16	10.3
# employed in public interest	8	5.1
# employed as judicial clerks	10	6.4
# employed in academia	3	1.9
Geographic Location		
# employed in state	72	46.2
# employed outside the US	1	0.6
# of states where employed	25	

Bar Passage Rates

First-time takers	172	Reporting %	86.63
Average school %	71.15	Average state %	76.76

Average pass difference −5.61

Jurisdiction	Takers	Passers	Pass %	State %	Diff %
Washington	100	67	67.00	74.42	−7.42
Utah	13	12	92.31	88.94	3.37
California	11	5	45.45	73.19	−27.74
Idaho	10	9	90.00	85.81	4.19
Others (2)	15	13	86.67		

GONZAGA UNIVERSITY SCHOOL OF LAW

PO Box 3528
Spokane, WA 99220-3528
Phone: 800.793.1710 or 509.313.5532; Fax: 509.313.3697
E-mail: admissions@lawschool.gonzaga.edu; Website: www.law.gonzaga.edu

Introduction

Gonzaga University School of Law belongs to a long and distinguished tradition of humanistic, Catholic, and Jesuit education. Founded in 1887, Gonzaga continues to maintain the tradition of academic excellence in education that is at the heart of the mission of the 450-year-old Jesuit order. The School of Law, established in 1912, is a member of the AALS and is approved by the ABA. Gonzaga University is committed to educating a diverse student community, including students of all backgrounds and beliefs.

The campus is located in Spokane, Washington, a four-season city with the Spokane River flowing through its center. Step outside the School of Law onto the Centennial Trail to enjoy the picturesque walk into beautiful downtown Spokane. The metropolitan area of approximately 400,000 people serves as the regional hub of the Inland Northwest, a large area running from the Cascade Mountains in the west to the Rockies in the east. Canada is a mere 100 miles to the north. For domestic and international travel, the Spokane International Airport is conveniently located 10 miles from the Gonzaga University campus.

Spokane is a cultural center for the area, with professional and amateur theater groups, a symphony, and numerous art galleries and other cultural offerings. Spokane also serves as a regional economic hub for health care, agriculture, light industry, as well as a recreational sports area abundant with lakes, mountains, and forests. In minutes you can get away from the city's robust, rapidly growing business community to the surrounding pine-covered hills.

Physical Facilities and Library

Rising from the banks of the beautiful Spokane River, Gonzaga University School of Law provides a stunning setting for research and learning. The law school offers a variety of classroom and library environments that support today's interactive teaching methods. Features throughout the building encourage students to greet each other and linger to talk and debate ideas in beautiful outdoor spaces, roof plazas, balconies, and comfortable lounges. Miles of state-of-the-art voice, data, and video cable provide the highway for audiovisual, computer, and telecommunications technology throughout the building. The mix of classrooms, rooms for simulations of various sizes, and clinical teaching space provides flexibility to preserve the best of traditional law teaching while introducing new methods. The Chastek Library is the largest legal research facility between Seattle and Minneapolis. With a collection of over 300,000 volumes and microform equivalents, plus an extensive array of electronic resources, the library provides access to legal materials and offers many services to support the instructional, research, and scholarly endeavors of the law school and university community. The School of Law library is equipped with a wireless network and has two computer labs. Librarians provide reference support and regularly teach sessions on legal research using both traditional and electronic resources.

Curriculum and Faculty

There is a deliberate and delicate balance to legal education at Gonzaga. The rigorous curriculum focuses on legal analysis, problem solving, values, and ethics. Equally as important is the emphasis on practical experience to develop real-world lawyering skills. The unique first-year program at Gonzaga that exposes students to simulated skills training in litigation and transactional work in the fall and spring semesters, respectively, evidences Gonzaga's commitment to these goals.

The term "teaching faculty" applies in a very special way to the School of Law faculty. The Jesuit tradition demands a high degree of student-professor interaction inside and outside the classroom, and this emphasis attracts exceptional faculty. Gonzaga's focus on the individual student, a favorable student-to-faculty ratio, and the promotion of positive rather than negative competition provides an atmosphere of success in which to study.

Special Programs

The first-year program at Gonzaga pairs two doctrinal courses each semester with a skills and professionalism lab that immediately begins the process of turning law students into lawyers. In the fall semester, Civil Procedure and Torts are paired with a lab that emphasizes the development of litigation skills. In addition, students are introduced to legal theory during the fall of first year, via a course emphasizing different perspectives on the law. In the spring, Contracts and Property are paired with a lab that exposes the students to the business law side of the profession. Both labs also include instruction and exercises that are designed to help our students begin to identify and develop the professional values and habits that will be a part of their lives as attorneys. All students are required to engage in experiential learning, either through working in a professional externship or in Gonzaga's legal clinic, during their final year of studies.

The Center for Law in Public Service supports the aspirations of students who study law in order to use their knowledge and skills for public service, whether they wish to make a full-time practice of public service law or to promote the public good through part-time pro bono legal work. The center provides curricular and extracurricular means for students to acquire the skills and substantive knowledge applicable to practicing public service law.

The Commercial Law Center imparts the legal and theoretical knowledge and teaches the lawyering skills needed to represent businesses and consumers in all manner of commercial transactions, including sales, leases, licenses, asset-based lending, and structured finance.

The Indian Law Program includes courses on federal and tribal Indian law, as well as Native American dispute resolution traditions, that equip students with the skills necessary to identify and understand legal and cultural issues relating to tribal sovereignty, tribal court procedures, and tribal government. The Indian Law Program includes clinical education opportunities for representation of tribal members in tribal courts as well as representation of Native Americans in the state court system. The Law School is committed to the recruitment of Native American students and the creation of an institutional environment that promotes their academic success.

Gonzaga offers three dual-degree programs leading to the JD/MBA, the JD/MAcc, and the JD/MSW degrees. These prepare students to enter fields that require, respectively, thorough knowledge of the law and business, accountancy, and social services.

Admission

The School of Law endeavors to attract students with ambitious minds, professional motivation, and commitment to the highest ethics and values of the legal profession and to public service. Consideration of applicants is not restricted to impersonal statistics, but includes recognition and review of the enriching qualities of applicants reflected in their personal statement, résumé, and letters of recommendation. Gonzaga seeks to enroll an ethnically and geographically diverse student body.

Student Activities

Gonzaga's educational philosophy is based on the centuries-old Ignatian model of educating the whole person—mind, body, and spirit. Students, therefore, find it easy to become involved in a broad range of activities at the School of Law. Gonzaga is a major player in national moot court competitions and fields a variety of moot court teams. The student-run *Gonzaga Law Review* is circulated throughout the country, and the *Gonzaga Journal of International Law*, the online international law journal, receives submissions from around the world. The Student Bar Association is a strong, active organization that encourages student involvement, and there is ample opportunity to participate in intraschool moot court competitions, legal fraternities, and other organizations and activities. Gonzaga's student organizations are diverse in nature and, whatever your interests or career goals, there are activities available that will enhance your knowledge and abilities, while contributing to the community.

Housing

The Gonzaga campus is in a residential area within close proximity to downtown Spokane. Housing is available within walking distance to the law school, and rental rates are reasonably priced compared to most large population centers. University owned on- and off-campus housing is available to law students on a space-available basis. For further information, please review the Gonzaga University Housing and Residence Office website: www.gonzaga.edu/Student-Life/Off-Campus-Living/GU-Owned.asp.

Financial Aid

Law school is a career investment. For students who need financial assistance to help fund this investment, we encourage filing the FAFSA. Gonzaga also provides more than $2 million in scholarship aid to entering law students, and your admission application will serve as your scholarship application. However, students who are interested in applying for the Thomas More Scholarship need to apply separately. Gonzaga awards up to five Thomas More Scholarships a year, covering 100 percent of tuition.

Career Services

The Career Services Office is committed to serving the needs of employers, students, and alumni. The office's priority is to match qualified students and alumni with employers. Recognizing that career development is a lifelong process, the office provides graduates access to career services throughout their professional lives. In addition, the office provides employers with timely and effective assistance to fill their organization's hiring needs. Employers are encouraged to utilize our recruitment services, including online job postings, job fairs, customized recruiting, and interviewing programs. Career services is focused on professional development, including up-to-date job listings, library resources, interview tools, workshops, career counseling, and presentations by attorneys discussing the practice of law. Prospective students are encouraged to meet with career counselors to learn more about legal opportunities.

APPLICANT PROFILE

Gonzaga University School of Law
This grid includes only applicants who earned 120–180 LSAT scores under standard administrations.

LSAT Score	3.75 +		3.50–3.74		3.25–3.49		3.00–3.24		2.75–2.99		2.50–2.74		2.25–2.49		2.00–2.24		Below 2.00		No GPA		Total	
	Apps	Adm	Apps	Adm	Apps	Adm	Apps	Adm	Apps	Adm	Apps	Adm	Apps	Adm	Apps	Adm	Apps	Adm	Apps	Adm	Apps	Adm
170–180	2	2	3	3	1	1	0	0	0	0	1	0	0	0	0	0	0	0	0	0	7	6
165–169	9	9	6	6	7	7	4	4	3	2	4	0	1	1	0	0	1	0	0	0	35	29
160–164	35	33	36	34	42	41	38	29	30	18	11	4	3	0	3	0	1	0	0	0	199	159
155–159	62	55	110	83	131	93	104	72	72	38	37	7	14	2	4	0	3	0	2	0	539	350
150–154	68	30	129	56	189	65	148	51	93	12	32	2	21	0	4	0	2	0	2	0	688	216
145–149	21	0	44	0	77	0	60	0	40	1	23	0	12	1	6	0	0	0	4	0	287	2
140–144	5	0	14	0	31	0	24	0	24	0	9	0	7	0	3	0	2	0	1	0	120	0
Below 140	2	0	2	0	4	0	8	0	9	0	6	0	3	0	4	1	1	0	2	0	41	1
Total	204	129	344	182	482	207	386	156	271	71	123	13	61	4	24	1	10	0	11	0	1916	763

Apps = Number of Applicants
Adm = Number Admitted
Reflects 99% of the total applicant pool; highest LSAT data reported.

HAMLINE UNIVERSITY SCHOOL OF LAW

1536 Hewitt Avenue
St. Paul, MN 55104
Phone: 651.523.2461, 800.388.3688; Fax: 651.523.3064
E-mail: lawadm@hamline.edu; Website: www.hamline.edu/law

ABA
Approved
Since
1975

The Basics

Type of school	Private
Term	Semester
Application deadline	4/1
Application fee	$35
Financial aid deadline	4/10
Can first year start other than fall?	No
Student to faculty ratio	15.1 to 1
# of housing spaces available restricted to law students	
graduate housing for which law students are eligible	60

Faculty and Administrators

	Total		Men		Women		Minorities	
	Spr	Fall	Spr	Fall	Spr	Fall	Spr	Fall
Full-time	33	33	18	19	15	14	5	3
Other full-time	0	1	0	1	0	0	0	0
Deans, librarians, & others who teach	8	9	2	2	6	7	2	3
Part-time	61	55	36	30	25	25	4	3
Total	102	98	56	52	46	46	11	9

Curriculum

	Full-Time	Part-Time
Typical first-year section size	60	40
Is there typically a "small section" of the first-year class, other than Legal Writing, taught by full-time faculty	No	No
If yes, typical size offered last year		
# of classroom course titles beyond first-year curriculum	175	

# of upper division courses, excluding seminars, with an enrollment:		
	Under 25	120
	25–49	61
	50–74	13
	75–99	2
	100+	0

# of seminars	17	
# of seminar positions available	282	
# of seminar positions filled	200	32
# of positions available in simulation courses	712	
# of simulation positions filled	401	160
# of positions available in faculty supervised clinical courses	77	
# of faculty supervised clinical positions filled	67	5
# involved in field placements	103	14
# involved in law journals	70	11
# involved in moot court or trial competitions	55	4
# of credit hours required to graduate	88	

JD Enrollment and Ethnicity

	Men #	Men %	Women #	Women %	Full-Time #	Full-Time %	Part-Time #	Part-Time %	1st-Year #	1st-Year %	Total #	Total %	JD Degs. Awd.
All Hispanics	10	3.2	15	4.4	15	3.3	10	5.1	7	3.1	25	3.8	6
Am. Ind./AK Nat.	2	0.6	3	0.9	2	0.4	3	1.5	1	0.4	5	0.8	1
Asian	16	5.1	25	7.4	31	6.8	10	5.1	17	7.5	41	6.3	9
Black/Af. Am.	4	1.3	18	5.3	15	3.3	7	3.6	13	5.7	22	3.4	13
Nat. Hl/Pac. Isl.	1	0.3	0	0.0	0	0.0	1	0.5	1	0.4	1	0.2	0
2 or more races	1	0.3	1	0.3	0	0.0	2	1.0	1	0.4	2	0.3	0
Subtotal (minor.)	34	10.9	62	18.3	63	13.8	33	16.8	40	17.6	96	14.7	29
Nonres. Alien	0	0.0	2	0.6	1	0.2	1	0.5	0	0.0	2	0.3	0
White/Cauc.	262	83.7	256	75.5	368	80.7	150	76.5	182	80.2	518	79.4	147
Unknown	17	5.4	19	5.6	24	5.3	12	6.1	5	2.2	36	5.5	18
Total	313	48.0	339	52.0	456	69.9	196	30.1	227	34.8	652		198

Transfers

Transfers in	3
Transfers out	10

Tuition and Fees

	Resident	Nonresident
Full-time	$33,506	$33,506
Part-time	$24,144	$24,144
Tuition Guarantee Program		N

Living Expenses

Estimated living expenses for singles

Living on campus	Living off campus	Living at home
$13,000	$17,660	$17,660

HAMLINE UNIVERSITY SCHOOL OF LAW

*ABA
Approved
Since
1975*

GPA and LSAT Scores

	Total	Full-Time	Part-Time
# of apps	1,350	1,108	242
# of offers	757	615	142
# of matrics	227	159	68
75% GPA	3.61	3.63	3.53
Median GPA	3.39	3.42	3.32
25% GPA	3.16	3.21	2.94
75% LSAT	156	156	156
Median LSAT	153	153	151
25% LSAT	149	149	146

Grants and Scholarships (from prior year)

	Total		Full-Time		Part-Time	
	#	%	#	%	#	%
Total # of students	650		468		182	
Total # receiving grants	340	52.3	267	57.1	73	40.1
Less than 1/2 tuition	129	19.8	89	19.0	40	22.0
Half to full tuition	131	20.2	102	21.8	29	15.9
Full tuition	77	11.8	73	15.6	4	2.2
More than full tuition	3	0.5	3	0.6	0	0.0
Median grant amount			$18,960		$9,438	

Informational and Library Resources

Total amount spent on library materials	$838,043
Study seating capacity inside the library	335
# of full-time equivalent professional librarians	7
Hours per week library is open	116
# of open, wired connections available to students	506
# of networked computers available for use by students	48
Has wireless network?	Y
Requires computer?	Y

JD Attrition (from prior year)

	Academic	Other	Total	
	#	#	#	%
1st year	4	2	6	2.9
2nd year	2	19	21	10.5
3rd year	0	0	0	0.0
4th year	0	0	0	0.0

Employment (9 months after graduation)

	Total	Percentage
Employment status known	227	97.0
Employment status unknown	7	3.0
Employed	192	84.6
Pursuing graduate degrees	5	2.2
Unemployed (seeking, not seeking, or studying for the bar)	10	4.4
Type of Employment		
# employed in law firms	73	38.0
# employed in business and industry	55	28.6
# employed in government	27	14.1
# employed in public interest	4	2.1
# employed as judicial clerks	17	8.9
# employed in academia	6	3.1
Geographic Location		
# employed in state	138	71.9
# employed outside the US	3	1.6
# of states where employed		15

Bar Passage Rates

First-time takers	243	Reporting %	73.66
Average school %	88.83	Average state %	89.58

Average pass difference −0.75

Jurisdiction	Takers	Passers	Pass %	State %	Diff %
Minnesota	179	159	88.83	89.58	−0.75

HAMLINE UNIVERSITY SCHOOL OF LAW

1536 Hewitt Avenue
St. Paul, MN 55104
Phone: 651.523.2461, 800.388.3688; Fax: 651.523.3064
E-mail: lawadm@hamline.edu; Website: www.hamline.edu/law

Introduction

Hamline University School of Law is a collaborative community where students work together to best serve clients and society. Hamline offers a full-time weekday and part-time weekend program, both of which provide a challenging curriculum, excellent faculty, and diverse experiential learning opportunities. Our expert faculty challenges students to realize their full potential through innovative educational experiences—both inside and outside the classroom. Hamline students graduate ready to practice law and inspired to use their legal education to solve problems and make a difference in the world.

The school also serves as a catalyst for reframing the legal landscape through distinguished guest speakers, thought-provoking symposia, and nationally recognized centers of excellence, such as Hamline's Dispute Resolution Institute and Health Law Institute. A Business Law Institute was added in 2010. Hamline's faculty includes nationally recognized experts in bioethics, intellectual property, international trade, corporate law, and dispute resolution. Other faculty members are renowned for scholarship and academic leadership in health law, criminal law, constitutional law, trial advocacy, and many other fields.

Hamline alumni are employed in all aspects of the law, which include private practice, government agencies, public and private corporate environments, as well as in the court system as prosecutors, public defenders, and members of the judiciary at the state and federal levels. Some alumni use their legal education as a backdrop for nontraditional legal employment outside the justice system. Hamline alumni are active and involved with the School of Law by serving as moot court competition judges, adjunct faculty, practicum supervisors, program and classroom speakers, and as mentors for individual students.

Library and Facilities

Located within the vibrant St. Paul-Minneapolis urban setting, the Hamline University School of Law is situated in the heart of Hamline University's 55-acre campus. The Law Library staff is readily available to provide support services, along with nearly 300,000 volumes and electronic databases—giving students access to the libraries of seven other colleges and universities through a consortium agreement. Hamline's Annette K. Levine Moot Court Room provides a technologically relevant setting for moot court competitions and for observing actual court proceedings.

Rigorous and Supportive Learning Environment

Hamline's core curriculum provides the analytical grounding necessary for success. In addition to a rich full-time program, Hamline offers a unique part-time weekend program that is taught by the same respected faculty members who teach in the day program. The law school also offers dual-degree and course exchange options, which allow students to combine their legal education with a second disciplinary focus in the areas of business administration, public administration, nonprofit management, creative writing, and organizational leadership.

Led by the internationally heralded Dispute Resolution Institute, our curriculum in negotiations, arbitration, and mediation is second to none. In addition, the Health Law Institute offers extensive academic and experiential learning opportunities for students interested in pursuing careers in the health law arena.

Hamline's rigorous offerings reflect considerable depth and innovation. Our newly reconfigured first-year curriculum includes International Law as well as Practice, Problem-Solving and Professionalism (P3), a new course designed to provide students with the context of legal practice and to frame lawyering as a broad profession grounded in problem-solving and dispute resolution. Hamline students may concentrate their studies in a variety of substantive areas: alternative dispute resolution, corporate/commercial law, child advocacy, criminal law, government and regulatory affairs, health law, intellectual property, international law, labor and employment, litigation and trial practice, property law, and public law and human rights.

At Hamline, professors move beyond traditional lectures to offer truly collaborative, student-centered classroom experiences while simultaneously conducting cutting-edge scholarship. Our accessible professors are dedicated to an open-door policy. An emphasis on seminars allows students to learn in small classes, make presentations, and create original research on topics of personal interest, ensuring that students work closely with Hamline's dedicated faculty throughout their law school experience. The Constance Bakken Fellows program provides funding for collaborative research between faculty and students.

Experiential Learning: At Home and Abroad

Hamline students further expand their skills by competing in appellate advocacy and negotiation competitions throughout the country and around the world. Hamline's 10 legal clinics give students real-world experience in the practice of health law, immigration law, small business planning, criminal law, child advocacy, alternative dispute resolution, education law, and trial practice. Each clinic operates as a small law office with students handling their own caseload and representing clients under the supervision of experienced in-house or adjunct faculty members.

Likewise, Hamline's externship program enables students to work directly with mentor attorneys and judges, and places students in private law firms, corporations, judges' chambers, public agencies, legislative offices, and businesses. In addition, all Hamline students must complete 24 pro bono service hours as a graduation requirement.

Through experiential learning opportunities, Hamline students absorb real-world legal lessons, gain a wealth of knowledge in case management and other lawyering skills, and establish valuable contacts in the professional legal community.

Hamline encourages international study for the development of a truly global perspective. Many students participate in an international exchange program with Hamline's European law school partners. Others compete in the Vienna International Moot Court Competition. Hamline provides conferences, classes, and training in London, Oslo, Budapest, and Jerusalem, among other foreign locations.

With international lawyers from around the world in our master of laws (LLM) program and our academic programs abroad, Hamline offers a truly global learning environment.

A Dynamic Student Community

Hamline attracts a dynamic and diverse student population. Students in our fall 2010 incoming class represented 28 states and 117 undergraduate institutions; 52 percent were women and 17.5 percent were students of color. Hamline also offers a graduate program leading to an LLM degree for lawyers holding a bachelor of laws (LLB) or equivalent degree from outside the United States. These students contribute to the cultural richness of the Hamline learning community.

Opportunities for student involvement abound at Hamline University School of Law. The *Hamline Law Review* and the *Hamline Journal of Public Law and Policy* are entirely staffed by law students. Hamline students also provide editorial assistance for the internationally respected *Journal of Law and Religion*. Hamline students can participate in more than 15 moot court teams, and with 35 active student organizations, students easily find professional, cultural and social connections to match their interests.

Hamline law students believe they can make a difference in their community, and frequently this passion can be seen through the innovative programs and initiatives they develop on campus. In recent years, for example, members of the Hamline Latino Law Student Association (LLSA) launched an annual event, Juris Fiesta, which raises funds for the Latino Law Student Scholarship and attracts national Latino legal leaders as keynote speakers. Another student organization, the Hamline Veteran's Association, has established an endowed annual scholarship for an eligible veteran.

Career Assistance

The Career Services Office (CSO) is committed to assisting all Hamline law students in career planning and job searches. Dedicated and experienced counselors provide informational programs, mock interviews, one-on-one career counseling, résumé assistance, and networking opportunities through an established mentoring program. They also organize on-campus interviews and work extensively with employers to advance Hamline law students and to solicit postings and information for the online job bank. Students are strongly encouraged to participate in Hamline's CSO programs and to build professional networks with alumni and other legal professionals.

Admission and Financial Aid

The School of Law maintains a selection process that emphasizes a rigorous but fair examination of each person as an individual, not merely as a set of credentials. In addition to the LSAT and undergraduate GPA, the admission committee gives significant weight to motivation, personal experiences, employment history, graduate education, maturity, letters of recommendation, and the ability to articulate one's interest in, and suitability for, the study of law. Hamline's admission policy is designed to enhance the academic rigor, professional dedication, social concern, and diversity of the student body, including cultural, economic, sexual orientation, racial, and ethnic composition. Hamline also provides a comprehensive financial aid program, which includes merit-based scholarships. At Hamline, 95 percent of law students qualify for need-based loans.

APPLICANT PROFILE

Hamline University School of Law
This grid includes only applicants with 120–180 LSAT scores earned under standard administrations.

LSAT Score	3.75 +		3.50–3.74		3.25–3.49		3.00–3.24		2.75–2.99		2.50–2.74		Below 2.50		No GPA		Totals	
	Apps	Adm	Apps	Adm	Apps	Adm	Apps	Adm	Apps	Adm	Apps	Adm	Apps	Adm	Apps	Adm	Apps	Adm
170–180	2	2	1	1	1	1	2	2	0	0	0	0	0	0	0	0	6	6
165–169	9	9	5	5	1	1	2	2	7	6	1	0	2	2	0	0	27	25
160–164	17	17	26	25	17	16	16	15	11	10	6	4	4	2	1	0	98	89
155–159	36	36	40	40	49	48	48	44	26	19	14	8	11	3	1	1	225	199
150–154	29	29	78	74	89	79	74	55	51	30	26	7	24	3	1	0	372	277
145–149	27	25	55	46	78	35	79	23	55	7	37	2	32	1	5	3	368	142
140–144	8	5	17	5	28	7	30	1	30	0	18	0	15	0	5	0	151	18
Below 140	4	0	2	0	10	0	18	0	18	0	20	0	18	0	12	0	102	0
Total	132	123	224	196	273	187	269	142	198	72	122	21	106	11	25	4	1349	756

Apps = Number of Applicants
Adm = Number Admitted
Reflects 99% of the total applicant pool; highest LSAT data reported.

HARVARD LAW SCHOOL

1515 Massachusetts Avenue, Austin Hall
Cambridge, MA 02138
Phone: 617.495.3109
E-mail: jdadmiss@law.harvard.edu; Website: www.law.harvard.edu

ABA
Approved
Since
1923

The Basics

Type of school	Private
Term	Semester
Application deadline	2/1
Application fee	$85
Financial aid deadline	4/1
Can first year start other than fall?	No
Student to faculty ratio	12.3 to 1
# of housing spaces available restricted to law students	603
graduate housing for which law students are eligible	3,211

Faculty and Administrators

	Total		Men		Women		Minorities	
	Spr	Fall	Spr	Fall	Spr	Fall	Spr	Fall
Full-time	119	115	96	90	23	25	15	14
Other full-time	26	26	14	15	12	11	4	4
Deans, librarians, & others who teach	13	13	8	8	5	5	5	5
Part-time	6	5	6	5	0	0	1	5
Total	164	159	124	118	40	41	25	28

Curriculum

		Full-Time	Part-Time
Typical first-year section size		80	0
Is there typically a "small section" of the first-year class, other than Legal Writing, taught by full-time faculty		No	No
If yes, typical size offered last year			
# of classroom course titles beyond first-year curriculum		331	
# of upper division	Under 25	104	
courses, excluding	25–49	67	
seminars, with	50–74	32	
an enrollment:	75–99	19	
	100+	21	
# of seminars		79	
# of seminar positions available		1,140	
# of seminar positions filled		1,106	0
# of positions available in simulation courses		1,069	
# of simulation positions filled		1,012	0
# of positions available in faculty supervised clinical courses		618	
# of faculty supervised clinical positions filled	519		0
# involved in field placements		233	0
# involved in law journals		1,000	0
# involved in moot court or trial competitions	350		0
# of credit hours required to graduate		84	

JD Enrollment and Ethnicity

	Men		Women		Full-Time		Part-Time		1st-Year		Total		JD Degs. Awd.
	#	%	#	%	#	%	#	%	#	%	#	%	
All Hispanics	68	7.5	69	8.3	137	7.9	0	0.0	48	8.6	137	7.9	31
Am. Ind./AK Nat.	7	0.8	3	0.4	10	0.6	0	0.0	2	0.4	10	0.6	3
Asian	42	4.7	45	5.4	87	5.0	0	0.0	5	0.9	87	5.0	56
Black/Af. Am.	87	9.6	108	13.0	195	11.3	0	0.0	60	10.7	195	11.3	71
Nat. HI/Pac. Isl.	53	5.9	77	9.3	130	7.5	0	0.0	80	14.3	130	7.5	0
2 or more races	5	0.6	6	0.7	11	0.6	0	0.0	9	1.6	11	0.6	0
Subtotal (minor.)	262	29.0	308	37.1	570	32.9	0	0.0	204	36.4	570	32.9	161
Nonres. Alien	3	0.3	6	0.7	9	0.5	0	0.0	0	0.0	9	0.5	0
White/Cauc.	504	55.9	435	52.3	939	54.2	0	0.0	312	55.7	939	54.2	315
Unknown	133	14.7	82	9.9	215	12.4	0	0.0	44	7.9	215	12.4	90
Total	902	52.0	831	48.0	1733	100.0	0	0.0	560	32.3	1733		593

Transfers

Transfers in	29
Transfers out	0

Tuition and Fees

	Resident	Nonresident
Full-time	$46,616	
Part-time		
Tuition Guarantee Program		N

Living Expenses

Estimated living expenses for singles

Living on campus	Living off campus	Living at home
$23,484	$23,484	$23,484

ABA
Approved
Since
1923

GPA and LSAT Scores

	Total	Full-Time	Part-Time
# of apps	7,574	7,574	0
# of offers	833	833	0
# of matrics	561	561	0
75% GPA	3.96	3.96	0.00
Median GPA	3.89	3.89	0.00
25% GPA	3.78	3.78	0.00
75% LSAT	176	176	0
Median LSAT	173	173	0
25% LSAT	171	171	0

Grants and Scholarships (from prior year)

	Total		Full-Time		Part-Time	
	#	%	#	%	#	%
Total # of students	1,765		1,765		0	
Total # receiving grants	892	50.5	892	50.5	0	0.0
Less than 1/2 tuition	601	34.1	601	34.1	0	0.0
Half to full tuition	267	15.1	267	15.1	0	0.0
Full tuition	14	0.8	14	0.8	0	0.0
More than full tuition	10	0.6	10	0.6	0	0.0
Median grant amount			$15,745		$0	

Informational and Library Resources

Total amount spent on library materials	$3,322,176
Study seating capacity inside the library	802
# of full-time equivalent professional librarians	32
Hours per week library is open	106
# of open, wired connections available to students	1,480
# of networked computers available for use by students	154
Has wireless network?	Y
Requires computer?	N

JD Attrition (from prior year)

	Academic	Other	Total	
	#	#	#	%
1st year	0	3	3	0.5
2nd year	0	0	0	0.0
3rd year	0	0	0	0.0
4th year	0	0	0	0.0

Employment (9 months after graduation)

	Total	Percentage
Employment status known	567	100.0
Employment status unknown	0	0.0
Employed	553	97.5
Pursuing graduate degrees	5	0.9
Unemployed (seeking, not seeking, or studying for the bar)	6	1.1
Type of Employment		
# employed in law firms	369	66.7
# employed in business and industry	22	4.0
# employed in government	15	2.7
# employed in public interest	30	5.4
# employed as judicial clerks	114	20.6
# employed in academia	3	0.5
Geographic Location		
# employed in state	64	11.6
# employed outside the US	15	2.7
# of states where employed	38	

Bar Passage Rates

First-time takers	541	Reporting %	91.50
Average school %	98.19	Average state %	85.37
Average pass difference	12.82		

Jurisdiction	Takers	Passers	Pass %	State %	Diff %
New York	271	267	98.52	86.51	12.01
Massachusetts	99	97	97.98	89.77	8.21
California	81	79	97.53	73.19	24.34
Illinois	44	43	97.73	90.89	6.84

HARVARD LAW SCHOOL

1515 Massachusetts Avenue, Austin Hall
Cambridge, MA 02138
Phone: 617.495.3109
E-mail: jdadmiss@law.harvard.edu; Website: www.law.harvard.edu

A Legal Metropolis

Harvard Law School combines the resources of the world's premier center for legal education and research with educational settings designed to enrich individual and interactive learning. The result is a uniquely vibrant and collaborative environment. Harvard's scope generates enormous vitality—an unparalleled breadth and depth of academic options, a wide array of research programs, a diverse student body drawn from across the nation and around the world, and a global network of distinguished alumni. Harvard Law School offers students a curriculum of unparalleled breadth: more than 350 courses, seminars, and reading groups that together reflect the remarkable range of the faculty's expertise and interests. Within this dynamic environment, law students have broad opportunities for intellectual engagement with faculty and classmates. Over 150 of our courses have fewer than 25 students enrolled; additionally, there are 80 seminars in which small groups of students work closely with faculty. First-year sections have 80 students, and opportunities to work directly with faculty members abound. For example, all first-year students may join intimate (fewer than 15 students), faculty-led reading groups on topics ranging from cyberlaw to climate change to terrorism. Harvard's extensive resources and collaborative approach create unmatched opportunities to prepare for leadership in public service, private practice, the judiciary, academia, business, or government.

Public Service

HLS strongly promotes public service. The school guarantees funding for summer public interest work, and over 500 JD students received funds to work in 34 countries and 35 states plus Washington, DC, in 2010. The Office of Public Interest Advising provides comprehensive services to students pursuing public service careers. The Low Income Protection Plan allows graduates substantial financial flexibility to pursue lower-paying employment, and a variety of fellowship programs provide additional support to graduates entering public service. Reflecting its public service commitment, HLS has a 40-hour minimum pro bono work requirement, with students actually completing an average of more than 550 hours of pro bono work during law school.

Faculty

The centerpiece of the HLS experience is working directly with scholars who shape the landscape of American and international law. The faculty includes leading specialists in every subject area. Beyond the classroom, students provide critical support to faculty producing cutting-edge research and influencing the development of the law and of societies around the world.

Programs of Study

To guide students as they move through the three years of law school and to create a tool for better coordination and collaboration between faculty members, the faculty has developed "programs of study." Students do not sign up for any program; nor should any student feel compelled to adhere to one. Instead, the programs of study reflect the best advice from faculty about how to approach particular subjects and potential careers. The six programs of study offer suggestions about how students can navigate our extensive course offerings with a sense of their relationship to different avenues of study and opportunities to move progressively through more advanced work before graduation. The programs of study can give students a picture of how different courses and seminars can relate to the work of practicing lawyers and academics, and how clinical work, summer opportunities, and fellowships also enhance your learning and development.

The six programs of study are:
- Criminal Justice
- International and Comparative Law
- Law and Business
- Law and Government
- Law and Social Change
- Law, Science, and Technology

International Scope

Harvard Law School presents students with tremendous opportunities to engage in the world. With students coming from more than 60 countries to study here and with hundreds of current students going abroad each year to work, study, engage in research, or advocate for change, HLS is truly a global crossroads. Each year, the Law School offers more than 75 courses, seminars, and reading groups taught with an international, foreign, or comparative law component. Research centers, such as the East Asian Legal Studies Program or the Program on International Financial Systems, offer students access to visiting scholars and cutting-edge ideas through colloquia, conferences, and research opportunities. Harvard's 5,000 alumni living outside the United States provide an unparalleled network of opportunity for potential collaboration and camaraderie for members of the community. In addition, scholars come to HLS from all over the world to make use of the incredible international collections housed in the law library.

Student Life

At HLS, a wide variety of extracurricular activities complement and enrich the classroom and clinical experiences. Whether exploring professional interests, serving the public, or merely socializing, students engage in an enormous range of activity on the HLS campus beyond the classroom. At present, there are more than 90 student organizations and journals at HLS. Student organizations based on social, political, service, or professional interests plan workshops, panels, concerts, networking opportunities, and conferences for almost every day of the academic year. Other activities planned by first-year social chairs, the second-year social committee, the third-year class marshals, as well as the Dean of Students Office, create a collegial and community-oriented environment on campus. Students are given a wide range of opportunities to create and implement ideas for activities and are encouraged to pursue their interests by forming new student organizations or planning one-time events.

Clinical Programs

The Clinical Legal Education Program is one of the most important and valued aspects of a Harvard Law School education, confirming our commitment to public service and to providing our students with the best possible educational experience. With dozens of in-house clinics and hundreds of externships, Harvard Law School has more clinical opportunities than any law school in the world. Some of the clinics include Mediation and Negotiation, Supreme Court Advocacy, Immigration, Human Rights, CyberLaw, Child Advocacy, Criminal Justice, Criminal Prosecution, Death Penalty, Disability Law, Domestic Violence, Education Law, Employment Civil Rights, Environmental Law, Estate Planning, Family Law, GLBT Law, Gender Violence, Government Lawyer, Health Law, Post-Foreclosure Eviction Defense, Predatory Lending/Consumer Protection, and Sports Law.

Clinical education at HLS helps to introduce and explore the roles and responsibilities of a lawyer. Taking a clinical course may aid students in thinking about what sort of law practice or lawyering work they like most. Mentored practice, in an educational setting, also helps students begin to understand their learning styles while getting a head start on learning the skills they will need when they begin their careers.

The Clinical Legal Education Program at Harvard Law School has three basic components:

- direct student responsibility for clients in a realistic practice setting;
- supervision and mentoring by an experienced practitioner; and
- companion classroom sessions in which clinical experience supports and contributes to further discussion and thought.

Seventy-five percent of the class of 2010 participated in clinical work. Clinical courses get enthusiastic reviews from student participants, most of whom find them challenging and educational. Many students find that this practical lawyering produces a sense of personal accomplishment as well as professional development because, in most cases, they are truly increasing access to justice for the most marginalized members of society. HLS also offers externship placements at various government agencies, nonprofits, and small firms. Students can also design independent clinical work projects that are tailored to unique interests. Finally, many students take advantage of the winter term, spending three to four weeks off campus in a clinical setting and then coming back to campus and continuing the work remotely for the following semester.

Employment After Graduation

More than 500 employers recruit on campus at HLS each year. Upon graduation, roughly 65 percent of HLS graduates enter private practice, about 20 percent enter judicial clerkships, and about 15 percent enter public interest or government work, business and industry, academia, or other unique pursuits. Virtually every year, the number of HLS graduates clerking for the US Supreme Court surpasses the number from any other law school. In fact, approximately one-fourth of all Supreme Court clerks over the last decade graduated from HLS. After clerkships, many HLS graduates pursue careers in public interest, government, and academia.

APPLICANT PROFILE

HLS does not provide a profile chart because it would be based solely upon undergraduate GPA and LSAT scores. Admission decisions are based on many factors beyond the GPA and LSAT. Each application is read thoroughly by our team of admissions professionals and faculty admissions committee members. Although most admitted candidates graduated near the top of their college classes and present LSAT scores in the top few percentiles, a significant proportion of candidates who meet these characterizations may not be offered admission. At the same time, some admitted candidates apply with lower GPA and LSAT credentials but offer combined academic and other achievements that impress the admissions committee. Candidates with higher grades and scores tend to be admitted at higher rates than candidates with lower grades and scores, but at no point on the GPA or LSAT scales are the chances for admission to Harvard Law School zero or 100 percent.

UNIVERSITY OF HAWAI'I AT MĀNOA | WILLIAM S. RICHARDSON SCHOOL OF LAW

2515 Dole Street
Honolulu, HI 96822-2350
Phone: 808.956.7966; Fax: 808.956.3813
E-mail: lawadm@hawaii.edu; Website: www.law.hawaii.edu

ABA
Approved
Since
1974

The Basics

Type of school	Public
Term	Semester
Application deadline	2/1
Application fee	$60
Financial aid deadline	3/1
Can first year start other than fall?	No
Student to faculty ratio	8.0 to 1
# of housing spaces available restricted to law students	
graduate housing for which law students are eligible	36

Faculty and Administrators

	Total		Men		Women		Minorities	
	Spr	Fall	Spr	Fall	Spr	Fall	Spr	Fall
Full-time	34	31	16	14	18	17	14	12
Other full-time	3	4	2	2	1	2	2	2
Deans, librarians, & others who teach	12	12	2	2	10	10	7	7
Part-time	44	22	34	13	10	9	15	13
Total	93	69	54	31	39	38	38	34

Curriculum

	Full-Time	Part-Time
Typical first-year section size	104	46
Is there typically a "small section" of the first-year class, other than Legal Writing, taught by full-time faculty	No	No
If yes, typical size offered last year		
# of classroom course titles beyond first-year curriculum	99	
# of upper division courses, excluding seminars, with an enrollment: Under 25	51	
25–49	11	
50–74	4	
75–99	4	
100+	0	
# of seminars	58	
# of seminar positions available	669	
# of seminar positions filled	432	18
# of positions available in simulation courses	154	
# of simulation positions filled	128	0
# of positions available in faculty supervised clinical courses	122	
# of faculty supervised clinical positions filled	109	1
# involved in field placements	40	0
# involved in law journals	39	0
# involved in moot court or trial competitions	39	0
# of credit hours required to graduate	89	

JD Enrollment and Ethnicity

	Men #	Men %	Women #	Women %	Full-Time #	Full-Time %	Part-Time #	Part-Time %	1st-Year #	1st-Year %	Total #	Total %	JD Degs. Awd.
All Hispanics	2	1.4	1	0.5	3	1.0	0	0.0	1	0.7	3	0.8	3
Am. Ind./AK Nat.	1	0.7	0	0.0	1	0.3	0	0.0	0	0.0	1	0.3	0
Asian	38	25.7	70	34.1	86	29.2	22	37.9	44	30.8	108	30.6	18
Black/Af. Am.	0	0.0	4	2.0	3	1.0	1	1.7	1	0.7	4	1.1	1
Nat. HI/Pac. Isl.	20	13.5	15	7.3	34	11.5	1	1.7	8	5.6	35	9.9	0
2 or more races	34	23.0	58	28.3	79	26.8	13	22.4	44	30.8	92	26.1	0
Subtotal (minor.)	95	64.2	148	72.2	206	69.8	37	63.8	98	68.5	243	68.8	52
Nonres. Alien	3	2.0	6	2.9	9	3.1	0	0.0	5	3.5	9	2.5	0
White/Cauc.	35	23.6	39	19.0	58	19.7	16	27.6	36	25.2	74	21.0	17
Unknown	15	10.1	12	5.9	22	7.5	5	8.6	4	2.8	27	7.6	14
Total	148	41.9	205	58.1	295	83.6	58	16.4	143	40.5	353		84

Transfers

Transfers in	2
Transfers out	2

Tuition and Fees

	Resident	Nonresident
Full-time	$16,421	$30,485
Part-time	$13,761	$25,481
Tuition Guarantee Program	N	

Living Expenses

Estimated living expenses for singles

Living on campus	Living off campus	Living at home
$12,285	$15,411	$6,117

UNIVERSITY OF HAWAI'I AT MĀNOA | WILLIAM S. RICHARDSON SCHOOL OF LAW

ABA Approved Since 1974

GPA and LSAT Scores

	Total	Full-Time	Part-Time
# of apps	1,250	1,093	337
# of offers	250	203	47
# of matrics	113	86	27
75% GPA	3.72	3.75	3.62
Median GPA	3.45	3.45	3.40
25% GPA	3.19	3.23	3.05
75% LSAT	159	159	156
Median LSAT	156	157	154
25% LSAT	153	154	151

Grants and Scholarships (from prior year)

	Total #	Total %	Full-Time #	Full-Time %	Part-Time #	Part-Time %
Total # of students	326		285		41	
Total # receiving grants	196	60.1	190	66.7	6	14.6
Less than 1/2 tuition	190	58.3	184	64.6	6	14.6
Half to full tuition	6	1.8	6	2.1	0	0.0
Full tuition	0	0.0	0	0.0	0	0.0
More than full tuition	0	0.0	0	0.0	0	0.0
Median grant amount			$5,000		$3,750	

Informational and Library Resources

Total amount spent on library materials	$671,422
Study seating capacity inside the library	431
# of full-time equivalent professional librarians	5
Hours per week library is open	96
# of open, wired connections available to students	282
# of networked computers available for use by students	37
Has wireless network?	Y
Requires computer?	Y

JD Attrition (from prior year)

	Academic #	Other #	Total #	Total %
1st year	0	2	2	1.3
2nd year	0	1	1	0.9
3rd year	1	0	1	1.5
4th year	0	0	0	0.0

Employment (9 months after graduation)

	Total	Percentage
Employment status known	84	95.5
Employment status unknown	4	4.5
Employed	76	90.5
Pursuing graduate degrees	7	8.3
Unemployed (seeking, not seeking, or studying for the bar)	1	1.2
Type of Employment		
# employed in law firms	28	36.8
# employed in business and industry	9	11.8
# employed in government	9	11.8
# employed in public interest	3	3.9
# employed as judicial clerks	25	32.9
# employed in academia	2	2.6
Geographic Location		
# employed in state	67	88.2
# employed outside the US	1	1.3
# of states where employed	6	

Bar Passage Rates

First-time takers	81	Reporting %	93.83
Average school %	88.16	Average state %	85.94
Average pass difference	2.22		

Jurisdiction	Takers	Passers	Pass %	State %	Diff %
Hawaii	76	67	88.16	85.94	2.22

The information on these pages was provided by the law school.

UNIVERSITY OF HAWAI'I AT MĀNOA | WILLIAM S. RICHARDSON SCHOOL OF LAW

2515 Dole Street
Honolulu, HI 96822-2350
Phone: 808.956.7966; Fax: 808.956.3813
E-mail: lawadm@hawaii.edu; Website: www.law.hawaii.edu

Introduction

The William S. Richardson School of Law at the University of Hawai'i is located at the foot of beautiful Mānoa Valley, minutes from sandy beaches and lush rain forests, as well as from the economic and legal center of urban Honolulu. We offer an excellent academic program with professors committed to outstanding teaching, scholarship, and community service. Our school is particularly noted for its collegial atmosphere, accessible faculty, and extraordinary cultural and ethnic diversity.

Placement after graduation is consistently very high. Our distinguished alumni serve as leaders in Hawai'i, as well as in national and international arenas. We are recognized particularly for our programs in environmental law, Native Hawaiian law, and international law with an Asian and Pacific focus. The William S. Richardson School of Law is fully accredited by the American Bar Association and is a member of the American Association of Law Schools.

Programs of Study

We offer a three-year, full-time JD program and an evening, part-time JD program. Law students may earn certificates in Environmental Law, Pacific-Asian Legal Studies, and Native Hawaiian Law. Summer courses are available as well as specialized short courses with distinguished visiting faculty in January (J Term). We also offer a one-year LLM program for foreign lawyers studying American law.

Environmental Law Program

The Law School's Environmental Law Program (ELP) was established in 1988 in recognition of the special challenges our state faces in developing an environmentally sustainable economy within a unique and fragile island environment. It has grown into a comprehensive program with a regional, national, and international reputation for excellence in teaching, scholarship, and public service. Thanks to its dedicated faculty, alumni, and friends throughout Hawai'i and the Pacific region, ELP offers unparalleled opportunities for students interested in focusing their studies in the environmental law field. The ELP has several components: (1) Certificate in Environmental Law; (2) faculty and student scholarship; (3) community outreach and education; (4) moot court; (5) Colloquia Series; (6) off-campus learning; (7) student-led Environmental Law Society; (8) career counseling and placement; and (9) Professional Service.

Pacific-Asian Legal Studies

Enhanced by Hawai'i's location, population, culture, and economic relationships, we offer an exceptional program in Pacific-Asian Legal Studies (PALS). The program has the two-fold purpose of conducting research and enriching the JD curriculum. Many faculty members have expertise in Pacific/Asian scholarship, teaching, and law reform. Recent course offerings in PALS have included, for example, Chinese Business Law, Chinese Law and Society, Pacific Island Legal Systems, Korean Law, Philippine Law, Japanese Law and Society, and US-Japan Business Transactions. The Certificate in Pacific-Asian Legal Studies allows students to focus their coursework and to earn recognition of their specialization in addition to the JD.

Selected students may do a full semester externship for academic credit in certain Pacific Island nations or, with approval, in agencies or entities in Asia or elsewhere. Students may also arrange a semester of study with law faculties in Asia.

Ka Huli Ao Center for Excellence in Native Hawaiian Law

Ka Huli Ao Center for Excellence in Native Hawaiian Law was established in 2005 by a federal grant administered by the US Department of Education. The Center focuses on education, research, community outreach, and the preservation of invaluable historical, legal, traditional, and customary materials. It offers new courses and supports Native Hawaiian law students as they pursue legal careers and leadership roles. Students may earn a certificate in Native Hawaiian Law.

Clinical Opportunities

All students are required to take at least one clinical course, and most students will take many such practical courses. We offer an extensive number of clinical and professional skills opportunities. Clinical courses teach and model excellent practice skills and stress a reflective method of looking at lawyering behavior. These courses are taught by full-time faculty as well as by some of Hawai'i's finest judges and lawyers who evaluate and mentor student efforts in presenting oral arguments, handling depositions, and negotiating for their clients in simulated sessions as well as with real clients. Skills taught in the various clinical courses include interviewing, counseling, drafting, fact investigation, negotiation, alternative dispute resolution, motion practice, trial practice, appellate practice, and legal writing. Our Clinical Program also directly addresses the legal problems faced by Hawai'i's most vulnerable people.

Community Service and Pro Bono

Our Pro Bono Program introduces students to public interest voluntary service and encourages them to respond directly to unmet needs in the community. Each student must do at least 60 hours of law-related work in one or more agencies or projects approved by the Law School pro bono advisor. In the past, students have worked for a wide variety of public service groups such as the Legal Aid Society of Hawai'i, Volunteer Legal Services, Native Hawaiian Legal Corporation, and the Earthjustice Legal Defense Fund.

JD Admission

Admission to both our full- and part-time JD programs is determined by an applicant's academic achievement, aptitude for the study of law, and professional promise. Preference is given to residents of Hawai'i and to nonresidents with strong ties to, or special interest in, Hawai'i, the Asia/Pacific region, environmental law, or other programs in the Law School. Approximately 20 percent of the student body are nonresidents.

In addition to the LSAT and undergraduate GPA, factors considered for admission include academic work beyond the bachelor's degree, work experience, writing ability, community service, diversity, overcoming adversity, and unusual accomplishments.

Applications from students wishing to transfer or from those wishing to visit for a semester or two are considered for both August and January admission.

LLM Admission

Our Master of Laws (LLM) Program is restricted to applicants who have earned a bachelor's degree in law, or its equivalent, from an institution outside the United States. Admission decisions are based upon a candidate's transcripts of previous law study, work experience, English writing ability, letters of recommendation, and TOEFL or IELTS scores. There is no LSAT requirement.

Student Activities

Student editorial boards publish the *University of Hawai'i Law Review* and the online *Asian-Pacific Law and Policy Journal*. Students also organize and participate in many facets of the moot court program, including competing in many national competitions. Student teams regularly perform very well, bringing home national and international titles and awards.

Most students are active in a variety of organizations within the Law School and in the Honolulu community. A sampling includes Advocates for Public Interest Law (APIL), student divisions of the American Bar Association, American Inns of Court, Phi Delta Phi and Delta Theta Phi, Hawai'i Women Lawyers, and the Environmental Law Society. Student affinity groups include the Filipino Law Students Association, Black Law Students Association, Hispanic Law Students Association, LAMBDA, and the 'Ahahui o Hawai'i, an organization for Native Hawaiian law students.

Library and Physical Facilities

The library assigns study carrels with wired and wireless Internet access. Seminar/discussion rooms are also available for study groups. The classroom building features a moot courtroom and an open courtyard for informal conversations and activities. Law students have full access to all facilities of the university, including the health, counseling, and computing centers, as well as extensive athletic facilities. The classroom building has wireless Internet access throughout for students, faculty, and staff.

Career Services

We assist students and alumni in obtaining part-time, summer, and associate positions in both the public and private sectors through our Career Development Office. Most students choose to remain in Hawai'i and the Asia/Pacific region, so that about 85 percent of our graduates work in Hawai'i after graduation. Many firms in Honolulu, government employers, and public interest organizations participate in on-campus interviews for second- and third-year students. Our students also are unusually successful in obtaining sought-after judicial clerkships upon graduation. Recent graduating classes have had an employment rate nine months after graduation varying from 85–100 percent.

APPLICANT PROFILE

University of Hawai'i at Mānoa | William S. Richardson School of Law
This grid includes only applicants who earned 120–180 LSAT scores under standard administrations.

LSAT Score	3.75 +		3.50–3.74		3.25–3.49		3.00–3.24		2.75–2.99		2.50–2.74		2.25–2.49		2.00–2.24		Below 2.00		No GPA		Totals	
	Apps	Adm	Apps	Adm	Apps	Adm	Apps	Adm	Apps	Adm	Apps	Adm	Apps	Adm	Apps	Adm	Apps	Adm	Apps	Adm	Apps	Adm
175–180	0	0	0	0	0	0	0	0	1	1	0	0	0	0	0	0	0	0	0	0	1	1
170–174	5	4	1	1	4	3	4	3	0	0	0	0	1	0	0	0	0	0	0	0	15	11
165–169	7	6	7	5	8	5	8	4	7	1	4	1	3	0	1	0	1	0	2	2	48	24
160–164	20	18	37	28	29	13	21	5	22	5	10	1	7	1	1	0	0	0	3	0	150	71
155–159	30	17	46	14	61	26	52	17	44	10	23	0	17	0	2	0	2	0	5	1	282	85
150–154	28	11	54	9	75	13	66	5	36	0	31	1	15	0	1	0	1	0	4	2	311	41
145–149	18	5	25	4	33	1	47	2	35	1	23	0	5	0	3	0	1	0	5	0	195	13
140–144	7	0	11	1	22	0	15	0	18	0	22	1	8	0	3	0	0	0	2	0	108	2
135–139	0	0	2	0	6	0	5	0	11	0	6	0	5	0	4	0	1	0	1	0	41	0
130–134	0	0	2	0	2	0	0	0	3	0	3	0	0	0	1	0	0	0	0	0	11	0
125–129	0	0	0	0	0	0	0	0	1	0	1	0	0	0	0	0	0	0	0	0	2	0
120–124	0	0	0	0	0	0	0	0	0	0	0	0	0	0	0	0	1	0	0	0	1	0
Total	115	61	185	62	240	61	218	36	178	18	123	4	61	1	16	0	7	0	22	5	1165	248

Apps = Number of Applicants
Adm = Number Admitted
Reflects 99% of the total applicant pool; highest LSAT data reported.

HOFSTRA UNIVERSITY SCHOOL OF LAW

121 Hofstra University
Hempstead, NY 11549
Phone: 516.463.5916; Fax: 516.463.6264
E-mail: lawadmissions@hofstra.edu; Website: http://law.hofstra.edu

The Basics

Type of school	Private
Term	Semester
Application deadline	4/15
Application fee	$0
Financial aid deadline	4/1
Can first year start other than fall?	No
Student to faculty ratio	14.3 to 1
# of housing spaces available restricted to law students	
graduate housing for which law students are eligible	225

Faculty and Administrators

	Total		Men		Women		Minorities	
	Spr	Fall	Spr	Fall	Spr	Fall	Spr	Fall
Full-time	63	60	42	36	21	24	11	8
Other full-time	0	0	0	0	0	0	0	0
Deans, librarians, & others who teach	3	2	0	1	3	1	1	1
Part-time	51	37	34	33	17	4	15	5
Total	117	99	76	70	41	29	27	14

Curriculum

	Full-Time	Part-Time
Typical first-year section size	94	0
Is there typically a "small section" of the first-year class, other than Legal Writing, taught by full-time faculty	Yes	Yes
If yes, typical size offered last year	32	
# of classroom course titles beyond first-year curriculum	155	

# of upper division courses, excluding seminars, with an enrollment:		
Under 25	63	
25–49	44	
50–74	10	
75–99	14	
100+	8	

# of seminars	48	
# of seminar positions available	941	
# of seminar positions filled	497	81
# of positions available in simulation courses	788	
# of simulation positions filled	473	184
# of positions available in faculty supervised clinical courses	140	
# of faculty supervised clinical positions filled	115	10
# involved in field placements	132	23
# involved in law journals	188	8
# involved in moot court or trial competitions	60	1
# of credit hours required to graduate	87	

JD Enrollment and Ethnicity

	Men #	Men %	Women #	Women %	Full-Time #	Full-Time %	Part-Time #	Part-Time %	1st-Year #	1st-Year %	Total #	Total %	JD Degs. Awd.
All Hispanics	25	4.4	37	7.5	48	5.1	14	12.1	8	2.2	62	5.8	33
Am. Ind./AK Nat.	2	0.4	2	0.4	4	0.4	0	0.0	1	0.3	4	0.4	0
Asian	53	9.3	65	13.2	106	11.2	12	10.3	36	9.9	118	11.1	15
Black/Af. Am.	27	4.8	62	12.6	74	7.8	15	12.9	33	9.1	89	8.4	31
Nat. Hl/Pac. Isl.	0	0.0	0	0.0	0	0.0	0	0.0	0	0.0	0	0.0	0
2 or more races	14	2.5	13	2.6	27	2.9	0	0.0	27	7.4	27	2.5	0
Subtotal (minor.)	121	21.3	179	36.2	259	27.4	41	35.3	105	28.9	300	28.3	79
Nonres. Alien	26	4.6	23	4.7	48	5.1	1	0.9	21	5.8	49	4.6	0
White/Cauc.	385	67.9	274	55.5	591	62.5	68	58.6	221	60.9	659	62.1	228
Unknown	35	6.2	18	3.6	47	5.0	6	5.2	16	4.4	53	5.0	41
Total	567	53.4	494	46.6	945	89.1	116	10.9	363	34.2	1061		351

Transfers

Transfers in	12
Transfers out	30

Tuition and Fees

	Resident	Nonresident
Full-time	$43,660	$43,660
Part-time	$32,669	$32,669
Tuition Guarantee Program		N

Living Expenses

Estimated living expenses for singles

Living on campus	Living off campus	Living at home
$23,398	$22,040	$9,519

HOFSTRA UNIVERSITY SCHOOL OF LAW

ABA
Approved
Since
1971

GPA and LSAT Scores

	Total	Full-Time	Part-Time
# of apps	5,434	4,851	583
# of offers	1,985	1,922	63
# of matrics	365	355	10
75% GPA	3.69	3.69	3.61
Median GPA	3.58	3.58	3.57
25% GPA	3.17	3.17	3.01
75% LSAT	160	160	159
Median LSAT	158	158	157
25% LSAT	156	156	151

Grants and Scholarships (from prior year)

	Total #	Total %	Full-Time #	Full-Time %	Part-Time #	Part-Time %
Total # of students	1,109		939		170	
Total # receiving grants	548	49.4	506	53.9	42	24.7
Less than 1/2 tuition	290	26.1	264	28.1	26	15.3
Half to full tuition	201	18.1	189	20.1	12	7.1
Full tuition	57	5.1	53	5.6	4	2.4
More than full tuition	0	0.0	0	0.0	0	0.0
Median grant amount			$20,000		$12,000	

Informational and Library Resources

Total amount spent on library materials	$1,469,502
Study seating capacity inside the library	464
# of full-time equivalent professional librarians	7
Hours per week library is open	101
# of open, wired connections available to students	164
# of networked computers available for use by students	114
Has wireless network?	Y
Requires computer?	N

JD Attrition (from prior year)

	Academic #	Other #	Total #	Total %
1st year	14	40	54	13.7
2nd year	6	8	14	4.4
3rd year	0	1	1	0.3
4th year	0	0	0	0.0

Employment (9 months after graduation)

	Total	Percentage
Employment status known	350	96.7
Employment status unknown	12	3.3
Employed	330	94.3
Pursuing graduate degrees	11	3.1
Unemployed (seeking, not seeking, or studying for the bar)	7	2.0
Type of Employment		
# employed in law firms	173	52.4
# employed in business and industry	58	17.6
# employed in government	43	13.0
# employed in public interest	11	3.3
# employed as judicial clerks	7	2.1
# employed in academia	15	4.5
Geographic Location		
# employed in state	279	84.5
# employed outside the US	0	0.0
# of states where employed		19

Bar Passage Rates

First-time takers	354	Reporting %	96.33
Average school %	76.54	Average state %	86.51

Average pass difference −9.97

Jurisdiction	Takers	Passers	Pass %	State %	Diff %
New York	341	261	76.54	86.51	−9.97

HOFSTRA UNIVERSITY SCHOOL OF LAW

121 Hofstra University
Hempstead, NY 11549
Phone: 516.463.5916; Fax: 516.463.6264
E-mail: lawadmissions@hofstra.edu; Website: http://law.hofstra.edu

Introduction

Hofstra Law School prepares motivated students to have an impact in the legal community and beyond. For 40 years, the Law School has provided an education rich in both the theory and skills needed to produce outstanding lawyers, business executives, and community leaders. Located on the campus of Hofstra University in Hempstead, New York, the Law School is 20 miles outside New York City in suburban Long Island. Hofstra Law School offers a JD program, as well as LLM graduate degrees in American Legal Studies (for foreign law graduates) and Family Law. Joint degrees are available in conjunction with the University's Frank G. Zarb School of Business (JD/MBA) and College of Liberal Arts and Sciences (JD/MA in Applied Social Research and Public Policy).

Vibrant Campus Life

Hofstra Law School, situated on the 240-acre Hofstra University main campus, provides a vibrant community for students studying the law. Few, if any, law schools can match the combination of Hofstra Law's green campus and its easy access to New York City, the hub of the nation's legal profession. Students living on campus in graduate housing enjoy a parklike setting that is home to one of the country's great arboretums. Yet, they can also take a free Hofstra shuttle bus to train stations that provide service to Manhattan in less than 40 minutes or drive just a few miles to world-class beaches.

Cutting-Edge Curriculum

As one of only a few US law schools to require Transnational Law as a first-year course, Hofstra Law is at the forefront of the changing realities of legal practice. This innovative course allows students to put their studies into a broader context by exploring the relationship between international law, foreign legal systems, and the US legal system. With the school offering more than 200 upper-level courses, students can explore practically any area of law and choose from newly designed concentrations in alternative dispute resolution, business law (honors concentration), criminal law and procedure, energy and environmental law, family law, and health law. Hofstra Law's advanced curriculum helps develop well-trained and practice-ready professionals. A survey of law firms conducted by the Hanover Research Council revealed that Hofstra Law graduates rate highly in a majority of competencies, including business knowledge, communication skills, advocacy skills, and general workplace skills.

Internationally Renowned Faculty

Hofstra Law School's full-time faculty consists of nearly 50 nationally and internationally recognized scholars who represent diverse fields. Faculty members have clerked for US Supreme Court justices, chaired major American Bar Association and law reform committees, received awards for scholarship and leadership in legal education and community affairs, and are recognized leaders in clinical and skills training. Their publications reflect a wide range of interests and expertise, ongoing participation in important scholarly debates, and significant contributions to the study and

teaching of law. The faculty's open-door policy creates an accessible and collegial environment and reflects its engagement with students.

Student Life

Hofstra Law students publish five journals: *Hofstra Law Review*, *Hofstra Labor and Employment Law Journal*, and *Journal of International Business and Law* are student-run; *ACTEC Law Journal* and *Family Court Review* are peer-reviewed and published under the auspices of the American College of Trust and Estate Counsel and the Association of Family and Conciliation Courts, respectively. There are more than 40 student organizations, ranging from Hofstra Law Women and the Black Law Students Association to the Public Justice Foundation and the International Law Society.

Professional Career Services

Hofstra Law provides a range of services to promote the career and professional growth of students. The Office of Career Services offers individual career and professional development counseling, educational programming, mock interviews, an extensive online employer database, and comprehensive on-campus interviewing. Hofstra Law also prepares students to succeed in a shifting legal marketplace by ensuring that they possess practice-ready skills and knowledge to meet the needs of employers and the expectations they have of new lawyers. These include interpersonal communication, client relations, and business cultivation—critical areas that influence the important yet subtle dynamics of legal practice. Through such events as the annual two-day Success Strategies Boot Camp, accomplished lawyers, academics, consultants, and law school administrators help students acquire knowledge and develop abilities that will differentiate them and help them transition smoothly into the workplace.

Revolutionary Clinical Program

Hofstra Law is widely recognized as a pioneer in fully integrating clinical education into a traditional law school curriculum. By the late 1970s, the school had one of the largest clinical programs in the nation. Over the years, its clinics have become well-known in legal circles in the metropolitan area. As students represent individuals facing real legal challenges, they gain valuable hands-on experience: they advocate in court, counsel clients, conduct fact investigations, and mediate disputes. Hofstra's current clinical opportunities are in Asylum, Child Advocacy, Community and Economic Development, Criminal Justice, Law Reform Advocacy, Mediation, and Securities Arbitration.

Training for Legal Practice

Recognizing that the well-rounded graduate needs to apply classroom theory to real-world situations, the Law School offers extensive skills and simulation-based training. The Externship Program provides an opportunity to gain substantive legal experience under the direct supervision and guidance of an experienced attorney. Other training tools include moot court competitions, conferences, workshops with accomplished attorneys, intensive pretrial and mediation courses, and a trial techniques program based on the curriculum of the National Institute for Trial Advocacy.

International Legal Education

Hofstra Law offers study-abroad summer sessions in Freiburg, Germany; Pisa, Italy; and Sydney, Australia, and a winter intersession in Curaçao. The school recently launched several new initiatives, including a language-development partnership with Rosetta Stone and an International Legal Practice Externship Program, and became a participant in the Public-Private Partnership for Justice Reform in Afghanistan. Hofstra Law is also a founding member of the European-American Consortium for Legal Education (EACLE), offering semester-long exchange programs with Erasmus University Rotterdam, Ghent University, the University of Helsinki, Parma University, and Warsaw University.

Engaging Centers and Institutes

Both nationally and internationally recognized, Hofstra Law School's centers and institutes attract thought leaders for research, debate, and the exchange of knowledge.

Center for Applied Legal Reasoning: This multidisciplinary center focuses on the study of theories of legal reasoning and the development of pedagogies to train students for the practice of law.

Center for Children, Families, and the Law: An interdisciplinary organization, this center is dedicated to education, research, and public service focused on children and families involved in the legal system.

Center for Legal Advocacy: This center features innovative programs aimed at improving client representation skills and enhancing the level of advocacy in the profession.

Institute for Health Law and Policy: Designed to train attorneys in the field of health law, this institute concentrates on the study and formulation of health care policy.

Institute for the Study of Conflict Transformation: This institute promotes the understanding of conflict processes and intervention from the transformative mediation framework.

Institute for the Study of Gender, Law, and Public Policy: The mission of this institute is to facilitate teaching, research, and scholarship concerning gender as it relates to law and public policy.

Institute for the Study of Legal Ethics: As a research center, this institute explores critical issues concerning lawyers' ethics and the legal profession.

Law, Logic and Technology Research Laboratory: The LLT Lab conducts empirical research on legal reasoning in substantive areas of law, using a logic-based analytical framework and state-of-the-art technology, to create knowledge, skills, and tools that enhance legal practice and legal education.

Rewarding Fellowships and Scholarships

Each year, the Law School awards fellowships to entering JD students based on their demonstrated commitment to advocacy in several areas. Fellowship recipients receive tuition assistance, gain valuable internship experience, and pursue a course of study that provides the knowledge and skills needed to make an impact in their chosen field. The **Child and Family Advocacy Fellowship** is awarded to individuals who plan to use their legal education to advocate for the interests of children and families. The **Health Law and Policy Fellowship** is awarded to individuals who want to represent medical providers, patients, and pharmaceutical companies and advance health law policy. The **Lesbian, Gay, Bisexual, and Transgender Rights Fellowship** is awarded to individuals who plan to use their legal education to advocate for the interests of the LGBT community. The **Dwight L. Greene Memorial Scholarship** is awarded to individuals who have a commitment to advocacy on behalf of minority groups. Other endowed scholarships are available for entering and continuing law students. Information about these opportunities is available at http://law.hofstra.edu.

APPLICANT PROFILE

The Admissions Committee reviews not only an applicant's academic record and LSAT performance, but the entire application to determine whether the applicant is likely to be successful at Hofstra Law. Hofstra Law seeks a diverse student body made up of individuals who will thrive in the school's experiential-learning program that trains them to make an impact in the legal profession, the business world, and society.

Hofstra University School of Law
This grid includes only applicants who earned 120–180 LSAT scores under standard administrations.

LSAT Score	GPA								
	3.75 +	3.50–3.74	3.25–3.49	3.00–3.24	2.75–2.99	2.50–2.74	2.25–2.49	2.00–2.24	Below 2.00
175–180									
170–174									
165–169									
160–164									
155–159									
150–154									
145–149									
140–144									
135–139									
130–134									
125–129									
120–124									

■ Good Possibility   ☐ Possible   ▨ Unlikely

UNIVERSITY OF HOUSTON LAW CENTER

100 Law Center
Houston, TX 77204-6060
Phone: 713.743.2280; Fax: 713.743.2194
E-mail: lawadmissions@uh.edu; Website: www.law.uh.edu

ABA
Approved
Since
1950

The Basics

Type of school	Public
Term	Semester
Application deadline	11/15 2/15 5/15
Application fee	$70
Financial aid deadline	4/1
Can first year start other than fall?	No
Student to faculty ratio	10.4 to 1
# of housing spaces available restricted to law students	
graduate housing for which law students are eligible	995

Faculty and Administrators

	Total		Men		Women		Minorities	
	Spr	Fall	Spr	Fall	Spr	Fall	Spr	Fall
Full-time	66	64	47	47	19	17	9	9
Other full-time	14	12	6	5	8	7	1	1
Deans, librarians, & others who teach	4	4	4	4	0	0	0	0
Part-time	89	71	65	46	24	25	70	53
Total	173	151	122	102	51	49	80	63

Curriculum

	Full-Time	Part-Time
Typical first-year section size	70	50
Is there typically a "small section" of the first-year class, other than Legal Writing, taught by full-time faculty	Yes	Yes
If yes, typical size offered last year	35	25
# of classroom course titles beyond first-year curriculum	223	
# of upper division courses, excluding seminars, with an enrollment: Under 25	144	
25–49	48	
50–74	24	
75–99	7	
100+	0	
# of seminars	24	
# of seminar positions available	346	
# of seminar positions filled	230	49
# of positions available in simulation courses	747	
# of simulation positions filled	480	75
# of positions available in faculty supervised clinical courses	186	
# of faculty supervised clinical positions filled	160	10
# involved in field placements	176	13
# involved in law journals	136	18
# involved in moot court or trial competitions	128	25
# of credit hours required to graduate	90	

JD Enrollment and Ethnicity

	Men		Women		Full-Time		Part-Time		1st-Year		Total		JD Degs. Awd.
	#	%	#	%	#	%	#	%	#	%	#	%	
All Hispanics	40	7.9	43	11.5	69	9.8	14	8.0	29	10.8	83	9.5	32
Am. Ind./AK Nat.	4	0.8	4	1.1	8	1.1	0	0.0	5	1.9	8	0.9	2
Asian	52	10.3	47	12.6	77	11.0	22	12.5	34	12.7	99	11.3	28
Black/Af. Am.	20	4.0	44	11.8	45	6.4	19	10.8	17	6.3	64	7.3	19
Nat. HI/Pac. Isl.	0	0.0	0	0.0	0	0.0	0	0.0	0	0.0	0	0.0	0
2 or more races	0	0.0	0	0.0	0	0.0	0	0.0	0	0.0	0	0.0	0
Subtotal (minor.)	116	23.0	138	37.0	199	28.4	55	31.3	85	31.7	254	29.0	81
Nonres. Alien	9	1.8	6	1.6	15	2.1	0	0.0	2	0.7	15	1.7	0
White/Cauc.	372	73.8	226	60.6	480	68.5	118	67.0	175	65.3	598	68.2	199
Unknown	7	1.4	3	0.8	7	1.0	3	1.7	6	2.2	10	1.1	2
Total	504	57.5	373	42.5	701	79.9	176	20.1	268	30.6	877		284

Transfers

Transfers in	0
Transfers out	3

Tuition and Fees

	Resident	Nonresident
Full-time	$26,731	$36,903
Part-time	$18,953	$25,735
Tuition Guarantee Program		N

Living Expenses

Estimated living expenses for singles

Living on campus	Living off campus	Living at home
$12,512	$15,456	$9,410

ABA
Approved
Since
1950

GPA and LSAT Scores

	Total	Full-Time	Part-Time
# of apps	3,929	3,279	650
# of offers	967	874	93
# of matrics	266	205	61
75% GPA	3.68	3.69	3.56
Median GPA	3.41	3.45	3.30
25% GPA	3.13	3.20	3.01
75% LSAT	164	164	161
Median LSAT	162	162	160
25% LSAT	159	160	157

Grants and Scholarships (from prior year)

	Total		Full-Time		Part-Time	
	#	%	#	%	#	%
Total # of students	898		715		183	
Total # receiving grants	411	45.8	411	57.5	0	0.0
Less than 1/2 tuition	345	38.4	345	48.3	0	0.0
Half to full tuition	50	5.6	50	7.0	0	0.0
Full tuition	0	0.0	0	0.0	0	0.0
More than full tuition	16	1.8	16	2.2	0	0.0
Median grant amount			$6,000		$0	

Informational and Library Resources

Total amount spent on library materials	$1,361,783
Study seating capacity inside the library	550
# of full-time equivalent professional librarians	11
Hours per week library is open	168
# of open, wired connections available to students	0
# of networked computers available for use by students	22
Has wireless network?	Y
Requires computer?	N

JD Attrition (from prior year)

	Academic	Other	Total	
	#	#	#	%
1st year	3	12	15	5.9
2nd year	5	2	7	2.4
3rd year	0	1	1	0.3
4th year	0	0	0	0.0

Employment (9 months after graduation)

	Total	Percentage
Employment status known	284	99.3
Employment status unknown	2	0.7
Employed	265	93.3
Pursuing graduate degrees	8	2.8
Unemployed (seeking, not seeking, or studying for the bar)	10	3.5
Type of Employment		
# employed in law firms	159	60.0
# employed in business and industry	51	19.2
# employed in government	31	11.7
# employed in public interest	9	3.4
# employed as judicial clerks	10	3.8
# employed in academia	5	1.9
Geographic Location		
# employed in state	236	89.1
# employed outside the US	1	0.4
# of states where employed	14	

Bar Passage Rates

First-time takers	269	Reporting %	97.77
Average school %	91.25	Average state %	85.48
Average pass difference	5.77		

Jurisdiction	Takers	Passers	Pass %	State %	Diff %
Texas	263	240	91.25	85.48	5.77

UNIVERSITY OF HOUSTON LAW CENTER

100 Law Center
Houston, TX 77204-6060
Phone: 713.743.2280; Fax: 713.743.2194
E-mail: lawadmissions@uh.edu; Website: www.law.uh.edu

Introduction

The University of Houston (UH) Law Center is located at the University of Houston, three miles south of downtown. The state-assisted UH Law Center, located in one of the nation's top 10 largest legal markets, is noted throughout the South and Southwest not only for its excellence, but also for its progressive and innovative approach to the teaching of law. The College of Law, the academic branch of the UH Law Center, is fully accredited by the American Bar Association and the American Association of Law Schools and has a chapter of the Order of the Coif, the national legal honorary scholastic society. The Law Center confers a Juris Doctor (JD) degree as a first degree in law and a Master of Laws (LLM) degree to students pursuing work beyond the JD degree.

Curriculum/Basic Program of Study

The first-year curriculum at the UH Law Center is prescribed. Students are also required to complete a course in professional responsibility, a practice-skills course, and one major piece of legal research and writing before graduation. While emphasis is placed on legal theory and the varying approaches to the law, there are many opportunities for hands-on learning.

Special Programs

The University of Houston Law Center emphasizes current legal and administrative problems confronting the region and nation, including intellectual property law, environmental law, energy law, tax law, health law, and international law. The UH Law Center is home to the Health Law and Policy Institute, a research and instruction center on interdisciplinary issues. The UH Law Center is also host to the Criminal Justice Institute; the Institute for Higher Education Law and Governance; the Institute for Intellectual Property and Information Law; the Center for Environment, Energy and Natural Resources Law; the Center for Children, Law, and Policy; the Blakely Advocacy Institute; and the Center for Consumer Law.

Clinical Programs and Trial Advocacy

The UH Law Center offers a wide variety of opportunities to gain hands-on experience. The UH Law Center houses several clinics, which gives students practice opportunities in providing legal services to indigent clients. The available clinics include the civil practice clinic, consumer law clinic, criminal practice clinic, immigration clinic, mediation clinic, and transactional clinic. Students can also choose from among different areas of concentration, such as externships focusing on health or environmental law or select an internship with a government agency or a court.

Practice skills courses coordinated through the Blakely Advocacy Institute are an integral part of the curriculum. Students can enhance their skills in trial, negotiation, pretrial, and appellate work through hands-on courses that simulate real-life situations. Several levels of courses are offered in civil and criminal advocacy. Intramural mock trial and moot court competitions are sponsored by the Advocates, an affiliated student organization. The institute also sponsors teams for criminal and civil interscholastic moot court and mock trial competitions, with UH Law Center students earning top honors in national and international competitions.

Activities

Extracurricular activities give voice to the diversity of the campus. Student groups represent special interests and provide important avenues to help law students succeed. Many arrange mentoring programs and match first-year students with second- or third-year students or working professionals. Others coordinate résumé-writing workshops, guest speaker forums, preregistration discussions of specific course offerings, or law-related charitable efforts that benefit the community.

The Student Bar Association (SBA) has input into every facet of student life at the UH Law Center. The SBA participates in the first-year orientation, organizes the annual charity Fun Run, aids in the selection of student representatives to sit on various faculty committees, and represents student attitudes and views both within and outside the UH Law Center.

Students are encouraged to become involved in one or more student organizations; to participate in the scholarly *Houston Law Review, Houston Journal of International Law, Houston Journal of Health Law and Policy, Houston Business and Tax Law Journal, Environmental and Energy Law and Policy Journal,* and the *Journal of Consumer and Commercial Law*; and to compete in tournaments ranging from moot court to mock trial, from mediation to negotiation.

UH Law Center students are active in a large number of student organizations including the Association of Women in Law, Black Law Students Association, Hispanic Law Students Association, Asian Law Students Association, Outlaw (GLBT student organization), Lex Judaica (Jewish students), Muslim Law Students Association, J. Reuben Clark Law Society, Christian Legal Society, Public Interest Law Organization, Health Law Organization, Intellectual Property Student Organization, Energy and Environmental Law Society, Federalist Society, International Law Society, American Constitution Society for Law and Policy, Phi Delta Phi, Phi Alpha Delta, Delta Theta Phi, and Sports and Entertainment Law Organization.

Career Development

The Office of Career Development strives for a creative approach in its job search partnership with students. The First Year Initiative exposes first-year students to a comprehensive career education series that surveys dozens of career opportunities. Students in small groups actively gather the information they need to make informed decisions on their career plans.

The Office of Career Development also presents a variety of panel discussions, receptions, and seminars with members of the Houston legal community to assist students in understanding law career options. Topics covered include duties and responsibilities of a law clerk, judicial clerkship opportunities, solo practice, and nontraditional uses of a law degree.

The office provides individual assistance in résumé preparation and interviewing techniques for all students and alumni. The annual On Campus Interview Program for second- and third-year students seeking summer clerkships and permanent positions to commence upon graduation attracts approximately 100 prospective employers to the campus.

Admission

The UH Law Center enrolls full-time (day) students and part-time (evening) students beginning in the fall semester, which starts in August. There is no spring or summer admission.

Demonstrated academic ability and strong LSAT scores are not the only criteria for admission. Consideration is also given to background, achievements, honors, extracurricular activities, service to others, unique abilities, hardships overcome, advanced degrees, employment, and leadership. The UH Law Center is also committed to diversity, and the UH System Board of Regents recognizes and endorses the benefits of diversity in the university setting. The Admissions Committee will consider the following additional factors: cultural history, ethnic origin, and race. These and other elements may be addressed in a personal statement of up to three pages, double-spaced.

APPLICANT PROFILE

University of Houston Law Center
This grid includes only applicants who earned 120–180 LSAT scores under standard administrations.

LSAT Score	GPA																
	3.75 +		3.50–3.74		3.25–3.49		3.00–3.24		2.75–2.99		2.50–2.74		Below 2.50		No GPA		Total
	Apps	Adm	Apps	Adm	Apps	Adm	Apps	Adm	Apps	Adm	Apps	Adm	Apps	Adm	Apps	Adm	Apps	Adm
170–180	15	14	15	14	18	17	9	8	4	4	0	0	4	0	0	0	65	57
165–169	64	61	63	59	61	59	43	43	26	23	16	9	10	8	3	3	286	265
160–164	134	105	196	149	184	117	134	81	72	24	32	10	20	5	12	9	784	500
155–159	135	35	189	27	252	15	191	8	73	0	50	1	47	0	29	1	966	87
150–154	72	11	151	9	180	10	177	5	120	2	59	0	47	0	17	2	823	39
145–149	32	3	77	2	122	3	99	0	93	1	47	1	55	0	14	0	539	10
140–144	14	0	22	1	47	0	63	0	59	0	42	0	40	0	11	0	298	1
Below 140	5	0	6	0	16	0	29	0	29	0	42	0	31	0	10	0	168	0
Total	471	229	719	261	880	221	745	145	476	54	288	21	254	13	96	15	3929	959

Apps = Number of Applicants
Adm = Number Admitted
Reflects 99% of the total applicant pool; highest LSAT data reported.

HOWARD UNIVERSITY SCHOOL OF LAW

Office of Admissions, 2900 Van Ness Street NW
Washington, DC 20008
Phone: 202.806.8008/8009; Fax: 202.806.8162
E-mail: admissions@law.howard.edu; Website: www.law.howard.edu

ABA
Approved
Since
1931

The Basics

Type of school	Private
Term	Semester
Application deadline	3/15
Application fee	$60
Financial aid deadline	2/15
Can first year start other than fall?	No
Student to faculty ratio	18.5 to 1
# of housing spaces available restricted to law students	
graduate housing for which law students are eligible	15

Faculty and Administrators

	Total		Men		Women		Minorities	
	Spr	Fall	Spr	Fall	Spr	Fall	Spr	Fall
Full-time	21	21	14	12	7	9	20	19
Other full-time	6	5	1	1	5	4	5	4
Deans, librarians, & others who teach	8	7	3	2	5	5	8	7
Part-time	31	34	20	24	11	10	26	30
Total	66	67	38	39	28	28	59	60

Curriculum

		Full-Time	Part-Time
Typical first-year section size		50	0
Is there typically a "small section" of the first-year class, other than Legal Writing, taught by full-time faculty		No	No
If yes, typical size offered last year			
# of classroom course titles beyond first-year curriculum		143	
# of upper division courses, excluding seminars, with an enrollment:	Under 25	64	
	25–49	19	
	50–74	13	
	75–99	0	
	100+	0	
# of seminars		33	
# of seminar positions available		495	
# of seminar positions filled		412	0
# of positions available in simulation courses		226	
# of simulation positions filled		226	0
# of positions available in faculty supervised clinical courses		136	
# of faculty supervised clinical positions filled		75	0
# involved in field placements		62	0
# involved in law journals		47	0
# involved in moot court or trial competitions		56	0
# of credit hours required to graduate		88	

JD Enrollment and Ethnicity

	Men #	Men %	Women #	Women %	Full-Time #	Full-Time %	Part-Time #	Part-Time %	1st-Year #	1st-Year %	Total #	Total %	JD Degs. Awd.
All Hispanics	8	4.1	14	5.0	22	4.7	0	0.0	9	5.6	22	4.7	3
Am. Ind./AK Nat.	1	0.5	1	0.4	2	0.4	0	0.0	1	0.6	2	0.4	4
Asian	7	3.6	10	3.6	17	3.6	0	0.0	6	3.7	17	3.6	8
Black/Af. Am.	153	78.9	224	80.3	377	79.7	0	0.0	123	76.4	377	79.7	106
Nat. HI/Pac. Isl.	2	1.0	1	0.4	3	0.6	0	0.0	2	1.2	3	0.6	0
2 or more races	0	0.0	0	0.0	0	0.0	0	0.0	0	0.0	0	0.0	0
Subtotal (minor.)	171	88.1	250	89.6	421	89.0	0	0.0	141	87.6	421	89.0	121
Nonres. Alien	2	1.0	9	3.2	11	2.3	0	0.0	4	2.5	11	2.3	0
White/Cauc.	15	7.7	17	6.1	32	6.8	0	0.0	12	7.5	32	6.8	9
Unknown	6	3.1	3	1.1	9	1.9	0	0.0	4	2.5	9	1.9	0
Total	194	41.0	279	59.0	473	100.0	0	0.0	161	34.0	473		133

Transfers

Transfers in	1
Transfers out	5

Tuition and Fees

	Resident	Nonresident
Full-time	$26,439	$26,439
Part-time		
Tuition Guarantee Program		N

Living Expenses

Estimated living expenses for singles

Living on campus	Living off campus	Living at home
N/A	$25,918	N/A

*ABA
Approved
Since
1931*

GPA and LSAT Scores

	Total	Full-Time	Part-Time
# of apps	1,836	1,836	0
# of offers	430	430	0
# of matrics	156	156	0
75% GPA	3.50	3.50	0.00
Median GPA	3.20	3.20	0.00
25% GPA	3.00	3.00	0.00
75% LSAT	156	156	0
Median LSAT	154	154	0
25% LSAT	151	151	0

Grants and Scholarships (from prior year)

	Total		Full-Time		Part-Time	
	#	%	#	%	#	%
Total # of students	468		468		0	
Total # receiving grants	251	53.6	251	53.6	0	0.0
Less than 1/2 tuition	130	27.8	130	27.8	0	0.0
Half to full tuition	115	24.6	115	24.6	0	0.0
Full tuition	0	0.0	0	0.0	0	0.0
More than full tuition	6	1.3	6	1.3	0	0.0
Median grant amount			$11,250		$0	

Informational and Library Resources

Total amount spent on library materials	$744,653
Study seating capacity inside the library	374
# of full-time equivalent professional librarians	7
Hours per week library is open	105
# of open, wired connections available to students	607
# of networked computers available for use by students	214
Has wireless network?	Y
Requires computer?	Y

JD Attrition (from prior year)

	Academic	Other	Total	
	#	#	#	%
1st year	8	6	14	8.5
2nd year	4	5	9	5.5
3rd year	0	0	0	0.0
4th year	0	0	0	0.0

Employment (9 months after graduation)

	Total	Percentage
Employment status known	121	91.7
Employment status unknown	11	8.3
Employed	109	90.1
Pursuing graduate degrees	1	0.8
Unemployed (seeking, not seeking, or studying for the bar)	7	5.8
Type of Employment		
# employed in law firms	52	47.7
# employed in business and industry	10	9.2
# employed in government	21	19.3
# employed in public interest	6	5.5
# employed as judicial clerks	15	13.8
# employed in academia	1	0.9
Geographic Location		
# employed in state	53	48.6
# employed outside the US	1	0.9
# of states where employed	19	

Bar Passage Rates

First-time takers	131	Reporting %	71.76
Average school %	63.82	Average state %	80.69

Average pass difference −16.87

Jurisdiction	Takers	Passers	Pass %	State %	Diff %
Maryland	39	25	64.10	78.20	−14.10
New York	36	27	75.00	86.51	−11.51
California	11	3	27.27	73.19	−45.92
Virginia	8	5	62.50	77.06	−14.56

HOWARD UNIVERSITY SCHOOL OF LAW

Office of Admissions, 2900 Van Ness Street NW
Washington, DC 20008
Phone: 202.806.8008/8009; Fax: 202.806.8162
E-mail: admissions@law.howard.edu; Website: www.law.howard.edu

Introduction

Howard University, a coeducational, private institution in Washington, DC, was chartered by the US Congress in 1867. Howard is historically (and continues to be) a majority African American institution that offers an educational experience of exceptional quality and value to students with high academic potential. Particular emphasis is placed on providing educational opportunities for promising African Americans and other persons of color who are underrepresented in the legal profession, as well as for nonminority persons with a strong interest in civil and human rights and public service. The main campus of Howard is located in northwest Washington, DC, on Georgia Avenue, and the law school is located on a separate 22-acre campus on Van Ness Street NW, adjacent to Connecticut Avenue, approximately three miles from the main campus.

The School of Law opened its doors in 1869. Originally, there was a great need to train lawyers with a strong commitment to helping black Americans secure and protect their newly established rights. Today, as a national law school, Howard is dedicated to protecting the rights of all Americans and understands that its place in the annals of legal history demands that it maintains and exemplifies truth, equality, and excellence in the pursuit of justice. The law school has a diverse student body and faculty. Howard University School of Law is fully accredited by the American Bar Association and the Association of American Law Schools, and certifies its graduates for bar examination in all jurisdictions of the United States.

Special Programs

The School of Law has a strong commitment to public service and to human and civil rights. Many programs and activities of the school reflect that fact. The school also provides an opportunity for clinical experience in civil and criminal litigation. Howard law school also offers a summer study-abroad program in comparative and international law at the University of the Western Cape in South Africa. The six-week program is approved by the ABA and offers constitutional, business, and trade law courses for credit. A student-exchange program has been established with Vermont Law School and Brigham Young University. Through the exchange program, a limited number of third-year JD students may spend a semester at one of these law schools to take advantage of curricular offerings that may be of specific interest to them.

The Institute for Intellectual Property and Social Justice (IIPSJ) is concerned with disparity of access to, and exploitation of, intellectual property as it relates to racial and economic inequities. IIPSJ's focus is on examining and utilizing intellectual property to advance social justice in this country and globally. IIPSJ sponsors numerous programs for students, attorneys, and judges; publishes papers; and supports externships for students.

Curriculum

The curriculum leading to the first degree in law covers three academic years of two semesters each. During the first two years, emphasis is on the fundamental analytical concepts and skills of the law and the system by which it is administered—the functions required of a lawyer within a legal system based

upon the common law. The curriculum in the third year provides diversified experience and a solid foundation of whatever specialization is desired.

Degree Programs

The School of Law offers programs leading to the Juris Doctor (JD), Master of Laws (LLM) for foreign law graduates, and Juris Doctor/Master in Business Administration (JD/MBA) degrees.

An applicant to the JD program must have a baccalaureate degree from an accredited college or university before enrolling in the Howard University School of Law. Competitive numerical predictors for admission to Howard University include a Law School Admission Test (LSAT) score of 153 and above and an undergraduate grade-point average (UGPA) of 3.4. In addition to the LSAT score and UGPA, we consider the rigor of an applicant's undergraduate course of study, letters of recommendation (particularly from faculty members who have taught the applicant), any graduate study, employment, extracurricular activities, and other indicators of potential for success in law school and excellence in the profession.

Applicants to the JD/MBA program must apply and meet the independent admission requirements of both schools, including completion of the GMAT.

The LLM program offers foreign law graduates an opportunity to further their legal studies through advanced study and research. To be admitted as a candidate for the LLM degree, applicants must be in high academic standing; have a degree in law from an accredited foreign university or its equivalent (as determined by the faculty of law); and have some experience in the judiciary, administrative establishment, bar, or law faculty.

Research Facilities

Howard University School of Law has a state-of-the-art, four-story, 76,000-square-foot law library. This facility provides space for a book collection of up to 215,000 volumes; seating for over 295 students (more than 70 percent of the student population), including 90 open carrels, with all locations wired for computer use; enlarged microfilm and audiovisual facilities; and distinctive rooms of wood and brick for special collections, newspaper and periodical reading, and the rare book collection.

The law library is both a working collection for law students and lawyers and a research institution for legal scholars. The civil rights archive contains briefs, working papers, and materials of the NAACP and other civil rights organizations. The library has a collection that emphasizes civil and political rights and literature to support study of the legal problems of the poor. Its collection has been expanded to also include considerable CD-ROM resources. The law library has an online catalogue system, e-mail capabilities, and Internet access.

Student Activities

The *Howard Law Journal* publishes legal materials for scholarly and professional interest. The national and international moot court teams, which sponsor intramural competition and participate in competitions nationwide, have won numerous honors. The Student Bar Association is the general student government organization. The *Barrister*, the student newspaper, publishes several issues a year. Other organizations represent students from diverse ethnic backgrounds, including African Americans, Latinos, Africans, Caribbean Islanders, and Asian Pacific Islanders.

Career Services

The Office of Career Services is an integral part of the law school. To assist students, the office offers workshops on job-search techniques and résumé writing, as well as seminars on career development and practice specialties. The office also maintains an extensive resource library with online employer research systems, newsletters, and updated listings of career opportunities. Each year, the Office of Career Services sponsors two on-campus interview programs, and more than 500 recruiters from law firms, government agencies, and corporations visit the law school with offers of employment for promising students and graduates. Approximately 4,500 interviews are scheduled annually. Graduates receive highly competitive and prestigious judicial clerkships and work for large and small private firms; federal, state, and local government agencies; public interest organizations; and public and private corporations throughout the United States.

APPLICANT PROFILE

Howard University School of Law
This grid includes only applicants who earned 120–180 LSAT scores under standard administrations.

LSAT Score	3.75 +		3.50–3.74		3.25–3.49		3.00–3.24		2.75–2.99		2.50–2.74		2.25–2.49		2.00–2.24		Below 2.00		No GPA		Totals	
	Apps	Adm	Apps	Adm	Apps	Adm	Apps	Adm	Apps	Adm	Apps	Adm	Apps	Adm	Apps	Adm	Apps	Adm	Apps	Adm	Apps	Adm
175–180	0	0	0	0	0	0	0	0	0	0	0	0	0	0	0	0	0	0	0	0	0	0
170–174	0	0	1	1	0	0	0	0	0	0	0	0	0	0	0	0	0	0	0	0	1	1
165–169	1	1	3	2	3	2	4	3	1	1	3	1	0	0	1	1	0	0	0	0	16	11
160–164	8	8	16	12	17	11	17	9	7	1	7	2	5	3	4	0	1	1	2	1	84	48
155–159	20	16	36	32	58	42	47	29	34	19	31	19	15	7	5	0	2	0	4	1	252	165
150–154	23	14	70	36	92	38	103	47	84	24	58	9	39	1	6	0	2	0	8	2	485	171
145–149	30	12	59	16	100	14	140	12	115	2	71	1	35	0	21	0	5	0	8	0	584	57
140–144	20	3	33	3	57	0	66	0	77	0	68	0	37	0	13	0	4	0	13	0	388	6
135–139	3	0	13	0	26	0	29	0	21	0	26	0	19	0	9	0	3	0	2	0	151	0
130–134	1	0	0	0	9	0	10	0	6	0	11	0	6	0	1	0	1	0	2	0	47	0
125–129	1	0	0	0	0	0	2	0	1	0	0	0	1	0	2	0	0	0	1	0	8	0
120–124	0	0	0	0	0	0	0	0	0	0	0	0	0	0	0	0	0	0	1	0	1	0
Total	107	54	231	102	362	107	418	100	346	47	275	32	157	11	62	1	18	1	41	4	2017	459

Apps = Number of Applicants
Adm = Number Admitted
Reflects 99% of the total applicant pool; highest LSAT data reported.

UNIVERSITY OF IDAHO COLLEGE OF LAW

PO Box 442321
Moscow, ID 83844-2321
Phone: 208.885.2300; Fax: 208.885.5709
E-mail: lawadmit@uidaho.edu; Website: www.law.uidaho.edu

ABA
Approved
Since
1925

The Basics

Type of school	Public
Term	Semester
Application deadline	2/15
Application fee	$50
Financial aid deadline	2/15
Can first year start other than fall?	No
Student to faculty ratio	15.7 to 1
# of housing spaces available restricted to law students graduate housing for which law students are eligible	300

Faculty and Administrators

	Total		Men		Women		Minorities	
	Spr	Fall	Spr	Fall	Spr	Fall	Spr	Fall
Full-time	18	17	12	10	6	7	2	2
Other full-time	6	4	1	0	5	4	0	0
Deans, librarians, & others who teach	8	8	3	3	5	5	1	1
Part-time	8	10	4	8	4	2	0	0
Total	40	39	20	21	20	18	3	3

Curriculum

	Full-Time	Part-Time
Typical first-year section size	57	0
Is there typically a "small section" of the first-year class, other than Legal Writing, taught by full-time faculty	No	No
If yes, typical size offered last year		
# of classroom course titles beyond first-year curriculum	89	

# of upper division courses, excluding seminars, with an enrollment:		
	Under 25	64
	25–49	10
	50–74	5
	75–99	8
	100+	1

# of seminars	17	
# of seminar positions available	379	
# of seminar positions filled	200	0
# of positions available in simulation courses	249	
# of simulation positions filled	172	0
# of positions available in faculty supervised clinical courses	192	
# of faculty supervised clinical positions filled	68	0
# involved in field placements	70	0
# involved in law journals	56	0
# involved in moot court or trial competitions	12	0
# of credit hours required to graduate	90	

JD Enrollment and Ethnicity

	Men #	Men %	Women #	Women %	Full-Time #	Full-Time %	Part-Time #	Part-Time %	1st-Year #	1st-Year %	Total #	Total %	JD Degs. Awd.
All Hispanics	10	4.8	14	9.9	24	6.9	0	0.0	14	10.7	24	6.9	7
Am. Ind./AK Nat.	5	2.4	3	2.1	8	2.3	0	0.0	3	2.3	8	2.3	0
Asian	5	2.4	2	1.4	7	2.0	0	0.0	4	3.1	7	2.0	7
Black/Af. Am.	4	1.9	1	0.7	5	1.4	0	0.0	2	1.5	5	1.4	0
Nat. HI/Pac. Isl.	0	0.0	0	0.0	0	0.0	0	0.0	0	0.0	0	0.0	0
2 or more races	10	4.8	3	2.1	13	3.7	0	0.0	6	4.6	13	3.7	0
Subtotal (minor.)	34	16.3	23	16.3	57	16.3	0	0.0	29	22.1	57	16.3	15
Nonres. Alien	1	0.5	1	0.7	2	0.6	0	0.0	2	1.5	2	0.6	0
White/Cauc.	158	76.0	109	77.3	267	76.5	0	0.0	95	72.5	267	76.5	74
Unknown	15	7.2	8	5.7	23	6.6	0	0.0	7	5.3	23	6.6	5
Total	208	59.6	141	40.4	349	100.0	0	0.0	133	37.5	349		94

Transfers

Transfers in	4
Transfers out	5

Tuition and Fees

	Resident	Nonresident
Full-time	$12,940	$24,532
Part-time		
Tuition Guarantee Program	N	

Living Expenses

Estimated living expenses for singles

Living on campus	Living off campus	Living at home
$16,718	$16,718	$10,870

UNIVERSITY OF IDAHO COLLEGE OF LAW

ABA
Approved
Since
1925

GPA and LSAT Scores

	Total	Full-Time	Part-Time
# of apps	862	862	0
# of offers	378	378	0
# of matrics	130	130	0
75% GPA	3.54	3.54	0.00
Median GPA	3.30	3.30	0.00
25% GPA	2.96	2.96	0.00
75% LSAT	157	157	0
Median LSAT	154	154	0
25% LSAT	151	151	0

Grants and Scholarships (from prior year)

	Total		Full-Time		Part-Time	
	#	%	#	%	#	%
Total # of students	322		319		3	
Total # receiving grants	97	30.1	97	30.4	0	0.0
Less than 1/2 tuition	61	18.9	61	19.1	0	0.0
Half to full tuition	19	5.9	19	6.0	0	0.0
Full tuition	12	3.7	12	3.8	0	0.0
More than full tuition	5	1.6	5	1.6	0	0.0
Median grant amount			$2,271		$0	

Informational and Library Resources

Total amount spent on library materials	$898,743
Study seating capacity inside the library	330
# of full-time equivalent professional librarians	4
Hours per week library is open	86
# of open, wired connections available to students	306
# of networked computers available for use by students	57
Has wireless network?	Y
Requires computer?	N

JD Attrition (from prior year)

	Academic	Other	Total	
	#	#	#	%
1st year	2	0	2	1.8
2nd year	0	7	7	6.5
3rd year	0	0	0	0.0
4th year	0	0	0	0.0

Employment (9 months after graduation)

	Total	Percentage
Employment status known	92	97.9
Employment status unknown	2	2.1
Employed	74	80.4
Pursuing graduate degrees	10	10.9
Unemployed (seeking, not seeking, or studying for the bar)	6	6.5
Type of Employment		
# employed in law firms	33	44.6
# employed in business and industry	8	10.8
# employed in government	8	10.8
# employed in public interest	1	1.4
# employed as judicial clerks	20	27.0
# employed in academia	1	1.4
Geographic Location		
# employed in state	45	60.8
# employed outside the US	0	0.0
# of states where employed		12

Bar Passage Rates

First-time takers	93	Reporting %	98.92
Average school %	83.70	Average state %	83.19
Average pass difference	.51		

Jurisdiction	Takers	Passers	Pass %	State %	Diff %
Idaho	53	48	90.57	85.81	4.76
Washington	13	7	53.85	74.42	−20.57
Utah	8	6	75.00	88.94	−13.94
California	5	3	60.00	73.19	−13.19
Others (8)	13	13	100.00		

UNIVERSITY OF IDAHO COLLEGE OF LAW

PO Box 442321
Moscow, ID 83844-2321
Phone: 208.885.2300; Fax: 208.885.5709
E-mail: lawadmit@uidaho.edu; Website: www.law.uidaho.edu

Introduction

The College of Law, established in 1909, has been a member of the AALS since 1914 and has been accredited by the ABA since 1925. As Idaho's leader in legal education, the College of Law emphasizes quality over quantity and is founded on collegiality and a dedication to the highest ideals of a noble profession.

College of Law students benefit from an attentive, dedicated, and accessible faculty as well as the unique opportunity to combine residential university community and metropolitan living and learning. The primary location of the College of Law is the Menard Law Building on the main campus of the University of Idaho in Moscow, Idaho. However, through the Semester in Practice and Third Year in Boise programs, third-year students may elect to engage in classroom and experiential learning in Boise, Idaho, one of America's fasting growing metropolitan areas.

Enrollment/Student Body

With an overall enrollment around 350, students at the College of Law have a wide variety of backgrounds and life experiences. Students come mostly from the West, representing almost 100 colleges and universities, 24 different states, and several foreign countries. Approximately 60 percent of our students are Idaho residents. The College of Law welcomes and actively seeks diversity, with particular attention to students of color and those who have overcome socioeconomic disadvantage. Due to our highly selective admission process and positive learning environment, including an academic support program run by a licensed attorney, academic attrition is less than 3 percent.

Technology, Library, and Physical Facilities

The College of Law occupies a building with full wireless Internet access and a newly renovated, state-of-the-art courtroom. The law library houses a collection of more than 240,000 volumes and volume-equivalents and more than 4,800 serial titles. The law library also provides a computer lab; LexisNexis, Westlaw, Dialog, and HeinOnline services; and the US Congressional Serial Set. Membership in the Western Library Network and the Inland Northwest Library Automation Network allows users to access holdings of libraries across the nation. Law students also have access to the other libraries of the University of Idaho and those at Washington State University, located 8 miles away in Pullman, Washington.

Curriculum

All first-year students are required to take courses in contract law, criminal law, tort law, legislation and regulation, property, civil procedure, legal research and writing, and constitutional law. After the first year, students may choose to pursue an area of emphasis (not required). The College of Law provides emphases in natural resources and environmental law, business law and entrepreneurship, advocacy and dispute resolution, and Native American law. In addition to the aforementioned areas of emphasis, the College of Law curriculum provides enrichments in a wide

variety of other substantive areas from ethics to international law. Upon graduation, our students have a broad and well-developed knowledge of the law.

Practical Skills

The College of Law places great importance on public service and the development of practical skills. Our distinctive Pro Bono Program, which requires all students to complete at least 40 hours of approved Pro Bono service before graduation, engages students in substantial, law-related public service and provides a learning experience outside the classroom.

There are eight live-client clinics available at the College of Law: (1) general practice clinic, (2) appellate clinic, (3) immigration clinic, (4) small business legal clinic, (5) tax clinic, (6) domestic violence and sexual assault clinic, (7) victims' rights clinic, and (8) mediation clinic.

Students may also sharpen their practical skills by participating in our Externship Program, completing a Semester in Practice and/or participating in a wide variety of faculty- and lawyer-supervised skills competitions.

Dual Degrees

Dual JD/MS/PhD degrees in water resources are offered as part of the one-of-a-kind Waters of the West initiative offered in cooperation with the University of Idaho College of Natural Resources. There are three options for emphasis: engineering and science; science and management; and law, management, and policy.

Dual JD/MS Environmental Science degrees are available in cooperation with the University of Idaho College of Graduate Studies Environmental Science Program.

Dual JD/Master of Accounting degrees in cooperation with the University of Idaho College of Business and Economics and Dual JD/Master of Accounting, Taxation Emphasis degrees in cooperation with Boise State University are also available. These programs are particularly valuable for students interested in practicing tax law.

Admission

Applications are accepted beginning in October preceding the year in which enrollment is desired. Our law program is full time. Although students have the option of spending all or part of their third year in Boise, Idaho, students must spend their first and second years in Moscow, Idaho. Applicants must submit college transcripts and letters of recommendation through LSAC's Credential Assembly Service (CAS). The application priority deadline is February 15, but we recommend late-fall application. Applications submitted after February 15 will be reviewed, but timely applications will receive priority consideration. The Admission Committee looks at each applicant holistically, including but not limited to LSAT score, academic record and background, writing ability, personal statement, work and life experiences, and recommendations.

Student Activities

Students belong to more than 30 active student organizations. The Student Bar Association represents student interests, both educational and social. The *Idaho Law Review*, which covers topics ranging from state and regional problems to national and international issues, and *The Crit* (an electronic journal of critical legal studies), give students valuable writing and editing experience. The Board of Student Advocates and the Law Students for Appropriate Dispute Resolution coordinate intramural competitions and provide opportunities for students to participate in national competitions that build professional skills. Other groups include the American Civil Liberties Union, Latino Law Caucus, the Federalist Society, Multicultural Law Caucus, Native American Law Students Association, OUTLaw, Black Law Students Association, J. Reuben Clark Society, and the Women's Law Caucus.

Career Development

The Career Development Office, run by a licensed attorney, facilitates students' career planning and their search for summer and permanent employment. The office actively promotes job opportunities, including arranging on-campus interview and recruit-by-mail programs. Historically, over 90 percent of graduates find employment within nine months of graduation or go on to advanced graduate study. The college has exceptional success placing students in federal and state judicial clerkships as the first step in their careers. A majority of students find employment in Idaho, although Utah, Washington, and Oregon are also popular. Idaho graduates are employed throughout the United States and several foreign countries.

APPLICANT PROFILE

University of Idaho College of Law
This grid includes only applicants who earned 120–180 LSAT scores under standard administrations.

LSAT Score	3.75 +		3.50–3.74		3.25–3.49		3.00–3.24		2.75–2.99		2.50–2.74		2.25–2.49		2.00–2.24		Below 2.00		No GPA		Total	
	Apps	Adm	Apps	Adm	Apps	Adm	Apps	Adm	Apps	Adm	Apps	Adm	Apps	Adm	Apps	Adm	Apps	Adm	Apps	Adm	Apps	Adm
175–180	0	0	0	0	0	0	0	0	0	0	0	0	0	0	0	0	0	0	0	0	0	0
170–174	2	2	1	1	0	0	0	0	1	1	2	2	0	0	0	0	0	0	0	0	6	6
165–169	5	5	1	1	2	2	1	1	1	1	0	0	0	0	0	0	0	0	0	0	10	10
160–164	16	16	9	9	16	16	16	13	9	9	6	6	1	1	1	1	0	0	1	0	75	71
155–159	17	16	27	26	42	38	36	30	23	18	16	10	6	4	4	3	1	0	1	1	173	146
150–154	32	19	42	16	67	24	54	17	47	11	16	2	14	1	4	2	2	1	3	1	281	94
145–149	13	5	22	7	39	6	35	2	30	5	17	1	6	1	4	1	1	0	4	3	171	31
140–144	4	1	9	0	14	1	19	3	24	2	14	2	4	0	0	0	0	0	5	1	93	10
135–139	0	0	5	0	4	0	2	0	4	0	3	0	0	0	0	0	0	0	3	0	21	0
130–134	1	0	0	0	1	0	3	0	3	0	4	0	2	0	2	0	1	0	0	0	17	0
125–129	0	0	0	0	0	0	0	0	0	0	0	0	1	0	1	0	0	0	1	0	3	0
120–124	0	0	0	0	0	0	0	0	0	0	0	0	0	0	0	0	0	0	0	0	0	0
Total	90	64	116	60	185	87	166	66	142	47	78	23	34	7	16	7	5	1	18	6	850	368

Apps = Number of Applicants
Adm = Number Admitted
Reflects 100% of the total applicant pool; highest LSAT data reported.

UNIVERSITY OF ILLINOIS COLLEGE OF LAW

504 East Pennsylvania Avenue
Champaign, IL 61820
Phone: 217.244.6415
E-mail: admissions@law.illinois.edu; Website: www.law.illinois.edu

ABA
Approved
Since
1923

The Basics

Type of school	Public
Term	Semester
Application deadline	3/15
Application fee	$0
Financial aid deadline	3/15
Can first year start other than fall?	No
Student to faculty ratio	12.8 to 1
# of housing spaces available restricted to law students	
graduate housing for which law students are eligible	1,914

Faculty and Administrators

	Total		Men		Women		Minorities	
	Spr	Fall	Spr	Fall	Spr	Fall	Spr	Fall
Full-time	40	41	29	24	11	17	9	9
Other full-time	8	8	3	2	5	6	0	1
Deans, librarians, & others who teach	11	11	6	6	5	5	0	0
Part-time	42	40	24	25	18	15	8	6
Total	101	100	62	57	39	43	17	16

Curriculum

	Full-Time	Part-Time
Typical first-year section size	57	0
Is there typically a "small section" of the first-year class, other than Legal Writing, taught by full-time faculty	Yes	No
If yes, typical size offered last year	38	
# of classroom course titles beyond first-year curriculum	134	

# of upper division courses, excluding seminars, with an enrollment:	Under 25	90
	25–49	42
	50–74	11
	75–99	4
	100+	3

# of seminars	53	
# of seminar positions available	1,045	
# of seminar positions filled	607	0
# of positions available in simulation courses	1,167	
# of simulation positions filled	840	0
# of positions available in faculty supervised clinical courses	48	
# of faculty supervised clinical positions filled	48	0
# involved in field placements	257	0
# involved in law journals	172	0
# involved in moot court or trial competitions	60	0
# of credit hours required to graduate	90	

JD Enrollment and Ethnicity

	Men		Women		Full-Time		Part-Time		1st-Year		Total		JD Degs. Awd.
	#	%	#	%	#	%	#	%	#	%	#	%	
All Hispanics	21	5.6	20	7.6	41	6.4	0	0.0	17	7.5	41	6.4	8
Am. Ind./AK Nat.	4	1.1	2	0.8	6	0.9	0	0.0	1	0.4	6	0.9	0
Asian	36	9.6	25	9.5	61	9.5	0	0.0	18	7.9	61	9.5	13
Black/Af. Am.	18	4.8	27	10.2	45	7.0	0	0.0	16	7.0	45	7.0	17
Nat. HI/Pac. Isl.	0	0.0	0	0.0	0	0.0	0	0.0	0	0.0	0	0.0	0
2 or more races	4	1.1	1	0.4	5	0.8	0	0.0	5	2.2	5	0.8	0
Subtotal (minor.)	83	22.1	75	28.4	158	24.7	0	0.0	57	25.1	158	24.7	38
Nonres. Alien	15	4.0	12	4.5	27	4.2	0	0.0	9	4.0	27	4.2	0
White/Cauc.	253	67.3	155	58.7	408	63.8	0	0.0	150	66.1	408	63.8	124
Unknown	25	6.6	22	8.3	47	7.3	0	0.0	11	4.8	47	7.3	20
Total	376	58.8	264	41.3	640	100.0	0	0.0	227	35.5	640		195

Transfers

Transfers in	6
Transfers out	6

Tuition and Fees

	Resident	Nonresident
Full-time	$36,420	$43,420
Part-time		
Tuition Guarantee Program		N

Living Expenses

Estimated living expenses for singles

Living on campus	Living off campus	Living at home
$16,086	$16,086	$16,086

ABA Approved Since 1923

GPA and LSAT Scores

	Total	Full-Time	Part-Time
# of apps	4,833	4,833	0
# of offers	984	984	0
# of matrics	228	228	0
75% GPA	3.90	3.90	0.00
Median GPA	3.80	3.80	0.00
25% GPA	3.30	3.30	0.00
75% LSAT	168	168	0
Median LSAT	167	167	0
25% LSAT	163	163	0

Grants and Scholarships (from prior year)

	Total		Full-Time		Part-Time	
	#	%	#	%	#	%
Total # of students	617		617		0	
Total # receiving grants	529	85.7	529	85.7	0	0.0
Less than 1/2 tuition	253	41.0	253	41.0	0	0.0
Half to full tuition	222	36.0	222	36.0	0	0.0
Full tuition	54	8.8	54	8.8	0	0.0
More than full tuition	0	0.0	0	0.0	0	0.0
Median grant amount			$12,500		$0	

Informational and Library Resources

Total amount spent on library materials	$1,410,887
Study seating capacity inside the library	331
# of full-time equivalent professional librarians	8
Hours per week library is open	102
# of open, wired connections available to students	802
# of networked computers available for use by students	42
Has wireless network?	Y
Requires computer?	N

JD Attrition (from prior year)

	Academic	Other	Total	
	#	#	#	%
1st year	0	11	11	4.8
2nd year	0	1	1	0.5
3rd year	0	0	0	0.0
4th year	0	0	0	0.0

Employment (9 months after graduation)

	Total	Percentage
Employment status known	192	100.0
Employment status unknown	0	0.0
Employed	165	85.9
Pursuing graduate degrees	15	7.8
Unemployed (seeking, not seeking, or studying for the bar)	1	0.5
Type of Employment		
# employed in law firms	110	66.7
# employed in business and industry	19	11.5
# employed in government	8	4.8
# employed in public interest	11	6.7
# employed as judicial clerks	11	6.7
# employed in academia	6	3.6
Geographic Location		
# employed in state	101	61.2
# employed outside the US	2	1.2
# of states where employed	24	

Bar Passage Rates

First-time takers	187	Reporting %	82.35
Average school %	95.45	Average state %	90.52
Average pass difference	4.93		

Jurisdiction	Takers	Passers	Pass %	State %	Diff %
Illinois	141	135	95.74	90.89	4.85
New York	13	12	92.31	86.51	5.80

UNIVERSITY OF ILLINOIS COLLEGE OF LAW

504 East Pennsylvania Avenue
Champaign, IL 61820
Phone: 217.244.6415
E-mail: admissions@law.illinois.edu; Website: www.law.illinois.edu

Introduction

Established over a century ago, the University of Illinois College of Law fosters excellence in legal education through a close community of faculty members and students, where teaching goes hand in hand with scholarship. The resources—intellectual, cultural, and recreational—of one of the world's largest and best universities are readily available to our law students, as is the appealing ambience of a university community. The college's comparatively low tuition makes the program an outstanding value.

Library and Physical Facilities

A hallmark of a great university and a great law school is its library. The University Library in Urbana-Champaign is the largest public university library in the country. The Jenner Law Library holds 750,000 volumes and provides access to an equally wide array of electronic resources. In addition to US legal materials, the Jenner Law Library has extensive holdings in foreign and international law and houses a world-class collection of rare legal materials. Equally significant is Jenner's professional staff. Ten of its 11 law librarians have JDs in addition to master's degrees in library science. Law librarians teach legal research and work closely with students to support research and learning.

Directly across the street from the law school is one of the country's largest physical education buildings, with indoor and outdoor swimming pools, tennis courts, four gyms, weight and exercise equipment, archery, and ball courts of all kinds. The facility is free for students.

Joint-Degree Programs

The College of Law administers 12 formal joint JD and master's or doctoral degree programs. The combined degrees available are JD-MBA, JD-MCS, JD-MEd, JD-EdM, JD-PhD, JD-MHRIR, JD-MA in Journalism, JD-MD, JD-MS in Chemistry, JD-MS in Natural Resources, JD-MUP, and JD-DVM.

Special Programs

Environmental Law—The college has an active program of environmental and planning studies. Beyond the first-year course in property, the college offers courses in environmental law, natural resources, and land-use planning.

Intellectual Property (IP)—The College of Law boasts a strong intellectual property curriculum and offers a rich array of courses taught by nationally known faculty and experienced practitioners. Students choose from a variety of offerings ranging from core patent, copyright, and trademark courses to cutting-edge classes like Law and Regulation of Cyberspace, Internet and Web Law, International Copyright Principles, and International IP Transfers. Beyond its own curriculum, the College of Law's intellectual property faculty capitalizes upon the university's highly regarded academic programs in science and engineering, as well as its National Center for Supercomputing Applications, recognized as the world's leader in computer design applications. The College of Law is currently collaborating with these premier university departments to develop joint-degree programs in the rapidly changing intellectual property arena.

Interdisciplinary Study—While the College of Law course offerings are so varied that it would take a student 12 years to sample all of them, students interested in related subjects outside the law school may receive up to 12 hours of credit for study in another discipline. This flexibility allows students to complement their legal education with advanced coursework in a highly regarded university.

International Legal Studies—Students pursuing international legal studies can choose from 15 international and comparative law courses. Faculty members have long-standing international connections, and some collaborate with international scholars and legal experts to teach these courses.

Public Interest Law and Public Policy—As one of the premier public law schools, the College of Law plays a special role in educating students to both serve the public interest and formulate public policy. The college's commitment to public interest law is demonstrated by the pro bono notation placed on diplomas of graduates who have performed at least 60 hours of unpaid legal work. In addition, students may choose from a variety of timely courses addressing public interest and policy issues.

Skills Training—The college offers four live-client clinics: Civil Litigation Clinic, International Human Rights Clinic, Transactions and Community Economic Development Clinic, and Employee Justice Clinic, as well as classes in legal drafting, business planning, advanced bankruptcy, environmental management, estate planning, and tax practice. All challenge students to solve concrete problems and draft legal documents in a variety of fields. Courses on computer applications in the law and quantitative methods in legal decision-making familiarize students with sophisticated techniques necessary in today's law practice; these include computerized methods of document preparation and information retrieval, statistical analysis, the use of computer simulations in litigation, and the calculation of damage awards.

Taxation—Illinois offers one of the strongest tax curricula in the country, with core courses that address all aspects of tax practice and advanced offerings that integrate tax problems with other fields of law.

Trial Advocacy Program—The college's Trial Advocacy Program is especially popular, enrolling about three-quarters of the third-year class. The yearlong program teaches the art of courtroom litigation and concludes with students conducting a daylong mock trial.

Housing

College of Law students live both off campus and in graduate- or married-student campus housing. For information concerning campus housing, contact the Graduate and Family Housing Department at 217.333.5656.

In addition, the Urbana-Champaign area has ample private rental opportunities available at relatively low cost. Most current College of Law students choose to live in private, off-campus housing due to its low cost and easy access to the award-winning Urbana-Champaign mass transit system, which is free for all University of Illinois students.

Student Activities

The small size and tight-knit community of the College of Law allow students to directly participate in an extensive variety of activities. Students run and write for the *University of Illinois Law Review*, the *Elder Law Journal*, the *University of Illinois Journal of Law, Technology, and Policy*, and the "Illinois Law Update" during their second and third years. In addition, second- and third-year students may participate in seven different moot court competitions that feature internal, external, and national contests, and several live-client legal clinics. First-year students also have many opportunities to get involved at the College of Law through the negotiation and client counseling competitions and several faculty-student committees. Finally, most students participate in at least one of the almost 35 student organizations. These organizations plan countless lectures, debates, charitable activities, sporting events, law firm visits, and social receptions, including the always anticipated annual formal ball.

Scholarships

The College of Law offers a number of scholarships, ranging from $1,000 to full tuition, awarded to students who show the greatest promise in the study of law. Previous academic success is a primary consideration; the committee also considers other relevant factors.

APPLICANT PROFILE

Our admission process takes into consideration many factors beyond the undergraduate GPA and the LSAT score. A statistical grid, as is typically provided here, only takes into consideration these two factors. Admission decisions at the University of Illinois College of Law are based on the Admission Committee's experienced judgment applied to individual cases. Consequently, we have chosen not to provide applicants with a grid that does not accurately portray our admission process.

INDIANA UNIVERSITY MAURER SCHOOL OF LAW—BLOOMINGTON

211 S. Indiana Avenue
Bloomington, IN 47405-7001
Phone: 812.855.4765; Fax: 812.855.1967
E-mail: lawadmis@indiana.edu; Website: www.law.indiana.edu

ABA
Approved
Since
1937

The Basics

Type of school	Public
Term	Semester
Application deadline	3/1
Application fee	$50
Financial aid deadline	3/10
Can first year start other than fall?	No
Student to faculty ratio	9.4 to 1
# of housing spaces available restricted to law students	
graduate housing for which law students are eligible	800

Faculty and Administrators

	Total		Men		Women		Minorities	
	Spr	Fall	Spr	Fall	Spr	Fall	Spr	Fall
Full-time	54	55	36	36	18	19	7	6
Other full-time	3	4	3	3	0	1	0	0
Deans, librarians, & others who teach	17	17	9	9	8	8	0	0
Part-time	20	10	15	9	5	1	1	0
Total	94	86	63	57	31	29	8	6

Curriculum

	Full-Time	Part-Time
Typical first-year section size	90	0
Is there typically a "small section" of the first-year class, other than Legal Writing, taught by full-time faculty	No	No
If yes, typical size offered last year		
# of classroom course titles beyond first-year curriculum	137	
# of upper division courses, excluding seminars, with an enrollment: Under 25	87	
25–49	22	
50–74	13	
75–99	4	
100+	4	
# of seminars	27	
# of seminar positions available	434	
# of seminar positions filled	319	0
# of positions available in simulation courses	603	
# of simulation positions filled	513	0
# of positions available in faculty supervised clinical courses	131	
# of faculty supervised clinical positions filled	131	0
# involved in field placements	258	0
# involved in law journals	156	0
# involved in moot court or trial competitions	475	0
# of credit hours required to graduate	88	

JD Enrollment and Ethnicity

	Men #	Men %	Women #	Women %	Full-Time #	Full-Time %	Part-Time #	Part-Time %	1st-Year #	1st-Year %	Total #	Total %	JD Degs. Awd.
All Hispanics	15	3.9	14	5.3	29	4.5	0	0.0	11	4.5	29	4.5	11
Am. Ind./AK Nat.	0	0.0	0	0.0	0	0.0	0	0.0	0	0.0	0	0.0	0
Asian	18	4.7	16	6.0	34	5.3	0	0.0	8	3.3	34	5.3	8
Black/Af. Am.	24	6.3	30	11.3	54	8.4	0	0.0	19	7.8	54	8.4	14
Nat. HI/Pac. Isl.	0	0.0	0	0.0	0	0.0	0	0.0	0	0.0	0	0.0	0
2 or more races	0	0.0	0	0.0	0	0.0	0	0.0	0	0.0	0	0.0	0
Subtotal (minor.)	57	15.0	60	22.6	117	18.1	0	0.0	38	15.5	117	18.1	33
Nonres. Alien	0	0.0	0	0.0	0	0.0	0	0.0	0	0.0	0	0.0	0
White/Cauc.	310	81.4	199	75.1	509	78.8	0	0.0	200	81.6	509	78.8	156
Unknown	14	3.7	6	2.3	20	3.1	0	0.0	7	2.9	20	3.1	7
Total	381	59.0	265	41.0	646	100.0	0	0.0	245	37.9	646		196

Transfers

Transfers in	0
Transfers out	14

Tuition and Fees

	Resident	Nonresident
Full-time	$26,904	$43,704
Part-time		
Tuition Guarantee Program	N	

Living Expenses

Estimated living expenses for singles

Living on campus	Living off campus	Living at home
$22,768	$22,768	N/A

INDIANA UNIVERSITY MAURER SCHOOL OF LAW—BLOOMINGTON

ABA
Approved
Since
1937

GPA and LSAT Scores

	Total	Full-Time	Part-Time
# of apps	3,441	3,441	0
# of offers	849	849	0
# of matrics	250	250	0
75% GPA	3.89	3.89	0.00
Median GPA	3.78	3.78	0.00
25% GPA	3.47	3.47	0.00
75% LSAT	164	164	0
Median LSAT	164	164	0
25% LSAT	156	156	0

Grants and Scholarships (from prior year)

	Total		Full-Time		Part-Time	
	#	%	#	%	#	%
Total # of students	622		620		2	
Total # receiving grants	572	92.0	572	92.3	0	0.0
Less than 1/2 tuition	318	51.1	318	51.3	0	0.0
Half to full tuition	121	19.5	121	19.5	0	0.0
Full tuition	53	8.5	53	8.5	0	0.0
More than full tuition	80	12.9	80	12.9	0	0.0
Median grant amount			$14,420		$0	

Informational and Library Resources

Total amount spent on library materials	$1,456,098
Study seating capacity inside the library	687
# of full-time equivalent professional librarians	10
Hours per week library is open	115
# of open, wired connections available to students	147
# of networked computers available for use by students	82
Has wireless network?	Y
Requires computer?	Y

JD Attrition (from prior year)

	Academic	Other	Total	
	#	#	#	%
1st year	0	7	7	3.2
2nd year	0	16	16	7.8
3rd year	0	0	0	0.0
4th year	0	0	0	0.0

Employment (9 months after graduation)

	Total	Percentage
Employment status known	193	99.0
Employment status unknown	2	1.0
Employed	174	90.2
Pursuing graduate degrees	9	4.7
Unemployed (seeking, not seeking, or studying for the bar)	5	2.6
Type of Employment		
# employed in law firms	71	40.8
# employed in business and industry	32	18.4
# employed in government	35	20.1
# employed in public interest	12	6.9
# employed as judicial clerks	13	7.5
# employed in academia	11	6.3
Geographic Location		
# employed in state	78	44.8
# employed outside the US	3	1.7
# of states where employed		29

Bar Passage Rates

First-time takers	173	Reporting %	74.57
Average school %	94.58	Average state %	84.82
Average pass difference	9.76		

Jurisdiction	Takers	Passers	Pass %	State %	Diff %
Indiana	96	92	95.83	82.74	13.09
Illinois	33	30	90.91	90.89	0.02

The information on these pages was provided by the law school.

INDIANA UNIVERSITY MAURER SCHOOL OF LAW—BLOOMINGTON

211 S. Indiana Avenue
Bloomington, IN 47405-7001
Phone: 812.855.4765; Fax: 812.855.1967
E-mail: lawadmis@indiana.edu; Website: www.law.indiana.edu

Introduction

The Indiana University Maurer School of Law—Bloomington provides the highest quality legal education in a relaxed, collegial setting. Founded in 1842, the law school is located on the beautifully wooded campus of one of the nation's largest teaching and research universities. The presence of the university, including the world-famous Jacobs School of Music, offers students cultural opportunities available in few urban areas, while retaining the advantages of a small university town. With a student body of fewer than 675 students, drawn from more than 200 undergraduate schools in the United States and abroad, the law school is small enough to retain its distinctive sense of community and collegiality, while large enough to facilitate a stimulating, cosmopolitan environment. The school is a charter member of the Association of American Law Schools (AALS) and is approved by the American Bar Association (ABA).

Library and Physical Facilities

With nearly 450,000 bound volumes, over 1.6 million microfilm pieces, and more than 34,000 electronic titles, the law library is one of the premier law libraries in the United States, the largest in the state of Indiana, and was named one of the top law school libraries in the nation by a national law school magazine. Law-trained librarians give instruction in research techniques and provide reference assistance. While continuing its commitment to a high-quality print collection, the library is a national leader in computer applications in legal education. Through Internet access (from the School of Law or their homes), students can utilize systems specific to law, such as LexisNexis and Westlaw, or access the rapidly expanding array of global information sources. All students are required to possess a laptop computer. Students may write their examinations using their laptops, but are not required to do so. The law school building features wireless access throughout, laptop-ready classrooms, and an outstanding law library where students can enjoy spectacular views of the wooded campus as they study. Recent renovations added three new classrooms to the second floor, new technology and seating in all classrooms, and several faculty offices. Across the street, a brand-new professional skills building houses additional classrooms and clinical space, including offices, student workspace, interview rooms, and more.

Curriculum

Indiana Law faculty recently adopted the most extensive first-year curriculum change in more than 20 years. In 2008–2009, first-year law students enrolled for the first time in the Legal Profession, an innovative new course on the economics and values of the profession—one that responds to the most important study on legal education in decades. In the four-credit spring course, students explore the economic and sociolegal structure and substance of the modern legal profession through in-depth ethnographic studies of—among others—solo and large firm practice, in-house counsel, government agencies, judges, and public interest practice. With this integrated first-year foundation as a guide, decisions regarding areas of study and career goals become more meaningful. Upper-level courses support a formative education that develops skills alongside traditional scholarship, culminating in a meaningful capstone course.

The school also offers traditional specialized courses, such as intellectual property, communications and Internet law, law and biomedical advances, immigration law, international business transactions, and environmental law. The school offers intensive training in litigation and dispute resolution. Students may participate in clinics that enable them to deal with client problems and, in some cases, represent clients in local courts, all under close faculty supervision.

Joint-Degree Programs

Formal joint-degree programs combine the award of a JD degree with a master's degree in business, accounting, public affairs, environmental science, journalism, telecommunications, or library science. The duration of most joint-degree programs is four years. However, the School of Law and the Kelley School of Business have recently established an intensive three-year JD/MBA program. Informal concurrent-degree programs with other disciplines (pursuing a JD and a master's or doctoral degree) are frequently designed to meet students' learning and career goals.

Opportunities to Study Abroad

The School of Law provides students with a wide variety of opportunities to study abroad. A limited number of second- and third-year students can take advantage of the unique opportunity to study in and immerse themselves in the legal education system and culture of another country. Semester-long opportunities are available through the London Law Consortium and exchange programs with Université Panthéon-Assas (Paris II) Law School; ESADE Law School in Barcelona, Spain; Bucerius Law School in Hamburg, Germany; China University of Political Science and Law in Beijing (CUPL); Friedrich-Schiller University in Jena, Germany; Warsaw University in Warsaw, Poland; the University of Auckland in Auckland, New Zealand; University of Hong Kong, Hong Kong; Zhejiang University in Hangzhou, China; and Peking University School of Transitional Law in Shenzhen, China. All classes, with the exception of those taken at Bucerius, Hong Kong, Auckland, and Zhejiang, are taught in the school's respective native language. Finally, the law school offers all students the opportunity to participate in summer study-abroad programs hosted by the Institute on International and Comparative Law in England, France, Italy, and Spain. All courses are taught in English.

Summer Start Program

A summer start program is offered for students who wish to begin their legal studies in the summer session. This program allows students to take one four-credit class in the summer in a small, intimate environment as they make the transition into the law school.

Admission

Generally, the quality and size of the applicant pool forces the Admissions Committee to rely heavily on the undergraduate grade-point average and the LSAT score. However, numerical indicators are not the only considerations used in evaluating applications. The committee considers the quality of the applicant's undergraduate institution, level and rigor of coursework, letters of recommendation (particularly those from faculty), graduate work, employment during and after college, extracurricular activities, potential for service to the profession, educational/geographic/socioeconomic diversity, and personal statement. Applicants are encouraged to explain matters that may have adversely affected their undergraduate performance. Applicants who feel they have been disadvantaged because of economic, educational, racial, or cultural factors are urged to bring this to the attention of the Admissions Committee.

Housing

The Bloomington area offers a variety of housing options for students. There are numerous apartments and houses available as off-campus rentals as well as on-campus housing. Information regarding off-campus housing options is provided to admitted students throughout the spring and summer.

Student Activities

A variety of student organizations present opportunities for involvement in groups focused on specialized areas of the law and public service. Some of the most active groups include the Black Law Student Association, Women's Law Caucus, Public Interest Law Foundation, Latino Law Student Association, and the Environmental Law Society. Students may also obtain practical experience through a number of clinical opportunities, including the Community Legal Clinic; Conservation Law Clinic; Criminal Law Externship; Disability Law Clinic; Elmore Entrepreneurship Law Clinic; Viola J. Taliaferro Children and Mediation Clinic; Inmate Legal Assistance Project; Tenant Assistance Project; Public Interest Internship Program; Federal Courts Clinic; Immigration Law Practicum; Indiana Legal Services Externship; Intellectual Property Practicum; Student Legal Services Externship, Washington, DC; Public Interest Program; and the Protective Order Project. Second- and third-year students are offered the opportunity to gain valuable writing, editing, and advocacy skills through participation in the Moot Court Competition or on one of our three journals. The *Indiana Law Journal* publishes articles by legal scholars, practitioners, jurists, and Indiana University law students. The *Federal Communications Law Journal* is the nation's oldest and largest-circulation communications law journal. The *Indiana Journal of Global Legal Studies* is a multidisciplinary journal that specializes in international and comparative law articles.

Career Placement

The Office of Career and Professional Development actively provides career planning and employment assistance to law students and alumni. Both on- and off-campus interviews are coordinated to facilitate contact between students and employers. In recent years, more than 96 percent of graduates have secured employment within nine months of graduation. More than one-half are located outside the state of Indiana. Graduates are found in all 50 states and in 31 foreign countries.

APPLICANT PROFILE

Indiana University Maurer School of Law—Bloomington
This grid includes only applicants who earned 120–180 LSAT scores under standard administrations.

LSAT Score	3.75 +		3.50–3.74		3.25–3.49		3.00–3.24		2.75–2.99		2.50–2.74		Below 2.50		No GPA		Total	
	Apps	Adm	Apps	Adm	Apps	Adm	Apps	Adm	Apps	Adm	Apps	Adm	Apps	Adm	Apps	Adm	Apps	Adm
175–180	5	2	6	4	4	0	1	0	4	2	0	0	0	0	1	0	21	8
170–174	48	20	38	8	40	10	20	2	11	4	5	1	9	1	0	0	166	45
165–169	174	140	149	62	129	64	103	32	48	21	24	6	34	8	10	4	647	331
160–164	324	130	321	68	205	30	116	19	54	17	17	1	29	1	25	2	1074	267
155–159	281	105	213	5	151	10	103	4	51	0	18	0	31	0	25	0	855	124
150–154	77	40	102	9	128	8	56	3	34	0	11	0	31	0	8	2	429	62
145–149	14	5	14	0	23	1	29	1	22	0	13	0	28	0	12	0	142	7
140–144	1	0	4	0	7	0	16	1	12	0	12	0	16	0	0	0	56	1
Below 140	3	0	2	0	5	0	6	0	7	0	6	0	13	0	3	0	39	0
Total	927	442	849	156	692	123	450	62	243	44	106	8	184	10	84	8	3429	845

Apps = Number of Applicants
Adm = Number Admitted
Reflects 99% of the total applicant pool; highest LSAT data reported.

INDIANA UNIVERSITY SCHOOL OF LAW—INDIANAPOLIS

530 West New York Street
Indianapolis, IN 46202-3225
Phone: 317.274.2459; Fax: 317.278.4780
E-mail: lawadmit@iupui.edu; Website: indylaw.indiana.edu

The Basics

Type of school	Public
Term	Semester
Application deadline	2/1 3/1
Application fee	$50
Financial aid deadline	3/10
Can first year start other than fall?	No
Student to faculty ratio	17.2 to 1

# of housing spaces available restricted to law students

graduate housing for which law students are eligible   288

Faculty and Administrators

	Total		Men		Women		Minorities	
	Spr	Fall	Spr	Fall	Spr	Fall	Spr	Fall
Full-time	39	38	21	20	18	18	4	5
Other full-time	4	3	4	3	0	0	0	0
Deans, librarians, & others who teach	14	14	7	7	7	7	1	1
Part-time	45	40	28	24	17	16	5	6
Total	102	95	60	54	42	41	10	12

Curriculum

	Full-Time	Part-Time
Typical first-year section size	96	94
Is there typically a "small section" of the first-year class, other than Legal Writing, taught by full-time faculty	No	No
If yes, typical size offered last year		
# of classroom course titles beyond first-year curriculum	138	

# of upper division courses, excluding seminars, with an enrollment:		
	Under 25	101
	25–49	66
	50–74	17
	75–99	12
	100+	2

# of seminars	13	
# of seminar positions available	240	
# of seminar positions filled	108	67
# of positions available in simulation courses	482	
# of simulation positions filled	335	111
# of positions available in faculty supervised clinical courses	75	
# of faculty supervised clinical positions filled	52	16
# involved in field placements	120	33
# involved in law journals	96	28
# involved in moot court or trial competitions	125	25
# of credit hours required to graduate	90	

JD Enrollment and Ethnicity

	Men		Women		Full-Time		Part-Time		1st-Year		Total		JD Degs. Awd.
	#	%	#	%	#	%	#	%	#	%	#	%	
All Hispanics	12	2.4	8	2.0	10	1.7	10	3.1	10	2.7	20	2.2	13
Am. Ind./AK Nat.	3	0.6	4	1.0	4	0.7	3	0.9	3	0.8	7	0.8	0
Asian	22	4.3	26	6.4	33	5.5	15	4.6	27	7.3	48	5.2	16
Black/Af. Am.	27	5.3	39	9.5	33	5.5	33	10.2	28	7.6	66	7.2	17
Nat. HI/Pac. Isl.	0	0.0	0	0.0	0	0.0	0	0.0	0	0.0	0	0.0	0
2 or more races	0	0.0	0	0.0	0	0.0	0	0.0	0	0.0	0	0.0	0
Subtotal (minor.)	64	12.6	77	18.8	80	13.4	61	18.9	68	18.4	141	15.4	46
Nonres. Alien	22	4.3	17	4.2	23	3.9	16	5.0	17	4.6	39	4.2	0
White/Cauc.	423	83.1	315	77.0	492	82.7	246	76.2	285	77.0	738	80.4	242
Unknown	0	0.0	0	0.0	0	0.0	0	0.0	0	0.0	0	0.0	0
Total	509	55.4	409	44.6	595	64.8	323	35.2	370	40.3	918		299

Transfers

Transfers in	25
Transfers out	12

Tuition and Fees

	Resident	Nonresident
Full-time	$20,554	$43,646
Part-time	$15,412	$32,545
Tuition Guarantee Program	N	

Living Expenses

Estimated living expenses for singles

Living on campus	Living off campus	Living at home
$21,124	$21,124	N/A

INDIANA UNIVERSITY SCHOOL OF LAW—INDIANAPOLIS

*ABA
Approved
Since
1944*

GPA and LSAT Scores

	Total	Full-Time	Part-Time
# of apps	1,900	1,628	272
# of offers	832	674	158
# of matrics	282	184	98
75% GPA	3.68	3.72	3.55
Median GPA	3.44	3.50	3.34
25% GPA	3.09	3.17	2.94
75% LSAT	159	160	155
Median LSAT	155	157	153
25% LSAT	151	153	149

Grants and Scholarships (from prior year)

	Total		Full-Time		Part-Time	
	#	%	#	%	#	%
Total # of students	944		625		319	
Total # receiving grants	378	40.0	296	47.4	82	25.7
Less than 1/2 tuition	327	34.6	269	43.0	58	18.2
Half to full tuition	35	3.7	23	3.7	12	3.8
Full tuition	10	1.1	0	0.0	10	3.1
More than full tuition	6	0.6	4	0.6	2	0.6
Median grant amount			$5,000		$2,000	

Informational and Library Resources

Total amount spent on library materials	$1,314,000
Study seating capacity inside the library	468
# of full-time equivalent professional librarians	10
Hours per week library is open	105
# of open, wired connections available to students	1,140
# of networked computers available for use by students	139
Has wireless network?	Y
Requires computer?	N

JD Attrition (from prior year)

	Academic	Other	Total	
	#	#	#	%
1st year	3	12	15	3.9
2nd year	4	12	16	5.7
3rd year	0	1	1	0.4
4th year	0	0	0	0.0

Employment (9 months after graduation)

	Total	Percentage
Employment status known	266	98.9
Employment status unknown	3	1.1
Employed	245	92.1
Pursuing graduate degrees	6	2.3
Unemployed (seeking, not seeking, or studying for the bar)	14	5.3
Type of Employment		
# employed in law firms	118	48.2
# employed in business and industry	36	14.7
# employed in government	56	22.9
# employed in public interest	5	2.0
# employed as judicial clerks	5	2.0
# employed in academia	9	3.7
Geographic Location		
# employed in state	198	80.8
# employed outside the US	0	0.0
# of states where employed		19

Bar Passage Rates

First-time takers	249	Reporting %	90.36
Average school %	82.67	Average state %	82.74

Average pass difference −0.07

Jurisdiction	Takers	Passers	Pass %	State %	Diff %
Indiana	225	186	82.67	82.74	−0.07

INDIANA UNIVERSITY SCHOOL OF LAW—INDIANAPOLIS

530 West New York Street
Indianapolis, IN 46202-3225
Phone: 317.274.2459; Fax: 317.278.4780
E-mail: lawadmit@iupui.edu; Website: indylaw.indiana.edu

Introduction

Founded in 1894 as the Indiana Law School, the IU School of Law—Indianapolis has emerged as a premier educational institution, located in the dynamic heart of Indiana on the Indianapolis campus of Indiana University—Purdue University. This campus is also home to the IU Schools of Medicine, Dentistry, Nursing, and Social Work. The law school building, Lawrence W. Inlow Hall, is a state-of-the-art facility, enabling the faculty to employ the latest technology and teaching methods. The building houses modern classrooms, private study areas, and an unparalleled law library. The school is just steps away from the state's courts, the legislature, and major law firms, giving students opportunities to observe the legal process in action and to participate in that process as law clerks, judicial externs, and legislative staff assistants. The school is the largest in the state of Indiana and one of the few Big Ten law schools to offer the cultural, recreational, and professional advantages of an urban educational environment.

Clinical Experiences

The law school offers several clinical programs. The Civil Practice Clinic allows students the opportunity to represent clients in a variety of cases, including housing, divorce, child support, consumer, and administrative matters. In the Civil Practice Disability Clinic, students represent school-age children with special needs, as well as persons who are afflicted with HIV, Alzheimer's disease, and AIDS. In the Criminal Defense Clinic, students represent clients in criminal cases involving a variety of misdemeanor or class D felony charges. Additional clinical opportunities include the Immigration Law Clinic, the Appellate Practice Clinic, and the Wrongful Conviction Clinic, which involves claims of innocence in postconviction proceedings.

Externships and Special Programs

The school's research centers and programs make significant contributions to the profession, both locally and nationally. The William S. and Christine S. Hall Center for Law and Health is considered one of the top health law programs in the nation. The center serves as a preeminent information resource on health law issues for the bar, government, and health care community. Through the center, students may pursue a concentration in law and health and participate in the *Indiana Health Law Review*.

The Program on Law and State Government enriches the dialogue between the academic legal community and state government policymakers. The program offers externships with more than 40 government offices and also sponsors a mediation course that qualifies students to become registered civil mediators. Additionally, the program sponsors a fellowship that allows students to host an academic event and write a publishable academic paper on critical legal or regulatory issues pertinent to state government.

The Center for Intellectual Property Law and Innovation provides experience for students in the fast-growing area of intellectual property.

The Court Externship Program provides externships with federal, state, and local courts. Externs work closely with judges and law clerks, learning about the legal process by experiencing it firsthand.

International Law Program

Because the school recognizes that international considerations touch all areas of the law from human rights to economic issues, it established the Center for International and Comparative Law. A wide variety of international courses, combined with opportunities for overseas experiences, demonstrate our commitment to a legal education with a world view. Our Program in International Human Rights Law has placed students in internships with human rights organizations in locations from Argentina to Zimbabwe.

The law school sponsors a summer program in cooperation with the University of Zagreb School of Law near the ancient Croatian city of Dubrovnik, as well as a program in China. Established in 1987, the Chinese Law Summer Program is hosted by Renmin (People's) University of China School of Law and introduces students to the Chinese legal and lawyering systems, its dispute resolution mechanisms, and Chinese constitutional law.

In addition to offering several courses and seminars in the area of international law, the school sponsors the *Indiana International and Comparative Law Review* and a student organization, the International Law Society. It is also home to the editorial offices of the *European Journal of Law Reform*.

Joint-Degree Programs

The school offers seven joint-degree options in cooperation with IU's School of Business, School of Public and Environmental Affairs, School of Medicine, School of Library and Information Science, School of Liberal Arts, and School of Social Work. Available degrees are the Doctor of Jurisprudence and Master of Business Administration (JD/MBA), Master of Health Administration (JD/MHA), Master of Public Affairs (JD/MPA), Master of Public Health (JD/MPH), Master of Library Science (JD/MLS), Master of Arts in Philosophy (JD/MPhil), and Master of Social Work (JD/MSW).

Special Summer Program

Summer admission is offered to a select group of applicants who can benefit from a rigorous, individualized summer course. Applicants who have either an LSAT score or GPA that is outside of the median range of accepted students, persons who are returning to school after several years outside of the classroom, and students for whom English is a second language may be considered for the summer program. Summer admittees earn two credits toward their JD degrees. Continuation in the fall is not contingent upon performance in the summer program. There is no special application procedure. Applicants who are not presumptively admitted and whose files are completed by February 1 may be considered for this program.

ICLEO

Additionally, the school strongly supports the Indiana Conference for Legal Education Opportunity (ICLEO) program, which provides those who are currently underrepresented in the legal profession or underrepresented in practice areas with assistance in preparing for law school through a six-week summer institute.

Admission

LSAT and LSAC's Credential Assembly Service are required.
The law school seeks to attain a culturally rich and diverse student body. To this end, admission decisions are based on a variety of factors in addition to the LSAT score and undergraduate GPA.

Indiana University School of Law—Indianapolis offers an early decision program. Early decision candidates must have their applications completed, with their Credential Assembly Service Law School Report, by November 15 and will be notified of the admission committee's decision by late December.

Academic Support Programs

The Student Affairs Office designs, manages, and implements academic support services, strategies, and outreach programs for students. Academic support programs currently offered include workshops on study skills, time management, exam preparation, bar exam advising, bar exam preparation, and sessions on academic advising topics and resources.

Students are offered assistance through the Dean's Tutorial Society. Supervised by a tenured faculty member, the tutorial society is staffed by academically distinguished students who offer individual tutoring as well as assistance in case briefing and exam preparation.

Student Activities

Students can participate in any of 30 different interest groups and organizations, ranging from Amnesty International to Sports and Entertainment Law Society. The school also offers an extensive moot court program, a client counseling program, and three law reviews.

Office of Professional Development

The Office of Professional Development provides career counseling and job-search assistance to students and alumni. Services include an on-campus interview program, a résumé review service, a mock interview program, and a variety of workshops and seminars.

APPLICANT PROFILE

Indiana University School of Law—Indianapolis
This grid includes only applicants who earned 120–180 LSAT scores under standard administrations.

LSAT Score	3.75 +		3.50–3.74		3.25–3.49		3.00–3.24		2.75–2.99		2.50–2.74		2.25–2.49		2.00–2.24		Below 2.00		No GPA		Total	
	Apps	Adm	Apps	Adm	Apps	Adm	Apps	Adm	Apps	Adm	Apps	Adm	Apps	Adm	Apps	Adm	Apps	Adm	Apps	Adm	Apps	Adm
170–180	6	6	2	2	4	4	1	1	2	2	1	1	0	0	1	0	0	0	0	0	17	16
165–169	10	10	9	9	11	11	9	7	6	6	1	1	3	1	0	0	1	0	1	1	51	46
160–164	50	48	55	54	50	47	46	45	24	24	12	12	6	3	0	0	0	0	7	5	250	238
155–159	97	84	116	81	126	64	75	36	73	34	22	6	11	3	4	1	1	0	12	4	537	313
150–154	68	41	101	36	137	29	93	22	71	16	29	1	19	1	7	0	2	0	20	5	547	151
145–149	24	10	41	16	76	17	60	11	57	8	32	2	7	2	13	0	0	0	18	2	328	68
140–144	5	3	13	7	17	3	26	5	24	1	13	1	9	0	4	0	0	0	8	0	119	20
Below 140	3	2	3	1	13	0	14	0	10	1	10	1	4	0	2	0	2	0	8	0	69	5
Total	263	204	340	206	434	175	324	127	267	92	120	25	59	10	31	1	6	0	74	17	1918	857

Apps = Number of Applicants
Adm = Number Admitted
Reflects 99% of the total applicant pool; highest LSAT data reported.

INTER AMERICAN UNIVERSITY SCHOOL OF LAW

PO Box 70351
San Juan, PR 00936-8351
Phone: 787.751.1912, exts. 2011, 2012
Website: www.derecho.inter.edu

ABA
Approved
Since
1969

The Basics

Type of school	Private
Term	Semester
Application deadline	
Application fee	$63
Financial aid deadline	9/28
Can first year start other than fall?	No
Student to faculty ratio	27.8 to 1
# of housing spaces available restricted to law students	
graduate housing for which law students are eligible	

Faculty and Administrators

	Total		Men		Women		Minorities	
	Spr	Fall	Spr	Fall	Spr	Fall	Spr	Fall
Full-time	21	23	14	14	7	9	21	23
Other full-time	1	1	0	0	1	1	1	1
Deans, librarians, & others who teach	4	4	2	2	2	2	4	4
Part-time	47	44	33	30	13	14	47	44
Total	73	72	49	46	23	26	73	72

Curriculum

	Full-Time	Part-Time
Typical first-year section size	45	60
Is there typically a "small section" of the first-year class, other than Legal Writing, taught by full-time faculty	Yes	Yes
If yes, typical size offered last year	7	6

# of classroom course titles beyond first-year curriculum		32
# of upper division courses, excluding seminars, with an enrollment:	Under 25	49
	25–49	33
	50–74	31
	75–99	0
	100+	0
# of seminars		0
# of seminar positions available		220
# of seminar positions filled	100	120
# of positions available in simulation courses		120
# of simulation positions filled	60	60
# of positions available in faculty supervised clinical courses		80
# of faculty supervised clinical positions filled	40	40
# involved in field placements	0	0
# involved in law journals	13	2
# involved in moot court or trial competitions	6	8
# of credit hours required to graduate		92

JD Enrollment and Ethnicity

	Men		Women		Full-Time		Part-Time		1st-Year		Total		JD Degs. Awd.
	#	%	#	%	#	%	#	%	#	%	#	%	
All Hispanics	390	100.0	476	100.0	474	100.0	392	100.0	256	100.0	866	100.0	235
Am. Ind./AK Nat.	0	0.0	0	0.0	0	0.0	0	0.0	0	0.0	0	0.0	0
Asian	0	0.0	0	0.0	0	0.0	0	0.0	0	0.0	0	0.0	0
Black/Af. Am.	0	0.0	0	0.0	0	0.0	0	0.0	0	0.0	0	0.0	0
Nat. HI/Pac. Isl.	0	0.0	0	0.0	0	0.0	0	0.0	0	0.0	0	0.0	0
2 or more races	0	0.0	0	0.0	0	0.0	0	0.0	0	0.0	0	0.0	0
Subtotal (minor.)	390	100.0	476	100.0	474	100.0	392	100.0	256	100.0	866	100.0	235
Nonres. Alien	0	0.0	0	0.0	0	0.0	0	0.0	0	0.0	0	0.0	0
White/Cauc.	0	0.0	0	0.0	0	0.0	0	0.0	0	0.0	0	0.0	0
Unknown	0	0.0	0	0.0	0	0.0	0	0.0	0	0.0	0	0.0	0
Total	390	45.0	476	55.0	474	54.7	392	45.3	256	29.6	866		235

Transfers

Transfers in	26
Transfers out	14

Tuition and Fees

	Resident	Nonresident
Full-time	$14,341	$14,341
Part-time	$11,142	$11,142
Tuition Guarantee Program		Y

Living Expenses

Estimated living expenses for singles

Living on campus	Living off campus	Living at home
N/A	$19,514	$14,782

INTER AMERICAN UNIVERSITY SCHOOL OF LAW

ABA
Approved
Since
1969

GPA and LSAT Scores

	Total	Full-Time	Part-Time
# of apps	909	561	348
# of offers	464	295	169
# of matrics	869	477	392
75% GPA	3.57	3.60	3.52
Median GPA	3.32	3.39	3.19
25% GPA	3.09	3.16	2.90
75% LSAT	142	142	141
Median LSAT	139	139	137
25% LSAT	135	136	134

Grants and Scholarships (from prior year)

	Total		Full-Time		Part-Time	
	#	%	#	%	#	%
Total # of students	848		430		418	
Total # receiving grants	50	5.9	30	7.0	20	4.8
Less than 1/2 tuition	3	0.4	0	0.0	3	0.7
Half to full tuition	3	0.4	1	0.2	2	0.5
Full tuition	42	5.0	28	6.5	14	3.3
More than full tuition	2	0.2	1	0.2	1	0.2
Median grant amount			$3,461		$3,719	

Informational and Library Resources

Total amount spent on library materials	$707,237
Study seating capacity inside the library	302
# of full-time equivalent professional librarians	7
Hours per week library is open	100
# of open, wired connections available to students	24
# of networked computers available for use by students	44
Has wireless network?	Y
Requires computer?	N

JD Attrition (from prior year)

	Academic	Other	Total	
	#	#	#	%
1st year	0	23	23	9.5
2nd year	11	1	12	4.8
3rd year	4	0	4	1.6
4th year	0	0	0	0.0

Employment (9 months after graduation)

	Total	Percentage
Employment status known	210	96.3
Employment status unknown	8	3.7
Employed	180	85.7
Pursuing graduate degrees	10	4.8
Unemployed (seeking, not seeking, or studying for the bar)	20	9.5
Type of Employment		
# employed in law firms	55	30.6
# employed in business and industry	80	44.4
# employed in government	29	16.1
# employed in public interest	2	1.1
# employed as judicial clerks	4	2.2
# employed in academia	10	5.6
Geographic Location		
# employed in state	166	92.2
# employed outside the US	0	0.0
# of states where employed	0	

Bar Passage Rates

First-time takers	228	Reporting %	175.44
Average school %	41.25	Average state %	50.28
Average pass difference	−9.03		

Jurisdiction	Takers	Passers	Pass %	State %	Diff %
Puerto Rico	400	165	41.25	50.28	−9.03

The information on these pages was provided by the law school.

INTER AMERICAN UNIVERSITY SCHOOL OF LAW

PO Box 70351
San Juan, PR 00936-8351
Phone: 787.751.1912, exts. 2011, 2012
Website: www.derecho.inter.edu

Introduction

The Inter American University School of Law is one of the 11 units of the Inter American University of Puerto Rico, a private nonprofit educational corporation accredited by the Middle States Association of Colleges and Secondary Schools, the Puerto Rico Council of Higher Education, and the Commonwealth of Puerto Rico Department of Education. The School of Law is approved by the ABA and is located in San Juan, the capital city of Puerto Rico. Since its founding, the School of Law has succeeded in meeting the needs of the legal profession, in particular, and Puerto Rico's society in general.

Enrollment/Student Body

The incoming class for academic year 2010–2011 was composed of 249 students. The student body comes mainly from Puerto Rico, although applicants from the mainland are encouraged to apply.

Library and Physical Facilities

The law school has developed its library into a center of access to traditional library services as well as computerized legal research services.

In 1993, the school was relocated to a new building that features seven classrooms equipped with air conditioning, accessibility for students with disabilities, state-of-the-art audiovisual equipment, seminar rooms, a library, a legal clinic, faculty offices, a conference room, a lounge, a Continuing Legal Education Program office, *Inter American School of Law Review* offices, student organization offices, administrative offices, a chapel, a student center, a cafeteria, a bookstore, an auditorium with a seating capacity of 310, parking, and more. The site has been landscaped to achieve a sense of serenity and beauty compatible with the building's functions.

In January 1990, the library signed a collaboration agreement to establish a consortium with the law school library of the Catholic University of Puerto Rico and the library of the Supreme Court of Puerto Rico, with the purpose of coordinating collection development and sharing its resources through an automated bibliographic network, interlibrary loans, and telecommunication services.

Curriculum

The JD program covers three years in the day division and four years in the evening division. Candidates must complete a minimum of 92 credit hours with a GPA of at least 2.5 to qualify for graduation.

Inter American University School of Law offers a three-week preparation course to be taken during the summer on a compulsory basis by students admitted to the school. Students who enter law school must be willing to make a heavy commitment.

For its part, Inter American University is willing to provide the best possible professional educational experience through the careful recruitment of a first-rate faculty, the development of a progressive curriculum, and a willingness to create new and exciting programs of clinical studies and research.

Admission

Proficiency in Spanish is essential to the program. Applicants must have a minimum grade-point average of 2.5, an immunization certificate (for students ages 21 and below), and a police department certificate of good conduct; those seeking admission may also be required to appear for a personal interview.

Candidates are required to take the Examen de Admisión a Estudios de Posgrado (EXADEP), the Aptitude Test for Graduate Education, and the Law School Admission Test (LSAT). Students should attain a 575 minimum score on the EXADEP and a minimum score of 130 on the LSAT. Application forms and other relevant information concerning the EXADEP may be obtained from Educational Testing Service, American International Plaza, 250 Muñoz Rivera Avenue, Suite 315, Hato Rey, PR 00918.

Housing

The university does not provide housing for law students. However, the areas surrounding the School of Law contain many private houses, apartments, and condominiums for rent.

Student Activities

Student organizations include the student council, an organization that represents the student body and participates in matters of administrative policy related to students' interests. Council representatives serve on various faculty committees as well as the university senate and the board of trustees.

Other student organizations are the Law Student Division of the American Bar Association; the Phi Alpha Delta legal fraternity (composed not only of law students, but also of distinguished honorary members who are supreme court justices, federal district court judges, and prominent attorneys); the National Association of Law Students; the Women Law Students Association; United Students Forging an Environmental Consciousness; the Law Student Division of the Inter-American Federation of Lawyers; the Association of Trial Lawyers of America; the Hispanic National Bar Association; the Federal Bar Association; the Student's Cooperative Bookstore; and the Hispanic Notarial Bar Association.

The *Inter American School of Law Review* is the official publication of the School of Law. Its members work under the supervision of an editorial board of four students chosen on the basis of merit and dedication to the *Law Review* and an academic advisor who is a faculty member appointed by the dean.

Clinical Programs

The faculty's Legal Aid Clinical Program is integrated with the Community Law Office through a combined effort of the US Legal Services Corporation and Inter American University. Law students are provided with the opportunity to learn skills such as interviewing, negotiation, counseling, fact gathering and analysis, legal research and drafting, decision making about alternative strategies, and preparation for trial and field practice. They also represent clients before administrative agencies and courts under the close supervision of the program's staff attorney-professors, pursuant to the rules of the Supreme Court of Puerto Rico. Students also gain practical experience by serving with Puerto Rico Legal Services, Inc.; the San Juan Community Law Office, Inc.; the Legal Aid Society of Puerto Rico; the district attorney's offices; and the Environmental Quality Board.

Career Services

The mission of the Career Placement Office is to prepare students and alumni for the legal job market by encouraging them to conduct self-assessments in an effort to focus their job searches, as well as to educate students and alumni on their legal and nonlegal options in today's competitive legal market. This is accomplished through a variety of services including, but not limited to, individual counseling, group seminars, self-assessment materials, interviewing programs, a career resource library, and the alumni network.

Continuing Legal Education Program

The Continuing Legal Education (CLE) Program offers advanced courses and seminars concerning different fields of law that may be of interest to practicing lawyers as well as to the community in general.

The CLE Program enjoys a good reputation and has been able to develop a consistent course offering, primarily in the following categories: courses designed for specialists; refresher courses for experienced lawyers; courses designed to provide information in nontraditional areas or stimulated by recent legislation, decisions, or agency rulings; and courses designed to develop lawyering skills.

Cost and Financial Aid

As of the date this report was published, the cost per credit is $457. Once admitted, the student pays $125 to reserve a place in the class and $435 for the preparatory course that takes place in July.

There is a deferred payment plan and financial aid options that include the Federal Guaranteed Loan Program, Stafford loans, the Commonwealth Education Fund, the Students Incentive Grant Program, the Institutional College Work-Study Program, and alternative loans for the regular academic program as well as for bar study (Alternative Bar Loans). The university also has an Honor Scholarship program for law students based on academic accomplishment and financial need.

Applicant Profile Not Available

THE UNIVERSITY OF IOWA COLLEGE OF LAW

320 Melrose Avenue
Iowa City, IA 52242
Phone: 800.553.4692, ext. 9095; 319.335.9095; Fax: 319.335.9646
E-mail: law-admissions@uiowa.edu; Website: www.law.uiowa.edu

ABA
Approved
Since
1923

The Basics

Type of school	Public
Term	Semester
Application deadline	3/1
Application fee	$60
Financial aid deadline	
Can first year start other than fall?	No
Student to faculty ratio	11.3 to 1
# of housing spaces available restricted to law students	
graduate housing for which law students are eligible	

Faculty and Administrators

	Total		Men		Women		Minorities	
	Spr	Fall	Spr	Fall	Spr	Fall	Spr	Fall
Full-time	41	43	27	26	14	17	6	6
Other full-time	2	3	2	3	0	0	0	0
Deans, librarians, & others who teach	13	13	5	6	8	7	2	2
Part-time	22	12	15	8	7	4	0	0
Total	78	71	49	43	29	28	8	8

Curriculum

	Full-Time	Part-Time
Typical first-year section size	70	0
Is there typically a "small section" of the first-year class, other than Legal Writing, taught by full-time faculty	Yes	No
If yes, typical size offered last year	40	
# of classroom course titles beyond first-year curriculum	63	

# of upper division courses, excluding seminars, with an enrollment:		
Under 25	56	
25–49	18	
50–74	10	
75–99	10	
100+	0	

# of seminars	24	
# of seminar positions available	301	
# of seminar positions filled	286	0
# of positions available in simulation courses	308	
# of simulation positions filled	269	0
# of positions available in faculty supervised clinical courses	80	
# of faculty supervised clinical positions filled	75	0
# involved in field placements	76	0
# involved in law journals	178	0
# involved in moot court or trial competitions	177	0
# of credit hours required to graduate	84	

JD Enrollment and Ethnicity

	Men		Women		Full-Time		Part-Time		1st-Year		Total		JD Degs. Awd.
	#	%	#	%	#	%	#	%	#	%	#	%	
All Hispanics	20	6.3	10	3.9	30	5.2	0	0.0	13	6.5	30	5.2	10
Am. Ind./AK Nat.	3	0.9	2	0.8	5	0.9	0	0.0	3	1.5	5	0.9	3
Asian	18	5.7	22	8.6	40	7.0	0	0.0	14	7.0	40	7.0	11
Black/Af. Am.	4	1.3	12	4.7	16	2.8	0	0.0	6	3.0	16	2.8	10
Nat. HI/Pac. Isl.	0	0.0	0	0.0	0	0.0	0	0.0	0	0.0	0	0.0	0
2 or more races	0	0.0	0	0.0	0	0.0	0	0.0	0	0.0	0	0.0	0
Subtotal (minor.)	45	14.2	46	17.9	91	15.9	0	0.0	36	18.0	91	15.9	34
Nonres. Alien	7	2.2	6	2.3	13	2.3	0	0.0	3	1.5	13	2.3	0
White/Cauc.	265	83.6	205	79.8	470	81.9	0	0.0	161	80.5	470	81.9	172
Unknown	0	0.0	0	0.0	0	0.0	0	0.0	0	0.0	0	0.0	0
Total	317	55.2	257	44.8	574	100.0	0	0.0	200	34.8	574		212

Transfers

Transfers in	4
Transfers out	5

Tuition and Fees

	Resident	Nonresident
Full-time	$24,154	$42,922
Part-time		
Tuition Guarantee Program		N

Living Expenses

Estimated living expenses for singles

Living on campus	Living off campus	Living at home
$16,885	$16,885	$8,785

THE UNIVERSITY OF IOWA COLLEGE OF LAW

ABA
Approved
Since
1923

GPA and LSAT Scores

	Total	Full-Time	Part-Time
# of apps	1,757	1,757	0
# of offers	692	692	0
# of matrics	203	203	0
75% GPA	3.77	3.77	0.00
Median GPA	3.59	3.59	0.00
25% GPA	3.41	3.41	0.00
75% LSAT	164	164	0
Median LSAT	161	161	0
25% LSAT	158	158	0

Grants and Scholarships (from prior year)

	Total		Full-Time		Part-Time	
	#	%	#	%	#	%
Total # of students	590		590		0	
Total # receiving grants	180	30.5	180	30.5	0	0.0
Less than 1/2 tuition	46	7.8	46	7.8	0	0.0
Half to full tuition	26	4.4	26	4.4	0	0.0
Full tuition	106	18.0	106	18.0	0	0.0
More than full tuition	2	0.3	2	0.3	0	0.0
Median grant amount			$20,146		$0	

Informational and Library Resources

Total amount spent on library materials	$3,179,599
Study seating capacity inside the library	679
# of full-time equivalent professional librarians	14
Hours per week library is open	105
# of open, wired connections available to students	503
# of networked computers available for use by students	99
Has wireless network?	Y
Requires computer?	N

JD Attrition (from prior year)

	Academic	Other	Total	
	#	#	#	%
1st year	1	8	9	4.6
2nd year	0	7	7	3.8
3rd year	0	0	0	0.0
4th year	0	0	0	0.0

Employment (9 months after graduation)

	Total	Percentage
Employment status known	206	100.0
Employment status unknown	0	0.0
Employed	189	91.7
Pursuing graduate degrees	11	5.3
Unemployed (seeking, not seeking, or studying for the bar)	3	1.5
Type of Employment		
# employed in law firms	101	53.4
# employed in business and industry	25	13.2
# employed in government	19	10.1
# employed in public interest	15	7.9
# employed as judicial clerks	14	7.4
# employed in academia	10	5.3
Geographic Location		
# employed in state	52	27.5
# employed outside the US	1	0.5
# of states where employed	30	

Bar Passage Rates

First-time takers	193	Reporting %	77.20	
Average school %	93.29	Average state %	89.57	
Average pass difference	3.72			

Jurisdiction	Takers	Passers	Pass %	State %	Diff %
Iowa	53	50	94.34	93.17	1.17
Illinois	32	31	96.88	90.89	5.99
Minnesota	18	18	100.00	89.58	10.42
California	14	11	78.57	73.19	5.38
Others (3)	32	29	90.63		

THE UNIVERSITY OF IOWA COLLEGE OF LAW

320 Melrose Avenue
Iowa City, IA 52242
Phone: 800.553.4692, ext. 9095; 319.335.9095; Fax: 319.335.9646
E-mail: law-admissions@uiowa.edu; Website: www.law.uiowa.edu

Introduction

The University of Iowa College of Law, founded in 1865, is the oldest law school in continuous operation west of the Mississippi River. Iowa enjoys a top national reputation, and its faculty is renowned for its outstanding scholarship and teaching.

The college is located in Iowa City, a cosmopolitan college town that is home to a dynamic teaching and research university and over 60,000 people. Students from all 50 states and roughly 100 countries attend the university. Iowa City offers a rich cultural life, Big Ten athletic events, and the world-famous Iowa Writers' Workshop.

The Boyd Law Building's central campus location on a bluff overlooking the Iowa River provides a professional enclave well-suited to the college's intensive style of education as well as easy access to the academic, cultural, social, and recreational resources of a major research university.

Admission

Iowa strives to enroll a student body that reflects the academic quality and diversity expected of a leading national law school. The college's numbers-plus policy looks beyond numerical indicators and utilizes a full file review to evaluate an applicant's potential contribution to enhancing classroom discussion. Factors such as maturity, work experience, ability to overcome adversity, and cultural background are considered.

Enrollment Date

Iowa offers only one starting date for entering students: August. All students may "accelerate" their course of study toward the JD degree by taking summer and intersession classes. The minimum time of study is no fewer than 27 months after the student has started law study at this law school or at a law school from which transfer credit has been accepted.

Curriculum

The students are the heart of our institution. A broad and wide-ranging curriculum, small classes, accessible professors, and caring administrators are just a few examples of Iowa's student-centered orientation.

Iowa's curriculum establishes a solid foundation for a lifetime of professional growth and personal development. Students take an active role in their professional training. We go the extra measure to ensure that our students have the proper resources and learning environment to maximize their individual development as professionals.

First-year students have at least one class each semester with approximately 40 students; courses taught in this small-section format allow extensive class participation and interaction with a faculty member. After completing the set of required first-year courses exploring fundamental legal concepts, students plan their own course of study from a rich menu of mainstream, specialized, and clinical offerings. Second- and third-year courses cover the range of specialties within the legal profession, allowing students to sample liberally and follow professional interests.

At Iowa, students benefit from the serious emphasis the college places on both interdisciplinary study and the study of international and comparative law. Interdisciplinary courses and research programs are actively encouraged; nearly one-third of the college's faculty members offer courses or conduct research in the international and comparative law fields.

Legal Analysis, Writing, and Research Program

The Legal Analysis, Writing, and Research (LAWR) Program at the College of Law is a two-semester, first-year course (two credits each semester), with classes of 20 students, and is designed to equip participants with effective skills in legal analysis, writing, and research.

Iowa Law Library

The University of Iowa College of Law Library is consistently recognized as one of the finest and largest law libraries anywhere. The library's international holdings are impressive; it includes a complete collection of United Nations documents since the UN's founding in 1945. The Law Library received significant and high praise in the 2010 *National Jurist* survey of law libraries that are located in the United States. Additionally, wireless Internet is available throughout the library.

Special Programs

The first writing center in the country established specifically for a law school community, Iowa's Writing Resource Center serves as an extension of the classroom and supplements the college's Legal Analysis, Writing, and Research Program. Members of the writing center's staff help law students with a broad range of writing, including class assignments, law journal articles, and résumés and cover letters. The center's staff teaches strategies for overcoming writer's block, adapting materials for various audiences, and generally improving the quality of students' writing.

The Academic Achievement Program (AAP) helps students achieve their full academic potential as they move from successful undergraduate careers to face the new challenges of law study. AAP presents a variety of programs, including a first-semester lecture series for new students. Individual study skills counseling is also available for all students.

Clinical Law Programs

The Clinical Law Programs give students opportunities to gain experience in many different areas of substantive law including criminal defense, disability rights, domestic violence, employment law, general civil, and immigration and asylum law. Externship opportunities are available with federal trial courts, the Iowa Attorney General, legal services offices, US Attorneys' offices, Federal Public Defenders' offices, and the Iowa City City Attorney, among others. Through the representation of real clients, students are able to develop and hone a diverse complement of lawyering skills from interviewing, counseling, and drafting court papers to trial practice, appellate advocacy, legislative lobbying, and policy development.

International Law

Iowa offers one of the nation's strongest programs for the study of international and comparative law. The school offers four study-abroad programs. Iowa is the stateside home of the London Law Consortium through which seven US law schools conduct a study-abroad program for a spring semester in London. The Iowa/Bordeaux Summer Program offers one month of intensive coursework in Arcachon, France. Students also have the opportunity to participate in an exchange program with Bucerius Law School in Germany as well as to study at Católica University in Lisbon, Portugal. In addition, students may receive credit for participating in other study-abroad programs offered by ABA-approved law schools.

Student Activities

Student activities at the law school include the American Constitution Society; the Asian American Law Students Association; the Black Law Students Association; the Christian Legal Society; Client Counseling; the Environmental Law Society; the Equal Justice Foundation; the Federalist Society; the Intellectual Property Law Society; the International Law Society; the Iowa Campaign for Human Rights; the *Iowa Law Review*; the Iowa Student Bar Association; the J. Reuben Clark Law Society; the Jewish Law Students Association; the *Journal of Corporation Law*; the *Journal of Gender, Race and Justice*; the *Journal of Transnational Law and Contemporary Problems*; the Latino Law Student Association; Law Students for Reproductive Justice; the Middle Eastern Law Students Association; Moot Court; the National Lawyers Guild; the Native American Law Students Association; the Order of the Coif; the Organization for Women Law Students and Staff; the Outlaws; Parents/Partners Weekend; Phi Alpha Delta; Phi Delta Phi; the *Pro Bono* Society; the Stephenson Competition; Supreme Court Day; and Trial Advocacy.

Expenses and Financial Aid

All admitted students are automatically considered for merit scholarships and fellowships based on their academic achievements. A separate application is not required. The college administers its substantial financial aid program to advance the goals of its selective admission policy. More than 90 percent of our students receive some form of financial aid. Grants, scholarships, work-study funds, and loans are awarded on a need or merit basis for the purpose of providing access to legal education for the talented and diverse students admitted to the college. A number of part-time employment opportunities are also available to second- and third-year students; nonresident students with a quarter-time research assistant position (10 hours per week) are classified as residents for tuition purposes. Eligibility for financial aid based on need is established by completion of the FAFSA, available at www.fafsa.ed.gov.

Career Services

Admitted students are strongly encouraged to pursue career counseling, which helps them clarify and articulate career and life plans with the JD or LLM; participate in internships, externships, summer associate positions, and other experiential legal opportunities; and develop strategic job-search plans for a wide range of legal careers. Each year, many 1Ls participate in the Partner for a Day program with alumni and employers, which helps them make career decisions and develop professional networks. To facilitate interviewing for summer and full-time employment, the Career Services Office provides students with access to national job fairs, résumé collections, video interviews, and on-campus interviews. The law school's participation in interview consortia on the East Coast and West Coast provides students with many interview opportunities outside of the Midwest. Finally, the Career Services Office offers continued services to alumni seeking career advice.

Applicant Profile Not Available

THE JOHN MARSHALL LAW SCHOOL

315 South Plymouth Court
Chicago, IL 60604
Phone: 800.537.4280; 312.987.1406; Fax: 312.427.5136
E-mail: admission@jmls.edu; Website: www.jmls.edu

The Basics

Type of school	Private
Term	Semester
Application deadline	3/1 11/1
Application fee	
Financial aid deadline	4/1
Can first year start other than fall?	Yes
Student to faculty ratio	16.3 to 1
# of housing spaces available restricted to law students	
graduate housing for which law students are eligible	

Faculty and Administrators

	Total		Men		Women		Minorities	
	Spr	Fall	Spr	Fall	Spr	Fall	Spr	Fall
Full-time	65	68	44	47	21	21	11	11
Other full-time	7	7	2	2	5	5	0	0
Deans, librarians, & others who teach	9	9	5	5	4	4	2	2
Part-time	152	160	104	112	48	48	8	13
Total	233	244	155	166	78	78	21	26

Curriculum

		Full-Time	Part-Time
Typical first-year section size		80	50
Is there typically a "small section" of the first-year class, other than Legal Writing, taught by full-time faculty		No	No
If yes, typical size offered last year			
# of classroom course titles beyond first-year curriculum		272	
# of upper division courses, excluding seminars, with an enrollment:	Under 25	240	
	25–49	68	
	50–74	36	
	75–99	15	
	100+	0	
# of seminars		41	
# of seminar positions available		1,025	
# of seminar positions filled		615	364
# of positions available in simulation courses		2,490	
# of simulation positions filled		1,050	617
# of positions available in faculty supervised clinical courses		90	
# of faculty supervised clinical positions filled		64	15
# involved in field placements		62	11
# involved in law journals		303	37
# involved in moot court or trial competitions		98	10
# of credit hours required to graduate		90	

JD Enrollment and Ethnicity

	Men		Women		Full-Time		Part-Time		1st-Year		Total		JD Degs. Awd.
	#	%	#	%	#	%	#	%	#	%	#	%	
All Hispanics	60	7.7	56	8.5	86	7.6	30	9.5	37	7.3	116	8.0	24
Am. Ind./AK Nat.	4	0.5	2	0.3	4	0.4	2	0.6	1	0.2	6	0.4	6
Asian	49	6.3	40	6.1	74	6.6	15	4.7	40	7.9	89	6.2	23
Black/Af. Am.	43	5.5	77	11.7	75	6.7	45	14.2	39	7.7	120	8.3	19
Nat. HI/Pac. Isl.	0	0.0	0	0.0	0	0.0	0	0.0	0	0.0	0	0.0	0
2 or more races	21	2.7	23	3.5	34	3.0	10	3.2	11	2.2	44	3.1	0
Subtotal (minor.)	177	22.6	198	30.0	273	24.3	102	32.2	128	25.1	375	26.0	81
Nonres. Alien	3	0.4	7	1.1	6	0.5	4	1.3	0	0.0	10	0.7	0
White/Cauc.	579	74.0	435	65.9	811	72.1	203	64.0	376	73.9	1014	70.3	283
Unknown	23	2.9	20	3.0	35	3.1	8	2.5	5	1.0	43	3.0	14
Total	782	54.2	660	45.8	1125	78.0	317	22.0	509	35.3	1442		384

Transfers

Transfers in	0
Transfers out	55

Tuition and Fees

	Resident	Nonresident
Full-time	$36,920	$36,920
Part-time	$26,400	$26,400
Tuition Guarantee Program	N	

Living Expenses

Estimated living expenses for singles

Living on campus	Living off campus	Living at home
$26,440	$26,440	$26,440

THE JOHN MARSHALL LAW SCHOOL

*ABA
Approved
Since
1951*

GPA and LSAT Scores

	Total	Full-Time	Part-Time
# of apps	3,523	2,941	582
# of offers	1,559	1,385	174
# of matrics	539	437	102
75% GPA	3.43	3.44	3.39
Median GPA	3.22	3.23	3.22
25% GPA	2.92	2.93	2.87
75% LSAT	157	157	155
Median LSAT	154	154	153
25% LSAT	151	152	151

Grants and Scholarships (from prior year)

	Total #	Total %	Full-Time #	Full-Time %	Part-Time #	Part-Time %
Total # of students	1,377		1,038		339	
Total # receiving grants	684	49.7	508	48.9	176	51.9
Less than 1/2 tuition	540	39.2	407	39.2	133	39.2
Half to full tuition	99	7.2	69	6.6	30	8.8
Full tuition	16	1.2	10	1.0	6	1.8
More than full tuition	29	2.1	22	2.1	7	2.1
Median grant amount			$10,000		$9,000	

Informational and Library Resources

Total amount spent on library materials	$1,257,886
Study seating capacity inside the library	754
# of full-time equivalent professional librarians	10
Hours per week library is open	96
# of open, wired connections available to students	12
# of networked computers available for use by students	67
Has wireless network?	Y
Requires computer?	N

JD Attrition (from prior year)

	Academic #	Other #	Total #	Total %
1st year	46	71	117	23.5
2nd year	4	11	15	3.6
3rd year	1	3	4	1.0
4th year	0	0	0	0.0

Employment (9 months after graduation)

	Total	Percentage
Employment status known	392	98.0
Employment status unknown	8	2.0
Employed	341	87.0
Pursuing graduate degrees	2	0.5
Unemployed (seeking, not seeking, or studying for the bar)	45	11.5
Type of Employment		
# employed in law firms	195	57.2
# employed in business and industry	75	22.0
# employed in government	46	13.5
# employed in public interest	4	1.2
# employed as judicial clerks	4	1.2
# employed in academia	17	5.0
Geographic Location		
# employed in state	308	90.3
# employed outside the US	2	0.6
# of states where employed	17	

Bar Passage Rates

First-time takers	398	Reporting %	94.47
Average school %	85.11	Average state %	90.89
Average pass difference	−5.78		

Jurisdiction	Takers	Passers	Pass %	State %	Diff %
Illinois	376	320	85.11	90.89	−5.78

The information on these pages was provided by the law school.

THE JOHN MARSHALL LAW SCHOOL

315 South Plymouth Court
Chicago, IL 60604
Phone: 800.537.4280; 312.987.1406; Fax: 312.427.5136
E-mail: admission@jmls.edu; Website: www.jmls.edu

Introduction

Since its founding in 1899, the John Marshall Law School has become one of the nation's largest free-standing institutions dedicated to the teaching of law. The school offers a curriculum, writing courses, and a trial advocacy program that prepare students in the theory and practice of law. Students attend both day and evening classes at the 315 South Plymouth Court location in Chicago's Loop.

The Law School's reputation has been built by alumni who work as attorneys in private practice, government, industry, and the judiciary. Among its graduates are the former US Secretary of Commerce, a member of the Illinois Supreme Court, and the chief judge of the Circuit Court of Cook County, the largest unified court system in the United States.

Students learn in rigorous classes taught by a highly regarded faculty and adjunct faculty. Coursework is supplemented with practical experience through clinical and externship programs. Located in the heart of Chicago's legal, financial, and commercial districts, the John Marshall Law School offers a location that is steps from the federal courthouse and blocks from the central offices of the Circuit Court of Cook County. Its students clerk or find positions with Chicago's top law firms, as well as with boutique firms.

The law school holds accreditations from the American Bar Association, the American Association of Law Schools, and the North Central Association. The ethnically and racially diverse student population reflects the law school's founding principles of access and opportunity.

Curriculum

The law school offers both day and evening programs for JD, MS, and LLM students. Students can be admitted into a joint JD/LLM curriculum after their second year. Students are admitted in both January and August. The law school's JD curriculum places major emphasis on legal foundation classes with required Lawyering Skills writing courses. Students have the option of earning a JD degree with a concentration in advocacy/dispute resolution, business, elder law, employee benefits, estate planning, general practice, information technology law, intellectual property law, international law, public interest law, or real estate law. Students also can earn a JD degree with a certificate of specialization in alternative dispute resolution, elder law, intellectual property law, international human rights law, or trial advocacy.

John Marshall offers students the option of earning a JD/MPA, JD/MA, or JD/MBA degree through relationships with area institutions. The law school also offers MS degrees for the nonlawyer in the areas of employee benefits, information technology and privacy law, real estate law, and tax law.

John Marshall offers the largest selection of LLM degrees in the Midwest. Lawyers interested in specializing in an area of law for an LLM degree can select from employee benefits, information technology and privacy law, intellectual property law, international business and trade law, real estate law, and tax law.

Clinics, Externships, and Special Programs

Clinical experience is one of the best hands-on learning techniques. John Marshall's Fair Housing Legal Clinic offers assistance to persons who have been discriminated against in their housing choices. Students learn interview techniques, claims investigation, pleadings, motions, and trial preparation.

The Patent Law Clinic gives students the opportunity to assist needy inventors in preparing and securing patents.

The Immigration Clinic gives students training through the Midwest Immigrant and Human Rights Center where they assist immigrants with asylum claims.

The Veterans Legal Support Center and Clinic gives students the opportunity to assist veterans filing medical and education claims with the United States Department of Veterans Affairs, as well as the opportunity to provide representation for veterans during the appeals process through a statewide network of pro bono attorneys.

The Post-Conviction and Innocence Claims Clinic, in conjunction with the Cook County Public Defender's Office, offers students the opportunity to assist public defenders as they review communications, past transcripts, and records; conduct legal research; and conduct field investigations in cases of appeal.

Students also can gain hands-on experience through externships. Students are paired with attorneys and judges through Judicial Externships, the Defenders Clinic, the Local Government Clinic, and the Prosecution Clinic.

Library

The recently renovated Louis L. Biro Law Library occupies the sixth through tenth floors of the law school's State Street building. A team of over 20 professional librarians and staff members work to serve the students during the 96 hours per week that the library is open. The library holds over 410,000 volumes and microform equivalents and provides on-campus and remote access to over 4,000 titles via our specialty electronic databases. Students have wireless access throughout the law school, and the library offers seating for 750, including eight group study rooms. In addition to supporting the research and instructional needs of the students, faculty, and staff of the law school, the library is also open to members of the Chicago Bar Association.

Admission

Students are admitted in August and January. Applications for August entrance may be filed between October 1 and March 1; for January entrance, between May 1 and October 15. The LSAT score is evaluated together with the cumulative grade-point average and other relevant factors, including difficulty of undergraduate program, postgraduate experience, leadership potential, business and professional background, and letters of recommendation. Applicants from disadvantaged groups will be given special consideration in cases where their overall records are competitive with other applicants. Minority representation in the class enrolled in 2010 was 30 percent. Applicants with a B+ average overall and an LSAT score in the 67th percentile may be presumed to be within the range for favorable consideration.

Student Activities

There are five honors programs: the *John Marshall Law Review*, the *Journal of Computer and Information Law*, the *Review of Intellectual Property Law* (an online journal), the Moot Court Honors Program, and the Trial Advocacy and Dispute Resolution Honors Program. John Marshall has a long-standing tradition of success in interscholastic competitions and sends teams to more than 30 moot court and mock trial competitions annually.

The student community at the John Marshall Law School includes more than 40 student organizations engaging in social awareness, community service, legal discussions, and social activities. Every student group at John Marshall reflects the diversity, highlights the talents, and enhances the opportunities of our total student body.

John Marshall welcomes numerous well-known visitors and scholars each year. In addition to giving lectures and presentations, our distinguished guests can be found meeting with individual classes or holding roundtable discussions with interested students and faculty.

Career Opportunities

The Career Services Office (CSO) offers personal assistance to help students assess and refine their career goals. The CSO sponsors more than 60 career-related programs each year, many featuring alumni as panelists and speakers. A robust Alumni Mentor Program has mentors meeting with students one-on-one to provide real-world advice on practice areas, law school courses, and the day-to-day practice of law. The CSO also aggressively promotes John Marshall students to employers. John Marshall graduates are employed at 34 of Chicago's 35 largest firms. Public service is another favored career path, with graduates serving as attorneys in the courts and government. Nearly one-fifth of all Illinois judges (circuit, appellate, and state supreme court) are John Marshall alumni.

Correspondence

We encourage you to visit our website at www.jmls.edu and to visit the law school. Tour arrangements can be made through our Office of Admission and visitors are welcome to sit in a class and talk with students and faculty. An admission counselor can explain the admission process and a representative from our Financial Aid Office can help you understand what loans and scholarships are available.

APPLICANT PROFILE

The John Marshall Law School
This grid includes only applicants who earned 120–180 LSAT scores under standard administrations.

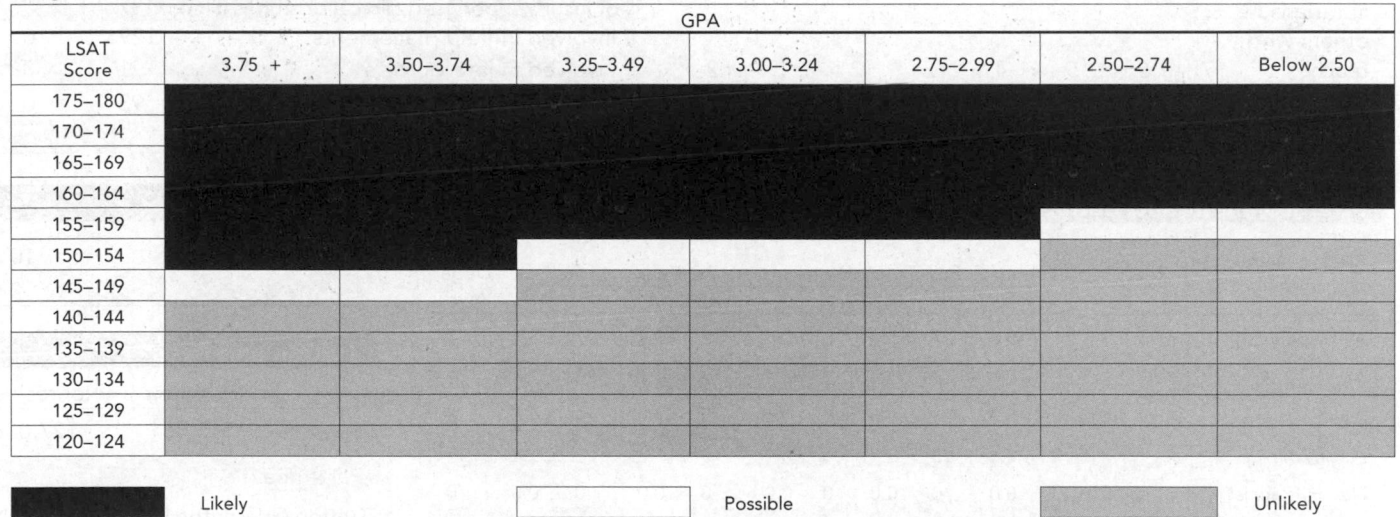

LSAT Score	GPA						
	3.75 +	3.50–3.74	3.25–3.49	3.00–3.24	2.75–2.99	2.50–2.74	Below 2.50
175–180							
170–174							
165–169							
160–164							
155–159							
150–154							
145–149							
140–144							
135–139							
130–134							
125–129							
120–124							

Likely   Possible   Unlikely

THE UNIVERSITY OF KANSAS SCHOOL OF LAW

1535 West 15th Street
Lawrence, KS 66045-7608
Phone: 866.220.3654 (toll free), 785.864.4378; Fax: 785.864.5054
E-mail: admitlaw@ku.edu; Website: www.law.ku.edu

ABA
Approved
Since
1923

The Basics

Type of school	Public
Term	Semester
Application deadline	3/15
Application fee	$55
Financial aid deadline	3/1
Can first year start other than fall?	Yes
Student to faculty ratio	12.9 to 1
# of housing spaces available restricted to law students	
graduate housing for which law students are eligible	550

Faculty and Administrators

	Total		Men		Women		Minorities	
	Spr	Fall	Spr	Fall	Spr	Fall	Spr	Fall
Full-time	31	32	18	20	13	12	4	3
Other full-time	3	3	0	0	3	3	0	0
Deans, librarians, & others who teach	7	6	5	4	2	2	1	2
Part-time	23	20	17	13	6	7	1	1
Total	64	61	40	37	24	24	6	6

Curriculum

	Full-Time	Part-Time
Typical first-year section size	59	0
Is there typically a "small section" of the first-year class, other than Legal Writing, taught by full-time faculty	Yes	No
If yes, typical size offered last year	21	
# of classroom course titles beyond first-year curriculum	102	

# of upper division courses, excluding seminars, with an enrollment:		
	Under 25	100
	25–49	28
	50–74	5
	75–99	4
	100+	1

# of seminars	18	
# of seminar positions available	354	
# of seminar positions filled	211	0
# of positions available in simulation courses	281	
# of simulation positions filled	259	0
# of positions available in faculty supervised clinical courses	202	
# of faculty supervised clinical positions filled	137	0
# involved in field placements	129	0
# involved in law journals	91	0
# involved in moot court or trial competitions	93	0
# of credit hours required to graduate	90	

JD Enrollment and Ethnicity

	Men		Women		Full-Time		Part-Time		1st-Year		Total		JD Degs. Awd.
	#	%	#	%	#	%	#	%	#	%	#	%	
All Hispanics	16	5.3	11	5.6	27	5.4	0	0.0	18	10.9	27	5.4	7
Am. Ind./AK Nat.	7	2.3	5	2.6	12	2.4	0	0.0	2	1.2	12	2.4	5
Asian	14	4.6	10	5.1	24	4.8	0	0.0	5	3.0	24	4.8	8
Black/Af. Am.	5	1.7	7	3.6	12	2.4	0	0.0	3	1.8	12	2.4	7
Nat. HI/Pac. Isl.	0	0.0	0	0.0	0	0.0	0	0.0	0	0.0	0	0.0	0
2 or more races	13	4.3	4	2.1	17	3.4	0	0.0	6	3.6	17	3.4	0
Subtotal (minor.)	55	18.2	37	19.0	92	18.5	0	0.0	34	20.6	92	18.5	29
Nonres. Alien	11	3.6	9	4.6	20	4.0	0	0.0	2	1.2	20	4.0	0
White/Cauc.	227	75.2	143	73.3	370	74.4	0	0.0	127	77.0	370	74.4	117
Unknown	9	3.0	6	3.1	15	3.0	0	0.0	2	1.2	15	3.0	15
Total	302	60.8	195	39.2	497	100.0	0	0.0	165	33.2	497		168

Transfers

Transfers in	10
Transfers out	2

Tuition and Fees

	Resident	Nonresident
Full-time	$15,561	$27,038

Part-time		
Tuition Guarantee Program		N

Living Expenses

Estimated living expenses for singles

Living on campus	Living off campus	Living at home
$16,606	$16,606	$16,606

THE UNIVERSITY OF KANSAS SCHOOL OF LAW

*ABA
Approved
Since
1923*

GPA and LSAT Scores

	Total	Full-Time	Part-Time
# of apps	1,120	1,120	0
# of offers	417	417	0
# of matrics	165	165	0
75% GPA	3.67	3.67	0.00
Median GPA	3.46	3.46	0.00
25% GPA	3.20	3.20	0.00
75% LSAT	160	160	0
Median LSAT	158	158	0
25% LSAT	155	155	0

Grants and Scholarships (from prior year)

	Total		Full-Time		Part-Time	
	#	%	#	%	#	%
Total # of students	499		499		0	
Total # receiving grants	386	77.4	386	77.4	0	0.0
Less than 1/2 tuition	292	58.5	292	58.5	0	0.0
Half to full tuition	75	15.0	75	15.0	0	0.0
Full tuition	11	2.2	11	2.2	0	0.0
More than full tuition	8	1.6	8	1.6	0	0.0
Median grant amount			$2,200		$0	

Informational and Library Resources

Total amount spent on library materials	$639,506
Study seating capacity inside the library	481
# of full-time equivalent professional librarians	8
Hours per week library is open	93
# of open, wired connections available to students	0
# of networked computers available for use by students	51
Has wireless network?	Y
Requires computer?	N

JD Attrition (from prior year)

	Academic	Other	Total	
	#	#	#	%
1st year	0	9	9	5.6
2nd year	0	4	4	2.3
3rd year	0	0	0	0.0
4th year	0	0	0	0.0

Employment (9 months after graduation)

	Total	Percentage
Employment status known	156	97.5
Employment status unknown	4	2.5
Employed	131	84.0
Pursuing graduate degrees	5	3.2
Unemployed (seeking, not seeking, or studying for the bar)	14	9.0
Type of Employment		
# employed in law firms	70	53.4
# employed in business and industry	28	21.4
# employed in government	18	13.7
# employed in public interest	7	5.3
# employed as judicial clerks	8	6.1
# employed in academia	0	0.0
Geographic Location		
# employed in state	66	50.4
# employed outside the US	2	1.5
# of states where employed	18	

Bar Passage Rates

First-time takers	183	Reporting %	71.58
Average school %	79.39	Average state %	87.31

Average pass difference –7.92

Jurisdiction	Takers	Passers	Pass %	State %	Diff %
Kansas	80	60	75.00	86.23	–11.23
Missouri	36	33	91.67	91.81	–0.14
Texas	6	4	66.67	85.48	–18.81
Colorado	5	5	100.00	85.67	14.33
California	4	2	50.00	73.19	–23.19

THE UNIVERSITY OF KANSAS SCHOOL OF LAW

1535 West 15th Street
Lawrence, KS 66045-7608
Phone: 866.220.3654 (toll free), 785.864.4378; Fax: 785.864.5054
E-mail: admitlaw@ku.edu; Website: www.law.ku.edu

Introduction

The University of Kansas (KU) School of Law is an excellent place to begin a legal career. It has a venerable history and a commitment to educating for the future. Legal education at KU began in 1878. The school was a charter member of the Association of American Law Schools, and since 1924, it has had a chapter of the Order of the Coif, a national law school honor society with chapters at leading law schools throughout the country. The law school is fully accredited by the American Bar Association.

The law school is on KU's main campus—one of the most beautiful in the country. It occupies Green Hall, named in honor of James Woods Green, first dean of the school. Green Hall is a five-story building with extensive clinical facilities, spacious and attractive classrooms, seminar rooms, a formal courtroom, and common areas. The school is equipped with a wireless network, allowing students to access the Internet and e-mail from anywhere in the law school.

The school's primary mission is to prepare its students to be outstanding members of the legal profession, well educated in the law, with a commitment to professional achievement and public service. The school educates students in both general principles of law and the skills needed for practice in a changing legal environment. Students develop technical competence, pride in legal craftsmanship, a sound sense of ethics and professionalism, and an appreciation for the role of law in society.

Faculty

KU Law faculty care about teaching. They are committed to excellence in the classroom and to serving as mentors for law students. This is the KU Law tradition. Students are encouraged to consult regularly with their teachers about their progress in the study of law as well as about career plans, job opportunities, and the professional responsibilities of lawyers. Law faculty offices are located throughout Green Hall, and doors are open to students.

Faculty members enrich their teaching by researching and writing about the areas of law they teach. They regularly participate in symposia, publish widely in legal journals, and enjoy national and international recognition for the quality of their scholarship. Many have written important treatises and casebooks used at law schools around the country.

Learning the Law

Entering students take basic courses that provide a solid foundation for upper-level classes and for the practice of law. The lawyering course focuses on the skills and values of the profession. Taught by faculty members with extensive practice experience, the course introduces students to the tools all lawyers use: an understanding of the legal system and legal institutions, case law and statutes, legal research and writing, and advocacy. First-year students take one of their other required courses in a small section of approximately 20 students, which provides an informal learning atmosphere and encourages in-depth discussions and critical analysis.

More than 100 courses are available to upper-level students, covering a broad range of practice areas from agricultural law to the law of cyberspace. Twelve clinical programs permit students, acting under faculty supervision, to develop legal skills and learn professional values in actual practice settings: the Criminal Prosecution Clinic, Paul E. Wilson Project for Innocence and Post-Conviction Remedies, Elder Law Clinic, Family Health Care Legal Services Clinic, Immigration/Asylum Clinic, Judicial Clerkship Clinic, Legal Aid Clinic, Legislative Clinic, Media Law Clinic, Public Policy Clinic, Tribal Judicial Support Clinic, and the Externship Clinic. The large number of clinical placements available means that every student can participate in at least one clinic and many participate in more than one.

The school's setting at the heart of a major university makes possible the 11 joint-degree programs open to law students. The most popular joint-degree programs are business, health services administration, and social welfare, but joint degrees are also available in East Asian languages and cultures, economics, indigenous nations studies, journalism, political science, philosophy, public administration, and urban planning. In addition, the school offers eight certification programs: advocacy, business and commercial law, elder law, environmental and natural resources law, international trade and finance, media law and policy, tax law, and tribal lawyering.

Library

The Wheat Law Library is the largest law library in Kansas. Its hallmark is excellent service for students and faculty. The law library is a wireless environment that allows students, faculty, and staff access to LexisNexis, Westlaw, CALI, HeinOnline, LLMC-Digital, the Internet, and numerous university-wide interdisciplinary databases. Access is also available on desktop computers in carrels and throughout the library. The law library's award-winning website, www.law.ku.edu/library/, is a comprehensive gateway that provides access to virtual resources beyond the scope of the physical collection as well as in-house topical research guides. Professional librarians and reference staff are eager to help with legal research ranging from the rich heritage of historical materials to cutting-edge digitized images.

Accelerated/Summer Program

The law school's unique summer school program is fully integrated with the curriculum of the fall and spring semesters. Students who begin law school in May and attend summer school each of the following two summers may complete degree requirements in just 27 months.

Student Life

Because the school seeks students with strong personal qualities in addition to high academic credentials, students learn the law with classmates who have the interpersonal skills, maturity, judgment, and ambition to succeed. The law school values diversity, and students have a wide range of education and work experience, enriching classroom discussions and student life.

KU Law students develop friendships that last a lifetime. They find as many opportunities for collaboration as for competition. They socialize and develop leadership skills and an appreciation for community service through membership in many student organizations. They hone research, writing, and editing skills through work on two student-edited publications: the *Kansas Law Review* and the *Kansas Journal of Law and Public Policy*. They participate regularly and successfully in moot court and mock trial competitions. Study abroad is available through the London Consortium, the school's Limerick and Istanbul programs, and other programs approved by the American Bar Association.

Career Services and Alumni

The school's Office of Career Services helps students define career goals and find employment that matches their interests. The office coordinates an extensive on-campus interviewing program, sponsors workshops exploring career options, and helps students develop job-seeking skills.

KU Law students and graduates are highly sought after by employers throughout the state, region, and nation. A majority of recent graduates chose employment in private law firms, but many chose government service, public interest work, the military, graduate study, and nontraditional careers. A considerable number of graduates accept judicial clerkships. Recent graduates have been law clerks at all levels, including the Supreme Court of the United States.

KU graduates have been highly successful in passing Kansas and Missouri bar examinations and have performed well on examinations in other states. The Office of Career Services provides up-to-date information on bar requirements for all states.

The school's 6,600-plus alumni live in all 50 states, the District of Columbia, Puerto Rico, and 17 foreign countries. Many participate in the law school's mentor program for first-year law students or in the Career Services Alumni Network, serving as sources of information about practice specialties and practice opportunities.

APPLICANT PROFILE

The University of Kansas School of Law
This grid includes applicants who earned 120–180 LSAT scores under standard administrations.

LSAT Score	GPA 3.75 +		3.50–3.74		3.25–3.49		3.00–3.24		2.75–2.99		2.50–2.74		2.25–2.49		2.00–2.24		Below 2.00		No GPA		Total	
	Apps	Adm	Apps	Adm	Apps	Adm	Apps	Adm	Apps	Adm	Apps	Adm	Apps	Adm	Apps	Adm	Apps	Adm	Apps	Adm	Apps	Adm
175–180	1	1	0	0	0	0	1	0	0	0	0	0	0	0	0	0	0	0	0	0	2	1
170–174	5	4	4	4	3	3	0	0	1	1	1	0	1	1	0	0	0	0	0	0	15	13
165–169	12	11	11	11	12	10	6	4	6	5	2	1	0	0	0	0	1	0	0	0	50	42
160–164	40	37	31	27	43	34	35	23	19	10	5	2	2	1	3	0	0	0	2	2	180	136
155–159	50	37	62	33	78	40	62	32	24	5	32	4	8	0	3	0	1	0	2	1	322	152
150–154	35	7	71	20	66	11	69	10	28	4	14	2	11	0	3	0	0	0	2	1	299	55
145–149	15	1	22	3	52	6	30	3	17	1	14	0	5	0	4	0	0	0	6	0	165	14
140–144	6	0	11	1	16	1	7	0	8	1	6	0	4	1	1	0	0	0	0	0	59	4
135–139	0	0	0	0	1	0	3	0	4	0	4	0	2	0	3	0	0	0	2	0	19	0
130–134	0	0	1	0	0	0	0	0	2	0	0	0	0	0	1	0	1	0	1	0	6	0
125–129	0	0	0	0	0	0	0	0	0	0	0	0	0	0	1	0	0	0	0	0	1	0
120–124	0	0	0	0	0	0	0	0	1	0	0	0	0	0	0	0	0	0	0	0	1	0
Total	164	98	213	99	271	105	213	72	109	27	79	9	33	3	19	0	3	0	16	4	1119	417

Apps = Number of Applicants
Adm = Number Admitted
Reflects 99% of the total applicant pool; highest LSAT data reported.

UNIVERSITY OF KENTUCKY COLLEGE OF LAW

209 Law Building, 620 South Limestone Street
Lexington, KY 40506-0048
Phone: 859.257.1678; Fax: 859.257-3140
E-mail: lawadmissions@email.uky.edu; Website: www.law.uky.edu

ABA
Approved
Since
1925

The Basics

Type of school	Public
Term	Semester
Application deadline	3/1
Application fee	$50
Financial aid deadline	4/1
Can first year start other than fall?	No
Student to faculty ratio	15.5 to 1
# of housing spaces available restricted to law students	
graduate housing for which law students are eligible	419

Faculty and Administrators

	Total		Men		Women		Minorities	
	Spr	Fall	Spr	Fall	Spr	Fall	Spr	Fall
Full-time	19	25	14	18	5	7	2	3
Other full-time	1	0	0	0	1	0	0	0
Deans, librarians, & others who teach	13	10	4	4	9	6	4	2
Part-time	18	17	11	13	7	4	10	9
Total	51	52	29	35	22	17	16	14

Curriculum

		Full-Time	Part-Time
Typical first-year section size		65	0
Is there typically a "small section" of the first-year class, other than Legal Writing, taught by full-time faculty		Yes	No
If yes, typical size offered last year		45	
# of classroom course titles beyond first-year curriculum		107	
# of upper division courses, excluding seminars, with an enrollment:	Under 25	53	
	25–49	32	
	50–74	11	
	75–99	0	
	100+	0	
# of seminars		10	
# of seminar positions available		160	
# of seminar positions filled		121	0
# of positions available in simulation courses		150	
# of simulation positions filled		82	0
# of positions available in faculty supervised clinical courses		33	
# of faculty supervised clinical positions filled		33	0
# involved in field placements		92	0
# involved in law journals		46	0
# involved in moot court or trial competitions		52	0
# of credit hours required to graduate		90	

JD Enrollment and Ethnicity

	Men #	Men %	Women #	Women %	Full-Time #	Full-Time %	Part-Time #	Part-Time %	1st-Year #	1st-Year %	Total #	Total %	JD Degs. Awd.
All Hispanics	6	2.5	0	0.0	6	1.4	0	0.0	1	0.7	6	1.4	1
Am. Ind./AK Nat.	3	1.2	0	0.0	3	0.7	0	0.0	1	0.7	3	0.7	0
Asian	5	2.1	1	0.6	6	1.4	0	0.0	2	1.5	6	1.4	0
Black/Af. Am.	18	7.4	21	11.9	39	9.3	0	0.0	12	8.9	39	9.3	7
Nat. HI/Pac. Isl.	0	0.0	2	1.1	2	0.5	0	0.0	0	0.0	2	0.5	0
2 or more races	0	0.0	0	0.0	0	0.0	0	0.0	0	0.0	0	0.0	0
Subtotal (minor.)	32	13.2	24	13.6	56	13.4	0	0.0	16	11.9	56	13.4	10
Nonres. Alien	0	0.0	0	0.0	0	0.0	0	0.0	0	0.0	0	0.0	0
White/Cauc.	208	85.6	152	86.4	360	85.9	0	0.0	116	85.9	360	85.9	110
Unknown	3	1.2	0	0.0	3	0.7	0	0.0	3	2.2	3	0.7	0
Total	243	58.0	176	42.0	419	100.0	0	0.0	135	32.2	419		120

Transfers

Transfers in	6
Transfers out	3

Tuition and Fees

	Resident	Nonresident
Full-time	$16,982	$29,424
Part-time		
Tuition Guarantee Program		N

Living Expenses

Estimated living expenses for singles

Living on campus	Living off campus	Living at home
$15,318	$15,318	$6,018

ABA
Approved
Since
1925

GPA and LSAT Scores

	Total	Full-Time	Part-Time
# of apps	1,191	1,191	0
# of offers	433	433	0
# of matrics	135	135	0
75% GPA	3.76	3.76	0.00
Median GPA	3.55	3.55	0.00
25% GPA	3.19	3.19	0.00
75% LSAT	162	162	0
Median LSAT	160	160	0
25% LSAT	157	157	0

Grants and Scholarships (from prior year)

	Total		Full-Time		Part-Time	
	#	%	#	%	#	%
Total # of students	406		406		0	
Total # receiving grants	266	65.5	266	65.5	0	0.0
Less than 1/2 tuition	163	40.1	163	40.1	0	0.0
Half to full tuition	93	22.9	93	22.9	0	0.0
Full tuition	1	0.2	1	0.2	0	0.0
More than full tuition	9	2.2	9	2.2	0	0.0
Median grant amount			$6,000		$0	

Informational and Library Resources

Total amount spent on library materials	$1,142,579
Study seating capacity inside the library	354
# of full-time equivalent professional librarians	8
Hours per week library is open	100
# of open, wired connections available to students	78
# of networked computers available for use by students	48
Has wireless network?	Y
Requires computer?	N

JD Attrition (from prior year)

	Academic	Other	Total	
	#	#	#	%
1st year	3	3	6	4.0
2nd year	0	0	0	0.0
3rd year	1	0	1	0.8
4th year	0	0	0	0.0

Employment (9 months after graduation)

	Total	Percentage
Employment status known	134	99.3
Employment status unknown	1	0.7
Employed	126	94.0
Pursuing graduate degrees	4	3.0
Unemployed (seeking, not seeking, or studying for the bar)	1	0.7
Type of Employment		
# employed in law firms	66	52.4
# employed in business and industry	10	7.9
# employed in government	11	8.7
# employed in public interest	12	9.5
# employed as judicial clerks	22	17.5
# employed in academia	3	2.4
Geographic Location		
# employed in state	101	80.2
# employed outside the US	0	0.0
# of states where employed	15	

Bar Passage Rates

First-time takers	135	Reporting %	85.19
Average school %	82.61	Average state %	85.92
Average pass difference	−3.31		

Jurisdiction	Takers	Passers	Pass %	State %	Diff %
Kentucky	115	95	82.61	85.92	−3.31

UNIVERSITY OF KENTUCKY COLLEGE OF LAW

209 Law Building, 620 South Limestone Street
Lexington, KY 40506-0048
Phone: 859.257.1678; Fax: 859.257-3140
E-mail: lawadmissions@email.uky.edu; Website: www.law.uky.edu

Introduction

The University of Kentucky College of Law is a small, state-supported law school on the main campus of the university in scenic Lexington, Kentucky, a city of approximately 250,000 in the center of the Bluegrass horse-farm region. Founded in 1908, the college has been a member of the AALS since 1912 and has been accredited by the ABA since 1925. The faculty has wide experience in law practice and government service, as well as teaching and research. UK Law has a strong tradition of faculty concern about their students' progress and success. The curriculum offers broad training in the law and legal methods, drawing upon sources from all jurisdictions. Accordingly, UK Law graduates are prepared to practice in any of the 50 states.

Library and Physical Facilities

The college is self-contained in a contemporary building that provides all facilities for a complete program of legal education. All classrooms have been renovated with the addition of state-of-the-art teaching technology. Classrooms provide for student use of laptop computers with wired and wireless Internet access. The law library is on the college's wireless network with a number of attractive study areas, and laptops are available for you to check out and use in the library.

Curriculum

UK Law offers a full-time program only, designed to be completed over three academic years or two and one-half years if you take classes during both summer sessions. Some first-year classes are divided into three sections to give you more individual attention, and you will be in a small legal writing section. As an upper-level student, you can select from a full range of elective courses in both traditional and newly-developing legal fields. After the first year, the only specific requirements are that you take a course in professional ethics, take at least one professional skills course, and complete a seminar involving substantial writing.

Legal Clinic

UK Law's Legal Clinic is located in its own building near the college. As a third-year student in the clinic course, you would represent low-income clients in a variety of civil legal matters. The clinic is supervised by a faculty member who was a very successful trial attorney for 10 years.

Externships

UK Law offers nine externships for course credit. The Judicial Clerkship Externship enables you to serve as a law clerk for a local state or federal judge. The Fayette Commonwealth Attorney's Office Externship enables you to participate in criminal prosecutions. The Federal Correctional Institute Externship permits you to counsel federal inmates in civil and criminal matters. In the Externship with the Kentucky Innocence Project, you work on selected criminal appeals where a claim of factual innocence is made. The Externship

with the US Attorney's Office gives you the opportunity to work on federal appellate briefs in both criminal and civil cases. The Children's Law Center Externship allows you to work on high-conflict custody cases representing children. The Department of Public Advocacy Externship enables you to work with the defense in criminal trials. The Externship with the UK HealthCare Risk Management Office gives you firsthand experience with hospital risk management issues and procedures. The Energy and Environment Cabinet Externship gives you insight into the legal and policy issues arising from energy development and environmental protection.

Joint Degrees

If you are interested in a career in international law, public or private law, international business, or in government service in the international sector, you should consider the four-year **JD/MA** dual-degree program with UK's Patterson School of Diplomacy and International Commerce. You must apply and be admitted to both programs.

The **JD/MBA** joint degree can be obtained in as little time as four years. You must apply and be admitted to both the UK College of Law and UK's Gatton College of Business and Economics.

If you are interested in a career in public administration, public service, or politics, you should consider the four-year **JD/MPA** joint-degree program with UK's Martin School of Public Policy. You must apply and be admitted to both programs.

Student Activities

There are a variety of cocurricular activities in which you may earn course credit. The *Kentucky Law Journal* is the 10th oldest American law review and is edited entirely by students, as is the *Kentucky Journal for Equine, Agricultural, and Natural Resources Law*. The college fields several moot court teams that participate in both national and international competitions. UK Law's Trial Advocacy Team advanced to national title competitions in six of the last seven years, placing second nationally in 2009. The Mock Trial Team for UK's Black Law Students Association won the Southeast Region of the Thurgood Marshall Moot Court Competition in both 2006 and 2008, placing second in the nation in 2006.

UK Law's Student Bar Association (SBA) serves as the law student governing body and student activities board. The SBA publishes a weekly online student newspaper and sponsors regular student social events and community service activities. UK's SBA was recognized by the ABA as the best student bar association in the nation in 2002.

The Student Public Interest Law Foundation, through grants and fundraising, sponsors 15–20 summer internships with public interest and public service organizations selected by the students who apply. Other active student groups include the Black Law Students Association, the Latino/a Law Student Association, the Asian-Pacific Islander Law Student Association, OUTLaw, the Women's Law Caucus, the Federalist Society, the American Constitutional Society, the Criminal Law Society, the International Law Society, the Environmental Law Society, the Equine Law Society, the

Health Law Society, the Intellectual Property Law Society, the Tax Law Society, the Libertarian Law Society, and the Student Animal Legal Defense Fund.

Admission

Admission is considered and granted by the faculty Admissions Committee. Each file is reviewed completely and is voted on by the full committee. While your undergraduate academic record and LSAT score(s) are the primary indicators for potential success in law school, all other factors you present will be considered. You are urged to read the full description of the admission process on our website and to provide full information about your intellectual and nonacademic achievements. The February LSAT is the last examination accepted by the Admissions Committee for that year. In most cases, the high LSAT score will be used by the Committee in making the admissions decision. Admission as a first-year student is for the fall term only.

Scholarships and Financial Aid

Over 60 percent of UK Law's 2010 entering class received some form of scholarship award. UK Law offers a number of three-year scholarships based on merit and/or contributions to diversity, for which you will be considered automatically after admission. For the largest and most prestigious award, the Bert Combs Scholarship, you must be selected for an interview. UK Law also offers three-year merit and diversity tuition-reduction fellowships for nonresidents of Kentucky.

You have the option of including a brief statement about your eligibility for merit and/or diversity awards with your admission application, but a separate scholarship application is not required. UK Law students are eligible for loan assistance through the Federal Direct Student Loan Program and federal graduate PLUS loan program, as well as through national private loan programs. Admitted candidates are mailed complete information on financial aid. To receive forms and information prior to admission, contact UK's Student Financial Aid Office, 128 Funkhouser Building, University of Kentucky, Lexington, KY 40506-0054.

Career Services

UK Law students have the benefit of a large on-campus job interview program for regional employers, as well as national placement through the college's participation in numerous off-campus interviewing conferences. The Career Services Office also uses alumni contacts to connect students with employers nationwide. Two UK Law graduates who are former practicing attorneys are on staff to offer advice and guidance to UK Law students and alumni.

UK Law's job placement rate consistently exceeds national averages. For the 2009 graduating class, 97 percent were employed or in advanced-degree programs within nine months after graduation. A majority of UK Law graduates choose private practice, with 15–25 percent of each graduating class selected for prestigious state and federal judicial clerkships.

APPLICANT PROFILE

University of Kentucky College of Law
Probability of admission to the University of Kentucky College of Law, based on admission decisions for the 2010 entering class.

LSAT Score	GPA								
	3.75–4.00	3.50–3.74	3.25–3.49	3.00–3.24	2.75–2.99	2.50–2.74	2.25–2.49	Below 2.25	GPA not scaled
165 & Above									
160–164									
157–159									
155–156									
153–154									
150–152									
145–149									
Below 145									

Probable ■　Very Competitive ■　Somewhat Competitive ■　Possible ■　Unlikely □

UNIVERSITY OF LA VERNE COLLEGE OF LAW

320 East D Street
Ontario, CA 91764
Phone: 877.858.4529; Fax: 909.460.2082
E-mail: lawadm@laverne.edu; Website: http://law.laverne.edu

Provisional *ABA Approved Since 2006*

The Basics

Type of school	Private
Term	Semester
Application deadline	7/1
Application fee	$50
Financial aid deadline	3/2
Can first year start other than fall?	Yes
Student to faculty ratio	16.0 to 1
# of housing spaces available restricted to law students	
graduate housing for which law students are eligible	

Faculty and Administrators

	Total		Men		Women		Minorities	
	Spr	Fall	Spr	Fall	Spr	Fall	Spr	Fall
Full-time	18	19	9	9	9	10	7	7
Other full-time	0	0	0	0	0	0	0	0
Deans, librarians, & others who teach	8	7	4	4	4	3	2	2
Part-time	22	22	15	12	7	10	4	11
Total	48	48	28	25	20	23	13	20

Curriculum

	Full-Time	Part-Time
Typical first-year section size	65	35
Is there typically a "small section" of the first-year class, other than Legal Writing, taught by full-time faculty	No	No
If yes, typical size offered last year		

# of classroom course titles beyond first-year curriculum		58
# of upper division courses, excluding seminars, with an enrollment:	Under 25	51
	25–49	35
	50–74	3
	75–99	0
	100+	0
# of seminars		6
# of seminar positions available		95
# of seminar positions filled	55	32
# of positions available in simulation courses		528
# of simulation positions filled	303	120
# of positions available in faculty supervised clinical courses		19
# of faculty supervised clinical positions filled	12	5
# involved in field placements	62	16
# involved in law journals	28	8
# involved in moot court or trial competitions	9	1
# of credit hours required to graduate		88

JD Enrollment and Ethnicity

	Men		Women		Full-Time		Part-Time		1st-Year		Total		JD Degs. Awd.
	#	%	#	%	#	%	#	%	#	%	#	%	
All Hispanics	32	13.7	38	19.7	53	17.0	17	14.9	26	15.8	70	16.4	14
Am. Ind./AK Nat.	4	1.7	2	1.0	5	1.6	1	0.9	4	2.4	6	1.4	0
Asian	25	10.7	30	15.5	38	12.2	17	14.9	23	13.9	55	12.9	17
Black/Af. Am.	5	2.1	7	3.6	9	2.9	3	2.6	5	3.0	12	2.8	3
Nat. HI/Pac. Isl.	0	0.0	0	0.0	0	0.0	0	0.0	0	0.0	0	0.0	0
2 or more races	0	0.0	0	0.0	0	0.0	0	0.0	0	0.0	0	0.0	0
Subtotal (minor.)	66	28.3	77	39.9	105	33.7	38	33.3	58	35.2	143	33.6	34
Nonres. Alien	5	2.1	4	2.1	9	2.9	0	0.0	2	1.2	9	2.1	0
White/Cauc.	122	52.4	82	42.5	147	47.1	57	50.0	85	51.5	204	47.9	58
Unknown	40	17.2	30	15.5	51	16.3	19	16.7	20	12.1	70	16.4	3
Total	233	54.7	193	45.3	312	73.2	114	26.8	165	38.7	426		95

Transfers

Transfers in	4
Transfers out	10

Tuition and Fees

	Resident	Nonresident
Full-time	$38,462	$38,462
Part-time	$29,062	$29,062
Tuition Guarantee Program		N

Living Expenses

Estimated living expenses for singles

Living on campus	Living off campus	Living at home
$23,104	$23,104	$23,104

ABA
Approved
Since
2006

GPA and LSAT Scores

	Total	Full-Time	Part-Time
# of apps	1,598	1,252	346
# of offers	666	559	107
# of matrics	166	127	39
75% GPA	3.33	3.35	3.17
Median GPA	3.05	3.06	2.91
25% GPA	2.74	2.82	2.64
75% LSAT	155	155	152
Median LSAT	152	153	151
25% LSAT	150	150	149

Grants and Scholarships (from prior year)

	Total		Full-Time		Part-Time	
	#	%	#	%	#	%
Total # of students	392		275		117	
Total # receiving grants	247	63.0	156	56.7	91	77.8
Less than 1/2 tuition	177	45.2	109	39.6	68	58.1
Half to full tuition	52	13.3	40	14.5	12	10.3
Full tuition	17	4.3	6	2.2	11	9.4
More than full tuition	1	0.3	1	0.4	0	0.0
Median grant amount			$15,375		$8,062	

Informational and Library Resources

Total amount spent on library materials	$1,000,935
Study seating capacity inside the library	300
# of full-time equivalent professional librarians	8
Hours per week library is open	96
# of open, wired connections available to students	100
# of networked computers available for use by students	35
Has wireless network?	Y
Requires computer?	N

JD Attrition (from prior year)

	Academic	Other	Total	
	#	#	#	%
1st year	8	22	30	21.0
2nd year	2	1	3	2.6
3rd year	1	0	1	0.9
4th year	0	0	0	0.0

Employment (9 months after graduation)

	Total	Percentage
Employment status known	76	100.0
Employment status unknown	0	0.0
Employed	48	63.2
Pursuing graduate degrees	7	9.2
Unemployed (seeking, not seeking, or studying for the bar)	3	3.9
Type of Employment		
# employed in law firms	31	64.6
# employed in business and industry	10	20.8
# employed in government	4	8.3
# employed in public interest	2	4.2
# employed as judicial clerks	0	0.0
# employed in academia	1	2.1
Geographic Location		
# employed in state	41	85.4
# employed outside the US	0	0.0
# of states where employed		6

Bar Passage Rates

First-time takers	72	Reporting %	100.00
Average school %	34.73	Average state %	74.29

Average pass difference −39.56

Jurisdiction	Takers	Passers	Pass %	State %	Diff %
California	64	19	29.69	73.19	−43.50
Utah	2	1	50.00	88.94	−38.94
District of Columbia	1	1	100.00	68.17	31.83
Florida	1	1	100.00	77.81	22.19
Others (4)	4	3	75.00		

UNIVERSITY OF LA VERNE COLLEGE OF LAW

320 East D Street
Ontario, CA 91764
Phone: 877.858.4529; Fax: 909.460.2082
E-mail: lawadm@laverne.edu; Website: http://law.laverne.edu

A Sense of Community

The University of La Verne College of Law, located in the heart of Southern California, prides itself on offering students not only an excellent legal education, but also a sense of community. At La Verne Law, you will be more than just a number. Our small class sizes and low student-to-faculty ratio ensure that you will get individualized attention from people who genuinely care about your success as both a student and a legal professional. Additionally, our excellent student body offers a spirit of collegiality, in which individuals work together toward a common goal: learning to become the best attorneys they can be. Come and see for yourself the La Verne Law difference.

Hit the Ground Running

At La Verne Law, we strive to ensure that you will have the skills you need to be a stellar attorney the moment you graduate. Our faculty are not only superb legal scholars, but also boast years of practical experience. This allows us to provide a curriculum that offers a solid foundation in legal theory as well as a strong focus on practical training. Our required Lawyering Skills Practicum (LSP) course is unique in offering law students the chance to simulate the practice of law under the guidance of accomplished attorneys. Many of our other course offerings will give you similar opportunities to hone your legal skills not just by hearing lectures but by actually using them.

La Verne Law also houses two campus-based clinics that allow you to actually work on legal issues with real-life clients. Our Disability Rights Legal Center (DRLC) focuses on disability civil rights litigation and special-education issues for low-income and minority families. Our Justice and Immigration Clinic (JIC) allows students to represent asylum applicants who cannot return to their home countries because of persecution based on race, religion, nationality, political opinion, or membership in a particular social group.

Outside of class, La Verne Law students have the opportunity to do externships with a multitude of regional organizations that provide them with the solid practical training they will need to be successful attorneys. Our students have participated in externships with the San Bernardino County District Attorney's Office, Inland County Legal Services, the Harriet Buhai Center for Family Law, and dozens of other organizations focusing on everything from the legal rights of Holocaust survivors to entertainment law.

A Focus on Your Career

La Verne Law's Career Services and Professional Development Office (CSPDO) is dedicated to ensuring that you have the resources and opportunities to make the most of your legal education and reach your career goals. As the only ABA-approved law school in the Inland Empire, an area severely underserved by attorneys, La Verne Law graduates are well-poised to take on the challenge of the new legal market.

In addition to a commitment to developing solid relationships with potential employers, CSPDO offers:
- Individualized career counseling and résumé and cover letter review for both students and alumni;
- Career and professional development workshops on topics ranging from interviewing skills to negotiating a job offer;
- On-campus interview and networking opportunities with representatives from law firms, corporations, government agencies, and public interest organizations;
- A constantly updated database of job postings featuring opportunities for law clerk positions, externships, judicial clerkships, and postgraduate positions;
- The opportunity, through our Mentor Program and Mock Interview Program, to connect with practicing attorneys who will give you advice, help you explore the areas of practice in which you are interested, and assist you in learning to put your best foot forward in an interview;
- Panels and receptions where students hear from and mingle with attorneys and potential employers from a huge variety of practice areas; and
- Career fairs and consortium events cosponsored with other Southern California ABA-approved law schools.

Our alumni have been successful in obtaining positions with large and small law firms, corporations, government agencies, and public interest organizations. Several have started their own thriving practices, and we are particularly proud of our alumni who currently sit or have sat on the bench.

A Commitment to Your Success

La Verne Law is committed to ensuring your success as both a law student and a legal professional. Our faculty are admired for their accessible demeanor and open-door policy, allowing you to obtain additional assistance with challenging subject matter. High-performing upper-level students offer free tutoring services, and our staff of bar exam professionals, all licensed attorneys, is dedicated to helping you prepare for the bar exam.

Location, Location, Location!

In addition to the amazing weather, La Verne Law students enjoy a wide variety of amenities due to the law school's location in the heart of Southern California. Where else can you lie in the sun in the morning and ski in the late afternoon with time for shopping in between? Located just east of Los Angeles and just north of Orange County, the Law School campus is less than an hour away from beautiful beaches, majestic mountains, world-class concert halls and museums, and much more. Disneyland and Knott's Berry Farm are only a short drive away, and students can even take the opportunity to unwind on the weekends by heading three hours north to Las Vegas. The Inland Empire itself offers a wide variety of entertainment opportunities from hot air balloon festivals to wine country tours, while boasting one of the lowest costs of living in Southern California.

Student Groups for Every Interest

La Verne Law students have the opportunity to participate in a wide variety of extra- and cocurricular activities. The *University of La Verne Law Review* is subscribed to by the United States Supreme Court, state and local courts, individuals, and academic law libraries throughout the world. Our traveling moot court and mock trial teams compete and place well in both regional and national competitions, focusing on such areas as criminal procedure, entertainment law, cybercrime, and international law. We also have a number of student organizations, both social and career-focused, such as the Student Bar Association, the Sports and Entertainment Law Society, the Public Interest Law Foundation, and many more. Collectively, they provide you with the opportunity to engage in community service, network among your peers, participate in professional events, or just take a well-deserved break from your studies.

Facilities to Enhance Your Law School Experience

La Verne Law's 64,000-square-foot building sits on a seven-acre site in the city of Ontario. The facility, designed to give students ready access to technology, includes a state-of-the-art computer lab and on-campus Internet access via a combination of hardwired and wireless connections. Classrooms are equipped with the latest audiovisual technologies, and La Verne Law's mock courtroom includes a custom-designed audiovideo system used for trial and appellate exercises. A large, grassy park provides shade trees where students can study, throw around a Frisbee, or just relax. Additionally, the campus includes a small picnic area where student groups often host barbecues and other events.

A Thriving Law Library

La Verne Law is proud of its excellent law library, which boasts 300,000-plus print and microform resources, including federal and California statutory law, court opinions, administrative rules and regulations, major treatises on a variety of legal topics, form and practice books, numerous legal periodicals, and access to a huge variety of electronic databases. The Law Library also serves as a selective depository for federal and California government documents, including legislative materials. Our law librarians are expert

legal researchers who hold both the JD and the MLS degrees, and they are available for assistance seven days a week. The Law Library staff also hosts a free series of short courses allowing law students the opportunity to obtain a Certificate in Legal Research.

Chart Your Own Academic Course

La Verne Law provides a variety of options to enhance your academic experience based on your own individual goals and needs. We offer both a full-time day and a part-time evening program in addition to summer classes. We also offer courses in a wide variety of subject areas spanning from the core first-year curriculum to a cutting-edge, first in the nation of its kind, course in computer game law.

Additionally, La Verne Law and the College of Business and Public Management offer dual Juris Doctor/Master of Business Administration (JD/MBA) and Juris Doctor/Master of Public Administration (JD/MPA) degree programs. Applicants must meet the admission standards of each degree program and should consult with each college for specific entrance requirements.

A Commitment to Diversity

La Verne Law believes that a diverse classroom is not only beneficial to all students but essential to a well-rounded learning experience. To that end, we strive to admit a class of students from a wide variety of cultural, ethnic, religious, and socioeconomic backgrounds, as well as students of diverse age, geographical origins, and academic and professional experience. To further ensure an accepting and welcoming campus, our students can participate in affinity groups such as the Black Law Students Association, the Hispanic National Bar Association, Pride Law Alliance, the J. Reuben Clark Society, and more.

APPLICANT PROFILE

At La Verne Law, we strive to provide you with the personalized attention you need to achieve your goals and become a successful member of the legal community. This philosophy extends to our admission process, during which we will consider you as an individual whose unique attributes should be evaluated independently from those of other applicants. Selection criteria include, but are not limited to, your educational and professional achievements, academic ability, motivation for entering the legal profession, individual

background, work ethic, letters of recommendation, leadership skills, dedication to community service, and core values. By evaluating each application on a case-by-case basis, we are able to shape our incoming class with diverse personalities and a collective aptitude for success in the law. If you seek a unique legal education tailored to your individual aspirations and providing you with all of the theoretical and practical skills you will need to succeed as an attorney, we invite you to visit us in person or on the web.

LEWIS & CLARK LAW SCHOOL

10015 SW Terwilliger Boulevard
Portland, OR 97219-7799
Phone: 800.303.4860 or 503.768.6613; Fax: 503.768.6793
E-mail: lawadmss@lclark.edu; Website: www.lclark.edu/law/

The Basics

Type of school	Private
Term	Semester
Application deadline	3/1
Application fee	$50
Financial aid deadline	3/1
Can first year start other than fall?	No
Student to faculty ratio	10.3 to 1
# of housing spaces available restricted to law students	22
graduate housing for which law students are eligible	

Faculty and Administrators

	Total		Men		Women		Minorities	
	Spr	Fall	Spr	Fall	Spr	Fall	Spr	Fall
Full-time	50	53	27	31	23	22	7	9
Other full-time	1	0	0	0	1	0	0	0
Deans, librarians, & others who teach	13	14	6	6	7	8	1	1
Part-time	51	38	34	24	17	14	10	9
Total	115	105	67	61	48	44	18	19

JD Enrollment and Ethnicity

	Men #	Men %	Women #	Women %	Full-Time #	Full-Time %	Part-Time #	Part-Time %	1st-Year #	1st-Year %	Total #	Total %	JD Degs. Awd.
All Hispanics	22	5.9	22	5.9	27	5.1	17	8.0	18	7.3	44	5.9	10
Am. Ind./AK Nat.	8	2.2	14	3.8	13	2.5	9	4.2	9	3.7	22	3.0	3
Asian	32	8.6	37	10.0	50	9.5	19	9.0	26	10.6	69	9.3	13
Black/Af. Am.	10	2.7	12	3.2	11	2.1	11	5.2	6	2.4	22	3.0	2
Nat. HI/Pac. Isl.	0	0.0	1	0.3	1	0.2	0	0.0	0	0.0	1	0.1	0
2 or more races	0	0.0	0	0.0	0	0.0	0	0.0	0	0.0	0	0.0	0
Subtotal (minor.)	72	19.5	86	23.2	102	19.3	56	26.4	59	24.1	158	21.3	28
Nonres. Alien	12	3.2	5	1.3	10	1.9	7	3.3	4	1.6	17	2.3	0
White/Cauc.	258	69.7	267	72.0	385	72.8	140	66.0	175	71.4	525	70.9	157
Unknown	28	7.6	13	3.5	32	6.0	9	4.2	7	2.9	41	5.5	10
Total	370	49.9	371	50.1	529	71.4	212	28.6	245	33.1	741		199

Curriculum

	Full-Time	Part-Time
Typical first-year section size	73	77
Is there typically a "small section" of the first-year class, other than Legal Writing, taught by full-time faculty	Yes	Yes
If yes, typical size offered last year	37	44

# of classroom course titles beyond first-year curriculum		137
# of upper division courses, excluding seminars, with an enrollment:	Under 25	113
	25–49	38
	50–74	14
	75–99	6
	100+	0
# of seminars		23
# of seminar positions available		423
# of seminar positions filled	201	100
# of positions available in simulation courses		584
# of simulation positions filled	304	151
# of positions available in faculty supervised clinical courses		195
# of faculty supervised clinical positions filled	122	54
# involved in field placements	46	30
# involved in law journals	97	42
# involved in moot court or trial competitions	85	41
# of credit hours required to graduate		89

Transfers

Transfers in	17
Transfers out	5

Tuition and Fees

	Resident	Nonresident
Full-time	$35,098	$35,098
Part-time	$26,334	$26,334
Tuition Guarantee Program		N

Living Expenses

Estimated living expenses for singles

Living on campus	Living off campus	Living at home
N/A	$18,150	$18,150

ABA Approved Since 1970

GPA and LSAT Scores

	Total	Full-Time	Part-Time
# of apps	3,427	3,223	204
# of offers	1,187	1,132	55
# of matrics	247	194	53
75% GPA	3.69	3.69	3.67
Median GPA	3.48	3.48	3.45
25% GPA	3.20	3.21	2.97
75% LSAT	164	164	163
Median LSAT	162	163	157
25% LSAT	157	160	152

Grants and Scholarships (from prior year)

	Total		Full-Time		Part-Time	
	#	%	#	%	#	%
Total # of students	715		521		194	
Total # receiving grants	293	41.0	250	48.0	43	22.2
Less than 1/2 tuition	224	31.3	194	37.2	30	15.5
Half to full tuition	66	9.2	53	10.2	13	6.7
Full tuition	3	0.4	3	0.6	0	0.0
More than full tuition	0	0.0	0	0.0	0	0.0
Median grant amount			$10,000		$9,500	

Informational and Library Resources

Total amount spent on library materials	$1,364,861
Study seating capacity inside the library	385
# of full-time equivalent professional librarians	8
Hours per week library is open	113
# of open, wired connections available to students	903
# of networked computers available for use by students	100
Has wireless network?	Y
Requires computer?	N

JD Attrition (from prior year)

	Academic	Other	Total	
	#	#	#	%
1st year	3	11	14	6.1
2nd year	2	5	7	3.1
3rd year	0	0	0	0.0
4th year	0	2	2	6.9

Employment (9 months after graduation)

	Total	Percentage
Employment status known	231	98.3
Employment status unknown	4	1.7
Employed	207	89.6
Pursuing graduate degrees	10	4.3
Unemployed (seeking, not seeking, or studying for the bar)	4	1.7
Type of Employment		
# employed in law firms	99	47.8
# employed in business and industry	25	12.1
# employed in government	32	15.5
# employed in public interest	27	13.0
# employed as judicial clerks	12	5.8
# employed in academia	12	5.8
Geographic Location		
# employed in state	156	75.4
# employed outside the US	4	1.9
# of states where employed	17	

Bar Passage Rates

First-time takers	218	Reporting %	85.32
Average school %	78.49	Average state %	76.85
Average pass difference	1.64		

Jurisdiction	Takers	Passers	Pass %	State %	Diff %
Oregon	186	146	78.49	76.85	1.64

LEWIS & CLARK LAW SCHOOL

10015 SW Terwilliger Boulevard
Portland, OR 97219-7799
Phone: 800.303.4860 or 503.768.6613; Fax: 503.768.6793
E-mail: lawadmss@lclark.edu; Website: www.lclark.edu/law/

Introduction

Lewis & Clark Law School believes in a balanced approach to legal education that ensures a solid theoretical foundation along with hands-on experience in practice. Situated next to a state park, the campus is one of the most beautiful in the nation. Students are only a moment away from an extensive trail system used by joggers, walkers, and bicyclists.

Enrollment/Student Body

The approximately 750 students attending the Law School represent a spectrum of ages, experiences, and priorities. Business executives, scientists, students of politics, musicians, and school teachers—people from many disciplines—meet at the Law School in a common pursuit. The atmosphere is one of mutual support during a time of academic challenge. Students and faculty can often be found discussing questions long after class has ended.

Faculty

The full-time faculty were educated at the nation's most distinguished law schools. They reflect a breadth of experience and interests that give depth and creative energy to their teaching. A number of faculty members have spent sabbaticals in recent years teaching in other countries; several have been Fulbright professors in such places as China, Greece, Germany, and Venezuela.

Library and Physical Facilities

The resources and staff of the Paul L. Boley Law Library, the largest law library in the state and the second largest in the Northwest, well exceed the standards set by the Association of American Law Schools.

Our collection includes extensive materials in environmental law, federal legislative history, tax law, commercial law, intellectual property, and legal history. We are also the only academic law library in the country to be a Patent and Trademark Depository Library. Supporting our collection is a sophisticated computer infrastructure of instruction labs and local area networks.

The Law School library is an exquisite study space with computer labs equipped with the latest technology. Wireless access is available on the entire campus.

Framed by majestic fir trees, the campus is composed of contemporary buildings with classrooms and a large state park within a moment's walk from the library. Traditional student needs and those of individuals with disabilities are met through a variety of facilities.

Curriculum

The Law School confers both the JD degree and a specialized LLM in Environmental and Natural Resources Law. Students may also apply for a joint JD/LLM degree. To earn a JD, a student must take a prescribed first-year set of courses. In the upper division, students must take a seminar, Constitutional Law II, and Professionalism, and fulfill two writing requirements. Students choose between a three-year day program and a four-year evening program. Admission criteria, faculty, academic opportunities, and graduation requirements are the same for each.

Because the Law School offers both a full-time and a part-time program, students have great flexibility in scheduling courses and in determining the pace at which they want to pursue law school. Classes are offered both during the day and in the evening. Many students transfer between divisions and use the summer school program to accelerate progress toward graduation. Regardless of the division in which a student is enrolled, students may select courses from either the day or evening schedule as they find appropriate.

Specific Special Programs

Certificates: By taking a group of upper-division courses approved by the faculty, and by maintaining a superior grade-point average in those courses, a student may earn a certificate showing a concentration in environmental and natural resources law, public interest law, global law, business law, tax law, intellectual property law, or criminal law.

The Law School has nationally recognized natural resources/environmental law and public interest law programs. The school is also home to an incredibly strong business and commercial law program. The intellectual property law program and global law program are particularly dynamic, and our criminal law program houses the first national organization in the United States to study and enhance the effectiveness of victim's rights law. Lewis & Clark is also a national leader of animal law programs and curriculums. All the traditional areas of legal study are fully covered. Students who do not wish to pursue a certificate may choose to study another area of particular interest.

Clinical Opportunities, Externships, and Simulations: A student may create a schedule with precisely the mix of practical skills courses that fit that student's interests and needs. Students may choose among live client clinical experience, externships and internships, or simulation courses. The legal clinic located in downtown Portland offers students the opportunity to interview and counsel real clients, prepare documents, conduct trials, negotiate settlements, and prepare appeals. Other established clinics at Lewis & Clark are the small business legal clinic, an environmental law clinic, an international environmental law clinic, a low-income taxpayer clinic, an animal law clinic, a crime victim advocacy clinic, and a business law practicum. Externships place a student in full-time work for a semester or for a summer and require a substantial research paper and attendance at a special seminar. Externs are placed throughout the United States and in foreign countries. Clinical internship seminars are similar to externships but the student works only part-time, attending other classes during the semester. Clinical internship seminars include placements with in-house counsel, government agencies, law firms, and public interest, nonprofit organizations. Other courses, such as moot courts, advanced advocacy, trial advocacy, criminal law seminar, estate planning seminar, corporate transactions seminar, and family mediation seminar, involve extensive simulations.

Admission

Lewis & Clark affirmatively seeks a diverse student body. The Admissions Committee makes a serious effort to consider each applicant as an individual. Factors such as college, program of study, length of time since the degree was obtained, experience, writing ability, and community activities are taken into consideration. Only those candidates with excellent professional promise are admitted. Academic attrition is low, averaging two to four percent.

Student Activities

Activities include three law reviews, *Environmental Law*, *Animal Law*, and *Lewis & Clark Law Review*; nine distinct moot court teams; numerous speakers on campus; programs that bring outstanding legal scholars to campus for lectures and seminars; and many student organizations reflecting the diverse makeup of the student body.

Expenses and Financial Aid

Approximately 40 percent of the students at Lewis & Clark receive some scholarship support during their law school career. The school annually awards renewable merit-based

Dean's Scholarships to incoming students. In addition, loan money and work-study funds are available. There is no separate application procedure for scholarship funds. Scholarship consideration is part of the admission process. Students are reviewed on the basis of undergraduate record, LSAT score, writing ability, and activities.

Students interested in loans need to apply for financial aid as early as possible and should not wait for an admission decision to begin the financial aid application. Applicants should submit the FAFSA (Free Application for Federal Student Aid) at www.fafsa.ed.gov.

Career Services

The Career Services Office maintains and runs an extraordinary number and variety of programs. In addition to posting clerk positions for law students and running the on-campus interviews, the office maintains an extensive mentoring program, runs dozens of panels each year on various areas of practice, and counsels individual students from the first year onward. The Career Services staff consists of experienced administrators, counselors, and professionals, including a full-time coordinator to assist public interest-minded students.

APPLICANT PROFILE

Lewis & Clark Law School
This grid includes only applicants who earned 120–180 LSAT scores under standard administrations.

LSAT Score	3.75 +		3.50–3.74		3.25–3.49		3.00–3.24		2.75–2.99		2.50–2.74		Below 2.50		No GPA		Total	
	Apps	Adm	Apps	Adm	Apps	Adm	Apps	Adm	Apps	Adm	Apps	Adm	Apps	Adm	Apps	Adm	Apps	Adm
170–180	24	22	27	25	21	21	15	13	5	4	8	1	3	2	1	1	104	89
165–169	83	76	79	72	76	66	46	40	38	25	18	8	8	3	5	4	353	294
160–164	150	111	273	185	226	138	155	74	78	35	33	8	14	0	11	5	940	556
155–159	125	46	230	63	229	26	183	14	89	8	46	4	26	1	12	3	940	165
150–154	64	9	118	16	142	15	113	11	65	1	37	2	29	0	8	4	576	58
145–149	17	3	44	6	58	5	62	2	46	3	25	0	18	0	8	1	278	20
140–144	5	1	11	0	24	1	16	0	21	0	14	0	11	0	4	1	106	3
Below 140	0	0	3	0	2	0	7	0	8	0	6	0	7	0	1	0	34	0
Total	468	268	785	367	778	272	597	154	350	76	187	23	116	6	50	19	3331	1185

Apps = Number of Applicants
Adm = Number Admitted
Reflects 100% of the total applicant pool; highest LSAT data reported.

LIBERTY UNIVERSITY SCHOOL OF LAW

1971 University Boulevard
Lynchburg, VA 24502
Phone: 434.592.5300; Fax: 434.592.5400
E-mail: lawadmissions@liberty.edu; Website: www.law.liberty.edu

ABA
Approved
Since
2006

The Basics

Type of school	Private
Term	Semester
Application deadline	5/1
Application fee	$50
Financial aid deadline	
Can first year start other than fall?	No
Student to faculty ratio	6.1 to 1
# of housing spaces available restricted to law students	
graduate housing for which law students are eligible	

Faculty and Administrators

	Total		Men		Women		Minorities	
	Spr	Fall	Spr	Fall	Spr	Fall	Spr	Fall
Full-time	17	18	12	12	5	6	5	6
Other full-time	1	1	1	1	0	0	0	0
Deans, librarians, & others who teach	7	7	5	5	2	2	1	1
Part-time	8	8	6	4	2	4	1	1
Total	33	34	24	22	9	12	7	8

Curriculum

	Full-Time	Part-Time
Typical first-year section size	60	0
Is there typically a "small section" of the first-year class, other than Legal Writing, taught by full-time faculty	No	No
If yes, typical size offered last year		

# of classroom course titles beyond first-year curriculum		43
# of upper division courses, excluding seminars, with an enrollment:	Under 25	28
	25–49	9
	50–74	19
	75–99	0
	100+	0
# of seminars		3
# of seminar positions available		45
# of seminar positions filled	22	0
# of positions available in simulation courses		445
# of simulation positions filled	387	0
# of positions available in faculty supervised clinical courses		8
# of faculty supervised clinical positions filled	5	0
# involved in field placements	21	0
# involved in law journals	44	0
# involved in moot court or trial competitions	17	0
# of credit hours required to graduate		90

JD Enrollment and Ethnicity

	Men		Women		Full-Time		Part-Time		1st-Year		Total		JD Degs. Awd.
	#	%	#	%	#	%	#	%	#	%	#	%	
All Hispanics	10	5.1	2	1.7	12	3.8	0	0.0	8	6.1	12	3.8	3
Am. Ind./AK Nat.	1	0.5	0	0.0	1	0.3	0	0.0	0	0.0	1	0.3	4
Asian	6	3.1	7	5.9	13	4.2	0	0.0	8	6.1	13	4.2	1
Black/Af. Am.	8	4.1	8	6.8	16	5.1	0	0.0	4	3.0	16	5.1	2
Nat. HI/Pac. Isl.	0	0.0	0	0.0	0	0.0	0	0.0	0	0.0	0	0.0	0
2 or more races	13	6.7	4	3.4	17	5.4	0	0.0	9	6.9	17	5.4	0
Subtotal (minor.)	38	19.5	21	17.8	59	18.8	0	0.0	29	22.1	59	18.8	10
Nonres. Alien	2	1.0	1	0.8	3	1.0	0	0.0	0	0.0	3	1.0	0
White/Cauc.	154	79.0	96	81.4	250	79.9	0	0.0	102	77.9	250	79.9	44
Unknown	1	0.5	0	0.0	1	0.3	0	0.0	0	0.0	1	0.3	3
Total	195	62.3	118	37.7	313	100.0	0	0.0	131	41.8	313		57

Transfers

Transfers in	1
Transfers out	3

Tuition and Fees

	Resident	Nonresident
Full-time	$29,120	
Part-time		
Tuition Guarantee Program	N	

Living Expenses

Estimated living expenses for singles

Living on campus	Living off campus	Living at home
$17,920	$17,920	$17,920

LIBERTY UNIVERSITY SCHOOL OF LAW

*ABA
Approved
Since
2006*

GPA and LSAT Scores

	Total	Full-Time	Part-Time
# of apps	459	459	0
# of offers	240	240	0
# of matrics	135	135	0
75% GPA	3.43	3.43	0.00
Median GPA	3.19	3.19	0.00
25% GPA	2.75	2.75	0.00
75% LSAT	153	153	0
Median LSAT	150	150	0
25% LSAT	148	148	0

Grants and Scholarships (from prior year)

	Total		Full-Time		Part-Time	
	#	%	#	%	#	%
Total # of students	267		267		0	
Total # receiving grants	266	99.6	266	99.6	0	0.0
Less than 1/2 tuition	130	48.7	130	48.7	0	0.0
Half to full tuition	103	38.6	103	38.6	0	0.0
Full tuition	33	12.4	33	12.4	0	0.0
More than full tuition	0	0.0	0	0.0	0	0.0
Median grant amount			$13,319		$0	

Informational and Library Resources

Total amount spent on library materials	$1,075,225
Study seating capacity inside the library	286
# of full-time equivalent professional librarians	5
Hours per week library is open	95
# of open, wired connections available to students	0
# of networked computers available for use by students	40
Has wireless network?	Y
Requires computer?	N

JD Attrition (from prior year)

	Academic	Other	Total	
	#	#	#	%
1st year	10	3	13	11.2
2nd year	0	3	3	3.2
3rd year	0	0	0	0.0
4th year	0	0	0	0.0

Employment (9 months after graduation)

	Total	Percentage
Employment status known	53	96.4
Employment status unknown	2	3.6
Employed	42	79.2
Pursuing graduate degrees	1	1.9
Unemployed (seeking, not seeking, or studying for the bar)	10	18.9
Type of Employment		
# employed in law firms	18	42.9
# employed in business and industry	8	19.0
# employed in government	10	23.8
# employed in public interest	2	4.8
# employed as judicial clerks	2	4.8
# employed in academia	2	4.8
Geographic Location		
# employed in state	16	38.1
# employed outside the US	0	0.0
# of states where employed	13	

Bar Passage Rates

First-time takers	51	Reporting %	100.00
Average school %	74.99	Average state %	79.45

Average pass difference −4.46

Jurisdiction	Takers	Passers	Pass %	State %	Diff %
Virginia	21	12	57.14	77.06	−19.92
North Carolina	9	5	55.56	76.79	−21.23
Tennessee	5	5	100.00	82.44	17.56
Florida	4	4	100.00	77.81	22.19
Others (11)	13	13	100.00		

The information on these pages was provided by the law school.

LIBERTY UNIVERSITY SCHOOL OF LAW

1971 University Boulevard
Lynchburg, VA 24502
Phone: 434.592.5300; Fax: 434.592.5400
E-mail: lawadmissions@liberty.edu; Website: www.law.liberty.edu

Introduction

Distinctively Christian, Liberty University School of Law has attracted national attention for its innovative program of legal education, competitive teams, and practice opportunities for its students. The student body will cap at approximately 450 to maintain the small classes and collegiality that students and faculty now enjoy. The law school and adjoining law library are advantageously located on one level in Liberty's million-square-foot Campus North complex. The 330-seat ceremonial courtroom features a nine-seat bench, which replicates the US Supreme Court bench. Two other mock trial courtrooms, all classrooms, and the law library feature the latest technologies. Liberty's 802.11n wireless network currently hosts approximately 950 wireless access points (WAPs) and distributes 16 streaming multichannels through a wireless connection known as Internet Protocol television (IPTV). The 6,500-acre campus rests in the eastern foothills of the Blue Ridge Mountains in Central Virginia, within easy driving distance of Washington, DC.

Program of Legal Education

Liberty's groundbreaking law program has three distinct but related components: foundations of law, substantive law courses, and lawyering skills. In keeping with the law school's mission "to equip future leaders in law with a superior legal education in fidelity to the Christian faith expressed through the Holy Scriptures," the foundations courses explore the thoughts and writings of those who shaped the American legal system. The Christian worldview permeates the curriculum. The six-semester skills program has two threads: a litigation thread and a planning thread. Each student moves a simulated case from the initial client interview to the court verdict and develops the practice skills essential to planning client affairs. While the core courses look much the same as at other law schools—same course names, same subject matter coverage, same casebooks—Liberty's distinction is in the linkage of the substantive law courses to the foundations and lawyering skills courses. The law faculty is highly accessible to students throughout each day. In addition to academic advising and support from faculty, many Liberty law students take advantage of the academic support program.

Academic Support

The Academic Support Program begins with an intensive four-day Barristers' Orientation for entering students. During the academic year, the program staff assists law students in achieving their full academic potential, helping them with class preparation, class participation, and examination strategies. Support includes post-class reviews prior to taking law school examinations and practice-exam workshops. The program director holds workshops on case briefing, note taking, time and stress management, outlining, exam preparation, and legal writing. All students may take advantage of one-on-one tutorials to help them assimilate course materials and apply classroom knowledge to law school examinations. The Academic Support Program also assists students with bar examination preparation.

Clinics, Externships, and Centers

The law school places a high priority on equipping students with the skills necessary to practice law, as evidenced in its Lawyering Skills Program. Its externship and clinical programs provide the next step in the continuum of classroom learning, from simulation to client- and real-life practice experience. The Constitutional Litigation Clinic works in conjunction with Liberty Counsel, a nonprofit legal organization specializing in constitutional law, which has offices on the Liberty University campus. Students work on live, real-time legal issues through current cases that address constitutional law challenges. The School of Law has formed a partnership with Liberty Counsel in founding the Liberty Center for Law and Policy. The center trains law students who have career plans and interests in public policy law with a focus on the legislative process, constitutional law, and religious liberty advocacy.

The law school engages in traditional externship placements through its Criminal Law Externship Program. This program places law students as externs in county and federal prosecutors' offices, and in public defenders' offices, under the supervision of experienced practitioners. Students are placed in a variety of field-study venues, including US attorneys' offices, commonwealth attorneys' offices, district attorneys' offices, and attorneys general offices; judicial clerkships at local, state, and federal courts; courts of appeal and state supreme courts; and in public interest organizations. The public service externship component gives students a wide variety of individualized experiences in public service law and pro bono legal assistance. In addition, Liberty law students obtain externships and summer positions in venues ranging from the White House and the Department of Homeland Security, to private law firms and corporations.

Cocurricular and Student Activities

In addition to the Student Bar Association (SBA) and many student organizations, the law school has nationally competitive teams in moot court, negotiation, and alternative dispute resolution, along with a developing transactional competition program. Students produce the *Liberty University Law Review* and the *Liberty Legal Journal*. Many law students volunteer their time in pro bono activities. The law school also matches students with private practitioners engaged in pro bono work and provides them opportunities to intern in legal aid offices, public defender offices, and prosecutorial offices. Student life includes attending the wide range of events on the campus of Liberty University and enjoying the sociability of the law school community. Law students have access to the university's many recreational facilities, which include the year-round Snowflex synthetic ski slope (the first of its kind in North America), ice rink, 112-acre lake, and equestrian center. Off campus, law students enjoy the rich history and natural beauty of Central Virginia.

Career Services

The Center for Career and Professional Development serves law students and alumni by providing tools to develop skills essential for career development, by cultivating a lifelong commitment to professionalism and community service, and by promoting regional and national awareness of the law school's distinctive program of legal study. The center cultivates internship and pro bono opportunities and works cooperatively with the school's clinical and externship programs to foster relationships with members of the bench and bar to the benefit of students and alumni. Alumni are working in all sectors of law practice. Placement statistics are available at the center.

Information Resources and Technologies

With many comfortable seating areas and close proximity to the classrooms, Ehrhorn Law Library provides an environment conducive to research, study, and writing. To its growing collection of nearly 300,000 volumes and volume equivalents, the law library is continually adding titles that support the curriculum and undergird the law school's mission. Along with its extensive microform archives, the law library provides access to law-related and general databases via the Internet through any web browser. These electronic databases are available to law students on or off campus. Reliable wired and wireless access to the Internet is provided throughout the law school facility. Every classroom has SMART technology. The law school community benefits from a high level of university support for its state-of-the-art computing, instructional, informational, and audiovisual technologies.

Admission and Financial Aid

Many law schools have developed courses of study that give expression to a particular jurisprudential perspective, be it law and economics, legal realism, or policy-oriented

jurisprudence. Liberty University School of Law has chosen to do the same, developing its curriculum and standards of conduct consistent with the Christian worldview. Its admission process is designed to identify those who desire to receive a legal education from this perspective. Each completed applicant file is reviewed by a law faculty committee. That committee gives careful attention to a full range of factors that indicate the applicant's likelihood of success in law school and the legal profession. It attempts to identify strengths and indicators of success that may not show up in test scores and to ensure that students make fully informed decisions in deciding to attend Liberty University School of Law. Written applications and letters of recommendation are used to identify applicants with strong communication skills, levels of interest, personal traits, and life experiences that exhibit a calling to law and potential for success in legal education and the practice of law. The personal statement, which addresses prescribed discussion points noted in the application for admission, is of particular importance in the admission decision.

Institutional scholarships are awarded on the basis of prior academic excellence and indicators of law school success, and for demonstrated leadership and service in keeping with the law school's mission. Committed to debt management, the law school assists each student with a financial aid package to meet individual needs.

The Office of Admissions and Financial Aid assists prospective students and law students with the law school admission process, financial aid, and other matters related to relocation and matriculation. To schedule a visit, call 434.592.5300 or e-mail lawadmissions@liberty.edu.

APPLICANT PROFILE

Liberty University School of Law recognizes that LSAT scores and undergraduate GPAs are important indicators of academic success, but that a number of other factors must be considered in making admission decisions. An important purpose of interviews and written applications is to identify applicants with particular communications skills, levels of interest, personal traits, and life experiences that evince a calling to law and potential for success in legal education. Factors providing predictors of success in law school may include: demonstrated leadership, highly motivated and successful employment history, proficiency in written and oral

communication skills, and a detailed explanation of personal reading and study habits, including the books having the greatest impact on the applicant's intellectual life. Breadth of intellectual interest and ability is an indicator of interest in, and appreciation for, the kind of education offered at the law school.

The law school looks at more than numbers. Questions asked on the application and during the interview process are designed to identify strengths that do not show up in test scores and to ensure that students are fully informed of the kind of legal education provided at Liberty.

LOUISIANA STATE UNIVERSITY, PAUL M. HEBERT LAW CENTER

202 Law Center
Baton Rouge, LA 70803
Phone: 225.578.8646; Fax: 225.578.8647
E-mail: admissions@law.lsu.edu; Website: www.law.lsu.edu

ABA
Approved
Since
1926

The Basics

Type of school	Public
Term	Semester
Application deadline	3/1
Application fee	$50
Financial aid deadline	
Can first year start other than fall?	No
Student to faculty ratio	17.0 to 1
# of housing spaces available restricted to law students	
graduate housing for which law students are eligible	

Faculty and Administrators

	Total		Men		Women		Minorities	
	Spr	Fall	Spr	Fall	Spr	Fall	Spr	Fall
Full-time	28	31	22	23	6	8	2	3
Other full-time	7	10	4	5	3	5	2	3
Deans, librarians, & others who teach	7	8	6	7	1	1	1	1
Part-time	32	26	30	22	2	4	4	1
Total	74	75	62	57	12	18	9	8

Curriculum

	Full-Time	Part-Time
Typical first-year section size	78	0
Is there typically a "small section" of the first-year class, other than Legal Writing, taught by full-time faculty	Yes	No
If yes, typical size offered last year	21	
# of classroom course titles beyond first-year curriculum	143	
# of upper division courses, excluding seminars, with an enrollment: Under 25	147	
25–49	36	
50–74	16	
75–99	8	
100+	1	
# of seminars	16	
# of seminar positions available	320	
# of seminar positions filled	191	0
# of positions available in simulation courses	533	
# of simulation positions filled	452	0
# of positions available in faculty supervised clinical courses	37	
# of faculty supervised clinical positions filled	37	0
# involved in field placements	95	0
# involved in law journals	48	0
# involved in moot court or trial competitions	57	0
# of credit hours required to graduate	94	

JD Enrollment and Ethnicity

	Men		Women		Full-Time		Part-Time		1st-Year		Total		JD Degs. Awd.
	#	%	#	%	#	%	#	%	#	%	#	%	
All Hispanics	16	4.3	16	6.1	32	5.2	0	0.0	10	4.5	32	5.1	10
Am. Ind./AK Nat.	4	1.1	4	1.5	8	1.3	0	0.0	2	0.9	8	1.3	1
Asian	11	3.0	5	1.9	16	2.6	0	0.0	5	2.2	16	2.5	3
Black/Af. Am.	24	6.5	25	9.5	47	7.6	2	11.8	30	13.5	49	7.7	7
Nat. HI/Pac. Isl.	0	0.0	0	0.0	0	0.0	0	0.0	0	0.0	0	0.0	0
2 or more races	2	0.5	4	1.5	6	1.0	0	0.0	4	1.8	6	0.9	0
Subtotal (minor.)	57	15.4	54	20.6	109	17.7	2	11.8	51	22.9	111	17.5	21
Nonres. Alien	0	0.0	0	0.0	0	0.0	0	0.0	0	0.0	0	0.0	0
White/Cauc.	287	77.4	197	75.2	470	76.3	14	82.4	165	74.0	484	76.5	141
Unknown	27	7.3	11	4.2	37	6.0	1	5.9	7	3.1	38	6.0	20
Total	371	58.6	262	41.4	616	97.3	17	2.7	223	35.2	633		182

Transfers

Transfers in	5
Transfers out	4

Tuition and Fees

	Resident	Nonresident
Full-time	$16,148	$30,228
Part-time		
Tuition Guarantee Program	N	

Living Expenses

Estimated living expenses for singles

Living on campus	Living off campus	Living at home
$15,904	$18,234	$10,082

LOUISIANA STATE UNIVERSITY, PAUL M. HEBERT LAW CENTER

ABA
Approved
Since
1926

GPA and LSAT Scores

	Total	Full-Time	Part-Time
# of apps	1,653	1,653	0
# of offers	585	585	0
# of matrics	222	222	0
75% GPA	3.60	3.60	0.00
Median GPA	3.38	3.38	0.00
25% GPA	3.14	3.14	0.00
75% LSAT	160	160	0
Median LSAT	158	158	0
25% LSAT	155	155	0

Grants and Scholarships (from prior year)

	Total		Full-Time		Part-Time	
	#	%	#	%	#	%
Total # of students	598		587		11	
Total # receiving grants	398	66.6	398	67.8	0	0.0
Less than 1/2 tuition	198	33.1	198	33.7	0	0.0
Half to full tuition	99	16.6	99	16.9	0	0.0
Full tuition	46	7.7	46	7.8	0	0.0
More than full tuition	55	9.2	55	9.4	0	0.0
Median grant amount			$5,361		$0	

Informational and Library Resources

Total amount spent on library materials	$865,834
Study seating capacity inside the library	468
# of full-time equivalent professional librarians	10
Hours per week library is open	104
# of open, wired connections available to students	60
# of networked computers available for use by students	40
Has wireless network?	Y
Requires computer?	N

JD Attrition (from prior year)

	Academic	Other	Total	
	#	#	#	%
1st year	1	14	15	6.4
2nd year	1	0	1	0.5
3rd year	0	0	0	0.0
4th year	0	0	0	0.0

Employment (9 months after graduation)

	Total	Percentage
Employment status known	178	97.8
Employment status unknown	4	2.2
Employed	158	88.8
Pursuing graduate degrees	4	2.2
Unemployed (seeking, not seeking, or studying for the bar)	14	7.9
Type of Employment		
# employed in law firms	88	55.7
# employed in business and industry	13	8.2
# employed in government	25	15.8
# employed in public interest	4	2.5
# employed as judicial clerks	27	17.1
# employed in academia	0	0.0
Geographic Location		
# employed in state	137	86.7
# employed outside the US	0	0.0
# of states where employed	11	

Bar Passage Rates

First-time takers	193	Reporting %	81.87
Average school %	89.24	Average state %	73.73
Average pass difference	15.51		

Jurisdiction	Takers	Passers	Pass %	State %	Diff %
Louisiana	158	141	89.24	73.73	15.51

LOUISIANA STATE UNIVERSITY, PAUL M. HEBERT LAW CENTER

202 Law Center
Baton Rouge, LA 70803
Phone: 225.578.8646; Fax: 225.578.8647
E-mail: admissions@law.lsu.edu; Website: www.law.lsu.edu

Introduction

The Louisiana State University (LSU) Law Center was originally established as the Louisiana State University Law School in 1906, pursuant to an authorization contained in the university charter. In 1979, the Law Center was renamed the Paul M. Hebert Law Center of Louisiana State University. The Law Center holds membership in the Association of American Law Schools (AALS) and is on the approved list of the American Bar Association (ABA).

Library and Physical Facilities

The Law Center, completed in October 1969, added extensive facilities to the original Law Center building, dedicated in 1938. Both buildings were vastly renovated over several years at a cost in excess of $17 million and were completed in 2004. The renovated complex provides classroom areas, seminar and discussion rooms, and meeting areas, as well as a courtroom and Law Clinic. The Law Clinic is a self-contained legal services office located in the Law Center where students are certified to practice law pursuant to Louisiana Supreme Court Rule XX. Separate offices for student research and student activities, such as the *Louisiana Law Review*, Moot Court Board, and Student Bar Association, are included in the facility. The law library, housed in the complex, provides one of the most complete collections of Roman and modern civil law reports and materials in the country. Library resources include reading and discussion rooms, study carrels, computer labs, and audiovisual facilities. Students also have access to other campus facilities, including the LSU Student Health Center, residential housing, and the Student Recreation Complex. The Law Center is located on the main campus of LSU in close proximity to the undergraduate campus and other units with which the Law Center has joint-degree or cocurricular programs.

Curriculum

The LSU Law Center has established a JD/DCL program through which all graduates receive the Juris Doctor (JD) degree and a Diploma in Comparative Law (DCL). First-year students follow a prescribed curriculum and, thereafter, may choose from a wide variety of courses to complete their degrees, including skills training courses and a newly expanded clinical program designed to take full advantage of the Law Center's location in Louisiana's capital city. The Law Center's dedication to the study of both civil and common law prepares its graduates to practice in any state and in many foreign countries. Six semesters of resident study are required for the degree. In addition to its full-time law faculty, the LSU Law Center invites a number of distinguished lecturers, including practicing attorneys and legal scholars, to teach courses in their areas of specialty each semester. A number of faculty members have law degrees from foreign countries.

Summer Session Abroad

The Law Center conducts a summer program in Lyon, France, and, when student interest warrants, in Buenos Aires,

Argentina. All classes are conducted in English and are designed to meet the requirements of the ABA and AALS.

Special Programs

A wide variety of courses afford each student the opportunity to participate in the preparation and trial of mock cases, both civil and criminal, and also to develop skills in legal negotiation and counseling. LSU sponsors and encourages student participation in national trial and appellate competitions throughout the school year.

In cooperation with the Center for Continuing Professional Development, the Law Center presents seminars, institutes, and conferences for practicing lawyers.

The LSU Law Center admits candidates for the degrees of Master of Laws (LLM) and Master of Civil Law (MCL). These programs are highly selective and admit students with exceptional ability.

Admission

The Admissions Committee considers many factors in reaching admission decisions. While the quantitative predictors of success in law school (performance on the LSAT and the undergraduate GPA of applicants) are typically the most important factors in the admission decision, the Admissions Committee considers many other factors, such as the ability to analyze and write well, as demonstrated by the personal statement and the written portion of the LSAT; two letters of recommendation from teachers or others who can express an opinion on the applicant's aptitude for the study of law; the rigor of the undergraduate program of study and grade trends; extracurricular activities; work experience or military service; social and economic background; and other evidence of an applicant's aptitude for the study of law and likely contribution to academic and community life. A baccalaureate degree from an accredited college or university is required for admission.

Applicants are advised to take the LSAT in October, and not later than December, prior to the year in which they seek admission to the Law Center. The Law Center admits students only in the fall and only for full-time study. There are no night courses offered. Transfer applications are considered.

Louisiana State University assures equal opportunity for all qualified persons without regard to race, color, religion, sexual orientation, national origin, age, disability, marital status, or veteran's status in the admission to, participation in, or employment in the programs and activities that the university operates.

Joint Programs

In addition to earning a JD/DCL, LSU Law students may also earn a Master of Mass Communication (MMC) degree through the LSU Manship School of Mass Communication, or a Master of Business Administration (MBA) or Master of Public Administration (MPA) through the LSU E.J. Ourso College of Business. The combined-degree programs are typically completed in four years. Applicants must apply to each institution separately.

Student Activities

The *Louisiana Law Review* was established to encourage high quality legal scholarship in the student body, to contribute to the development of the law through scholarly criticism and analysis, and to serve the bar of Louisiana through comments and discussion of current cases and legal problems. It is edited by a board of student editors with faculty cooperation.

The Louisiana Chapter of the Order of the Coif, a national honorary law fraternity, was established at the Law Center in 1942. Election to the Order of the Coif is recognized as the highest honor a law student may receive.

Because a large number of graduates of the Law Center go directly into practice, the LSU Law Center has an extensive Trial Advocacy Program in which moot court training is offered both for trial work and in appellate argument.

Students have an opportunity to join student organizations representing a variety of interests, including, but not limited to, the Public Interest Law Society (PILS), the International Law Society, the Federalist Society, the American Constitution Society, the Environmental Law Society, and the Tax Club.

All students at the Law Center are members of the Student Bar Association. This association promotes and coordinates student activities within the Law Center and serves as an instructional medium for postgraduate bar association activities.

Expenses and Financial Aid

The Scholarship Committee automatically considers all admitted students for scholarship support. Most scholarships range in size from $2,000 to full-tuition awards. Awards are offered to applicants whom the committee believes will best contribute to the academic and community life of the Law Center.

A number of loan funds are available to help deserving students who need financial assistance to continue their education. All such funds are subject to the policies and regulations authorized by the LSU Student Loan Fund Committee. Detailed information on all loan funds may be secured by contacting the Student Loan Section, LSU Office of Financial Aid and Scholarships, 1146 Pleasant Hall, Baton Rouge, LA 70803.

Career Services

The Career Services Office is dedicated to enhancing the personal growth and professional opportunities for law students and alumni through individual counseling, workshops, and resources. More than 1,000 employers in the United States, including private firms, government agencies, judges, nonprofits, and corporations, recruit students yearly from the LSU Law Center through visits to the campus, consortiums, job fairs, and electronic postings. More than 165 legal employers from Louisiana, Texas, Georgia, Tennessee, Mississippi, Alabama, Florida, New York, and Washington, DC, visit the school each year to recruit LSU Law Center students.

APPLICANT PROFILE

Louisiana State University, Paul M. Hebert Law Center
This grid includes only applicants who earned 120–180 LSAT scores under standard administrations.

LSAT Score	3.75 +		3.50–3.74		3.25–3.49		3.00–3.24		2.75–2.99		2.50–2.74		2.25–2.49		2.00–2.24		Below 2.00		No GPA		Total	
	Apps	Adm	Apps	Adm	Apps	Adm	Apps	Adm	Apps	Adm	Apps	Adm	Apps	Adm	Apps	Adm	Apps	Adm	Apps	Adm	Apps	Adm
175–180	1	1	0	0	0	0	0	0	0	0	0	0	0	0	0	0	0	0	0	0	1	1
170–174	2	2	3	3	0	0	1	1	0	0	0	0	0	0	0	0	0	0	0	0	6	6
165–169	12	11	10	10	12	11	8	7	5	5	2	1	2	1	1	0	1	0	0	0	53	46
160–164	35	31	36	35	68	57	39	36	14	11	16	4	10	2	5	0	0	0	0	0	223	176
155–159	66	51	113	80	138	71	90	43	62	12	36	5	13	0	5	0	0	0	5	1	528	263
150–154	44	17	97	13	115	18	105	8	66	5	27	3	16	1	6	0	1	0	8	1	485	66
145–149	14	2	28	6	63	7	57	10	42	2	25	2	9	0	3	0	0	0	1	0	242	29
140–144	9	0	3	0	8	0	19	0	20	0	11	0	8	0	5	0	0	0	1	0	84	0
135–139	0	0	4	0	3	0	6	0	3	0	10	0	4	0	3	0	0	0	1	0	34	0
130–134	0	0	0	0	1	0	1	0	1	0	0	0	0	0	3	0	1	0	1	0	8	0
125–129	0	0	0	0	0	0	0	0	0	0	0	0	0	0	0	0	0	0	0	0	0	0
120–124	0	0	0	0	0	0	0	0	0	0	0	0	0	0	0	0	0	0	0	0	0	0
Total	183	115	294	147	408	164	326	105	213	35	127	15	62	4	31	0	3	0	17	2	1664	587

Apps = Number of Applicants
Adm = Number Admitted
Reflects 99% of the total applicant pool; highest LSAT data reported.

UNIVERSITY OF LOUISVILLE'S BRANDEIS SCHOOL OF LAW

University of Louisville
Louisville, KY 40292
Phone: 502.852.6364; Fax: 502.852.8971
E-mail: lawadmissions@louisville.edu; Website: www.law.louisville.edu

ABA
Approved
Since
1931

The Basics

Type of school	Public
Term	Semester
Application deadline	3/15
Application fee	$50
Financial aid deadline	5/1
Can first year start other than fall?	No
Student to faculty ratio	15.0 to 1
# of housing spaces available restricted to law students graduate housing for which law students are eligible	102

Faculty and Administrators

	Total		Men		Women		Minorities	
	Spr	Fall	Spr	Fall	Spr	Fall	Spr	Fall
Full-time	22	23	12	14	10	9	20	20
Other full-time	3	3	1	1	2	2	3	3
Deans, librarians, & others who teach	8	9	5	6	3	3	7	7
Part-time	16	8	12	6	3	2	9	6
Total	49	43	30	27	18	16	39	36

Curriculum

	Full-Time	Part-Time
Typical first-year section size	68	0
Is there typically a "small section" of the first-year class, other than Legal Writing, taught by full-time faculty	No	No
If yes, typical size offered last year		
# of classroom course titles beyond first-year curriculum	75	
# of upper division courses, excluding seminars, with an enrollment: Under 25	59	
25–49	19	
50–74	17	
75–99	0	
100+	0	
# of seminars	23	
# of seminar positions available	414	
# of seminar positions filled	209	101
# of positions available in simulation courses	285	
# of simulation positions filled	99	107
# of positions available in faculty supervised clinical courses	19	
# of faculty supervised clinical positions filled	16	0
# involved in field placements	148	6
# involved in law journals	49	5
# involved in moot court or trial competitions	58	3
# of credit hours required to graduate	90	

JD Enrollment and Ethnicity

	Men		Women		Full-Time		Part-Time		1st-Year		Total		JD Degs. Awd.
	#	%	#	%	#	%	#	%	#	%	#	%	
All Hispanics	7	3.0	6	3.2	12	3.2	1	2.1	5	3.3	13	3.1	3
Am. Ind./AK Nat.	0	0.0	0	0.0	0	0.0	0	0.0	0	0.0	0	0.0	0
Asian	2	0.8	7	3.7	9	2.4	0	0.0	3	2.0	9	2.1	3
Black/Af. Am.	6	2.5	10	5.3	16	4.2	0	0.0	8	5.3	16	3.8	9
Nat. HI/Pac. Isl.	0	0.0	0	0.0	0	0.0	0	0.0	0	0.0	0	0.0	0
2 or more races	4	1.7	4	2.1	7	1.8	1	2.1	4	2.6	8	1.9	0
Subtotal (minor.)	19	8.0	27	14.3	44	11.6	2	4.3	20	13.2	46	10.8	15
Nonres. Alien	1	0.4	2	1.1	3	0.8	0	0.0	1	0.7	3	0.7	0
White/Cauc.	213	89.9	160	84.7	328	86.5	45	95.7	131	86.2	373	87.6	109
Unknown	4	1.7	0	0.0	4	1.1	0	0.0	1	0.7	4	0.9	3
Total	237	55.6	189	44.4	379	89.0	47	11.0	153	35.7	426		129

Transfers

Transfers in	4
Transfers out	2

Tuition and Fees

	Resident	Nonresident
Full-time	$15,760	$30,300
Part-time	$7,960	$15,230
Tuition Guarantee Program	N	

Living Expenses

Estimated living expenses for singles

Living on campus	Living off campus	Living at home
$18,380	$18,380	$9,938

UNIVERSITY OF LOUISVILLE'S BRANDEIS SCHOOL OF LAW

ABA
Approved
Since
1931

GPA and LSAT Scores

	Total	Full-Time	Part-Time
# of apps	1,769	1,644	125
# of offers	538	526	12
# of matrics	143	135	8
75% GPA	3.67	3.68	3.35
Median GPA	3.39	3.40	3.28
25% GPA	3.10	3.08	3.27
75% LSAT	160	159	160
Median LSAT	157	157	157
25% LSAT	155	154	155

Grants and Scholarships (from prior year)

	Total #	Total %	Full-Time #	Full-Time %	Part-Time #	Part-Time %
Total # of students	435		368		67	
Total # receiving grants	180	41.4	164	44.6	16	23.9
Less than 1/2 tuition	152	34.9	137	37.2	15	22.4
Half to full tuition	28	6.4	27	7.3	1	1.5
Full tuition	0	0.0	0	0.0	0	0.0
More than full tuition	0	0.0	0	0.0	0	0.0
Median grant amount			$5,000		$4,000	

Informational and Library Resources

Total amount spent on library materials	$1,456,011
Study seating capacity inside the library	370
# of full-time equivalent professional librarians	6
Hours per week library is open	89
# of open, wired connections available to students	5
# of networked computers available for use by students	35
Has wireless network?	Y
Requires computer?	N

JD Attrition (from prior year)

	Academic #	Other #	Total #	Total %
1st year	10	6	16	10.9
2nd year	1	2	3	2.1
3rd year	0	0	0	0.0
4th year	0	0	0	0.0

Employment (9 months after graduation)

	Total	Percentage
Employment status known	111	98.2
Employment status unknown	2	1.8
Employed	106	95.5
Pursuing graduate degrees	4	3.6
Unemployed (seeking, not seeking, or studying for the bar)	1	0.9
Type of Employment		
# employed in law firms	61	57.5
# employed in business and industry	15	14.2
# employed in government	12	11.3
# employed in public interest	8	7.5
# employed as judicial clerks	8	7.5
# employed in academia	2	1.9
Geographic Location		
# employed in state	84	79.2
# employed outside the US	1	0.9
# of states where employed		14

Bar Passage Rates

First-time takers	109	Reporting %	88.99
Average school %	85.57	Average state %	85.92
Average pass difference	−0.35		

Jurisdiction	Takers	Passers	Pass %	State %	Diff %
Kentucky	97	83	85.57	85.92	−0.35

UNIVERSITY OF LOUISVILLE'S BRANDEIS SCHOOL OF LAW

University of Louisville
Louisville, KY 40292
Phone: 502.852.6364; Fax: 502.852.8971
E-mail: lawadmissions@louisville.edu; Website: www.law.louisville.edu

Introduction

Founded in 1846, the University of Louisville's Brandeis School of Law is Kentucky's oldest law school and America's fifth oldest law school in continuous operation. Heir to the legacy of Justice Louis D. Brandeis, the school is distinguished by a rich history, national outreach, and profound dedication to public service. UofL Law is an integral part of the University of Louisville, a premier research institution founded in 1798.

UofL Law is exceptional in many ways. We boast a strong core curriculum, enhanced by specialized and interdisciplinary studies. We offer a full-time program (three years) and a part-time program (four or five years). Faculty members dedicated to both teaching and research guide students with strong academic skills and diverse backgrounds. From a supportive legal community, we draw in job opportunities and adjuncts who bring their real-world expertise to the classroom. International exchanges, for faculty and for students, expose our school to global opportunities.

The metropolitan area, with a population of approximately one million, combines a gracious ambience of southern hospitality with cultural, aesthetic, and recreational attractions, including historic Churchill Downs, the Actors Theatre of Louisville, the Speed Art Museum, the brand new state-of-the-art KFC Yum! Center, and the Muhammad Ali Institute for Peace and Justice. UofL Law is located minutes away from the largest legal community in the region. Our expansive alumni network spanning 49 states and six countries is invaluable to your success.

Enrollment/Student Body

The School of Law enrolls first-year students beginning in the fall semester, which starts in August. Candidates may apply for admission to either the full-time (three-year) division or the part-time (four-to-five-year) division.

Candidates must have completed a bachelor's degree at an accredited college or university prior to enrollment. All undergraduate majors are acceptable, with courses that emphasize critical reasoning, writing, and communication skills recognized as good preparation for the study of law. With an entering class of 140–150 each fall, first-year class sizes seldom exceed 70 students. Basic Legal Skills (the first-year writing course) is broken down into smaller class sizes of around 22 students.

The entire student body, composed of almost as many women as men, numbers around 400, allowing every student the opportunity to develop close relationships with his or her professors.

Faculty

Professors at UofL Law are masters of the intellectual and practical skills central to success in the legal profession. Many UofL Law professors have practiced law, worked in government, or clerked for federal judges. Our faculty excels in teaching, scholarship, and service to the community. They collaborate with colleagues at other law schools and in other departments at the University of Louisville. Public officials throughout the United States often rely on their expertise.

With 33 full-time faculty members (including 12 women and 4 faculty members of color) and numerous part-time or adjunct teachers, the faculty-to-student ratio is 1 to 14. Students have the opportunity to explore issues important to them through close cooperation with individual members of the faculty.

Curriculum

The law school's full-time and part-time divisions are both daytime programs, with all classes occurring between the hours of 8:00 AM and 5:00 PM. Both divisions share the same curriculum, faculty, and academic standards. The foundational classes during the first year are laid out for students. After completing the first-year curriculum, students choose from core courses in doctrinal subjects, advanced research and writing, and professional responsibility. Students may also take advantage of a rich variety of specialized and interdisciplinary electives.

A highly successful Academic Success Program directed by Kimberly Ballard, a magna cum laude graduate of UofL Law, offers structured study groups, academic success seminars, a library with study aids, and individual academic counseling. The Academic Success Office at UofL Law is committed to helping every student achieve his or her full potential.

Samuel L. Greenebaum Public Service Program

Reflecting the spirit of Justice Louis D. Brandeis, UofL Law was one of America's first five law schools to adopt public service as part of the prescribed course of study. Through this public service work, students develop practical skills, serve their communities, and establish professional values. All students are required to complete 30 hours of pro bono services as a condition of graduation.

During the 2009–2010 academic year, over 100 placements were maintained, 11 of which were new to the program. Within these 100 placements existed over 200 service opportunities, which allowed each student to be matched to a public service choice that was of the most interest.

Library and Physical Facilities

The law school is housed in Wilson W. Wyatt Hall, a gracious colonial-style building overlooking the formal entrance to the University of Louisville's Belknap Campus—a traditional college campus located in an urban setting.

The school's law library houses a collection of more than 400,000 volumes and microform volume equivalents, carefully selected to aid student instruction and promote research. The library still receives original briefs of the US Supreme Court—a rare distinction for a law school and a practice originated by Justice Brandeis that continues today.

State-of-the-art instructional and research technologies; two computer labs; the Allen Courtroom's contemporary litigation environment; wireless access in the library, classrooms, and common areas; and a full-time technology staff provide a wealth of services to every law student. The school's website serves as our community bulletin board. Students can download course syllabi, assignments, handouts, old exams, and other materials; browse job listings from the Career

Services Office; review the Academic Support Program's catalog of study aids; and get news, calendars, schedules, and more. Technology is increasingly part of legal teaching and learning as the faculty continue to incorporate presentations and Internet resources into the classroom experience.

Special Programs

The School of Law offers seven dual-degree programs designed to enhance the students' understanding, skills, and career opportunities in both areas of study. Each program requires application and admission to both participating schools. Programs include the Juris Doctor/Master of Business Administration (JD/MBA), Juris Doctor/Master of Arts in Political Science (JD/MAPS), Juris Doctor/Master of Arts in Bioethics and Medical Humanities (JD/MA), Juris Doctor/Master of Arts in Humanities (JD/MAH), Juris Doctor/Master of Divinity (JD/MDiv) at the Louisville Presbyterian Theological Seminary, Juris Doctor/Master of Science in Social Work (JD/MSSW), and Juris Doctor/Master of Urban Planning (JD/MUP).

The school also operates clinical externship programs in which upper-class students, with supervision, represent clients and appear in court. A third-year student may receive credit by working in the criminal arena (DA or PD), the tax arena (IRS), the judicial branch (various judges), family law (Center for Women and Families or Legal Aid Society), or technology (University of Louisville Office of Technology Transfer).

The law school operates a live-client clinic, housed in the same building as the Legal Aid Society. Under the direction and supervision of faculty, students in the clinic gain experience interacting with and representing clients.

International experience is another unique opportunity. The Brandeis School offers faculty or student exchanges with law schools in France, England, Germany, Finland, Australia, and South Africa.

Practical Success

Participating annually in about a dozen moot court and professional skills competitions, the law school has won several regional and national championships, including, most recently, the New York University Immigration Moot Court Competition.

Real clients, real cases, real problems, and real solutions are what you'll find at the UofL Law Clinic. Law students gain practical experience applying their newly acquired legal skills to public housing and domestic violence cases. Students act as primary attorneys under the supervision of the clinic's director.

Students are also actively involved in writing for and publishing the *University of Louisville Law Review*, the Journal of Law and Education, and the *Journal of Animal and Environmental Law*. Graduates of the University of Louisville's Brandeis School of Law consistently achieve high employment rates.

Admission

Applicants may apply beginning October 1 and prior to March 15. Both full-time and part-time first-year students must start classes in the fall semester.

For the best chance of consideration, it is recommended that the LSAT be taken no later than December. Scores from LSATs taken in June, prior to the first semester of enrollment, will be considered only under extraordinary circumstances.

APPLICANT PROFILE

University of Louisville's Brandeis School of Law
This grid includes only applicants who earned 120–180 LSAT scores under standard administrations.

LSAT Score	3.75 +		3.50–3.74		3.25–3.49		3.00–3.24		2.75–2.99		2.50–2.74		2.25–2.49		2.00–2.24		Below 2.00		No GPA		Total	
	Apps	Adm	Apps	Adm	Apps	Adm	Apps	Adm	Apps	Adm	Apps	Adm	Apps	Adm	Apps	Adm	Apps	Adm	Apps	Adm	Apps	Adm
175–180	0	0	0	0	0	0	0	0	0	0	0	0	0	0	0	0	0	0	0	0	0	0
170–174	2	2	2	2	2	2	2	2	0	0	1	0	1	0	0	0	0	0	0	0	10	8
165–169	4	3	6	6	2	2	9	8	6	3	8	2	3	0	0	0	1	0	0	0	39	24
160–164	25	24	34	34	35	31	31	29	17	13	14	7	5	2	6	0	1	0	3	3	171	143
155–159	57	53	86	73	93	50	89	48	75	11	47	6	20	3	7	0	1	0	3	2	478	246
150–154	61	29	84	17	106	6	107	8	83	4	45	1	14	3	10	0	0	0	5	2	515	70
145–149	27	18	35	10	59	5	65	1	59	2	35	0	15	0	9	0	2	0	4	0	310	36
140–144	6	1	12	2	32	3	26	2	26	0	20	0	17	0	9	0	1	0	3	0	152	8
135–139	0	0	4	0	6	0	9	0	14	0	7	0	6	0	3	0	2	0	3	0	54	0
130–134	0	0	1	0	1	0	4	0	4	0	8	0	1	0	2	0	0	0	0	0	21	0
125–129	0	0	0	0	0	0	0	0	2	0	0	0	1	0	4	0	1	0	0	0	8	0
120–124	0	0	0	0	0	0	1	0	0	0	1	0	0	0	0	0	1	0	0	0	3	0
Total	182	130	264	144	336	99	343	98	286	33	186	16	83	8	50	0	10	0	21	7	1761	535

Apps = Number of Applicants
Adm = Number Admitted
Reflects 99% of the total applicant pool; highest LSAT data reported.

LOYOLA LAW SCHOOL, LOYOLA MARYMOUNT UNIVERSITY

919 Albany Street
Los Angeles, CA 90015
Phone: 213.736.1074; Fax: 213.736.6523
E-mail: admissions@lls.edu; Website: www.lls.edu

ABA
Approved
Since
1935

The Basics

Type of school	Private
Term	Semester
Application deadline	2/1 4/15
Application fee	
Financial aid deadline	3/14
Can first year start other than fall?	No
Student to faculty ratio	15.0 to 1
# of housing spaces available restricted to law students	
graduate housing for which law students are eligible	

Faculty and Administrators

	Total		Men		Women		Minorities	
	Spr	Fall	Spr	Fall	Spr	Fall	Spr	Fall
Full-time	65	66	34	35	31	31	11	12
Other full-time	1	0	1	0	0	0	0	0
Deans, librarians, & others who teach	15	15	8	8	7	7	5	5
Part-time	82	72	62	57	20	15	41	29
Total	163	153	105	100	58	53	57	46

Curriculum

		Full-Time	Part-Time
Typical first-year section size		86	58
Is there typically a "small section" of the first-year class, other than Legal Writing, taught by full-time faculty		No	No
If yes, typical size offered last year			
# of classroom course titles beyond first-year curriculum		155	
# of upper division courses, excluding seminars, with an enrollment:	Under 25	152	
	25–49	47	
	50–74	11	
	75–99	10	
	100+	7	
# of seminars		46	
# of seminar positions available		854	
# of seminar positions filled		336	180
# of positions available in simulation courses		1,525	
# of simulation positions filled		655	478
# of positions available in faculty supervised clinical courses		280	
# of faculty supervised clinical positions filled		201	58
# involved in field placements		200	44
# involved in law journals		193	21
# involved in moot court or trial competitions		67	15
# of credit hours required to graduate		87	

JD Enrollment and Ethnicity

	Men		Women		Full-Time		Part-Time		1st-Year		Total		JD Degs. Awd.
	#	%	#	%	#	%	#	%	#	%	#	%	
All Hispanics	72	11.2	86	13.3	124	12.2	34	12.3	47	11.5	158	12.3	41
Am. Ind./AK Nat.	1	0.2	3	0.5	2	0.2	2	0.7	1	0.2	4	0.3	1
Asian	92	14.4	133	20.5	182	18.0	43	15.6	69	17.0	225	17.5	87
Black/Af. Am.	26	4.1	24	3.7	36	3.6	14	5.1	19	4.7	50	3.9	11
Nat. HI/Pac. Isl.	2	0.3	0	0.0	2	0.2	0	0.0	0	0.0	2	0.2	0
2 or more races	33	5.1	35	5.4	45	4.4	23	8.3	34	8.4	68	5.3	0
Subtotal (minor.)	226	35.3	281	43.4	391	38.6	116	42.0	170	41.8	507	39.3	158
Nonres. Alien	6	0.9	9	1.4	13	1.3	2	0.7	7	1.7	15	1.2	0
White/Cauc.	368	57.4	310	47.8	532	52.5	146	52.9	220	54.1	678	52.6	197
Unknown	41	6.4	48	7.4	77	7.6	12	4.3	10	2.5	89	6.9	26
Total	641	49.7	648	50.3	1013	78.6	276	21.4	407	31.6	1289		388

Transfers

Transfers in	43
Transfers out	12

Tuition and Fees

	Resident	Nonresident
Full-time	$41,840	$41,840
Part-time	$28,035	$28,035
Tuition Guarantee Program		N

Living Expenses

Estimated living expenses for singles

Living on campus	Living off campus	Living at home
N/A	$25,908	$13,950

ABA
Approved
Since
1935

GPA and LSAT Scores

	Total	Full-Time	Part-Time
# of apps	5,550	5,303	2,566
# of offers	1,589	1,485	104
# of matrics	403	340	63
75% GPA	3.70	3.72	3.61
Median GPA	3.56	3.57	3.38
25% GPA	3.31	3.33	3.09
75% LSAT	163	163	161
Median LSAT	161	161	159
25% LSAT	158	159	155

Grants and Scholarships (from prior year)

	Total		Full-Time		Part-Time	
	#	%	#	%	#	%
Total # of students	1,287		1,002		285	
Total # receiving grants	421	32.7	380	37.9	41	14.4
Less than 1/2 tuition	177	13.8	159	15.9	18	6.3
Half to full tuition	222	17.2	203	20.3	19	6.7
Full tuition	0	0.0	0	0.0	0	0.0
More than full tuition	22	1.7	18	1.8	4	1.4
Median grant amount			$21,000		$15,000	

Informational and Library Resources

Total amount spent on library materials	$2,472,646
Study seating capacity inside the library	550
# of full-time equivalent professional librarians	13
Hours per week library is open	108
# of open, wired connections available to students	300
# of networked computers available for use by students	175
Has wireless network?	Y
Requires computer?	N

JD Attrition (from prior year)

	Academic	Other	Total	
	#	#	#	%
1st year	24	31	55	13.8
2nd year	2	3	5	1.2
3rd year	0	4	4	1.0
4th year	0	1	1	1.4

Employment (9 months after graduation)

	Total	Percentage
Employment status known	396	100.0
Employment status unknown	0	0.0
Employed	370	93.4
Pursuing graduate degrees	4	1.0
Unemployed (seeking, not seeking, or studying for the bar)	21	5.3
Type of Employment		
# employed in law firms	232	62.7
# employed in business and industry	51	13.8
# employed in government	11	3.0
# employed in public interest	56	15.1
# employed as judicial clerks	12	3.2
# employed in academia	8	2.2
Geographic Location		
# employed in state	356	96.2
# employed outside the US	1	0.3
# of states where employed	8	

Bar Passage Rates

First-time takers	375	Reporting %	100.00
Average school %	82.93	Average state %	73.19
Average pass difference	9.74		

Jurisdiction	Takers	Passers	Pass %	State %	Diff %
California	375	311	82.93	73.19	9.74

LOYOLA LAW SCHOOL, LOYOLA MARYMOUNT UNIVERSITY

919 Albany Street
Los Angeles, CA 90015
Phone: 213.736.1074; Fax: 213.736.6523
E-mail: admissions@lls.edu; Website: www.lls.edu

Law School and Campus

Loyola Law School was founded in 1920 and is one of California's largest law schools. Having graduated more than 16,000 men and women, Loyola has had a profound effect on the legal profession and on American history. Known best for producing many of our nation's most exciting and influential attorneys, Loyola instills in its graduates a deep commitment to public service and ethical practice while emphasizing the philosophical, analytical, and professional skills essential to the lawyering process.

The Law School, a division of Loyola Marymount University (LMU), includes nearly 1,300 full-time day and part-time evening students, nearly 140 full-time and adjunct faculty, and 110 administrative and technical staff. Housed on a modern, innovative campus, including eight buildings, a spacious parking facility, green lawns, and athletic courts, Loyola encompasses an entire city block in downtown Los Angeles. The academic and social spaces are dedicated solely to the law school community—the environment is warm and welcoming. World-renowned architect Frank Gehry has received national and international recognition for the campus design.

The cornerstone of the campus, the William M. Rains Law Library, is one of the largest private law libraries in the western United States, providing extensive research capabilities with a collection of over 600,000 volumes and the latest advances in information technology.

Our central location, just minutes away from many courts, major law firms, and public interest agencies, provides excellent opportunities for our students. Students also have easy access to LA Live, an entertainment and sports venue that includes the Staples Center, Nokia Theatre, Grammy Museum, a movie theater, and restaurants.

Juris Doctor

The Juris Doctor prepares students to be effective lawyers and judges in any jurisdiction in the United States. Loyola recognizes that a quality education must do more than simply prepare a student to file a lawsuit or draft a contract. The program is designed to teach students to think and reason critically. The faculty strives to instill in students a respect and appreciation for the law and a desire to improve the society in which we live. The Juris Doctor is offered in both a full-time, three-year day division and a part-time, four-year evening division.

JD/MBA

Loyola Law School and the Graduate Program of the College of Business Administration of Loyola Marymount University offer a dual-degree program in law and business. Graduates of the program receive the Juris Doctor degree (JD) and the Master of Business Administration (MBA). A graduate certificate in International Business can also be earned with the MBA.

The dual-degree program provides for the achievement of both degrees in four years instead of the five normally required to complete the degree programs separately. The program is only open to full-time day students. Students may receive up to 12 units of business classes toward the 87 units required to

earn a JD, and may be allowed to count up to 12 units of law classes toward the 54 units required to earn an MBA.

Applicants must apply and be accepted separately to the Law School and the MBA program. Applicants must also apply and be accepted to the JD/MBA program. Applications for the JD/MBA program may be submitted after the first year of law school. Interested applicants should contact the LMU College of Business Administration to request an application for the MBA program and the Law School Office of Admissions to request an application for the JD/MBA program.

Master of Laws in Taxation and JD/Tax LLM

Loyola also offers the Master of Laws (LLM) degree in Taxation. This degree distinguishes tax specialists by its advanced legal theory, tax policy, and scholarship. Students may earn both the JD degree and the LLM in Taxation in three years (rather than the four years typically required to complete the degree programs separately) by completing an intensive summer tax session and by taking advanced tax courses that count for double credit toward both the Juris Doctor and the LLM in Taxation.

Faculty

The faculty is composed of scholars who publish innovative theories, influencing the development and direction of the legal profession. They draft hundreds of scholarly articles and books, advise law firms and agencies on recent developments, and lecture at universities around the world. They also include seasoned attorneys with extensive and varied practice experience as United States Supreme Court clerks, public interest lawyers, agency chiefs, and law firm partners. But most importantly, the Loyola faculty are exceptional teachers who maintain an open door policy to encourage free and continuous interaction with their students.

Curriculum

The curriculum is designed to provide the knowledge and skills that will enable students to become excellent practicing lawyers. The curriculum integrates traditional instruction in legal doctrine and theory with a special commitment to the development of legal skills.

The Law School has a wide variety of course offerings and seminars in business/corporate law, commercial law, constitutional and civil rights law, criminal law, environmental law, entertainment/sports law, health care law, intellectual property law, international law, law and social policy, litigation and legal skills, public interest law, and tax law.

Innovative Programs, Centers, and Clinics

Loyola demonstrates its commitment to public service by requiring all students to donate 40 hours to working in the public interest sector. The **Public Interest Law Department** coordinates public interest activities, counsels students about law practice and fellowships, and administers five public service programs. The law school also houses several clinical programs, among them the **Disability Rights Legal Center**, the **Center for Juvenile Law and Policy,** and the **Center for**

Conflict Resolution. Students have many opportunities through these programs to work with clients, practice their skills, and receive individualized feedback from faculty members and directors.

As part of our new **Advocacy Institute**, students can earn a certificate in civil litigation and advocacy or criminal justice advocacy. Our excellent **trial advocacy programs** also allow upper-division students to compete in noted trial competitions. Loyola students have won numerous awards at international and national trial advocacy and moot court competitions in recent years. Students interested in spending the summer abroad may attend one of our **international programs** in Costa Rica, China, Cyprus, Italy, or London.

Other opportunities include the **Entertainment Law Practicum** which allows students to get hands-on experience through field placements at television networks, major movie studios, record companies, talent agencies, and entertainment law firms. Loyola's **Business Law Practicum** offers an innovative approach to educating business lawyers with practical, real-world training. Through the **Immigration Justice Practicum** students cover substantive immigration law issues in a fall semester class and work in the spring semester for an organization that handles immigration issues. Finally, our **externship program** exposes students to **many other areas of practice** as they work for government offices, public interest organizations, or private corporations.

Admission and Financial Aid/Scholarships

Admission to the law school is based on a comprehensive evaluation that includes LSAT performance, undergraduate academic record, the personal statement, and letters of recommendation. Professional experience, extracurricular activities, community involvement, and qualities such as motivation, maturity, and focus are also closely evaluated. A prospective student may also submit a résumé.

Applications for admission are accepted on a rolling basis. The committee begins reading complete files in December. Deadlines are **February 1** for the day program and **April 15** for the evening program. Early applicants have greater prospects for gaining admission and receiving scholarship awards.

All admitted students are considered for our scholarship programs. The committee uses the merits of the file to evaluate the admitted student's potential to contribute to our community. In addition to the general scholarship program, Loyola offers the **Public Interest Scholars Program** for students interested in having a career in public service. For graduates working at public interest organizations or with government agencies, a **Loan Repayment Assistance Program** is also available. Entering students can work with our dedicated financial aid staff to find other sources (primarily loans) to help fund their educational and personal expenses.

Career Services

The Office of Career Services offers a wealth of services, programs, and resources to students and alumni. A large professional staff counsels and assists students and graduates in the job development process. Hundreds of national, international, and regional employers recruit from Loyola annually. Graduates are employed by the nation's most prestigious private and public legal organizations. Overall placement figures are consistently strong—recent classes have employment rates (within nine months of graduation) above 90 percent.

APPLICANT PROFILE

Loyola Law School, Loyola Marymount University
This grid includes only applicants who earned 120–180 LSAT scores under standard administrations.

LSAT Score	GPA 3.75 +		3.50–3.74		3.25–3.49		3.00–3.24		2.75–2.99		2.50–2.74		2.25–2.49		2.00–2.24		Below 2.00		No GPA		Total	
	Apps	Adm	Apps	Adm	Apps	Adm	Apps	Adm	Apps	Adm	Apps	Adm	Apps	Adm	Apps	Adm	Apps	Adm	Apps	Adm	Apps	Adm
175–180	1	1	3	3	5	4	3	1	3	1	1	0	0	0	0	0	0	0	1	1	17	11
170–174	12	12	31	27	18	16	13	8	12	6	6	2	2	0	2	0	1	0	1	1	98	72
165–169	93	89	116	102	112	75	85	44	42	16	25	2	8	0	2	0	1	0	6	2	490	330
160–164	243	220	377	319	344	149	236	78	112	20	57	5	26	0	5	0	0	0	13	6	1413	797
155–159	180	105	340	131	388	43	244	16	150	10	85	2	35	0	9	0	3	0	19	3	1453	310
150–154	81	12	204	30	269	15	263	4	138	3	62	1	41	0	15	0	1	0	23	0	1097	65
145–149	19	0	77	1	121	0	144	0	91	0	62	0	23	0	11	0	2	0	6	0	556	1
140–144	10	0	24	0	44	0	62	0	45	0	49	0	19	0	7	0	1	0	9	0	270	0
135–139	3	0	4	0	17	0	17	0	22	0	19	0	12	0	7	0	2	0	4	0	107	0
130–134	0	0	2	0	1	0	4	0	11	0	5	0	5	0	5	0	1	0	1	0	35	0
125–129	0	0	0	0	0	0	0	0	0	0	1	0	0	0	0	0	0	0	0	0	1	0
120–124	0	0	0	0	0	0	0	0	0	0	0	0	0	0	0	0	0	0	0	0	0	0
Total	642	439	1178	613	1319	302	1071	151	626	56	372	12	171	0	63	0	12	0	83	13	5537	1586

Apps = Number of Applicants
Adm = Number Admitted
Represents 99% of applicant pool; highest LSAT data reported.

LOYOLA UNIVERSITY CHICAGO SCHOOL OF LAW

25 East Pearson Street, Suite 1208
Chicago, IL 60611
Phone: 312.915.7170; Fax: 312.915.7906
E-mail: law-admissions@luc.edu; Website: www.luc.edu/law

ABA
Approved
Since
1925

The Basics

Type of school	Private
Term	Semester
Application deadline	3/1
Application fee	$0
Financial aid deadline	3/1
Can first year start other than fall?	No
Student to faculty ratio	13.4 to 1
# of housing spaces available restricted to law students	96
graduate housing for which law students are eligible	106

Faculty and Administrators

	Total		Men		Women		Minorities	
	Spr	Fall	Spr	Fall	Spr	Fall	Spr	Fall
Full-time	48	50	29	32	19	18	5	7
Other full-time	8	10	4	6	4	4	1	2
Deans, librarians, & others who teach	15	15	5	5	10	10	2	2
Part-time	90	99	45	52	45	47	7	10
Total	161	174	83	95	78	79	15	21

Curriculum

	Full-Time	Part-Time
Typical first-year section size	83	43
Is there typically a "small section" of the first-year class, other than Legal Writing, taught by full-time faculty	Yes	No
If yes, typical size offered last year	20	
# of classroom course titles beyond first-year curriculum	186	

# of upper division courses, excluding seminars, with an enrollment:		
	Under 25	108
	25–49	44
	50–74	13
	75–99	3
	100+	0

# of seminars	50	
# of seminar positions available	1,048	
# of seminar positions filled	640	162
# of positions available in simulation courses	879	
# of simulation positions filled	538	135
# of positions available in faculty supervised clinical courses	117	
# of faculty supervised clinical positions filled	101	5
# involved in field placements	77	10
# involved in law journals	190	21
# involved in moot court or trial competitions	56	1
# of credit hours required to graduate	86	

JD Enrollment and Ethnicity

	Men		Women		Full-Time		Part-Time		1st-Year		Total		JD Degs. Awd.
	#	%	#	%	#	%	#	%	#	%	#	%	
All Hispanics	19	4.4	30	7.2	42	6.1	7	4.4	24	8.2	49	5.8	17
Am. Ind./AK Nat.	0	0.0	1	0.2	0	0.0	1	0.6	1	0.3	1	0.1	4
Asian	15	3.5	21	5.0	25	3.6	11	6.9	11	3.8	36	4.2	18
Black/Af. Am.	22	5.1	38	9.1	42	6.1	18	11.3	30	10.3	60	7.1	14
Nat. HI/Pac. Isl.	0	0.0	0	0.0	0	0.0	0	0.0	0	0.0	0	0.0	0
2 or more races	1	0.2	14	3.3	13	1.9	2	1.3	15	5.2	15	1.8	0
Subtotal (minor.)	57	13.2	104	24.8	122	17.6	39	24.5	81	27.8	161	18.9	53
Nonres. Alien	5	1.2	5	1.2	9	1.3	1	0.6	5	1.7	10	1.2	0
White/Cauc.	355	82.2	294	70.2	534	77.2	115	72.3	205	70.4	649	76.3	188
Unknown	15	3.5	16	3.8	27	3.9	4	2.5	0	0.0	31	3.6	22
Total	432	50.8	419	49.2	692	81.3	159	18.7	291	34.2	851		266

Transfers

Transfers in	15
Transfers out	15

Tuition and Fees

	Resident	Nonresident
Full-time	$38,086	$38,086
Part-time	$28,766	$28,766
Tuition Guarantee Program		N

Living Expenses

Estimated living expenses for singles

Living on campus	Living off campus	Living at home
$19,900	$19,900	$19,900

LOYOLA UNIVERSITY CHICAGO SCHOOL OF LAW

*ABA
Approved
Since
1925*

GPA and LSAT Scores

	Total	Full-Time	Part-Time
# of apps	5,452	4,751	701
# of offers	1,638	1,510	128
# of matrics	292	243	49
75% GPA	3.59	3.59	3.58
Median GPA	3.41	3.41	3.40
25% GPA	3.13	3.13	3.12
75% LSAT	162	163	159
Median LSAT	161	161	157
25% LSAT	157	158	153

Grants and Scholarships (from prior year)

	Total		Full-Time		Part-Time	
	#	%	#	%	#	%
Total # of students	840		652		188	
Total # receiving grants	531	63.2	460	70.6	71	37.8
Less than 1/2 tuition	398	47.4	331	50.8	67	35.6
Half to full tuition	119	14.2	115	17.6	4	2.1
Full tuition	13	1.5	13	2.0	0	0.0
More than full tuition	1	0.1	1	0.2	0	0.0
Median grant amount			$11,000		$6,000	

Informational and Library Resources

Total amount spent on library materials	$930,451
Study seating capacity inside the library	451
# of full-time equivalent professional librarians	10
Hours per week library is open	101
# of open, wired connections available to students	328
# of networked computers available for use by students	64
Has wireless network?	Y
Requires computer?	N

JD Attrition (from prior year)

	Academic	Other	Total	
	#	#	#	%
1st year	1	2	3	1.1
2nd year	0	15	15	5.5
3rd year	0	0	0	0.0
4th year	0	1	1	2.3

Employment (9 months after graduation)

	Total	Percentage
Employment status known	299	97.4
Employment status unknown	8	2.6
Employed	274	91.6
Pursuing graduate degrees	14	4.7
Unemployed (seeking, not seeking, or studying for the bar)	7	2.3
Type of Employment		
# employed in law firms	145	52.9
# employed in business and industry	52	19.0
# employed in government	46	16.8
# employed in public interest	14	5.1
# employed as judicial clerks	12	4.4
# employed in academia	5	1.8
Geographic Location		
# employed in state	221	80.7
# employed outside the US	2	0.7
# of states where employed	18	

Bar Passage Rates

First-time takers	295	Reporting %	88.14
Average school %	93.08	Average state %	90.88
Average pass difference	2.20		

Jurisdiction	Takers	Passers	Pass %	State %	Diff %
Illinois	253	235	92.89	90.89	2.00
Wisconsin	7	7	100.00	90.80	9.20

The information on these pages was provided by the law school.

LOYOLA UNIVERSITY CHICAGO SCHOOL OF LAW

25 East Pearson Street, Suite 1208
Chicago, IL 60611
Phone: 312.915.7170; Fax: 312.915.7906
E-mail: law-admissions@luc.edu; Website: www.luc.edu/law

Introduction

The School of Law is located on the Water Tower Campus of the university, a few blocks north of the Chicago Loop. This campus adjoins Michigan Avenue at the historical Water Tower, a Chicago landmark, in approximately the center of the renowned Magnificent Mile, a commercial center over which the John Hancock Center towers. This location provides ready access to the state and federal courts and to the offices of most other institutions of federal, state, and local government, as well as the cultural centers of Chicago. The school is a member of the AALS and is approved by the ABA. The School of Law celebrated its 100th anniversary in 2008.

Library and Facilities

The Philip H. Corboy Law Center, at 25 East Pearson Street, provides Loyola's law students with a modern and enhanced learning environment. The School of Law library is located on floors 3–5 of the Law Center. More than 400,000 volumes enhance Loyola's broad-based law curriculum and support the varied research needs of students and faculty. Offering custom-designed furnishings and custom carrels, the 43,900-square-foot facility creates a comfortable and accommodating atmosphere for users. The library is open 100 hours each week, with expanded hours during examination periods. The law library is fully staffed with professional librarians and paraprofessionals to assist students and faculty.

Across the street from the Law Center is a 25-story, 600-bed residence hall, Baumhart Hall, which opened in fall 2006. This structure enables graduate, professional, and undergraduate student residents to experience contemporary living in fully furnished apartments. Amenities include a 24-hour security staff, a food court and late-night café, a state-of-the-art fitness center, wireless access in apartment bedrooms and public areas, a laundry room equipped with "smart system" washers and dryers, and rent includes all utilities, heat and air-conditioning, cable, and high-speed Internet access.

Foreign Study Programs

Since 1983, the School of Law has offered a program of international and comparative law courses at the Rome Center for Liberal Arts, the university's campus in Rome, Italy. Each summer, for approximately four weeks, law students can take one or more of the courses offered in Rome by members of Loyola's law faculty. In 2009, Supreme Court Justice Ruth Bader Ginsberg participated in the Rome Program. In 2010, Supreme Court Justice Antonin Scalia conducted a two-week class on the Constitution.

In 1997, the law school added a program in Strasbourg, France. This one-week optional field study follows the summer program in Rome.

In summer 2008, Loyola inaugurated a three-week program in China. In addition to time in the classroom, students hear from guest lecturers and experience guided excursions to sites in Beijing and the surrounding areas.

In 1989, Loyola inaugurated its London Comparative Advocacy Program in which students travel to London between semesters for approximately 15 days to become immersed in the world of the British barrister.

In spring 2003, Loyola inaugurated an immersion program at Universidad Alberto Hurtado, a Jesuit law school in Santiago, Chile.

Clinical Legal Education

For students, faculty, and alumni, Loyola's four legal clinics represent a valuable bridge between theory and practice, classroom and career. Through the clinics, the School of Law offers service to others in a way that gives them dignity while providing students with practical legal experience. In spring 2003, the law school celebrated the 20th anniversary of its clinical program that began with the founding of its Community Law Center Clinic, followed later by the Federal Tax Clinic, Child and Family Law Clinic, the Business Law Clinic, the Life After Innocence Project, and the Health Justice Project.

Special Opportunities

The School of Law has dual-degree programs with the School of Social Work, the Department of Political Science, the School of Education, and the Graduate School of Business. Automatic acceptance into the master's of political science program is granted to candidates admitted to the law school. Provisional admission to the MBA program is granted based upon LSAT score and law school grades. The multidegree programs are structured to allow completion after four years. Loyola offers accelerated LLM programs in health law, child and family law, and taxation to JD students who fulfill program requirements. Recognizing the increasing need for specialization in legal education and practice, the school offers specialized curricula in five key areas: International Law and Practice, Health Law, Child and Family Law, Advocacy, and Tax Law.

Child and Family Law Center

The Loyola ChildLaw Center was created in 1993 to prepare law students to represent abused and neglected children. The center is the first of its kind at any American law school; it was the recipient of the National Association of Counsel for Children 1996 Outstanding Legal Advocacy Award, and it draws on the full resources of Loyola University, including the schools of medicine, social work, and education. The program includes an LLM degree and a master's degree program for nonlawyers.

The Center houses our renowned ChildLaw and Education Institute, offering students an integrated curriculum in education law, interdisciplinary research, and outreach experiences, with the opportunity to represent children confronting barriers to educational equality. Law students also may obtain a unique dual degree with the School of Education, which will result in a JD and MA in Comparative Education.

The law school and Teach for America (TFA) have entered into a partnership. TFA corps members who are interested in using their legal education to advocate for children's legal interests and well-being will receive matching AmeriCorps Awards.

Annually, Child and Family Law Fellows are selected from the entering law class. One fellowship is reserved for a TFA corps member. Each fellow receives financial support.

Institute for Health Law

The Beazley Institute for Health Law was created in 1984 in recognition of the need for an academic forum to study the field of health law and to act as a vehicle to foster dialogue between the law and the health sciences. Through the institute, the law school offers an SJD in Health Law and Policy and an LLM in Health Law. In addition, it offers the first Master of Jurisprudence (MJ) in Health Law and Doctor of Law (DLaw) in Health Law and Policy, providing health care professionals with an intensive overview in health law. More than two dozen health law classes are offered at the law school.

Institute for Consumer Antitrust Studies

The Institute for Consumer Antitrust Studies is an independent, academically-based institute designed to explore the effect of antitrust and consumer law enforcement on the individual consumer and the general public. The institute was founded by a grant from the US District Court for the Northern District of Illinois and is supported by Loyola and private donors.

Advocacy

Loyola prepares its students for careers of leadership at the bar and on the bench. For over 100 years, Loyola's tradition of educating and training top litigators has produced some of the country's most accomplished and recognized trial attorneys and judges. The Dan K. Webb Center for Advocacy is composed of a second-year required course in advocacy, courses in beginning and advanced trial advocacy, numerous moot court competitions, the Corboy Fellowship Program in Trial Advocacy for mock trial competitions, and a wide variety of litigation-related courses and an extensive curriculum in alternative dispute resolution.

A certificate in advocacy is available for students who complete a menu of advocacy courses.

Symbolic of our advocacy success is our selection by the National Institute for Trial Advocacy as the site for two of its largest advocacy training programs, the Midwest Regional Trial Advocacy Program and the Midwest Regional Deposition Training Program.

Admission

Factors other than LSAT scores and college grades are considered. Such factors include work experience, personal goals, specialized education, and other evidence of the ability to contribute invaluable insight to law classes.

Career Services

The Career Resources Office assists students and alumni with career planning and employment selection. Seminars by practicing attorneys and alumni, résumé preparation, interviewing techniques, individual counseling, and job-search strategies are just some of the programs administered by the Career Resources Office.

A year-round, on-campus employer interview and recruitment program provides employment opportunities.

The School of Law is a member of NALP.

Cocurricular Activities

Students are encouraged to participate in cocurricular activities. There are six student-edited publications, including the *Annals of Health Law*, *Children's Legal Rights Journal*, *Consumer Law Review*, *International Law Review*, *Loyola University Chicago Law Journal*, and *Public Interest Law Reporter*. Students compete in more than 20 moot court and mock trial national and international competitions. All students are members of the Loyola Student Bar Association, the principal instrument of student government. There are over 30 student organizations devoted to legal practice, ethnic groups, or law student chapters of professional bar associations.

APPLICANT PROFILE

Loyola University Chicago School of Law
This grid includes only applicants who earned 120–180 LSAT scores under standard administrations.

LSAT Score	3.75 +		3.50–3.74		3.25–3.49		3.00–3.24		2.50–2.99		2.00–2.49		Below 2.00		No GPA		Total	
	Apps	Adm	Apps	Adm	Apps	Adm	Apps	Adm	Apps	Adm	Apps	Adm	Apps	Adm	Apps	Adm	Apps	Adm
165–180	61	59	95	92	73	69	41	40	56	42	21	9	1	0	3	2	351	313
160–164	175	161	276	257	250	213	170	135	136	91	29	10	0	0	14	7	1050	874
155–159	203	76	351	127	352	42	278	27	235	16	59	7	2	0	18	3	1498	298
145–154	148	15	334	31	512	34	442	38	457	17	126	2	9	0	29	2	2057	139
120–144	24	0	55	1	79	0	96	0	200	0	72	0	5	0	18	0	549	1
Total	611	311	1111	508	1266	358	1027	240	1084	166	307	28	17	0	82	14	5505	1625

Apps = Number of Applicants
Adm = Number Admitted
Reflects 99% of the total applicant pool; highest LSAT data reported.

LOYOLA UNIVERSITY NEW ORLEANS COLLEGE OF LAW

7214 St. Charles Avenue, Box 904
New Orleans, LA 70118
Phone: 504.861.5575; Fax: 504.861.5772
E-mail: ladmit@loyno.edu; Website: http://law.loyno.edu/

ABA
Approved
Since
1931

The Basics

Type of school	Private
Term	Semester
Application deadline	
Application fee	$40
Financial aid deadline	
Can first year start other than fall?	No
Student to faculty ratio	17.0 to 1
# of housing spaces available restricted to law students	55
graduate housing for which law students are eligible	55

Faculty and Administrators

	Total		Men		Women		Minorities	
	Spr	Fall	Spr	Fall	Spr	Fall	Spr	Fall
Full-time	37	41	23	23	14	18	11	12
Other full-time	11	9	6	4	5	5	1	0
Deans, librarians, & others who teach	4	3	3	2	1	1	0	0
Part-time	27	23	21	19	6	4	3	2
Total	79	76	53	48	26	28	15	14

Curriculum

	Full-Time	Part-Time
Typical first-year section size	81	67
Is there typically a "small section" of the first-year class, other than Legal Writing, taught by full-time faculty	No	No
If yes, typical size offered last year		
# of classroom course titles beyond first-year curriculum	189	

# of upper division courses, excluding seminars, with an enrollment:		
	Under 25	45
	25–49	31
	50–74	22
	75–99	9
	100+	2

# of seminars	44	
# of seminar positions available	921	
# of seminar positions filled	467	177
# of positions available in simulation courses	92	
# of simulation positions filled	54	9
# of positions available in faculty supervised clinical courses	174	
# of faculty supervised clinical positions filled	149	10
# involved in field placements	22	2
# involved in law journals	119	9
# involved in moot court or trial competitions	24	1
# of credit hours required to graduate	90	

JD Enrollment and Ethnicity

	Men		Women		Full-Time		Part-Time		1st-Year		Total		JD Degs. Awd.
	#	%	#	%	#	%	#	%	#	%	#	%	
All Hispanics	43	10.2	32	7.8	65	9.5	10	6.5	28	10.4	75	9.0	23
Am. Ind./AK Nat.	5	1.2	2	0.5	3	0.4	4	2.6	4	1.5	7	0.8	3
Asian	17	4.0	17	4.1	31	4.6	3	2.0	11	4.1	34	4.1	11
Black/Af. Am.	38	9.0	83	20.1	106	15.6	15	9.8	29	10.8	121	14.5	31
Nat. HI/Pac. Isl.	0	0.0	1	0.2	1	0.1	0	0.0	0	0.0	1	0.1	0
2 or more races	0	0.0	0	0.0	0	0.0	0	0.0	0	0.0	0	0.0	0
Subtotal (minor.)	103	24.4	135	32.8	206	30.2	32	20.9	72	26.8	238	28.5	69
Nonres. Alien	3	0.7	2	0.5	4	0.6	1	0.7	4	1.5	5	0.6	0
White/Cauc.	290	68.7	254	61.7	432	63.4	112	73.2	175	65.1	544	65.2	194
Unknown	26	6.2	21	5.1	39	5.7	8	5.2	18	6.7	47	5.6	19
Total	422	50.6	412	49.4	681	81.7	153	18.3	269	32.3	834		282

Transfers

Transfers in	11
Transfers out	14

Tuition and Fees

	Resident	Nonresident
Full-time	$36,196	$36,196
Part-time	$24,476	$24,476
Tuition Guarantee Program	N	

Living Expenses

Estimated living expenses for singles

Living on campus	Living off campus	Living at home
$20,400	$20,400	$15,100

LOYOLA UNIVERSITY NEW ORLEANS COLLEGE OF LAW

ABA
Approved
Since
1931

GPA and LSAT Scores

	Total	Full-Time	Part-Time
# of apps	1,913	1,745	168
# of offers	860	765	95
# of matrics	246	200	46
75% GPA	3.59	3.61	3.44
Median GPA	3.34	3.38	3.22
25% GPA	3.09	3.13	2.95
75% LSAT	157	157	154
Median LSAT	153	154	151
25% LSAT	150	151	149

Grants and Scholarships (from prior year)

	Total		Full-Time		Part-Time	
	#	%	#	%	#	%
Total # of students	882		726		156	
Total # receiving grants	355	40.2	327	45.0	28	17.9
Less than 1/2 tuition	182	20.6	163	22.5	19	12.2
Half to full tuition	144	16.3	136	18.7	8	5.1
Full tuition	28	3.2	27	3.7	1	0.6
More than full tuition	1	0.1	1	0.1	0	0.0
Median grant amount			$16,600		$10,125	

Informational and Library Resources

Total amount spent on library materials	$1,266,406
Study seating capacity inside the library	366
# of full-time equivalent professional librarians	1
Hours per week library is open	106
# of open, wired connections available to students	40
# of networked computers available for use by students	74
Has wireless network?	Y
Requires computer?	N

JD Attrition (from prior year)

	Academic	Other	Total	
	#	#	#	%
1st year	12	21	33	10.1
2nd year	3	1	4	1.7
3rd year	1	0	1	0.3
4th year	0	0	0	0.0

Employment (9 months after graduation)

	Total	Percentage
Employment status known	226	91.5
Employment status unknown	21	8.5
Employed	193	85.4
Pursuing graduate degrees	20	8.8
Unemployed (seeking, not seeking, or studying for the bar)	0	0.0
Type of Employment		
# employed in law firms	105	54.4
# employed in business and industry	25	13.0
# employed in government	30	15.5
# employed in public interest	4	2.1
# employed as judicial clerks	27	14.0
# employed in academia	2	1.0
Geographic Location		
# employed in state	151	78.2
# employed outside the US	0	0.0
# of states where employed		21

Bar Passage Rates

First-time takers	249	Reporting %	72.69
Average school %	70.17	Average state %	73.73
Average pass difference	−3.56		

Jurisdiction	Takers	Passers	Pass %	State %	Diff %
Louisiana	181	127	70.17	73.73	−3.56

LOYOLA UNIVERSITY NEW ORLEANS COLLEGE OF LAW

7214 St. Charles Avenue, Box 904
New Orleans, LA 70118
Phone: 504.861.5575; Fax: 504.861.5772
E-mail: ladmit@loyno.edu; Website: http://law.loyno.edu/

Introduction

It is a rare combination of wide-ranging programs of study, real-life opportunities, and a commitment to the community that makes Loyola University New Orleans College of Law stand apart. It is an institution that trains lawyers to think critically and be advocates for social justice. The entire Loyola law school community provides an atmosphere for our students to excel, succeed, and become productive members of legal communities across the country. It is a school where students have the opportunity to learn from a prestigious faculty, participate in many extracurricular activities to hone their practical lawyering skills, and serve the New Orleans community through our many clinical offerings.

Loyola New Orleans is a Catholic institution of higher learning in the Jesuit tradition. The College of Law was established in 1914, approved by the ABA in 1931, and has been a member of the AALS since 1934. The College of Law is committed to excellence in legal education in the tradition of its spiritual heritage, with the goal being wisdom, not mere technical competence. The law school welcomes all persons who strive for the truth and who are prepared to challenge all assumptions in light of this commitment.

Physical Facilities and Library

Loyola University has two campuses, both located approximately five miles from the historic French Quarter. The 20-acre main campus, in the heart of the uptown residential community, faces the nationally recognized Audubon Park and Zoo. The 4.2-acre Broadway campus is the home of the College of Law, including the new 16,000-square-foot wing that was dedicated in April 2007, providing more classroom, office, and library space. Renovation of the new home of our clinic offices and Office of Career Services will be completed in 2011.

The law library's collection of 385,000 volumes and microform equivalents supports the curriculum and research needs of the students. In addition to conventional resources, the library has extensive computer facilities in place to access information outside its confines. The Online Catalog Library Center service permits the library to access a national bibliographic database of over 10 million publications. The law library houses two computer labs equipped with 59 personal computers on a network with access to the Internet, LexisNexis, Westlaw, e-mail, and other computer resources; remote-controlled viewing/listening rooms; and a computerized legal research room.

Curriculum and Special Programs

The curricula at Loyola New Orleans have been shaped by Louisiana's unique role as the only state in the union that has a legal system based on significant elements of both the civil law and common law traditions. The civil law was imported into Louisiana during the eighteenth century, when it was first a colony of France, and later, Spain. As a result of Louisiana's unique legal heritage, Loyola New Orleans has developed three separate curricula: two full-time divisions—civil law and common law; and a part-time civil law division. It is important to note that the Loyola New Orleans JD degree will allow a

graduate to sit for the bar in any of the 50 states, without regard for the curriculum chosen. Loyola offers a Certificate in Common Law Studies and a Certificate in Civil Law Studies for students who wish to acquire a foundation in both disciplines. Full-time students are required to be in residence for a minimum of six full semesters. The normal time frame for part-time students is eight semesters and one summer session. At the graduate level, the law school offers an LLM for International Students for graduates of non-US law schools.

Practical Lawyering Skills Program—Loyola has one of the most unique and far-reaching professional lawyering skills programs in the country. Recognizing hands-on, learn-by-doing opportunities that develop the future practitioner's skills to be as important as traditional academic studies, the curriculum incorporates specialized courses and the expertise of attorneys and judges. Currently, over 100 members of the bench and bar teach in the skills curriculum. Skills courses are offered tuition-free, and students are required to complete eight skills credits but may complete as many above those required as they choose.

International Law—Loyola has summer sessions on four continents and in six countries, established ties with a number of important foreign law schools, sent its professors to teach or lecture at law schools in more than a dozen foreign countries, and hosted lectures by a number of professors from non-US law schools. Summer courses are taught in special five-week, summer-abroad sessions in Mexico and Eastern Europe (Russia, Hungary, and Austria). There are also two- and three-week sessions offered each summer in Brazil or Costa Rica. Students may obtain a Certificate in International Legal Studies. There are also seminar courses that have short trips abroad to Austria, Italy, and Turkey.

Public Interest Law—As part of Loyola's Jesuit commitment to social justice, the law school provides many courses and activities as part of this specialty, including the very active Law Clinic and Center for Social Justice. Most of the public interest focus falls under the umbrella of the Gillis Long Poverty Law Center. A loan forgiveness program is available for graduates working in eligible public interest employment.

Environmental Law—Loyola received a $2 million grant to establish a faculty chair for environmental law. A nationally renowned scholar was hired to head the Loyola Center for Environmental Law and Land Use. The center was created to address legal issues relative to economic development, environmental protection, and the public's role in environmental policy issues. A certificate in environmental law was established as part of this specialty.

Tax Law—Loyola recently established a certificate program designed to certify students in this area of law and assist those students who may choose to pursue an LLM in tax upon graduation.

Other Areas of Significant Emphasis—Other areas of significant emphasis include corporate law and maritime law.

Clinical Education—The law clinic is a vital component of the law school. Students chosen to participate in the senior-year program will be assigned cases, both civil and criminal, and will be expected to prepare them for trial prior to actually participating in the trial process. The areas of law practiced in the clinic are criminal (both prosecution and defense), immigration, family law, civil rights, and landlord/tenant. Additionally, the Katrina clinic and construction fraud mediation clinic give our students special opportunities to help our community. Upper-division students also have an opportunity to serve as judicial clerks in the federal extern program.

Joint-Degree Programs—Loyola offers three combined degrees: JD/Master of Business Administration, JD/Master of Public Administration, and JD/Master of Urban and Regional Planning.

Scholarly Publications and Student Activities

The *Loyola Law Review* is published by a student editorial board and includes student work and articles written by specialists from the practicing bar and academic community. Staff membership is based on scholarship and interest in legal writing.

The *Loyola University New Orleans Journal of Public Interest Law* is devoted to issues faced by the poor, children, the elderly, and all others who are unable to afford legal representation.

The *Loyola Intellectual Property and High Technology Law Annual* is a scholarly publication focusing on current legal issues in patents, copyrights, trademarks, and technology law.

The *Loyola Maritime Law Journal* provides an avenue for research and writing in the field of maritime law. Staff membership is based on scholarship.

The Moot Court Board, selected from prior years' competitions, is responsible for the Moot Court Program. Teams are entered each year in competitions. Loyola teams have an impressive winning record in a wide variety of local, regional, national, and international competitions.

There are a number of student organizations, including but not limited to three legal fraternities as well as the Intellectual Property Law Society, Sports and Entertainment Law Society, and the Health Care Law Society.

Admission

The law school begins processing applications for admission on September 1 each year. The first decision letters are generally released in December. The admission decision is based on an initial evaluation of a combination of the LSAT score and the undergraduate cumulative grade-point average. Additionally, the undergraduate institution attended, the undergraduate major, and any grade trends will be taken into consideration. Also included in the evaluation will be the required personal statement, letters of recommendation, and résumés, all of which may present a more illuminating portrait of the applicant's skills and accomplishments. Competition for acceptance to the law school is high, thus all information provided is used to make the final admission decision.

Career Services

The College of Law Office of Career Services offers a variety of services to both students and alumni. The office maintains and operates a career-planning center, assists students in preparing résumés, videotapes mock interviews, and conducts seminars on career planning, employment opportunities, and interviewing techniques. The office actively solicits job opportunities for summer and school-term clerkships, as well as employment options for each year's graduating class.

APPLICANT PROFILE

Loyola University New Orleans College of Law
This grid includes only applicants who earned 120–180 LSAT scores under standard administrations.

LSAT Score	GPA								
	3.75 +	3.50–3.74	3.25–3.49	3.00–3.24	2.75–2.99	2.50–2.74	2.25–2.49	2.00–2.24	Below 2.00
175–180									
170–174									
165–169									
160–164									
155–159									
150–154									
145–149									
140–144									
135–139									
130–134									
125–129									
120–124									

■ Excellent   ▨ Possible   □ Unlikely

The College of Law considers many factors beyond LSAT score and GPA. This chart should be used only as a general guide.

UNIVERSITY OF MAINE SCHOOL OF LAW

246 Deering Avenue
Portland, ME 04102
Phone: 207.780.4341; Fax: 207.780.4018
E-mail: mainelaw@usm.maine.edu; Website: http://mainelaw.maine.edu

The Basics

Type of school	Public
Term	Semester
Application deadline	3/1
Application fee	$50
Financial aid deadline	2/15
Can first year start other than fall?	No
Student to faculty ratio	15.0 to 1
# of housing spaces available restricted to law students	
graduate housing for which law students are eligible	275

Faculty and Administrators

	Total		Men		Women		Minorities	
	Spr	Fall	Spr	Fall	Spr	Fall	Spr	Fall
Full-time	16	14	11	9	5	5	0	0
Other full-time	1	2	1	1	0	1	0	0
Deans, librarians, & others who teach	7	7	3	3	4	4	0	0
Part-time	14	12	10	10	4	2	0	0
Total	38	35	25	23	13	12	0	0

Curriculum

	Full-Time	Part-Time
Typical first-year section size	96	0
Is there typically a "small section" of the first-year class, other than Legal Writing, taught by full-time faculty	Yes	No
If yes, typical size offered last year	46	
# of classroom course titles beyond first-year curriculum	80	

# of upper division courses, excluding seminars, with an enrollment:		
Under 25	26	
25–49	15	
50–74	4	
75–99	1	
100+	0	

# of seminars	24	
# of seminar positions available	375	
# of seminar positions filled	196	0
# of positions available in simulation courses	144	
# of simulation positions filled	117	0
# of positions available in faculty supervised clinical courses	56	
# of faculty supervised clinical positions filled	56	0
# involved in field placements	25	0
# involved in law journals	49	0
# involved in moot court or trial competitions	24	0
# of credit hours required to graduate	90	

JD Enrollment and Ethnicity

	Men		Women		Full-Time		Part-Time		1st-Year		Total		JD Degs. Awd.
	#	%	#	%	#	%	#	%	#	%	#	%	
All Hispanics	6	4.1	4	3.1	10	3.6	0	0.0	3	3.2	10	3.6	0
Am. Ind./AK Nat.	3	2.0	1	0.8	4	1.4	0	0.0	0	0.0	4	1.4	0
Asian	2	1.4	0	0.0	2	0.7	0	0.0	0	0.0	2	0.7	1
Black/Af. Am.	0	0.0	6	4.6	6	2.2	0	0.0	1	1.1	6	2.2	0
Nat. HI/Pac. Isl.	0	0.0	6	4.6	6	2.2	0	0.0	2	2.1	6	2.2	0
2 or more races	0	0.0	0	0.0	0	0.0	0	0.0	0	0.0	0	0.0	0
Subtotal (minor.)	11	7.4	17	13.1	28	10.1	0	0.0	6	6.3	28	10.1	1
Nonres. Alien	1	0.7	2	1.5	3	1.1	0	0.0	0	0.0	3	1.1	0
White/Cauc.	136	91.9	111	85.4	247	88.8	0	0.0	89	93.7	247	88.8	81
Unknown	0	0.0	0	0.0	0	0.0	0	0.0	0	0.0	0	0.0	0
Total	148	53.2	130	46.8	278	100.0	0	0.0	95	34.2	278		82

Transfers

Transfers in	4
Transfers out	0

Tuition and Fees

	Resident	Nonresident
Full-time	$21,994	$32,824

Part-time		
Tuition Guarantee Program		N

Living Expenses

Estimated living expenses for singles

Living on campus	Living off campus	Living at home
$16,024	$16,024	$7,636

UNIVERSITY OF MAINE SCHOOL OF LAW

ABA
Approved
Since
1962

GPA and LSAT Scores

	Total	Full-Time	Part-Time
# of apps	1,171	1,171	0
# of offers	446	446	0
# of matrics	95	95	0
75% GPA	3.62	3.62	0.00
Median GPA	3.41	3.41	0.00
25% GPA	3.18	3.18	0.00
75% LSAT	159	159	0
Median LSAT	156	156	0
25% LSAT	153	153	0

Grants and Scholarships (from prior year)

	Total #	Total %	Full-Time #	Full-Time %	Part-Time #	Part-Time %
Total # of students	264		264		0	
Total # receiving grants	85	32.2	85	32.2	0	0.0
Less than 1/2 tuition	73	27.7	73	27.7	0	0.0
Half to full tuition	5	1.9	5	1.9	0	0.0
Full tuition	7	2.7	7	2.7	0	0.0
More than full tuition	0	0.0	0	0.0	0	0.0
Median grant amount			$3,751		$0	

Informational and Library Resources

Total amount spent on library materials	$626,438
Study seating capacity inside the library	237
# of full-time equivalent professional librarians	6
Hours per week library is open	97
# of open, wired connections available to students	0
# of networked computers available for use by students	12
Has wireless network?	Y
Requires computer?	N

JD Attrition (from prior year)

	Academic #	Other #	Total #	Total %
1st year	1	5	6	6.7
2nd year	1	0	1	1.1
3rd year	0	0	0	0.0
4th year	0	0	0	0.0

Employment (9 months after graduation)

	Total	Percentage
Employment status known	93	100.0
Employment status unknown	0	0.0
Employed	73	78.5
Pursuing graduate degrees	6	6.5
Unemployed (seeking, not seeking, or studying for the bar)	13	14.0
Type of Employment		
# employed in law firms	33	45.2
# employed in business and industry	18	24.7
# employed in government	9	12.3
# employed in public interest	6	8.2
# employed as judicial clerks	5	6.8
# employed in academia	2	2.7
Geographic Location		
# employed in state	51	69.9
# employed outside the US	0	0.0
# of states where employed	10	

Bar Passage Rates

First-time takers	81	Reporting %	83.95
Average school %	82.35	Average state %	82.49

Average pass difference –0.14

Jurisdiction	Takers	Passers	Pass %	State %	Diff %
Maine	68	56	82.35	82.49	–0.14

The information on these pages was provided by the law school.

UNIVERSITY OF MAINE SCHOOL OF LAW

246 Deering Avenue
Portland, ME 04102
Phone: 207.780.4341; Fax: 207.780.4018
E-mail: mainelaw@usm.maine.edu; Website: http://mainelaw.maine.edu

Introduction

Maine Law is a vibrant and distinctive place to study law. Students study law in a supportive and personalized environment and are prepared for success in today's global economy.

Maine Law holds a pivotal place in state and regional affairs and is a destination point for students, scholars, and civic leaders from near and far. The state's only law school, and one of the smallest in the nation, Maine Law fosters educational and scholarly excellence, professionalism, and public service through a close community of faculty members and students. Our location in the vibrant coastal city of Portland, Maine—the largest city in the state and two hours north of Boston—allows students to benefit from a multitude of hands-on training opportunities offered through clinical programs, externships, community service projects, and employment. We have a tradition of training remarkably distinguished graduates—governors, federal and state judges, prominent lawyers, and civic leaders—who remain close to the law school. We are the law school of the University of Maine System and an administrative unit of the University of Southern Maine (USM).

Location

The law school is located in Portland, one of the most livable cities in the United States, and the largest city in Maine. It has the charm of a small town with the cultural activities of a large city. Opportunities to participate in year-round outdoor activities are abundant.

Faculty

Faculty members are well-regarded for their commitment to teaching, for their accessibility to students, and for their cutting-edge scholarship. They come from a variety of backgrounds and have extensive experience in private practice and public service. They make significant contributions to legislative, judicial, and professional institutions; community organizations; and policy and economic development initiatives. Their research spans matters of state, national, and international interest and examines topics as varied as international treaty practice, Maine tort law, coastal zone management, federal tax elections, constitutional controls over the military, intellectual property, and commercial practice.

Curriculum

Maine Law offers a broad-based curriculum that helps prepare students for practice in all states. The school's strengths are in business and commercial law, environmental and marine law, international law, intellectual property, clinical training, and trial advocacy. Ninety credit hours are required for graduation.

The first-year curriculum is a prescribed program consisting of courses that allow students to develop legal analytical skills as well as the ability to read and understand cases and statutory material. The program provides the foundation course in legal research and writing, including a moot court experience. Most courses after the first year are elective. All students are required to complete Professional Responsibility, Constitutional Law II, and a perspective course—one that places the law in a broader philosophical, historical, or comparative context. Each student must fulfill an upper-level writing requirement through a substantial research paper under the direction of a member of the faculty, through a seminar or independent study, or through membership on the *Maine Law Review* or *Ocean and Coastal Law Journal*. Maine Law's practical skills program includes courses in trial practice, negotiation, and alternative dispute resolution. The course in advanced trial advocacy has fielded award-winning teams.

Special Programs

Cumberland Legal Aid Clinic—Third-year students represent clients under faculty supervision in this approved legal assistance office. Students work on family law and domestic matters, juvenile justice, and criminal, consumer, housing, employment, and probate issues at both the trial and appellate levels. The clinic also provides representation for prisoners in a variety of civil matters. All clinical courses work with the state's domestic violence project.

Intellectual Property Law Clinic—Students have the rare opportunity to work with clients involved with developing new products and businesses. Under the supervision of intellectual property lawyers at the Center for Law and Innovation, students work directly with independent inventors, entrepreneurs, and research scientists engaged in technology transfer.

Externships—Students have access to numerous clinical externship opportunities, for academic credit, in many areas. Externships are available with government agencies and nonprofit organizations.

Center for Law and Innovation—The Center for Law and Innovation provides students with courses, conferences, and hands-on experiences to enhance their understanding of the role of law in the development of technological progress and innovation. In addition to offering courses in intellectual property and Internet law, the center provides summer-session technology law courses that bring distinguished scholars and practitioners to the school. Externship opportunities are available with the Maine Patent Program, a unique service program established by the Maine legislature to provide education and legal assistance regarding the patent process to Maine inventors, entrepreneurs, and businesses.

Marine Law Institute (MLI)—The MLI is an ocean and coastal law program that conducts research on laws and policies affecting ocean and coastal resources. The program also supports a student-edited journal and offers courses and seminars in coastal zone law, marine resources law, port security, law of the sea, and admiralty.

Pro Bono Program—The faculty has established a voluntary standard of 80 hours of pro bono legal service for each student during his or her three years of law school and has instituted a means of encouraging students to fulfill that standard while recognizing those who follow through with it.

Joint-Degree Programs—Maine Law and the University of Southern Maine offer the following joint-degree programs: JD/MCP in Community Planning and Development, JD/MS in

Health Policy and Management, JD/MA in Public Policy and Management with the Edmund S. Muskie School of Public Service, and a JD/MBA with the School of Business.

International-Exchange Programs—Semester-exchange programs are available with Dalhousie University Schulich School of Law, University of New Brunswick Faculty of Law, National University of Ireland, Université du Maine, and University of Buckingham.

Student Activities

The Student Bar Association performs the varied functions of student government and acts as an umbrella organization of other student organizations, such as the American Constitution Society, Animal Legal Defense Fund, Black Law Students Association, Business Law Association, Environmental Law Society, Federalist Society, Health Law Association, International Law Society, Latino/Latina Law Students Association, Lesbian/Gay/Bisexual Law Caucus, Maine Association for Public Interest Law, Maine Law and Technology Association, National Lawyers Guild, Native American Law Association, Prisoner Justice Project, Sports and Entertainment Law Society, and the Women's Law Association.

The *Maine Law Review* and the *Ocean and Coastal Law Journal* are scholarly journals managed, edited, and published by students. Students interested in developing written and oral advocacy skills participate in Moot Court and/or the Trial Advocacy Team.

Career Services

The Career Services Office provides a full range of services, including counseling; career resource materials; specific summer, full-time, part-time, and work-study job listings; and extensive on-campus recruiting. The small size of the law school ensures services tailored to meet the specific needs of its students. A number of workshops, speakers, and panel discussions throughout the year assist students in learning about the diverse opportunities available to them.

Expenses, Financial Aid, and Housing

Maine Law offers a reasonable tuition charge to both residents and nonresidents. The FAFSA priority deadline is February 15. A number of scholarships are available for entering students. Candidates for admission will automatically be considered for all scholarships for which they are eligible. There are no dorms for law students, however, there are plenty of rental properties situated around the law school. There is also a privately owned and operated student housing complex located less than five minutes from the law school. For tuition rates for the current year, please visit our website, www.mainelaw.maine.edu.

APPLICANT PROFILE

University of Maine School of Law
This grid includes only applicants who earned 120–180 LSAT scores under standard administrations.

LSAT Score	3.75 +		3.50–3.74		3.25–3.49		3.00–3.24		2.75–2.99		2.50–2.74		2.25–2.49		2.00–2.24		Below 2.00		No GPA		Total	
	Apps	Adm	Apps	Adm	Apps	Adm	Apps	Adm	Apps	Adm	Apps	Adm	Apps	Adm	Apps	Adm	Apps	Adm	Apps	Adm	Apps	Adm
175–180	0	0	1	1	0	0	0	0	0	0	0	0	0	0	0	0	0	0	0	0	1	1
170–174	0	0	1	1	2	2	0	0	0	0	0	0	0	0	0	0	0	0	0	0	3	3
165–169	5	5	4	4	6	6	7	7	2	1	5	5	2	1	0	0	1	0	1	1	33	30
160–164	16	15	28	26	25	22	16	13	10	5	13	4	0	0	0	0	2	0	0	0	110	85
155–159	20	18	70	62	67	54	62	42	54	18	23	6	9	2	3	0	0	0	0	0	308	202
150–154	27	20	76	35	91	24	86	18	57	4	29	2	4	0	3	0	1	0	5	1	379	104
145–149	12	3	41	7	62	7	54	2	42	0	22	1	3	0	2	0	1	0	12	0	251	20
140–144	2	0	6	0	14	0	9	0	11	0	6	0	6	0	0	0	0	0	2	0	56	0
135–139	0	0	0	0	2	0	2	0	3	0	2	0	1	0	1	0	0	0	2	0	13	0
130–134	1	0	0	0	0	0	1	0	0	0	2	0	0	0	0	0	0	0	1	0	5	0
125–129	0	0	0	0	0	0	0	0	0	0	2	0	0	0	0	0	0	0	0	0	2	0
120–124	0	0	0	0	0	0	0	0	0	0	1	0	0	0	0	0	0	0	0	0	1	0
Total	83	61	227	136	269	115	237	82	179	28	105	18	25	3	9	0	5	0	23	2	1162	445

Apps = Number of Applicants
Adm = Number Admitted
Reflects 99% of the total applicant pool; highest LSAT data reported.

MARQUETTE UNIVERSITY LAW SCHOOL

Office of Admissions, PO Box 1881, 1215 West Michigan Street
Milwaukee, WI 53201-1881
Phone: 414.288.6767; Fax: 414.288.0676
E-mail: law.admission@marquette.edu; Website: http://law.marquette.edu

ABA
Approved
Since
1925

The Basics

Type of school	Private	
Term	Semester	
Application deadline	4/1	6/1
Application fee	$50	
Financial aid deadline	3/1	
Can first year start other than fall?	No	
Student to faculty ratio	16.7 to 1	
# of housing spaces available restricted to law students		
graduate housing for which law students are eligible		

Faculty and Administrators

	Total		Men		Women		Minorities	
	Spr	Fall	Spr	Fall	Spr	Fall	Spr	Fall
Full-time	35	33	21	20	14	13	5	5
Other full-time	6	6	0	0	6	6	0	0
Deans, librarians, & others who teach	11	10	4	3	7	7	1	1
Part-time	42	30	30	21	12	9	5	3
Total	94	79	55	44	39	35	11	9

Curriculum

	Full-Time	Part-Time
Typical first-year section size	80	35
Is there typically a "small section" of the first-year class, other than Legal Writing, taught by full-time faculty	Yes	Yes
If yes, typical size offered last year	46	35
# of classroom course titles beyond first-year curriculum	155	
# of upper division courses, excluding seminars, with an enrollment: Under 25	95	
25–49	45	
50–74	12	
75–99	7	
100+	0	
# of seminars	28	
# of seminar positions available	420	
# of seminar positions filled	259	76
# of positions available in simulation courses	544	
# of simulation positions filled	397	117
# of positions available in faculty supervised clinical courses	77	
# of faculty supervised clinical positions filled	54	16
# involved in field placements	196	58
# involved in law journals	104	31
# involved in moot court or trial competitions	22	6
# of credit hours required to graduate	90	

JD Enrollment and Ethnicity

	Men		Women		Full-Time		Part-Time		1st-Year		Total		JD Degs. Awd.
	#	%	#	%	#	%	#	%	#	%	#	%	
All Hispanics	28	6.5	17	5.2	39	6.7	6	3.5	14	5.5	45	5.9	9
Am. Ind./AK Nat.	4	0.9	2	0.6	4	0.7	2	1.2	1	0.4	6	0.8	2
Asian	14	3.2	11	3.4	15	2.6	10	5.8	7	2.7	25	3.3	8
Black/Af. Am.	13	3.0	24	7.3	31	5.3	6	3.5	14	5.5	37	4.9	13
Nat. HI/Pac. Isl.	0	0.0	0	0.0	0	0.0	0	0.0	0	0.0	0	0.0	0
2 or more races	0	0.0	0	0.0	0	0.0	0	0.0	0	0.0	0	0.0	0
Subtotal (minor.)	59	13.7	54	16.5	89	15.2	24	13.9	36	14.1	113	14.9	32
Nonres. Alien	0	0.0	2	0.6	1	0.2	1	0.6	0	0.0	2	0.3	0
White/Cauc.	370	85.8	271	82.9	493	84.3	148	85.5	218	85.5	641	84.6	201
Unknown	2	0.5	0	0.0	2	0.3	0	0.0	1	0.4	2	0.3	1
Total	431	56.9	327	43.1	585	77.2	173	22.8	255	33.6	758		234

Transfers

Transfers in	23
Transfers out	7

Tuition and Fees

	Resident	Nonresident
Full-time	$36,300	$36,300
Part-time	$21,750	$21,750
Tuition Guarantee Program		N

Living Expenses

Estimated living expenses for singles

Living on campus	Living off campus	Living at home
$18,890	$18,890	$18,890

ABA Approved Since 1925

GPA and LSAT Scores

	Total	Full-Time	Part-Time
# of apps	2,282	2,054	228
# of offers	957	905	52
# of matrics	247	208	39
75% GPA	3.64	3.64	3.63
Median GPA	3.46	3.46	3.30
25% GPA	3.14	3.14	3.05
75% LSAT	159	159	160
Median LSAT	157	157	157
25% LSAT	154	154	153

Grants and Scholarships (from prior year)

	Total		Full-Time		Part-Time	
	#	%	#	%	#	%
Total # of students	743		563		180	
Total # receiving grants	302	40.6	247	43.9	55	30.6
Less than 1/2 tuition	228	30.7	178	31.6	50	27.8
Half to full tuition	61	8.2	58	10.3	3	1.7
Full tuition	9	1.2	8	1.4	1	0.6
More than full tuition	4	0.5	3	0.5	1	0.6
Median grant amount			$8,000		$4,000	

Informational and Library Resources

Total amount spent on library materials	$1,450,968
Study seating capacity inside the library	150
# of full-time equivalent professional librarians	9
Hours per week library is open	113
# of open, wired connections available to students	92
# of networked computers available for use by students	63
Has wireless network?	Y
Requires computer?	N

JD Attrition (from prior year)

	Academic	Other	Total	
	#	#	#	%
1st year	2	14	16	7.3
2nd year	1	3	4	1.8
3rd year	2	0	2	0.8
4th year	0	0	0	0.0

Employment (9 months after graduation)

	Total	Percentage
Employment status known	209	98.6
Employment status unknown	3	1.4
Employed	184	88.0
Pursuing graduate degrees	6	2.9
Unemployed (seeking, not seeking, or studying for the bar)	16	7.7
Type of Employment		
# employed in law firms	115	62.5
# employed in business and industry	25	13.6
# employed in government	14	7.6
# employed in public interest	11	6.0
# employed as judicial clerks	11	6.0
# employed in academia	8	4.3
Geographic Location		
# employed in state	141	76.6
# employed outside the US	1	0.5
# of states where employed	17	

Bar Passage Rates

First-time takers	212	Reporting %	100.00
Average school %	100.00	Average state %	90.80
Average pass difference	9.20		

Jurisdiction	Takers	Passers	Pass %	State %	Diff %
Wisconsin	212	212	100.00	90.80	9.20

MARQUETTE UNIVERSITY LAW SCHOOL

The information on these pages was provided by the law school.

Office of Admissions, PO Box 1881, 1215 West Michigan Street
Milwaukee, WI 53201-1881
Phone: 414.288.6767; Fax: 414.288.0676
E-mail: law.admission@marquette.edu; Website: http://law.marquette.edu

Introduction

For more than a century, Marquette University Law School has been committed to training men and women to serve the public interest by becoming highly skilled and ethical attorneys. Traditionally, the curriculum has emphasized the practical aspects of legal education. In recent years, that emphasis has expanded to include particular excellence in the areas of intellectual property, dispute resolution, sports law, labor and employment law, criminal law, family law, and litigation-related courses. The National Sports Law Institute, the premier sports law program in the United States, is a part of the Law School. Our nearly 7,000 alumni serve in a broad range of legal, public, and corporate positions throughout the US.

The Law School is located on the university campus—two blocks from the Milwaukee County Courthouse and a short walk from the federal courthouse and downtown Milwaukee. Marquette is the only law school in southeast Wisconsin. Marquette—a Catholic, Jesuit, and urban university—is the largest private university in the state. The Catholic and Jesuit nature of the school translates into a specific concern for the well-being of each individual, whether he or she is a student, a legal client, or the victim of a crime. Persons of all religious backgrounds attend Marquette, serve on our faculty, and are valued in our community. The Law School is committed to academic freedom, the broadest possible scope of inquiry, and the examination of any subject.

Milwaukee is a lively city on Lake Michigan, 90 miles north of Chicago. Wisconsin's largest city, with a metropolitan-area population of about 1.5 million, Milwaukee retains the appeal of a small town. Clean and well run, it is known for its many ethnic festivals and the variety of its cuisine.

Enrollment/Student Body

Within the Marquette Law School community, people know and care about one another. Our students come together from nearly 220 different colleges and universities, and hail from almost 40 different states, as well as from a handful of foreign countries. Our faculty includes 40 full-time professors in addition to prominent practicing attorneys and judges who serve as adjunct professors.

Law students at Marquette represent a broad range of backgrounds, beliefs, and life experiences. Our minority enrollment is about 15 percent of the student body. We respect our different traditions and believe diversity enriches the legal education we offer.

Library and Physical Facilities

In summer 2010, the Law School moved into an entirely new structure, Eckstein Hall. This state-of-the-art "green" building is roughly twice the size of the former facility. Eckstein Hall features the latest technology and houses a full-service café, a conference center, a fitness center, and two courtrooms. For more information on the Law School's new home, including the path-breaking four-level "library without borders," please visit www.marquette.edu/law.

Curriculum

The Law School offers full- and part-time programs leading to the JD degree. The Law School's curriculum is rooted in core courses that include consideration of the theoretical underpinnings of the law as well as the practical application of substantive legal concepts. The curriculum is national in focus and scope and emphasizes the skills and values necessary to be a competent and ethical lawyer as well as a contributing citizen and community leader. Our adjunct faculty includes many of the state's outstanding practitioners who supplement required and core courses by teaching a broad range of electives.

Students may earn a **JD/MBA** through the Law School and the College of Business Administration; of special note is the JD/MBA with a **sports business** concentration. Joint programs with the graduate school allow students to earn a **JD/MA** in **international affairs**, the **history of philosophy**, **social and applied philosophy**, or **political science**. The Law School offers a joint program with Marquette University's graduate program in dispute resolution that allows a student to graduate with a **JD** and a **certificate in dispute resolution**. In conjunction with the Medical College of Wisconsin, we offer the **JD/MA** in **bioethics**. Each joint-degree program requires meeting all requirements of both the Law School and the other degree-granting institution; typically, each program can be completed in four years. As an alternative to a joint degree, law students may take up to six hours of coursework in a related graduate program at Marquette, such as public policy, sociology, philosophy, or history.

Special Programs

Our comprehensive trial practice courses provide an exceptional opportunity for students to develop trial skills. Distinctive clinics include the prosecutor and defender clinics, judicial internships, and numerous supervised field work opportunities.

Marquette University Law School's sports law program provides a comprehensive offering of sports law courses and student internships with sports organizations, as well as opportunities for membership on the Marquette Sports Law Review and the sports law moot court team. Our broad, well-rounded curriculum is designed to provide students with both theoretical and practical education concerning legal regulation of the amateur and professional sports industries. Law students who fulfill certain requirements are eligible to earn a **sports law certificate** in addition to the JD. More information on the program and the certificate may be found at http://law.marquette.edu/jw/sports.

The Law School's Restorative Justice Initiative (RJI) gives law students the opportunity to work with victims of crime, offenders, and community members toward repairing the harm that crime has caused. More information on the RJI may be found at http://law.marquette.edu/jw/restorative.

Admission and Financial Aid

Review of completed applications begins after October 1 and continues through the spring. Although the applicant's LSAT score and academic record are important considerations in the selection process, the Admissions Committee also considers qualitative factors, such as letters of recommendation, essays, work experience, extracurricular activities, and personal accomplishments and characteristics that contribute to the diversity of the school, the legal community, and the profession. Admitted applicants are required to submit nonrefundable tuition deposits in April and June. These deposits are applied to the student's fall semester tuition. Interviews are not part of the application process.

Although most students finance their educations through a combination of loan programs, all applicants offered admission are considered for available merit scholarship awards. Additionally, the Law School has established a Loan Repayment Assistance Program (LRAP) to help graduates in government service or public interest practice repay the cost of their educational loans. More information on LRAP may be found at http://law.marquette.edu/jw/lrap.

Diploma Privilege

Since 1933, graduates of the Law School who qualify have been admitted to the practice of law in Wisconsin without having to take the Wisconsin Bar Examination. Marquette graduates are entitled to sit for bar examinations in any American jurisdiction.

Student Activities

The Law School publishes the *Marquette Law Review*, the *Marquette Sports Law Review*, the *Marquette Intellectual Property Law Review*, and the *Marquette Elder's Advisor* (elder law journal). Students may develop advocacy skills in moot court competitions. Marquette moot court teams have won regional titles and championships in national competitions. A wide variety of student organizations are active at the Law School. A listing of student groups and descriptions of their activities may be found on the Law School's website.

Career Services

The Career Planning Center (CPC) processes hundreds of listings of employment opportunities, coordinates campus interviews, and provides counseling assistance to students—helping them to assess career options, tailor job search strategies, and navigate the competitive job market in a personal way. The CPC will help students network with Marquette alumni and other potential resource persons. The Law School's employment rate consistently exceeds the national average. Our goals are to keep our placement rate high and to ensure a good fit and job satisfaction for all our graduates.

Housing

Ample, affordable housing is available throughout Milwaukee and its suburbs. Information and assistance on securing housing may be obtained from the Office of University Apartments and Off-Campus Student Services; telephone: 414.288.7281, web: www.marquette.edu/orl/apartments/services.shtml.

APPLICANT PROFILE

Marquette University Law School
This grid includes only applicants who earned 120–180 LSAT scores under standard administrations.

LSAT Score	3.75 +		3.50–3.74		3.25–3.49		3.00–3.24		2.75–2.99		2.50–2.74		2.25–2.49		2.00–2.24		Below 2.00		No GPA		Total	
	Apps	Adm	Apps	Adm	Apps	Adm	Apps	Adm	Apps	Adm	Apps	Adm	Apps	Adm	Apps	Adm	Apps	Adm	Apps	Adm	Apps	Adm
175–180	0	0	0	0	0	0	0	0	0	0	0	0	0	0	0	0	0	0	0	0	0	0
170–174	2	2	2	2	4	4	1	1	5	5	0	0	1	0	0	0	0	0	0	0	15	14
165–169	8	7	6	6	12	11	12	11	10	8	3	2	5	2	1	0	1	0	1	1	59	48
160–164	44	42	74	67	75	65	48	40	36	22	30	16	16	1	3	1	2	0	1	1	329	255
155–159	94	86	172	143	173	103	139	70	109	42	31	4	12	1	8	0	3	0	7	4	748	453
150–154	78	36	145	69	179	34	122	10	82	12	42	5	16	1	6	0	1	0	4	3	675	170
145–149	16	2	31	3	56	5	74	5	38	1	26	1	13	1	9	0	0	0	5	0	268	18
140–144	6	0	11	0	19	0	34	0	24	0	10	0	12	0	4	0	0	0	1	0	121	0
135–139	4	0	1	0	3	0	7	0	8	0	6	0	7	0	1	0	1	0	5	0	43	0
130–134	0	0	3	0	2	0	7	0	7	0	2	0	3	0	3	0	1	0	0	0	28	0
125–129	0	0	1	0	1	0	1	0	0	0	0	0	0	0	1	0	0	0	2	0	6	0
120–124	0	0	0	0	0	0	0	0	0	0	0	0	0	0	0	0	0	0	0	0	0	0
Total	252	175	446	290	524	222	445	137	319	90	150	28	85	6	36	1	9	0	26	9	2292	958

Apps = Number of Applicants
Adm = Number Admitted
Reflects 100% of the total applicant pool; highest LSAT data reported.

UNIVERSITY OF MARYLAND SCHOOL OF LAW

500 West Baltimore Street
Baltimore, MD 21201-1786
Phone: 410.706.3492; Fax: 410.706.1793
E-mail: admissions@law.umaryland.edu; Website: www.law.umaryland.edu

ABA
Approved
Since
1930

The Basics

Type of school	Public
Term	Semester
Application deadline	4/1
Application fee	$70
Financial aid deadline	3/1
Can first year start other than fall?	No
Student to faculty ratio	11.2 to 1
# of housing spaces available restricted to law students	
graduate housing for which law students are eligible	425

Faculty and Administrators

	Total		Men		Women		Minorities	
	Spr	Fall	Spr	Fall	Spr	Fall	Spr	Fall
Full-time	65	62	30	30	35	32	15	13
Other full-time	1	1	0	0	1	1	0	0
Deans, librarians, & others who teach	13	13	5	5	8	8	3	3
Part-time	81	50	55	34	26	16	3	5
Total	160	126	90	69	70	57	21	21

Curriculum

	Full-Time	Part-Time
Typical first-year section size	78	74
Is there typically a "small section" of the first-year class, other than Legal Writing, taught by full-time faculty	Yes	Yes
If yes, typical size offered last year	26	25
# of classroom course titles beyond first-year curriculum	223	
# of upper division courses, excluding seminars, with an enrollment: Under 25	148	
25–49	35	
50–74	13	
75–99	2	
100+	2	
# of seminars	87	
# of seminar positions available	1,185	
# of seminar positions filled	859	166
# of positions available in simulation courses	706	
# of simulation positions filled	568	108
# of positions available in faculty supervised clinical courses	385	
# of faculty supervised clinical positions filled	351	20
# involved in field placements	230	25
# involved in law journals	184	12
# involved in moot court or trial competitions	75	2
# of credit hours required to graduate	85	

JD Enrollment and Ethnicity

	Men		Women		Full-Time		Part-Time		1st-Year		Total		JD Degs. Awd.
	#	%	#	%	#	%	#	%	#	%	#	%	
All Hispanics	36	7.2	45	9.7	70	9.5	11	4.7	32	10.8	81	8.4	22
Am. Ind./AK Nat.	2	0.4	1	0.2	1	0.1	2	0.9	0	0.0	3	0.3	2
Asian	46	9.1	44	9.5	63	8.6	27	11.6	27	9.1	90	9.3	36
Black/Af. Am.	38	7.6	65	14.0	71	9.7	32	13.7	27	9.1	103	10.7	36
Nat. Hl/Pac. Isl.	0	0.0	1	0.2	0	0.0	1	0.4	0	0.0	1	0.1	0
2 or more races	7	1.4	9	1.9	13	1.8	3	1.3	6	2.0	16	1.7	0
Subtotal (minor.)	129	25.6	165	35.6	218	29.7	76	32.6	92	31.1	294	30.4	102
Nonres. Alien	6	1.2	2	0.4	6	0.8	2	0.9	3	1.0	8	0.8	0
White/Cauc.	357	71.0	286	61.6	491	66.9	152	65.2	185	62.5	643	66.5	170
Unknown	11	2.2	11	2.4	19	2.6	3	1.3	16	5.4	22	2.3	3
Total	503	52.0	464	48.0	734	75.9	233	24.1	296	30.6	967		281

Transfers

Transfers in	24
Transfers out	16

Tuition and Fees

	Resident	Nonresident
Full-time	$25,350	$36,629
Part-time	$19,385	$27,844
Tuition Guarantee Program		N

Living Expenses

Estimated living expenses for singles

Living on campus	Living off campus	Living at home
$22,086	$27,756	$16,596

UNIVERSITY OF MARYLAND SCHOOL OF LAW

 ABA Approved Since 1930

GPA and LSAT Scores

	Total	Full-Time	Part-Time
# of apps	3,853	3,338	515
# of offers	683	552	131
# of matrics	296	223	73
75% GPA	3.70	3.68	3.62
Median GPA	3.50	3.51	3.40
25% GPA	3.30	3.34	3.24
75% LSAT	163	163	160
Median LSAT	161	161	157
25% LSAT	157	158	155

Grants and Scholarships (from prior year)

	Total		Full-Time		Part-Time	
	#	%	#	%	#	%
Total # of students	953		723		230	
Total # receiving grants	428	44.9	351	48.5	77	33.5
Less than 1/2 tuition	358	37.6	281	38.9	77	33.5
Half to full tuition	69	7.2	69	9.5	0	0.0
Full tuition	0	0.0	0	0.0	0	0.0
More than full tuition	1	0.1	1	0.1	0	0.0
Median grant amount			$4,000		$3,729	

Informational and Library Resources

Total amount spent on library materials	$1,496,298
Study seating capacity inside the library	509
# of full-time equivalent professional librarians	12
Hours per week library is open	107
# of open, wired connections available to students	1,209
# of networked computers available for use by students	193
Has wireless network?	Y
Requires computer?	Y

JD Attrition (from prior year)

	Academic	Other	Total	
	#	#	#	%
1st year	1	18	19	6.3
2nd year	0	2	2	0.6
3rd year	0	0	0	0.0
4th year	0	0	0	0.0

Employment (9 months after graduation)

	Total	Percentage
Employment status known	240	98.4
Employment status unknown	4	1.6
Employed	230	95.8
Pursuing graduate degrees	1	0.4
Unemployed (seeking, not seeking, or studying for the bar)	1	0.4
Type of Employment		
# employed in law firms	92	40.0
# employed in business and industry	43	18.7
# employed in government	32	13.9
# employed in public interest	10	4.3
# employed as judicial clerks	32	13.9
# employed in academia	21	9.1
Geographic Location		
# employed in state	153	66.5
# employed outside the US	3	1.3
# of states where employed	19	

Bar Passage Rates

First-time takers	234	Reporting %	77.35
Average school %	85.08	Average state %	78.20
Average pass difference	6.88		

Jurisdiction	Takers	Passers	Pass %	State %	Diff %
Maryland	181	154	85.08	78.20	6.88

UNIVERSITY OF MARYLAND SCHOOL OF LAW

500 West Baltimore Street
Baltimore, MD 21201-1786
Phone: 410.706.3492; Fax: 410.706.1793
E-mail: admissions@law.umaryland.edu; Website: www.law.umaryland.edu

Introduction

The University of Maryland School of Law was established in 1816, making it one of the oldest law schools in the nation. Currently, its innovative programs, renowned faculty, and superb student body make it one of the liveliest, most vibrant, and diverse law schools today.

Maryland School of Law offers a wide range of course offerings that incorporate cutting-edge legal issues into a well-established and nationally recognized legal curriculum. The law school offers a variety of highly regarded programs and initiatives, including environmental, health care, business, and international law. Additionally, Maryland has an institutional commitment to preparing students for career success, and a welcoming community dedicated to developing each student's talents fully. The law school is also committed to instilling a spirit of public service in all its students and provides unparalleled opportunities for experiential learning in pursuit of the public interest. The law school's new, state-of-the-art facility is ideally located in the Baltimore-Washington corridor, presenting a broad range of educational and career opportunities.

Maryland students are recruited by many of the nation's most respected law firms. They assume positions of leadership as lawyers and judges, business executives and community advocates, legislators and policymakers, and other agents of social, political, and economic progress.

Maryland School of Law is fully accredited by the ABA, is a member of the AALS, and has a chapter of the Order of the Coif.

Community of Students, Faculty, and Alumni

At Maryland, entering students quickly become part of a supportive community. We are diverse in age, gender, race, academic background, and prior employment, and this diversity is reflected in our students and in our faculty and deans. Our faculty are national leaders in a wide range of subject areas, and they are readily available to support and advise students. Smaller classes and an 11:1 student-to-faculty ratio enable close working relationships to develop in a professional and intellectually vibrant setting.

Many resources are available to students to ease their transition to law school. Students also directly benefit from a wide network of engaged alumni who occupy positions of professional leadership throughout the state, region, and nation. By acting as mentors, volunteer judges, and adjunct faculty, alumni help connect each student's law school experience with the professional life of the surrounding legal community.

Location

Maryland Law's location in the Baltimore-Washington corridor is among our greatest assets. Our state-of-the-art facility sits just a few blocks from Baltimore's beautiful Inner Harbor and Camden Yards, and—along with the rest of the burgeoning University of Maryland, Baltimore (UMB) campus—is playing a vital role in the city's downtown renaissance.

The law school is also a short commute from Capitol Hill and Maryland's capital in Annapolis, providing our students unique access to all levels of the federal and state government and judiciary. Students take full advantage of our proximity to Washington, DC, pursuing externships and careers with leading national law firms, public interest groups, government agencies, and other organizations of prominence.

Our proximity to the other professional schools on the UMB campus allows us to offer an array of interdisciplinary courses and joint-degree programs. These offerings produce sophisticated graduates who are prepared to practice in an environment of increasing complexity.

Law School Complex and Library

The School of Law and the Thurgood Marshall Law Library occupy a state-of-the-art complex that supports the school's programs integrating classroom and experiential learning. The facility boasts three courtrooms, including the Ceremonial Courtroom, where state and federal trial and appellate courts regularly sit in session to hear cases. Our classrooms and courtrooms are equipped with the latest in educational technology, as well as wired and wireless Internet access for student use. In addition to their own notebook computers, students can use public computers located throughout the facility for writing and research.

The Thurgood Marshall Law Library houses a collection of about 520,270 volumes and equivalents accessible through the online catalog. A staff of 26, including 12 librarians, provides customized reference and consulting services to faculty and students. In addition to LexisNexis and Westlaw, the library offers an extensive array of legal and nonlegal web-based electronic databases. Seating in the library includes carrels, tables in attractive reading rooms, and comfortable lounge areas, all located in spaces full of natural light.

Curriculum and Specialty Programs

The rigorous core curriculum at Maryland forms the basis for more specialized study through over 200 elective courses, seminars, independent studies, simulations, clinics, and externships. Also, each student must satisfy an advanced writing requirement by producing a substantial paper based on extensive research. Full-time students generally complete the Juris Doctor curriculum in three years; evening students typically complete the program in four years.

Maryland Law is home to several nationally recognized specialty programs. These programs are a magnet for leading faculty from across the country as they provide opportunities for in-depth scholarship and teaching. Three of our specialty programs—Law and Health Care, Environmental Law, and Clinical Law—have established national reputations for excellence. Our other specialty areas include Business Law; Intellectual Property Law; International and Comparative Law; and Women, Leadership, and Equality.

Regardless of what course of study they pursue, students can expect a challenging law school experience that will cultivate depth of understanding and clarity of thought, the hallmarks of the most successful lawyers.

Clinical Law Program

Through the Cardin Requirement, named after our alumnus US Senator Benjamin Cardin, each full-time day student gains hands-on legal experience by representing actual clients who would otherwise lack access to justice.

Our legal clinic is among the best and largest in the nation. In addition to in-house clinical work, students may gain experience in public and private nonprofit externships in the Baltimore-Washington region.

Dual Degrees and Interdisciplinary Study

Today's lawyer must practice in an environment of increasing sophistication. Maryland Law offers several dual-degree programs in partnership with other leading academic institutions in the region. Dual-degree programs include Business Administration, Community Planning, Criminal Justice, Ethics, Liberal Arts, Pharmacy, Public Policy, Public Health, Public Management, Nursing, and Social Work.

Admission

Maryland School of Law's faculty believe that the quality of legal education is directly affected by the diversity of our students. The admission committee selects applicants who have the greatest potential for succeeding in law school studies and whose background, character, and experience will contribute to the diversity that we believe is important.

The factors we consider in the admission file evaluation process include geographic origin, cultural and language background, barriers overcome, and extracurricular pursuits, work, leadership activities, and service or social experiences. The personal statement and letters of recommendation are the primary means for candidates to convey this information.

First-year students are admitted only in the fall. The School of Law uses a rolling admission process, reviewing applications in the order in which files are completed. Applications should be filed as early as possible after September 1 of the year preceding enrollment and before March 1. Applicants are encouraged to complete the application early; applications completed later may be at a competitive disadvantage. Residency may be a factor in close cases. Applicants are encouraged to visit the school, but interviews are not part of the admission process.

Student Activities

The law school is home to more than 40 active and diverse student-run organizations. Students enforce the law school's honor code, participate in inter- and intraschool advocacy competitions, and volunteer in the local community and in gulf regions affected by Hurricane Katrina. Students can further their writing and editing expertise by participating in one of the five student-edited scholarly journals or serving as a writing center fellow. The Office of Student Affairs provides group and one-on-one academic advising to students at all stages of their legal education, leadership education to student leaders, and financial literacy workshops for all interested students.

Scholarships and Need-Based Financial Assistance

The School of Law offers a number of scholarships and traditional need-based financial aid assistance. All applicants are considered for the scholarship program based on the totality of the information available in the applicant's admission file and evidence of potential unique contributions to the academic and cocurricular programs, as well as student life. Such potential should be clearly described in the personal statement, résumé, and other admission documents. All admitted applicants **must** file the FAFSA as soon after January 1 as possible in order to be considered for scholarships or need-based financial assistance.

Career Development

Students at Maryland benefit from extensive connections to the bar, judiciary, business and industry, government, and community organizations in Maryland; Washington, DC; and beyond. Our Career Development Office offers a multitude of expert services and professional resources to help students and alumni launch their legal careers.

In the most recent survey, 96 percent of our 2009 graduates whose employment status is known were employed, and 3 percent were pursuing advanced degrees or not seeking immediate employment. Graduates chose a variety of professional positions: 40 percent were in private practice, 19 percent in business and industry, 14 percent in judicial clerkships, 14 percent in government and other public service, 9 percent in academia, and 4 percent in public interest organizations.

APPLICANT PROFILE

The University of Maryland School of Law's admission policy focuses on the academic potential of applicants coupled with a flexible assessment of applicants' talents, experiences, and potential to contribute to the learning of those around them. Each applicant is evaluated on the basis of all the information available in his or her file, including UGPA, LSAT score, a personal statement, letters of recommendation, résumé, advanced degrees, professional accomplishments, and other related information.

THE UNIVERSITY OF MEMPHIS—CECIL C. HUMPHREYS SCHOOL OF LAW

One North Front Street
Memphis, TN 38103-2189
Phone: 901.678.5403; Fax: 901.678.0741
E-mail: lawadmissions@memphis.edu; Website: www.memphis.edu/law

ABA
Approved
Since
1965

The Basics

Type of school	Public
Term	Semester
Application deadline	3/1
Application fee	$25
Financial aid deadline	3/1
Can first year start other than fall?	No
Student to faculty ratio	18.1 to 1
# of housing spaces available restricted to law students	
graduate housing for which law students are eligible	125

Faculty and Administrators

	Total		Men		Women		Minorities	
	Spr	Fall	Spr	Fall	Spr	Fall	Spr	Fall
Full-time	20	18	12	12	8	6	19	18
Other full-time	1	0	0	0	1	0	1	0
Deans, librarians, & others who teach	3	3	2	2	1	1	3	3
Part-time	28	31	20	23	8	8	5	9
Total	52	52	34	37	18	15	28	30

Curriculum

	Full-Time	Part-Time
Typical first-year section size	75	0
Is there typically a "small section" of the first-year class, other than Legal Writing, taught by full-time faculty	No	No
If yes, typical size offered last year		
# of classroom course titles beyond first-year curriculum	75	
# of upper division courses, excluding seminars, with an enrollment: Under 25	44	
25–49	19	
50–74	17	
75–99	2	
100+	1	
# of seminars	9	
# of seminar positions available	108	
# of seminar positions filled	93	0
# of positions available in simulation courses	222	
# of simulation positions filled	196	0
# of positions available in faculty supervised clinical courses	42	
# of faculty supervised clinical positions filled	42	0
# involved in field placements	38	0
# involved in law journals	60	0
# involved in moot court or trial competitions	27	0
# of credit hours required to graduate	90	

JD Enrollment and Ethnicity

	Men		Women		Full-Time		Part-Time		1st-Year		Total		JD Degs. Awd.
	#	%	#	%	#	%	#	%	#	%	#	%	
All Hispanics	4	1.6	4	2.3	8	2.0	0	0.0	3	1.8	8	1.9	1
Am. Ind./AK Nat.	4	1.6	0	0.0	3	0.7	1	4.2	2	1.2	4	0.9	0
Asian	3	1.2	5	2.8	6	1.5	2	8.3	3	1.8	8	1.9	3
Black/Af. Am.	15	5.9	20	11.3	22	5.4	13	54.2	20	12.2	35	8.1	15
Nat. HI/Pac. Isl.	0	0.0	0	0.0	0	0.0	0	0.0	0	0.0	0	0.0	0
2 or more races	0	0.0	0	0.0	0	0.0	0	0.0	0	0.0	0	0.0	0
Subtotal (minor.)	26	10.2	29	16.4	39	9.6	16	66.7	28	17.1	55	12.7	19
Nonres. Alien	0	0.0	0	0.0	0	0.0	0	0.0	0	0.0	0	0.0	0
White/Cauc.	220	86.3	143	80.8	355	87.0	8	33.3	136	82.9	363	84.0	107
Unknown	9	3.5	5	2.8	14	3.4	0	0.0	0	0.0	14	3.2	2
Total	255	59.0	177	41.0	408	94.4	24	5.6	164	38.0	432		128

Transfers

Transfers in	4
Transfers out	1

Tuition and Fees

	Resident	Nonresident
Full-time	$14,298	$36,170
Part-time	$14,138	$36,010
Tuition Guarantee Program		N

Living Expenses

Estimated living expenses for singles

Living on campus	Living off campus	Living at home
$14,832	$14,832	$9,183

THE UNIVERSITY OF MEMPHIS—CECIL C. HUMPHREYS SCHOOL OF LAW

ABA
Approved
Since
1965

GPA and LSAT Scores

	Total	Full-Time	Part-Time
# of apps	964	964	0
# of offers	313	301	12
# of matrics	158	148	10
75% GPA	3.56	3.56	3.09
Median GPA	3.29	3.31	2.91
25% GPA	3.03	3.06	2.67
75% LSAT	157	158	152
Median LSAT	155	156	149
25% LSAT	153	154	145

Grants and Scholarships (from prior year)

	Total		Full-Time		Part-Time	
	#	%	#	%	#	%
Total # of students	420		392		28	
Total # receiving grants	114	27.1	110	28.1	4	14.3
Less than 1/2 tuition	39	9.3	35	8.9	4	14.3
Half to full tuition	66	15.7	66	16.8	0	0.0
Full tuition	8	1.9	8	2.0	0	0.0
More than full tuition	1	0.2	1	0.3	0	0.0
Median grant amount			$6,774		$4,466	

Informational and Library Resources

Total amount spent on library materials	$754,991
Study seating capacity inside the library	327
# of full-time equivalent professional librarians	3
Hours per week library is open	168
# of open, wired connections available to students	0
# of networked computers available for use by students	65
Has wireless network?	Y
Requires computer?	N

JD Attrition (from prior year)

	Academic	Other	Total	
	#	#	#	%
1st year	5	2	7	4.4
2nd year	7	2	9	7.0
3rd year	0	0	0	0.0
4th year	0	0	0	0.0

Employment (9 months after graduation)

	Total	Percentage
Employment status known	113	95.8
Employment status unknown	5	4.2
Employed	103	91.2
Pursuing graduate degrees	2	1.8
Unemployed (seeking, not seeking, or studying for the bar)	7	6.2
Type of Employment		
# employed in law firms	60	58.3
# employed in business and industry	12	11.7
# employed in government	14	13.6
# employed in public interest	4	3.9
# employed as judicial clerks	11	10.7
# employed in academia	1	1.0
Geographic Location		
# employed in state	87	84.5
# employed outside the US	0	0.0
# of states where employed	14	

Bar Passage Rates

First-time takers	119	Reporting %		92.44
Average school %	88.18	Average state %		82.44
Average pass difference	5.74			

Jurisdiction	Takers	Passers	Pass %	State %	Diff %
Tennessee	110	97	88.18	82.44	5.74

THE UNIVERSITY OF MEMPHIS—CECIL C. HUMPHREYS SCHOOL OF LAW

One North Front Street
Memphis, TN 38103-2189
Phone: 901.678.5403; Fax: 901.678.0741
E-mail: lawadmissions@memphis.edu; Website: www.memphis.edu/law

History of the School of Law

The Cecil C. Humphreys School of Law at the University of Memphis was established in response to widespread interest in developing a full-time accredited law program to serve Memphis and West Tennessee. The Cecil C. Humphreys School of Law opened in 1962 and was accredited by the American Bar Association (ABA) in 1965. The school was named in honor of Cecil C. Humphreys, then-president of Memphis State University and an educator of great distinction. Dr. Humphreys led the group that worked with the state legislature and the ABA to accredit the law school. The school also is an active member of the Association of American Law Schools (AALS).

Since its inception, the School of Law has graduated over 5,000 students and continues its tradition of preparing competent and ethical attorneys. Our graduates can be found throughout the United States, employed in private practice, federal and state judiciaries, corporate boardrooms, government agencies, and public service organizations.

Memphis and the School of Law

Memphis is one of the South's largest, most beautiful, and most diverse cities. Memphis has one of the lowest cost-of-living rates of any major US city, and its temperate climate provides ample opportunity for year-round activities. Memphis has a rich history and an unmatched musical heritage.

The School of Law brings together unique individuals with a wide variety of cultural, geographical, employment, and academic backgrounds. Many of its students come to law school immediately after finishing their undergraduate education; however, a significant number have been in the workforce or have completed advanced degrees. The diversity within the student body enriches the classroom experience for all students and enhances the overall quality of the educational program.

In 2010, the School of Law received a "best value" rating by *preLaw* magazine, recognizing that Memphis is among schools that can boast a high bar exam passage rate, a strong job placement rate for graduates, and an affordable tuition. The School of Law has been cited elsewhere for "quality of life," reflecting student responses to questions about building aesthetics, sense of community, location, classroom facilities, social life, and library staff.

In January 2010, the School of Law began classes in the newly renovated US Custom House and Post Office located in the heart of legal, business, and cultural districts in downtown Memphis. This beautiful state-of-the-art building offers a magnificent view of the Mississippi River and is within blocks of numerous law offices and both state and federal courthouses.

The University of Memphis

The University of Memphis serves as a regional center for education, service, and research, and is linked historically, intellectually, and emotionally with its community. It is a learner-centered metropolitan research university that enrolls over 21,000 students and is accredited by the Commission on Colleges of the Southern Association of Colleges and Schools.

Curriculum

The School of Law offers a full-time day program and a part-time day program. The challenging curriculum prepares our students for the practice of law. The curriculum reflects a commitment to traditional legal education, and academic emphasis is placed on fundamental lawyering skills and areas of knowledge.

Lawyering Skills, Legal Clinics, and Externships

The School of Law provides the opportunity to take upper-level courses in lawyering skills, including trial advocacy, appellate advocacy, and alternative dispute resolution. Upper-division students may receive academic credit and practical experience through our Externship and Clinic Programs. Externship placements are offered in the US District Court, Federal Bankruptcy Court, US Attorney's Office, Federal Public Defender's Office, state appellate judicial offices, National Labor Relations Board, Shelby County District Attorney's Office, Shelby County Public Defender's Office, and the Memphis Area Legal Services Office. Spring 2011 clinic offerings include Child and Family Litigation, Civil Litigation, Elder Law, and Immigration Law. Students enrolled in the legal clinic courses are either specially admitted to practice by the Tennessee Supreme Court or by the US Immigration Court. They represent indigent clients referred through Memphis Area Legal Services or by the Community Legal Center as well as children in abuse and neglect cases, terminations of parental rights cases, adoptions, and other civil legal matters as referred through appointment by the courts.

Joint- and Dual-Degree Programs

The School of Law and the Fogelman College of Business and Economics offer a coordinated degree program leading to both the JD and MBA degrees. The purpose of this program is to allow students to study business management and law. This joint degree enables students to complete the JD and MBA in considerably less time than would be required to complete each degree separately.

The School of Law and the Department of Political Science offer a dual degree leading to both the JD and MA degrees. Credit toward degrees in these disciplines can be earned simultaneously if admission and curricula are carefully structured. Students can complete both degrees in less time than would normally be required to complete each degree separately.

Library and Information Technology

The University of Memphis law library serves students, faculty, the legal community, and the public with reference services and access to its collection of print and electronic resources. The law library occupies five levels of the historic School of Law building and offers students many options for study—from study rooms to a three-sided glass reading room overlooking the Mississippi River. Students have access to computers in labs and open study areas. There is wireless access throughout the building.

THE UNIVERSITY OF MEMPHIS—CECIL C. HUMPHREYS SCHOOL OF LAW

Student Programs and Activities

The *University of Memphis Law Review* is a scholarly journal edited and staffed entirely by students. Law review members have numerous opportunities to improve their legal research, writing, and editing skills.

The Moot Court Board is composed of 20 third-year students who are dedicated to the development of advocacy skills. In addition to intraschool competitions, the law school fields several teams in national moot court and mock trial competitions. In recent years, University of Memphis teams have earned national recognition for their performances in major national moot court and mock trial competitions. This national recognition garnered an invitation to participate in the Moot Court National Championship in 2009 and 2010.

The Student Bar Association (SBA) is the student government of the law school. The SBA coordinates a wide variety of activities, ranging from social events to a speaker series. Students can also choose from many other student groups, ranging from legal fraternities to special interest and service organizations.

Admission

Applicants initially are evaluated by the Admissions Office based on a weighed combination of LSAT score and cumulative undergraduate GPA as calculated by the Law School Admission Council. Those not admitted, or denied, as a result of this evaluation will be reviewed by the Faculty Admission Committee using nonquantifiable factors such as quality of the applicant's undergraduate institution, level and rigor of coursework, letters of recommendation, graduate work, employment during and after college, extracurricular activities, educational diversity, and state of residence. In an attempt to attract a diverse student population, the school has developed a selection process that reviews the merits of all qualified applicants but assures that admission is based on a comprehensive range of criteria demonstrated to be predictive of success in law school.

Career Services

The Career Services Office actively assists students and alumni by helping them develop their interest in specific areas of the law, enhancing their professional skills, and providing information about opportunities for legal employment. A comprehensive national Internet job bank as well as a network of alumni mentors are available to help students who are interested in law careers beyond the Memphis area.

In addition to hosting a large number of firms, corporations, and public interest/governmental employers for on-campus interviewing and seminars, the School of Law is a member of several organizations that conduct annual recruiting conferences.

Employment for Memphis law graduates has remained consistently high during the last decade. Of those known graduates seeking legal employment in the graduating class of 2009, 93.75 percent were employed within nine months of graduation, as reported to the Association for Legal Career Professionals (NALP). Memphis has graduates practicing in all 50 states and in several foreign countries.

Tennessee Institute for Pre-Law

Applicants from Tennessee as well as applicants from Crittenden County, Arkansas, and applicants from De Soto, Marshall, Tate, and Tunica counties in Mississippi are eligible to apply for the Tennessee Institute for Pre-Law (TIP) program, which facilitates law school admission for students from diverse backgrounds who do not meet traditional academic standards for admission. Participants who successfully complete the program will be guaranteed admission to the law school. The TIP program is available to all applicants who will have met the requirements for a bachelor's degree prior to the start of the program. The TIP program is a five-week program of classroom instruction that simulates the first-year law school curriculum.

APPLICANT PROFILE

The University of Memphis—Cecil C. Humphreys School of Law
This grid includes only applicants who earned 120–180 LSAT scores under standard administrations.

LSAT Score	3.75 +		3.50–3.74		3.25–3.49		3.00–3.24		2.75–2.99		2.50–2.74		2.25–2.49		2.00–2.24		Below 2.00		No GPA		Total	
	Apps	Adm	Apps	Adm	Apps	Adm	Apps	Adm	Apps	Adm	Apps	Adm	Apps	Adm	Apps	Adm	Apps	Adm	Apps	Adm	Apps	Adm
175–180	0	0	0	0	0	0	0	0	0	0	0	0	0	0	0	0	0	0	0	0	0	0
170–174	1	1	0	0	0	0	1	1	1	1	0	0	0	0	0	0	0	0	0	0	3	3
165–169	3	3	0	0	3	3	4	4	4	4	3	1	0	0	1	1	0	0	0	0	18	16
160–164	14	10	15	13	18	16	17	15	9	7	4	1	4	1	4	2	0	0	1	1	86	66
155–159	25	19	40	32	49	33	43	26	27	14	22	3	6	1	2	1	1	0	2	1	217	130
150–154	31	16	51	18	57	20	58	15	41	12	20	2	10	1	5	0	0	0	0	0	273	84
145–149	13	2	16	3	40	0	42	1	28	2	20	1	10	0	5	0	2	0	2	0	178	9
140–144	0	0	7	0	18	1	21	0	19	1	16	1	7	0	6	0	4	0	0	0	98	3
135–139	1	0	0	0	7	0	7	0	15	0	9	0	8	0	4	0	1	0	1	0	53	0
130–134	0	0	0	0	1	0	2	0	3	0	4	0	3	0	2	0	0	0	3	0	18	0
125–129	0	0	0	0	0	0	0	0	2	0	1	0	0	0	0	0	0	0	0	0	3	0
120–124	0	0	0	0	0	0	0	0	0	0	0	0	1	0	0	0	2	0	0	0	4	0
Total	88	51	129	66	194	73	195	62	149	41	99	9	49	3	29	4	10	0	9	2	951	311

Apps = Number of Applicants
Adm = Number Admitted
Reflects 99% of the total applicant pool; highest LSAT data reported.

MERCER UNIVERSITY—WALTER F. GEORGE SCHOOL OF LAW

Office of Admissions, 1021 Georgia Avenue
Macon, GA 31207
Phone: 478.301.2605; Fax: 478.301.2989
E-mail: martin_sv@law.mercer.edu; Website: www.law.mercer.edu

ABA Approved Since 1925

The Basics

Type of school	Private
Term	Semester
Application deadline	3/15
Application fee	$50
Financial aid deadline	4/1
Can first year start other than fall?	No
Student to faculty ratio	12.9 to 1
# of housing spaces available restricted to law students	
graduate housing for which law students are eligible	32

Faculty and Administrators

	Total		Men		Women		Minorities	
	Spr	Fall	Spr	Fall	Spr	Fall	Spr	Fall
Full-time	29	27	20	18	9	9	3	3
Other full-time	0	0	0	0	0	0	0	0
Deans, librarians, & others who teach	8	8	4	5	4	3	0	0
Part-time	35	21	28	17	7	4	2	2
Total	72	56	52	40	20	16	5	5

Curriculum

	Full-Time	Part-Time
Typical first-year section size	80	0
Is there typically a "small section" of the first-year class, other than Legal Writing, taught by full-time faculty	Yes	No
If yes, typical size offered last year	27	

# of classroom course titles beyond first-year curriculum		112
# of upper division courses, excluding seminars, with an enrollment:	Under 25	147
	25–49	21
	50–74	6
	75–99	5
	100+	0
# of seminars		16
# of seminar positions available		240

# of seminar positions filled	158	0
# of positions available in simulation courses		876
# of simulation positions filled	723	0
# of positions available in faculty supervised clinical courses		36
# of faculty supervised clinical positions filled	26	0
# involved in field placements	111	0
# involved in law journals	46	0
# involved in moot court or trial competitions	68	0
# of credit hours required to graduate		91

JD Enrollment and Ethnicity

	Men		Women		Full-Time		Part-Time		1st-Year		Total		JD Degs. Awd.
	#	%	#	%	#	%	#	%	#	%	#	%	
All Hispanics	10	4.0	2	1.0	12	2.7	0	0.0	8	4.8	12	2.7	1
Am. Ind./AK Nat.	2	0.8	4	2.1	6	1.4	0	0.0	4	2.4	6	1.4	1
Asian	17	6.9	4	2.1	21	4.8	0	0.0	4	2.4	21	4.8	6
Black/Af. Am.	11	4.5	31	16.1	42	9.6	0	0.0	18	10.9	42	9.6	11
Nat. HI/Pac. Isl.	1	0.4	0	0.0	1	0.2	0	0.0	1	0.6	1	0.2	0
2 or more races	0	0.0	0	0.0	0	0.0	0	0.0	0	0.0	0	0.0	0
Subtotal (minor.)	41	16.6	41	21.4	82	18.7	0	0.0	35	21.2	82	18.7	19
Nonres. Alien	0	0.0	0	0.0	0	0.0	0	0.0	0	0.0	0	0.0	0
White/Cauc.	183	74.1	138	71.9	321	73.1	0	0.0	111	67.3	321	73.1	109
Unknown	23	9.3	13	6.8	36	8.2	0	0.0	19	11.5	36	8.2	14
Total	247	56.3	192	43.7	439	100.0	0	0.0	165	37.6	439		142

Transfers

Transfers in	3
Transfers out	13

Tuition and Fees

	Resident	Nonresident
Full-time	$35,695	$35,695
Part-time		
Tuition Guarantee Program		N

Living Expenses

Estimated living expenses for singles

Living on campus	Living off campus	Living at home
$16,000	$16,000	$16,000

MERCER UNIVERSITY—WALTER F. GEORGE SCHOOL OF LAW

ABA
Approved
Since
1925

GPA and LSAT Scores

	Total	Full-Time	Part-Time
# of apps	1,915	1,915	0
# of offers	609	609	0
# of matrics	166	166	0
75% GPA	3.62	3.62	0.00
Median GPA	3.41	3.41	0.00
25% GPA	3.03	3.03	0.00
75% LSAT	158	158	0
Median LSAT	156	156	0
25% LSAT	153	153	0

Grants and Scholarships (from prior year)

	Total		Full-Time		Part-Time	
	#	%	#	%	#	%
Total # of students	431		431		0	
Total # receiving grants	143	33.2	143	33.2	0	0.0
Less than 1/2 tuition	54	12.5	54	12.5	0	0.0
Half to full tuition	36	8.4	36	8.4	0	0.0
Full tuition	33	7.7	33	7.7	0	0.0
More than full tuition	20	4.6	20	4.6	0	0.0
Median grant amount			$25,000		$0	

Informational and Library Resources

Total amount spent on library materials	$783,959
Study seating capacity inside the library	422
# of full-time equivalent professional librarians	5
Hours per week library is open	68
# of open, wired connections available to students	748
# of networked computers available for use by students	33
Has wireless network?	Y
Requires computer?	Y

JD Attrition (from prior year)

	Academic	Other	Total	
	#	#	#	%
1st year	2	5	7	4.4
2nd year	0	15	15	11.5
3rd year	0	0	0	0.0
4th year	0	0	0	0.0

Employment (9 months after graduation)

	Total	Percentage
Employment status known	159	100.0
Employment status unknown	0	0.0
Employed	123	77.4
Pursuing graduate degrees	9	5.7
Unemployed (seeking, not seeking, or studying for the bar)	24	15.1
Type of Employment		
# employed in law firms	68	55.3
# employed in business and industry	16	13.0
# employed in government	23	18.7
# employed in public interest	7	5.7
# employed as judicial clerks	7	5.7
# employed in academia	2	1.6
Geographic Location		
# employed in state	96	78.0
# employed outside the US	1	0.8
# of states where employed		10

Bar Passage Rates

First-time takers	159	Reporting %	79.25
Average school %	87.30	Average state %	86.28
Average pass difference	1.02		

Jurisdiction	Takers	Passers	Pass %	State %	Diff %
Georgia	126	110	87.30	86.28	1.02

MERCER UNIVERSITY—WALTER F. GEORGE SCHOOL OF LAW

Office of Admissions, 1021 Georgia Avenue
Macon, GA 31207
Phone: 478.301.2605; Fax: 478.301.2989
E-mail: martin_sv@law.mercer.edu; Website: www.law.mercer.edu

Introduction

The Walter F. George School of Law of Mercer University is located in Macon, Georgia, about 80 miles south of Atlanta. Founded in 1873, it is one of the oldest private law schools in the nation. Named for a distinguished alumnus who served as a United States senator for 36 years, the school became a member of AALS in 1923 and has been ABA-approved since 1925. With its distinctive Woodruff curriculum and a total student body of roughly 440, Mercer Law School provides an educational environment that fosters in-depth learning, a candid and lively exchange of views, and a genuine sense of community and collegiality.

Admission

Mercer University's Walter F. George School of Law accepts applications between September 1 and March 15 from prospective students wishing to begin their studies in the fall semester. Applicants must have completed a bachelor's degree prior to law school enrollment. They must register with the Credential Assembly Service (CAS) and take the LSAT, preferably in the summer or fall before application is made. Applicants must submit two letters of recommendation, an application fee, and a personal statement candidly discussing their strengths and weaknesses as prospective law students.

LSAT score and undergraduate GPA figure significantly into the admission decision, but the Admissions Committee considers an array of other factors in arriving at an overall judgment of the applicant's likely contribution to the educational enterprise and his or her potential for success in the profession. Such factors as the applicant's employment history, community and military service, advanced degrees, leadership ability, personal hardships, and other relevant background information will be evaluated.

Library Facilities

The Furman Smith Law Library is the primary resource center of the law school. The law library and computing facilities are accessible to students 24 hours a day. The library's collection of over 350,000 volumes is enhanced by a wide array of online services. Students are able to access network resources from any of the numerous network drops and wireless access points throughout the law school. In addition, each first-year student receives a laptop computer to use during his or her legal education at Mercer Law School. The law library staff of 15 includes 5 professional law librarians who teach legal research courses and provide superior service to students, faculty, and the legal community.

Curriculum

Mercer's Woodruff Curriculum and the atmosphere of the law school work together to provide students with a thorough intellectual foundation, strong practical skills, professional relationships, and a commitment to ethical behavior. Mercer is one of a few select schools in the country to receive the prestigious Gambrell Professionalism Award from the American Bar Association. The award cites the depth and excellence of the Woodruff Curriculum and its serious commitment to professionalism.

The Woodruff Curriculum helps students develop essential problem-solving, counseling, and trial and appellate advocacy skills. It also helps ensure that they acquire the level of understanding of law and the legal system needed to excel in any of the various forms of legal practice that they may choose to enter—law firm, legal aid office, in-house corporate counsel, government legal employment, etc.

All students take research and writing courses during at least four semesters of law study, and many take a research or writing course each term. Mercer is the first law school in the nation to offer a Certificate in Advanced Legal Writing, Research, and Drafting. Students are selected for the Certificate Program through an application process. In 2003, in recognition of Mercer's nationally known Legal Writing Program, the Legal Writing Institute selected Mercer as its host school. The Legal Writing Institute is the world's largest organization of lawyers, judges, and law professors devoted to improving legal writing.

Joint JD/MBA Program

Mercer's School of Law and Mercer's School of Business and Economics offer a joint program leading to both the Juris Doctor and Master of Business Administration degrees. An applicant to the program should indicate on the application to the law school his or her intent to also apply to the School of Business and Economics. The applicant must be admitted separately to each school.

Business Certificate Program

Students in good standing in the Walter F. George School of Law may choose to take up to three graduate courses in the School of Business and Economics without applying for admission to the MBA program. Currently, two specific combinations of courses can be taken for a Certificate in Practice Management or a Certificate in Corporate Finance.

Special Programs

Law school provides a foundation upon which lawyers build successful careers and meaningful lives. At Mercer Law, that foundation includes rigorous intellectual training anchored by nationally recognized programs in legal writing, ethics and professionalism, and public service.

The Law and Public Service Program offers students the opportunity to earn academic credit while helping to represent clients in one of the law school's clinics, such as the Habeas Project or Public Defender's Clinic, in judges' chambers through the Judicial Field Placement Program, and summer externships through various agencies. Students may also be selected as fellows through the Public Interest Fellowship Program. After completing the fellowship, the fellows are offered a one-time loan forgiveness grant conditional on their making a two-year commitment to a public interest employer in Georgia after graduation.

Since 1985, the National Criminal Defense College (NCDC) has held its Summer Trial Practice Institute every year on the Mercer Law School campus. NCDC conducts two, two-week trial skills sessions for nearly 200 public defenders and criminal defense attorneys from across the country.

Student Activities

At Mercer University's Walter F. George School of Law, excellence is measured by more than what happens inside the classroom. You will find a broad array of activities outside the classroom that have been designed to engage the members of our academic community and enable our students to stand out once they enter the professional world.

In Mercer's moot court and mock trial programs, students improve their written and oral advocacy, negotiation, and client counseling skills. Recently, Mercer Law's Moot Court program was ranked among the top 20 in the nation, based on our record of wins in national competitions. In addition, Mercer Law's Mock Trial Team won the 2009 ABA National Criminal Justice Trial Advocacy Competition.

The *Mercer Law Review* (the oldest continually published law review in Georgia) has been edited and published quarterly by law students since 1949.

Students may also gain editorial experience in connection with the *Journal of Southern Legal History*, which is published by the law school.

In addition to moot court and *Law Review*, Mercer offers its students the opportunity to participate in over two dozen student organizations where they can gain valuable leadership and relationship-building experiences.

Financial Aid

Mercer awards over $3 million in scholarship aid every year to students whose academic records, LSAT scores, and personal achievements demonstrate the potential for outstanding performance in the study of law. The priority deadline for scholarship consideration is January 1.

Two of our most prestigious scholarships are the George W. Woodruff Scholarship (full tuition plus a $5,000 stipend) and the Walter F. George Foundation Public Service Scholarship (full tuition plus a $6,000 summer community service stipend). In order to be considered for the George W. Woodruff scholarship, you must have your admission application and scholarship application completed and received in our office no later than January 15. The Woodruff Scholarship application may be found online at www.law.mercer.edu/admissions. Click on the scholarships link. You may also apply online through LSAC's website, LSAC.org.

In addition to scholarship aid, students may qualify for student loans, and work-study is available after the first year of law school.

Career Services

Mercer Law School has an active career services office. Alumni and faculty members support students in their efforts to find satisfying employment. The office assists students in obtaining permanent, summer, and part-time employment.

Services of the office include arranging on-campus interviews with employers, career-planning seminars, and off-campus interviewing consortia. Individual career counseling and résumé and cover-letter writing workshops also comprise much of the work of the office. An extensive library of career resources is available for student use.

The Office of Career Services reports that 83.02 percent of the Class of 2009 was employed or pursuing LLM degrees within six to nine months after graduation.

APPLICANT PROFILE

Mercer University—Walter F. George School of Law
This grid includes only applicants who earned 120–180 LSAT scores under standard administrations.

LSAT Score	3.75 +		3.50–3.74		3.25–3.49		3.00–3.24		2.75–2.99		2.50–2.74		2.25–2.49		2.00–2.24		Below 2.00		No GPA		Total	
	Apps	Adm	Apps	Adm	Apps	Adm	Apps	Adm	Apps	Adm	Apps	Adm	Apps	Adm	Apps	Adm	Apps	Adm	Apps	Adm	Apps	Adm
175–180	1	1	0	0	0	0	0	0	0	0	0	0	0	0	0	0	0	0	0	0	1	1
170–174	1	1	0	0	1	1	0	0	1	1	0	0	0	0	0	0	0	0	0	0	3	3
165–169	10	10	4	3	4	4	3	3	6	6	4	3	1	1	0	0	0	0	0	0	32	30
160–164	21	21	29	29	37	34	22	20	13	12	12	10	7	7	2	0	0	0	1	1	144	134
155–159	38	37	60	54	86	72	72	50	60	36	48	31	16	7	6	2	0	0	3	2	389	291
150–154	44	31	102	47	112	27	110	13	83	11	43	1	8	1	2	0	2	0	3	1	509	132
145–149	26	1	53	5	111	5	112	2	71	0	66	0	15	0	9	0	0	0	1	0	464	13
140–144	13	0	20	0	48	0	57	0	64	0	50	0	11	0	7	0	1	0	6	0	277	0
135–139	4	0	7	0	8	0	8	0	11	0	19	0	8	0	2	0	0	0	0	0	67	0
130–134	2	0	0	0	5	0	4	0	2	0	8	0	3	0	6	0	3	0	2	0	35	0
125–129	0	0	1	0	0	0	1	0	1	0	2	0	0	0	0	0	0	0	0	0	5	0
120–124	0	0	1	0	0	0	1	0	0	0	1	0	0	0	0	0	0	0	0	0	3	0
Total	160	102	277	138	412	143	390	88	312	66	253	45	69	16	34	2	6	0	16	4	1929	604

Apps = Number of Applicants
Adm = Number Admitted
Reflects 99% of the total applicant pool; highest LSAT data reported.

UNIVERSITY OF MIAMI SCHOOL OF LAW

PO Box 248087
Coral Gables, FL 33124-8087
Phone: 305.284.2523; Fax: 305.284.3084
E-mail: admissions@law.miami.edu; Website: www.law.miami.edu

ABA
Approved
Since
1941

The Basics

Type of school	Private
Term	Semester
Application deadline	7/31
Application fee	$60
Financial aid deadline	3/1
Can first year start other than fall?	No
Student to faculty ratio	14.6 to 1
# of housing spaces available restricted to law students	
graduate housing for which law students are eligible	

Faculty and Administrators

	Total		Men		Women		Minorities	
	Spr	Fall	Spr	Fall	Spr	Fall	Spr	Fall
Full-time	69	82	42	42	27	40	21	25
Other full-time	0	0	0	0	0	0	0	0
Deans, librarians, & others who teach	16	18	4	4	12	14	5	6
Part-time	124	86	90	63	32	22	28	15
Total	209	186	136	109	71	76	54	46

Curriculum

	Full-Time	Part-Time
Typical first-year section size	100	0
Is there typically a "small section" of the first-year class, other than Legal Writing, taught by full-time faculty	Yes	No
If yes, typical size offered last year	50	

# of classroom course titles beyond first-year curriculum		93
# of upper division courses, excluding seminars, with an enrollment:	Under 25	44
	25–49	44
	50–74	16
	75–99	12
	100+	17

# of seminars		44
# of seminar positions available		660
# of seminar positions filled	375	0
# of positions available in simulation courses	1,300	
# of simulation positions filled	923	0
# of positions available in faculty supervised clinical courses	135	
# of faculty supervised clinical positions filled	116	0
# involved in field placements	267	0
# involved in law journals	195	0
# involved in moot court or trial competitions	82	0
# of credit hours required to graduate		88

JD Enrollment and Ethnicity

	Men		Women		Full-Time		Part-Time		1st-Year		Total		JD Degs. Awd.
	#	%	#	%	#	%	#	%	#	%	#	%	
All Hispanics	99	12.7	107	18.7	202	15.1	4	21.1	81	16.9	206	15.2	55
Am. Ind./AK Nat.	3	0.4	4	0.7	7	0.5	0	0.0	4	0.8	7	0.5	0
Asian	23	2.9	28	4.9	51	3.8	0	0.0	14	2.9	51	3.8	23
Black/Af. Am.	48	6.2	51	8.9	97	7.3	2	10.5	29	6.0	99	7.3	26
Nat. HI/Pac. Isl.	0	0.0	1	0.2	1	0.1	0	0.0	1	0.2	1	0.1	0
2 or more races	2	0.3	2	0.3	4	0.3	0	0.0	4	0.8	4	0.3	0
Subtotal (minor.)	175	22.4	193	33.7	362	27.1	6	31.6	133	27.7	368	27.2	104
Nonres. Alien	13	1.7	13	2.3	22	1.6	4	21.1	4	0.8	26	1.9	0
White/Cauc.	523	67.1	330	57.6	847	63.5	6	31.6	298	62.1	853	63.0	308
Unknown	69	8.8	37	6.5	103	7.7	3	15.8	45	9.4	106	7.8	40
Total	780	57.6	573	42.4	1334	98.6	19	1.4	480	35.5	1353		462

Transfers

Transfers in	6
Transfers out	15

Tuition and Fees

	Resident	Nonresident
Full-time	$38,024	$38,024
Part-time		
Tuition Guarantee Program		N

Living Expenses

Estimated living expenses for singles

Living on campus	Living off campus	Living at home
$22,034	$22,034	$10,910

ABA
Approved
Since
1941

GPA and LSAT Scores

	Total	Full-Time	Part-Time
# of apps	4,909	4,909	0
# of offers	2,311	2,311	0
# of matrics	489	489	0
75% GPA	3.60	3.60	0.00
Median GPA	3.40	3.40	0.00
25% GPA	3.16	3.16	0.00
75% LSAT	160	160	0
Median LSAT	158	158	0
25% LSAT	156	156	0

Grants and Scholarships (from prior year)

	Total		Full-Time		Part-Time	
	#	%	#	%	#	%
Total # of students	1,384		1,351		33	
Total # receiving grants	461	33.3	461	34.1	0	0.0
Less than 1/2 tuition	192	13.9	192	14.2	0	0.0
Half to full tuition	250	18.1	250	18.5	0	0.0
Full tuition	7	0.5	7	0.5	0	0.0
More than full tuition	12	0.9	12	0.9	0	0.0
Median grant amount			$20,000		$0	

Informational and Library Resources

Total amount spent on library materials	$2,382,489
Study seating capacity inside the library	698
# of full-time equivalent professional librarians	10
Hours per week library is open	111
# of open, wired connections available to students	28
# of networked computers available for use by students	165
Has wireless network?	Y
Requires computer?	N

JD Attrition (from prior year)

	Academic	Other	Total	
	#	#	#	%
1st year	9	31	40	7.6
2nd year	1	0	1	0.3
3rd year	0	0	0	0.0
4th year	0	0	0	0.0

Employment (9 months after graduation)

	Total	Percentage
Employment status known	354	94.7
Employment status unknown	20	5.3
Employed	308	87.0
Pursuing graduate degrees	22	6.2
Unemployed (seeking, not seeking, or studying for the bar)	9	2.5
Type of Employment		
# employed in law firms	205	66.6
# employed in business and industry	33	10.7
# employed in government	22	7.1
# employed in public interest	21	6.8
# employed as judicial clerks	11	3.6
# employed in academia	8	2.6
Geographic Location		
# employed in state	190	61.7
# employed outside the US	3	1.0
# of states where employed		22

Bar Passage Rates

First-time takers	384	Reporting %	84.90
Average school %	82.52	Average state %	79.57
Average pass difference	2.95		

Jurisdiction	Takers	Passers	Pass %	State %	Diff %
Florida	260	210	80.77	77.81	2.96
New York	66	59	89.39	86.51	2.88

UNIVERSITY OF MIAMI SCHOOL OF LAW

PO Box 248087
Coral Gables, FL 33124-8087
Phone: 305.284.2523; Fax: 305.284.3084
E-mail: admissions@law.miami.edu; Website: www.law.miami.edu

Introduction

The University of Miami School of Law is on the main campus of one of the largest private research universities in the United States. The surrounding South Florida region is one of a kind in one of the most dynamic areas of international trade and commerce. Students attend law school in a beautiful, subtropical setting while taking advantage of the opportunities available in the surrounding legal community. Miami Law is accredited by the ABA, is a member of the AALS, and has a chapter of the prestigious scholastic society, the Order of the Coif.

Faculty

The faculty have exceptional credentials. They are graduates of the world's top universities and law schools, have completed prestigious judicial clerkships, and have significant work experience in private practice and government. They are leading scholars in their fields and are renowned for combining their scholarly distinction and real-world experience with an enthusiastic approach to teaching. Their expertise is especially strong in international and foreign law (half have written or taught in those fields), arbitration, taxation, securities regulation, immigration, human rights, the Internet, legal theory, evidence, and ethics.

Library

With nearly 600,000 volumes and a wide array of electronic resources, Miami Law's library is one of the most comprehensive resources for legal research in the Southeast. The library has liberal hours, a full-time staff of 28, computer labs, and ample seating for individual and group study. The campus is wireless.

Curriculum

The school provides a solid foundation in all the traditional subjects basic to understanding and practicing the law. In addition, the school is constantly expanding its offerings to ensure they reflect the opportunities of the changing world.

Choosing from more than 160 courses, workshops, and seminars, students ordinarily complete the JD degree in three years of full-time study. Summer sessions are available. Miami's course offerings in inter-American, international, arbitration, and transnational law are outstanding. Joint JD/Master's programs are offered in business administration, public health, music business, and marine affairs and policy. In addition, JD/LLM degrees are offered in taxation, real property development, international law, inter-American law, transnational law, international arbitration, and ocean and coastal law. The school also offers a triple degree option where students who were undergraduate business majors can earn a JD, an MBA, and an LLM in tax or real property in four years.

Master of Laws (LLM) programs include inter-American law, international arbitration, international law, ocean and coastal law, taxation, estate planning, real property development, and transnational law. A JD degree (or equivalent degree from a foreign law school) is required for entrance into an LLM program.

Special Programs

The school has ten clinics in Immigration, Human Rights, Tenants' Rights, Federal Appellate, Children and Youth Law, Health and Elder Law, Community Lawyering, and Bankruptcy Assistance. In addition, there is the Miami Innocence Project and the Capital Defense Project. These clinics enable students to participate in environmental protection advocacy; work toward the exoneration of prisoners wrongfully convicted; or represent neglected children, immigrants, and the elderly in need of health care who are facing complicated legal issues. They can assist prisoners appealing federal sentencing rulings, tenants caught up in housing disputes, and can advocate for community legal needs in economically challenged neighborhoods.

The Center for Ethics and Public Service is an interdisciplinary project teaching the values of ethical judgment, professional responsibility, and public service and includes the nationally-known STREET LAW program.

HOPE (Helping Others Through Pro Bono Efforts) is the law school's public interest resource center. This center helps students understand the array of public interest opportunities at Miami Law and provides guidance and training to law students dedicated to community service and advocacy. It links students, faculty, and alumni with projects, lectures, clinics, and fellowships in the public sector. The school also has a dedicated Assistant Dean of Pro Bono and Public Interest.

Miami Law offers one of the most comprehensive and sophisticated Litigation Skills training programs in the nation, integrating trial, pretrial, litigation, and clinical experiences. Directed by a full-time faculty member, distinguished trial attorneys and judges from both state and federal courts assist with the trial and pretrial courses and help supervise the externship placements.

Study-abroad options consist of programs in Germany, Israel, France, Africa, and Switzerland. Through these programs, students can focus on specific interests such as international law, arbitration of international business disputes, comparative law issues in international business, foreign legal systems, and human rights. In addition, the school has an International Moot Court Program where students participate in one international moot court competition and take a workshop, obtaining course credit.

Admission

Admission is competitive. Undergraduate grade-point averages are used in the review process. While all LSAT scores are considered, the highest score is given the greatest weight. Two letters of recommendation or two evaluations (or combination thereof) are required and a personal statement is strongly encouraged. Work experience, extracurricular activities, special skills, and background are also considered. First-year students are admitted only in the fall semester. Applicants are urged to apply as early as possible after September 1. Applications received after February 1 will be considered on a space-available basis until July 31.

The Student Body and Student Life

Miami's student body is highly talented and exceptionally diverse. The school is consistently among the leaders in numbers of Hispanic, African American, and foreign students graduated from its JD program.

The school's many student activities include an active Student Bar Association, Honor Council, Moot Court Board, and more than 55 diverse student organizations. These provide members personal, academic, and career support. All encourage student leadership and involvement in pro bono activities, assist in recruiting students, and provide networking and career opportunities with alumni and other members of the legal community. The school's leadership works closely with student organizations and facilitates or cosponsors a broad array of special programs and events throughout the year. The school's organizations include the Black, Hispanic, Caribbean, South Asian, Middle Eastern, and Asian/Pacific American law student organizations; OUTLaw; Miami Law Women; Federalist Society; International Law Society; Entertainment and Sports Law Society; the Student Animal Legal Defense Fund; and many more. Miami's law journals include the *University of Miami Law Review*, the *University of Miami Inter-American Law Review*, the *University of Miami International and Comparative Law Review*, the *Black Law Review*, the *Business Law Review*, *National Security and Armed Conflict Law Review*, and *Psychology, Public Policy, and Law Review*.

Expenses and Financial Aid

Scholarship aid available through the school does not exceed the cost of tuition. Most scholarships are merit based, although need is sometimes considered. Admitted applicants are automatically considered for most scholarship awards. Applicants who wish to be considered for a merit scholarship should complete their admission files prior to January 4. Most scholarships are awarded on a rolling basis. Those admitted by February 1 are considered for the prestigious Harvey T. Reid and Soia Mentschikoff scholarships. In addition, admitted students are eligible to apply for the public interest-related Miami Scholars Program, which requires a separate application with a deadline of March 1.

The law school assists and encourages all students to apply for federal aid (loans) prior to considering private educational loans. Federal loans may be applied for by first completing the FAFSA online at www.fafsa.gov. Our Federal School Code is E00532. Any additional financial aid information can be found on our website at www.law.miami.edu/finaid.

Career Services

The Career Development Office (CDO) offers extraordinary individual career counseling to law students and alumni, with attorneys in different areas of specialty providing guidance. The CDO offers a wide range of job-related programming and job fairs, networking opportunities with attorneys in varied practice areas, and access to a resource library and national job postings via the Internet. The On-Campus Interview Program attracts national and local employers, providing opportunities with law firms, government agencies, public service organizations, corporate counsel, and the judiciary.

APPLICANT PROFILE

University of Miami School of Law
This grid includes only applicants who earned 120–180 LSAT scores under standard administrations.

LSAT Score	GPA									
	3.75 +	3.50–3.74	3.25–3.49	3.00–3.24	2.75–2.99	2.50–2.74	2.25–2.49	2.00–2.24	Below 2.00	No GPA
175–180										
170–174										
165–169										
160–164										
155–159										
150–154										
145–149										
140–144										
135–139										
130–134										
125–129										
120–124										

■ Good Possibility   □ Possible   ▧ Unlikely

When reviewing the grid, it is important to note that admission to the school is based upon all aspects of an applicant's background, and not limited to the LSAT and undergraduate grade-point average.

THE UNIVERSITY OF MICHIGAN LAW SCHOOL

Hutchins Hall, 625 South State Street
Ann Arbor, MI 48109-1215
Phone: 734.764.1358
E-mail: law.jd.admissions@umich.edu; Website: www.law.umich.edu

ABA
Approved
Since
1923

The Basics

Type of school	Public
Term	Semester
Application deadline	11/15 2/15
Application fee	$75
Financial aid deadline	
Can first year start other than fall?	Yes
Student to faculty ratio	10.7 to 1
# of housing spaces available restricted to law students	258
graduate housing for which law students are eligible	1,200

Faculty and Administrators

	Total		Men		Women		Minorities	
	Spr	Fall	Spr	Fall	Spr	Fall	Spr	Fall
Full-time	90	87	61	61	29	26	17	15
Other full-time	5	5	1	1	4	4	1	1
Deans, librarians, & others who teach	4	4	3	3	1	1	0	0
Part-time	35	31	27	22	8	9	3	2
Total	134	127	92	87	42	40	21	18

JD Enrollment and Ethnicity

	Men #	Men %	Women #	Women %	Full-Time #	Full-Time %	Part-Time #	Part-Time %	1st-Year #	1st-Year %	Total #	Total %	JD Degs. Awd.
All Hispanics	21	3.3	26	5.1	47	4.1	0	0.0	15	4.0	47	4.1	20
Am. Ind./AK Nat.	4	0.6	1	0.2	5	0.4	0	0.0	2	0.5	5	0.4	2
Asian	38	6.1	80	15.8	118	10.4	0	0.0	35	9.3	118	10.4	36
Black/Af. Am.	14	2.2	18	3.6	32	2.8	0	0.0	11	2.9	32	2.8	20
Nat. HI/Pac. Isl.	0	0.0	0	0.0	0	0.0	0	0.0	0	0.0	0	0.0	0
2 or more races	24	3.8	20	4.0	44	3.9	0	0.0	14	3.7	44	3.9	0
Subtotal (minor.)	101	16.1	145	28.7	246	21.7	0	0.0	77	20.4	246	21.7	97
Nonres. Alien	14	2.2	12	2.4	26	2.3	0	0.0	8	2.1	26	2.3	0
White/Cauc.	453	72.1	319	63.0	772	68.1	0	0.0	257	68.2	772	68.1	228
Unknown	60	9.6	30	5.9	90	7.9	0	0.0	35	9.3	90	7.9	33
Total	628	55.4	506	44.6	1134	100.0	0	0.0	377	33.2	1134		377

Curriculum

	Full-Time	Part-Time
Typical first-year section size	93	0
Is there typically a "small section" of the first-year class, other than Legal Writing, taught by full-time faculty	Yes	No
If yes, typical size offered last year	47	
# of classroom course titles beyond first-year curriculum	188	

# of upper division courses, excluding seminars, with an enrollment:		
	Under 25	93
	25–49	40
	50–74	16
	75–99	8
	100+	6

# of seminars	77	
# of seminar positions available	1,127	
# of seminar positions filled	963	0
# of positions available in simulation courses	357	
# of simulation positions filled	303	0
# of positions available in faculty supervised clinical courses	289	
# of faculty supervised clinical positions filled	287	0
# involved in field placements	41	0
# involved in law journals	470	0
# involved in moot court or trial competitions	55	0
# of credit hours required to graduate	82	

Transfers

Transfers in	24
Transfers out	2

Tuition and Fees

	Resident	Nonresident
Full-time	$44,600	$47,600
Part-time		
Tuition Guarantee Program	N	

Living Expenses

Estimated living expenses for singles

Living on campus	Living off campus	Living at home
$17,500	$17,500	$7,000

*ABA
Approved
Since
1923*

GPA and LSAT Scores

	Total	Full-Time	Part-Time
# of apps	6,311	6,311	0
# of offers	1,171	1,171	0
# of matrics	376	376	0
75% GPA	3.85	3.85	0.00
Median GPA	3.73	3.73	0.00
25% GPA	3.57	3.57	0.00
75% LSAT	171	171	0
Median LSAT	169	169	0
25% LSAT	168	168	0

Grants and Scholarships (from prior year)

	Total		Full-Time		Part-Time	
	#	%	#	%	#	%
Total # of students	1,117		1,117		0	
Total # receiving grants	685	61.3	685	61.3	0	0.0
Less than 1/2 tuition	624	55.9	624	55.9	0	0.0
Half to full tuition	26	2.3	26	2.3	0	0.0
Full tuition	15	1.3	15	1.3	0	0.0
More than full tuition	20	1.8	20	1.8	0	0.0
Median grant amount			$12,000		$0	

Informational and Library Resources

Total amount spent on library materials	$2,912,889
Study seating capacity inside the library	854
# of full-time equivalent professional librarians	9
Hours per week library is open	112
# of open, wired connections available to students	337
# of networked computers available for use by students	202
Has wireless network?	Y
Requires computer?	N

JD Attrition (from prior year)

	Academic	Other	Total	
	#	#	#	%
1st year	0	3	3	0.8
2nd year	2	4	6	1.6
3rd year	1	2	3	0.8
4th year	0	0	0	0.0

Employment (9 months after graduation)

	Total	Percentage
Employment status known	410	99.5
Employment status unknown	2	0.5
Employed	397	96.8
Pursuing graduate degrees	7	1.7
Unemployed (seeking, not seeking, or studying for the bar)	2	0.5
Type of Employment		
# employed in law firms	288	72.5
# employed in business and industry	11	2.8
# employed in government	10	2.5
# employed in public interest	32	8.1
# employed as judicial clerks	54	13.6
# employed in academia	1	0.3
Geographic Location		
# employed in state	46	11.6
# employed outside the US	8	2.0
# of states where employed	37	

Bar Passage Rates

First-time takers	390	Reporting %	82.05
Average school %	94.35	Average state %	84.59
Average pass difference	9.76		

Jurisdiction	Takers	Passers	Pass %	State %	Diff %
New York	133	123	92.48	86.51	5.97
Illinois	66	65	98.48	90.89	7.59
California	57	53	92.98	73.19	19.79
Michigan	36	34	94.44	86.87	7.57
Others (6)	28	27	96.43		

The information on these pages was provided by the law school.

THE UNIVERSITY OF MICHIGAN LAW SCHOOL

Hutchins Hall, 625 South State Street
Ann Arbor, MI 48109-1215
Phone: 734.764.1358
E-mail: law.jd.admissions@umich.edu; Website: www.law.umich.edu

Introduction

The University of Michigan Law School, founded in 1859, is one of the nation's finest institutions of legal education. The school's distinguished and diverse faculty, many preeminent in their fields, have a history of devotion to both scholarship and teaching. Our students come from around the globe to contribute their remarkable talents and accomplishments and make the Law School a collegial community that exudes a sense of serious purpose, academic achievement, and social commitment. Never restricted to the privileged, in 1870, Michigan—then the largest law school in the country—became the second American university to confer a law degree on an African American. That same year, Michigan became the first major law school to admit a woman, and in 1871, its graduate, Sarah Killgore, became the first woman with a law degree in the nation to be admitted to the bar.

Faculty

Michigan has almost 80 full-time faculty members, with many distinguished visiting scholars further enhancing course offerings. While maintaining a long tradition of eminence in constitutional, criminal, international, and comparative law, the interdisciplinary breadth of the faculty is reflected in an extraordinary range of expertise, including classics, economics, feminist theory, history, life sciences, philosophy, political theory, and public policy. We offer depth as well, whether measured by the number of professors who are also voting faculty members of a world-class department in another discipline, or the number with PhDs in cognate disciplines, or the number who are Fellows of the American Academy of Arts and Sciences.

Physical Facilities and Library

The location of residential and academic buildings within the strikingly beautiful Gothic architecture of the William W. Cook Law Quadrangle fosters the integration of activities for both students and faculty. Construction of a new four-story, 100,000-square-foot building south of the quad, and a 16,000-square-foot commons that will become the quad's vibrant new heart, was begun in Summer 2009; completion is anticipated by January 2012.

With over one million volumes, the Law Library's comprehensive collection covers Anglo-American, foreign, comparative, and international law, and includes legislation, court reports, and administrative material from all US jurisdictions, Great Britain, Europe, and most Asian and South American countries. In 1957, the library became the first depository of EU documents at an American university. It is also a selective depository for US government publications, and extensively collects documents of international intergovernmental organizations. There is special depth in the collections relating to indigenous peoples. Law students also have access to all other university libraries.

Curriculum

Recognized as preeminent in interdisciplinary legal studies, the insights and methods of many other fields are apparent throughout our broad curriculum. Formal dual-degree programs are available in 13 disciplines, while others are created ad hoc, sometimes with other institutions. Alternatively, students may count 12 credits of graduate-level work in other departments toward their JD. With the Law School located at the center of the university, it is easy for students to take advantage of these options, and about 15 percent of second- and third-year students do so.

A key component of the first year is our exceptional Legal Practice Program. This comprehensive class provides individualized instruction in legal writing, research, and oral advocacy by full-time faculty to first-year students.

Particularly renowned for international scholarship, Michigan's leadership is evident in its requirement that all students complete Transnational Law—the first elite law school to so recognize the centrality of the field to modern lawyering. The Geneva Externship Program provides 20 students annually with a unique "in" to extremely competitive jobs in the public international field, while other programs, such as the South Africa externship program, the Program for Cambodian Law and Development, and our AIRE Centre internships provide students with advanced training in international areas of interest.

Bottom line, as one of the leaders in American legal education, Michigan's curriculum is strong across the board. Students with interest in business, corporate, and securities; intellectual property; criminal; international; environmental; and public interest law should pay special attention to Michigan's extensive offerings.

Clinical Opportunities

Michigan is committed to the union of theory and practice, and our clinical practice program, with more than 30 years of experience, is unquestionably one of the nation's best. Michigan is one of only two states to allow students to appear in court as early as second year, meaning that our students have more opportunities to represent clients selected from a rich pool of cases—often in smaller jurisdictions, where a faster timetable allows students to handle many cases from beginning to end. Beyond the General Clinic, where students are involved in civil and criminal trial work, as well as immigration and refugee cases, our diverse offerings include litigation clinics in Child Advocacy Law, Juvenile Justice, Criminal Appellate Practice, Human Trafficking, as well as our groundbreaking non-DNA Innocence Clinic; transactional clinics such as Urban Communities, International Transactions, and Low Income Tax; the interdisciplinary medicolegal Pediatric Advocacy Clinic; an Environmental Law Clinic run in cooperation with the National Wildlife Federation; and a Mediation Clinic. Students can also participate in the Family Law Project, a student-run advocacy program for victims of domestic violence, as well as a variety of practicums, in fields ranging from copyright to bankruptcy, in which real cases are dissected in a classroom setting.

Admission and Student Body

Please refer to Applicant Profile for more information.

Student Activities

Approximately 450 students participate in six journals: the *Michigan Law Review*, the *Journal of Law Reform*, the *Michigan Journal of International Law*, the *Michigan Journal of Gender and Law*, the *Michigan Telecommunications and Technology Law Review*, and the *Michigan Journal of Race and Law*. Students interested in honing advocacy skills may choose to enter numerous moot court competitions. The Law School Student Senate funds more than 50 student organizations dedicated to affinity group membership and legal interests; students also participate in groups throughout the larger University community. Our voluntary Pro Bono Pledge gives students yet one more outlet to serve the world outside the Law School with their developing legal skills; projects range from local to global in providing underrepresented individuals with valuable expertise.

Financial Aid

Our financial aid resources are substantial, and we distribute more than $3.5 million in grants annually to each entering class. Grants range in size from $5,000 to as much as full tuition plus a stipend, and average about $15,000 annually. Our resources are divided between grants made with reference to financial need, and merit awards made to outstanding candidates who are remarkable for their anticipated contribution to the Law School and the profession.

Michigan's generous and progressive Debt Management Program (Loan Repayment Assistance Program—LRAP) provides graduates with the flexibility to choose jobs from an unlimited range of law-related opportunities, including lower-paying public interest positions, while still maintaining a reasonable lifestyle.

Career Services/Public Service

Repeatedly rated by multiple publications among the top law schools for career prospects, Michigan offers unparalleled opportunity. Our location in the center of the country means that employers from all major markets target our graduates, and our on-campus recruiting program is consistently one of the largest in the country, even in comparison to other top schools—both in absolute numbers of employers recruiting and in relative terms of interviews per student. While the majority of our graduates go to the best and largest private-sector firms across the nation, the range of work performed by our alumni is truly extraordinary. Michigan has, for example, the third largest number of state and federal judges, the third largest number of legal academics, and the fourth largest number of Skadden Fellows; we are also leaders in judicial clerkships (about 15 percent of each class obtains positions in federal, state, and international courts), as well as government and public-interest employment (on average, about 10 percent). And as one of only a handful of schools regularly sending its graduates to more than 30 states and abroad, our students have confidence that their degree will be portable wherever they choose to live. The largest number of our graduates go to New York City and Chicago, followed closely by California and Washington, DC. Our reach extends well beyond these cities, though; the most recent class sent graduates to markets ranging from Seattle to Miami, London to Madrid, and to Hanoi, to name just a few.

Our six attorney-counselors have experience across the legal spectrum, and can advise students about the full range of professional opportunities. Both when the market is flourishing and when it contracts, the breadth of Michigan's recruiting program and depth of its counselors' expertise serves students exceptionally well.

Housing

Ann Arbor combines ease of living with superb cultural, athletic, and entertainment offerings. Approximately half of our first-year students (along with some upper-class and LLM students) reside in the Lawyers Club, enjoying the easy access and camaraderie of life in the Law Quad. High-quality, off-campus housing is available in a wide variety of choices. Economical University family housing is also available a short (and free) bus ride away, in northeast Ann Arbor.

APPLICANT PROFILE

We choose not to provide an applicant profile because we do not believe a grid based on undergraduate GPA and LSAT scores can accurately reflect our comprehensive admission process, which focuses on many elements in an application in order to determine an applicant's particular intellectual strengths, nonacademic achievements, and unique personal circumstances. We view our student body as one of our greatest assets, and our goal is to admit a group of students who, individually and collectively, are among the best applying to US law schools in a given year. We seek a mix of students with varying backgrounds and experiences who will respect and learn from each other. Our most general measures are an applicant's LSAT score and undergraduate GPA. As measured by those statistics, Michigan is among a handful of the most selective law schools in the country. However, each of these measures is far from perfect. Even the highest possible scores will not guarantee admission, and low scores will likewise not automatically result in a denial, as both circumstances may have significant offsetting considerations.

MICHIGAN STATE UNIVERSITY COLLEGE OF LAW

Office of Admissions and Financial Aid, 300 Law College Building
East Lansing, MI 48824-1300
Phone: 800.844.9352, 517.432.0222; Fax: 517.432.0098
E-mail: admiss@law.msu.edu; Website: www.law.msu.edu

ABA
Approved
Since
1941

The Basics

Type of school	Private
Term	Semester
Application deadline	4/30
Application fee	$60
Financial aid deadline	4/1
Can first year start other than fall?	No
Student to faculty ratio	15.6 to 1
# of housing spaces available restricted to law students	
graduate housing for which law students are eligible	1, 049

Faculty and Administrators

	Total		Men		Women		Minorities	
	Spr	Fall	Spr	Fall	Spr	Fall	Spr	Fall
Full-time	43	49	25	25	18	24	6	7
Other full-time	5	3	1	1	4	2	0	0
Deans, librarians, & others who teach	20	21	10	10	10	11	2	2
Part-time	59	63	46	46	13	17	9	8
Total	127	136	82	82	45	54	17	17

Curriculum

		Full-Time	Part-Time
Typical first-year section size		75	75
Is there typically a "small section" of the first-year class, other than Legal Writing, taught by full-time faculty		No	No
If yes, typical size offered last year			
# of classroom course titles beyond first-year curriculum		188	
# of upper division courses, excluding seminars, with an enrollment:	Under 25	121	
	25–49	41	
	50–74	24	
	75–99	8	
	100+	3	
# of seminars		65	
# of seminar positions available		1,215	
# of seminar positions filled		702	34
# of positions available in simulation courses		1,249	
# of simulation positions filled		893	40
# of positions available in faculty supervised clinical courses		225	
# of faculty supervised clinical positions filled		141	8
# involved in field placements		352	18
# involved in law journals		163	3
# involved in moot court or trial competitions		65	0
# of credit hours required to graduate		88	

JD Enrollment and Ethnicity

	Men		Women		Full-Time		Part-Time		1st-Year		Total		JD Degs. Awd.
	#	%	#	%	#	%	#	%	#	%	#	%	
All Hispanics	10	2.0	20	5.3	22	2.7	8	10.0	14	4.8	30	3.4	8
Am. Ind./AK Nat.	4	0.8	8	2.1	11	1.4	1	1.3	5	1.7	12	1.4	6
Asian	15	3.0	10	2.6	24	3.0	1	1.3	4	1.4	25	2.8	16
Black/Af. Am.	23	4.6	38	10.0	47	5.8	14	17.5	21	7.2	61	6.9	8
Nat. HI/Pac. Isl.	1	0.2	0	0.0	1	0.1	0	0.0	0	0.0	1	0.1	0
2 or more races	1	0.2	6	1.6	7	0.9	0	0.0	4	1.4	7	0.8	0
Subtotal (minor.)	54	10.7	82	21.6	112	13.9	24	30.0	48	16.5	136	15.4	38
Nonres. Alien	36	7.1	24	6.3	59	7.3	1	1.3	18	6.2	60	6.8	0
White/Cauc.	376	74.6	253	66.6	576	71.6	53	66.3	204	70.1	629	71.2	273
Unknown	38	7.5	21	5.5	57	7.1	2	2.5	21	7.2	59	6.7	20
Total	504	57.0	380	43.0	804	91.0	80	9.0	291	32.9	884		349

Transfers

Transfers in	18
Transfers out	14

Tuition and Fees

	Resident	Nonresident
Full-time	$34,045	$34,045
Part-time	$28,220	$28,220
Tuition Guarantee Program		N

Living Expenses

Estimated living expenses for singles

Living on campus	Living off campus	Living at home
$15,174	$15,174	$15,174

MICHIGAN STATE UNIVERSITY COLLEGE OF LAW

*ABA
Approved
Since
1941*

GPA and LSAT Scores

	Total	Full-Time	Part-Time
# of apps	3,471	3,275	204
# of offers	1,212	1,172	40
# of matrics	299	276	23
75% GPA	3.74	3.74	3.79
Median GPA	3.52	3.52	3.59
25% GPA	3.24	3.24	3.38
75% LSAT	159	159	167
Median LSAT	157	157	163
25% LSAT	152	152	158

Grants and Scholarships (from prior year)

	Total		Full-Time		Part-Time	
	#	%	#	%	#	%
Total # of students	957		892		65	
Total # receiving grants	349	36.5	331	37.1	18	27.7
Less than 1/2 tuition	65	6.8	62	7.0	3	4.6
Half to full tuition	154	16.1	150	16.8	4	6.2
Full tuition	130	13.6	119	13.3	11	16.9
More than full tuition	0	0.0	0	0.0	0	0.0
Median grant amount			$22,055		$15,134	

Informational and Library Resources

Total amount spent on library materials	$1,084,446
Study seating capacity inside the library	455
# of full-time equivalent professional librarians	8
Hours per week library is open	109
# of open, wired connections available to students	1,059
# of networked computers available for use by students	66
Has wireless network?	Y
Requires computer?	Y

JD Attrition (from prior year)

	Academic	Other	Total	
	#	#	#	%
1st year	7	18	25	8.8
2nd year	0	1	1	0.3
3rd year	0	0	0	0.0
4th year	0	0	0	0.0

Employment (9 months after graduation)

	Total	Percentage
Employment status known	246	97.2
Employment status unknown	7	2.8
Employed	230	93.5
Pursuing graduate degrees	12	4.9
Unemployed (seeking, not seeking, or studying for the bar)	4	1.6
Type of Employment		
# employed in law firms	99	43.0
# employed in business and industry	58	25.2
# employed in government	21	9.1
# employed in public interest	7	3.0
# employed as judicial clerks	8	3.5
# employed in academia	32	13.9
Geographic Location		
# employed in state	125	54.3
# employed outside the US	6	2.6
# of states where employed	29	

Bar Passage Rates

First-time takers	254	Reporting %	72.44
Average school %	93.49	Average state %	87.57
Average pass difference	5.92		

Jurisdiction	Takers	Passers	Pass %	State %	Diff %
Michigan	133	126	94.74	86.87	7.87
Illinois	34	33	97.06	90.89	6.17
New York	17	13	76.47	86.51	–10.04

MICHIGAN STATE UNIVERSITY COLLEGE OF LAW

Office of Admissions and Financial Aid, 300 Law College Building
East Lansing, MI 48824-1300
Phone: 800.844.9352, 517.432.0222; Fax: 517.432.0098
E-mail: admiss@law.msu.edu; Website: www.law.msu.edu

Introduction

With a broad and rigorous curriculum that provides extensive opportunities for students to gain valuable practical experience, Michigan State University (MSU) College of Law successfully prepares graduates for legal employment in settings across the nation—litigation, transactional law, business and industry, alternative dispute resolution, and public interest—to mention just a few.

As a law school with a 100-plus year tradition of graduating outstanding lawyers, judges, and entrepreneurs, students at MSU Law benefit from the college's status as a private law school located in the heart of a Big 10, world-class research university. The College of Law's location in East Lansing provides students with convenient access to externships and employment with state and federal agencies and courts, and an array of law firms and corporations. MSU Law is fully accredited by the ABA and is a member of the AALS.

Academic Programs

The College of Law curriculum provides a thorough education in all principal areas of law and practice. A total of 88 credit hours is required for graduation, with 40 of these credits being proscribed by the College of Law. The Law College teaches core legal skills, supplemented with academic concentrations, programmatic initiatives, and scholarly research and exchanges. The educational program of the college teaches and reinforces the ethical core of good lawyering, the values of professionalism and service, the art of client representation and trial advocacy, and the understanding of legal principles, private rights, and public policy.

The Law College strives to continuously strengthen academic quality in all programs and activities of the college. The college is committed to fostering flexible opportunities for professional growth, innovation, research, and scholarship by the faculty. The faculty is committed to excellence in instruction, to making significant contributions to legal research, and to engaging in public service and community outreach. The staff is committed to providing necessary service, support, and creativity.

The elective and required curriculum of the Law College integrates theory and practice, thereby helping to ensure that graduates of MSU Law are well prepared for their first professional positions and the professional responsibilities for decades to come.

Focus Areas: Law students at MSU have the opportunity to choose a focus area or certificate program when selecting elective courses. Focus areas include Alternative Dispute Resolution (ADR), Corporate Law, Criminal Law, Environmental and Natural Resource Law, Family Law, Health Law, Intellectual Property and Communications Law, International and Comparative Law, Public Law and Regulation, and Taxation Law.

Certificate Programs: MSU Law students may elect to participate in one of three certificate programs, thereby developing greater expertise in an area of law. MSU Law certificate programs are Child and Family Advocacy, Trial Practice at the Geoffrey Fieger Trial Practice Institute, and Indigenous Law.

Canadian and American Law Degree Program: MSU Law students who rank in the top half of the class may enroll in the dual-degree program with the University of Ottawa Faculty of Law, thereby earning both a US and a Canadian law degree in four years.

Study-Abroad Programs: The MSU Law Canadian study-abroad program provides students with the opportunity to study US-Canadian and international law and gain legal work experience in Ottawa. Additionally, the Law College offers study-abroad programs in Japan and Poland.

Dual-Degree Options: Law students with an interest in broadening their skills set have the opportunity to pursue a dual degree with another graduate program at Michigan State University. Dual degrees are established with more than a dozen graduate programs, with the typical dual-degree student being able to earn the law degree and a master's degree in just four years.

Master of Laws (LLM) Program: An LLM is offered for foreign lawyers. An LLM/MJ (Master of Jurisprudence) is offered in Intellectual Property and Communications Law for domestic and foreign students.

Experiential Learning

MSU Law Clinics: The Law College operates law clinics to benefit area residents and to give law students an opportunity to put their legal knowledge into practice. Students in the clinics may handle cases from start to finish and gain much satisfaction—as well as résumé-building experience—from their clinical experiences, all while helping members of their own community. Law clinics available to students are the First Amendment Clinic, Housing Clinic, Immigration Clinic, Plea and Sentencing Clinic, Small Business and Nonprofit Law Clinic, Tax Clinic, and the Chance at Childhood Law and Social Work Clinic.

Spring Semester in Washington, DC: The Law College's Washington, DC, Semester Program provides the opportunity for 25 students to spend a full spring semester in our nation's capital, working 24 hours weekly for federal agencies while also enrolling in several law courses taught by MSU Law faculty. The DC program provides valuable practical experience and insights into employment with the federal government.

Externships: Externships, which are field placements that provide practical legal training under the supervision of practicing attorneys and faculty members, may be completed with a variety of legal employers—judicial, legal aid, nonprofit, and governmental. Two of the most innovative and exciting externship opportunities are in Washington, DC, and Ottawa, Canada.

MSU Law Journals: *Michigan State Law Review, Journal of International Law, Journal of Medicine and Law, Journal of Business and Securities Law, Journal of Gender Law,* and *MSU Entertainment and Sports Law Journal.*

Trial Practice Institute: MSU Law alumnus Geoffrey N. Fieger has partnered with the Law College to establish a premier trial practice institute, designed specifically to train law students as successful trial lawyers. Students interview at the end of their first year of law school, and selected students start the program at the beginning of their second year. The institute offers hands-on learning experiences through clinics, externships, field placements, and simulations.

Career Services

Graduates of the College of Law can be found in all regions of the country and abroad. In a typical year, graduates accept employment in 25 or more states. The most common career path of recent graduates is private practice, with graduates accepting employment with law firms of all sizes. Other recent MSU Law graduates have accepted judicial clerkships (4–8 percent), employment in business or industry (15–25 percent), governmental employment (10–15 percent), and public interest work (3–5 percent). Placement rates for new graduates consistently exceed 90 percent.

Admission

MSU Law has an admission process designed to identify individuals who have the potential to excel in their legal studies and the practice of law. The College of Law seeks to enroll students who are academically talented and who bring to the classroom a diversity of personal and professional experiences and perspectives. The Law College's Admission Committee considers many variables in addition to the applicant's undergraduate grade-point average and score on the LSAT.

The Admission Committee encourages candidates for the Juris Doctor program to apply for admission at the earliest possible date after October 1 and prior to March 1. The Admission Office accepts applications through late spring, with a final deadline of April 30. Candidates whose applications are received prior to February 1 will be given priority consideration for scholarship assistance. Applications for admission are reviewed on a rolling-admission basis beginning in early November and continuing through late spring. Applications generally are reviewed according to the date they are complete with all supporting materials. Admission to Michigan State University College of Law is granted for the fall term only for both the full-time and part-time programs.

Scholarship Assistance

The College of Law offers one of the most generous scholarship programs among law schools nationally, with as many as 60 full-tuition scholarships awarded to members of each incoming class. Additionally, the Law College annually awards 50 scholarships ranging in value up to $25,000. Every applicant who is offered admission to the Law College is considered for scholarship assistance, though grants based on financial need require an application. Law students who achieve a GPA of 3.60 or higher at the end of their first year of full-time studies at MSU Law automatically qualify for scholarship assistance that covers one-half, three-quarters, or 100 percent of tuition.

APPLICANT PROFILE

Michigan State University College of Law
This grid includes only applicants who earned 120–180 LSAT scores under standard administrations.

LSAT Score	GPA 3.75 +		3.50–3.74		3.25–3.49		3.00–3.24		2.75–2.99		2.50–2.74		2.25–2.49		2.00–2.24		Below 2.00		No GPA		Total	
	Apps	Adm	Apps	Adm	Apps	Adm	Apps	Adm	Apps	Adm	Apps	Adm	Apps	Adm	Apps	Adm	Apps	Adm	Apps	Adm	Apps	Adm
170–180	9	6	4	3	1	1	4	1	1	1	0	0	0	0	1	0	0	0	0	0	20	12
165–169	29	23	34	24	10	8	13	6	13	8	4	4	4	0	0	0	1	0	1	0	109	73
160–164	94	64	98	72	94	66	51	31	18	13	16	8	6	3	7	1	3	0	5	3	392	261
155–159	151	125	218	146	193	107	147	69	97	42	57	18	33	6	11	1	3	0	13	8	923	522
150–154	92	64	178	90	243	50	234	29	147	7	66	2	30	3	13	0	4	0	12	3	1019	248
145–149	33	18	103	27	121	5	126	3	101	4	60	1	34	1	14	0	3	0	19	2	614	61
140–144	13	0	17	0	43	3	44	0	37	1	35	2	20	0	12	0	1	0	8	0	230	6
Below 140	6	2	9	1	14	0	27	0	27	0	16	0	13	0	10	0	6	0	11	0	139	3
Total	427	302	661	363	719	240	646	139	441	76	254	35	140	13	68	2	21	0	69	16	3446	1186

Apps = Number of Applicants
Adm = Number Admitted
Reflects 99% of the total applicant pool; highest LSAT data reported.

UNIVERSITY OF MINNESOTA LAW SCHOOL

290 Walter F. Mondale Hall, 229 19th Avenue South
Minneapolis, MN 55455
Phone: 612.625.3487; Fax: 612.626.1874
E-mail: jdadmissions@umn.edu; Website: www.law.umn.edu

ABA
Approved
Since
1923

The Basics

Type of school	Public
Term	Semester
Application deadline	4/1
Application fee	$75
Financial aid deadline	5/1
Can first year start other than fall?	No
Student to faculty ratio	10.9 to 1
# of housing spaces available restricted to law students	
graduate housing for which law students are eligible	

Faculty and Administrators

	Total		Men		Women		Minorities	
	Spr	Fall	Spr	Fall	Spr	Fall	Spr	Fall
Full-time	59	55	36	32	23	23	5	4
Other full-time	4	3	3	3	1	0	0	0
Deans, librarians, & others who teach	10	9	4	3	5	5	1	1
Part-time	172	133	92	75	80	57	75	63
Total	245	200	135	113	109	85	81	68

Curriculum

		Full-Time	Part-Time
Typical first-year section size		88	0
Is there typically a "small section" of the first-year class, other than Legal Writing, taught by full-time faculty		Yes	No
If yes, typical size offered last year		44	
# of classroom course titles beyond first-year curriculum		181	
# of upper division courses, excluding seminars, with an enrollment:	Under 25	55	
	25–49	20	
	50–74	13	
	75–99	7	
	100+	3	
# of seminars		66	
# of seminar positions available		761	
# of seminar positions filled		742	0
# of positions available in simulation courses		300	
# of simulation positions filled		297	0
# of positions available in faculty supervised clinical courses		350	
# of faculty supervised clinical positions filled		348	0
# involved in field placements		122	0
# involved in law journals		165	0
# involved in moot court or trial competitions		191	0
# of credit hours required to graduate		88	

JD Enrollment and Ethnicity

	Men		Women		Full-Time		Part-Time		1st-Year		Total		JD Degs. Awd.
	#	%	#	%	#	%	#	%	#	%	#	%	
All Hispanics	13	3.0	16	5.1	29	3.9	0	0.0	7	2.7	29	3.9	3
Am. Ind./AK Nat.	4	0.9	3	1.0	7	0.9	0	0.0	0	0.0	7	0.9	5
Asian	32	7.3	24	7.6	56	7.4	0	0.0	17	6.6	56	7.4	26
Black/Af. Am.	16	3.7	8	2.5	24	3.2	0	0.0	9	3.5	24	3.2	5
Nat. HI/Pac. Isl.	1	0.2	1	0.3	2	0.3	0	0.0	2	0.8	2	0.3	0
2 or more races	7	1.6	9	2.9	16	2.1	0	0.0	16	6.2	16	2.1	0
Subtotal (minor.)	73	16.7	61	19.4	134	17.8	0	0.0	51	19.7	134	17.8	39
Nonres. Alien	10	2.3	9	2.9	19	2.5	0	0.0	5	1.9	19	2.5	7
White/Cauc.	324	74.1	235	74.6	559	74.3	0	0.0	194	74.9	559	74.3	222
Unknown	30	6.9	10	3.2	40	5.3	0	0.0	9	3.5	40	5.3	16
Total	437	58.1	315	41.9	752	100.0	0	0.0	259	34.4	752		284

Transfers

Transfers in	31
Transfers out	6

Tuition and Fees

	Resident	Nonresident
Full-time	$31,882	$40,388
Part-time		
Tuition Guarantee Program	N	

Living Expenses

Estimated living expenses for singles

Living on campus	Living off campus	Living at home
N/A	$14,262	$7,286

ABA
Approved
Since
1923

GPA and LSAT Scores

	Total	Full-Time	Part-Time
# of apps	3,866	3,866	0
# of offers	1,031	1,031	0
# of matrics	260	260	0
75% GPA	3.84	3.84	0.00
Median GPA	3.71	3.71	0.00
25% GPA	3.36	3.36	0.00
75% LSAT	168	168	0
Median LSAT	167	167	0
25% LSAT	159	159	0

Grants and Scholarships (from prior year)

	Total #	Total %	Full-Time #	Full-Time %	Part-Time #	Part-Time %
Total # of students	766		766		0	
Total # receiving grants	480	62.7	480	62.7	0	0.0
Less than 1/2 tuition	312	40.7	312	40.7	0	0.0
Half to full tuition	141	18.4	141	18.4	0	0.0
Full tuition	6	0.8	6	0.8	0	0.0
More than full tuition	21	2.7	21	2.7	0	0.0
Median grant amount			$10,000		$0	

Informational and Library Resources

Total amount spent on library materials	$2,237,325
Study seating capacity inside the library	773
# of full-time equivalent professional librarians	12
Hours per week library is open	81
# of open, wired connections available to students	0
# of networked computers available for use by students	86
Has wireless network?	Y
Requires computer?	Y

JD Attrition (from prior year)

	Academic #	Other #	Total #	Total %
1st year	0	10	10	4.7
2nd year	0	7	7	2.7
3rd year	0	2	2	0.7
4th year	0	0	0	0.0

Employment (9 months after graduation)

	Total	Percentage
Employment status known	255	100.0
Employment status unknown	0	0.0
Employed	240	94.1
Pursuing graduate degrees	6	2.4
Unemployed (seeking, not seeking, or studying for the bar)	3	1.2
Type of Employment		
# employed in law firms	113	47.1
# employed in business and industry	29	12.1
# employed in government	25	10.4
# employed in public interest	28	11.7
# employed as judicial clerks	27	11.2
# employed in academia	1	0.4
Geographic Location		
# employed in state	122	50.8
# employed outside the US	4	1.7
# of states where employed	27	

Bar Passage Rates

First-time takers	251	Reporting %	80.88
Average school %	92.12	Average state %	87.44
Average pass difference	4.68		

Jurisdiction	Takers	Passers	Pass %	State %	Diff %
Minnesota	140	135	96.43	89.58	6.85
New York	25	22	88.00	86.51	1.49
California	23	15	65.22	73.19	–7.97
Illinois	15	15	100.00	90.89	9.11

UNIVERSITY OF MINNESOTA LAW SCHOOL

290 Walter F. Mondale Hall, 229 19th Avenue South
Minneapolis, MN 55455
Phone: 612.625.3487; Fax: 612.626.1874
E-mail: jdadmissions@umn.edu; Website: www.law.umn.edu

Introduction

The University of Minnesota Law School, founded in 1888, is one of the country's premier law schools. Under the leadership of international scholar Dean David Wippman, the quality of Minnesota's faculty, the academic credentials of its students, and the caliber of its library and physical facilities are the strongest in the history of the school. For over 120 years, the school's tradition of excellence and innovation in legal education has made it among the best in the nation. In keeping with its Midwestern traditions, the Law School provides a personal, collegial environment for the study of law. At the same time, the school's location in the midst of a thriving cosmopolitan area provides a variety of academic, employment, cultural, and recreational opportunities. Students have easy access to the resources of a world-class research university and to the Twin Cities of Minneapolis and St. Paul, one of the most progressive and livable metropolitan communities in the country.

Faculty

The faculty's wide-ranging expertise allows students to choose from an academically rich and innovative curriculum that integrates theory and doctrine with skills, ethics, and practice.

Faculty members are prolific and influential scholars, having published over 250 books and close to 2,500 articles. Thirty-six percent of the tenured faculty are invited members of the prestigious American Law Institute, and 68 percent of them have been honored with chair-level appointments. Members of the faculty include a recent chair of the United Nations Sub-Commission on the Promotion and Protection of Human Rights (the first US citizen to chair the commission since Eleanor Roosevelt), a member of the American Academy of Arts and Sciences, and a former counselor on international law for the US Department of State.

But while the faculty's scholarship has earned them national acclaim, their equally energetic passion for teaching and mentoring, along with a 10:1 student-to-faculty ratio, have earned them the respect and appreciation of their students.

Student Body/Admission

With 260 students in the entering class, the student body is large enough to enjoy the benefits of diverse backgrounds, perspectives, and interests, while remaining small enough to foster the kind of collegial and supportive community that is a hallmark of Minnesota life.

Although the atmosphere and camaraderie reflect distinctly Minnesotan values, 41 states, 11 countries, and over 200 undergraduate institutions are represented in the current JD student body. The admissions committee looks beyond a simple evaluation of LSAT and undergraduate GPA to compose a class that will produce leaders in the legal profession. Many students have advanced degrees and prior work experience.

Library and Physical Facilities

The award-winning Walter F. Mondale Hall was substantially expanded in 2001. The building houses all faculty offices, 8 law school research institutes, model classrooms in varying sizes, a beautiful auditorium, the law clinics, a cafeteria, the law school bookstore, student lockers, offices for student organizations and publications, a variety of lounge areas, and a computer lab. All incoming JD students are issued laptops, and wireless access is available in all student areas of the building.

Mondale Hall also houses the law library, which is the seventh largest in the United States with over one million volumes. The library offers students 24-hour access. The professional staff takes pride in the outstanding collection of materials and in the individualized service it provides to students and faculty.

Curriculum

Minnesota is implementing curriculum innovations that are designed to merge traditionally doctrinal pedagogy with clinical instruction. Beginning in the first year, students will build on basic lawyering skills, doctrinal concepts, and ethical considerations to craft professional solutions to realistic problems in the new Practice and Professionalism class. First-year students will also enjoy Minnesota's rich curriculum with the opportunity to choose an elective in their second semester. Minnesota continues to be one of only a handful of schools with three years of writing requirements and enjoys one of the smallest first-year writing section sizes, with 10 to 12 students per section. Second-year students are required to participate in a journal or competitive moot court.

Drawing on the strength of a world-class university, qualified students may pursue dual or joint degrees with a myriad of nationally ranked graduate and professional schools. Especially noteworthy is Minnesota's unique joint-degree program in law, health, and the life sciences. Students also enjoy the opportunity to specialize in various subject areas. Currently, concentrations are available in health law and bioethics, human rights, and labor and employment law.

Clinical Programs

With 22 separate clinics, Minnesota has one of the country's largest and most active clinical programs. Through the clinics, students represent real clients under the close tutelage of the clinic faculty. Over 50 percent of the student body participates in a live-client clinic prior to graduation, providing more than 18,000 hours of pro bono legal work for the Twin Cities community each year.

Special Programs

Minnesota hosts international exchange programs in France, Germany, Ireland, Italy, the Netherlands, Spain, Sweden, and Uruguay, and a six-week Summer Study-Abroad Program in Beijing, China. These programs enable interested students to study abroad and allow students to benefit from the international perspectives students from these countries bring to the classroom.

Through the Law School Public Service Program, students are asked to perform 50 hours of pro bono legal service for low-income and disadvantaged Minnesotans. Those who complete at least 50 hours of service are recognized for their dedication with a notation on their transcript and at the graduation ceremony.

Eight major research institutes are housed in the law school: the Human Rights Center; Institute on Race and Poverty; Center for Business Law; Consortium on Law and Values in Health, Environment, and the Life Sciences; Institute on Crime and Public Policy; Institute on Law and Economics; Institute on Law and Politics; and the Institute on Law and Rationality. These institutes enrich the school's intellectual life, contribute to policy debate and formation, and provide research and employment opportunities for selected law students.

Student Activities

Minnesota hosts seven student-edited journals: *ABA Journal of Labor and Employment Law; Constitutional Commentary; Crime and Justice; Law and Inequality: A Journal of Theory and Practice; Minnesota Journal of International Law; Minnesota Journal of Law, Science, and Technology;* and *Minnesota Law Review.* Students receive academic credit for their journal work.

Students also receive credit for moot court participation. The breadth of Minnesota's moot court program is unusual, with eight programs spanning a wide variety of subject areas: Civil Rights Moot Court, Intellectual Property Moot Court, International Moot Court, Environmental Moot Court, Wagner Labor Law Moot Court, National Moot Court, ABA Moot Court, and Maynard Pirsig Moot Court.

Student extracurricular activities include 50 separate student organizations, spanning the full spectrum of political viewpoints, social interests, and intellectual and recreational activities (not to mention a full-blown musical theater production).

Expenses and Financial Aid

In recent years, over 90 percent of the student body has received financial aid and approximately 65 percent of each incoming class received a scholarship of some kind. Second- and third-year students also may apply for research assistantships.

Career and Professional Development

With alumni in all 50 states and over 260 federal and state court judges nationwide, Minnesota graduates are leaders in the judiciary, government, law practice, business, and academics. Employers interview on campus, at regional interview programs sponsored by the Career Center, and at job fairs for nearly 700 offices, including law firms, corporations, and governmental agencies from around the United States. Employers nationwide regularly solicit résumés from students for job postings. Each year, 15 to 20 percent of the graduates accept prestigious judicial clerkships, and approximately 98 percent are employed within nine months of graduation.

APPLICANT PROFILE

University of Minnesota Law School
This grid includes only applicants who earned 120–180 LSAT scores under standard administrations.

LSAT Score	GPA																					
	3.75 +		3.50–3.74		3.25–3.49		3.00–3.24		2.75–2.99		2.50–2.74		2.25–2.49		2.00–2.24		Below 2.00		No GPA		Total	
	Apps	Adm	Apps	Adm	Apps	Adm	Apps	Adm	Apps	Adm	Apps	Adm	Apps	Adm	Apps	Adm	Apps	Adm	Apps	Adm	Apps	Adm
175–180	11	11	17	10	16	9	5	4	5	3	2	1	0	0	1	0	1	0	3	2	61	40
170–174	102	80	101	70	83	55	39	23	21	12	13	6	7	3	3	0	1	0	14	7	384	256
165–169	263	161	294	148	210	87	149	65	52	14	34	4	10	1	4	1	1	0	23	9	1040	490
160–164	215	64	317	37	235	6	131	1	58	1	28	1	13	0	2	0	0	0	28	0	1027	110
155–159	128	44	175	12	152	4	93	2	62	2	33	0	13	0	3	0	0	0	22	1	681	65
150–154	80	30	114	15	91	1	55	1	31	2	17	0	9	0	7	0	1	0	6	0	411	49
145–149	20	3	26	1	39	0	26	0	19	0	10	1	4	0	1	0	0	0	6	1	151	6
140–144	2	0	6	0	10	0	16	0	6	0	7	0	5	0	2	0	1	0	1	0	56	0
135–139	0	0	2	0	3	0	4	0	7	0	3	0	1	0	1	0	0	0	3	0	24	0
130–134	0	0	0	0	3	0	0	0	2	0	1	0	2	0	0	0	1	0	1	0	10	0
125–129	0	0	1	0	0	0	0	0	0	0	1	0	0	0	0	0	0	0	1	0	3	0
120–124	0	0	0	0	0	0	0	0	0	0	0	0	0	0	1	0	0	0	0	0	1	0
Total	821	393	1053	293	842	162	518	96	263	34	149	13	64	4	25	1	6	0	108	20	3849	1016

Apps = Number of Applicants
Adm = Number Admitted
Reflects 99% of the total applicant pool; highest LSAT data reported.

THE UNIVERSITY OF MISSISSIPPI SCHOOL OF LAW

Robert C. Khayat Law Center, PO Box 1848
University, MS 38677
Phone: Admission: 662.915.6910, Main: 662.915.7361; Fax: 662.915.1289
E-mail: lawmiss@olemiss.edu; Website: www.law.olemiss.edu

ABA
Approved
Since
1930

The Basics

Type of school	Public
Term	Semester
Application deadline	3/1
Application fee	$40
Financial aid deadline	3/1
Can first year start other than fall?	No
Student to faculty ratio	15.2 to 1
# of housing spaces available restricted to law students	
graduate housing for which law students are eligible	

Faculty and Administrators

	Total		Men		Women		Minorities	
	Spr	Fall	Spr	Fall	Spr	Fall	Spr	Fall
Full-time	28	26	19	17	9	9	8	7
Other full-time	5	5	5	5	0	0	1	1
Deans, librarians, & others who teach	8	8	6	6	2	2	1	1
Part-time	14	15	10	9	4	6	1	1
Total	55	54	40	37	15	17	11	10

Curriculum

	Full-Time	Part-Time
Typical first-year section size	58	0
Is there typically a "small section" of the first-year class, other than Legal Writing, taught by full-time faculty	No	No
If yes, typical size offered last year		

# of classroom course titles beyond first-year curriculum		81
# of upper division courses, excluding seminars, with an enrollment:	Under 25	35
	25–49	12
	50–74	4
	75–99	2
	100+	0
# of seminars		14
# of seminar positions available		252
# of seminar positions filled	193	0
# of positions available in simulation courses		110
# of simulation positions filled	103	0
# of positions available in faculty supervised clinical courses		80
# of faculty supervised clinical positions filled	74	0
# involved in field placements	39	0
# involved in law journals	80	0
# involved in moot court or trial competitions	70	0
# of credit hours required to graduate		90

JD Enrollment and Ethnicity

	Men		Women		Full-Time		Part-Time		1st-Year		Total		JD Degs. Awd.
	#	%	#	%	#	%	#	%	#	%	#	%	
All Hispanics	8	2.8	3	1.3	11	2.1	0	0.0	8	4.0	11	2.1	1
Am. Ind./AK Nat.	4	1.4	2	0.9	6	1.2	0	0.0	3	1.5	6	1.2	1
Asian	1	0.3	3	1.3	4	0.8	0	0.0	2	1.0	4	0.8	3
Black/Af. Am.	16	5.6	44	19.2	60	11.6	0	0.0	20	10.1	60	11.6	19
Nat. Hl/Pac. Isl.	0	0.0	0	0.0	0	0.0	0	0.0	0	0.0	0	0.0	0
2 or more races	0	0.0	0	0.0	0	0.0	0	0.0	0	0.0	0	0.0	0
Subtotal (minor.)	29	10.1	52	22.7	81	15.7	0	0.0	33	16.6	81	15.7	25
Nonres. Alien	2	0.7	0	0.0	2	0.4	0	0.0	2	1.0	2	0.4	0
White/Cauc.	256	89.2	177	77.3	433	83.9	0	0.0	164	82.4	433	83.9	137
Unknown	0	0.0	0	0.0	0	0.0	0	0.0	0	0.0	0	0.0	0
Total	287	55.6	229	44.4	516	100.0	0	0.0	199	38.6	516		162

Transfers

Transfers in	1
Transfers out	3

Tuition and Fees

	Resident	Nonresident
Full-time	$10,275	$22,470
Part-time		
Tuition Guarantee Program		N

Living Expenses

Estimated living expenses for singles

Living on campus	Living off campus	Living at home
$18,574	$18,574	$18,574

THE UNIVERSITY OF MISSISSIPPI SCHOOL OF LAW

ABA
Approved
Since
1930

GPA and LSAT Scores

	Total	Full-Time	Part-Time
# of apps	1,602	1,602	0
# of offers	532	532	0
# of matrics	199	199	0
75% GPA	3.69	3.69	0.00
Median GPA	3.51	3.51	0.00
25% GPA	3.26	3.26	0.00
75% LSAT	158	158	0
Median LSAT	156	156	0
25% LSAT	151	151	0

Grants and Scholarships (from prior year)

	Total		Full-Time		Part-Time	
	#	%	#	%	#	%
Total # of students	495		495		0	
Total # receiving grants	153	30.9	153	30.9	0	0.0
Less than 1/2 tuition	48	9.7	48	9.7	0	0.0
Half to full tuition	77	15.6	77	15.6	0	0.0
Full tuition	1	0.2	1	0.2	0	0.0
More than full tuition	27	5.5	27	5.5	0	0.0
Median grant amount			$6,826		$0	

Informational and Library Resources

Total amount spent on library materials	$787,966
Study seating capacity inside the library	297
# of full-time equivalent professional librarians	7
Hours per week library is open	105
# of open, wired connections available to students	777
# of networked computers available for use by students	57
Has wireless network?	Y
Requires computer?	N

JD Attrition (from prior year)

	Academic	Other	Total	
	#	#	#	%
1st year	1	5	6	3.5
2nd year	0	1	1	0.6
3rd year	0	0	0	0.0
4th year	0	0	0	0.0

Employment (9 months after graduation)

	Total	Percentage
Employment status known	153	94.4
Employment status unknown	9	5.6
Employed	137	89.5
Pursuing graduate degrees	6	3.9
Unemployed (seeking, not seeking, or studying for the bar)	8	5.2
Type of Employment		
# employed in law firms	81	59.1
# employed in business and industry	12	8.8
# employed in government	21	15.3
# employed in public interest	3	2.2
# employed as judicial clerks	17	12.4
# employed in academia	0	0.0
Geographic Location		
# employed in state	72	52.6
# employed outside the US	0	0.0
# of states where employed		17

Bar Passage Rates

First-time takers	160	Reporting %	84.38
Average school %	91.11	Average state %	84.93
Average pass difference	6.18		

Jurisdiction	Takers	Passers	Pass %	State %	Diff %
Mississippi	106	96	90.57	85.21	5.36
Tennessee	18	18	100.00	82.44	17.56
Georgia	11	9	81.82	86.28	−4.46

THE UNIVERSITY OF MISSISSIPPI SCHOOL OF LAW

Robert C. Khayat Law Center, PO Box 1848
University, MS 38677
Phone: Admission: 662.915.6910, Main: 662.915.7361; Fax: 662.915.1289
E-mail: lawmiss@olemiss.edu; Website: www.law.olemiss.edu

Introduction

In 1854, recognizing the need for formal law instruction in the state of Mississippi, the legislature established the Department of Law at the University of Mississippi. In 2011, the School of Law moved into a $50 million LEED certified facility, the Robert C. Khayat Law Center.

Oxford, a small town of approximately 19,000 people, lies nestled in the quiet hills of North Mississippi, just 75 miles southeast of bustling Memphis, Tennessee, and 180 miles north of the state capital of Jackson.

The new building has traditional Greek Revival architecture to match the architectural style of the campus, and it is state-of-the-art in terms of instructional space.

The University of Mississippi is the fourth oldest state-supported law school in the nation. The School of Law is fully approved by the American Bar Association and is a long-standing member of the Association of American Law Schools.

Library and Physical Facilities

The library houses one of the most extensive federal, state, and international law collections in the Southeast. The library's experienced, service-oriented staff is available to assist patrons with these materials and to provide training in all aspects of traditional and computer-assisted legal research. Other library features include open stacks, an online catalog, two state-of-the-art computer labs, and private study rooms and carrels that may be reserved. The library has a strong commitment to new information technologies and has recently added additional multimedia support, along with enhanced wired and wireless network access for patrons.

Admission

Admission to law school is gained by committee approval based upon an applicant's credentials. These credentials include a satisfactory LSAT score and an acceptable academic record at the undergraduate level. A bachelor's degree from an accredited school is required before an applicant can register for law school.

There are no prelaw requisites. Every applicant must take the LSAT and register with LSAC's Credential Assembly Service. An LSAT score obtained more than three years before application is not valid, and the applicant will be required to retake the test. Applications are available the September preceding admission, with the application completion deadline for both summer and fall enrollment being March 1. However, early application is encouraged. Applicants who file late risk being placed on a waiting list.

Although the LSAT and GPA are the most important factors in the admission process, other considerations are (1) grade patterns and progression; (2) quality of undergraduate institution; (3) difficulty of major field of study; (4) number of years since bachelor's degree was earned; (5) job experience; (6) social, personal, or economic circumstances that may have affected college grades or performance on the LSAT or academic record; (7) nonacademic achievements; (8) letters of recommendation; and (9) residency.

Entrance Dates

Students are given the option to enter in the summer or fall of each admission year. Because summer and fall enrollees are considered as one class, the same standards are applied in the decision-making process.

Curriculum

First-year students complete a predetermined curriculum that focuses on the development of analytical skills and a foundation of substantive knowledge. Largely, second- and third-year students are free to select their own courses of study and emphasis, although a number of courses are recommended to ensure a broad-based substantive and procedural background. Students may select from a large number of elective courses, including seminars, clinical, and trial advocacy courses. The elective curriculum offers generous opportunities for students to pursue special interests such as constitutional and individual rights, business and commercial transactions, federal taxation, international law, and environmental law.

Clinical Programs

Civil Legal Clinic—Under the supervision of the director of the clinic, students provide legal counseling for low-income clients on civil matters. The program includes clinical units in Elder Law, Consumer Law, Child Advocacy, Legislation, and Domestic Violence.

Criminal Appeals Clinic—The Criminal Appeals Clinic was established by the National Center for Justice and the Rule of Law. The course of study is designed to give students practical experience representing clients in criminal appellate cases and includes direct student participation in the pro bono representation of indigent persons in their cases on appeal.

Prosecution Externship Program—The Prosecution Externship was established by the National Center for Justice and the Rule of Law. It is designed to prepare law students for careers in criminal law by combining academic training with placements as externs in local, state, and federal prosecutor offices.

Student Activities

The *Mississippi Law Journal,* edited and published by law students three times each year, includes articles by distinguished professors, judges, and practitioners.

The *Journal of Space Law* is the oldest journal dedicated to space law and is the only one of its kind in the United States. The National Center for Remote Sensing, Air and Space Law faculty regularly supervise an editorial team of 15 to 18 law student editors, staff, and authors on this journal.

The **Moot Court Board** oversees several moot court competitions, including the Steen, Reynolds, and Dalehite trial competition each fall and the McGlinchey Stafford oral-advocacy competition each spring.

Summer-Abroad Programs

The School of Law offers an opportunity to earn up to six semester credit hours in its summer session held annually in England at Downing College, Cambridge University. Classes offered are for full academic credit and are subject to the same academic standards maintained in the domestic program.

Special Programs

One of the most active organizations is the **Public Interest Law Foundation**. The student-run organization focuses its efforts on community groups that need legal assistance—victims of domestic violence, children, and defendants who cannot afford an attorney. The organization raises money to support students working in public interest jobs.

The **National Center for Justice and the Rule of Law** is a component of the law center funded by a multimillion dollar grant from the Department of Justice. The center works cooperatively with agencies in sponsoring research, hosting international and national conferences, and presenting educational programs on issues related to criminal justice, such as international and domestic terrorism, drug-trafficking, and the role of the proposed International Criminal Court. Advanced courses in criminal law and procedure are offered to students who may choose a criminal law concentration and receive official recognition of that achievement upon graduation.

The **National Center for Remote Sensing, Air and Space Law** is funded by a grant from NASA. The only center of its kind in the United States, it serves as a research, advisory, and training resource for the emerging commercial geospatial industry, the international legal community, and related user groups. A concentration in remote sensing, air and space law is available through the center. Courses include US Space Law, International Space Law, Remote Sensing Law, Independent Study, US Aviation Law, International Aviation Law, and the *Journal of Space Law*.

Mississippi Innocence Project—Established in 2007 and housed at the School of Law, the Mississippi Innocence Project is committed to providing the highest quality legal representation to its clients: state prisoners serving significant periods of incarceration who have cognizable claims of wrongful conviction.

Housing

The majority of law students live off campus in rental units. On-campus housing is available, and students who are interested in living on campus should make early application to the Housing Office.

Career Services

A full-time director of career services assists students in finding employment. Seventy-five to 100 law firms and other prospective employers interview at the law school each year. Approximately 60 percent of graduating seniors are employed prior to graduation, with the remaining number being placed within six months of graduation. The law school is an active member of the National Association for Law Placement (NALP) and annually participates in the Atlanta Legal Hiring Conference, the Equal Justice Works Public Interest Career Fair, the Patent Law Interview Program, and the Southeastern Minority Job Fair.

APPLICANT PROFILE

The University of Mississippi School of Law
This grid includes only applicants who earned 120–180 LSAT scores under standard administrations.

LSAT Score	GPA																				
	3.75 +		3.50–3.74		3.25–3.49		3.00–3.24		2.75–2.99		2.50–2.74		2.25–2.49		2.00–2.24		Below 2.00		No GPA		Total	
	Apps	Adm	Apps	Adm	Apps	Adm	Apps	Adm	Apps	Adm	Apps	Adm	Apps	Adm	Apps	Adm	Apps	Adm	Apps	Adm	Apps	Adm
175–180	0	0	0	0	0	0	0	0	0	0	0	0	0	0	0	0	0	0	0	0	0	0
170–174	2	2	0	0	1	1	0	0	0	0	1	1	1	0	0	0	0	0	0	0	5	4
165–169	10	9	3	3	5	4	5	4	7	6	1	0	0	0	1	0	1	0	0	0	33	26
160–164	25	24	19	18	38	35	27	16	22	10	17	3	8	3	4	0	0	0	1	1	161	110
155–159	56	56	78	75	114	62	86	26	60	9	44	3	18	2	8	0	0	0	0	0	464	233
150–154	62	41	91	32	108	20	111	8	63	1	33	0	14	0	5	0	1	0	0	0	488	102
145–149	20	8	37	16	62	6	54	3	43	2	26	1	18	0	5	0	0	0	2	0	267	36
140–144	8	5	11	4	14	2	36	3	13	1	17	2	6	0	2	0	2	0	2	0	111	17
135–139	0	0	3	0	7	0	8	0	11	0	8	0	5	0	4	0	1	0	1	0	48	0
130–134	0	0	0	0	1	0	2	0	2	0	1	0	1	0	0	0	1	0	0	0	8	0
125–129	0	0	0	0	0	0	2	0	1	0	0	0	0	0	0	0	0	0	0	0	3	0
120–124	0	0	0	0	0	0	0	0	0	0	0	0	0	0	0	0	1	0	0	0	1	0
Total	183	145	242	148	350	130	331	60	222	29	148	10	71	5	29	0	7	0	6	1	1589	528

Apps = Number of Applicants
Adm = Number Admitted
Reflects 99% of the total applicant pool; highest LSAT data reported.

MISSISSIPPI COLLEGE SCHOOL OF LAW

151 E. Griffith Street
Jackson, MS 39201
Phone: 601.925.7152; Fax: 601.925.7166
E-mail: lawadmissions@mc.edu; Website: http://law.mc.edu

The Basics

Type of school	Private
Term	Semester
Application deadline	6/1
Application fee	$0
Financial aid deadline	6/1
Can first year start other than fall?	No
Student to faculty ratio	17.3 to 1
# of housing spaces available restricted to law students	
graduate housing for which law students are eligible	

Faculty and Administrators

	Total		Men		Women		Minorities	
	Spr	Fall	Spr	Fall	Spr	Fall	Spr	Fall
Full-time	25	26	11	12	14	14	4	4
Other full-time	0	0	0	0	0	0	0	0
Deans, librarians, & others who teach	8	7	5	4	3	3	1	1
Part-time	28	77	28	40	0	36	1	6
Total	61	110	44	56	17	53	6	11

Curriculum

	Full-Time	Part-Time
Typical first-year section size	70	0
Is there typically a "small section" of the first-year class, other than Legal Writing, taught by full-time faculty	Yes	No
If yes, typical size offered last year	52	
# of classroom course titles beyond first-year curriculum		81

# of upper division courses, excluding seminars, with an enrollment:		
	Under 25	88
	25–49	29
	50–74	12
	75–99	7
	100+	0

# of seminars		19
# of seminar positions available		285
# of seminar positions filled	213	0
# of positions available in simulation courses		810
# of simulation positions filled	715	0
# of positions available in faculty supervised clinical courses		55
# of faculty supervised clinical positions filled	37	0
# involved in field placements	170	0
# involved in law journals	48	0
# involved in moot court or trial competitions	74	0
# of credit hours required to graduate		90

JD Enrollment and Ethnicity

	Men		Women		Full-Time		Part-Time		1st-Year		Total		JD Degs. Awd.
	#	%	#	%	#	%	#	%	#	%	#	%	
All Hispanics	5	1.5	0	0.0	4	0.7	1	9.1	2	0.9	5	0.9	1
Am. Ind./AK Nat.	1	0.3	0	0.0	1	0.2	0	0.0	0	0.0	1	0.2	1
Asian	4	1.2	1	0.5	3	0.6	2	18.2	2	0.9	5	0.9	3
Black/Af. Am.	19	5.8	31	14.1	49	9.1	1	9.1	17	7.9	50	9.1	11
Nat. HI/Pac. Isl.	0	0.0	0	0.0	0	0.0	0	0.0	0	0.0	0	0.0	0
2 or more races	0	0.0	0	0.0	0	0.0	0	0.0	0	0.0	0	0.0	0
Subtotal (minor.)	29	8.9	32	14.5	57	10.6	4	36.4	21	9.8	61	11.2	16
Nonres. Alien	0	0.0	0	0.0	0	0.0	0	0.0	0	0.0	0	0.0	0
White/Cauc.	294	89.9	179	81.4	466	86.9	7	63.6	190	88.8	473	86.5	152
Unknown	4	1.2	9	4.1	13	2.4	0	0.0	3	1.4	13	2.4	3
Total	327	59.8	220	40.2	536	98.0	11	2.0	214	39.1	547		171

Transfers

Transfers in	0
Transfers out	15

Tuition and Fees

	Resident	Nonresident
Full-time	$28,070	
Part-time		
Tuition Guarantee Program	Y	

Living Expenses

Estimated living expenses for singles

Living on campus	Living off campus	Living at home
N/A	$21,225	$21,225

MISSISSIPPI COLLEGE SCHOOL OF LAW

ABA Approved Since 1980

GPA and LSAT Scores

	Total	Full-Time	Part-Time
# of apps	1,357	1,356	1
# of offers	735	734	1
# of matrics	212	212	0
75% GPA	3.58	3.58	0.00
Median GPA	3.24	3.24	0.00
25% GPA	2.94	2.94	0.00
75% LSAT	154	154	0
Median LSAT	150	150	0
25% LSAT	147	147	0

Grants and Scholarships (from prior year)

	Total		Full-Time		Part-Time	
	#	%	#	%	#	%
Total # of students	536		521		15	
Total # receiving grants	182	34.0	182	34.9	0	0.0
Less than 1/2 tuition	104	19.4	104	20.0	0	0.0
Half to full tuition	32	6.0	32	6.1	0	0.0
Full tuition	22	4.1	22	4.2	0	0.0
More than full tuition	24	4.5	24	4.6	0	0.0
Median grant amount			$9,000		$0	

Informational and Library Resources

Total amount spent on library materials	$1,029,053
Study seating capacity inside the library	394
# of full-time equivalent professional librarians	5
Hours per week library is open	108
# of open, wired connections available to students	0
# of networked computers available for use by students	27
Has wireless network?	Y
Requires computer?	N

JD Attrition (from prior year)

	Academic	Other	Total	
	#	#	#	%
1st year	3	23	26	13.1
2nd year	2	1	3	1.7
3rd year	1	0	1	0.6
4th year	0	0	0	0.0

Employment (9 months after graduation)

	Total	Percentage
Employment status known	151	88.8
Employment status unknown	19	11.2
Employed	136	90.1
Pursuing graduate degrees	5	3.3
Unemployed (seeking, not seeking, or studying for the bar)	10	6.6
Type of Employment		
# employed in law firms	81	59.6
# employed in business and industry	13	9.6
# employed in government	23	16.9
# employed in public interest	3	2.2
# employed as judicial clerks	16	11.8
# employed in academia	0	0.0
Geographic Location		
# employed in state	79	58.1
# employed outside the US	1	0.7
# of states where employed		15

Bar Passage Rates

First-time takers	165	Reporting %	72.12
Average school %	79.83	Average state %	85.34

Average pass difference −5.51

Jurisdiction	Takers	Passers	Pass %	State %	Diff %
Mississippi	107	83	77.57	85.21	−7.64
Alabama	12	12	100.00	86.51	13.49

MISSISSIPPI COLLEGE SCHOOL OF LAW

151 E. Griffith Street
Jackson, MS 39201
Phone: 601.925.7152; Fax: 601.925.7166
E-mail: lawadmissions@mc.edu; Website: http://law.mc.edu

Introduction to MC Law School

Mississippi College School of Law (MC Law) is located in downtown Jackson, Mississippi, and serves as a state-of-the-art legal center for the mid-South region. Jackson is the state capital, boasts a metropolitan population of 480,000, and is the political, cultural, and commercial center of Mississippi. Forty percent of all Mississippi attorneys work in the Jackson metro area.

MC Law's innovative campus includes an administrative building, an 18,000-square-foot classroom building with high-tech teaching centers, modern courtrooms, a nationally recognized law library, and a student center. A safe and convenient student parking lot is located next to the law school. Within walking distance of the law school lies a vibrant legal community, as well as the legislature, federal and state administrative agencies, and federal and state courts.

MC Law is part of Mississippi College—a university located in nearby Clinton, Mississippi, that has a liberal arts undergraduate program, nursing school, graduate school, physician assistant school, business school, and law school. MC Law is accredited by the American Bar Association and holds memberships in the Association of American Law Schools, the International Association of Law Schools, and the American Society of Comparative Law. Graduates of MC Law are eligible to take the bar examination in all 50 states.

Admission Procedures

When admitting students, the Admissions Office uses a "whole-person" concept and considers undergraduate GPA, LSAT score, and personal or academic achievements and honors. Every applicant must take the LSAT and may register for the Credential Assembly Service (CAS) prior to being considered for admission. There is no application fee if an online application is used. The school makes admission decisions on a rolling basis to permit early notification. Decisions are made without discrimination on the basis of race, religion, gender, orientation, age, military service, or national origin. The application deadline is June 1. When an applicant is accepted, a deposit of $250 is required to reserve a seat in the entering class. A second deposit of $250 must be received by June 1. Upon enrollment, these nonrefundable payments are credited to the applicant's tuition. Tuition is locked in so that a student pays the same tuition throughout law school with no subsequent increase. All applicants are automatically considered for merit-based scholarships that exceed $2 million.

Dynamic Learning Environment

The diversity of the student body adds to the learning environment. Over 60 percent of our students come from outside Mississippi. Many students have work experience, military service, or advanced degrees. This diversity fosters an exciting exchange of ideas inside and outside the classroom. Our students receive one-on-one attention and interaction with professors that extend beyond the classroom. The school is dedicated to maintaining a supportive learning environment. Because of our size and collegial atmosphere, students form lasting relationships with one another, collaborate on team projects, and are active in a variety of cocurricular and extracurricular activities.

Curriculum and Course Offerings

MC Law offers a broad curriculum. Our course of study integrates the theoretical aspects of the law with practical, hands-on training. First-year law students are required to take fundamental courses that focus on the major doctrinal areas of law, as well as development of legal writing and research skills. MC Law offers a broad range of second- and third-year elective courses. Our curriculum emphasizes the following disciplines: litigation and dispute resolution, family law, business and tax law, bioethics and health law, international law, and advocacy. MC Law offers a Louisiana Civil Law Certificate program for those who want to practice in Louisiana or to study comparative law. The law school operates on a semester basis. Students may begin their studies in June or August. A summer term is available to second- and third-year students who wish to accelerate or enrich their studies. An Executive Program allows students to attend on a part-time basis.

Faculty

Teaching is our strength. Our faculty members have impeccable credentials and are leaders in their fields of study. From insurance to international law and from constitutional law to ethics, our professors are regularly cited in courts, scholarly journals, and the media. MC Law is renowned for the extraordinary level of interaction between faculty and students. Because of our strategic location, federal and state judges and some of the best legal practitioners teach as adjunct professors, giving our students valuable practical training and helpful networking opportunities.

Legal Centers at MC Law

MC Law maintains legal centers to allow a subject area to be developed through course offerings, speakers, moot court teams, student organizations, externships, and cocurricular activities. MC Law supports these centers: Family and Children's Law, Bioethics and Health Law, Litigation and Dispute Resolution, Business and Tax Law, Public Service Law, and International and Comparative Law.

International and Comparative Law Center

The International and Comparative Law Center permits our students to take a global focus in their legal education. In addition to the international law-related courses the center oversees, students can participate in summer legal studies in Merida, Mexico; Seoul, South Korea; and Berlin, Germany. The Center coordinates a series of speakers and programs with an international theme.

Externship Skills Training Program

At MC Law, classroom theory and practical application go hand in hand. In addition to courses in legal doctrine, a wide range of instruction in the skills of modern practice is offered to second- and third-year students. Student externs work alongside practicing attorneys in government offices and public interest organizations. Depending on the particular externship, students present cases in court, interview witnesses, prepare pleadings, take depositions, negotiate with opposing parties, research legal issues, and draft court opinions. This program allows students to practice in the real world what they have learned in more traditional law school classes and gain experience prior to graduation. Students may take an externship in their home state. Many students secure employment as a result of this extern program.

Student Activities

The *Mississippi College Law Review* is a legal journal edited and published by law students who are selected on the basis of grades and the ability to do creative, scholarly research and writing. Membership on the *Law Review* staff is recognized as both an honor and a unique educational experience. The law school also provides an appellate advocacy program administered by the Moot Court Board, composed of second- and third-year students. This required program provides students with instruction and practice in both brief writing and oral argument. The school's legal aid office allows students to acquire client interviewing skills and substantive practical experience while providing a valuable pro bono service.

The Law Student Bar Association is the organized student government of the law school. Other student activities include two national legal fraternity chapters, Phi Alpha Delta and Phi Delta Phi; student chapters of the Mississippi Association for Justice and the Defense Lawyers Association; the Women's Student Bar Association; the Federal Bar Association; BLSA; and the Environmental Law Association.

Career Services

The Career Services Office assists in job placement and career development. In addition to the traditional on-campus interviews, the law school participates in regional interviews and offers a series of workshops throughout the year. Students are encouraged to work in local or national public interest or government agencies through the MC Law/Federal Work-Study public interest program. Graduates are employed by major law firms, corporations, and government agencies throughout the United States, with a primary focus in the

Southeast. Students have received clerkships with the United States Court of Appeals, United States District Courts, and the appellate and trial courts of various states. A number of graduates serve as JAG officers in the military services.

Minority Student Program

The law school offers a variety of programs to assist minority students: scholarships/stipends, student organizations, and an academic support program. Minority students are strongly encouraged to apply, and each applicant's entire record will be carefully considered. We are interested in students who have overcome challenges in life and who are the first in their family to attend law school. The Black Law Students Association (BLSA) chapter is an active contributor to student life and reaches out to the local community.

Library

The law library has a collection of more than 360,000 volumes and is committed to acquiring materials for both the immediate and the long-term needs of the law school. Emphasis is placed on development of the collections of statutes, legal periodicals, federal and state legislative materials, reports of federal and state appellate courts, federal administrative agency materials, specialized loose-leaf services, and microforms and treatises that support our teaching and scholarship. The library is a member of the American Association of Law Libraries. The technology division supports a WiFi system and a computer help desk for students. Newly constructed study rooms are available for group use.

Advocacy

MC Law sends 30 teams to regional and national trial and appellate advocacy moot court competitions. Preparation for these competitions flows from intraschool competitions in the 1L year and from a required appellate advocacy course in the 2L year. These programs, coupled with other coursework, give MC Law students skills and confidence that serve them well in practice.

APPLICANT PROFILE

Mississippi College School of Law
This grid includes only applicants who earned 120–180 LSAT scores under standard administrations.

LSAT Score	GPA								
	3.75 +	3.50–3.74	3.25–3.49	3.00–3.24	2.75–2.99	2.50–2.74	2.25–2.49	2.00–2.24	Below 2.00
175–180									
170–174									
165–169									
160–164									
155–159									
150–154									
145–149									
140–144									
135–139									
130–134									
125–129									
120–124									

■ Good Possibility   ☐ Possibility   ▨ Unlikely

UNIVERSITY OF MISSOURI SCHOOL OF LAW

Office of Admissions, 103 Hulston Hall
Columbia, MO 65211
Phone: 573.882.6042, toll-free: 888.MULaw4U; Fax: 573.882.9625
E-mail: mulawadmissions@missouri.edu; Website: www.law.missouri.edu

ABA
Approved
Since
1923

ABA
AMERICAN BAR ASSOCIATION
Section of Legal Education
and Admissions to the Bar

The Basics

Type of school	Public
Term	Semester
Application deadline	3/1
Application fee	$55
Financial aid deadline	3/1
Can first year start other than fall?	No
Student to faculty ratio	14.1 to 1
# of housing spaces available restricted to law students	
graduate housing for which law students are eligible	

Faculty and Administrators

	Total Spr	Total Fall	Men Spr	Men Fall	Women Spr	Women Fall	Minorities Spr	Minorities Fall
Full-time	24	28	18	20	6	8	3	4
Other full-time	0	0	0	0	0	0	0	0
Deans, librarians, & others who teach	14	14	9	9	5	5	2	2
Part-time	16	10	9	6	7	4	0	0
Total	54	52	36	35	18	17	5	6

Curriculum

		Full-Time	Part-Time
Typical first-year section size		75	0
Is there typically a "small section" of the first-year class, other than Legal Writing, taught by full-time faculty		Yes	No
If yes, typical size offered last year		35	
# of classroom course titles beyond first-year curriculum		118	
# of upper division courses, excluding seminars, with an enrollment:	Under 25	84	
	25–49	28	
	50–74	11	
	75–99	2	
	100+	0	
# of seminars		3	
# of seminar positions available		70	
# of seminar positions filled		64	0
# of positions available in simulation courses		305	
# of simulation positions filled		221	0
# of positions available in faculty supervised clinical courses		46	
# of faculty supervised clinical positions filled		47	0
# involved in field placements		81	0
# involved in law journals		103	0
# involved in moot court or trial competitions		170	0
# of credit hours required to graduate		89	

JD Enrollment and Ethnicity

	Men #	Men %	Women #	Women %	Full-Time #	Full-Time %	Part-Time #	Part-Time %	1st-Year #	1st-Year %	Total #	Total %	JD Degs. Awd.
All Hispanics	8	2.9	6	3.6	14	3.2	0	0.0	2	1.3	14	3.1	2
Am. Ind./AK Nat.	0	0.0	1	0.6	1	0.2	0	0.0	0	0.0	1	0.2	2
Asian	5	1.8	7	4.2	11	2.5	1	25.0	3	2.0	12	2.7	3
Black/Af. Am.	15	5.4	13	7.7	27	6.1	1	25.0	15	9.9	28	6.3	11
Nat. HI/Pac. Isl.	0	0.0	0	0.0	0	0.0	0	0.0	0	0.0	0	0.0	0
2 or more races	5	1.8	1	0.6	6	1.4	0	0.0	6	4.0	6	1.3	0
Subtotal (minor.)	33	11.9	28	16.7	59	13.3	2	50.0	26	17.2	61	13.7	19
Nonres. Alien	0	0.0	2	1.2	2	0.5	0	0.0	1	0.7	2	0.4	0
White/Cauc.	232	83.5	134	79.8	364	82.4	2	50.0	116	76.8	366	82.1	117
Unknown	13	4.7	4	2.4	17	3.8	0	0.0	8	5.3	17	3.8	6
Total	278	62.3	168	37.7	442	99.1	4	0.9	151	33.9	446		142

Transfers

Transfers in	7
Transfers out	0

Tuition and Fees

	Resident	Nonresident
Full-time	$16,759	$31,986
Part-time		
Tuition Guarantee Program		N

Living Expenses

Estimated living expenses for singles

Living on campus	Living off campus	Living at home
$15,890	$15,890	$15,890

ABA
Approved
Since
1923

GPA and LSAT Scores

	Total	Full-Time	Part-Time
# of apps	1,024	1,024	0
# of offers	393	393	0
# of matrics	148	148	0
75% GPA	3.76	3.76	0.00
Median GPA	3.43	3.43	0.00
25% GPA	3.06	3.06	0.00
75% LSAT	161	161	0
Median LSAT	159	159	0
25% LSAT	157	157	0

Grants and Scholarships (from prior year)

	Total		Full-Time		Part-Time	
	#	%	#	%	#	%
Total # of students	445		441		4	
Total # receiving grants	232	52.1	232	52.6	0	0.0
Less than 1/2 tuition	199	44.7	199	45.1	0	0.0
Half to full tuition	23	5.2	23	5.2	0	0.0
Full tuition	10	2.2	10	2.3	0	0.0
More than full tuition	0	0.0	0	0.0	0	0.0
Median grant amount			$5,000		$0	

Informational and Library Resources

Total amount spent on library materials	$815,321
Study seating capacity inside the library	472
# of full-time equivalent professional librarians	7
Hours per week library is open	70
# of open, wired connections available to students	6
# of networked computers available for use by students	52
Has wireless network?	Y
Requires computer?	N

JD Attrition (from prior year)

	Academic	Other	Total	
	#	#	#	%
1st year	2	2	4	2.6
2nd year	0	4	4	2.8
3rd year	0	0	0	0.0
4th year	0	0	0	0.0

Employment (9 months after graduation)

	Total	Percentage
Employment status known	144	95.4
Employment status unknown	7	4.6
Employed	113	78.5
Pursuing graduate degrees	7	4.9
Unemployed (seeking, not seeking, or studying for the bar)	10	6.9
Type of Employment		
# employed in law firms	72	63.7
# employed in business and industry	8	7.1
# employed in government	18	15.9
# employed in public interest	2	1.8
# employed as judicial clerks	11	9.7
# employed in academia	1	0.9
Geographic Location		
# employed in state	87	77.0
# employed outside the US	1	0.9
# of states where employed	11	

Bar Passage Rates

First-time takers	152	Reporting %	83.55
Average school %	92.13	Average state %	91.81
Average pass difference	0.32		

Jurisdiction	Takers	Passers	Pass %	State %	Diff %
Missouri	127	117	92.13	91.81	0.32

UNIVERSITY OF MISSOURI SCHOOL OF LAW

Office of Admissions, 103 Hulston Hall
Columbia, MO 65211
Phone: 573.882.6042, toll-free: 888.MULaw4U; Fax: 573.882.9625
E-mail: mulawadmissions@missouri.edu; Website: www.law.missouri.edu

Introduction

The University of Missouri School of Law (MU) is a dynamic and collegial community. Founded in 1839, MU was the first state university west of the Mississippi River. Established in 1872, the School of Law has had an enviable history of service to the state and the nation. Graduates include judges, governors, attorneys general, and legislators who serve locally and nationwide. The law school is a charter member of the Association of American Law Schools (AALS) and is fully accredited.

Located in Columbia, MU is 35 miles from Jefferson City, the state capital. The location provides law students with easy access to the legislature, the Supreme Court, and the various offices of state government. In addition to living and studying in one of America's most livable cities, students are within two hours of the cultural, athletic, and entertainment centers of St. Louis and Kansas City. Students and their families enjoy Columbia's Midwestern friendliness. It combines a small town feel with the diversity and opportunities often found only in larger cities. Columbia truly offers something for everyone.

Faculty

The faculty at MU is strong and vibrant. The faculty focus is on teaching, research, and service. MU is among the top 10 percent of law schools in American Law Institute membership. Multiple members of the faculty serve as commissioners and reporters for the National Conference of Commissioners on Uniform State Laws. Faculty maintain an open-door policy for students. Faculty scholarship regularly appears in the finest national law publications.

Enrollment/Student Body

The law school student body is composed of students from numerous states and foreign countries. This diverse and collegial group of students provides a wealth of experience and fosters a stimulating learning environment. MU maintains a smaller incoming class size to foster greater interaction with faculty and peers.

Curriculum

The academic program leading to the JD degree traditionally consists of six semesters of study. One seven-week semester is offered each summer. The first-year curriculum is proscribed, as is a portion of the second-year curriculum.

To graduate, students must complete 89 semester hours, including a writing requirement and a professional perspectives requirement. Students must have a minimum average of 77.5 on a scale of 65 to 100 to graduate.

Library and Physical Facilities

John K. Hulston Hall is dominated by windows, skylights, and large open spaces. It is a magnificent laboratory in which to study the law. The law school is part of the campus wireless network and law students can access the Internet and computer-assisted legal services throughout Hulston Hall or anywhere on campus. Exams are offered on laptop computers.

The law library houses an extensive collection of legal volumes and reference materials and a significant rare book collection. Specialized librarians, researchers, and computer support personnel are available to assist students. Faculty and students have 24-hour access to the law library.

Special Programs: Alternative Dispute Resolution

The Center for the Study of Dispute Resolution is a unique feature of the law school and provides national leadership in this rapidly developing area of the law. First-year law students are exposed to an overview of dispute resolution processes. MU also offers a variety of dispute resolution courses and other educational opportunities for second- and third-year students.

One of the first programs of its kind in the country, the center houses a Master of Laws in Dispute Resolution degree program.

Dual-Degree Programs

The School of Law offers several dual-degree programs, including Business Administration (JD/MBA), Public Affairs (JD/MPA), Health Administration (JD/MHA), Library Science (JD/MLS), and Journalism (JD/MA and JD/PhD). The law school has established other dual-degree programs to meet individual interests. Traditionally, dual-degree students spend their first year in the School of Law. (Students must fulfill the entrance requirements of both schools.)

Certificate Programs

The law school offers a certificate in Alternative Dispute Resolution. Students can complete this certificate by concentrating their elective hours in this area of the law.

In addition, a certificate in Journalism, the Digital Globe, or the European Union is available to law students through the Graduate School.

MU hosts one of the TransAtlantic Centers in the United States. The Center is working to develop a better understanding of the transatlantic agenda between the EU and the United States.

Study-Abroad Programs

The MU School of Law offers opportunities to study abroad in South Africa, Austria, and London. Since 2004, MU has conducted a summer program in Cape Town, South Africa, in cooperation with the University of the Western Cape. The program consists of three two-credit courses in different areas of comparative law and includes field trips to the Cape of Good Hope, Stellenbosch wine region, Robben Island (prison home of Nelson Mandela), and other scenic and historical locations.

In cooperation with Georgia State University, MU offers a Summer Academy in International Commercial Arbitration. Based at Johannes Kepler University in Linz, Austria, the program includes field trips to Vienna, Salzburg, Budapest, Venice, and other locations in Central and Eastern Europe.

MU is also part of the London Law Consortium. This group of six ABA-approved schools offers second- and third-year students a culturally enriching spring semester in London. With law school approval, students can also obtain academic credit while studying in another ABA-approved law school's international program.

Clinics and Externships

MU provides students with practical experience to enhance lawyering skills and to promote awareness of ethical issues. An active externship and judicial clerkship program and five clinical programs—the Criminal Prosecution Clinic, Family Violence Clinic, Legislative Clinic, Mediation Clinic, and the Innocence Clinic—have been developed to enrich student skills. Students, subject to the rules of the Missouri Supreme Court, are able to practice law in these programs.

Student Activities

All students are eligible to participate in the writing competition for membership on the *Missouri Law Review*, the *Journal of Dispute Resolution*, or the *Missouri Environmental Law and Policy Review*. Also open to all students, the Board of Advocates sponsors a wide variety of advocacy competitions. The school has chapters of the Order of Barristers, the Student Bar Association, and two legal fraternities. In addition, MU is one of only 75 law schools with a chapter of the Order of the Coif, the national law school honor society. Other student organizations, encompassing almost every aspect of social and academic life, are also offered.

Admission

A faculty committee reviews all applications. In many cases, factors other than the GPA or LSAT score have proven to be determinative. If the LSAT is repeated, the committee will consider all scores in its evaluation. Applications from disadvantaged students are especially encouraged.

Students are encouraged to apply early and to visit the law school. The Admissions Office can arrange for students to meet with an admission counselor, attend a class, and tour the facility.

Expenses and Financial Aid

Law school is a career investment. MU offers an outstanding value for the cost, and the accompanying housing, utility, and related living expenses in Columbia are low when compared to more urban settings.

Financial assistance is available to students.

Career Development

The Office of Career and Professional Development serves as a liaison between students or alumni and prospective employers. Students are taught to use their analytical and advocacy skills to achieve career goals. Workshops, seminars, and individual counseling are offered to help students successfully employ their lawyering skills. Typically, between 90 and 95 percent of each graduating class accepts employment within nine months of graduation.

APPLICANT PROFILE

University of Missouri School of Law
This grid includes only applicants who earned 120–180 LSAT scores under standard administrations.

LSAT Score	GPA								
	3.75 +	3.50–3.74	3.25–3.49	3.00–3.24	2.75–2.99	2.50–2.74	2.25–2.49	2.00–2.24	Below 2.00
175–180									
170–174									
165–169									
160–164									
155–159									
150–154									
145–149									
140–144									
135–139									
130–134									
125–129									
120–124									

■ Good Possibility ▨ Possible ☐ Unlikely

This chart is to be used as a general guide only. Nonnumerical factors are strongly considered for all applicants.

UNIVERSITY OF MISSOURI—KANSAS CITY SCHOOL OF LAW

5100 Rockhill Road
Kansas City, MO 64110
Phone: 816.235.1644; Fax: 816.235.5276
E-mail: law@umkc.edu; Website: www.law.umkc.edu

ABA
Approved
Since
1936

Section of Legal Education
and Admissions to the Bar

The Basics

Type of school	Public
Term	Semester
Application deadline	3/1
Application fee	$60
Financial aid deadline	3/1
Can first year start other than fall?	No
Student to faculty ratio	13.3 to 1
# of housing spaces available restricted to law students	
graduate housing for which law students are eligible	500

Faculty and Administrators

	Total		Men		Women		Minorities	
	Spr	Fall	Spr	Fall	Spr	Fall	Spr	Fall
Full-time	30	29	19	17	11	12	4	4
Other full-time	5	5	4	3	1	2	0	0
Deans, librarians, & others who teach	8	8	4	4	4	4	0	0
Part-time	25	12	20	9	5	3	0	0
Total	68	54	47	33	21	21	4	4

Curriculum

		Full-Time	Part-Time
Typical first-year section size		56	56
Is there typically a "small section" of the first-year class, other than Legal Writing, taught by full-time faculty		No	No
If yes, typical size offered last year			
# of classroom course titles beyond first-year curriculum		133	
# of upper division courses, excluding seminars, with an enrollment:	Under 25	83	
	25–49	31	
	50–74	11	
	75–99	8	
	100+	0	
# of seminars		16	
# of seminar positions available		255	
# of seminar positions filled		171	0
# of positions available in simulation courses		555	
# of simulation positions filled		436	0
# of positions available in faculty supervised clinical courses		127	
# of faculty supervised clinical positions filled		95	0
# involved in field placements		72	0
# involved in law journals		190	0
# involved in moot court or trial competitions		44	0
# of credit hours required to graduate		91	

JD Enrollment and Ethnicity

	Men		Women		Full-Time		Part-Time		1st-Year		Total		JD Degs. Awd.
	#	%	#	%	#	%	#	%	#	%	#	%	
All Hispanics	11	3.7	8	4.2	19	4.1	0	0.0	8	4.4	19	3.9	5
Am. Ind./AK Nat.	2	0.7	1	0.5	3	0.7	0	0.0	0	0.0	3	0.6	1
Asian	8	2.7	6	3.2	13	2.8	1	4.2	4	2.2	14	2.9	3
Black/Af. Am.	7	2.4	18	9.5	23	5.0	2	8.3	11	6.0	25	5.2	9
Nat. HI/Pac. Isl.	0	0.0	0	0.0	0	0.0	0	0.0	0	0.0	0	0.0	0
2 or more races	0	0.0	0	0.0	0	0.0	0	0.0	0	0.0	0	0.0	0
Subtotal (minor.)	28	9.5	33	17.5	58	12.6	3	12.5	23	12.6	61	12.6	19
Nonres. Alien	4	1.4	4	2.1	7	1.5	1	4.2	3	1.6	8	1.7	0
White/Cauc.	233	79.3	140	74.1	355	77.3	18	75.0	150	82.0	373	77.2	118
Unknown	29	9.9	12	6.3	39	8.5	2	8.3	7	3.8	41	8.5	22
Total	294	60.9	189	39.1	459	95.0	24	5.0	183	37.9	483		159

Transfers

Transfers in	15
Transfers out	5

Tuition and Fees

	Resident	Nonresident
Full-time	$15,550	$29,500
Part-time	$8,542	$15,982
Tuition Guarantee Program	N	

Living Expenses

Estimated living expenses for singles

Living on campus	Living off campus	Living at home
$28,712	$29,471	$20,720

UNIVERSITY OF MISSOURI—KANSAS CITY SCHOOL OF LAW

ABA
Approved
Since
1936

GPA and LSAT Scores

	Total	Full-Time	Part-Time
# of apps	974	915	59
# of offers	392	386	6
# of matrics	156	152	4
75% GPA	3.53	3.53	3.35
Median GPA	3.25	3.27	3.16
25% GPA	2.94	2.94	3.11
75% LSAT	158	158	152
Median LSAT	156	156	150
25% LSAT	154	154	148

Grants and Scholarships (from prior year)

	Total #	Total %	Full-Time #	Full-Time %	Part-Time #	Part-Time %
Total # of students	515		489		26	
Total # receiving grants	159	30.9	150	30.7	9	34.6
Less than 1/2 tuition	90	17.5	88	18.0	2	7.7
Half to full tuition	52	10.1	45	9.2	7	26.9
Full tuition	12	2.3	12	2.5	0	0.0
More than full tuition	5	1.0	5	1.0	0	0.0
Median grant amount			$6,975		$5,726	

Informational and Library Resources

Total amount spent on library materials	$710,738
Study seating capacity inside the library	417
# of full-time equivalent professional librarians	8
Hours per week library is open	100
# of open, wired connections available to students	46
# of networked computers available for use by students	55
Has wireless network?	Y
Requires computer?	N

JD Attrition (from prior year)

	Academic #	Other #	Total #	Total %
1st year	7	12	19	10.2
2nd year	0	0	0	0.0
3rd year	0	0	0	0.0
4th year	0	0	0	0.0

Employment (9 months after graduation)

	Total	Percentage
Employment status known	150	100.0
Employment status unknown	0	0.0
Employed	137	91.3
Pursuing graduate degrees	3	2.0
Unemployed (seeking, not seeking, or studying for the bar)	7	4.7
Type of Employment		
# employed in law firms	73	53.3
# employed in business and industry	29	21.2
# employed in government	17	12.4
# employed in public interest	5	3.6
# employed as judicial clerks	13	9.5
# employed in academia	0	0.0
Geographic Location		
# employed in state	99	72.3
# employed outside the US	0	0.0
# of states where employed	10	

Bar Passage Rates

First-time takers	152	Reporting %	87.50
Average school %	94.74	Average state %	91.81
Average pass difference	2.93		

Jurisdiction	Takers	Passers	Pass %	State %	Diff %
Missouri	133	126	94.74	91.81	2.93

UNIVERSITY OF MISSOURI—KANSAS CITY SCHOOL OF LAW

5100 Rockhill Road
Kansas City, MO 64110
Phone: 816.235.1644; Fax: 816.235.5276
E-mail: law@umkc.edu; Website: www.law.umkc.edu

Introduction

The University of Missouri—Kansas City School of Law (UMKC) takes pride in being the urban public law school with the small liberal arts feel. UMKC serves and collaborates with the legal communities in two major metropolitan areas of the states of Missouri and Kansas. Students, faculty, and alumni actively lead and participate in professional activities with area bar associations, lawyers, and law firms, as well as government agencies and the judiciary.

UMKC law school graduates hold important positions in legal arenas across the country, distinguishing themselves in private practice, government service, academia, and corporate roles. UMKC is one of only six law schools to have educated both a president of the United States and a US Supreme Court justice. Many other UMKC alumni currently serve as judges at the federal, state, and local levels.

UMKC School of Law is committed to providing a high-quality legal education in a professional and supportive environment, concentrating always on the foundations of good lawyering: respect for people, knowledge, ideas, and justice. UMKC is one of the most student-friendly law schools in the country, with outstanding student-faculty interaction and alumni providing mentoring to our students through the UMKC Inns of Court program.

Founded in 1895, the school is accredited by the American Bar Association (ABA) and is a member of the Association of American Law Schools (AALS).

Faculty

Our faculty are outstanding scholars who have extensive practice experience and national renown. For example, Professor Doug Linder's Famous Trials website, www.umkc.edu/famoustrials, receives seven to nine million hits per month. Professor Bill Eckhardt was the chief prosecutor in the My Lai massacre case, while Professor Bill Black's experience and expertise in bank regulation has led him to major roles in a Barack Obama campaign documentary and a Michael Moore film about America's financial crisis.

Faculty at UMKC are actively engaged with students both inside and outside the classroom—in competitions as well as activities and events. Under faculty supervision, students write and edit a substantial portion of the *UMKC Law Review*, a scholarly legal journal, and also serve as assistant editors of *The Urban Lawyer*, published by the ABA Section of State and Local Government Law, and the national and international *Journal of the American Academy of Matrimonial Lawyers*.

Library and Physical Facilities

Office suites shared by faculty and students are designed to foster the exchange of ideas and to promote collegiality between faculty and students. The school has over 121,000 square feet of usable space, which includes wireless computer access throughout the building, and a newly remodeled courtroom with state-of-the-art technology and an innovative viewing theater.

The Leon E. Bloch Law Library combines the traditions of print media with emerging electronic media in preparing the lawyer for the future and supporting the legal community.

Curriculum

Courses are taught in a variety of formats. Many of the substantive courses include problem solving, simulations, service learning, and the development of skills components essential to the practice of law. The first-year JD program offers a year-long intensive Introduction to Law and Lawyering Processes. The upper-level program includes a combination of required courses, as well as a broad selection of elective courses.

All first-year sections have 60 or fewer students, and first-year legal research and writing classes have approximately 25 students each. Among the 114 upper division courses offered each year, 84 have an enrollment of fewer than 25 students, and 19 more have an enrollment of between 25 and 49 students. A law school strategies program that includes supervised, structured study groups, lecture series, and weekly workshops is open to all students. Additional opportunities include a week-long summer program, which is available on a limited basis.

While the school's innovative Solo and Small Firm Initiative prepares students for general practice, those seeking more focused study can pursue one of our five emphasis areas: Litigation; Business and Entrepreneurial Law; Urban, Land Use and Environmental Law; International, Comparative, and Foreign Law, and Law in Service to Children and Families. These emphases build on our long-standing tradition of excellence in these areas and prepare students to enter the job market with specialized knowledge and skills.

A part-time day program is available for those students with family or career responsibilities who are unable to enroll on a full-time basis. Full-time students may graduate in two and one-half years by attending two summer sessions.

JD/MBA and JD/MPA Programs

The School of Law has established dual-degree programs with the Henry W. Bloch School of Business and Public Administration. The program allows students to earn a JD degree and a Master of Business Administration or Master of Public Administration degree on an accelerated basis through cross-acceptance of some credit hours. Applicants must satisfy the admission requirements of each school.

JD/LLM and Combined-Degree Programs

The School of Law has adopted combined-degree programs that allow qualified JD students to apply, with approval, up to 12 credit hours of UMKC tax or estate planning courses toward an LLM on an accelerated basis, generally requiring only one additional semester (or two summer sessions) beyond that required for the JD degree.

Student Activities

The law school's location in a metropolitan area provides many opportunities for students to engage in real-life representation of clients in clinical programs. More than 50 percent of our students take advantage of internships and clinics that include UMKC's Child and Family Services Clinic, Tax Clinic, Entrepreneurial Legal Services Clinic, and the

Innocence Project Clinic. The school also offers a number of field placements. Students may also participate in our Pro Bono/Public Service Program designed to instill a sense of civic responsibility and meet the needs of those with limited means in the community.

Students obtain advanced skills development in trial and appellate advocacy through sequenced upper-level courses and competition participation. Students also participate in client counseling and negotiation competitions. UMKC teams frequently win regional and national honors in these competitions. UMKC has the best record of any law school in the country in advancing its teams to the national finals of the Negotiation Competition.

UMKC benefits from an active Student Bar Association, which represents students and plays an important role in establishing school policy. Three national legal fraternities have chapters at the school, as do Black Law Students, Hispanic Law Students, Jewish Law Students, Asian Pacific Islander Law Students, Women Law Students, and Nontraditional Law Students. Additional student organizations specialize in many areas of interest, with over 30 total student groups. Students also have the opportunity to participate in study-abroad programs that visit China, Ireland, and Oxford. The school provides many opportunities for development of personal relationships that will last throughout one's career.

Admission

The School of Law restricts the number of students admitted each year to achieve a favorable faculty-to-student ratio, providing the best possible legal education for each student enrolled. Because many more people apply to the law school than there are seats available, admission is highly competitive. While substantial weight is given to the LSAT score and undergraduate GPA, the law school and its faculty believe that using factors in addition to the LSAT and GPA contribute to an intellectually stimulating and diverse environment. These factors include racial, ethnic, cultural, gender, age, or other forms of diversity; triumphs over challenges and barriers based on societal discrimination or economic disadvantage; outstanding leadership qualities; serious and sustained commitment to significant public or community service; advanced or specialized educational achievements; accomplishments or qualities indicative of potential for contributing to scholarly and creative initiatives; and potential to provide high-quality legal services to clients.

Students may be admitted with a bachelor's degree from an approved institution, or in appropriate cases, with 90 hours of acceptable academic work. Arrangements can be made to meet with students and faculty, visit a class, or tour the school.

Career Services

The Office of Career Services assists law students in exploring and defining career options. It also provides advice and assistance in résumé preparation and interviewing skills. The office sponsors a series of programs to introduce students to a variety of career opportunities. Participants in the school's Judicial Clerkship Initiative have enjoyed a high placement rate in pursuing clerkships with state and federal judges.

APPLICANT PROFILE

University of Missouri—Kansas City School of Law

LSAT Score	GPA								
	3.75 +	3.50–3.74	3.25–3.49	3.00–3.24	2.75–2.99	2.50–2.74	2.25–2.49	2.00–2.24	Below 2.00
175–180	■	■	■	■	■	□	□	▓	
170–174	■	■	■	■	■	□	□	▓	
165–169	■	■	■	■	■	□	□	▓	
160–164	■	■	■	■	■	□	□	▓	
155–159	■	■	■	■	□	□	□	▓	
150–154	■	■	■	■	□	□	□	▓	
145–149	▓	▓	▓	▓	▓	▓	▓	▓	
140–144	▓	▓	▓	▓	▓	▓	▓	▓	
135–139	▓	▓	▓	▓	▓	▓	▓	▓	
130–134	▓	▓	▓	▓	▓	▓	▓	▓	
125–129	▓	▓	▓	▓	▓	▓	▓	▓	
120–124	▓	▓	▓	▓	▓	▓	▓	▓	

■ Good Possibility   □ Possible   ▓ Unlikely

UNIVERSITY OF MONTANA SCHOOL OF LAW

32 Campus Drive
Missoula, MT 59812
Phone: 406.243.4311
E-mail: lawadmis@umontana.edu; Website: www.umt.edu/law

The Basics

Type of school	Public
Term	Semester
Application deadline	3/15
Application fee	$60
Financial aid deadline	3/1
Can first year start other than fall?	No
Student to faculty ratio	13.1 to 1
# of housing spaces available restricted to law students	
graduate housing for which law students are eligible	251

Faculty and Administrators

	Total		Men		Women		Minorities	
	Spr	Fall	Spr	Fall	Spr	Fall	Spr	Fall
Full-time	15	17	7	8	8	9	4	4
Other full-time	2	2	1	1	1	1	0	0
Deans, librarians, & others who teach	7	6	2	2	5	4	0	0
Part-time	14	8	10	7	4	1	1	0
Total	38	33	20	18	18	15	5	4

Curriculum

	Full-Time	Part-Time
Typical first-year section size	42	0
Is there typically a "small section" of the first-year class, other than Legal Writing, taught by full-time faculty	No	No
If yes, typical size offered last year		
# of classroom course titles beyond first-year curriculum	67	
# of upper division courses, excluding seminars with an enrollment: Under 25	22	
25–49	6	
50–74	0	
75–99	0	
100+	0	
# of seminars	0	
# of seminar positions available	400	
# of seminar positions filled	361	0
# of positions available in simulation courses	81	
# of simulation positions filled	81	0
# of positions available in faculty supervised clinical courses	25	
# of faculty supervised clinical positions filled	19	0
# involved in field placements	58	0
# involved in law journals	41	0
# involved in moot court or trial competitions	30	0
# of credit hours required to graduate	90	

JD Enrollment and Ethnicity

	Men #	Men %	Women #	Women %	Full-Time #	Full-Time %	Part-Time #	Part-Time %	1st-Year #	1st-Year %	Total #	Total %	JD Degs. Awd.
All Hispanics	4	2.7	2	1.8	6	2.3	0	0.0	3	3.5	6	2.3	2
Am. Ind./AK Nat.	8	5.5	3	2.7	11	4.3	0	0.0	4	4.7	11	4.3	3
Asian	0	0.0	3	2.7	3	1.2	0	0.0	0	0.0	3	1.2	0
Black/Af. Am.	1	0.7	0	0.0	1	0.4	0	0.0	0	0.0	1	0.4	0
Nat. HI/Pac. Isl.	0	0.0	0	0.0	0	0.0	0	0.0	0	0.0	0	0.0	0
2 or more races	1	0.7	2	1.8	3	1.2	0	0.0	3	3.5	3	1.2	0
Subtotal (minor.)	14	9.6	10	9.1	24	9.4	0	0.0	10	11.8	24	9.4	5
Nonres. Alien	1	0.7	0	0.0	1	0.4	0	0.0	1	1.2	1	0.4	0
White/Cauc.	131	89.7	100	90.9	231	90.2	0	0.0	74	87.1	231	90.2	71
Unknown	0	0.0	0	0.0	0	0.0	0	0.0	0	0.0	0	0.0	0
Total	146	57.0	110	43.0	256	100.0	0	0.0	85	33.2	256		76

Transfers

Transfers in	4
Transfers out	3

Tuition and Fees

	Resident	Nonresident
Full-time	$11,062	$26,186
Part-time		
Tuition Guarantee Program		N

Living Expenses

Estimated living expenses for singles

Living on campus	Living off campus	Living at home
$12,000	$12,000	$9,600

ABA
Approved
Since
1923

GPA and LSAT Scores

	Total	Full-Time	Part-Time
# of apps	527	527	0
# of offers	197	197	0
# of matrics	85	85	0
75% GPA	3.75	3.75	0.00
Median GPA	3.42	3.42	0.00
25% GPA	3.14	3.14	0.00
75% LSAT	158	158	0
Median LSAT	155	155	0
25% LSAT	153	153	0

Grants and Scholarships (from prior year)

	Total #	Total %	Full-Time #	Full-Time %	Part-Time #	Part-Time %
Total # of students	248		248		0	
Total # receiving grants	99	39.9	99	39.9	0	0.0
Less than 1/2 tuition	88	35.5	88	35.5	0	0.0
Half to full tuition	8	3.2	8	3.2	0	0.0
Full tuition	0	0.0	0	0.0	0	0.0
More than full tuition	3	1.2	3	1.2	0	0.0
Median grant amount			$2,400		$0	

Informational and Library Resources

Total amount spent on library materials	$782,758
Study seating capacity inside the library	360
# of full-time equivalent professional librarians	3
Hours per week library is open	98
# of open, wired connections available to students	226
# of networked computers available for use by students	25
Has wireless network?	Y
Requires computer?	N

JD Attrition (from prior year)

	Academic #	Other #	Total #	Total %
1st year	0	3	3	3.6
2nd year	1	2	3	3.5
3rd year	0	0	0	0.0
4th year	0	0	0	0.0

Employment (9 months after graduation)

	Total	Percentage
Employment status known	76	96.2
Employment status unknown	3	3.8
Employed	66	86.8
Pursuing graduate degrees	5	6.6
Unemployed (seeking, not seeking, or studying for the bar)	4	5.3
Type of Employment		
# employed in law firms	32	48.5
# employed in business and industry	3	4.5
# employed in government	7	10.6
# employed in public interest	7	10.6
# employed as judicial clerks	17	25.8
# employed in academia	0	0.0
Geographic Location		
# employed in state	50	75.8
# employed outside the US	0	0.0
# of states where employed	9	

Bar Passage Rates

First-time takers	73	Reporting %	91.78
Average school %	94.03	Average state %	88.64
Average pass difference	5.39		

Jurisdiction	Takers	Passers	Pass %	State %	Diff %
Montana	67	63	94.03	88.64	5.39

UNIVERSITY OF MONTANA SCHOOL OF LAW

32 Campus Drive
Missoula, MT 59812
Phone: 406.243.4311
E-mail: lawadmis@umontana.edu; Website: www.umt.edu/law

The information on these pages was provided by the law school.

Introduction

The University of Montana (UM) School of Law is located in Missoula on the west slopes of the Rocky Mountains. Missoula is situated halfway between Yellowstone and Glacier national parks and is surrounded by several of the largest designated wilderness areas in the continental United States. The city is known for its outdoor opportunities and quality of life.

The School of Law was established in 1911 and serves as a legal center for the state. It has been accredited by the Association of American Law Schools (AALS) since 1914 and by the American Bar Association (ABA) since 1923. As one of the smallest law schools in the nation, the University of Montana School of Law offers students a congenial academic, intellectual, and social environment.

As the School of Law enters its second century of preparing students for the practice of law and community leadership, we have expanded and substantially renovated our building. Students now enjoy new classrooms, formal and informal study spaces, clinic and student-group offices, and community areas.

UM's Program

The University of Montana School of Law integrates theory and practice throughout its curriculum to instill entry-level practice and competence in its graduates. The School of Law's curriculum, teaching methodology, and assessment techniques are designed to address the following components of a lawyer's work: (1) knowledge of the law, (2) ability to apply legal rules to solve problems, (3) ability to use lawyering skills (e.g., negotiation and client counseling), (4) perspective on the societal role and responsibility of lawyers, and (5) sensitivity to the dynamics of social and interpersonal interaction.

The school has created three distinctive programs to acquaint first-year students with the ways lawyers think and work: (1) the Introductory Program, (2) the Lawyer Skills Program, and (3) the Law Firm Program. In the Introductory Program, students are initiated into the legal culture by surveying legal history, the American legal system, the litigation process, legal writing, and legal analysis and jurisprudence. The School of Law is one of the few to introduce first-year students to the skills involved in dispute resolution, including client counseling, legal document drafting, and oral argument. UM's program encourages students to cooperate and collaborate rather than compete as they begin to think and work as lawyers. Entering students belong to *law firms*—groups of seven students directed by upper-class students.

The school has long emphasized performance in its curriculum. The school's Legal Writing and Dispute Resolution programs represent a comprehensive approach to lawyering skills. Students master specific transactional skills such as planning an estate, drafting a contract, and creating a small business.

The upper-division clinical training program provides students with a wide range of opportunities to earn required academic credit by working on cases under the supervision of faculty and practicing attorneys in Missoula. The clinical offerings include ACLU, Associated Students of UM Legal

Services, Child Support Enforcement Division, Criminal Defense, DNRC Forestry and Trust Land Management Divisions, Federal Judicial, Indian Law, Innocence Project, Land Use, Mediation, Missoula City Attorney's Office, Missoula County Attorney's Office, Montana Legal Services Association, National Wildlife Federation, Natural Resource, Office of State Public Defender, Rocky Mountain Elk Foundation, UM Legal Counsel, USDA General Counsel, and US Department of Justice.

Special Programs

The School of Law offers three certificate programs: (1) Environmental and Natural Resource Law and the opportunity to participate in natural resource clinics, the *Public Land and Resources Law Review*, the Environmental Law Group, and the Environmental Law Moot Court Team; (2) Alternative Dispute Resolution and the opportunity to participate in the Mediation Clinic; and (3) American Indian Law and the opportunity to participate in the Indian Law Clinic, the Native American Law Student Association (NALSA), and the NALSA Moot Court Team.

In conjunction with the School of Law, UM's graduate school offers a certificate in Natural Resources Conflict Resolution. It is the only graduate-level certificate program in the Rocky Mountain West specifically designed to provide students with a working knowledge of the theory and practice of collaboration, consensus building, and conflict resolution as they apply to natural resources and the environment.

The School of Law offers three joint-degree programs. Students can combine their law degrees with a Master of Science in Environmental Studies, a Master of Business Administration, or a Master of Public Administration. These programs can lead to completion of the joint degree in as little as three years. The School of Law also offers concentrations in the areas of Trial Advocacy, Business, and Tax Law.

Admission

A committee of law faculty reviews applications. Candidates must be of good moral character, have intellectual promise, and have a baccalaureate degree from an approved college or university prior to matriculation. Applicants are considered in resident or nonresident pools. The School of Law seeks a diverse student body and welcomes applications from members of groups historically underrepresented in the legal profession.

The School of Law recommends that you submit your application as soon as possible. We begin reviewing completed applications as they are submitted. Applications are not considered complete until all application materials, including the LSAC Law School Report, are received. If your file is completed by February 15, you will be notified of a decision (admit, deny, or retain for further review) by March 15. If your file is completed by March 15, you will be notified of a decision by April 15. Files completed after March 15 may be considered on a space-available basis.

The most important admission criteria are the cumulative undergraduate GPA and the LSAT score. If the LSAT is repeated, all scores will be used in evaluating the applicant.

The admission committee weighs such factors as writing ability; college attended; trend in grades; quality of work in difficult courses; experience prior to application to law school, including graduate study; ability to overcome economic or other disadvantages; and change in performance after an absence from school.

The school recognizes a commitment to provide full opportunities for the study of law and entry into the legal profession of qualified members of groups (notably racial and ethnic minorities) who have been victims of discrimination.

Student Activities

All students are members of the Student Bar Association (SBA). The SBA contributes to the professional development and the social life of the student body. Other student organizations include the American Association for Justice (AAJ), ACLU, Animal Legal Defense Fund, Christian Legal Society, Environmental Law Group, Federalist Society, International Law Student Association, Military Law Society, Montana Public Interest Law Coalition, Native American Law Student Association, Clayberg Inn of Phi Delta Phi national law fraternity, Rural Advocacy League, and Women's Law Caucus. The *Montana Law Review* and the *Public Land and Resources Law Review* afford supplementary training in analyzing legal problems precisely and presenting legal issues cogently.

The School of Law is proud of its performance in interscholastic competitions. Nearly every year, the School of Law fields teams that compete at the national level. Most recently, UM won the 2000 National Moot Court Competition championship. UM won the ATLA trial competition national championship in 1992 and the national ABA Client Counseling Competition championship in 1990. Additionally, the Environmental Law Moot Court Team, which competes at the National Environmental Law Moot Court Competition each year, won the Best Oralist Award in 2002, and competed in the final round in 2005. Likewise, the Indian Law and Jessup International Law Moot Court teams have won oralist and brief honors in their respective national and, in the case of the Jessup team, international competitions.

APPLICANT PROFILE

University of Montana School of Law

LSAT Score	GPA								
	3.75 +	3.50–3.74	3.25–3.49	3.00–3.24	2.75–2.99	2.50–2.74	2.25–2.49	2.00–2.24	Below 2.00
175–180	■	■	■	■	■			▨	▨
170–174	■	■	■	■	■			▨	▨
165–169	■	■	■	■	■			▨	▨
160–164	■	■	■	■	■			▨	▨
155–159	■	■	■	■	■			▨	▨
150–154	■	■	■	■			▨	▨	▨
145–149					▨	▨	▨	▨	▨
140–144			▨	▨	▨	▨	▨	▨	▨
135–139	▨	▨	▨	▨	▨	▨	▨	▨	▨
130–134	▨	▨	▨	▨	▨	▨	▨	▨	▨
125–129	▨	▨	▨	▨	▨	▨	▨	▨	▨
120–124	▨	▨	▨	▨	▨	▨	▨	▨	▨

■ Good Possibility   □ Possible   ▨ Unlikely

UNIVERSITY OF NEBRASKA COLLEGE OF LAW

PO Box 830902
Lincoln, NE 68583-0902
Phone: 402.472.2161; Fax: 402.472.5185
E-mail: lawadm@unl.edu; Website: http://law.unl.edu/

ABA
Approved
Since
1923

The Basics

Type of school	Public
Term	Semester
Application deadline	3/1
Application fee	$25
Financial aid deadline	5/1
Can first year start other than fall?	No
Student to faculty ratio	13.3 to 1
# of housing spaces available restricted to law students	
graduate housing for which law students are eligible	295

Faculty and Administrators

	Total		Men		Women		Minorities	
	Spr	Fall	Spr	Fall	Spr	Fall	Spr	Fall
Full-time	25	25	21	18	4	7	1	2
Other full-time	1	1	1	1	0	0	0	0
Deans, librarians, & others who teach	11	10	5	5	6	5	1	0
Part-time	27	23	19	16	8	7	0	0
Total	64	59	46	40	18	19	2	2

JD Enrollment and Ethnicity

	Men		Women		Full-Time		Part-Time		1st-Year		Total		JD Degs. Awd.
	#	%	#	%	#	%	#	%	#	%	#	%	
All Hispanics	6	2.3	1	0.7	7	1.7	0	0.0	1	0.7	7	1.7	2
Am. Ind./AK Nat.	2	0.8	2	1.3	4	1.0	0	0.0	2	1.4	4	1.0	0
Asian	6	2.3	3	2.0	9	2.2	0	0.0	3	2.1	9	2.2	2
Black/Af. Am.	7	2.7	3	2.0	10	2.4	0	0.0	1	0.7	10	2.4	2
Nat. HI/Pac. Isl.	0	0.0	0	0.0	0	0.0	0	0.0	0	0.0	0	0.0	0
2 or more races	0	0.0	0	0.0	0	0.0	0	0.0	0	0.0	0	0.0	0
Subtotal (minor.)	21	8.0	9	5.9	30	7.3	0	0.0	7	4.8	30	7.2	6
Nonres. Alien	2	0.8	0	0.0	2	0.5	0	0.0	1	0.7	2	0.5	0
White/Cauc.	238	91.2	144	94.1	380	92.2	2	100.0	138	94.5	382	92.3	115
Unknown	0	0.0	0	0.0	0	0.0	0	0.0	0	0.0	0	0.0	0
Total	261	63.0	153	37.0	412	99.5	2	0.5	146	35.3	414		122

Curriculum

	Full-Time	Part-Time
Typical first-year section size	70	0
Is there typically a "small section" of the first-year class, other than Legal Writing, taught by full-time faculty	Yes	No
If yes, typical size offered last year	47	
# of classroom course titles beyond first-year curriculum		83
# of upper division courses, excluding seminars, with an enrollment: Under 25		51
25–49		22
50–74		12
75–99		0
100+		0
# of seminars		10
# of seminar positions available		140
# of seminar positions filled	137	0
# of positions available in simulation courses		466
# of simulation positions filled	360	0
# of positions available in faculty supervised clinical courses		62
# of faculty supervised clinical positions filled	59	0
# involved in field placements	20	0
# involved in law journals	33	0
# involved in moot court or trial competitions	57	0
# of credit hours required to graduate		93

Transfers

Transfers in	2
Transfers out	2

Tuition and Fees

	Resident	Nonresident
Full-time	$13,337	$28,649
Part-time		
Tuition Guarantee Program		N

Living Expenses

Estimated living expenses for singles

Living on campus	Living off campus	Living at home
$13,786	$13,358	$7,586

ABA
Approved
Since
1923

GPA and LSAT Scores

	Total	Full-Time	Part-Time
# of apps	678	677	1
# of offers	364	363	1
# of matrics	145	144	1
75% GPA	3.84	3.84	0.00
Median GPA	3.60	3.61	2.47
25% GPA	3.35	3.35	0.00
75% LSAT	160	160	0
Median LSAT	156	156	157
25% LSAT	153	153	0

Grants and Scholarships (from prior year)

	Total #	Total %	Full-Time #	Full-Time %	Part-Time #	Part-Time %
Total # of students	394		394		0	
Total # receiving grants	173	43.9	173	43.9	0	0.0
Less than 1/2 tuition	90	22.8	90	22.8	0	0.0
Half to full tuition	35	8.9	35	8.9	0	0.0
Full tuition	0	0.0	0	0.0	0	0.0
More than full tuition	48	12.2	48	12.2	0	0.0
Median grant amount			$8,000		$0	

Informational and Library Resources

Total amount spent on library materials	$795,653
Study seating capacity inside the library	372
# of full-time equivalent professional librarians	6
Hours per week library is open	109
# of open, wired connections available to students	15
# of networked computers available for use by students	15
Has wireless network?	Y
Requires computer?	N

JD Attrition (from prior year)

	Academic #	Other #	Total #	Total %
1st year	5	0	5	3.6
2nd year	0	4	4	3.0
3rd year	0	0	0	0.0
4th year	0	0	0	0.0

Employment (9 months after graduation)

	Total	Percentage
Employment status known	132	98.5
Employment status unknown	2	1.5
Employed	118	89.4
Pursuing graduate degrees	3	2.3
Unemployed (seeking, not seeking, or studying for the bar)	8	6.1
Type of Employment		
# employed in law firms	71	60.2
# employed in business and industry	16	13.6
# employed in government	18	15.3
# employed in public interest	2	1.7
# employed as judicial clerks	7	5.9
# employed in academia	3	2.5
Geographic Location		
# employed in state	88	74.6
# employed outside the US	0	0.0
# of states where employed		17

Bar Passage Rates

First-time takers	122	Reporting %	81.15
Average school %	90.91	Average state %	86.86
Average pass difference	4.05		

Jurisdiction	Takers	Passers	Pass %	State %	Diff %
Nebraska	65	60	92.31	87.93	4.38
Colorado	12	9	75.00	85.67	–10.67
Iowa	7	7	100.00	93.17	6.83
Texas	6	5	83.33	85.48	–2.15
Others (2)	9	9	100.00		

UNIVERSITY OF NEBRASKA COLLEGE OF LAW

PO Box 830902
Lincoln, NE 68583-0902
Phone: 402.472.2161; Fax: 402.472.5185
E-mail: lawadm@unl.edu; Website: http://law.unl.edu/

Introduction

Founded in 1888, the University of Nebraska College of Law offers an excellent legal education at a reasonable cost. It is large enough to provide students with a diverse curriculum, yet small enough to ensure that students are not lost in the crowd. Nebraska Law is a charter member of the AALS and is accredited by the ABA. It is located on the University of Nebraska's East Campus in the state's capital, Lincoln, with a population of approximately 251,000 and a vibrant array of opportunities.

Curriculum

Nebraska Law's academic year runs from late August to early May. A two-day orientation before the beginning of the fall semester introduces first-year students to the college. Each incoming student is assigned a faculty advisor who can answer questions about law school, course selections, and career goals. The first-year curriculum is 18 hours the first semester and 15 hours the second semester and includes civil procedure, contracts, criminal law, legal writing, property, and torts. Courses in the second and third years are elective, with the exception of required courses in constitutional law, professional responsibility, a research seminar, and a professional skills course. The curriculum encompasses a broad range of subjects, and offers particular depth in the areas of litigation, alternative dispute resolution, taxation, environmental, employment, international, space and telecommunications, and corporate and commercial law. Students who wish to focus on a particular area of the law may pursue the Litigation Skills Program of Concentrated Studies or the Business Program of Concentrated Studies or develop an individualized program of concentrated study.

The College of Law provides an Academic Resource Program for first-year students to assist them in developing and improving fundamental skills such as note taking, briefing cases, legal analysis, outlining, and writing examinations. The program provides weekly skills classes as well as a series of lectures and individual academic counseling.

Although completing the requirements for a JD degree normally takes three years, it is possible to graduate in two and one-half years by attending summer school. The college offers no night classes and rarely accepts part-time students. Students receiving the JD degree are qualified to practice in any state upon passage of that state's bar examination.

Skills and Clinical Education

Nebraska Law recognizes that becoming a lawyer involves more than learning legal theory. Students need to develop practical skills to effectively represent clients and function as lawyers. The College of Law has offered courses that emphasize "learning by doing" since the early 1970s. Professional skills courses offered include pretrial litigation, trial advocacy, appellate advocacy, mediation, negotiations, alternative dispute resolution, client interviewing and counseling, construction law, business planning, civil law, and criminal law. These classes allow second- and third-year students to develop lawyering skills in simulated settings or in the handling of real cases for actual clients. In the Civil Clinic, third-year students represent clients in and out of court in matters such as bankruptcy, domestic relations, immigration, and landlord-tenant disputes. Students in the Criminal Clinic prosecute misdemeanor cases in Lancaster County.

Joint-Degree Programs

The College's interdisciplinary program in law and psychology is recognized as one of the finest in the nation. Nebraska Law also participates in seven other joint-degree programs and will work with students to individually design programs in disciplines not covered by a formal program. In each program, students will earn two degrees with fewer credit hours and in less time than if the degrees were pursued separately. The formal joint-degree programs include JD/MBA (Business), JD/MPA (Accounting), JD/PhD (Psychology), JD/MA (Political Science), JD/MA or MS (Economics), JD/MCRP (Community and Regional Planning), JD/PhD (Educational Administration), and JD/MA (Journalism).

Library and Physical Facilities

The Schmid Law Library has a collection of about 395,000 volumes and a full complement of the latest developments in information technology. The library provides seating for 335 students and has 14 group-study rooms, each with full access to power and fast data connections, both wired and wireless, for the best access to the Internet from any place in the library. The five professional librarians and the staff strive to create a service-oriented environment for legal research and scholarship. All these attributes combine to make the Schmid Law Library not only the largest, but the most effective, efficient, and friendliest law library in the region.

In addition to the library, Nebraska Law's classrooms, Hamann Auditorium, and Welpton Courtroom feature attractive decor, adjustable chairs, laptop compatibility, and state-of-the-art technology.

Student Activities

The *Nebraska Law Review*, published by a student editorial board, publishes leading articles from well-known authorities in their fields, as well as student notes and comments. Other extracurricular academic programs include the National Moot Court Competition, Client Counseling Competition, and National Trial Competition.

Students can become involved in over 25 activities and organizations, including the Student Bar Association, Women's Law Caucus, Black Law Students Association, Nebraska Entertainment and Sports Law Association, Equal Justice Society, Federalist Society, Multicultural Legal Society, and two national legal fraternities.

Career Services

The College of Law operates its own Career Services Office for students seeking full-time employment or summer clerkships. The office provides students with a variety of placement-related services and also organizes on-campus interviews by private law firms, governmental agencies, corporations, and other potential employers.

Admission

Admission decisions are made on a rolling basis. Students are required to have a bachelor's degree from an accredited institution, take the LSAT, and register with LSAC's Credential Assembly Service. In making its decisions, the Admissions Committee seeks to identify those individuals who have the ability to compete successfully in a rigorous academic environment. The major factors that the committee considers are the applicant's LSAT score and the applicant's undergraduate grade-point average. However, admission decisions are not simply a function of the numbers. The committee also takes into account any upward (or downward) trend in the applicant's academic performance over time, quality of the applicant's undergraduate institution, course of study, personal statement, work experience, graduate study, extracurricular activities, letters of recommendation, and other information supplied by the applicant.

Nebraska Law will waive the application fee upon demonstration of financial need. To visit a law class, meet with admission personnel, or tour the law college, contact the admission office.

APPLICANT PROFILE

The University of Nebraska College of Law has opted not to include a detailed applicant profile that isolates the undergraduate grade-point average and LSAT score for applied and admitted students. While these credentials are important, the Admissions Committee reviews all information supplied by the applicant and considers many factors beyond the LSAT score and undergraduate grade-point average in making admission decisions.

UNIVERSITY OF NEVADA, LAS VEGAS, WILLIAM S. BOYD SCHOOL OF LAW

4505 Maryland Parkway, Box 451003
Las Vegas, NV 89154-1003
Phone: 702.895.2440; Fax: 702.895.2414
E-mail: request@law.unlv.edu; Website: www.law.unlv.edu

The Basics

Type of school	Public
Term	Semester
Application deadline	3/15
Application fee	$50
Financial aid deadline	2/1
Can first year start other than fall?	No
Student to faculty ratio	13.4 to 1
# of housing spaces available restricted to law students	
graduate housing for which law students are eligible	

Faculty and Administrators

	Total		Men		Women		Minorities	
	Spr	Fall	Spr	Fall	Spr	Fall	Spr	Fall
Full-time	28	25	12	10	16	15	6	5
Other full-time	3	1	2	0	1	1	0	0
Deans, librarians, & others who teach	10	10	5	4	5	6	2	2
Part-time	16	12	12	11	3	0	1	1
Total	57	48	31	25	25	22	9	8

Curriculum

		Full-Time	Part-Time
Typical first-year section size		56	34
Is there typically a "small section" of the first-year class, other than Legal Writing, taught by full-time faculty		No	No
If yes, typical size offered last year			
# of classroom course titles beyond first-year curriculum		82	
# of upper division courses, excluding seminars, with an enrollment:	Under 25	87	
	25–49	21	
	50–74	10	
	75–99	2	
	100+	0	
# of seminars		11	
# of seminar positions available		176	
# of seminar positions filled		111	35
# of positions available in simulation courses		184	
# of simulation positions filled		138	19
# of positions available in faculty supervised clinical courses		78	
# of faculty supervised clinical positions filled		75	13
# involved in field placements		125	8
# involved in law journals		53	8
# involved in moot court or trial competitions		24	4
# of credit hours required to graduate		89	

JD Enrollment and Ethnicity

	Men		Women		Full-Time		Part-Time		1st-Year		Total		JD Degs. Awd.
	#	%	#	%	#	%	#	%	#	%	#	%	
All Hispanics	21	7.9	32	15.3	39	11.2	14	10.9	19	13.0	53	11.2	13
Am. Ind./AK Nat.	5	1.9	5	2.4	10	2.9	0	0.0	5	3.4	10	2.1	5
Asian	26	9.8	22	10.5	37	10.7	11	8.6	13	8.9	48	10.1	19
Black/Af. Am.	14	5.3	18	8.6	21	6.1	11	8.6	11	7.5	32	6.7	6
Nat. HI/Pac. Isl.	0	0.0	0	0.0	0	0.0	0	0.0	0	0.0	0	0.0	0
2 or more races	0	0.0	0	0.0	0	0.0	0	0.0	0	0.0	0	0.0	0
Subtotal (minor.)	66	24.8	77	36.8	107	30.8	36	28.1	48	32.9	143	30.1	43
Nonres. Alien	0	0.0	1	0.5	0	0.0	1	0.8	0	0.0	1	0.2	0
White/Cauc.	185	69.5	119	56.9	222	64.0	82	64.1	92	63.0	304	64.0	89
Unknown	15	5.6	12	5.7	18	5.2	9	7.0	6	4.1	27	5.7	13
Total	266	56.0	209	44.0	347	73.1	128	26.9	146	30.7	475		146

Transfers

Transfers in	6
Transfers out	5

Tuition and Fees

	Resident	Nonresident
Full-time	$20,838	$34,238
Part-time	$13,606	$22,228
Tuition Guarantee Program		N

Living Expenses

Estimated living expenses for singles

Living on campus	Living off campus	Living at home
$16,790	$18,920	$11,000

UNIVERSITY OF NEVADA, LAS VEGAS, WILLIAM S. BOYD SCHOOL OF LAW

ABA
Approved
Since
2000

GPA and LSAT Scores

	Total	Full-Time	Part-Time
# of apps	1,745	1,504	241
# of offers	322	269	53
# of matrics	145	107	38
75% GPA	3.70	3.72	3.50
Median GPA	3.46	3.52	3.22
25% GPA	3.15	3.29	2.87
75% LSAT	161	161	159
Median LSAT	159	159	156
25% LSAT	156	157	153

Grants and Scholarships (from prior year)

	Total		Full-Time		Part-Time	
	#	%	#	%	#	%
Total # of students	484		366		118	
Total # receiving grants	157	32.4	144	39.3	13	11.0
Less than 1/2 tuition	79	16.3	76	20.8	3	2.5
Half to full tuition	73	15.1	66	18.0	7	5.9
Full tuition	0	0.0	0	0.0	0	0.0
More than full tuition	5	1.0	2	0.5	3	2.5
Median grant amount			$10,000		$9,800	

Informational and Library Resources

Total amount spent on library materials	$1,153,817
Study seating capacity inside the library	313
# of full-time equivalent professional librarians	6
Hours per week library is open	101
# of open, wired connections available to students	1,215
# of networked computers available for use by students	54
Has wireless network?	Y
Requires computer?	N

JD Attrition (from prior year)

	Academic	Other	Total	
	#	#	#	%
1st year	0	12	12	7.5
2nd year	0	1	1	0.7
3rd year	0	0	0	0.0
4th year	0	0	0	0.0

Employment (9 months after graduation)

	Total	Percentage
Employment status known	140	100.0
Employment status unknown	0	0.0
Employed	132	94.3
Pursuing graduate degrees	1	0.7
Unemployed (seeking, not seeking, or studying for the bar)	1	0.7
Type of Employment		
# employed in law firms	80	60.6
# employed in business and industry	6	4.5
# employed in government	6	4.5
# employed in public interest	10	7.6
# employed as judicial clerks	27	20.5
# employed in academia	3	2.3
Geographic Location		
# employed in state	114	86.4
# employed outside the US	1	0.8
# of states where employed	8	

Bar Passage Rates

First-time takers	151	Reporting %	90.07
Average school %	80.15	Average state %	73.00
Average pass difference	7.15		

Jurisdiction	Takers	Passers	Pass %	State %	Diff %
Nevada	136	109	80.15	73.00	7.15

UNIVERSITY OF NEVADA, LAS VEGAS, WILLIAM S. BOYD SCHOOL OF LAW

4505 Maryland Parkway, Box 451003
Las Vegas, NV 89154-1003
Phone: 702.895.2440; Fax: 702.895.2414
E-mail: request@law.unlv.edu; Website: www.law.unlv.edu

Introduction

The William S. Boyd School of Law, the first and only public law school in Nevada history, commenced classes in fall 1998 and now has graduated over 1,200 students. Located in a unique, dynamic, and continually growing metropolitan area, BSL offers its students an evolving social climate in which to study the law and observe and participate in its application. The law school is fully accredited by the American Bar Association and is a member of the Association of American Law Schools.

Faculty

The full-time faculty consists of experienced, accomplished, and well-respected legal educators. All faculty members have excellent credentials, experience, and reputations; all are people for whom teaching and mentoring of students is very important; and all are people who are eager to serve their community through scholarship, civic involvement, and various outreach programs. The law school also taps into the wealth of talent in the local bar for adjunct faculty who teach a variety of specialized courses.

Curriculum

The Boyd School of Law offers and encourages its students to undertake a generalist curriculum. Specific course offerings are constantly reviewed and revised as societal needs, student interest, and faculty resources change. The curriculum generally emphasizes the responsibilities, skills, and values required of members of the legal profession. This emphasis comes to the fore in Lawyering Process, a three-semester required course that offers students the opportunity to examine the relationship between legal analysis and other legal skills such as research, writing, oral advocacy, and client interviewing and counseling, with significant emphasis on professionalism and ethics.

Programs of Study

The law school offers a traditional three-year, full-time JD program, as well as a four-year, part-time JD program during evening hours and a four-year, part-time JD program during day hours. Additionally, three dual-degree programs have been established: Juris Doctor/Master of Business Administration, Juris Doctor/Master of Social Work, and Juris Doctor/PhD in Education.

Community Service

A unique aspect of a Boyd education is an early focus on service learning. Under the supervision of attorneys from Legal Aid Center of Southern Nevada, Nevada Legal Services, and the law school, all first-year students participate in a community service program directing informational workshops and providing legal information to those in need on the subjects of bankruptcy, foreclosure mediation, small claims, family law, paternity custody, immigration, mediation, and guardianship. After the first year, in our Partners in Pro Bono program, students work one-on-one with attorney mentors on pro bono cases. These programs are intended to acquaint students with the large unmet need for legal services and to instill a lasting commitment to community service and pro bono work.

Hands-on Experience

The Thomas and Mack Legal Clinic houses the school's "law firm" and offers an integrated academic and practice-based educational experience that teaches students to be reflective practitioners and community-oriented professionals. The clinic has focused on seven specific areas: appellate litigation, education, family justice, innocence, immigration, juvenile justice, and mediation. Additionally, the law school provides an extensive externship program. Working closely with the legal community, the law school has established a year-round program offering opportunities for students to extern with the federal and state judiciary, government and public service agencies, and Nevada and US legislatures.

Saltman Center for Conflict Resolution

The Saltman Center for Conflict Resolution was established in 2003 to provide a venue for advanced study of the nature of conflict and the methods through which conflicts may be resolved. The work of the center encompasses conflicts arising out of regional, national, and international concerns, in both the public and private sectors. Recognizing that a sophisticated understanding of conflict necessarily requires insights derived from disciplines other than law, the center places particular emphasis on interdisciplinary approaches to understanding and resolving disputes. The center's faculty teach courses on mediation, negotiations, alternative dispute resolution, and arbitration as well as a clinical offering in the area of mediation.

Student Activities

The *Nevada Law Journal* is a publication devoted to scholarly research on the subject of national legal interest as well as on issues of particular interest to the Nevada legal community.

The *UNLV Gaming Law Journal* is a journal of legal scholarship published by the students and dedicated to analyzing the law and policy implications of gaming case law, legislation, administrative regulations, and important gaming legal events.

The Society of Advocates is the school's appellate and trial forensic program. The society consists of an executive board and team members who participate in interscholastic competitions. Teams compete in mock trial, client counseling, negotiation, mediation, and alternative dispute resolution competitions, as well as traditional appellate advocacy. Boyd's teams have been very successful in winning regional, national, and international competitions.

Students also participate in over 20 student organizations.

Career Services

The Department of Career Services offers personalized career counseling, employment workshops, a job opportunity board, on-campus interviewing programs, and a state-of-the-art online job-search program to assist students.

Academic Success Program

The Boyd School of Law Academic Success Program provides students a comprehensive network of presentations, activities, tutorials, and workshops designed to stimulate learning and to amplify the classroom experience. The program supplements the curriculum with opportunities to enhance learning skills and develop more efficient and effective methods of studying, comprehending, and writing. As part of this program, the student-operated Center for Academic Success and Enrichment (CASE) offers students mentoring, advising, and tutoring.

Facility

The Boyd School of Law facility includes the William S. Boyd Hall, the James E. Rogers Center for Administration and Justice, and the Thomas and Mack Moot Court Facility. Classrooms include state-of-the art technology for presentations using PowerPoint, video, and document cameras, and are equipped to facilitate video conferencing and distance learning. Classroom, lounge, and study space offer students indoor and outdoor wireless access seating areas where they can make productive use of their time between classes.

Library

The Wiener-Rogers Law Library holds the most substantial collection of legal materials in the state of Nevada. The library is staffed by excellent, service-oriented librarians who have come from major libraries across the country. Patrons and students have access to a core collection of important material in printed and micro formats. The library offers one computer lab and provides numerous carrels for individual study, as well as group study rooms. The growing library collection now exceeds 350,000 volumes and microform volume equivalents.

Admission

The Boyd School of Law seeks to enroll an academically well-qualified, accomplished, and diverse group of individuals who will contribute to the vitality of the school's educational program, the community, and the legal profession after graduation. Applicants for admission may demonstrate qualification and accomplishment through distinguished academic records as undergraduate or graduate students, successful careers, meaningful contributions to their communities, or successful efforts to meet challenges associated with race, ethnicity, gender, economic status, or disability. Students of diverse backgrounds, attitudes, and interests contribute to the breadth and quality of the classroom and nonclassroom dialogues which are critical elements of legal education.

APPLICANT PROFILE

The Boyd School of Law has elected not to publish an applicant profile based on LSAT score and undergraduate GPA. Those two factors, while certainly important, are not the only factors taken into consideration. The Boyd School of Law uses no form of indexing system in reaching its admission decisions. Each completed application file is reviewed in its entirety.

NEW ENGLAND LAW | BOSTON

154 Stuart Street
Boston, MA 02116
Phone: 617.422.7210; Fax: 617.422.7201
E-mail: admit@nesl.edu; Website: www.nesl.edu

The Basics

Type of school	Private
Term	Semester
Application deadline	3/15
Application fee	$65
Financial aid deadline	4/7
Can first year start other than fall?	No
Student to faculty ratio	21.9 to 1
# of housing spaces available restricted to law students	
graduate housing for which law students are eligible	

Faculty and Administrators

	Total		Men		Women		Minorities	
	Spr	Fall	Spr	Fall	Spr	Fall	Spr	Fall
Full-time	37	38	25	25	12	12	33	33
Other full-time	0	2	0	1	0	1	0	0
Deans, librarians, & others who teach	6	6	3	3	3	3	4	4
Part-time	50	45	31	34	19	11	4	4
Total	93	91	59	63	34	27	41	41

Curriculum

		Full-Time	Part-Time
Typical first-year section size		105	95
Is there typically a "small section" of the first-year class, other than Legal Writing, taught by full-time faculty		No	No
If yes, typical size offered last year			
# of classroom course titles beyond first-year curriculum		118	
# of upper division courses, excluding seminars, with an enrollment:	Under 25	105	
	25–49	41	
	50–74	18	
	75–99	5	
	100+	5	
# of seminars		43	
# of seminar positions available		857	
# of seminar positions filled		350	245
# of positions available in simulation courses		812	
# of simulation positions filled		285	296
# of positions available in faculty supervised clinical courses		70	
# of faculty supervised clinical positions filled		53	6
# involved in field placements		160	28
# involved in law journals		121	20
# involved in moot court or trial competitions		10	0
# of credit hours required to graduate		86	

JD Enrollment and Ethnicity

	Men		Women		Full-Time		Part-Time		1st-Year		Total		JD Degs. Awd.
	#	%	#	%	#	%	#	%	#	%	#	%	
All Hispanics	12	2.4	14	2.2	20	2.5	6	1.8	8	2.0	26	2.3	9
Am. Ind./AK Nat.	0	0.0	0	0.0	0	0.0	0	0.0	0	0.0	0	0.0	3
Asian	19	3.8	30	4.7	39	4.9	10	3.0	14	3.6	49	4.3	11
Black/Af. Am.	5	1.0	11	1.7	13	1.6	3	0.9	5	1.3	16	1.4	7
Nat. HI/Pac. Isl.	0	0.0	0	0.0	0	0.0	0	0.0	0	0.0	0	0.0	0
2 or more races	14	2.8	8	1.3	12	1.5	10	3.0	22	5.6	22	1.9	0
Subtotal (minor.)	50	10.0	63	10.0	84	10.6	29	8.6	49	12.5	113	10.0	30
Nonres. Alien	3	0.6	4	0.6	6	0.8	1	0.3	3	0.8	7	0.6	0
White/Cauc.	366	73.3	454	71.7	583	73.2	237	70.5	269	68.8	820	72.4	220
Unknown	80	16.0	112	17.7	123	15.5	69	20.5	70	17.9	192	17.0	36
Total	499	44.1	633	55.9	796	70.3	336	29.7	391	34.5	1132		292

Transfers

Transfers in	0
Transfers out	18

Tuition and Fees

	Resident	Nonresident
Full-time	$39,990	$39,990
Part-time	$29,990	$29,990
Tuition Guarantee Program	N	

Living Expenses

Estimated living expenses for singles

Living on campus	Living off campus	Living at home
N/A	$17,780	$9,800

ABA Approved Since 1969

GPA and LSAT Scores

	Total	Full-Time	Part-Time
# of apps	3,210	2,734	765
# of offers	2,073	1,680	393
# of matrics	393	301	92
75% GPA	3.45	3.49	3.27
Median GPA	3.21	3.24	3.02
25% GPA	2.95	3.02	2.72
75% LSAT	154	154	154
Median LSAT	153	153	151
25% LSAT	151	151	149

Grants and Scholarships (from prior year)

	Total #	Total %	Full-Time #	Full-Time %	Part-Time #	Part-Time %
Total # of students	1,096		737		359	
Total # receiving grants	563	51.4	450	61.1	113	31.5
Less than 1/2 tuition	409	37.3	349	47.4	60	16.7
Half to full tuition	90	8.2	60	8.1	30	8.4
Full tuition	64	5.8	41	5.6	23	6.4
More than full tuition	0	0.0	0	0.0	0	0.0
Median grant amount			$7,500		$10,000	

Informational and Library Resources

Total amount spent on library materials	$1,216,344
Study seating capacity inside the library	473
# of full-time equivalent professional librarians	9
Hours per week library is open	104
# of open, wired connections available to students	159
# of networked computers available for use by students	51
Has wireless network?	Y
Requires computer?	N

JD Attrition (from prior year)

	Academic #	Other #	Total #	Total %
1st year	20	34	54	13.5
2nd year	2	16	18	5.5
3rd year	0	0	0	0.0
4th year	0	2	2	2.5

Employment (9 months after graduation)

	Total	Percentage
Employment status known	297	94.9
Employment status unknown	16	5.1
Employed	234	78.8
Pursuing graduate degrees	14	4.7
Unemployed (seeking, not seeking, or studying for the bar)	45	15.2
Type of Employment		
# employed in law firms	108	46.2
# employed in business and industry	68	29.1
# employed in government	34	14.5
# employed in public interest	3	1.3
# employed as judicial clerks	16	6.8
# employed in academia	4	1.7
Geographic Location		
# employed in state	149	63.7
# employed outside the US	1	0.4
# of states where employed		22

Bar Passage Rates

First-time takers	311	Reporting %	77.17
Average school %	85.84	Average state %	89.36

Average pass difference −3.52

Jurisdiction	Takers	Passers	Pass %	State %	Diff %
Massachusetts	210	181	86.19	89.77	−3.58
New York	30	25	83.33	86.51	−3.18

The information on these pages was provided by the law school.

NEW ENGLAND LAW | BOSTON

154 Stuart Street
Boston, MA 02116
Phone: 617.422.7210; Fax: 617.422.7201
E-mail: admit@nesl.edu; Website: www.nesl.edu

Introduction

New England Law | Boston offers an exceptional academic program; an engaged, welcoming community; and a menu of experiential learning opportunities that's among the most varied in the nation—all in the heart of Boston's legal community. Founded in 1908 as Portia Law School, the first law school in the nation exclusively for women, New England Law has been coeducational since 1938.

The law school officially announced the shortening of its name from New England School of Law to New England Law | Boston during its centennial celebrations in 2008. The law school is accredited by the American Bar Association (ABA) and is a member of the Association of American Law Schools (AALS).

The Faculty

The faculty brings elite academic credentials, a wealth of legal practice experience, and a strong desire to help students reach their goals. Because of the school's location in the heart of the legal community, the school's adjunct professors are drawn from a pool of outstanding practitioners, including more than a dozen judges.

Even US Supreme Court justices have provided their points of view in the school's classrooms, with visits in the 2008–2009 academic year from four High Court justices. During her visit, Justice Sandra Day O'Connor (retired) remarked: "It's a tremendous honor to be here to celebrate the start of the second hundred years of this amazing law school, and it's a privilege to be here with America's favorite dean. In a real sense this is a pioneering law school..."

Academic Program

Whether it's a placement at the attorney general's office, with a district attorney, or at the EPA, among many others, the law school offers one of the most wide-ranging, experiential-learning programs in the country. Through 16 clinics, three academic centers, and multiple cocurricular activities, students gain hands-on experience with the benefit of consistent faculty supervision. Programs include a variety of judicial clerkship opportunities.

The law school is one of a handful in the country to place students regularly at a variety of international criminal tribunals (International Criminal Tribunals for the former Yugoslavia and Rwanda-The Hague, Netherlands; Special Court for Sierra Leone-The Hague; Extraordinary Chambers in the Courts of Cambodia-Phnom Penh, International Criminal Court-The Hague) and at UN headquarters.

The law school has three nationally distributed journals, the New England Law Review, the New England Journal on Criminal and Civil Confinement, and the Journal of International and Comparative Law. The curriculum at New England Law prepares students to practice in any jurisdiction in the United States.

Academic Centers

The law school has three academic centers.

The Center for International Law and Policy provides students with the opportunity to move beyond the walls of the classroom, confront critical social and legal issues, interact directly with senior international officials and victims of international crises, and apply what they are learning to actual cases. Recently, students have been working on the preparation of issue briefs related to the work of the United Nations Human Rights Council. Students provide legal research and analysis to international prosecutors on issues pending before the international tribunals, from the contours of command responsibility to the interpretation of the Genocide Convention.

The Center for Law and Social Responsibility engages students and faculty in public interest work in areas such as the environment, children and families, and wrongful convictions. Some recent projects include representing townspeople who are fighting the construction of a carbon-polluting power plant near an elementary school, and investigating potential wrongful conviction cases.

The Center for Business Law offers a wide range of challenging opportunities, with placements at organizations like NASDAQ, FINRA, and insurance giant Liberty Mutual. One project involved research for a book on corporate governance.

Diversity

The law school's earliest alumnae broke major barriers blocking the entry of women into the legal profession. (Blanche Braxton '21, for example, was the first African American woman admitted to the Massachusetts Bar.) The school's pioneering roots are evident today as it continues to offer a quality legal education to students from a broad range of backgrounds. The school is one of only a few in the United States offering a program that provides parents with primary child-rearing responsibilities an opportunity to pursue a legal education.

New England Law fosters a comfortable and supportive atmosphere for students of color. A cornerstone of that commitment is the Charles Hamilton Houston Enrichment Program. The program seeks to address racial bias in the legal profession and the law, promote diversity in the student body, and reduce isolation. The program combines discussion groups with guest speakers and community-building activities.

Study Options

Students may enroll in the full-time day division, the part-time day or evening divisions, or the Special Part-time Program. New England Law accepts foreign lawyers in an advanced placement JD program or an LLM program in Advanced Legal Studies.

Study Abroad

Students may study in summer-abroad programs in Galway, Ireland; London; Malta; Chile; or Prague; or in semester-abroad programs in Denmark, the Netherlands, Tanzania, Switzerland, Nepal, Paris X-Nanterre, or Cambodia. An international criminal process clinic in The Hague enrolls students for a summer or semester.

Financial Aid

Our generous financial aid program consists of a combination of federal loan programs, private loans, institutional need-based grants, and merit scholarships. Federal work-study funding is also available.

Student Activities

New England Law has a Student Bar Association, which oversees more than two dozen student groups. These organizations sponsor speakers, social events, and volunteer activities during the year. Student representatives sit on most faculty committees.

Career Services

The Career Services Office (CSO) provides students with individual career counseling, job-search resources, and career programs and workshops. The office maintains an extensive resource library and an online Recruitment and Programming Center with services that include a searchable job-posting database, employer recruitment programs, an e-mail service that sends students job postings, an alumni networking and mentoring program, and postings of job-related programs sponsored by the CSO and outside organizations.

As a member of the Massachusetts Law School Consortium, New England Law participates in recruitment programs with the state's six other ABA-accredited law schools. The school is also a member of the Northeast Law School Consortium and participates in recruitment programs with eight ABA-accredited law schools in the region.

Most students take the Massachusetts bar exam, while many take exams in New York, the District of Columbia, Florida, New Hampshire, and New Jersey.

APPLICANT PROFILE

New England Law | Boston
This grid includes only applicants who earned 120–180 LSAT scores under standard administrations.

LSAT Score	GPA 3.75 +		3.50–3.74		3.25–3.49		3.00–3.24		2.75–2.99		2.50–2.74		2.25–2.49		2.00–2.24		Below 2.00		No GPA		Total	
	Apps	Adm	Apps	Adm	Apps	Adm	Apps	Adm	Apps	Adm	Apps	Adm	Apps	Adm	Apps	Adm	Apps	Adm	Apps	Adm	Apps	Adm
175–180	0	0	0	0	0	0	0	0	0	0	0	0	0	0	0	0	0	0	0	0	0	0
170–174	0	0	0	0	3	3	2	2	0	0	1	1	0	0	0	0	0	0	0	0	6	6
165–169	2	2	5	4	7	7	3	3	5	5	7	7	3	3	1	0	2	0	0	0	35	31
160–164	19	18	51	50	27	27	36	36	25	25	18	16	6	5	5	4	1	0	0	0	188	181
155–159	43	43	104	102	117	113	134	129	79	69	60	54	37	23	7	4	5	0	9	6	595	543
150–154	80	74	159	150	255	243	287	260	183	138	108	79	67	36	21	10	4	1	10	2	1174	993
145–149	41	25	109	42	149	29	213	42	118	20	97	8	35	2	17	0	4	0	14	2	797	170
140–144	8	0	26	0	51	0	59	0	52	0	36	0	16	0	5	0	0	0	8	0	261	0
135–139	1	0	8	0	13	0	22	0	17	0	18	0	8	0	9	0	4	0	3	0	103	0
130–134	0	0	2	0	8	0	8	0	5	0	10	0	5	0	0	0	0	0	5	0	43	0
125–129	1	0	0	0	0	0	1	0	0	0	1	0	1	0	0	0	2	0	0	0	6	0
120–124	0	0	0	0	0	0	0	0	0	0	0	0	0	0	1	0	1	0	0	0	2	0
Total	195	162	464	348	630	422	765	472	484	257	356	165	178	69	66	18	23	1	49	10	3210	1924

Apps = Number of Applicants
Adm = Number Admitted
Reflects 99% of the total applicant pool; highest LSAT data reported.

UNIVERSITY OF NEW HAMPSHIRE SCHOOL OF LAW

Two White Street
Concord, NH 03301
Phone: 603.228.9217; Fax: 603.229.0425
E-mail: admissions@law.unh.edu; Website: www.law.unh.edu

ABA
Approved
Since
1974

AMERICAN BAR ASSOCIATION
Section of Legal Education
and Admissions to the Bar

The Basics

Type of school	Private
Term	Semester
Application deadline	4/1
Application fee	$55
Financial aid deadline	3/31
Can first year start other than fall?	No
Student to faculty ratio	14.9 to 1
# of housing spaces available restricted to law students	3
graduate housing for which law students are eligible	

Faculty and Administrators

	Total Spr	Total Fall	Men Spr	Men Fall	Women Spr	Women Fall	Minorities Spr	Minorities Fall
Full-time	22	25	13	14	9	11	1	2
Other full-time	7	8	4	4	3	4	0	0
Deans, librarians, & others who teach	8	8	4	4	4	4	0	0
Part-time	35	27	23	15	12	12	2	2
Total	72	68	44	37	28	31	3	4

Curriculum

	Full-Time	Part-Time
Typical first-year section size	75	0
Is there typically a "small section" of the first-year class, other than Legal Writing, taught by full-time faculty	Yes	No
If yes, typical size offered last year	15	
# of classroom course titles beyond first-year curriculum	92	

# of upper division courses, excluding seminars, with an enrollment:		
Under 25	108	
25–49	16	
50–74	14	
75–99	3	
100+	0	

# of seminars	15	
# of seminar positions available	253	
# of seminar positions filled	166	0
# of positions available in simulation courses	864	
# of simulation positions filled	672	0
# of positions available in faculty supervised clinical courses	243	
# of faculty supervised clinical positions filled	178	0
# involved in field placements	91	0
# involved in law journals	41	0
# involved in moot court or trial competitions	44	0
# of credit hours required to graduate	85	

JD Enrollment and Ethnicity

	Men #	Men %	Women #	Women %	Full-Time #	Full-Time %	Part-Time #	Part-Time %	1st-Year #	1st-Year %	Total #	Total %	JD Degs. Awd.
All Hispanics	11	4.5	10	5.7	21	5.0	0	0.0	5	3.8	21	5.0	3
Am. Ind./AK Nat.	0	0.0	1	0.6	1	0.2	0	0.0	0	0.0	1	0.2	0
Asian	21	8.6	24	13.6	45	10.7	0	0.0	13	9.9	45	10.7	9
Black/Af. Am.	7	2.9	11	6.3	18	4.3	0	0.0	4	3.1	18	4.3	6
Nat. HI/Pac. Isl.	0	0.0	0	0.0	0	0.0	0	0.0	0	0.0	0	0.0	0
2 or more races	8	3.3	2	1.1	10	2.4	0	0.0	3	2.3	10	2.4	0
Subtotal (minor.)	47	19.3	48	27.3	95	22.7	0	0.0	25	19.1	95	22.7	18
Nonres. Alien	7	2.9	10	5.7	17	4.1	0	0.0	5	3.8	17	4.1	8
White/Cauc.	189	77.8	118	67.0	307	73.3	0	0.0	101	77.1	307	73.3	86
Unknown	0	0.0	0	0.0	0	0.0	0	0.0	0	0.0	0	0.0	15
Total	243	58.0	176	42.0	419	100.0	0	0.0	131	31.3	419		127

Transfers

Transfers in	1
Transfers out	9

Tuition and Fees

	Resident	Nonresident
Full-time	$37,000	$37,000
Part-time		
Tuition Guarantee Program		N

Living Expenses

Estimated living expenses for singles

Living on campus	Living off campus	Living at home
$20,647	$20,647	$20,647

UNIVERSITY OF NEW HAMPSHIRE SCHOOL OF LAW

ABA
Approved
Since
1974

GPA and LSAT Scores

	Total	Full-Time	Part-Time
# of apps	1,308	1,308	0
# of offers	608	608	0
# of matrics	132	132	0
75% GPA	3.58	3.58	0.00
Median GPA	3.34	3.34	0.00
25% GPA	3.03	3.03	0.00
75% LSAT	158	158	0
Median LSAT	153	153	0
25% LSAT	150	150	0

Grants and Scholarships (from prior year)

	Total		Full-Time		Part-Time	
	#	%	#	%	#	%
Total # of students	430		429		1	
Total # receiving grants	242	56.3	242	56.4	0	0.0
Less than 1/2 tuition	208	48.4	208	48.5	0	0.0
Half to full tuition	33	7.7	33	7.7	0	0.0
Full tuition	1	0.2	1	0.2	0	0.0
More than full tuition	0	0.0	0	0.0	0	0.0
Median grant amount			$8,000		$0	

Informational and Library Resources

Total amount spent on library materials	$1,039,637
Study seating capacity inside the library	306
# of full-time equivalent professional librarians	8
Hours per week library is open	105
# of open, wired connections available to students	307
# of networked computers available for use by students	26
Has wireless network?	Y
Requires computer?	N

JD Attrition (from prior year)

	Academic	Other	Total	
	#	#	#	%
1st year	1	16	17	11.1
2nd year	0	0	0	0.0
3rd year	0	0	0	0.0
4th year	0	0	0	0.0

Employment (9 months after graduation)

	Total	Percentage
Employment status known	127	92.0
Employment status unknown	11	8.0
Employed	104	81.9
Pursuing graduate degrees	5	3.9
Unemployed (seeking, not seeking, or studying for the bar)	16	12.6
Type of Employment		
# employed in law firms	62	59.6
# employed in business and industry	18	17.3
# employed in government	6	5.8
# employed in public interest	8	7.7
# employed as judicial clerks	5	4.8
# employed in academia	5	4.8
Geographic Location		
# employed in state	21	20.2
# employed outside the US	1	1.0
# of states where employed	24	

Bar Passage Rates

First-time takers	153	Reporting %	73.86
Average school %	78.76	Average state %	85.70
Average pass difference	−6.94		

Jurisdiction	Takers	Passers	Pass %	State %	Diff %
New Hampshire	36	33	91.67	86.84	4.83
Massachusetts	32	26	81.25	89.77	−8.52
New York	23	18	78.26	86.51	−8.25
Virginia	22	12	54.55	77.06	−22.51

UNIVERSITY OF NEW HAMPSHIRE SCHOOL OF LAW

Two White Street
Concord, NH 03301
Phone: 603.228.9217; Fax: 603.229.0425
E-mail: admissions@law.unh.edu; Website: www.law.unh.edu

Introduction

UNH Law, formerly Franklin Pierce Law Center, is known throughout the world as an innovative leader in legal education, providing its students with the skills to lead and serve, and to meet the emerging needs of a global society. UNH Law emphasizes individually tailored legal programs and a broad range of learning settings, including lectures and seminars, real-client clinics, independent study, and externships in law firms, in courts, and in private and public agencies. In addition, we promote a community spirit of caring and compassion, with a close working relationship between students and faculty. Self-reliant students who know their own strengths and objectives thrive at UNH Law and find the focus on personal pride and responsibility more motivating than fear or competition.

UNH Law is one of the smallest law schools in the United States. The University of New Hampshire affiliation provides the resources of a major research university. Each entering class numbers approximately 150 students, allowing for a 14:1 student-to-teacher ratio. Classes are small, especially after the first year; 75 of the 109 elective courses enroll 35 or fewer students.

Located in New Hampshire's capital city of Concord (45,000 population), UNH Law is ideally situated one hour from Boston, the Atlantic seacoast, the state's Lakes Region, and the White Mountains.

Special Programs

- **Intellectual Property**—The internationally recognized intellectual property specialization (patents, licensing, technology transfer, trade secrets, trademarks, cyberlaw, and copyrights) is supported by 14 full-time faculty members, all intellectual property lawyers. Training includes learning to advise clients regarding intellectual property protection, infringement, and technology transfer. Students with technical backgrounds may focus on patent law, many passing the patent bar prior to graduation. Other intellectual property areas do not require a technical background.
- **Commerce and Technology Law**—The business curriculum prepares students for traditional types of practice and brings new opportunities for students choosing to confront the legal issues involving electronic commerce. The business and e-commerce curriculum also integrates well with the intellectual property curriculum, particularly for students interested in business and legal innovations associated with the Internet.
- **Social Justice Institute**—This hands-on professional training program prepares students for public interest law in private practice, governmental service, social policy advocacy, and criminal practice. Clinic students represent clients in cases involving misdemeanor and felony defense; predatory lending; bankruptcy and consumer fraud; unemployment compensation; as well as trademark, copyright, and small business transactions. In addition, students have the opportunity to assist in projects with the Institute for Health, Law, and Ethics.
- **Criminal Law**—Our criminal law curriculum offers courses, individual mentoring, clinics, and externships to prepare students for careers in prosecution or defense. Criminal Practice Clinic students represent clients charged with misdemeanor and juvenile offenses at the district court level. In the Appellate Defender Program, students prepare briefs for the New Hampshire Supreme Court in criminal cases. Externship opportunities are available in prosecutorial positions at the local, state, and federal level, and in defense positions with law firms and governmental agencies.
- **International Criminal Law and Justice**—This program is designed to prepare the next generation of lawyers, peacekeepers, policy makers, and law enforcement professionals who will be confronting global issues of criminal law and justice. The program includes a one-week seminar in Washington, DC; explores legal responses to terrorism, counterfeiting, intellectual property crimes, human trafficking; and more.

International Summer Institutes in China and Ireland

- The Intellectual Property Summer Institute at Tsinghua University in Beijing offers an overview of China's patent, copyright, and trademark laws, as well as an introduction to some of the major international instruments and institutions regulating international trade and intellectual property.
- The eLaw Summer Institute at University College Cork, Ireland, focuses on law and emerging policy of the information age.

Academic Opportunities

The *Daniel Webster Scholar Honors Program* is a comprehensive, practice-based program focused on making law students client-ready. Admission to the program is competitive; application is made at the end of the 1L year. Second- and third-year students complete a range of courses, demonstrate their developing professional skills and judgment, and compile a portfolio of work. Students who successfully complete the program will be certified as having passed the New Hampshire bar examination, subject to passing character and fitness requirements.

The UNH Law *Externship Program* exchanges a full-credit semester in the classroom for a real-life experience working in an active legal position. Externs work with experienced attorneys and judges while under the close supervision of a faculty member.

Joint-Degree Programs and LLM

UNH Law offers three dual-degree programs: JD/Master of Laws (LLM) in Intellectual Property, JD/LLM in Commerce and Technology, and JD/LLM in International Criminal Law and Justice. Summer programs enable students to earn additional credits needed to complete joint-degree programs in three years. The three LLM degrees are designed for law graduates who wish to examine the legally sophisticated intellectual property issues that often arise in policy making and teaching.

Student Activities

Students prepare notes and comments for *IDEA: The Intellectual Property Law Review* and *UNH Law Review*. Students organize and participate in a wide variety of formal organizations and informal activities and events throughout the year.

Career Services

The Career Services Office works with students and alumni to find the best match to meet their skills and interests in changing legal markets. The office provides extensive individual counseling and guidance; brings attorneys to campus to provide firsthand information about the practice of law; advises students of all resources through weekly publications and job boards; coordinates the efforts of faculty, staff, and student groups to provide information about opportunities to gain experience; and conducts outreach to employers. More than 75 percent of our graduates secure positions outside New Hampshire.

Clinics

- Intellectual Property and Business Transaction Clinic
- Administrative Law and Advocacy Clinic
- UNH Law Innocence Project
- Consumer and Commercial Law Clinic
- Criminal Practice Clinic
- Appellate Defender Program
- Street Law Project
- Intellectual Property Amicus Clinic
- International Technology Transfer Institute

Admission

While LSAT scores and grade-point average are factors that must be considered in the decision-making process, neither alone determines admission. Every application receives a thorough and thoughtful review. The candidate's personal statement, letters of recommendation, and résumé are evaluated along with the numbers. Community service, employment during college, and other nonacademic accomplishments are given weight to the extent that they reflect initiative, social responsibility, focus, and maturity.

APPLICANT PROFILE

The University of New Hampshire School of Law seeks to admit students who will make a contribution to the law school community, to the legal profession, and to society. Admission is based on a whole-person review of each application, including academic ability and aptitude, demonstration of academic success, relevant experience that addresses the school's mission or areas of excellence, leadership, diversity, moral character, community service, and other qualitative personal attributes. UNH Law values diverse opinions, backgrounds, and perspectives; this enrichment within the classroom and community is core to the educational experience.

THE UNIVERSITY OF NEW MEXICO SCHOOL OF LAW

MSC11-6070, 1 University of New Mexico
Albuquerque, NM 87131-0001
Phone: 505.277.2146; Fax: 505.277.9958
E-mail: admissions@law.unm.edu; Website: http://lawschool.unm.edu

ABA
Approved
Since
1948

The Basics

Type of school	Public
Term	Semester
Application deadline	2/15
Application fee	$50
Financial aid deadline	3/1
Can first year start other than fall?	No
Student to faculty ratio	12.4 to 1
# of housing spaces available restricted to law students	
graduate housing for which law students are eligible	

Faculty and Administrators

	Total		Men		Women		Minorities	
	Spr	Fall	Spr	Fall	Spr	Fall	Spr	Fall
Full-time	23	23	9	9	14	14	10	10
Other full-time	3	5	1	2	2	3	0	0
Deans, librarians, & others who teach	13	12	7	6	6	6	4	4
Part-time	40	36	21	18	19	18	8	13
Total	79	76	38	35	41	41	22	27

Curriculum

	Full-Time	Part-Time
Typical first-year section size	38	0
Is there typically a "small section" of the first-year class, other than Legal Writing, taught by full-time faculty	Yes	No
If yes, typical size offered last year	16	

# of classroom course titles beyond first-year curriculum		99
# of upper division courses, excluding seminars, with an enrollment:	Under 25	54
	25–49	17
	50–74	5
	75–99	0
	100+	0

# of seminars		12
# of seminar positions available		148
# of seminar positions filled	126	0
# of positions available in simulation courses		142
# of simulation positions filled	128	0
# of positions available in faculty supervised clinical courses		124
# of faculty supervised clinical positions filled	114	0
# involved in field placements	55	0
# involved in law journals	67	0
# involved in moot court or trial competitions	26	0
# of credit hours required to graduate		86

JD Enrollment and Ethnicity

	Men #	Men %	Women #	Women %	Full-Time #	Full-Time %	Part-Time #	Part-Time %	1st-Year #	1st-Year %	Total #	Total %	JD Degs. Awd.
All Hispanics	51	30.9	49	26.3	100	28.5	0	0.0	29	25.4	100	28.5	33
Am. Ind./AK Nat.	5	3.0	21	11.3	26	7.4	0	0.0	7	6.1	26	7.4	11
Asian	1	0.6	2	1.1	3	0.9	0	0.0	1	0.9	3	0.9	4
Black/Af. Am.	6	3.6	9	4.8	15	4.3	0	0.0	3	2.6	15	4.3	0
Nat. Hl/Pac. Isl.	1	0.6	4	2.2	5	1.4	0	0.0	2	1.8	5	1.4	0
2 or more races	1	0.6	0	0.0	1	0.3	0	0.0	0	0.0	1	0.3	0
Subtotal (minor.)	65	39.4	85	45.7	150	42.7	0	0.0	42	36.8	150	42.7	48
Nonres. Alien	1	0.6	0	0.0	1	0.3	0	0.0	1	0.9	1	0.3	0
White/Cauc.	86	52.1	84	45.2	170	48.4	0	0.0	65	57.0	170	48.4	59
Unknown	13	7.9	17	9.1	30	8.5	0	0.0	6	5.3	30	8.5	5
Total	165	47.0	186	53.0	351	100.0	0	0.0	114	32.5	351		112

Transfers

Transfers in	3
Transfers out	0

Tuition and Fees

	Resident	Nonresident
Full-time	$13,660	$30,604
Part-time		
Tuition Guarantee Program		N

Living Expenses

Estimated living expenses for singles

Living on campus	Living off campus	Living at home
$13,666	$14,656	$8,576

ABA Approved Since 1948

GPA and LSAT Scores

	Total	Full-Time	Part-Time
# of apps	1,147	1,147	0
# of offers	242	242	0
# of matrics	116	116	0
75% GPA	3.60	3.60	0.00
Median GPA	3.40	3.40	0.00
25% GPA	3.10	3.10	0.00
75% LSAT	159	159	0
Median LSAT	156	156	0
25% LSAT	153	153	0

Grants and Scholarships (from prior year)

	Total		Full-Time		Part-Time	
	#	%	#	%	#	%
Total # of students	351		351		0	
Total # receiving grants	102	29.1	102	29.1	0	0.0
Less than 1/2 tuition	62	17.7	62	17.7	0	0.0
Half to full tuition	15	4.3	15	4.3	0	0.0
Full tuition	23	6.6	23	6.6	0	0.0
More than full tuition	2	0.6	2	0.6	0	0.0
Median grant amount			$5,000		$0	

Informational and Library Resources

Total amount spent on library materials	$711,894
Study seating capacity inside the library	292
# of full-time equivalent professional librarians	7
Hours per week library is open	93
# of open, wired connections available to students	330
# of networked computers available for use by students	76
Has wireless network?	Y
Requires computer?	Y

JD Attrition (from prior year)

	Academic	Other	Total	
	#	#	#	%
1st year	0	0	0	0.0
2nd year	0	1	1	0.9
3rd year	0	1	1	0.9
4th year	0	0	0	0.0

Employment (9 months after graduation)

	Total	Percentage
Employment status known	113	100.0
Employment status unknown	0	0.0
Employed	104	92.0
Pursuing graduate degrees	2	1.8
Unemployed (seeking, not seeking, or studying for the bar)	3	2.7
Type of Employment		
# employed in law firms	50	48.1
# employed in business and industry	4	3.8
# employed in government	21	20.2
# employed in public interest	14	13.5
# employed as judicial clerks	9	8.7
# employed in academia	3	2.9
Geographic Location		
# employed in state	87	83.7
# employed outside the US	2	1.9
# of states where employed	12	

Bar Passage Rates

First-time takers	103	Reporting %	93.20
Average school %	94.79	Average state %	90.58
Average pass difference	4.21		

Jurisdiction	Takers	Passers	Pass %	State %	Diff %
New Mexico	96	91	94.79	90.58	4.21

THE UNIVERSITY OF NEW MEXICO SCHOOL OF LAW

MSC11-6070, 1 University of New Mexico
Albuquerque, NM 87131-0001
Phone: 505.277.2146; Fax: 505.277.9958
E-mail: admissions@law.unm.edu; Website: http://lawschool.unm.edu

Introduction

Located in Albuquerque, the School of Law is known for its small classes, easy student-faculty interaction, and programs in clinical law, natural resources law, and Indian law. The excellent student-to-faculty ratio, one of the best in the country, facilitates a sense of community in the educational experience. It also allows the school to offer more courses with smaller enrollments. The school is a member of the Association of American Law Schools (AALS) and is approved by the American Bar Association (ABA). The University of New Mexico is the state's flagship institution, with approximately 33,000 students on its main and branch campuses.

Curriculum

The Juris Doctor (JD) program offers a full-time day curriculum. Students normally complete the required 86 hours of law credit for the JD degree in three academic years (six semesters). A limited number of entering students may be admitted to the Flexible Time Program, which allows students to take fewer credit hours per semester and graduate in five academic years. All students must take the standard first-year curriculum, including basic courses in torts, contracts, civil procedure, property, criminal law, and constitutional law. Emphasis is also placed on the skills of advocacy: legal writing, oral argument, litigation, counseling, and negotiation. First-year classes range in size from approximately 13 to 59 students. After completion of the first-year curriculum, courses are elective except for Ethics and a clinical program. Typically, one-half of the electives have fewer than 15 students. Every student must complete the advanced writing requirement.

Special Programs

Clinical Law. UNM's program in Clinical Law is regarded as one of the finest practical lawyering programs in the country and includes the Law Practice Clinic, the Business and Tax Clinic, the Community Lawyering Clinic, and the Southwest Indian Law Clinic. Students may participate in the extern placement program and elect assignment to a judge's office, the public defender's office, federal and state administrative offices, and private practitioners. The school also offers an innovative course in Criminal Law in Practice, in which students receive hands-on experience in either prosecution or defense of criminal cases at both the misdemeanor and felony levels. Unlike most other law schools, UNM requires six credit hours of clinical work for graduation. In 1970, the New Mexico Supreme Court adopted a rule permitting students to practice before state courts.

Indian Law. UNM has long been a leader in Indian law and has developed one of the most comprehensive programs in the country. The school offers students the Southwest Indian Law Clinic, the *Tribal Law Journal*, the Indian Law Certificate (ILC), scholarly research, guest lectures, seminars, and social activities. An ILC student completes the JD while enrolling in 21 hours of required and elective Indian law courses.

Natural Resources Law. The UNM School of Law is widely known for its strength in the areas of natural resources and environmental law and offers a number of electives in these subjects. Students who want to gain a more comprehensive understanding of resource problems may participate in the Natural Resources Certificate Program, which may include work on the *Natural Resources Journal*, an internationally recognized quarterly.

Business Law. UNM's Economic Development Program gives students the training they need to become well-prepared business lawyers. An enhanced curriculum includes the Business and Tax Clinic, which offers services to small businesses, start-ups, nonprofit organizations, and economic development programs. Students learn how to advise entrepreneurs on a wide range of business issues.

International Law. The school has developed a variety of programs and courses that provide opportunities for students interested in international law. Students may expand their experience through coursework at the law school and through the study-abroad and exchange programs.

- *Guanajuato Summer Law Institute.* The School of Law, in conjunction with the Universidad de Guanajuato, Southwestern University, and Texas Tech University, offers four to six weeks of summer law study in Guanajuato, Mexico. The institute features an introduction to Mexican law and international law subjects related to Latin America. The institute is ABA-approved.
- *Visiting Programs.* In conjunction with the University of New Mexico's Office of International Programs, law students can take advantage of UNM-sponsored exchange programs throughout Central and South America, Europe, Asia, and Africa.

Dual-Degree Programs

Three established dual JD and master's degree programs are offered: the JD and MPA in Public Administration, the JD and MBA, and the JD and MA in Latin American Studies. Students can also earn the JD degree and an MA, MS, or PhD in other academic fields. Students must satisfy the admission and academic requirements of both the School of Law and the graduate school.

Facilities

The School of Law, a state-of-the-art facility, is located on the northern edge of the UNM campus. The building is wireless and laptop friendly. The law school includes classroom and seminar rooms, all faculty offices, student organization and publication offices, a computer lab, the Clinical Program, and the law library. The law school is also home to the American Indian Law Center, Inc., the Utton Transboundary Resources Center, and the Institute of Public Law. Adjacent to the law school is the Albuquerque branch of the New Mexico Court of Appeals.

Law Library. The UNM Law Library is the largest legal research facility in New Mexico. The library offers a wide variety of electronic products, and its book and microform collection of 417,000 includes special collections in American Indian law, Mexican and Latin American law, land grant law, and natural resources law. The library's 48,646 square feet of space provides 359 seats, including 106 student carrels and 253 noncarrel seats, plus numerous areas for study, lounging, and browsing. Wireless Internet broadcasters, group study rooms equipped with audiovisual equipment, photocopy facilities, the school's computer lab for student use, and a classroom for legal research instruction are found in the library. The library is also home to the Governor Bruce King Archives and Reading Room, which serves as a meeting space for special events.

Career Services. The school's smaller size allows for individualized attention in all aspects of career development and job-search methodology. Regular workshops are provided on résumé and cover letter writing, interviewing, and job-search strategies. In addition, the law school sponsors on-campus interviews, a mock interview program, and presentations on various practice opportunities.

Student Activities

Extracurricular activities include the *Natural Resources Journal*, the *New Mexico Law Review*, the *Tribal Law Journal*, and several moot court and mock trial competitions. All law students are members of the University's Graduate/Professional Student Association and the Student Bar Association. Students may participate in over 30 law student organizations.

Admission and Financial Aid

Applicants must take the LSAT, register for the LSAC Credential Assembly Service, and have a bachelor's degree from an accredited university or college before registration in the fall. A five-member committee reviews applications. Substantial weight is given to the applicant's personal statement, prior work experience, extracurricular activities, letters of recommendation, and other information supplied by the applicant. Applications from New Mexico residents are given a preference. Students apply for financial aid by filing the FAFSA. Types of financial aid include loans, grants, and work study. The school awards grants to students based on the Access Group's Need Access application.

Albuquerque

The Albuquerque metropolitan area has a population of approximately 750,000. Situated along the Rio Grande, the city is located at a high desert elevation of 5,000–7,000 feet and is surrounded by the Sandia Mountains.

From golf to skiing to hiking to fly-fishing, students have access to outdoor New Mexico. In addition, students have the opportunity to visit museums and art galleries and take in concerts and theater. The combination of multiple cultures reflected in food, music, art, architecture, and local customs heightens Albuquerque's appeal.

APPLICANT PROFILE

The University of New Mexico School of Law
This grid includes only applicants who earned 120–180 LSAT scores under standard administrations.

LSAT Score	3.75 +		3.50–3.74		3.25–3.49		3.00–3.24		2.75–2.99		2.50–2.74		2.25–2.49		2.00–2.24		Below 2.00		No GPA		Total	
	Apps	Adm	Apps	Adm	Apps	Adm	Apps	Adm	Apps	Adm	Apps	Adm	Apps	Adm	Apps	Adm	Apps	Adm	Apps	Adm	Apps	Adm
175–180	0	0	0	0	0	0	0	0	0	0	0	0	0	0	0	0	0	0	0	0	0	0
170–174	2	2	2	2	2	2	1	1	0	0	0	0	1	0	0	0	0	0	0	0	8	7
165–169	5	5	4	4	9	5	2	0	3	1	0	0	2	1	1	0	0	0	0	0	26	16
160–164	17	13	26	19	25	21	14	3	12	3	7	1	2	0	6	0	2	1	1	0	112	61
155–159	27	14	48	24	56	22	49	12	41	10	18	2	7	2	2	0	1	0	2	0	251	86
150–154	34	13	63	13	83	11	65	8	47	5	29	4	19	2	3	0	2	0	5	0	350	56
145–149	16	2	38	3	48	2	45	1	34	3	19	1	12	0	7	0	0	0	4	0	223	12
140–144	9	0	14	0	19	2	20	0	32	1	20	0	7	1	2	0	0	0	5	0	129	4
135–139	4	0	4	0	6	0	13	0	6	0	9	0	4	0	4	0	0	0	6	0	56	0
130–134	0	0	1	0	1	0	4	0	1	0	1	0	1	0	0	0	1	0	0	0	10	0
125–129	0	0	0	0	0	0	0	0	0	0	3	0	2	0	0	0	1	0	0	0	6	0
120–124	0	0	0	0	0	0	0	0	0	0	0	0	0	0	1	0	0	0	0	0	1	0
Total	114	49	200	65	249	65	213	25	176	23	106	8	57	6	26	0	8	1	23	0	1172	242

Apps = Number of Applicants
Adm = Number Admitted
Reflects 99% of the total applicant pool; highest LSAT data reported.

NEW YORK LAW SCHOOL

185 West Broadway
New York, NY 10013
Phone: 212.431.2888; Fax: 212.966.1522
E-mail: admissions@nyls.edu; Website: www.nyls.edu

ABA
Approved
Since
1954

The Basics

Type of school	Private
Term	Semester
Application deadline	4/1
Application fee	$0
Financial aid deadline	4/1
Can first year start other than fall?	No
Student to faculty ratio	23.1 to 1
# of housing spaces available	
restricted to law students	99
graduate housing for which law students are eligible	99

Faculty and Administrators

	Total		Men		Women		Minorities	
	Spr	Fall	Spr	Fall	Spr	Fall	Spr	Fall
Full-time	58	65	40	44	18	21	7	9
Other full-time	6	6	4	3	2	3	0	0
Deans, librarians, & others who teach	16	15	6	6	10	9	0	0
Part-time	123	111	71	71	52	40	10	11
Total	203	197	121	124	82	73	17	20

Curriculum

	Full-Time	Part-Time
Typical first-year section size	103	103
Is there typically a "small section" of the first-year class, other than Legal Writing, taught by full-time faculty	Yes	Yes
If yes, typical size offered last year	34	34

		Full-Time	Part-Time
# of classroom course titles beyond first-year curriculum		243	
# of upper division courses, excluding seminars, with an enrollment:	Under 25	221	
	25–49	45	
	50–74	26	
	75–99	15	
	100+	39	
# of seminars		110	
# of seminar positions available		1,729	
# of seminar positions filled		797	306
# of positions available in simulation courses		1,707	
# of simulation positions filled		1,020	315
# of positions available in faculty supervised clinical courses		108	
# of faculty supervised clinical positions filled		78	0
# involved in field placements		259	17
# involved in law journals		227	25
# involved in moot court or trial competitions		129	8
# of credit hours required to graduate		86	

JD Enrollment and Ethnicity

	Men		Women		Full-Time		Part-Time		1st-Year		Total		JD Degs. Awd.
	#	%	#	%	#	%	#	%	#	%	#	%	
All Hispanics	103	11.0	121	12.3	166	11.1	58	13.5	105	16.3	224	11.6	35
Am. Ind./AK Nat.	9	1.0	1	0.1	3	0.2	7	1.6	3	0.5	10	0.5	1
Asian	27	2.9	36	3.7	49	3.3	14	3.2	15	2.3	63	3.3	46
Black/Af. Am.	46	4.9	93	9.5	89	6.0	50	11.6	48	7.5	139	7.2	21
Nat. HI/Pac. Isl.	1	0.1	0	0.0	1	0.1	0	0.0	0	0.0	1	0.1	0
2 or more races	12	1.3	18	1.8	25	1.7	5	1.2	12	1.9	30	1.6	0
Subtotal (minor.)	198	21.1	269	27.4	333	22.3	134	31.1	183	28.4	467	24.3	103
Nonres. Alien	0	0.0	0	0.0	0	0.0	0	0.0	0	0.0	0	0.0	0
White/Cauc.	631	67.1	595	60.5	978	65.5	248	57.5	424	65.8	1226	63.8	269
Unknown	111	11.8	119	12.1	181	12.1	49	11.4	37	5.7	230	12.0	67
Total	940	48.9	983	51.1	1492	77.6	431	22.4	644	33.5	1923		439

Transfers

Transfers in	13
Transfers out	37

Tuition and Fees

	Resident	Nonresident
Full-time	$46,460	$46,460
Part-time	$35,700	$35,700
Tuition Guarantee Program		Y

Living Expenses

Estimated living expenses for singles

Living on campus	Living off campus	Living at home
$22,898	$22,898	$10,074

ABA
Approved
Since
1954

GPA and LSAT Scores

	Total	Full-Time	Part-Time
# of apps	4,520	3,685	835
# of offers	2,100	1,821	279
# of matrics	641	520	121
75% GPA	3.48	3.49	3.44
Median GPA	3.28	3.30	3.14
25% GPA	3.00	3.03	2.86
75% LSAT	157	157	155
Median LSAT	155	155	153
25% LSAT	153	153	151

Grants and Scholarships (from prior year)

	Total		Full-Time		Part-Time	
	#	%	#	%	#	%
Total # of students	1,856		1,408		448	
Total # receiving grants	662	35.7	570	40.5	92	20.5
Less than 1/2 tuition	590	31.8	503	35.7	87	19.4
Half to full tuition	63	3.4	60	4.3	3	0.7
Full tuition	9	0.5	7	0.5	2	0.4
More than full tuition	0	0.0	0	0.0	0	0.0
Median grant amount			$10,000		$7,500	

Informational and Library Resources

Total amount spent on library materials	$1,558,042
Study seating capacity inside the library	700
# of full-time equivalent professional librarians	14
Hours per week library is open	98
# of open, wired connections available to students	95
# of networked computers available for use by students	120
Has wireless network?	Y
Requires computer?	N

JD Attrition (from prior year)

	Academic	Other	Total	
	#	#	#	%
1st year	21	56	77	10.6
2nd year	1	4	5	0.9
3rd year	0	0	0	0.0
4th year	0	0	0	0.0

Employment (9 months after graduation)

	Total	Percentage
Employment status known	412	93.8
Employment status unknown	27	6.2
Employed	364	88.3
Pursuing graduate degrees	19	4.6
Unemployed (seeking, not seeking, or studying for the bar)	24	5.8
Type of Employment		
# employed in law firms	162	44.5
# employed in business and industry	84	23.1
# employed in government	29	8.0
# employed in public interest	57	15.7
# employed as judicial clerks	12	3.3
# employed in academia	11	3.0
Geographic Location		
# employed in state	275	75.5
# employed outside the US	5	1.4
# of states where employed	12	

Bar Passage Rates

First-time takers	419	Reporting %	96.18
Average school %	81.14	Average state %	86.51
Average pass difference	−5.37		

Jurisdiction	Takers	Passers	Pass %	State %	Diff %
New York	403	327	81.14	86.51	−5.37

NEW YORK LAW SCHOOL

185 West Broadway
New York, NY 10013
Phone: 212.431.2888; Fax: 212.966.1522
E-mail: admissions@nyls.edu; Website: www.nyls.edu

Introduction

New York Law School has developed a unique approach to legal education that it calls *The Right Program for Each Student*. At its core is an acknowledgment that different practice settings require different levels of training. For example, students working in larger organizations with extensive in-house training programs have less need for hands-on training than those who will open a solo practice. Those in larger organizations may need training in a specialized area, while those in general practice may need more breadth and less specialized expertise. The following components of *The Right Program for Each Student* are described on our website: Harlan Scholars Honors Program, Individual Program, Comprehensive Curriculum, and the Professional Development Project.

Founded in 1891, New York Law School is one of the oldest independent law schools in the country. The school is fully accredited by the American Bar Association and is a member of the Association of American Law Schools.

Location/Physical Facilities/Library

New York Law School is located in the historic TriBeCa district in Lower Manhattan. It is an extraordinary setting for the study of law and one of the city's most colorful and dynamic neighborhoods. Lower Manhattan is the site of New York's largest concentration of government agencies, courts, law firms, banks, corporate headquarters, and securities exchanges. Federal Courts, New York State Civil and Criminal Courts, Family Court, and the Court of International Trade are within a four-block radius of the Law School.

The opening of a striking new building during the 2009–2010 academic year doubles the size of the school's facilities and provides the most modern and technologically advanced law building in New York City. This new building houses a four story library—containing more than 500,000 volumes and periodicals, individual and group study space, an auditorium, classrooms, student activity space, and a penthouse dining facility for students.

Student Life

We are committed to giving students a first-rate law school experience—in and out of the classroom. In return, we demand of them the seriousness of purpose necessary to become ethical professionals—the kind of lawyers sought by clients, law firms, government agencies, advocacy groups, and corporations.

New York Law School has a long-standing and continuing interest in enrolling students from varied backgrounds, including older students, minority students, women, career-changers, and public servants. Students range in age from 20 to 62, with the average age being 25.

Faculty

The Law School's distinguished full-time faculty is composed of productive scholars who are dedicated educators and who share a strong commitment to the school's vision and philosophy embodied in its core values: embracing innovation, fostering integrity and professionalism, and advancing justice for a diverse society. A national survey of law faculty scholarship includes them among the 50 most prolific law faculties in the country and notes the significant number of their books that are published by university presses. Leading jurists and attorneys who work in nearby offices are members of the adjunct faculty.

Curriculum and Special Programs

The required curriculum, composed of the entire first year and part of the second year, provides a foundation in legal reasoning and in areas of law that are considered indispensable building blocks of a legal education. In the second year and thereafter, students may design their programs with elective courses chosen from an extraordinarily rich array.

Elements such as legal analysis and legal writing, counseling, interviewing, negotiating, advocacy, planning, and strategizing form the core subject areas of the school's Lawyering Skills Program. Five clinical programs offer students the opportunity to represent real clients.

Externship and judicial internship programs permit students to do actual lawyering work in law offices.

Admission

In the admission process, a number of factors are taken into account, including the applicant's academic record and LSAT scores. The admission committee also looks for those applicants who have demonstrated leadership ability, motivation, and a sense of service and responsibility to society. Excellence in a particular field of study, progression of grades, strength of undergraduate curriculum, work and community service experience, graduate study in other disciplines, and extracurricular activities all are considered as well. Writing ability receives particular attention, and the admission committee strongly urges applicants to submit the optional writing sample.

The school seeks to enroll students who, through their diversity of backgrounds, experiences, perspectives, and ambitions, promise to enrich the law school community and, ultimately, the larger society. We do not charge an application fee.

Academic Centers

The Institute for Information Law and Policy is the home for the study of technology, intellectual property, and information law. It includes our Media Law Center and the Program on Law and Journalism. The Institute offers a certificate of mastery in law office technology and a patent bar preparation curriculum.

The Center for New York City Law focuses on governmental and legal processes in the urban setting.

The Center for International Law focuses on legal issues relating to international trade and finance.

The Justice Action Center seeks to develop students' expertise in civil rights and civil liberties law and international human rights.

The Center on Business Law and Policy focuses on business and corporate law.

The Center on Financial Services Law focuses on law in financial services including regulatory reforms and other current issues in this global industry.

The Center for Professional Values serves as a vehicle through which to examine the role of the legal profession and alternative approaches to the practice of law.

The Center for Real Estate Studies enables students to study both the private practice and public regulation of real estate.

The Diane Abbey Law Center for Children and Families exists to ensure that children and the families who care for them receive the legal assistance they need to remain safe and secure, and to thrive.

Moot Court/Law Journals/Student Organizations

New York Law School students exhibit well-honed courtroom skills, in recent years winning outright three national moot court competitions and earning awards in many others. The school's annual Robert F. Wagner Sr. Labor and Employment Law Competition is one of the nation's largest student-run moot court competitions.

The Law School currently has three scholarly publications, edited and staffed by students, which are an integral part of the Law School's program: *Law Review*, *Journal of*

International and Comparative Law, and *Journal of Human Rights*.

Students have established some 35 interest organizations as well.

Expenses and Financial Aid

New York Law School has established a program of financial aid to assist students in meeting the costs of a legal education through grants, scholarships, work-study awards, and loans. Scholarships are awarded on the basis of academic merit and financial need.

Office of Professional Development

The Office of Professional Development brings together three key student services: Student Life, Career Services, and Public Interest and Community Service. This innovative structure allows us to offer students personal attention from their first day of study to help them pursue their professional goals. The Career Services Office offers a wide array of services, including individual career counseling, on-campus interview programs, career panels and workshops, alumni network and mentoring programs, online employer databases, and information on summer, full- and part-time positions, and alternative career opportunities.

APPLICANT PROFILE

New York Law School
This grid includes only applicants who earned 120–180 LSAT scores under standard administrations.

LSAT Score	3.75 +		3.50–3.74		3.25–3.49		3.00–3.24		2.75–2.99		2.50–2.74		Below 2.50		No GPA		Total	
	Apps	Adm	Apps	Adm	Apps	Adm	Apps	Adm	Apps	Adm	Apps	Adm	Apps	Adm	Apps	Adm	Apps	Adm
170–180	4	3	3	2	2	2	2	2	5	5	0	0	0	0	0	0	16	14
165–169	9	9	9	8	11	11	14	14	9	9	8	7	5	2	2	2	67	62
160–164	53	51	76	73	101	100	80	74	51	48	32	26	27	16	7	4	427	392
155–159	93	90	166	162	225	220	213	200	139	126	81	57	77	22	21	17	1015	894
150–154	95	62	232	166	309	178	313	105	204	51	118	15	79	8	30	6	1380	591
145–149	49	7	110	22	155	24	191	16	165	24	92	6	70	1	23	0	855	100
140–144	17	0	37	0	67	3	74	4	76	2	56	3	51	0	17	0	395	12
Below 140	9	0	12	0	27	0	35	0	39	0	33	0	36	0	10	0	201	0
Total	329	222	645	433	897	538	922	415	688	265	420	114	345	49	110	29	4356	2065

Apps = Number of Applicants
Adm = Number Admitted
Reflects 99% of the total applicant pool; highest LSAT data reported.

NEW YORK UNIVERSITY SCHOOL OF LAW

40 Washington Square South
New York, NY 10012
Phone: 212.998.6060; Fax: 212.995.4527
E-mail: law.moreinfo@nyu.edu; Website: www.law.nyu.edu

ABA
Approved
Since
1930

The Basics

Type of school	Private
Term	Semester
Application deadline	2/1
Application fee	$75
Financial aid deadline	4/15
Can first year start other than fall?	No
Student to faculty ratio	9.2 to 1
# of housing spaces available restricted to law students	810
graduate housing for which law students are eligible	

Faculty and Administrators

	Total		Men		Women		Minorities	
	Spr	Fall	Spr	Fall	Spr	Fall	Spr	Fall
Full-time	120	135	85	98	35	37	17	19
Other full-time	13	16	4	6	9	10	1	2
Deans, librarians, & others who teach	13	14	5	5	8	9	1	1
Part-time	111	74	78	49	33	25	7	5
Total	257	239	172	158	85	81	26	27

Curriculum

		Full-Time	Part-Time
Typical first-year section size		89	0
Is there typically a "small section" of the first-year class, other than Legal Writing, taught by full-time faculty		No	No
If yes, typical size offered last year			
# of classroom course titles beyond first-year curriculum		329	
# of upper division courses, excluding seminars, with an enrollment:	Under 25	121	
	25–49	84	
	50–74	39	
	75–99	12	
	100+	17	
# of seminars		153	
# of seminar positions available		3,569	
# of seminar positions filled		2,600	0
# of positions available in simulation courses		74	
# of simulation positions filled		74	0
# of positions available in faculty supervised clinical courses		202	
# of faculty supervised clinical positions filled		186	0
# involved in field placements		175	0
# involved in law journals		623	0
# involved in moot court or trial competitions		146	0
# of credit hours required to graduate		83	

JD Enrollment and Ethnicity

	Men		Women		Full-Time		Part-Time		1st-Year		Total		JD Degs. Awd.
	#	%	#	%	#	%	#	%	#	%	#	%	
All Hispanics	51	6.2	52	8.5	103	7.2	0	0.0	37	7.8	103	7.2	34
Am. Ind./AK Nat.	3	0.4	0	0.0	3	0.2	0	0.0	0	0.0	3	0.2	0
Asian	80	9.7	65	10.7	145	10.1	0	0.0	50	10.5	145	10.1	59
Black/Af. Am.	36	4.4	74	12.2	110	7.7	0	0.0	48	10.1	110	7.7	25
Nat. HI/Pac. Isl.	0	0.0	0	0.0	0	0.0	0	0.0	0	0.0	0	0.0	0
2 or more races	1	0.1	0	0.0	1	0.1	0	0.0	0	0.0	1	0.1	0
Subtotal (minor.)	171	20.8	191	31.4	362	25.3	0	0.0	135	28.4	362	25.3	118
Nonres. Alien	26	3.2	26	4.3	52	3.6	0	0.0	16	3.4	52	3.6	0
White/Cauc.	432	52.6	272	44.7	704	49.2	0	0.0	260	54.6	704	49.2	241
Unknown	193	23.5	120	19.7	313	21.9	0	0.0	65	13.7	313	21.9	129
Total	822	57.4	609	42.6	1431	100.0	0	0.0	476	33.3	1431		497

Transfers

Transfers in	58
Transfers out	3

Tuition and Fees

	Resident	Nonresident
Full-time	$48,213	
Part-time		
Tuition Guarantee Program		N

Living Expenses

Estimated living expenses for singles

Living on campus	Living off campus	Living at home
$22,601	$22,601	$22,601

NEW YORK UNIVERSITY SCHOOL OF LAW

*ABA
Approved
Since
1930*

GPA and LSAT Scores

	Total	Full-Time	Part-Time
# of apps	8,461	8,461	0
# of offers	1,771	1,771	0
# of matrics	476	476	0
75% GPA	3.86	3.86	0.00
Median GPA	3.71	3.71	0.00
25% GPA	3.57	3.57	0.00
75% LSAT	175	175	0
Median LSAT	172	172	0
25% LSAT	169	169	0

Grants and Scholarships (from prior year)

	Total		Full-Time		Part-Time	
	#	%	#	%	#	%
Total # of students	1,427		1,427		0	
Total # receiving grants	657	46.0	657	46.0	0	0.0
Less than 1/2 tuition	507	35.5	507	35.5	0	0.0
Half to full tuition	48	3.4	48	3.4	0	0.0
Full tuition	102	7.1	102	7.1	0	0.0
More than full tuition	0	0.0	0	0.0	0	0.0
Median grant amount			$16,500		$0	

Informational and Library Resources

Total amount spent on library materials	$2,662,940
Study seating capacity inside the library	850
# of full-time equivalent professional librarians	39
Hours per week library is open	101
# of open, wired connections available to students	790
# of networked computers available for use by students	185
Has wireless network?	Y
Requires computer?	Y

JD Attrition (from prior year)

	Academic	Other	Total	
	#	#	#	%
1st year	0	7	7	1.6
2nd year	0	9	9	1.9
3rd year	0	1	1	0.2
4th year	0	0	0	0.0

Employment (9 months after graduation)

	Total	Percentage
Employment status known	471	100.0
Employment status unknown	0	0.0
Employed	457	97.0
Pursuing graduate degrees	9	1.9
Unemployed (seeking, not seeking, or studying for the bar)	2	0.4
Type of Employment		
# employed in law firms	327	71.6
# employed in business and industry	10	2.2
# employed in government	19	4.2
# employed in public interest	47	10.3
# employed as judicial clerks	49	10.7
# employed in academia	5	1.1
Geographic Location		
# employed in state	291	63.7
# employed outside the US	10	2.2
# of states where employed	27	

Bar Passage Rates

First-time takers	479	Reporting %	80.38
Average school %	96.88	Average state %	86.51
Average pass difference	10.37		

Jurisdiction	Takers	Passers	Pass %	State %	Diff %
New York	385	373	96.88	86.51	10.37

NEW YORK UNIVERSITY SCHOOL OF LAW

40 Washington Square South
New York, NY 10012
Phone: 212.998.6060; Fax: 212.995.4527
E-mail: law.moreinfo@nyu.edu; Website: www.law.nyu.edu

Introduction

Founded in 1835, New York University School of Law has a long record of academic excellence, national scholarly influence, and innovative achievements. It has long been a pacesetter in legal education, pioneering new approaches to practical skills training and the early recognition that law has an increasingly global dimension, to which all students should be exposed in the classroom. Its innovative Lawyering and Clinical and Advocacy Programs, interdisciplinary colloquia, public interest initiatives, and law and business transaction courses have all served as models for others. The law school has a proud history of fairness and openness: More than 100 years ago, NYU Law became one of the first law schools to routinely admit women and other groups discriminated against by many other institutions, and it continues to offer opportunities to exceptional students from groups historically underrepresented in the profession. The law school's location in the financial and cultural capital of the world provides students ready access to the very best practitioners and policy makers, including top executives in business and finance, as well as leaders of international, governmental, and public interest organizations. Through its numerous clinics, centers, and institutes, the law school provides unparalleled professional experience for students who graduate to pursue careers in government, business, and, of course, the legal profession.

Curriculum

The curriculum at NYU School of Law is designed to offer students the best possible foundation in legal theory and practice, and to empower them with the skills they need to be successful lawyers—and leaders—in the twenty-first century. Taught by top-tier faculty, the curriculum is distinguished by its depth and breadth across all traditional areas of legal study, interdisciplinary strength, and global perspective. The law school is committed to providing students with a sophisticated understanding of how US law interacts with—and is informed by—the regimes of other nations and the international community, and to educating lawyers who will use their degrees to become leaders of the profession and of society.

In recent years, the law school has implemented several significant innovations in the curriculum, including the addition of a first-year Administrative and Regulatory State course, and a first-year elective that allows students to choose among constitutional law, corporations, international law, tax, or property. The Lawyering Program, recognized by the Carnegie Foundation as the best of its kind, complements the theoretical and doctrinal courses offered in the first year, and sets the foundation for more than 32 fieldwork clinics that students can take in the upper years, including new offerings in business law, tax, and federal regulation.

Students take classes from faculty who are leaders in their fields, including international, environmental, and criminal law experts, as well as the foremost scholars in civil procedure, torts, and administrative law and policy. NYU Law has a distinguished interdisciplinary curriculum, including its law and philosophy program and a robust business and law program that offers unique transactional courses that teach students how lawyers can add value to the strategic development, design, negotiation, and implementation of deals in law, finance, real estate, entertainment, tax, and business. Students enjoy intellectual and pedagogical diversity, mixing traditional classes with a choice of courses in cutting-edge fields such as the law of democracy and law and security, as well as colloquia, clinics, independent research, journal work, study abroad, fellowships, and more.

Faculty

NYU Law's preeminent faculty are not only engaged in high-level scholarly inquiry and teaching, they can also be found contributing to the world beyond the classroom, advising international tribunals, testifying before Congress, authoring briefs in important cases, or working to protect the rights of immigrants and children. The faculty actively mentor their students, involving them in important work and helping them to develop their own scholarship. The faculty has expanded significantly in recent years, with 38 new members joining since 2002—resulting in total growth of 25 percent. More than merely increasing the faculty's size and its diversity, these additions have expanded the breadth and depth of its scholarly interests. Recent additions have brought expertise across the curriculum as well as in interdisciplinary fields, such as empirical legal studies, legal history, law and politics, law and economics, and law and philosophy. The law school also attracts leading academics as visitors who bring fresh perspectives and further enhance the robust intellectual life of the community.

Institutes and Centers

A rich intellectual life outside the classroom is sustained by more than 25 institutes and centers, including the Brennan Center for Justice, the Hauser Global Law School Program, the Institute for International Law and Justice, the Frank J. Guarini Center on Environmental and Land Use Law, the Institute for Policy and Integrity, and the Pollack Center for Law and Business. These enterprises bring together leading faculty and professional teams of lawyers, economists, and policy experts to produce research and commentary that influences the real world of law, policy, and business. They also provide students unique opportunities to work on sophisticated projects in the areas of national security, real estate, criminal justice, human rights, and international law, among many others.

Library and Physical Facilities

NYU School of Law's library contains one of the largest academic law collections in the world. Located in charming Greenwich Village, the law school's campus includes the recently renovated Vanderbilt Hall and its neighbor, Furman Hall, finished in 2004. In the fall of 2010, the law school opened a new academic facility, Wilf Hall, which, along with a newly restored townhouse at 22 Washington Square North, houses the law school's many centers and institutes. D'Agostino Hall, Mercer Residence, and two low-rise, on-campus apartment buildings provide housing for more than 800 law students.

Student Journals and Activities

There are eight student-edited publications as well as writing opportunities through the Moot Court Board. There are more than 65 student organizations, including the Law Students for Human Rights, the award-winning Suspension Representation Project, and the law school's own student government group, the Student Bar Association.

Career Services

NYU School of Law has an extensive career services program. Career planning for first-year students includes personal career counseling, workshops on all aspects of the job search, specialty panels featuring speakers from all areas of practice, and a videotape mock interview program. Each year, more than 500 private law firms, public interest organizations, government agencies, corporations, and public accounting firms visit the law school to interview students. More than 70 percent of these employers are from outside New York.

The Public Interest Law Center provides students interested in public service with comprehensive support, including advice on courses and career opportunities. The Public Interest Summer Funding Program guarantees funding to all first- and second-year students who work in public interest positions. The Public Interest Law Center, in conjunction with other area law schools, also sponsors an annual public interest legal career fair, the largest event of its kind in the country.

Admission

The admission process is highly selective, seeking men and women of exceptional ability with diverse experiences, backgrounds, and points of view. The Committee on

Admissions reviews each undergraduate transcript closely, with attention to factors such as trends in the applicant's grades, class rank, the ratio of pass/fail to graded courses, the diversity and depth of coursework, and the length of time since graduation.

Other aspects of the application influence the decision; the committee evaluates work experience and extracurricular and community activities for evidence of advancement, leadership, and capacity for assuming responsibility. Factors other than undergraduate grades and LSAT scores may be particularly significant for applicants who have experienced educational or socioeconomic disadvantage.

Financial Aid

NYU School of Law has several full-tuition scholarship programs. The flagship Root-Tilden-Kern Scholarship Program selects entering students for their intellectual potential and demonstrated commitment to public service through law. AnBryce Scholarships are awarded to outstanding students who are among the first in their immediate families to pursue a graduate degree. The Furman Academic Scholarships are given to students who show promise in becoming legal academics. Scholarships are also available in the areas of business law, criminal law, environmental law, housing and urban policy, intellectual property, international law, Latino human rights, and law and economics. A limited number of other awards are also made on the basis of intellectual potential or evidence that the student will enrich the law school's educational environment. Federal and private loans also provide funding. Graduates who pursue careers in public service may be eligible for postgraduation benefits through the school's generous and groundbreaking Loan Repayment Assistance Program.

APPLICANT PROFILE

NYU School of Law does not provide a profile chart because we believe that while an applicant's undergraduate record and LSAT scores are important, they are not the sole determinants for admission to the law school. No index or cut-off is used in reviewing applications. There is no particular combination of grades or scores that assures admittance or

guarantees rejection. The Committee on Admissions simply aims to enroll an entering class with the strongest combination of qualifications and the greatest potential to contribute to the vibrant intellectual life at NYU School of Law, to the legal profession as a whole, and more broadly, to society in general.

UNIVERSITY OF NORTH CAROLINA SCHOOL OF LAW

Campus Box 3380, 5026 Van Hecke-Wettach Hall
Chapel Hill, NC 27599-3380
Phone: 919.962.5109; Fax: 919.843.7939
E-mail: law_admissions@unc.edu; Website: www.law.unc.edu

The Basics

Type of school	Public
Term	Semester
Application deadline	3/1
Application fee	$70
Financial aid deadline	3/1
Can first year start other than fall?	No
Student to faculty ratio	15.2 to 1
# of housing spaces available restricted to law students	
graduate housing for which law students are eligible	120

Faculty and Administrators

	Total		Men		Women		Minorities	
	Spr	Fall	Spr	Fall	Spr	Fall	Spr	Fall
Full-time	42	42	27	25	15	17	7	5
Other full-time	0	0	0	0	0	0	0	0
Deans, librarians, & others who teach	12	13	5	8	7	5	1	2
Part-time	33	31	21	20	12	11	6	3
Total	87	86	53	53	34	33	14	10

JD Enrollment and Ethnicity

	Men		Women		Full-Time		Part-Time		1st-Year		Total		JD Degs. Awd.
	#	%	#	%	#	%	#	%	#	%	#	%	
All Hispanics	37	9.7	40	10.1	77	9.9	0	0.0	25	9.8	77	9.9	6
Am. Ind./AK Nat.	9	2.4	5	1.3	14	1.8	0	0.0	3	1.2	14	1.8	6
Asian	10	2.6	14	3.5	24	3.1	0	0.0	16	6.3	24	3.1	16
Black/Af. Am.	18	4.7	39	9.8	57	7.3	0	0.0	20	7.8	57	7.3	18
Nat. Hl/Pac. Isl.	7	1.8	5	1.3	12	1.5	0	0.0	0	0.0	12	1.5	0
2 or more races	11	2.9	15	3.8	26	3.3	0	0.0	9	3.5	26	3.3	0
Subtotal (minor.)	92	24.1	118	29.8	210	27.0	0	0.0	73	28.6	210	27.0	46
Nonres. Alien	6	1.6	5	1.3	11	1.4	0	0.0	1	0.4	11	1.4	0
White/Cauc.	238	62.3	243	61.4	481	61.8	0	0.0	158	62.0	481	61.8	133
Unknown	46	12.0	30	7.6	76	9.8	0	0.0	23	9.0	76	9.8	58
Total	382	49.1	396	50.9	778	100.0	0	0.0	255	32.8	778		237

Curriculum

	Full-Time	Part-Time
Typical first-year section size	87	0

Is there typically a "small section" of the first-year class, other than Legal Writing, taught by full-time faculty	Yes	No
If yes, typical size offered last year	29	

# of classroom course titles beyond first-year curriculum		119
# of upper division courses, excluding seminars, with an enrollment:	Under 25	54
	25–49	35
	50–74	9
	75–99	3
	100+	6
# of seminars		28
# of seminar positions available		412
# of seminar positions filled	354	0
# of positions available in simulation courses		1,108
# of simulation positions filled	1,009	0
# of positions available in faculty supervised clinical courses		54
# of faculty supervised clinical positions filled	54	0
# involved in field placements	155	0
# involved in law journals	238	0
# involved in moot court or trial competitions	62	0
# of credit hours required to graduate		86

Transfers

Transfers in	13
Transfers out	2

Tuition and Fees

	Resident	Nonresident
Full-time	$17,068	$31,218
Part-time		
Tuition Guarantee Program		N

Living Expenses

Estimated living expenses for singles

Living on campus	Living off campus	Living at home
$20,470	$20,470	$8,354

UNIVERSITY OF NORTH CAROLINA SCHOOL OF LAW

ABA
Approved
Since
1923

GPA and LSAT Scores

	Total	Full-Time	Part-Time
# of apps	3,044	3,044	0
# of offers	546	546	0
# of matrics	254	254	0
75% GPA	3.73	3.73	0.00
Median GPA	3.51	3.51	0.00
25% GPA	3.34	3.34	0.00
75% LSAT	165	165	0
Median LSAT	163	163	0
25% LSAT	159	159	0

Grants and Scholarships (from prior year)

	Total		Full-Time		Part-Time	
	#	%	#	%	#	%
Total # of students	765		765		0	
Total # receiving grants	653	85.4	653	85.4	0	0.0
Less than 1/2 tuition	555	72.5	555	72.5	0	0.0
Half to full tuition	79	10.3	79	10.3	0	0.0
Full tuition	3	0.4	3	0.4	0	0.0
More than full tuition	16	2.1	16	2.1	0	0.0
Median grant amount			$4,407		$0	

Informational and Library Resources

Total amount spent on library materials	$1,894,920
Study seating capacity inside the library	530
# of full-time equivalent professional librarians	11
Hours per week library is open	109
# of open, wired connections available to students	580
# of networked computers available for use by students	105
Has wireless network?	Y
Requires computer?	N

JD Attrition (from prior year)

	Academic	Other	Total	
	#	#	#	%
1st year	4	6	10	3.9
2nd year	0	2	2	0.8
3rd year	0	1	1	0.4
4th year	0	0	0	0.0

Employment (9 months after graduation)

	Total	Percentage
Employment status known	222	97.8
Employment status unknown	5	2.2
Employed	206	92.8
Pursuing graduate degrees	4	1.8
Unemployed (seeking, not seeking, or studying for the bar)	5	2.3
Type of Employment		
# employed in law firms	114	55.3
# employed in business and industry	22	10.7
# employed in government	19	9.2
# employed in public interest	29	14.1
# employed as judicial clerks	19	9.2
# employed in academia	3	1.5
Geographic Location		
# employed in state	135	65.5
# employed outside the US	0	0.0
# of states where employed	22	

Bar Passage Rates

First-time takers	208	Reporting %	75.48
Average school %	89.81	Average state %	77.59
Average pass difference	12.22		

Jurisdiction	Takers	Passers	Pass %	State %	Diff %
North Carolina	144	128	88.89	76.79	12.10
New York	13	13	100.00	86.51	13.49

UNIVERSITY OF NORTH CAROLINA SCHOOL OF LAW

Campus Box 3380, 5026 Van Hecke-Wettach Hall
Chapel Hill, NC 27599-3380
Phone: 919.962.5109; Fax: 919.843.7939
E-mail: law_admissions@unc.edu; Website: www.law.unc.edu

Introduction

The University of North Carolina, the first state university chartered in the United States, has offered degrees in law since 1845. The School of Law has been a member of the American Association of Law Schools since 1920 and has been an approved law school since the American Bar Association began its accreditation activities in 1923. The School of Law is one of the outstanding institutions in the United States, and the University of North Carolina is recognized as being among the nation's leaders in graduate and professional education. The programs at the School of Law reflect a powerful, active commitment to the goals of teaching, scholarship, and public service. The town of Chapel Hill, a university community, is close to the Research Triangle Park, the metropolitan and industrial centers of Greensboro and Durham, and the state capital, Raleigh. The immediate area offers an attractive blend of a strong academic atmosphere in a multicultural, cosmopolitan setting.

Library and Physical Facilities

Housed on five floors within the law school, the library provides critical support to the school's academic program and to lawyers and members of the public throughout the state. Its collection, which totals over 547,000 volumes, includes court reports for American and English appellate courts, current codes and session laws for all states, and other primary legal materials. Within the library, a university computer lab provides Internet access, electronic mail, word processing capabilities, and is easily accessible to law students. Additionally, students may bring their own laptop computers and connect to the university's network in many of the high-technology classrooms, library study carrels, and other areas in the building.

The School of Law aims to provide a quality legal education that will prepare students to practice successfully in any jurisdiction. The three-year Juris Doctor program begins with a first-year core curriculum designed to provide a theoretical and analytical foundation for law students. The second-year curriculum provides an important bridge between the core instruction of the first year and the culminating electives, seminars, and skills-oriented instruction of the third year. Finally, in the third year, the curriculum is designed to provide a capstone for students' legal education and begin the transition into practice.

Dual-Degree Programs/Certificate Programs

Ten formal dual JD and master's degree programs are available: JD/MPP (in conjunction with Duke University), JD/MBA, JD/MPA, JD/MPH, JD/MRP, JD/MSW, JD/MASA, JD/MAMC, JD/MSLS, or MSIS.

The Nonprofit Leadership Certificate Program prepares graduate students for leadership roles in North Carolina's rapidly growing nonprofit sector. The program provides an in-depth examination of leadership issues within human services, education, the arts, and other nonprofit organizations.

International Study Opportunities

In addition to the regularly taught courses in international business and human rights and the *International Law Journal*, students interested in international law can enhance their legal experience further with foreign study during the school year in France, the Netherlands, Mexico, England, and Scotland. Additionally, after the first year, students may also participate in the school's Summer Law Programs in Sydney, Australia; Augsburg, Germany; or Sorrento, Italy.

Centers and Initiatives

Carolina boasts nationally recognized centers in banking and financial services; civil rights; poverty, work, and opportunity; our new Center for Law, Environment, Adaptation and Resources (CLEAR); and the Center for Law and Government. All are key areas tied to our history and the unique opportunities unfolding in North Carolina, the South, and the world. These centers and initiatives expand and enliven our curriculum, push the frontiers of teaching and research, and open new channels of scholarship for students.

Student Activities

Outside of the classroom, student organizations provide a forum for the enormous talent and energy characteristic of Carolina law students. Students can write for five prominent student publications—the *North Carolina Law Review*, the *North Carolina Journal of International Law and Commercial Regulation*, the *North Carolina Banking Institute Journal*, the *First Amendment Law Review*, and the *North Carolina Journal of Law and Technology*. The Student Bar Association sponsors a full range of professional, athletic, and social events; a speakers program; minority recruitment events; a legal research service for practicing lawyers; and participation in school governance. The Moot Court Program is student operated and fields a number of successful teams in regional, national, and international competitions. Over 50 student organizations are active in the School of Law, including the Black Law Students Association, Parents as Law Students, the Federalist Society, the Hispanic/Latino Law Students Association, the Native American Law Students Association, ACLU, Women in Law, American Constitution Society, and our nationally recognized Pro Bono Program.

Expenses and Financial Aid

Full-time tuition and fees—North Carolina resident, $17,068; nonresident, $31,218. Estimated additional expenses—$19,740. Chancellors' Scholars Program scholarships are available, as well as other merit-based scholarships. Need-based assistance is awarded on the basis of FAFSA information. Students must submit parental information to FAFSA to be considered for need-based grants.

Admitted applicants are automatically considered for merit-based scholarships. Awards range from $5,000 to full tuition. Scholarship offers are made beginning in February.

Housing

There are graduate dormitories near the law school for single students; however, most students live off campus. University student family housing and private apartments are available. Information may be obtained from the University Housing Office, Carr Building CB 5500, Chapel Hill, NC 27399-5580; 919.962.5401.

Career Services Office

The Career Services Office staff assists students and alumni with summer and permanent positions. Each year, approximately 200 employers from across the nation interview at the School of Law. Of those 2009 graduates reporting to the Career Services Office, 93 percent had accepted employment or were in graduate school within nine months of graduation. Of those 2009 graduates who entered into the practice arena, 55 percent entered private practice; 15 percent entered public sector work, including public interest; 9 percent accepted judicial clerkships; 11 percent entered business/corporate-related practice; and 2 percent entered academia. Regarding job location, 66 percent were employed in North Carolina; 7 percent were employed in New York, New Jersey, and Pennsylvania; and 2 percent were employed in Alaska, California, Hawaii, Oregon, and Washington. Almost 83 percent of our students are employed in the South Atlantic region of the country, which includes Delaware; Washington, DC; Florida; Georgia; Maryland; North Carolina; South Carolina; Virginia; and West Virginia.

APPLICANT PROFILE

University of North Carolina School of Law
This grid includes only applicants who earned 120–180 LSAT scores under standard administrations.

LSAT Score	3.75 +		3.50–3.74		3.25–3.49		3.00–3.24		2.75–2.99		2.50–2.74		2.25–2.49		2.00–2.24		Below 2.00		No GPA		Total	
	Apps	Adm	Apps	Adm	Apps	Adm	Apps	Adm	Apps	Adm	Apps	Adm	Apps	Adm	Apps	Adm	Apps	Adm	Apps	Adm	Apps	Adm
175–180	3	2	3	2	1	0	0	0	3	0	0	0	0	0	0	0	0	0	1	0	11	4
170–174	21	16	29	16	22	10	13	3	6	0	4	0	1	0	1	0	0	0	0	0	97	45
165–169	96	64	89	30	92	29	54	7	18	5	9	0	1	0	4	1	0	0	7	0	370	136
160–164	241	57	315	70	275	48	107	16	40	1	20	2	7	0	2	0	2	0	11	0	1020	194
155–159	187	31	228	29	197	35	114	8	49	0	18	0	16	0	3	0	1	0	17	0	830	103
150–154	76	6	83	4	92	10	71	2	37	1	16	0	7	0	7	0	1	0	8	0	398	23
145–149	19	0	35	1	41	0	42	0	25	0	13	0	6	0	9	1	0	0	5	0	195	2
140–144	7	0	16	0	12	0	12	0	8	0	12	0	1	0	2	0	1	0	5	0	76	0
135–139	1	0	2	0	5	0	6	0	7	0	2	0	5	0	0	0	1	0	3	0	32	0
130–134	1	0	3	0	2	0	1	0	0	0	0	0	2	0	0	0	0	0	2	0	11	0
125–129	0	0	0	0	0	0	0	0	0	0	0	0	0	0	0	0	1	0	0	0	1	0
120–124	0	0	0	0	0	0	0	0	0	0	0	0	0	0	0	0	0	0	0	0	0	0
Total	652	176	803	152	739	132	420	36	193	7	94	2	46	0	28	2	7	0	59	0	3041	507

Apps = Number of Applicants
Adm = Number Admitted
Reflects 99% of the total applicant pool; highest LSAT data reported.

NORTH CAROLINA CENTRAL UNIVERSITY SCHOOL OF LAW

640 Nelson Street
Durham, NC 27707
Phone: 919.530.6333; Fax: 919.530.6339
E-mail: sbrownb@nccu.edu; Website: www.nccu.edu/law

ABA
Approved
Since
1950

The Basics

Type of school	Public
Term	Semester
Application deadline	3/31
Application fee	$40
Financial aid deadline	4/1
Can first year start other than fall?	No
Student to faculty ratio	13.4 to 1
# of housing spaces available restricted to law students	
graduate housing for which law students are eligible	32

Faculty and Administrators

	Total		Men		Women		Minorities	
	Spr	Fall	Spr	Fall	Spr	Fall	Spr	Fall
Full-time	34	34	13	13	21	21	20	21
Other full-time	7	8	4	5	3	3	4	5
Deans, librarians, & others who teach	10	10	2	2	8	8	7	7
Part-time	17	18	7	8	10	10	11	10
Total	68	70	26	28	42	42	42	43

Curriculum

		Full-Time	Part-Time
Typical first-year section size		55	35
Is there typically a "small section" of the first-year class, other than Legal Writing, taught by full-time faculty		No	No
If yes, typical size offered last year			
# of classroom course titles beyond first-year curriculum		91	
# of upper division courses, excluding seminars, with an enrollment:	Under 25	108	
	25–49	23	
	50–74	10	
	75–99	11	
	100+	1	
# of seminars		20	
# of seminar positions available		551	
# of seminar positions filled		229	11
# of positions available in simulation courses		442	
# of simulation positions filled		315	56
# of positions available in faculty supervised clinical courses		308	
# of faculty supervised clinical positions filled	231	11
# involved in field placements		63	2
# involved in law journals		64	4
# involved in moot court or trial competitions	34	0
# of credit hours required to graduate		88	

JD Enrollment and Ethnicity

	Men		Women		Full-Time		Part-Time		1st-Year		Total		JD Degs. Awd.
	#	%	#	%	#	%	#	%	#	%	#	%	
All Hispanics	5	2.0	6	1.7	7	1.4	4	3.6	2	1.0	11	1.8	8
Am. Ind./AK Nat.	3	1.2	2	0.6	5	1.0	0	0.0	2	1.0	5	0.8	1
Asian	10	4.1	8	2.2	13	2.6	5	4.5	7	3.4	18	3.0	9
Black/Af. Am.	103	42.0	191	53.5	269	54.8	25	22.5	106	51.7	294	48.8	84
Nat. Hl/Pac. Isl.	0	0.0	0	0.0	0	0.0	0	0.0	0	0.0	0	0.0	0
2 or more races	0	0.0	2	0.6	2	0.4	0	0.0	2	1.0	2	0.3	0
Subtotal (minor.)	121	49.4	209	58.5	296	60.3	34	30.6	119	58.0	330	54.8	102
Nonres. Alien	8	3.3	13	3.6	15	3.1	6	5.4	5	2.4	21	3.5	0
White/Cauc.	112	45.7	122	34.2	167	34.0	67	60.4	82	40.0	234	38.9	75
Unknown	4	1.6	13	3.6	13	2.6	4	3.6	4	2.0	17	2.8	3
Total	245	40.7	357	59.3	491	81.6	111	18.4	210	34.1	602		180

Transfers

Transfers in	2
Transfers out	5

Tuition and Fees

	Resident	Nonresident
Full-time	$9,961	$23,222
Part-time	$9,961	$23,222
Tuition Guarantee Program		N

Living Expenses

Estimated living expenses for singles

Living on campus	Living off campus	Living at home
$14,256	$19,750	$10,000

NORTH CAROLINA CENTRAL UNIVERSITY SCHOOL OF LAW

ABA
Approved
Since
1950

GPA and LSAT Scores

	Total	Full-Time	Part-Time
# of apps	2,214	2,097	868
# of offers	461	360	101
# of matrics	206	172	34
75% GPA	3.55	3.54	3.63
Median GPA	3.26	3.19	3.43
25% GPA	2.91	2.87	3.18
75% LSAT	150	149	156
Median LSAT	146	145	148
25% LSAT	143	142	145

Grants and Scholarships (from prior year)

	Total		Full-Time		Part-Time	
	#	%	#	%	#	%
Total # of students	601		480		121	
Total # receiving grants	258	42.9	248	51.7	10	8.3
Less than 1/2 tuition	152	25.3	142	29.6	10	8.3
Half to full tuition	40	6.7	40	8.3	0	0.0
Full tuition	52	8.7	52	10.8	0	0.0
More than full tuition	14	2.3	14	2.9	0	0.0
Median grant amount			$4,500		$0	

Informational and Library Resources

Total amount spent on library materials	$1,022,181
Study seating capacity inside the library	325
# of full-time equivalent professional librarians	6
Hours per week library is open	100
# of open, wired connections available to students	96
# of networked computers available for use by students	449
Has wireless network?	Y
Requires computer?	N

JD Attrition (from prior year)

	Academic	Other	Total	
	#	#	#	%
1st year	22	4	26	12.6
2nd year	2	1	3	1.7
3rd year	0	0	0	0.0
4th year	0	0	0	0.0

Employment (9 months after graduation)

	Total	Percentage
Employment status known	123	68.0
Employment status unknown	58	32.0
Employed	104	84.6
Pursuing graduate degrees	2	1.6
Unemployed (seeking, not seeking, or studying for the bar)	15	12.2
Type of Employment		
# employed in law firms	54	51.9
# employed in business and industry	9	8.7
# employed in government	20	19.2
# employed in public interest	14	13.5
# employed as judicial clerks	4	3.8
# employed in academia	1	1.0
Geographic Location		
# employed in state	88	84.6
# employed outside the US	0	0.0
# of states where employed		10

Bar Passage Rates

First-time takers	186	Reporting %	87.63
Average school %	81.59	Average state %	77.27
Average pass difference	4.32		

Jurisdiction	Takers	Passers	Pass %	State %	Diff %
North Carolina	149	120	80.54	76.79	3.75
New York	7	7	100.00	86.51	13.49
Maryland	7	6	85.71	78.20	7.51

NORTH CAROLINA CENTRAL UNIVERSITY SCHOOL OF LAW

640 Nelson Street
Durham, NC 27707
Phone: 919.530.6333; Fax: 919.530.6339
E-mail: sbrownb@nccu.edu; Website: www.nccu.edu/law

Introduction

The mission of the North Carolina Central University School of Law is to produce competent and socially responsible members of the legal profession. NCCU School of Law accomplishes its mission by providing a challenging and broad-based educational program that stimulates intellectual inquiry of the highest order and that fosters in each student a deep sense of professional responsibility and personal integrity. Founded in 1939 to provide an opportunity for a legal education to African Americans, the School of Law now provides this opportunity to one of the most diverse student bodies in the nation. This environment of diversity better prepares our students to effect positive change in the broader society.

The School of Law has been accredited by the North Carolina State Bar Council and the ABA since 1950. Today, NCCU School of Law remains one of the most affordable and diverse in the country. The School of Law offers two programs leading to the Juris Doctor degree: a full-time day program and the oldest ABA-accredited part-time evening program between Atlanta, Georgia, and Washington, DC. The School of Law participates in an interinstitutional agreement with Duke University and the University of North Carolina at Chapel Hill that permits students to enroll in electives at any member law school without an increase in tuition.

Facilities, Library, and Technology

The Albert L. Turner Law School building is a state-of-the-art facility that provides the law school community with an attractive, comfortable, and technology-friendly environment in which to work and study. The entire building is wireless. Students are provided a laptop and software for use throughout their matriculation. All classrooms are equipped with state-of-the-art multimedia resources, including smart boards, video and teleconferencing capabilities, and lectern computers with Internet access. The School of Law has several state-of-the-art group-study rooms, a moot courtroom, and a Great Hall for gatherings.

The law library, with more than 378,233 volumes and volume equivalents, provides the resources needed to support the Juris Doctor program, the JD/MLS and JD/MBA dual-degree programs, and the legal community. The law library is a selective North Carolina and United States government depository and has a special collection in civil rights law.

Special Academic Programs

- **Joint-Degree Options**—There are two joint-degree programs available to Day Program students. The joint-degree JD/MBA Program allows students who are interested in a career in law and business to receive both degrees in four years. The joint-degree JD/MLS Program allows students who are interested in a career in law librarianship to simultaneously pursue both degrees. Students must apply and be accepted to each program separately.
- **Evening Program**—The Evening Program is a four-year, year-round program that offers a unique opportunity for motivated professionals to pursue a legal education while maintaining their current daytime work commitments.
- **Academic Support Program**—The Academic Support Program is available to assist students with the rigors of law school. Through the tutorial program, workshops, one-on-one guidance, and readily available resources, all students have access to information to enable them to become effective and successful law students.
- **Faculty Advising Program**—Each student is assigned a faculty advisor who is available to discuss questions or problems related to the School of Law experience, career choices, and personal problems that might affect academic performance. They also advise students on taking appropriate classes and monitor their progress.
- **Clinical Program**—The award-winning Clinical Program is rated highly by *National Jurist* magazine. It operates year-round from a state-of-the-art model law office. The program offers as many as 13 innovative clinical experiences that provide law students with the opportunity to gain practical skills in the area of law that interests them the most. It is the most comprehensive program of any law school in the state. In-house clinical professors teach skills courses and supervise clinical students who represent real clients with real legal issues.
- **Invest in Success Program**—This bar preparation program is a joint effort with the faculty and academic support staff. Various faculty members conduct weekly substantive law reviews during the summer. The Office of Academic Support conducts workshops on various topics and works with students to improve their essay exam writing skills. Special attention is given to those students who underperformed in NC Distinctions, the School of Law's bar-prep-for-credit course.
- **Institutes**—The law school offers special programs and certificates through our Biotechnology and Pharmaceutical Law Institute and the Dispute Resolution Institute.

Admission

Admission to the School of Law is competitive, with approximately 3,000 applicants competing for approximately 180–190 seats in the Day Program and 40–45 seats in the Evening Program. Students are admitted for the Fall semester only on a rolling admission basis. Applicants are evaluated for admission based on a range of attributes, including academic achievement, performance on the LSAT, personal and professional experiences, intelligence and reasoning ability, individuality of thought and creativity, initiative and motivation, judgment and maturity, oral and written communication skills, integrity, leadership ability, and their potential contribution to the legal profession.

Because it is presumed that Evening Program students will have full-time employment, the Admissions Committee places greater weight on the quantifiable performance predictors for applicants to the Evening Program. Electronic applications for admission are accepted from October 1 through March 31 via our website at www.nccu.edu/law or the Law School Admission Council's website at www.LSAC.org.

Please note: Prospective applicants should view the School of Law website at www.nccu.edu/law for information regarding the School of Law.

Performance-Based Admission Program (PBAP)

As part of its commitment to the school's mission, North Carolina Central University School of Law offers prospective students opportunities to gain admission through its Performance-Based Admission Program (PBAP). The PBAP enables applicants whose numerical predictors fall below the presumptively admissible range to demonstrate their ability through a rigorous two-week, noncredit program in the spring. The Office of Admissions selects PBAP participants based on a number of factors, including, but not limited to, a history of below-average standardized test scores followed by academic achievement, work experience, a significant time lapse between the undergraduate degree and law school application, and students who come from socially disadvantaged backgrounds. Students who successfully complete PBAP are then offered admission to NCCU's School of Law Day or Evening Program.

Student Organizations

The *North Carolina Central Law Review* is devoted to a broad range of legal topics submitted by legal scholars, attorneys, and law students. Students are selected for membership based upon GPA and performance in the annual Law Review Writing Competition. The School of Law also has a student-run *Biotechnology and Pharmaceutical Law Review*. The Moot Court Board consists of upper-class students who have demonstrated exceptional ability in appellate skills. The Trial Advocacy Board consists of student teams who participate in mock jury trial competitions. The board has gained regional and national recognition for its excellence in trial advocacy. Other student organizations include the Black Law Students Association, Christian Legal Society, Environmental Law Society, Hispanic Law Student Association, Innocence Project, Native American Law Student Association, OutLaw Alliance, Public Interest Law Organization, Sports and Entertainment Law Society, Women's Caucus, and various legal fraternities.

Career Services

The Office of Career Services offers a range of career planning and development services, including career counseling, résumé workshops, interview preparation, job postings and information sessions, and panel discussions on legal careers. Graduates find employment in law firms, corporations, state and federal government agencies, public interest organizations, the judiciary, and the military.

Financial Aid

For information about financial aid, please visit our website at www.nccu.edu/law/admissions/financial.html.

Tuition and Expenses

NCCU School of Law provides one of the most cost effective legal educations in the country. For information on tuition, fees, and expenses, please visit our website at www.nccu.edu/law/admissions/expenses.html or contact Student Accounting at 919.530.5071.

Housing

Limited on-campus housing is available for single law students. Write the Department of Residential Life, North Carolina Central University, PO Box 19382, Durham, NC 27707, or call 919.530.6227.

APPLICANT PROFILE

North Carolina Central University School of Law
This grid includes only applicants with 120–180 LSAT scores earned under standard administrations.

LSAT Score	3.75 +		3.50–3.74		3.25–3.49		3.00–3.24		2.75–2.99		2.50–2.74		2.25–2.49		2.00–2.24		Below 2.00		No GPA		Totals	
	Apps	Adm	Apps	Adm	Apps	Adm	Apps	Adm	Apps	Adm	Apps	Adm	Apps	Adm	Apps	Adm	Apps	Adm	Apps	Adm	Apps	Adm
175–180	0	0	0	0	0	0	0	0	1	0	0	0	0	0	0	0	0	0	0	0	1	0
170–174	3	2	0	0	0	0	1	0	2	0	1	0	0	0	0	0	0	0	0	0	7	2
165–169	3	2	1	1	6	1	1	0	2	0	2	0	0	0	2	0	0	0	1	1	18	5
160–164	8	5	16	7	14	4	12	5	11	1	7	1	7	1	1	0	2	0	0	0	78	24
155–159	17	6	26	12	39	12	31	9	25	8	23	6	16	2	6	0	1	0	2	0	186	55
150–154	30	12	47	15	62	21	88	16	73	14	47	8	31	0	19	1	4	0	5	0	406	87
145–149	27	12	69	19	141	43	134	31	134	20	95	4	46	3	25	0	5	0	10	0	686	132
140–144	31	11	52	19	94	21	128	18	118	10	119	5	53	1	20	1	5	0	16	2	636	88
135–139	13	6	23	6	38	3	38	2	47	1	43	1	25	0	12	0	13	0	10	1	262	20
130–134	2	0	6	1	15	0	18	0	11	0	14	0	17	0	5	0	3	0	3	0	94	1
125–129	0	0	2	0	1	0	0	0	4	0	1	0	0	0	3	0	0	0	1	0	12	0
120–124	0	0	0	0	0	0	0	0	0	0	0	0	0	0	1	0	0	0	0	0	1	0
Total	134	56	242	80	410	105	451	81	428	54	352	25	195	7	94	2	33	0	48	4	2387	414

Apps = Number of Applicants
Adm = Number Admitted
Reflects 99% of the total applicant pool; highest LSAT data reported.

UNIVERSITY OF NORTH DAKOTA SCHOOL OF LAW

215 Centennial Drive, Stop 9003
Grand Forks, ND 58202
Phone: 701.777.2104; Fax: 701.777.6447
E-mail: hoffman@law.und.edu; Website: www.law.und.edu

ABA
Approved
Since
1923

The Basics

Type of school	Public
Term	Semester
Application deadline	7/31
Application fee	$35
Financial aid deadline	4/15
Can first year start other than fall?	No
Student to faculty ratio	19.6 to 1
# of housing spaces available restricted to law students	
graduate housing for which law students are eligible	235

Faculty and Administrators

	Total		Men		Women		Minorities	
	Spr	Fall	Spr	Fall	Spr	Fall	Spr	Fall
Full-time	10	11	7	8	3	3	2	2
Other full-time	1	1	0	1	1	0	0	0
Deans, librarians, & others who teach	7	7	2	2	5	5	0	0
Part-time	9	9	6	7	3	2	0	0
Total	27	28	15	18	12	10	2	2

Curriculum

	Full-Time	Part-Time
Typical first-year section size	85	0
Is there typically a "small section" of the first-year class, other than Legal Writing, taught by full-time faculty	No	No
If yes, typical size offered last year		
# of classroom course titles beyond first-year curriculum	66	
# of upper division courses, excluding seminars, with an enrollment: Under 25	27	
25–49	15	
50–74	7	
75–99	1	
100+	0	
# of seminars	6	
# of seminar positions available	102	
# of seminar positions filled	56	0
# of positions available in simulation courses	169	
# of simulation positions filled	117	0
# of positions available in faculty supervised clinical courses	33	
# of faculty supervised clinical positions filled	11	0
# involved in field placements	25	0
# involved in law journals	28	0
# involved in moot court or trial competitions	12	0
# of credit hours required to graduate	90	

JD Enrollment and Ethnicity

	Men		Women		Full-Time		Part-Time		1st-Year		Total		JD Degs. Awd.
	#	%	#	%	#	%	#	%	#	%	#	%	
All Hispanics	6	4.3	3	2.6	9	3.5	0	0.0	4	4.8	9	3.5	2
Am. Ind./AK Nat.	5	3.6	5	4.3	10	3.9	0	0.0	2	2.4	10	3.9	3
Asian	4	2.9	2	1.7	6	2.3	0	0.0	3	3.6	6	2.3	0
Black/Af. Am.	4	2.9	4	3.4	8	3.1	0	0.0	3	3.6	8	3.1	0
Nat. HI/Pac. Isl.	0	0.0	0	0.0	0	0.0	0	0.0	0	0.0	0	0.0	0
2 or more races	1	0.7	1	0.9	2	0.8	0	0.0	2	2.4	2	0.8	0
Subtotal (minor.)	20	14.3	15	12.9	35	13.7	0	0.0	14	16.9	35	13.7	5
Nonres. Alien	14	10.0	10	8.6	24	9.4	0	0.0	10	12.0	24	9.4	0
White/Cauc.	92	65.7	80	69.0	172	67.2	0	0.0	38	45.8	172	67.2	67
Unknown	14	10.0	11	9.5	25	9.8	0	0.0	21	25.3	25	9.8	0
Total	140	54.7	116	45.3	256	100.0	0	0.0	83	32.4	256		76

Transfers

Transfers in	3
Transfers out	1

Tuition and Fees

	Resident	Nonresident
Full-time	$10,163	$22,323
Part-time		
Tuition Guarantee Program		N

Living Expenses

Estimated living expenses for singles

Living on campus	Living off campus	Living at home
$14,400	$14,400	$14,000

UNIVERSITY OF NORTH DAKOTA SCHOOL OF LAW

ABA
Approved
Since
1923

GPA and LSAT Scores

	Total	Full-Time	Part-Time
# of apps	536	536	0
# of offers	206	206	0
# of matrics	83	83	0
75% GPA	3.61	3.61	0.00
Median GPA	3.39	3.39	0.00
25% GPA	3.14	3.14	0.00
75% LSAT	154	154	0
Median LSAT	151	151	0
25% LSAT	148	148	0

Grants and Scholarships (from prior year)

	Total		Full-Time		Part-Time	
	#	%	#	%	#	%
Total # of students	247		247		0	
Total # receiving grants	93	37.7	93	37.7	0	0.0
Less than 1/2 tuition	51	20.6	51	20.6	0	0.0
Half to full tuition	30	12.1	30	12.1	0	0.0
Full tuition	2	0.8	2	0.8	0	0.0
More than full tuition	10	4.0	10	4.0	0	0.0
Median grant amount			$4,300		$0	

Informational and Library Resources

Total amount spent on library materials	$623,126
Study seating capacity inside the library	222
# of full-time equivalent professional librarians	5
Hours per week library is open	99
# of open, wired connections available to students	174
# of networked computers available for use by students	21
Has wireless network?	Y
Requires computer?	N

JD Attrition (from prior year)

	Academic	Other	Total	
	#	#	#	%
1st year	0	1	1	1.2
2nd year	0	1	1	1.2
3rd year	0	0	0	0.0
4th year	0	0	0	0.0

Employment (9 months after graduation)

	Total	Percentage
Employment status known	71	88.7
Employment status unknown	9	11.2
Employed	60	84.5
Pursuing graduate degrees	4	5.6
Unemployed (seeking, not seeking, or studying for the bar)	6	8.5
Type of Employment		
# employed in law firms	34	56.7
# employed in business and industry	8	13.3
# employed in government	7	11.7
# employed in public interest	1	1.7
# employed as judicial clerks	9	15.0
# employed in academia	0	0.0
Geographic Location		
# employed in state	42	70.0
# employed outside the US	2	3.3
# of states where employed	11	

Bar Passage Rates

First-time takers	79	Reporting %	94.94
Average school %	85.33	Average state %	87.03
Average pass difference	−1.70		

Jurisdiction	Takers	Passers	Pass %	State %	Diff %
North Dakota	50	43	86.00	86.76	−0.76
Minnesota	19	17	89.47	89.58	−0.11
Wisconsin	2	2	100.00	90.80	9.20
Arizona	2	1	50.00	79.76	−29.76
Nevada	2	1	50.00	73.00	−23.00

UNIVERSITY OF NORTH DAKOTA SCHOOL OF LAW

215 Centennial Drive, Stop 9003
Grand Forks, ND 58202
Phone: 701.777.2104; Fax: 701.777.6447
E-mail: hoffman@law.und.edu; Website: www.law.und.edu

Introduction

Founded in 1899, the University of North Dakota (UND) School of Law blends quality, opportunity, and a sense of community in its education of approximately 245 students. The school is a fully accredited graduate professional school awarding the JD degree. It has been a member of the AALS since 1910 and was approved by the ABA in 1923. UND Law is part of a highly respected, nationally recognized university, located in Grand Forks, North Dakota. Grand Forks, a community of nearly 60,000, is in the heart of the Red River Valley on the North Dakota/Minnesota border. It offers a small-town feel with all the opportunities of an urban area and has a large legal community including county, state, and federal trial courts.

Library and Physical Facilities

The Thormodsgard Law Library manages a growing collection of comprehensive resources necessary for the study of law and provides a home for students. The school and library are linked everywhere with high-speed Ethernet and wireless access points. The Computer Services office supports the web, e-mail, file sharing, database, group scheduling, servers, and the in-house video system, as well as student laptops. The elegant, traditionally appointed Baker Courtroom provides facilities for trial and appellate arguments and is used by the North Dakota Supreme Court and occasionally by other federal and district courts.

Curriculum

The curriculum of the School of Law covers a period of three full academic years. All the work of the first year is prescribed. Courses in the second and third years are elective, except for the course in Professional Responsibility.

Special Programs

The size of the student body is ideally suited for close professional contact with faculty, the visiting courts, legal professionals, and alumni. Students are given ample opportunity to participate in the governance of the school. Elected members of the Student Bar Association attend regularly scheduled faculty meetings and are active voting participants in most law school committees.

In consultation with area tribes and Indian leaders, the UND School of Law has established the region's first Northern Plains Indian Law Center. The center is a clearinghouse for American Indian legal materials and provides a forum for discussing and resolving legal issues confronting Indian tribes, the states, and the federal government. It also supports tribal advocacy training programs. Among the center's programs are the Tribal Judicial Institute, the Institute for the Study of Tribal Gaming Law and Policy, the Native American Law Project, and the Tribal Environmental Law Project.

The Clinical Education Program of the UND School of Law provides students with the opportunity to integrate the theory and practice of law in a real law office setting. In the clinic, students assume the role of lawyers and, in doing so, move beyond the classroom into the world of law practice. In the course of representing their clients, students gain firsthand experience with substantive law, the many skills of lawyering, and the rules of professional ethics. Students reflect on their experiences during clinic class discussions, "case-rounds" sessions, one-on-one faculty supervision, and legal research and writing assignments.

A comprehensive Externship Program allows students an opportunity to earn academic credit while gaining practical experience in a variety of placements. Externship students receive local and state field placements throughout the academic year, as well as during the summer in the Federal Externship Program.

The school has an extensive Trial Advocacy Program in which students learn trial skills in a simulated advocacy setting under the close supervision of experienced trial lawyers. Each student in this course is responsible, with one student advocate cocounsel, for the trial of at least one full civil or criminal case during the semester.

During sessions of the state legislature, selected students serve as legislative interns at the North Dakota state capital in Bismarck.

Central Legal Research (CLR) provides select students with opportunities to work with attorneys and judges across North Dakota on the issues and problems faced in practice. Focusing primarily on criminal law and procedure issues, CLR students work closely with an experienced lawyer and with each other, honing their skills by writing, researching, analyzing, and discussing their individual projects. CLR students receive a full in-state tuition waiver and develop a broad writing portfolio.

UND offers a joint Juris Doctor/Master of Business Administration (JD/MBA) as well as a Juris Doctor/Master of Public Administration (JD/MPA) degree. Utilizing free summer time, these joint-degree programs could be completed in four years or less.

The UND School of Law is one of approximately 80 law schools throughout the United States that have a chapter of the national legal honorary society, the Order of the Coif. The Order of the Coif was founded to encourage legal scholarship and advance the ethical standards of the legal profession.

UND law students may receive credit for summer law study at the University of Oslo Faculty of Law, Oslo, Norway. The program provides six weeks of instruction and offers students specialized instruction in such areas as the Norwegian legal system, comparative criminal justice, and European law. As part of this exchange program, up to 15 Norwegian law students also attend the UND School of Law during the spring semester.

Admission

The School of Law has no specific undergraduate course prerequisites and agrees with the observations in the introduction to this guide. The school admits students only in August and only for full-time study. Applications are available upon request. The policy of the faculty of the School of Law is to admit those applicants who, in the determination of the faculty, will be able to satisfactorily complete the law school program. The admission committee utilizes the following criteria to achieve this goal: (1) LSAT score; (2) undergraduate GPA; (3) past performance in an academic environment; (4) past performance in activities that would tend to predict the applicant's ability to complete successfully the law school program; and (5) other evidence relevant to predicted success and prospective professional responsibility. The total number of students admitted is, of course, limited by considerations involving space and faculty courseload.

The law school does not have a nonresident quota; however, preference is given to residents.

Students who have begun the study of law in other accredited law schools may be admitted in exceptional circumstances to advanced standing, provided they have fulfilled the requirements for admission to the University of North Dakota School of Law. Ordinarily, no transfer credit will be allowed for more than two semesters of work completed elsewhere, nor will transfer credit be given for any courses in which an unsatisfactory or failing grade has been received. Moreover, admission may be conditioned upon meeting such additional requirements as the faculty may prescribe. No student will be admitted as a transfer student with advanced standing who is not eligible to continue as a student at his or her present law school.

Student Activities

The *North Dakota Law Review* provides research and writing opportunities. Students participate in various moot court activities, with the North Dakota Supreme Court judging the moot court finals. Student organizations include the Environmental Law Society, Law Women's Caucus, Native American Law Students Association, Public Interest Law Students Association, Student Trial Lawyers Association, and an active Student Bar Association. One of the more popular activities during the year is the Malpractice Bowl, pitting law students against medical school students in an annual football game. The School of Law also has chapters of the Order of the Coif and legal fraternities.

Expenses and Financial Aid

Tuition and fees per semester for students averaging 15 credit hours in 2010–2011 are $5,081.50 for in-state resident, $6,902 for contiguous states, and $11,162 for nonresident. The semester fees include student activity and university fees totaling $559.64 and an $800 per semester professional fee. The student activity and university fees cover payment for health services, the university center, campus publications, and drama and athletic events. The professional fee is assessed by the School of Law and is used to support and improve the law school program. Fees are subject to change without notice. Loan funds for all qualified students are available through the university Student Financial Aid Office, PO Box 8371, Grand Forks, ND 58202.

Housing

The university has a comprehensive housing system with options including family housing facilities, student apartment housing, and traditional residence halls for single students. For more detailed information, visit www.housing.und.edu.

Career Services

The Career Services Office serves students and alumni by assisting with the job-search process and employment information, and provides job seekers with knowledge about types of employment, specific employers, positions available, and wage and salary information. The office also assists in job-search strategies and skills such as résumé writing, interviewing techniques, and electronic job-search strategies. More than 94 percent of graduates find employment within six months of graduation. While a majority choose employment in North Dakota and Minnesota, graduates are employed nationally and internationally.

APPLICANT PROFILE

University of North Dakota School of Law
This grid includes only applicants who earned 120–180 LSAT scores under standard administrations.

LSAT Score	3.75 +		3.50–3.74		3.25–3.49		3.00–3.24		2.75–2.99		2.50–2.74		2.25–2.49		2.00–2.24		Below 2.00		No GPA		Total	
	Apps	Adm	Apps	Adm	Apps	Adm	Apps	Adm	Apps	Adm	Apps	Adm	Apps	Adm	Apps	Adm	Apps	Adm	Apps	Adm	Apps	Adm
175–180	0	0	0	0	0	0	0	0	0	0	0	0	0	0	0	0	0	0	0	0	0	0
170–174	0	0	0	0	0	0	0	0	0	0	0	0	0	0	0	0	0	0	0	0	0	0
165–169	2	2	0	0	1	1	0	0	0	0	0	0	0	0	0	0	0	0	0	0	3	3
160–164	1	1	1	1	3	3	2	2	3	3	2	2	0	0	1	0	1	0	2	0	16	12
155–159	8	7	9	9	8	8	9	7	8	6	6	1	3	0	2	0	0	0	0	0	53	38
150–154	10	10	20	16	28	18	33	24	21	10	8	3	8	1	3	0	0	0	2	1	133	83
145–149	20	12	29	16	33	9	45	12	35	4	15	1	10	0	1	0	3	0	5	2	196	56
140–144	10	4	5	1	10	0	14	0	13	2	9	0	2	0	5	1	0	0	3	1	71	9
135–139	1	0	2	0	1	1	3	0	8	0	3	0	3	0	4	0	0	0	2	0	27	1
130–134	0	0	0	0	4	0	2	0	3	0	1	0	2	0	0	0	1	0	0	0	13	0
125–129	0	0	0	0	0	0	1	0	0	0	0	0	0	0	1	0	0	0	1	0	3	0
120–124	0	0	0	0	0	0	0	0	0	0	0	0	0	0	0	0	0	0	0	0	0	0
Total	52	36	66	43	88	40	109	45	91	25	44	7	28	1	17	1	5	0	15	4	515	202

Apps = Number of Applicants
Adm = Number Admitted
Reflects 100% of the total applicant pool; highest LSAT data reported.

NORTHEASTERN UNIVERSITY SCHOOL OF LAW

400 Huntington Avenue, 101 Knowles Center
Boston, MA 02115
Phone: 617.373.2395; Fax: 617.373.8865
E-mail: lawadmissions@neu.edu; Website: www.northeastern.edu/law

The Basics

Type of school	Private
Term	Quarter
Application deadline	11/15 3/1
Application fee	$75
Financial aid deadline	2/1
Can first year start other than fall?	No
Student to faculty ratio	14.3 to 1
# of housing spaces available restricted to law students	46
graduate housing for which law students are eligible	

Faculty and Administrators

	Total		Men		Women		Minorities	
	Spr	Fall	Spr	Fall	Spr	Fall	Spr	Fall
Full-time	35	36	17	16	18	20	8	9
Other full-time	0	0	0	0	0	0	0	0
Deans, librarians, & others who teach	8	7	1	0	7	7	1	1
Part-time	33	43	18	22	15	21	4	10
Total	76	86	36	38	40	48	13	20

Curriculum

	Full-Time	Part-Time
Typical first-year section size	70	0

	Yes	No
Is there typically a "small section" of the first-year class, other than Legal Writing, taught by full-time faculty	Yes	No
If yes, typical size offered last year	13	

# of classroom course titles beyond first-year curriculum		99

# of upper division courses, excluding seminars, with an enrollment:		
	Under 25	59
	25–49	32
	50–74	8
	75–99	2
	100+	0

# of seminars		14
# of seminar positions available		202
# of seminar positions filled	181	0
# of positions available in simulation courses		263
# of simulation positions filled	237	0
# of positions available in faculty supervised clinical courses		104
# of faculty supervised clinical positions filled	89	0
# involved in field placements	483	0
# involved in law journals	110	0
# involved in moot court or trial competitions	45	0
# of credit hours required to graduate		87

JD Enrollment and Ethnicity

	Men #	Men %	Women #	Women %	Full-Time #	Full-Time %	Part-Time #	Part-Time %	1st-Year #	1st-Year %	Total #	Total %	JD Degs. Awd.
All Hispanics	22	8.7	39	10.4	61	9.7	0	0.0	17	7.8	61	9.7	21
Am. Ind./AK Nat.	1	0.4	7	1.9	8	1.3	0	0.0	2	0.9	8	1.3	1
Asian	16	6.3	44	11.7	60	9.5	0	0.0	27	12.3	60	9.5	22
Black/Af. Am.	18	7.1	58	15.5	76	12.1	0	0.0	29	13.2	76	12.1	15
Nat. HI/Pac. Isl.	0	0.0	0	0.0	0	0.0	0	0.0	0	0.0	0	0.0	0
2 or more races	0	0.0	0	0.0	0	0.0	0	0.0	0	0.0	0	0.0	0
Subtotal (minor.)	57	22.4	148	39.5	205	32.6	0	0.0	75	34.2	205	32.6	59
Nonres. Alien	1	0.4	0	0.0	1	0.2	0	0.0	1	0.5	1	0.2	0
White/Cauc.	152	59.8	169	45.1	321	51.0	0	0.0	105	47.9	321	51.0	102
Unknown	44	17.3	58	15.5	102	16.2	0	0.0	38	17.4	102	16.2	31
Total	254	40.4	375	59.6	629	100.0	0	0.0	219	34.8	629		192

Transfers

Transfers in	9
Transfers out	1

Tuition and Fees

	Resident	Nonresident
Full-time	$41,066	
Part-time		
Tuition Guarantee Program	N	

Living Expenses

Estimated living expenses for singles

Living on campus	Living off campus	Living at home
$19,500	$19,500	$9,420

*ABA
Approved
Since
1969*

GPA and LSAT Scores

	Total	Full-Time	Part-Time
# of apps	4,311	4,311	0
# of offers	1,360	1,360	0
# of matrics	220	220	0
75% GPA	3.70	3.70	0.00
Median GPA	3.53	3.53	0.00
25% GPA	3.31	3.31	0.00
75% LSAT	164	164	0
Median LSAT	161	161	0
25% LSAT	155	155	0

Grants and Scholarships (from prior year)

	Total		Full-Time		Part-Time	
	#	%	#	%	#	%
Total # of students	604		602		2	
Total # receiving grants	490	81.1	490	81.4	0	0.0
Less than 1/2 tuition	475	78.6	475	78.9	0	0.0
Half to full tuition	10	1.7	10	1.7	0	0.0
Full tuition	5	0.8	5	0.8	0	0.0
More than full tuition	0	0.0	0	0.0	0	0.0
Median grant amount			$8,500		$0	

Informational and Library Resources

Total amount spent on library materials	$1,070,492
Study seating capacity inside the library	337
# of full-time equivalent professional librarians	8
Hours per week library is open	88
# of open, wired connections available to students	370
# of networked computers available for use by students	55
Has wireless network?	Y
Requires computer?	N

JD Attrition (from prior year)

	Academic	Other	Total	
	#	#	#	%
1st year	1	6	7	3.3
2nd year	1	0	1	0.5
3rd year	1	0	1	0.5
4th year	0	0	0	0.0

Employment (9 months after graduation)

	Total	Percentage
Employment status known	214	96.8
Employment status unknown	7	3.2
Employed	202	94.4
Pursuing graduate degrees	4	1.9
Unemployed (seeking, not seeking, or studying for the bar)	8	3.7
Type of Employment		
# employed in law firms	86	42.6
# employed in business and industry	20	9.9
# employed in government	34	16.8
# employed in public interest	21	10.4
# employed as judicial clerks	11	5.4
# employed in academia	30	14.9
Geographic Location		
# employed in state	129	63.9
# employed outside the US	2	1.0
# of states where employed	22	

Bar Passage Rates

First-time takers	207	Reporting %	78.74
Average school %	95.09	Average state %	89.77
Average pass difference	5.32		

Jurisdiction	Takers	Passers	Pass %	State %	Diff %
Massachusetts	163	155	95.09	89.77	5.32

NORTHEASTERN UNIVERSITY SCHOOL OF LAW

400 Huntington Avenue, 101 Knowles Center
Boston, MA 02115
Phone: 617.373.2395; Fax: 617.373.8865
E-mail: lawadmissions@neu.edu; Website: www.northeastern.edu/law

Introduction

"Experiential" and "collaborative" are today's hot buttons in legal education. But for one school, those buttons have been hot for more than 40 years. At Northeastern University School of Law, we developed our practical learning education model in 1968. Central to it is our Cooperative Legal Education Program, which allows students to graduate with four, quarter-long, full-time jobs on their résumés. Combining classroom theory and rigorous academics with work experience, Northeastern law students receive their JD degrees in the same three-year period as students at other schools, but graduate with at least 1,500 hours of full-time work experience. We walk the walk in terms of collaboration, too. Instead of grades, students get written evaluations from their professors and co-op employers. Without a class rank to compete for, students are free to work together and take intellectual risks. The school cultivates a culture of cooperation, collaboration, and mutual respect. Our talented students, graduates, and faculty understand what it is lawyers do, how they should do it, and the difference they can make in the lives of others. Consistently recognized as one of the best public interest programs in the nation, the school's commitment to social justice extends through the curriculum, co-op program, clinics and institutes, and student group activism. The law school provides financial support through several public interest initiatives, from the Loan Deferral and Forgiveness Program to co-op stipends to the generous Public Interest Law Scholarship.

Northeastern law students are people who believe that if you don't agree with the system—change it. They're risk takers who enjoy using the law—and even their careers—in nontraditional ways. They're team players who thrive on learning together as opposed to learning at the expense of others. They're realists who believe practical experience is critical to the legal education process. And best of all, they're passionate idealists who truly believe they can change the world.

Learning Through Experience

Northeastern's **Cooperative Legal Education Program** guarantees all students four, full-time work experiences (co-ops) prior to graduation. Students alternate periods of academic study with equal periods of workplace experience during their second and third years of law school. During the first year, students follow a traditional, two-semester, full-time academic schedule. At the end of the first year, students switch to a year-round, quarter system. During the summer, half of the class begins the first academic quarter of their second year. The other half of the class starts their first co-op. For the remaining two years, students alternate every three months between working full time on co-op and attending classes. By participating in four, full-time co-op placements with four different legal employers, students are provided with an extraordinary opportunity to experience the actual practice of law and to determine their career paths based on practical training.

More than 900 employers worldwide currently participate in the co-op program, representing virtually every practice area, including law firms of all sizes, trial and appellate judges in federal and state courts, public defender and legal services organizations, government agencies, corporate and union

legal departments, and a variety of advocacy groups. Students work with employers in more than 40 states and countries. In recent years, students have increasingly developed their own co-ops in the United States and abroad. All students are required to successfully complete four, full-time legal work experiences in order to graduate.

Students may be paid on co-op with salaries ranging from minimal compensation for public interest employers to more than $3,100 per week for large private firms. Some students may be eligible for federal Work-Study funding; additionally, every qualified law student is guaranteed one $2,500 stipend to support an unfunded government or public interest law co-op.

Clinics and Institutes

Northeastern offers students the opportunity to engage in advocacy on behalf of individuals and community organizations often unacknowledged or underrepresented by the justice system. Together, the clinics, institutes, and special programs reflect and fulfill a commitment to social and economic justice that distinguishes Northeastern as one of the nation's foremost public interest law schools. Students can participate with faculty and staff in the work of the following outstanding research and service centers: the **Civil Rights and Restorative Justice Project**, the **Domestic Violence Institute**, the **Public Health Advocacy Institute**, and the **Program on Human Rights and the Global Economy**. Northeastern also offers five clinics: Criminal Advocacy, Domestic Violence, Poverty Law and Practice, Prisoners' Rights, and Public Health. The clinics differ from one another by substantive legal focus, advocacy experience, and the primary skills each seeks to impart. Students engage in challenging legal practice with the support of clinical faculty who provide the requisite training, close supervision, and opportunity for reflection.

Putting Public Service Into Practice

Nationally recognized as a leader in public interest law, Northeastern shares, supports, and encourages our students' passion for justice. About 85 percent of our students fulfill our public interest law graduation requirement through a public interest co-op, and half of our students participate in our clinics providing legal assistance to underserved communities. In addition, every first-year student participates in **Legal Skills in Social Context**, a one-of-a-kind, year-long signature course introducing the central skills of effective lawyering: legal research, objective and persuasive legal writing, client representation, critical analysis, and oral skills—all heavily grounded in the social contexts in which the law is practiced. "Law offices" of about 14 first-year students plan and execute a social justice project—an extensive real-world legal research project on behalf of a community-based or public service organization.

Student Life

The School of Law has one of the most diverse student bodies in the country. Sixty percent of the students in the first-year class are women, 34 percent are people of color, 12 percent identify as LGBT, and 9 percent hold advanced degrees. Our first-year students range in age from 20 to 50 and approximately 75 percent have taken one or more years after graduation from college before enrolling in law school. They come from 32 different states and over 120 various undergraduate institutions. Students are active participants in the law school community, serving on all of the school's standing committees, including the Admissions Committee. Students also run a wide variety of more than 30 organizations, ranging from the American Civil Liberties Union to the Queer Caucus to the Northeastern University Law Journal.

Dual-Degree Programs

Northeastern offers six dual-degree programs. In cooperation with Tufts University School of Medicine, students may pursue a JD/MPH program. Completion of the dual-degree program takes three and one-half years, rather than the average five years if the degrees were obtained sequentially. The School of Law has also partnered with Brandeis University's Heller School of Social Policy and Management to offer a JD/MA in Sustainable International Development. This accelerated four-year program includes combined law/international development co-ops. For students interested in environmental law, the School of Law, in conjunction with Vermont Law School, offers its law students the opportunity to earn both a JD and a master's degree in Environmental Law and Policy (MELP) in the same three-year period it would take to earn just the JD. Dual-degrees are also available from other schools and colleges at Northeastern University, including a JD/MBA, JD/MSA/MBA, and JD/MS/PhD-Law, Policy, and Society.

Career Services

The Office of Career Services actively assists students and graduates in their pursuit of professionally rewarding careers.

APPLICANT PROFILE

Northeastern University School of Law does not provide an applicant profile based solely upon LSAT scores and undergraduate GPAs. The Admissions Committee at Northeastern seeks to enroll a diverse, talented, and passionate student body that is eager to make a difference in the world. In keeping with the school's collaborative community spirit, the School of Law incorporates students, staff, and faculty in its admissions process as members of the

Students generally find their postgraduate employment prospects to be substantially enhanced through the co-op program; on average, 40 percent accept postgraduate employment with one of their former co-op employers. Northeastern graduates are employed throughout the world in every practice area. They may be found teaching at distinguished law schools, sitting on the bench at both the state and federal levels, practicing as partners in prominent law firms, and serving as directors of legal aid and public defender programs throughout the nation. Graduates of Northeastern enter public service careers at a rate that is three times the national average. In addition, graduates have been awarded prestigious postgraduate fellowships, including those granted by Skadden, Equal Justice Works, Georgetown, and the Center for Constitutional Rights.

Financing Your Education

Northeastern is committed to providing access to all admitted students. Each year, the School of Law awards more than $1.5 million to first-year students based on a combination of need and merit. Scholarships include the Dean's Scholarship, Academic Excellence Scholarship, Public Interest Law Scholarship, Social Justice Scholarship, Peace Corps Scholarship, Teach For America Scholarship, and Designated Law Scholarship. These scholarships represent a three-year commitment, with awards guaranteed for the upper-level years as long as the student remains in good academic standing. The law school also provides co-op stipends, endowed scholarships for upper-level students, and a Loan Deferral and Forgiveness Program for graduates pursuing careers in public interest.

school's Admissions Committee. The Admissions Committee considers academic criteria, including undergraduate grades and LSAT score, as well as other accomplishments, work experience, life experience, community involvement, the essays, recommendations from individuals who know the candidate well, and any other relevant information in making its decisions.

NORTHERN ILLINOIS UNIVERSITY COLLEGE OF LAW

Swen Parson Hall, Room 151
DeKalb, IL 60115-2890
Phone: 800.892.3050 or 815.753.8595; Fax: 815.753.5680
E-mail: Lawadm@niu.edu; Website: www.niu.edu/law

ABA
Approved
Since
1978

The Basics

Type of school	Public
Term	Semester
Application deadline	4/1
Application fee	$50
Financial aid deadline	3/1
Can first year start other than fall?	No
Student to faculty ratio	18.1 to 1

# of housing spaces available
  restricted to law students
    graduate housing for which law students are eligible   300

Faculty and Administrators

	Total		Men		Women		Minorities	
	Spr	Fall	Spr	Fall	Spr	Fall	Spr	Fall
Full-time	14	15	8	8	6	7	5	7
Other full-time	4	4	1	1	3	3	1	1
Deans, librarians, & others who teach	11	11	8	8	3	3	1	1
Part-time	5	10	2	8	3	2	1	1
Total	34	40	19	25	15	15	8	10

Curriculum

	Full-Time	Part-Time
Typical first-year section size	65	0
Is there typically a "small section" of the first-year class, other than Legal Writing, taught by full-time faculty	No	No
If yes, typical size offered last year		

# of classroom course titles beyond first-year curriculum		42
# of upper division courses, excluding seminars, with an enrollment:	Under 25	41
	25–49	13
	50–74	1
	75–99	5
	100+	0

# of seminars		6	
# of seminar positions available		84	
# of seminar positions filled	84		0
# of positions available in simulation courses		150	
# of simulation positions filled	139		0
# of positions available in faculty supervised clinical courses		40	
# of faculty supervised clinical positions filled	28		0
# involved in field placements	46		0
# involved in law journals	40		0
# involved in moot court or trial competitions	25		0
# of credit hours required to graduate		90	

JD Enrollment and Ethnicity

	Men		Women		Full-Time		Part-Time		1st-Year		Total		JD Degs. Awd.
	#	%	#	%	#	%	#	%	#	%	#	%	
All Hispanics	18	9.4	6	4.3	24	7.5	0	0.0	9	6.5	24	7.2	9
Am. Ind./AK Nat.	1	0.5	0	0.0	1	0.3	0	0.0	0	0.0	1	0.3	0
Asian	3	1.6	11	7.8	13	4.0	1	9.1	4	2.9	14	4.2	10
Black/Af. Am.	8	4.2	16	11.3	24	7.5	0	0.0	14	10.1	24	7.2	9
Nat. HI/Pac. Isl.	0	0.0	1	0.7	1	0.3	0	0.0	0	0.0	1	0.3	0
2 or more races	3	1.6	2	1.4	4	1.2	1	9.1	5	3.6	5	1.5	0
Subtotal (minor.)	33	17.3	36	25.5	67	20.9	2	18.2	32	23.0	69	20.8	28
Nonres. Alien	0	0.0	0	0.0	0	0.0	0	0.0	0	0.0	0	0.0	0
White/Cauc.	142	74.3	99	70.2	233	72.6	8	72.7	106	76.3	241	72.6	64
Unknown	16	8.4	6	4.3	21	6.5	1	9.1	2	1.4	22	6.6	7
Total	191	57.5	141	42.5	321	96.7	11	3.3	140	41.9	332		99

Transfers

Transfers in	0
Transfers out	4

Tuition and Fees

	Resident	Nonresident
Full-time	$17,268	$30,960
Part-time		
Tuition Guarantee Program		N

Living Expenses

Estimated living expenses for singles

Living on campus	Living off campus	Living at home
$15,972	$15,972	$5,312

NORTHERN ILLINOIS UNIVERSITY COLLEGE OF LAW

ABA
Approved
Since
1978

GPA and LSAT Scores

	Total	Full-Time	Part-Time
# of apps	1,216	1,141	75
# of offers	594	572	22
# of matrics	135	132	3
75% GPA	3.55	3.54	3.57
Median GPA	3.28	3.26	3.53
25% GPA	3.04	3.04	3.39
75% LSAT	155	155	156
Median LSAT	153	153	149
25% LSAT	150	150	148

Grants and Scholarships (from prior year)

	Total		Full-Time		Part-Time	
	#	%	#	%	#	%
Total # of students	309		298		11	
Total # receiving grants	153	49.5	151	50.7	2	18.2
Less than 1/2 tuition	10	3.2	10	3.4	0	0.0
Half to full tuition	30	9.7	28	9.4	2	18.2
Full tuition	107	34.6	107	35.9	0	0.0
More than full tuition	6	1.9	6	2.0	0	0.0
Median grant amount			$12,504		$5,470	

Informational and Library Resources

Total amount spent on library materials	$783,106
Study seating capacity inside the library	213
# of full-time equivalent professional librarians	6
Hours per week library is open	98
# of open, wired connections available to students	14
# of networked computers available for use by students	43
Has wireless network?	Y
Requires computer?	N

JD Attrition (from prior year)

	Academic	Other	Total	
	#	#	#	%
1st year	4	9	13	11.9
2nd year	0	0	0	0.0
3rd year	0	1	1	1.0
4th year	0	0	0	0.0

Employment (9 months after graduation)

	Total	Percentage
Employment status known	83	90.2
Employment status unknown	9	9.8
Employed	61	73.5
Pursuing graduate degrees	1	1.2
Unemployed (seeking, not seeking, or studying for the bar)	17	20.5
Type of Employment		
# employed in law firms	36	59.0
# employed in business and industry	6	9.8
# employed in government	10	16.4
# employed in public interest	4	6.6
# employed as judicial clerks	0	0.0
# employed in academia	5	8.2
Geographic Location		
# employed in state	43	70.5
# employed outside the US	0	0.0
# of states where employed	7	

Bar Passage Rates

First-time takers	85	Reporting %	87.06
Average school %	79.73	Average state %	90.89

Average pass difference −11.16

Jurisdiction	Takers	Passers	Pass %	State %	Diff %
Illinois	74	59	79.73	90.89	−11.16

NORTHERN ILLINOIS UNIVERSITY COLLEGE OF LAW

Swen Parson Hall, Room 151
DeKalb, IL 60115-2890
Phone: 800.892.3050 or 815.753.8595; Fax: 815.753.5680
E-mail: Lawadm@niu.edu; Website: www.niu.edu/law

Introduction

Northern Illinois University was founded in 1895, and the College of Law was established in 1978. The College of Law seeks to prepare its graduates not only for the traditional role of lawyers, but also for the tasks we can assume will be performed in the future by lawyers. The school has a diverse and professionally distinguished faculty dedicated to teaching and scholarship.

Our Campus

The College of Law is located in DeKalb, a community conveniently located approximately 65 miles west of Chicago and 25 miles from the suburban area on the Ronald Reagan Memorial Tollway (I-88). DeKalb is close enough to the Chicago metropolitan area to draw on its many resources, yet retain its own college town flavor—a safe and affordable environment with a high quality of life.

The university's main campus is set on 755 acres of rolling country land. The lush campus features two lagoons, museums, and a vast variety of cultural opportunities. It ultimately provides an excellent environment for the study of law.

Though on a relatively large campus with all of the associated activities and opportunities, the College of Law is a small oasis at its center.

Libraries

The David C. Shapiro Memorial Law Library provides one of the best ratios of library materials to students of any American law school. The law library offers in-depth, research-level coverage of more than 32 areas of American law and study-level coverage of almost all other areas. Coverage of international, European Union, and British law is provided at study level. As a federally designated depository, the law library also receives selected government documents. In addition to its physical collection of over 262,000 volumes and volume equivalents, the library also offers access to Westlaw, LexisNexis, and a wide range of other web-based legal resources. Laptop users enjoy convenient access to these electronic products anywhere in the law school through the College of Law's wireless network. Access to most of these resources is available off campus as well. The library also features a student computer lab that offers desktop high-speed Internet access and laser printing.

Further research support is provided through Founders Memorial Library, the university's main library, which is conveniently located adjacent to the College of Law. Founders Memorial Library contains over 2 million volumes and an additional 1.3 million federal, state, and international government documents. It also subscribes to diverse collections of nonlegal web-based resources that may be accessed either on or off campus.

Enrollment/Student Body

The student body represents universities from coast to coast and reflects a broad spectrum of ethnic, cultural, and geographic diversity. Our low student-to-faculty ratio, which is normally 15 to 1, facilitates a supportive environment with a lively exchange of ideas. The law school provides an atmosphere of shared goals and achievement and a genuine sense of community.

Curriculum and Clinical Experience Opportunities

The College of Law provides its students with a curriculum that will make them well-rounded legal professionals. The first-year program consists of the traditional ABA-required courses. After the first year, the only required courses are Constitutional Law II, Professional Responsibility, Introduction to Lawyering Skills, and a seminar; the remaining courses may be selected from a wide range of electives. A total of 90 credit hours are required to graduate from the College of Law. Northern offers an Academic Support Program during the first year of classes. The ultimate goal is to help students succeed.

During the summer, electives are offered on the main campus. Also during the summer, NIU offers an international law program in France. During this program, students receive six hours of credit in international and comparative law.

The clinical lawyering skills programs offer students the opportunity to acquire essential techniques needed in pretrial and trial work through structured simulations and experiences in an array of legal settings. The externship programs provide students with sound experience under the supervision of a highly qualified practicing attorney or the opportunity to be a law clerk for a state or federal judge. The Zeke Giorgi Legal Clinic in Rockford gives students the opportunity to apply legal theory by representing clients and resolving disputes in a real-world setting.

Admission

Considering the College of Law's small entering class size of between 110 and 120 out of an applicant pool ranging from 1,200 to 1,500, we are a relatively selective institution. The College of Law grants admission on a competitive basis through an evaluation of an applicant's aptitude and professional promise. Factors of most importance to the admission committee are the applicant's undergraduate record, LSAT score, reasons for seeking admission, school or community activities and accomplishments, employment background, and ability to add diversity to the law school community and the legal profession.

Applicants may submit their application online at the Law School Admission Council's (LSAC) website at LSAC.org. In addition to the application, prospective students must submit a personal statement, résumé, and application fee directly through LSAC.org. The College of Law requires applicants to use the LSAC Credential Assembly Service (CAS). International students who do not have a degree from a United States institution must submit all foreign transcripts and TOEFL scores to CAS. In order for Northern to receive LSAT scores, applicants need to submit official undergraduate and graduate transcripts as well as two letters of recommendation to CAS. Applicants are encouraged to submit their application early, even if the LSAT has not yet been taken, due to the limited number of seats in each entering class.

Student Activities

Students are offered a wide variety of educational and professionally oriented activities. Among these are the *Northern Illinois University Law Review*, a forum for the expression of serious legal scholarship, and the Moot Court Society. Students compete in a wide selection of moot court and alternative dispute resolution competitions. Organizations range from the Asian American Law Student Organization to the Women's Law Caucus.

Expenses and Financial Aid

The College of Law offers its students small class sizes and a quality legal education at a relatively affordable cost. For the 2010–2011 academic year, in-state tuition and fees equal $17,268 and out-of-state tuition and fees equal $30,460. Out-of-state residents may apply and qualify for in-state tuition within six months. Accordingly, relatively few second- and third-year students are classified as out-of-state residents.

Scholarships and grants are available for students from a variety of sources. After the first year, students may qualify for research assistantships or graduate assistantships.

Information on scholarships, grants, and loans is available on our website at www.niu.edu/law. The priority deadline for the FAFSA application is March 1.

Career Opportunities

The Career Opportunities Office has a strong track record in assisting and preparing our graduates for rewarding careers through references to prospective employers and on-campus interviews. The office assists current students in obtaining enriching summer legal employment. Due to Northern's small class size, personalized counseling is a reality.

Housing

Affordable housing is available both on and off campus. Handicap-accessible housing is also available. For information about on-campus housing, prospective students may telephone 815.753.5125, or visit the student housing website at www.shds.niu.edu/housing.

Many moderately priced apartments are available close to the university. The housing budget is $10,660. Prospective students may contact off-campus housing at 815.753.9999 or visit the website at www.niu.edu/comnontrad/housing/index.shtml.

Correspondence

We encourage you to visit our law school community and our website. Check our admission web pages for activities and programming or call us toll free at 815.753.8595.

APPLICANT PROFILE

Northern Illinois University College of Law
This grid includes only applicants who earned 120–180 LSAT scores under standard administrations.

LSAT Score	3.75 +		3.50–3.74		3.25–3.49		3.00–3.24		2.75–2.99		2.50–2.74		2.25–2.49		2.00–2.24		Below 2.00		No GPA		Total	
	Apps	Adm	Apps	Adm	Apps	Adm	Apps	Adm	Apps	Adm	Apps	Adm	Apps	Adm	Apps	Adm	Apps	Adm	Apps	Adm	Apps	Adm
170–180	1	1	1	1	2	2	0	0	0	0	0	0	0	0	0	0	0	0	0	0	4	4
165–169	1	1	0	0	1	1	0	0	0	0	0	0	1	1	0	0	1	0	0	0	4	3
160–164	13	13	17	17	12	12	15	14	8	6	4	4	3	3	1	0	0	0	0	0	73	69
155–159	22	21	35	33	48	45	43	38	31	29	19	14	18	7	3	1	4	0	1	1	224	189
150–154	33	28	70	59	77	67	93	56	73	28	37	19	21	2	3	0	2	0	4	1	413	260
145–149	18	14	37	24	46	11	48	8	56	7	39	2	25	0	13	1	1	0	5	0	288	67
140–144	9	1	15	0	20	0	32	0	24	0	18	0	14	0	7	0	2	0	2	0	143	1
Below 140	1	0	1	0	5	0	14	0	15	0	14	0	11	0	5	0	4	0	1	0	71	0
Total	98	79	176	134	211	138	245	116	207	70	131	39	93	13	32	2	14	0	13	2	1220	593

Apps = Number of Applicants
Adm = Number Admitted
Reflects 99% of the total applicant pool; highest LSAT data reported.

NORTHERN KENTUCKY UNIVERSITY—SALMON P. CHASE COLLEGE OF LAW

Nunn Hall, Nunn Drive
Highland Heights, KY 41099
Phone: 859.572.5490; Fax: 859.572.6081
E-mail: chaseadmissions@nku.edu; Website: http://chaselaw.nku.edu/

ABA
Approved
Since
1954

The Basics

Type of school	Public
Term	Semester
Application deadline	2/1 4/1 7/1
Application fee	$40
Financial aid deadline	3/1
Can first year start other than fall?	No
Student to faculty ratio	15.8 to 1
# of housing spaces available restricted to law students	
graduate housing for which law students are eligible	

Faculty and Administrators

	Total		Men		Women		Minorities	
	Spr	Fall	Spr	Fall	Spr	Fall	Spr	Fall
Full-time	27	28	19	19	8	9	4	4
Other full-time	1	0	0	0	1	0	0	0
Deans, librarians, & others who teach	7	10	2	4	5	6	0	0
Part-time	10	24	5	13	5	11	1	1
Total	45	62	26	36	19	26	5	5

Curriculum

		Full-Time	Part-Time
Typical first-year section size		65	60
Is there typically a "small section" of the first-year class, other than Legal Writing, taught by full-time faculty		No	No
If yes, typical size offered last year			
# of classroom course titles beyond first-year curriculum		89	
# of upper division courses, excluding seminars, with an enrollment:	Under 25	48	
	25–49	14	
	50–74	6	
	75–99	5	
	100+	1	
# of seminars		8	
# of seminar positions available		190	
# of seminar positions filled		115	41
# of positions available in simulation courses		204	
# of simulation positions filled		130	57
# of positions available in faculty supervised clinical courses		8	
# of faculty supervised clinical positions filled		6	2
# involved in field placements		29	4
# involved in law journals		35	6
# involved in moot court or trial competitions		30	7
# of credit hours required to graduate		90	

JD Enrollment and Ethnicity

	Men		Women		Full-Time		Part-Time		1st-Year		Total		JD Degs. Awd.
	#	%	#	%	#	%	#	%	#	%	#	%	
All Hispanics	6	1.7	5	1.9	7	1.9	4	1.7	5	2.5	11	1.8	4
Am. Ind./AK Nat.	0	0.0	2	0.7	1	0.3	1	0.4	1	0.5	2	0.3	1
Asian	5	1.4	7	2.6	8	2.1	4	1.7	3	1.5	12	2.0	3
Black/Af. Am.	8	2.3	19	7.1	17	4.5	10	4.2	6	3.0	27	4.4	6
Nat. HI/Pac. Isl.	0	0.0	0	0.0	0	0.0	0	0.0	0	0.0	0	0.0	0
2 or more races	1	0.3	1	0.4	1	0.3	1	0.4	1	0.5	2	0.3	0
Subtotal (minor.)	20	5.8	34	12.7	34	9.1	20	8.4	16	8.1	54	8.8	14
Nonres. Alien	0	0.0	0	0.0	0	0.0	0	0.0	0	0.0	0	0.0	0
White/Cauc.	303	87.3	220	82.4	317	84.5	206	86.2	175	88.8	523	85.2	134
Unknown	24	6.9	13	4.9	24	6.4	13	5.4	6	3.0	37	6.0	0
Total	347	56.5	267	43.5	375	61.1	239	38.9	197	32.1	614		148

Transfers

Transfers in	3
Transfers out	3

Tuition and Fees

	Resident	Nonresident
Full-time	$15,124	$32,882
Part-time	$10,492	$33,208
Tuition Guarantee Program	N	

Living Expenses

Estimated living expenses for singles

Living on campus	Living off campus	Living at home
$10,324	$16,942	$16,942

NORTHERN KENTUCKY UNIVERSITY—SALMON P. CHASE COLLEGE OF LAW

ABA
Approved
Since
1954

GPA and LSAT Scores

	Total	Full-Time	Part-Time
# of apps	1,145	959	186
# of offers	550	451	99
# of matrics	199	137	62
75% GPA	3.63	3.57	3.72
Median GPA	3.28	3.32	3.20
25% GPA	3.05	3.05	2.95
75% LSAT	157	157	156
Median LSAT	155	155	153
25% LSAT	152	153	150

Grants and Scholarships (from prior year)

	Total		Full-Time		Part-Time	
	#	%	#	%	#	%
Total # of students	609		374		235	
Total # receiving grants	171	28.1	140	37.4	31	13.2
Less than 1/2 tuition	35	5.7	30	8.0	5	2.1
Half to full tuition	59	9.7	49	13.1	10	4.3
Full tuition	77	12.6	61	16.3	16	6.8
More than full tuition	0	0.0	0	0.0	0	0.0
Median grant amount			$12,000		$10,000	

Informational and Library Resources

Total amount spent on library materials	$718,867
Study seating capacity inside the library	255
# of full-time equivalent professional librarians	7
Hours per week library is open	168
# of open, wired connections available to students	31
# of networked computers available for use by students	46
Has wireless network?	Y
Requires computer?	N

JD Attrition (from prior year)

	Academic	Other	Total	
	#	#	#	%
1st year	19	0	19	10.0
2nd year	10	3	13	6.5
3rd year	2	0	2	1.1
4th year	0	0	0	0.0

Employment (9 months after graduation)

	Total	Percentage
Employment status known	130	97.0
Employment status unknown	4	3.0
Employed	119	91.5
Pursuing graduate degrees	0	0.0
Unemployed (seeking, not seeking, or studying for the bar)	8	6.2
Type of Employment		
# employed in law firms	50	42.0
# employed in business and industry	32	26.9
# employed in government	17	14.3
# employed in public interest	8	6.7
# employed as judicial clerks	6	5.0
# employed in academia	6	5.0
Geographic Location		
# employed in state	68	57.1
# employed outside the US	0	0.0
# of states where employed	9	

Bar Passage Rates

First-time takers	118	Reporting %	83.05
Average school %	85.71	Average state %	85.97
Average pass difference	−0.26		

Jurisdiction	Takers	Passers	Pass %	State %	Diff %
Kentucky	56	49	87.50	85.92	1.58
Ohio	42	35	83.33	86.03	−2.70

NORTHERN KENTUCKY UNIVERSITY—SALMON P. CHASE COLLEGE OF LAW

Nunn Hall, Nunn Drive
Highland Heights, KY 41099
Phone: 859.572.5490; Fax: 859.572.6081
E-mail: chaseadmissions@nku.edu; Website: http://chaselaw.nku.edu/

Introduction

Founded in 1893, NKU Chase College of Law is located on the main campus of Northern Kentucky University, a metropolitan university just seven miles south of Cincinnati, Ohio. The region supports a thriving legal and business community in which more than 370 Fortune 500 companies have a presence. Chase offers both full-time and part-time programs of study. It is accredited by the American Bar Association and is a member of the Association of American Law Schools.

Evening Division

For the past 117 years, NKU Chase has been providing legal education to working professionals through its evening division. Evening division students generally attend class three evenings per week from 6:30 PM to 9:15 PM.

Centers for Excellence

Center for Excellence in Advocacy: The Center for Excellence in Advocacy continues NKU Chase's tradition of innovative advocacy skills training. Students learn the practical aspects of pretrial procedures, negotiations, mediations, trial techniques, appellate advocacy, and legislation. At the same time, a sharp focus on legal ethics and professionalism is maintained.

Transactional Law Practice Center: The Transactional Law Practice Center provides students with multiple opportunities to develop the skill sets and knowledge employed by lawyers involved in the practice of business and transactional law. The center offers training in interviewing, negotiating, drafting, business planning, and client counseling. The center also offers specialized courses and workshops in related disciplines including accounting, corporate finance, general business concepts, and economics, which enables students to understand the business aspects, as well as the legal aspects, of a corporate transaction.

Local Government Law Center: The Local Government Law Center is one of the very few centers nationwide devoted primarily to state and local government law, and it is the only one based in a public law school. The center promotes the development and study of government law through teaching, scholarship, and continuing education; offers law students clinical opportunities to gain practical experience in state and local government law; provides technical assistance and support to local governments; and serves the public through its newsletter, website, public speaking engagements, and community outreach.

Certificates and Concentrations

Certificate programs enable Chase students to focus their studies on particular skill sets or law subjects. Students earn certificates by completing course work and participating in extracurricular learning opportunities and externships. Both the Center for Excellence in Advocacy and the Transactional Law Practice Center offer students the ability to earn a certificate signifying excellence in each respective skill set. Concentration programs provide students an opportunity to "major" in a particular law subject while simultaneously

obtaining a well-rounded legal education. At Chase, we offer concentrations in Tax or Employment and Labor Law.

Pro Bono Service Program

The Pro Bono Service Program requires students to complete 50 hours of pro bono service prior to graduation. Pro bono work is broadly defined as law-related work performed in legal service organizations, government agencies, private law firms (pro bono cases), nonprofit organizations, and legislative offices. Students select from a variety of organizations designated as approved placement sites, or they design their own pro bono projects. In addition, Chase offers several pro bono projects based at the law school. Service could include interviewing clients about legal problems, researching issues for public interest lawyers, engaging in legislative or policy analysis, teaching at-risk youth about the law, providing income tax assistance to low-income clients, or participating in legal aid clinics.

Clinics and Externships

Small Business and Nonprofit Law Clinic: The Small Business and Nonprofit Law Clinic provides students with unique, practical experience in transactional law, while providing affordable legal services to entrepreneurs, small businesses, and nonprofit entities. Chase law students staff the clinic under the supervision of a full-time clinic director and licensed attorney. Students interact directly with clients to provide legal advice on a wide range of business-law issues, including entity formation, intellectual property, and contracts.

Hybrid Clinics: Chase works in conjunction with the Kentucky Department of Public Advocacy and the Ohio Justice and Policy Center to provide students with opportunities to work on real cases as part of the Kentucky Innocence Project, the Constitutional Litigation Clinic, and the Indigent Defense Clinic.

Externships: An abundance of additional opportunities for study outside the classroom are also provided to allow students to develop their practical and professional skills as well as to deepen their knowledge of particular areas of law. Externships are available in a wide variety of settings, including criminal prosecution and defense, civil family and poverty law, juvenile law, and tax law, as well as in both federal and state judicial settings and settings specifically tailored to the individual student's interests.

Joint-Degree Program

NKU Chase offers a Juris Doctor/Master of Business Administration (JD/MBA) degree program, which is an attractive alternative for those who wish to practice law or business in a complex environment. Courses at Chase serve as electives for the MBA degree, and vice-versa. Thus, the credit hours required to obtain both degrees through the JD/MBA program are fewer than the credit hours required to complete each degree separately.

Student Activities

Competition Teams: NKU Chase offers a wide variety of national competition teams that provide students with myriad opportunities to learn-by-doing in a competitive yet collaborative environment. Moot Court simulates appellate advocacy and strengthens skills in legal research, brief writing, and oral advocacy. The National Trial Advocacy Team simulates lower court trials and hones trial-related skills. The Arbitration Team simulates an arbitration hearing and, like the Trial Team, develops trial-related skills. The Client Counseling Team hones skills related to interviewing and counseling and helps students learn the norms of professional responsibility. The Negotiation Team conducts legal negotiations, which is a skill critical to all types of legal practice.

Law Review: The *Northern Kentucky Law Review* is an independent journal published by NKU Chase students and includes scholarly legal writings by law professors, practitioners, jurists, and students.

Organizations: Student organizations bring prominent local, regional, and national speakers to campus to speak on topics of interest to the NKU Chase community, the university, and the community at large. Our student organizations also provide many opportunities for community service. These organizations include:

- American Constitution Society for Law and Policy
- Black Law Students Association
- Chase Intellectual Property Society
- Chase Latino Law Association
- Chase Public Interest Group
- Chase Student Advocacy Society
- Environmental Law Society
- The Federalist Society for Law and Public Policy Studies
- International Law Student Association
- The Legal Association of Women
- Phi Alpha Delta Law Fraternity International
- Sports and Entertainment Law Group
- Student Bar Association
- Transactional Law Practice Group

Scholars Program

The NKU Chase Scholars Program recognizes the achievements of outstanding students and provides financial assistance that will allow them to explore a variety of professional opportunities after graduation.

- **Salmon P. Chase Scholars:** Full-tuition scholarship each year plus a paid research assistantship in the second or third year of study.
- **Henry Clay Scholars:** Scholarship award amounts begin at $10,000 per year.
- **John Marshall Harlan Diversity Scholars:** Scholarship award amounts range from $3,000 to full tuition. Diversity is defined as "the ability to enhance the multicultural and socioeconomic diversity at the college of law through such characteristics as ethnicity, race, gender, age, abilities/limitations, and/or multicultural and socioeconomic background."

Career Development

The Career Development Office assists students and alumni with career planning, networking, and developing job-search skills and strategies. The office schedules fall and spring on-campus interviews; posts job notices daily; sends out e-newsletters to students; manages a student résumé database; conducts mock interviews; and holds seminars, workshops, and networking events to prepare students for the job market. Additionally, the office assists students with participation in a variety of local, regional, and national job fairs and recruiting programs throughout the country. Throughout the year, the office also coordinates information sessions with attorneys, which enable students to network and learn about a wide variety of legal specialties and career options. In addition to summer employment, many of our students also obtain legal work experience for pay during the school year.

Admission

NKU Chase seeks to admit applicants who have the best prospect of high-quality academic work. The Admissions Committee relies heavily on undergraduate grades and performance on the LSAT. Additional factors considered include academic performance, including course selection patterns, upward trends in grades, and post-undergraduate work completed; achievements made in another profession or vocation; community involvement and volunteerism; cultural, educational, or sociological diversity; demonstrated leadership and professionalism; employment background including working while attending college; and letters of recommendation.

APPLICANT PROFILE

Northern Kentucky University—Salmon P. Chase College of Law
This grid includes only applicants who earned 120–180 LSAT scores under standard administrations.

LSAT Score	GPA 3.75 +		3.50–3.74		3.25–3.49		3.00–3.24		2.75–2.99		2.50–2.74		Below 2.50		No GPA		Total	
	Apps	Adm	Apps	Adm	Apps	Adm	Apps	Adm	Apps	Adm	Apps	Adm	Apps	Adm	Apps	Adm	Apps	Adm
170–180	0	0	0	0	0	0	1	1	1	1	0	0	0	0	0	0	2	2
165–169	3	3	3	3	0	0	3	2	0	0	1	1	1	1	0	0	11	10
160–164	25	23	20	20	15	15	24	23	9	9	5	5	6	3	0	0	104	98
155–159	25	24	41	40	51	47	59	56	34	26	34	22	27	9	2	2	273	226
150–154	44	40	53	44	73	35	72	30	63	14	33	4	30	2	2	2	370	171
145–149	18	4	23	8	51	7	50	8	40	5	30	1	20	1	6	2	238	36
140–144	4	1	11	0	18	0	15	2	22	0	13	0	4	1	1	0	88	4
Below 140	0	0	1	0	7	0	9	0	14	0	11	0	11	0	2	0	55	0
Total	119	95	152	115	215	104	233	122	183	55	127	33	99	17	13	6	1141	547

Apps = Number of Applicants   Adm = Number Admitted   Reflects 100% of the total applicant pool; highest LSAT data reported.

NORTHWESTERN UNIVERSITY SCHOOL OF LAW

375 East Chicago Avenue
Chicago, IL 60611-3069
Phone: 312.503.3100; Fax: 312.503.0178
E-mail: admissions@law.northwestern.edu; Website: www.law.northwestern.edu

ABA
Approved
Since
1923

The Basics

Type of school	Private
Term	Semester
Application deadline	1/15 2/15
Application fee	$100
Financial aid deadline	2/15 3/1
Can first year start other than fall?	Yes
Student to faculty ratio	8.5 to 1
# of housing spaces available restricted to law students	
graduate housing for which law students are eligible	42

Faculty and Administrators

	Total		Men		Women		Minorities	
	Spr	Fall	Spr	Fall	Spr	Fall	Spr	Fall
Full-time	80	79	45	45	35	34	10	9
Other full-time	19	20	7	7	12	13	3	2
Deans, librarians, & others who teach	11	10	7	6	4	4	0	0
Part-time	88	68	68	55	20	13	20	17
Total	198	177	127	113	71	64	33	28

Curriculum

	Full-Time	Part-Time
Typical first-year section size	63	0
Is there typically a "small section" of the first-year class, other than Legal Writing, taught by full-time faculty	No	No
If yes, typical size offered last year		

# of classroom course titles beyond first-year curriculum		210	
# of upper division courses, excluding seminars, with an enrollment:	Under 25	160	
	25–49	68	
	50–74	30	
	75–99	0	
	100+	0	
# of seminars		67	
# of seminar positions available		1,439	
# of seminar positions filled	1,055		0
# of positions available in simulation courses		1,200	
# of simulation positions filled	1,054		0
# of positions available in faculty supervised clinical courses		345	
# of faculty supervised clinical positions filled	343		0
# involved in field placements	263		0
# involved in law journals	387		0
# involved in moot court or trial competitions	29		0
# of credit hours required to graduate		84	

JD Enrollment and Ethnicity

	Men		Women		Full-Time		Part-Time		1st-Year		Total		JD Degs. Awd.
	#	%	#	%	#	%	#	%	#	%	#	%	
All Hispanics	28	6.3	33	8.8	61	7.5	0	0.0	8	2.9	61	7.5	21
Am. Ind./AK Nat.	1	0.2	6	1.6	7	0.9	0	0.0	0	0.0	7	0.9	3
Asian	75	16.9	78	20.9	153	18.7	0	0.0	47	17.2	153	18.7	38
Black/Af. Am.	34	7.7	33	8.8	67	8.2	0	0.0	18	6.6	67	8.2	20
Nat. HI/Pac. Isl.	0	0.0	0	0.0	0	0.0	0	0.0	0	0.0	0	0.0	0
2 or more races	11	2.5	11	2.9	22	2.7	0	0.0	22	8.0	22	2.7	0
Subtotal (minor.)	149	33.6	161	43.0	310	37.9	0	0.0	95	34.7	310	37.9	82
Nonres. Alien	30	6.8	26	7.0	56	6.9	0	0.0	10	3.6	56	6.9	0
White/Cauc.	264	59.6	187	50.0	451	55.2	0	0.0	169	61.7	451	55.2	158
Unknown	0	0.0	0	0.0	0	0.0	0	0.0	0	0.0	0	0.0	64
Total	443	54.2	374	45.8	817	100.0	0	0.0	274	33.5	817		304

Transfers

Transfers in	38
Transfers out	7

Tuition and Fees

	Resident	Nonresident
Full-time	$49,714	
Part-time		
Tuition Guarantee Program		N

Living Expenses

Estimated living expenses for singles

Living on campus	Living off campus	Living at home
$22,048	$22,048	$22,048

ABA Approved Since 1923

GPA and LSAT Scores

	Total	Full-Time	Part-Time
# of apps	4,480	4,480	0
# of offers	813	813	0
# of matrics	274	274	0
75% GPA	3.90	3.90	0.00
Median GPA	3.80	3.80	0.00
25% GPA	3.40	3.40	0.00
75% LSAT	171	171	0
Median LSAT	170	170	0
25% LSAT	166	166	0

Grants and Scholarships (from prior year)

	Total #	Total %	Full-Time #	Full-Time %	Part-Time #	Part-Time %
Total # of students	814		814		0	
Total # receiving grants	260	31.9	260	31.9	0	0.0
Less than 1/2 tuition	141	17.3	141	17.3	0	0.0
Half to full tuition	112	13.8	112	13.8	0	0.0
Full tuition	7	0.9	7	0.9	0	0.0
More than full tuition	0	0.0	0	0.0	0	0.0
Median grant amount			$20,000		$0	

Informational and Library Resources

Total amount spent on library materials	$871,385
Study seating capacity inside the library	629
# of full-time equivalent professional librarians	12
Hours per week library is open	96
# of open, wired connections available to students	161
# of networked computers available for use by students	102
Has wireless network?	Y
Requires computer?	Y

JD Attrition (from prior year)

	Academic #	Other #	Total #	Total %
1st year	0	12	12	4.4
2nd year	0	2	2	0.8
3rd year	0	0	0	0.0
4th year	0	0	0	0.0

Employment (9 months after graduation)

	Total	Percentage
Employment status known	258	99.2
Employment status unknown	2	0.8
Employed	247	95.7
Pursuing graduate degrees	5	1.9
Unemployed (seeking, not seeking, or studying for the bar)	0	0.0
Type of Employment		
# employed in law firms	189	76.5
# employed in business and industry	14	5.7
# employed in government	4	1.6
# employed in public interest	7	2.8
# employed as judicial clerks	23	9.3
# employed in academia	8	3.2
Geographic Location		
# employed in state	98	39.7
# employed outside the US	5	2.0
# of states where employed	23	

Bar Passage Rates

First-time takers	258	Reporting %	78.29
Average school %	90.60	Average state %	89.19
Average pass difference	1.41		

Jurisdiction	Takers	Passers	Pass %	State %	Diff %
Illinois	124	118	95.16	90.89	4.27
New York	78	65	83.33	86.51	–3.18

NORTHWESTERN UNIVERSITY SCHOOL OF LAW

375 East Chicago Avenue
Chicago, IL 60611-3069
Phone: 312.503.3100; Fax: 312.503.0178
E-mail: admissions@law.northwestern.edu; Website: www.law.northwestern.edu

Introduction

Guided by a visionary strategic plan and its recent update, "Plan 2008: Building Great Leaders for the Changing World," Northwestern University School of Law, founded in 1859, advances the understanding of law and produces graduates prepared to excel in a rapidly changing world. Northwestern Law uniquely blends a rigorous intellectual environment with a collegial and supportive community. With one of the lowest student-to-faculty ratios in the country—9:1—our students have exceptional access to their full-time professors, who comprise the most highly credentialed and interdisciplinary law faculty in the nation. The law school's lakefront location in the heart of downtown Chicago provides a wealth of part-time employment options for students while in school, and a spectacular setting in which to study law. Northwestern Law's proximity to courts, commerce, and public interest activities enables students to experience the practice of law, as well as its theory, in one of the most vibrant legal and business communities in the world.

Enrollment and Admission

Northwestern Law's close-knit community fosters collaborative learning, which enables students to develop outstanding leadership, team, organizational, and professional skills. We seek students with a wide variety of experience and backgrounds, and our Admissions Committee considers many factors beyond test scores and GPAs when evaluating applicants. Currently, more than 95 percent of entering JD students have at least one year of full-time work experience; approximately 85 percent have two years of experience; and approximately 60 percent have three or more years of experience. Through a unique interviewing program, Northwestern Law ensures it enrolls students with strong academic credentials as well as the interpersonal skills and maturity needed to thrive in the law school community.

Faculty

Our faculty is composed of world-class scholars, diverse in background and perspective, whose research and writing contribute to resolving significant academic and public policy issues. Northwestern Law has a higher percentage of PhD-trained professors than any other law school, making it the most highly credentialed and interdisciplinary faculty in the country. The faculty includes scholars with advanced degrees in economics, history, philosophy, and political science, as well as law. It includes a former US Ambassador-at-Large for War Crimes Issues; a leading expert on race, gender, and the law; an author of more than 50 books on tax law; the coauthor of the most frequently cited book within legal scholarship; the first American attorney to argue before the European Court of Human Rights; and the senior author for the most widely used casebook on American legal history. The full-time research faculty is supplemented by a distinguished group of clinical professors who lead students in simulations, in representing clients, and in efforts to reform our legal system; as well as senior lecturers and adjunct professors, who teach a wide variety of specialized courses.

Curriculum

In the rigorous first year of study, Northwestern Law provides a superior foundation in legal reasoning, analysis, and writing, as well as a thorough understanding of the structures and policies of the law. Communication, teamwork, cross-training in business, and experiential learning are also hallmarks of Northwestern Law. The law school's size enables students to have one-on-one relationships with professors, with required first-year courses taught in sections of approximately 60 students. The JD program requires 83 semester hours of credit. The broad and flexible curriculum gives upper-level students the opportunity to specialize in particular areas, to pursue advanced research in legal theory, or to pursue a range of hands-on simulation, externship, and live-client opportunities. The Owen L. Coon/James A. Rahl Senior Research Program enables third-year students to do individual research under the supervision of a professor, using library, field, and interdisciplinary research methods.

Special Degree and International Programs

A limited number of highly motivated students are enrolled in Northwestern Law's Accelerated JD program—the first such program offered by a top law school. Accelerated JD students complete the same number of credit hours as traditional three-year JD students in five semesters over the course of two calendar years.

A combined program in law and business, jointly offered with Northwestern's Kellogg School of Management, enables students to earn both a JD from the law school and an MBA degree from Kellogg after only three years of study. Students may also enroll in a highly integrated six-year JD-PhD program with the law school and one of the graduate school departments.

Northwestern Law is the only top law school in the country to offer a four-year joint-degree program leading to both a JD and an LLM in International Human Rights (JD-LLM IHR). JD-LLM IHR students receive a thorough grounding in the norms and mechanisms of international human rights law and international criminal law. A distinctive feature of the new JD-LLM IHR program is a requirement that students complete a semester-long externship with one of a number of designated international and hybrid criminal tribunals, foreign supreme courts, and international human rights organizations.

Students who wish to specialize in the study of tax law can earn an LLM in Taxation or jointly pursue a JD and an LLM in Taxation at the same time. Students educated outside the United States can earn an LLM through a nine-month program of advanced study, or an LLM degree and a certificate in business administration from Kellogg through a twelve-month program in law and business. In addition, international lawyers also have the option to earn an LLM in 15 weeks over the summer in Northwestern Law's new Accelerated Summer LLM program. Legal and business professionals abroad can earn an LLM degree from Northwestern through our Executive LLM Programs in Seoul, South Korea; Madrid, Spain; and Tel Aviv, Israel.

Clinical Programs

In Northwestern Law's comprehensive clinical program, students learn strong litigation and negotiation skills and gain direct experience with representing clients and reforming laws.

The innovative simulation-based curriculum, including the Program on Advocacy and Professionalism and the Program on Negotiation and Mediation, gives students the skills they need to negotiate and communicate effectively, solve problems, prepare briefs, examine witnesses, present evidence, and argue cases.

The **Bluhm Legal Clinic** is widely recognized as the best legal clinic facility in the country. The clinic centers—Fred Bartlit Center for Trial Strategy, Children and Family Justice Center, Small Business Opportunity Center, Center for International Human Rights, Center on Wrongful Convictions, Roderick MacArthur Justice Center, and Investor Protection Center—are nationally recognized for their direct involvement in legal reform.

Students represent underserved clients as well as challenge the fairness of our legal institutions and propose solutions for reform. Working in teams, they assist small business owners and prepare cases in juvenile justice, immigration and asylum, and criminal matters. In addition to fine-tuning their skills as advocates, they often effect change in the law and legal institutions.

Library and Facilities

With more than a half million volumes and access to a wide range of electronic resources, the Pritzker Legal Research Center is one of the country's largest law libraries. It also provides students access to the 3.7 million volumes of the combined Northwestern University libraries.

Our modern facilities and recent additions support collaboration and interaction. Wireless technology is available throughout the law school, and recent renovations include a new 22,000-square-foot clinic center, more than 10 state-of-the-art classrooms and seminar rooms, and upgraded lighting.

Student Activities

Northwestern Law students take an intense and energetic interest in their community and education. Six scholarly journals are available for research, writing, and editing. Students automatically belong to the Student Bar Association, which gives them a voice in curriculum and administration, and they have an opportunity to participate in more than 50 student organizations. Our students also enjoy Chicago's sophisticated yet friendly atmosphere, along with its world-class cultural, sports, and entertainment offerings. Northwestern's 20-acre Chicago campus is nestled between the shores of Lake Michigan, the energy of Michigan Avenue's Magnificent Mile, and the elegant Gold Coast residential area.

Career Services

The Center for Career Strategy and Advancement proactively cultivates relationships with potential employers while assisting students in focusing their goals and developing short- and long-term career strategies. Traditionally, more than 700 national employers recruit our students. Nearly 80 percent of the recruiters are based in regions outside the Midwest.

Expenses and Financial Aid

Northwestern Law annually awards $6 million in grants and scholarships in addition to long-term, low-interest institutional loans. These resources enable the law school to cover 100 percent of a student's calculated financial need. Approximately 85 percent of our currently enrolled students receive financial aid.

APPLICANT PROFILE

At Northwestern Law, emphasis on teamwork, communication, and interpersonal skills begins during the admission process, in which every applicant is urged to interview. Currently, more than 75 percent of applicants are interviewed, and college seniors must be interviewed. We also place a heavy emphasis on work experience, which contributes to an environment where students learn a great deal from not only faculty, but also each other.

NOTRE DAME LAW SCHOOL

Admissions Office, 1329 Biolchini Hall
Notre Dame, IN 46556
Phone: 574.631.6626; Fax: 574.631.5474
E-mail: lawadmit@nd.edu; Website: http://law.nd.edu

ABA
Approved
Since
1925

The Basics

Type of school	Private
Term	Semester
Application deadline	2/15
Application fee	$65
Financial aid deadline	2/28
Can first year start other than fall?	No
Student to faculty ratio	10.3 to 1
# of housing spaces available restricted to law students	
graduate housing for which law students are eligible	148

Faculty and Administrators

	Total		Men		Women		Minorities	
	Spr	Fall	Spr	Fall	Spr	Fall	Spr	Fall
Full-time	40	45	29	33	11	12	6	8
Other full-time	1	1	0	0	1	1	0	0
Deans, librarians, & others who teach	12	12	7	7	5	5	2	2
Part-time	47	40	27	26	20	14	13	10
Total	100	98	63	66	37	32	21	20

Curriculum

	Full-Time	Part-Time
Typical first-year section size	63	0
Is there typically a "small section" of the first-year class, other than Legal Writing, taught by full-time faculty	No	No
If yes, typical size offered last year		
# of classroom course titles beyond first-year curriculum	117	

# of upper division courses, excluding seminars, with an enrollment:		
	Under 25	84
	25–49	33
	50–74	11
	75–99	4
	100+	3

# of seminars	25	
# of seminar positions available	478	
# of seminar positions filled	355	0
# of positions available in simulation courses	212	
# of simulation positions filled	185	0
# of positions available in faculty supervised clinical courses	122	
# of faculty supervised clinical positions filled	108	0
# involved in field placements	51	0
# involved in law journals	174	0
# involved in moot court or trial competitions	92	0
# of credit hours required to graduate	90	

JD Enrollment and Ethnicity

	Men		Women		Full-Time		Part-Time		1st-Year		Total		JD Degs. Awd.
	#	%	#	%	#	%	#	%	#	%	#	%	
All Hispanics	36	10.9	26	11.1	62	11.0	0	0.0	28	16.3	62	11.0	13
Am. Ind./AK Nat.	5	1.5	2	0.9	7	1.2	0	0.0	2	1.2	7	1.2	1
Asian	16	4.9	29	12.3	45	8.0	0	0.0	9	5.2	45	8.0	11
Black/Af. Am.	14	4.3	15	6.4	29	5.1	0	0.0	10	5.8	29	5.1	8
Nat. HI/Pac. Isl.	1	0.3	0	0.0	1	0.2	0	0.0	0	0.0	1	0.2	0
2 or more races	8	2.4	6	2.6	14	2.5	0	0.0	10	5.8	14	2.5	0
Subtotal (minor.)	80	24.3	78	33.2	158	28.0	0	0.0	59	34.3	158	28.0	33
Nonres. Alien	2	0.6	6	2.6	8	1.4	0	0.0	4	2.3	8	1.4	0
White/Cauc.	226	68.7	138	58.7	364	64.5	0	0.0	103	59.9	364	64.5	112
Unknown	21	6.4	13	5.5	34	6.0	0	0.0	6	3.5	34	6.0	27
Total	329	58.3	235	41.7	564	100.0	0	0.0	172	30.5	564		172

Transfers

Transfers in	19
Transfers out	4

Tuition and Fees

	Resident	Nonresident
Full-time	$40,805	$40,805
Part-time		
Tuition Guarantee Program		N

Living Expenses

Estimated living expenses for singles

Living on campus	Living off campus	Living at home
$16,700	$16,700	$16,700

NOTRE DAME LAW SCHOOL

*ABA
Approved
Since
1925*

GPA and LSAT Scores

	Total	Full-Time	Part-Time
# of apps	4,022	4,022	0
# of offers	661	661	0
# of matrics	172	172	0
75% GPA	3.73	3.73	0.00
Median GPA	3.57	3.57	0.00
25% GPA	3.39	3.39	0.00
75% LSAT	168	168	0
Median LSAT	167	167	0
25% LSAT	162	162	0

Grants and Scholarships (from prior year)

	Total		Full-Time		Part-Time	
	#	%	#	%	#	%
Total # of students	548		548		0	
Total # receiving grants	423	77.2	423	77.2	0	0.0
Less than 1/2 tuition	350	63.9	350	63.9	0	0.0
Half to full tuition	69	12.6	69	12.6	0	0.0
Full tuition	2	0.4	2	0.4	0	0.0
More than full tuition	2	0.4	2	0.4	0	0.0
Median grant amount			$14,000		$0	

Informational and Library Resources

Total amount spent on library materials	$1,319,758
Study seating capacity inside the library	585
# of full-time equivalent professional librarians	9
Hours per week library is open	95
# of open, wired connections available to students	86
# of networked computers available for use by students	95
Has wireless network?	Y
Requires computer?	N

JD Attrition (from prior year)

	Academic	Other	Total	
	#	#	#	%
1st year	0	6	6	3.3
2nd year	0	0	0	0.0
3rd year	0	0	0	0.0
4th year	0	0	0	0.0

Employment (9 months after graduation)

	Total	Percentage
Employment status known	198	100.0
Employment status unknown	0	0.0
Employed	185	93.4
Pursuing graduate degrees	4	2.0
Unemployed (seeking, not seeking, or studying for the bar)	2	1.0
Type of Employment		
# employed in law firms	97	52.4
# employed in business and industry	17	9.2
# employed in government	21	11.4
# employed in public interest	14	7.6
# employed as judicial clerks	28	15.1
# employed in academia	7	3.8
Geographic Location		
# employed in state	18	9.7
# employed outside the US	0	0.0
# of states where employed	29	

Bar Passage Rates

First-time takers	195	Reporting %	98.97
Average school %	87.59	Average state %	83.75
Average pass difference	3.84		

Jurisdiction	Takers	Passers	Pass %	State %	Diff %
Illinois	41	40	97.56	90.89	6.67
California	29	19	65.52	73.19	−7.67
New York	21	20	95.24	86.51	8.73
Indiana	14	12	85.71	82.74	2.97
Others (24)	88	78	88.64		

NOTRE DAME LAW SCHOOL

Admissions Office, 1329 Biolchini Hall
Notre Dame, IN 46556
Phone: 574.631.6626; Fax: 574.631.5474
E-mail: lawadmit@nd.edu; Website: http://law.nd.edu

Introduction

With a rich history that dates to its founding in 1869, Notre Dame Law School today enjoys a national and international reputation for preparing consummate professionals—men and women who are extraordinarily competent in their professional endeavors and who commit themselves to serve their clients and the profession effectively and honorably. Distinctive among nationally regarded law schools as a result of the school's and the university's Catholic heritage and tradition, faith and values, and community spirit, the Law School inspires students to examine their practice of law within the context of their responsibilities as members of the bar, as leaders within their respective fields, and as citizens of the world community.

Enrollment/Student Body

The student body represents the national stature and international nature of the programs of the Law School and the university. Our student body of approximately 575 students represents nearly all states and a number of foreign countries. The small size of the student body fosters a sense of community and allows significant interaction between faculty and students.

Faculty

Faculty members come to Notre Dame Law School with experience in private practice and government service, and represent a wide range of undergraduate institutions, law schools, and state bars. Members of the faculty are well regarded for their commitment to teaching, as well as their accessibility to students outside of the classroom as advisors and mentors. At the same time, these premier scholars publish in leading journals and are invited to participate in academic conferences around the world.

Library and Physical Facilities

In January 2009, the Law School moved into the Eck Hall of Law, a beautiful and spacious, three-story, 85,000-square-foot building. It is connected to the existing building by a covered walkway and chapel, with a common area above. The design captures the Law School's commitment to shaping the minds, hearts, and souls of the next generation of Notre Dame lawyers. In June 2010, the equally beautiful gothic structure that has been home to the Law School since 1930, reopened after undergoing a major renovation. Bilochini Hall houses an expanded Kresge Law Library, several administrative offices, four journal offices, and additional classroom space.

The Kresge Law Library is among the top American law school research libraries. The staff of 29 is noted for its service to law school faculty, students, and staff, and the larger university community.

The Law School provides significant computing support for students and other members of the law school community. Five full-time technology professionals offer assistance for both hardware and software, in addition to other computing and technology needs.

Curriculum

The JD curriculum provides a strong foundation in those areas that have proven to be fundamental to the actual practice of law in every American jurisdiction, while giving students the opportunity to tailor coursework to particular career aspirations. Required courses, those that are critical to a mastery of specialized areas of the law, total 42 of the 90 credit hours needed for graduation. In addition to the JD degree, the Law School confers three graduate law degrees: an LLM in International and Comparative Law, an LLM in International Human Rights, and a JSD (also in International Human Rights). The LLM in International and Comparative Law is offered exclusively at the Law School's London Law Centre.

London Programs

Notre Dame Law School recognizes that today's legal practice increasingly involves problems that the law of no one nation can resolve. Hence, JD candidates may augment their legal education by participating in one of two programs offered by the Law School through its London Law Centre. Second-year students who wish to immerse themselves in comparative and international law, as well as in the traditions of the American and British common-law systems, can study in the only year-long overseas program offered by an American law school. Students who desire a shorter international-study experience and who have completed their first year of law school can spend six weeks in London during Notre Dame's summer program.

Student Life

The sense of community and the quality of student life at Notre Dame have developed out of long-standing traditions that make the Notre Dame Law School experience different: admission policies that emphasize the importance of qualitative factors such as service to others; a mission that focuses on teaching, scholarship, and service in the legal and Judeo-Christian traditions; and an emphasis on forming and nurturing collegial relationships between students and faculty. The Law School is centrally located on the Notre Dame campus, and law students fully participate in athletic, cultural, religious, and social events on the campus. Law students also manage to find a comfortable balance between their studies and involvement in the Law School's four law journals and any of 30 organizations that reflect the professional and personal interests of the student body.

Expenses and Financial Aid

Notre Dame is committed to providing a legal education of the highest quality at a tuition structure that compares favorably to other nationally regarded private law schools. Additionally, law students benefit from the low cost of living in northern Indiana.

In recent years, scholarship assistance has been provided annually to approximately 60–70 percent of entering students on the basis of merit, commitment to the Law School's mission, and financial need. Fellowships range from $5,000 to full tuition and are renewable for all three years of legal study.

Housing

Many single law students choose to live on campus in graduate-student housing. Married students with children can live in the unfurnished University Village apartments. Students who wish to live off campus can find reasonably priced accommodations near the campus and can secure on-campus parking for a nominal additional charge.

Career Services

Notre Dame Law School graduates have, in recent years, found rewarding work all over the country and in a wide variety of practice areas. Historically, the employment rate has been at or above 95 percent within nine months of graduation. Employers participate in interviews exclusive to Notre Dame law students in Los Angeles; Washington, DC; and New York, as well as on campus. Employers are interested in interviewing Notre Dame law students because of the Law School's reputation for preparing extraordinarily competent lawyers. A national network of over 8,000 Law School alumni and friends assists students and graduates in finding employment opportunities across the country.

Graduates of Notre Dame Law School have been successful in terms of obtaining judicial clerkships, with 10–15 percent of recent graduating classes choosing this career option. These highly sought-after positions provide graduates with a unique opportunity to learn firsthand about the inner workings of the judicial system, while at the same time allowing them to hone important legal skills and problem-solving abilities.

The Career Services Office (CSO) also coordinates a variety of initiatives to encourage students who wish to be employed in public interest work following graduation. These include a variety of informational programs and services, including participation in our campus-wide, nonprofit career night. The CSO also participates in public interest law career fairs across the country and is a sponsoring and coordinating school for the Midwest Public Interest Law Career Conference in Chicago. Additionally, the office coordinates a comprehensive summer stipend program that provides funding for over 100 students working in public interest positions each summer. The Law School's Loan Repayment Assistance Program (LRAP) assists eligible law school graduates who choose to work in public interest, public service, or other similar positions after graduation. The Law School seeks to help reduce the financial pressures that can discourage graduates from pursuing positions in public interest and public service employment.

Please visit our website for the most current employment information.

APPLICANT PROFILE

Each year the Law School Admissions Committee employs a whole-person review philosophy to create a class from a large number of highly qualified applicants. We seek to enroll multidimensional students with a wide range of talents, backgrounds, experiences, accomplishments, and points of view. Academic ability, as reflected in the LSAT score and academic performance in college are important; however, the committee considers a broad array of elements in addition to these two quantitative measures. Notre Dame Law School officials involved in the admission process are mindful of the school's objective to produce lawyers who are competent, compassionate, and committed to serving their clients with integrity. The admission process is highly selective and seeks to enroll men and women of exceptional ability. We do not provide an applicant profile grid because it would be based solely on LSAT and GPA.

NOVA SOUTHEASTERN UNIVERSITY—SHEPARD BROAD LAW CENTER

3305 College Avenue
Fort Lauderdale, FL 33314-7721
Phone: 954.262.6117; Fax: 954.262.3844
E-mail: admission@nsu.law.nova.edu; Website: www.nsulaw.nova.edu

ABA
Approved
Since
1975

The Basics

Type of school	Private
Term	Semester
Application deadline	4/1
Application fee	$50
Financial aid deadline	4/15
Can first year start other than fall?	No
Student to faculty ratio	15.9 to 1
# of housing spaces available restricted to law students	30
graduate housing for which law students are eligible	429

Faculty and Administrators

	Total		Men		Women		Minorities	
	Spr	Fall	Spr	Fall	Spr	Fall	Spr	Fall
Full-time	52	51	30	28	22	23	12	11
Other full-time	9	9	3	3	6	6	4	4
Deans, librarians, & others who teach	9	8	4	3	5	5	3	3
Part-time	40	46	32	31	8	15	9	9
Total	110	114	69	65	41	49	28	27

Curriculum

		Full-Time	Part-Time
Typical first-year section size		65	67
Is there typically a "small section" of the first-year class, other than Legal Writing, taught by full-time faculty		No	No
If yes, typical size offered last year			
# of classroom course titles beyond first-year curriculum		137	
# of upper division courses, excluding seminars, with an enrollment:	Under 25	144	
	25–49	45	
	50–74	26	
	75–99	17	
	100+	0	
# of seminars		20	
# of seminar positions available		400	
# of seminar positions filled		223	52
# of positions available in simulation courses		1,334	
# of simulation positions filled		901	266
# of positions available in faculty supervised clinical courses		110	
# of faculty supervised clinical positions filled		29	2
# involved in field placements		69	6
# involved in law journals		100	10
# involved in moot court or trial competitions		72	5
# of credit hours required to graduate		90	

JD Enrollment and Ethnicity

	Men #	Men %	Women #	Women %	Full-Time #	Full-Time %	Part-Time #	Part-Time %	1st-Year #	1st-Year %	Total #	Total %	JD Degs. Awd.
All Hispanics	90	17.2	122	21.1	153	17.1	59	28.6	76	19.3	212	19.3	49
Am. Ind./AK Nat.	2	0.4	5	0.9	3	0.3	4	1.9	2	0.5	7	0.6	0
Asian	18	3.4	25	4.3	39	4.4	4	1.9	17	4.3	43	3.9	10
Black/Af. Am.	17	3.3	47	8.1	42	4.7	22	10.7	25	6.4	64	5.8	15
Nat. HI/Pac. Isl.	5	1.0	6	1.0	10	1.1	1	0.5	0	0.0	11	1.0	0
2 or more races	0	0.0	0	0.0	0	0.0	0	0.0	0	0.0	0	0.0	0
Subtotal (minor.)	132	25.2	205	35.5	247	27.6	90	43.7	120	30.5	337	30.6	75
Nonres. Alien	6	1.1	11	1.9	12	1.3	5	2.4	14	3.6	17	1.5	0
White/Cauc.	333	63.7	305	52.9	548	61.3	90	43.7	209	53.2	638	58.0	193
Unknown	52	9.9	56	9.7	87	9.7	21	10.2	52	13.2	108	9.8	17
Total	523	47.5	577	52.5	894	81.3	206	18.7	395	35.7	1100		285

Transfers

Transfers in	9
Transfers out	26

Tuition and Fees

	Resident	Nonresident
Full-time	$32,607	$32,607
Part-time	$24,579	$24,579
Tuition Guarantee Program		N

Living Expenses

Estimated living expenses for singles

Living on campus	Living off campus	Living at home
$20,064	$26,118	$12,429

NOVA SOUTHEASTERN UNIVERSITY—SHEPARD BROAD LAW CENTER

ABA
Approved
Since
1975

GPA and LSAT Scores

	Total	Full-Time	Part-Time
# of apps	2,794	2,349	445
# of offers	1,099	991	108
# of matrics	386	322	64
75% GPA	3.42	3.46	3.29
Median GPA	3.16	3.19	3.03
25% GPA	2.94	2.96	2.86
75% LSAT	153	153	151
Median LSAT	150	151	149
25% LSAT	148	148	145

Grants and Scholarships (from prior year)

	Total		Full-Time		Part-Time	
	#	%	#	%	#	%
Total # of students	1,092		903		189	
Total # receiving grants	173	15.8	138	15.3	35	18.5
Less than 1/2 tuition	119	10.9	95	10.5	24	12.7
Half to full tuition	20	1.8	14	1.6	6	3.2
Full tuition	33	3.0	29	3.2	4	2.1
More than full tuition	1	0.1	0	0.0	1	0.5
Median grant amount			$12,000		$9,500	

Informational and Library Resources

Total amount spent on library materials	$1,211,520
Study seating capacity inside the library	532
# of full-time equivalent professional librarians	12
Hours per week library is open	104
# of open, wired connections available to students	4
# of networked computers available for use by students	10
Has wireless network?	Y
Requires computer?	Y

JD Attrition (from prior year)

	Academic	Other	Total	
	#	#	#	%
1st year	55	29	84	18.5
2nd year	13	11	24	7.8
3rd year	0	7	7	2.3
4th year	0	0	0	0.0

Employment (9 months after graduation)

	Total	Percentage
Employment status known	253	99.2
Employment status unknown	2	0.8
Employed	198	78.3
Pursuing graduate degrees	17	6.7
Unemployed (seeking, not seeking, or studying for the bar)	25	9.9
Type of Employment		
# employed in law firms	139	70.2
# employed in business and industry	23	11.6
# employed in government	20	10.1
# employed in public interest	7	3.5
# employed as judicial clerks	5	2.5
# employed in academia	4	2.0
Geographic Location		
# employed in state	175	88.4
# employed outside the US	1	0.5
# of states where employed		16

Bar Passage Rates

First-time takers	258	Reporting %	96.12
Average school %	83.87	Average state %	77.81
Average pass difference	6.06		

Jurisdiction	Takers	Passers	Pass %	State %	Diff %
Florida	248	208	83.87	77.81	6.06

NOVA SOUTHEASTERN UNIVERSITY—SHEPARD BROAD LAW CENTER

3305 College Avenue
Fort Lauderdale, FL 33314-7721
Phone: 954.262.6117; Fax: 954.262.3844
E-mail: admission@nsu.law.nova.edu; Website: www.nsulaw.nova.edu

Introduction

NSU Law Center is one of 16 graduate and professional schools of Nova Southeastern University, the largest private independent university in Florida and the sixth largest in the United States. NSU Law is accredited by the ABA and is a member of the AALS. The Law Center is located in the suburbs of Fort Lauderdale, in the heart of South Florida's fast-growing Broward, Miami-Dade, Palm Beach area. We encourage applicants to tour the campus and speak with the staff of the Admissions Office.

Curriculum and Special Academic/Professional Programs

The Law Center offers a rigorous traditional academic program in three-year day and four-year evening versions. NSU Law prides itself on preparing graduates to make a smooth transition from the classroom to the courtroom or boardroom.

Lawyering Skills and Values (LSV)—Every student completes a four-semester LSV sequence that combines traditional legal reasoning, writing, and research with an introduction to lawyer interviewing, counseling, negotiating, mediating, advocating, and other critical skills in a simulated law firm experience.

Clinical Opportunities—Clinical education is an important part of the NSU Law experience. The Law Center offers students a pioneering combination of academics and clinical experience which gives students the knowledge and skills they need to hit the ground running and launch a successful career in the highly competitive legal marketplace. Students have an opportunity to participate in numerous supervised clinical and externship experiences in the Alternative Dispute Resolution, Business Practice, Children and Families Law, Criminal Justice, Environmental and Land Use Law, International Practice, or Personal Injury Litigation clinics. During the clinical program, students are introduced to a practice specialty under the guidance of a seasoned mentor. Each clinical semester begins with intensive classes that focus on advanced substantive law and lawyering skills in the clinic specialty plus interdisciplinary topics. For the rest of the term, faculty members supervise the students' representation of clients in Law Center clinics, government agencies, nonprofit organizations, and private law offices.

International Dual-Degree Opportunities—NSU Law students have an opportunity to study both common law and civil law through our dual-degree program with the University of Barcelona. With successful completion of the program and the appropriate bar requirements, students can qualify for admission to the bar in both Spain and the United States. As lawyers, dual-degree graduates will have an opportunity to practice in the United States and Spain, and to practice transactional law in the European Union. The dual degree will also assist those wishing to practice in Latin America. Opportunities are also available in the Czech Republic and Italy.

Joint Degrees—NSU Law offers students opportunities to earn a second graduate degree in a complementary discipline and in a compressed time frame.

Internships—In addition to an award-winning pro bono service program, the Law Center operates judicial internship, mediation, street law, consumer protection, and dependency workshop programs that provide valuable real-world experiences.

Two Admission Programs

The Law Center's Admissions Committee oversees two separate programs. The Regular Admission Program combines each applicant's undergraduate grades and LSAT score according to a weighted formula based on the academic success of NSU Law students. The committee also values the applicant's personal statement, writing sample, work experience, and letters of recommendation. While no single factor is determinative, if the LSAT/UGPA combination does not demonstrate the promise of academic achievement, an applicant is unlikely to be offered regular admission.

Selected applicants who are denied regular admission will be offered the opportunity to earn admission to the Law Center by successful performance in NSU Law's unique Alternative Admission Model Program for Legal Education (AAMPLE). In the 32 years of AAMPLE's operation, more than 1,000 students have qualified for admission. AAMPLE students who enroll in a six-week summer session and earn a C+ average in the two courses are offered admission to the Law Center. AAMPLE is presented in two formats, the traditional on-campus program and an innovative online model.

Approximately 43 percent of our applicants are offered seats through the Regular Admission Program. Another 34 percent are invited to the AAMPLE Program. Applicants are encouraged to review the charts that follow this narrative to evaluate the likelihood of being admitted to the Law Center via the Regular Admission or the AAMPLE Program. NSU Law's two admission programs produce a diverse student body. Recent classes were nearly evenly divided between men and women, with members of minority groups comprising approximately 34 percent of the class.

The Admissions Committee awards partial tuition scholarships on the basis of academic merit to approximately 35 percent of students admitted through the Regular Admission Program.

Faculty

NSU Law professors have a long tradition of teaching excellence. The faculty's open-door policy is enhanced by our sophisticated wireless communications system and pioneering laptop program. Limits on the size of first-year sections result in more individualized feedback. The faculty's expertise is reflected in rich classroom discussion and a wide range of scholarly publications and professional service.

Library and Physical Facilities

Nova Southeastern has been a technology pioneer for more than a decade. NSU Law Center installed the first wireless system in a law school in 1996 and was the first US law school to provide totally wireless access to all faculty, staff, and students. NSU Law leads the way in the use of technology in legal education.

The Law Library's extensive holdings include special collections in tax, criminal law, law and popular culture, admiralty, and international law. With more than 340,000 volume/volume equivalents, the Law Library provides access to primary and secondary sources of US law as well as case-finding and updating tools. The Law Library and Technology Center is designated as a United Nations depository and as a depository for US and Florida government documents.

Leo Goodwin Sr. Hall, which houses the Law Center, has two courtrooms used by students in the school's trial advocacy and moot court programs as well as by the National Institute for Trial Advocacy and state appellate court judges.

Student Activities

The Law Center is home to three significant publications: the *Nova Law Review*, the *Journal of International and Comparative Law*, and the *International Citator and Research Project*.

The Moot Court Society sponsors intramural competitions. Members of the society compete in major national events. The Association of Trial Lawyers of America and other student advocacy groups field teams in competitions around the country.

Students shape the life of the Law Center through their involvement in a wide range of service organizations and social clubs. Extremely active groups include the Asian Pacific American Law Students Association, Black Law Students Association, Jewish Law Students Association, Hispanic Law Student Association, Lambda, Student Bar Association, Florida Association for Women Lawyers, National Association for Public Interest Law, International Law Society, Native American Law Students Association, and a variety of practice specialty and sports clubs. Students also guide chapters of national legal fraternities, participate with lawyers and judges in the Inns of Court, and serve on faculty committees.

Career Services

Our Career Development Office assists students and alumni with career counseling and the employment process. In addition to facilitating on-campus interviews and résumé distributions, the director coordinates career-option seminars and interviewing workshops. The office also sponsors skill courses and assists students in finding pro bono experiences with law firms and legal agencies throughout the country.

APPLICANT PROFILE

Nova Southeastern University—Shepard Broad Law Center
Regular Admission Program

LSAT Score	GPA								
	3.75 +	3.50–3.74	3.25–3.49	3.00–3.24	2.75–2.99	2.50–2.74	2.25–2.49	2.00–2.24	Below 2.00
165–180									
160–164									
155–159									
150–154									
145–149									
140–144									
135–139									
130–134									
Below 130									

■ Good Possibility   □ Possible   ■ Unlikely

Please use this chart as a general guide in determining admission chances for the Regular Admission Program. Nonnumerical factors are also considered during the file evaluation process.

AAMPLE
Enrolled/Successful

LSAT Score	GPA								
	3.75 +	3.50–3.74	3.25–3.49	3.00–3.24	2.75–2.99	2.25–2.74	2.00–2.24	Below 2.00	Unknown GPA
150–159					1/0	2/1	1/1		
145–149		2/2	6/3	11/8	10/9	24/16	3/1		1/0
140–144	2/2	6/4	13/8	16/10	14/7	13/5			
135–139	1/0		2/2	1/1	1/0				
130–134					1/0				

Please use this chart to determine the possibility of being admitted through AAMPLE (Alternative Admission Model Program for Legal Education). The chart reflects admission data for the Summer 2010 AAMPLE combined, including both on campus and online AAMPLE programs. Overall, there were 100 students enrolled in on-campus AAMPLE, with 63 successful, and 31 enrolled in online AAMPLE, 17 of whom were successful in 2010.

OHIO NORTHERN UNIVERSITY—CLAUDE W. PETTIT COLLEGE OF LAW

525 South Main Street
Ada, OH 45810
Phone: 877.452.9668, 419.772.2211; Fax: 419.772.3042
E-mail: lawadmissions@onu.edu; Website: www.law.onu.edu

ABA
Approved
Since
1948

AMERICAN BAR ASSOCIATION
Section of Legal Education
and Admissions to the Bar

The Basics

Type of school	Private
Term	Semester
Application deadline	
Application fee	
Financial aid deadline	6/1
Can first year start other than fall?	No
Student to faculty ratio	11.8 to 1
# of housing spaces available restricted to law students	52
graduate housing for which law students are eligible	52

Faculty and Administrators

	Total		Men		Women		Minorities	
	Spr	Fall	Spr	Fall	Spr	Fall	Spr	Fall
Full-time	21	22	12	14	9	8	5	4
Other full-time	0	0	0	0	0	0	0	0
Deans, librarians, & others who teach	7	7	5	5	2	2	1	1
Part-time	12	11	9	8	3	3	0	0
Total	40	40	26	27	14	13	6	5

Curriculum

	Full-Time	Part-Time
Typical first-year section size	60	0
Is there typically a "small section" of the first-year class, other than Legal Writing, taught by full-time faculty	No	No
If yes, typical size offered last year		

# of classroom course titles beyond first-year curriculum		80
# of upper division courses, excluding seminars, with an enrollment:	Under 25	42
	25–49	20
	50–74	3
	75–99	3
	100+	0
# of seminars		12
# of seminar positions available		144

# of seminar positions filled	123	0
# of positions available in simulation courses	435	
# of simulation positions filled	313	0
# of positions available in faculty supervised clinical courses	75	
# of faculty supervised clinical positions filled	26	0
# involved in field placements	82	0
# involved in law journals	43	0
# involved in moot court or trial competitions	26	0
# of credit hours required to graduate	90	

JD Enrollment and Ethnicity

	Men #	Men %	Women #	Women %	Full-Time #	Full-Time %	Part-Time #	Part-Time %	1st-Year #	1st-Year %	Total #	Total %	JD Degs. Awd.
All Hispanics	2	1.0	1	0.9	3	1.0	0	0.0	2	1.7	3	1.0	1
Am. Ind./AK Nat.	2	1.0	0	0.0	2	0.6	0	0.0	1	0.8	2	0.6	1
Asian	2	1.0	2	1.7	4	1.3	0	0.0	0	0.0	4	1.3	6
Black/Af. Am.	8	4.1	15	12.9	23	7.3	0	0.0	8	6.7	23	7.3	8
Nat. HI/Pac. Isl.	0	0.0	0	0.0	0	0.0	0	0.0	0	0.0	0	0.0	0
2 or more races	0	0.0	0	0.0	0	0.0	0	0.0	0	0.0	0	0.0	0
Subtotal (minor.)	14	7.1	18	15.5	32	10.2	0	0.0	11	9.2	32	10.2	16
Nonres. Alien	1	0.5	8	6.9	9	2.9	0	0.0	1	0.8	9	2.9	0
White/Cauc.	171	86.8	85	73.3	256	81.8	0	0.0	100	83.3	256	81.8	83
Unknown	11	5.6	5	4.3	16	5.1	0	0.0	8	6.7	16	5.1	2
Total	197	62.9	116	37.1	313	100.0	0	0.0	120	38.3	313		101

Transfers

Transfers in	2
Transfers out	5

Tuition and Fees

	Resident	Nonresident
Full-time	$31,264	$31,264
Part-time		
Tuition Guarantee Program		N

Living Expenses

Estimated living expenses for singles

Living on campus	Living off campus	Living at home
$16,255	$16,255	$16,255

OHIO NORTHERN UNIVERSITY—CLAUDE W. PETTIT COLLEGE OF LAW

ABA
Approved
Since
1948

GPA and LSAT Scores

	Total	Full-Time	Part-Time
# of apps	1,291	1,291	0
# of offers	484	484	0
# of matrics	120	120	0
75% GPA	3.70	3.70	0.00
Median GPA	3.49	3.49	0.00
25% GPA	2.94	2.94	0.00
75% LSAT	156	156	0
Median LSAT	154	154	0
25% LSAT	149	149	0

Grants and Scholarships (from prior year)

	Total		Full-Time		Part-Time	
	#	%	#	%	#	%
Total # of students	307		307		0	
Total # receiving grants	167	54.4	167	54.4	0	0.0
Less than 1/2 tuition	39	12.7	39	12.7	0	0.0
Half to full tuition	121	39.4	121	39.4	0	0.0
Full tuition	7	2.3	7	2.3	0	0.0
More than full tuition	0	0.0	0	0.0	0	0.0
Median grant amount			$20,000		$0	

Informational and Library Resources

Total amount spent on library materials	$858,506
Study seating capacity inside the library	308
# of full-time equivalent professional librarians	4
Hours per week library is open	113
# of open, wired connections available to students	288
# of networked computers available for use by students	68
Has wireless network?	Y
Requires computer?	N

JD Attrition (from prior year)

	Academic	Other	Total	
	#	#	#	%
1st year	7	10	17	14.9
2nd year	0	0	0	0.0
3rd year	0	0	0	0.0
4th year	0	0	0	0.0

Employment (9 months after graduation)

	Total	Percentage
Employment status known	84	87.5
Employment status unknown	12	12.5
Employed	78	92.9
Pursuing graduate degrees	1	1.2
Unemployed (seeking, not seeking, or studying for the bar)	4	4.8
Type of Employment		
# employed in law firms	39	50.0
# employed in business and industry	10	12.8
# employed in government	9	11.5
# employed in public interest	4	5.1
# employed as judicial clerks	6	7.7
# employed in academia	3	3.8
Geographic Location		
# employed in state	40	51.3
# employed outside the US	0	0.0
# of states where employed	14	

Bar Passage Rates

First-time takers	101	Reporting %	71.29
Average school %	79.17	Average state %	86.01

Average pass difference −6.84

Jurisdiction	Takers	Passers	Pass %	State %	Diff %
Ohio	52	41	78.85	86.03	−7.18
Indiana	9	8	88.89	82.74	6.15
Illinois	6	5	83.33	90.89	−7.56
Kentucky	5	3	60.00	85.92	−25.92

OHIO NORTHERN UNIVERSITY—CLAUDE W. PETTIT COLLEGE OF LAW

525 South Main Street
Ada, OH 45810
Phone: 877.452.9668, 419.772.2211; Fax: 419.772.3042
E-mail: lawadmissions@onu.edu; Website: www.law.onu.edu

Introduction

Founded in 1885, the Ohio Northern University Pettit College of Law is the second oldest of the nine Ohio law schools. The college is accredited by the American Bar Association and is a member of the Association of American Law Schools. Annually, the college enrolls more than 320 students from more than 40 states in its full-time Juris Doctor degree and LLM programs. Dedicated to the rigorous pursuits of teaching and practicing law, the college's esteemed faculty is committed to fostering an open-door policy and a strong mentoring program to students with a passion for legal scholastic excellence. The College of Law is located in Ada, Ohio, with an off-campus legal clinic in Lima, Ohio.

The College and the University

The Claude W. Pettit College of Law is accredited by the American Bar Association and is a member of the Association of American Law Schools. The college is centered in newly renovated Tilton Hall, a modern building that houses all law classes and the Taggart Law Library.

The College of Law lies at the center of the tree-lined campus. The university's facilities are readily available to all law students and are located only steps away from the law building. These facilities include walking and biking trails, a sports center, and the Freed Center for the Performing Arts. Law students may bowl, swim, and play handball, racquet sports, and basketball all year round in indoor and outdoor facilities. The sports center houses a wide variety of modern fitness machines and one of the best indoor tracks in the Midwest.

Student Life

Community is part of your law school experience.

Your involvement in cocurricular activities plays an important role in your law school experience. By participating in any of more than 20 different student organizations, you will quickly see your communication, social, and leadership skills develop, and you'll build long-lasting relationships with peers and faculty. These activities also showcase your drive for excellence to prospective employers.

Improve your oral advocacy and brief writing skills by participating in moot court. The *Ohio Northern University Law Review*, a highly respected law journal of the College of Law, is edited and published by students three times a year.

While taking a break from studying, you'll discover the cultural side of the university. Theatre, dance, music, and other programs are hosted regularly at the acclaimed Freed Center for the Performing Arts. Permanent and provisional art collections are on display at the Elzay Gallery of Art. If sports are more your interest, you can attend a game at Dial-Roberson Stadium or participate in a number of intramural sports activities at King-Horn Sports Center. You can also watch Ohio Northern athletes compete in 21 varsity sports.

Faculty

With a 10:1 student-to-faculty ratio, our professors and staff will know you by name and interact with you on a personal level.

From the moment you arrive on campus, you will notice something different about our faculty. They are engaged in your education and truly interested in seeing you succeed. This is individualized attention you won't encounter at a larger school. Our goal is not only to educate, but also to ensure the development of practical skills, morals, and leadership needed to be successful in the practice of law.

Our professors have studied at some of the most prestigious schools in the United States—including Harvard, Columbia, Yale, and Duke—and practiced at some of the largest firms in the country. More than 50 percent of the faculty holds a PhD or LLM degree in addition to their JD degree. You learn your craft from renowned experts specializing in international law, law of war, commercial law, business law, bankruptcy law, criminal law, and tax law.

Curriculum

Ohio Northern takes learning beyond traditional theory and brings the practice of law to life in the classroom.

During your first year, your studies will focus on the foundations of the law. The school's innovative first-year curriculum, however, will also introduce you to modern practice. During the first year January term, practicing lawyers will demonstrate how legal theory shapes what they do in courtrooms and boardrooms. A court of appeals will actually hear cases in the law building during the term, giving you a chance to interact with the judges and lawyers. In the second and third years of study, students have the opportunity to take a wide array of electives.

CONCURRENT JD AND LLM: Our concurrent JD and LLM in Democratic Governance and Rule of Law degree is designed for students who have a passion for bringing democracy and law reform to developing countries. You will build valuable international relationships through domestic and overseas externships. You will graduate in three years with both your Juris Doctor and a Master of Legal Letters (LLM) degree.

INTERNATIONAL LLM: Our one-year International LLM in Democratic Governance and Rule of Law provides an opportunity for young lawyers from transitional democracies to study democracy and law at Ohio Northern. Each year, a group of lawyers travel from across the globe to study international law alongside our JD students in an effort to implement law reforms that can support democracy and the rule of law in their home countries.

PHARMACY/LAW DUAL DEGREE: Our pharmacy and law dual degree joins together two of ONU's elite programs into a combined seven-year curriculum. Following substantial educational, practice, and research experiences in both pharmacy and law, you will graduate with your doctor of pharmacy and Juris Doctor degrees.

Practical Skills

Get involved, apply your learning in a real-life scenario, and compete on a national stage.

CLINIC: By participating in a clinic, you can enhance your writing, analytical, and communication skills and garner valuable courtroom and client experience. Nearly 70 percent of ONU students choose to take advantage of this unique opportunity and participate in a clinic study before they graduate.

EXPERIENTIAL LEARNING: Inside and outside of the classroom, our academic and nonacademic experiential learning activities provide a valuable opportunity to engage in the practice of law prior to graduation.

Career Services

Exceeding the national average in job placement, for the past eight years ONU has a 94 percent employment rate nine months after graduation.

We realize legal training is only part of the equation; your ultimate goal is to find a job. Our skilled staff in the Office of Career Services is here to help. We provide workshops and coordinate individual meetings to help you with résumé preparation, interviewing skills, professional image, and other career development techniques. We also tap into our more than 4,500 distinguished alumni to offer networking options and further strengthen our recruiting channels across the country.

Each year, more than 600 employers look to ONU for assistance in hiring law clerks, summer associates, and attorneys. Whether you want to pursue a career in private practice, government, business, or judicial clerkships, ONU will prepare you for a successful career and work with you to find the right job.

Admission and Financial Aid

Ohio Northern University is committed to a culturally and socially diverse student body. While Ohio Northern gives significant weight to the LSAT and undergraduate GPA, the Admissions Committee may consider other factors such as candidates' undergraduate programs, grade trends, completion of other graduate degrees, professional accomplishments, and socioeconomic or cultural barriers faced by the applicant. Although letters of recommendation are not required, letters from persons who have a basis to assess the candidate's intellectual ability and potential for success in law school, such as former professors or employers, are strongly recommended.

The Summer Starter Program is an opportunity for students whose outstanding undergraduate performance indicates probable academic success in law school, despite disproportionate LSAT scores. Candidates who qualify for the program, based on their application, will be invited to interview for the program on campus.

The College of Law also provides scholarship awards for students whose undergraduate records demonstrate academic excellence. Scholarship amounts range from $5,000 to $32,000 and are renewable provided the student maintains a 3.0 cumulative GPA at the end of the first year. Additionally, substantial scholarships are awarded to students who excel in their first year of law school. In order to foster diversity in the student body and the legal profession, the university awards grants-in-aid to eligible students. The college generally awards approximately $4 million of institutional aid annually to all three classes.

Students are encouraged to schedule a campus visit where they can sit in on a class, meet with a financial aid counselor, tour the facilities, and talk with current students. Contact lawadmissions@onu.edu to make arrangements.

Facilities and Technology

The college contains state-of-the-art facilities including two moot courtrooms, a technology classroom, wireless capabilities throughout the building, and classrooms equipped with plasma televisions and SMART Board technology.

The Taggart Law Library features an outstanding collection of federal, state, and international legal materials. In addition, the technology research center is available for research, training, and printing. The library is open seven days a week and provides seating for up to 303 students. The reading rooms of the library offer ideal locations for both quiet and group study.

APPLICANT PROFILE

Ohio Northern University—Claude W. Pettit College of Law
This grid includes only applicants who earned 120–180 LSAT scores under standard administrations.

LSAT Score	GPA								
	3.75 +	3.50–3.74	3.25–3.49	3.00–3.24	2.75–2.99	2.50–2.74	2.25–2.49	2.00–2.24	Below 2.00
175–180									
170–174									
165–169									
160–164									
155–159									
150–154									
145–149									
140–144									
135–139									
130–134									
125–129									
120–124									

■ Good Possibility   □ Possible   ▨ Unlikely

THE OHIO STATE UNIVERSITY MORITZ COLLEGE OF LAW

John Deaver Drinko Hall, 55 West 12th Avenue
Columbus, OH 43210-1391
Phone: 614.292.8810; Fax: 614.292.1492
E-mail: lawadmit@osu.edu; Website: www.moritzlaw.osu.edu

*ABA
Approved
Since
1923*

The Basics

Type of school	Public
Term	Semester
Application deadline	3/15
Application fee	$60
Financial aid deadline	3/1
Can first year start other than fall?	No
Student to faculty ratio	15.5 to 1
# of housing spaces available restricted to law students graduate housing for which law students are eligible	927

Faculty and Administrators

	Total		Men		Women		Minorities	
	Spr	Fall	Spr	Fall	Spr	Fall	Spr	Fall
Full-time	40	33	24	19	16	14	9	4
Other full-time	9	9	6	6	3	3	0	1
Deans, librarians, & others who teach	11	11	9	9	2	2	7	7
Part-time	22	17	15	15	7	2	3	1
Total	82	70	54	49	28	21	19	13

Curriculum

	Full-Time	Part-Time
Typical first-year section size	70	0
Is there typically a "small section" of the first-year class, other than Legal Writing, taught by full-time faculty	Yes	No
If yes, typical size offered last year	40	
# of classroom course titles beyond first-year curriculum	116	

# of upper division courses, excluding seminars, with an enrollment:		
	Under 25	77
	25–49	30
	50–74	15
	75–99	7
	100+	0

# of seminars		22	
# of seminar positions available		440	
# of seminar positions filled	373		0
# of positions available in simulation courses		250	
# of simulation positions filled	240		0
# of positions available in faculty supervised clinical courses		142	
# of faculty supervised clinical positions filled	138		0
# involved in field placements	67		0
# involved in law journals	297		0
# involved in moot court or trial competitions	81		0
# of credit hours required to graduate		88	

JD Enrollment and Ethnicity

	Men		Women		Full-Time		Part-Time		1st-Year		Total		JD Degs. Awd.
	#	%	#	%	#	%	#	%	#	%	#	%	
All Hispanics	15	3.8	21	7.1	36	5.2	0	0.0	12	5.2	36	5.2	10
Am. Ind./AK Nat.	2	0.5	3	1.0	5	0.7	0	0.0	2	0.9	5	0.7	0
Asian	20	5.0	23	7.8	43	6.2	0	0.0	15	6.6	43	6.2	14
Black/Af. Am.	24	6.0	24	8.1	48	6.9	0	0.0	15	6.6	48	6.9	21
Nat. HI/Pac. Isl.	1	0.3	0	0.0	1	0.1	0	0.0	1	0.4	1	0.1	0
2 or more races	5	1.3	3	1.0	8	1.2	0	0.0	2	0.9	8	1.2	0
Subtotal (minor.)	67	16.8	74	25.1	141	20.3	0	0.0	47	20.5	141	20.3	45
Nonres. Alien	8	2.0	8	2.7	16	2.3	0	0.0	4	1.7	16	2.3	0
White/Cauc.	295	74.1	197	66.8	492	71.0	0	0.0	164	71.6	492	71.0	136
Unknown	28	7.0	16	5.4	44	6.3	0	0.0	14	6.1	44	6.3	24
Total	398	57.4	295	42.6	693	100.0	0	0.0	229	33.0	693		205

Transfers

Transfers in	11
Transfers out	6

Tuition and Fees

	Resident	Nonresident
Full-time	$24,468	$39,418
Part-time		
Tuition Guarantee Program		N

Living Expenses

Estimated living expenses for singles

Living on campus	Living off campus	Living at home
$19,844	$19,844	$19,844

THE OHIO STATE UNIVERSITY MORITZ COLLEGE OF LAW

ABA Approved Since 1923

GPA and LSAT Scores

	Total	Full-Time	Part-Time
# of apps	2,703	2,703	0
# of offers	962	962	0
# of matrics	230	230	0
75% GPA	3.82	3.82	0.00
Median GPA	3.66	3.66	0.00
25% GPA	3.45	3.45	0.00
75% LSAT	164	164	0
Median LSAT	163	163	0
25% LSAT	160	160	0

Grants and Scholarships (from prior year)

	Total		Full-Time		Part-Time	
	#	%	#	%	#	%
Total # of students	669		669		0	
Total # receiving grants	527	78.8	527	78.8	0	0.0
Less than 1/2 tuition	415	62.0	415	62.0	0	0.0
Half to full tuition	94	14.1	94	14.1	0	0.0
Full tuition	4	0.6	4	0.6	0	0.0
More than full tuition	14	2.1	14	2.1	0	0.0
Median grant amount			$8,500		$0	

Informational and Library Resources

Total amount spent on library materials	$1,522,355
Study seating capacity inside the library	695
# of full-time equivalent professional librarians	8
Hours per week library is open	107
# of open, wired connections available to students	0
# of networked computers available for use by students	112
Has wireless network?	Y
Requires computer?	N

JD Attrition (from prior year)

	Academic	Other	Total	
	#	#	#	%
1st year	0	0	0	0.0
2nd year	0	8	8	3.3
3rd year	0	0	0	0.0
4th year	0	0	0	0.0

Employment (9 months after graduation)

	Total	Percentage
Employment status known	233	100.0
Employment status unknown	0	0.0
Employed	216	92.7
Pursuing graduate degrees	9	3.9
Unemployed (seeking, not seeking, or studying for the bar)	3	1.3
Type of Employment		
# employed in law firms	112	51.9
# employed in business and industry	37	17.1
# employed in government	34	15.7
# employed in public interest	4	1.9
# employed as judicial clerks	14	6.5
# employed in academia	15	6.9
Geographic Location		
# employed in state	121	56.0
# employed outside the US	2	0.9
# of states where employed		25

Bar Passage Rates

First-time takers	207	Reporting %	76.81
Average school %	94.35	Average state %	86.09
Average pass difference	8.26		

Jurisdiction	Takers	Passers	Pass %	State %	Diff %
Ohio	139	130	93.53	86.03	7.50
New York	20	20	100.00	86.51	13.49

THE OHIO STATE UNIVERSITY MORITZ COLLEGE OF LAW

John Deaver Drinko Hall, 55 West 12th Avenue
Columbus, OH 43210-1391
Phone: 614.292.8810; Fax: 614.292.1492
E-mail: lawadmit@osu.edu; Website: www.moritzlaw.osu.edu

Introduction

Founded in 1891, the Ohio State University Moritz College of Law has played a leading role in the legal profession through countless contributions made by graduates and faculty. The administration of the College of Law is committed to advancing the quality and reputation of the college through ongoing improvements to the academic program and student services, thereby creating a learning environment that is second to none.

Ohio State's 9,600 law alumni are central to the college's national reputation. Graduates of the college include justices of the Ohio Supreme Court, governors, current and former US senators and representatives, managing partners in law firms, chief executive officers, professors, and attorneys with nonprofit organizations and public interest law firms.

The comprehensive scope of the university and its location in the state capital provide law students with access to a wealth of educational, professional, cultural, and recreational resources and opportunities. Law students are able to pursue joint degrees with one of the university's more than 100 graduate programs and also may extern with federal and state judges or find employment with one of the more than 500 law firms located in central Ohio.

Academic Program

With approximately 140 classes offered annually, Ohio State students have a rich array of courses from which to choose. The curriculum is designed to provide a strong theoretical and analytical foundation, as well as multiple opportunities for developing and honing lawyering skills.

Alternative Dispute Resolution—The College of Law is widely regarded as having one of the nation's finest programs in the area of Alternative Dispute Resolution. The program emphasizes training in an array of dispute resolution methods beyond litigation, including negotiation, mediation, and arbitration. Students with an especially strong interest may want to serve as a member or editor of the *Ohio State Journal on Dispute Resolution* or pursue a certificate in Dispute Resolution.

Clinical Opportunities—The College of Law offers an extensive selection of clinics in civil law, criminal law, children's issues, mediation, and legislation. Students enrolled in a clinic course benefit from working with real clients, the court, or other parties while receiving intensive feedback and supervision from one of the college's 15 clinical faculty members. The fieldwork component of each clinic course is augmented by a classroom component in which topics such as lawyering skills, legal doctrine, and ethical and strategic issues are addressed.

Judicial Externship Program—Ohio State law students have the opportunity to gain first-hand insight into the judicial system through the college's Judicial Externship Program. As externs, students earn academic credit for conducting legal research and drafting legal documents for justices of the Ohio Supreme Court and for judges at the federal and county levels.

A Global Perspective on the Law—Students with an interest in international law may select from a menu of approximately 20 courses that have an international law or comparative law focus, including semester-long and summer study-abroad programs in Oxford, England. The College of Law awards a Certificate in International Trade and Development to students who combine their law coursework with select courses in international economics, politics, history, culture, and foreign language.

Faculty

One of the most frequently cited strengths of the College of Law is the quality of the faculty. Faculty members are consistently recognized for the experiences they bring to the classroom, for the clarity of their teaching, and for their accessibility to students outside of the classroom. As a group, they are highly regarded for being committed teachers who care about students. Members of the Ohio State law faculty also have earned a reputation within the profession for their expertise in specific areas of the law. Faculty are regularly cited in court and in the national media; they serve on legal reform commissions, help draft model statutes, and provide testimony before Congress.

Moritz Law Library

The Moritz Law Library provides Ohio State law students with one of the largest collections among law school libraries in the nation and access to a vast array of electronic databases. Law students with a laptop and network card can tap into online resources from virtually any point within the Moritz Law Library or the law building. All classrooms are wired for use of laptop computers.

Extracurricular Opportunities

Learning Outside of the Classroom—Recognizing that a student's legal education rests on what occurs in the classroom as well as the intellectual interchange and professional development outside of the classroom, the College of Law strives to provide an environment that is rich with extracurricular and cocurricular opportunities. Each year, the college brings to campus more than 100 speakers to address students, law faculty, and members of the bar.

The Program on Law and Leadership seeks to increase the awareness and understanding of leadership development among lawyers as well as excite and equip students for future leadership roles both in and beyond the profession. It has multiple components: education, a speaker series, skills workshops, scholarships, career assessment, and mentoring.

Ohio State law students have the opportunity to refine their legal writing skills through participation in one of the college's five highly regarded law journals: the *Ohio State Law Journal*, the *Ohio State Journal on Dispute Resolution*, the *Ohio State Journal of Criminal Law*, the *I/S: A Journal of Law and Policy for the Information Society*, and the *Entrepreneurial Business Law Journal*. Students are able to refine their skills in the areas of oral advocacy and legal writing through a variety of intramural and interscholastic competitions. In recent years, Ohio State law students have competed in approximately 14 interscholastic moot court competitions including the National Moot Court Competition, the Jessup International Law Moot Court Competition, the Frederick Douglass Moot Court

Competition, the National Health Law Moot Court Competition, the Civil Rights Moot Court Competition, the Corporate Law Competition, and the Criminal Procedure Moot Court Competition.

Service to the Public—The College of Law enjoys a strong reputation for its commitment to public service as part of the educational mission of the college. Ohio State law students are encouraged to become involved in the Leadership Program or in one or more of the college's many public interest initiatives, such as the Pro Bono Research Group. To encourage Ohio State law students to accept low-paying or volunteer positions with public interest organizations during the summer, the college and the Public Interest Law Foundation annually offer several student-funded fellowships.

Placement Opportunities

Moritz College of Law students and graduates are provided with an array of career and professional development services by a staff of six full- and part-time professionals, three of whom have JDs. Students and alumni have access to an online job-posting system and a wide variety of programs, workshops, and events. All programming and counseling services are designed to teach skills and to provide a foundation for gaining legal and professional career experience. The on-campus recruiting program, which brings over 120 employers to campus to interview students annually, is conducted through a state-of-the-art web-based recruiting system that allows students access at all hours. Alumni and practitioners interact with students through many avenues,

including a practice interview program and a mentoring program. Each year, students find employment across the country. Ohio State is a member of the National Law School Consortium, which hosts job fairs and events in a number of major legal markets nationwide. Cutting-edge technology, current resources, talented staff, and creative initiatives give College of Law students a sound professional development foundation.

Admission and Financial Aid

The Moritz College of Law is committed to enrolling highly motivated men and women who have excelled academically and who bring to the College of Law a diversity of personal and professional backgrounds. In selecting members of each entering class, the Admissions Committee seeks to enroll individuals who represent all segments of society, as well as those who, as attorneys, will respect the profession's public service obligations.

An Ohio State legal education offers one of the best values among nationally regarded law schools. The annual cost of tuition for residents of Ohio is roughly half the tuition charged by comparably ranked private law schools. Columbus also boasts a cost of living that compares favorably to major cities across the country. Nonresidents of Ohio who relocate to the state may be reclassified as Ohio residents after residing in the state for 12 months. Each year, the College of Law awards more than $3 million in need-based and merit-based financial aid to members of the student body.

APPLICANT PROFILE

The Ohio State University Moritz College of Law
This grid includes only applicants who earned 120–180 LSAT scores under standard administrations.

LSAT Score	3.75 +		3.50–3.74		3.25–3.49		3.00–3.24		2.75–2.99		2.50–2.74		2.25–2.49		2.00–2.24		Below 2.00		No GPA		Total	
	Apps	Adm	Apps	Adm	Apps	Adm	Apps	Adm	Apps	Adm	Apps	Adm	Apps	Adm	Apps	Adm	Apps	Adm	Apps	Adm	Apps	Adm
175–180	1	1	4	4	1	1	3	3	1	0	1	0	0	0	0	0	0	0	0	0	11	9
170–174	34	32	20	20	12	11	10	10	3	2	3	0	1	0	2	1	0	0	0	0	85	76
165–169	88	85	91	89	81	65	36	18	17	2	11	0	2	0	0	0	0	0	2	1	328	260
160–164	224	181	266	164	197	92	99	24	33	4	15	0	3	0	2	0	0	0	19	5	858	470
155–159	175	46	184	33	146	19	83	4	43	0	15	0	9	0	1	0	0	0	13	1	669	103
150–154	89	14	93	14	84	9	52	2	30	0	21	0	8	0	4	0	2	0	4	0	387	39
145–149	28	0	25	1	54	1	42	0	32	0	13	0	18	0	6	0	0	0	12	0	230	2
140–144	6	0	8	0	17	0	22	0	8	0	16	0	5	0	2	0	0	0	2	0	86	0
135–139	3	0	4	0	3	0	6	0	5	0	3	0	0	0	2	0	0	0	3	0	29	0
130–134	0	0	2	0	3	0	2	0	2	0	5	0	1	0	1	0	0	0	1	0	17	0
125–129	0	0	0	0	0	0	3	0	0	0	0	0	1	0	1	0	0	0	0	0	5	0
120–124	0	0	0	0	0	0	0	0	0	0	0	0	0	0	0	0	0	0	1	0	1	0
Total	648	359	697	325	598	198	358	61	174	8	103	0	48	0	21	1	2	0	57	7	2706	959

Apps = Number of Applicants
Adm = Number Admitted
Reflects 100% of total applicant pool; highest LSAT data reported.

UNIVERSITY OF OKLAHOMA COLLEGE OF LAW

Andrew M. Coats Hall, 300 Timberdell Road
Norman, OK 73019
Phone: 405.325.4726; Fax: 405.325.0502
E-mail: admissions@law.ou.edu; Website: www.law.ou.edu

ABA
Approved
Since
1923

The Basics

Type of school	Public
Term	Semester
Application deadline	3/15
Application fee	$50
Financial aid deadline	3/1
Can first year start other than fall?	No
Student to faculty ratio	14.0 to 1
# of housing spaces available restricted to law students	
graduate housing for which law students are eligible	537

Faculty and Administrators

	Total Spr	Total Fall	Men Spr	Men Fall	Women Spr	Women Fall	Minorities Spr	Minorities Fall
Full-time	32	34	19	23	13	11	3	6
Other full-time	1	0	0	0	1	0	0	0
Deans, librarians, & others who teach	5	5	4	4	1	1	0	0
Part-time	19	16	14	13	5	3	2	2
Total	57	55	37	40	20	15	5	8

Curriculum

	Full-Time	Part-Time
Typical first-year section size	43	0
Is there typically a "small section" of the first-year class, other than Legal Writing, taught by full-time faculty	No	No
If yes, typical size offered last year		

# of classroom course titles beyond first-year curriculum		113
# of upper division courses, excluding seminars, with an enrollment:	Under 25	53
	25–49	29
	50–74	15
	75–99	4
	100+	1
# of seminars		11
# of seminar positions available		176

# of seminar positions filled	167	0
# of positions available in simulation courses	232	
# of simulation positions filled	228	0
# of positions available in faculty supervised clinical courses	53	
# of faculty supervised clinical positions filled	51	0
# involved in field placements	61	0
# involved in law journals	120	0
# involved in moot court or trial competitions	87	0
# of credit hours required to graduate	90	

JD Enrollment and Ethnicity

	Men #	Men %	Women #	Women %	Full-Time #	Full-Time %	Part-Time #	Part-Time %	1st-Year #	1st-Year %	Total #	Total %	JD Degs. Awd.
All Hispanics	14	4.7	7	2.9	21	3.9	0	0.0	8	4.6	21	3.9	5
Am. Ind./AK Nat.	25	8.4	18	7.5	43	8.0	0	0.0	13	7.5	43	8.0	18
Asian	13	4.4	15	6.3	28	5.2	0	0.0	7	4.0	28	5.2	4
Black/Af. Am.	11	3.7	9	3.8	20	3.7	0	0.0	7	4.0	20	3.7	10
Nat. HI/Pac. Isl.	0	0.0	0	0.0	0	0.0	0	0.0	0	0.0	0	0.0	0
2 or more races	0	0.0	1	0.4	1	0.2	0	0.0	1	0.6	1	0.2	0
Subtotal (minor.)	63	21.2	50	20.8	113	21.0	0	0.0	36	20.8	113	21.0	37
Nonres. Alien	0	0.0	1	0.4	1	0.2	0	0.0	0	0.0	1	0.2	0
White/Cauc.	230	77.4	183	76.3	413	76.9	0	0.0	130	75.1	413	76.9	139
Unknown	4	1.3	6	2.5	10	1.9	0	0.0	7	4.0	10	1.9	0
Total	297	55.3	240	44.7	537	100.0	0	0.0	173	32.2	537		177

Transfers

Transfers in	6
Transfers out	3

Tuition and Fees

	Resident	Nonresident
Full-time	$18,105	$28,034
Part-time		
Tuition Guarantee Program	N	

Living Expenses

Estimated living expenses for singles

Living on campus	Living off campus	Living at home
$15,824	$17,923	$12,034

UNIVERSITY OF OKLAHOMA COLLEGE OF LAW

ABA
Approved
Since
1923

GPA and LSAT Scores

	Total	Full-Time	Part-Time
# of apps	1,111	1,111	0
# of offers	335	335	0
# of matrics	174	174	0
75% GPA	3.70	3.70	0.00
Median GPA	3.46	3.46	0.00
25% GPA	3.20	3.20	0.00
75% LSAT	161	161	0
Median LSAT	159	159	0
25% LSAT	157	157	0

Grants and Scholarships (from prior year)

	Total		Full-Time		Part-Time	
	#	%	#	%	#	%
Total # of students	550		550		0	
Total # receiving grants	408	74.2	408	74.2	0	0.0
Less than 1/2 tuition	312	56.7	312	56.7	0	0.0
Half to full tuition	83	15.1	83	15.1	0	0.0
Full tuition	0	0.0	0	0.0	0	0.0
More than full tuition	13	2.4	13	2.4	0	0.0
Median grant amount			$4,000		$0	

Informational and Library Resources

Total amount spent on library materials	$801,795
Study seating capacity inside the library	442
# of full-time equivalent professional librarians	7
Hours per week library is open	99
# of open, wired connections available to students	105
# of networked computers available for use by students	119
Has wireless network?	Y
Requires computer?	N

JD Attrition (from prior year)

	Academic	Other	Total	
	#	#	#	%
1st year	1	8	9	4.6
2nd year	0	2	2	1.2
3rd year	0	1	1	0.5
4th year	0	0	0	0.0

Employment (9 months after graduation)

	Total	Percentage
Employment status known	165	100.0
Employment status unknown	0	0.0
Employed	149	90.3
Pursuing graduate degrees	3	1.8
Unemployed (seeking, not seeking, or studying for the bar)	7	4.2
Type of Employment		
# employed in law firms	87	58.4
# employed in business and industry	25	16.8
# employed in government	25	16.8
# employed in public interest	4	2.7
# employed as judicial clerks	3	2.0
# employed in academia	5	3.4
Geographic Location		
# employed in state	108	72.5
# employed outside the US	1	0.7
# of states where employed	13	

Bar Passage Rates

First-time takers	161	Reporting %	76.40
Average school %	95.12	Average state %	86.76
Average pass difference	8.36		

Jurisdiction	Takers	Passers	Pass %	State %	Diff %
Oklahoma	123	117	95.12	86.76	8.36

UNIVERSITY OF OKLAHOMA COLLEGE OF LAW

Andrew M. Coats Hall, 300 Timberdell Road
Norman, OK 73019
Phone: 405.325.4726; Fax: 405.325.0502
E-mail: admissions@law.ou.edu; Website: www.law.ou.edu

Introduction

The University of Oklahoma College of Law is located on the main campus of the university in Norman, a city of approximately 100,000 adjacent to the Oklahoma City metropolitan area. The college was founded in 1909 and joined the membership of the Association of American Law Schools in 1911. The law school has been accredited by the American Bar Association's Section of Legal Education and Admissions to the Bar since that list was first published in 1923.

The College of Law is housed in beautiful Andrew M. Coats Hall, located on the south part of the university campus. A substantial addition to the existing building was completed in 2002. It has the most significant law library in Oklahoma and houses three courtrooms for training and enrichment purposes. The entering class is approximately 175 students so that the first-year sections consist of 45 students. Admission is very competitive. More than 95 percent of the students admitted will graduate. More than 95 percent will pass the bar exam on their first try, and more than 95 percent will have employment using their legal skills within nine months of graduation.

The College of Law benefits from being part of a strong university community. The University of Oklahoma, the state's flagship university, is a major doctoral degree-granting research university. Founded in 1890, the university has 18 colleges.

Admission

The College of Law utilizes a rolling admission process. A faculty committee meets regularly throughout the academic year to review applications. Admission to the College of Law is highly competitive, and many factors are considered in the selection process. Although considerable weight is given to undergraduate grade-point average and performance on the LSAT, thoughtful attention is also given to an applicant's extracurricular activities, employment experience, graduate studies, military service, adjustments to personal difficulties, and other relevant factors.

In addition to the regular fall entering class, the College of Law conducts a special Early Admission Program each summer. Admission is offered to a select group of approximately 20 students who have demonstrated a probable capacity for success in the study and practice of law. Students in the program typically receive five hours of credit for the summer study and then join the fall class.

International Programs

For the 37th year, the College of Law will conduct a summer program at Oxford University for American law students. The program affords students an opportunity to live and study in stimulating and beautiful surroundings under the guidance of American and English legal educators. Other opportunities exist for foreign study abroad in almost any country in which a student wishes to study.

Library and Physical Facilities

Andrew M. Coats Hall provides 170,000 square feet of instructional space for its programs. The modern facility provides wireless Internet access and multimedia technology in classrooms, the library, and student areas. The building features three courtrooms, one of which has seating for 250 persons and is equipped with the latest in technological innovations. The library offers access to electronic web-based services, maintains over 350,000 volumes and equivalents, and also contains one of the nation's largest Native People's collections.

Student Activities

The College of Law sponsors three major student-directed journals, the *Oklahoma Law Review*, the *American Indian Law Review*, and the *Oklahoma Journal of Law and Technology*, an online review, which focuses on intellectual property law.

Since 1948, the *Oklahoma Law Review* has been published quarterly to give expression to legal scholarship nationally and to serve the profession and the public with timely discussion of important legal issues.

The *American Indian Law Review*, published biannually, serves as a nationwide scholarly forum for the presentation of important developments in Indian law and affairs. The *Review* offers in-depth articles written by nationally recognized experts on a wide range of issues in the rapidly expanding field of Indian law.

The *Oklahoma Journal of Law and Technology* is a web-based collection of important articles on the various aspects of intellectual property. The student Board of Editors continually monitors and updates the articles and other material on the website.

The College of Law provides opportunities for students to participate in a wide range of extracurricular interscholastic appellate moot court, counseling and interviewing, negotiation, and trial advocacy competitions. The student Board of Advocates works closely with the students to facilitate participation in these competitions and provide intramural competitions for 1L and upper-level students.

All students at the College of Law may join a wide variety of organizations and participate in many kinds of extracurricular activities. The law school has an active Student Bar Association, affiliated with the Law Student Division of the American Bar Association. The student-elected Board of Governors supervises student activities and works with the faculty and administration of the law school.

Career Services

The College of Law's Office of Professional and Career Development provides comprehensive professional planning and placement services to all students. The director and the associate director work personally with students on the entire range of career development services, including offering workshops on interviewing and résumé and cover letter writing, using web-based resources, scheduling on-campus interviews, and providing individual counseling. The office works closely with law firms, government agencies, judges, and alumni around the country to expand employment opportunities for graduates.

Employment opportunities have continually expanded for University of Oklahoma law graduates, and the market placement has been very strong. In recent years, over 95 percent of graduates consistently are employed within nine months of graduation, placing the College of Law among the upper echelon of schools nationally. Approximately two-thirds

of the college's graduates practice in Oklahoma. The other one-third are found in all 50 states and 14 foreign countries, with concentrations in Texas; Washington, DC; and California. In addition to traditional legal careers as attorneys, prosecutors, and judges, University of Oklahoma law graduates work in areas such as corporate management, banking, journalism, public service, government, entrepreneurial enterprises, teaching, and academia.

APPLICANT PROFILE

University of Oklahoma College of Law
This grid includes only applicants who earned 120–180 LSAT scores under standard administrations.

LSAT Score	GPA															
	3.75 +		3.50–3.74		3.25–3.49		3.00–3.24		2.75–2.99		2.50–2.74		Below 2.50		No GPA		Total	
	Apps	Adm	Apps	Adm	Apps	Adm	Apps	Adm	Apps	Adm	Apps	Adm	Apps	Adm	Apps	Adm	Apps	Adm
170–180	3	2	4	4	4	3	1	1	1	1	0	0	0	0	0	0	13	11
165–169	13	12	10	10	8	6	6	5	8	5	4	2	1	1	0	0	50	41
160–164	35	32	42	33	35	25	21	15	15	12	5	4	2	1	2	0	157	122
155–159	60	41	65	33	85	32	52	22	29	4	18	1	9	0	6	0	324	133
150–154	52	12	65	11	71	9	48	4	37	1	22	2	16	0	3	0	314	39
145–149	19	1	17	0	36	2	29	0	26	0	12	0	11	0	9	0	159	3
140–144	7	1	8	0	5	0	10	0	8	0	8	0	10	0	1	0	57	1
Below 140	2	0	2	0	5	0	3	0	6	0	12	0	5	0	6	0	41	0
Total	191	101	213	91	249	77	170	47	130	23	81	9	54	2	27	0	1115	350

Apps = Number of Applicants
Adm = Number Admitted
Reflects 100% of the total applicant pool; highest LSAT data reported.

OKLAHOMA CITY UNIVERSITY SCHOOL OF LAW

2501 North Blackwelder Avenue
Oklahoma City, OK 73106-1493
Phone: 866.529.6281 or 405.208.5354
E-mail: lawquestions@okcu.edu; Website: http://law.okcu.edu/

ABA
Approved
Since
1960

The Basics

Type of school	Private
Term	Semester
Application deadline	8/1
Application fee	$50
Financial aid deadline	3/1
Can first year start other than fall?	No
Student to faculty ratio	16.6 to 1
# of housing spaces available restricted to law students	
graduate housing for which law students are eligible	30

Faculty and Administrators

	Total		Men		Women		Minorities	
	Spr	Fall	Spr	Fall	Spr	Fall	Spr	Fall
Full-time	28	31	16	18	12	13	4	4
Other full-time	3	3	2	2	1	1	0	0
Deans, librarians, & others who teach	6	6	3	3	3	3	2	2
Part-time	29	23	17	16	12	7	2	4
Total	66	63	38	39	28	24	8	10

Curriculum

	Full-Time	Part-Time
Typical first-year section size	78	72
Is there typically a "small section" of the first-year class, other than Legal Writing, taught by full-time faculty	No	No
If yes, typical size offered last year		
# of classroom course titles beyond first-year curriculum	117	
# of upper division courses, excluding seminars, with an enrollment: Under 25	123	
25–49	34	
50–74	15	
75–99	10	
100+	0	
# of seminars	13	
# of seminar positions available	182	
# of seminar positions filled	148	9
# of positions available in simulation courses	398	
# of simulation positions filled	232	22
# of positions available in faculty supervised clinical courses	28	
# of faculty supervised clinical positions filled	23	0
# involved in field placements	48	0
# involved in law journals	49	5
# involved in moot court or trial competitions	22	1
# of credit hours required to graduate	90	

JD Enrollment and Ethnicity

	Men		Women		Full-Time		Part-Time		1st-Year		Total		JD Degs. Awd.
	#	%	#	%	#	%	#	%	#	%	#	%	
All Hispanics	21	5.6	12	4.6	29	5.1	4	5.6	13	5.8	33	5.2	9
Am. Ind./AK Nat.	12	3.2	22	8.4	26	4.6	8	11.1	14	6.2	34	5.3	5
Asian	10	2.7	8	3.0	17	3.0	1	1.4	7	3.1	18	2.8	4
Black/Af. Am.	11	2.9	10	3.8	20	3.5	1	1.4	6	2.7	21	3.3	4
Nat. HI/Pac. Isl.	0	0.0	0	0.0	0	0.0	0	0.0	0	0.0	0	0.0	0
2 or more races	10	2.7	8	3.0	16	2.8	2	2.8	7	3.1	18	2.8	0
Subtotal (minor.)	64	17.2	60	22.8	108	19.1	16	22.2	47	20.9	124	19.5	26
Nonres. Alien	3	0.8	3	1.1	4	0.7	2	2.8	1	0.4	6	0.9	0
White/Cauc.	303	81.2	199	75.7	451	80.0	51	70.8	176	78.2	502	78.9	133
Unknown	3	0.8	1	0.4	1	0.2	3	4.2	1	0.4	4	0.6	1
Total	373	58.6	263	41.4	564	88.7	72	11.3	225	35.4	636		161

Transfers

Transfers in	3
Transfers out	10

Tuition and Fees

	Resident	Nonresident
Full-time	$33,925	$33,925
Part-time	$22,640	$22,640
Tuition Guarantee Program	N	

Living Expenses

Estimated living expenses for singles

Living on campus	Living off campus	Living at home
$16,450	$16,450	$16,450

OKLAHOMA CITY UNIVERSITY SCHOOL OF LAW

ABA
Approved
Since
1960

GPA and LSAT Scores

	Total	Full-Time	Part-Time
# of apps	1,361	1,262	99
# of offers	625	605	20
# of matrics	224	213	11
75% GPA	3.49	3.48	3.66
Median GPA	3.14	3.12	3.37
25% GPA	2.86	2.86	3.17
75% LSAT	153	153	154
Median LSAT	150	150	149
25% LSAT	149	149	148

Grants and Scholarships (from prior year)

	Total		Full-Time		Part-Time	
	#	%	#	%	#	%
Total # of students	623		533		90	
Total # receiving grants	226	36.3	219	41.1	7	7.8
Less than 1/2 tuition	149	23.9	145	27.2	4	4.4
Half to full tuition	61	9.8	58	10.9	3	3.3
Full tuition	2	0.3	2	0.4	0	0.0
More than full tuition	14	2.2	14	2.6	0	0.0
Median grant amount			$12,000		$10,000	

Informational and Library Resources

Total amount spent on library materials	$704,348
Study seating capacity inside the library	381
# of full-time equivalent professional librarians	8
Hours per week library is open	103
# of open, wired connections available to students	147
# of networked computers available for use by students	68
Has wireless network?	Y
Requires computer?	N

JD Attrition (from prior year)

	Academic	Other	Total	
	#	#	#	%
1st year	17	17	34	14.8
2nd year	4	2	6	3.0
3rd year	0	0	0	0.0
4th year	0	0	0	0.0

Employment (9 months after graduation)

	Total	Percentage
Employment status known	164	98.8
Employment status unknown	2	1.2
Employed	139	84.8
Pursuing graduate degrees	1	0.6
Unemployed (seeking, not seeking, or studying for the bar)	14	8.5
Type of Employment		
# employed in law firms	77	55.4
# employed in business and industry	32	23.0
# employed in government	15	10.8
# employed in public interest	11	7.9
# employed as judicial clerks	0	0.0
# employed in academia	3	2.2
Geographic Location		
# employed in state	87	62.6
# employed outside the US	0	0.0
# of states where employed		19

Bar Passage Rates

First-time takers	164	Reporting %	75.00
Average school %	83.74	Average state %	86.53
Average pass difference	−2.79		

Jurisdiction	Takers	Passers	Pass %	State %	Diff %
Oklahoma	101	84	83.17	86.76	−3.59
Texas	22	19	86.36	85.48	0.88

OKLAHOMA CITY UNIVERSITY SCHOOL OF LAW

2501 North Blackwelder Avenue
Oklahoma City, OK 73106-1493
Phone: 866.529.6281 or 405.208.5354
E-mail: lawquestions@okcu.edu; Website: http://law.okcu.edu/

Introduction

At Oklahoma City University School of Law (OCU LAW) we introduce students to an educational philosophy that purposefully and carefully blends the theory and practice of law in all of its forms. Located within minutes of some of Oklahoma's largest law firms, corporations, banks, city and state government agencies, the state capital, and state and federal courts, our location enables our students to gain valuable experience before graduation.

Oklahoma City, the capital of Oklahoma, boasts a metropolitan population that numbers over one million and covers 625 square miles. In the past 10 years, Oklahoma City has undergone a revitalization resulting in a new NBA team, a new AAA baseball stadium, the establishment of Bricktown as a premier historic entertainment district, a new public library, creation of a new riverfront recreation area, and increased investment in public schools. It is considered an easy, comfortable, and friendly place to live.

Faculty

The faculty at OCU LAW are committed to the intellectual and professional growth of every student. They hold law degrees from a variety of law schools, including the nation's most prestigious. Many faculty members also hold advanced degrees in law and other fields of study, and most have significant practice-based experience.

Library and Physical Facilities

Classes at OCU LAW are held in the Sarkeys Law Center. It houses two moot courtrooms and classrooms equipped with contemporary technology. The building features several common areas that foster interaction between students and faculty. The OCU LAW Library, located in the nearby historic Gold Star Memorial Building, houses a collection of over 321,561 volumes and volume equivalents and features computer labs with access to all online research databases. A wireless network is available in all law school facilities.

Scheduling Options

The School of Law offers a full-time JD program with either a traditional day or sunset (late afternoon/early evening) schedule. Our part-time program is available with sunset classes. By attending summer sessions, full-time students may complete their degree requirements (90 semester hours) in as little as two-and-a-half years and part-time students in three-and-a-half years.

Special Programs

In Oklahoma, students who have completed just 45 course hours are eligible for a limited license, and those who qualify may appear in court under certain circumstances. As a companion to this state licensing policy, OCU LAW has created a range of externship opportunities where academic credit can be earned in a variety of practice placement sites with field supervisors, operating under the guidance of a full-time director of externship programs.

The School of Law operates three legal centers for its students and the legal community. The Center on Alternative Dispute Resolution provides coherence and structure for the varied activities of OCU LAW in the areas of negotiation, mediation, and arbitration. The Native American Legal Resource Center focuses on Native American law and provides legal services to tribes and tribal courts, frequently through federal grants. The Center for the Study of State Constitutional Law and Government promotes scholarship and discussion on important issues relating to state government.

OCU LAW cosponsors (with Stetson University) summer international programs in Buenos Aires, Argentina; Granada, Spain; Freiberg, Germany; The Hague, the Netherlands; and Tianjin, China.

Office of Admission

OCU LAW seeks serious, motivated students who value education and demonstrate a commitment to the values and ethics of the legal profession. Many factors are considered in the evaluation of applications. Reviewers look for evidence of analytical and critical thinking, as well as reading, research, and writing skills that suggest the applicant is prepared for law school. Additionally, the committee considers factors such as work and life experience, cultural and economic background, advanced degrees, and extracurricular and community activities.

The Alternate Summer Admission Program (ASAP) offers a limited number of applicants who do not meet traditional admission requirements an opportunity to demonstrate their capacity for law study and to earn admission for the fall by attending and passing two summer classes. Any applicant not offered direct admission will automatically be considered for admission through the summer program.

OCU LAW uses a rolling admission review process and will review applications until the class is filled. Applications received by February 1, with LSAT scores on record, will receive priority consideration for admission and scholarship assistance. To be eligible for priority review, applicants should take the June, October, or December LSAT in the year prior to which they are applying.

Scholarships

Each year OCU LAW awards over 1.5 million in scholarships. New applicants are evaluated and encouraged to apply for our generous scholarships ranging from $5,000 to full-tuition awards. The Hatton W. Sumners Scholarship, for example, is a full-tuition award that includes a book and living expense stipend. The Sumners Scholarships are competitive and awarded based on academic and leadership potential demonstrated within the scholarship application and during an on-campus interview. Applications for the Sumners award are due February 1. Additional scholarship assistance is available to returning upper-division students based on academic performance.

Student Services

OCU LAW actively provides law students with opportunities to be engaged with the larger legal community. Numerous guest speakers, programs, and activities are sponsored to provide students with exposure to local, state, and national leaders; scholars; and legal professionals.

The entire staff at the law school is committed to assisting law students. The associate dean for students offers broad support to students and student organizations. An in-house financial aid advisor provides loan and debt management counseling, and a student technology coordinator assists students with their computing needs. A very accessible professional library staff, which includes five librarians with JD degrees, aids students in the development of important research skills.

Professional and Career Development Center

The Professional and Career Development Center (PCDC) hosts a wide range of workshops and guest speakers in addition to offering personal career counseling and employer cultivation efforts. The center seeks to expose law students to various areas of the law, to provide the resources needed to successfully conduct an employment search, and to guide them in developing the skills, ethics, and values of a legal professional. Details of services provided, contact information for career counselors, and a list of programs and workshops are available on the Professional and Career Development section of the OCU LAW website.

Curriculum

The School of Law offers a joint JD/MBA program and specialized certificate programs in alternative dispute resolution, public law, and business law (with concentrations in e-commerce or in financial services and commercial law). The core curriculum for every OCU LAW student includes a purposeful balance of legal theory and practical application. It provides a well-grounded foundation in the basic doctrines, functions, and ethical principles that underlie law and law practice, and is designed to produce graduates who have a breadth of understanding that enables them to become leaders in law, business, government, and civic life.

APPLICANT PROFILE

Oklahoma City University School of Law
This grid includes only applicants who earned 120–180 LSAT scores under standard administrations.

LSAT Score	3.75 +		3.50–3.74		3.25–3.49		3.00–3.24		2.75–2.99		2.50–2.74		2.25–2.49		2.00–2.24		Below 2.00		No GPA		Total	
	Apps	Adm	Apps	Adm	Apps	Adm	Apps	Adm	Apps	Adm	Apps	Adm	Apps	Adm	Apps	Adm	Apps	Adm	Apps	Adm	Apps	Adm
175–180	0	0	0	0	0	0	0	0	0	0	0	0	0	0	0	0	0	0	0	0	0	0
170–174	0	0	0	0	1	1	0	0	1	1	0	0	0	0	0	0	0	0	0	0	2	2
165–169	4	4	1	0	2	2	0	0	2	2	0	0	0	0	0	0	0	0	0	0	9	8
160–164	10	10	5	5	10	10	11	11	5	5	2	2	0	0	2	2	0	0	0	0	45	45
155–159	12	12	25	25	15	15	23	20	17	14	17	14	16	11	3	1	1	0	3	0	132	112
150–154	20	20	42	40	65	61	63	57	49	43	29	20	25	13	16	3	2	1	3	2	314	260
145–149	30	19	55	34	81	35	101	43	85	35	55	17	38	3	13	0	7	1	8	1	473	188
140–144	15	2	25	2	39	2	42	0	62	0	45	0	29	0	11	0	5	0	5	0	278	6
135–139	2	0	1	0	6	0	10	0	9	0	9	0	12	0	7	0	5	0	4	0	65	0
130–134	1	0	0	0	2	0	2	0	4	0	2	0	2	0	2	0	1	0	3	0	19	0
125–129	0	0	1	0	0	0	1	0	0	0	1	0	2	0	1	0	0	0	0	0	6	0
120–124	0	0	0	0	0	0	0	0	0	0	0	0	0	0	0	0	0	0	0	0	0	0
Total	94	67	155	106	221	126	253	131	234	100	160	53	124	27	55	6	21	2	26	3	1343	621

Apps = Number of Applicants
Adm = Number Admitted
Reflects 99% of the total applicant pool; highest LSAT data reported.

UNIVERSITY OF OREGON SCHOOL OF LAW

Office of Admissions, 1221 University of Oregon
Eugene, OR 97403-1221
Phone: 541.346.3846; Fax: 541.346.3984
E-mail: admissions@law.uoregon.edu; Website: www.law.uoregon.edu

The Basics

Type of school	Public
Term	Semester
Application deadline	3/1
Application fee	$50
Financial aid deadline	3/1
Can first year start other than fall?	No
Student to faculty ratio	15.7 to 1
# of housing spaces available restricted to law students	
graduate housing for which law students are eligible	72

Faculty and Administrators

	Total		Men		Women		Minorities	
	Spr	Fall	Spr	Fall	Spr	Fall	Spr	Fall
Full-time	27	29	14	16	13	13	5	7
Other full-time	4	6	0	1	4	5	0	2
Deans, librarians, & others who teach	5	5	1	1	4	4	0	0
Part-time	34	25	20	13	14	12	3	1
Total	70	65	35	31	35	34	8	10

Curriculum

		Full-Time	Part-Time
Typical first-year section size		61	0
Is there typically a "small section" of the first-year class, other than Legal Writing, taught by full-time faculty		No	No
If yes, typical size offered last year			
# of classroom course titles beyond first-year curriculum		102	
# of upper division courses, excluding seminars, with an enrollment:	Under 25	89	
	25–49	25	
	50–74	7	
	75–99	5	
	100+	1	
# of seminars		15	
# of seminar positions available		333	
# of seminar positions filled		240	0
# of positions available in simulation courses		576	
# of simulation positions filled		478	0
# of positions available in faculty supervised clinical courses		184	
# of faculty supervised clinical positions filled		128	0
# involved in field placements		106	0
# involved in law journals		124	0
# involved in moot court or trial competitions		26	0
# of credit hours required to graduate		85	

JD Enrollment and Ethnicity

	Men		Women		Full-Time		Part-Time		1st-Year		Total		JD Degs. Awd.
	#	%	#	%	#	%	#	%	#	%	#	%	
All Hispanics	10	3.4	6	2.6	16	3.0	0	0.0	5	2.8	16	3.0	6
Am. Ind./AK Nat.	4	1.4	3	1.3	7	1.3	0	0.0	1	0.6	7	1.3	4
Asian	15	5.1	24	10.3	39	7.4	0	0.0	11	6.3	39	7.4	20
Black/Af. Am.	10	3.4	5	2.1	15	2.9	0	0.0	5	2.8	15	2.9	4
Nat. HI/Pac. Isl.	1	0.3	0	0.0	1	0.2	0	0.0	0	0.0	1	0.2	0
2 or more races	7	2.4	5	2.1	12	2.3	0	0.0	8	4.5	12	2.3	0
Subtotal (minor.)	47	16.1	43	18.4	90	17.1	0	0.0	30	17.0	90	17.1	34
Nonres. Alien	6	2.1	3	1.3	9	1.7	0	0.0	4	2.3	9	1.7	0
White/Cauc.	222	76.0	181	77.4	403	76.6	0	0.0	137	77.8	403	76.6	122
Unknown	17	5.8	7	3.0	24	4.6	0	0.0	5	2.8	24	4.6	26
Total	292	55.5	234	44.5	526	100.0	0	0.0	176	33.5	526		182

Transfers

Transfers in	1
Transfers out	10

Tuition and Fees

	Resident	Nonresident
Full-time	$24,031	$29,953
Part-time		
Tuition Guarantee Program	N	

Living Expenses

Estimated living expenses for singles

Living on campus	Living off campus	Living at home
$14,460	$14,460	$7,026

UNIVERSITY OF OREGON SCHOOL OF LAW

ABA
Approved
Since
1923

GPA and LSAT Scores

	Total	Full-Time	Part-Time
# of apps	2,285	2,285	0
# of offers	902	902	0
# of matrics	177	177	0
75% GPA	3.66	3.66	0.00
Median GPA	3.43	3.43	0.00
25% GPA	3.18	3.18	0.00
75% LSAT	161	161	0
Median LSAT	159	159	0
25% LSAT	157	157	0

Grants and Scholarships (from prior year)

	Total #	Total %	Full-Time #	Full-Time %	Part-Time #	Part-Time %
Total # of students	544		544		0	
Total # receiving grants	305	56.1	305	56.1	0	0.0
Less than 1/2 tuition	276	50.7	276	50.7	0	0.0
Half to full tuition	23	4.2	23	4.2	0	0.0
Full tuition	0	0.0	0	0.0	0	0.0
More than full tuition	6	1.1	6	1.1	0	0.0
Median grant amount			$5,000		$0	

Informational and Library Resources

Total amount spent on library materials	$1,127,809
Study seating capacity inside the library	333
# of full-time equivalent professional librarians	8
Hours per week library is open	107
# of open, wired connections available to students	1,354
# of networked computers available for use by students	26
Has wireless network?	Y
Requires computer?	Y

JD Attrition (from prior year)

	Academic #	Other #	Total #	Total %
1st year	1	15	16	8.7
2nd year	0	2	2	1.1
3rd year	0	0	0	0.0
4th year	0	0	0	0.0

Employment (9 months after graduation)

	Total	Percentage
Employment status known	153	93.9
Employment status unknown	10	6.1
Employed	134	87.6
Pursuing graduate degrees	9	5.9
Unemployed (seeking, not seeking, or studying for the bar)	10	6.5
Type of Employment		
# employed in law firms	62	46.3
# employed in business and industry	8	6.0
# employed in government	20	14.9
# employed in public interest	19	14.2
# employed as judicial clerks	21	15.7
# employed in academia	4	3.0
Geographic Location		
# employed in state	85	63.4
# employed outside the US	3	2.2
# of states where employed	13	

Bar Passage Rates

First-time takers	160	Reporting %	71.25
Average school %	82.46	Average state %	76.85
Average pass difference	5.61		

Jurisdiction	Takers	Passers	Pass %	State %	Diff %
Oregon	114	94	82.46	76.85	5.61

The information on these pages was provided by the law school.

UNIVERSITY OF OREGON SCHOOL OF LAW

Office of Admissions, 1221 University of Oregon
Eugene, OR 97403-1221
Phone: 541.346.3846; Fax: 541.346.3984
E-mail: admissions@law.uoregon.edu; Website: www.law.uoregon.edu

In Brief

The University of Oregon School of Law is Oregon's state-supported law school. In 1923, Oregon Law became one of the first law schools to be approved by the American Bar Association. It is the only law school in the state with membership in Order of the Coif. Oregon Law is housed in the William W. Knight Law Center on the university's historic 295-acre campus in Eugene, the state's second largest city. The award-winning Knight Law Center, which includes the John E. Jaqua Law Library, is home to three academic programs: the Doctor of Jurisprudence (JD) program, the Oregon LLM in Environmental and Natural Resources Law, and the Master's in Conflict and Dispute Resolution, an interdisciplinary program of the University of Oregon Graduate School. The Green Business Initiative (GBI) and the Portland Externships programs are law school initiatives based at the University of Oregon in downtown Portland. Though one of the West's smallest law schools, with just 180 first-year students, Oregon Law offers program options that support a diversity of professional interests and career goals.

Our Students and Faculty

Oregon Law is a small community of interesting students who are also smart, friendly, and energetic. Among the characteristics that distinguish the first-year class: 42 percent lived, worked, or studied abroad prior to law school. Almost 25 percent speak more than one language. Seventeen percent of students were the first in their family to graduate from college. Over 100 colleges and universities are represented in the class. Just 18 percent majored in political science as undergraduates. Twenty-one percent graduated with a double major, and 7 percent came to law school with a master's or doctoral degree. Fifteen percent were college athletes, many of whom were attracted to the university for its athletic heritage. Perhaps, most significantly, 84 percent were engaged in public interest or public service employment or activities prior to law school. That passion and dedication flourishes at Oregon Law. For eight of the last nine years, Oregon Law has finished first in the annual Oregon State Bar Pro Bono Challenge, garnering the most pro bono hours among the state's three law schools.

Full-time faculty form the core of a respected community of scholars and teachers at Oregon Law. Engaged nationally on important issues in their fields, innovative in their classrooms, and passionate about the law, our faculty earned Oregon Law membership in the academy's honorary scholastic society, the Order of the Coif. A select group of adjunct faculty—practicing members of the bar—also contribute to broadening the professional network of our students. Finally, critical to the development of legal research and writing skills is our Law Library faculty. They oversee vast information resources that support the work of both faculty and students. At Oregon Law, our faculty challenge students with a rigorous classroom experience, but they also generously give of their time outside of the classroom.

Curriculum

Though a small school, Oregon Law is able to offer students many program options, enabling different goals and interests to be met. Broad faculty expertise, a range of specialized centers and programs, and the additional resources that only a law school on the campus of a major research university can provide are what make these program options possible. All students at Oregon Law are engaged in full-time study.

- **Centers and Programs** fuel much of the academic energy among students and faculty at Oregon Law. These include the Appropriate Dispute Resolution (ADR) Center, Environmental and Natural Resources Law (ENR) Center, Center for Law and Entrepreneurship, Ocean and Coastal Law Center, the University of Oregon School of Law Portland Program, Public Interest Public Service Program (PIPS), and the Wayne Morse Center for Law and Politics. The Oregon Child Advocacy Project is also housed in the School of Law. Several of the programs offer opportunities for fellowships.
- Oregon Law presently offers three **concurrent JD/master's degree** programs with other University of Oregon departments, as well as one with the Graduate School. A concurrent degree arrangement enables students to earn a master's degree with only one additional year of study, rather than the traditional two years. Students apply separately to the master's program of their choice. These include business administration with the Lundquist College of Business (JD/MBA), environmental studies with the Environmental Studies Program (JD/MA or JD/MS), international studies with the Department of International Studies (JD/MA), and conflict and dispute resolution with the Graduate School (JD/MA or JD/MS). Through a special arrangement, an Oregon Law student can earn a master's degree in water resources (JD/MS) at Oregon State University in Corvallis.
- About one-third of Oregon Law students concentrate their legal studies on a specialized area of interest. Following a prescribed set of electives, students can earn a **"statement of completion"** in one of 12 areas. These include business law, criminal law, dispute resolution, environmental and natural resources law, estate planning, intellectual property law, international law, law and entrepreneurship, ocean and coastal law, public interest and public service law, sustainable business law, and tax law.
- More than 80 percent of Oregon Law students graduate with "real world" experience, completing at least one for-credit **clinic or externship** as part of their legal training. The clinics include a mediation clinic, small business clinic, civil practice and advanced civil practice clinics, criminal defense clinic, prosecution and advanced prosecution clinics, environmental law and advanced environmental law clinics, and domestic violence and advanced domestic violence clinics. Externships include the Office of the United States Trustee Externship, Portland In-House Counsel Externships, environmental law externships, child advocacy externships, domestic violence externships, local government externships, and judicial externships.
- A semester-long **foreign exchange program** with the University of Adelaide School of Law, situated in South Australia's capital, is another program option for students, particularly those focusing on some aspect of international law. Many international study programs sponsored by other ABA law schools also are open to Oregon Law students for degree credit.
- The Oregon **LLM** in Environmental and Natural Resources Law is an advanced law degree program offered at Oregon

Law. The cohort that participates in this one-year program is a small and select group of US law school graduates and international lawyers seeking more specialized training in environmental and natural resources law.

Admission Decisions

Oregon Law receives applications from many more qualified applicants than there are seats in the class. The fact that the first-year class is small makes the admission process a little more competitive. However, our admissions committee reads each applicant's file in a comprehensive and holistic way. To ensure fair consideration of a breadth of applicants, our admissions committee is comprised of faculty, both senior and new; program administrators; a law student; and admission officers. The committee is charged with determining, primarily through numerical (though with the consideration of nonnumerical) factors, if an applicant is prepared to succeed academically in law school. The committee also assesses to what extent an applicant's interests and goals match those reflected in our curriculum and in our community. That is why we ask a range of questions on our application (including those related to conduct), request that you provide us with a résumé of your professional experiences, ask for letters of recommendation, and spend time evaluating the quality of your personal statement. No specific LSAT score or combination of LSAT score and undergraduate GPA ensures admission. While Oregon is a state-supported law school, we welcome applications from nonresidents. Both residents and nonresidents are considered for scholarships at the time of admission.

Student Life

Students come to Eugene, Oregon, from all over the country. More than 30 states are usually represented in the first-year class. In this city of 150,000, life is pretty laid back and interactions are less formal. The cost of living is low. Most Oregon Law graduates work in major urban centers, but the preference to go to law school in a more relaxed setting is a common theme among alumni and students.

There are about 40 student organizations promoting events throughout the year. Among them is Land, Air, and Water (LAW), which annually hosts PIELC, the largest public interest environmental law conference in the world. There is an active women law students group, five multicultural organizations, and an LGBTQ organization. The School of Law supports three student-run publications: *Oregon Law Review*, *Journal of Environmental Law and Litigation*, and *Oregon Review of International Law*. The Moot Court Board sponsors five in-house school competitions. There are numerous public interest fundraisers and community outreach and mentoring programs. Students also participate on all committees of the law school, including faculty hiring, dean's advisory, diversity, and others.

Careers

The staff of the Career Services Office (CSO) provides comprehensive and personalized career counseling to law students. The Oregon CSO utilizes a network of more than 5,500 alumni and oversees a busy on-campus interview program. Students take advantage of the popular Portland Interview Program and the Portland Mentorship Program. More than half of the most recent graduating class chose to remain in Oregon, but alumni work on Wall Street; in Washington, DC; and throughout the West. Graduates have risen to prominent positions, particularly in Portland and Seattle and in the federal and state courts. For 11 of the last 12 years, Oregon graduates have passed the Oregon state bar examination at rates that have met or exceeded the state average. An associate director of public service initiatives helps develop public interest externship opportunities, works on fundraising initiatives for our loan repayment assistance program (LRAP), and works in conjunction with the CSO to assist public interest students in their job searches.

APPLICANT PROFILE

University of Oregon School of Law

LSAT Score	GPA								
	3.75 +	3.50–3.74	3.25–3.49	3.00–3.24	2.75–2.99	2.50–2.74	2.25–2.49	2.00–2.24	Below 2.00
175–180									
170–174									
165–169									
160–164									
155–159									
150–154									
145–149									
140–144									
135–139									
130–134									
125–129									
120–124									

■ Good Possibility □ Possible ▨ Unlikely

PACE UNIVERSITY SCHOOL OF LAW

78 North Broadway
White Plains, NY 10603
Phone: 914.422.4210; Fax: 914.989.8714
E-mail: admissions@law.pace.edu; Website: www.law.pace.edu

ABA
Approved
Since
1978

The Basics

Type of school	Private
Term	Semester
Application deadline	11/14 3/1
Application fee	$65
Financial aid deadline	2/15
Can first year start other than fall?	Yes
Student to faculty ratio	13.2 to 1
# of housing spaces available restricted to law students	
graduate housing for which law students are eligible	110

Faculty and Administrators

	Total		Men		Women		Minorities	
	Spr	Fall	Spr	Fall	Spr	Fall	Spr	Fall
Full-time	45	44	28	27	17	17	7	7
Other full-time	2	3	2	3	0	0	0	0
Deans, librarians, & others who teach	11	10	6	4	5	6	1	0
Part-time	36	45	22	31	14	14	5	1
Total	94	102	58	65	36	37	13	8

Curriculum

	Full-Time	Part-Time
Typical first-year section size	53	53
Is there typically a "small section" of the first-year class, other than Legal Writing, taught by full-time faculty	Yes	Yes
If yes, typical size offered last year	20	18
# of classroom course titles beyond first-year curriculum	172	

# of upper division courses, excluding seminars, with an enrollment:		
	Under 25	157
	25–49	44
	50–74	11
	75–99	3
	100+	0

# of seminars	40	
# of seminar positions available	620	
# of seminar positions filled	454	164
# of positions available in simulation courses	276	
# of simulation positions filled	197	58
# of positions available in faculty supervised clinical courses	114	
# of faculty supervised clinical positions filled	79	27
# involved in field placements	189	38
# involved in law journals	98	26
# involved in moot court or trial competitions	51	12
# of credit hours required to graduate	88	

JD Enrollment and Ethnicity

	Men		Women		Full-Time		Part-Time		1st-Year		Total		JD Degs. Awd.
	#	%	#	%	#	%	#	%	#	%	#	%	
All Hispanics	15	4.4	26	5.8	26	4.2	15	8.6	9	3.4	41	5.2	12
Am. Ind./AK Nat.	1	0.3	1	0.2	2	0.3	0	0.0	1	0.4	2	0.3	0
Asian	19	5.5	25	5.6	33	5.4	11	6.3	11	4.1	44	5.6	22
Black/Af. Am.	6	1.7	22	4.9	22	3.6	6	3.4	4	1.5	28	3.6	6
Nat. HI/Pac. Isl.	0	0.0	0	0.0	0	0.0	0	0.0	0	0.0	0	0.0	0
2 or more races	4	1.2	7	1.6	11	1.8	0	0.0	3	1.1	11	1.4	0
Subtotal (minor.)	45	13.1	81	18.2	94	15.3	32	18.4	28	10.5	126	16.0	40
Nonres. Alien	2	0.6	5	1.1	7	1.1	0	0.0	2	0.7	7	0.9	0
White/Cauc.	201	58.6	264	59.3	359	58.5	106	60.9	126	47.2	465	59.0	169
Unknown	95	27.7	95	21.3	154	25.1	36	20.7	111	41.6	190	24.1	12
Total	343	43.5	445	56.5	614	77.9	174	22.1	267	33.9	788		222

Transfers

Transfers in	5
Transfers out	12

Tuition and Fees

	Resident	Nonresident
Full-time	$39,794	$39,794
Part-time	$29,858	$29,858
Tuition Guarantee Program	N	

Living Expenses

Estimated living expenses for singles

Living on campus	Living off campus	Living at home
$19,674	$20,776	$7,864

PACE UNIVERSITY SCHOOL OF LAW

*ABA
Approved
Since
1978*

GPA and LSAT Scores

	Total	Full-Time	Part-Time
# of apps	3,082	2,639	443
# of offers	1,167	1,065	102
# of matrics	299	265	34
75% GPA	3.57	3.58	3.52
Median GPA	3.40	3.40	3.34
25% GPA	3.12	3.13	3.01
75% LSAT	156	156	156
Median LSAT	154	154	153
25% LSAT	152	152	149

Grants and Scholarships (from prior year)

	Total		Full-Time		Part-Time	
	#	%	#	%	#	%
Total # of students	747		562		185	
Total # receiving grants	511	68.4	408	72.6	103	55.7
Less than 1/2 tuition	354	47.4	278	49.5	76	41.1
Half to full tuition	123	16.5	99	17.6	24	13.0
Full tuition	34	4.6	31	5.5	3	1.6
More than full tuition	0	0.0	0	0.0	0	0.0
Median grant amount			$9,000		$8,000	

Informational and Library Resources

Total amount spent on library materials	$1,231,381
Study seating capacity inside the library	545
# of full-time equivalent professional librarians	9.95
Hours per week library is open	101
# of open, wired connections available to students	320
# of networked computers available for use by students	85
Has wireless network?	Y
Requires computer?	N

JD Attrition (from prior year)

	Academic	Other	Total	
	#	#	#	%
1st year	6	19	25	9.6
2nd year	3	8	11	4.9
3rd year	0	1	1	0.5
4th year	0	0	0	0.0

Employment (9 months after graduation)

	Total	Percentage
Employment status known	244	96.8
Employment status unknown	8	3.2
Employed	215	88.1
Pursuing graduate degrees	15	6.1
Unemployed (seeking, not seeking, or studying for the bar)	14	5.7
Type of Employment		
# employed in law firms	91	42.3
# employed in business and industry	39	18.1
# employed in government	21	9.8
# employed in public interest	11	5.1
# employed as judicial clerks	13	6.0
# employed in academia	38	17.7
Geographic Location		
# employed in state	154	71.6
# employed outside the US	3	1.4
# of states where employed		12

Bar Passage Rates

First-time takers	258	Reporting %	91.09
Average school %	84.26	Average state %	86.51
Average pass difference	–2.25		

Jurisdiction	Takers	Passers	Pass %	State %	Diff %
New York	235	198	84.26	86.51	–2.25

PACE UNIVERSITY SCHOOL OF LAW

78 North Broadway
White Plains, NY 10603
Phone: 914.422.4210; Fax: 914.989.8714
E-mail: admissions@law.pace.edu; Website: www.law.pace.edu

A Well-Rounded Legal Education

Pace Law School is a national law school ranked among the top environmental law schools in the country. Students can explore a range of subject matters or pursue one of our sixteen curriculum concentrations. Pace Law School also offers a variety of clinics, centers, externships, and simulation courses for hands-on practical experience. White Plains, New York, home to Pace Law School, not only ranks in the top ten nationwide for income and standard of living but is also just 20 miles north of the heart—and pulse—of New York City.

Founded in 1976, Pace Law School benefits from its network of more than 7,000 alumni throughout the world. Pace Law School offers full-time and part-time day programs, the Master of Laws in Environmental Law—including the nation's first Climate Change track, the Land Use and Sustainable Development track, Comparative Legal Studies, and a Doctor of Laws in Environmental Law. The school is part of Pace University, a comprehensive, independent, and diversified university with campuses in New York City and Westchester County.

A Varied Curriculum

The JD program provides students with the fundamental skills necessary for the practice of law nationally, and the flexibility to shape their elective coursework based on particular career goals. The curriculum is based on the concept that rigorous standards and high-quality teaching can coexist with an atmosphere congenial to learning and enjoyment. Students can obtain certificates in Environmental Law and in International Law by completing a sequence of courses with a specified GPA in the applicable area. Pace offers the opportunity to pursue joint degrees in the JD/MBA and JD/MPA programs, as well as the JD/MEM with Yale University School of Forestry, the JD/MS in Environmental Policy with Bard College, and the JD/MA in Women's History with Sarah Lawrence College. Graduate law degrees, an LLM in Comparative Legal Studies or Environmental Law and an SJD in Environmental Law, attract attorneys from around the world. Pace JD candidates taking 12 credits of environmental law may earn LLM degrees in one additional semester.

The majority of elective classes have fewer than 25 students, which enables close faculty-student relationships. The range of scholarship reflects a faculty of diverse interests, and the curriculum offers courses in traditional areas of legal study, legal theory, and specialized studies. Curricular concentrations include constitutional law, commercial law, corporate law, civil litigation and dispute resolution, criminal law and criminal procedure, evidence, family law, intellectual property, real estate law, women's justice, and land use law. Faculty scholarship also covers such specialized areas as the Americans with Disabilities Act, children's legal representation, environmental and toxic torts, equal pay, hazardous waste, health care fraud, international commercial law, land use, legal and ethical issues in health care, nonprofit organizations, prosecutorial and judicial ethics, racially motivated violence, securities fraud, and white-collar crime.

Renowned Centers and Programs

Pace Law School offers many clinics, simulation courses, and externships through our on-campus centers, institutes, and lawyering skills programs.

Students can represent the underserved through the Family Court Externship with the Pace Women's Justice Center, preserve individual liberties through our John Jay Legal Services Immigration Justice Clinic, or work side-by-side with Assistant District Attorneys through a prosecution externship preparing and prosecuting criminal cases.

In the popular and growing field of environmental law, students work on conservation and development matters through the Land Use Law Center; help accelerate the world's transition to clean, efficient, and renewable energy alternatives through the Pace Energy and Climate Center; extern with a federal agency in Washington, DC; and help nation-states develop climate change policies through the country's only United Nations Environmental Diplomacy Externship.

Pace Law School's international programs allow students to spend a summer abroad with one of the United Nations War Crimes Tribunals, or intern locally through an international trade with law firms and corporate legal departments handling international trade matters. Students may also spend the spring semester abroad through our Pace London Law Program.

Judicial externship programs allow students to hone their writing skills in a mentoring program with a faculty member and in the chambers of a state or United States district or circuit court judge.

Whatever your interests, Pace Law School has the facilities and resources to help you pursue them.

Modern Library and Physical Facilities

The Pace Law Library is housed in an airy, modern facility. The law library contains an extensive collection of law and law-related publications, provides access to materials in other libraries in metropolitan New York and throughout the United States, and subscribes to national online research systems such as LexisNexis, Westlaw, HeinOnline and BNA's Law School Professional Information Center. Pace Law students have free access to these databases from computer terminals distributed throughout the law library as well as in the student lounge, and from their home computers. A wireless network is available in the law library, classroom buildings, and throughout the campus. The library was recently renovated and features attractive, comfortable space in which students can study individually or in groups.

Financial Aid

A comprehensive aid program has been developed to include scholarships, need-based grants, employment, loans, and a loan forgiveness program for graduates who choose a public interest career. Over $1.6 million has been allocated for first-year students. These funds may be available on the basis of financial need and academic merit.

Supportive Career Development Services

The Center for Career Development and the Public Interest Law Center offer a number of services to students and alumni, including one-on-one counseling and résumé review; panels and programs regarding the many areas of legal practice; specific job, internship, and fellowship opportunities (provided through our website); and on-campus interview and résumé collection programs. The centers publish dozens of career guides, available online, which provide an overview of practice specialties and related legal employment markets, descriptions of the various types of legal employers, and specific legal recruiting information. The centers also produce a monthly online newsletter and provide sample résumés and cover letters. The staff actively solicits and identifies employment opportunities through an on-campus career fair, targeted mailings, and other outreach activities, as well as develops and maintains an extensive collection of resources for students and alumni to use in their job searches. Respondents to the 2009 class survey reported 88.1 percent employment within the nine months following graduation.

Student Activities

Pace Law School publishes three law reviews, the *Pace Law Review*, the *Pace Environmental Law Review*, and the *Pace International Law Review*. Students also work on the *Journal of Court Innovations*, a joint journal created by Pace Law School and the New York State Judicial Institute, and *GreenLaw*, an online blog published by the Pace Law Center for Environmental Legal Studies. Students compete in interscholastic moot court competitions, host the largest environmental moot court competition in the country (the National Environmental Moot Court Competition), and participate in the Pace-sponsored and directed Willem C. Vis International Commercial Arbitration Moot, the first and largest international commercial arbitration moot court competition of its kind, in Vienna, Austria. The school also sponsors 26 active student organizations, focusing on professional interests, diversity, politics, and social action.

Admission/Visits to Campus

Pace seeks students with demonstrated potential to contribute meaningfully to the diversity of the law school community and legal profession. Full-time students may apply to enter in September or January. The January entry program allows students to complete the program through an accelerated two-and-a-half-year program.

The law school hosts several open house programs which include tours; discussions with faculty, administrators, and students; and information regarding the admission process, financial aid, placement, and life at Pace Law School. For a complete list of our on-campus events, visit our website at www.law.pace.edu.

APPLICANT PROFILE

Pace University School of Law
This grid includes only applicants who earned 120–180 LSAT scores under standard administrations.

LSAT Score	3.75 +		3.50–3.74		3.25–3.49		3.00–3.24		2.75–2.99		2.50–2.74		2.25–2.49		2.00–2.24		Below 2.00		No GPA		Total	
	Apps	Adm	Apps	Adm	Apps	Adm	Apps	Adm	Apps	Adm	Apps	Adm	Apps	Adm	Apps	Adm	Apps	Adm	Apps	Adm	Apps	Adm
175–180	1	1	0	0	0	0	0	0	1	1	0	0	0	0	0	0	0	0	0	0	2	2
170–174	6	6	1	1	3	2	1	1	0	0	0	0	0	0	0	0	0	0	0	0	11	10
165–169	7	7	13	13	13	10	10	8	8	6	6	3	3	0	2	0	0	0	2	0	64	47
160–164	43	35	51	41	67	48	47	32	34	19	15	4	10	2	4	1	0	0	4	2	275	184
155–159	67	55	117	96	148	121	147	103	87	45	42	17	30	4	14	0	2	0	7	6	661	447
150–154	80	62	156	112	219	121	216	70	112	14	59	1	38	0	9	0	4	0	15	3	908	383
145–149	36	8	102	19	130	10	135	1	91	0	55	0	24	0	9	0	2	0	17	0	601	38
140–144	15	0	26	0	48	0	65	0	51	0	29	0	27	0	7	0	0	0	13	0	281	0
135–139	3	0	13	0	14	0	24	0	17	0	19	0	11	0	7	0	3	0	5	0	116	0
130–134	0	0	1	0	2	0	5	0	2	0	11	0	2	0	4	0	0	0	2	0	29	0
125–129	0	0	0	0	0	0	2	0	3	0	4	0	0	0	0	0	0	0	0	0	9	0
120–124	0	0	0	0	0	0	0	0	0	0	0	0	0	0	0	0	0	0	0	0	0	0
Total	258	174	480	282	644	312	652	215	406	85	240	25	145	6	56	1	11	0	65	11	2957	1111

Apps = Number of Applicants
Adm = Number Admitted
Reflects 99% of the total applicant pool; highest LSAT data reported.

UNIVERSITY OF THE PACIFIC, MCGEORGE SCHOOL OF LAW

3200 Fifth Avenue
Sacramento, CA 95817
Phone: 916.739.7105; Fax: 916.739.7301
E-mail: mcgeorge@pacific.edu; Website: www.mcgeorge.edu

ABA
Approved
Since
1969

The Basics

Type of school	Private
Term	Semester
Application deadline	5/1
Application fee	$50
Financial aid deadline	
Can first year start other than fall?	No
Student to faculty ratio	12.7 to 1
# of housing spaces available restricted to law students	167
graduate housing for which law students are eligible	167

Faculty and Administrators

	Total		Men		Women		Minorities	
	Spr	Fall	Spr	Fall	Spr	Fall	Spr	Fall
Full-time	58	60	34	37	24	23	15	16
Other full-time	3	3	2	3	1	0	2	0
Deans, librarians, & others who teach	24	24	10	10	14	14	1	1
Part-time	41	28	27	20	14	8	5	3
Total	126	115	73	70	53	45	23	20

Curriculum

	Full-Time	Part-Time
Typical first-year section size	83	94
Is there typically a "small section" of the first-year class, other than Legal Writing, taught by full-time faculty	Yes	Yes
If yes, typical size offered last year	41	47
# of classroom course titles beyond first-year curriculum	178	
# of upper division courses, excluding seminars, with an enrollment: Under 25	101	
25–49	43	
50–74	14	
75–99	16	
100+	1	
# of seminars	17	
# of seminar positions available	337	
# of seminar positions filled	208	64
# of positions available in simulation courses	908	
# of simulation positions filled	573	257
# of positions available in faculty supervised clinical courses	181	
# of faculty supervised clinical positions filled	112	48
# involved in field placements	209	77
# involved in law journals	95	16
# involved in moot court or trial competitions	32	8
# of credit hours required to graduate	88	

JD Enrollment and Ethnicity

	Men		Women		Full-Time		Part-Time		1st-Year		Total		JD Degs. Awd.
	#	%	#	%	#	%	#	%	#	%	#	%	
All Hispanics	27	5.1	32	6.5	45	6.2	14	4.6	10	2.9	59	5.8	32
Am. Ind./AK Nat.	5	0.9	14	2.8	15	2.1	4	1.3	10	2.9	19	1.9	3
Asian	71	13.4	76	15.4	110	15.2	37	12.3	54	15.7	147	14.3	46
Black/Af. Am.	9	1.7	18	3.6	13	1.8	14	4.6	5	1.5	27	2.6	8
Nat. Hl/Pac. Isl.	0	0.0	0	0.0	0	0.0	0	0.0	0	0.0	0	0.0	0
2 or more races	0	0.0	0	0.0	0	0.0	0	0.0	0	0.0	0	0.0	0
Subtotal (minor.)	112	21.1	140	28.3	183	25.3	69	22.8	79	23.0	252	24.6	89
Nonres. Alien	8	1.5	8	1.6	11	1.5	5	1.7	6	1.7	16	1.6	0
White/Cauc.	411	77.4	347	70.1	530	73.2	228	75.5	258	75.2	758	73.9	219
Unknown	0	0.0	0	0.0	0	0.0	0	0.0	0	0.0	0	0.0	0
Total	531	51.8	495	48.2	724	70.6	302	29.4	343	33.4	1026		308

Transfers

Transfers in	9
Transfers out	28

Tuition and Fees

	Resident	Nonresident
Full-time	$39,989	$39,989
Part-time	$26,603	$26,603
Tuition Guarantee Program		N

Living Expenses

Estimated living expenses for singles

Living on campus	Living off campus	Living at home
$20,694	$20,694	$20,694

UNIVERSITY OF THE PACIFIC, MCGEORGE SCHOOL OF LAW

*ABA
Approved
Since
1969*

GPA and LSAT Scores

	Total	Full-Time	Part-Time
# of apps	3,175	2,878	297
# of offers	1,333	1,249	84
# of matrics	346	298	48
75% GPA	3.55	3.55	3.51
Median GPA	3.38	3.38	3.33
25% GPA	3.07	3.09	2.82
75% LSAT	160	160	159
Median LSAT	158	158	155
25% LSAT	155	155	152

Grants and Scholarships (from prior year)

	Total		Full-Time		Part-Time	
	#	%	#	%	#	%
Total # of students	1,037		660		377	
Total # receiving grants	555	53.5	408	61.8	147	39.0
Less than 1/2 tuition	502	48.4	368	55.8	134	35.5
Half to full tuition	46	4.4	34	5.2	12	3.2
Full tuition	7	0.7	6	0.9	1	0.3
More than full tuition	0	0.0	0	0.0	0	0.0
Median grant amount			$11,250		$5,900	

Informational and Library Resources

Total amount spent on library materials	$1,453,747
Study seating capacity inside the library	94
# of full-time equivalent professional librarians	7
Hours per week library is open	108
# of open, wired connections available to students	271
# of networked computers available for use by students	59
Has wireless network?	Y
Requires computer?	N

JD Attrition (from prior year)

	Academic	Other	Total	
	#	#	#	%
1st year	5	7	12	3.6
2nd year	2	33	35	12.0
3rd year	1	4	5	1.6
4th year	0	0	0	0.0

Employment (9 months after graduation)

	Total	Percentage
Employment status known	253	98.8
Employment status unknown	3	1.2
Employed	225	88.9
Pursuing graduate degrees	6	2.4
Unemployed (seeking, not seeking, or studying for the bar)	5	2.0
Type of Employment		
# employed in law firms	105	46.7
# employed in business and industry	24	10.7
# employed in government	46	20.4
# employed in public interest	25	11.1
# employed as judicial clerks	8	3.6
# employed in academia	5	2.2
Geographic Location		
# employed in state	184	81.8
# employed outside the US	1	0.4
# of states where employed	11	

Bar Passage Rates

First-time takers	256	Reporting %	93.36
Average school %	77.41	Average state %	73.19
Average pass difference	4.22		

Jurisdiction	Takers	Passers	Pass %	State %	Diff %
California	239	185	77.41	73.19	4.22

UNIVERSITY OF THE PACIFIC, MCGEORGE SCHOOL OF LAW

3200 Fifth Avenue
Sacramento, CA 95817
Phone: 916.739.7105; Fax: 916.739.7301
E-mail: mcgeorge@pacific.edu; Website: www.mcgeorge.edu

Overview

The University of the Pacific, McGeorge School of Law is in Sacramento, California, capital of the nation's most populous state and one of the world's leading economies. The school is a member of the AALS, is accredited by the ABA, and has a chapter of the Order of the Coif.

Day- and evening-division programs provide the flexibility to earn a JD degree in three, four, or five years of study. More than 1,000 students pursue a JD, LLM, or JSD on Pacific McGeorge's unique 13-acre, law-school-only campus. The school's reputation for educating well-prepared, practice-ready lawyers grows from the vitality of students and faculty working together. The diversity of the student body is reflected in the 150 or more colleges and universities that students attended as undergraduates, the 50 or more major fields, the range in years from age 20 to over 60, and the gender and ethnic diversity represented annually by the growing number of students from a wide range of ethnic and cultural heritages.

Library and Physical Facilities

Pacific McGeorge's students study on a campus designed exclusively for legal education that includes class and seminar rooms, a student center, a technologically equipped trial courtroom; a lecture hall; a clinical legal education center; a law library and computer center; administrative, faculty, and student services offices; recreational facilities; and student apartments.

The Gordon D. Schaber Law Library is a comprehensive legal research facility of over 500,000 volumes. The library includes a new state-of-the-art student study area, computer lab, group study rooms, and wireless Internet capabilities. Pacific McGeorge librarians are experts in legal research methodology and assist students in using the library's electronic and traditional resources.

Curriculum

Pacific McGeorge offers more than 100 advanced elective course offerings, ranging from comprehensive courses in traditional areas such as business, constitutional law, criminal justice, and family and juvenile law, to a wide variety of courses in specialty areas such as environmental (both US and international), entertainment, labor, intellectual property, mass media, banking, and elder law. Certificate and concentration curricula are offered for those with specific career interests.

Clinical Experience: Pacific McGeorge believes that clinical education—working in a practice setting while guided by a faculty mentor—is a key part of the law school experience. On-campus clinics include Community Legal Services, Business and Community Development, Administrative Adjudication, Parole Representation, Victim's Rights, Civil Practice, Bankruptcy, Immigration, and Legislative Process. Off campus, the internship program makes available more than 125 placements.

Certificate Programs

- **Advocacy:** Advocacy is an integral part of the law, including representing clients in civil and criminal litigation, at administrative hearings, or applying alternative dispute-resolution techniques to negotiate business matters or to avoid litigation. The Advocacy certificate especially prepares those interested in pursuing courtroom advocacy. Additionally, a one-year LLM in Experiential Law Teaching empowers international and domestic lawyers and law professors to implement advocacy principles in their practices and classrooms.
- **International Legal Studies:** Law and accounting firms, government agencies, and corporations require lawyers savvy in international law. The International Legal Studies curriculum balances public international law and private international law. Study-abroad opportunities include a Summer Institute in Salzburg, Austria, as well as opportunities to pursue an LLM in Transnational Business Practice, or an LLM or JSD in International Water Resources Law.
- **Public Law & Policy:** The Public Law & Policy certificate prepares students for private or public service careers in government. Students benefit from hands-on experience and develop networking contacts with governmental entities. Graduates practice as consultants, lobbyists, in-house counsel, or in staff and policy positions with legislative branches, executive departments, or administrative agencies. A one- or two-year LLM program in Public Law & Policy is also available.

Concentrations

- **Business Law:** The demands and complexities of a global economy require a strong basis in business law. The Business Law concentration prepares students to pursue general business law practice or specialized law practice in entertainment law, employment law, banking law, real estate law, and more.
- **Criminal Justice:** The Criminal Justice concentration offers wide-ranging electives, including sentencing and postconviction remedies, white-collar crime, capital punishment, criminal pretrial litigation, evidence courses, juvenile law, family violence, and problems in criminal justice. Internship and specialization opportunities provide hands-on training.
- **Environmental Law:** Local, national, and international laws govern myriad aspects of environmental law and vary from an extremely specific to a very broad focus. The Environmental Law concentration provides the foundation necessary to pursue careers working in environmental issues or environmental law.
- **Intellectual Property:** The diverse Intellectual Property concentration prepares graduates to practice in areas such as the entertainment industry; music and theater law; intellectual property litigation; sports; trademark and domain-name law; patent and biotechnology law; and computer and Internet law.
- **Tax:** The Tax concentration offers a specialized curriculum and a variety of elective tax courses to prepare graduates to work as tax, business, or estate planning specialists.

Student Activities

Over 40 professional, social, and academic student organizations at Pacific McGeorge represent the breadth of interests and diversity of the student community. Student staffs manage, edit, and write for the *McGeorge Law Review* and the *Pacific McGeorge Global Business and Development Law Journal*. Pacific McGeorge competition teams compete with notable success in a wide range of trial, appellate, counseling, and dispute-resolution competitions on the regional and national levels, as well as at the Willem C. Vis International Commercial Arbitration Moot Competition in Vienna, Austria.

Admission and Financial Aid

Admission is competitive. Prelegal education includes at least a bachelor's degree or senior standing from an accredited college or university. An applicant's undergraduate record and LSAT results are important factors in the decision process. When there are multiple LSAT scores, the highest may be accorded significant weight. Other factors considered are grade patterns or trends, employment and career accomplishments, graduate work, and extracurricular or community activities. Ethnic, cultural, and experiential backgrounds that contribute to student-body diversity are valued. Strong merit- and need-based financial aid programs provide scholarship awards and grants to entering and advanced students. A knowledgeable financial aid staff provides counseling to assist students in minimizing student loan indebtedness.

Housing

Pacific McGeorge has 150 on-campus apartments, furnished and unfurnished, including one- and two-bedroom units, studios, and townhouses. Early application is advised. The school's full-time housing coordinator also assists in locating off-campus accommodations that are readily available in Sacramento.

Career Services

The Pacific McGeorge Career Development Office (CDO) provides comprehensive career search assistance for permanent, part-time, and summer employment. The CDO staff is available to help students identify their interests, introduce them to the vast array of career development and employment opportunity resources, and assist with career decision making. The CDO focuses on career counseling, individualized review and critique of résumés and cover letters, and job search strategy development.

Pacific McGeorge faculty and alumni play a major role in our programs, sharing their experience and offering advice to students seeking career opportunities in their fields of expertise. Alumni participate in a Day in the Life Speakers Series, the Alumni Mentor Program, and mock interviews. In addition, the CDO hosts employer on-campus interviews for students and maintains up-to-date listings of specific employment opportunities, as well as an extensive library of resource materials.

APPLICANT PROFILE

University of the Pacific, McGeorge School of Law
This grid includes only applicants who earned 120–180 LSAT scores under standard administrations.

LSAT Score	3.75 +		3.50–3.74		3.25–3.49		3.00–3.24		2.75–2.99		2.50–2.74		2.25–2.49		2.00–2.24		Below 2.00		No GPA		Total	
	Apps	Adm	Apps	Adm	Apps	Adm	Apps	Adm	Apps	Adm	Apps	Adm	Apps	Adm	Apps	Adm	Apps	Adm	Apps	Adm	Apps	Adm
175–180	0	0	0	0	0	0	2	2	1	0	0	0	0	0	0	0	0	0	0	0	3	2
170–174	5	5	3	3	8	6	6	5	3	1	4	3	1	1	1	1	0	0	0	0	31	25
165–169	15	15	10	9	17	17	20	16	22	16	18	10	2	2	2	1	1	0	0	0	107	86
160–164	43	43	82	80	109	105	108	89	64	54	55	35	9	6	5	0	2	0	3	3	480	415
155–159	78	75	169	161	255	187	231	91	130	47	67	19	32	6	9	0	3	0	11	10	985	596
150–154	56	37	158	101	195	46	227	9	107	0	63	1	29	0	16	0	2	0	11	1	864	195
145–149	19	3	46	1	76	0	98	0	69	0	44	0	18	0	9	0	3	0	6	0	388	4
140–144	6	0	16	1	34	0	38	0	38	0	29	0	20	0	10	0	1	0	6	0	198	1
135–139	2	0	3	0	7	0	18	0	13	0	11	0	7	0	4	0	3	0	2	0	70	0
130–134	0	0	1	0	2	0	2	0	5	0	4	0	3	0	2	0	0	0	3	0	22	0
125–129	0	0	1	0	0	0	0	0	0	0	1	0	2	0	1	0	1	0	0	0	6	0
120–124	0	0	0	0	0	0	0	0	0	0	0	0	0	0	0	0	0	0	0	0	0	0
Total	224	178	489	356	703	361	750	212	452	118	296	68	123	15	59	2	16	0	42	14	3154	1324

Apps = Number of Applicants
Adm = Number Admitted
Reflects 99% of the total applicant pool; highest LSAT data reported.

PENN STATE UNIVERSITY, THE DICKINSON SCHOOL OF LAW

Lewis Katz Building, University Park, PA 16802-1017; Phone: 814.867.1251; Fax: 814.867.0405
333 West South Street, Carlisle, PA 17013-2899; Phone: 717.240.5207; Fax: 717.241.3503
E-mail: admissions@law.psu.edu; Website: www.law.psu.edu; Phone: 800.840.1122

ABA Approved Since 1931

The Basics

Type of school	Public
Term	Semester
Application deadline	3/31
Application fee	$60
Financial aid deadline	3/1
Can first year start other than fall?	No
Student to faculty ratio	9.4 to 1
# of housing spaces available restricted to law students	10
graduate housing for which law students are eligible	424

Faculty and Administrators

	Total		Men		Women		Minorities	
	Spr	Fall	Spr	Fall	Spr	Fall	Spr	Fall
Full-time	52	54	30	30	22	24	9	8
Other full-time	4	3	4	3	0	0	2	1
Deans, librarians, & others who teach	16	13	8	7	8	6	1	1
Part-time	20	19	12	11	8	8	1	2
Total	92	89	54	51	38	38	13	12

Curriculum

	Full-Time	Part-Time
Typical first-year section size	41	0
Is there typically a "small section" of the first-year class, other than Legal Writing, taught by full-time faculty	No	No
If yes, typical size offered last year		
# of classroom course titles beyond first-year curriculum	106	
# of upper division courses, excluding seminars, with an enrollment: Under 25	148	
25–49	20	
50–74	13	
75–99	1	
100+	0	
# of seminars	26	
# of seminar positions available	520	
# of seminar positions filled	330	0
# of positions available in simulation courses	463	
# of simulation positions filled	349	0
# of positions available in faculty supervised clinical courses	134	
# of faculty supervised clinical positions filled	97	0
# involved in field placements	85	0
# involved in law journals	163	0
# involved in moot court or trial competitions	37	0
# of credit hours required to graduate	88	

JD Enrollment and Ethnicity

	Men		Women		Full-Time		Part-Time		1st-Year		Total		JD Degs. Awd.
	#	%	#	%	#	%	#	%	#	%	#	%	
All Hispanics	10	2.8	9	3.4	19	3.1	0	0.0	1	0.4	19	3.1	17
Am. Ind./AK Nat.	0	0.0	0	0.0	0	0.0	0	0.0	0	0.0	0	0.0	0
Asian	12	3.4	22	8.4	34	5.5	0	0.0	15	6.6	34	5.5	12
Black/Af. Am.	11	3.1	14	5.3	25	4.1	0	0.0	12	5.3	25	4.0	18
Nat. Hi/Pac. Isl.	0	0.0	0	0.0	0	0.0	0	0.0	0	0.0	0	0.0	0
2 or more races	5	1.4	5	1.9	10	1.6	0	0.0	3	1.3	10	1.6	0
Subtotal (minor.)	38	10.7	50	19.1	88	14.3	0	0.0	31	13.6	88	14.2	49
Nonres. Alien	6	1.7	6	2.3	12	1.9	0	0.0	4	1.8	12	1.9	0
White/Cauc.	295	82.9	194	74.0	488	79.1	1	100.0	184	80.7	489	79.1	125
Unknown	17	4.8	12	4.6	29	4.7	0	0.0	9	3.9	29	4.7	21
Total	356	57.6	262	42.4	617	99.8	1	0.2	228	36.9	618		201

Transfers

Transfers in	8
Transfers out	8

Tuition and Fees

	Resident	Nonresident
Full-time	$36,816	$36,816
Part-time		
Tuition Guarantee Program	N	

Living Expenses

Estimated living expenses for singles

Living on campus	Living off campus	Living at home
$22,300	$22,300	$22,300

PENN STATE UNIVERSITY, THE DICKINSON SCHOOL OF LAW

ABA
Approved
Since
1931

GPA and LSAT Scores

	Total	Full-Time	Part-Time
# of apps	5,326	5,326	0
# of offers	1,551	1,551	0
# of matrics	228	228	0
75% GPA	3.80	3.80	0.00
Median GPA	3.60	3.60	0.00
25% GPA	3.40	3.40	0.00
75% LSAT	161	161	0
Median LSAT	159	159	0
25% LSAT	157	157	0

Grants and Scholarships (from prior year)

	Total #	Total %	Full-Time #	Full-Time %	Part-Time #	Part-Time %
Total # of students	597		586		11	
Total # receiving grants	318	53.3	318	54.3	0	0.0
Less than 1/2 tuition	263	44.1	263	44.9	0	0.0
Half to full tuition	54	9.0	54	9.2	0	0.0
Full tuition	1	0.2	1	0.2	0	0.0
More than full tuition	0	0.0	0	0.0	0	0.0
Median grant amount			$8,000		$0	

Informational and Library Resources

Total amount spent on library materials	$1,622,117
Study seating capacity inside the library	395
# of full-time equivalent professional librarians	7
Hours per week library is open	96
# of open, wired connections available to students	0
# of networked computers available for use by students	123
Has wireless network?	Y
Requires computer?	N

JD Attrition (from prior year)

	Academic #	Other #	Total #	Total %
1st year	11	16	27	13.2
2nd year	2	3	5	2.7
3rd year	0	0	0	0.0
4th year	0	0	0	0.0

Employment (9 months after graduation)

	Total	Percentage
Employment status known	193	96.0
Employment status unknown	8	4.0
Employed	168	87.0
Pursuing graduate degrees	10	5.2
Unemployed (seeking, not seeking, or studying for the bar)	7	3.6
Type of Employment		
# employed in law firms	67	39.9
# employed in business and industry	24	14.3
# employed in government	32	19.0
# employed in public interest	2	1.2
# employed as judicial clerks	29	17.3
# employed in academia	6	3.6
Geographic Location		
# employed in state	70	41.7
# employed outside the US	3	1.8
# of states where employed	23	

Bar Passage Rates

First-time takers	218	Reporting %	88.53
Average school %	82.38	Average state %	85.48

Average pass difference −3.10

Jurisdiction	Takers	Passers	Pass %	State %	Diff %
Pennsylvania	107	95	88.78	85.69	3.10
New York	47	34	72.34	86.51	−14.17
New Jersey	39	30	76.92	83.64	−6.72

PENN STATE UNIVERSITY, THE DICKINSON SCHOOL OF LAW

Lewis Katz Building, University Park, PA 16802-1017; Phone: 814.867.1251; Fax: 814.867.0405
333 West South Street, Carlisle, PA 17013-2899; Phone: 717.240.5207; Fax: 717.241.3503
E-mail: admissions@law.psu.edu; Website: www.law.psu.edu; Phone: 800.840.1122

Introduction

Founded in 1834, Penn State Law is the oldest law school in Pennsylvania and the fifth oldest in the nation. The law school embraces the university's mission to improve the lives of the people of Pennsylvania, the nation, and the world through legal teaching, scholarship, and service.

Our law school is an engaged, diverse, and multidisciplinary intellectual community that challenges students to research, think, and act like lawyers—and to ascend to new heights of academic excellence. Through an intensive and comprehensive program of study that includes both classroom-based and experiential learning, our students are prepared to practice law at the highest level in an increasingly global world. As part of a world-class research university, Penn State Law students have access to extensive academic and programmatic resources to enhance their learning experience. Courses are offered at Penn State's University Park campus in State College, Pennsylvania, and at the law school's traditional home in Carlisle, Pennsylvania.

Faculty

Penn State's faculty includes one of the nation's leading scholars of corporate mergers and acquisitions, the world's preeminent expert on Russian law, leading scholars of commercial arbitration, renowned scholars of antitrust and law and economics, former law clerks to United States Supreme Court Justices, a leading scholar of international banking and finance, the first legal counsel to the African Union, the legal counsel to the Greek Presidency of the European Union, and other active and influential teachers and scholars in a wide range of substantive areas.

Our faculty scholars value academic rigor and are committed to sharing their knowledge, engaging students, and sustaining an intense and comprehensive legal program. They encourage students to participate in vigorous in-class discussion and provide abundant opportunities for thoughtful discourse and research outside of the classroom.

Curriculum

Our curriculum is designed to produce leaders and lawyers with high professional and ethical standards and the ability to navigate legal, policy, and social developments in all areas of human endeavor. After completing required first-year coursework, students can explore professional and intellectual interests by choosing elective courses in a variety of areas, including criminal law, trial advocacy, government and politics, and science and intellectual property. Experiential learning programs, moot court teams, concentrated research opportunities, and law journals enhance the curriculum by providing opportunities for students to distinguish themselves and explore their strengths.

Academic Programs and Activities

Experiential Learning: The law school's curriculum includes a wide range of experiential learning opportunities, including semester-long government agency externships in Washington, DC, and clinics that focus on child advocacy,

immigrants' rights, appellate civil rights litigation, rural economic development, disability law, elder and consumer protection law, and family law. Clinical professors include the former deputy director of the Lawyers' Committee for Civil Rights Under Law and the former deputy director of the National Immigration Forum.

Centers: Students can pursue focused scholarship through academic centers that include the Center for the Study of Mergers and Acquisitions; Institute for Sports Law, Policy, and Research; Institute of Arbitration Law and Practice; Center for Government Law and Public Policy Studies; Center on Children and the Law; and Agricultural Law Resource and Reference Center.

Joint Degrees: Students can pursue joint-degree programs and other forms of multidisciplinary study with other graduate departments within the university, including the School of International Affairs, Smeal College of Business, College of Education, and College of Agricultural Sciences.

Public Interest: In addition to our clinics, students can explore service-oriented careers through field placements with legal services, public defenders, and nonprofit public interest offices. Our Miller Center for Public Interest Advocacy works with a network of attorneys to enable students to participate in pro bono cases.

International Programs

As citizens of a global society, we provide a rich and evocative international curriculum—complete with significant opportunities for immersion in international cultures and legal systems. Our relationship with Penn State's School of International Affairs has enriched the intellectual life of our law school and particularly our curriculum, which offers ever expanding opportunities for international interactions and cross-border, interdisciplinary studies. Penn State law students may take electives from the School of International Affairs and learn from a faculty of former diplomats, national leaders, and government analysts, as well as scholars of international economics, agricultural development, and business.

Many of our law faculty have exceptional depth in international issues, enabling the law school to offer advanced coursework in comparative and international commercial law, constitutional law, corporate law, and humanitarian law, among other areas. Additionally, we have established student exchange programs with the University of Cape Town in South Africa, the University of Maastricht Faculty of Law in the Netherlands, and Yeditepe University in Turkey.

The law school also offers one of the oldest and most prestigious master of laws programs for foreign-trained lawyers, whose presence at the law school enriches the diversity of our educational experience.

Physical Facilities, Technology, and Library

The university has invested more than $120 million in new and renovated facilities for the law school in Carlisle and University Park. Our buildings reflect the serious academic nature of the study of law, with state-of-the-art libraries, classrooms, and gathering spaces that enhance opportunities for learning, spontaneous discussion, and passionate debate.

Our facilities are reciprocally designed and equipped with sophisticated and pervasive audiovisual technologies that provide our students with appropriate exposure to technology, allow for the real-time delivery of classes and programs between Carlisle and University Park, and enable us to conduct courses and other collaborative projects with schools and institutions worldwide. In addition to modern electronic courtrooms, our facilities feature class and seminar rooms equipped with integrated high-definition video, personal video systems to complement the teaching experience, and advanced recording technologies. Consistent with Penn State's commitment to sustainability and "green" design, the law school buildings are also designed to meet Leadership in Energy and Environmental Design (LEED) certification requirements and to encourage efficient energy use.

With holdings of more than a half-million volumes and access to a wealth of electronic resources, the Penn State Law Library fully supports the research and study activities of students, faculty, and members of the bar. Additionally, legal and interdisciplinary research is greatly enhanced through access to the vast print and electronic collections held by other university libraries.

Our building initiatives, combined with an additional several million dollars annually for faculty and program development, represent one of the largest investments ever made in an American law school.

Student Activities

Law students may pursue activities in legal scholarship, trial advocacy, and public service to refine their legal skills and develop their leadership styles. Law students edit and publish four journals: the *Penn State Law Review*, the *Penn State Environmental Law Review*, the *Penn State International Law Review*, and the *Yearbook on Arbitration and Mediation*. Second- and third-year students can also pursue valuable trial experience by engaging in moot court team competitions at both the regional and national levels. Our vibrant student body supports more than 40 active student groups that organize social events, serve the underrepresented, host speakers, and establish professional networks. Law students are also welcome to participate in the hundreds of organizations, events, and activities available at Penn State's flagship University Park campus.

Career Services

Dedicated to keeping in touch with a profession that is both fast-paced and nuanced, our Career Services Office offers a dynamic menu of programs and high-quality individual counseling sessions and programming to assist students in identifying and achieving their career goals. Our career services professionals maintain contact with employers across the country, resulting in two formal, on-campus interview programs and the posting of more than 1,500 positions annually. Students can participate in more than 20 job fairs, including one in the District of Columbia, two exclusively devoted to public interest, several minority job fairs, and one exclusively devoted to patent law.

Admission and Financial Aid

You can apply online at www.law.psu.edu. Admitted students may choose to attend first-year classes in University Park or Carlisle, Pennsylvania.

The Financial Aid Office works with accepted students to obtain the funding necessary to finance their education. All admitted students are considered for scholarship opportunities.

APPLICANT PROFILE

Penn State University, The Dickinson School of Law
This grid includes only applicants who earned 120–180 LSAT scores under standard administrations.

LSAT Score	GPA															
	3.75 +		3.50–3.74		3.25–3.49		3.00–3.24		2.75–2.99		2.50–2.74		Below 2.50		No GPA		Total	
	Apps	Adm	Apps	Adm	Apps	Adm	Apps	Adm	Apps	Adm	Apps	Adm	Apps	Adm	Apps	Adm	Apps	Adm
170–180	10	8	12	10	9	9	3	3	9	6	3	1	6	1	0	0	52	38
165–169	49	46	54	52	35	33	50	35	36	19	23	4	18	2	4	4	269	195
160–164	189	184	244	232	282	245	211	105	107	11	62	8	37	3	21	10	1153	798
155–159	215	120	400	175	430	90	312	20	168	7	91	2	64	1	42	5	1722	420
150–154	153	13	295	35	310	23	242	13	125	1	78	0	54	0	26	0	1283	85
145–149	36	0	90	0	95	0	109	0	66	0	41	0	29	0	21	0	487	0
140–144	12	0	26	0	53	0	56	0	49	0	17	0	17	0	7	0	237	0
Below 140	4	0	4	0	7	0	14	0	19	0	24	0	14	0	5	0	91	0
Total	668	371	1125	504	1221	400	997	176	579	44	339	15	239	7	126	19	5294	1536

Apps = Number of Applicants
Adm = Number Admitted
Reflects 99% of the total applicant pool; highest LSAT data reported.

UNIVERSITY OF PENNSYLVANIA LAW SCHOOL

3400 Chestnut Street
Philadelphia, PA 19104-6204
Phone: 215.898.7400; Fax: 215.898.9606
E-mail: admissions@law.upenn.edu; Website: www.law.upenn.edu

The Basics

Type of school	Private
Term	Semester
Application deadline	2/15
Application fee	$80
Financial aid deadline	3/1
Can first year start other than fall?	No
Student to faculty ratio	10.2 to 1
# of housing spaces available restricted to law students	
graduate housing for which law students are eligible	999

Faculty and Administrators

	Total		Men		Women		Minorities	
	Spr	Fall	Spr	Fall	Spr	Fall	Spr	Fall
Full-time	62	67	48	51	14	16	12	10
Other full-time	10	8	1	0	9	8	1	2
Deans, librarians, & others who teach	4	1	3	1	1	0	0	0
Part-time	48	40	41	29	7	11	6	4
Total	124	116	93	81	31	35	19	16

Curriculum

	Full-Time	Part-Time
Typical first-year section size	85	0
Is there typically a "small section" of the first-year class, other than Legal Writing, taught by full-time faculty	Yes	No
If yes, typical size offered last year	42	
# of classroom course titles beyond first-year curriculum	161	

# of upper division courses, excluding seminars, with an enrollment:		
	Under 25	79
	25–49	39
	50–74	16
	75–99	11
	100+	4

# of seminars	59	
# of seminar positions available	826	
# of seminar positions filled	725	0
# of positions available in simulation courses	576	
# of simulation positions filled	526	0
# of positions available in faculty supervised clinical courses	149	
# of faculty supervised clinical positions filled	143	0
# involved in field placements	29	0
# involved in law journals	386	0
# involved in moot court or trial competitions	145	0
# of credit hours required to graduate	89	

JD Enrollment and Ethnicity

	Men		Women		Full-Time		Part-Time		1st-Year		Total		JD Degs. Awd.
	#	%	#	%	#	%	#	%	#	%	#	%	
All Hispanics	21	5.0	16	4.2	37	4.6	0	0.0	12	4.8	37	4.6	25
Am. Ind./AK Nat.	0	0.0	0	0.0	0	0.0	0	0.0	0	0.0	0	0.0	1
Asian	50	11.9	63	16.5	113	14.1	0	0.0	34	13.7	113	14.1	37
Black/Af. Am.	28	6.7	32	8.4	60	7.5	0	0.0	19	7.6	60	7.5	18
Nat. HI/Pac. Isl.	0	0.0	0	0.0	0	0.0	0	0.0	0	0.0	0	0.0	0
2 or more races	12	2.9	21	5.5	33	4.1	0	0.0	8	3.2	33	4.1	0
Subtotal (minor.)	111	26.4	132	34.6	243	30.3	0	0.0	73	29.3	243	30.3	81
Nonres. Alien	15	3.6	10	2.6	25	3.1	0	0.0	9	3.6	25	3.1	0
White/Cauc.	282	67.0	227	59.4	508	63.3	0	0.0	141	56.6	508	63.4	179
Unknown	13	3.1	13	3.4	26	3.2	0	0.0	26	10.4	26	3.2	12
Total	421	52.4	382	47.6	802	99.9	0	0.0	249	31.0	802		276

Transfers

Transfers in	25
Transfers out	7

Tuition and Fees

	Resident	Nonresident
Full-time	$48,362	$48,362

Part-time		
Tuition Guarantee Program		N

Living Expenses

Estimated living expenses for singles

Living on campus	Living off campus	Living at home
$19,788	$19,788	$13,132

UNIVERSITY OF PENNSYLVANIA LAW SCHOOL

ABA
Approved
Since
1923

GPA and LSAT Scores

	Total	Full-Time	Part-Time
# of apps	6,003	6,003	0
# of offers	866	866	0
# of matrics	250	250	0
75% GPA	3.90	3.90	0.00
Median GPA	3.85	3.85	0.00
25% GPA	3.54	3.54	0.00
75% LSAT	171	171	0
Median LSAT	170	170	0
25% LSAT	166	166	0

Grants and Scholarships (from prior year)

	Total		Full-Time		Part-Time	
	#	%	#	%	#	%
Total # of students	790		790		0	
Total # receiving grants	338	42.7	338	42.8	0	0.0
Less than 1/2 tuition	274	34.6	274	34.7	0	0.0
Half to full tuition	43	5.4	43	5.4	0	0.0
Full tuition	20	2.5	20	2.5	0	0.0
More than full tuition	1	0.1	1	0.1	0	0.0
Median grant amount			$14,000		$0	

Informational and Library Resources

Total amount spent on library materials	$1,451,722
Study seating capacity inside the library	524
# of full-time equivalent professional librarians	16
Hours per week library is open	115
# of open, wired connections available to students	26
# of networked computers available for use by students	140
Has wireless network?	Y
Requires computer?	N

JD Attrition (from prior year)

	Academic	Other	Total	
	#	#	#	%
1st year	0	0	0	0.0
2nd year	0	7	7	2.6
3rd year	0	0	0	0.0
4th year	0	0	0	0.0

Employment (9 months after graduation)

	Total	Percentage
Employment status known	258	100.0
Employment status unknown	0	0.0
Employed	252	97.7
Pursuing graduate degrees	4	1.6
Unemployed (seeking, not seeking, or studying for the bar)	2	0.8
Type of Employment		
# employed in law firms	186	73.8
# employed in business and industry	10	4.0
# employed in government	10	4.0
# employed in public interest	6	2.4
# employed as judicial clerks	38	15.1
# employed in academia	2	0.8
Geographic Location		
# employed in state	41	16.3
# employed outside the US	4	1.6
# of states where employed	24	

Bar Passage Rates

First-time takers	255	Reporting %	73.33
Average school %	95.72	Average state %	86.12
Average pass difference	9.60		

Jurisdiction	Takers	Passers	Pass %	State %	Diff %
New York	124	119	95.97	86.51	9.46
Pennsylvania	53	51	96.23	85.69	10.54
New Jersey	10	9	90.00	83.64	6.36

UNIVERSITY OF PENNSYLVANIA LAW SCHOOL

3400 Chestnut Street
Philadelphia, PA 19104-6204
Phone: 215.898.7400; Fax: 215.898.9606
E-mail: admissions@law.upenn.edu; Website: www.law.upenn.edu

Introduction

The hallmarks of the Penn Law experience are an extraordinary cross-disciplinary legal education and a vibrant and collegial community. Penn Law is one of the nation's leading law schools and takes advantage of its position at the University of Pennsylvania, one of the world's preeminent research universities. Penn Law faculty collaborate with world-renowned scholars throughout the University, and students enrich their legal education with study in other disciplines via courses, certificate programs (including programs at the Wharton School), and formal joint-degree programs.

Penn Law has a well-deserved reputation as a school where collegiality trumps competitiveness. We pride ourselves on the supportive environment we provide for students as they engage in the rigors of legal study. Students develop close relationships with their faculty and colleagues.

Minutes from downtown Philadelphia, Penn Law enjoys a university campus neighborhood and close proximity to one of the nation's most lively urban areas, providing an exciting, invigorating, and affordable experience.

Faculty

Penn Law faculty are unparalleled in the depth and breadth of their intellectual interests, the quality of their scholarship, and their teaching excellence. More than 70 percent hold advanced degrees in addition to their JDs, and close to 50 percent hold secondary appointments or have an affiliation with other schools throughout the university.

The Law School has a low student-to-faculty ratio that fosters the development of close personal and professional relationships. Faculty employ an open-door policy and encourage students to join in their research endeavors. It has become a Penn Law tradition for professors to host dinner parties at their homes for first-year students and to invite students to small group lunches at neighborhood restaurants.

Libraries

Biddle Law Library, one of the world's premier law libraries, overlooks the Penn Law courtyard. It is a modern complex with expansive areas encompassing rooms for study groups, computer labs, and places for quiet study. Librarians teach legal research courses and work closely with students and faculty in identifying and accessing the legal and interdisciplinary materials that support their scholarship.

Curriculum

Penn Law's first-year curriculum includes foundational courses plus two electives. Students receive individualized legal writing and research instruction in small group courses. In the upper years, students choose from electives that range from standards, such as corporations and evidence, to introductory courses in specialized areas of the law, to seminars in emerging fields. Students may supplement their legal education with up to four courses at Penn's other esteemed graduate and professional schools as part of their JD degree.

Penn Law offers students a wide choice of clinical courses in which to develop their applied-lawyering skills under intensive faculty supervision. Students also enjoy participating in Penn's ABA award-winning mandatory pro bono program, which allows them to gain practical experience while working on behalf of underserved populations.

Penn Law's Center on Professionalism provides a unique program for students to develop professional skills to complement their classroom learning. The Center gives students insight into their professional foundations and expands their knowledge of the skills necessary for leadership in the profession.

In addition to the JD, Penn Law offers the Master of Laws (LLM), Master of Comparative Law (LLCM), and Doctor of Juridical Science (SJD).

Special Programs

Penn Law's cross-disciplinary program is unrivaled among the leading law schools. Law students may take classes and earn certificates or joint degrees throughout the university.

Penn's three-year JD/MBA (Wharton) is the country's first fully integrated three-year program offered on one campus by elite law and business schools. Additional three-year interdisciplinary degrees include the JD/MSEd, JD/MES (Environmental), JD/MPA, JD/MA (International), JD/MBE (Bioethics), MA/MS (Criminology), JD/MSW (with a BSW), JD/LLM (Hong Kong University), and JD/MS (Social Policy). Other programs include the JD/MCP, JD/MPH, JD/AM (Islamic Studies), JD/MA (Global Business Law), JD/PhD (American Legal History, Philosophy), JD/MD, JD/MS (Historic Preservation), JD/MA (Philosophy), and JD/EdD.

Students can also earn certificates in programs such as Business and Public Policy, Environmental Policy, Environmental Science, Cross-Sector Innovation, Gender and Sexuality Studies, International Business and Law (ESADE), East Asian Studies, Middle East and Islamic Studies, Nonprofit Management, and other ad hoc programs.

Penn Law's international and comparative law program offers formal study abroad in Tokyo, Hamburg, Beijing, Tel Aviv, Barcelona, Paris, and Hong Kong; a Transnational Clinic; numerous courses, including an extensive international research seminar with field research; and the Penn Law Global Initiative, which offers summer-abroad opportunities throughout the world.

Student Body

Students come from all over the country and from more than 200 undergraduate institutions, creating one of the nation's most diverse student bodies. About 11 percent hold advanced degrees and, on average, 68 percent have taken one or more years of graduate studies before enrolling in law school. Over one-third of the student body is composed of students of color. The diversity of the community creates a dynamic and engaging classroom environment and enriches every aspect of the school.

Student Activities

Over 90 student groups provide myriad opportunities for students to work and socialize together. Activities cover a wide spectrum of academic interest areas, identity groups, political affiliations, sports, journals, moot court and mock trial programs, and service organizations.

The *University of Pennsylvania Law Review* is the nation's oldest law review journal and among its most distinguished. Today, Penn Law's tradition of exceptional journal scholarship also includes the *Journal of Constitutional Law*, *Journal of International Law*, *Journal of Business Law*, and *Journal of Law and Social Change*, as well as the student-published *East Asia Law Review*.

Penn Law's Moot Court program is nationally recognized and supported by faculty who appreciate its immense value to participants. Our Mock Trial Team travels for competitions throughout the country and invites trial professionals to lecture on trial advocacy.

Admission

The demand for a Penn Law legal education has risen dramatically in recent years. In the 2009–2010 admission cycle, over 6,000 applicants sought admission for the JD program. Fourteen percent of applicants were accepted, with a median LSAT score in the 97th percentile.

The Law School evaluates each application holistically. While academic excellence is of primary importance, we take all factors in each application into consideration and do not apply numeric cutoffs for LSAT or GPA. Instead, each individual file is read by two members of the Admissions Committee. In addition to an applicant's academic history, the committee considers letters of recommendation, a personal statement, a supplemental essay, and a résumé to develop a full picture of each applicant.

We begin processing applications on October 1. Applications received by December 1, and completed by December 15, will be considered for our early decision (binding) program; these applicants receive a decision by the end of December. The regular admission deadline is February 15. Our program is limited to fall semester, full-time students.

Current first-year JD students enrolled in a full-time program who have achieved excellent records at other law schools may apply as transfer students after completion of their first year only; we do not accept mid-semester or second-year transfer students. All applicants must apply by July 1. Transfer decisions are made on a rolling basis, beginning in mid-June.

Housing

Penn Law is located in a city that is both vibrant and affordable. Students select from a wide range of living arrangements on campus or in private housing.

Expenses and Financial Aid

The Law School maintains a substantial program of need-based grant and loan aid, with approximately 80 percent of the student body receiving financial assistance.

Penn Law extends merit-based scholarships to a select group of applicants. Every applicant admitted to the Law School is automatically considered for merit-based aid.

Penn Law nominates students with a demonstrated previous involvement in public service and a commitment to public sector employment following graduation for the Toll Public Interest Scholarship. We also have a strong loan forgiveness program to assist graduates who choose public sector work.

Career Services

The Career Planning and Professionalism Office has a successful record of assisting law students in finding employment coast-to-coast and counseling students and alumni on career opportunities. The office offers specialized counseling for public interest, government, first-year job searches, judicial clerkships, international law practice, and non-traditional careers.

Penn Law graduates proceed to productive careers in every conceivable arena of practice, business, and advocacy. In recent years, 70–75 percent of graduates began their careers in private practice, 15–20 percent in judicial clerkships, 4–8 percent in government or public interest positions, 1–2 percent in university or law school teaching or study, and 3–4 percent in the business world.

APPLICANT PROFILE

Penn Law has chosen not to include an applicant profile because LSAT and GPA figures alone do not capture the qualities that make our students so dynamic. We value our students' diverse backgrounds, rich life experiences, leadership, community service, professional accomplishments, advanced degrees and coursework, motivation, initiative, and exemplary writing skills. While admission to Penn Law requires an excellent academic record, the Admissions Committee approaches each application holistically and takes all of these factors into consideration.

PEPPERDINE UNIVERSITY SCHOOL OF LAW

24255 Pacific Coast Highway
Malibu, CA 90263
Phone: 310.506.4611; Fax: 310.506.7668
E-mail: soladmis@pepperdine.edu; Website: http://law.pepperdine.edu

ABA Approved Since 1972

The Basics

Type of school	Private	
Term	Semester	
Application deadline	2/1	4/1
Application fee	$60	
Financial aid deadline	4/1	
Can first year start other than fall?	No	
Student to faculty ratio	15.6 to 1	
# of housing spaces available restricted to law students		
graduate housing for which law students are eligible		251

Faculty and Administrators

	Total		Men		Women		Minorities	
	Spr	Fall	Spr	Fall	Spr	Fall	Spr	Fall
Full-time	34	34	23	22	11	12	4	5
Other full-time	1	1	1	1	0	0	0	0
Deans, librarians, & others who teach	11	10	7	6	4	4	0	0
Part-time	54	60	43	49	11	11	3	4
Total	100	105	74	78	26	27	7	9

JD Enrollment and Ethnicity

	Men #	Men %	Women #	Women %	Full-Time #	Full-Time %	Part-Time #	Part-Time %	1st-Year #	1st-Year %	Total #	Total %	JD Degs. Awd.
All Hispanics	12	3.5	25	7.7	37	5.5	0	0.0	18	8.1	37	5.5	7
Am. Ind./AK Nat.	0	0.0	1	0.3	1	0.1	0	0.0	0	0.0	1	0.1	2
Asian	27	7.9	26	8.0	53	7.9	0	0.0	23	10.4	53	7.9	22
Black/Af. Am.	7	2.0	18	5.6	25	3.7	0	0.0	4	1.8	25	3.7	5
Nat. HI/Pac. Isl.	0	0.0	0	0.0	0	0.0	0	0.0	0	0.0	0	0.0	0
2 or more races	8	2.3	9	2.8	17	2.5	0	0.0	17	7.7	17	2.5	0
Subtotal (minor.)	54	15.7	79	24.4	133	19.9	0	0.0	62	27.9	133	19.9	36
Nonres. Alien	0	0.0	0	0.0	0	0.0	0	0.0	0	0.0	0	0.0	0
White/Cauc.	207	60.3	177	54.6	384	57.6	0	0.0	121	54.5	384	57.6	120
Unknown	82	23.9	68	21.0	150	22.5	0	0.0	39	17.6	150	22.5	48
Total	343	51.4	324	48.6	667	100.0	0	0.0	222	33.3	667		204

Curriculum

	Full-Time	Part-Time
Typical first-year section size	75	0
Is there typically a "small section" of the first-year class, other than Legal Writing, taught by full-time faculty	No	No
If yes, typical size offered last year		
# of classroom course titles beyond first-year curriculum	129	

# of upper division courses, excluding seminars, with an enrollment:	Under 25	127
	25–49	35
	50–74	14
	75–99	8
	100+	5

# of seminars	26	
# of seminar positions available	500	
# of seminar positions filled	395	0
# of positions available in simulation courses	2,105	
# of simulation positions filled	1,756	0
# of positions available in faculty supervised clinical courses	74	
# of faculty supervised clinical positions filled	53	0
# involved in field placements	199	0
# involved in law journals	205	0
# involved in moot court or trial competitions	62	0
# of credit hours required to graduate	88	

Transfers

Transfers in	6
Transfers out	10

Tuition and Fees

	Resident	Nonresident
Full-time	$41,210	$41,210
Part-time		
Tuition Guarantee Program		N

Living Expenses

Estimated living expenses for singles

Living on campus	Living off campus	Living at home
$24,468	$24,468	$24,468

ABA
Approved
Since
1972

GPA and LSAT Scores

	Total	Full-Time	Part-Time
# of apps	3,422	3,422	0
# of offers	965	965	0
# of matrics	222	222	0
75% GPA	3.75	3.75	0.00
Median GPA	3.62	3.62	0.00
25% GPA	3.31	3.31	0.00
75% LSAT	165	165	0
Median LSAT	163	163	0
25% LSAT	159	159	0

Grants and Scholarships (from prior year)

	Total #	Total %	Full-Time #	Full-Time %	Part-Time #	Part-Time %
Total # of students	667		667		0	
Total # receiving grants	373	55.9	373	55.9	0	0.0
Less than 1/2 tuition	215	32.2	215	32.2	0	0.0
Half to full tuition	134	20.1	134	20.1	0	0.0
Full tuition	6	0.9	6	0.9	0	0.0
More than full tuition	18	2.7	18	2.7	0	0.0
Median grant amount			$9,000		$0	

Informational and Library Resources

Total amount spent on library materials	$872,314
Study seating capacity inside the library	433
# of full-time equivalent professional librarians	9
Hours per week library is open	106
# of open, wired connections available to students	80
# of networked computers available for use by students	33
Has wireless network?	Y
Requires computer?	N

JD Attrition (from prior year)

	Academic #	Other #	Total #	Total %
1st year	8	13	21	9.1
2nd year	0	0	0	0.0
3rd year	0	0	0	0.0
4th year	0	0	0	0.0

Employment (9 months after graduation)

	Total	Percentage
Employment status known	199	100.0
Employment status unknown	0	0.0
Employed	179	89.9
Pursuing graduate degrees	10	5.0
Unemployed (seeking, not seeking, or studying for the bar)	5	2.5
Type of Employment		
# employed in law firms	113	63.1
# employed in business and industry	29	16.2
# employed in government	16	8.9
# employed in public interest	2	1.1
# employed as judicial clerks	9	5.0
# employed in academia	10	5.6
Geographic Location		
# employed in state	136	76.0
# employed outside the US	4	2.2
# of states where employed	21	

Bar Passage Rates

First-time takers	199	Reporting %	87.94
Average school %	80.00	Average state %	73.19
Average pass difference	6.81		

Jurisdiction	Takers	Passers	Pass %	State %	Diff %
California	175	140	80.00	73.19	6.81

PEPPERDINE UNIVERSITY SCHOOL OF LAW

24255 Pacific Coast Highway
Malibu, CA 90263
Phone: 310.506.4611; Fax: 310.506.7668
E-mail: soladmis@pepperdine.edu; Website: http://law.pepperdine.edu

Introduction

Pepperdine School of Law is located in Malibu, California, just 30 miles from downtown Los Angeles, making it a conducive environment for the intense study of law. Malibu offers an almost rural setting, yet it is an integral part of greater Los Angeles, providing access to one of the largest legal communities in the world. Pepperdine is a Christian university committed to the highest standards of academic excellence and Christian values, where students are strengthened for lives of purpose, service, and leadership.

Student Body

Pepperdine students bring a broad spectrum of backgrounds. They share a strong desire to attain high levels of achievement in academics, in their personal lives, and in their careers. Students come to Pepperdine from diverse socioeconomic, cultural, and religious backgrounds for the emphasis on integrity, service, and justice with a desire to become trusted leaders.

Faculty

Although the faculty have distinguished themselves through scholarly research and writing as well as leadership positions in prestigious legal organizations, the faculty's primary mission is to teach—to help students see the structure of legal thought and to be available as professional examples of a multifaceted profession. They demonstrate to their students that lawyers should be people-oriented individuals with strong moral character, capable of guiding their clients toward what is just and honorable as well as what is legally permissible.

Library and Physical Facilities

The School of Law occupies the Odell McConnell Law Center, located on the university's 830-acre campus overlooking the Pacific Ocean. The Jerene Appleby Harnish Library is the focal point of the school, housing a collection of over 400,000 volumes and volume equivalents. Students enjoy access to a multitude of leading online legal research services. Wireless network access is available throughout the Law Center. The facility contains two high-tech courtrooms, as well as lecture halls, seminar rooms, a bookstore, student dining area, and lounges.

Curriculum

Pepperdine offers a three-year, full-time JD program; four-year, full-time JD/MBA and JD/MPP dual-degree programs; a five-year, full-time JD/MDiv dual-degree program; a concurrent JD/MDR-degree program; and an LLM in Dispute Resolution. A student enrolled full time in a summer session can accelerate graduation by one semester. The required core courses are complemented by an extensive selection of elective courses.

The Palmer Center for Entrepreneurship and the Law

Unique in the nation, the Palmer Center prepares students for the modern hybrid role of lawyer, business consultant, financial strategist, and venture capitalist, and equips them with credentials and options in the field of entrepreneurship. Through carefully tailored coursework, the Palmer Center integrates multifaceted law and business disciplines into a distinctive and dynamic certificate program that supplements and complements the traditional JD degree.

Straus Institute for Dispute Resolution

The Straus Institute is the most comprehensive program of its type in the nation. Students studying in the field of dispute resolution can complete a special certificate program as part of their Juris Doctor degree program or a Master of Dispute Resolution. The LLM in Dispute Resolution began January 2003.

Nootbaar Institute on Law, Religion, and Ethics

The Nootbaar Institute was created to explore the nexus between these three disciplines, with particular emphasis on religion and the practice of law. While affirming Pepperdine's Christian identity, the institute draws from the largest possible pool of religious voices, seeking dialogue and common ground with other faith traditions.

Wm. Matthew Byrne Jr. Judicial Clerkship Institute

Each year, Pepperdine University School of Law brings law students from across the country to its campus for the Wm. Matthew Byrne Jr. Judicial Clerkship Institute (Byrne JCI). Through the Byrne JCI, students who have been accepted into federal judicial clerkship positions have the opportunity to gain distinctive, comprehensive training by federal judges.

Clinical Education

Clinical law programs provide students with the opportunity to refine their skills under the supervision of faculty, lawyers, and judges. The majority of clinical law opportunities are with the district attorneys, public defenders, and state and federal court judges. There are a number of programs offering experience in corporate and securities law, tax law, juvenile law, family law, labor law, consumer protection, environmental law, and trade regulation. Placements are also available within the film, television, and music industries.

Public Interest Opportunities

Pepperdine has partnered with the Los Angeles Union Rescue Mission to develop the Pepperdine/Union Rescue Mission Legal Aid Clinic. Located in downtown Los Angeles, the mission provides emergency food and shelter, health services, recovery programs, education, job training, and counseling within a Christian context. Students volunteer at the mission, where they meet with residents regarding legal concerns. The Pepperdine/Union Rescue Mission Family Law Clinic helps clients resolve issues such as child custody and support. The Special Education Advocacy Clinic gives students an opportunity to gain valuable experience advocating for children with disabilities.

Asylum Clinic

The Asylum Clinic, under the direction of retired United States immigration judge and now Pepperdine professor, Bruce J. Einhorn, provides law student representation to indigent and near-indigent foreign-born individuals who seek to legalize their status in the United States based on their fear of religious and other persecution abroad. The clinic provides students real-world experience in immigration law and litigation, and also provides advocacy for persons of faith as well as other vulnerable persons.

London Program

Students have the opportunity to study law in London at Pepperdine's university-owned facility in the museum district of South Kensington. While in London, students may serve as externs in clinical placements.

Exchange Programs

Students have the opportunity to participate in exchange programs with the University of Copenhagen and the University of Augsburg. Classes are taught in English in both programs.

Career Development Office

The Career Development Office is committed to helping law students explore, define, and achieve their career goals through career-related workshops, guest-speaker programs, and one-on-one counseling sessions. The office also manages on-campus recruiting programs and cosponsors with the Alumni Office a robust Alumni Mentoring Program. Over 300 employers participated in Pepperdine's most recent fall recruiting programs.

Student Activities

Pepperdine has earned a national reputation for excellence in appellate advocacy and trial advocacy competitions. Editorial and staff positions are awarded with the *Pepperdine Law Review, Pepperdine Dispute Resolution Law Journal, National Association of Administrative Law Judges Journal,* and the *Journal of Business, Entrepreneurship, and the Law.*

Admission

Admission is based on the applicant's academic record, LSAT score, a written personal statement, as well as a response to the university's mission statement, and other information that reflects outstanding academic and professional promise. Applications are also evaluated on the basis of employment experience, extracurricular activities, community involvement, commitment to high standards of morality and ethics, maturity, initiative, and motivation. The admission process is guided by the view that a student body that reflects diversity provides a superior educational environment. Admission decisions may be based on consideration of factors that include racial and ethnic origin, unique work or service experience, a history of overcoming disadvantage, or unusual life experiences. First-year students are admitted only in the fall.

Expenses and Financial Aid

Pepperdine's active financial aid program provides over 85 percent of the student body with some type of assistance. Scholarships and grants are available to students with outstanding academic credentials and to those with demonstrated financial need. The deadline for completed applications for financial aid is April 1 of the entering year.

Housing

The George Page Residential Complex is located directly across the street from the Law Center. The 72-unit complex houses graduate students in four-bedroom apartments. The Admission Office also provides an extensive housing referral service.

APPLICANT PROFILE

Pepperdine University School of Law
This grid includes only applicants who earned 120–180 LSAT scores under standard administrations.

LSAT Score	GPA																
	3.75 +		3.50–3.74		3.25–3.49		3.00–3.24		2.75–2.99		2.50–2.74		Below 2.50		No GPA		Total	
	Apps	Adm	Apps	Adm	Apps	Adm	Apps	Adm	Apps	Adm	Apps	Adm	Apps	Adm	Apps	Adm	Apps	Adm
175–180	5	5	3	3	0	0	1	1	1	1	0	0	0	0	0	0	10	10
170–174	22	21	23	22	13	10	7	6	7	2	0	0	4	0	0	0	76	61
165–169	90	84	82	76	59	52	41	35	26	12	17	4	7	0	4	2	326	265
160–164	166	147	269	186	238	121	139	43	64	2	33	1	12	0	9	1	930	501
155–159	139	45	234	43	226	6	138	3	78	3	43	0	28	0	7	0	893	100
150–154	58	6	134	15	136	3	117	0	80	0	33	0	35	1	13	0	606	25
Below 150	30	0	55	1	109	1	126	0	96	0	71	0	50	0	14	0	551	2
Total	510	308	800	346	781	193	569	88	352	20	197	5	136	1	47	3	3392	964

Apps = Number of Applicants
Adm = Number Admitted
Reflects 99% of the total applicant pool; highest LSAT data reported.

PHOENIX SCHOOL OF LAW

4041 North Central Avenue
Phoenix, AZ 85012
Phone: 602.682.6800; Fax: 602.682.6999
E-mail: admissions@phoenixlaw.edu; Website: www.phoenixlaw.edu

ABA
Approved
Since
2007

The Basics

Type of school	Private
Term	Semester
Application deadline	
Application fee	$50
Financial aid deadline	
Can first year start other than fall?	Yes
Student to faculty ratio	14.4 to 1
# of housing spaces available restricted to law students	
graduate housing for which law students are eligible	

Faculty and Administrators

	Total		Men		Women		Minorities	
	Spr	Fall	Spr	Fall	Spr	Fall	Spr	Fall
Full-time	27	28	15	12	12	16	6	8
Other full-time	3	4	0	0	3	4	0	0
Deans, librarians, & others who teach	5	7	2	2	3	5	2	4
Part-time	18	25	13	19	5	6	2	4
Total	53	64	30	33	23	31	10	16

Curriculum

	Full-Time	Part-Time
Typical first-year section size	46	40

Is there typically a "small section" of the first-year class, other than Legal Writing, taught by full-time faculty	Yes	No
If yes, typical size offered last year	10	

# of classroom course titles beyond first-year curriculum		31
# of upper division courses, excluding seminars, with an enrollment:	Under 25	45
	25–49	23
	50–74	5
	75–99	1
	100+	0

# of seminars		2
# of seminar positions available		20
# of seminar positions filled	15	1
# of positions available in simulation courses		40
# of simulation positions filled	9	9
# of positions available in faculty supervised clinical courses		59
# of faculty supervised clinical positions filled	36	4
# involved in field placements	45	9
# involved in law journals	56	12
# involved in moot court or trial competitions	5	0
# of credit hours required to graduate		87

JD Enrollment and Ethnicity

	Men		Women		Full-Time		Part-Time		1st-Year		Total		JD Degs. Awd.
	#	%	#	%	#	%	#	%	#	%	#	%	
All Hispanics	41	10.4	48	14.6	65	12.6	24	11.4	62	13.1	89	12.3	11
Am. Ind./AK Nat.	3	0.8	3	0.9	6	1.2	0	0.0	5	1.1	6	0.8	0
Asian	20	5.1	20	6.1	29	5.6	11	5.2	25	5.3	40	5.5	0
Black/Af. Am.	18	4.5	24	7.3	32	6.2	10	4.8	34	7.2	42	5.8	2
Nat. HI/Pac. Isl.	0	0.0	0	0.0	0	0.0	0	0.0	0	0.0	0	0.0	0
2 or more races	4	1.0	2	0.6	5	1.0	1	0.5	6	1.3	6	0.8	0
Subtotal (minor.)	86	21.7	97	29.6	137	26.7	46	21.9	132	27.8	183	25.3	14
Nonres. Alien	1	0.3	4	1.2	5	1.0	0	0.0	5	1.1	5	0.7	0
White/Cauc.	265	66.9	199	60.7	326	63.4	138	65.7	295	62.1	464	64.1	48
Unknown	44	11.1	28	8.5	46	8.9	26	12.4	43	9.1	72	9.9	7
Total	396	54.7	328	45.3	514	71.0	210	29.0	475	65.6	724		69

Transfers

Transfers in	5
Transfers out	30

Tuition and Fees

	Resident	Nonresident
Full-time	$36,036	$36,036
Part-time	$29,156	$29,156
Tuition Guarantee Program		N

Living Expenses

Estimated living expenses for singles

Living on campus	Living off campus	Living at home
N/A	$26,280	N/A

PHOENIX SCHOOL OF LAW

ABA
Approved
Since
2007

GPA and LSAT Scores

	Total	Full-Time	Part-Time
# of apps	2,692	2,350	342
# of offers	1,875	1,682	193
# of matrics	392	290	102
75% GPA	3.37	3.37	3.47
Median GPA	3.04	3.02	3.11
25% GPA	2.70	2.69	2.75
75% LSAT	153	153	153
Median LSAT	150	149	150
25% LSAT	148	148	146

Grants and Scholarships (from prior year)

	Total		Full-Time		Part-Time	
	#	%	#	%	#	%
Total # of students	537		352		185	
Total # receiving grants	278	51.8	219	62.2	59	31.9
Less than 1/2 tuition	259	48.2	210	59.7	49	26.5
Half to full tuition	19	3.5	9	2.6	10	5.4
Full tuition	0	0.0	0	0.0	0	0.0
More than full tuition	0	0.0	0	0.0	0	0.0
Median grant amount			$7,000		$7,000	

Informational and Library Resources

Total amount spent on library materials	$831,151
Study seating capacity inside the library	212
# of full-time equivalent professional librarians	6
Hours per week library is open	107
# of open, wired connections available to students	0
# of networked computers available for use by students	46
Has wireless network?	Y
Requires computer?	Y

JD Attrition (from prior year)

	Academic	Other	Total	
	#	#	#	%
1st year	26	37	63	17.6
2nd year	0	15	15	19.0
3rd year	0	3	3	5.9
4th year	0	0	0	0.0

Employment (9 months after graduation)

	Total	Percentage
Employment status known	57	100.0
Employment status unknown	0	0.0
Employed	54	94.7
Pursuing graduate degrees	1	1.8
Unemployed (seeking, not seeking, or studying for the bar)	2	3.5
Type of Employment		
# employed in law firms	24	44.4
# employed in business and industry	14	25.9
# employed in government	8	14.8
# employed in public interest	3	5.6
# employed as judicial clerks	1	1.9
# employed in academia	4	7.4
Geographic Location		
# employed in state	50	92.6
# employed outside the US	0	0.0
# of states where employed		3

Bar Passage Rates

First-time takers	55	Reporting %	100.00
Average school %	69.10	Average state %	80.11

Average pass difference −11.01

Jurisdiction	Takers	Passers	Pass %	State %	Diff %
Arizona	51	34	66.67	79.76	−13.09
Colorado	1	1	100.00	85.67	14.33
Florida	1	1	100.00	77.81	22.19
Ohio	1	1	100.00	86.03	13.97
Utah	1	1	100.00	88.94	11.06

PHOENIX SCHOOL OF LAW

4041 North Central Avenue
Phoenix, AZ 85012
Phone: 602.682.6800; Fax: 602.682.6999
E-mail: admissions@phoenixlaw.edu; Website: www.phoenixlaw.edu

Introduction to Phoenix School of Law

At PhoenixLaw, our overarching commitment is to our students. Our faculty, staff, students, and alumni are passionate about our three-part mission:

(1) An educational experience that is focused on student-centered outcomes.

Our faculty, staff, students, and alumni share a responsibility to help students develop the values, skills, and knowledge required of legal professionals. Recognizing the rigors of a legal education, PhoenixLaw expects every member of its community to contribute to an intellectually demanding, supportive, multicultural learning environment. PhoenixLaw also endeavors to foster a culture of humility, transparency, dignity, fairness, and respect.

(2) Outcome-driven programs and experiences that yield professionally-prepared graduates.

In addition to the traditional emphasis on doctrine, critical thinking, and writing skills, at PhoenixLaw we impart real world experience. By focusing on the practical skills and methodologies of law practice, combined with the faculty and staff's accountability for market-leading student outcomes, we prepare our students to be effective lawyers and give them a head start in legal practice.

(3) A commitment to serving underserved communities and student populations.

This premise has a broad spectrum, and begins with the location of PhoenixLaw in a community that historically has been underserved by legal education. It continues by immersing PhoenixLaw students in a culture that encourages service to individuals and groups that have historically been underserved by the legal profession. We impart to our students the understanding that the ability to interact effectively with persons of diverse backgrounds and experiences is a significant skill necessary for their success.

A community of accomplished students, notable alumni, distinguished faculty, and experienced staff, PhoenixLaw is continually advancing. We believe that we provide an exceptional law school education and experience; setting ourselves apart on the basis of our outcomes and our culture. We welcome all to join our dynamic community.

Full- and Part-Time Programs

At Phoenix School of Law, students have the flexibility of three program options to pursue their legal education: full-time day, part-time day, and part-time evening. Full-time faculty members teach all program options. All students can also benefit from the law practitioners in the Phoenix metro area who share their practical knowledge as adjunct professors. In addition to the fall, spring, and optional summer semester, Phoenix School of Law offers students the opportunity to take elective courses during three, one-week intersession semesters.

Admission

Phoenix School of Law admits students after a careful and thorough application evaluation. The initial measurement for admission is the undergraduate GPA and LSAT. Highly qualified applicants typically are admitted first. Admission decisions may include attention to factors that enhance the educational experience of the entire student body. The Admissions Committee weighs all characteristics bearing upon the ability of an applicant to study law successfully. Undergraduate grades and majors, the difficulty of the undergraduate field of study, LSAT scores, personal statements, and letters of recommendation are important. Phoenix School of Law also evaluates other criteria, such as experience, accomplishments, graduate study and degrees, the LSAT writing sample, and other factors that may provide meaningful insight into potential.

Curriculum

The faculty and administration at the Phoenix School of Law believe that in order to create law graduates who are professionally prepared, they must be exposed to traditional theory, practical skills, and ethical instruction in a variety of different ways: externships, workshops, classes, and mentoring. This practical experience helps develop our students to be professionally prepared upon graduation. At PhoenixLaw, there are several main areas of focus for experiential learning:

Infusion of Skills and Values

Since the School's inception, faculty members have taken a coordinated approach to teaching key skills and values as part of their courses. PhoenixLaw faculty members have assumed responsibility for teaching 17 specific skills throughout the core curriculum.

General Practice Skills

As a requirement for graduation, all students must satisfactorily complete a capstone course—the General Practice Skills (GPS) course. The course's objective is to infuse skills and values essential to the practice of law for the final year course curriculum. The course is taught by adjunct professors who are all working attorneys in the legal community.

Clinical and Externship Programs

The goals of these programs include teaching practice-ready professional skills and values, promoting pro bono service to underserved segments of the community, and providing students with opportunities to engage in small group/collaborative work, while exposing students to the rich tapestry of legal service opportunities. An additional goal is that through the clinical and externship experience, each student will demonstrate improved skills of learning from practice and will have developed a strong commitment to the value of lifelong learning in the practice of law. PhoenixLaw Clinics include the Mediation Clinic, Veterans' Community Services Clinic, Veterans' Tax Clinic, Human Rights and Immigration Clinic, American Indian Law Clinic, and the Prosecution Clinic.

Faculty

The faculty at the Phoenix School of Law is an extraordinary and diverse staff of professors who are dedicated to providing every student with accessibility, academic support, and mentorship. Educated at some of the best law schools around the nation, they have a wide range of special interests and have worked in large private firms, government agencies, public interest organizations, and as judicial clerks. Our faculty also includes several retired judges. The PhoenixLaw faculty is actively involved in scholarship and public service, but their first priority is teaching our students.

Mentoring Programs

Upon starting classes at PhoenixLaw, each student is assigned a faculty mentor. This mentor helps guide the student through their law school experience and develop a professional relationship that extends beyond the classroom and to their career. They act as an advisor, assisting the student in understanding and applying policies and procedures, accessing information, and pursuing appropriate avenues to obtain information and approvals. Mentoring is also provided via various student organizations, where 2L and 3L students assist the 1Ls by guiding them through their first year of law school.

Academic Success and Bar Exam Preparation

Helping students to succeed in law school is the goal of PhoenixLaw's Academic Success Program. The staff of Academic Success provides classes and workshops, as well as small-group and individual academic support counseling to assist students in:

- adjusting to a rigorous legal learning environment;
- constructing time management and stress management skills to meet the personal tasks and academic demands of law school;
- identifying individualized learning style preferences to enhance efficiency and effectiveness in academics and practice;
- developing the necessary study skills, classroom preparation, and exam preparation tools to succeed in law school;
- maximizing effective writing, analytical, oratory, and legal reasoning skills;
- passing the bar examination with a comprehensive bar strategies course to ensure that students understand the bar review and exam process.

Career Services

PhoenixLaw's Center for Professional Development (CPD) is a full-service career counseling and resource center, committed to assisting each student in identifying, developing, and attaining his or her individual career goals. Students meet with a member of the CPD staff in their first year to discuss unique career planning goals and to develop effective job search strategies. Individual counseling sessions are supplemented by career planning workshops and programs throughout the semester including résumé and cover letter workshops, interview skills workshops, networking skills workshops, career panels, and mock interview programs, to name a few.

CPD offers a comprehensive recruitment program that brings students together with employers and provides them with opportunities to gain practical experience. Each semester CPD hosts employers for on-campus interviews, performs résumé collections, and distributes weekly job postings. The variety of recruitment opportunities for employers has resulted in the placement of PhoenixLaw graduates in large and regional private firms, judicial clerkships, government agencies, public interest groups, and the business sector.

The CPD's "PSL Career Blog," contains numerous online resources, and apprises students and alumni on the national legal economy and networking opportunities.

Library and Information Technology

The PhoenixLaw Library houses an expansive physical collection of legal resources, as well as several electronic databases. The law library is continuously expanding its collection, including multiple formats, such as print, electronic, and audio, to best accommodate each student's learning style and maximize results.

Several workshops are offered throughout the year to supplement research skills that students learn in their legal writing courses and other classes.

PhoenixLaw employs the latest technology to make learning more effective for our students. From state-of-the-art classrooms, intranet, and wireless technology, to smartboards and podcasting, our Information Technology Department is continually implementing new ways to enhance the learning experience.

APPLICANT PROFILE

Phoenix School of Law

LSAT Score	GPA									
	3.75 +	3.50–3.74	3.25–3.49	3.00–3.24	2.75–2.99	2.50–2.74	2.25–2.49	2.00–2.24	Below 2.00	No GPA
175–180	■	■	■	■	■	■	■	▨		
170–174	■	■	■	■	■	■	■	▨		
165–169	■	■	■	■	■	■	■	▨		
160–164	■	■	■	■	■	■	■	▨		
157–159	■	■	■	■	■	■	▨			
154–156	■	■	■	■	■	■	▨			
150–153	■	■	■	■	■	▨				
145–149	▨	▨	▨	▨	▨	▨	▨			
140–144										
135–139										
130–134										
125–129										
120–124										

■ Highly Possible   ▨ Possible   ☐ Unlikely

The information contained in this chart should be used as an estimated guide as to the likelihood of admission. The Admissions Committee engages in a holistic review of all information submitted by candidates for admission. LSAT and UGPA are not the sole determinants for admission.

UNIVERSITY OF PITTSBURGH SCHOOL OF LAW

3900 Forbes Avenue, Barco Law Building
Pittsburgh, PA 15260
Phone: 412.648.1413; Fax: 412.648.1318
E-mail: admitlaw@pitt.edu; Website: www.law.pitt.edu

ABA
Approved
Since
1923

The Basics

Type of school	Public
Term	Semester
Application deadline	3/1
Application fee	$55
Financial aid deadline	3/1 4/1
Can first year start other than fall?	No
Student to faculty ratio	13.8 to 1
# of housing spaces available restricted to law students	
graduate housing for which law students are eligible	

Faculty and Administrators

	Total		Men		Women		Minorities	
	Spr	Fall	Spr	Fall	Spr	Fall	Spr	Fall
Full-time	41	45	24	25	17	20	7	9
Other full-time	1	2	1	2	0	0	0	1
Deans, librarians, & others who teach	10	10	3	3	7	7	1	1
Part-time	61	51	44	35	16	15	5	7
Total	113	108	72	65	40	42	13	18

JD Enrollment and Ethnicity

	Men		Women		Full-Time		Part-Time		1st-Year		Total		JD Degs. Awd.
	#	%	#	%	#	%	#	%	#	%	#	%	
All Hispanics	12	2.8	10	3.2	22	3.0	0	0.0	8	3.1	22	3.0	5
Am. Ind./AK Nat.	1	0.2	1	0.3	2	0.3	0	0.0	1	0.4	2	0.3	0
Asian	21	5.0	27	8.5	48	6.5	0	0.0	17	6.6	48	6.5	0
Black/Af. Am.	20	4.7	30	9.5	50	6.8	0	0.0	18	6.9	50	6.8	12
Nat. HI/Pac. Isl.	0	0.0	0	0.0	0	0.0	0	0.0	0	0.0	0	0.0	0
2 or more races	1	0.2	2	0.6	3	0.4	0	0.0	3	1.2	3	0.4	0
Subtotal (minor.)	55	13.0	70	22.1	125	16.9	0	0.0	47	18.1	125	16.9	29
Nonres. Alien	0	0.0	0	0.0	0	0.0	0	0.0	0	0.0	0	0.0	0
White/Cauc.	282	66.8	198	62.5	480	65.0	0	0.0	163	62.9	480	65.0	136
Unknown	85	20.1	49	15.5	134	18.1	0	0.0	49	18.9	134	18.1	44
Total	422	57.1	317	42.9	739	100.0	0	0.0	259	35.0	739		209

Curriculum

	Full-Time	Part-Time
Typical first-year section size	86	0
Is there typically a "small section" of the first-year class, other than Legal Writing, taught by full-time faculty	No	No
If yes, typical size offered last year		
# of classroom course titles beyond first-year curriculum	195	

# of upper division courses, excluding seminars, with an enrollment:	Under 25	120
	25–49	27
	50–74	11
	75–99	6
	100+	2

# of seminars	22	
# of seminar positions available	275	
# of seminar positions filled	240	0
# of positions available in simulation courses	224	
# of simulation positions filled	188	0
# of positions available in faculty supervised clinical courses	174	
# of faculty supervised clinical positions filled	144	0
# involved in field placements	122	0
# involved in law journals	185	0
# involved in moot court or trial competitions	96	0
# of credit hours required to graduate	88	

Transfers

Transfers in	12
Transfers out	10

Tuition and Fees

	Resident	Nonresident
Full-time	$26,550	$34,176
Part-time		
Tuition Guarantee Program	N	

Living Expenses

Estimated living expenses for singles

Living on campus	Living off campus	Living at home
$16,584	$16,584	$16,584

UNIVERSITY OF PITTSBURGH SCHOOL OF LAW

ABA
Approved
Since
1923

GPA and LSAT Scores

	Total	Full-Time	Part-Time
# of apps	2,756	2,756	0
# of offers	954	954	0
# of matrics	259	259	0
75% GPA	3.63	3.63	0.00
Median GPA	3.38	3.38	0.00
25% GPA	3.07	3.07	0.00
75% LSAT	161	161	0
Median LSAT	160	160	0
25% LSAT	158	158	0

Grants and Scholarships (from prior year)

	Total		Full-Time		Part-Time	
	#	%	#	%	#	%
Total # of students	682		682		0	
Total # receiving grants	365	53.5	365	53.5	0	0.0
Less than 1/2 tuition	260	38.1	260	38.1	0	0.0
Half to full tuition	93	13.6	93	13.6	0	0.0
Full tuition	6	0.9	6	0.9	0	0.0
More than full tuition	6	0.9	6	0.9	0	0.0
Median grant amount			$10,800		$0	

Informational and Library Resources

Total amount spent on library materials	$1,334,860
Study seating capacity inside the library	425
# of full-time equivalent professional librarians	14
Hours per week library is open	101
# of open, wired connections available to students	80
# of networked computers available for use by students	69
Has wireless network?	Y
Requires computer?	N

JD Attrition (from prior year)

	Academic	Other	Total	
	#	#	#	%
1st year	1	14	15	6.4
2nd year	0	1	1	0.4
3rd year	0	0	0	0.0
4th year	0	0	0	0.0

Employment (9 months after graduation)

	Total	Percentage
Employment status known	228	99.1
Employment status unknown	2	0.9
Employed	196	86.0
Pursuing graduate degrees	6	2.6
Unemployed (seeking, not seeking, or studying for the bar)	19	8.3
Type of Employment		
# employed in law firms	112	57.1
# employed in business and industry	33	16.8
# employed in government	26	13.3
# employed in public interest	6	3.1
# employed as judicial clerks	17	8.7
# employed in academia	1	0.5
Geographic Location		
# employed in state	122	62.2
# employed outside the US	1	0.5
# of states where employed	23	

Bar Passage Rates

First-time takers	218	Reporting %	79.36
Average school %	91.91	Average state %	85.69
Average pass difference	6.22		

Jurisdiction	Takers	Passers	Pass %	State %	Diff %
Pennsylvania	173	159	91.91	85.69	6.22

UNIVERSITY OF PITTSBURGH SCHOOL OF LAW

3900 Forbes Avenue, Barco Law Building
Pittsburgh, PA 15260
Phone: 412.648.1413; Fax: 412.648.1318
E-mail: admitlaw@pitt.edu; Website: www.law.pitt.edu

Introduction

The University of Pittsburgh School of Law (Pitt Law), founded in 1895, is a leader in legal education. It features a broad and varied curriculum, an internationally accomplished faculty, state-of-the-art physical facilities, and a talented and diverse student body hailing from all over the globe. Pitt Law is located in its own six-story building on campus in Oakland, the cultural and educational center of Pittsburgh. State and federal courts, major corporate headquarters, and hundreds of law firms are located nearby in downtown Pittsburgh, only minutes from campus. The dynamic Oakland area is home to four colleges and universities, the world-renowned, multihospital University of Pittsburgh Medical Center, numerous scientific and high-tech offices and research centers, museums, art galleries, coffee houses, and libraries. The Pitt campus abuts a beautiful 429-acre city park. Desirable and affordable residential areas are situated nearby and all mass transit in the city is free to Pitt students.

Faculty

Without question, one of the most invigorating aspects of attending Pitt Law is the faculty. Students have the opportunity to work with and alongside some of the finest legal scholars in the world. While Pitt Law's faculty are known nationally and internationally for their legal scholarship, Pitt Law students appreciate how accessible and committed to teaching they are.

Library and Physical Facilities

The Barco Law Library is an attractive, 450,000-volume, open-stack research facility, housed on three floors of the School of Law building. Classrooms with state-of-the-art technology are located on the first and ground floors of the School of Law building.

In Spring 2011, construction will be completed on the student lounge which will provide a multipurpose space for students to study, socialize, and relax between classes. The new space will contain a Starbucks coffee kiosk with "grab-n-go" food items, ample seating, a new student organization office suite that offers both collaborative and private work environments, new student lockers to better accommodate books and personal items, comfortable couches and chairs that promote student gathering, soft lighting, and increased electrical access for laptop use. This newly built-out space is adjacent to the Teplitz Memorial Courtroom where moot court sessions are held.

Curricular and Special Programs

Unlike the harsh, competitive stereotype of law school, Pitt Law fosters a spirit of personal achievement and collaboration. The courses are challenging and the standards are high, but students find the professors are encouraging and motivating. Rather than a culture that thrives on creating stress, Pitt Law offers an educational atmosphere of creativity, openness, growth, and excellence.

- *Clinical Programs*—Academics and reality meet head-on in our legal clinics. Pitt Law students have the opportunity to obtain hands-on experience in several clinical programs, including a Tax Clinic; an Environmental Law Clinic; a Civil Practice Clinic with a focus on either Health Law or Elder Law; a Family Law Clinic; and an Immigration Law Clinic. With a supervising attorney, students do it all: pretrial preparation, negotiation, litigation, and counseling real-life clients about real-life legal concerns.
- *Programs of Specialized Study*—One way to prepare for law practice in an increasingly complex society is to develop specialized expertise. Pitt Law students may seize that advantage through participation in diverse programs of specialized study that permits students to focus their studies in high-demand areas of practice. Pitt Law has such programs in the areas of civil litigation; environmental law, science, and policy; health law; international and comparative law; and intellectual property and technology law.
- *Joint-Degree Programs*—Prompted by the recognized value of attorneys who work effectively across disciplines, we offer several joint-degree programs that provide rigorous, integrated training, effectively merging law and a number of allied fields. They include the JD/MBA with both Pitt and Carnegie Mellon University; the JD/MPH with our Graduate School of Public Health; the JD/MPA, JD/MPIA, and JD/MID with our Graduate School of Public and International Affairs; the JD/MA (Bioethics); the JD/MSW (Social Work); and the JD/MSPPM and JD/MAM with the Heinz College at Carnegie Mellon University.
- *Semester in DC*—Pitt Law students can spend a semester working for a nonprofit or government agency in Washington, DC, while earning a full semester's worth of academic credit. The DC Externship Program allows students to combine supervised field work with a government or nonprofit employer, a related academic seminar, and the option of earning additional credit by pursuing an independent study related to the externship. Members of the Pitt Law alumni network are eager to serve as mentors to Pitt Law students, and many DC area employers are interested in receiving externship applications from Pitt Law students.
- *Innovation Practice Institute (IPI)*—Pitt Law is uniquely situated amid some of the world's leading innovators in fields ranging from regenerative medicine to robotics, to entertainment technology, to alternative energy and green building. Taking advantage of this environment, IPI gives Pitt Law students the opportunity to immerse themselves in experiential, cross-disciplinary, project-based learning to develop the skills and confidence to participate as professionals in the innovation culture and economy.

Center for International Legal Education (CILE)

In today's world, legal problems regularly involve many nations and many sets of laws. Today's global lawyer understands the political, cultural, and social influences on the legal systems of other countries and uses that knowledge for the benefit of his or her clients. CILE faculty prepare Pitt Law students for successful futures in tomorrow's world. Students study the workings of foreign legal systems and explore the wide array of issues facing practicing attorneys in the global marketplace. The center also coordinates international programs at Pitt with the University Center for International Studies and affiliated area studies programs, and it supervises a number of specialized language classes, for example, French for Lawyers, Spanish for Lawyers, German for Lawyers, and Chinese for Lawyers.

Student Activities

The *University of Pittsburgh Law Review*, the *Journal of Law and Commerce*, and the *Journal of Technology Law and Policy* are among the journals published by law students. More than 30 law student organizations thrive at Pitt Law, reflecting the diverse social and intellectual interests and experiences of our students. They include the Asian Law Students Association, the Black Law Students Association, the Environmental Law Council, the Federalist Society, the Hispanic Law Society, the Jewish Law Students Association, the Lesbian-Gay Rights Organization (OUTLAW), the Pitt Law Women's Association, and the Pitt Legal Income Sharing Foundation, among others.

Career Services

The Career Services Office provides year-round assistance to Pitt Law students and graduates. The office serves as a clearinghouse for information on summer, part-time, and permanent work with law firms, corporations, accounting firms, government agencies, judges, and other legal employers. It also helps students develop practical job-search strategies, helps demystify the dynamics of the legal job market, offers strategies for finding the perfect job in that market, and offers information and counseling regarding nontraditional careers utilizing professional skills gained in law school. The CSO works closely with Pitt Law's Alumni Office to create opportunities for students to connect with our large network of alumni.

Admission and Financial Aid

Pitt Law has a highly competitive admission process and decision-making is based upon several factors; the GPA and LSAT scores serve as the most important of those. When evaluating an undergraduate degree, the admission committee pays careful attention to the strength of the major field of study, looking specifically for a prospective student to have shown evidence of discipline and ability to handle a

rigorous and demanding program. The same assessment is made of graduate and professional work. A required personal statement provides a view into the nonacademic world of the applicant. This is critical to Pitt Law's ability to enroll a diverse class—students with various backgrounds and a range of experiences. Similarly, letters of recommendation and résumés provide a broader view of the applicant's accomplishments. Applicants are reviewed on a rolling notification basis. Pitt Law assists accepted students in securing the financial resources needed to cover the cost of their legal education. Approximately half of the student body receives merit or need-based scholarships. Pitt Law also offers a Public Interest Scholarship and numerous named scholarships. All students admitted to Pitt Law are automatically considered for scholarships and notifications of awards are included in their acceptance letters.

The City of Pittsburgh

Today Pittsburgh is spectacular—a thriving business center and a high-tech hotbed rated America's most livable city in 2010! Our campus is at the center of it all. We are a stroll away from wonderfully diverse neighborhoods, acres of parks, scores of restaurants and shops, three major league sports arenas, movies, museums, galleries, dance clubs, coffee houses, and riverside cafés, and that's just the short list. A quick commute on your bike takes you to the nucleus of the law and business community in downtown Pittsburgh. You'll also find the heart of the cultural district downtown, offering world-class theater, opera, symphony, ballet, and dance. For a law student, Pittsburgh is a lot more than a livable city—it's a context for building a strong career. There is no finer preparation for law than learning in a setting that gives you a wealth of opportunity to put theory into practice. Pittsburgh is the global headquarters for Fortune 500 corporations, home to one of the nation's largest medical centers, a hub of public policy interest, and host to more than 2,500 high technology companies—all served by a robust and sophisticated practicing bar. Pitt Law's location near the heart of the legal community makes practitioners accessible as mentors in the classroom and models in the field and permits many students to get real legal experience while still in school.

APPLICANT PROFILE

University of Pittsburgh School of Law
This grid includes only applicants who earned 120–180 LSAT scores under standard administrations.

LSAT Score	3.75 +		3.50–3.74		3.25–3.49		3.00–3.24		2.75–2.99		2.50–2.74		Below 2.50		No GPA		Total	
	Apps	Adm	Apps	Adm	Apps	Adm	Apps	Adm	Apps	Adm	Apps	Adm	Apps	Adm	Apps	Adm	Apps	Adm
165–180	42	35	60	42	38	29	39	27	19	13	9	3	12	7	2	1	221	157
160–164	125	98	167	113	195	127	120	82	39	28	25	13	9	4	8	6	688	471
155–159	123	54	205	75	256	75	155	37	86	14	31	7	25	1	18	4	899	267
150–154	72	5	117	10	127	16	133	14	61	4	22	2	16	0	9	0	557	51
145–149	19	0	36	1	40	1	58	0	35	0	18	0	9	0	11	0	226	2
Below 145	8	0	15	0	27	0	32	0	28	2	25	0	12	0	6	0	153	2
Total	389	192	600	241	683	248	537	160	268	61	130	25	83	12	54	11	2744	950

Apps = Number of Applicants
Adm = Number Admitted
Reflects 99% of the total applicant pool; highest LSAT data reported.

PONTIFICAL CATHOLIC UNIVERSITY OF PUERTO RICO SCHOOL OF LAW

2250 Avenida Las Americas, Suite 633
Ponce, PR 00717-9997
Phone: 787.841.2000, exts. 1836, 1837; Fax: 787.841.4620
E-mail: derecho@email.pucpr.edu; Website: www.pucpr.edu/derecho

ABA
Approved
Since
1967

The Basics

Type of school	Private
Term	Semester
Application deadline	4/15 9/30
Application fee	
Financial aid deadline	
Can first year start other than fall?	Yes
Student to faculty ratio	33.2 to 1
# of housing spaces available restricted to law students	
graduate housing for which law students are eligible	

Faculty and Administrators

	Total		Men		Women		Minorities	
	Spr	Fall	Spr	Fall	Spr	Fall	Spr	Fall
Full-time	16	17	12	12	4	5	16	17
Other full-time	4	4	3	3	1	1	4	4
Deans, librarians, & others who teach	8	8	5	5	3	3	8	8
Part-time	27	25	15	15	12	10	27	25
Total	55	54	35	35	20	19	55	54

Curriculum

		Full-Time	Part-Time
Typical first-year section size		51	39
Is there typically a "small section" of the first-year class, other than Legal Writing, taught by full-time faculty		Yes	Yes
If yes, typical size offered last year		22	22
# of classroom course titles beyond first-year curriculum		96	
# of upper division courses, excluding seminars, with an enrollment:	Under 25	60	
	25–49	68	
	50–74	21	
	75–99	2	
	100+	0	
# of seminars		18	
# of seminar positions available		388	
# of seminar positions filled		40	270
# of positions available in simulation courses		203	
# of simulation positions filled		101	78
# of positions available in faculty supervised clinical courses		7	
# of faculty supervised clinical positions filled		6	1
# involved in field placements		0	0
# involved in law journals		46	12
# involved in moot court or trial competitions		0	0
# of credit hours required to graduate		94	

Transfers

Transfers in	1
Transfers out	27

Tuition and Fees

	Resident	Nonresident
Full-time	$14,126	
Part-time	$10,766	
Tuition Guarantee Program		N

JD Enrollment and Ethnicity

	Men		Women		Full-Time		Part-Time		1st-Year		Total		JD Degs. Awd.
	#	%	#	%	#	%	#	%	#	%	#	%	
All Hispanics	436	99.8	397	100.0	534	99.8	299	100.0	270	99.6	833	99.9	156
Am. Ind./AK Nat.	0	0.0	0	0.0	0	0.0	0	0.0	0	0.0	0	0.0	0
Asian	0	0.0	0	0.0	0	0.0	0	0.0	0	0.0	0	0.0	0
Black/Af. Am.	0	0.0	0	0.0	0	0.0	0	0.0	0	0.0	0	0.0	0
Nat. HI/Pac. Isl.	0	0.0	0	0.0	0	0.0	0	0.0	0	0.0	0	0.0	0
2 or more races	0	0.0	0	0.0	0	0.0	0	0.0	0	0.0	0	0.0	0
Subtotal (minor.)	436	99.8	397	100.0	534	99.8	299	100.0	270	99.6	833	99.9	156
Nonres. Alien	0	0.0	0	0.0	0	0.0	0	0.0	0	0.0	0	0.0	0
White/Cauc.	1	0.2	0	0.0	1	0.2	0	0.0	1	0.4	1	0.1	0
Unknown	0	0.0	0	0.0	0	0.0	0	0.0	0	0.0	0	0.0	0
Total	437	52.4	397	47.6	535	64.1	299	35.9	271	32.5	834		156

Living Expenses

Estimated living expenses for singles

Living on campus	Living off campus	Living at home
$22,421	$24,469	$20,845

PONTIFICAL CATHOLIC UNIVERSITY OF PUERTO RICO SCHOOL OF LAW

ABA
Approved
Since
1967

GPA and LSAT Scores

	Total	Full-Time	Part-Time
# of apps	579	393	186
# of offers	342	228	114
# of matrics	289	190	99
75% GPA	3.58	3.62	3.50
Median GPA	3.30	3.30	3.12
25% GPA	2.97	3.00	2.89
75% LSAT	138	137	136
Median LSAT	135	134	133
25% LSAT	132	127	131

Grants and Scholarships (from prior year)

	Total		Full-Time		Part-Time	
	#	%	#	%	#	%
Total # of students	696		474		222	
Total # receiving grants	69	9.9	46	9.7	23	10.4
Less than 1/2 tuition	40	5.7	32	6.8	8	3.6
Half to full tuition	16	2.3	9	1.9	7	3.2
Full tuition	13	1.9	5	1.1	8	3.6
More than full tuition	0	0.0	0	0.0	0	0.0
Median grant amount			$2,500		$3,140	

Informational and Library Resources

Total amount spent on library materials	$662,202
Study seating capacity inside the library	184
# of full-time equivalent professional librarians	4
Hours per week library is open	98
# of open, wired connections available to students	102
# of networked computers available for use by students	30
Has wireless network?	Y
Requires computer?	N

JD Attrition (from prior year)

	Academic	Other	Total	
	#	#	#	%
1st year	14	27	41	15.8
2nd year	2	0	2	1.0
3rd year	3	0	3	1.6
4th year	0	0	0	0.0

Employment (9 months after graduation)

	Total	Percentage
Employment status known	0	0.0
Employment status unknown	0	0.0
Employed	0	0.0
Pursuing graduate degrees	0	0.0
Unemployed (seeking, not seeking, or studying for the bar)	0	0.0
Type of Employment		
# employed in law firms	0	0.0
# employed in business and industry	0	0.0
# employed in government	0	0.0
# employed in public interest	0	0.0
# employed as judicial clerks	0	0.0
# employed in academia	0	0.0
Geographic Location		
# employed in state	0	0.0
# employed outside the US	0	0.0
# of states where employed		0

Bar Passage Rates

First-time takers	140	Reporting %	100.00
Average school %	36.43	Average state %	50.28
Average pass difference	−13.85		

Jurisdiction	Takers	Passers	Pass %	State %	Diff %
Puerto Rico	140	51	36.43	50.28	−13.85

PONTIFICAL CATHOLIC UNIVERSITY OF PUERTO RICO SCHOOL OF LAW

2250 Avenida Las Americas, Suite 633
Ponce, PR 00717-9997
Phone: 787.841.2000, exts. 1836, 1837; Fax: 787.841.4620
E-mail: derecho@email.pucpr.edu; Website: www.pucpr.edu/derecho

Introduction

The School of Law of the Pontifical Catholic University of Puerto Rico was founded in 1961. It is located within the main campus of the Pontifical Catholic University of Puerto Rico, on the southern part of the island in the historical city of Ponce, one of the most beautiful places in Puerto Rico.

The primary objective of the Pontifical Catholic University School of Law is the formation of lawyers imbued with a deep love and concern for their Catholic faith and imbedded in the redeeming truths of Christian philosophy and ethics. The law school of the Pontifical Catholic University of Puerto Rico hopes to contribute to upholding the high ethical, cultural, and literary accomplishments of the Puerto Rican bar, which historically represents a tradition of moral austerity, intellectual achievement, and professional competence.

Library and Physical Facilities

The School of Law occupies the Spellman Building. Its location on the campus of Pontifical Catholic University of Puerto Rico enables students to study related academic disciplines, to participate in the intellectual life, and to enjoy many other facilities of the university.

Among the materials in the library is a comprehensive and growing collection of legal treatises, tests, monographs, and periodicals, including the most important and recent publications in civil, common, and comparative law. Modern audiovisual equipment and computerized services are also available. The library is an authorized depository for United Nations documents as well as for United States government documents. In addition, it offers the services of the Westlaw and LexisNexis systems, which permit computer-assisted legal research.

Curriculum

The required subjects are:
- Administrative Law
- Advanced Legal Analysis
- Civil Procedure
- Constitutional Law
- Contracts
- Corporations
- Criminal Procedure
- Evidence
- Family Law
- Federal Jurisdiction
- Fundamentals of Research, Analysis, and Writing
- Intermediate Research, Analysis, and Writing
- Introduction to Law
- Legal Aid Clinic
- Legal Ethics and Professional Responsibility
- Mercantile Law
- Mortgages
- Notarial Law
- Obligations
- Penal Law
- Property Law
- Successions and Donations
- Theology
- Torts
- Trial Practice
- Workshop Bar Preparation

The basic program covers three years in the day division or four years in the evening division.

The school curriculum includes a clinical program for third-year students. Pursuant to a rule approved by the Supreme Court of the Commonwealth of Puerto Rico in 1974, students practice trial advocacy under the supervision of law school professors in the Courts of First Instance and in administrative agencies.

The Pontifical Catholic University of Puerto Rico also offers a combined JD/MBA degree. For the combined degree, students are required to complete 85 credit hours at the School of Law (79 required credits and 6 elective credits), plus 9 credit hours in electives completed at the Graduate Program of the School of Business Administration, for a total of 94 credit hours. In addition, the students must complete 34 credit hours at the School of Business Administration (31 required credits and 3 electives) and an additional 9 approved elective credits in JD, for a total of 43 credits, plus 4 hours of Theology.

Admission

Application for admission is open to men and women of good character who have received a bachelor's degree from a qualified institution and have obtained a 2.5 grade-point average.

The required forms for application for admission and all other information may be obtained from the registrar of the law school and should be filed with all supporting documents before April 15. The School of Law admits beginning students in August and January for both the full-time and part-time programs.

Applicants are required to take both the LSAT and the Examen de Admisión a Estudios de Posgrado (EXADEP) (formerly PAEG).

Test scores are not the only factor considered. Besides the objective factors, there are many intangible and personal considerations, such as strong motivation, disadvantaged circumstances, evidence of improving performance, and relevant work experience. A personal interview of the applicant by a committee is essential before a decision is made. Applicants of both sexes and from all religious, racial, social, and ethnic backgrounds are encouraged to apply.

All courses are offered only in Spanish. Consequently, students are required to be proficient in Spanish.

Student Activities

The law review, *Revista de Derecho Puertorriqueño*, is devoted to scholarly analysis and discussion of development of the law. It publishes student notes, comments, and surveys, as well as articles of outstanding quality submitted by attorneys, judges, and other members of the legal profession. The school has a student council, a chapter of the National Association of Law Students of Puerto Rico, and an Association for Women's Rights. Local chapters of Phi Alpha Delta international law fraternity, the Delta Theta Phi law fraternity, and the Law Student Division of the ABA are also active and well organized in the law school.

Housing

Students live either in university residences or private housing. Inquiries concerning housing facilities should be addressed to the Housing Office, Pontifical Catholic University of Puerto Rico, 2250 Avenida Las Americas, Suite 545, Ponce, PR 00717-9997.

Expenses and Financial Aid

There is a deferred plan for students who have financial difficulties at the time of registration. The university has made available for law students several full-tuition scholarships to be awarded on the basis of scholastic excellence. The university also has an office for student loans and other types of financial services.

Applicant Profile Not Available

UNIVERSITY OF PUERTO RICO SCHOOL OF LAW

PO Box 23349, UPR Station
San Juan, PR 00931-3349
Phone: 787.999.9553; Fax: 787.999.9564
E-mail: admisiones@law.upr.edu; Website: www.law.upr.edu

ABA
Approved
Since
1945

AMERICAN BAR ASSOCIATION
Section of Legal Education
and Admissions to the Bar

The Basics

Type of school	Public
Term	Semester
Application deadline	2/15
Application fee	$20
Financial aid deadline	5/31
Can first year start other than fall?	No
Student to faculty ratio	23.0 to 1
# of housing spaces available	
restricted to law students	18
graduate housing for which law students are eligible	18

Faculty and Administrators

	Total		Men		Women		Minorities	
	Spr	Fall	Spr	Fall	Spr	Fall	Spr	Fall
Full-time	24	24	17	16	7	8	23	23
Other full-time	4	4	4	3	0	1	2	4
Deans, librarians, & others who teach	15	15	5	5	10	10	15	15
Part-time	60	61	38	37	21	20	57	58
Total	103	104	64	61	38	39	97	100

Curriculum

		Full-Time	Part-Time
Typical first-year section size		75	40
Is there typically a "small section" of the first-year class, other than Legal Writing, taught by full-time faculty		No	No
If yes, typical size offered last year			
# of classroom course titles beyond first-year curriculum		108	
# of upper division courses, excluding seminars, with an enrollment:	Under 25	128	
	25–49	42	
	50–74	25	
	75–99	17	
	100+	0	
# of seminars		43	
# of seminar positions available		645	
# of seminar positions filled		283	209
# of positions available in simulation courses		274	
# of simulation positions filled		145	49
# of positions available in faculty supervised clinical courses		420	
# of faculty supervised clinical positions filled		267	124
# involved in field placements		3	2
# involved in law journals		29	0
# involved in moot court or trial competitions		2	1
# of credit hours required to graduate		92	

JD Enrollment and Ethnicity

	Men		Women		Full-Time		Part-Time		1st-Year		Total		JD Degs. Awd.
	#	%	#	%	#	%	#	%	#	%	#	%	
All Hispanics	0	0.0	0	0.0	0	0.0	0	0.0	0	0.0	0	0.0	0
Am. Ind./AK Nat.	0	0.0	0	0.0	0	0.0	0	0.0	0	0.0	0	0.0	0
Asian	0	0.0	0	0.0	0	0.0	0	0.0	0	0.0	0	0.0	0
Black/Af. Am.	0	0.0	0	0.0	0	0.0	0	0.0	0	0.0	0	0.0	0
Nat. HI/Pac. Isl.	0	0.0	0	0.0	0	0.0	0	0.0	0	0.0	0	0.0	0
2 or more races	0	0.0	0	0.0	0	0.0	0	0.0	0	0.0	0	0.0	0
Subtotal (minor.)	0	0.0	0	0.0	0	0.0	0	0.0	0	0.0	0	0.0	4
Nonres. Alien	94	28.4	99	24.4	1	0.2	192	100.0	93	24.6	193	26.2	0
White/Cauc.	0	0.0	0	0.0	0	0.0	0	0.0	0	0.0	0	0.0	0
Unknown	237	71.6	307	75.6	544	99.8	0	0.0	285	75.4	544	73.8	192
Total	331	44.9	406	55.1	545	73.9	192	26.1	378	51.3	737		196

Transfers

Transfers in	0
Transfers out	0

Tuition and Fees

	Resident	Nonresident
Full-time	$7,611	$9,437
Part-time	$6,341	$11,643
Tuition Guarantee Program		Y

Living Expenses

Estimated living expenses for singles

Living on campus	Living off campus	Living at home
$10,895	$15,155	$10,455

UNIVERSITY OF PUERTO RICO SCHOOL OF LAW

*ABA
Approved
Since
1945*

GPA and LSAT Scores

	Total	Full-Time	Part-Time
# of apps	597	243	188
# of offers	221	162	59
# of matrics	197	147	50
75% GPA	3.80	3.83	3.75
Median GPA	3.59	3.59	3.56
25% GPA	3.34	3.34	3.15
75% LSAT	150	145	149
Median LSAT	146	143	146
25% LSAT	142	141	143

Grants and Scholarships (from prior year)

	Total		Full-Time		Part-Time	
	#	%	#	%	#	%
Total # of students	740		527		213	
Total # receiving grants	0	0.0	0	0.0	0	0.0
Less than 1/2 tuition	0	0.0	0	0.0	0	0.0
Half to full tuition	0	0.0	0	0.0	0	0.0
Full tuition	0	0.0	0	0.0	0	0.0
More than full tuition	0	0.0	0	0.0	0	0.0
Median grant amount			$0		$0	

Informational and Library Resources

Total amount spent on library materials	$1,222,254
Study seating capacity inside the library	437
# of full-time equivalent professional librarians	9
Hours per week library is open	112
# of open, wired connections available to students	170
# of networked computers available for use by students	49
Has wireless network?	Y
Requires computer?	N

JD Attrition (from prior year)

	Academic	Other	Total	
	#	#	#	%
1st year	5	0	5	1.3
2nd year	2	0	2	1.7
3rd year	3	0	3	1.5
4th year	0	0	0	0.0

Employment (9 months after graduation)

	Total	Percentage
Employment status known	30	16.6
Employment status unknown	151	83.4
Employed	23	76.7
Pursuing graduate degrees	2	6.7
Unemployed (seeking, not seeking, or studying for the bar)	5	16.7
Type of Employment		
# employed in law firms	10	43.5
# employed in business and industry	6	26.1
# employed in government	2	8.7
# employed in public interest	0	0.0
# employed as judicial clerks	3	13.0
# employed in academia	2	8.7
Geographic Location		
# employed in state	21	91.3
# employed outside the US	0	0.0
# of states where employed	0	

Bar Passage Rates

First-time takers	172	Reporting %	100.00
Average school %	64.53	Average state %	50.28
Average pass difference	14.25		

Jurisdiction	Takers	Passers	Pass %	State %	Diff %
Puerto Rico	172	111	64.53	50.28	14.25

UNIVERSITY OF PUERTO RICO SCHOOL OF LAW

PO Box 23349, UPR Station
San Juan, PR 00931-3349
Phone: 787.999.9553; Fax: 787.999.9564
E-mail: admisiones@law.upr.edu; Website: www.law.upr.edu

The information on these pages was provided by the law school.

Introduction

The University of Puerto Rico School of Law was founded in 1913 at its present site on the University Campus at Río Piedras, within the metropolitan area of San Juan in the heart of the Caribbean. The University of Puerto Rico is accredited by the Middle States Colleges Association. The School of Law has been accredited by the American Bar Association since 1945 and by the Association of American Law Schools since 1948. It is also accredited by the Council on Higher Education and the Puerto Rico Supreme Court.

Academic and Special Programs

The Academic Program: The guiding principle behind our academic program is to increase and diversify the learning and development experiences of our students. That is the reason why half of our study program is elective. Our students can take courses ranging from theoretical to practical, to issues pertaining to civil rights, technology, feminism, business, international relations, and comparative law. In addition, our students, as part of their program, have to participate in a clinical program.

The study program consists of 92 credit hours. The majority of the courses are taught in Spanish.

Degree Offered: Juris Doctor
Joint-Degree Programs:
- Dual Juris Doctor and Law Degree Program (Licenciatura en Derecho) with the University of Barcelona, Spain
- Juris Doctor and Master of Business Administration with the University of Puerto Rico Graduate School of Business Administration
- Juris Doctor and Doctor of Medicine with the University of Puerto Rico School of Medicine
- Juris Doctor and Master of Public Policy with the Humphrey School of Public Affairs at the University of Minnesota

Graduate: LLM for Latin American and Caribbean lawyers
Special Programs: The School of Law has student exchange programs with the University of Arizona James E. Rogers College of Law, the University of Connecticut School of Law, the University of Palermo in Argentina, the University of Chile Law School, the University of Ottawa Faculty of Law in Canada, and the University of Amberes in Belgium. Under these programs, students register at their home institution but will take a full course load at the host institution. The credits and grades earned during a single semester will be awarded by the home institution according to the standard procedure of the home law school. Students also have a chance to participate in a summer law program at the University of Barcelona, Spain. Also, the school has a winter-exchange program with the University of Ottawa Faculty of Law in Canada, through which students can earn four credits studying Law and Technology or Law, Technology, and Feminism for one week in Canada and two weeks in Puerto Rico.

Clinical Program

In March 1974, the Puerto Rico Supreme Court approved rules for the local courts to allow students to practice law and participate in judicial proceedings. The US District Court followed suit in 1991. Our curriculum requires that students in their last year of study complete a two-semester clinical program. The clinical program stands as clear testimony of our school's commitment to community service. The Legal Aid Clinic handles over 1,300 cases per year, offering assistance to those in need of legal aid. Our clinic offers our students the opportunity to practice law in a wide range of areas in an environment resembling the facilities of a modern, medium-sized law firm.
- Cyber Law
- Community Economic Development
- Criminal Law (federal and state)
- Family Law
- Mediation
- Gay and Lesbian Rights
- Civil Rights
- Environmental Law
- Employment Law
- Civil Cases (in general)
- Juvenile Law
- Health Rights for Women Inmates

Admission

In order to be admitted to the University of Puerto Rico School of Law, applicants must take two aptitude tests: the Law School Admission Test (LSAT) and the Examen de Admisión a Estudios de Posgrado (EXADEP). The tests must be taken no later than February of the year of application. Applicants must also have a bachelor's degree from an accredited institution before enrolling.

The entering class is selected by converting the LSAT, the EXADEP, and the GPA into the student's admission index and making offers of admission to those with the 200 highest admission indexes. However, 7 percent of the new class is chosen from those with 201–260 indexes based on a complete profile of the applicant, taking into consideration his or her ability to study law, his or her past accomplishments, and his or her disadvantages in receiving a postsecondary education.

Applicants who cannot take the required aptitude tests because of disability are considered individually by the admission committee. The University of Puerto Rico does not discriminate against students on the basis of race, color, religion, gender, age, marital status, national origin, or disability.

Expenses and Financial Aid

Resident law students pay tuition and fees amounting to $127 per credit each semester. Nonresident students who are US citizens pay the same amount that would be required from Puerto Rican students if they were to study in the state from which the nonresidents come, thus establishing a reciprocity principle. Nonresident students who are not US citizens pay additional tuition and fees amounting approximately to $2,327.50 for eight or more credits for each semester.

All financial aid for the University of Puerto Rico School of Law is administered by the school's Office of Financial Aid. Each student is considered on his or her own merit and need. Awards are made only after an applicant has been admitted.

Alumni

Our student body is made up of graduates from public and private universities in Puerto Rico and the states, as well as foreign institutions. They come from a wide range of academic backgrounds and social experiences, providing a unique atmosphere in the classroom and outside. Our alumni are leaders in the legal field and in the public arena serving as governors, US ambassadors, partners in major law firms, Puerto Rico Supreme Court Justices, attorneys general, presidents of the University of Puerto Rico, and chief executive officers in the banking industry.

Library and Physical Facilities

The School of Law's library is the largest law library in the Caribbean. Its collection encompasses both the Romano-Germanic civil law and Anglo-American common law traditions. Also, our library has been designated as a European Documentation Center by the European Union and a selective depository for US government documents. Our school is equipped with state-of-the-art technology, smart classrooms, courtroom-classrooms, and wireless connections for the students.

APPLICANT PROFILE

University of Puerto Rico School of Law
This grid includes only applicants who earned 120–180 LSAT scores under standard administrations.

LSAT Score	3.75 +		3.50–3.74		3.25–3.49		3.00–3.24		2.75–2.99		2.50–2.74		2.25–2.49		2.00–2.24		Below 2.00		No GPA		Total	
	Apps	Adm	Apps	Adm	Apps	Adm	Apps	Adm	Apps	Adm	Apps	Adm	Apps	Adm	Apps	Adm	Apps	Adm	Apps	Adm	Apps	Adm
175–180	0	0	0	0	0	0	0	0	0	0	0	0	0	0	0	0	0	0	0	0	0	0
170–174	0	0	0	0	0	0	0	0	0	0	0	0	1	1	0	0	0	0	0	0	1	1
165–169	1	1	1	1	0	0	0	0	0	0	0	0	0	0	0	0	0	0	0	0	2	2
160–164	4	4	1	1	5	5	1	1	0	0	1	1	0	0	0	0	0	0	0	0	12	12
155–159	7	7	0	0	1	1	1	1	0	0	0	0	2	1	0	0	0	0	0	0	11	10
150–154	7	7	10	10	7	7	6	5	3	3	1	1	1	1	0	0	2	2	0	0	37	36
145–149	17	16	23	20	22	21	19	9	13	4	6	2	1	1	2	0	1	0	3	2	107	75
140–144	22	21	28	20	39	20	24	4	20	1	12	1	6	1	2	0	0	0	5	0	158	68
135–139	17	9	37	6	40	2	17	0	17	0	9	0	1	0	3	0	2	0	1	0	144	17
130–134	8	0	12	0	17	0	15	0	15	0	5	0	6	0	2	0	1	0	4	0	85	0
125–129	4	0	6	0	8	0	7	0	3	0	1	0	2	0	1	0	1	0	0	0	33	0
120–124	0	0	0	0	0	0	0	0	0	0	0	0	0	0	0	0	0	0	3	0	3	0
Total	87	65	118	58	139	56	90	20	71	8	35	5	20	5	10	0	7	2	16	2	593	221

Apps = Number of Applicants
Adm = Number Admitted
Reflects 99% of the total applicant pool; highest LSAT data reported.

QUINNIPIAC UNIVERSITY SCHOOL OF LAW

275 Mount Carmel Avenue
Hamden, CT 06518
Phone: 203.582.3400; Fax: 203.582.3339
E-mail: ladm@quinnipiac.edu; Website: http://law.quinnipiac.edu

The Basics

Type of school	Private
Term	Semester
Application deadline	3/1
Application fee	$65
Financial aid deadline	
Can first year start other than fall?	No
Student to faculty ratio	13.0 to 1
# of housing spaces available restricted to law students	
graduate housing for which law students are eligible	

Faculty and Administrators

	Total		Men		Women		Minorities	
	Spr	Fall	Spr	Fall	Spr	Fall	Spr	Fall
Full-time	25	26	15	15	10	11	2	2
Other full-time	6	6	5	5	1	1	0	0
Deans, librarians, & others who teach	3	3	2	2	1	1	0	0
Part-time	39	34	20	26	19	8	1	1
Total	73	69	42	48	31	21	3	3

Curriculum

	Full-Time	Part-Time
Typical first-year section size	56	45
Is there typically a "small section" of the first-year class, other than Legal Writing, taught by full-time faculty	No	Yes
If yes, typical size offered last year		22
# of classroom course titles beyond first-year curriculum	120	
# of upper division courses, excluding seminars, with an enrollment: Under 25	118	
25–49	18	
50–74	4	
75–99	1	
100+	0	
# of seminars	12	
# of seminar positions available	352	
# of seminar positions filled	82	41
# of positions available in simulation courses	306	
# of simulation positions filled	61	163
# of positions available in faculty supervised clinical courses	84	
# of faculty supervised clinical positions filled	36	20
# involved in field placements	92	0
# involved in law journals	40	16
# involved in moot court or trial competitions	10	5
# of credit hours required to graduate	86	

JD Enrollment and Ethnicity

	Men		Women		Full-Time		Part-Time		1st-Year		Total		JD Degs. Awd.
	#	%	#	%	#	%	#	%	#	%	#	%	
All Hispanics	4	1.6	13	5.8	13	3.8	4	3.1	5	3.1	17	3.6	3
Am. Ind./AK Nat.	1	0.4	1	0.4	1	0.3	1	0.8	0	0.0	2	0.4	0
Asian	6	2.5	16	7.1	15	4.4	7	5.5	10	6.1	22	4.7	6
Black/Af. Am.	4	1.6	7	3.1	6	1.8	5	3.9	2	1.2	11	2.4	4
Nat. HI/Pac. Isl.	0	0.0	0	0.0	0	0.0	0	0.0	0	0.0	0	0.0	0
2 or more races	0	0.0	2	0.9	2	0.6	0	0.0	2	1.2	2	0.4	0
Subtotal (minor.)	15	6.2	39	17.4	37	10.9	17	13.4	19	11.7	54	11.6	13
Nonres. Alien	5	2.1	6	2.7	8	2.4	3	2.4	4	2.5	11	2.4	0
White/Cauc.	207	85.2	166	74.1	269	79.1	104	81.9	130	79.8	373	79.9	81
Unknown	16	6.6	13	5.8	26	7.6	3	2.4	10	6.1	29	6.2	5
Total	243	52.0	224	48.0	340	72.8	127	27.2	163	34.9	467		99

Transfers

Transfers in	4
Transfers out	8

Tuition and Fees

	Resident	Nonresident
Full-time	$42,740	$42,740
Part-time	$30,180	$30,180
Tuition Guarantee Program	N	

Living Expenses

Estimated living expenses for singles

Living on campus	Living off campus	Living at home
N/A	$20,174	$13,976

ABA
Approved
Since
1992

GPA and LSAT Scores

	Total	Full-Time	Part-Time
# of apps	2,490	2,260	249
# of offers	1,092	1,010	82
# of matrics	163	123	40
75% GPA	3.62	3.61	3.64
Median GPA	3.42	3.43	3.38
25% GPA	3.13	3.13	3.11
75% LSAT	159	160	155
Median LSAT	157	157	153
25% LSAT	154	155	152

Grants and Scholarships (from prior year)

	Total		Full-Time		Part-Time	
	#	%	#	%	#	%
Total # of students	415		291		124	
Total # receiving grants	289	69.6	237	81.4	52	41.9
Less than 1/2 tuition	156	37.6	104	35.7	52	41.9
Half to full tuition	107	25.8	107	36.8	0	0.0
Full tuition	26	6.3	26	8.9	0	0.0
More than full tuition	0	0.0	0	0.0	0	0.0
Median grant amount			$20,000		$4,500	

Informational and Library Resources

Total amount spent on library materials	$919,532
Study seating capacity inside the library	350
# of full-time equivalent professional librarians	5
Hours per week library is open	93
# of open, wired connections available to students	264
# of networked computers available for use by students	103
Has wireless network?	Y
Requires computer?	N

JD Attrition (from prior year)

	Academic	Other	Total	
	#	#	#	%
1st year	1	11	12	7.6
2nd year	0	3	3	2.4
3rd year	0	1	1	0.9
4th year	0	0	0	0.0

Employment (9 months after graduation)

	Total	Percentage
Employment status known	107	97.3
Employment status unknown	3	2.7
Employed	101	94.4
Pursuing graduate degrees	0	0.0
Unemployed (seeking, not seeking, or studying for the bar)	6	5.6
Type of Employment		
# employed in law firms	46	45.5
# employed in business and industry	25	24.8
# employed in government	17	16.8
# employed in public interest	1	1.0
# employed as judicial clerks	8	7.9
# employed in academia	1	1.0
Geographic Location		
# employed in state	72	71.3
# employed outside the US	0	0.0
# of states where employed		11

Bar Passage Rates

First-time takers	112	Reporting %	77.68
Average school %	89.66	Average state %	85.56
Average pass difference	4.10		

Jurisdiction	Takers	Passers	Pass %	State %	Diff %
Connecticut	87	78	89.66	85.56	4.10

QUINNIPIAC UNIVERSITY SCHOOL OF LAW

275 Mount Carmel Avenue
Hamden, CT 06518
Phone: 203.582.3400; Fax: 203.582.3339
E-mail: ladm@quinnipiac.edu; Website: http://law.quinnipiac.edu

Introduction

Excellent law schools share many common traits—faculty renowned for their scholarship and commitment to teaching; academically rigorous courses; loyal, successful alumni; and motivated, focused students. All of these are essential components of Quinnipiac Law's identity. However, what sets Quinnipiac apart is its personal, student-centered approach to the law school experience. Contributing to this identity is a favorable 13:1 student-to-faculty ratio, the extraordinary accessibility of the faculty, and an environment that both challenges and supports its students as they prepare for careers in law.

Nestled among the hills, woods, and waterways of Connecticut on one of the most beautiful campuses in New England, yet just 75 miles from New York City, Quinnipiac's setting and location are ideal. The beautiful, state-of-the-art law center opened in 1995. Wireless computer access throughout provides students with a modern, relaxed, and safe environment for study.

Faculty

Our faculty's academic credentials span the nation's leading institutions from Harvard, Yale, and Berkeley to Chicago, Michigan, and Columbia. They combine excellence in scholarship and teaching with exceptional accessibility. The care with which faculty members demonstrate their interest in each student's progress and success is a distinguishing characteristic of Quinnipiac Law. Most faculty have an open-door policy and generously share their expertise, insight, and time. The low student-to-faculty ratio (13:1) allows students to work closely with faculty, and this translates into a different kind of law school experience.

Library and Physical Facilities

The 50,000-square-foot law library is at the center of the School of Law complex. With a collection of more than 450,000 volumes, it also provides comprehensive access to numerous electronic resources and databases such as LexisNexis, Westlaw/Dialog, JSTOR, and other web-based services. Its interlibrary loan network makes it possible to obtain materials from any library in the world. The beautiful facility features spacious public areas, numerous reading rooms, and individual study carrels, providing a comfortable and relaxing environment for research and study.

Curriculum

The law school is fully approved by the ABA and is a member of AALS. Full-time day and part-time evening programs are offered beginning each fall. The academic program is designed to prepare students to be generalists or specialists. The program provides a dynamic blend of traditional classroom instruction and extensive practical learning opportunities.

Students who wish to focus on a specific area of study may choose from six different concentrations—**Civil Advocacy and Dispute Resolution**, **Criminal Law and Advocacy**, **Family Law**, **Health Law**, **Intellectual Property**, and **Tax**. About one-third of our students choose a focus in one of the above concentrations. However, one may develop an informal concentration in a variety of other fields with the advice and assistance of a faculty member.

The law school also offers a joint JD/MBA degree (with a health care management track) and a summer study-abroad program with Trinity College in Dublin, Ireland.

Special Programs

Quinnipiac is recognized as having one of the premier clinical and externship programs in the country, and students often cite their experiences in these programs as one of the highlights of their law school career. Every student is guaranteed participation in at least one of these practical learning opportunities that allow students to bridge the gap between theory and practice. A total of 15 clinical and externship programs are available to students.

The six clinical programs include **Civil**, **Tax**, **Advanced**, **Evening** (for part-time students), **Defense Appellate**, and **Prosecution Appellate**. The **Civil Clinic** typically deals with the following types of cases or issues: Education, Employment, Health, Housing, Family and Children, Immigration, Law Reform, and Poverty. The nine externship programs are **Corporate Counsel**, **Criminal Justice**, **Family and Juvenile Law**, **Judicial**, **Legal Services**, **Legislative**, **Mediation**, **Public Interest**, and **Field Placement II**.

Quinnipiac has established two centers in specialized fields of law—the **Center for Health Law and Policy** and the **Center on Dispute Resolution**—both of which draw on the considerable academic strengths and resources within the law school community.

Admission

Admission is competitive and based upon a variety of factors: undergraduate academic record, LSAT scores, personal statement, letters of recommendation, résumé, and other evidence such as advanced degrees, life and work experience, and extracurricular activities. Applications are welcomed from students of color, nontraditional students, and all students who add to the diversity of the student body. A rolling admission system is employed; however, the priority application deadline for admission and scholarship consideration is March 1. *Candidates for the full-tuition Dean's Fellows awards must apply by February 1.*

Student Activities

Quinnipiac students often comment about the strong sense of community that permeates the law school. That sense of community is enhanced by the numerous and varied opportunities for students to participate in cocurricular activities, including a dynamic Student Bar Association, more than 25 different student organizations, a thriving Moot Court Society, a Mock Trial team, an active *Quinnipiac Law Review*, and two student journals—the *Health Law Journal* and the *Probate Law Journal*.

Expenses and Financial Aid

Approximately 90 percent of the student body receives some form of financial assistance. Every applicant is considered for merit-based scholarships that range from $3,000 to full tuition per year. March 1 is the application deadline for most merit awards. However, candidates for the full-tuition Dean's Fellows scholarships must submit applications by February 1. Total institutional scholarships and grants for the 2010–2011 academic year totaled approximately $5.2 million.

Housing

Campus housing for graduate and professional students is not available. However, there is ample, affordable housing available near the campus and throughout New Haven county. The School of Law Admissions Office maintains a housing website and roommate locator online for its admitted students and also provides personal assistance in securing off-campus accommodations.

Career Services

The Office of Career Services provides students and graduates with the expert guidance necessary to make informed career decisions. It offers substantial support through individual counseling and workshops on topics such as writing résumés and interviewing techniques.

The office coordinates on- and off-campus recruitment programs. Students interview with employers for a variety of summer internships and permanent jobs in the private and public sector.

Over the past six years, more than 90 percent of our graduates have been employed within nine months of graduation. The graduating class of 2009 had a 94 percent placement rate and found employment as follows: 46 percent entered private practice, 25 percent took positions in business and industry, 17 percent chose government service work, 8 percent received judicial clerkships, 1 percent went into public interest work, and 1 percent were studying for advanced degrees. The remainder went into other fields of employment.

APPLICANT PROFILE

Quinnipiac University School of Law
This grid includes only applicants who earned 120–180 LSAT scores under standard administrations.

LSAT Score	3.75 +		3.50–3.74		3.25–3.49		3.00–3.24		2.75–2.99		2.50–2.74		Below 2.50		No GPA		Total	
	Apps	Adm	Apps	Adm	Apps	Adm	Apps	Adm	Apps	Adm	Apps	Adm	Apps	Adm	Apps	Adm	Apps	Adm
170–180	6	5	2	2	3	3	2	2	4	2	1	0	1	1	0	0	19	15
165–169	24	20	13	12	14	13	13	11	11	8	3	3	10	1	1	1	89	69
160–164	58	53	92	80	94	86	73	59	37	30	30	16	16	5	4	2	404	331
155–159	89	80	166	149	158	135	134	103	57	37	42	11	35	3	5	2	686	520
150–154	68	28	140	42	169	30	163	20	121	7	43	2	45	1	7	0	756	130
145–149	17	5	45	5	61	5	72	0	46	0	34	0	24	0	3	0	302	15
140–144	8	0	12	0	18	0	21	0	21	0	11	0	16	0	5	0	112	0
Below 140	3	0	4	0	8	0	7	0	10	0	21	0	17	0	3	0	73	0
Total	273	191	474	290	525	272	485	195	307	84	185	32	164	11	28	5	2441	1080

Apps = Number of Applicants
Adm = Number Admitted
Reflects 99% of the total applicant pool; highest LSAT data reported.

REGENT UNIVERSITY SCHOOL OF LAW

1000 Regent University Drive, RH239
Virginia Beach, VA 23464
Phone: 757.352.4584; Fax: 757.352.4139
E-mail: lawschool@regent.edu; Website: www.regent.edu/law

ABA
Approved
Since
1989

The Basics

Type of school	Private
Term	Semester
Application deadline	6/1
Application fee	$50
Financial aid deadline	6/1
Can first year start other than fall?	No
Student to faculty ratio	16.1 to 1
# of housing spaces available restricted to law students	
graduate housing for which law students are eligible	860

Faculty and Administrators

	Total		Men		Women		Minorities	
	Spr	Fall	Spr	Fall	Spr	Fall	Spr	Fall
Full-time	21	21	14	14	7	7	4	4
Other full-time	3	4	3	3	0	1	0	1
Deans, librarians, & others who teach	9	9	6	6	3	3	1	1
Part-time	15	18	14	16	1	2	0	2
Total	48	52	37	39	11	13	5	8

JD Enrollment and Ethnicity

	Men		Women		Full-Time		Part-Time		1st-Year		Total		JD Degs. Awd.
	#	%	#	%	#	%	#	%	#	%	#	%	
All Hispanics	6	2.7	10	5.0	16	3.9	0	0.0	9	5.4	16	3.7	2
Am. Ind./AK Nat.	6	2.7	6	3.0	12	2.9	0	0.0	7	4.2	12	2.8	1
Asian	8	3.5	16	7.9	24	5.9	0	0.0	11	6.5	24	5.6	4
Black/Af. Am.	8	3.5	15	7.4	20	4.9	3	15.8	7	4.2	23	5.4	7
Nat. HI/Pac. Isl.	0	0.0	0	0.0	0	0.0	0	0.0	0	0.0	0	0.0	0
2 or more races	0	0.0	0	0.0	0	0.0	0	0.0	0	0.0	0	0.0	0
Subtotal (minor.)	28	12.4	47	23.3	72	17.6	3	15.8	34	20.2	75	17.5	14
Nonres. Alien	1	0.4	2	1.0	3	0.7	0	0.0	0	0.0	3	0.7	0
White/Cauc.	189	83.6	145	71.8	319	78.0	15	78.9	130	77.4	334	78.0	105
Unknown	8	3.5	8	4.0	15	3.7	1	5.3	4	2.4	16	3.7	4
Total	226	52.8	202	47.2	409	95.6	19	4.4	168	39.3	428		124

Curriculum

	Full-Time	Part-Time
Typical first-year section size	80	80
Is there typically a "small section" of the first-year class, other than Legal Writing, taught by full-time faculty	Yes	Yes
If yes, typical size offered last year	40	40
# of classroom course titles beyond first-year curriculum	78	
# of upper division courses, excluding seminars, with an enrollment: Under 25	78	
25–49	17	
50–74	9	
75–99	6	
100+	0	
# of seminars	2	
# of seminar positions available	24	
# of seminar positions filled	18	0
# of positions available in simulation courses	480	
# of simulation positions filled	315	8
# of positions available in faculty supervised clinical courses	56	
# of faculty supervised clinical positions filled	21	3
# involved in field placements	57	2
# involved in law journals	71	1
# involved in moot court or trial competitions	56	0
# of credit hours required to graduate	90	

Transfers

Transfers in	2
Transfers out	4

Tuition and Fees

	Resident	Nonresident
Full-time	$31,410	$31,410
Part-time	$24,235	$24,235
Tuition Guarantee Program	N	

Living Expenses

Estimated living expenses for singles

Living on campus	Living off campus	Living at home
$19,840	$19,840	$19,840

REGENT UNIVERSITY SCHOOL OF LAW

ABA
Approved
Since
1989

GPA and LSAT Scores

	Total	Full-Time	Part-Time
# of apps	699	674	25
# of offers	330	321	9
# of matrics	168	164	4
75% GPA	3.54	3.54	3.29
Median GPA	3.32	3.32	2.96
25% GPA	2.97	2.97	2.86
75% LSAT	156	156	158
Median LSAT	152	152	156
25% LSAT	150	150	154

Grants and Scholarships (from prior year)

	Total		Full-Time		Part-Time	
	#	%	#	%	#	%
Total # of students	417		394		23	
Total # receiving grants	337	80.8	321	81.5	16	69.6
Less than 1/2 tuition	245	58.8	229	58.1	16	69.6
Half to full tuition	70	16.8	70	17.8	0	0.0
Full tuition	18	4.3	18	4.6	0	0.0
More than full tuition	4	1.0	4	1.0	0	0.0
Median grant amount			$5,000		$2,000	

Informational and Library Resources

Total amount spent on library materials	$642,413
Study seating capacity inside the library	324
# of full-time equivalent professional librarians	10
Hours per week library is open	109
# of open, wired connections available to students	218
# of networked computers available for use by students	61
Has wireless network?	Y
Requires computer?	N

JD Attrition (from prior year)

	Academic	Other	Total	
	#	#	#	%
1st year	25	10	35	21.6
2nd year	1	1	2	1.6
3rd year	0	0	0	0.0
4th year	0	0	0	0.0

Employment (9 months after graduation)

	Total	Percentage
Employment status known	129	95.6
Employment status unknown	6	4.4
Employed	114	88.4
Pursuing graduate degrees	1	0.8
Unemployed (seeking, not seeking, or studying for the bar)	12	9.3
Type of Employment		
# employed in law firms	62	54.4
# employed in business and industry	19	16.7
# employed in government	12	10.5
# employed in public interest	2	1.8
# employed as judicial clerks	10	8.8
# employed in academia	7	6.1
Geographic Location		
# employed in state	43	37.7
# employed outside the US	2	1.8
# of states where employed	26	

Bar Passage Rates

First-time takers	139	Reporting %	72.66
Average school %	76.24	Average state %	78.72

Average pass difference −2.48

Jurisdiction	Takers	Passers	Pass %	State %	Diff %
Virginia	54	41	75.93	77.06	−1.13
Texas	9	9	100.00	85.48	14.52
South Carolina	9	7	77.78	78.19	−0.41
New York	6	5	83.33	86.51	−3.18
Others (4)	23	15	65.22		

REGENT UNIVERSITY SCHOOL OF LAW

1000 Regent University Drive, RH239
Virginia Beach, VA 23464
Phone: 757.352.4584; Fax: 757.352.4139
E-mail: lawschool@regent.edu; Website: www.regent.edu/law

Introduction

Regent Law is unique among ABA-approved law schools in offering a nationally recognized, rigorous academic experience in the context of a Christian worldview. Its 2,500-plus alumni, which include Virginia Governor Bob McDonnell '89, exemplify Regent Law's motto—"Law is more than a profession. It's a calling."—by providing excellent and principled legal counsel. The law school is composed of approximately 420 students and is situated on a stately, Georgian-style campus in Virginia Beach, Virginia, minutes from the Atlantic Ocean, less than a two-hour drive from Richmond, and less than four hours from Washington, DC.

Rigorous Academics and Christian Worldview

As demonstrated by an internationally recognized faculty; recent all-time-high bar pass rates; and alumni judicial clerkships and employment (top law firms, federal and state courts, etc.) at or above the national average; Regent Law is academically excellent. While affirming the faith of individual students, the school embraces a Christian worldview, encouraging students to see law as a vocation, or "calling." Regent's worldview provides a platform for developing the highest ethical standards in its students; it also helps make Regent a diverse and richly supportive academic community. Regent was recently cited as one of the best law schools for quality of life.

Academic Program/Legal Skills

Regent's Center for Advocacy Skills develops practical lawyering skills through clinical practica including a civil litigation clinic, a robust legal research and writing curriculum, a partnership with the American Center for Law and Justice (the nation's foremost public interest law firm defending religious liberties), extensive externship opportunities, and highly successful student Moot Court, Negotiation, and Trial Advocacy teams. Recent national team awards include the 2010 NBLSA International Negotiation Championship; 2009 National Pretrial Competition (with Best Brief and Best Oralist awards); 2009/08 Spong Moot Court Championships; and ABA National Negotiation and National Moot Court titles in 2007 and 2006, respectively.

Center for Global Justice, Human Rights, and the Rule of Law

Regent's new Center for Global Justice is a comprehensive response to the plight of the enslaved, oppressed, and trafficked worldwide. Through hands-on international summer internships, a unique global justice curriculum, and an annual symposium, the Center for Global Justice equips Regent Law students with the tools they need to be advocates for the oppressed around the world. See www.regent.edu/globaljustice for more information.

Full- and Part-Time Programs

The School of Law offers full- and part-time 90-semester-hour Juris Doctor programs, in-residence only. Students in the full-time program normally complete their degrees in three years; part-time students complete their degrees in four to five years.

Admission and the Bar

Applicants are required to submit a Regent-specific personal statement as part of the admission process. This personal statement is considered very carefully along with the applicant's LSAT score(s), undergraduate record, résumé, and letters of recommendation. Regent is committed to considering the entire application in the decision process, ultimately offering admission to prospective students who present a strong likelihood for success in law school. This commitment has resulted in a diverse student body. Applications from prospective students with LSAT scores of 150 and above and UGPAs above 3.0 are especially encouraged, as the School of Law has evidence that such students are very likely to succeed in law school and are also very likely to pass the bar exam on their first attempt. At the time of printing, Regent's first-time bar passage rate for all 2010 graduates was 89 percent, those with LSAT scores at or above 155 had a 95 percent pass rate, and those with scores at or above 160 had a 100 percent pass rate.

Academic Assistance

Regent Law is on the cutting edge of legal pedagogy in offering academic assistance to its students. Regent employs two faculty members, a director and associate director of academic success, who oversee the three components of the school's Academic Success Program. Under the first component, the school invites selected first-year students to attend a two-week program as a condition for admission into the school. The program helps students develop excellent law school study skills and introduces them to selected areas of the law in small sections taught by members of the full-time faculty. Under the second component, the school offers study skills workshops during the spring and fall semesters. As the third component, the associate director meets one-on-one with students to provide individualized counseling on how to improve their study strategies. The second and third components are available to all students. Student feedback on the school's Academic Success Program has been very positive.

The Law Library

Immediately adjacent to the School of Law and occupying the entire third floor of the library building, the newly renovated law library features 140 carrels in secluded study areas, as well as areas for group interaction, with both LAN and WiFi connections throughout for accessing essential legal research databases. With holdings of over 396,000 volumes and equivalents, the library's collection strengths are constitutional law and history, legal history, jurisprudence, law and faith, philosophy of law, international human rights, and family law.

International Law and Summer-Abroad/Exchange Programs

The School of Law has established the *Regent Journal of International Law* and has a very active International Law Society. The *Journal* is jointly edited by students from Regent Law and its Korean sister school, Handong International Law School, making it truly an international journal. In addition, the law school hosts a summer program in Strasbourg, France, focusing on international law and human rights. A summer program in Haifa and Jerusalem, Israel, focuses on issues of international law and the State of Israel, and provides a hermeneutical comparison of Biblical and Qur'anic law. Regent also offers semester-abroad opportunities. Students may spend a semester studying international law at Handong International Law School in South Korea. The School of Law has created student-exchange programs with Spanish universities in Barcelona and Madrid. Students are able to spend a semester in Spain and take subjects such as civil law and international private law. The School of Law has also approved a study-abroad agreement with Shantou University in China. Under the agreement, Regent students will be able to study law in English at Shantou and Regent will welcome visiting students from Shantou.

Housing

Regent Law students may choose from a variety of on- and off-campus housing options. Regent Village and Regent Commons offer convenient and quality housing within walking distance to the law school. Regent's on-campus housing provides a safe, friendly atmosphere and includes the following options: efficiency, quad, and one-, two-, and three-bedroom apartments. Housing applications are provided to admitted candidates only. Rates are comparable to or less than similar apartment complexes in the vicinity.

Financial Aid

The School of Law is committed to helping students finance their legal education by awarding approximately $3.4 million in scholarships and grants, ranging from $500 to full tuition. In recent years, approximately 92 percent of law students received some type of financial aid; 70 percent received scholarships or grants. Typically, admitted candidates with LSAT scores greater than or equal to 160, UGPAs greater than or equal to 3.0, and personal goals evidencing a calling toward Christian leadership and service have been awarded academic merit scholarships ranging from 80 to 100 percent of tuition costs. Other scholarships are awarded on the basis of academic promise and other factors indicative of potential for law school success. Regent also provides grant assistance for qualified students who are called to serve minority communities upon graduation. Students not awarded financial assistance the first year of law school may qualify for assistance in future years based on academic performance. Residents of Virginia may also qualify for the Virginia Tuition Assistance Grant. Regent provides a student loan repayment assistance program (LRAP) for qualified graduates practicing in the area of public interest law. A variety of loan options, including Stafford and Graduate PLUS, are available to meet the tuition and living expenses related to law school.

Campus Visitations

Campus visitation event schedule: www.regent.edu/lawvisitation.

The Office of Admissions encourages prospective student visits. To RSVP for campus visitations or to arrange a visit to the law school, please e-mail lawschool@regent.edu or telephone 757.352.4584.

APPLICANT PROFILE

Regent University School of Law
This grid includes only applicants who earned 120–180 LSAT scores under standard administrations.

LSAT Score	GPA								
	3.75 +	3.50–3.74	3.25–3.49	3.00–3.24	2.75–2.99	2.50–2.74	2.25–2.49	2.00–2.24	Below 2.00
175–180									
170–174									
165–169									
160–164									
155–159									
150–154									
146–149									
120–145									

Strong Possibility   Possible   Unlikely

This grid is intended to provide prospective applicants a general sense of our admission standards, as based upon competition for entry into recent classes entering the law school. This grid does not adequately describe the numerous nonquantifiable factors that are considered by our Admission Committee. Prospective applicants are encouraged to review our admission materials for a fuller understanding of the admission review standards used by Regent University School of Law.

UNIVERSITY OF RICHMOND SCHOOL OF LAW

28 Westhampton Way
University of Richmond, VA 23173
Phone: 804.289.8189; Fax: 804.287.6516
E-mail: lawadmissions@richmond.edu; Website: http://law.richmond.edu

The Basics

Type of school	Private
Term	Semester
Application deadline	3/1
Application fee	$35
Financial aid deadline	3/1
Can first year start other than fall?	Yes
Student to faculty ratio	14.0 to 1
# of housing spaces available	
restricted to law students	8
graduate housing for which law students are eligible	8

Faculty and Administrators

	Total Spr	Total Fall	Men Spr	Men Fall	Women Spr	Women Fall	Minorities Spr	Minorities Fall
Full-time	24	30	17	20	7	10	2	2
Other full-time	7	6	3	2	4	4	1	1
Deans, librarians, & others who teach	16	14	6	5	10	9	0	0
Part-time	58	46	35	33	21	13	0	3
Total	105	96	61	60	42	36	3	6

Curriculum

		Full-Time	Part-Time
Typical first-year section size		55	0
Is there typically a "small section" of the first-year class, other than Legal Writing, taught by full-time faculty		No	No
If yes, typical size offered last year			
# of classroom course titles beyond first-year curriculum		102	
# of upper division courses, excluding seminars, with an enrollment:	Under 25	102	
	25–49	27	
	50–74	7	
	75–99	5	
	100+	0	
# of seminars		19	
# of seminar positions available		337	
# of seminar positions filled	245		0
# of positions available in simulation courses		485	
# of simulation positions filled	420		0
# of positions available in faculty supervised clinical courses		58	
# of faculty supervised clinical positions filled	47		0
# involved in field placements	70		0
# involved in law journals	188		0
# involved in moot court or trial competitions	36		0
# of credit hours required to graduate		86	

JD Enrollment and Ethnicity

	Men #	Men %	Women #	Women %	Full-Time #	Full-Time %	Part-Time #	Part-Time %	1st-Year #	1st-Year %	Total #	Total %	JD Degs. Awd.
All Hispanics	2	0.8	2	1.0	4	0.9	0	0.0	1	0.7	4	0.9	1
Am. Ind./AK Nat.	2	0.8	3	1.5	5	1.1	0	0.0	2	1.4	5	1.1	0
Asian	13	5.1	16	7.8	27	6.0	2	25.0	11	7.5	29	6.3	9
Black/Af. Am.	24	9.4	18	8.7	41	9.1	1	12.5	10	6.8	42	9.1	9
Nat. HI/Pac. Isl.	1	0.4	0	0.0	1	0.2	0	0.0	1	0.7	1	0.2	0
2 or more races	0	0.0	0	0.0	0	0.0	0	0.0	0	0.0	0	0.0	0
Subtotal (minor.)	42	16.5	39	18.9	78	17.3	3	37.5	25	17.1	81	17.6	19
Nonres. Alien	4	1.6	2	1.0	6	1.3	0	0.0	2	1.4	6	1.3	0
White/Cauc.	208	81.9	164	79.6	367	81.2	5	62.5	118	80.8	372	80.9	136
Unknown	0	0.0	1	0.5	1	0.2	0	0.0	1	0.7	1	0.2	0
Total	254	55.2	206	44.8	452	98.3	8	1.7	146	31.7	460		155

Transfers

Transfers in	12
Transfers out	9

Tuition and Fees

	Resident	Nonresident
Full-time	$34,070	$34,070
Part-time		
Tuition Guarantee Program		N

Living Expenses

Estimated living expenses for singles

Living on campus	Living off campus	Living at home
$14,200	$15,650	$6,350

UNIVERSITY OF RICHMOND SCHOOL OF LAW

ABA
Approved
Since
1928

GPA and LSAT Scores

	Total	Full-Time	Part-Time
# of apps	2,105	2,105	0
# of offers	558	558	0
# of matrics	146	146	0
75% GPA	3.63	3.63	0.00
Median GPA	3.47	3.47	0.00
25% GPA	3.16	3.16	0.00
75% LSAT	163	163	0
Median LSAT	162	162	0
25% LSAT	159	159	0

Grants and Scholarships (from prior year)

	Total #	Total %	Full-Time #	Full-Time %	Part-Time #	Part-Time %
Total # of students	465		465		0	
Total # receiving grants	226	48.6	226	48.6	0	0.0
Less than 1/2 tuition	189	40.6	189	40.6	0	0.0
Half to full tuition	36	7.7	36	7.7	0	0.0
Full tuition	0	0.0	0	0.0	0	0.0
More than full tuition	1	0.2	1	0.2	0	0.0
Median grant amount			$10,000		$0	

Informational and Library Resources

Total amount spent on library materials	$1,596,332
Study seating capacity inside the library	675
# of full-time equivalent professional librarians	7
Hours per week library is open	106
# of open, wired connections available to students	809
# of networked computers available for use by students	65
Has wireless network?	Y
Requires computer?	Y

JD Attrition (from prior year)

	Academic #	Other #	Total #	Total %
1st year	0	9	9	6.0
2nd year	0	0	0	0.0
3rd year	0	0	0	0.0
4th year	0	0	0	0.0

Employment (9 months after graduation)

	Total	Percentage
Employment status known	150	98.0
Employment status unknown	3	2.0
Employed	140	93.3
Pursuing graduate degrees	3	2.0
Unemployed (seeking, not seeking, or studying for the bar)	4	2.7
Type of Employment		
# employed in law firms	53	37.9
# employed in business and industry	29	20.7
# employed in government	17	12.1
# employed in public interest	5	3.6
# employed as judicial clerks	29	20.7
# employed in academia	0	0.0
Geographic Location		
# employed in state	109	77.9
# employed outside the US	0	0.0
# of states where employed		15

Bar Passage Rates

First-time takers	152	Reporting %	83.55
Average school %	82.68	Average state %	77.06
Average pass difference	5.62		

Jurisdiction	Takers	Passers	Pass %	State %	Diff %
Virginia	127	105	82.68	77.06	5.62

UNIVERSITY OF RICHMOND SCHOOL OF LAW

28 Westhampton Way
University of Richmond, VA 23173
Phone: 804.289.8189; Fax: 804.287.6516
E-mail: lawadmissions@richmond.edu; Website: http://law.richmond.edu

Introduction

The University of Richmond School of Law, founded in 1870, enjoys an established reputation for preparing its graduates for legal careers. Accredited by the ABA and a member of the AALS, its graduates are qualified to seek admission to the bar in all 50 states and the District of Columbia.

Situated on the university's 350-acre suburban campus, the school is only a 20-minute drive from downtown Richmond and its thriving legal community. In addition to being home to a number of international law firms, Richmond is the capital of the Commonwealth of Virginia, with numerous state and federal offices, and is the seat of both the Supreme Court of Virginia and the US Court of Appeals for the Fourth Circuit.

Library and Physical Facilities

The law school, located in a collegiate, gothic-style building, includes a moot courtroom that is the site of many classes, events, and mock trials, and where a panel of federal judges from the Fourth Circuit hears oral arguments once a year. The building has both wired and wireless connections, with almost 900 wired network connections. Every student has an individual study carrel, bearing his/her name, which functions as a personal office in the law library. The library offers a comprehensive collection of both electronic and print resources.

Curriculum

Courses in contracts, torts, criminal law, civil procedure, property, constitutional law, and a choice of one elective comprise the first-year curriculum. Required upper-level courses include professional responsibility and a third-year writing seminar. Elective courses in a variety of areas are available. In addition, all students complete a comprehensive, two-year program in legal reasoning, writing, research, and fundamental lawyering skills and values.

Academic Success Program and Bar Passage

Richmond Law has a comprehensive Academic Success Program geared toward assisting students to achieve at their highest possible academic level. The program also supports students in preparing for the bar exam, in whatever jurisdiction they choose to take it. Richmond Law consistently has one of the highest bar passage rates among first-time test takers in the Commonwealth of Virginia.

Special Programs

Several dual-degree programs allow students to earn the JD degree as well as a master's degree in a related discipline. Dual-degree programs are available in business administration, health administration, social work, urban studies and planning, and public administration, as well as others.

The law school operates the Children's Law Center through which students may participate in the Delinquency Clinic, the Disability Clinic, the Juvenile Law and Policy Clinic, the Family Law Clinic, and the Advanced Children's Clinic.

Exciting clinical placements are arranged for academic credit in various legal arenas, including civil, criminal, judicial, corporate, and nonprofit placements. Students receive credit while obtaining valuable work experience in courts, law offices, corporations, and government and public interest agencies.

The Intellectual Property Institute has developed a curriculum to enable students to obtain a Certificate of Concentration in Intellectual Property Law. Students may also participate in the Intellectual Property and Transactional Law Clinic, through which they can represent for-profit and nonprofit organizations, business start-ups, artists, authors, and inventors.

The National Center for Family Law fosters research, scholarship, reports, conferences, symposia, legislative testimony, and other public participation and discourse on issues related to Family Law. Students may earn a Certificate of Concentration in Family Law.

The Robert R. Merhige Jr. Center for Environmental Studies engages in research, instruction, and public outreach on energy and environmental issues in the Mid-Atlantic region and beyond. The center hosts conferences, symposia, and speakers on pressing environmental issues, generating dialogue for policy solutions.

The Institute for Actual Innocence (IAI) works to identify, investigate, and exonerate wrongfully convicted individuals in the Commonwealth of Virginia. Students, with hands-on involvement by faculty and practicing lawyers, conduct reinvestigations of cases where credible evidence of actual innocence is present. Students learn the subtleties and pitfalls involved in interviewing witnesses, inmates, and other parties central to criminal cases. They learn to analyze a criminal trial or appellate record for new evidentiary perspectives. The IAI offers an environment for students to express their problem-solving, interpersonal, and analytical skills.

"University of Richmond Downtown," a satellite campus in the heart of the city of Richmond, serves as a hub of community-based service, learning, research, and collaboration with nonprofit and government partners. UR Downtown aims to address pressing community needs through a combination of pro bono legal services provided by law students and attorneys, and community-based research and services provided by undergraduates and faculty.

International Programs

Richmond Law offers an extremely popular summer program at Emmanuel College in Cambridge, England, and an exchange program with the University of Paris, as well as with more than 20 universities worldwide, 9 of which have acclaimed law programs.

Student Activities

A student board publishes the *University of Richmond Law Review* on a quarterly basis. The *Richmond Journal of Law and Technology*, the first student-edited scholarly journal in the world to be published exclusively in electronic form, went online April 10, 1995. The *Richmond Journal of Law and the Public Interest* is a second online journal published by our students as an interdisciplinary journal dedicated to current and often controversial issues affecting the public. The *Richmond Journal of Global Law and Business* provides scholarly and practical insight into major legal and business issues affecting our global economy.

Richmond's moot court activities allow students to test their research, brief-writing, trial, negotiation, and appellate advocacy skills. Beginning in their 1L year, students participate in intraschool tournaments that lead to membership on the Moot Court Board, the Trial Advocacy Board (TAB), and the Client Counseling and Negotiation Board (CCNB). Moot Court, TAB, and CCNB teams represent the law school in regional, national, and international competitions.

Admission

Applications are reviewed as they become complete. All decisions are released by March 31. The admission committee considers the UGPA and LSAT as two important items, although extracurricular and community service activities and employment experience are also of interest. The law school provides an equal educational opportunity without regard to race, color, national origin, sex, disability, or religion.

We encourage class visits and, in keeping with our very personal approach to admission, we also encourage you to take advantage of meeting with a law student. Law students are available to give tours Monday through Saturday and may be reached at LSAR@richmond.edu.

Expenses and Financial Aid

Institutional aid in the form of grants and scholarships is available on the basis of need and merit. Financial Aid decisions are often made based on submission of the FAFSA and we recommend filing this form by February 25 to get the fullest consideration of all available aid. Parental income is not considered in determining financial aid for students who are considered to be independent by the law school.

John Marshall Scholars Program—The law school's most prestigious awards offer $10,000 annual stipends in addition to

$20,000 merit scholarships, as well as other honors, and are renewable annually if criteria are met. If invited to compete for these awards, a separate application must be submitted. Committee consideration for these scholarships is based solely on merit and personal attributes. Some applicants may be able to demonstrate the required attributes by having successfully overcome serious disadvantages or obstacles. John Marshall Scholars will be awarded institutional grants and scholarships in addition to their JM Scholarship, and will be invited to participate in a specially designed John Marshall Scholar seminar.

Housing

Limited on-campus housing is available on a first-come, first-served basis. Richmond offers an abundance of good, affordable housing in proximity to the law school. For information on housing, contact the Admissions Office.

Career Services

The Career Services Office works closely with law students and alumni in obtaining employment by helping to align their interests and talents with a desired career path, as well as assisting them with developing the skills and the knowledge necessary to conduct successful job searches. The office conducts a comprehensive, on-campus interview program which includes law firms and government and public interest employers, and it participates in a number of national job fairs. It also maintains an extensive employment database and organizes regular informational programs and networking opportunities for students.

Richmond has more types of courts than any city in the United States outside of Washington, DC, or Boston, which provide a myriad of opportunities for externships and part-time employment while students are in their second and third years of study, thereby giving our students the benefit of gaining crucial legal experience and producing income for educational purposes.

APPLICANT PROFILE

University of Richmond School of Law
This grid includes only applicants who earned 120–180 LSAT scores under standard administrations.

LSAT Score	3.75 +		3.50–3.74		3.25–3.49		3.00–3.24		2.75–2.99		2.50–2.74		2.25–2.49		2.00–2.24		Below 2.00		No GPA		Total	
	Apps	Adm	Apps	Adm	Apps	Adm	Apps	Adm	Apps	Adm	Apps	Adm	Apps	Adm	Apps	Adm	Apps	Adm	Apps	Adm	Apps	Adm
175–180	0	0	1	1	1	0	0	0	0	0	0	0	0	0	0	0	0	0	0	0	2	1
170–174	5	3	3	1	3	2	4	1	0	0	0	0	4	2	0	0	0	0	0	0	19	9
165–169	12	5	19	9	16	10	37	19	12	9	8	7	2	1	1	1	0	0	2	1	109	62
160–164	67	64	93	86	144	91	96	62	45	16	25	13	12	6	8	4	0	0	5	4	495	346
155–159	79	21	160	53	155	10	121	8	58	3	52	2	27	0	4	0	0	0	3	1	659	98
150–154	41	8	81	10	99	9	94	4	52	2	29	0	18	2	5	0	2	0	6	1	427	36
145–149	17	0	29	0	38	0	42	0	43	0	16	0	7	0	7	0	1	0	2	0	202	0
140–144	2	0	10	1	20	0	20	0	16	0	27	0	11	0	3	0	0	0	4	0	113	1
135–139	1	0	8	1	2	0	8	0	9	0	4	0	5	0	3	0	1	0	1	0	42	1
130–134	1	0	0	0	2	0	4	0	6	0	5	0	1	0	2	0	0	0	1	0	22	0
125–129	0	0	0	0	0	0	0	0	0	0	1	0	0	0	1	0	0	0	0	0	2	0
120–124	0	0	0	0	0	0	0	0	0	0	0	0	0	0	0	0	0	0	0	0	0	0
Total	225	101	404	162	480	122	426	94	241	30	167	22	87	11	34	5	4	0	24	7	2092	554

Apps = Number of Applicants
Adm = Number Admitted
Reflects 99% of the total applicant pool; highest LSAT data reported.

ROGER WILLIAMS UNIVERSITY SCHOOL OF LAW

Ten Metacom Avenue
Bristol, RI 02809-5171
Phone: 401.254.4555 or 800.633.2727; Fax: 401.254.4516
E-mail: admissions@rwu.edu; Website: http://law.rwu.edu

ABA
Approved
Since
1995

The Basics

Type of school	Private
Term	Semester
Application deadline	3/15
Application fee	$60
Financial aid deadline	2/15
Can first year start other than fall?	No
Student to faculty ratio	16.4 to 1
# of housing spaces available restricted to law students	
graduate housing for which law students are eligible	72

Faculty and Administrators

	Total		Men		Women		Minorities	
	Spr	Fall	Spr	Fall	Spr	Fall	Spr	Fall
Full-time	29	26	17	14	12	12	4	5
Other full-time	1	1	0	0	1	1	0	0
Deans, librarians, & others who teach	10	10	4	4	6	6	0	0
Part-time	29	32	21	24	8	8	2	3
Total	69	69	42	42	27	27	6	8

Curriculum

	Full-Time	Part-Time
Typical first-year section size	70	0
Is there typically a "small section" of the first-year class, other than Legal Writing, taught by full-time faculty	No	No
If yes, typical size offered last year		

# of classroom course titles beyond first-year curriculum		111
# of upper division courses, excluding seminars, with an enrollment: Under 25		42
25–49		20
50–74		15
75–99		6
100+		0
# of seminars		41
# of seminar positions available		769
# of seminar positions filled	529	0
# of positions available in simulation courses		225
# of simulation positions filled	197	0
# of positions available in faculty supervised clinical courses		75
# of faculty supervised clinical positions filled	62	0
# involved in field placements	59	0
# involved in law journals	50	0
# involved in moot court or trial competitions	38	0
# of credit hours required to graduate		90

JD Enrollment and Ethnicity

	Men #	Men %	Women #	Women %	Full-Time #	Full-Time %	Part-Time #	Part-Time %	1st-Year #	1st-Year %	Total #	Total %	JD Degs. Awd.
All Hispanics	2	0.7	12	4.5	14	2.6	0	0.0	1	0.5	14	2.6	11
Am. Ind./AK Nat.	2	0.7	0	0.0	2	0.4	0	0.0	1	0.5	2	0.4	2
Asian	6	2.2	8	3.0	14	2.6	0	0.0	8	3.9	14	2.6	4
Black/Af. Am.	5	1.8	10	3.7	15	2.8	0	0.0	7	3.4	15	2.8	5
Nat. HI/Pac. Isl.	0	0.0	0	0.0	0	0.0	0	0.0	0	0.0	0	0.0	0
2 or more races	1	0.4	1	0.4	2	0.4	0	0.0	2	1.0	2	0.4	0
Subtotal (minor.)	16	5.9	31	11.5	47	8.7	0	0.0	19	9.3	47	8.7	22
Nonres. Alien	1	0.4	2	0.7	3	0.6	0	0.0	1	0.5	3	0.6	0
White/Cauc.	222	81.9	207	77.0	429	79.4	0	0.0	164	80.4	429	79.4	125
Unknown	32	11.8	29	10.8	61	11.3	0	0.0	20	9.8	61	11.3	23
Total	271	50.2	269	49.8	540	100.0	0	0.0	204	37.8	540		171

Transfers

Transfers in	9
Transfers out	9

Tuition and Fees

	Resident	Nonresident
Full-time	$38,010	$38,010
Part-time		
Tuition Guarantee Program		N

Living Expenses

Estimated living expenses for singles

Living on campus	Living off campus	Living at home
$20,134	$20,134	$20,134

ABA Approved Since 1995

GPA and LSAT Scores

	Total	Full-Time	Part-Time
# of apps	1,501	1,501	0
# of offers	949	949	0
# of matrics	198	198	0
75% GPA	3.50	3.50	0.00
Median GPA	3.30	3.30	0.00
25% GPA	3.00	3.00	0.00
75% LSAT	154	154	0
Median LSAT	151	151	0
25% LSAT	149	149	0

Grants and Scholarships (from prior year)

	Total		Full-Time		Part-Time	
	#	%	#	%	#	%
Total # of students	550		550		0	
Total # receiving grants	255	46.4	255	46.4	0	0.0
Less than 1/2 tuition	138	25.1	138	25.1	0	0.0
Half to full tuition	56	10.2	56	10.2	0	0.0
Full tuition	58	10.5	58	10.5	0	0.0
More than full tuition	3	0.5	3	0.5	0	0.0
Median grant amount			$12,500		$0	

Informational and Library Resources

Total amount spent on library materials	$854,476
Study seating capacity inside the library	403
# of full-time equivalent professional librarians	6
Hours per week library is open	110
# of open, wired connections available to students	196
# of networked computers available for use by students	83
Has wireless network?	Y
Requires computer?	N

JD Attrition (from prior year)

	Academic	Other	Total	
	#	#	#	%
1st year	5	14	19	8.7
2nd year	1	1	2	1.3
3rd year	0	0	0	0.0
4th year	0	0	0	0.0

Employment (9 months after graduation)

	Total	Percentage
Employment status known	159	85.5
Employment status unknown	27	14.5
Employed	130	81.8
Pursuing graduate degrees	15	9.4
Unemployed (seeking, not seeking, or studying for the bar)	12	7.5
Type of Employment		
# employed in law firms	62	47.7
# employed in business and industry	20	15.4
# employed in government	14	10.8
# employed in public interest	9	6.9
# employed as judicial clerks	19	14.6
# employed in academia	3	2.3
Geographic Location		
# employed in state	52	40.0
# employed outside the US	1	0.8
# of states where employed	19	

Bar Passage Rates

First-time takers	218	Reporting %	75.23
Average school %	88.42	Average state %	83.41
Average pass difference	5.01		

Jurisdiction	Takers	Passers	Pass %	State %	Diff %
Rhode Island	79	75	94.94	79.92	15.02
New York	32	24	75.00	86.51	−11.51
Massachusetts	22	20	90.91	89.77	1.14
New Jersey	16	14	87.50	83.64	3.86
Connecticut	15	12	80.00	85.56	−5.56

ROGER WILLIAMS UNIVERSITY SCHOOL OF LAW

Ten Metacom Avenue
Bristol, RI 02809-5171
Phone: 401.254.4555 or 800.633.2727; Fax: 401.254.4516
E-mail: admissions@rwu.edu; Website: http://law.rwu.edu

Introduction

Roger Williams University School of Law offers a world-class faculty, a strong and diverse student body and an extraordinarily close and symbiotic relationship with the local bench and bar. The faculty hail from the nation's top law schools, boasting an impressive academic productivity, while bringing a wealth of hands-on experience—regional, national and international—in virtually every area of the law to the student-teacher experience. Students reap the benefits of this dynamic through high bar-pass rates and excellent professional placements. By attending Rhode Island's only law school, they gain unparalleled access to the state's most sought-after judicial internships and the undivided attention of a state bar that functions in many ways as a de facto extension of a fast-growing alumni base. Students are regularly exposed to top legal minds. Leading members of the state and federal bench and bar teach here as adjuncts. Nationally known legal experts lecture at the law school, both as permanent faculty and distinguished guests. Each year, the Rhode Island Supreme Court hears final arguments in our internal moot court competition. RWU Law offers a rigorous and competitive legal education in a warm, open, and supportive environment.

Location

Located in picturesque Bristol, Rhode Island, on the banks of Mount Hope Bay, RWU Law offers idyllic walking trails and easy waterfront access. Bristol is a classic New England village, complete with tree-lined streets, a town green and waterfront parks—as well as gourmet restaurants that stand alongside lively pubs and whimsical shops. In the summer, local waterways come alive with swimmers and boaters, while thousands throng to the town's famous Independence Day parade, established in 1785. A half-hour north is Providence, a city of artistic and intellectual ambiance, bustling with theaters, museums, art galleries, antique shops, bookstores, and a mélange of ethnic neighborhoods, restaurants, and cultural events. Providence is also the seat of Rhode Island's legal culture, with the beautiful Frank Licht Judicial Complex anchoring the divide between the busy downtown and the bohemian atmosphere of College Hill, home to Brown University and the Rhode Island School of Design. The seaside city of Newport is a short drive south, boasting spectacular Gilded Age mansions, renowned jazz, folk, and classical music festivals, the International Tennis Hall of Fame and some of New England's finest beaches. Boston is just an hour north, New York City less than three hours south, and the all-seasons attractions of Maine, New Hampshire, and Vermont within easy reach.

Library and Physical Facilities

Our Law Library is dedicated to providing the best possible resources for legal research. With a collection of more than 300,000 volumes and an ever-expanding menu of nearly 4,000 serial subscriptions, the Law Library houses one of the region's finest collections of printed legal materials, while also providing access to numerous online services and free Internet sources. Its 35,000-square-foot facility includes 16 private group-study rooms, several of them A/V equipped, and scores of computer workstations with ample wireless and wired network connections. In addition to its director, the Law Library offers five highly qualified law librarians and six support staff members to assist and advance the pedagogical and research needs of students and faculty. RWU Law offers an attractive learning environment, with plenty of comfortable sofas, chairs and tables, and many quiet study nooks sprinkled through the law school building. In addition to the Law School Bistro, law students can grab a meal at the RWU Dining Commons, a new facility offering dining options for every taste and appetite, with a focus on organic and locally grown foods. Many law students also enjoy working out in RWU's state-of-the-art Recreation Center, featuring a fully equipped gym, squash courts, yoga and relaxation classes, basketball courts, and an indoor swimming pool.

Curriculum

The curriculum integrates intellectual theory, case analysis, and practical lawyering skills. The fundamental building blocks of effective lawyering constitute the first- and second-year curriculum. Students learn the skills of traditional legal analysis and the ability to elicit and convey information that every lawyer must master. The Legal Methods program and other required courses prepare students to become problem solvers; to comprehend, analyze, and synthesize complex material; and to communicate their positions effectively. In the latter years of their education, students gain expertise in legal specialties through clustering elective courses in particular fields of interest.

Joint-Degree Programs

Roger Williams University offers a JD/Master of Science in Criminal Justice. This program is designed to prepare graduates to formulate system policy and serve effectively as administrators to United States justice system agencies. The School of Law also offers two joint-degree programs in conjunction with the University of Rhode Island. The JD/Master of Marine Affairs program is geared toward students interested in maritime, admiralty, and environmental law. The JD/Master of Science in Labor Relations and Human Resources program is designed for students interested in issues relating to employment and labor relations.

Special Programs

Marine Affairs Institute—The institute is recognized as a distinguished focal point for the exploration of legal, economic, and policy issues raised by the development of the oceans and coastal zone. Students take elective courses in traditional admiralty law and practice, pollution and environmental regulation, coastal zoning, fisheries, and the international law of the sea.

Feinstein Institute—The school believes that lawyers should serve the communities that support them. Introducing students to volunteerism and public service as part of their legal education, therefore, sets the stage for a lifetime of commitment. Thus, students are required to complete 50 hours of community service.

Honors Program

The Honors Program is a three-year program of seminars, clinics, and externships. Scholarships of $20,000 to full tuition are awarded to students selected for the Honors Program. The Admissions Committee selects students, evaluating them on their academic records, LSAT scores, and recommendations.

Practical Experience

The School of Law operates a Criminal Defense Clinic and an Immigration Clinic in Providence. These clinics provide a service to the community by helping indigent clients and, at the same time, provide an excellent opportunity for students to represent clients before courts and agencies under the supervision of a faculty member. The School of Law also operates a Mediation Clinic in Bristol. As the only law school in Rhode Island, externship opportunities abound. Students may engage in a semester-long supervised clerkship in a judge's chambers or in a public interest or governmental law office for academic credit.

Study Abroad

The London Program on Comparative Advocacy internship combines classroom learning at the Inner Temple (one of the four Inns of Court) with a unique and privileged opportunity for students to be trained in English common law trial techniques with a barrister or judge. The School of Law also offers programs in Tianjin, China, and Buenos Aires, Argentina, through a partnership with Stetson University College of Law.

Admission

Admission is competitive and is based on the undergraduate grade-point average (UGPA) and the Law School Admission Test (LSAT) score, as well as other indicators of probable success in the study of law, such as graduate degree, work experience, undergraduate extracurricular activities, and community service. Applicants must register with LSAC's Credential Assembly Service. A personal statement and the $60 fee must accompany all applications. One letter of recommendation is required.

Financial Aid

Merit-based scholarships of up to full tuition are available; no separate application is required. Federal and state governmental agencies, as well as private lenders, offer students loans at comparative rates and flexible repayment terms. Students must file the Free Application for Federal Student Aid (FAFSA) to be considered for federal loans.

Student Activities

Law Review—Membership on the *Roger Williams University Law Review* is considered one of the most valuable and prestigious student activities available. The *Law Review* is staffed and primarily administered by students who are selected based upon superior academic achievement and writing ability.

Moot Court Board—The Moot Court Board is composed of students possessing superior appellate advocacy and writing ability. This prestigious organization sponsors speakers and programs on appellate advocacy, an intraschool competition, and moot court teams.

Extracurricular Activities—Student organizations include, but are not limited to, the Multicultural Law Students Association, Women's Law Association, the Alliance (LGBT), Black Law Students Association, Latino Law Students Association, Asian Pacific American Law Students Association, Older Wiser Law Students, Maritime Law Society, Sports and Entertainment Law Society, International Law Society, Association for Public Interest Law, and Association of Trial Lawyers of America.

Career Services

The Office of Career Services is dedicated to serving the needs of law students, alumni, and the legal community. The office features a welcoming suite for career research, on-campus interviews, and mock interviews. All of these tools help to prepare students to take advantage of the versatility of the Juris Doctor degree.

APPLICANT PROFILE

Roger Williams University School of Law

LSAT Score	GPA								
	3.75 +	3.50–3.74	3.25–3.49	3.00–3.24	2.75–2.99	2.50–2.74	2.25–2.49	2.00–2.24	Below 2.00
175–180	■	■	■	■	■	▨	▨		
170–174	■	■	■	■	■	▨	▨		
165–169	■	■	■	■	■	▨	▨		
160–164	■	■	■	■	■	▨	▨		
155–159	■	■	■	■	■	▨	▨		
150–154	▨	▨	▨	▨	▨	▨	▨		
145–149	▨	▨	▨	▨	▨	▨	▨		
140–144									
135–139									
130–134									
125–129									
120–124									

■ Good Possibility ▨ Possible ☐ Unlikely

This chart is to be used as a general guide only. Nonnumerical factors are strongly considered for all applicants.

RUTGERS—THE STATE UNIVERSITY OF NEW JERSEY—SCHOOL OF LAW—CAMDEN

217 North Fifth Street
Camden, NJ 08102
Phone: 856.225.6102 or 800.466.7561; Fax: 856.969.7903
E-mail: admissions@camlaw.rutgers.edu; Website: www.camlaw.rutgers.edu

ABA
Approved
Since
1950

The Basics

Type of school	Public
Term	Semester
Application deadline	3/1 4/15 6/15
Application fee	$65
Financial aid deadline	7/15
Can first year start other than fall?	Yes
Student to faculty ratio	11.6 to 1
# of housing spaces available restricted to law students	
graduate housing for which law students are eligible	224

Faculty and Administrators

	Total		Men		Women		Minorities	
	Spr	Fall	Spr	Fall	Spr	Fall	Spr	Fall
Full-time	53	51	35	33	18	18	5	5
Other full-time	3	3	0	0	3	3	1	1
Deans, librarians, & others who teach	14	14	5	5	9	9	2	2
Part-time	56	43	34	30	22	13	6	1
Total	126	111	74	68	52	43	14	9

Curriculum

	Full-Time	Part-Time
Typical first-year section size	79	34
Is there typically a "small section" of the first-year class, other than Legal Writing, taught by full-time faculty	No	No
If yes, typical size offered last year		
# of classroom course titles beyond first-year curriculum	193	
# of upper division courses, excluding seminars, with an enrollment: Under 25	100	
25–49	38	
50–74	7	
75–99	7	
100+	1	
# of seminars	40	
# of seminar positions available	675	
# of seminar positions filled	447	64
# of positions available in simulation courses	722	
# of simulation positions filled	510	113
# of positions available in faculty supervised clinical courses	209	
# of faculty supervised clinical positions filled	137	44
# involved in field placements	101	16
# involved in law journals	147	17
# involved in moot court or trial competitions	21	2
# of credit hours required to graduate	84	

JD Enrollment and Ethnicity

	Men		Women		Full-Time		Part-Time		1st-Year		Total		JD Degs. Awd.
	#	%	#	%	#	%	#	%	#	%	#	%	
All Hispanics	26	5.5	17	5.4	36	6.3	7	3.2	17	6.3	43	5.4	10
Am. Ind./AK Nat.	3	0.6	1	0.3	3	0.5	1	0.5	2	0.7	4	0.5	1
Asian	38	8.0	29	9.2	47	8.2	20	9.3	25	9.3	67	8.5	29
Black/Af. Am.	18	3.8	24	7.6	29	5.1	13	6.0	9	3.3	42	5.3	18
Nat. HI/Pac. Isl.	0	0.0	1	0.3	0	0.0	1	0.5	1	0.4	1	0.1	0
2 or more races	0	0.0	0	0.0	0	0.0	0	0.0	0	0.0	0	0.0	0
Subtotal (minor.)	85	17.9	72	22.9	115	20.1	42	19.4	54	20.1	157	19.9	58
Nonres. Alien	5	1.1	1	0.3	5	0.9	1	0.5	0	0.0	6	0.8	0
White/Cauc.	384	81.0	242	76.8	453	79.1	173	80.1	215	79.9	626	79.3	230
Unknown	0	0.0	0	0.0	0	0.0	0	0.0	0	0.0	0	0.0	0
Total	474	60.1	315	39.9	573	72.6	216	27.4	269	34.1	789		288

Transfers

Transfers in	38
Transfers out	13

Tuition and Fees

	Resident	Nonresident
Full-time	$22,382	$33,173
Part-time	$18,816	$27,853
Tuition Guarantee Program		N

Living Expenses

Estimated living expenses for singles

Living on campus	Living off campus	Living at home
$15,673	$20,413	$7,643

RUTGERS—THE STATE UNIVERSITY OF NEW JERSEY—SCHOOL OF LAW—CAMDEN

ABA Approved Since 1950

GPA and LSAT Scores

	Total	Full-Time	Part-Time
# of apps	2,013	2,013	N/A
# of offers	633	633	N/A
# of matrics	269	127	142
75% GPA	3.60	3.60	3.60
Median GPA	3.40	3.40	3.40
25% GPA	3.10	3.00	3.20
75% LSAT	161	163	160
Median LSAT	160	161	159
25% LSAT	157	158	155

Grants and Scholarships (from prior year)

	Total		Full-Time		Part-Time	
	#	%	#	%	#	%
Total # of students	810		619		191	
Total # receiving grants	207	25.6	197	31.8	10	5.2
Less than 1/2 tuition	198	24.4	188	30.4	10	5.2
Half to full tuition	9	1.1	9	1.5	0	0.0
Full tuition	0	0.0	0	0.0	0	0.0
More than full tuition	0	0.0	0	0.0	0	0.0
Median grant amount			$4,000		$1,500	

Informational and Library Resources

Total amount spent on library materials	$810,184
Study seating capacity inside the library	396
# of full-time equivalent professional librarians	7
Hours per week library is open	103
# of open, wired connections available to students	130
# of networked computers available for use by students	50
Has wireless network?	Y
Requires computer?	Y

JD Attrition (from prior year)

	Academic	Other	Total	
	#	#	#	%
1st year	0	23	23	8.5
2nd year	1	0	1	0.4
3rd year	0	0	0	0.0
4th year	1	0	1	2.2

Employment (9 months after graduation)

	Total	Percentage
Employment status known	237	98.7
Employment status unknown	3	1.2
Employed	202	85.2
Pursuing graduate degrees	8	3.4
Unemployed (seeking, not seeking, or studying for the bar)	22	9.3
Type of Employment		
# employed in law firms	81	40.1
# employed in business and industry	30	14.9
# employed in government	5	2.5
# employed in public interest	3	1.5
# employed as judicial clerks	72	35.6
# employed in academia	8	4.0
Geographic Location		
# employed in state	131	64.9
# employed outside the US	0	0.0
# of states where employed	13	

Bar Passage Rates

First-time takers	239	Reporting %	87.87
Average school %	80.00	Average state %	83.64
Average pass difference	−3.64		

Jurisdiction	Takers	Passers	Pass %	State %	Diff %
New Jersey	210	168	80.00	83.64	−3.64

RUTGERS—THE STATE UNIVERSITY OF NEW JERSEY—SCHOOL OF LAW—CAMDEN

217 North Fifth Street
Camden, NJ 08102
Phone: 856.225.6102 or 800.466.7561; Fax: 856.969.7903
E-mail: admissions@camlaw.rutgers.edu; Website: www.camlaw.rutgers.edu

Introduction

Chartered in 1766 by George III of Great Britain as the Queen's College, Rutgers—The State University of New Jersey is one of the oldest and largest state higher educational systems in the nation. The law school at the Camden campus is proud to continue this national reputation of excellence. With more than 100 faculty and staff members, the law school is a leading center of legal education. Noted for excellence in scholarship and rigor in training of new lawyers, the law school faculty is internationally recognized in fields as diverse as international law, health law, family and women's rights law, state constitutional law, and legal history.

Located at the base of the Benjamin Franklin Bridge, just minutes from the Liberty Bell and Independence Hall in Philadelphia, the law school is in one of the nation's largest legal markets. With its thriving, 40-acre, tree-lined urban campus in Camden, New Jersey, Rutgers is a handsome blend of converted Victorian buildings and newly constructed facilities. The Susquehanna Bank Center at the Waterfront, an indoor/outdoor concert venue; the Adventure Aquarium; the USS Battleship New Jersey; the renovated, historic Victor building with its upscale apartments; the new River LINE rail system; and Campbell's Field (the minor league baseball stadium), just a few blocks from the law school, are centerpieces for the ongoing development of Camden's waterfront. Camden, which is the county seat, has federal and local courts adjacent to the law school. A member of the Association of American Law Schools, the school is included on the list of approved schools of the American Bar Association.

Faculty

Faculty scholarship has been cited by numerous courts, including the United States Supreme Court, and faculty members have authored numerous casebooks and significant legal works. Faculty members have testified before Congress and serve as consultants and reporters for the American Bar Association, the American Law Institute, and several federal and state commissions, and act as counsel in important public interest litigation.

Library and Physical Facilities

The law school opened the doors to its new law building in 2008. A 2,300 square-foot courtroom and lobby with the new addition of 53,000 square feet almost doubles the size of the existing law building. The $40 million construction project has created state-of-the art classrooms, renovated two 100–150 seat lecture theaters and multiple seminar rooms, and expanded space for student organizations and social life at the law school. A magnificent two-story glass bridge and art display houses a student lounge and Law Café and welcomes visitors crossing the Benjamin Franklin Bridge from Philadelphia into New Jersey. A selective federal repository, the law library, with more than 445,000 bibliographic units, is one of the largest in the state. In addition to having access to traditional materials, students are trained on a number of computerized research systems, including a myriad of databases available on the Internet.

Curriculum and Special Programs

The first-year curriculum includes the traditional core legal courses. Central to the curriculum is the lawyering program that engages students in simulated lawyering activities and practical applications of the law. Upper-class students can typically choose from more than 100 exciting elective courses each year, including electronic commerce, trial advocacy, sports law, children's law, and international business transactions.

An outstanding Externship Program offers third-year students the opportunity to work with federal and state judges, public agencies, and public interest organizations. Other students participate in the Civil Practice Clinic and pro bono programs at the law school. Live client experiences include the Domestic Violence Project, the Pro Bono Bankruptcy Project, the Immigration Project, the Mediation Project, and the Elder Law Clinic, or representing clients in connection with the LEAP Charter School. Each of these programs constitutes a comprehensive initiative that reflects the law school's commitment to public service.

Students may pursue their legal studies in the full-time day program as well as the part-time program, available day or evening. Both programs are subject to the same rigorous admission and academic standards.

Joint-Degree Programs

Eight formal joint JD and master's or doctoral degree programs are available with the University of Medicine and Dentistry, Graduate School of Business, Bloustein School of Planning and Public Policy, School of Social Work, and Graduate School—Camden, including the JD/MD, JD/DO, JD/MPA, JD/MBA, JD/MPH, JD/MPAP, JD/MSW, and JD/MCRP. Upon approval of the faculty, students may also pursue self-designed joint-degree programs within Rutgers University or with other graduate institutions.

Admission

Although admission is highly competitive, the Committee on Admissions does consider each applicant's file individually, and special qualities may occasionally overcome lower numbers. Important factors to the committee include LSAT score, undergraduate and graduate grade-point average, undergraduate and graduate institutions, work experience, and letters of recommendation. Typically, half of the full-time entering class scores in the top quartile on the LSAT (160 or higher) with a median GPA of 3.5. The entering class size each fall is about 225 full- and part-time day and 45 part-time evening students. The law school draws from 34 states and 4 foreign countries. More than 250 colleges and universities are represented in the student body. Decisions are made on a rolling basis beginning in early December. The law school has rolling admission and will consider candidates who take the February or June LSAT. However, early applicants have an enhanced opportunity for admission. Applicants may also apply for advanced standing as transfer students but are only eligible upon completion of one year of law study. Students may request an application from the law school or apply online at www.camlaw.rutgers.edu/.

Housing

Air-conditioned and carpeted law school apartments are located on campus; and nearby, the renovated, historic Victor building, with its spectacular views of the Philadelphia skyline, provides upscale apartment living. There are also abundant housing opportunities in the nearby suburbs and excellent public transportation systems. First-year admitted students are invited to utilize the law school's housing webpage and to attend the Dean's Law and Housing Day in the spring.

Financial Aid

In the 2009–2010 academic year, over $22 million was distributed to law students through fellowships, grants, loans, and employment. The average financial aid package was approximately $32,235, with 89 percent of the student body receiving some form of assistance. The William D. Ford Federal Direct Loan Program, the largest financial aid program, provided more than $18.7 million to our law students in the last academic year. For fall consideration, the FAFSA should be submitted by March 1. Merit-based scholarships are also available for outstanding academic performance.

Career Services

As a direct result of the quality of legal education at Rutgers, for the last five years the school has averaged an employment rate of over 90 percent in the legal profession within nine months of graduation. All major Philadelphia, New Jersey, and Delaware firms recruit from Rutgers, as do prestigious firms from New York City, California, and Washington, DC. The school's more than 9,000 alumni are leading members of the judiciary, government, and bar throughout this nation. The average salary of an associate who joins a private law firm is in excess of $108,000, with top students typically making in excess of $160,000. The school's placement rate is one of the best in the country (36 percent of last year's class) for highly desirable state and federal clerkships.

Student Activities

Among the numerous student organizations are the Latino Law Students Association, Asian/Pacific American Law Students Association, Association for Public Interest Law, Black Law Students Association, Christian Legal Society, Community Outreach Group, Cyberlaw, Environmental Law Students Association, Francis Deak International Law Society, OUTLAW Student Bar Association, Health Law Society, Italian-American Law Students Organization, Jewish Law Students Association, Law Journal (publishes the *Rutgers Law Journal*), *Journal of Law and Public Policy*, *Rutgers Journal of Law and Religion*, Phi Alpha Delta law fraternity, Pro Bono/Public Interest Steering Committee, and the Women's Law Caucus.

APPLICANT PROFILE

Rutgers—The State University of New Jersey—School of Law—Camden
This grid includes only applicants who earned 120–180 LSAT scores under standard administrations.

LSAT Score	GPA								
	3.75 +	3.50–3.74	3.25–3.49	3.00–3.24	2.75–2.99	2.50–2.74	2.25–2.49	2.00–2.24	Below 2.00
170–180									
165–169									
161–164									
158–160									
155–157									
150–154									
Below 150									

■ Very Likely   ■ Likely   ■ Possible   ☐ Unlikely*

*Special attributes may sometimes overcome lower scores/GPAs.
This chart is to be used as a general guide only. Nonnumerical factors are strongly considered for all applicants.

RUTGERS UNIVERSITY SCHOOL OF LAW—NEWARK

Center for Law and Justice, 123 Washington Street
Newark, NJ 07102
Phone: 973.353.5554; Fax: 973.353.3459
E-mail: lawinfo@andromeda.rutgers.edu; Website: www.law.newark.rutgers.edu

ABA
Approved
Since
1941

The Basics

Type of school	Public
Term	Semester
Application deadline	3/15
Application fee	$65
Financial aid deadline	3/15
Can first year start other than fall?	No
Student to faculty ratio	17.8 to 1
# of housing spaces available restricted to law students	
graduate housing for which law students are eligible	110

Faculty and Administrators

	Total		Men		Women		Minorities	
	Spr	Fall	Spr	Fall	Spr	Fall	Spr	Fall
Full-time	32	38	18	22	14	16	11	12
Other full-time	0	2	0	0	0	2	0	0
Deans, librarians, & others who teach	15	16	8	9	7	7	5	6
Part-time	37	32	25	24	11	8	1	0
Total	84	88	51	55	32	33	17	18

Curriculum

		Full-Time	Part-Time
Typical first-year section size		60	70
Is there typically a "small section" of the first-year class, other than Legal Writing, taught by full-time faculty		Yes	Yes
If yes, typical size offered last year		32	34
# of classroom course titles beyond first-year curriculum		103	
# of upper division courses, excluding seminars, with an enrollment:	Under 25	64	
	25–49	33	
	50–74	9	
	75–99	10	
	100+	2	
# of seminars		21	
# of seminar positions available		420	
# of seminar positions filled		225	76
# of positions available in simulation courses		375	
# of simulation positions filled		223	111
# of positions available in faculty supervised clinical courses		204	
# of faculty supervised clinical positions filled		175	12
# involved in field placements		78	14
# involved in law journals		178	25
# involved in moot court or trial competitions		65	6
# of credit hours required to graduate		84	

JD Enrollment and Ethnicity

	Men		Women		Full-Time		Part-Time		1st-Year		Total		JD Degs. Awd.
	#	%	#	%	#	%	#	%	#	%	#	%	
All Hispanics	45	9.7	40	10.6	61	10.0	24	10.5	29	10.3	85	10.1	25
Am. Ind./AK Nat.	1	0.2	2	0.5	2	0.3	1	0.4	1	0.4	3	0.4	0
Asian	56	12.1	48	12.8	73	12.0	31	13.5	39	13.9	104	12.4	24
Black/Af. Am.	59	12.7	73	19.4	89	14.6	43	18.8	40	14.2	132	15.7	29
Nat. HI/Pac. Isl.	0	0.0	0	0.0	0	0.0	0	0.0	0	0.0	0	0.0	0
2 or more races	3	0.6	3	0.8	5	0.8	1	0.4	5	1.8	6	0.7	0
Subtotal (minor.)	164	35.4	166	44.1	230	37.7	100	43.7	114	40.6	330	39.3	78
Nonres. Alien	4	0.9	7	1.9	9	1.5	2	0.9	2	0.7	11	1.3	0
White/Cauc.	295	63.7	203	54.0	371	60.8	127	55.5	165	58.7	498	59.4	177
Unknown	0	0.0	0	0.0	0	0.0	0	0.0	0	0.0	0	0.0	0
Total	463	55.2	376	44.8	610	72.7	229	27.3	281	33.5	839		258

Transfers

Transfers in	12
Transfers out	10

Tuition and Fees

	Resident	Nonresident
Full-time	$24,977	$35,897
Part-time	$16,274	$23,554
Tuition Guarantee Program		N

Living Expenses

Estimated living expenses for singles

Living on campus	Living off campus	Living at home
$16,013	$20,753	$7,983

RUTGERS UNIVERSITY SCHOOL OF LAW—NEWARK

ABA
Approved
Since
1941

GPA and LSAT Scores

	Total	Full-Time	Part-Time
# of apps	3,336	2,598	738
# of offers	945	817	128
# of matrics	283	220	63
75% GPA	3.57	3.60	3.54
Median GPA	3.32	3.36	3.22
25% GPA	3.01	3.06	2.93
75% LSAT	161	161	161
Median LSAT	158	159	157
25% LSAT	155	155	154

Grants and Scholarships (from prior year)

	Total		Full-Time		Part-Time	
	#	%	#	%	#	%
Total # of students	835		593		242	
Total # receiving grants	275	32.9	240	40.5	35	14.5
Less than 1/2 tuition	226	27.1	197	33.2	29	12.0
Half to full tuition	37	4.4	32	5.4	5	2.1
Full tuition	8	1.0	7	1.2	1	0.4
More than full tuition	4	0.5	4	0.7	0	0.0
Median grant amount			$6,000		$4,000	

Informational and Library Resources

Total amount spent on library materials	$775,433
Study seating capacity inside the library	532
# of full-time equivalent professional librarians	18
Hours per week library is open	95
# of open, wired connections available to students	570
# of networked computers available for use by students	180
Has wireless network?	Y
Requires computer?	N

JD Attrition (from prior year)

	Academic	Other	Total	
	#	#	#	%
1st year	2	22	24	9.3
2nd year	2	9	11	4.2
3rd year	0	2	2	0.8
4th year	0	0	0	0.0

Employment (9 months after graduation)

	Total	Percentage
Employment status known	241	99.2
Employment status unknown	2	0.8
Employed	220	91.3
Pursuing graduate degrees	2	0.8
Unemployed (seeking, not seeking, or studying for the bar)	18	7.5
Type of Employment		
# employed in law firms	94	42.7
# employed in business and industry	37	16.8
# employed in government	15	6.8
# employed in public interest	2	0.9
# employed as judicial clerks	70	31.8
# employed in academia	2	0.9
Geographic Location		
# employed in state	143	65.0
# employed outside the US	1	0.5
# of states where employed	10	

Bar Passage Rates

First-time takers	235	Reporting %	94.04
Average school %	81.45	Average state %	83.64
Average pass difference	−2.19		

Jurisdiction	Takers	Passers	Pass %	State %	Diff %
New Jersey	221	180	81.45	83.64	−2.19

RUTGERS UNIVERSITY SCHOOL OF LAW—NEWARK

Center for Law and Justice, 123 Washington Street
Newark, NJ 07102
Phone: 973.353.5554; Fax: 973.353.3459
E-mail: lawinfo@andromeda.rutgers.edu; Website: www.law.newark.rutgers.edu

Introduction

Rutgers University School of Law—Newark has been a pioneer in legal education for more than 100 years. Few law schools can match our contributions to the advancement of legal theory and practice, the diversity of our faculty and student body, the accomplishments of our public interest programs, and our reputation for outstanding academic quality and a progressive tradition. Our law professors are prominent scholars and experts in established and emerging areas of law who challenge students in an intense yet supportive environment. Our students come to us from around the world, bringing wide-ranging backgrounds and perspectives that enrich discourse in the classroom and throughout the law school community. Our clinical program offers invaluable hands-on instruction by noted litigators and teachers and the opportunity to provide service to the underserved. Our dual-degree program with several academic disciplines within the university and with the state's medical school enables students to add an interdisciplinary perspective to their study of law. The law school is located in the heart of New Jersey's largest city, which is home to leading law firms, courts, and government agencies, major cultural institutions, Fortune 100 companies, entrepreneurial ventures, and public interest groups that offer numerous learning, internship, and volunteer opportunities.

The Center for Law and Justice

The law school is housed in the Center for Law and Justice, one of the finest law school buildings in the country. Highlights include a light-filled library boasting over 780,000 volumes and volume-equivalents and five computer labs; lecture rooms with excellent acoustics, sight lines, and power lines at every seat; an attractive courtroom complex where the Appellate Division of the Superior Court regularly hears cases; and numerous lounge and study areas. Wireless Internet access is available throughout the building and in all classrooms. The Center opens onto a pedestrian plaza and a garden terrace—favorite gathering spots for students and faculty.

Faculty

The faculty contribute to every aspect of the law school experience. Faculty members examine, shape, and resolve new and developing issues of law. Particular concentrations of academic strength lie in the fields of criminal law, constitutional law, intellectual property, legal history, and international law, with notable expertise as well in family law, race and the law, and labor and employment law. Faculty engage students through teaching styles that range from traditional Socratic method to interactive problem-solving. The faculty is diverse, ensuring the kind of intellectual inquiry that provides a rich foundation for a career in law.

Curriculum

The rigorous curriculum ensures the development of professional skills and values within a theoretical framework that promotes intellectual growth and a commitment to justice.

First-year students learn the essential conceptual, analytical, and research methods to be effective lawyers in complex environments. Upper-level students build on those skills through our extensive curriculum of over 200 class, clinic, and seminar options. The faculty review the curriculum regularly to ensure that the offerings prepare students for a rapidly changing legal environment.

An accredited semester of study abroad sends students to Leiden University in the Netherlands for an intensive program in international law, European Union law, comparative law, legal history, and law and international economics. The Rutgers Division of Global Affairs, located in our building, also serves as a nexus for students interested in the international dimension.

Joint-degree programs are available with the Rutgers Graduate Schools of Business, Planning and Public Policy, Criminal Justice, and Social Work, as well as with the University of Medicine and Dentistry of New Jersey. Students are encouraged to take advantage of the rich curriculum offerings throughout the university through cross-disciplinary registration. The Foreign Lawyer Program permits persons with foreign law degrees to earn a JD in two years.

Centers, institutes, and programs integrate faculty scholarship and activity, student interests and participation, and outreach to the larger university, legal, and other communities. As one example, the Center for Law, Science, and Technology supports faculty and student interest in intellectual property law, as well as in the intersection of law and science more generally. Among other activities, the Center holds an annual conference on patent law involving leaders from the judiciary, practice, industry, and the academic community.

Clinics and Public Service

The 43-year-old clinical program offers students extensive opportunities for hands-on legal experience in real cases involving underrepresented clients, communities, or causes. Guided by talented and accomplished faculty with expertise in litigation, legislation, mediation, or transactional practice, our clinics are noted for their diversity, breadth, and comprehensiveness of experiences, as well as for their involvement in cases and projects of social and community impact. Clinical students provide corporate, transactional, and intellectual property legal services to nonprofit corporations and start-up, for-profit businesses; litigate important constitutional and international human rights issues; provide representation to low-income children and their families; assist low-income clients on tax matters; and participate in a wide range of community education and outreach efforts. Other opportunities include pro bono work, internships, fellowships, and summer placements. The Loan Repayment Assistance Program, one of the largest in the country, assists graduates pursuing careers in public service.

Students and Student Life

Rutgers enrolls students of extraordinary academic and professional promise who enrich the community with their intellectual strength and significant life and work experience. Many students have earned advanced degrees while others provide a global perspective to the classroom.

Diversity of views enlivens the classroom and creates an inclusive environment. Our Minority Student Program reflects the faculty's long-standing commitment to preserve the diversity of the law school and to improve diversity in the legal profession. Student-run organizations reflect myriad interests, political positions, and backgrounds, from the Women's Law Forum to the Entertainment and Sports Law Society. Student publications include the *Rutgers Law Review*, *Rutgers Computer and Technology Law Journal*, *Women's Rights Law Reporter*, *Rutgers Race and the Law Review*, and the online *Rutgers Law Record*.

Admission

The faculty believe that diverse perspectives and backgrounds are essential to a complete understanding of the law and its relation to contemporary society. The law school seeks and attracts a talented student body with a breadth of experience and provides unparalleled opportunities for those who have been historically excluded from the legal profession.

The Admissions Committee considers a broad range of factors, including, but not limited to, educational and employment experiences, community service, LSAT score, UGPA, race, ethnicity, socioeconomic background, and

extraordinary family circumstances. Every applicant can choose to compete for admission with primary emphasis placed on numerical indicators (LSAT score and UGPA) or nonnumerical indicators (experiences and accomplishments).

In each entering class, 35–40 percent of our students are people of color. All regions of the country and more than two dozen foreign countries are represented.

Housing

On-campus graduate housing is located in close proximity to the law school. The recent addition of a new residence hall has increased the availability of on-campus housing for law students. Nearby suburban communities offer a variety of housing options. Public transportation is widely available.

Career Development

The Office of Career Services provides traditional and innovative services and programs, helping students and graduates develop career goals and conduct successful job searches. Individual counseling, skills training programs, panels, workshops, networking events, and on- and off-campus interview programs that attract many of the nation's leading law firms are a few of the myriad of services offered. The office also works closely with prospective employers to maximize recruitment opportunities.

APPLICANT PROFILE

Rutgers University School of Law—Newark

LSAT Score	GPA									
	3.75 +	3.50–3.74	3.25–3.49	3.00–3.24	2.75–2.99	2.50–2.74	2.25–2.49	2.00–2.24	Below 2.00	No GPA
175–180										
170–174										
165–169										
160–164										
157–159										
154–156										
150–153										
145–149										
140–144										
135–139										
130–134										
125–129										
120–124										

■ Highly Possible   ▨ Possible   □ Unlikely

The information contained in this grid should be used as an approximate gauge as to the likelihood of admission. The Admissions Committee gives considerable weight to individual accomplishments and other nonnumerical factors in the admissions process. LSAT and UGPA are not the sole determinants for admission.

ST. JOHN'S UNIVERSITY SCHOOL OF LAW

8000 Utopia Parkway
Queens, NY 11439
Phone: 718.990.6474; Fax: 718.990.2526
E-mail: lawinfo@stjohns.edu; Website: www.law.stjohns.edu

ABA
Approved
Since
1937

ABA
AMERICAN BAR ASSOCIATION
Section of Legal Education
and Admissions to the Bar

The Basics

Type of school	Private
Term	Semester
Application deadline	4/1
Application fee	$60
Financial aid deadline	4/1
Can first year start other than fall?	No
Student to faculty ratio	15.8 to 1
# of housing spaces available restricted to law students	69
graduate housing for which law students are eligible	69

Faculty and Administrators

	Total		Men		Women		Minorities	
	Spr	Fall	Spr	Fall	Spr	Fall	Spr	Fall
Full-time	44	47	23	27	21	20	8	8
Other full-time	4	3	1	0	3	3	1	0
Deans, librarians, & others who teach	7	8	4	5	3	3	0	0
Part-time	77	73	64	55	13	18	7	4
Total	132	131	92	87	40	44	16	12

Curriculum

	Full-Time	Part-Time
Typical first-year section size	82	64
Is there typically a "small section" of the first-year class, other than Legal Writing, taught by full-time faculty	No	No
If yes, typical size offered last year		
# of classroom course titles beyond first-year curriculum	242	

# of upper division courses, excluding seminars, with an enrollment:		
	Under 25	149
	25–49	34
	50–74	14
	75–99	8
	100+	1

# of seminars	36	
# of seminar positions available	713	
# of seminar positions filled	335	58
# of positions available in simulation courses	999	
# of simulation positions filled	612	77
# of positions available in faculty supervised clinical courses	220	
# of faculty supervised clinical positions filled	179	6
# involved in field placements	196	16
# involved in law journals	93	4
# involved in moot court or trial competitions	77	4
# of credit hours required to graduate	86	

JD Enrollment and Ethnicity

	Men		Women		Full-Time		Part-Time		1st-Year		Total		JD Degs. Awd.
	#	%	#	%	#	%	#	%	#	%	#	%	
All Hispanics	38	7.3	50	12.0	66	8.6	22	12.5	36	10.6	88	9.4	25
Am. Ind./AK Nat.	0	0.0	0	0.0	0	0.0	0	0.0	0	0.0	0	0.0	0
Asian	20	3.8	19	4.6	30	3.9	9	5.1	19	5.6	39	4.1	9
Black/Af. Am.	25	4.8	28	6.7	34	4.5	19	10.8	17	5.0	53	5.6	17
Nat. HI/Pac. Isl.	6	1.1	4	1.0	8	1.0	2	1.1	0	0.0	10	1.1	0
2 or more races	20	3.8	21	5.0	35	4.6	6	3.4	14	4.1	41	4.4	0
Subtotal (minor.)	109	20.8	122	29.3	173	22.6	58	33.0	86	25.4	231	24.6	70
Nonres. Alien	9	1.7	3	0.7	11	1.4	1	0.6	0	0.0	12	1.3	0
White/Cauc.	343	65.6	250	60.0	499	65.3	94	53.4	211	62.2	593	63.1	189
Unknown	62	11.9	42	10.1	81	10.6	23	13.1	42	12.4	104	11.1	31
Total	523	55.6	417	44.4	764	81.3	176	18.7	339	36.1	940		292

Transfers

Transfers in	6
Transfers out	4

Tuition and Fees

	Resident	Nonresident
Full-time	$44,280	$44,280
Part-time	$33,210	$33,210
Tuition Guarantee Program	N	

Living Expenses

Estimated living expenses for singles

Living on campus	Living off campus	Living at home
$23,250	$23,250	$9,950

ST. JOHN'S UNIVERSITY SCHOOL OF LAW

ABA Approved Since 1937

GPA and LSAT Scores

	Total	Full-Time	Part-Time
# of apps	4,510	3,673	837
# of offers	1,596	1,391	205
# of matrics	341	267	74
75% GPA	3.72	3.71	3.79
Median GPA	3.55	3.50	3.63
25% GPA	3.19	3.14	3.43
75% LSAT	162	163	157
Median LSAT	161	161	155
25% LSAT	156	158	153

Grants and Scholarships (from prior year)

	Total		Full-Time		Part-Time	
	#	%	#	%	#	%
Total # of students	915		737		178	
Total # receiving grants	353	38.6	336	45.6	17	9.6
Less than 1/2 tuition	128	14.0	117	15.9	11	6.2
Half to full tuition	92	10.1	89	12.1	3	1.7
Full tuition	132	14.4	129	17.5	3	1.7
More than full tuition	1	0.1	1	0.1	0	0.0
Median grant amount			$27,500		$10,000	

Informational and Library Resources

Total amount spent on library materials	$1,469,798
Study seating capacity inside the library	596
# of full-time equivalent professional librarians	8
Hours per week library is open	100
# of open, wired connections available to students	0
# of networked computers available for use by students	91
Has wireless network?	Y
Requires computer?	N

JD Attrition (from prior year)

	Academic	Other	Total	
	#	#	#	%
1st year	12	1	13	4.2
2nd year	0	4	4	1.5
3rd year	0	1	1	0.3
4th year	0	0	0	0.0

Employment (9 months after graduation)

	Total	Percentage
Employment status known	277	97.5
Employment status unknown	7	2.5
Employed	228	82.3
Pursuing graduate degrees	6	2.2
Unemployed (seeking, not seeking, or studying for the bar)	28	10.1
Type of Employment		
# employed in law firms	144	63.2
# employed in business and industry	30	13.2
# employed in government	23	10.1
# employed in public interest	3	1.3
# employed as judicial clerks	8	3.5
# employed in academia	19	8.3
Geographic Location		
# employed in state	207	90.8
# employed outside the US	1	0.4
# of states where employed	13	

Bar Passage Rates

First-time takers	279	Reporting %	99.28
Average school %	91.34	Average state %	86.51
Average pass difference	4.83		

Jurisdiction	Takers	Passers	Pass %	State %	Diff %
New York	277	253	91.34	86.51	4.83

ST. JOHN'S UNIVERSITY SCHOOL OF LAW

8000 Utopia Parkway
Queens, NY 11439
Phone: 718.990.6474; Fax: 718.990.2526
E-mail: lawinfo@stjohns.edu; Website: www.law.stjohns.edu

Introduction

St. John's University School of Law is a forceful presence and an integral part of the New York metropolitan area. It imparts to its students training and competency in the basic skills and techniques of the legal profession, a grasp of the history and the system of common law, and a familiarity with important statutes and decisions in federal and state jurisdictions.

The law school is a state-of-the-art facility with a gross total square footage of 179,400, one of the highest space-per-student ratios in the country. Some highlights of the facility include a new high-tech clinical suite, alumni function areas, a student lounge, faculty offices, classrooms for teaching clinical and lawyering skills, and a state-of-the-art moot courtroom.

St. John's School of Law is approved by the ABA and is a member of the AALS.

Physical Facilities and Library

The showpiece of the law school building is its beautiful law library, which incorporates the most recent advances in law library science and technology. It contains a computer laboratory and several study rooms for student conferences. The library occupies approximately 50,000 square feet on five of the eight building levels. It has been designated a depository library for US government and UN documents.

The School of Law has recently completed a major renovation of its moot court, producing a beautiful, state-of-the-art facility that incorporates technologies that further the teaching and research missions of St. John's. In addition, the School of Law has completed renovations of first-year classrooms, clinic offices, the professional skills center, the writing center, and the faculty library.

New York City

The School of Law is located on the Queens Campus of St. John's University. Situated on almost 100 rolling acres in a residential area, the campus boasts a spectacular view of the Manhattan skyline. The campus is easily accessible to Manhattan and all of New York City, and the location provides opportunities and access to the world's largest law firms, businesses, government agencies, and courts.

Clinical and Externship Programs

Elective clinical programs and externships are available to second- and third-year students.

Externships: Civil, Criminal Justice, Judicial, Special Education, Judicial/Matrimonial Alternative Dispute Resolution (ADR), Street Law.

Clinics: Elder Law, Securities Arbitration, Child Advocacy, Domestic Violence, Refugee and Immigration Rights, Prosecution, Immigrant Tenant Advocacy, Criminal Defense, Bankruptcy Advocacy, Economic Justice, and Bread and Life: Bridge to Justice.

Vincentian Scholarship Program

The mission statement of St. John's University School of Law calls for the law school "to provide a superior legal education for a diverse population of students with special awareness for economic fairness and equal opportunity, consistent with and in fulfillment of the Vincentian tradition and mission." In furtherance of this Vincentian tradition and mission, the School of Law provides five full-tuition Vincentian scholarships each year in its ongoing effort to achieve a diverse student body.

Student Activities

Publications—*St. John's Law Review/St. Thomas More Institute for Research, Journal of Catholic Legal Studies, Journal of Civil Rights and Economic Development, New York International Law Review, American Bankruptcy Institute Law Review, N.Y. Litigator,* and *N.Y. Real Property Law Journal.*

Mock Trial and Appellate Activities—Moot Court Honor Society, Frank S. Polestino Trial Advocacy Institute. In the 2009 National Institute for Trial Advocacy (NITA) Tournament of Champions, St. John's Law claimed the traveling trophy for the "best of the best" mock trial team in the country.

Specialized Legal Activities—Student Bar Association, Admiralty Law Society, Women's Law Association, Bankruptcy Law Society, Environmental Law Club, Entertainment and Sports Club, International Law Society, Intellectual Property, Labor and Employment Club, Real Property Club, Black Law Students Association, South Asian Law Students Association, Asian Pacific American Law Students Association, Latino American Law Students Association, and Client Counseling Competition. The school also maintains chapters in two legal societies, Phi Delta Phi and Phi Alpha Delta.

Special Diversity Admission Program

The School of Law sponsors a program for individuals who have faced the challenges of discrimination, chronic financial hardship, or other social, educational, or physical disadvantages to such an extent that their undergraduate performance or LSAT score would not otherwise warrant unconditional acceptance into the entering class. This Summer Institute Program consists of a substantive course taught and graded according to the same qualitative standard applied to all first-year courses, as well as a legal writing course. The program enables individuals whose LSAT scores and GPAs are not reliable predictors of their success to demonstrate their ability to succeed in the study of law.

Centers

Hugh L. Carey Center for Dispute Resolution; Ronald H. Brown Center for Civil Rights and Economic Development; Center for Bankruptcy Studies; Center for International and Comparative Law; Center for Labor and Employment Law; Center for Law, Religion and the Global Community; Writing Center; Center for Professional Skills; and Public Interest Law Center.

Academic Support

The Writing Center is a place where students can brainstorm about ideas, practice writing exam essays, edit scholarly pieces, submit papers to writing competitions, find publication sources for articles, polish briefs and memoranda for use as writing samples, practice proper citation form, hone grammar skills, or get help with any general writing problems. The Writing Center was recently renovated, is located on the first floor of the law school building, and is staffed by some of the law school's best writers.

Career Services

Career Services provides an array of services, including résumé and cover letter critiquing, mock interview coaching, job and judicial clerkship postings, newsletters, lists of prospective employers, interview programs, and career education panels. Recent graduates have obtained employment in many areas of the legal profession. Approximately 5 percent accept federal and state judicial clerkships. For the class of 2009, the employment rate (nine months after graduation) was 89 percent.

Alumni of the law school are currently practicing throughout the United States and its territories. Many have achieved positions of prominence in executive and legislative branches of the government, as members of the judiciary, and in both private and corporate practice. Two recent governors of New York, a congressman for New York, a recent governor of the US Virgin Islands, and a former governor of California were graduates of St. John's School of Law.

Financial Aid and Housing

The School of Law provides extensive financial scholarship aid to students annually. There are new university housing facilities, and many students find other suitable living accommodations in the vicinity of the university. In addition, the Admission Office coordinates a housing network for students.

Summer Study-Abroad Programs

Each summer, St. John's University offers study-abroad programs as a way to enjoy the experience of learning in a different setting. Students have the pleasure of learning and gaining credits toward graduation in Rome, Paris, and Barcelona. Courses in International or Comparative Law are traditionally offered in a four-week program (for up to six credits for each program). US and foreign law students are allowed to apply. They also have the opportunity to visit top Italian, French, and Spanish legal institutions and develop networking connections for future reference. Limited externships are available after each program.

LLM in Bankruptcy and LLM in US Legal Studies

LLM in Bankruptcy—St. John's has the nation's first master's program in bankruptcy. It is designed to meet an important and special educational need in the field of bankruptcy law. Matriculating students will be required to complete 30 credits, including the preparation and defense of a major thesis on a current significant bankruptcy topic. Students may matriculate on a full- or part-time basis.

LLM in US Legal Studies—St. John's offers an LLM Program tailored exclusively for foreign law school graduates. The program is one year in residence and requires the completion of 24 credits. Students may enroll on a full- or part-time basis.

APPLICANT PROFILE

St. John's University School of Law

LSAT Score	GPA								
	3.75 +	3.50–3.74	3.25–3.49	3.00–3.24	2.75–2.99	2.50–2.74	2.25–2.49	2.00–2.24	Below 2.00
175–180									
170–174									
165–169									
160–164									
155–159									
150–154									
145–149									
140–144									
135–139									
130–134									
125–129									
120–124									

■ Good Possibility   ▧ Possible   ▢ Unlikely

Average LSAT data reported.

SAINT LOUIS UNIVERSITY SCHOOL OF LAW

3700 Lindell Boulevard
St. Louis, MO 63108
Phone: 314.977.2800; Fax: 314.977.1464
E-mail: admissions@law.slu.edu; Website: http://law.slu.edu

The Basics

Type of school	Private
Term	Semester
Application deadline	3/1
Application fee	$55
Financial aid deadline	3/1
Can first year start other than fall?	No
Student to faculty ratio	14.8 to 1
# of housing spaces available restricted to law students	
graduate housing for which law students are eligible	

Faculty and Administrators

	Total		Men		Women		Minorities	
	Spr	Fall	Spr	Fall	Spr	Fall	Spr	Fall
Full-time	47	52	26	28	21	24	5	6
Other full-time	13	13	1	1	12	12	1	1
Deans, librarians, & others who teach	15	17	5	5	10	12	1	1
Part-time	61	39	39	28	22	11	15	7
Total	136	121	71	62	65	59	22	15

Curriculum

	Full-Time	Part-Time
Typical first-year section size	85	48
Is there typically a "small section" of the first-year class, other than Legal Writing, taught by full-time faculty	Yes	Yes
If yes, typical size offered last year	25	37
# of classroom course titles beyond first-year curriculum	168	

# of upper division courses, excluding seminars, with an enrollment:		
	Under 25	210
	25–49	49
	50–74	25
	75–99	5
	100+	6

# of seminars	36	
# of seminar positions available	441	
# of seminar positions filled	294	65
# of positions available in simulation courses	1,397	
# of simulation positions filled	975	173
# of positions available in faculty supervised clinical courses	149	
# of faculty supervised clinical positions filled	132	15
# involved in field placements	118	17
# involved in law journals	117	7
# involved in moot court or trial competitions	46	10
# of credit hours required to graduate	91	

JD Enrollment and Ethnicity

	Men		Women		Full-Time		Part-Time		1st-Year		Total		JD Degs. Awd.
	#	%	#	%	#	%	#	%	#	%	#	%	
All Hispanics	12	2.4	18	4.1	25	3.1	5	3.6	11	3.4	30	3.2	10
Am. Ind./AK Nat.	2	0.4	2	0.5	3	0.4	1	0.7	0	0.0	4	0.4	0
Asian	12	2.4	23	5.3	29	3.6	6	4.3	4	1.2	35	3.7	10
Black/Af. Am.	13	2.6	34	7.8	38	4.8	9	6.5	11	3.4	47	5.0	19
Nat. HI/Pac. Isl.	0	0.0	0	0.0	0	0.0	0	0.0	0	0.0	0	0.0	0
2 or more races	11	2.2	7	1.6	16	2.0	2	1.4	9	2.8	18	1.9	0
Subtotal (minor.)	50	10.0	84	19.2	111	13.9	23	16.7	35	10.7	134	14.3	54
Nonres. Alien	3	0.6	4	0.9	5	0.6	2	1.4	5	1.5	7	0.7	0
White/Cauc.	437	87.2	341	78.0	671	83.9	107	77.5	279	85.3	778	82.9	251
Unknown	11	2.2	8	1.8	13	1.6	6	4.3	8	2.4	19	2.0	13
Total	501	53.4	437	46.6	800	85.3	138	14.7	327	34.9	938		318

Transfers

Transfers in	4
Transfers out	15

Tuition and Fees

	Resident	Nonresident
Full-time	$35,475	$35,475
Part-time	$25,815	$25,815
Tuition Guarantee Program		N

Living Expenses

Estimated living expenses for singles

Living on campus	Living off campus	Living at home
$22,886	$22,886	$22,886

*ABA
Approved
Since
1924*

GPA and LSAT Scores

	Total	Full-Time	Part-Time
# of apps	2,307	2,159	405
# of offers	1,187	1,081	106
# of matrics	334	297	37
75% GPA	3.70	3.70	3.74
Median GPA	3.44	3.45	3.27
25% GPA	3.14	3.18	3.03
75% LSAT	159	159	157
Median LSAT	156	156	155
25% LSAT	153	153	151

Grants and Scholarships (from prior year)

	Total		Full-Time		Part-Time	
	#	%	#	%	#	%
Total # of students	967		771		196	
Total # receiving grants	360	37.2	330	42.8	30	15.3
Less than 1/2 tuition	268	27.7	238	30.9	30	15.3
Half to full tuition	60	6.2	60	7.8	0	0.0
Full tuition	32	3.3	32	4.2	0	0.0
More than full tuition	0	0.0	0	0.0	0	0.0
Median grant amount			$17,090		$6,000	

Informational and Library Resources

Total amount spent on library materials	$967,492
Study seating capacity inside the library	505
# of full-time equivalent professional librarians	10
Hours per week library is open	103
# of open, wired connections available to students	601
# of networked computers available for use by students	65
Has wireless network?	Y
Requires computer?	N

JD Attrition (from prior year)

	Academic	Other	Total	
	#	#	#	%
1st year	5	16	21	6.4
2nd year	0	18	18	6.4
3rd year	1	2	3	1.0
4th year	0	0	0	0.0

Employment (9 months after graduation)

	Total	Percentage
Employment status known	303	100.0
Employment status unknown	0	0.0
Employed	267	88.1
Pursuing graduate degrees	3	1.0
Unemployed (seeking, not seeking, or studying for the bar)	17	5.6
Type of Employment		
# employed in law firms	151	56.6
# employed in business and industry	52	19.5
# employed in government	22	8.2
# employed in public interest	27	10.1
# employed as judicial clerks	12	4.5
# employed in academia	3	1.1
Geographic Location		
# employed in state	185	69.3
# employed outside the US	0	0.0
# of states where employed		21

Bar Passage Rates

First-time takers	300	Reporting %	76.33
Average school %	95.20	Average state %	91.65
Average pass difference	3.55		

Jurisdiction	Takers	Passers	Pass %	State %	Diff %
Missouri	189	181	95.77	91.81	3.96
Illinois	40	37	92.50	90.89	1.61

SAINT LOUIS UNIVERSITY SCHOOL OF LAW

3700 Lindell Boulevard
St. Louis, MO 63108
Phone: 314.977.2800; Fax: 314.977.1464
E-mail: admissions@law.slu.edu; Website: http://law.slu.edu

Introduction

The mission of Saint Louis University School of Law (SLU Law) is to advance the understanding and development of law, and prepare students to achieve professional success and personal satisfaction through leadership and service to others. The school is guided by the Jesuit tradition of academic excellence, freedom of inquiry, and respect for individual differences.

Located in scenic midtown St. Louis, SLU Law is perfectly positioned to provide students with unparalleled exposure to the legal world. St. Louis boasts an impressive array of law firms, corporate offices, and governmental agencies, in addition to local, state, and federal courthouses throughout the city and surrounding counties, including the tallest federal courthouse in the United States.

With an accomplished, accessible faculty and a diverse curriculum, SLU Law provides a challenging yet collegial environment designed to foster success for dedicated students. Whatever the interest—corporate and finance, criminal, health, international, intellectual property, tax, securities, real estate, labor and employment, or litigation—the school can help students achieve their desired career goals.

First-year, full-time law students benefit from the school's unique small-section program, where two of their five classes have 25–35 students. This allows for individualized instruction and focused student interaction and, most importantly, builds a sense of community among classmates. The remaining classes are formed by combining different small sections to allow students to get to know others in their entering class.

For those who work full time and are unable to attend classes during the day, SLU Law offers a challenging **Part-Time Program**—the only program of its kind in the state of Missouri. Through this program, students can earn their law degree in four years with summer attendance or five years without summer attendance.

Special Academic Programs

Centers for Excellence—The school features one of the premier health law studies programs in the nation, along with specialized centers in employment law and international and comparative law.

- The **Center for Health Law Studies** boasts a nationally recognized faculty, an unparalleled curriculum, and some of the country's finest health law publications.
- The **Wefel Center for Employment Law** specializes in issues of labor disputes, benefits, hiring and discharging, and arbitration.
- The **Center for International and Comparative Law** offers a specialized program of study in areas such as public international law, international criminal law, and international corporate law. Students receive instruction from faculty who have experienced and studied foreign legal systems.

Concentrations—In addition to our three certificate programs through our Centers for Excellence, the School of Law offers concentrations in the following areas: Business Transactional Law; Civil Litigation Skills; Criminal Litigation Skills; Taxation; Urban Development, Land Use, and Environmental Law; and Intellectual Property.

Study Abroad and Exchange Programs—Through the Center for International and Comparative Law, students can study law at Saint Louis University's campus in **Madrid, Spain**, earning up to six credit hours of comparative law with foreign and American professors who have extensive experience in the fields of foreign and American criminal law, civil law, and global human rights. SLU Law also has study abroad opportunities in the following locations: Bern, Switzerland; Cork, Ireland; Paris or Orleans, France; and Southeast Asia.

Dual-Degree Programs—The School of Law offers intensive dual-degree programs in cooperation with other university schools, including the Schools of Business, Public Health, and Public Policy. Candidates in a dual-degree program must complete the first-year law curriculum before beginning the dual program. The dual-degree programs available are JD/MBA, JD/MHA, JD/MA in Public Administration, JD/MA in Urban Affairs, JD/MPH, JD/MPH in Health Policy, JD/MSW, JD/MA in Sociology and Criminal Justice, and JD/PhD in Health Care Ethics.

Public Service

SLU Law has a strong commitment to public service and a faculty pro bono director. Starting with orientation and continuing throughout the year, SLU Law sponsors and participates in public service events and projects. Some of the programs include Make a Difference Day—Homeward Bound, Habitat for Humanity, Court Appointed Special Advocates, Stand Down for Homeless Veterans, and the Tax Assistance Program.

Professional Skills Training

Students participate in courses that focus on lawyering skills through simulated client situations or live client representation under the supervision of a faculty member. **Legal Clinics** allow students to represent clients in a variety of settings, from court appearances to appeals to real estate matters. Students in the judicial clerkship programs clerk for area judges. Externships allow students to work in outside placements ranging from government agencies to large health care systems. Simulated professional skills experiences include the **Trial Advocacy Program**, **Moot Court**, and **Appellate Advocacy Program**, as well as multiple drafting courses. Drafting courses are offered in a variety of specialized areas such as intellectual property, health law, real estate, and secured transactions. Courses such as Client Counseling and Negotiations provide students with the tools necessary for skillful client interaction and the art of effective negotiation in client representation. Many of the competitions and cocurricular activities also allow students to apply legal theory to simulated client representation.

Cocurricular Activities

SLU Law allows students to perfect their writing and editing skills by working on one of **three law journals**—*Saint Louis University Law Journal*, *Saint Louis University Public Law Review*, and the *Journal of Health Law and Policy*. Qualifying students are invited to write and edit the collections of scholarly work submitted by lawyers and law professors across the world. A broad spectrum of student competitions at the local, regional, and national levels allows students to further their skills. **Moot Court Competitions** hone a student's skills in the appellate phase of litigation, including research, analysis, writing, and oral argument before judges. SLU Law students regularly compete in the National Health Law Moot Court Competition, the ABA Moot Court Competition, the Frederick Douglass Moot Court Competition, the Jessup Moot Court Competition (International Law), the Intellectual Property Moot Court Competition, and the National Environmental Law Moot Court Competition. Numerous **Trial Advocacy Competitions** allow SLU Law students to practice the skills necessary for trying cases before a jury. Each year students participate in the Texas Young Lawyers Association Trial Advocacy Competition, the ABA Employment Law Trial Advocacy Competition, and the Thurgood Marshall Mock Trial Competition. Other competitions include the ABA's Client Counseling and Negotiations competitions.

Financial Aid/Scholarships

The Saint Louis University School of Law awards a substantial number of merit-based scholarships to a select group of highly qualified admitted students, including 10 full-tuition scholarships through the 1843 Scholars program. The school has a variety of ways to help students meet their financial goals. Contact the School of Law's Financial Aid Coordinator at fin_aid@law.slu.edu.

Library

The Omer Poos Law Library serves as the center for legal and interdisciplinary research. SLU Law's databases allow students to access a wide variety of legal materials at any time from anywhere. The library provides a state-of-the-art research environment with access to scores of electronic resources and a collection of over 600,000 volumes. Research librarians hold both law and library science degrees and are available during the day and evening to assist students with research. The SLU Law library faculty and staff take pride in providing personal attention and service to students.

Career Services

The Career Services Office, staffed by licensed attorneys and a licensed professional counselor, assists students in identifying their career goals. Students with differing backgrounds and career goals benefit from the personalized assistance that the office provides. Historically, graduating classes have outpaced the national employment average by approximately five percent each year. Across the nation, SLU Law alumni work at large and small firms, excel as CEOs and in-house counsel, and serve in national, state, and local government organizations.

APPLICANT PROFILE

Saint Louis University School of Law
This grid includes only applicants who earned 120–180 LSAT scores under standard administrations.

LSAT Score	3.75 +		3.50–3.74		3.25–3.49		3.00–3.24		2.75–2.99		2.50–2.74		2.25–2.49		2.00–2.24		Below 2.00		No GPA		Total	
	Apps	Adm	Apps	Adm	Apps	Adm	Apps	Adm	Apps	Adm	Apps	Adm	Apps	Adm	Apps	Adm	Apps	Adm	Apps	Adm	Apps	Adm
175–180	1	1	0	0	1	1	0	0	0	0	0	0	0	0	0	0	0	0	0	0	2	2
170–174	6	2	5	4	6	5	4	2	2	1	2	2	1	0	0	0	0	0	0	0	26	16
165–169	26	16	25	21	12	9	10	8	10	7	3	1	3	0	1	0	1	0	3	1	94	63
160–164	93	70	93	82	71	65	70	62	26	13	18	6	10	2	2	0	0	0	7	4	390	304
155–159	108	105	140	127	129	106	97	68	66	29	36	11	18	6	5	1	2	0	9	4	610	457
150–154	80	65	137	73	174	77	119	34	64	6	28	2	17	1	6	0	1	0	12	2	638	260
145–149	22	9	43	15	78	11	61	4	45	0	35	1	20	1	3	0	0	0	11	0	318	41
140–144	2	0	10	0	19	1	28	0	21	0	19	0	9	1	3	0	1	0	2	0	114	2
135–139	1	0	4	0	7	0	16	0	10	0	8	0	10	0	6	0	1	0	3	0	66	0
130–134	0	0	1	0	2	0	5	0	4	0	5	0	4	0	5	0	0	0	1	0	27	0
125–129	0	0	0	0	0	0	0	0	1	0	0	0	1	0	3	0	0	0	0	0	5	0
120–124	0	0	0	0	0	0	0	0	1	0	0	0	0	0	0	0	0	0	0	0	1	0
Total	339	268	458	322	499	275	410	178	250	56	154	23	93	11	34	1	6	0	48	11	2291	1145

Apps = Number of Applicants
Adm = Number Admitted
Reflects 99% of the total applicant pool; highest LSAT data reported.

ST. MARY'S UNIVERSITY SCHOOL OF LAW

One Camino Santa Maria
San Antonio, TX 78228-8601
Phone: 210.436.3523; Toll-free: 866.639.5831; Fax: 210.431.4202
E-mail: lawadmissions@stmarytx.edu; Website: http://law.stmarytx.edu

ABA
Approved
Since
1948

The Basics

Type of school	Private
Term	Semester
Application deadline	3/1
Application fee	$55
Financial aid deadline	3/31
Can first year start other than fall?	No
Student to faculty ratio	22.4 to 1
# of housing spaces available restricted to law students	
graduate housing for which law students are eligible	108

Faculty and Administrators

	Total		Men		Women		Minorities	
	Spr	Fall	Spr	Fall	Spr	Fall	Spr	Fall
Full-time	31	28	19	17	12	11	6	5
Other full-time	7	8	5	2	2	6	2	3
Deans, librarians, & others who teach	13	14	9	10	4	4	6	6
Part-time	53	52	28	32	25	20	8	6
Total	104	102	61	61	43	41	22	20

Curriculum

	Full-Time	Part-Time
Typical first-year section size	76	61
Is there typically a "small section" of the first-year class, other than Legal Writing, taught by full-time faculty	No	No
If yes, typical size offered last year		

# of classroom course titles beyond first-year curriculum		107
# of upper division courses, excluding seminars, with an enrollment:	Under 25	47
	25–49	29
	50–74	12
	75–99	19
	100+	0
# of seminars		12
# of seminar positions available		156

	Full-Time	Part-Time
# of seminar positions filled	116	7
# of positions available in simulation courses	313	
# of simulation positions filled	164	35
# of positions available in faculty supervised clinical courses	64	
# of faculty supervised clinical positions filled	59	5
# involved in field placements	22	4
# involved in law journals	73	7
# involved in moot court or trial competitions	90	0
# of credit hours required to graduate	90	

JD Enrollment and Ethnicity

	Men		Women		Full-Time		Part-Time		1st-Year		Total		JD Degs. Awd.
	#	%	#	%	#	%	#	%	#	%	#	%	
All Hispanics	128	26.4	86	25.0	167	24.7	47	30.7	81	22.5	214	25.8	60
Am. Ind./AK Nat.	4	0.8	3	0.9	4	0.6	3	2.0	1	0.3	7	0.8	0
Asian	15	3.1	10	2.9	20	3.0	5	3.3	4	1.1	25	3.0	14
Black/Af. Am.	10	2.1	21	6.1	22	3.3	9	5.9	13	3.6	31	3.7	7
Nat. HI/Pac. Isl.	0	0.0	0	0.0	0	0.0	0	0.0	0	0.0	0	0.0	0
2 or more races	5	1.0	1	0.3	4	0.6	2	1.3	6	1.7	6	0.7	0
Subtotal (minor.)	162	33.5	121	35.2	217	32.1	66	43.1	105	29.2	283	34.2	81
Nonres. Alien	0	0.0	0	0.0	0	0.0	0	0.0	0	0.0	0	0.0	0
White/Cauc.	322	66.5	223	64.8	458	67.9	87	56.9	196	54.4	545	65.8	160
Unknown	0	0.0	0	0.0	0	0.0	0	0.0	0	0.0	0	0.0	0
Total	484	58.5	344	41.5	675	81.5	153	18.5	301	43.5	828		241

Transfers

Transfers in	2
Transfers out	10

Tuition and Fees

	Resident	Nonresident
Full-time	$28,160	$28,160
Part-time	$17,120	$17,120
Tuition Guarantee Program	N	

Living Expenses

Estimated living expenses for singles

Living on campus	Living off campus	Living at home
$15,424	$15,424	$15,424

ABA
Approved
Since
1948

GPA and LSAT Scores

	Total	Full-Time	Part-Time
# of apps	1,965	1,718	247
# of offers	848	768	80
# of matrics	301	255	46
75% GPA	3.36	3.40	3.21
Median GPA	3.03	3.07	2.87
25% GPA	2.68	2.72	2.48
75% LSAT	156	156	154
Median LSAT	153	154	151
25% LSAT	151	151	149

Grants and Scholarships (from prior year)

	Total		Full-Time		Part-Time	
	#	%	#	%	#	%
Total # of students	863		681		182	
Total # receiving grants	348	40.3	238	34.9	110	60.4
Less than 1/2 tuition	337	39.0	229	33.6	108	59.3
Half to full tuition	11	1.3	9	1.3	2	1.1
Full tuition	0	0.0	0	0.0	0	0.0
More than full tuition	0	0.0	0	0.0	0	0.0
Median grant amount			$2,014		$0	

Informational and Library Resources

Total amount spent on library materials	$1,036,421
Study seating capacity inside the library	390
# of full-time equivalent professional librarians	6
Hours per week library is open	108
# of open, wired connections available to students	562
# of networked computers available for use by students	77
Has wireless network?	Y
Requires computer?	N

JD Attrition (from prior year)

	Academic	Other	Total	
	#	#	#	%
1st year	11	5	16	4.4
2nd year	4	11	15	5.7
3rd year	0	1	1	0.4
4th year	0	0	0	0.0

Employment (9 months after graduation)

	Total	Percentage
Employment status known	200	97.6
Employment status unknown	5	2.4
Employed	175	87.5
Pursuing graduate degrees	2	1.0
Unemployed (seeking, not seeking, or studying for the bar)	12	6.0
Type of Employment		
# employed in law firms	120	68.6
# employed in business and industry	16	9.1
# employed in government	23	13.1
# employed in public interest	4	2.3
# employed as judicial clerks	6	3.4
# employed in academia	3	1.7
Geographic Location		
# employed in state	160	91.4
# employed outside the US	0	0.0
# of states where employed	7	

Bar Passage Rates

First-time takers	195	Reporting %	96.92
Average school %	83.60	Average state %	85.48
Average pass difference	−1.88		

Jurisdiction	Takers	Passers	Pass %	State %	Diff %
Texas	189	158	83.60	85.48	−1.88

ST. MARY'S UNIVERSITY SCHOOL OF LAW

One Camino Santa Maria
San Antonio, TX 78228-8601
Phone: 210.436.3523; Toll-free: 866.639.5831; Fax: 210.431.4202
E-mail: lawadmissions@stmarytx.edu; Website: http://law.stmarytx.edu

Introduction

St. Mary's University School of Law was founded in 1927 as part of the oldest and largest Catholic university in the Southwest. St. Mary's is located in the beautiful, unique, and legendary city of San Antonio. San Antonio combines a diverse blend of historic sites, natural beauty, charming vistas, and urban amenities. With its culturally rich population and environment, San Antonio is the perfect backdrop for the mission and goals of the School of Law. Enriched by the spirit of the Society of Mary (Marianists), the school imparts to its students the knowledge and attributes of mind and character essential to public service. St. Mary's is vigilant of the need to preserve a tradition of excellence in legal education with the development of new programs and methodologies for the changing world, and now offers a **part-time evening program** in addition to its traditional full-time day program.

Library and Physical Facilities

The Sarita Kenedy East Law Library is the largest legal information center in San Antonio and its surrounding area. The library is housed in a spacious, bright, and beautiful building. There is ample study-table seating and large private study carrels. Small conference rooms accommodate groups for discussion and collaboration. A federal depository library, the collection consists of print, microfilm, and multimedia items totaling over 400,000 volumes (or equivalent), which cover a wide range of subjects, including US federal and state laws, and foreign, comparative, and international law. The collection and resources are cataloged and searchable through an automated library information system. The library subscribes to LexisNexis, Westlaw, Loislaw, HeinOnline, LLMC-Digital, the Center for Computer-Assisted Legal Instruction (CALI), the Index to Legal Periodicals Full Text, Congressional Universe, AccessUN, the United Nations Treaty Series, and other information databases. Computers and Internet access, both wired and wireless, are available and supported throughout the library facilities. The library is staffed with eight degreed librarians and about eight paraprofessionals who provide friendly, quality service.

The Law Classroom Building contains four amphitheater-style classrooms with electronically retractable walls and a newly renovated and technologically advanced modern courtroom at its center. Electrical outlets and data ports are located at each student's seat, and the public lounges provide wireless access.

The law school's four primary buildings are located around an oak-shaded quadrangle, forming a central gathering spot. The recently completed Alumni Athletic and Convocation Center offers 135,000 square feet of wellness and fitness options. The center provides for ceremonial facilities as well as athletic endeavors.

Curriculum

Required full-time, first-year courses are Constitutional Law, Contracts, Criminal Law, Legal Research and Writing, Civil Procedure, Property, and Torts. All students must also take the required courses of Professional Responsibility, Evidence, and Texas Civil Procedure (only required of those planning to take the Texas bar examination), as well as a specified number of courses from a menu-style core curriculum. Students must also complete a research paper.

Clinical Legal Education

The Clinical Program at St. Mary's offers three clinical classes: Civil Justice, Criminal Justice, and Immigration/Human Rights. The clinics teach substantive law, lawyering skills, and responsibilities through the supervised representation of low-income clients and the development of community-based projects. The Civil Justice Clinic represents persons who are homeless; victims of violent crimes; persons who are undocumented, primarily in family law; social security claims; consumer issues; and tax controversies. The Criminal Justice Clinic accepts representation of individuals of any age in misdemeanor and low felony cases as well as some innocence claims. Immigration/Human Rights students represent indigent foreign nationals and refugees in Immigration Court and assist clients with applications for asylum, T and U (trafficking and violent crime victim) visas, and benefits under the Violence Against Women Act.

International Law

The **St. Mary's Institute on World Legal Problems** is conducted at the University of Innsbruck in Austria during July and August. The program is designed to provide law students with a broader understanding of global issues and the role law can play in their peaceful resolution.

Seven justices of the United States Supreme Court have participated in the program as distinguished visiting jurists—former Chief Justice William H. Rehnquist; current Chief Justice John G. Roberts, Jr.; Justice Antonin Scalia; Justice Samuel A. Alito, Jr.; Justice Ruth Bader Ginsburg; former Justice Sandra Day O'Connor; and former Justice John Paul Stevens. The program draws students and faculty from all parts of the United States and abroad. It has included students from at least 100 American law schools as well as from Austria, Hungary, China, and Russia. More than 40 visiting professors from law schools in the United States and several foreign countries have also participated.

The Innsbruck Institute is part of the law school's program in international and comparative law.

The **St. Mary's University School of Law Institute on Chinese Law and Business** is a new program of legal studies that prepares law students for the challenges of representing clients doing business with Chinese partners. This summer program is conducted with the cooperation of Beihang University in Beijing.

St. Mary's houses a **Center for Terrorism Law**, a nonpartisan, nonprofit institution dedicated to the study of legal issues associated with terrorism, with particular emphasis on cyberspace and information assurance technologies.

Judicial Internships

St. Mary's students may participate in a wide range of pregraduation judicial internships with outstanding state and federal courts. Students work under the supervision of a judge or staff attorney, performing legal research and writing projects which often include the drafting of orders that will be used to decide pending cases, the composition of jury instructions, the researching of evidentiary questions, or attendance at settlement conferences.

Admission Standards

St. Mary's goal is to create an intellectually stimulating student body composed of persons with diverse backgrounds who share a desire for academic excellence and accomplishment in the practice of law. In addition to academic ability, St. Mary's seeks evidence of qualities such as leadership ability, maturity, community organization skills, knowledge of other languages and cultures, a history of overcoming disadvantage, public interest accomplishments, or success in a previous career. A faculty committee reviews all applications. No one is automatically rejected. All files are read.

Student Activities

St. Mary's has over 30 active student organizations. Student organizations are a key part of the collegial environment of the law school.

St. Mary's has two law reviews—the *St. Mary's Law Journal* and *The Scholar: St. Mary's Law Review on Minority Issues*. The reviews offer students excellent opportunities to develop advanced legal research and writing skills. The *Law Journal* has been cited as a persuasive authority in hundreds of court decisions.

St. Mary's students are active in moot court and mock trial competitions. During the spring semester, first-year students participate in a school-wide moot court competition. Second- and third-year students can compete in on-campus tournaments and in St. Mary's External Advocacy Program

(EAP). St. Mary's EAP students travel throughout the US to attend the ABA National Moot Court, National Mock Trial, ATLA Mock Trial, and negotiation competitions.

Career Services

The role of the Office of Career Services is to assist law students and graduates with their career searches by informing them of career options and job-search strategies and connecting them with potential employers. Career Services does so by sponsoring programs and job fairs designed to educate, facilitate, and connect students with potential employers during and after law school.

One-on-one confidential strategy sessions with the assistant dean provide a unique opportunity for students to develop a personal plan to assess and meet their career goals. The office maintains a job bank and a résumé bank. The Student Resource Center offers an extensive and up-to-date library of career resources and directories of attorneys, as well as computer terminals with Internet resources, to help students direct and begin their careers in legal and nontraditional positions. Students have extensive opportunities to interact with alumni, who assist with career programming and networking events throughout the year.

For the students in the class of 2009 who reported employment status, 89 percent are employed, with almost all of them working in the legal field.

LLM Degrees

St. Mary's offers both an LLM Degree in American Legal Studies and another in International Comparative Law.

APPLICANT PROFILE

St. Mary's University School of Law
This grid includes only applicants who earned 120–180 LSAT scores under standard administrations.

LSAT Score	3.75 + Apps	Adm	3.50–3.74 Apps	Adm	3.25–3.49 Apps	Adm	3.00–3.24 Apps	Adm	2.75–2.99 Apps	Adm	2.50–2.74 Apps	Adm	2.25–2.49 Apps	Adm	2.00–2.24 Apps	Adm	Below 2.00 Apps	Adm	No GPA Apps	Adm	Total Apps	Adm
175–180	0	0	0	0	0	0	0	0	0	0	0	0	0	0	0	0	0	0	0	0	0	0
170–174	2	2	1	1	1	1	1	1	0	0	0	0	0	0	0	0	0	0	0	0	5	5
165–169	2	2	3	3	3	3	5	5	1	1	2	2	1	1	0	0	0	0	0	0	17	17
160–164	6	6	27	27	33	33	28	28	15	15	11	11	6	6	6	5	0	0	1	1	133	132
155–159	35	35	36	34	68	65	68	67	44	44	44	41	24	23	10	10	3	2	2	2	334	323
150–154	35	23	95	72	103	65	118	68	102	51	59	25	39	20	20	7	5	1	4	0	580	332
145–149	35	1	65	4	102	9	91	6	95	7	62	2	35	2	19	1	5	0	5	0	514	32
140–144	7	0	15	0	26	1	57	1	46	0	44	0	21	0	8	0	1	0	5	0	230	2
135–139	3	0	3	0	7	0	13	0	17	0	22	0	17	0	5	0	1	0	3	0	91	0
130–134	0	0	2	0	2	0	7	0	3	0	9	0	3	0	1	0	1	0	2	0	30	0
125–129	0	0	0	0	1	0	2	0	1	0	0	0	2	0	0	0	0	0	0	0	6	0
120–124	0	0	0	0	1	0	0	0	0	0	0	0	0	0	0	0	0	0	0	0	1	0
Total	125	69	247	141	347	177	390	176	324	118	253	81	148	52	69	23	16	3	22	3	1941	843

Apps = Number of Applicants
Adm = Number Admitted
Reflects 99% of the total applicant pool; highest LSAT data reported.

UNIVERSITY OF ST. THOMAS SCHOOL OF LAW—MINNEAPOLIS

1000 LaSalle Avenue
Minneapolis, MN 55403
Phone: 651.962.4895
E-mail: lawschool@stthomas.edu; Website: www.stthomas.edu/law

The Basics

Type of school	Private
Term	Semester
Application deadline	7/1
Application fee	
Financial aid deadline	7/1
Can first year start other than fall?	No
Student to faculty ratio	17.3 to 1
# of housing spaces available restricted to law students	
graduate housing for which law students are eligible	

Faculty and Administrators

	Total		Men		Women		Minorities	
	Spr	Fall	Spr	Fall	Spr	Fall	Spr	Fall
Full-time	19	26	12	18	7	8	4	5
Other full-time	4	3	2	1	2	2	1	1
Deans, librarians, & others who teach	13	10	5	4	8	6	1	0
Part-time	66	56	44	38	22	18	7	6
Total	102	95	63	61	39	34	13	12

Curriculum

	Full-Time	Part-Time
Typical first-year section size	85	0
Is there typically a "small section" of the first-year class, other than Legal Writing, taught by full-time faculty	Yes	No
If yes, typical size offered last year	43	
# of classroom course titles beyond first-year curriculum	86	

# of upper division courses, excluding seminars, with an enrollment:		
	Under 25	127
	25–49	23
	50–74	8
	75–99	4
	100+	0

# of seminars	14	
# of seminar positions available	195	
# of seminar positions filled	190	0
# of positions available in simulation courses	422	
# of simulation positions filled	378	0
# of positions available in faculty supervised clinical courses	73	
# of faculty supervised clinical positions filled	71	0
# involved in field placements	609	0
# involved in law journals	78	0
# involved in moot court or trial competitions	31	0
# of credit hours required to graduate	88	

JD Enrollment and Ethnicity

	Men		Women		Full-Time		Part-Time		1st-Year		Total		JD Degs. Awd.
	#	%	#	%	#	%	#	%	#	%	#	%	
All Hispanics	4	1.5	5	2.4	9	1.9	0	0.0	1	0.6	9	1.9	5
Am. Ind./AK Nat.	2	0.7	0	0.0	2	0.4	0	0.0	2	1.2	2	0.4	0
Asian	12	4.5	17	8.2	29	6.1	0	0.0	10	6.0	29	6.1	11
Black/Af. Am.	7	2.6	8	3.9	15	3.2	0	0.0	4	2.4	15	3.2	9
Nat. HI/Pac. Isl.	0	0.0	1	0.5	1	0.2	0	0.0	1	0.6	1	0.2	0
2 or more races	0	0.0	1	0.5	1	0.2	0	0.0	1	0.6	1	0.2	0
Subtotal (minor.)	25	9.3	32	15.5	57	12.0	0	0.0	19	11.3	57	12.0	25
Nonres. Alien	0	0.0	0	0.0	0	0.0	0	0.0	0	0.0	0	0.0	0
White/Cauc.	217	81.0	155	74.9	372	78.3	0	0.0	132	78.6	372	78.3	107
Unknown	26	9.7	20	9.7	46	9.7	0	0.0	17	10.1	46	9.7	22
Total	268	56.4	207	43.6	475	100.0	0	0.0	168	35.4	475		155

Transfers

Transfers in	6
Transfers out	10

Tuition and Fees

	Resident	Nonresident
Full-time	$36,313	
Part-time		
Tuition Guarantee Program		N

Living Expenses

Estimated living expenses for singles		
Living on campus	Living off campus	Living at home
N/A	$18,585	$18,585

UNIVERSITY OF ST. THOMAS SCHOOL OF LAW—MINNEAPOLIS

ABA Approved Since 2003

GPA and LSAT Scores

	Total	Full-Time	Part-Time
# of apps	1,801	1,801	0
# of offers	917	917	0
# of matrics	168	168	0
75% GPA	3.52	3.52	0.00
Median GPA	3.24	3.24	0.00
25% GPA	3.01	3.01	0.00
75% LSAT	161	161	0
Median LSAT	156	156	0
25% LSAT	154	154	0

Grants and Scholarships (from prior year)

	Total		Full-Time		Part-Time	
	#	%	#	%	#	%
Total # of students	459		457		2	
Total # receiving grants	272	59.3	272	59.5	0	0.0
Less than 1/2 tuition	93	20.3	93	20.4	0	0.0
Half to full tuition	73	15.9	73	16.0	0	0.0
Full tuition	106	23.1	106	23.2	0	0.0
More than full tuition	0	0.0	0	0.0	0	0.0
Median grant amount			$20,000		$0	

Informational and Library Resources

Total amount spent on library materials	$797,065
Study seating capacity inside the library	379
# of full-time equivalent professional librarians	5
Hours per week library is open	83
# of open, wired connections available to students	595
# of networked computers available for use by students	67
Has wireless network?	Y
Requires computer?	N

JD Attrition (from prior year)

	Academic	Other	Total	
	#	#	#	%
1st year	0	1	1	0.6
2nd year	0	10	10	7.2
3rd year	0	0	0	0.0
4th year	0	0	0	0.0

Employment (9 months after graduation)

	Total	Percentage
Employment status known	144	100.0
Employment status unknown	0	0.0
Employed	129	89.6
Pursuing graduate degrees	4	2.8
Unemployed (seeking, not seeking, or studying for the bar)	9	6.2
Type of Employment		
# employed in law firms	43	33.3
# employed in business and industry	42	32.6
# employed in government	15	11.6
# employed in public interest	9	7.0
# employed as judicial clerks	14	10.9
# employed in academia	4	3.1
Geographic Location		
# employed in state	94	72.9
# employed outside the US	0	0.0
# of states where employed	20	

Bar Passage Rates

First-time takers	141	Reporting %	78.01
Average school %	90.91	Average state %	89.58
Average pass difference	1.33		

Jurisdiction	Takers	Passers	Pass %	State %	Diff %
Minnesota	110	100	90.91	89.58	1.33

UNIVERSITY OF ST. THOMAS SCHOOL OF LAW—MINNEAPOLIS

1000 LaSalle Avenue
Minneapolis, MN 55403
Phone: 651.962.4895
E-mail: lawschool@stthomas.edu; Website: www.stthomas.edu/law

Introduction

The University of St. Thomas integrates faith and reason in the search for truth through a focus on morality and social justice. The close-knit community, drawn together by this unique mission, shares a distinctive vision of what law and the legal profession can be. The School of Law attracts students from across the country who want to be servant leaders and who understand their responsibility to serve their clients, the community, and those who are most in need of, and least able to pay for, legal assistance.

Curriculum

The School of Law offers more than 85 advanced, elective courses in addition to 15 required courses.

The University of St. Thomas offers a unique, nationally recognized, structured mentor externship integrated into the curriculum that matches each student with an experienced lawyer or judge for each year of law school. Mentors introduce students to a range of lawyering tasks. In addition to gaining practical knowledge, students talk with their mentors about the intellectual, ethical, and moral challenges facing attorneys.

Students can also pursue one of five joint-degree programs, including Business Administration (JD/MBA), Catholic Studies (JD/MA), Public Policy (JD/MA), Professional Psychology (JD/MA), and Social Work (JD/MSW).

Special Programs

At the Interprofessional Center for Counseling and Legal Services (IPC), law students work side by side with students from graduate programs in social work and professional psychology. The IPC is among the first in the country to forge an equal partnership among the three disciplines. The IPC gives students experience working with actual clients on active cases.

The Holloran Center for Ethical Leadership unites leaders from a range of professions who work together to pursue practical solutions and create effective tools in confronting the challenge of creating ethical leaders. The center hosts an annual national professionals conference, business and law roundtables on ethical governance, and Trusted Adviser Seminars, in which servant leaders from the Twin Cities discuss issues with students in the professional schools.

The Terrence J. Murphy Institute for Catholic Thought, Law and Public Policy is a collaboration between the Center for Catholic Studies and the School of Law. The institute explores the various interactions between law and Catholic thought on topics ranging from workers' rights, to criminal law, to marriage and family.

The Area

The University of St. Thomas School of Law is located in downtown Minneapolis, the regional center for business and culture. Minneapolis and the nearby capital city of St. Paul make up the core of the Twin Cities metropolitan area—a metro area of more than 3.5 million residents. The Twin Cities are home to a vibrant business community that features 12 of

Fortune 500's largest corporations. The Twin Cities are also home to a lively legal community that has embraced the School of Law through the mentor externship and summer employment opportunities.

The seemingly limitless recreational opportunities and distinctive beauty of the region add immeasurably to the quality of life. The Twin Cities boast 949 lakes in the metropolitan area. Outdoor enthusiasts have plenty of options from which to choose.

Admission

The School of Law seeks to identify students who show the potential to distinguish themselves academically and to integrate the fundamental characteristics of faith and values into their professional character and identity.

The Admissions Committee reviews applications with the goal of understanding the strengths, skills, and unique perspectives of each applicant. While the committee examines quantitative criteria such as LSAT scores and undergraduate transcripts, it also focuses on qualitative factors, such as writing skills, leadership experience, motivation, public service orientation, and commitment to our mission of exploring the integration of faith and reason.

The committee carefully examines all materials submitted to determine whether the School of Law and the student are a good fit. A student's personal statement, letters of recommendation, and other subjective information play an important role in assisting the committee with its goal.

Faculty

The faculty are a distinguished group of scholars with an impressive mixture of skills, expertise, and experience. Faculty members are nationally recognized for their professional and scholarly proficiency; all have experience as teachers and as practicing lawyers or expert witnesses, and 16 have advanced degrees in other disciplines.

Of equal importance, faculty members have demonstrated a commitment to service and leadership. All have developed reputations as caring, accessible mentors for students, and each has an inspiring record of service to the community. Faculty members share a strong commitment to our mission and a dedication to assisting each student in his or her formation as an accomplished servant leader.

Each academic year, the full-time faculty is supplemented by over 75 practicing attorneys and judges who serve as adjunct professors.

Enrollment/Student Body

The student body is diverse. In the fall 2010 entering class, students represented 29 states and 84 undergraduate institutions. While many students come to the School of Law directly from undergraduate institutions, others have earned postgraduate degrees or have work experience.

Library and Physical Facilities

The School of Law occupies a new building, of over 150,000 square feet, in downtown Minneapolis, near the federal courthouse and major laws firms and businesses. The building has several defining features that make it "quite simply breathtaking," as described by an ABA site-evaluation team. These include the dramatic four-story Schultz Grand Atrium, used for lectures, conferences, and social gatherings; the Frey Moot Courtroom, which provides a striking setting in which to learn lawyering skills or hear moot court arguments; and the beautiful Chapel of St. Thomas More.

Modern technology enhances the classrooms, library, groups study areas, moot courtroom, and private offices. A computer lab and a computer training center accommodate student research needs.

The library, with its ample seating, 12 group study rooms, and 3 AV viewing rooms, provides an attractive, functional environment for group or individual study. The library's strong electronic collection provides convenient access to many resources from both on and off campus.

Financial Aid

St. Thomas is committed to making high-quality legal education available to students by offering scholarships, grants, employment, and loans. The School of Law administers two scholarship programs that acknowledge applicants who have outstanding academic records, who contribute to our dedicated diversity effort, or who are particularly likely to contribute to the school's mission. All incoming students are automatically considered for scholarship awards.

The UST Loan Repayment Assistance Program (UST-LRAP) provides up to $6,000 in annual assistance for up to 10 years for qualifying applicants. In general, graduates with financial need who undertake public service jobs benefiting the poor and underserved will be eligible to receive assistance with repaying loans for law school tuition.

Career Services

Alumni and students work with federal and state judges; international, national, and local public interest organizations; corporations; banks; and law firms of all sizes.

The Office of Career and Professional Development supports students and alumni wherever they are in their career paths and encourages them to consider how their career choices complement their spiritual and ethical beliefs. Available resources include résumé and cover letter writing workshops and individual review, interviewing skills seminars, mock interviews, an online job center, a resource center, practice area panel discussions with local attorneys, networking events, career fairs, and on-campus interviewing.

Student Activities

Students are encouraged to form and join student organizations that help them integrate their faith or passion for social justice with their image of themselves as lawyers. Students have created several unique student organizations dedicated to integrating faith and reason in the search for truth with an emphasis on social justice.

The *University of St. Thomas Law Journal* gives students the opportunity to contribute to the development of legal scholarship and further hone their research, analytical, and writing abilities. The Board of Advocates oversees interscholastic competitions in moot court, trial advocacy, client counseling, and negotiation.

All students are required to perform 50 hours of community service work, exploring a variety of ways in which their interests, skills, and talents can best serve the public. The Public Service Board administers the School of Law's public service requirement, and maintains and distributes information about public service opportunities.

APPLICANT PROFILE

University of St. Thomas School of Law—Minneapolis
This grid includes only applicants who earned 120–180 LSAT scores under standard administrations.

LSAT Score	3.75 +		3.50–3.74		3.25–3.49		3.00–3.24		2.75–2.99		2.50–2.74		2.25–2.49		2.00–2.24		Below 2.00		No GPA		Total	
	Apps	Adm	Apps	Adm	Apps	Adm	Apps	Adm	Apps	Adm	Apps	Adm	Apps	Adm	Apps	Adm	Apps	Adm	Apps	Adm	Apps	Adm
175–180	0	0	0	0	0	0	0	0	0	0	0	0	0	0	0	0	0	0	0	0	0	0
170–174	3	3	4	4	4	4	1	1	0	0	0	0	0	0	0	0	0	0	0	0	12	12
165–169	17	17	8	8	8	7	6	5	7	6	4	3	6	6	0	0	0	0	1	1	57	53
160–164	34	32	64	61	46	46	35	32	18	18	10	10	5	5	3	3	1	1	3	2	219	210
155–159	56	56	69	63	91	86	78	71	51	45	28	23	22	13	3	0	1	0	5	5	404	362
150–154	50	33	91	57	116	62	84	40	66	21	39	8	24	7	8	1	2	0	8	3	488	232
145–149	19	4	56	12	75	9	74	13	45	5	38	1	21	1	11	0	2	0	6	1	347	46
140–144	6	1	18	0	26	0	39	1	26	0	19	0	14	0	2	0	1	0	3	0	154	2
135–139	2	0	1	0	4	0	8	0	16	0	8	0	13	0	6	0	2	0	4	0	64	0
130–134	0	0	0	0	0	0	6	0	6	0	5	0	3	0	1	0	1	0	3	0	31	0
125–129	0	0	0	0	0	0	1	0	0	0	3	0	1	0	3	0	0	0	3	0	12	0
120–124	0	0	0	0	0	0	0	0	0	0	0	0	0	0	1	0	0	0	0	0	1	0
Total	187	146	311	205	376	214	332	163	236	95	154	45	109	32	38	4	10	1	36	12	1789	917

Apps = Number of Applicants
Adm = Number Admitted
Reflects 99% of the total applicant pool; highest LSAT data reported.

ST. THOMAS UNIVERSITY SCHOOL OF LAW

16401 NW 37th Avenue
Miami Gardens, FL 33054
Phone: 800.245.4569, 305.623.2310; Fax: 305.623.2357
E-mail: admitme@stu.edu; Website: www.stu.edu/lawschool

ABA
Approved
Since
1988

The Basics

Type of school	Private
Term	Semester
Application deadline	6/1
Application fee	$60
Financial aid deadline	4/1
Can first year start other than fall?	No
Student to faculty ratio	19.7 to 1
# of housing spaces available restricted to law students	
graduate housing for which law students are eligible	100

Faculty and Administrators

	Total		Men		Women		Minorities	
	Spr	Fall	Spr	Fall	Spr	Fall	Spr	Fall
Full-time	31	28	17	13	14	15	6	5
Other full-time	1	0	0	0	1	0	0	0
Deans, librarians, & others who teach	11	10	7	7	4	3	4	4
Part-time	33	30	27	22	6	8	9	10
Total	76	68	51	42	25	26	19	19

Curriculum

	Full-Time	Part-Time
Typical first-year section size	60	0
Is there typically a "small section" of the first-year class, other than Legal Writing, taught by full-time faculty	No	No
If yes, typical size offered last year		
# of classroom course titles beyond first-year curriculum	116	

# of upper division courses, excluding seminars, with an enrollment:		
	Under 25	148
	25–49	34
	50–74	21
	75–99	3
	100+	0

# of seminars	14	
# of seminar positions available	224	
# of seminar positions filled	173	0
# of positions available in simulation courses	275	
# of simulation positions filled	259	0
# of positions available in faculty supervised clinical courses	82	
# of faculty supervised clinical positions filled	82	0
# involved in field placements	158	0
# involved in law journals	129	0
# involved in moot court or trial competitions	70	0
# of credit hours required to graduate	90	

JD Enrollment and Ethnicity

	Men		Women		Full-Time		Part-Time		1st-Year		Total		JD Degs. Awd.
	#	%	#	%	#	%	#	%	#	%	#	%	
All Hispanics	120	30.8	151	44.0	271	37.0	0	0.0	110	40.3	271	37.0	71
Am. Ind./AK Nat.	2	0.5	1	0.3	3	0.4	0	0.0	2	0.7	3	0.4	0
Asian	10	2.6	9	2.6	19	2.6	0	0.0	7	2.6	19	2.6	12
Black/Af. Am.	20	5.1	29	8.5	49	6.7	0	0.0	15	5.5	49	6.7	18
Nat. HI/Pac. Isl.	0	0.0	0	0.0	0	0.0	0	0.0	0	0.0	0	0.0	0
2 or more races	15	3.8	16	4.7	31	4.2	0	0.0	15	5.5	31	4.2	0
Subtotal (minor.)	167	42.8	206	60.1	373	50.9	0	0.0	149	54.6	373	50.9	112
Nonres. Alien	4	1.0	8	2.3	12	1.6	0	0.0	0	0.0	12	1.6	0
White/Cauc.	219	56.2	129	37.6	348	47.5	0	0.0	124	45.4	348	47.5	90
Unknown	0	0.0	0	0.0	0	0.0	0	0.0	0	0.0	0	0.0	0
Total	390	53.2	343	46.8	733	100.0	0	0.0	273	37.2	733		202

Transfers

Transfers in	6
Transfers out	16

Tuition and Fees

	Resident	Nonresident
Full-time	$33,082	$33,082
Part-time		
Tuition Guarantee Program	N	

Living Expenses

Estimated living expenses for singles

Living on campus	Living off campus	Living at home
$21,932	$22,543	$10,722

ST. THOMAS UNIVERSITY SCHOOL OF LAW

*ABA
Approved
Since
1988*

GPA and LSAT Scores

	Total	Full-Time	Part-Time
# of apps	2,165	2,165	0
# of offers	1,094	1,094	0
# of matrics	275	275	0
75% GPA	3.37	3.37	0.00
Median GPA	3.01	3.01	0.00
25% GPA	2.72	2.72	0.00
75% LSAT	153	153	0
Median LSAT	150	150	0
25% LSAT	148	148	0

Grants and Scholarships (from prior year)

	Total		Full-Time		Part-Time	
	#	%	#	%	#	%
Total # of students	682		682		0	
Total # receiving grants	249	36.5	249	36.5	0	0.0
Less than 1/2 tuition	177	26.0	177	26.0	0	0.0
Half to full tuition	71	10.4	71	10.4	0	0.0
Full tuition	0	0.0	0	0.0	0	0.0
More than full tuition	1	0.1	1	0.1	0	0.0
Median grant amount			$15,808		$0	

Informational and Library Resources

Total amount spent on library materials	$644,307
Study seating capacity inside the library	480
# of full-time equivalent professional librarians	6
Hours per week library is open	106
# of open, wired connections available to students	70
# of networked computers available for use by students	36
Has wireless network?	Y
Requires computer?	N

JD Attrition (from prior year)

	Academic	Other	Total	
	#	#	#	%
1st year	32	21	53	22.2
2nd year	4	3	7	3.0
3rd year	0	0	0	0.0
4th year	0	0	0	0.0

Employment (9 months after graduation)

	Total	Percentage
Employment status known	176	97.8
Employment status unknown	4	2.2
Employed	122	69.3
Pursuing graduate degrees	16	9.1
Unemployed (seeking, not seeking, or studying for the bar)	38	21.6
Type of Employment		
# employed in law firms	78	63.9
# employed in business and industry	22	18.0
# employed in government	6	4.9
# employed in public interest	8	6.6
# employed as judicial clerks	4	3.3
# employed in academia	1	0.8
Geographic Location		
# employed in state	81	66.4
# employed outside the US	2	1.6
# of states where employed	13	

Bar Passage Rates

First-time takers	182	Reporting %	79.12
Average school %	73.61	Average state %	77.81

Average pass difference −4.20

Jurisdiction	Takers	Passers	Pass %	State %	Diff %
Florida	144	106	73.61	77.81	−4.20

ST. THOMAS UNIVERSITY SCHOOL OF LAW

16401 NW 37th Avenue
Miami Gardens, FL 33054
Phone: 800.245.4569, 305.623.2310; Fax: 305.623.2357
E-mail: admitme@stu.edu; Website: www.stu.edu/lawschool

Introduction

St. Thomas University School of Law, fully accredited by the American Bar Association and the prestigious Association of American Law Schools, was founded in 1984 and is one of the most culturally diverse and technologically advanced law schools in the country. St. Thomas emphasizes professional ethics throughout its programs, provides intensive academic support on an individual and small-group basis, and offers a broad curriculum, including an array of clinical experiences.

St. Thomas University is located on a 140-acre campus several miles northwest of Miami. Fifteen miles southeast, in downtown Miami, stands the federal courthouse, the location of the United States District Court for the Southern District of Florida. State trial and appellate courts are several blocks away. Approximately 20 miles to the north of the law school is the city of Ft. Lauderdale, another venue for state and appellate courts.

Library and Physical Facilities

The Alex A. Hanna Law Library at St. Thomas University School of Law furnishes students with an online catalog to assist them in locating both digital content and traditional materials. The Library meets the needs of students in the twenty-first century by providing them with a wide array of online databases to assist with their research and allow them to pursue their interests in scholarship. Moreover, the library has a large microform collection to provide added depth of resources. A wireless network enables students, through their laptops or one of 20 library workstations, to access digital information resources from anywhere on campus. Students may also access most of the databases from home through the school's proxy server. Professional reference staff provides instruction in performing online and traditional research. Reference services are also available to assist students in the evenings and on weekends.

Clinical Legal Education Programs

St. Thomas University School of Law requires six credits of professional skills courses to graduate. Students are eligible to participate in any of the law school's 10 clinical offerings in an effort to meet that requirement.

Bankruptcy Clinic—The Bankruptcy Clinic offers a comprehensive set of legal services focused on assisting and empowering low-income individuals in their interaction with the bankruptcy system.

Family Court Clinic—This clinic allows third-year students an opportunity to represent clients in both Family Court and the Domestic Violence Court. The Family Court Clinic is a two-semester, two-track, four-credits-per-semester course. The family division track allows students to learn about family law matters, including the dissolution of marriage, paternity, custody, and adoption cases. In the domestic violence division, students are given the opportunity to provide in-court representation to victims of domestic violence in civil permanent injunction hearings.

Appellate Litigation Clinic—This is a year-long clinical program open to third-year students that provides experience in handling criminal cases in state appellate courts. Each student will have primary responsibility for at least two cases from inception through record preparation, all

relevant motions, and the writing of briefs and oral arguments. The program also features a weekly seminar in the appellate process.

Immigration Clinic—Third-year law students will represent asylum seekers, battered spouses and children who have fled their native country, and other noncitizens seeking immigration relief in Immigration Court before the Board of Immigration Appeals and the Department of Homeland Security (formerly the INS).

Judicial Internship—Judicial internships provide an opportunity for students to hear arguments, discuss cases with judges, and apply research and writing skills to real facts. Interns will work closely with supervising staff attorneys and judges.

Tax Clinic—The Tax Clinic, offered to second- and third-year students, is one of the components of the law school's skills training program. The student represents clients before the Internal Revenue Service (IRS), the District Counsel, and the United States Tax Court. In addition, the student is expected to attend conferences with the IRS, job fairs in the community, and Tax Court sessions.

Civil Practice Clinic—This course can be taken full time or part time in one semester and is available to second- and third-year students. Those students whose placement requires they be a Certified Legal Intern must be in their third year. Typical placements include Legal Aid, City Attorney, County Attorney, Attorney General, or other public sector agencies handling civil matters.

Criminal Practice Clinic—This course can be taken full time or part time in one semester and is only available to incoming third-year students. Typical placements include the offices of the State Attorney, US Attorney, and Public Defender. The externship also contains a classroom component in which students discuss their cases and review relevant law.

Students learn through a combination of actual trial practice and classroom work. Under the supervision of an assistant state attorney, the students engage in plea bargain negotiations and try cases.

Placement in the Public Defender's office provides students with the opportunity to defend indigent adults and minors charged with felonies and misdemeanor crimes.

Elder Law Clinic—This course covers the growing legal needs of the elderly. Students will work with the Probate Division of the Circuit Court and members of the Elder Law Bar on case management issues and strategies to deal with a continually aging population.

Florida Supreme Court—For one semester, the intern will function as a law clerk to an individual justice or as a central staff law clerk working for all of the justices.

Graduate-Degree Programs

The **LLM Program in Intercultural Human Rights** offers in-depth instruction on a critical issue of our time: the protection of human dignity across political, cultural, and religious lines. The faculty of global distinction includes top-level United Nations experts, outstanding scholars, judges, and practitioners in the field. This program of global renown has attracted students from over 65 countries since its inception in 2001. A one-year 24-credit program, it offers mostly one-week compact courses in intercultural human rights. It features human rights law and complaint procedures; international law; humanitarian law;

human rights and terrorism; issues of refugees, women, and children; indigenous peoples; religion; criminal law; and international trade, taught by eminent faculty from the United Nations and prominent centers of scholarship.

The **JSD Program in Intercultural Human Rights** provides a premier opportunity for human rights scholars to make a lasting contribution to this dynamic and action-oriented field. The JSD degree is conferred upon successful completion of a dissertation in the field, the passing of the rigorosum, and proof of publication of the dissertation.

Special Programs

- **Summer-in-Spain Program**—Law students have the opportunity to take six credits at the Royal College University Escorial María Cristina, a part of the University of Madrid. The program is designed to prepare participants for practicing law in the globalized twenty-first century.
- **Summer Conditional Program**—Applicants who may not have strong academic credentials, but nonetheless possess the abilities necessary to succeed in a rigorous program of legal study, may be invited to participate in a summer conditional program. Students who successfully complete the summer conditional program are offered admission to the fall entering class. This program is usually offered each year but, under special circumstances, may not be available.
- **Joint-Degree Programs**—The law school offers four joint-degree programs in cooperation with other graduate divisions of the university. A JD/MBA in Accounting couples lawyering skills with those traditionally in great demand in the corporate, tax, and accounting worlds. The joint JD/MBA in International Business opens the burgeoning field of international transactional law to the new attorney. The JD/MS in Marriage and Family Counseling, one of the only programs of its kind in the country, fills a serious need in the family lawyer's repertory of skills. A joint JD/MS in Sports Administration prepares participants for a diverse set of positions in the world of sports.
- **Academic Support Program**—The law school is committed to the success of its students and offers a comprehensive

support system, including Dean's Fellows, tutors, practice examinations, lectures, a director for academic support, and a program to assist graduates with the bar examination.

Career Services

The Office of Career Services is dedicated to assisting students in identifying and attaining their professional goals. It offers a range of traditional and innovative services, including a career services resource center, on-campus interviews with major law firms and government agencies, and speakers drawn from various areas of legal practice.

Student Activities

The *St. Thomas Law Review* is a student-operated scholarly journal, publishing articles submitted by law faculty and members of the bench and bar nationwide. Membership is determined on the basis of academic excellence and demonstrated writing ability.

The Student Bar Association sponsors various social and educational programs for the student body and otherwise represents student interests. In the student-run Moot Court Program, teams of student advocates compete in interscholastic tournaments across the country, preparing written briefs and presenting oral arguments in simulated appellate cases presided over by members of the bench and bar. Numerous student organizations are active on campus.

Housing

Law students can reserve on-campus housing at the University Inn or Villanova Hall, which offer private rooms with private baths and a choice of meal plans.

For law students desiring to live off campus, numerous apartment complexes are located within minutes of the law school.

APPLICANT PROFILE

St. Thomas University School of Law
This grid includes only applicants who earned 120–180 LSAT scores under standard administrations.

LSAT Score	3.75 +		3.50–3.74		3.25–3.49		3.00–3.24		2.75–2.99		2.50–2.74		2.25–2.49		2.00–2.24		Below 2.00		No GPA		Total	
	Apps	Adm	Apps	Adm	Apps	Adm	Apps	Adm	Apps	Adm	Apps	Adm	Apps	Adm	Apps	Adm	Apps	Adm	Apps	Adm	Apps	Adm
175–180	0	0	0	0	0	0	0	0	0	0	0	0	0	0	0	0	0	0	0	0	0	0
170–174	1	1	0	0	0	0	0	0	0	0	0	0	0	0	0	0	0	0	0	0	1	1
165–169	1	1	0	0	2	2	1	1	0	0	0	0	0	0	0	0	0	0	0	0	4	4
160–164	6	6	6	5	11	11	4	4	5	5	3	2	4	4	2	2	0	0	0	0	41	39
155–159	13	13	29	28	29	25	39	36	26	23	23	22	22	17	5	3	4	1	1	0	191	168
150–154	30	28	53	53	79	76	101	92	85	73	85	76	51	33	19	13	3	0	5	4	511	448
145–149	19	17	82	57	119	64	199	90	172	74	112	36	78	6	31	1	9	0	14	4	835	349
140–144	13	3	24	1	78	3	118	2	94	2	89	0	57	1	29	0	7	0	13	2	522	14
135–139	10	0	8	0	19	0	39	0	31	0	31	0	17	0	9	0	5	0	7	0	176	0
130–134	0	0	2	0	5	0	6	0	12	0	14	0	11	0	7	0	1	0	2	0	60	0
125–129	0	0	0	0	0	0	0	0	0	0	1	0	1	0	2	0	1	0	2	0	7	0
120–124	0	0	0	0	0	0	1	0	0	0	0	0	0	0	0	0	0	0	0	0	1	0
Total	93	69	204	144	342	181	508	225	425	177	358	136	241	61	104	19	30	1	44	10	2349	1023

Apps = Number of Applicants
Adm = Number Admitted
Reflects 99% of the total applicant pool; highest LSAT data reported.

SAMFORD UNIVERSITY, CUMBERLAND SCHOOL OF LAW

800 Lakeshore Drive
Birmingham, AL 35229
Phone: 800.888.7213; Fax: 205.726.2057
E-mail: lawadm@samford.edu; Website: www.cumberland.samford.edu

ABA Approved Since 1949

The Basics

Type of school	Private
Term	Semester
Application deadline	12/31 2/28
Application fee	$50
Financial aid deadline	3/1
Can first year start other than fall?	No
Student to faculty ratio	17.9 to 1
# of housing spaces available restricted to law students	
graduate housing for which law students are eligible	

Faculty and Administrators

	Total		Men		Women		Minorities	
	Spr	Fall	Spr	Fall	Spr	Fall	Spr	Fall
Full-time	22	23	16	17	6	6	4	5
Other full-time	0	0	0	0	0	0	0	0
Deans, librarians, & others who teach	11	11	5	5	6	6	2	2
Part-time	34	23	28	15	6	8	1	2
Total	67	57	49	37	18	20	7	9

Curriculum

		Full-Time	Part-Time
Typical first-year section size		57	0
Is there typically a "small section" of the first-year class, other than Legal Writing, taught by full-time faculty		No	No
If yes, typical size offered last year			
# of classroom course titles beyond first-year curriculum		102	
# of upper division courses, excluding seminars, with an enrollment:	Under 25	73	
	25–49	36	
	50–74	14	
	75–99	0	
	100+	0	
# of seminars		13	
# of seminar positions available		201	
# of seminar positions filled		150	0
# of positions available in simulation courses		417	
# of simulation positions filled		352	0
# of positions available in faculty supervised clinical courses		0	
# of faculty supervised clinical positions filled		0	0
# involved in field placements		54	0
# involved in law journals		87	0
# involved in moot court or trial competitions		48	0
# of credit hours required to graduate		90	

JD Enrollment and Ethnicity

	Men #	Men %	Women #	Women %	Full-Time #	Full-Time %	Part-Time #	Part-Time %	1st-Year #	1st-Year %	Total #	Total %	JD Degs. Awd.
All Hispanics	3	1.1	6	2.8	9	1.8	0	0.0	5	3.0	9	1.8	1
Am. Ind./AK Nat.	2	0.7	3	1.4	5	1.0	0	0.0	1	0.6	5	1.0	0
Asian	3	1.1	2	0.9	5	1.0	0	0.0	3	1.8	5	1.0	0
Black/Af. Am.	9	3.3	19	8.8	28	5.7	0	0.0	12	7.2	28	5.7	10
Nat. HI/Pac. Isl.	0	0.0	1	0.5	1	0.2	0	0.0	1	0.6	1	0.2	0
2 or more races	6	2.2	5	2.3	11	2.2	0	0.0	9	5.4	11	2.2	0
Subtotal (minor.)	23	8.3	36	16.7	59	12.0	0	0.0	31	18.7	59	12.0	12
Nonres. Alien	0	0.0	4	1.9	4	0.8	0	0.0	0	0.0	4	0.8	0
White/Cauc.	223	80.8	158	73.5	381	77.6	0	0.0	131	78.9	381	77.6	114
Unknown	30	10.9	17	7.9	47	9.6	0	0.0	4	2.4	47	9.6	31
Total	276	56.2	215	43.8	491	100.0	0	0.0	166	33.8	491		157

Transfers

Transfers in	8
Transfers out	10

Tuition and Fees

	Resident	Nonresident
Full-time	$33,155	$33,155
Part-time	$19,695	$19,695
Tuition Guarantee Program	N	

Living Expenses

Estimated living expenses for singles

Living on campus	Living off campus	Living at home
N/A	$22,180	$22,180

SAMFORD UNIVERSITY, CUMBERLAND SCHOOL OF LAW

ABA Approved Since 1949

GPA and LSAT Scores

	Total	Full-Time	Part-Time
# of apps	1,678	1,678	0
# of offers	561	561	0
# of matrics	166	166	0
75% GPA	3.55	3.55	0.00
Median GPA	3.32	3.32	0.00
25% GPA	3.06	3.06	0.00
75% LSAT	158	158	0
Median LSAT	155	155	0
25% LSAT	153	153	0

Grants and Scholarships (from prior year)

	Total #	Total %	Full-Time #	Full-Time %	Part-Time #	Part-Time %
Total # of students	493		493		0	
Total # receiving grants	146	29.6	146	29.6	0	0.0
Less than 1/2 tuition	67	13.6	67	13.6	0	0.0
Half to full tuition	38	7.7	38	7.7	0	0.0
Full tuition	28	5.7	28	5.7	0	0.0
More than full tuition	13	2.6	13	2.6	0	0.0
Median grant amount			$20,000		$0	

Informational and Library Resources

Total amount spent on library materials	$920,889
Study seating capacity inside the library	474
# of full-time equivalent professional librarians	7
Hours per week library is open	105
# of open, wired connections available to students	200
# of networked computers available for use by students	71
Has wireless network?	Y
Requires computer?	N

JD Attrition (from prior year)

	Academic #	Other #	Total #	Total %
1st year	1	19	20	11.2
2nd year	0	1	1	0.6
3rd year	0	0	0	0.0
4th year	0	0	0	0.0

Employment (9 months after graduation)

	Total	Percentage
Employment status known	160	98.2
Employment status unknown	3	1.8
Employed	144	90.0
Pursuing graduate degrees	6	3.7
Unemployed (seeking, not seeking, or studying for the bar)	7	4.4
Type of Employment		
# employed in law firms	102	70.8
# employed in business and industry	17	11.8
# employed in government	14	9.7
# employed in public interest	1	0.7
# employed as judicial clerks	8	5.6
# employed in academia	2	1.4
Geographic Location		
# employed in state	97	67.4
# employed outside the US	1	0.7
# of states where employed	12	

Bar Passage Rates

First-time takers	150	Reporting %	70.00
Average school %	92.38	Average state %	86.51
Average pass difference	5.87		

Jurisdiction	Takers	Passers	Pass %	State %	Diff %
Alabama	105	97	92.38	86.51	5.87

The information on these pages was provided by the law school.

SAMFORD UNIVERSITY, CUMBERLAND SCHOOL OF LAW

800 Lakeshore Drive
Birmingham, AL 35229
Phone: 800.888.7213; Fax: 205.726.2057
E-mail: lawadm@samford.edu; Website: www.cumberland.samford.edu

Introduction

Cumberland School of Law, established in 1847 as a part of Cumberland University in Lebanon, Tennessee, is one of the oldest law schools in the country. The law school was acquired by Samford University in 1961. Today, Samford University is the largest privately supported and fully accredited institution of higher learning in Alabama. Samford's beautiful 300 acre campus is located in a suburban area of Birmingham, the state's largest industrial, business, and cultural center. Cumberland School of Law has been a member of the Association of American Law Schools (AALS) since 1952 and has been accredited by the American Bar Association (ABA) since 1949.

Advocacy and Skills Training

Cumberland's emphasis on teaching students the art and science of courtroom advocacy begins in the first-year curriculum. Lawyering and Legal Reasoning is a six-credit, two-semester course that provides students with hands-on, practical instruction in prelitigation skills, such as client interviewing, counseling, memorandum preparation, and negotiation; pretrial skills, including summary judgment motions and making compelling oral arguments; and appellate litigation skills. This intensive course prepares students to work effectively in their first summer clerkships, where they are expected to research cases and write briefs.

The state-of-the-art Advanced Trial Advocacy Courtroom provides students with access to the modern technology found in most courtrooms across the country. In Cumberland's Advanced Trial Advocacy course, students learn how to reproduce evidence with three-dimensional digital presenters, video, and DVD reenactments. By mastering this technology and completing the hands-on training in the Advanced Trial Advocacy course, students will be equipped for success in any courtroom.

Cumberland has an exceptional record of recent trial advocacy competition victories. It won the 2008 American Association for Justice National Championship (finishing as a runner-up in 2009) and both the ABA and Association of Trial Lawyers of America national championships (including several national second- and third-place awards). To date, Cumberland has also won 39 regional championships and the coveted American College of Trial Lawyers' Emil Gumpert Award for Excellence in Teaching Trial Advocacy. The law school also offers a Certificate in Trial Advocacy to recognize students' achievements. Cumberland students have the chance to get class credit and professional experience working for Birmingham's major law firms, judges' offices, and corporate legal departments. The clinical curriculum offers second- and third-year students judicial and corporate externships, as well as externships in the offices of the IRS, US Attorney, and organizations that serve underrepresented or economically disadvantaged groups. In addition, the Alabama Third-Year Practice Rule gives third-year students a chance to practice law under the supervision of a licensed attorney.

Library and Physical Facilities

The Lucille Stewart Beeson Law Library, a freestanding Georgian structure, is visually stunning, as well as superbly functional. The building's design is intended to make all facilities easily accessible to students with disabilities. All study carrels and conference rooms are wired for data transmission. In addition, law students have full access to the university's four campus libraries, as well as six computer labs. Wireless Internet access is available here and in many areas around campus.

Center for Biotechnology, Law, and Ethics (CBLE)

As one of the first of its kind in the United States, the CBLE is dedicated to furthering practical training in the legal disciplines critical to biotechnology. Cumberland's unique program builds on a base of intellectual property, health care, environmental, tort, and natural resources law. The CBLE highlights issues related to the medical, pharmaceutical, and agricultural sectors, and offers students research opportunities. In addition, the CBLE hosts an annual symposium during which experts from around the world speak on such topics.

Center for Community Mediation and Public Interest Law Project

The Cumberland Community Mediation Center (CCMC) emphasizes a commitment to public service, an important attribute of the education received at Cumberland. The CCMC provides free and confidential mediation services to the Birmingham community. Students completing the Mediator Practice course are eligible to volunteer as mediators. The mission of the Public Interest Law Project is to promote, encourage, and complete community service and legal public interest projects in the Birmingham community. Each year, Cumberland partners with the Alabama State Bar to hold a number of legal clinics throughout the state to help senior citizens and the underprivileged.

Joint-Degree Programs

To broaden their perspective and prepare them for careers in special fields, Cumberland students may pursue seven different joint degrees: JD/Master of Accountancy, JD/MBA, JD/MPH, JD/MPA, JD/Master of Divinity, JD/Master of Theological Studies, and JD/MS in Environmental Management. Some of these joint-degree programs can be completed in three years.

Admission

The law school seeks a diverse student body that will make a contribution to the law school and the legal profession. To that end, every applicant's file is thoroughly reviewed for admission. In addition to the LSAT and GPA, difficulty of major, personal challenges overcome, graduate work completed, scholarly achievements, and volunteer and work experience are also considered. Applications are evaluated on a rolling basis, so it is important to apply early.

Applications for fall admission are accepted from September 1 to February 28.

Flex-Time Option

Cumberland's flex-time option allows students a maximum of five years to complete their studies. Flex students are required to take a minimum of eight credit hours each semester. Flex students attend classes during the day and pay an hourly tuition rate.

Scholarships

Generous merit-based scholarship assistance is awarded to Cumberland's entering and current law students annually. In addition, numerous other scholarships are provided to those students who distinguish themselves academically, make outstanding contributions through leadership in the law school, or demonstrate financial need.

Student Activities

The Student Bar Association functions as the first professional organization of a law student's career. In addition to the more than two dozen outstanding organizations, students may also be invited to join one of three national legal fraternities and be inducted into two honorary societies, Order of the Barrister and Curia Honoris. Student-run publications include *Cumberland Law Review* and *American Journal of Trial Advocacy*.

International Law

Cumberland conducts an ABA-approved international summer program that is offered at Sidney Sussex College, Cambridge, England. There is also a cooperative arrangement between Samford University and NALSAR University of Law in Hyderabad, India. The graduate degree of Master of Comparative Law is offered to international law school graduates. Each year, two Cumberland graduates are awarded full-tuition scholarships for studies toward an LLM degree at Norwich Law School in England.

Career Development

The Office of Career Development provides the training, resources, and guidance to enable Cumberland students and alumni to make well-informed career choices, secure employment as quickly and efficiently as possible, and forge rewarding careers. To help students and graduates achieve these goals, the office provides career counseling, résumé editing, practice interviews, on-campus interview programs, job fairs, job listings, instructional handouts, a resource library, and extensive educational programming. In addition to educational programs on résumé drafting, interviewing skills, networking, and job searching, Career Development also presents a "Lunch with a Lawyer" series, in which Cumberland alumni and other law school graduates come to campus to discuss the practical aspects of their work in various traditional and nontraditional legal jobs. All programs are taught by the attorneys on the Career Development staff and by Cumberland alumni and other attorneys.

APPLICANT PROFILE

Samford University, Cumberland School of Law

LSAT Score	GPA								
	3.75 +	3.50–3.74	3.25–3.49	3.00–3.24	2.75–2.99	2.50–2.74	2.25–2.49	2.00–2.24	Below 2.00
175–180									
170–174									
165–169									
160–164									
155–159									
150–154									
145–149									
140–144									
135–139									
130–134									
125–129									
120–124									

■ Good Possibility   □ Possible   ▨ Unlikely

UNIVERSITY OF SAN DIEGO SCHOOL OF LAW

Warren Hall Room 203, 5998 Alcalá Park
San Diego, CA 92110-2492
Phone: 619.260.4528; Fax: 619.260.2218
E-mail: jdinfo@sandiego.edu; Website: www.law.sandiego.edu

ABA
Approved
Since
1961

AMERICAN BAR ASSOCIATION
Section of Legal Education
and Admissions to the Bar

The Basics

Type of school	Private
Term	Semester
Application deadline	2/1
Application fee	$50
Financial aid deadline	3/2
Can first year start other than fall?	No
Student to faculty ratio	13.6 to 1
# of housing spaces available restricted to law students	
graduate housing for which law students are eligible	45

Faculty and Administrators

	Total		Men		Women		Minorities	
	Spr	Fall	Spr	Fall	Spr	Fall	Spr	Fall
Full-time	56	57	43	43	13	14	5	9
Other full-time	8	9	1	2	7	7	1	2
Deans, librarians, & others who teach	9	9	4	4	5	5	1	1
Part-time	44	53	33	38	11	15	5	7
Total	117	128	81	87	36	41	12	19

Curriculum

	Full-Time	Part-Time
Typical first-year section size	75	40
Is there typically a "small section" of the first-year class, other than Legal Writing, taught by full-time faculty	No	No
If yes, typical size offered last year		
# of classroom course titles beyond first-year curriculum	153	
# of upper division courses, excluding seminars, with an enrollment: Under 25	225	
25–49	51	
50–74	28	
75–99	35	
100+	2	
# of seminars	33	
# of seminar positions available	573	
# of seminar positions filled	309	119
# of positions available in simulation courses	1,035	
# of simulation positions filled	524	214
# of positions available in faculty supervised clinical courses	363	
# of faculty supervised clinical positions filled	223	69
# involved in field placements	117	130
# involved in law journals	173	25
# involved in moot court or trial competitions	70	6
# of credit hours required to graduate	85	

JD Enrollment and Ethnicity

	Men		Women		Full-Time		Part-Time		1st-Year		Total		JD Degs. Awd.
	#	%	#	%	#	%	#	%	#	%	#	%	
All Hispanics	55	10.4	51	10.6	91	11.0	15	8.5	40	12.3	106	10.5	27
Am. Ind./AK Nat.	1	0.2	2	0.4	2	0.2	1	0.6	0	0.0	3	0.3	0
Asian	73	13.8	82	17.1	133	16.0	22	12.5	53	16.3	155	15.4	43
Black/Af. Am.	5	0.9	7	1.5	10	1.2	2	1.1	5	1.5	12	1.2	7
Nat. HI/Pac. Isl.	0	0.0	2	0.4	1	0.1	1	0.6	0	0.0	2	0.2	0
2 or more races	12	2.3	30	6.3	40	4.8	2	1.1	23	7.1	42	4.2	0
Subtotal (minor.)	146	27.7	174	36.3	277	33.3	43	24.4	121	37.2	320	31.8	83
Nonres. Alien	3	0.6	4	0.8	5	0.6	2	1.1	1	0.3	7	0.7	0
White/Cauc.	364	68.9	286	59.7	523	62.9	127	72.2	192	59.1	650	64.5	229
Unknown	15	2.8	15	3.1	26	3.1	4	2.3	11	3.4	30	3.0	6
Total	528	52.4	479	47.6	831	82.5	176	17.5	325	32.3	1007		318

Transfers

Transfers in	19
Transfers out	5

Tuition and Fees

	Resident	Nonresident
Full-time	$41,414	$41,414
Part-time	$29,904	$29,904
Tuition Guarantee Program		N

Living Expenses

Estimated living expenses for singles

Living on campus	Living off campus	Living at home
$21,686	$21,686	$11,763

UNIVERSITY OF SAN DIEGO SCHOOL OF LAW

ABA
Approved
Since
1961

GPA and LSAT Scores

	Total	Full-Time	Part-Time
# of apps	5,179	4,789	390
# of offers	1,622	1,541	81
# of matrics	330	293	37
75% GPA	3.63	3.64	3.63
Median GPA	3.49	3.49	3.45
25% GPA	3.30	3.31	3.16
75% LSAT	163	163	164
Median LSAT	161	161	159
25% LSAT	159	159	158

Grants and Scholarships (from prior year)

	Total		Full-Time		Part-Time	
	#	%	#	%	#	%
Total # of students	1,000		816		184	
Total # receiving grants	441	44.1	374	45.8	67	36.4
Less than 1/2 tuition	176	17.6	153	18.8	23	12.5
Half to full tuition	217	21.7	183	22.4	34	18.5
Full tuition	22	2.2	12	1.5	10	5.4
More than full tuition	26	2.6	26	3.2	0	0.0
Median grant amount			$21,000		$16,200	

Informational and Library Resources

Total amount spent on library materials	$1,437,452
Study seating capacity inside the library	602
# of full-time equivalent professional librarians	9
Hours per week library is open	112
# of open, wired connections available to students	240
# of networked computers available for use by students	63
Has wireless network?	Y
Requires computer?	N

JD Attrition (from prior year)

	Academic	Other	Total	
	#	#	#	%
1st year	5	18	23	7.1
2nd year	0	0	0	0.0
3rd year	0	4	4	1.2
4th year	0	0	0	0.0

Employment (9 months after graduation)

	Total	Percentage
Employment status known	318	97.5
Employment status unknown	8	2.5
Employed	276	86.8
Pursuing graduate degrees	23	7.2
Unemployed (seeking, not seeking, or studying for the bar)	6	1.9
Type of Employment		
# employed in law firms	164	59.4
# employed in business and industry	37	13.4
# employed in government	25	9.1
# employed in public interest	16	5.8
# employed as judicial clerks	8	2.9
# employed in academia	25	9.1
Geographic Location		
# employed in state	221	80.1
# employed outside the US	5	1.8
# of states where employed	15	

Bar Passage Rates

First-time takers	332	Reporting %	100.00
Average school %	76.48	Average state %	74.24
Average pass difference	2.24		

Jurisdiction	Takers	Passers	Pass %	State %	Diff %
California	297	225	75.76	73.19	2.57
New York	10	8	80.00	86.51	−6.51
Texas	5	3	60.00	85.48	−25.48
Utah	3	3	100.00	88.94	11.06
Others (11)	17	15	88.24		

UNIVERSITY OF SAN DIEGO SCHOOL OF LAW

Warren Hall Room 203, 5998 Alcalá Park
San Diego, CA 92110-2492
Phone: 619.260.4528; Fax: 619.260.2218
E-mail: jdinfo@sandiego.edu; Website: www.law.sandiego.edu

Introduction

As one of the most selective law schools in the country, the University of San Diego (USD) School of Law is a leading center of academic excellence. The school's internationally regarded faculty of scholars and expert practitioners create a demanding, yet welcoming, environment that emphasizes individualized legal education. The school is also known as a leader in creating programs and courses to prepare future lawyers to practice in a rapidly changing world marked by globalization and dramatic advancements in technology. Founded in 1954, the law school is part of the University of San Diego, a private, nonprofit, independent Roman Catholic university. The university is located on a 182-acre campus overlooking Mission Bay and the Pacific Ocean, featuring Spanish Renaissance architecture and well-maintained, garden-like grounds.

Admission

USD School of Law strives to draw talented students from all regions of the country and from different ethnic and social backgrounds. The university is committed to advancing academic excellence, expanding legal and professional knowledge, creating a diverse and inclusive community, and preparing leaders dedicated to ethical conduct and compassionate service.

Accreditation and Membership

Accredited—American Bar Association (ABA), Committee of Bar Examiners—State of California.

Membership—Association of American Law Schools (AALS), Order of the Coif.

Legal Research Center (LRC)

The Pardee Legal Research Center offers a full range of traditional printed and state-of-the-art electronic services. Computer legal research systems include those of BNA, CCH, HeinOnline, LegalTrac, LexisNexis, and Westlaw. Among all law libraries at ABA-accredited schools, USD is in the top one-third in collection size with over half a million volumes.

Special Programs

Summer Law Study Abroad Program—USD School of Law, in cooperation with foreign universities, conducts summer law study programs in England, France, Italy, and Spain. The programs introduce American law students to foreign law and legal institutions and provide intensive study during four- to five-week sessions. Classes abroad sensitize students to the cultural differences that influence effective international dealing and expose students to the perspectives of foreign experts.

Clinical Education Program—This program is recognized as one of the most extensive and successful in the nation, including client-based clinics and placement clinics as well as an externship/internship program. In the legal clinics, which close about 600 cases each year, students represent low-income clients in nine areas of law under the supervision of a clinical professor who is a licensed attorney specializing in that area.

Research and Advocacy Institutes—Recently, the school launched two new research institutes: the Center for Corporate and Securities Law and the Center for Intellectual Property Law and Markets. USD also houses the Center for Public Interest Law, Children's Advocacy Institute, Institute for Law and Philosophy, Center for the Study of Constitutional Originalism, Energy Policy Initiatives Center, and Center for Education Policy and Law.

Concurrent Degrees—Students desiring to concentrate in business or international relations may concurrently pursue the JD/MBA, JD/International MBA, or JD/MA in International Relations.

Lawyering Skills—Students receive extensive training in a variety of legal skills, including first-year legal writing and research, interviewing, counseling, discovery, trial advocacy, and alternative dispute resolution.

Oral Advocacy—USD's National Moot Court and National Mock Trial teams consistently rank among the finest teams in the nation. The Mock Trial team has taken first place in the prestigious American Inns of Court's National Tournament of Champions. The Mock Trial team has won the Western Regional Championship of the Association of Trial Lawyers of America nine times and has been selected as the best team in the Ninth Circuit for seven of the last nine years.

Campus Highlights

The law school buildings sit directly across from the new Student Life Pavilion, a 62,000-square-foot expansion of the Hahn University Center (UC), the nexus of the USD campus. The UC now offers 134,000 square feet of office space for student organizations and multiuse areas, including a bakery, deli, grill, mini-grocery store, pizza parlor, and the university's main dining hall.

Student Activities

With more than 40 different groups available, student organizations not only serve the various interests of our students but also develop a sense of community among their members. The active groups promote leadership, conduct orientation programs, provide study assistance, represent group concerns, sponsor speaker programs, and promote community relations. The school's four law journals, the *San Diego International Law Journal*, the *Journal of Contemporary Legal Issues*, the *San Diego Law Review*, and the *San Diego Journal of Climate and Energy Law*, each offer opportunities to be on the inside of developing legal scholarship.

Financial Aid

The School of Law is committed to providing all possible financial assistance to eligible students whose personal resources are insufficient to meet their educational expenses. Sources of financial aid include over 430 need/merit, merit, and diversity-based scholarships; federal plans, such as work-study programs; the Perkins, Direct, and Graduate PLUS federal loan programs; and institutional loans. Private loan programs are also available to assist law students with supplemental financing.

Career Services

USD Law's Career Services office is committed to supporting all students in achieving their diverse career objectives. Throughout their law school years, students are offered opportunities to explore career options with private law firms, government agencies, and public interest organizations, and to obtain internships, fellowships, and clerkships with federal and state courts nationwide. Traditionally, more than 250 interviewers each year interview USD students on and off campus as part of an extensive recruiting process.

USD's law graduates practice in 50 states, the District of Columbia, and at least 50 foreign countries. For the graduating class of 2009, within nine months of graduation, approximately 96 percent were employed or enrolled in a full-time degree program. For the class of 2009, approximately 59 percent accepted positions with law firms and 18 percent began their careers in public service, including local, state, and federal government; federal courts; and public interest agencies. Others pursued careers in a range of business and corporate positions. The median salary for graduates in private practice was $97,000. The median salary for graduates working in the public sectors was $57,000.

Housing

The USD Department of Residential Life and the School of Law Office of Admissions assist in providing information and resources in locating on- and off-campus accommodations.

APPLICANT PROFILE

University of San Diego School of Law
(Note: This chart is to be used as a general guide only. Nonnumerical factors are also considered.)

LSAT Score	GPA								
	3.75 +	3.50–3.74	3.25–3.49	3.00–3.24	2.75–2.99	2.50–2.74	2.25–2.49	2.00–2.24	Below 2.00
175–180	■	■	■	■	■	■	▦		
170–174	■	■	■	■	■	■	▦		
165–169	■	■	■	■	■	▦			
160–164	■	■	■	■	■	▦			
155–159	■	■	▦	▦	■	■			
150–154	▦	▦							
145–149									
140–144									
135–139									
130–134									
125–129									
120–124									

■ Very Likely   ▦ Possible   ▢ Unlikely

UNIVERSITY OF SAN FRANCISCO SCHOOL OF LAW

USF School of Law, 2130 Fulton Street
San Francisco, CA 94117-1080
Phone: 415.422.6586; Fax: 415.422.5442
E-mail: lawadmissions@usfca.edu; Website: www.law.usfca.edu

ABA
Approved
Since
1935

AMERICAN BAR ASSOCIATION
Section of Legal Education
and Admissions to the Bar

The Basics

Type of school	Private
Term	Semester
Application deadline	2/1
Application fee	$60
Financial aid deadline	2/15
Can first year start other than fall?	No
Student to faculty ratio	15.3 to 1
# of housing spaces available restricted to law students	
graduate housing for which law students are eligible	25

Faculty and Administrators

	Total		Men		Women		Minorities	
	Spr	Fall	Spr	Fall	Spr	Fall	Spr	Fall
Full-time	35	37	18	20	17	17	14	16
Other full-time	0	0	0	0	0	0	0	0
Deans, librarians, & others who teach	6	6	3	3	3	3	0	0
Part-time	41	48	30	34	11	14	9	11
Total	82	91	51	57	31	34	23	27

Curriculum

	Full-Time	Part-Time
Typical first-year section size	114	45
Is there typically a "small section" of the first-year class, other than Legal Writing, taught by full-time faculty	No	No
If yes, typical size offered last year		
# of classroom course titles beyond first-year curriculum	98	
# of upper division courses, excluding seminars, with an enrollment: Under 25	70	
25–49	29	
50–74	11	
75–99	4	
100+	0	
# of seminars	16	
# of seminar positions available	320	
# of seminar positions filled	185	28
# of positions available in simulation courses	538	
# of simulation positions filled	282	42
# of positions available in faculty supervised clinical courses	120	
# of faculty supervised clinical positions filled	93	15
# involved in field placements	130	13
# involved in law journals	79	5
# involved in moot court or trial competitions	86	1
# of credit hours required to graduate	86	

JD Enrollment and Ethnicity

	Men		Women		Full-Time		Part-Time		1st-Year		Total		JD Degs. Awd.
	#	%	#	%	#	%	#	%	#	%	#	%	
All Hispanics	38	11.2	43	10.8	66	11.2	15	10.0	30	12.0	81	11.0	19
Am. Ind./AK Nat.	2	0.6	6	1.5	3	0.5	5	3.3	4	1.6	8	1.1	1
Asian	44	13.0	59	14.8	82	13.9	21	14.0	45	17.9	103	13.9	43
Black/Af. Am.	26	7.7	30	7.5	35	5.9	21	14.0	18	7.2	56	7.6	18
Nat. HI/Pac. Isl.	1	0.3	2	0.5	3	0.5	0	0.0	1	0.4	3	0.4	0
2 or more races	5	1.5	12	3.0	14	2.4	3	2.0	3	1.2	17	2.3	0
Subtotal (minor.)	116	34.2	152	38.0	203	34.5	65	43.3	101	40.2	268	36.3	84
Nonres. Alien	3	0.9	9	2.3	11	1.9	1	0.7	2	0.8	12	1.6	0
White/Cauc.	156	46.0	178	44.5	272	46.2	62	41.3	112	44.6	334	45.2	86
Unknown	64	18.9	61	15.3	103	17.5	22	14.7	36	14.3	125	16.9	35
Total	339	45.9	400	54.1	589	79.7	150	20.3	251	34.0	739		209

Transfers

Transfers in	0
Transfers out	7

Tuition and Fees

	Resident	Nonresident
Full-time	$38,800	$38,800
Part-time	$27,745	$27,745
Tuition Guarantee Program		N

Living Expenses

Estimated living expenses for singles		
Living on campus	Living off campus	Living at home
$21,824	$20,660	$10,060

ABA Approved Since 1935

GPA and LSAT Scores

	Total	Full-Time	Part-Time
# of apps	4,697	4,163	534
# of offers	1,478	1,350	128
# of matrics	251	184	67
75% GPA	3.62	3.63	3.58
Median GPA	3.45	3.46	3.28
25% GPA	3.09	3.16	2.82
75% LSAT	161	161	160
Median LSAT	159	159	156
25% LSAT	155	155	153

Grants and Scholarships (from prior year)

	Total		Full-Time		Part-Time	
	#	%	#	%	#	%
Total # of students	706		574		132	
Total # receiving grants	296	41.9	245	42.7	51	38.6
Less than 1/2 tuition	209	29.6	166	28.9	43	32.6
Half to full tuition	84	11.9	76	13.2	8	6.1
Full tuition	3	0.4	3	0.5	0	0.0
More than full tuition	0	0.0	0	0.0	0	0.0
Median grant amount			$18,500		$6,500	

Informational and Library Resources

Total amount spent on library materials	$1,431,247
Study seating capacity inside the library	428
# of full-time equivalent professional librarians	6
Hours per week library is open	98
# of open, wired connections available to students	1,030
# of networked computers available for use by students	81
Has wireless network?	Y
Requires computer?	N

JD Attrition (from prior year)

	Academic	Other	Total	
	#	#	#	%
1st year	20	14	34	12.7
2nd year	2	7	9	4.1
3rd year	1	1	2	1.1
4th year	0	0	0	0.0

Employment (9 months after graduation)

	Total	Percentage
Employment status known	189	96.4
Employment status unknown	7	3.6
Employed	176	93.1
Pursuing graduate degrees	0	0.0
Unemployed (seeking, not seeking, or studying for the bar)	7	3.7
Type of Employment		
# employed in law firms	56	31.8
# employed in business and industry	28	15.9
# employed in government	8	4.5
# employed in public interest	4	2.3
# employed as judicial clerks	2	1.1
# employed in academia	19	10.8
Geographic Location		
# employed in state	86	48.9
# employed outside the US	0	0.0
# of states where employed	8	

Bar Passage Rates

First-time takers	189	Reporting %	95.24
Average school %	78.33	Average state %	73.19
Average pass difference	5.14		

Jurisdiction	Takers	Passers	Pass %	State %	Diff %
California	180	141	78.33	73.19	5.14

UNIVERSITY OF SAN FRANCISCO SCHOOL OF LAW

USF School of Law, 2130 Fulton Street
San Francisco, CA 94117-1080
Phone: 415.422.6586; Fax: 415.422.5442
E-mail: lawadmissions@usfca.edu; Website: www.law.usfca.edu

Introduction

Founded in 1912, the University of San Francisco (USF) School of Law is located on a hilltop campus in a quiet residential neighborhood overlooking Golden Gate Park, the Pacific Ocean, and downtown San Francisco.

The San Francisco Bay Area is an extension of the campus and plays a vital role in the educational experience. The law school is located minutes away from the Civic Center, home to federal, state, and local government agencies, as well as federal and state courts, including the California Supreme Court. The city and its surrounding communities provide unsurpassed learning, practice, placement, and service opportunities to complement the academic program. Students represent clients in law school clinics, intern year-round in the city's many major national and international law firms, clerk for judges, and work in public interest organizations.

The USF School of Law is fully accredited by the American Bar Association and is a member of the Association of American Law Schools.

Educating for Justice

The USF School of Law offers a rigorous education with a global perspective in a diverse, supportive community. Our graduates are skilled, ethical professionals prepared for any legal career, with a commitment to social justice as their enduring foundation. Our inclusive Jesuit mission of educating minds and hearts to change the world integrates humanity and ethical conduct into the practice of law. Evidence of this mission in action includes our extensive list of programs dedicated to serving communities throughout the United States and around the globe and our unique curriculum focused on ethics and professional responsibility.

Degree Programs

The USF School of Law offers full- and part-time Juris Doctor (JD) programs that empower students to develop their analytical abilities, master legal writing and research skills, acquire a firm foundation of basic law, explore an array of specialties, and refine their skills in practical settings. The full-time program requires three years of study, while the part-time program can be completed in four years. Students entering the part-time program may accelerate their studies and complete the degree in seven semesters or they may convert to the full-time program after the first year and graduate in three years. In conjunction with the USF School of Business and Professional Studies, the law school offers a four-year, full-time concurrent JD/MBA degree program. The law school also offers a Master of Laws (LLM) in International Transactions and Comparative Law for foreign lawyers and a Master of Laws in Intellectual Property and Technology Law for foreign and US lawyers.

Facilities

The USF School of Law is housed in the Koret Law Center and comprises Kendrick Hall, where classrooms and faculty offices are located, and the Dorraine Zief Law Library. Kendrick Hall, built in the 1960s and recently renovated, features a rotunda skylight, spiral stairways, and circular configurations that enhance natural light and offer informal gathering spaces for students and faculty. Students prepare for trial practice in a new, 70-seat moot courtroom. Classrooms offer power and wireless connections at every seat. Administrative offices are located in Kendrick Hall to provide easy access to services and staff. Office space for student organizations and clinical programs, a student lounge, and a café are all found here as well.

Linked to Kendrick Hall by a soaring glass atrium, the Dorraine Zief Law Library, which opened in 2000, is a modern, technologically advanced study environment. It houses an extensive collection and connects to countless online resources. The library also features individual and group study rooms equipped with audiovisual equipment, computer classrooms, and research rooms.

By being part of a larger campus community, USF law students benefit from the amenities and facilities one expects to find at a major urban university, including the outstanding recreational and fitness facilities of USF's award-winning Koret Health and Recreation Center. The university's 55-acre campus also features a main library, bookstore, student center, and dining facilities.

The Curriculum

The core curriculum, concentrated in the first year of the full-time program and the first and second years of the part-time program, includes courses essential to a solid understanding of dominant legal concepts. The core curriculum is complemented by a rich offering of courses and programs providing almost unlimited opportunities for specialized study and practical experience. Elective courses are constantly updated to reflect changes in the law, to meet the pace of technological change, and to match student interest.

JD certificate programs and elective clusters offer concentrated study for students who wish to pursue particular career objectives or develop specialized skills. Notable among these are courses in international and comparative law, public interest law, advocacy and alternative dispute resolution, business law, and intellectual property and cyberspace law. There are also opportunities for participation in unique clinical programs, including a Mediation Clinic, an Investor Justice Clinic, a Criminal and Juvenile Justice Law Clinic, a Child Advocacy Clinic, an Internet and Intellectual Property Justice Clinic, and an International Human Rights Law Clinic.

International Programs

Our extensive menu of international programs provides exceptional opportunities to study and intern abroad. Traditional summer study-abroad programs are offered in Mexico, Dublin, and Prague, and externship and service opportunities are offered in India, Vietnam, China, Cambodia, Argentina, and the Philippines, among other countries. USF's innovative Frank C. Newman International Human Rights Law Clinic affords many students the opportunity to personally present their research and policy proposals to the United Nations Commission on Human Rights in Geneva or the Commission on the Status of Women in New York. The Center for Law and Global Justice acquaints students with differing legal traditions and provides opportunities for international externships and service learning. The center is a resource for international programming and courses, and creates opportunities for students to conduct research on critical human rights issues.

Student Activities

Much of a USF law student's education takes place outside the classroom. Students expand their scholarship interests by writing, editing, and publishing several law journals, including the *USF Law Review*, the *USF Maritime Law Journal*, and the *Intellectual Property Law Bulletin*. Opportunities to hone advocacy and leadership skills abound. Students participate in the annual Advocate of the Year Competition, compete in interschool moot court and trial advocacy competitions, and also take part in countless externship and clinical opportunities available at the law school. The representative student government, the Student Bar Association (SBA), works with more than 35 student organizations that reflect the diversity and varied interests of USF law students. The USF Public Interest Law Foundation's annual gala auction, which raises funds for students working in unpaid summer internships in the public interest and public sector, is one example of the many student-sponsored events held each year.

Frequent panels, guest speakers, special programs, and symposia provide students with regular opportunities for intellectual interchange with faculty, alumni, members of the bench and bar, and visiting dignitaries. Examples of recent symposia topics include Clean Technology and the Law: The Legal Infrastructure for Promoting the Development and Dissemination of Clean Technologies; Litigation, Settlement and the Public Interest: Fluid Recovery and Cy Pres Relief; the Emerging Role of Intellectual Property Protection in the (Digital) Cloud; the Future of Same-Sex Marriage; and the

award-winning California Water Law Symposium "Who Controls the Water? Reforming California Water Law Governance in the Age of Scarcity."

The Law Student Pro Bono Project and the Law in Motion Service Program offer opportunities for service, sponsoring a variety of legal and nonlegal community outreach and pro bono projects.

Faculty

USF School of Law professors bring to the classroom the highest educational credentials, substantial practical experience, and an underlying dedication to teaching, scholarship, and service. They are respected authors, researchers, and legal theorists who write books, casebooks, practice guides, law review articles, and book reviews. Faculty members have achieved numerous scholastic accomplishments, graduating from the most elite law schools, earning honors, and serving as editors of prestigious law journals. Almost all have substantial practical experience and continue to be involved in service to the community and the profession. Their zeal for teaching comes to life in the classroom, in clinics, and in informal conversations with students. They create an intellectually challenging but supportive atmosphere in which each student thrives.

The full-time faculty is complemented by approximately 60 adjunct professors, including federal and state court judges, attorneys from many public agencies, and other distinguished members of the bar in private practice. Our location in the dynamic San Francisco Bay Area legal community allows the law school to expand its curriculum with specialized courses and provides students access to a wealth of practical expertise.

APPLICANT PROFILE

University of San Francisco School of Law
This grid includes only applicants who earned 120–180 LSAT scores under standard administrations.

LSAT Score	3.75 +		3.50–3.74		3.25–3.49		3.00–3.24		2.75–2.99		2.50–2.74		2.25–2.49		2.00–2.24		Below 2.00		No GPA		Total	
	Apps	Adm	Apps	Adm	Apps	Adm	Apps	Adm	Apps	Adm	Apps	Adm	Apps	Adm	Apps	Adm	Apps	Adm	Apps	Adm	Apps	Adm
175–180	2	2	0	0	2	2	0	0	0	0	0	0	0	0	0	0	0	0	0	0	4	4
170–174	7	7	16	16	9	8	6	4	4	2	6	2	2	0	1	1	1	0	0	0	52	40
165–169	25	24	31	31	50	43	38	30	29	18	12	4	11	6	2	0	2	0	9	7	209	163
160–164	93	90	184	176	211	181	187	111	89	30	67	24	17	5	4	0	1	0	11	7	864	624
155–159	112	99	283	238	348	73	285	35	170	17	96	4	58	3	11	0	2	0	24	5	1389	474
150–154	79	36	214	70	237	12	265	14	167	6	87	5	38	0	15	0	4	0	19	1	1125	144
145–149	35	7	75	6	120	9	135	2	117	2	64	1	24	1	15	0	3	0	14	0	602	28
140–144	9	0	31	0	50	0	50	0	42	0	45	0	29	0	8	0	2	0	8	0	274	0
135–139	6	0	5	0	12	0	24	0	24	0	14	0	15	0	7	0	0	0	2	0	109	0
130–134	0	0	2	0	0	0	1	0	6	0	5	0	3	0	4	0	2	0	3	0	26	0
125–129	0	0	1	0	0	0	0	0	0	0	5	0	2	0	1	0	0	0	0	0	9	0
120–124	0	0	0	0	0	0	0	0	0	0	0	0	0	0	0	0	0	0	0	0	0	0
Total	368	265	842	537	1039	328	991	196	648	75	401	40	199	15	68	1	17	0	90	20	4663	1477

Apps = Number of Applicants
Adm = Number Admitted
Reflects 99% of the total applicant pool; highest LSAT data reported.

SANTA CLARA UNIVERSITY SCHOOL OF LAW

500 El Camino Real
Santa Clara, CA 95053
Phone: 408.554.5048; Fax: 408.554.7897
E-mail: LawAdmissions@scu.edu; Website: http://law.scu.edu

*ABA
Approved
Since
1937*

The Basics

Type of school	Private
Term	Semester
Application deadline	2/1
Application fee	$75
Financial aid deadline	3/1
Can first year start other than fall?	No
Student to faculty ratio	12.4 to 1
# of housing spaces available restricted to law students	
graduate housing for which law students are eligible	68

Faculty and Administrators

	Total		Men		Women		Minorities	
	Spr	Fall	Spr	Fall	Spr	Fall	Spr	Fall
Full-time	57	63	28	33	29	30	13	14
Other full-time	1	2	0	0	1	2	0	1
Deans, librarians, & others who teach	11	12	4	5	7	7	7	8
Part-time	57	37	36	18	21	19	11	8
Total	126	114	68	56	58	58	31	31

Curriculum

		Full-Time	Part-Time
Typical first-year section size		77	78
Is there typically a "small section" of the first-year class, other than Legal Writing, taught by full-time faculty		Yes	Yes
If yes, typical size offered last year		39	39
# of classroom course titles beyond first-year curriculum		170	
# of upper division courses, excluding seminars, with an enrollment:	Under 25	131	
	25–49	49	
	50–74	19	
	75–99	17	
	100+	1	
# of seminars		102	
# of seminar positions available		1,879	
# of seminar positions filled		1,530	0
# of positions available in simulation courses		329	
# of simulation positions filled		301	0
# of positions available in faculty supervised clinical courses		266	
# of faculty supervised clinical positions filled		238	0
# involved in field placements		382	0
# involved in law journals		104	0
# involved in moot court or trial competitions		42	0
# of credit hours required to graduate		86	

JD Enrollment and Ethnicity

	Men		Women		Full-Time		Part-Time		1st-Year		Total		JD Degs. Awd.
	#	%	#	%	#	%	#	%	#	%	#	%	
All Hispanics	49	9.3	34	7.4	71	9.5	12	5.1	28	8.6	83	8.4	22
Am. Ind./AK Nat.	6	1.1	3	0.7	6	0.8	3	1.3	1	0.3	9	0.9	1
Asian	123	23.4	128	27.9	172	23.0	79	33.8	76	23.3	251	25.5	88
Black/Af. Am.	17	3.2	10	2.2	20	2.7	7	3.0	9	2.8	27	2.7	11
Nat. HI/Pac. Isl.	4	0.8	5	1.1	6	0.8	3	1.3	0	0.0	9	0.9	0
2 or more races	13	2.5	12	2.6	18	2.4	7	3.0	25	7.7	25	2.5	0
Subtotal (minor.)	212	40.4	192	41.9	293	39.1	111	47.4	139	42.6	404	41.1	126
Nonres. Alien	11	2.1	17	3.7	23	3.1	5	2.1	9	2.8	28	2.8	0
White/Cauc.	302	57.5	249	54.4	433	57.8	118	50.4	178	54.6	551	56.1	181
Unknown	0	0.0	0	0.0	0	0.0	0	0.0	0	0.0	0	0.0	0
Total	525	53.4	458	46.6	749	76.2	234	23.8	326	33.2	983		307

Transfers

Transfers in	42
Transfers out	13

Tuition and Fees

	Resident	Nonresident
Full-time	$39,360	$39,360
Part-time	$27,552	$27,552
Tuition Guarantee Program		N

Living Expenses

Estimated living expenses for singles

Living on campus	Living off campus	Living at home
$21,972	$21,972	$21,972

SANTA CLARA UNIVERSITY SCHOOL OF LAW

*ABA
Approved
Since
1937*

GPA and LSAT Scores

	Total	Full-Time	Part-Time
# of apps	4,959	4,511	448
# of offers	2,081	1,846	235
# of matrics	314	238	76
75% GPA	3.53	3.55	3.47
Median GPA	3.32	3.35	3.24
25% GPA	3.08	3.14	2.94
75% LSAT	162	162	161
Median LSAT	160	160	159
25% LSAT	158	158	157

Grants and Scholarships (from prior year)

	Total		Full-Time		Part-Time	
	#	%	#	%	#	%
Total # of students	1,001		749		252	
Total # receiving grants	391	39.1	314	41.9	77	30.6
Less than 1/2 tuition	328	32.8	280	37.4	48	19.0
Half to full tuition	40	4.0	22	2.9	18	7.1
Full tuition	23	2.3	12	1.6	11	4.4
More than full tuition	0	0.0	0	0.0	0	0.0
Median grant amount			$10,000		$10,000	

Informational and Library Resources

Total amount spent on library materials	$1,226,999
Study seating capacity inside the library	500
# of full-time equivalent professional librarians	9
Hours per week library is open	106
# of open, wired connections available to students	922
# of networked computers available for use by students	62
Has wireless network?	Y
Requires computer?	N

JD Attrition (from prior year)

	Academic	Other	Total	
	#	#	#	%
1st year	26	26	52	16.3
2nd year	0	1	1	0.4
3rd year	0	0	0	0.0
4th year	0	0	0	0.0

Employment (9 months after graduation)

	Total	Percentage
Employment status known	256	98.5
Employment status unknown	4	1.5
Employed	220	85.9
Pursuing graduate degrees	2	0.8
Unemployed (seeking, not seeking, or studying for the bar)	11	4.3
Type of Employment		
# employed in law firms	94	42.7
# employed in business and industry	34	15.5
# employed in government	20	9.1
# employed in public interest	13	5.9
# employed as judicial clerks	7	3.2
# employed in academia	7	3.2
Geographic Location		
# employed in state	130	59.1
# employed outside the US	1	0.5
# of states where employed	8	

Bar Passage Rates

First-time takers	274	Reporting %	84.67
Average school %	81.47	Average state %	73.19
Average pass difference	8.28		

Jurisdiction	Takers	Passers	Pass %	State %	Diff %
California	232	189	81.47	73.19	8.28

The information on these pages was provided by the law school.

SANTA CLARA UNIVERSITY SCHOOL OF LAW

500 El Camino Real
Santa Clara, CA 95053
Phone: 408.554.5048; Fax: 408.554.7897
E-mail: LawAdmissions@scu.edu; Website: http://law.scu.edu

Introduction

Santa Clara Law, just 40 miles south of San Francisco, is located on the lush, historic, 105-acre campus of Santa Clara University, California's oldest operating institution of higher learning. The university was founded by the Jesuits in 1851 on the site of the Mission Santa Clara de Asís, one of California's original 21 missions. Established in 1911, Santa Clara Law has fostered an exceptional academic program based on the Jesuit tradition for more than 100 years. Approved by the ABA, Santa Clara Law is a member of the Order of the Coif and the AALS.

Santa Clara Law students are committed to excellence, ethics, and social justice. The school strives to prepare its students to serve as lawyers who lead in any field, and offers students ample opportunities to apply their skills in internships, clinics, field placements, and community involvement.

Location

Santa Clara Law is located in the heart of Silicon Valley, one of the most vibrant and exciting economies in the world, and home to leading national and international law firms as well as companies such as Google, Apple, eBay, Intel, and Yahoo!

Our location enhances the curriculum, including the nationally acclaimed high-tech and intellectual property program, which features experienced Silicon Valley executives and attorneys who share their experience in courses, workshops, and lectures. In addition, students benefit from the location through internship and job opportunities, lectures, and networking events.

The San Francisco Bay Area is one of the most beautiful regions in the US, and the Mediterranean climate boasts sun more than 300 days a year. North of Santa Clara are the world-class cities of Berkeley, Oakland, and San Francisco. Southwest are the coastal towns of Santa Cruz, Monterey, Carmel, and Big Sur.

Diversity

Santa Clara Law is one of the most diverse law schools in the country, and the school offers an array of programs that encourage and support diversity. Santa Clara Law students learn with students from all 50 states and numerous foreign countries, and they are taught by a diverse and talented group of faculty members who are committed to an inclusive learning experience. Forty-four percent of applicants for fall 2010 were from outside California, and the 2010 entering class included 45 percent minorities and 48 percent women.

Library and Physical Facilities

Towering palm trees, spacious lawns, and vibrant flower gardens surround the Heafey Law Library. A traditional moot courtroom provides the setting for advocacy training and activities of the Edwin A. Heafey Jr. Center for Trial and Appellate Advocacy. Other facilities include the Bergin Hall faculty office building and Bannan Hall, where our law career services, Academic Success Program, and many other programs are located. Students also have access to the full array of campus facilities, including computer labs; the Cowell Student Health Center; Benson Memorial Center; and the Pat Malley Fitness Center, which includes a well-equipped weight room, fitness classes, an outdoor pool, locker rooms with steam rooms and saunas, and courts for basketball, volleyball, and racquetball.

Curriculum

Santa Clara Law offers full-time and part-time programs (with day and evening classes), extensive diversity outreach programs, and an Academic Success Program. More than 200 courses are available, and 86 semester units are required to graduate. The degrees available include JD, JD/MBA, JD/MSIS, LLM in International Law, LLM in US Law for Foreign Attorneys, and LLM in Intellectual Property. An academic orientation introduces first-year students to the study of law. The first-year curriculum is prescribed.

The JD/MBA and the JD/MSIS combined-degree programs are a powerful union of Santa Clara's nationally recognized School of Law and Leavey School of Business. Students earn both degrees in a full-time program lasting three and one-half to four years.

International Law Certificate

The International Law Program sponsors summer law study programs in more locations than any other American law school, including programs in: Munich, Germany; Strasbourg, France; Geneva, Switzerland; Oxford, England; Hong Kong; Singapore; Shanghai, China; The Hague, the Netherlands; Istanbul, Turkey; San Jose, Costa Rica; Tokyo, Japan; Vienna; Budapest; Sydney, Australia; and Seoul, Korea. Nearly all programs offer internships with law offices, corporations, or groups particularly suited to allow students on-site observation and participation in areas of international law. Students may earn a certificate in International Law.

Computer and High-Technology Law Certificate

With its central Silicon Valley location, **Santa Clara Law is one of the top places in the country to study intellectual property and high-tech law** for good reasons. Students learn from a dozen full-time faculty members with expertise in every aspect of intellectual property (IP) and high-tech law plus two dozen part-time faculty members working in IP and high-tech law at leading Silicon Valley firms and companies. Students have unparalleled internship opportunities with leading high-tech companies and law firms. The IP and high-tech curriculum is one of the largest in the country, and students can create a highly personalized course of study, including a certificate in High Tech Law or International High Tech Law.

Public Interest and Social Justice Law Certificate

The Santa Clara Law community has a true commitment to social justice, and students serve the poor and the marginalized in many ways while in law school, including work for the Center for Social Justice and Public Service, which offers an array of resources for students who want to focus on this area during their legal education and in practice. Santa Clara Law takes seriously the charge of graduating lawyers who lead with a commitment to a more humane and just world, and many students choose to earn a certificate in Public Interest.

Clinical Programs

At Santa Clara Law's Katharine and George Alexander Community Law Center, experienced attorneys mentor students as they participate in all phases of a case from the initial client interview through the trial. Students can earn credit for work as law clerks with public agencies such as the district attorney or public defender, with legal aid offices, or with private law offices. Students may also work as judges' clerks in appellate courts, including the California Supreme Court, or trial courts, including the United States District Court and local superior court. Another clinical opportunity is the Northern California Innocence Project (NCIP), in which students work under the supervision of experienced legal and forensic staff to evaluate case histories and work with prisoners, crime and evidence labs, law enforcement, defense attorneys, and prosecutors to help prove claims of innocence.

Student Activities

Santa Clara Law has 35 student groups, including an extensive array of minority student organizations and national and international moot court teams. The school's quarterly, *Santa Clara Law Review*, is published by a student editorial board. The *Computer and High Technology Law Journal* provides a practical resource for the high-tech industry and

legal community. The *Journal of International Law* is a respected, peer-reviewed scholarly journal. Through the Student Bar Association and student-faculty committees, students participate in the decision processes of the school.

Admission

A faculty committee reviews all applications. No one is automatically accepted or rejected. When the LSAT is repeated, the highest score received is used.

Santa Clara Law has a policy for special admission, and applicants may request special consideration because of race, disadvantaged background, or other factors.

Applicants are encouraged to visit Santa Clara Law. Arrangements can be made through the Admissions Office to tour the campus, attend a class, or meet with an admission counselor.

Career Services

Law Career Services offers several workshops, presentations, and services to help students launch a career; these include on-campus interviewing, job fairs, mock interviews, diversity receptions, and speed networking. Each year, a number of law firms, companies, and public and government agencies interview on campus or request résumés from our students. A high percentage of our graduates are employed within nine months of graduation in positions throughout the United States.

APPLICANT PROFILE

Santa Clara University School of Law
This grid includes only applicants who earned 120–180 LSAT scores under standard administrations.

LSAT Score	3.75 +		3.50–3.74		3.25–3.49		3.00–3.24		2.75–2.99		2.50–2.74		2.25–2.49		2.00–2.24		Below 2.00		No GPA		Total	
	Apps	Adm	Apps	Adm	Apps	Adm	Apps	Adm	Apps	Adm	Apps	Adm	Apps	Adm	Apps	Adm	Apps	Adm	Apps	Adm	Apps	Adm
175–180	1	1	2	2	8	8	2	2	1	1	0	0	0	0	0	0	1	1	0	0	15	15
170–174	17	17	24	24	19	19	18	18	15	13	4	2	4	0	3	1	2	0	4	3	110	97
165–169	87	87	82	81	89	87	65	63	47	36	24	10	13	5	5	0	3	1	12	11	427	381
160–164	184	178	316	308	324	297	231	197	86	47	56	19	19	2	6	0	0	0	17	15	1239	1063
155–159	184	107	346	163	366	116	285	48	123	17	65	5	33	2	6	1	1	0	27	5	1436	464
150–154	110	17	218	14	267	17	252	9	99	4	47	3	31	0	8	0	1	0	20	0	1053	64
145–149	27	0	66	2	84	0	100	0	78	0	46	0	16	0	8	0	2	0	11	0	438	2
140–144	9	0	16	0	26	0	37	0	31	0	24	0	21	0	3	0	0	0	5	0	172	0
135–139	3	0	3	0	6	0	15	0	15	0	9	0	10	0	5	0	2	0	3	0	71	0
130–134	0	0	1	0	3	0	5	0	4	0	3	0	2	0	3	0	1	0	0	0	22	0
125–129	0	0	1	0	0	0	0	0	0	0	3	0	0	0	1	0	1	0	1	0	7	0
120–124	0	0	0	0	0	0	0	0	0	0	0	0	0	0	1	0	0	0	0	0	1	0
Total	622	407	1075	594	1192	544	1010	337	499	118	281	39	149	9	49	2	14	2	100	34	4991	2086

Apps = Number of Applicants
Adm = Number Admitted
Reflects 99% of the total applicant pool; highest LSAT data reported.

SEATTLE UNIVERSITY SCHOOL OF LAW

901 12th Avenue, Sullivan Hall
Seattle, WA 98122-1090
Phone: 206.398.4200; Fax: 206.398.4058
E-mail: lawadmis@seattleu.edu; Website: www.law.seattleu.edu

ABA
Approved
Since
1994

The Basics

Type of school	Private
Term	Semester
Application deadline	3/1
Application fee	$60
Financial aid deadline	
Can first year start other than fall?	Yes
Student to faculty ratio	12.3 to 1
# of housing spaces available restricted to law students	
graduate housing for which law students are eligible	

Faculty and Administrators

	Total		Men		Women		Minorities	
	Spr	Fall	Spr	Fall	Spr	Fall	Spr	Fall
Full-time	60	65	32	37	28	28	14	15
Other full-time	1	1	1	1	0	0	1	1
Deans, librarians, & others who teach	11	11	4	5	7	6	2	3
Part-time	53	59	39	44	14	15	9	3
Total	125	136	76	87	49	49	26	22

Curriculum

		Full-Time	Part-Time
Typical first-year section size		90	61
Is there typically a "small section" of the first-year class, other than Legal Writing, taught by full-time faculty		No	No
If yes, typical size offered last year			
# of classroom course titles beyond first-year curriculum		170	
# of upper division courses, excluding seminars, with an enrollment:	Under 25	131	
	25–49	57	
	50–74	23	
	75–99	6	
	100+	0	
# of seminars		41	
# of seminar positions available		814	
# of seminar positions filled		410	104
# of positions available in simulation courses		681	
# of simulation positions filled		363	215
# of positions available in faculty supervised clinical courses		126	
# of faculty supervised clinical positions filled		86	32
# involved in field placements		145	10
# involved in law journals		99	9
# involved in moot court or trial competitions		29	2
# of credit hours required to graduate		90	

JD Enrollment and Ethnicity

	Men		Women		Full-Time		Part-Time		1st-Year		Total		JD Degs. Awd.
	#	%	#	%	#	%	#	%	#	%	#	%	
All Hispanics	21	4.2	39	7.6	50	6.2	10	4.9	26	8.1	60	5.9	16
Am. Ind./AK Nat.	2	0.4	8	1.6	9	1.1	1	0.5	5	1.6	10	1.0	3
Asian	49	9.9	46	8.9	72	8.9	23	11.3	22	6.9	95	9.4	30
Black/Af. Am.	13	2.6	19	3.7	24	3.0	8	3.9	8	2.5	32	3.2	8
Nat. HI/Pac. Isl.	8	1.6	9	1.8	15	1.9	2	1.0	2	0.6	17	1.7	0
2 or more races	17	3.4	20	3.9	28	3.5	9	4.4	17	5.3	37	3.7	0
Subtotal (minor.)	110	22.1	141	27.4	198	24.5	53	26.1	80	25.0	251	24.8	80
Nonres. Alien	5	1.0	4	0.8	9	1.1	0	0.0	4	1.3	9	0.9	0
White/Cauc.	359	72.2	356	69.3	571	70.7	144	70.9	226	70.6	715	70.7	224
Unknown	23	4.6	13	2.5	30	3.7	6	3.0	10	3.1	36	3.6	12
Total	497	49.2	514	50.8	808	79.9	203	20.1	320	31.7	1011		320

Transfers

Transfers in	14
Transfers out	6

Tuition and Fees

	Resident	Nonresident
Full-time	$37,330	$37,330
Part-time	$31,098	$31,098
Tuition Guarantee Program		N

Living Expenses

Estimated living expenses for singles

Living on campus	Living off campus	Living at home
$17,942	$17,942	$9,941

SEATTLE UNIVERSITY SCHOOL OF LAW

ABA Approved Since 1994

GPA and LSAT Scores

	Total	Full-Time	Part-Time
# of apps	2,892	2,633	259
# of offers	1,013	925	88
# of matrics	324	266	58
75% GPA	3.58	3.60	3.33
Median GPA	3.33	3.35	3.01
25% GPA	3.07	3.14	2.69
75% LSAT	160	161	159
Median LSAT	158	158	157
25% LSAT	155	156	153

Grants and Scholarships (from prior year)

	Total		Full-Time		Part-Time	
	#	%	#	%	#	%
Total # of students	1,036		808		228	
Total # receiving grants	536	51.7	452	55.9	84	36.8
Less than 1/2 tuition	523	50.5	440	54.5	83	36.4
Half to full tuition	7	0.7	6	0.7	1	0.4
Full tuition	6	0.6	6	0.7	0	0.0
More than full tuition	0	0.0	0	0.0	0	0.0
Median grant amount			$9,000		$8,000	

Informational and Library Resources

Total amount spent on library materials	$1,191,452
Study seating capacity inside the library	429
# of full-time equivalent professional librarians	9
Hours per week library is open	119
# of open, wired connections available to students	2,287
# of networked computers available for use by students	16
Has wireless network?	Y
Requires computer?	Y

JD Attrition (from prior year)

	Academic	Other	Total	
	#	#	#	%
1st year	3	22	25	7.6
2nd year	0	4	4	1.3
3rd year	0	1	1	0.3
4th year	0	0	0	0.0

Employment (9 months after graduation)

	Total	Percentage
Employment status known	337	100.0
Employment status unknown	0	0.0
Employed	294	87.2
Pursuing graduate degrees	14	4.2
Unemployed (seeking, not seeking, or studying for the bar)	19	5.6
Type of Employment		
# employed in law firms	137	46.6
# employed in business and industry	69	23.5
# employed in government	42	14.3
# employed in public interest	23	7.8
# employed as judicial clerks	16	5.4
# employed in academia	7	2.4
Geographic Location		
# employed in state	255	86.7
# employed outside the US	3	1.0
# of states where employed	15	

Bar Passage Rates

First-time takers	323	Reporting %	90.09
Average school %	75.60	Average state %	74.42
Average pass difference	1.18		

Jurisdiction	Takers	Passers	Pass %	State %	Diff %
Washington	291	220	75.60	74.42	1.18

SEATTLE UNIVERSITY SCHOOL OF LAW

901 12th Avenue, Sullivan Hall
Seattle, WA 98122-1090
Phone: 206.398.4200; Fax: 206.398.4058
E-mail: lawadmis@seattleu.edu; Website: www.law.seattleu.edu

Introduction

Seattle University School of Law, the largest and most diverse law school in the Pacific Northwest, is dedicated to the twin goals of academic excellence and education for justice.

The School of Law is home to leading academic programs, including the country's top-ranked Legal Writing Program and the Ronald A. Peterson Law Clinic, as well as distinguished centers and institutes. These programs and a superb faculty support the law school's mission to educate outstanding lawyers to be leaders for a just and humane world.

The school enrolls just over 1,000 students representing more than 250 undergraduate schools and drawn from the top third of the national law school applicant pool. We serve an impressive body of students, whose diversity encompasses age, life experience, and cultural heritage. The law school is recognized nationally for its diverse faculty and welcoming environment. It is the only Washington law school with a part-time program geared to meet the needs of working professionals.

The law school is accredited by the ABA and holds membership in the AALS. Students may pursue a Juris Doctor or one of many joint degrees.

Location

Located in the heart of dynamic Seattle, the law school is a vital part of the community. It is located on the beautiful urban campus of Seattle University in the lively Capitol Hill neighborhood just steps from downtown Seattle. The area offers a mix of exciting, professional, cultural, and recreational opportunities.

One of the most beautiful and livable cities in the United States, Seattle is a legal, business, technological, and cultural hub that provides law students access to summer and school-year employment with major players in the economy, multinational law firms, and public agencies.

Sullivan Hall, home to the law school, is an award-winning, state-of-the-art facility with the latest technology throughout its impressive library, classrooms, courtroom, and study and activity areas. The School of Law Annex is a modern building less than a block from Sullivan Hall, which was built to accommodate the growing law school. It houses the clinical and externship programs, student journals, and additional classrooms.

Focus Area and First-Year Curriculum

Our innovative first-year studies are rigorous, emphasizing sound legal analytical skills while allowing students to choose an elective course in the second semester. Our Focus Area Curriculum allows students to select a primary area of interest and supports that with enrollment in a prescribed range of courses. Students may focus their upper-division legal studies in one of 14 substantive areas, including Civil Advocacy, Criminal Practice, Environmental Law, Health Law, Labor and Employment, or Real Estate Law.

Faculty

Seattle University School of Law is home to an outstanding faculty of committed teacher-scholars. Our professors do not choose between scholarship and teaching, but rather are experts in their fields who are drawn to share their knowledge with students.

A primary mission that drives the academic program is the faculty's desire to prepare students to practice the law with competence, honor, and commitment to public service. Our talented faculty members teach students to analyze problems and construct policy arguments, as well as train them to write and speak with clarity and precision.

The teaching is both demanding and humane. It blends legal theory, doctrinal analysis, and comprehensive practical-skills training. Reflecting the Jesuit tradition of open inquiry, social responsibility, and concern for personal growth, the law school values freedom of conscience, thought, and speech.

Since 2000, law school faculty members have authored or coauthored 117 books, 130 book chapters, and more than 901 articles that have appeared in prestigious law reviews and specialized journals. Articles by our faculty are among the most read on Social Sciences Research Network (SSRN).

Academic Enrichment Programs

Access to Justice Institute (ATJI)—The mission of ATJI is to inspire all law students toward a lifelong commitment to equal justice. The institute connects students to public interest opportunities that fulfill unmet legal needs, facilitates advocacy and legal skills training, hosts social justice forums and events, counsels students in public interest career exploration, and collaborates with local, state, and national efforts to promote equal justice.

Center for Law and Equality—The Fred T. Korematsu Center for Law and Equality aims to advance social justice by fostering critical thinking about discrimination in US society and through targeted advocacy to promote equality and freedom. The center's work is divided into three units: research, advocacy, and education projects.

International Initiatives—Seattle University School of Law is a leader in global legal education and has expanded its international reach to offer students and faculty a greater world view. Among the many compelling programs are the International and Comparative Law Program, the Center for Global Justice, and Mexico/Latin America Initiatives.

Adolf A. Berle Jr. Center on Corporations, Law and Society—The Berle Center facilitates the study of the constantly evolving American and global economic system; the ongoing struggle for power between and among corporations, governments, individuals, and society; and the role of law in mediating and shaping the nature of our economic relations and institutions.

Admission and Financial Aid

In admission decisions, the law school places equal emphasis on three factors: (1) LSAT performance; (2) the undergraduate academic record; and (3) personal achievements, especially talents or factors that contribute to our law school community in special and significant ways.

We also admit a limited group of applicants annually through our **Access Admission Program**, which addresses those cases in which traditional admission criteria are inadequate predictors of success in law school and in the practice of law. Members of historically disadvantaged, underrepresented, or physically challenged groups are among those individuals considered for this program (limited to no more than 10 percent of the entering class).

The law school's **Scholarship Program** is among the most ambitious in the region, awarding over $3 million per year to approximately 350 students. Its objectives are twofold: to offer to all students—regardless of economic or social background—the advantages of a private legal education, and to recognize and reward—regardless of financial need—the achievements and outstanding potential of the most highly qualified students in the applicant pool. Upon admission, all entering students are automatically considered for scholarships. The School of Law offers a **Loan Repayment Assistance Program** to support graduates who choose full-time public interest legal careers as licensed attorneys doing law-related, public interest work. It offers two annual full-tuition **Scholars for Justice Awards** to outstanding students committed to social justice work, a full-tuition **Native American Scholarship** to an enrolled member of a federally recognized tribe, and the **Adolf A. Berle Scholarship** to a student committed to studying corporate governance.

APPLICANT PROFILE

Seattle University School of Law
This grid includes only applicants who earned 120–180 LSAT scores under standard administrations.

LSAT Score	3.75 +		3.50–3.74		3.25–3.49		3.00–3.24		2.75–2.99		2.50–2.74		2.25–2.49		2.00–2.24		Below 2.00		No GPA		Total	
	Apps	Adm	Apps	Adm	Apps	Adm	Apps	Adm	Apps	Adm	Apps	Adm	Apps	Adm	Apps	Adm	Apps	Adm	Apps	Adm	Apps	Adm
175–180	0	0	0	0	0	0	0	0	0	0	1	1	0	0	0	0	0	0	0	0	1	1
170–174	4	3	6	6	7	5	3	3	5	4	2	1	1	0	1	1	0	0	1	1	30	24
165–169	20	17	26	22	25	21	16	12	13	7	8	6	4	1	1	0	1	0	3	2	117	88
160–164	72	58	119	98	137	106	79	57	53	27	25	12	7	0	4	0	3	0	6	3	505	361
155–159	107	76	203	113	198	96	170	70	88	28	50	9	21	2	7	1	3	1	13	6	860	402
150–154	63	14	139	22	185	37	160	17	91	9	42	5	32	0	8	1	2	1	15	5	737	111
145–149	23	1	55	5	80	12	100	3	62	1	37	1	15	10	6	0	2	0	14	0	394	23
140–144	5	0	20	1	34	1	37	1	35	0	20	0	13	0	7	0	2	0	2	0	175	3
135–139	1	0	2	0	10	0	8	0	13	0	4	0	7	0	3	0	0	0	0	0	48	0
130–134	0	0	0	0	0	0	3	0	2	0	4	0	0	0	3	0	2	0	2	0	16	0
125–129	0	0	1	0	0	0	0	0	0	0	1	0	1	0	1	0	0	0	0	0	4	0
120–124	0	0	0	0	0	0	0	0	0	0	0	0	0	0	0	0	0	0	0	0	0	0
Total	295	169	571	267	676	278	576	163	362	76	194	35	101	13	41	3	15	2	56	17	2887	1013

Apps = Number of Applicants
Adm = Number Admitted
Reflects 99% of the total applicant pool; highest LSAT data reported.

SETON HALL UNIVERSITY SCHOOL OF LAW

Office of Admissions, One Newark Center
Newark, NJ 07102-5210
Phone: 888.415.7271, 973.642.8747; Fax: 973.642.8876
E-mail: admitme@shu.edu; Website: http://law.shu.edu

ABA
Approved
Since
1951

The Basics

Type of school	Private
Term	Semester
Application deadline	4/1
Application fee	$65
Financial aid deadline	4/1
Can first year start other than fall?	No
Student to faculty ratio	14.0 to 1
# of housing spaces available restricted to law students	
graduate housing for which law students are eligible	

Faculty and Administrators

	Total		Men		Women		Minorities	
	Spr	Fall	Spr	Fall	Spr	Fall	Spr	Fall
Full-time	53	57	32	34	21	23	10	9
Other full-time	2	2	0	0	2	2	0	0
Deans, librarians, & others who teach	16	16	3	3	13	13	2	2
Part-time	102	83	68	49	34	34	9	6
Total	173	158	103	86	70	72	21	17

Curriculum

	Full-Time	Part-Time
Typical first-year section size	75	65
Is there typically a "small section" of the first-year class, other than Legal Writing, taught by full-time faculty	No	No
If yes, typical size offered last year		

# of classroom course titles beyond first-year curriculum		143
# of upper division courses, excluding seminars, with an enrollment:	Under 25	242
	25–49	43
	50–74	47
	75–99	19
	100+	0
# of seminars		24
# of seminar positions available		400

# of seminar positions filled	214	148
# of positions available in simulation courses	1,290	
# of simulation positions filled	728	408
# of positions available in faculty supervised clinical courses	117	
# of faculty supervised clinical positions filled	111	4
# involved in field placements	134	42
# involved in law journals	163	10
# involved in moot court or trial competitions	37	0
# of credit hours required to graduate	88	

JD Enrollment and Ethnicity

	Men		Women		Full-Time		Part-Time		1st-Year		Total		JD Degs. Awd.
	#	%	#	%	#	%	#	%	#	%	#	%	
All Hispanics	31	5.5	27	5.6	29	4.1	29	8.3	23	6.4	58	5.5	15
Am. Ind./AK Nat.	2	0.4	0	0.0	1	0.1	1	0.3	1	0.3	2	0.2	0
Asian	40	7.0	50	10.3	49	7.0	41	11.7	34	9.5	90	8.5	17
Black/Af. Am.	16	2.8	21	4.3	14	2.0	23	6.6	12	3.3	37	3.5	8
Nat. HI/Pac. Isl.	0	0.0	0	0.0	0	0.0	0	0.0	0	0.0	0	0.0	0
2 or more races	4	0.7	6	1.2	3	0.4	7	2.0	2	0.6	10	0.9	0
Subtotal (minor.)	93	16.4	104	21.4	96	13.6	101	28.9	72	20.1	197	18.7	40
Nonres. Alien	4	0.7	1	0.2	2	0.3	3	0.9	5	1.4	5	0.5	0
White/Cauc.	471	82.9	380	78.4	606	86.1	245	70.2	282	78.6	851	80.8	276
Unknown	0	0.0	0	0.0	0	0.0	0	0.0	0	0.0	0	0.0	0
Total	568	53.9	485	46.1	704	66.9	349	33.1	359	34.1	1053		320

Transfers

Transfers in	10
Transfers out	22

Tuition and Fees

	Resident	Nonresident
Full-time	$45,048	$45,048
Part-time	$33,981	$33,981
Tuition Guarantee Program		N

Living Expenses

Estimated living expenses for singles

Living on campus	Living off campus	Living at home
N/A	$20,402	$10,007

ABA Approved Since 1951

GPA and LSAT Scores

	Total	Full-Time	Part-Time
# of apps	4,033	3,179	854
# of offers	1,849	1,580	269
# of matrics	358	249	109
75% GPA	3.65	3.69	3.54
Median GPA	3.43	3.51	3.30
25% GPA	3.17	3.26	3.00
75% LSAT	161	162	156
Median LSAT	159	160	153
25% LSAT	155	158	150

Grants and Scholarships (from prior year)

	Total		Full-Time		Part-Time	
	#	%	#	%	#	%
Total # of students	1,090		723		367	
Total # receiving grants	433	39.7	368	50.9	65	17.7
Less than 1/2 tuition	250	22.9	200	27.7	50	13.6
Half to full tuition	142	13.0	127	17.6	15	4.1
Full tuition	41	3.8	41	5.7	0	0.0
More than full tuition	0	0.0	0	0.0	0	0.0
Median grant amount			$20,000		$7,500	

Informational and Library Resources

Total amount spent on library materials	$1,025,511
Study seating capacity inside the library	579
# of full-time equivalent professional librarians	8
Hours per week library is open	81
# of open, wired connections available to students	62
# of networked computers available for use by students	167
Has wireless network?	Y
Requires computer?	Y

JD Attrition (from prior year)

	Academic	Other	Total	
	#	#	#	%
1st year	18	26	44	12.4
2nd year	10	3	13	3.9
3rd year	0	0	0	0.0
4th year	0	0	0	0.0

Employment (9 months after graduation)

	Total	Percentage
Employment status known	308	100.0
Employment status unknown	0	0.0
Employed	290	94.2
Pursuing graduate degrees	0	0.0
Unemployed (seeking, not seeking, or studying for the bar)	18	5.8
Type of Employment		
# employed in law firms	112	38.6
# employed in business and industry	31	10.7
# employed in government	10	3.4
# employed in public interest	8	2.8
# employed as judicial clerks	116	40.0
# employed in academia	6	2.1
Geographic Location		
# employed in state	187	64.5
# employed outside the US	0	0.0
# of states where employed	13	

Bar Passage Rates

First-time takers	305	Reporting %	87.21
Average school %	90.23	Average state %	83.64
Average pass difference	6.59		

Jurisdiction	Takers	Passers	Pass %	State %	Diff %
New Jersey	266	240	90.23	83.64	6.59

The information on these pages was provided by the law school.

SETON HALL UNIVERSITY SCHOOL OF LAW

Office of Admissions, One Newark Center
Newark, NJ 07102-5210
Phone: 888.415.7271, 973.642.8747; Fax: 973.642.8876
E-mail: admitme@shu.edu; Website: http://law.shu.edu

Introduction

Founded in 1951, Seton Hall University School of Law is the only private law school in the state of New Jersey. While it values its Catholic identity, the law school is a pluralistic community representing a diversity of racial, cultural, religious, and socioeconomic backgrounds. The school is consistently recognized for its outstanding teaching and high level of student satisfaction.

One Newark Center, Our Home

Rich in history and culture, Newark is a city to explore. Whatever your interest, you'll find it here—the performing and visual arts, sports, great food, and captivating architecture are within easy reach. The law school is a block from Newark's Penn Station, from which a 20-minute train ride takes students to Manhattan and the world's largest law firms. Students can walk to Newark's major law firms, government agencies, and the federal and state courthouses. Housing options are extensive. Students enjoy living in nearby historic buildings and, with its expansive network of train lines, Newark is within easy reach of New York City, Hoboken, Jersey City, and many suburban communities. The law school's open, welcoming design is a reflection of the faculty and administration's commitment to students. Offices, classrooms, moot courtrooms, and the library are interconnected by balconies overlooking a striking five-story, glass-encased atrium. The entire law school complex is saturated with Wi-Fi Internet connectivity, including access to wireless printing. The building has unusually large student space, including newly renovated student journal and organization offices, lounges, meeting rooms, a chapel, and a cafeteria. The Peter W. Rodino Jr. Law Library is located on three floors and accommodates 600 students and 100 terminals for student use. The Law Library's collection contains more than 425,000 volumes covering a wide array of law and law-related subjects. Health Law and Intellectual Property Law are areas of particular strength. The Rodino Library is a depository for US government documents and for New Jersey state documents.

Curriculum

The JD requires 88 credits to graduate and may be completed as a full-time or a part-time program. The school offers both a day and an evening program following a semester calendar. The program emphasizes humanistic principles and encourages their synthesis with knowledge of the law and professional responsibility. The law school is committed to in-depth training in legal writing and research.

In addition to the core required courses, more than 200 courses are offered in a wide range of areas grouped as follows: Constitutional Law, Corporate Law, Criminal Law and Procedure, Health and Drug Law, Intellectual Property and Entertainment Law, International Legal Studies, Labor and Employment Law, Personal and Family Law, Property and Estates Law, Public Interest, and Taxation. Externships, journals, pro bono, and moot court programs are also included in the school's offerings.

Master of Laws (LLM) and a Master of Science in Jurisprudence (MSJ) are also offered in the areas of health, science, and technology law.

Public Interest

Seton Hall School of Law is committed to public interest and clinical education. Through the Seton Hall Law Center for Social Justice, students are provided with one of the most comprehensive clinical and pro bono programs offered by any New York area law school. The school's clinics presently represent more than 3,000 disadvantaged and underrepresented clients each year in a wide range of litigation such as civil litigation, family law, impact litigation, immigration and human rights, immigrant workers rights, juvenile justice, and civil rights and constitutional litigation. Clinical projects include International Human Rights/Rule of Law and Urban Revitalization. The Center for Social Justice provides services in the public's interest while training and mentoring future attorneys whose careers will be dedicated in whole or in part to public interest work. Students can take part in various programs geared toward public interest beginning as early as their first year, including clinical programs, externships, and pro bono assignments. Scholarship and other financial assistance are available through the Distinguished Public Interest Scholarship, Summer Public Interest Law Fellowship, and Public Interest Loan Repayment Assistance Program.

Special Programs

Internships—The law school offers judicial internships with justices of the New Jersey Supreme Court, judges of the New Jersey Appellate Division, Chancery and Law Courts, the Third Circuit Court of Appeals, the US District Courts, and the US Bankruptcy Courts. There are myriad internship programs with nonprofit and government agencies.

Externships—Externship offerings include environmental law; health law; entertainment law; international organizations, the European Court of Justice or Court of First Instance; the Federal Public Defender; Securities and Exchange Commission; New York Stock Exchange; Internal Revenue Service; National Labor Relations Board; and US Attorney.

Concentrations—The law school offers concentrations in Health Law and Intellectual Property Law that allow students to study a specialized curriculum developed by faculty in consultation with attorneys and government officials working in the field. The breadth and depth of both curricula is unparalleled. In addition to coursework, students have the opportunity to participate in externships and take part in frequent symposia and colloquia.

Joint-Degree Programs—**JD/MBA**—a four-year program with Seton Hall University Stillman School of Business; **JD/MADIR**—a four-year program with Seton Hall University Whitehead School of Diplomacy and International Relations; **JD/MD**—a six-year program with the Robert Wood Johnson Medical School of the University of Medicine and Dentistry of New Jersey; **MSJ/MD**—a five-year program with the Robert Wood Johnson Medical School of the University of Medicine and Dentistry of New Jersey.

Journals—The law school offers students an opportunity to advance legal scholarship through four student journals—the *Seton Hall Law Review, Seton Hall Legislative Journal, Circuit Review*, and the *Journal of Sports and Entertainment Law*.

International Study—The law school offers two summer programs for the study of law in the Middle East at the American University of Cairo in Egypt and at the University of Jordan in Amman. Additionally, a summer program in Leuven, Belgium, and Geneva, Switzerland, focusing on intellectual property is offered. Seton Hall's Zanzibar program is the only ABA-approved winter-intersession program focusing on modern-day slavery and human trafficking. And, a winter-intersession program in Chamonix, France, focuses on international human rights.

LLM and MSJ Degrees—Seton Hall offers LLM degrees in Health Law and Intellectual Property. Seton Hall also offers a Master of Science in Jurisprudence (MSJ) degree in Health Law, Science, and Technology, which provides professionals with a solid foundation in legal aspects of health care and intellectual property regulation. Such a concentrated exposure to health law issues can be vital to medical directors, regulatory and contract compliance officers, risk and case managers, employee benefits personnel, lobbyists, and pharmaceutical employees. Full- and part-time programs are available for both the LLM and MSJ degrees.

Moot Court Program—Students represent the law school in the National Moot Court competition as well as in 10 interschool competitions focusing on specific areas of law.

LEO Institute—The Monsignor Thomas Fahy Legal Education Opportunities Institute provides an intense summer classroom experience for educationally disadvantaged students. Applicants from disadvantaged groups, regardless of race, religion, age, sex, sexual orientation, or national origin, may wish to inquire about this program.

Student Activities

There are more than 35 student organizations at Seton Hall Law, representing various personal and professional interests. The Student Bar Association (SBA) and other student organizations sponsor a variety of practical, social, and educational events. The SBA plays a major role in orientation, coordinates the first-year mentoring program, and sponsors a holiday party each November in Newark and a Barristers' Ball in the spring. Organizations sponsor career seminars focused on different areas of the law, host symposiums and panel discussions that focus on current legal and societal issues, and plan annual banquets and networking receptions during the year.

Committed to Your Success

At Seton Hall you will find a school committed to your success. The majority of our students participate in hands-on clinical training or externships, and 94 percent of our students are employed within nine months of graduation. Seton Hall Law maintains a proactive Career Services Office staffed by full-time counselors who assist students in defining their career objectives and goals and establishing contact with employers. Each fall and spring, law firms, accounting firms, and public interest and governmental employers conduct interviews through the school's On-Campus Interview Program. Alumni are practicing nationwide.

APPLICANT PROFILE

Seton Hall University School of Law
This grid includes only applicants who earned 120–180 LSAT scores under standard administrations.

LSAT Score	3.75 +		3.50–3.74		3.25–3.49		3.00–3.24		2.75–2.99		2.50–2.74		2.25–2.49		2.00–2.24		Below 2.00		No GPA		Total	
	Apps	Adm	Apps	Adm	Apps	Adm	Apps	Adm	Apps	Adm	Apps	Adm	Apps	Adm	Apps	Adm	Apps	Adm	Apps	Adm	Apps	Adm
170–180	3	3	8	6	9	9	6	6	6	5	1	1	1	0	1	0	0	0	0	0	35	30
165–169	34	31	36	34	35	35	26	24	11	9	10	8	6	2	2	0	1	0	2	2	163	145
160–164	153	147	205	201	228	219	185	169	89	61	47	22	31	12	16	3	0	0	13	7	967	841
155–159	165	137	334	249	279	153	194	88	109	26	55	6	40	5	8	1	4	1	14	3	1202	669
150–154	89	21	151	35	176	23	195	16	112	5	61	4	31	1	12	0	4	0	16	1	847	106
145–149	29	1	68	8	85	7	119	3	79	5	53	2	25	1	10	0	3	0	10	1	481	28
140–144	15	1	31	1	44	0	52	1	38	1	28	0	16	1	7	0	3	0	7	0	241	5
Below 140	2	0	9	0	22	0	20	0	24	0	25	0	12	0	8	0	6	0	5	0	133	0
Total	490	341	842	534	878	446	797	307	468	112	280	43	162	22	64	4	21	1	67	14	4069	1824

Apps = Number of Applicants
Adm = Number Admitted
Reflects 99% of the total applicant pool; highest LSAT data reported.

SMU DEDMAN SCHOOL OF LAW

Office of Admissions, PO Box 750110
Dallas, TX 75275-0110
Phone: 214.768.2550, 888.768.5291; Fax: 214.768.2549
E-mail: lawadmit@smu.edu; Website: www.law.smu.edu

The Basics

Type of school	Private
Term	Semester
Application deadline	11/1 2/15
Application fee	$75
Financial aid deadline	11/1 2/15
Can first year start other than fall?	No
Student to faculty ratio	15.7 to 1
# of housing spaces available restricted to law students	
graduate housing for which law students are eligible	

Faculty and Administrators

	Total		Men		Women		Minorities	
	Spr	Fall	Spr	Fall	Spr	Fall	Spr	Fall
Full-time	41	41	27	27	14	14	10	9
Other full-time	4	5	3	3	1	2	1	1
Deans, librarians, & others who teach	7	7	5	5	2	2	0	0
Part-time	48	45	37	35	8	7	9	13
Total	100	98	72	70	25	25	20	23

Curriculum

	Full-Time	Part-Time
Typical first-year section size	89	75
Is there typically a "small section" of the first-year class, other than Legal Writing, taught by full-time faculty	No	No
If yes, typical size offered last year		
# of classroom course titles beyond first-year curriculum	132	

# of upper division courses, excluding seminars, with an enrollment:		
	Under 25	95
	25–49	54
	50–74	9
	75–99	15
	100+	1

# of seminars	18	
# of seminar positions available	354	
# of seminar positions filled	210	89
# of positions available in simulation courses	1,328	
# of simulation positions filled	658	268
# of positions available in faculty supervised clinical courses	328	
# of faculty supervised clinical positions filled	133	63
# involved in field placements	51	37
# involved in law journals	150	51
# involved in moot court or trial competitions	41	12
# of credit hours required to graduate	87	

JD Enrollment and Ethnicity

	Men		Women		Full-Time		Part-Time		1st-Year		Total		JD Degs. Awd.
	#	%	#	%	#	%	#	%	#	%	#	%	
All Hispanics	32	6.8	46	11.1	50	9.1	28	8.3	17	6.7	78	8.8	25
Am. Ind./AK Nat.	12	2.5	5	1.2	10	1.8	7	2.1	5	2.0	17	1.9	1
Asian	31	6.6	33	8.0	34	6.2	30	8.9	30	11.9	64	7.2	23
Black/Af. Am.	17	3.6	30	7.2	24	4.4	23	6.8	11	4.3	47	5.3	11
Nat. Hl/Pac. Isl.	0	0.0	0	0.0	0	0.0	0	0.0	0	0.0	0	0.0	0
2 or more races	1	0.2	3	0.7	3	0.5	1	0.3	4	1.6	4	0.5	0
Subtotal (minor.)	93	19.7	117	28.3	121	22.0	89	26.3	67	26.5	210	23.7	60
Nonres. Alien	2	0.4	1	0.2	3	0.5	0	0.0	1	0.4	3	0.3	0
White/Cauc.	343	72.5	272	65.7	392	71.4	223	66.0	181	71.5	615	69.3	194
Unknown	35	7.4	24	5.8	33	6.0	26	7.7	4	1.6	59	6.7	0
Total	473	53.3	414	46.7	549	61.9	338	38.1	253	28.5	887		259

Transfers

Transfers in	35
Transfers out	1

Tuition and Fees

	Resident	Nonresident
Full-time	$40,186	$40,186
Part-time	$30,140	$30,140
Tuition Guarantee Program		N

Living Expenses

Estimated living expenses for singles

Living on campus	Living off campus	Living at home
$19,072	$19,072	$19,072

SMU DEDMAN SCHOOL OF LAW

ABA
Approved
Since
1927

GPA and LSAT Scores

	Total	Full-Time	Part-Time
# of apps	2,596	2,327	765
# of offers	729	566	163
# of matrics	254	177	77
75% GPA	3.82	3.86	3.71
Median GPA	3.67	3.75	3.50
25% GPA	3.29	3.38	3.00
75% LSAT	165	166	163
Median LSAT	163	164	160
25% LSAT	156	157	159

Grants and Scholarships (from prior year)

	Total		Full-Time		Part-Time	
	#	%	#	%	#	%
Total # of students	903		524		379	
Total # receiving grants	607	67.2	393	75.0	214	56.5
Less than 1/2 tuition	378	41.9	178	34.0	200	52.8
Half to full tuition	199	22.0	185	35.3	14	3.7
Full tuition	9	1.0	9	1.7	0	0.0
More than full tuition	21	2.3	21	4.0	0	0.0
Median grant amount			$20,000		$6,000	

Informational and Library Resources

Total amount spent on library materials	$1,376,696
Study seating capacity inside the library	716
# of full-time equivalent professional librarians	6
Hours per week library is open	104
# of open, wired connections available to students	0
# of networked computers available for use by students	107
Has wireless network?	Y
Requires computer?	N

JD Attrition (from prior year)

	Academic	Other	Total	
	#	#	#	%
1st year	3	8	11	4.3
2nd year	0	3	3	1.1
3rd year	0	0	0	0.0
4th year	0	0	0	0.0

Employment (9 months after graduation)

	Total	Percentage
Employment status known	307	100.0
Employment status unknown	0	0.0
Employed	274	89.3
Pursuing graduate degrees	14	4.6
Unemployed (seeking, not seeking, or studying for the bar)	8	2.6
Type of Employment		
# employed in law firms	185	67.5
# employed in business and industry	53	19.3
# employed in government	19	6.9
# employed in public interest	4	1.5
# employed as judicial clerks	11	4.0
# employed in academia	2	0.7
Geographic Location		
# employed in state	256	93.4
# employed outside the US	0	0.0
# of states where employed		16

Bar Passage Rates

First-time takers	307	Reporting %	95.77
Average school %	89.46	Average state %	85.48
Average pass difference	3.98		

Jurisdiction	Takers	Passers	Pass %	State %	Diff %
Texas	294	263	89.46	85.48	3.98

SMU DEDMAN SCHOOL OF LAW

Office of Admissions, PO Box 750110
Dallas, TX 75275-0110
Phone: 214.768.2550, 888.768.5291; Fax: 214.768.2549
E-mail: lawadmit@smu.edu; Website: www.law.smu.edu

Introduction

Founded in 1925, SMU Dedman School of Law is located on a magnificent tree-lined campus in a beautiful residential neighborhood just five miles north of downtown Dallas. SMU offers an intimate learning community within a vibrant urban center.

With a relatively small entering class size, an outstanding teaching faculty, and distinguished guest lecturers, SMU offers a scholarly community with fantastic opportunities both inside and outside the classroom. SMU also has a well-rounded, diverse student body from approximately 200 colleges and universities, 30 states, and 20 countries.

Law School Campus

SMU offers a beautiful setting in which to pursue legal studies. The Law School Quadrangle, a six-acre, self-contained corner of the campus, offers students convenient access to all law school facilities. The larger SMU campus offers students a variety of housing options, a childcare facility, a health center, and a new fitness/wellness center.

SMU recently completed a multimillion-dollar renovation of all of the law school classrooms. A four-story parking garage with 500 spaces is available exclusively for law student parking, and a new dining hall opened in 2005.

Curriculum

SMU offers seven degree programs: JD (full-time day or part-time evening), JD/MBA, JD/MA in Economics, LLM (General), LLM (Taxation), LLM (for foreign attorneys), and SJD.

Students find a sophisticated curriculum that complements SMU's wide breadth of class offerings with extensive depth of focus. The JD curriculum is designed to achieve the goal of producing lawyers who are capable and responsible professionals through its emphasis on providing substantive knowledge, ethical and moral training, and practical skills to serve clients in local, national, and global communities.

Each JD student must complete 87 credit hours. Thirty-one of these hours comprise the mandatory first-year curriculum. After the first year, students must complete a course in professional responsibility and two upper-level writing courses (including an edited writing seminar in which an extensive scholarly, expository writing project is reviewed and critiqued by the professor).

SMU offers many small classes in which students will get to know their classmates and professors. Each entering class is divided into three sections (two full-time day and one part-time evening) of approximately 90 students each. Each semester, first-year students are assigned to a legal research, writing, and advocacy class of approximately 25 students. Over one-half of SMU's upper-division courses have fewer than 25 students, and approximately three-quarters have fewer than 50 students.

SMU's rich upper-division curricular offerings, with over 165 upper-division courses per year, provide students with a wide range of courses and the freedom to tailor a program of study that furthers their professional and personal goals. With traditional strengths in business, litigation, tax, and international law, the curriculum extends to many areas, including intellectual property, health care, environmental, and family law.

SMU's LLM programs are intended to enhance careers in the private practice of law, teaching, and public service by providing the opportunity for students who already have their basic law degree to increase their understanding of legal theory and policies. The LLM program for foreign attorneys is the largest graduate program, enrolling approximately 40 students from about 20 countries each year. SMU has over 1,400 international alumni from over 70 countries, including many who hold significant positions in major international corporations, in the highest courts of their nations, and in other key government and private entities.

Student Activities and Law Reviews

Students are able to enhance their legal education by participating in numerous programs and conferences sponsored by various faculty and student groups and centers. Selected law students serve on five major journals for which they receive academic credit. Law students are able to expand their legal education experience by participating in over 20 moot court, trial advocacy, client counseling, and negotiation competitions held at the local, regional, national, and international level, and by becoming active members in over 30 student organizations.

Externships and Clinics

Externships offer students the opportunity to work at a government agency for up to two hours of course credit. Popular externships include those with the US Attorney, the SEC, and the EPA.

Clinics offer students an opportunity to engage in the practice of law for up to six hours of course credit. Currently SMU has eight clinical opportunities: civil litigation, criminal defense, criminal prosecution, death penalty, federal taxation, small business, consumer law, and child advocacy.

Public Service

All students are required to perform 30 hours of public service before graduating. This model public service program not only allows the student to learn in a hands-on setting, but also provides an early exposure to pro bono practice, which is integral to the US legal system. SMU professors voluntarily hold themselves to this same requirement.

Overseas Study

SMU offers students an opportunity to study law for six weeks at University College at Oxford University in England.

Career Services and Bar Passage

SMU provides students with job placement assistance throughout their legal careers. The Career Services Office helps students develop their job search and career development skills, and partners with students in locating summer and permanent job opportunities.

SMU graduates fare very well in the legal market. Within nine months of graduation, approximately 97 percent of the class of 2009 was employed. They had an average starting salary of over $115,000 in the private sector and an average starting salary of over $107,000 overall.

In July 2009, 91 percent of SMU first-time test takers passed the Texas bar exam. The statewide pass rate was approximately 83 percent.

Admission

SMU looks for excellent, well-rounded students with strong academic backgrounds, life experiences, and perspectives that will enrich its educational community. Each application is considered in its entirety: LSAT score, undergraduate performance, graduate studies, work experience, activities, personal statement, and letters of recommendation are all read and evaluated. Applications can be downloaded from the web.

Scholarships

SMU provides approximately 50 percent of its entering class with scholarship assistance. SMU law scholarships, including several full-tuition Hutchison scholarships, are awarded on the basis of the admission application, including the applicant's answer to an optional question. In addition, two private foundations, the Hatton W. Sumners Foundation and the Dallas Bar Foundation, fund and select five to nine additional full-tuition scholarships per entering class. Both foundations require a separate scholarship application, available from the SMU Admissions Office. The Sarah T. Hughes Scholarships, sponsored by the Dallas Bar Foundation, are awarded to outstanding minority applicants. The Sumners Scholars are selected from a competitive pool of applicants with strong academics and extracurricular activities. Both foundations require that the SMU application, the respective scholarship application, and all supporting documents be submitted by February 15.

APPLICANT PROFILE

SMU Dedman School of Law
This grid includes only applicants who earned 120–180 LSAT scores under standard administrations.

LSAT Score	3.75 +		3.50–3.74		3.25–3.49		3.00–3.24		2.75–2.99		2.50–2.74		2.25–2.49		2.00–2.24		Below 2.00		No GPA		Total	
	Apps	Adm	Apps	Adm	Apps	Adm	Apps	Adm	Apps	Adm	Apps	Adm	Apps	Adm	Apps	Adm	Apps	Adm	Apps	Adm	Apps	Adm
175–180	3	3	2	2	0	0	0	0	0	0	0	0	0	0	0	0	0	0	0	0	5	5
170–174	8	7	12	11	16	12	6	4	2	1	0	0	2	1	0	0	0	0	0	0	46	36
165–169	56	52	56	44	55	43	40	29	19	6	16	7	6	2	2	2	1	0	3	3	254	188
160–164	135	86	172	53	154	33	79	30	49	16	22	8	12	5	1	0	0	0	5	3	629	234
155–159	115	67	164	23	158	2	113	2	62	1	33	2	15	0	8	0	1	0	19	1	688	98
150–154	58	32	108	14	126	8	108	6	73	2	35	1	17	1	2	0	0	0	9	1	536	65
145–149	32	20	45	7	71	3	56	0	50	1	35	0	17	0	8	0	3	0	13	3	330	34
140–144	9	2	15	2	20	0	28	0	15	0	14	0	12	0	6	0	0	0	3	0	122	4
135–139	2	0	2	0	8	0	3	0	7	0	14	0	7	0	4	0	0	0	3	0	50	0
130–134	0	0	1	0	2	1	0	0	2	0	5	0	1	0	1	0	1	0	2	1	15	2
125–129	0	0	0	0	0	0	0	0	0	0	0	0	2	0	1	0	0	0	0	0	3	0
120–124	0	0	0	0	0	0	0	0	0	0	0	0	0	0	1	0	0	0	0	0	1	0
Total	418	269	577	156	610	102	433	71	279	27	174	18	91	9	34	2	6	0	57	12	2679	666

Apps = Number of Applicants
Adm = Number Admitted
Reflects 92% of the total applicant pool; highest LSAT data reported.

UNIVERSITY OF SOUTH CAROLINA SCHOOL OF LAW

701 South Main Street
Columbia, SC 29208
Phone: 803.777.6605; Fax: 803.777.2847
E-mail: usclaw@law.sc.edu; Website: www.law.sc.edu

ABA
Approved
Since
1925

AMERICAN BAR ASSOCIATION
Section of Legal Education
and Admissions to the Bar

The Basics

Type of school	Public
Term	Semester
Application deadline	3/1
Application fee	$60
Financial aid deadline	3/1
Can first year start other than fall?	No
Student to faculty ratio	15.9 to 1
# of housing spaces available restricted to law students	
graduate housing for which law students are eligible	429

Faculty and Administrators

	Total		Men		Women		Minorities	
	Spr	Fall	Spr	Fall	Spr	Fall	Spr	Fall
Full-time	36	35	21	20	15	15	5	6
Other full-time	1	1	1	1	0	0	0	0
Deans, librarians, & others who teach	12	12	5	5	7	7	0	0
Part-time	19	18	15	15	4	3	0	2
Total	68	66	42	41	26	25	5	8

Curriculum

		Full-Time	Part-Time
Typical first-year section size		80	0
Is there typically a "small section" of the first-year class, other than Legal Writing, taught by full-time faculty		No	No
If yes, typical size offered last year			
# of classroom course titles beyond first-year curriculum		119	
# of upper division courses, excluding seminars, with an enrollment:	Under 25	63	
	25–49	32	
	50–74	14	
	75–99	13	
	100+	0	
# of seminars		23	
# of seminar positions available		418	
# of seminar positions filled		363	0
# of positions available in simulation courses		544	
# of simulation positions filled		477	0
# of positions available in faculty supervised clinical courses		71	
# of faculty supervised clinical positions filled		66	0
# involved in field placements		5	0
# involved in law journals		178	0
# involved in moot court or trial competitions		47	0
# of credit hours required to graduate		90	

JD Enrollment and Ethnicity

	Men		Women		Full-Time		Part-Time		1st-Year		Total		JD Degs. Awd.
	#	%	#	%	#	%	#	%	#	%	#	%	
All Hispanics	12	3.0	5	1.8	17	2.5	0	0.0	7	3.0	17	2.5	5
Am. Ind./AK Nat.	0	0.0	3	1.1	3	0.4	0	0.0	3	1.3	3	0.4	0
Asian	6	1.5	6	2.2	12	1.8	0	0.0	4	1.7	12	1.8	3
Black/Af. Am.	14	3.5	31	11.2	45	6.6	0	0.0	17	7.2	45	6.6	18
Nat. HI/Pac. Isl.	0	0.0	0	0.0	0	0.0	0	0.0	0	0.0	0	0.0	0
2 or more races	8	2.0	6	2.2	14	2.1	0	0.0	3	1.3	14	2.1	0
Subtotal (minor.)	40	9.9	51	18.3	91	13.4	0	0.0	34	14.3	91	13.3	29
Nonres. Alien	0	0.0	0	0.0	0	0.0	0	0.0	0	0.0	0	0.0	0
White/Cauc.	362	89.6	225	80.9	586	86.0	1	100.0	202	85.2	587	86.1	181
Unknown	2	0.5	2	0.7	4	0.6	0	0.0	1	0.4	4	0.6	4
Total	404	59.2	278	40.8	681	99.9	1	0.1	237	34.8	682		214

Transfers

Transfers in	5
Transfers out	8

Tuition and Fees

	Resident	Nonresident
Full-time	$20,236	$40,494
Part-time		
Tuition Guarantee Program		N

Living Expenses

Estimated living expenses for singles

Living on campus	Living off campus	Living at home
$16,517	$16,517	$8,259

ABA Approved Since 1925

GPA and LSAT Scores

	Total	Full-Time	Part-Time
# of apps	2,185	2,185	0
# of offers	751	751	0
# of matrics	239	239	0
75% GPA	3.64	3.64	0.00
Median GPA	3.39	3.39	0.00
25% GPA	3.04	3.04	0.00
75% LSAT	161	161	0
Median LSAT	159	159	0
25% LSAT	156	156	0

Grants and Scholarships (from prior year)

	Total #	Total %	Full-Time #	Full-Time %	Part-Time #	Part-Time %
Total # of students	685		685		0	
Total # receiving grants	377	55.0	377	55.0	0	0.0
Less than 1/2 tuition	335	48.9	335	48.9	0	0.0
Half to full tuition	39	5.7	39	5.7	0	0.0
Full tuition	2	0.3	2	0.3	0	0.0
More than full tuition	1	0.1	1	0.1	0	0.0
Median grant amount			$17,488		$0	

Informational and Library Resources

Total amount spent on library materials	$1,436,222
Study seating capacity inside the library	506
# of full-time equivalent professional librarians	10
Hours per week library is open	99
# of open, wired connections available to students	42
# of networked computers available for use by students	42
Has wireless network?	Y
Requires computer?	Y

JD Attrition (from prior year)

	Academic #	Other #	Total #	Total %
1st year	5	7	12	5.0
2nd year	0	11	11	4.8
3rd year	1	0	1	0.5
4th year	0	0	0	0.0

Employment (9 months after graduation)

	Total	Percentage
Employment status known	232	94.7
Employment status unknown	13	5.3
Employed	206	88.8
Pursuing graduate degrees	8	3.4
Unemployed (seeking, not seeking, or studying for the bar)	17	7.3
Type of Employment		
# employed in law firms	109	52.9
# employed in business and industry	18	8.7
# employed in government	31	15.0
# employed in public interest	7	3.4
# employed as judicial clerks	38	18.4
# employed in academia	3	1.5
Geographic Location		
# employed in state	156	75.7
# employed outside the US	1	0.5
# of states where employed	15	

Bar Passage Rates

First-time takers	239	Reporting %	79.50
Average school %	85.26	Average state %	78.19
Average pass difference	7.07		

Jurisdiction	Takers	Passers	Pass %	State %	Diff %
South Carolina	190	162	85.26	78.19	7.07

UNIVERSITY OF SOUTH CAROLINA SCHOOL OF LAW

701 South Main Street
Columbia, SC 29208
Phone: 803.777.6605; Fax: 803.777.2847
E-mail: usclaw@law.sc.edu; Website: www.law.sc.edu

Introduction

The University of South Carolina School of Law, established in 1867, is located in Columbia, South Carolina. With a metropolitan population approaching 700,000, Columbia combines the advantages of a progressive, growing area with the pace of a smaller city. The School of Law is located two blocks from the state capitol building. As the seat of state government, Columbia is home to the South Carolina Supreme Court, Court of Appeals, federal district and bankruptcy courts, South Carolina criminal and civil courts, and courts of special jurisdiction. As part of a major research university, law students can take advantage of rich interdisciplinary opportunities and a lively social and athletic scene. Columbia residents enjoy easy access to the mountains and the beautiful South Carolina low country and coastal region. The School of Law is accredited by the American Bar Association and has been a member of the Association of American Law Schools since 1924.

Library and Academic Programs

Since its founding, the School of Law has provided outstanding preparation for law students. The curriculum combines traditional teaching methods and courses with modern, state-of-the-art instruction. The School of Law houses a major research library with a collection of more than 500,000 volumes and extensive computer-assisted research capabilities, including LexisNexis, Westlaw, Loislaw, HeinOnline, BNA, SSRN, and the online catalog. The library also includes the South Carolina Legal History Collection. Law students and faculty have access to the collection of the main university library, the Thomas Cooper Library. A highly skilled staff of librarians provides assistance and instruction in research and reference techniques. The library is open approximately 100 hours per week and for extended hours during the examination period. The computer lab and an electronic learning facility are also located within the library. Individual closed study carrels are available for assignment to students, and larger study rooms and open carrels are also available. A wireless computer network is available throughout the building and the law center.

The School of Law offers a full-time-only day program leading to the Juris Doctor degree. In order to earn the JD, a student must successfully complete 90 semester hours of coursework. In each semester, a student must register for a minimum of 12 credit hours. The School of Law offers one seven-week summer session each year.

In addition to all first-year courses, students are required to take Criminal Procedure, Professional Responsibility, a professional skills course, and a perspective course, and to satisfy an upper-level writing requirement. The School of Law offers advanced courses that allow detailed study in corporate and commercial law, tax and estate planning, environmental law, family law, international law, and litigation. The peer-assistance tutoring program provides academic support to first-year students, and numerous resources are available to assist students in succeeding academically.

Dual-Degree Programs

The School of Law, in cooperation with other graduate programs at USC, currently offers dual JD and master's degrees in the following: International Business Administration, Human Resources, Accountancy, Economics, Public Administration, Criminology and Criminal Justice, Social Work, Earth and Environmental Resources Management, Mass Communication, and Health Services Policy and Management. The USC School of Law and Vermont Law School offer a dual degree in environmental law and policy, in which students may earn a JD from USC and a Master of Environmental Law and Policy degree from Vermont Law School in only three years.

Clinics, Public Service, and Special Programs

The School of Law recognizes that experiential learning in the area of professional skills is essential to a well-rounded legal education. Under special court rule, third-year law students in South Carolina may represent clients and appear in court when enrolled in a clinical legal education course. The clinical education program offers courses designed to develop critical lawyering skills. The program offers training in trial advocacy, interviewing, counseling, negotiation, alternative dispute resolution, and legal drafting. Clinics include criminal practice, veterans' rights, bankruptcy, federal litigation, and nonprofit organizations. Externships are available in children's law and foreign practice.

The Pro Bono Program, one of the longest operating programs of its type, has an outstanding national and local reputation. Under the leadership of a full-time director and a student board, the program offers students opportunities to work with a wide range of public interest organizations, including CASA, Volunteer Lawyers for the Arts, the Homeless Legal Clinic, juvenile arbitration, the Greater Columbia Literacy Project, Project Ayuda, the Legal Justice Center, the public defenders' office, the South Carolina Department of Consumer Affairs, the South Carolina Office of Indigent Defense, and volunteer income tax assistance, among others.

The Law School's Children's Law Center provides training to professionals who work with children in the juvenile and family courts. The Nelson Mullins Riley and Scarborough Center on Professionalism at the Law School provides a professionalism series for first-year students and is a national leader in the development of mentoring programs to assist in the transition from law school to law practice. The National Advocacy Center and the National College of District Attorneys are located on the USC campus. The Advocacy Center, operated by the US Department of Justice, provides intensive training to approximately 15,000 federal prosecutors and attorneys from across the country. The National College of District Attorneys provides training to nearly 2,000 prosecutors.

Admission

The School of Law seeks to enroll qualified students who will enhance and embrace the school's rigorous educational environment and, as graduates, make positive societal contributions to South Carolina, the region, and the nation.

In making decisions, the Faculty Committee on Admissions employs a holistic approach, taking into account all information available about each candidate. No single factor is conclusive. While undergraduate grades and the Law School Admission Test (LSAT) are important, the committee's decision is also influenced by other factors, including the applicant's personal statement, graduate study, military service, leadership and community service, employment or other life experience, residency, letters of recommendation, and potential for contribution to a diverse educational environment.

Scholarships and Financial Aid

While many students depend on federal and private student loans to help finance their legal education, the School of Law does offer scholarship assistance based both on merit and on financial need. Merit-based scholarships may range from $1,000 to full tuition. Awards are made on a rolling basis, typically beginning in March of each year. Candidates who want priority consideration for merit-based scholarships should make sure that the completed application and all supporting materials are received in the Office of Admissions no later than February 1. There is no separate application for merit-based scholarships. Applicants who wish to be considered for need-based scholarships or loans should submit the FAFSA.

Office of Career Services

The Office of Career Services serves as liaison between students and legal employers and offers services to equip students with the skills and information necessary for a successful employment search. The Career Services Office uses Symplicity. Services available include individual counseling, résumé writing and interviewing seminars, on-campus interviews, and participation in job fairs. The School of Law regularly participates in the Southeastern Law Placement Consortium in Atlanta; the Mid-Atlantic Legal Recruiting Conference in Washington, DC; the Southeastern Minority Job Fair; the Patent Law Interview Program in Chicago; the Southeastern Legal Hiring Conference; and the National Public Interest Career Fair.

Student Activities

The School of Law publishes the *South Carolina Law Review*; the *ABA Real Property, Trust and Estate Law Journal*; the *Southeastern Environmental Law Journal*; the *Journal of Law and Education*; and the *South Carolina Journal of International Law and Business*. Moot court and mock trial teams are sponsored in national, international, ABA, and various other competitions. Students who have obtained high academic achievement are eligible for membership in the Order of the Coif, a national legal honorary society, and the Order of the Wig and Robe, a local scholastic organization founded in 1935. The Peer Mentoring Program pairs each first-year student with upper-class students to help with the transition to law school. Student organizations include the Student Bar Association; Black Law Students Association; Women in Law; SALSA, the Hispanic Law Students Association; APALSA, the Asian Pacific Law Students Association; Christian Legal Society; Environmental Law Society; Children's Advocacy Law Society; Federalist Society; Health Law Society; Intellectual Property Law Society; James L. Petigru Public Interest Law Society; Just Democracy; International Law Society; OutLaw; Sports and Entertainment Law Society; Law School Democrats; Law School Republicans; national law fraternities Phi Alpha Delta and Phi Delta Phi; Service Members and Veterans in Law; and the American Constitution Society, among others.

APPLICANT PROFILE

University of South Carolina School of Law
This grid includes only applicants who earned 120–180 LSAT scores under standard administrations.

LSAT Score	GPA																					
	3.75 +		3.50–3.74		3.25–3.49		3.00–3.24		2.75–2.99		2.50–2.74		2.25–2.49		2.00–2.24		Below 2.00		No GPA		Total	
	Apps	Adm	Apps	Adm	Apps	Adm	Apps	Adm	Apps	Adm	Apps	Adm	Apps	Adm	Apps	Adm	Apps	Adm	Apps	Adm	Apps	Adm
170–180	6	6	4	3	2	2	2	2	0	0	0	0	1	0	0	0	0	0	0	0	15	13
165–169	19	18	13	13	19	18	7	7	10	8	9	8	5	3	1	0	1	0	1	1	85	76
160–164	68	62	84	83	96	92	79	67	55	47	26	15	10	4	8	3	1	1	0	0	427	374
155–159	83	68	133	65	151	41	122	27	81	8	48	6	15	4	2	0	1	0	6	3	642	222
150–154	52	13	117	11	121	8	124	10	75	3	25	2	15	0	9	0	2	0	4	0	544	47
145–149	25	4	40	2	55	5	71	7	40	2	32	1	12	0	8	0	0	0	6	2	289	23
140–144	6	2	16	0	21	0	26	0	14	0	20	0	11	0	4	0	0	0	1	0	119	2
Below 140	1	0	5	0	7	0	14	0	11	0	10	0	5	0	7	0	0	0	5	0	65	0
Total	260	173	412	177	472	166	445	120	286	68	170	32	74	11	39	3	5	1	23	6	2186	757

Apps = Number of Applicants
Adm = Number Admitted
Reflects 100% of the total applicant pool; highest LSAT data reported.

THE UNIVERSITY OF SOUTH DAKOTA SCHOOL OF LAW

414 E. Clark
Vermillion, SD 57069-2390
Phone: 605.677.5443; Fax: 605.677.5417
E-mail: law@usd.edu; Website: www.usd.edu/law

The Basics

Type of school	Public
Term	Semester
Application deadline	3/1
Application fee	$35
Financial aid deadline	3/15
Can first year start other than fall?	No
Student to faculty ratio	13.2 to 1
# of housing spaces available restricted to law students	
graduate housing for which law students are eligible	188

Faculty and Administrators

	Total		Men		Women		Minorities	
	Spr	Fall	Spr	Fall	Spr	Fall	Spr	Fall
Full-time	13	13	9	9	4	4	0	1
Other full-time	1	1	1	1	0	0	0	0
Deans, librarians, & others who teach	1	1	1	1	0	0	0	0
Part-time	3	7	1	5	2	2	1	0
Total	18	22	12	16	6	6	1	1

Curriculum

	Full-Time	Part-Time
Typical first-year section size	79	0

	Yes	No
Is there typically a "small section" of the first-year class, other than Legal Writing, taught by full-time faculty	Yes	No
If yes, typical size offered last year	40	

# of classroom course titles beyond first-year curriculum		44
# of upper division courses, excluding seminars, with an enrollment:	Under 25	34
	25–49	8
	50–74	6
	75–99	0
	100+	0
# of seminars		0
# of seminar positions available		0
# of seminar positions filled	0	0
# of positions available in simulation courses		149
# of simulation positions filled	138	0
# of positions available in faculty supervised clinical courses		0
# of faculty supervised clinical positions filled	0	0
# involved in field placements	13	0
# involved in law journals	25	0
# involved in moot court or trial competitions	36	0
# of credit hours required to graduate		90

JD Enrollment and Ethnicity

	Men		Women		Full-Time		Part-Time		1st-Year		Total		JD Degs. Awd.
	#	%	#	%	#	%	#	%	#	%	#	%	
All Hispanics	2	1.8	1	1.1	3	1.5	0	0.0	1	1.3	3	1.5	0
Am. Ind./AK Nat.	4	3.6	3	3.2	7	3.4	0	0.0	0	0.0	7	3.4	0
Asian	1	0.9	0	0.0	1	0.5	0	0.0	0	0.0	1	0.5	0
Black/Af. Am.	2	1.8	4	4.3	6	3.0	0	0.0	3	4.0	6	2.9	0
Nat. HI/Pac. Isl.	0	0.0	0	0.0	0	0.0	0	0.0	0	0.0	0	0.0	0
2 or more races	1	0.9	2	2.1	3	1.5	0	0.0	3	4.0	3	1.5	0
Subtotal (minor.)	10	9.0	10	10.6	20	9.9	0	0.0	7	9.3	20	9.8	0
Nonres. Alien	0	0.0	0	0.0	0	0.0	0	0.0	0	0.0	0	0.0	0
White/Cauc.	100	90.1	84	89.4	182	89.7	2	100.0	67	89.3	184	89.8	65
Unknown	1	0.9	0	0.0	1	0.5	0	0.0	1	1.3	1	0.5	0
Total	111	54.1	94	45.9	203	99.0	2	1.0	75	36.6	205		65

Transfers

Transfers in	0
Transfers out	0

Tuition and Fees

	Resident	Nonresident
Full-time	$11,208	$21,960
Part-time	$5,435	$10,638
Tuition Guarantee Program		N

Living Expenses

Estimated living expenses for singles

Living on campus	Living off campus	Living at home
$11,118	$13,632	N/A

THE UNIVERSITY OF SOUTH DAKOTA SCHOOL OF LAW

ABA
Approved
Since
1923

GPA and LSAT Scores

	Total	Full-Time	Part-Time
# of apps	449	449	0
# of offers	220	220	0
# of matrics	75	75	0
75% GPA	3.72	3.72	0.00
Median GPA	3.38	3.38	0.00
25% GPA	3.12	3.12	0.00
75% LSAT	154	154	0
Median LSAT	150	150	0
25% LSAT	149	149	0

Grants and Scholarships (from prior year)

	Total #	Total %	Full-Time #	Full-Time %	Part-Time #	Part-Time %
Total # of students	204		202		2	
Total # receiving grants	73	35.8	73	36.1	0	0.0
Less than 1/2 tuition	69	33.8	69	34.2	0	0.0
Half to full tuition	0	0.0	0	0.0	0	0.0
Full tuition	2	1.0	2	1.0	0	0.0
More than full tuition	2	1.0	2	1.0	0	0.0
Median grant amount			$1,477		$0	

Informational and Library Resources

Total amount spent on library materials	$546,547
Study seating capacity inside the library	227
# of full-time equivalent professional librarians	2
Hours per week library is open	168
# of open, wired connections available to students	268
# of networked computers available for use by students	37
Has wireless network?	Y
Requires computer?	N

JD Attrition (from prior year)

	Academic #	Other #	Total #	Total %
1st year	2	2	4	5.0
2nd year	2	0	2	3.4
3rd year	0	0	0	0.0
4th year	0	0	0	0.0

Employment (9 months after graduation)

	Total	Percentage
Employment status known	73	100.0
Employment status unknown	0	0.0
Employed	62	84.9
Pursuing graduate degrees	3	4.1
Unemployed (seeking, not seeking, or studying for the bar)	6	8.2
Type of Employment		
# employed in law firms	28	45.2
# employed in business and industry	8	12.9
# employed in government	3	4.8
# employed in public interest	5	8.1
# employed as judicial clerks	14	22.6
# employed in academia	1	1.6
Geographic Location		
# employed in state	45	72.6
# employed outside the US	0	0.0
# of states where employed	11	

Bar Passage Rates

First-time takers	67	Reporting %	95.52
Average school %	96.88	Average state %	89.85
Average pass difference	7.03		

Jurisdiction	Takers	Passers	Pass %	State %	Diff %
South Dakota	58	56	96.55	89.77	6.78
Iowa	4	4	100.00	93.17	6.83
Colorado	2	2	100.00	85.67	14.33

THE UNIVERSITY OF SOUTH DAKOTA SCHOOL OF LAW

The information on these pages was provided by the law school.

414 E. Clark
Vermillion, SD 57069-2390
Phone: 605.677.5443; Fax: 605.677.5417
E-mail: law@usd.edu; Website: www.usd.edu/law

Introduction

The University of South Dakota School of Law (USD Law), located on the University of South Dakota campus in Vermillion, is noted for its contributions in training distinguished leaders for the bench, the bar, and the lawmaking bodies of the state and region. Established in 1901, USD Law is approved by the ABA and is a member of the AALS. The law school offers a strong American Indian Law Program, and the Legal Writing Program is becoming among the best in the nation. The city of Vermillion, with a population of about 11,000 and located in the southeastern corner of South Dakota along the Missouri National Recreational River, provides a small-town atmosphere. The professional community setting at USD Law provides students with opportunities for individual attention by professors. USD Law offers an extraordinary experience in legal education at a remarkably reasonable tuition rate for both residents and nonresidents. More than 75 percent of upper-level courses have 25 or fewer students enrolled.

Library and Physical Facilities

The three-level McKusick Law Library is equipped to meet the research needs of students, faculty, and members of the bar. Students, staff, and faculty have access to the law school facility seven days a week, 24 hours a day through swipe-card access. It is South Dakota's largest and most complete law library, providing essential research services to the courts, legislature, government agencies, lawyers, private citizens, and students conducting interdisciplinary research. The book and microform collections include court reports, statutes, and other legal authorities.

The School of Law building was completed in 1981 and features a balconied courtroom in the middle of the building as the architectural focal point. The courtroom is fully equipped with state-of-the-art videoconferencing technologies and has an adjoining audiovisual control room and judges' chambers. The building also contains two large classrooms; two smaller classrooms; a seminar room; a computer laboratory; a student lounge, locker, and lunch area, and suites of offices for faculty, administration, and student organizations. The law school building is equipped for both wired and wireless network connectivity. The student organization suites contain study carrels for member use. The law library has 227 study seats, including 166 carrels assigned to members of the student body.

Curriculum

Ninety semester credits are required for the JD degree. The first-year curriculum is required of all students. In the second and third years, electives are available in addition to required courses. During the summer, an externship program is offered for six credit hours. Externs learn by doing under the close supervision of an attorney and the externship director. Skills training is also provided to second- and third-year students in the trial techniques course, negotiations, and other courses, each of which utilizes to the fullest extent the technological capabilities of the law school.

Special Programs

- Joint-Degree Programs—There are nine programs with other graduate departments, with master's degrees available in professional accountancy, business administration, history, English, psychology, education administration, political science, public administration, and administrative studies. Students may transfer nine hours of approved interdisciplinary coursework for JD credit and can complete both programs in three years and receive maximum credit.
- Interdisciplinary Study—For upper-division students not in a joint-degree program, up to six graduate credits in other university divisions may be taken and applied toward the hours required for the JD degree. This allows a law student to broaden the educational experience by the pursuit of new disciplines.
- Areas of Curricular Emphases—The American Indian Law Program provides students with the knowledge, skills, and experiences necessary to meet the challenges and opportunities in working with sovereign tribes and native people. Nationally recognized professors direct a unique and extensive curriculum with a concentration in the study of American Indian law. Nine American Indian reservations are located within the borders of South Dakota. The law school hosts the longest running biennial Indian Law Symposium in the United States, supports the Native American Law Student Association (twice named national chapter of the year), and works closely on the USD campus with the American Indian Studies Department and the Institute of American Indian Studies, directed by a law professor.
- The USD School of Law and Vermont Law School offer a dual degree in environmental law. Students earn a JD from USD and a Master of Science in Environmental Law (MSEL) from Vermont Law School.

Admission Options

- Flex-Time Program—This program permits certain well-qualified students to take less than the normal load of credits each semester and obtain a JD in five years instead of three. The program admits a limited number of students who could not attend law school on a full-time basis. The law school does not offer evening or weekend courses.
- Accelerated Admission—An applicant may apply for accelerated admission, and be admitted to and enroll in law school without final completion of the requirements for the applicant's undergraduate degree. The undergraduate degree must be attained by the applicant prior to graduation from law school.
- Law Honors Scholars Program—High school seniors who are accepted as USD undergraduate Honors Scholars may apply for and receive provisional (automatic) admission to the law school upon successful completion of their undergraduate degree in four years with a 3.5 GPA, fulfillment of the University Honors Program requirements, and completion of the LSAT for statistical purposes only.
- Law Screening Program—Applicants who are not regularly admitted may be invited to participate in the Law Screening Program. The summer program consists of two

courses offered in five weeks of lectures and finals during the sixth week. Participants are admitted or denied admission on the basis of their performance on final exams, which are graded anonymously.

Student Activities

The *South Dakota Law Review* publishes articles by legal scholars, lawyers, jurists, and students three times a year. The *Sustainable Development Law Journal* publishes articles on a variety of law topics, including environmental law and natural resources. Other cocurricular activities include a Moot Court Board, Alternative Dispute Resolution Board, and Trial Advocacy teams. Boards successfully compete at the intramural, regional, and national levels. The school is active in the Law Student Division of the ABA. Other organizations include Student Bar Association, Women in Law, Black Law Students Association, Christian Legal Society, Environmental Law Society, Law School Democrats, Federalist Society, American Constitution Society, Delta Theta Phi, Phi Alpha Delta, Phi Delta Phi, Trial Advocacy Group, Legal Assistance Group, and Corporate and Business Law Association. The Native American Law Student Association (NALSA) USD chapter is represented nationally and hosted the national NALSA Moot Court Tournament in spring 2010.

SD Supreme Court—Each spring, USD Law hosts the three-day March term of the Supreme Court of South Dakota, which provides an extraordinary opportunity for law and undergraduate students, faculty, and the public to observe oral arguments before the state's highest appeals court. The law school also works closely with Access to Justice, the pro bono office of the State Bar of South Dakota.

Pro bono Opportunities—The Law School provides substantial pro bono experiences for students assisting people with their legal needs by working closely with Access to Justice and AmeriCorps, the South Dakota Bar's pro bono office, as well as an Elder Law Program, R.D. Hurd Volunteer Society, area legal services offices, South Dakota Innocence Project, Equal Justice Works, Volunteer Income Tax Assistance (VITA) program, and the Domestic Violence Legal Program, among others.

Career Services

The placement opportunities for third-year law students are excellent in South Dakota, the surrounding areas, and throughout the United States. Approximately 23 percent of the graduates are placed in judicial clerkships, and one-third are employed outside South Dakota. The law school has an active program to place first- and second-year students in summer internship programs with law firms.

APPLICANT PROFILE

The University of South Dakota School of Law

LSAT Score	GPA								
	3.75 +	3.50–3.74	3.25–3.49	3.00–3.24	2.75–2.99	2.50–2.74	2.25–2.49	2.00–2.24	– 2.00
165 +	■	■	■	■	■	■	▨	▨	
160–164	■	■	■	■	■	▨	▨	▨	
155–159	■	■	■	■	■	▨	▨		
150–154	■	■	■	■	▨	▨			
145–149	▨	▨	▨	▨					
140–144									
– 140									

■ Good Possibility   ▨ Possible   ☐ Unlikely

USD School of Law considers many factors beyond LSAT score and GPA. This chart should be used only as a general rule.

For fall 2010:

Applicants:	449
Completed applications:	449
Standard full-time admits:	210
Accepted from Law Screening or PLSI:	10
Total admitted:	220
Matriculated full-time:	75

Stats for the 210 standard admits:	LSAT	GPA
75th:	156	3.72
Median:	153	3.44
25th:	150	3.17

SOUTH TEXAS COLLEGE OF LAW

1303 San Jacinto Street
Houston, TX 77002-7006
Phone: 713.659.8040; Fax: 713.646.2906
E-mail: admissions@stcl.edu; Website: www.stcl.edu

ABA
Approved
Since
1959

The Basics

Type of school	Private
Term	Semester
Application deadline	2/15 10/1
Application fee	$55
Financial aid deadline	5/1 10/1
Can first year start other than fall?	Yes
Student to faculty ratio	21.0 to 1
# of housing spaces available restricted to law students	
graduate housing for which law students are eligible	

Faculty and Administrators

	Total		Men		Women		Minorities	
	Spr	Fall	Spr	Fall	Spr	Fall	Spr	Fall
Full-time	49	44	32	28	17	16	4	6
Other full-time	0	0	0	0	0	0	0	0
Deans, librarians, & others who teach	5	6	3	4	2	2	1	1
Part-time	41	41	30	27	11	14	4	6
Total	95	91	65	59	30	32	9	13

JD Enrollment and Ethnicity

	Men		Women		Full-Time		Part-Time		1st-Year		Total		JD Degs. Awd.
	#	%	#	%	#	%	#	%	#	%	#	%	
All Hispanics	79	11.4	96	15.7	134	13.3	41	13.9	106	15.7	175	13.4	35
Am. Ind./AK Nat.	4	0.6	3	0.5	6	0.6	1	0.3	2	0.3	7	0.5	1
Asian	46	6.6	67	11.0	88	8.7	25	8.4	54	8.0	113	8.7	40
Black/Af. Am.	17	2.4	28	4.6	22	2.2	23	7.8	24	3.6	45	3.4	18
Nat. HI/Pac. Isl.	1	0.1	2	0.3	2	0.2	1	0.3	0	0.0	3	0.2	0
2 or more races	22	3.2	13	2.1	33	3.3	2	0.7	21	3.1	35	2.7	0
Subtotal (minor.)	169	24.3	209	34.3	285	28.2	93	31.4	207	30.6	378	29.0	96
Nonres. Alien	1	0.1	3	0.5	4	0.4	0	0.0	3	0.4	4	0.3	0
White/Cauc.	525	75.5	398	65.2	720	71.4	203	68.6	466	68.9	923	70.7	275
Unknown	0	0.0	0	0.0	0	0.0	0	0.0	0	0.0	0	0.0	0
Total	695	53.3	610	46.7	1009	77.3	296	22.7	676	51.8	1305		373

Curriculum

		Full-Time	Part-Time
Typical first-year section size		95	70
Is there typically a "small section" of the first-year class, other than Legal Writing, taught by full-time faculty		No	No
If yes, typical size offered last year			
# of classroom course titles beyond first-year curriculum		160	
# of upper division courses, excluding seminars, with an enrollment:	Under 25	158	
	25–49	48	
	50–74	20	
	75–99	22	
	100+	0	
# of seminars		25	
# of seminar positions available		524	
# of seminar positions filled		271	97
# of positions available in simulation courses		514	
# of simulation positions filled		346	119
# of positions available in faculty supervised clinical courses		208	
# of faculty supervised clinical positions filled		75	50
# involved in field placements		96	44
# involved in law journals		205	50
# involved in moot court or trial competitions		67	13
# of credit hours required to graduate		90	

Transfers

Transfers in	3
Transfers out	13

Tuition and Fees

	Resident	Nonresident
Full-time	$26,340	$26,340
Part-time	$17,760	$17,760
Tuition Guarantee Program		N

Living Expenses

Estimated living expenses for singles

Living on campus	Living off campus	Living at home
N/A	$23,700	$23,700

ABA
Approved
Since
1959

GPA and LSAT Scores

	Total	Full-Time	Part-Time
# of apps	2,436	2,129	307
# of offers	1,095	961	134
# of matrics	461	381	80
75% GPA	3.45	3.47	3.38
Median GPA	3.24	3.26	3.10
25% GPA	2.99	3.02	2.87
75% LSAT	156	157	154
Median LSAT	153	154	152
25% LSAT	151	151	150

Grants and Scholarships (from prior year)

	Total #	Total %	Full-Time #	Full-Time %	Part-Time #	Part-Time %
Total # of students	1,278		973		305	
Total # receiving grants	455	35.6	389	40.0	66	21.6
Less than 1/2 tuition	426	33.3	363	37.3	63	20.7
Half to full tuition	27	2.1	26	2.7	1	0.3
Full tuition	0	0.0	0	0.0	0	0.0
More than full tuition	2	0.2	0	0.0	2	0.7
Median grant amount			$2,600		$1,300	

Informational and Library Resources

Total amount spent on library materials	$1,666,733
Study seating capacity inside the library	877
# of full-time equivalent professional librarians	11
Hours per week library is open	106
# of open, wired connections available to students	1,380
# of networked computers available for use by students	105
Has wireless network?	Y
Requires computer?	N

JD Attrition (from prior year)

	Academic #	Other #	Total #	Total %
1st year	28	17	45	7.2
2nd year	5	2	7	1.9
3rd year	0	0	0	0.0
4th year	0	0	0	0.0

Employment (9 months after graduation)

	Total	Percentage
Employment status known	338	89.9
Employment status unknown	38	10.1
Employed	299	88.5
Pursuing graduate degrees	6	1.8
Unemployed (seeking, not seeking, or studying for the bar)	17	5.0
Type of Employment		
# employed in law firms	184	61.5
# employed in business and industry	58	19.4
# employed in government	37	12.4
# employed in public interest	2	0.7
# employed as judicial clerks	10	3.3
# employed in academia	7	2.3
Geographic Location		
# employed in state	282	94.3
# employed outside the US	0	0.0
# of states where employed		10

Bar Passage Rates

First-time takers	391	Reporting %	97.19
Average school %	86.84	Average state %	85.48
Average pass difference	1.36		

Jurisdiction	Takers	Passers	Pass %	State %	Diff %
Texas	380	330	86.84	85.48	1.36

The information on these pages was provided by the law school.

SOUTH TEXAS COLLEGE OF LAW

1303 San Jacinto Street
Houston, TX 77002-7006
Phone: 713.659.8040; Fax: 713.646.2906
E-mail: admissions@stcl.edu; Website: www.stcl.edu

Introduction

South Texas College of Law, situated at the very core of Houston's vibrant downtown legal and financial centers, is a private, nonprofit, independent law school founded in 1923. South Texas is the oldest law school in Houston, one of the largest in the nation, is accredited by the American Bar Association, and is a member of the AALS. The college offers full- and part-time programs leading to the Doctor of Jurisprudence degree.

Admission

Full- and part-time students are admitted to South Texas in the fall semester, while only full-time students are admitted in the spring. Admission application deadlines are February 15 for fall consideration and October 1 for spring. Early application is encouraged. A bachelor's degree is required. Applicants must also take the LSAT and register with LSAC's Credential Assembly Service.

Students are admitted primarily on the basis of their LSAT score and undergraduate GPA. However, a significant percentage of each incoming class is selected on the basis of additional factors. Every attempt is made to evaluate each applicant as an individual, a prospective student, and a future professional.

Curriculum

The curriculum at South Texas combines traditional classroom instruction with a broad range of innovative simulated and clinical courses. The college offers a class scheduling system whereby students may select convenient class times rather than have to choose between day and evening divisions. To accommodate part-time working students, a complete curriculum of classes is scheduled after 5:30 PM, with a few classes also scheduled on Saturdays. For students interested in the increased globalization of law, South Texas offers a variety of study-abroad programs throughout the year. Two ABA-approved cooperative exchange programs allow students to study for a semester in the Netherlands or Denmark. Summer programs are offered in Malta, Turkey, Ireland, England, Chile, the Czech Republic, and Italy.

JD/MBA Cooperative Program

Through a special cooperative program, students in the JD program at South Texas College of Law are eligible to apply for admission to the MBA program at Mays Business School, Texas A&M University. Upon acceptance into the MBA program, students are granted a leave of absence after their second year of law studies to attain their MBA and then return to South Texas to complete their JD degree.

Special Programs

Development of strong legal and advocacy skills is important at South Texas, as evidenced by its four Centers of Excellence and its skills and clinical programs.

Since 1980, the **Advocacy Program** has outperformed all other law school teams in the nation by winning an array of state, regional, and national championship victories. The **Frank Evans Center for Conflict Resolution** allows students to learn from and interact with practicing attorneys who specialize in mediation and arbitration. The **Corporate Compliance Center** involves students who are interested in working as in-house counsel, corporate counsel, outside counsel, and business lawyers. The center explores issues such as how companies promote policies and procedures that ensure legal and ethical behavior and how companies detect and deter wrongdoing. The **Transactional Practice Center** is designed to teach students the fundamental elements of completing a business transaction such as purchasing or developing real estate, buying or selling a corporation, or creating a partnership.

South Texas offers academic internships that place students in the real world of lawyering, including state and federal trial and appellate court chambers, prosecutors' and defenders' offices, public interest legal service providers, and state and federal government agencies. In the **International Process Clinic**, students work with defenders involved with the United Nations' ad hoc International Criminal Tribunal for the former Yugoslavia. In the **Direct Representation Clinics**, students work in an on-site clinic while providing direct representation for clients in a variety of administrative and state court settings.

Academic Assistance and Counseling. Students are encouraged to participate in the varied programs and services offered, which are designed to help them reach their full academic potential.

The **Langdell Scholar Program**, conducted by course-proficient upperclassmen, continues to benefit students in mastering the framework of legal analysis, while garnering a proficiency in effective outlining, study skills, and exam-taking techniques. Students attend these valuable sessions voluntarily or are selected into the program based on their LSAT performance, undergraduate GPA, and academic assistance diagnostic test.

Student Activities

Students at South Texas have the opportunity to become members of approximately 40 active student organizations representing a wide range of interests.

Scholarly Publications

South Texas College of Law students participate in journals on the basis of outstanding scholarship and writing ability. Our students edit and publish a variety of scholarly publications, including the *South Texas Law Review, Currents: International Trade Law Journal,* and the *Corporate Counsel Review;* and coedit the *Construction Law Journal* and *Texas Business Journal* in conjunction with each journal's respective state bar section.

Library and Physical Facilities

Recent additions to the South Texas campus ensure that students have access to and are trained with state-of-the-art tools now used in the legal profession. The T. Gerald Treece Courtroom houses a nine-seat judges' bench and boasts the very latest courtroom technology available to trial attorneys. The courtroom is heavily used by the school's nationally recognized advocacy program for practice and competitions. It is also available to the members of Houston's legal community, including the judiciary.

The Fred Parks Law Library encompasses more than 72,000 square feet. Each of the 870-plus seats in the six-story facility is wired for data and power and is also Internet accessible through wireless connectivity. The building is crowned with a conference center and rooftop terrace that is perfect for congregating students as well as for campus events.

The college is also the home of the First and Fourteenth Texas Courts of Appeals, distinguishing South Texas as one of only two American law schools housing appellate courts on a permanent basis.

Financial Assistance

South Texas offers an extensive financial aid program, in terms of both scholarships and outside funding options. Depending on their qualifications, Texas residents are eligible for state and federal tuition assistance grants, which have amounted to as much as several thousand dollars in prior years. In addition, the Office of Scholarships and Financial Aid administers financial assistance through the Federal Work-Study Program, federal and private loans, and a variety of scholarship offerings.

Incoming students are considered for merit scholarships based on UGPA and LSAT. Continuing students are eligible for both merit- and need-based scholarships. Contact the Office of Scholarships and Financial Aid for eligibility and documentation requirements at 713.646.1820.

Career Services

In light of today's competitive job market, the Career Resources Center (CRC) continues to provide South Texas students and graduates with a full range of services to assist in their employment search, while at the same time being responsive to the changes in hiring trends and patterns. The office serves as a counseling and resource center for students seeking employment on either a full- or part-time basis and assists graduates pursuing permanent employment. In addition to on-campus recruiting, the CRC also offers an array of professional development programs and career panels designed to assist students in their job-search preparation and networking. The objective of the CRC staff is to aid students in exploring career options, while helping them build valuable job-search skills utilizing their strengths and abilities. By taking advantage of the many programs and services offered by the CRC, students are better equipped to maximize their career-planning opportunities.

APPLICANT PROFILE

South Texas College of Law
This grid includes only applicants who earned 120–180 LSAT scores under standard administrations.

LSAT Score	3.75 +		3.50–3.74		3.25–3.49		3.00–3.24		2.75–2.99		2.50–2.74		2.25–2.49		2.00–2.24		Below 2.00		No GPA		Total	
	Apps	Adm	Apps	Adm	Apps	Adm	Apps	Adm	Apps	Adm	Apps	Adm	Apps	Adm	Apps	Adm	Apps	Adm	Apps	Adm	Apps	Adm
170–180	1	1	0	0	4	4	1	1	0	0	0	0	1	0	0	0	0	0	0	0	7	6
165–169	2	2	2	2	9	8	8	8	3	3	2	2	3	0	1	0	0	0	1	0	31	25
160–164	14	14	34	33	46	45	29	29	26	16	12	5	8	3	4	1	0	0	2	1	175	147
155–159	42	41	67	64	93	84	96	86	40	32	42	22	18	5	11	3	4	0	6	1	419	338
150–154	39	34	105	90	122	111	143	90	120	51	65	15	38	6	12	1	5	0	4	3	653	401
145–149	30	6	58	13	124	19	106	5	95	10	54	2	36	0	17	1	2	0	7	0	529	56
140–144	9	0	18	0	41	1	45	1	47	0	43	1	18	1	9	0	2	0	8	0	240	4
Below 140	5	0	8	0	10	0	32	0	22	0	29	0	16	0	10	0	2	0	9	0	143	0
Total	142	98	292	202	449	272	460	220	353	112	247	47	138	15	64	6	15	0	37	5	2197	977

Apps = Number of Applicants
Adm = Number Admitted
Reflects 99% of the total applicant pool; highest LSAT data reported.

UNIVERSITY OF SOUTHERN CALIFORNIA, GOULD SCHOOL OF LAW

699 Exposition Boulevard
Los Angeles, CA 90089-0074
Phone: 213.740.2523; Fax: 213.740.4570
E-mail: admissions@law.usc.edu; Website: www.law.usc.edu

ABA
Approved
Since
1924

The Basics

Type of school	Private
Term	Semester
Application deadline	2/1
Application fee	$75
Financial aid deadline	3/1
Can first year start other than fall?	No
Student to faculty ratio	12.8 to 1
# of housing spaces available restricted to law students	1
graduate housing for which law students are eligible	46

Faculty and Administrators

	Total		Men		Women		Minorities	
	Spr	Fall	Spr	Fall	Spr	Fall	Spr	Fall
Full-time	42	41	27	25	15	16	12	9
Other full-time	1	2	0	0	1	2	0	0
Deans, librarians, & others who teach	18	16	6	6	12	10	5	4
Part-time	73	50	50	30	23	20	17	13
Total	134	109	83	61	51	48	34	26

JD Enrollment and Ethnicity

	Men		Women		Full-Time		Part-Time		1st-Year		Total		JD Degs. Awd.
	#	%	#	%	#	%	#	%	#	%	#	%	
All Hispanics	36	10.6	31	9.9	67	10.3	0	0.0	20	9.2	67	10.3	21
Am. Ind./AK Nat.	3	0.9	0	0.0	3	0.5	0	0.0	2	0.9	3	0.5	3
Asian	57	16.8	75	24.0	132	20.3	0	0.0	34	15.6	132	20.3	34
Black/Af. Am.	17	5.0	31	9.9	48	7.4	0	0.0	19	8.7	48	7.4	15
Nat. HI/Pac. Isl.	0	0.0	0	0.0	0	0.0	0	0.0	0	0.0	0	0.0	0
2 or more races	5	1.5	13	4.2	18	2.8	0	0.0	10	4.6	18	2.8	0
Subtotal (minor.)	118	34.8	150	48.1	268	41.2	0	0.0	85	39.0	268	41.2	79
Nonres. Alien	3	0.9	6	1.9	9	1.4	0	0.0	2	0.9	9	1.4	0
White/Cauc.	179	52.8	126	40.4	305	46.9	0	0.0	120	55.0	305	46.9	96
Unknown	39	11.5	30	9.6	69	10.6	0	0.0	11	5.0	69	10.6	15
Total	339	52.1	312	47.9	651	100.0	0	0.0	218	33.5	651		196

Curriculum

	Full-Time	Part-Time
Typical first-year section size	70	0
Is there typically a "small section" of the first-year class, other than Legal Writing, taught by full-time faculty	Yes	No
If yes, typical size offered last year	35	
# of classroom course titles beyond first-year curriculum	111	

# of upper division courses, excluding seminars, with an enrollment:	Under 25	77
	25–49	33
	50–74	7
	75–99	4
	100+	8

# of seminars	36	
# of seminar positions available	420	
# of seminar positions filled	219	0
# of positions available in simulation courses	483	
# of simulation positions filled	388	0
# of positions available in faculty supervised clinical courses	74	
# of faculty supervised clinical positions filled	69	0
# involved in field placements	133	0
# involved in law journals	163	0
# involved in moot court or trial competitions	56	0
# of credit hours required to graduate	88	

Transfers

Transfers in	18
Transfers out	8

Tuition and Fees

	Resident	Nonresident
Full-time	$48,434	$48,434
Part-time		
Tuition Guarantee Program	N	

Living Expenses

Estimated living expenses for singles

Living on campus	Living off campus	Living at home
$21,768	$21,768	$10,968

UNIVERSITY OF SOUTHERN CALIFORNIA, GOULD SCHOOL OF LAW

*ABA
Approved
Since
1924*

GPA and LSAT Scores

	Total	Full-Time	Part-Time
# of apps	6,587	6,587	0
# of offers	1,435	1,435	0
# of matrics	220	220	0
75% GPA	3.73	3.73	0.00
Median GPA	3.64	3.64	0.00
25% GPA	3.46	3.46	0.00
75% LSAT	169	169	0
Median LSAT	167	167	0
25% LSAT	166	166	0

Grants and Scholarships (from prior year)

	Total		Full-Time		Part-Time	
	#	%	#	%	#	%
Total # of students	618		618		0	
Total # receiving grants	379	61.3	379	61.3	0	0.0
Less than 1/2 tuition	335	54.2	335	54.2	0	0.0
Half to full tuition	31	5.0	31	5.0	0	0.0
Full tuition	8	1.3	8	1.3	0	0.0
More than full tuition	5	0.8	5	0.8	0	0.0
Median grant amount			$12,100		$0	

Informational and Library Resources

Total amount spent on library materials	$1,100,036
Study seating capacity inside the library	230
# of full-time equivalent professional librarians	9
Hours per week library is open	100
# of open, wired connections available to students	42
# of networked computers available for use by students	110
Has wireless network?	Y
Requires computer?	N

JD Attrition (from prior year)

	Academic	Other	Total	
	#	#	#	%
1st year	1	1	2	0.9
2nd year	0	9	9	4.2
3rd year	0	0	0	0.0
4th year	0	0	0	0.0

Employment (9 months after graduation)

	Total	Percentage
Employment status known	205	98.1
Employment status unknown	4	1.9
Employed	195	95.1
Pursuing graduate degrees	2	1.0
Unemployed (seeking, not seeking, or studying for the bar)	4	2.0
Type of Employment		
# employed in law firms	153	78.5
# employed in business and industry	11	5.6
# employed in government	10	5.1
# employed in public interest	6	3.1
# employed as judicial clerks	8	4.1
# employed in academia	6	3.1
Geographic Location		
# employed in state	168	86.2
# employed outside the US	1	0.5
# of states where employed	9	

Bar Passage Rates

First-time takers	205	Reporting %	90.24
Average school %	90.81	Average state %	73.19
Average pass difference	17.62		

Jurisdiction	Takers	Passers	Pass %	State %	Diff %
California	185	168	90.81	73.19	17.62

UNIVERSITY OF SOUTHERN CALIFORNIA, GOULD SCHOOL OF LAW

699 Exposition Boulevard
Los Angeles, CA 90089-0074
Phone: 213.740.2523; Fax: 213.740.4570
E-mail: admissions@law.usc.edu; Website: www.law.usc.edu

Introduction

The University of Southern California, Gould School of Law is a private, highly selective national law school with over a 105-year history and a reputation for academic excellence. Under the leadership of a stellar, energetic faculty, the school's rigorous, interdisciplinary program focuses on the law as an expression of social values and an instrument for implementing social goals. USC is known for its diverse student body, its leadership in clinical education, and its tight-knit alumni network composed of national leaders in the legal profession, business, and the public sector. With 210 entering students in each class, the school is small, informal, and collegial.

USC Law School is located on the beautiful 226-acre main campus of the University of Southern California, just south of downtown Los Angeles and in the heart of the city's exciting Arts and Entertainment Corridor. The campus offers a lush, park-like atmosphere within a bustling urban setting. A dynamic laboratory for legal training, Los Angeles is a center of state, national, and international commerce and government, and the city's legal market is among the most extensive in the world. The law school is housed in a five-level facility that provides a superb setting for professional training and sophisticated legal research.

Curriculum

USC's curriculum is comprehensive, uniquely interdisciplinary, and designed to challenge. Courses provide a solid foundation in all substantive areas of law as well as extensive opportunities to explore specializations in traditional and emerging fields. Many faculty members have expertise in both law and other disciplines, such as economics, communication, public policy, medicine, history, psychology, and philosophy. The first-year curriculum consists of courses that examine the foundation of the legal system. The second and third years of study allow students to pursue individual interests in areas such as international law, intellectual property, entertainment law, corporations and business-government relationships, taxation, bioethics, civil rights and liberties, and judicial administration.

Special Programs

Dual Degrees: The law school offers 15 dual-degree programs in coordination with USC graduate and professional schools, the California Institute of Technology, and the London School of Economics. These programs enable qualified students to earn a law degree and a master's degree in the following fields: Business Administration, Business Taxation, Economics, Communications Management, Gerontology, International Relations, Philosophy, Political Science, Public Administration, Public Policy, Real Estate Development, and Social Work. A JD/PharmD program and a JD/PhD program in Social Science with the California Institute of Technology, as well as a JD/LLM with the London School of Economics, are also offered.

Legal Clinics: The nationally recognized Post-Conviction Justice Project, the Employer Legal Advice Clinic, the Small Business Clinic, and the Immigration Clinic enable students to gain valuable advocacy and lawyering skills by representing real clients under faculty supervision. Students in the Intellectual Property and Technology Law Clinic review

technology contracts, engage in patent evaluation and application, assist with litigation, and perform film clearance work. Students in the International Human Rights Clinic work on projects and cases both locally and internationally that confront the most pressing human rights concerns of our day.

Public Service Programs: The Office of Public Service provides comprehensive opportunities and coordination for all external service learning and community service. These opportunities include more than 60 clinical field placements, allowing students to earn academic credit while engaging in service learning at government and public interest agencies and with federal and state judges, as well as pro bono and community service in the surrounding Los Angeles neighborhoods.

International Programs: USC offers students several opportunities to study abroad. Students can participate in the law school's semester abroad exchange program with the University of Hong Kong, Bocconi University (Italy), University Jean Moulin Lyon 3 (France), and Bond University (Australia). The law school also offers a one-year dual-degree program (JD/LLM) with the London School of Economics. Moreover, students may participate in programs offered around the world by other ABA-approved law schools.

Research Centers: Law students participate in the scholarly activities of several interdisciplinary research centers: the Pacific Center for Health Policy and Ethics; Saks Institute for Mental Health Law, Policy, and Ethics; the Center in Law, Economics, and Organization; the USC-Caltech Center for the Study of Law and Politics; the Center for Law, History, and Culture; and the Center for Law and Philosophy.

Continuing Legal Education: Students help coordinate the law school's practice-oriented programs and serve as research assistants for the Institute on Entertainment Law and Business, Institute on Taxation, Institute on Trusts and Estates, Real Estate Law and Business Conference, Corporate Counsel Institute, and the Intellectual Property Institute.

Student Activities and Cocurricular Programs

Academic life is exciting and fast-paced, and students are often engaged in numerous scholarly pursuits and cocurricular programs. The *Southern California Law Review* has one of the largest circulations in the country. Students also publish the *Southern California Interdisciplinary Law Journal* and the *Southern California Review of Law and Social Justice.* The Moot Court Honors Program sends participants to national and state competitions.

Public service activities abound. The Public Interest Law Foundation is one of the largest in the country, providing summer grants for public service employment as well as the Irmas Fellowship for public interest law, which awards a year's salary to a third-year student committed to postgraduate work in public interest.

The diversity of USC Law School's student population is reflected in nearly 40 political, religious, social, cultural, and ethnic organizations. Our students play an active and valued role in the day-to-day operation of the law school, including service on faculty committees. Students are given a wide range of opportunities to create and implement ideas for activities and are encouraged to pursue their interests by forming new student organizations or planning social or academic events. Asian, African American, Muslim, Middle

Eastern, Jewish, and Latino law students are represented by associations. Other student organizations include the Student Bar Association, international and entertainment law societies, Art Law Society, Women's Law Association, OUTLaw, Legal Aid Alternative Breaks Project, Christian Legal Society, Public Interest Law Foundation, Health Law and Bioethics Society, Corporate Law Society, Intellectual Property and Technology Law Society, Street Law, Sports Law, Trial Lawyers, and chapters of the ACLU and the Federalist Society.

Professional Careers

USC graduates accept job offers in all regions of the country, with New York and Washington, DC, being the most popular placement locations outside the West Coast. A number of graduates begin their professional careers as judicial law clerks to federal and state judges. Each year, several hundred private firms, government agencies, public interest organizations, and corporations from throughout the country come to USC to recruit students for summer and permanent employment. An off-campus recruiting program helps coordinate interviews with East Coast employers. The school's enthusiastic network of alumni is a valuable tool in the job-search process. The Alumni Mentor Lunch provides first-year students with the opportunity to meet graduates who practice in the student's field of interest, and other programs bring alumni from a range of fields to campus to discuss career opportunities. Overall placement statistics are consistently strong; historically, more than 96 percent of each graduating class finds employment within nine months of graduation. Average starting salaries are among the highest in the nation.

Housing

Graduate law housing is available in an apartment-style residence located within easy walking distance of the law school for a limited number of incoming students. The two-bedroom apartments are fully furnished and equipped with Internet access. A roommate referral service is available to help incoming students arrange shared housing in various Los Angeles neighborhoods.

Admission and Financial Aid

Admission decisions are made on the basis of the student's academic record, LSAT score and writing sample, personal statement, letters of recommendation, résumé, extracurricular activities, and other information in the file. The Admissions Committee gives primary consideration to outstanding academic and professional promise and to qualities that will enhance the diversity of the student body or enrich the law school educational environment. Two letters of recommendation are required; applicants are strongly urged to submit at least one academic recommendation letter. The law school operates on a semester basis and admits only full-time students. USC is committed to helping students successfully finance their legal education. In addition to various loan programs, the law school offers substantial scholarship awards to a large percentage of the incoming class. Most scholarships are based on merit as evidenced by strong academic credentials and test scores. In addition, the school offers a Loan Repayment Assistance Program which assists graduates who accept employment with governmental agencies and public interest organizations that traditionally offer lower pay than private firms.

APPLICANT PROFILE

University of Southern California, Gould School of Law
This grid includes only applicants who earned 120–180 LSAT scores under standard administrations.

LSAT Score	3.75 +		3.50–3.74		3.25–3.49		3.00–3.24		2.75–2.99		Below 2.75		No GPA		Total	
	Apps	Adm	Apps	Adm	Apps	Adm	Apps	Adm	Apps	Adm	Apps	Adm	Apps	Adm	Apps	Adm
175–180	58	54	39	34	31	8	12	0	5	1	2	0	2	1	149	98
170–174	221	200	244	188	127	36	63	7	29	0	13	0	13	2	710	433
165–169	584	367	657	327	340	45	176	10	56	2	30	1	29	0	1872	752
160–164	428	38	576	35	407	25	202	8	66	2	42	0	39	1	1760	109
155–159	165	10	255	16	220	11	137	1	56	0	52	0	19	0	904	38
150–154	63	0	127	0	122	0	105	0	80	0	56	0	17	0	570	0
Below 150	26	0	74	0	123	0	133	0	90	0	123	0	24	0	593	0
Total	1545	669	1972	600	1370	125	828	26	382	5	318	1	143	4	6558	1430

Apps = Number of Applicants
Adm = Number Admitted
Reflects 99% of the total applicant pool; highest LSAT data reported.

SOUTHERN ILLINOIS UNIVERSITY SCHOOL OF LAW

School of Law Welcome Center, 1209 W. Chautauqua, Mailcode 6811
Carbondale, IL 62901
Phone: 800.739.9187 or 618.453.8858; Fax: 618.453.8921
E-mail: lawadmit@siu.edu; Website: www.law.siu.edu

ABA
Approved
Since
1974

The Basics

Type of school	Public
Term	Semester
Application deadline	4/1
Application fee	
Financial aid deadline	4/1
Can first year start other than fall?	No
Student to faculty ratio	12.2 to 1
# of housing spaces available restricted to law students	
graduate housing for which law students are eligible	360

Faculty and Administrators

	Total		Men		Women		Minorities	
	Spr	Fall	Spr	Fall	Spr	Fall	Spr	Fall
Full-time	24	26	10	13	14	13	3	4
Other full-time	0	1	0	0	0	1	0	0
Deans, librarians, & others who teach	8	8	6	5	2	3	1	1
Part-time	10	6	6	3	4	3	0	0
Total	42	41	22	21	20	20	4	5

Curriculum

	Full-Time	Part-Time
Typical first-year section size	68	0
Is there typically a "small section" of the first-year class, other than Legal Writing, taught by full-time faculty	No	No
If yes, typical size offered last year		
# of classroom course titles beyond first-year curriculum	72	

# of upper division courses, excluding seminars, with an enrollment:		
	Under 25	77
	25–49	23
	50–74	11
	75–99	0
	100+	0

# of seminars	10	
# of seminar positions available	123	
# of seminar positions filled	88	0
# of positions available in simulation courses	540	
# of simulation positions filled	276	
# of positions available in faculty supervised clinical courses	56	
# of faculty supervised clinical positions filled	44	0
# involved in field placements	94	0
# involved in law journals	59	0
# involved in moot court or trial competitions	30	0
# of credit hours required to graduate	90	

JD Enrollment and Ethnicity

	Men #	Men %	Women #	Women %	Full-Time #	Full-Time %	Part-Time #	Part-Time %	1st-Year #	1st-Year %	Total #	Total %	JD Degs. Awd.
All Hispanics	5	2.1	1	0.7	6	1.6	0	0.0	3	2.1	6	1.6	5
Am. Ind./AK Nat.	2	0.8	3	2.1	5	1.3	0	0.0	4	2.8	5	1.3	1
Asian	7	3.0	5	3.4	12	3.2	0	0.0	6	4.2	12	3.1	4
Black/Af. Am.	4	1.7	6	4.1	10	2.6	0	0.0	3	2.1	10	2.6	3
Nat. HI/Pac. Isl.	1	0.4	0	0.0	1	0.3	0	0.0	1	0.7	1	0.3	0
2 or more races	0	0.0	0	0.0	0	0.0	0	0.0	0	0.0	0	0.0	0
Subtotal (minor.)	19	8.0	15	10.3	34	8.9	0	0.0	17	11.8	34	8.9	13
Nonres. Alien	0	0.0	0	0.0	0	0.0	0	0.0	0	0.0	0	0.0	0
White/Cauc.	204	86.1	120	82.8	322	84.7	2	100.0	119	82.6	324	84.8	118
Unknown	14	5.9	10	6.9	24	6.3	0	0.0	8	5.6	24	6.3	4
Total	237	62.0	145	38.0	380	99.5	2	0.5	144	37.7	382		135

Transfers

Transfers in	4
Transfers out	6

Tuition and Fees

	Resident	Nonresident
Full-time	$14,746	$33,097
Part-time		
Tuition Guarantee Program		N

Living Expenses

Estimated living expenses for singles

Living on campus	Living off campus	Living at home
$14,546	$14,546	$5,322

ABA Approved Since 1974

GPA and LSAT Scores

	Total	Full-Time	Part-Time
# of apps	658	658	0
# of offers	364	364	0
# of matrics	144	144	0
75% GPA	3.60	3.60	0.00
Median GPA	3.30	3.30	0.00
25% GPA	3.00	3.00	0.00
75% LSAT	157	157	0
Median LSAT	153	153	0
25% LSAT	151	151	0

Grants and Scholarships (from prior year)

	Total		Full-Time		Part-Time	
	#	%	#	%	#	%
Total # of students	383		382		1	
Total # receiving grants	171	44.6	171	44.8	0	0.0
Less than 1/2 tuition	109	28.5	109	28.5	0	0.0
Half to full tuition	46	12.0	46	12.0	0	0.0
Full tuition	12	3.1	12	3.1	0	0.0
More than full tuition	4	1.0	4	1.0	0	0.0
Median grant amount			$5,110		$0	

Informational and Library Resources

Total amount spent on library materials	$773,272
Study seating capacity inside the library	349
# of full-time equivalent professional librarians	5
Hours per week library is open	78
# of open, wired connections available to students	12
# of networked computers available for use by students	53
Has wireless network?	Y
Requires computer?	N

JD Attrition (from prior year)

	Academic	Other	Total	
	#	#	#	%
1st year	3	14	17	12.6
2nd year	1	0	1	0.9
3rd year	0	0	0	0.0
4th year	0	0	0	0.0

Employment (9 months after graduation)

	Total	Percentage
Employment status known	113	100.0
Employment status unknown	0	0.0
Employed	83	73.5
Pursuing graduate degrees	10	8.8
Unemployed (seeking, not seeking, or studying for the bar)	20	17.7
Type of Employment		
# employed in law firms	49	59.0
# employed in business and industry	8	9.6
# employed in government	15	18.1
# employed in public interest	3	3.6
# employed as judicial clerks	5	6.0
# employed in academia	3	3.6
Geographic Location		
# employed in state	46	55.4
# employed outside the US	0	0.0
# of states where employed		15

Bar Passage Rates

First-time takers	114	Reporting %	76.32
Average school %	90.80	Average state %	91.03
Average pass difference	−0.23		

Jurisdiction	Takers	Passers	Pass %	State %	Diff %
Illinois	74	67	90.54	90.89	−0.35
Missouri	13	12	92.31	91.81	0.50

SOUTHERN ILLINOIS UNIVERSITY SCHOOL OF LAW

School of Law Welcome Center, 1209 W. Chautauqua, Mailcode 6811
Carbondale, IL 62901
Phone: 800.739.9187 or 618.453.8858; Fax: 618.453.8921
E-mail: lawadmit@siu.edu; Website: www.law.siu.edu

Introduction

The School of Law is located on the campus of Southern Illinois University Carbondale, a 142-year-old university with a tradition of excellence as well as a diverse, multicultural student body of approximately 20,000. Carbondale, a community of 27,000 people, is one of the most scenic areas of Illinois. National forests, state parks, historic sites, campgrounds, theaters, festivals, and cultural events make Carbondale's quality of life among the highest in small cities in Illinois. The 12:1 student-to-faculty ratio at the School of Law is among the best in the nation. The School of Law is fully accredited by the ABA and is a member of the AALS.

Curriculum

All students have a uniform first-year curriculum. A broad range of courses are offered in the second and third years. The School of Law is at the forefront of legal education in providing a strong **Writing Across the Curriculum** program. Our students acquire strong legal writing skills by practicing those skills in every course in the law school and receiving substantial constructive critiques of their work throughout the three-year curriculum.

An innovative and **nationally recognized first-year Lawyering Skills Program** gives students a solid foundation in basic lawyering skills, including legal research and writing, oral advocacy, client interviewing and counseling, and negotiation. In addition, the school has a strong health law curriculum and is the site for the National Health Law Moot Court Competition as well as a Center for Health Law and Policy. The school also has groups of courses in trial/litigation skills, intellectual property, and criminal, labor, corporate, family, international, and environmental law.

After three years of intensive education in **theory and skills**, graduates are prepared to not only pass the bar, but also to begin their careers with confidence in the skills they have learned and practiced while in law school.

Special Programs

Clinical programs enable senior law students to represent clients under the supervision of licensed attorneys. The Civil Practice/Elder Clinic provides direct legal assistance to persons 60 years of age and older in the 13 southernmost counties of Illinois. Students may participate in the Public Interest or Judicial Externship Program and obtain academic credit while working at nonprofit, local, state, federal legal, or judicial offices. The Domestic Violence Clinic provides legal assistance to victims of domestic violence. Students can also gain valuable experience through work in the award-winning Self Help Legal Center.

Three semester-away programs allow second- and third-year students the opportunity to spend a semester living and working in different locations. The **Law and Government** program, located in the Illinois state capital of Springfield, focuses on state and local government. The **Criminal Trial Practice Program**, located in southeast Missouri, provides hands-on experience with the Missouri Public Defender System. The **Health Law and Policy Program** offers students the opportunity to engage with state and not-for-profit entities in the health care field in Springfield, Illinois.

The school provides a comprehensive **trial and appellate moot court** program with teams that have successfully competed in the McGee National Civil Rights Moot Court, ABA Moot Court, and Darras Disability Law Moot Court competitions. The school also holds an annual intramural Appellate Moot Court Competition.

All entering law students are assigned to a study group and an upper-level law student tutor as part of the **Academic Success** program and participate in the **Professionalism and the Law** class. Both programs give students additional tools and skills necessary in the legal profession. The Professionalism class grew out of the SIU School of Law Professional Development program, which was awarded the coveted E. Smythe Gambrell Award from the American Bar Association. The law school was recognized for its design and implementation of a model professionalism program for law students.

The School of Law sponsors two annual **lecture series**: the Hiram H. Lesar Distinguished Lecture Series and the Dr. Arthur Grayson Distinguished Lecture Series. Past speakers include Governor Douglas Wilder, Morris Dees, and Hans Blix. In addition, the school cosponsors an annual health law symposium and the Health Policy Institute, that attract health law policy experts from across the country.

The School of Law has partnered with the University of Missouri—Kansas City to offer students a four-week study-abroad program in Ireland. The program allows students to receive six elective credit hours and the chance to study at some of Ireland's preeminent institutions.

A variety of **concurrent JD/master's degree programs** in accountancy, business administration, education, electrical and computer engineering, public administration, and social work are offered in conjunction with the graduate school. A concurrent PhD program is available in political science. A six-year program offered in cooperation with the School of Medicine permits students to concurrently obtain JD and MD degrees.

A Master of Legal Studies (MLS) program and Master of Laws (LLM) program are also available.

Library and Physical Facilities

Southern Illinois University School of Law's primary facility is the Lesar Law Building, housing the classrooms, courtroom, auditorium, faculty offices, and law library. Because the number of activities and services has expanded since the main building was completed in 1981, some offices are located in two nearby buildings. Both additional facilities are in immediate proximity to the Lesar Law Building, creating an informal law school campus within the broader university grounds. All together, the facilities offer over 100,000 square feet of space.

Law students enjoy **24-hour access to the law library**, which has ample study space. In addition to a rich print and microform collection, the law library has evolved to meet the changing nature of legal research and user expectations by providing wireless access to a wide array of electronic legal materials. Law students also have virtual as well as physical access to the university's Morris Library, which houses a major research collection and is located within walking distance of the law school. The law library employs a friendly and welcoming staff who interact on a first-name basis with law students. The law librarians are committed to teaching law students the fundamentals of legal research formally, by co-teaching the Lawyering Skills first-year course, and informally, through their interactions at the reference desk. Additionally, the law librarians offer an advanced legal research course for upper-level students.

Student Activities

The school publishes the *SIU Law Journal*, which provides editorial and writing experience for a number of upper-class students. Students with a particular interest in health law can also publish articles in the *Journal of Legal Medicine*. As mentioned in the Special Programs section, the school provides a comprehensive **trial and appellate moot court** program as well as an annual intramural Appellate Moot Court Competition.

All students belong to the Student Bar Association (SBA). The SBA serves as a channel of communication between students and faculty. In addition to providing services to its members, SBA schedules lectures and coordinates two major social events annually including Barristers Ball and Chili Trivia. Students play an active role in law school governance, serving on most faculty committees. Past and current student organizations include Equal Justice Works, Phi Alpha Delta, International Law Society, Women's Law Forum, Environmental Law Society, Parents as Law Students, Animal Legal Defense Fund, Business Law Society, Black Law Student Association, Federalist Society, Law School Democrats, Law School Republicans, Media Law Society, Lesbian and Gay Law Students and Supporters, Sports Law Society, Phi Delta Phi, Law and Medicine Society, Christian Legal Society, Decalogue Society, Employment and Labor Law Association, Justinian Society, Military Law Society, Hispanic Law Student Association, Asian American Law Student Association, Alternative Dispute Resolution Student Society, J. Reuben Clark Law Society, and law student divisions of the Illinois State Bar Association and the American Bar Association.

Career Services

School of Law graduates find employment nationwide, with **alumni in 49 states and several foreign countries**, including

Austria, Belgium, Canada, Hong Kong, Japan, Puerto Rico, Ukraine, and the Virgin Islands. School of Law graduates continue to excel with average bar passage rates at or above the state and national averages. The Office of Career Services provides services for both enrolled students and alumni, including individual career counseling, on-campus interviews, career workshops, and more. Students have the opportunity to participate in a variety of regional and national job fairs and career conferences. The Career Library contains diverse career materials, including national and international directories, judicial clerkship information, and government and public interest job information. Students can contact the Office of Career Services at 618.453.8707 or by e-mail at lawjobs@siu.edu.

Expenses, Scholarships, and Financial Aid

Financial support from the State of Illinois combined with a generous program of scholarships for both incoming and current students allow graduates of the SIU School of Law to enjoy an **average debt load** that is **below the national law school average**. Students can qualify for the in-state resident tuition rate after they have been an Illinois resident for six consecutive months. Student loans and work study opportunities are administered by the university's Financial Aid Office. Information concerning in-state resident applications, loans, and financial aid procedures may be obtained from the Office of Admission at 618.453.8858 or by e-mail at lawadmit@siu.edu.

Admission

Admission decisions are based on a number of factors. Although the LSAT score and undergraduate GPA are important, non-numerical factors are considered as well. For repeat test takers, the **highest LSAT score** is used for both admission and scholarship purposes. Other factors considered by the Admission Committee include trends in academic performance, writing ability, leadership and maturity, letters of recommendation, work experience, community and public service, and obstacles imposed by religious, ethnic, gender, or disability discrimination.

APPLICANT PROFILE

Southern Illinois University School of Law
This grid includes only applicants who earned 120–180 LSAT scores under standard administrations.

LSAT Score	GPA							
	3.75 or Above	3.50–3.74	3.25–3.49	3.00–3.24	2.75–2.99	2.50–2.74	2.25–2.49	2.24 or Below
165 or Above								
160–164								
158–159								
156–157								
155								
154								
153								
152								
Below 152								

■ Probable   ▨ Competitive   ☐ Unlikely

This grid reflects the highest LSAT score of the applicant.

SOUTHERN UNIVERSITY LAW CENTER

Admission Office, PO Box 9294
Baton Rouge, LA 70813
Phone: 225.771.4976 or 800.537.1135; Fax: 225.771.2121
E-mail: admission@sulc.edu; Website: www.sulc.edu

ABA Approved Since 1953

The Basics

Type of school	Public
Term	Semester
Application deadline	2/28 5/1
Application fee	$25
Financial aid deadline	4/15
Can first year start other than fall?	No
Student to faculty ratio	14.1 to 1
# of housing spaces available restricted to law students	
graduate housing for which law students are eligible	5

Faculty and Administrators

	Total		Men		Women		Minorities	
	Spr	Fall	Spr	Fall	Spr	Fall	Spr	Fall
Full-time	34	34	15	15	19	19	21	21
Other full-time	1	1	0	0	1	1	1	1
Deans, librarians, & others who teach	5	5	4	4	1	1	5	5
Part-time	20	22	14	12	6	9	12	13
Total	60	62	33	31	27	30	39	40

Curriculum

		Full-Time	Part-Time
Typical first-year section size		55	38
Is there typically a "small section" of the first-year class, other than Legal Writing, taught by full-time faculty		Yes	Yes
If yes, typical size offered last year		20	20
# of classroom course titles beyond first-year curriculum		50	
# of upper division courses, excluding seminars, with an enrollment:	Under 25	12	
	25–49	27	
	50–74	9	
	75–99	0	
	100+	0	
# of seminars		9	
# of seminar positions available		148	
# of seminar positions filled		132	16
# of positions available in simulation courses		224	
# of simulation positions filled		182	42
# of positions available in faculty supervised clinical courses		134	
# of faculty supervised clinical positions filled		69	55
# involved in field placements		9	0
# involved in law journals		40	5
# involved in moot court or trial competitions		8	4
# of credit hours required to graduate		96	

JD Enrollment and Ethnicity

	Men		Women		Full-Time		Part-Time		1st-Year		Total		JD Degs. Awd.
	#	%	#	%	#	%	#	%	#	%	#	%	
All Hispanics	18	5.5	33	8.4	13	2.7	38	16.2	51	15.9	51	7.1	3
Am. Ind./AK Nat.	2	0.6	0	0.0	2	0.4	0	0.0	2	0.6	2	0.3	0
Asian	3	0.9	2	0.5	2	0.4	3	1.3	1	0.3	5	0.7	0
Black/Af. Am.	160	49.1	251	63.5	288	59.3	123	52.3	171	53.4	411	57.0	72
Nat. HI/Pac. Isl.	0	0.0	0	0.0	0	0.0	0	0.0	0	0.0	0	0.0	0
2 or more races	1	0.3	0	0.0	1	0.2	0	0.0	1	0.3	1	0.1	0
Subtotal (minor.)	184	56.4	286	72.4	306	63.0	164	69.8	226	70.6	470	65.2	75
Nonres. Alien	0	0.0	0	0.0	0	0.0	0	0.0	0	0.0	0	0.0	0
White/Cauc.	139	42.6	108	27.3	176	36.2	71	30.2	90	28.1	247	34.3	59
Unknown	3	0.9	1	0.3	4	0.8	0	0.0	4	1.3	4	0.6	0
Total	326	45.2	395	54.8	486	67.4	235	32.6	320	44.4	721		134

Transfers

Transfers in	1
Transfers out	9

Tuition and Fees

	Resident	Nonresident
Full-time	$8,478	$13,080
Part-time	$7,168	$11,768
Tuition Guarantee Program	Y	

Living Expenses

Estimated living expenses for singles

Living on campus	Living off campus	Living at home
$18,450	$18,450	$18,450

*ABA
Approved
Since
1953*

GPA and LSAT Scores

	Total	Full-Time	Part-Time
# of apps	1,330	1,077	253
# of offers	520	397	123
# of matrics	320	229	91
75% GPA	3.08	3.14	3.04
Median GPA	2.69	2.86	2.77
25% GPA	2.56	2.61	2.45
75% LSAT	148	148	148
Median LSAT	145	145	144
25% LSAT	143	143	142

Grants and Scholarships (from prior year)

	Total		Full-Time		Part-Time	
	#	%	#	%	#	%
Total # of students	598		431		167	
Total # receiving grants	156	26.1	156	36.2	0	0.0
Less than 1/2 tuition	89	14.9	89	20.6	0	0.0
Half to full tuition	43	7.2	43	10.0	0	0.0
Full tuition	0	0.0	0	0.0	0	0.0
More than full tuition	24	4.0	24	5.6	0	0.0
Median grant amount			$1,756		$0	

Informational and Library Resources

Total amount spent on library materials	$756,153
Study seating capacity inside the library	285
# of full-time equivalent professional librarians	3
Hours per week library is open	99
# of open, wired connections available to students	4
# of networked computers available for use by students	43
Has wireless network?	Y
Requires computer?	N

JD Attrition (from prior year)

	Academic	Other	Total	
	#	#	#	%
1st year	30	22	52	21.8
2nd year	0	0	0	0.0
3rd year	0	1	1	0.5
4th year	0	0	0	0.0

Employment (9 months after graduation)

	Total	Percentage
Employment status known	124	100.0
Employment status unknown	0	0.0
Employed	114	91.9
Pursuing graduate degrees	2	1.6
Unemployed (seeking, not seeking, or studying for the bar)	8	6.5
Type of Employment		
# employed in law firms	50	43.9
# employed in business and industry	15	13.2
# employed in government	27	23.7
# employed in public interest	4	3.5
# employed as judicial clerks	16	14.0
# employed in academia	2	1.8
Geographic Location		
# employed in state	92	80.7
# employed outside the US	1	0.9
# of states where employed	10	

Bar Passage Rates

First-time takers	104	Reporting %	100.00
Average school %	63.46	Average state %	73.73
Average pass difference	−10.27		

Jurisdiction	Takers	Passers	Pass %	State %	Diff %
Louisiana	104	66	63.46	73.73	−10.27

SOUTHERN UNIVERSITY LAW CENTER

Admission Office, PO Box 9294
Baton Rouge, LA 70813
Phone: 225.771.4976 or 800.537.1135; Fax: 225.771.2121
E-mail: admission@sulc.edu; Website: www.sulc.edu

Introduction

In September 1947, the Southern University school of law was officially opened, and it was redesignated as a law center in 1985. Accredited by the American Bar Association, the Supreme Court of Louisiana, and the Southern Association of Colleges and Secondary Schools, the Law Center maintains a high standard of professional education. It is fully approved by the Veterans Administration for the training of eligible veterans. The Southern University Law Center adheres to the principle of equal opportunity without regard to ethnicity, gender, creed, national origin, age, disability, or marital status.

The Law Center is located in Baton Rouge, the capital of Louisiana. With a population of over 600,000, this seat of state government includes state agencies and courts. As a hub of legal activity, Baton Rouge offers law students many opportunities to participate in state government through interaction with the legislature, state agencies, and private law firms.

Library

The law library contains more than 450,000 volumes, 1,000,000 microfiche, 40,000 rolls of microfilm, and 800 law reviews. The library offers research assistance and reference services to students, faculty, and the public. Its collection adequately supports the curriculum and conforms to the standards of the American Bar Association. Both federal and Louisiana state governments have designated Southern University Law Center Library as an official depository for government documents. A complete collection of Louisiana legal materials, including continuing legal education materials of the Louisiana Bar Association, is provided in the library. Although library acquisitions reflect the civil law tradition of Louisiana, sufficient materials for research in the common law and a substantial number of basic legal reference works are available. Media equipment in the library includes copying machines for printed materials and microform.

The library occupies a 30,000-square-foot area, which includes computer and multimedia law learning labs. Cooperative arrangements with the Louisiana State University Law Center Library provide access to one of the largest Anglo-American and civil law resource collections in the southern region. Interlibrary loans from other libraries can be made through the Southern University Law Library.

Curriculum

The program of study is designed to give students a comprehensive knowledge of both the civil law and the common law. While emphasis is given to the substantive and procedural law of Louisiana with its French and Spanish origins, Anglo-American law is strongly integrated into the curriculum. Fundamental differences in method and approach, and the results reached in the two systems, are analyzed.

The civil law system of Louisiana offers the law student a unique educational opportunity. The program of instruction examines the historical background of the Anglo-American setting. Students are trained in the art of advocacy, legal research, and the sources and social purposes of legal principles. Techniques to discipline the students' minds in legal reasoning are an integral part of the educational objectives of the Law Center. Students are instructed in the ethics of the legal profession and the professional responsibility of the lawyer to society.

The Juris Doctor (JD) degree is offered at the Southern University Law Center through a full-time and a part-time day/evening program. The JD program has a three-year curriculum requiring 96 hours of academic credits. The part-time program requires enrollment in at least eight credit hours each semester and can be completed in four years. A JD and Master of Public Administration (JD/MPA) joint degree is also offered by the Law Center and the Southern University Nelson Mandela School of Public Policy and Urban Affairs. The JD/MPA joint-degree program requires 123 hours of academic credit and can be completed in four years.

Admission

The Law Center does not prescribe any prelegal courses but strongly recommends a foundation in such courses as English, speech, political science, history, economics, psychology, logic, mathematics, analytical courses, and science.

Students beginning the study of law are admitted only in the fall semester. Applicants are advised to take the LSAT prior to the February test date of the expected year of enrollment. Under no circumstances will a score received on a test administered more than three years prior to the anticipated date of acceptance be considered. All applications for admission are reviewed by a special committee. Many variables are taken into consideration for admission, including, but not limited to, the undergraduate grade-point average and the LSAT. Work experience and past pursuits are also reviewed.

Completed application forms, in addition to two letters of recommendation and one copy of an official transcript showing degree earned, should be filed with the admission office during the fall semester prior to the year in which admission is sought.

Student Activities

Third-year law students are eligible to enroll in the Clinical Education Program, which allows students to handle cases under the direct supervision of a full-time faculty member of the Law Center.

The *Southern University Law Review* is a scholarly periodical published under the auspices of the Southern University Law Center. Editorial administration and managerial responsibilities are handled by the student members of the *Law Review* staff with guidance from a faculty advisor. Students who complete the first year with at least 29 credit hours and are ranked in the top 7 percent of their class at the end of the spring semester shall be invited to membership. Students who complete the first year with at least 29 credit hours and a cumulative undergraduate grade-point average of 3.0 may participate in the "write-on" competition.

Law Review membership provides eligible students with a wealth of experience in legal research and writing.

The Student Bar Association (SBA), an affiliate of the American Law Student Association, is a self-governing organization that receives full cooperation of the Law Center faculty. Any student in good standing enrolled at the Law Center is eligible for membership.

The purpose of the Student Bar Association is to promote the general welfare of the Law Center, encourage among its members high scholarship, and cultivate rapport and cooperation among the students, faculty, and members of the legal profession.

Housing

Limited dormitory accommodations are available for law students. All students desiring to live in campus housing are required to submit an application to the Housing Office, in addition to a security deposit of $50. Applications should be made to the Director of Housing, Southern University, as early as possible.

Other Student Organizations

Other student organizations include the Moot Court Board; Law Student Division, ABA; Black Law Students Association; Delta Theta Phi Law Fraternity International; Phi Alpha Delta Law Fraternity, International; Women in Law; Environmental Law Society; Sports and Entertainment Legal Association; Louisiana Trial Lawyers Association; Christians at Law Society; International Law Students Association; Southern Student Association of Criminal Defense Lawyers; Public Interest Law Society; Phi Delta Phi International Legal Fraternity; Business Entrepreneurship Leadership Association; and the Thurgood Marshall Club.

Career Services

The Office of Career Counseling and Development assists students and alumni in obtaining meaningful employment opportunities. Information on part-time employment before graduation is available through this office. The office maintains a resource center directed toward résumé and cover letter writing, interview skills, and legal career opportunities. The Law Center is a member of the National Association for Legal Career Professionals (formerly National Association for Law Placement) and subscribes to its standards for promoting career planning and development activities.

Applicant Profile Not Available

SOUTHWESTERN LAW SCHOOL

3050 Wilshire Boulevard
Los Angeles, CA 90010-1106
Phone: 213.738.6834; Fax: 213.383.1688
E-mail: admissions@swlaw.edu; Website: www.swlaw.edu

ABA
Approved
Since
1970

The Basics

Type of school	Private
Term	Semester
Application deadline	4/1
Application fee	$60
Financial aid deadline	6/1
Can first year start other than fall?	No
Student to faculty ratio	14.3 to 1
# of housing spaces available restricted to law students	
graduate housing for which law students are eligible	

Faculty and Administrators

	Total		Men		Women		Minorities	
	Spr	Fall	Spr	Fall	Spr	Fall	Spr	Fall
Full-time	55	54	31	31	24	23	13	12
Other full-time	2	3	2	2	0	1	0	1
Deans, librarians, & others who teach	9	10	4	4	5	6	0	1
Part-time	43	28	26	20	17	8	9	7
Total	109	95	63	57	46	38	22	21

Curriculum

	Full-Time	Part-Time
Typical first-year section size	82	87
Is there typically a "small section" of the first-year class, other than Legal Writing, taught by full-time faculty	No	No
If yes, typical size offered last year		

# of classroom course titles beyond first-year curriculum		143
# of upper division courses, excluding seminars, with an enrollment:	Under 25	138
	25–49	41
	50–74	33
	75–99	4
	100+	0
# of seminars		18
# of seminar positions available		366

# of seminar positions filled	194	59
# of positions available in simulation courses	1,085	
# of simulation positions filled	631	183
# of positions available in faculty supervised clinical courses	54	
# of faculty supervised clinical positions filled	48	6
# involved in field placements	267	42
# involved in law journals	88	15
# involved in moot court or trial competitions	87	15
# of credit hours required to graduate	87	

JD Enrollment and Ethnicity

	Men		Women		Full-Time		Part-Time		1st-Year		Total		JD Degs. Awd.
	#	%	#	%	#	%	#	%	#	%	#	%	
All Hispanics	59	11.2	95	16.8	98	13.2	56	15.8	51	12.6	154	14.1	28
Am. Ind./AK Nat.	4	0.8	2	0.4	4	0.5	2	0.6	1	0.2	6	0.5	3
Asian	57	10.8	86	15.2	104	14.0	39	11.0	46	11.4	143	13.1	49
Black/Af. Am.	29	5.5	39	6.9	29	3.9	39	11.0	17	4.2	68	6.2	18
Nat. Hl/Pac. Isl.	2	0.4	1	0.2	1	0.1	2	0.6	1	0.2	3	0.3	0
2 or more races	10	1.9	9	1.6	17	2.3	2	0.6	11	2.7	19	1.7	0
Subtotal (minor.)	161	30.5	232	40.9	253	34.1	140	39.5	127	31.4	393	35.9	98
Nonres. Alien	2	0.4	3	0.5	5	0.7	0	0.0	2	0.5	5	0.5	0
White/Cauc.	290	54.9	261	46.0	380	51.3	171	48.3	228	56.4	551	50.3	133
Unknown	75	14.2	71	12.5	103	13.9	43	12.1	47	11.6	146	13.3	70
Total	528	48.2	567	51.8	741	67.7	354	32.3	404	36.9	1095		301

Transfers

Transfers in	16
Transfers out	24

Tuition and Fees

	Resident	Nonresident
Full-time	$39,110	$39,110
Part-time	$23,546	$23,546
Tuition Guarantee Program	N	

Living Expenses

Estimated living expenses for singles

Living on campus	Living off campus	Living at home
N/A	$26,819	$13,094

SOUTHWESTERN LAW SCHOOL

*ABA
Approved
Since
1970*

GPA and LSAT Scores

	Total	Full-Time	Part-Time
# of apps	3,949	3,383	566
# of offers	1,155	980	175
# of matrics	410	295	115
75% GPA	3.54	3.56	3.37
Median GPA	3.35	3.43	3.15
25% GPA	3.13	3.22	2.83
75% LSAT	158	158	156
Median LSAT	155	156	152
25% LSAT	152	153	151

Grants and Scholarships (from prior year)

	Total		Full-Time		Part-Time	
	#	%	#	%	#	%
Total # of students	1,052		729		323	
Total # receiving grants	332	31.6	256	35.1	76	23.5
Less than 1/2 tuition	172	16.3	130	17.8	42	13.0
Half to full tuition	123	11.7	100	13.7	23	7.1
Full tuition	13	1.2	10	1.4	3	0.9
More than full tuition	24	2.3	16	2.2	8	2.5
Median grant amount			$18,000		$9,508	

Informational and Library Resources

Total amount spent on library materials	$1,531,074
Study seating capacity inside the library	610
# of full-time equivalent professional librarians	9
Hours per week library is open	108
# of open, wired connections available to students	326
# of networked computers available for use by students	142
Has wireless network?	Y
Requires computer?	N

JD Attrition (from prior year)

	Academic	Other	Total	
	#	#	#	%
1st year	14	22	36	9.3
2nd year	7	24	31	11.0
3rd year	0	0	0	0.0
4th year	0	0	0	0.0

Employment (9 months after graduation)

	Total	Percentage
Employment status known	277	95.8
Employment status unknown	12	4.2
Employed	258	93.1
Pursuing graduate degrees	3	1.1
Unemployed (seeking, not seeking, or studying for the bar)	4	1.4
Type of Employment		
# employed in law firms	146	56.6
# employed in business and industry	70	27.1
# employed in government	20	7.8
# employed in public interest	12	4.7
# employed as judicial clerks	3	1.2
# employed in academia	6	2.3
Geographic Location		
# employed in state	226	87.6
# employed outside the US	2	0.8
# of states where employed		11

Bar Passage Rates

First-time takers	286	Reporting %	96.50
Average school %	61.23	Average state %	73.19

Average pass difference −11.96

Jurisdiction	Takers	Passers	Pass %	State %	Diff %
California	276	169	61.23	73.19	−11.96

The information on these pages was provided by the law school.

SOUTHWESTERN LAW SCHOOL

3050 Wilshire Boulevard
Los Angeles, CA 90010-1106
Phone: 213.738.6834; Fax: 213.383.1688
E-mail: admissions@swlaw.edu; Website: www.swlaw.edu

100 Years of Innovative Legal Education

With a long-standing emphasis on diversity, public service, innovative programs, and a mid-city campus featuring a world-renowned Art Deco landmark, Southwestern Law School reflects the vibrancy of Los Angeles and provides an ideal setting for law study. Founded 100 years ago as an independent, nonprofit, nonsectarian institution, Southwestern is fully approved by the ABA and is a member of the AALS. It is the only law school to offer four JD courses of study that differ in scheduling and instructional approach, including traditional full- and part-time programs, as well as a unique two-year accelerated curriculum. Concurrent 3- and 4-year JD/MBA programs are also available. Southwestern's 10,000 alumni include prominent public officials—from members of Congress to mayors, and over 200 judges—as well as founders of major law firms and general counsels of multinational corporations. The law school has strong ties to the legal, business, and civic sectors, and its Biederman Entertainment and Media Law Institute is closely linked to the entertainment industry in Hollywood and internationally.

Diverse and Talented Student Body

There is a strong sense of community among the students who come to Southwestern from virtually every state and a dozen foreign countries, and represent over 250 undergraduate institutions. About two-thirds have prior work experience or have already completed advanced degrees in diverse disciplines from accounting to urban planning. In the most recent entering class, women and men are equally represented, while minorities make up 39 percent, and students report fluency in over 20 foreign languages. The average age is 26, with a range from 21 to 60.

Distinguished Faculty

Southwestern's faculty focus on enhancing the classroom experience and providing personal attention to each student. The full-time faculty include internationally recognized experts in alternative dispute resolution, antitrust, civil rights, criminal justice, entertainment and media, environmental, ethics, human rights, intellectual property, international and urban development, among other areas of the law. The adjunct faculty of distinguished judges and attorneys are known for their expertise in specialized practices and enjoy sharing their real-world knowledge with students in stimulating elective courses.

Award-Winning Campus Facilities

Southwestern has created a welcoming student-centered oasis within a campus that encompasses nearly two city blocks in the heart of Los Angeles. The recent $29 million campus expansion includes the extraordinary Bullocks Wilshire Building, which is listed on the National Register of Historic Places. The award-winning facilities feature state-of-the-art multimedia technology in the classrooms, courtrooms, and clinics; wireless Internet access; spacious dining facilities and student lounges in restored historic areas; large terraces with panoramic city views; tranquil

student commons and promenade plazas; as well as a 10,000-square-foot, spa-quality fitness center. At over 83,000 square feet, Southwestern's Taylor Law Library is the second largest academic law library facility in California. The law school's Julian C. Dixon Courtroom and Advocacy Center is the most technologically sophisticated center of its kind.

Two-, Three-, and Four-Year JD Programs

Four JD programs are offered: a three-year, full-time day program; a four-year, part-time evening program; PLEAS— a four-year, part-time day program for students with child or elder-care responsibilities; and SCALE—an accelerated two-year, full-time program featuring small classes, practical skills training, and real-world experience. Southwestern has also established exciting new dual-degree affiliations with the Drucker Graduate School of Management of Claremont Graduate University for a JD/MBA and JD/MA in Management, as well as California State University, Dominguez Hills, for a unique JD/MA in Negotiation, Conflict Resolution, and Peacebuilding. LLM programs are offered in individualized law studies and in entertainment and media law.

Comprehensive Curriculum

Recognized by the Carnegie Foundation for innovation, Southwestern's cutting-edge, first-year curriculum provides a unique opportunity for students to choose one of three tracks in their legal research and writing course—appellate, negotiation, or trial advocacy—and to take an elective as early as their second semester. Recent upper-division enhancements include a January intersession, capstone courses, and special "mini-term" courses taught by international legal experts. The required traditional curriculum includes 17 courses, while more than 200 elective courses, 150 externship placements, and three clinical programs allow students to design a broad-based legal education or emphasize an area of law. Southwestern's location, faculty expertise, alumni presence in the profession, and history have enabled the law school to develop a reputation as a leader, particularly in entertainment and media law, international law, criminal law, and trial advocacy/litigation. Southwestern sponsors summer law programs in Argentina, Canada, England, and Mexico. A wide array of academic support programs and individualized counseling is provided by the Dean of Students and Diversity Affairs, the Director of Academic Support and Bar-Related Programs, and the Writing Center to ensure student success.

Entertainment and Media Law Institute

Southwestern was the first law school to establish a center focused on entertainment and media law. The internationally recognized Biederman Entertainment and Media Law Institute features the largest contingent of full-time entertainment and media law faculty of any law school, and benefits from an extensive network of alumni and adjunct faculty who hold prominent positions in these industries. The institute sponsors over 45 courses, 60 externships, the Biederman Scholars program, a special law firm practicum, a scholarly journal, and summer programs in Los Angeles and London, in addition to lectures and symposia with industry leaders. Southwestern also established the first LLM program in Entertainment and Media Law.

Student Activities

Southwestern's interscholastic Moot Court Honors Program, Negotiation Honors Program, Trial Advocacy Honors Program, and client counseling teams consistently earn top awards in competitions around the country. Students demonstrate their outstanding research, writing, and editing skills through service on the *Southwestern Law Review* and the *Southwestern Journal of International Law*, as well as the *Journal of International Media and Entertainment Law* published in conjunction with the ABA Forums on Communications Law and the Entertainment and Sports Industries. The Student Bar Association sponsors award-winning student welfare and community outreach programs and oversees over 50 student organizations, including three legal fraternities; minority, cultural, political, and religious groups; and societies focused on specific areas of law.

Public Interest Opportunities

Southwestern encourages, recognizes, and rewards students' public interest involvement through its Public Service Policy and a variety of programs: the Children's Rights, Immigration Law, and Street Law clinics; special scholarship funds; the Public Interest Service Award; the Silbert Public Interest Fellowship Program; Public Interest Summer Grants for students working with public service agencies; extensive student volunteer work with local schools and community organizations; and a large selection of externships. During the annual Public Interest Law Week, the entire law school community rallies to raise awareness and funds supporting public interest activities.

Career Services and Alumni Network

The Career Services Office offers individualized career counseling and coordinates a full calendar of workshops, networking events, mock interviews, and panel presentations, as well as the Alumni Resource Network to help students prepare for and secure legal employment. The office sponsors intensive on- and off-campus interview programs and provides web-based access to extensive job listings and on-campus interview opportunities through Symplicity. Although the majority of Southwestern graduates choose to practice in California, alumni can be found in 47 states and 17 foreign countries.

Admission Criteria

Admission to Southwestern is highly selective, with an average acceptance rate over the past five years of under 30 percent. While emphasis is placed on undergraduate GPA and LSAT scores earned within the past three years, community involvement, work experience, motivation, recommendations, and diversity are also major factors. Transfer applications are considered from students who have successfully completed at least one year at another ABA-approved law school.

Financial Aid/Scholarships

About 90 percent of Southwestern's students receive some form of financial aid that may include scholarships, grants, loans, and work-study funds. Among the more than 80 institutional scholarship funds is the Wildman/Schumacher Scholarship Program, which provides up to full-tuition renewable scholarships to members of the first-year entering class who demonstrate exceptional academic and leadership potential.

APPLICANT PROFILE

Southwestern Law School
Prospects for Admission

| | LSAT Score | | | | | | |
GPA	120–144	145–149	150–154	155–159	160–164	165–169	170 +
3.75 +							
3.50–3.74							
3.25–3.49							
3.00–3.24							
2.75–2.99							
2.50–2.74							
2.25–2.49							
2.00–2.24							

☐ Unlikely   ☐ Possible   ■ Likely

Note: This chart is to be used as a general guide only in determining chances for admittance. Nonnumerical factors are seriously considered for all applicants.

STANFORD UNIVERSITY LAW SCHOOL

Office of Admissions, 559 Nathan Abbott Way
Stanford, CA 94305-8610
Phone: 650.723.4985; Fax: 650.723.0838
E-mail: Admissions@law.stanford.edu; Website: www.law.stanford.edu

The Basics

Type of school	Private
Term	Quarter
Application deadline	2/1
Application fee	$100
Financial aid deadline	3/15
Can first year start other than fall?	No
Student to faculty ratio	7.5 to 1
# of housing spaces available restricted to law students	
graduate housing for which law students are eligible	638

Faculty and Administrators

	Total		Men		Women		Minorities	
	Spr	Fall	Spr	Fall	Spr	Fall	Spr	Fall
Full-time	63	62	38	37	25	25	14	14
Other full-time	6	6	1	1	5	5	2	2
Deans, librarians, & others who teach	17	18	11	11	6	7	3	3
Part-time	63	25	35	19	28	6	10	3
Total	149	111	85	68	64	43	29	22

Curriculum

	Full-Time	Part-Time
Typical first-year section size	60	0
Is there typically a "small section" of the first-year class, other than Legal Writing, taught by full-time faculty	Yes	No
If yes, typical size offered last year	30	
# of classroom course titles beyond first-year curriculum	181	

# of upper division courses, excluding seminars, with an enrollment:		
	Under 25	168
	25–49	33
	50–74	15
	75–99	4
	100+	1

# of seminars	63	
# of seminar positions available	1,005	
# of seminar positions filled	636	0
# of positions available in simulation courses	388	
# of simulation positions filled	346	0
# of positions available in faculty supervised clinical courses	265	
# of faculty supervised clinical positions filled	242	0
# involved in field placements	28	0
# involved in law journals	383	0
# involved in moot court or trial competitions	44	0
# of credit hours required to graduate	111	

JD Enrollment and Ethnicity

	Men		Women		Full-Time		Part-Time		1st-Year		Total		JD Degs. Awd.
	#	%	#	%	#	%	#	%	#	%	#	%	
All Hispanics	29	9.2	29	11.3	58	10.2	0	0.0	22	12.2	58	10.2	19
Am. Ind./AK Nat.	7	2.2	2	0.8	9	1.6	0	0.0	0	0.0	9	1.6	3
Asian	31	9.9	25	9.7	56	9.8	0	0.0	13	7.2	56	9.8	26
Black/Af. Am.	25	8.0	33	12.8	58	10.2	0	0.0	14	7.8	58	10.2	12
Nat. HI/Pac. Isl.	0	0.0	0	0.0	0	0.0	0	0.0	0	0.0	0	0.0	0
2 or more races	9	2.9	8	3.1	17	3.0	0	0.0	12	6.7	17	3.0	0
Subtotal (minor.)	101	32.2	97	37.7	198	34.7	0	0.0	61	33.9	198	34.7	64
Nonres. Alien	5	1.6	5	1.9	10	1.8	0	0.0	2	1.1	10	1.8	0
White/Cauc.	184	58.6	133	51.8	317	55.5	0	0.0	96	53.3	317	55.5	98
Unknown	24	7.6	22	8.6	46	8.1	0	0.0	21	11.7	46	8.1	9
Total	314	55.0	257	45.0	571	100.0	0	0.0	180	31.5	571		173

Transfers

Transfers in	15
Transfers out	0

Tuition and Fees

	Resident	Nonresident
Full-time	$46,581	$46,581
Part-time		
Tuition Guarantee Program		N

Living Expenses

Estimated living expenses for singles

Living on campus	Living off campus	Living at home
$24,954	$26,754	N/A

STANFORD UNIVERSITY LAW SCHOOL

ABA
Approved
Since
1923

GPA and LSAT Scores

	Total	Full-Time	Part-Time
# of apps	4,248	4,248	0
# of offers	379	379	0
# of matrics	180	180	0
75% GPA	3.94	3.94	0.00
Median GPA	3.88	3.88	0.00
25% GPA	3.74	3.74	0.00
75% LSAT	173	173	0
Median LSAT	170	170	0
25% LSAT	167	167	0

Grants and Scholarships (from prior year)

	Total		Full-Time		Part-Time	
	#	%	#	%	#	%
Total # of students	557		557		0	
Total # receiving grants	340	61.0	340	61.0	0	0.0
Less than 1/2 tuition	157	28.2	157	28.2	0	0.0
Half to full tuition	172	30.9	172	30.9	0	0.0
Full tuition	7	1.3	7	1.3	0	0.0
More than full tuition	4	0.7	4	0.7	0	0.0
Median grant amount			$23,592		$0	

Informational and Library Resources

Total amount spent on library materials	$932,780
Study seating capacity inside the library	508
# of full-time equivalent professional librarians	10
Hours per week library is open	103
# of open, wired connections available to students	90
# of networked computers available for use by students	66
Has wireless network?	Y
Requires computer?	Y

JD Attrition (from prior year)

	Academic	Other	Total	
	#	#	#	%
1st year	0	2	2	1.1
2nd year	0	1	1	0.5
3rd year	0	1	1	0.5
4th year	0	0	0	0.0

Employment (9 months after graduation)

	Total	Percentage
Employment status known	181	100.0
Employment status unknown	0	0.0
Employed	172	95.0
Pursuing graduate degrees	4	2.2
Unemployed (seeking, not seeking, or studying for the bar)	4	2.2
Type of Employment		
# employed in law firms	108	62.8
# employed in business and industry	4	2.3
# employed in government	5	2.9
# employed in public interest	7	4.1
# employed as judicial clerks	45	26.2
# employed in academia	3	1.7
Geographic Location		
# employed in state	74	43.0
# employed outside the US	3	1.7
# of states where employed	24	

Bar Passage Rates

First-time takers	180	Reporting %	77.22
Average school %	94.24	Average state %	76.54
Average pass difference	17.70		

Jurisdiction	Takers	Passers	Pass %	State %	Diff %
California	104	97	93.27	73.19	20.08
New York	35	34	97.14	86.51	10.63

STANFORD UNIVERSITY LAW SCHOOL

Office of Admissions, 559 Nathan Abbott Way
Stanford, CA 94305-8610
Phone: 650.723.4985; Fax: 650.723.0838
E-mail: Admissions@law.stanford.edu; Website: www.law.stanford.edu

Introduction

Stanford Law School is part of one of the world's leading research institutions, providing plentiful opportunities for interdisciplinary cooperation. Stanford University is a private university located in the heart of Silicon Valley, just 35 miles south of San Francisco. The university's 8,180 acres stretch between the foothills of the Santa Cruz Mountains and the cities of Palo Alto and Menlo Park, in a part of the country that offers an ideal, Mediterranean climate of dry, warm summers and wet, but temperate winters.

Current enrollment at the university is approximately 15,000 students, of whom about 8,000 are graduate students. The law school is small, with about 571 JD students, 63 LLM and JSM students, and approximately 50 permanent faculty members. The school has teaching and research ties with schools and departments across campus. Law School courses are taught in 16 multimedia classrooms with full wireless Internet connectivity.

Stanford Law School offers a unique combination of the classic and cutting edge in legal education. The school is preparing its students for a rich and varied professional life in an era of great excitement and rapid change—much of it generated by the remarkable innovations in information technology pioneered in Silicon Valley—and for careers in an increasingly global community.

Faculty

Stanford Law School's faculty is distinguished not only for its scholarship, but also for its commitment to teaching and curricular innovation. The school's unusually low student-to-faculty ratio of 7.5 to 1 creates an intimate, collegial environment that fosters students' intellectual and professional development both in and out of the classroom. Students have many opportunities to work closely with faculty members as research assistants on scholarly projects, and the faculty encourages interested students to develop their own scholarship for future academic careers. The relationships formed between Stanford Law faculty and students often last a lifetime.

Instruction at Stanford Law takes place primarily in small classes and seminars and through individually directed research. It also takes place via a diverse range of legal clinics, which offer students experience with real cases and clients and personalized feedback.

The faculty is continually engaged in developing new teaching methods to complement curricular innovations. Case studies, similar to those of business schools, challenge students to consider the interaction of legal and nonlegal factors involved in a given situation. Numerous interdisciplinary opportunities allow faculty and students from the law school and other parts of the university, joined by practitioners and policymakers, to engage in applied research.

Library and Physical Facilities

Housed within Crown Quadrangle is the Robert Crown Law Library, which holds an excellent collection of print materials and a vast collection of online resources. Popular with the law students are the library's spacious reading rooms. An entire floor of the library, with its comfortable reading room and technology-enabled meeting rooms and classroom, is available 24 hours a day, 7 days a week. The 27 friendly and service-minded staff members are dedicated to helping students, faculty, and staff with all their research needs.

Special Programs

Joint-Degree Programs—Stanford Law School is actively expanding its joint-degree programs, leveraging the highly rated graduate schools and academic programs across Stanford University. To facilitate interdisciplinary study and scholarship, and simplify the pursuit of joint degrees, Stanford Law has adapted the law school calendar to be compatible with that of the wider university. The school offers more than 20 formal joint-degree programs in such areas as Bioengineering, Business, Computer Science, Economics, Education, Electrical Engineering, Environment and Resources, Health Research and Policy, History, International and Comparative Area Studies, International Policy Studies, Management Science and Engineering, Philosophy, Political Science, Psychology, Public Policy, and Sociology. Joint-degree programs are also offered with Princeton's Woodrow Wilson School of Public and International Affairs and Johns Hopkins' School of Advanced International Studies. For students with specialized career aspirations, opportunities to customize a joint degree are limitless.

Programs and Centers—Stanford Law School's 20-plus innovative academic programs and centers give students the opportunity for concentrated study and close interaction with faculty. Students may engage in graduate-level research and policy-oriented study through centers and programs such as the Stanford Constitutional Law Center; Stanford Criminal Justice Center; Environmental and Natural Resources Law and Policy Program; Stanford Center on International Conflict and Negotiation; Rule of Law Program; Stanford Program in International Law; Arthur and Toni Rembe Rock Center for Corporate Governance; John M. Olin Program in Law and Economics; Stanford Program in Law, Science and Technology; Center for E-Commerce; the Center for Internet and Society; Center for Law and the Biosciences; Transatlantic Technology Law Forum; CodeX: Stanford Center for Computers and Law; Stanford Center on the Legal Profession; Martin Daniel Gould Center for Conflict Resolution; Gould Negotiation and Mediation Program; and John and Terry Levin Center for Public Service and Public Interest Law.

Team-Taught Courses and Concentration—Stanford Law now offers 14 team-oriented, problem-solving courses, many of which are cotaught by law school faculty and faculty from Stanford's other top-rated schools and departments. Classes are open to students from a variety of disciplines.

Clinical Program—Stanford Law is a leader in the development of clinical teaching and has expanded its clinical program to include 10 clinics that offer students the opportunity to undertake, under the close supervision of experienced practitioners, the roles and responsibilities of practicing lawyers. Students engage in witness examination, depositions, discovery, negotiations, drafting pleadings and memos, oral arguments, and analysis of tactical and ethical problems. Clinics include the Criminal Defense Clinic, Criminal Prosecution Clinic, Cyberlaw Clinic, Environmental

Law Clinic, Immigrants' Rights Clinic, International Human Rights and Development Clinic, Organizations and Transactions Clinic, Stanford Community Law Clinic, Supreme Court Litigation Clinic, and Youth and Education Law Project.

Housing

Stanford provides a variety of housing options for law students. Students may choose from furnished single rooms to four bedroom apartments equipped with full kitchens. A new residence built specifically for law students and other graduate students from around campus—and adjacent to the law school—intensifies the interdisciplinary learning experience. The university also lists off-campus housing opportunities. More information about housing is available at the Housing Assignment Services website: www.stanford.edu/dept/hds/has/.

Student Activities

More than 50 student organizations plus nine journals and a film documentary project enrich the law school experience. Opportunities for scholarly work are provided through the *Stanford Law Review* and journals focused on civil rights and civil liberties; international law; law, business, and finance; law and policy; technology law; environmental law; animal law and policy; and law, science, and policy. Advocacy skills are developed in moot court and mock trial.

Students who are female, Asian, African American, Latino, Native American, Christian, or LGBT will all find groups that share their particular concerns. Other organizations focus on environmental law, international law, law and technology, and public interest law. Local affiliates of the Federalist Society, the American Constitution Society, and the National Lawyers Guild are present.

Expenses and Financial Aid

Estimated expenses are as follows: for 2010–2011, full-time tuition is $44,880, with additional expenses including housing estimated at $26,655 for single students living on campus and $28,455 for single students living off campus. Scholarships are awarded on the basis of financial need. The purpose of financial aid is to assist students who would otherwise be unable to pursue a legal education at Stanford. Approximately 80 percent of the student body receives tuition fellowship or loan assistance.

Stanford law students planning public service careers may apply for Public Service Fellowships for their second and third years of school. The school also offers funding to students who dedicate a law school summer to qualified public service work. And for graduates who take low-paying public interest jobs and have substantial educational debt, the school has an excellent loan repayment assistance program—the Miles and Nancy Rubin Loan Repayment Assistance Program.

Career Services

The Office of Career Services, together with the John and Terry Levin Center for Public Service and Public Interest Law, helps students find employment. Approximately 250 employers representing over 500 offices worldwide participate in the spring and fall on-campus interview programs. The office also offers counseling and information on traditional and nontraditional careers and employers. The school encourages students to consider public interest and public sector employment and assists students to secure such positions.

A survey of students graduating in the class of 2009 shows the following employment patterns: law firm associates, 62.5 percent; judicial clerks, 26 percent; business (legal and nonlegal), 2.5 percent; public interest, government, or law teaching, 9 percent.

APPLICANT PROFILE

Our admission process takes into consideration many factors besides the undergraduate GPA and LSAT score. A statistical grid, as is typically provided here, only takes into consideration these two factors. We have chosen not to provide applicants with such a grid because our admission process would not be accurately portrayed.

STETSON UNIVERSITY COLLEGE OF LAW

1401 61st Street South
Gulfport, FL 33707
Phone: 727.562.7802; Fax: 727.343.0136
E-mail: lawadmit@law.stetson.edu; Website: www.law.stetson.edu

ABA
Approved
Since
1930

ABA AMERICAN BAR ASSOCIATION
Section of Legal Education
and Admissions to the Bar

The Basics

Type of school	Private
Term	Semester
Application deadline	3/15
Application fee	$55
Financial aid deadline	8/1
Can first year start other than fall?	No
Student to faculty ratio	15.4 to 1
# of housing spaces available restricted to law students	211
graduate housing for which law students are eligible	

Faculty and Administrators

	Total		Men		Women		Minorities	
	Spr	Fall	Spr	Fall	Spr	Fall	Spr	Fall
Full-time	50	54	26	28	24	26	8	11
Other full-time	9	5	8	4	1	1	2	1
Deans, librarians, & others who teach	4	4	2	1	2	3	0	0
Part-time	47	54	33	36	14	18	1	3
Total	110	117	69	69	41	48	11	15

Curriculum

	Full-Time	Part-Time
Typical first-year section size	70	70
Is there typically a "small section" of the first-year class, other than Legal Writing, taught by full-time faculty	No	No
If yes, typical size offered last year		
# of classroom course titles beyond first-year curriculum	172	

# of upper division courses, excluding seminars, with an enrollment:	Under 25	253
	25–49	52
	50–74	30
	75–99	3
	100+	0

# of seminars	23	
# of seminar positions available	398	
# of seminar positions filled	256	34
# of positions available in simulation courses	1,316	
# of simulation positions filled	902	164
# of positions available in faculty supervised clinical courses	212	
# of faculty supervised clinical positions filled	76	4
# involved in field placements	267	16
# involved in law journals	84	9
# involved in moot court or trial competitions	85	5
# of credit hours required to graduate	88	

JD Enrollment and Ethnicity

	Men #	Men %	Women #	Women %	Full-Time #	Full-Time %	Part-Time #	Part-Time %	1st-Year #	1st-Year %	Total #	Total %	JD Degs. Awd.
All Hispanics	42	8.1	50	8.9	76	8.8	16	7.5	35	9.7	92	8.5	38
Am. Ind./AK Nat.	1	0.2	8	1.4	5	0.6	4	1.9	1	0.3	9	0.8	1
Asian	13	2.5	17	3.0	22	2.5	8	3.7	7	1.9	30	2.8	9
Black/Af. Am.	24	4.6	48	8.6	62	7.2	10	4.7	27	7.5	72	6.7	27
Nat. HI/Pac. Isl.	0	0.0	0	0.0	0	0.0	0	0.0	0	0.0	0	0.0	0
2 or more races	8	1.5	13	2.3	18	2.1	3	1.4	5	1.4	21	1.9	0
Subtotal (minor.)	88	16.9	136	24.2	183	21.1	41	19.2	75	20.8	224	20.7	81
Nonres. Alien	4	0.8	3	0.5	7	0.8	0	0.0	6	1.7	7	0.6	0
White/Cauc.	387	74.4	388	69.2	613	70.7	162	75.7	259	71.7	775	71.7	231
Unknown	41	7.9	34	6.1	64	7.4	11	5.1	21	5.8	75	6.9	22
Total	520	48.1	561	51.9	867	80.2	214	19.8	361	33.4	1081		337

Transfers

Transfers in	7
Transfers out	20

Tuition and Fees

	Resident	Nonresident
Full-time	$33,220	$33,220
Part-time	$23,020	$23,020
Tuition Guarantee Program		N

Living Expenses

Estimated living expenses for singles

Living on campus	Living off campus	Living at home
$23,664	$23,664	$23,664

ABA
Approved
Since
1930

GPA and LSAT Scores

	Total	Full-Time	Part-Time
# of apps	2,991	2,663	333
# of offers	1,120	1,002	118
# of matrics	360	290	70
75% GPA	3.66	3.67	3.50
Median GPA	3.42	3.44	3.26
25% GPA	3.17	3.22	3.07
75% LSAT	158	159	156
Median LSAT	156	156	154
25% LSAT	154	154	152

Grants and Scholarships (from prior year)

	Total		Full-Time		Part-Time	
	#	%	#	%	#	%
Total # of students	1,084		876		208	
Total # receiving grants	268	24.7	234	26.7	34	16.3
Less than 1/2 tuition	78	7.2	66	7.5	12	5.8
Half to full tuition	80	7.4	65	7.4	15	7.2
Full tuition	70	6.5	63	7.2	7	3.4
More than full tuition	40	3.7	40	4.6	0	0.0
Median grant amount			$17,025		$7,000	

Informational and Library Resources

Total amount spent on library materials	$1,453,751
Study seating capacity inside the library	867
# of full-time equivalent professional librarians	10
Hours per week library is open	93
# of open, wired connections available to students	1,595
# of networked computers available for use by students	117
Has wireless network?	Y
Requires computer?	Y

JD Attrition (from prior year)

	Academic	Other	Total	
	#	#	#	%
1st year	0	9	9	2.3
2nd year	2	23	25	8.3
3rd year	0	5	5	1.4
4th year	0	1	1	3.1

Employment (9 months after graduation)

	Total	Percentage
Employment status known	315	97.8
Employment status unknown	7	2.2
Employed	281	89.2
Pursuing graduate degrees	11	3.5
Unemployed (seeking, not seeking, or studying for the bar)	9	2.9
Type of Employment		
# employed in law firms	154	54.8
# employed in business and industry	37	13.2
# employed in government	41	14.6
# employed in public interest	21	7.5
# employed as judicial clerks	17	6.0
# employed in academia	5	1.8
Geographic Location		
# employed in state	247	87.9
# employed outside the US	0	0.0
# of states where employed		21

Bar Passage Rates

First-time takers	299	Reporting %	95.32
Average school %	81.05	Average state %	77.81
Average pass difference	3.24		

Jurisdiction	Takers	Passers	Pass %	State %	Diff %
Florida	285	231	81.05	77.81	3.24

STETSON UNIVERSITY COLLEGE OF LAW

1401 61st Street South
Gulfport, FL 33707
Phone: 727.562.7802; Fax: 727.343.0136
E-mail: lawadmit@law.stetson.edu; Website: www.law.stetson.edu

Introduction

Founded in 1900, Stetson University College of Law is Florida's first law school. The college's main campus is in Gulfport, a suburb of St. Petersburg. Located in a former resort hotel, the campus provides an outstanding environment in which to study law. A satellite campus in downtown Tampa hosts some classes in our part-time and full-time JD programs and houses judges on Florida's Second District Court of Appeal. Stetson is fully accredited by the American Bar Association and has been an Association of American Law Schools member since 1931. The college is an equal opportunity educational institution. For additional information, visit www.law.stetson.edu.

Dolly and Homer Hand Law Library and Physical Facilities

Stetson's amazing facilities boast seven courtrooms—including the nation's first elder-friendly courtroom—and modern classrooms designed to enhance the learning experience. The Student Center features organizational offices, interviewing rooms, gym, pool, and nearby athletic fields. The Hand Law Library in Gulfport and the satellite library in Tampa form one of the Southeast's most advanced research and communications technology centers. Housing more than 420,000 volumes and providing 50 group-study rooms, this library system offers 24/7 swipe card access, wireless access to many online databases, and outstanding legal reference assistance with 10 professional librarians on staff. There is a laptop requirement for all students.

Admission

Last year, Stetson received 3,024 applications, offered admission to 1,120 applicants, and enrolled 360 first-year students: 290 full-time and 70 part-time. The 2010 entering class included 20 percent minority students and 51 percent women; 120 undergraduate institutions, 29 states, and 7 countries were represented within the group of new students. These numbers represent the fall full-time and part-time 2010 entering classes. We no longer offer a spring JD start date. The student body consists of approximately 856 full-time and 216 part-time JD students, 17 students in the International Law LLM program (from 7 countries), and 37 Elder Law LLM students (online program). Our students, faculty, and staff work together toward one common goal: preparing our students to be the best lawyers and leaders possible.

Faculty

The intellectual exchange among students and faculty is continuous, both inside and outside the classroom. The 55 full-time professors are engaged in projects that bring them regional, national, and international prominence, but make teaching and working with students their top priority. Each semester, the full-time faculty is supplemented by approximately 50 practicing attorneys and judges who serve as adjunct professors in specialized areas.

Curriculum

Academic Success Programs: Stetson offers many programs, including academic advising, an academic orientation, bar exam preparation offered by a full-time director of bar preparation services, and a semester-long academic skills workshop, designed to assist all students in achieving their academic potential.

Lawyering Skills: Stetson's academic program focuses on the lawyering process. Stetson is a pioneer and a national leader in advocacy and clinical training.

Public Service: All JD students must complete a pro bono graduation requirement. Each year, all students participate in a Professionalism Day to learn more about the profession and serve the community.

Additional Academic Offerings: Stetson offers a part-time JD program that allows a student to earn a law degree in four years (including summers) by taking classes in the evenings; part-time students must take classes at both the Gulfport and Tampa campuses. Qualified foreign attorneys may receive advanced standing to complete the JD program in two years. Stetson offers three domestic dual-degree programs (JD/MBA, JD/MD, and JD/MPH). A new dual-degree program is available with a Spanish law school, as are semester exchange programs in Mexico and Spain. Study-abroad opportunities are also available in Argentina, China, the Netherlands, Spain, Switzerland, and the Cayman Islands. A rotating one-week experience is also offered; the 2011 trip is to Greece. A semester-abroad program in London is offered each fall. Stetson has Centers for Excellence in Advocacy, Elder Law, Higher Education Law and Policy, and International Law. The school also hosts the National Clearinghouse for Science, Technology and the Law; the Institute for Biodiversity Law and Policy; and the Institute for Caribbean Law and Policy. Students may participate in a Civil Rights Bus Tour in the summer.

Expenses and Financial Aid

Full-time tuition for 2010–2011 (fall/spring) was $33,000, and part-time tuition for 2010–2011 (fall/spring/summer) was $28,420. Partial- and full-merit and diversity scholarships are offered on a competitive basis. Need and merit scholarships are offered for continuing students. There is no financial aid deadline. Stetson offers a public service scholarship for third-year students and is a proud Yellow Ribbon Scholarship Program participant.

Special Programs

Advocacy: Stetson is recognized as one of the best law schools for advocacy. Stetson's teams routinely win international, national, regional, and state mock trial, moot court, and alternative dispute resolution competitions.

Clinics and Internships: Stetson offers upper-level students a wide variety of opportunities to work closely with attorneys and judges, and, in some cases, actually represent clients and try cases. Clinical opportunities include Immigration, Civil Poverty Law, Elder Law, Local Government, Prosecution, Public Defender, and Veterans Appellate Rights. Internships include American/Caribbean Law, Bankruptcy Judicial, Elder and Disability Law, Elder Consumer Protection, Employment

Discrimination, Environmental Law, EEOC, Family Law, Federal Agency, Federal and State Judicial (Tampa Bay/Tallahassee), Florida Department of State, Homeless Advocacy, In-House Counsel, Intellectual Property, Labor Law, Municipal and Administrative Law, Private Practice, State and Federal Litigation, State Supreme Court, and the US Court of Appeals for Veterans Claims (DC). Stetson also offers a summer Law and Policy internship program in Washington, DC.

Certificates of Concentration: Students can apply to a certificate program in which they focus their elective credits on advocacy, elder law, or international law. The JD/MBA program offers a concentration in Eco-Asset Management.

Law Review: The *Stetson Law Review* publishes three issues each year. Stetson also publishes the *Journal of International Aging Law and Policy* in cooperation with AARP and the *Journal of International Wildlife Law and Policy*.

Honors Program: Full-time students who rank in the top 15 percent of their entering class after their first or second semester and part-time students who rank in the top 15 percent of their entering class after their first or second year are invited to interview for a spot in the Honors Program, which features a special colloquium and seminar. Honors Program students also are invited to attend faculty colloquia and other special events.

Continuing Legal Education and High-Profile Speakers: Students are encouraged to attend the numerous seminars and conferences sponsored by the College of Law for practicing attorneys, judges, and other professionals. Recent featured speakers include US Supreme Court Justices Antonin Scalia and Clarence Thomas, former US Attorney General Janet Reno, Innocence Project founder Barry Scheck, and civil rights icon Representative John Lewis.

Residential Life

Stetson offers a variety of housing opportunities on and near campus including 49 dorm rooms, some of which are designated for special needs students. The university also owns 42 single-family homes and a 32-unit apartment complex, all located within a few blocks of the campus. A wait-list is maintained for these spaces. The Office of Residential Life also maintains a roommates-wanted list and a general listing of other rental opportunities in the local area, although these rentals are not formally affiliated with Stetson.

Career Development

Stetson's commitment to helping students achieve their goals is reflected in its strong career development program. The Office of Career Development assists students and alumni in securing all types of legal and law-related employment and provides group seminars and individual counseling on subjects ranging from interviewing techniques to résumé writing. More than 92 percent of the 2009 graduating class reported that they found employment within nine months of graduation. Approximately 89 percent of recent Stetson graduates practice within Florida; however, alumni are located in 48 states and 22 countries.

Office of Student Life

The Office of Student Life offers student activities that support Stetson's academic mission and enrich the law school experience, such as cultural programs, experiential education trips, pro bono service opportunities, and monthly leadership luncheons. Stetson has more than 45 diverse and active student organizations. The Student Bar Association is the umbrella organization under which all others are coordinated. The Stetson Chapter of the American Bar Association (ABA) Law Student Division has been recognized regionally and nationally as one of the largest and best, and the Student Leadership Development Program was awarded the ABA's prestigious E. Smythe Gambrell Professionalism Award for excellence in professionalism programming. A strong Office of Student Life presence on campus allows students many opportunities to hone their leadership and communication skills, network socially with their peers and legal professionals, and grow interpersonally as strong future members of the legal profession.

APPLICANT PROFILE

Stetson University College of Law
This grid includes only applicants who earned 120–180 LSAT scores under standard administrations.

LSAT Score	GPA																					
	3.75 +		3.50–3.74		3.25–3.49		3.00–3.24		2.75–2.99		2.50–2.74		2.25–2.49		2.00–2.24		Below 2.00		No GPA		Total	
	Apps	Adm	Apps	Adm	Apps	Adm	Apps	Adm	Apps	Adm	Apps	Adm	Apps	Adm	Apps	Adm	Apps	Adm	Apps	Adm	Apps	Adm
175–180	0	0	0	0	2	2	0	0	0	0	0	0	0	0	0	0	0	0	0	0	2	2
170–174	4	4	1	1	3	3	2	2	1	1	1	0	2	1	1	0	0	0	0	0	15	12
165–169	11	11	10	10	11	10	12	12	7	3	6	2	7	4	2	1	0	0	0	0	66	53
160–164	43	39	55	53	66	58	57	51	28	21	25	7	7	1	1	0	0	0	3	3	285	233
155–159	97	97	155	150	173	136	135	89	81	22	55	12	30	1	6	0	2	0	6	4	740	511
150–154	109	72	176	85	216	65	198	30	152	14	78	2	40	0	11	0	2	1	6	4	988	273
145–149	42	2	76	10	117	6	129	5	73	1	47	0	23	0	7	0	1	0	8	3	523	27
140–144	14	0	25	0	38	0	57	0	46	0	30	0	20	0	7	0	1	0	3	0	241	0
135–139	2	0	3	0	10	0	18	0	19	0	18	0	14	0	6	0	2	0	8	0	100	0
130–134	0	0	0	0	5	0	5	0	6	0	5	0	7	0	2	0	1	0	3	0	34	0
125–129	0	0	0	0	0	0	0	0	2	0	0	0	0	0	0	0	1	0	0	0	4	0
120–124	0	0	0	0	0	0	0	0	0	0	0	0	1	0	0	0	0	0	0	0	1	0
Total	322	225	501	309	641	280	614	189	415	62	265	23	151	7	43	1	10	1	37	14	2999	1111

Apps = Number of Applicants
Adm = Number Admitted
Reflects 99% of the total applicant pool; highest LSAT data reported.

SUFFOLK UNIVERSITY LAW SCHOOL

David J. Sargent Hall, 120 Tremont Street
Boston, MA 02108-4977
Phone: 617.573.8144; Fax: 617.523.1367
E-mail: lawadm@suffolk.edu; Website: www.law.suffolk.edu

ABA Approved Since 1953

The Basics

Type of school	Private
Term	Semester
Application deadline	3/1
Application fee	$60
Financial aid deadline	3/1
Can first year start other than fall?	No
Student to faculty ratio	17.0 to 1

# of housing spaces available
  restricted to law students
  graduate housing for which law students are eligible

Faculty and Administrators

	Total		Men		Women		Minorities	
	Spr	Fall	Spr	Fall	Spr	Fall	Spr	Fall
Full-time	67	76	39	46	28	30	13	12
Other full-time	4	4	2	2	2	2	0	0
Deans, librarians, & others who teach	17	18	10	10	7	8	1	1
Part-time	64	59	46	44	18	15	5	4
Total	152	157	97	102	55	55	19	17

JD Enrollment and Ethnicity

	Men		Women		Full-Time		Part-Time		1st-Year		Total		JD Degs. Awd.
	#	%	#	%	#	%	#	%	#	%	#	%	
All Hispanics	25	2.8	40	5.1	39	3.6	26	4.4	23	4.4	65	3.9	20
Am. Ind./AK Nat.	2	0.2	2	0.3	2	0.2	2	0.3	1	0.2	4	0.2	3
Asian	42	4.7	84	10.6	91	8.3	35	5.9	50	9.6	126	7.5	31
Black/Af. Am.	17	1.9	27	3.4	35	3.2	9	1.5	15	2.9	44	2.6	9
Nat. HI/Pac. Isl.	0	0.0	0	0.0	0	0.0	0	0.0	0	0.0	0	0.0	0
2 or more races	12	1.3	9	1.1	16	1.5	5	0.8	12	2.3	21	1.2	0
Subtotal (minor.)	98	11.0	162	20.5	183	16.8	77	13.0	101	19.3	260	15.5	64
Nonres. Alien	15	1.7	24	3.0	22	2.0	17	2.9	9	1.7	39	2.3	0
White/Cauc.	751	84.3	579	73.3	855	78.4	475	80.4	413	79.0	1330	79.1	363
Unknown	27	3.0	25	3.2	30	2.8	22	3.7	0	0.0	52	3.1	42
Total	891	53.0	790	47.0	1090	64.8	591	35.2	523	31.1	1681		486

Curriculum

	Full-Time	Part-Time
Typical first-year section size	84	100

Is there typically a "small section" of the first-year class, other than Legal Writing, taught by full-time faculty	Yes	No
If yes, typical size offered last year	42	

# of classroom course titles beyond first-year curriculum	297	

# of upper division courses, excluding seminars, with an enrollment:		
Under 25	111	
25–49	65	
50–74	27	
75–99	9	
100+	24	

# of seminars	62	
# of seminar positions available	1,150	
# of seminar positions filled	602	296
# of positions available in simulation courses	1,112	
# of simulation positions filled	678	334
# of positions available in faculty supervised clinical courses	109	
# of faculty supervised clinical positions filled	93	16
# involved in field placements	84	10
# involved in law journals	141	22
# involved in moot court or trial competitions	140	19
# of credit hours required to graduate	84	

Transfers

Transfers in	18
Transfers out	20

Tuition and Fees

	Resident	Nonresident
Full-time	$41,120	$41,120
Part-time	$30,914	$30,914
Tuition Guarantee Program	N	

Living Expenses

Estimated living expenses for singles

Living on campus	Living off campus	Living at home
N/A	$22,113	$15,497

*ABA
Approved
Since
1953*

GPA and LSAT Scores

	Total	Full-Time	Part-Time
# of apps	3,356	2,727	629
# of offers	1,844	1,459	385
# of matrics	531	328	203
75% GPA	3.50	3.50	3.40
Median GPA	3.20	3.30	3.10
25% GPA	2.90	3.00	2.90
75% LSAT	158	159	156
Median LSAT	156	157	153
25% LSAT	152	155	151

Grants and Scholarships (from prior year)

	Total		Full-Time		Part-Time	
	#	%	#	%	#	%
Total # of students	1,682		1,079		603	
Total # receiving grants	695	41.3	558	51.7	137	22.7
Less than 1/2 tuition	495	29.4	379	35.1	116	19.2
Half to full tuition	166	9.9	145	13.4	21	3.5
Full tuition	29	1.7	29	2.7	0	0.0
More than full tuition	5	0.3	5	0.5	0	0.0
Median grant amount			$15,000		$6,500	

Informational and Library Resources

Total amount spent on library materials	$2,077,718
Study seating capacity inside the library	880
# of full-time equivalent professional librarians	15
Hours per week library is open	103
# of open, wired connections available to students	3,750
# of networked computers available for use by students	280
Has wireless network?	Y
Requires computer?	N

JD Attrition (from prior year)

	Academic	Other	Total	
	#	#	#	%
1st year	10	21	31	5.8
2nd year	2	2	4	0.8
3rd year	0	0	0	0.0
4th year	0	0	0	0.0

Employment (9 months after graduation)

	Total	Percentage
Employment status known	464	96.7
Employment status unknown	16	3.3
Employed	385	83.0
Pursuing graduate degrees	8	1.7
Unemployed (seeking, not seeking, or studying for the bar)	66	14.2
Type of Employment		
# employed in law firms	193	50.1
# employed in business and industry	77	20.0
# employed in government	53	13.8
# employed in public interest	10	2.6
# employed as judicial clerks	18	4.7
# employed in academia	17	4.4
Geographic Location		
# employed in state	301	78.2
# employed outside the US	1	0.3
# of states where employed	22	

Bar Passage Rates

First-time takers	459	Reporting %	89.76
Average school %	88.11	Average state %	89.77
Average pass difference	−1.66		

Jurisdiction	Takers	Passers	Pass %	State %	Diff %
Massachusetts	412	363	88.11	89.77	−1.66

SUFFOLK UNIVERSITY LAW SCHOOL

David J. Sargent Hall, 120 Tremont Street
Boston, MA 02108-4977
Phone: 617.573.8144; Fax: 617.523.1367
E-mail: lawadm@suffolk.edu; Website: www.law.suffolk.edu

Introduction

Suffolk University Law School has produced some of the nation's most distinguished legal professionals. Suffolk Law's curriculum combines a strong academic foundation with expertise in an array of specialty areas, and a nationally known faculty provides superior preparation for practice. Through clinical, internship, and public service opportunities, students earn credit while experiencing how the law works in the real world. Suffolk Law is an unmatched place to launch a successful career in the law.

Technology and Physical Facilities

Every seat in Sargent Hall's classrooms, library, and common areas has direct access to a high-speed network. Sargent Hall is wireless accessible throughout and all classrooms contain multimedia capabilities. A central media control room provides the ability to conduct videoconferencing and webcasting from any of the Law School's classrooms.

Concentrations and Joint-Degree Programs

Students may enroll in one of five concentrations: Business Law and Financial Services, Civil Litigation, Health and Biomedical Law, Intellectual Property (which includes a specialization in Patent Law), or International Law. Suffolk Law offers five, four-year, joint-degree programs that combine a Juris Doctor with a Master of Business Administration, Public Administration, International Economics, Finance, or Criminal Justice, as well as a three-year JD/MBA program.

Clinical and Internship Programs

Students are encouraged to enroll in one of our clinical programs. Suffolk Law's clinics include the Battered Women's Advocacy Program, Child Advocacy, Education Advocacy, Evening Landlord-Tenant, Family Advocacy, Health, Housing, Immigration, Investor Advocacy, Juvenile Internship Program, Juvenile Justice Center, Suffolk Defenders, and Suffolk Prosecutors. Additionally, students can participate in the Civil and Judicial Internship Program, interning in a variety of legal settings, including state and federal courts; federal, state, and local government agencies; legal aid organizations; public defenders' offices; and private law firms and companies.

Foreign and Graduate Programs

Suffolk Law, in conjunction with the University of Lund, offers a summer study-abroad program held in Lund, Sweden. The program combines the strengths of our international law curriculum with the expertise offered by the University of Lund law faculty and the Swedish Bar and Judiciary.

Suffolk Law has an exclusive agreement with the Center for International Legal Studies (CILS) in Salzburg, Austria, to offer internships to US law students and externships to graduates with law degrees. International internships are available to JD students, and international externships are offered to LLM students and other postgraduates with law degrees. Internships are available at law firms, businesses, and nonprofit organizations in almost every country of the world.

Suffolk Law offers two LLM degree programs. One is in Global Law and Technology, which offers specializations in Intellectual Property and Information Technology Law, Biotechnology and Health Law, International Law and Business, and US Law and Legal Methods, and is held in Boston, Massachusetts. Full-time and part-time schedules are offered. The second program offers an LLM in US and Global Business Law to lawyers from international jurisdictions and to US JD law graduates. This executive-style LLM program is administered at law schools abroad only.

Academic Support Programs

The goal of the Academic Support Program (ASP) is to help students make the most of their abilities. To accomplish this goal, the faculty conducts weekly classes on such diverse topics as legal analysis and writing, course outlining, and time management. These optional classes are open to all first-year students. In addition, ASP professors are always available to meet with individual or small groups of students in order to address specific questions or issues. The ASP also has a lending library containing study aids and material on substantive legal topics. Additionally, the ASP library contains exercises on grammar, legal writing, and analysis. All students are encouraged to stop by and take advantage of these resources.

Scholarships and Loans

Suffolk Law participates in student financial aid programs to assist students in financing the cost of their legal education. Both need-based and merit-based aid is available. Financial aid awards (scholarships, grants, loans, and employment awards) are made to assist students in financing educational costs when their personal and family resources may not be sufficient. Merit-based scholarships are awarded by the law school's Admissions Committee at the time a candidate is admitted. These awards are made to students based on outstanding academic achievement.

In addition to the need-based grant and merit-based scholarship programs, Suffolk Law offers Sargent Scholarships ranging from $20,000 to full tuition to entering students with significant financial need and exceptional academic strength. All admitted students who apply for need-based financial aid are considered for an award.

Suffolk Law also has a Loan Repayment Assistance Program for students who, upon graduation, pursue low-income, public service, law-related employment.

Student Activities, Publications, and Opportunities

Students have a number of opportunities to develop legal skills outside of the classroom through participation in the *Suffolk University Law Review*, the *Suffolk Transnational Law Review*, the *Journal of High Technology Law* (www.jhtl.org), and the *Suffolk Journal of Health and Biomedical Law*. Students can also participate in the Moot Court Board (which also publishes the *Suffolk Journal of Trial and Appellate Advocacy*) as well as on moot court competition teams such as the National Trial Competition Team, ATLA Trial Team,

Constitutional Law Team, Information Technology and Privacy Law Team, Intellectual Property Law Team, Jessup International Law Team, National Invitational Trial Tournament of Champions, National Moot Court Team, Securities Law Team, Sports Law Team, and Tax Law Team. Students can also join one of more than 40 student organizations or participate in the Student Bar Association.

Career Development Office

Suffolk University Law School is committed to preparing students to serve diverse clients and communities. Suffolk Law graduates can be found in private practice; corporations; public interest organizations; the military; the executive, judicial, and legislative branches of government; and in rewarding careers outside the legal realm. The Career Development Office coordinates on- and off-campus recruitment programs and résumé collections throughout the academic year, and also maintains an extensive online job database, a resource library, and employment websites. Job searching support begins with a comprehensive career-based curriculum provided to first-year students and extends throughout students' time at the Law School and throughout graduates' professional careers. The Career Development Office offers one-on-one career counseling and coaching, résumé and cover letter critiques, mock interviews, and innovative programs, panels, workshops, and information sessions. Professional staff conduct employer visits and related job cultivation nationwide. The Career Development Office prides itself on connecting with students through personalized outreach and cutting-edge technology and makes sure all students are supported in their job searches and career development endeavors.

Peer Mentoring Program

This program helps nontraditional students achieve their full potential as law students. Suffolk Law defines nontraditional students as those who have been historically excluded or marginalized from the law school community based on any of the following factors: (1) race, (2) ethnicity, (3) socioeconomic disadvantage, or (4) history of low performance on standardized tests.

The program starts with a two-week summer session that begins two weeks before orientation. Participating students attend classes on criminal law and contracts and receive extensive training in case briefing, legal analysis, outlining, exam preparation, and exam writing. Students also receive feedback on case briefs and practice exams and, at the end of each class, an upper-class student mentor leads a small group discussion regarding the class material.

Building on the summer session, the program holds weekly seminars during the academic year to help students master the skills to perform well on both multiple-choice and essay exams. Students have the opportunity to meet individually on an ongoing basis with both an upper-class student mentor and the program director. The purpose of both the weekly seminars and the individual meetings is to help students develop and adhere to sound time management practices, effective study habits, and critical thinking skills.

Rappaport Center for Law and Public Service

The Rappaport Center for Law and Public Service was established in 2006, with the generous support of Phyllis and Jerry Rappaport and The Phyllis and Jerome Lyle Rappaport Foundation. Leveraging Suffolk Law School's ideal downtown location, and rich tradition of public service, the Rappaport Center brings together elected officials, senior policymakers, community advocates, private sector leaders, faculty, and students to engage in dialogue around important public policy issues. The center also provides career advising to students interested in public service, administers the law school's pro bono program, and is home to the highly competitive Rappaport Fellows Program in Law and Public Policy. For more information about the Rappaport Center, please visit www.rappaportcenter.org.

APPLICANT PROFILE

Suffolk University Law School

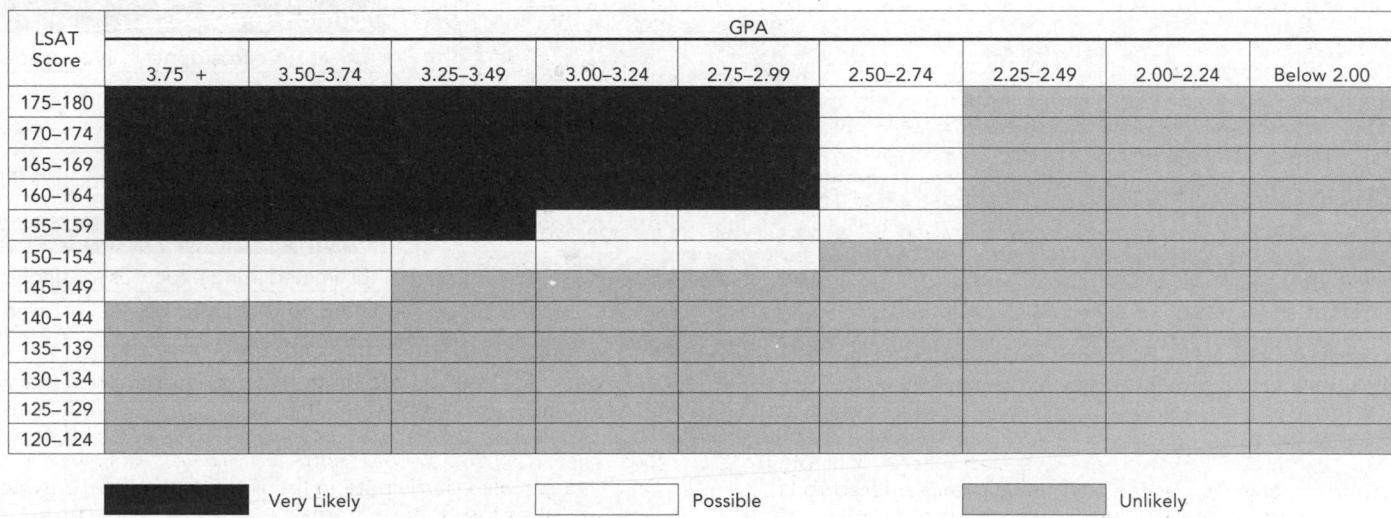

LSAT Score	GPA								
	3.75 +	3.50–3.74	3.25–3.49	3.00–3.24	2.75–2.99	2.50–2.74	2.25–2.49	2.00–2.24	Below 2.00
175–180									
170–174									
165–169									
160–164									
155–159									
150–154									
145–149									
140–144									
135–139									
130–134									
125–129									
120–124									

■ Very Likely ☐ Possible ▨ Unlikely

SYRACUSE UNIVERSITY COLLEGE OF LAW

Office of Admissions and Financial Aid, Suite 340
Syracuse, NY 13244-1030
Phone: 315.443.1962; Fax: 315.443.9568
E-mail: admissions@law.syr.edu; Website: www.law.syr.edu

ABA
Approved
Since
1923

The Basics

Type of school	Private
Term	Semester
Application deadline	4/1
Application fee	$75
Financial aid deadline	2/15
Can first year start other than fall?	No
Student to faculty ratio	11.9 to 1
# of housing spaces available restricted to law students	
graduate housing for which law students are eligible	150

Faculty and Administrators

	Total		Men		Women		Minorities	
	Spr	Fall	Spr	Fall	Spr	Fall	Spr	Fall
Full-time	41	45	27	31	14	14	9	9
Other full-time	17	15	8	6	9	9	2	2
Deans, librarians, & others who teach	6	6	3	3	3	3	1	1
Part-time	21	16	16	12	5	4	3	1
Total	85	82	54	52	31	30	15	13

Curriculum

	Full-Time	Part-Time
Typical first-year section size	65	0
Is there typically a "small section" of the first-year class, other than Legal Writing, taught by full-time faculty	Yes	No
If yes, typical size offered last year	45	
# of classroom course titles beyond first-year curriculum	115	

# of upper division courses, excluding seminars, with an enrollment:	Under 25	120
	25–49	27
	50–74	6
	75–99	2
	100+	0

# of seminars		12
# of seminar positions available		192
# of seminar positions filled	122	0
# of positions available in simulation courses		565
# of simulation positions filled	405	0
# of positions available in faculty supervised clinical courses		155
# of faculty supervised clinical positions filled	154	0
# involved in field placements	108	0
# involved in law journals	77	0
# involved in moot court or trial competitions	51	0
# of credit hours required to graduate		87

JD Enrollment and Ethnicity

	Men		Women		Full-Time		Part-Time		1st-Year		Total		JD Degs. Awd.
	#	%	#	%	#	%	#	%	#	%	#	%	
All Hispanics	16	4.2	12	4.6	27	4.3	1	33.3	7	2.8	28	4.4	8
Am. Ind./AK Nat.	0	0.0	1	0.4	1	0.2	0	0.0	0	0.0	1	0.2	2
Asian	33	8.7	30	11.6	63	9.9	0	0.0	17	6.8	63	9.9	21
Black/Af. Am.	13	3.4	6	2.3	19	3.0	0	0.0	5	2.0	19	3.0	6
Nat. HI/Pac. Isl.	0	0.0	1	0.4	1	0.2	0	0.0	0	0.0	1	0.2	0
2 or more races	9	2.4	7	2.7	16	2.5	0	0.0	15	6.0	16	2.5	0
Subtotal (minor.)	71	18.7	57	22.0	127	20.0	1	33.3	44	17.5	128	20.1	37
Nonres. Alien	10	2.6	5	1.9	15	2.4	0	0.0	3	1.2	15	2.4	0
White/Cauc.	250	66.0	164	63.3	413	65.0	1	33.3	198	78.9	414	64.9	100
Unknown	48	12.7	33	12.7	80	12.6	1	33.3	6	2.4	81	12.7	40
Total	379	59.4	259	40.6	635	99.5	3	0.5	251	39.3	638		189

Transfers

Transfers in	5
Transfers out	14

Tuition and Fees

	Resident	Nonresident
Full-time	$45,126	$45,126
Part-time		
Tuition Guarantee Program		N

Living Expenses

Estimated living expenses for singles

Living on campus	Living off campus	Living at home
$18,574	$18,574	$18,574

SYRACUSE UNIVERSITY COLLEGE OF LAW

ABA Approved Since 1923

GPA and LSAT Scores

	Total	Full-Time	Part-Time
# of apps	2,332	2,332	0
# of offers	962	962	0
# of matrics	252	252	0
75% GPA	3.57	3.57	0.00
Median GPA	3.32	3.32	0.00
25% GPA	3.12	3.12	0.00
75% LSAT	157	157	0
Median LSAT	155	155	0
25% LSAT	153	153	0

Grants and Scholarships (from prior year)

	Total #	Total %	Full-Time #	Full-Time %	Part-Time #	Part-Time %
Total # of students	603		598		5	
Total # receiving grants	446	74.0	446	74.6	0	0.0
Less than 1/2 tuition	363	60.2	363	60.7	0	0.0
Half to full tuition	77	12.8	77	12.9	0	0.0
Full tuition	0	0.0	0	0.0	0	0.0
More than full tuition	6	1.0	6	1.0	0	0.0
Median grant amount			$7,500		$0	

Informational and Library Resources

Total amount spent on library materials	$1,406,410
Study seating capacity inside the library	398
# of full-time equivalent professional librarians	10
Hours per week library is open	106
# of open, wired connections available to students	19
# of networked computers available for use by students	76
Has wireless network?	Y
Requires computer?	Y

JD Attrition (from prior year)

	Academic #	Other #	Total #	Total %
1st year	8	21	29	13.2
2nd year	0	4	4	2.1
3rd year	0	1	1	0.5
4th year	0	0	0	0.0

Employment (9 months after graduation)

	Total	Percentage
Employment status known	203	93.5
Employment status unknown	14	6.5
Employed	176	86.7
Pursuing graduate degrees	15	7.4
Unemployed (seeking, not seeking, or studying for the bar)	6	3.0
Type of Employment		
# employed in law firms	78	44.3
# employed in business and industry	36	20.5
# employed in government	25	14.2
# employed in public interest	14	8.0
# employed as judicial clerks	18	10.2
# employed in academia	5	2.8
Geographic Location		
# employed in state	89	50.6
# employed outside the US	2	1.1
# of states where employed	25	

Bar Passage Rates

First-time takers	222	Reporting %	75.68
Average school %	87.49	Average state %	86.42
Average pass difference	1.07		

Jurisdiction	Takers	Passers	Pass %	State %	Diff %
New York	150	131	87.33	86.51	0.82
Pennsylvania	18	16	88.89	85.69	3.20

SYRACUSE UNIVERSITY COLLEGE OF LAW

Office of Admissions and Financial Aid, Suite 340
Syracuse, NY 13244-1030
Phone: 315.443.1962; Fax: 315.443.9568
E-mail: admissions@law.syr.edu; Website: www.law.syr.edu

Introduction

Syracuse University College of Law was established in 1895. The College of Law is a charter member of the AALS and is fully approved by the ABA. Embedded in a dynamic teaching and research university, the College of Law is one of the oldest of the 11 schools and colleges comprising Syracuse University. The College of Law complex is located on the 200-acre SU main campus overlooking scenic Central New York and the city of Syracuse.

Curriculum

Syracuse University College of Law's mission is guided by the philosophy that the best way to educate lawyers to practice in today's world is to engage them in a process of interdisciplinary learning while teaching them to apply what they learn in the classroom to real legal issues, problems, and clients. Beginning in the first year and continuing throughout the curriculum, students are exposed to educational settings that integrate opportunities to acquire a better understanding of legal theory and doctrine, develop professional skills, and gain exposure to the values and ethics of the legal profession. As a result, Syracuse students are better prepared for the practice of law.

Interdisciplinary Learning Opportunities

- **Disability Law and Policy Program**—Students may pursue a joint degree in law and disability studies and certificate programs in disability law and policy. Coursework, internships, and the Disability Rights Clinic push the boundaries of a traditional legal education and engage students in hands-on learning for the public good.
- **Institute for National Security and Counterterrorism (INSCT)**—The institute, a joint enterprise of the College of Law and the Maxwell School of Citizenship and Public Affairs, is dedicated to interdisciplinary teaching, research, and public service focused on important national and global problems of security and terrorism. INSCT students pursuing professional and doctoral degrees engage in advanced coursework toward specialty certificates in security and terrorism studies. The institute's research portfolio is broad and deep, ranging from faculty-supervised student working papers and research reports, to significant articles and books for academic journals and presses, to sponsorship of major workshops and conferences designed to further a research agenda in security or terrorism. While all INSCT research advances knowledge in the field, many projects are conducted on behalf of, or in consultation with, agencies, municipalities, and other public entities, thus providing direct public service.
- **Technology Commercialization Law Program**—The program is a course concentration within the law curriculum that provides an interdisciplinary and applied approach to the study of commercial development of new technologies. The program combines classroom courses, case study problem-solving, negotiation and drafting exercises, and applied research projects.
- **Family Law and Social Policy Center**—The center prepares students for a career in family law by engaging them in interdisciplinary research, providing them with applied learning experiences, and connecting them with the community to provide services that benefit families and children. The center offers opportunities that blend interdisciplinary theory and practice in the field of family law in challenging and rewarding ways. These combined experiences allow students to emerge from the program with the professional skills and experiences necessary to launch successful and satisfying careers in family law.
- **Center for Global Law and Practice**—The center provides students with specialized foreign, comparative, and international courses as well as cocurricular offerings. Students are exposed to the myriad ways in which the process of globalization increasingly impacts trade and commerce; the environment; national, regional, and local governments; individual rights and welfare; and even the legal profession itself. A summer-abroad program is offered in London.
- **Center for Indigenous Law, Governance, and Citizenship**—The center is a research-based law and policy institute focused on indigenous nations, their development, and their interaction with the US and Canadian governments.
- **Institute for the Study of the Judiciary, Politics, and the Media (IJPM)**—The institute is a collaborative effort between Syracuse University's College of Law, Maxwell School of Citizenship and Public Affairs, and the S. I. Newhouse School of Public Communications. The institute is devoted to the study of issues at the intersection of law, politics, and the media. The institute sponsors lectures, conferences, and symposia designed to foster discussion and debate among legal scholars, sitting judges, and working journalists.
- **Center on Property, Citizenship, and Social Entrepreneurism**—The center brings together experts from a variety of fields and institutions to discuss and explore issues related to modern real estate transactions and finance; community development and housing; global property law systems; and access to ownership for inclusion of the elderly, the poor, and persons with disabilities.
- **Burton Blatt Institute (BBI) Centers of Innovation on Disability**—Through research and scholarship in action, the institute will advance the civic, economic, and social participation of persons with disabilities in a global society. The institute seeks to create a collaborative environment—with entrepreneurial innovation and best business practices—to foster public-private dialogue, and create the capacity to transform policy, systems, and people through inclusive education, the workforce, and communities.

Other Opportunities for Specialization

- **Clinical Programs**—Legal concepts learned in the classroom come to life for students who participate in the in-house clinics and externship program. Students work with lawyers in law offices, becoming immersed in the actual practice of law through their work on real cases affecting real clients. Students provide much-needed legal services to our community, as many of our clients are unable to afford private counsel. Diverse clinical opportunities at the College of Law include the Criminal

Defense Law Clinic, the Community Development Law Clinic, the Children's Rights and Family Law Clinic, the Disability Rights Clinic, the Elder Law Clinic, the Low Income Taxpayer Law Clinic, and the Securities Arbitration Clinic/Consumer Law Clinic. In addition, the externship program provides opportunities for students to work in government offices, judges' chambers, university-based programs, and public interest organizations.

- **Joint-Degree Programs**—Students who desire a greater degree of specialization may select from a number of joint-degree opportunities. Formal joint-degree programs exist in public administration, international relations, business administration or accounting, communications, environmental law, education (disability studies), social work, and engineering. Joint degrees may also be designed to fit special career objectives.
- **Advocacy Skills**—Syracuse Law is recognized for its exceptional advocacy programs. Students are actively involved, and have been highly successful, in national and regional moot court competitions. Syracuse students participate in intraschool programs throughout the year in trial and appellate competitions covering a wide variety of areas.

Library

The law library's four spacious levels within the College of Law complex house more than 473,000 volumes in print and microform; 2,200 serials; and extensive audio, video, and electronic holdings—all accessible through the university-wide online library catalog. On the main floor, the circulation and reference desks offer conveniently located services and research support in close proximity to the Electronic Research Center. The library adds approximately 2,500 new titles to its catalog each year, including a growing number of licensed electronic databases.

Admission

History reveals that undergraduate grades and LSAT scores are reliable measures, in most cases, for predicting probable success in law study. Thus, an index combining grades and test scores becomes a factor in most admission decisions. However, recognizing that numerical indicators are not always the best predictors of success in law school—even when considered in combination with other factors—the college admits a limited number of students each year through its Legal Education Opportunity (LEO) Program. The program's dual objectives are to recruit and admit persons who may have been deprived of equal education opportunities for reasons of race, gender, poverty, or other factors beyond their control; and to recruit and admit persons with unusual accomplishments, backgrounds, and experiences that suggest traditional admission criteria may be inadequate predictors of likely success in law study.

Financial Aid

The college is committed to assisting students in financing their legal education through a comprehensive financial aid program. Awards are made from a variety of sources, including merit-based scholarships; need-based tuition grants; and from federal sources, including the work-study program and the Perkins and Direct Loan programs.

Professional and Career Development

The Office of Professional and Career Development provides a full range of career-oriented services to students, including a broad mix of innovative and traditional support. Programming is designed to prepare students for leadership, service, and professionalism, while developing their ability to deal with lifelong career planning. The Professional and Career Development staff work one-on-one with students assisting them in crafting job search strategies that focus on their interests and capitalize on their strengths.

APPLICANT PROFILE

Syracuse University College of Law
This grid includes only applicants who earned 120–180 LSAT scores under standard administrations.

LSAT Score	GPA																				
	3.75 +		3.50–3.74		3.25–3.49		3.00–3.24		2.75–2.99		2.50–2.74		2.25–2.49		2.00–2.24		Below 2.00		No GPA		Total	
	Apps	Adm	Apps	Adm	Apps	Adm	Apps	Adm	Apps	Adm	Apps	Adm	Apps	Adm	Apps	Adm	Apps	Adm	Apps	Adm	Apps	Adm
170–180	1	1	3	3	5	5	4	3	1	1	0	0	0	0	0	0	0	0	0	0	14	13
165–169	4	4	2	2	1	1	1	1	2	2	4	3	2	0	1	0	1	0	0	0	18	13
160–164	16	16	32	31	40	38	37	36	20	19	16	9	7	2	3	0	1	0	0	0	172	151
155–159	46	42	82	80	111	104	129	119	74	44	53	11	24	0	8	0	2	0	9	4	538	404
150–154	62	42	151	73	204	100	231	91	109	17	48	5	31	0	12	0	3	0	15	1	866	329
145–149	20	1	75	8	101	8	111	5	80	0	39	0	19	0	3	0	2	0	13	0	463	22
120–144	9	0	21	0	49	0	59	0	43	0	31	0	14	0	9	0	3	0	9	0	247	0
Total	158	106	366	197	511	256	572	255	329	83	191	28	97	2	36	0	12	0	46	5	2318	932

Apps = Number of Applicants
Adm = Number Admitted
Reflects 99% of the total applicant pool; highest LSAT data reported.

TEMPLE UNIVERSITY—JAMES E. BEASLEY SCHOOL OF LAW

1719 North Broad Street
Philadelphia, PA 19122
Phone: 800.560.1428; Fax: 215.204.9319
E-mail: lawadmis@temple.edu; Website: www.law.temple.edu

The Basics

Type of school	Public
Term	Semester
Application deadline	3/1
Application fee	$60
Financial aid deadline	3/1
Can first year start other than fall?	No
Student to faculty ratio	12.6 to 1
# of housing spaces available restricted to law students	
graduate housing for which law students are eligible	

Faculty and Administrators

	Total		Men		Women		Minorities	
	Spr	Fall	Spr	Fall	Spr	Fall	Spr	Fall
Full-time	58	61	34	36	24	25	14	15
Other full-time	1	2	1	2	0	0	1	1
Deans, librarians, & others who teach	12	12	4	5	8	7	2	2
Part-time	122	94	81	59	41	35	13	13
Total	193	169	120	102	73	67	30	31

Curriculum

	Full-Time	Part-Time
Typical first-year section size	60	60
Is there typically a "small section" of the first-year class, other than Legal Writing, taught by full-time faculty	No	No
If yes, typical size offered last year		
# of classroom course titles beyond first-year curriculum	179	
# of upper division courses, excluding seminars, with an enrollment: Under 25	192	
25–49	55	
50–74	19	
75–99	14	
100+	0	
# of seminars	51	
# of seminar positions available	754	
# of seminar positions filled	526	92
# of positions available in simulation courses	1,169	
# of simulation positions filled	861	142
# of positions available in faculty supervised clinical courses	74	
# of faculty supervised clinical positions filled	64	1
# involved in field placements	215	14
# involved in law journals	161	2
# involved in moot court or trial competitions	36	3
# of credit hours required to graduate	87	

JD Enrollment and Ethnicity

	Men #	Men %	Women #	Women %	Full-Time #	Full-Time %	Part-Time #	Part-Time %	1st-Year #	1st-Year %	Total #	Total %	JD Degs. Awd.
All Hispanics	38	6.8	36	8.5	67	8.4	7	3.8	32	9.8	74	7.5	5
Am. Ind./AK Nat.	7	1.3	2	0.5	8	1.0	1	0.5	1	0.3	9	0.9	1
Asian	31	5.6	54	12.7	70	8.8	15	8.1	24	7.3	85	8.6	29
Black/Af. Am.	30	5.4	41	9.6	61	7.7	10	5.4	22	6.7	71	7.2	20
Nat. HI/Pac. Isl.	0	0.0	0	0.0	0	0.0	0	0.0	0	0.0	0	0.0	0
2 or more races	4	0.7	3	0.7	7	0.9	0	0.0	7	2.1	7	0.7	0
Subtotal (minor.)	110	19.7	136	31.9	213	26.7	33	17.7	86	26.3	246	25.0	55
Nonres. Alien	1	0.2	3	0.7	4	0.5	0	0.0	1	0.3	4	0.4	0
White/Cauc.	442	79.4	281	66.0	574	72.0	149	80.1	238	72.8	723	73.6	228
Unknown	4	0.7	6	1.4	6	0.8	4	2.2	1	0.3	10	1.0	7
Total	557	56.7	426	43.3	797	81.1	186	18.9	326	33.3	983		295

Transfers

Transfers in	0
Transfers out	11

Tuition and Fees

	Resident	Nonresident
Full-time	$18,206	$31,220
Part-time	$14,692	$25,108
Tuition Guarantee Program	N	

Living Expenses

Estimated living expenses for singles

Living on campus	Living off campus	Living at home
$20,260	$20,260	$15,016

TEMPLE UNIVERSITY—JAMES E. BEASLEY SCHOOL OF LAW

ABA
Approved
Since
1933

GPA and LSAT Scores

	Total	Full-Time	Part-Time
# of apps	4,682	4,279	403
# of offers	1,813	1,696	117
# of matrics	326	271	55
75% GPA	3.63	3.64	3.54
Median GPA	3.44	3.47	3.28
25% GPA	3.20	3.24	3.03
75% LSAT	164	164	161
Median LSAT	161	162	159
25% LSAT	159	160	157

Grants and Scholarships (from prior year)

	Total #	Total %	Full-Time #	Full-Time %	Part-Time #	Part-Time %
Total # of students	976		784		192	
Total # receiving grants	434	44.5	408	52.0	26	13.5
Less than 1/2 tuition	308	31.6	282	36.0	26	13.5
Half to full tuition	56	5.7	56	7.1	0	0.0
Full tuition	70	7.2	70	8.9	0	0.0
More than full tuition	0	0.0	0	0.0	0	0.0
Median grant amount			$7,500		$3,750	

Informational and Library Resources

Total amount spent on library materials	$1,407,603
Study seating capacity inside the library	664
# of full-time equivalent professional librarians	17
Hours per week library is open	96
# of open, wired connections available to students	425
# of networked computers available for use by students	118
Has wireless network?	Y
Requires computer?	N

JD Attrition (from prior year)

	Academic #	Other #	Total #	Total %
1st year	0	12	12	3.9
2nd year	1	19	20	6.3
3rd year	0	0	0	0.0
4th year	0	0	0	0.0

Employment (9 months after graduation)

	Total	Percentage
Employment status known	284	99.6
Employment status unknown	1	0.4
Employed	249	87.7
Pursuing graduate degrees	10	3.5
Unemployed (seeking, not seeking, or studying for the bar)	21	7.4
Type of Employment		
# employed in law firms	117	47.0
# employed in business and industry	31	12.4
# employed in government	26	10.4
# employed in public interest	19	7.6
# employed as judicial clerks	38	15.3
# employed in academia	15	6.0
Geographic Location		
# employed in state	169	67.9
# employed outside the US	1	0.4
# of states where employed	18	

Bar Passage Rates

First-time takers	285	Reporting %	78.60
Average school %	95.09	Average state %	85.69
Average pass difference	9.40		

Jurisdiction	Takers	Passers	Pass %	State %	Diff %
Pennsylvania	224	213	95.09	85.69	9.40

TEMPLE UNIVERSITY—JAMES E. BEASLEY SCHOOL OF LAW

1719 North Broad Street
Philadelphia, PA 19122
Phone: 800.560.1428; Fax: 215.204.9319
E-mail: lawadmis@temple.edu; Website: www.law.temple.edu

Introduction

Temple Law School is recognized both nationally and internationally as a leader in legal education. We offer both day and evening programs, and students may enroll on either a full- or part-time basis. Our innovative student-centered curriculum integrates both critical thinking and practical legal skills and has been developed in response to new realities and new challenges, such as globalization, technology, and interdisciplinary studies. Students at Temple build lawyering skills both in the classroom and in the law firms, courts, public service agencies, and financial institutions of Philadelphia, a major legal, commercial, and cultural center. Our students, faculty, and alumni are shaping the law at every level and are making an impact in Philadelphia, the United States, and around the world.

Temple students are bright, dynamic, and diverse. They come from a variety of backgrounds and disciplines. Many have traveled and lived in other countries, and their real-life experiences vitalize classroom discussion. A recent entering class hailed from 136 colleges and universities, and from 31 states and foreign countries. Ten percent had earned advanced degrees, and nearly 75 percent had at least one year of work experience before entering law school.

The faculty is an extraordinary group who are recognized throughout the world as legal experts, scholars, and policy makers. Their breadth of experience in virtually every area of practice brings a rich and distinctive quality to classroom discussions. While their accomplishments are many, it is their commitment to teaching that many students note as their greatest achievement.

The Study of Law at Temple

Trial skills enhance every lawyer's abilities in areas that intersect all aspects of practice, and Temple students benefit from one of the most advanced **trial advocacy** programs in the nation. Experienced faculty, innovative teaching methods, and extensive clinical offerings set Temple's program above the rest. The trial advocacy curriculum includes the innovative Integrated Program, which combines the teaching of trial advocacy, evidence, and civil procedure in a year-long course. Temple's record in law school trial competitions is unmatched, having won an unparalleled 21 consecutive National Trial Competition regional championships, 5 national championships, and 15 invitational tournaments. Consistently recognized for its prizewinning trial advocacy programs, Temple has the distinction of being the only two-time winner of the American College of Trial Lawyers' Emil Gumpert Award for Excellence in Teaching Trial Advocacy.

Temple students have access to an extensive array of programs to prepare them to practice law in an increasingly global society. Temple's strength in **international law** includes opportunities for summer study in Rome, Italy, as well as semester-abroad programs in Tokyo, Japan; Beijing, China; Cork, Ireland; Tel Aviv, Israel; Utrecht, the Netherlands; and Muenster, Germany. Additionally, Temple offers a Master of Laws program for international students holding foreign law degrees and has many active student organizations, such as an international law journal, the International Law Society, and the Jessup International Moot

Court team. Temple's strong reputation in international law has been enhanced by the JD/LLM in Transnational Law for American law students; an LLM program in Beijing, China, in which Chinese lawyers study American law; and the creation of the Institute for International Law and Public Policy. Students may also design individualized study-abroad options at law schools around the world.

Temple is a pioneer in **intellectual property and technology law**, preparing students to learn and succeed in the virtual world. Temple has expanded the boundaries of traditional intellectual property law by integrating bodies of law that focus on the rapid expansion of the Internet, electronic commerce, biotechnologies, and other newly emerging legal issues. With faculty members who are experts in the field, and through hands-on activities outside the classroom, such as writing for a journal specializing in technology law or participating on the Intellectual Property Law Moot Court Team, students learn how to meet the challenges of practicing law in a world without borders.

Temple offers superior training in **business and tax law**, including a creative program that combines the teaching of professional responsibility, substantive law courses, and business skills, such as interviewing, negotiating, and drafting. Prospective business lawyers can also pursue a JD/LLM in Taxation or, in conjunction with the Fox School of Business and Management, pursue a dual JD/MBA degree, or earn a certificate in business law.

Public service is a Temple tradition. The Office of Public Interest Programs is the focal point for public interest activities at the law school. Students provide legal services in the Philadelphia area through the extensive clinical program, the Temple Legal Aid Office, and various volunteer and community outreach programs. Public interest careers are supported by the Student Public Interest Network, which provides grants for summer internships; the Public Interest Scholars Program, which provides scholarships to entering students with a demonstrated commitment to public service; and the Barrack Public Interest Fellowships, a loan repayment assistance program for graduates in public interest jobs.

The curriculum is anchored by the first-year **legal research and writing program**. Instruction in law schools is founded on the notion of teaching each student to think like an attorney. Temple's legal research and writing program is a year-long course of study that teaches the basics of writing and speaking like a lawyer. Students learn basic legal research techniques and the fundamentals of legal writing. It is one of the most intensive and advanced programs of its kind in the country and is rated as one of the best in the nation.

Technology and Facilities

Located in the heart of a thriving, urban university, the law school complex consists of three recently renovated buildings designed to provide students with a state-of-the-art educational environment. "Smart" classrooms equipped with cutting-edge technology, including video, audio, and Internet access, allow faculty to use technology in all of the classrooms and the law school's "anytime, anywhere" computer access program includes a combination of wired and wireless network access. The faculty and administration regularly communicate with students via e-mail, and the law school uses a sophisticated course management system that allows the faculty to post assignments, syllabi, announcements, and links to a variety of additional resources for each class.

Student Activities

Students are an integral part of policy making and governance at the law school. The Student Bar Association is the governing organization that oversees the more than 30 student groups that flourish at Temple, including the Black Law Students Association, the Latino Law Students Association, the Asian/Pacific Islander American Law Student Association, the Women's Law Caucus, and OUTLaw. Student publications include the *Temple Law Review;* the *Temple Journal of Science, Technology, and Environmental Law;* the *Temple International and Comparative Law Journal;* and the *Temple Political and Civil Rights Law Review.* Students who excel in advocacy may participate in the National Trial Team or the Moot Court Honor Society.

Career Planning

Temple students are poised and ready to succeed in every sector of the legal job market, having acquired unique practical training that other schools don't offer. As graduates, they carry a strong reputation for being able to hit the ground running, confident and prepared to practice law in the field of their choice. The Career Planning Office assists students with the development of strategies for securing employment and provides the resources necessary to supplement each student's individualized job search. Through the school's online career planning manager, students can search job postings,

participate in various recruiting programs, and apply for jobs. In addition, one-on-one career counseling is available, and workshops and programs are offered to assist students in sharpening their job-search skills, including résumé writing, networking, and interviewing. Temple alumni are working in all 50 states and around the world and in a variety of legal fields.

Admission and Financial Aid

Temple's highly competitive admission process is designed to look at the whole person. The faculty Admissions Committee carefully evaluates each application and is committed to admitting the very best from a pool of talented applicants. In keeping with Temple's commitment to diversity and its mission of offering opportunities to students who might otherwise be precluded from pursuing a high-quality legal education, the committee may consider an application under Sp.A.C.E, its discretionary admission process. Through this process, the committee carefully selects applicants who have outstanding performance records and exceptional aptitudes for the study and practice of law that are not necessarily reflected by grades and LSAT scores alone.

The financial aid program supports the admission process with a combination of loans and both need- and merit-based scholarships, including the Beasley Scholars program, Conwell Law Scholarships, Law Faculty Scholarships, the Rubin-Presser Public Interest Scholars program, and First Year Scholar Awards.

APPLICANT PROFILE

Temple University—James E. Beasley School of Law
This grid includes only applicants who earned 120–180 LSAT scores under standard administrations.

LSAT Score	3.75 +		3.50–3.74		3.25–3.49		3.00–3.24		2.75–2.99		2.50–2.74		2.25–2.49		2.00–2.24		Below 2.00		No GPA		Total	
	Apps	Adm	Apps	Adm	Apps	Adm	Apps	Adm	Apps	Adm	Apps	Adm	Apps	Adm	Apps	Adm	Apps	Adm	Apps	Adm	Apps	Adm
170–180	25	23	35	30	36	31	16	11	9	4	6	0	0	0	0	0	0	0	0	0	127	99
165–169	92	90	124	119	108	106	83	59	30	21	18	11	7	3	1	0	0	0	4	0	467	409
160–164	240	211	354	292	393	278	257	139	98	45	36	11	20	4	5	1	0	0	13	8	1416	989
155–159	147	42	281	69	305	67	232	51	120	27	45	7	16	2	5	0	2	0	16	5	1169	270
150–154	77	6	149	6	177	13	167	11	96	1	49	0	22	0	5	0	3	0	12	0	757	37
145–149	29	0	58	1	78	0	90	0	64	0	41	0	15	0	4	0	1	0	14	0	394	1
140–144	12	0	19	0	36	0	46	0	36	0	33	0	18	0	7	0	0	0	7	0	214	0
Below 140	5	0	12	0	18	0	31	0	22	0	30	0	15	0	7	0	2	0	6	0	148	0
Total	627	372	1032	517	1151	495	922	271	475	98	258	29	113	9	34	1	8	0	72	13	4692	1805

Apps = Number of Applicants
Adm = Number Admitted
Reflects 99% of the total applicant pool; highest LSAT data reported.

UNIVERSITY OF TENNESSEE COLLEGE OF LAW

Admissions Office, 1505 W. Cumberland Avenue, Suite 161
Knoxville, TN 37996-1810
Phone: 865.974.4131; Fax: 865.974.1572
E-mail: lawadmit@utk.edu; Website: www.law.utk.edu

The Basics

Type of school	Public
Term	Semester
Application deadline	2/15
Application fee	$15
Financial aid deadline	3/1
Can first year start other than fall?	No
Student to faculty ratio	15.3 to 1
# of housing spaces available restricted to law students	
graduate housing for which law students are eligible	

Faculty and Administrators

	Total		Men		Women		Minorities	
	Spr	Fall	Spr	Fall	Spr	Fall	Spr	Fall
Full-time	25	27	18	18	7	9	2	3
Other full-time	1	3	0	2	1	1	0	0
Deans, librarians, & others who teach	14	15	5	5	9	10	1	1
Part-time	41	35	25	22	16	13	0	0
Total	81	80	48	47	33	33	3	4

Curriculum

		Full-Time	Part-Time
Typical first-year section size		55	0
Is there typically a "small section" of the first-year class, other than Legal Writing, taught by full-time faculty		No	No
If yes, typical size offered last year			
# of classroom course titles beyond first-year curriculum		131	
# of upper division courses, excluding seminars, with an enrollment:	Under 25	90	
	25–49	15	
	50–74	15	
	75–99	0	
	100+	0	
# of seminars		25	
# of seminar positions available		468	
# of seminar positions filled		364	0
# of positions available in simulation courses		576	
# of simulation positions filled		520	0
# of positions available in faculty supervised clinical courses		167	
# of faculty supervised clinical positions filled		166	0
# involved in field placements		42	0
# involved in law journals		168	0
# involved in moot court or trial competitions		147	0
# of credit hours required to graduate		89	

JD Enrollment and Ethnicity

	Men		Women		Full-Time		Part-Time		1st-Year		Total		JD Degs. Awd.
	#	%	#	%	#	%	#	%	#	%	#	%	
All Hispanics	14	5.1	12	5.7	26	5.4	0	0.0	15	8.9	26	5.4	6
Am. Ind./AK Nat.	1	0.4	1	0.5	2	0.4	0	0.0	0	0.0	2	0.4	2
Asian	8	2.9	17	8.1	25	5.2	0	0.0	9	5.3	25	5.2	5
Black/Af. Am.	22	8.1	34	16.3	56	11.6	0	0.0	15	8.9	56	11.6	16
Nat. HI/Pac. Isl.	0	0.0	0	0.0	0	0.0	0	0.0	0	0.0	0	0.0	0
2 or more races	9	3.3	4	1.9	13	2.7	0	0.0	2	1.2	13	2.7	0
Subtotal (minor.)	54	19.8	68	32.5	122	25.3	0	0.0	41	24.3	122	25.3	31
Nonres. Alien	1	0.4	2	1.0	3	0.6	0	0.0	2	1.2	3	0.6	0
White/Cauc.	216	79.1	137	65.6	353	73.2	0	0.0	125	74.0	353	73.2	134
Unknown	2	0.7	2	1.0	4	0.8	0	0.0	1	0.6	4	0.8	2
Total	273	56.6	209	43.4	482	100.0	0	0.0	169	35.1	482		168

Transfers

Transfers in	5
Transfers out	1

Tuition and Fees

	Resident	Nonresident
Full-time	$14,462	$33,206
Part-time		
Tuition Guarantee Program	N	

Living Expenses

Estimated living expenses for singles

Living on campus	Living off campus	Living at home
$18,252	$18,252	$12,914

UNIVERSITY OF TENNESSEE COLLEGE OF LAW

ABA
Approved
Since
1925

GPA and LSAT Scores

	Total	Full-Time	Part-Time
# of apps	1,508	1,508	0
# of offers	410	410	0
# of matrics	169	169	0
75% GPA	3.81	3.81	0.00
Median GPA	3.60	3.60	0.00
25% GPA	3.38	3.38	0.00
75% LSAT	162	162	0
Median LSAT	160	160	0
25% LSAT	156	156	0

Grants and Scholarships (from prior year)

	Total		Full-Time		Part-Time	
	#	%	#	%	#	%
Total # of students	471		471		0	
Total # receiving grants	292	62.0	292	62.0	0	0.0
Less than 1/2 tuition	223	47.3	223	47.3	0	0.0
Half to full tuition	52	11.0	52	11.0	0	0.0
Full tuition	5	1.1	5	1.1	0	0.0
More than full tuition	12	2.5	12	2.5	0	0.0
Median grant amount			$5,000		$0	

Informational and Library Resources

Total amount spent on library materials	$956,968
Study seating capacity inside the library	437
# of full-time equivalent professional librarians	8
Hours per week library is open	96
# of open, wired connections available to students	94
# of networked computers available for use by students	94
Has wireless network?	Y
Requires computer?	N

JD Attrition (from prior year)

	Academic	Other	Total	
	#	#	#	%
1st year	0	2	2	1.3
2nd year	0	1	1	0.7
3rd year	0	0	0	0.0
4th year	0	0	0	0.0

Employment (9 months after graduation)

	Total	Percentage
Employment status known	138	98.6
Employment status unknown	2	1.4
Employed	128	92.8
Pursuing graduate degrees	4	2.9
Unemployed (seeking, not seeking, or studying for the bar)	5	3.6
Type of Employment		
# employed in law firms	80	62.5
# employed in business and industry	8	6.2
# employed in government	19	14.8
# employed in public interest	2	1.6
# employed as judicial clerks	16	12.5
# employed in academia	3	2.3
Geographic Location		
# employed in state	103	80.5
# employed outside the US	0	0.0
# of states where employed	13	

Bar Passage Rates

First-time takers	143	Reporting %	90.91
Average school %	88.46	Average state %	82.44
Average pass difference	6.02		

Jurisdiction	Takers	Passers	Pass %	State %	Diff %
Tennessee	130	115	88.46	82.44	6.02

UNIVERSITY OF TENNESSEE COLLEGE OF LAW

Admissions Office, 1505 W. Cumberland Avenue, Suite 161
Knoxville, TN 37996-1810
Phone: 865.974.4131; Fax: 865.974.1572
E-mail: lawadmit@utk.edu; Website: www.law.utk.edu

Introduction

For more than a century, the University of Tennessee College of Law has offered a strong combination of practical and theoretical legal training. Established in 1890, the College of Law is a charter member of the AALS and is ABA approved.

Enrollment/Student Body

The College of Law enrolls a small, selective, and diverse class each August. The 2010 entering class was composed of 169 students, of which 41 percent were women, 59 percent were men, and 24 percent were students of color. Entering students were graduates of 82 colleges and universities across the nation and around the world, and were residents of 19 states and 2 foreign countries. Although many members of each entering class are pursuing a law degree directly from undergraduate school, a number of law students have advanced degrees and have had careers in fields as diverse as engineering, teaching, medicine, journalism, and business. In the 2010–2011 academic year, the student population of the College of Law is 482, of which 23 percent are students of color.

Faculty

The quality of our faculty is evidenced by their legal training at some of the finest law schools in the United States, the significance of their scholarly writings, their activity in professional associations, and their involvement with public service. Current students at UT tell potential candidates for admission that they find the faculty to be excellent teachers—accessible and caring.

College of Law, Library, and Physical Facilities

The law center at the University of Tennessee—a melding of the old with the new—is an exceptional setting for education in the twenty-first century. The 110,000-square-foot facility was completed in 1997 and is located on Cumberland Avenue, just across from the University Center, in the heart of the campus. The law center includes the Joel A. Katz Law Library, dedicated to a distinguished corporate and entertainment lawyer and alumnus.

Location

The College of Law is located on the main campus of the University of Tennessee. Knoxville is the largest city in eastern Tennessee and the third largest in the state. More than 28,000 students attend UTK. Knoxville has the natural advantage of being located in the foothills of the Great Smoky Mountains, making hiking, biking, golf, and fishing popular and accessible activities. Knoxville is close to major legal markets in the Southeast, including Atlanta, Nashville, Birmingham, and Charlotte.

Curriculum

First-year students begin law school with a week-long introductory period in which a series of minicourses introduce students to the study of law. Second- and third-year students may choose from over 80 elective courses. Two dual-degree programs are offered—the JD/MBA and the JD/MPA (Master of Public Administration).

The College of Law offers two optional concentrations for students. The **James L. Clayton Center for Entrepreneurial Law** offers integrated upper-division courses that expose students to facets of law that affect business deals and provide hands-on experience in negotiating and documenting transactions with insight into the needs and concerns of the business community. A **Business Clinic** is offered for students seeking practical experience working with business clients.

The **Center for Advocacy and Dispute Resolution** allows interested students to focus their second- and third-year experience toward a career in advocacy (commonly known as litigation or trial practice) with an expanded emphasis on alternative forms of dispute resolution. UT was recognized by the American College of Trial Lawyers for the 1996 Emil Gumpert Award for Excellence in Teaching Trial Advocacy.

The **Charles H. Miller Legal Clinic** is the site for UT's clinical programs. Established in 1947, this is one of the oldest continually operating clinical programs in the United States and is nationally recognized for excellence in teaching. UT also offers a Mediation Clinic, in which students work in teams to mediate real civil and misdemeanor cases in the lower courts. Other clinical programs focus on business, domestic violence, and environmental issues.

UT offers three **Externships**—judicial, prosecutorial, and public defender. The Prosecutorial Externship Program enables students to prosecute real cases on behalf of the state under the supervision of experienced district attorneys in Knox County.

Student Activities and Programs

Students can choose from a variety of student programs, activities, publications, and organizations. A complete listing is available on our website.

Participation in UT's Moot Court program enables students to compete in intracollege and national competitions. A UT team placed second in the 2011 National Moot Court Competition. In 2010, Tennessee fielded the national championship team in the Giles Sutherland Rich Memorial intellectual property moot court competition and placed first in the Region VII National Moot Court Competition. UT won three Jerome Prince Evidence Moot Court national championships and was the first team in the history of that competition to win back-to-back titles in 2000 and 2001.

The *Tennessee Law Review* offers participants an excellent opportunity to conduct legal research and produce writings of a scholarly and practical nature. *Transactions* provides an opportunity for students to write about topical issues and legal developments of interest to the business bar. Students participating in the *Tennessee Journal of Law and Policy* analyze the latest developments in law and public decision making. The Student Bar Association and various other student organizations offer numerous programs, services, and special events. The national honor society, Order of the Coif, and two leading professional fraternities, Phi Delta Phi and Phi Alpha Delta, have local chapters here.

UT Pro Bono is a student-directed, community service organization. Working with local attorneys and legal aid organizations, UT Pro Bono serves as a resource by providing law students for research, educational, and investigatory assistance. UT Pro Bono currently operates programs working with the homeless and low income populations, immigrant assistance, animal law, and volunteer income tax assistance projects.

Admission

The College of Law strives to craft a class of diverse individuals, whose life experiences will enrich the law school community. Admission to the College of Law is competitive. The Admissions Committee places substantial emphasis on traditional indicators of performance—UGPA and LSAT score. The committee also considers factors such as improvement in undergraduate grades and graduate school performance, strength of undergraduate institution and major course of study, extracurricular activities, community service, and employment and professional experience. Also considered are circumstances that may have affected an applicant's grades or LSAT score; economic, social, or cultural background; and success in overcoming social or economic disadvantage. Applicants are required to submit two letters of recommendation and write a personal statement and an essay.

The College of Law recognizes its obligation to assure legal education to qualified applicants who are members of historically underrepresented groups in the legal profession and encourages applications from such students.

Successful completion of the CLEO Summer Institute may also be considered by the Admissions Committee.

Expenses, Financial Aid, and Housing

The College of Law offers a number of scholarships for entering students. Scholarships may be based on academic credentials (LSAT score and UGPA), records of leadership and community service, or other factors as established by the scholarship donor. Several scholarships may be awarded for which financial need, as established by the university after the FAFSA process is complete, is a primary criterion. Candidates

for admission should complete the FAFSA process as soon as possible after the first of the year to be considered for scholarships in which financial need is a factor. Candidates for admission will automatically be considered for all scholarships for which they are eligible. Please check our website or our Applicant Guide for more information and application guidelines. Campus apartment housing is open to law students. Knoxville also offers ample private apartment housing at a reasonable cost within walking distance or a short drive from the law school.

Career Center

Recruiting and hiring practices in the legal job market suggest that making career decisions should be an ongoing, developmental process that begins in the first year of law school and continues through and after graduation. UT students acquire the skills and knowledge necessary to research, select, and seek the right career path for them and gain necessary information about the professional areas in which a law degree can be used.

The staff of the Bettye B. Lewis Career Center offers a comprehensive menu of services for employers who seek to recruit Tennessee students through formal and informal recruitment methods, off-campus job fairs, and recruiting consortia. First-year students are introduced to career development and job-search strategies through individual counseling and small group resource training sessions called the IL Career Integration Program. Students are coached in the development of individual job-search strategy plans throughout their law school careers.

These efforts have contributed to a consistently high employment rate for UT graduates that is well above the national average. Most graduates choose to stay in the southeastern United States, but graduates accept positions across the country. For detailed information, please see the College of Law website at www.law.utk.edu.

APPLICANT PROFILE

University of Tennessee College of Law
This grid includes only applicants who earned 120–180 LSAT scores under standard administrations.

LSAT Score	GPA 3.75 +		3.50–3.74		3.25–3.49		3.00–3.24		2.75–2.99		2.50–2.74		2.25–2.49		2.00–2.24		Below 2.00		No GPA		Total	
	Apps	Adm	Apps	Adm	Apps	Adm	Apps	Adm	Apps	Adm	Apps	Adm	Apps	Adm	Apps	Adm	Apps	Adm	Apps	Adm	Apps	Adm
175–180	0	0	0	0	0	0	1	1	0	0	0	0	0	0	0	0	0	0	0	0	1	1
170–174	6	5	1	1	0	0	2	1	0	0	0	0	0	0	0	0	0	0	0	0	9	7
165–169	16	16	20	15	18	16	11	8	9	6	1	0	2	0	1	0	0	0	0	0	78	61
160–164	63	56	71	59	80	49	46	15	23	8	13	5	7	0	2	0	0	0	3	0	308	192
155–159	92	51	115	26	114	16	61	6	36	2	23	3	8	1	2	0	0	0	4	1	455	106
150–154	46	9	79	9	70	8	66	4	38	1	21	0	10	1	4	0	2	0	2	0	338	32
145–149	24	3	25	6	44	6	45	0	21	0	15	0	5	0	9	0	1	0	1	0	190	16
140–144	2	0	11	1	16	1	18	0	9	0	12	0	1	0	4	0	3	0	2	0	78	2
135–139	1	0	2	0	1	0	7	0	6	0	8	0	4	0	1	0	0	0	2	0	32	0
130–134	0	0	0	0	2	0	0	0	3	0	4	0	1	0	1	0	0	0	1	0	12	0
125–129	0	0	0	0	0	0	0	0	2	0	1	0	2	0	3	0	0	0	0	0	8	0
120–124	0	0	0	0	0	0	0	0	0	0	0	0	0	0	0	0	0	0	1	0	1	0
Total	250	140	324	117	345	96	257	36	147	17	98	8	40	2	27	0	6	0	16	1	1510	417

Apps = Number of Applicants
Adm = Number Admitted
Reflects 100% of the total applicant pool; highest LSAT data reported.

THE UNIVERSITY OF TEXAS SCHOOL OF LAW

727 East Dean Keeton Street
Austin, TX 78705
Phone: 512.232.1200; Fax: 512.471.2765
E-mail: admissions@law.utexas.edu; Website: www.utexas.edu/law/

ABA
Approved
Since
1923

The Basics

Type of school	Public
Term	Semester
Application deadline	11/1 2/1
Application fee	$70
Financial aid deadline	3/31
Can first year start other than fall?	No
Student to faculty ratio	10.9 to 1
# of housing spaces available restricted to law students	
graduate housing for which law students are eligible	

Faculty and Administrators

	Total		Men		Women		Minorities	
	Spr	Fall	Spr	Fall	Spr	Fall	Spr	Fall
Full-time	89	84	53	50	36	34	14	13
Other full-time	19	19	10	11	9	8	1	2
Deans, librarians, & others who teach	8	8	3	3	5	5	1	1
Part-time	74	55	60	38	14	17	19	9
Total	190	166	126	102	64	64	35	25

Curriculum

		Full-Time	Part-Time
Typical first-year section size		96	0
Is there typically a "small section" of the first-year class, other than Legal Writing, taught by full-time faculty		Yes	No
If yes, typical size offered last year		24	
# of classroom course titles beyond first-year curriculum		180	
# of upper division courses, excluding seminars, with an enrollment:	Under 25	224	
	25–49	54	
	50–74	15	
	75–99	10	
	100+	8	
# of seminars		68	
# of seminar positions available		823	
# of seminar positions filled		655	0
# of positions available in simulation courses		412	
# of simulation positions filled		333	0
# of positions available in faculty supervised clinical courses		329	
# of faculty supervised clinical positions filled		264	0
# involved in field placements		216	0
# involved in law journals		610	0
# involved in moot court or trial competitions		97	0
# of credit hours required to graduate		86	

JD Enrollment and Ethnicity

	Men		Women		Full-Time		Part-Time		1st-Year		Total		JD Degs. Awd.
	#	%	#	%	#	%	#	%	#	%	#	%	
All Hispanics	94	15.2	89	16.6	183	15.9	0	0.0	60	15.2	183	15.9	61
Am. Ind./AK Nat.	3	0.5	2	0.4	5	0.4	0	0.0	1	0.3	5	0.4	1
Asian	28	4.5	34	6.3	62	5.4	0	0.0	16	4.1	62	5.4	35
Black/Af. Am.	22	3.6	34	6.3	56	4.9	0	0.0	16	4.1	56	4.9	30
Nat. HI/Pac. Isl.	1	0.2	0	0.0	1	0.1	0	0.0	1	0.3	1	0.1	0
2 or more races	4	0.6	9	1.7	13	1.1	0	0.0	9	2.3	13	1.1	0
Subtotal (minor.)	152	24.6	168	31.3	320	27.7	0	0.0	103	26.1	320	27.7	127
Nonres. Alien	5	0.8	8	1.5	13	1.1	0	0.0	6	1.5	13	1.1	0
White/Cauc.	391	63.3	325	60.6	716	62.0	0	0.0	238	60.4	716	62.0	212
Unknown	70	11.3	35	6.5	105	9.1	0	0.0	47	11.9	105	9.1	53
Total	618	53.6	536	46.4	1154	100.0	0	0.0	394	34.1	1154		392

Transfers

Transfers in	9
Transfers out	8

Tuition and Fees

	Resident	Nonresident
Full-time	$28,669	$44,638
Part-time		
Tuition Guarantee Program		N

Living Expenses

Estimated living expenses for singles

Living on campus	Living off campus	Living at home
$15,392	$15,530	$7,388

ABA Approved Since 1923

GPA and LSAT Scores

	Total	Full-Time	Part-Time
# of apps	5,815	5,815	0
# of offers	1,316	1,316	0
# of matrics	389	389	0
75% GPA	3.84	3.84	0.00
Median GPA	3.71	3.71	0.00
25% GPA	3.57	3.57	0.00
75% LSAT	169	169	0
Median LSAT	167	167	0
25% LSAT	164	164	0

Grants and Scholarships (from prior year)

	Total #	Total %	Full-Time #	Full-Time %	Part-Time #	Part-Time %
Total # of students	1,182		1,182		0	
Total # receiving grants	1078	91.2	1078	91.2	0	0.0
Less than 1/2 tuition	906	76.6	906	76.6	0	0.0
Half to full tuition	142	12.0	142	12.0	0	0.0
Full tuition	9	0.8	9	0.8	0	0.0
More than full tuition	21	1.8	21	1.8	0	0.0
Median grant amount			$8,078		$0	

Informational and Library Resources

Total amount spent on library materials	$1,429,617
Study seating capacity inside the library	1,039
# of full-time equivalent professional librarians	12
Hours per week library is open	107
# of open, wired connections available to students	248
# of networked computers available for use by students	94
Has wireless network?	Y
Requires computer?	N

JD Attrition (from prior year)

	Academic #	Other #	Total #	Total %
1st year	0	7	7	1.8
2nd year	0	12	12	3.0
3rd year	0	1	1	0.2
4th year	0	0	0	0.0

Employment (9 months after graduation)

	Total	Percentage
Employment status known	433	100.0
Employment status unknown	0	0.0
Employed	402	92.8
Pursuing graduate degrees	0	0.0
Unemployed (seeking, not seeking, or studying for the bar)	10	2.3
Type of Employment		
# employed in law firms	256	63.7
# employed in business and industry	23	5.7
# employed in government	43	10.7
# employed in public interest	28	7.0
# employed as judicial clerks	47	11.7
# employed in academia	4	1.0
Geographic Location		
# employed in state	273	67.9
# employed outside the US	4	1.0
# of states where employed	26	

Bar Passage Rates

First-time takers	374	Reporting %	91.44
Average school %	92.98	Average state %	84.42
Average pass difference	8.56		

Jurisdiction	Takers	Passers	Pass %	State %	Diff %
Texas	279	260	93.19	85.48	7.71
California	32	29	90.63	73.19	17.43
New York	31	29	93.55	86.51	7.04

THE UNIVERSITY OF TEXAS SCHOOL OF LAW

727 East Dean Keeton Street
Austin, TX 78705
Phone: 512.232.1200; Fax: 512.471.2765
E-mail: admissions@law.utexas.edu; Website: www.utexas.edu/law/

Introduction

The School of Law is located at The University of Texas at Austin. This location in the heart of the capital city provides ready access to the state legislature, the Supreme Court of Texas, the federal trial and appellate court, the offices of state and federal agencies, and the libraries and other main campus facilities. Recognized for its distinguished faculty and rich academic program, the law school has been a member of the AALS since 1907, was approved by the ABA in 1923, and is fully accredited.

Situated on the banks of the Colorado River, Austin is an eclectic city noted for its politics, scholars, rolling hills, film industry, and live music and restaurant scene. The University of Texas plays an important role in this metropolitan area of over one million people, and many entertainment and cultural activities cater to the student population.

Library and Physical Facilities

The Tarlton Law Library in the Joseph D. Jamail Center for Legal Research is one of the leading academic law libraries in the United States and one of the finest legal research centers in the Southwest. The library serves an academic community of over 1,300 full-time law students and 100 faculty members. In addition to the library's large print collection of over one million volumes, students also have access to databases, e-books, and electronic journals.

In 2010, the newly constructed Susman Academic Center was dedicated as part of the extensive renovation of the Tarlton Library. The fifth and sixth floors of the library were transformed into the Academic Center, which houses 54 faculty offices; 38 additional offices illuminated with natural light via skylights; 2 large, high-tech equipped meeting rooms, each of which can be flexibly subdivided into 2 or 3 separate areas; an expansive commons area with a two-story atrium; 2 faculty research areas; 6 additional conference rooms; and 4 seminar classrooms. The Susman Academic Center expands the Law School's available office and public spaces, and creates attractive, light-filled spaces for faculty and students to work and collaborate.

Faculty

The University of Texas School of Law has long had one of the most outstanding faculties in the nation, both in terms of scholarly distinction of the faculty members and their success in the classroom. More than one-third of the faculty is elected to the American Law Institute, one of the highest percentage memberships in the nation. Texas is also one of nine schools with four faculty elected to the American Academy of Arts and Sciences, the nation's most prestigious learned society. The law school has consistently hired the best and brightest young scholars, including eight former clerks for justices of the United States Supreme Court.

Texas enjoys a leadership position in many areas of legal study. The breadth and depth of offerings in several areas—constitutional law, environmental law, wills and estates, admiralty and maritime law, torts and product liability, labor law, jurisprudence, and philosophy—is matched by few schools in the country. With one of the largest faculties in the country, Texas is able to offer students coverage of all fields of law and exposure to truly diverse scholarly perspectives on legal questions.

Enrollment/Student Body

As a public institution of higher education, the School of Law's nonresident enrollment is limited by the Texas Legislature to 35 percent. We currently have over 133 undergraduate institutions and 32 states represented in our student body. Please refer to the statistical information for details regarding the competitiveness of our student body.

Special Programs

The school offers clinical education courses for credit in such fields as actual innocence, capital punishment, children's rights, community development, criminal defense, domestic violence, environmental, housing, immigration, juvenile justice, legislative lawyering, mediation, mental health, national security, Supreme Court, and transnational worker rights. Internships are available to qualified students with the Texas Supreme Court, the Texas Court of Criminal Appeals, and the Third Court of Appeals. A limited number of internships are available for credit in the public service area. The law school also has an extensive trial-advocacy program boasting several national championships. There are a number of joint-degree programs—JD/MPAff; JD/MBA; JD/Master of Arts in Latin American Studies; JD/Master of Arts in Middle Eastern Studies; JD/Master of Arts in Russian, East European, and Eurasian Studies; JD/Master of Science in Community and Regional Planning; JD/Master of Global Policy Studies; JD/Master of Science in Social Work; and JD/Master of Science in Information Studies—in addition to several combined programs with a PhD.

Curriculum

All first-year students are required to take a full courseload, averaging 15 hours per week, in contracts, property, torts, civil procedure, criminal law, constitutional law, brief writing and oral advocacy, and legal research and writing. After the first year, the only required courses are professional responsibility, advanced constitutional law, a writing and research seminar, and a skills class. A student may design his or her course of study from an array of course offerings in many fields of law. These offerings include interdisciplinary and advanced public and private law courses.

Student-Edited Journals

The School of Law offers many student-administered, cocurricular activities that enhance the law students' regular studies. Student-edited journals include the *American Journal of Criminal Law; Texas Environmental Law Journal; Texas Hispanic Journal of Law and Policy; Texas Intellectual Property Law Journal; Texas International Law Journal; Texas Journal of Oil, Gas, and Energy Law; Texas Journal of Women and the Law; Texas Journal on Civil Liberties and Civil Rights; Texas Law Review; Texas Review of Entertainment and Sports*

Law; Texas Review of Law and Politics; and The *Review of Litigation.*

Admission

Admission to the JD program at UT Law is competitive. For the entering class of 2010, approximately 5,815 applicants competed for 400 available seats. As a general rule, there are no presumptive numbers. Every application completed and submitted is reviewed in its entirety. Each applicant must take the LSAT and have earned a baccalaureate degree from an accredited college or university with a minimum grade-point average of 2.2 as calculated by the Law School Admission Council (LSAC), or have completed the equivalent of six semesters and expect to graduate during the current academic year. Each candidate must complete all application forms and fulfill all mandatory attachments as described in the application.

Financial Aid

A limited number of scholarships are available for first-year students on the basis of merit and financial need. The prestigious Townes-Rice Scholarship is offered to eight outstanding law students with full tuition and fees plus a $5,000 stipend for all three years of law school. The law school also offers an Equal Justice Scholarship for an entering student interested in a career in public interest. Scholarships and research assistantships are available for second- and third-year students. The law school administers several short-term and long-term loan funds for students with financial need, and the university offers substantial federally funded loan programs.

Housing

Approximately 95 percent of all law students live off campus. The Division of Housing and Food Services (PO Box 7666, University Station, Austin, TX 78713; telephone: 512.471.3136) has information regarding on-campus living. Other sources of information are classified ads in the student newspaper, the *Daily Texan;* apartment management services; rental agencies; and current students.

Career Services

Each year, nearly 500 employers participate in career services programs and recruit our students for summer and full-time positions through on-campus interviews, recruit-by-mail opportunities, and off-campus job fairs. Over 50 percent of on-campus employers are from outside the state of Texas. For the past three years, 98 percent of graduates who were actively seeking employment have secured it within nine months of graduation.

APPLICANT PROFILE

The University of Texas School of Law
This grid includes only applicants who earned 120–180 LSAT scores under standard administrations.

LSAT Score	3.75 +		3.50–3.74		3.25–3.49		3.00–3.24		2.75–2.99		2.50–2.74		2.25–2.49		2.00–2.24		Below 2.00		No GPA		Total	
	Apps	Adm	Apps	Adm	Apps	Adm	Apps	Adm	Apps	Adm	Apps	Adm	Apps	Adm	Apps	Adm	Apps	Adm	Apps	Adm	Apps	Adm
175–180	62	59	37	28	28	3	16	0	4	0	1	0	0	0	0	0	1	0	1	1	150	91
170–174	229	212	209	138	122	18	49	1	26	0	6	0	1	0	0	0	0	0	10	8	652	377
165–169	529	410	539	208	317	22	152	4	39	2	22	0	8	0	1	0	2	0	26	6	1635	652
160–164	433	66	524	53	329	20	160	3	58	3	16	0	10	0	3	0	0	0	36	3	1569	148
155–159	183	19	207	13	186	5	122	3	46	0	28	0	17	0	7	0	0	0	15	0	811	40
150–154	75	2	96	0	118	1	99	0	64	0	39	0	12	0	3	0	1	0	9	0	516	3
145–149	21	0	41	0	72	0	47	0	41	0	25	0	17	0	7	0	2	0	6	0	279	0
140–144	8	0	25	0	10	0	27	0	17	0	12	0	4	0	0	0	0	0	4	0	107	0
135–139	1	0	2	0	2	0	5	0	9	0	8	0	7	0	5	0	0	0	1	0	40	0
130–134	0	0	1	0	2	0	0	0	3	0	6	0	2	0	1	0	0	0	1	0	16	0
125–129	0	0	0	0	0	0	0	0	0	0	0	0	1	0	0	0	0	0	0	0	1	0
120–124	0	0	0	0	0	0	0	0	0	0	0	0	0	0	0	0	0	0	0	0	0	0
Total	1541	768	1681	440	1186	69	677	11	307	5	163	0	79	0	27	0	6	0	109	18	5776	1311

Apps = Number of Applicants
Adm = Number Admitted
Reflects 99% of the total applicant pool; highest LSAT data reported.

TEXAS SOUTHERN UNIVERSITY—THURGOOD MARSHALL SCHOOL OF LAW

Office of Admissions, 3100 Cleburne
Houston, TX 77004
Phone: 713.313.7114 or 713.313.7115; Fax: 713.313.7297
E-mail: erene@tmslaw.tsu.edu; Website: www.tsulaw.edu

The Basics

Type of school	Public
Term	Semester
Application deadline	4/1
Application fee	$55
Financial aid deadline	4/15
Can first year start other than fall?	No
Student to faculty ratio	14.1 to 1
# of housing spaces available restricted to law students	
graduate housing for which law students are eligible	

Faculty and Administrators

	Total Spr	Total Fall	Men Spr	Men Fall	Women Spr	Women Fall	Minorities Spr	Minorities Fall
Full-time	34	30	13	12	21	18	27	23
Other full-time	1	0	1	0	0	0	0	0
Deans, librarians, & others who teach	17	16	9	8	8	8	16	15
Part-time	23	13	18	7	5	6	22	11
Total	75	59	41	27	34	32	65	49

Curriculum

	Full-Time	Part-Time
Typical first-year section size	60	0
Is there typically a "small section" of the first-year class, other than Legal Writing, taught by full-time faculty	No	No
If yes, typical size offered last year		
# of classroom course titles beyond first-year curriculum	71	
# of upper division courses, excluding seminars, with an enrollment: Under 25	90	
25–49	47	
50–74	43	
75–99	1	
100+	0	
# of seminars	31	
# of seminar positions available	611	
# of seminar positions filled	386	0
# of positions available in simulation courses	200	
# of simulation positions filled	168	0
# of positions available in faculty supervised clinical courses	119	
# of faculty supervised clinical positions filled	119	0
# involved in field placements	63	0
# involved in law journals	11	0
# involved in moot court or trial competitions	4	0
# of credit hours required to graduate	90	

JD Enrollment and Ethnicity

	Men #	Men %	Women #	Women %	Full-Time #	Full-Time %	Part-Time #	Part-Time %	1st-Year #	1st-Year %	Total #	Total %	JD Degs. Awd.
All Hispanics	82	30.7	77	25.3	159	27.8	0	0.0	63	29.9	159	27.8	26
Am. Ind./AK Nat.	1	0.4	2	0.7	3	0.5	0	0.0	2	0.9	3	0.5	1
Asian	23	8.6	18	5.9	41	7.2	0	0.0	17	8.1	41	7.2	11
Black/Af. Am.	100	37.5	154	50.7	254	44.5	0	0.0	75	35.5	254	44.5	69
Nat. HI/Pac. Isl.	0	0.0	0	0.0	0	0.0	0	0.0	0	0.0	0	0.0	0
2 or more races	0	0.0	2	0.7	2	0.4	0	0.0	2	0.9	2	0.4	0
Subtotal (minor.)	206	77.2	253	83.2	459	80.4	0	0.0	159	75.4	459	80.4	107
Nonres. Alien	7	2.6	3	1.0	10	1.8	0	0.0	3	1.4	10	1.8	0
White/Cauc.	54	20.2	48	15.8	102	17.9	0	0.0	49	23.2	102	17.9	31
Unknown	0	0.0	0	0.0	0	0.0	0	0.0	0	0.0	0	0.0	0
Total	267	46.8	304	53.2	571	100.0	0	0.0	211	37.0	571		141

Transfers

Transfers in	2
Transfers out	6

Tuition and Fees

	Resident	Nonresident
Full-time	$13,065	$16,815
Part-time		
Tuition Guarantee Program	N	

Living Expenses

Estimated living expenses for singles

Living on campus	Living off campus	Living at home
$18,492	$18,492	$18,492

TEXAS SOUTHERN UNIVERSITY—THURGOOD MARSHALL SCHOOL OF LAW

ABA Approved Since 1949

GPA and LSAT Scores

	Total	Full-Time	Part-Time
# of apps	2,228	2,228	0
# of offers	667	667	0
# of matrics	212	212	0
75% GPA	3.33	3.33	0.00
Median GPA	3.01	3.01	0.00
25% GPA	2.74	2.74	0.00
75% LSAT	149	149	0
Median LSAT	148	148	0
25% LSAT	145	145	0

Grants and Scholarships (from prior year)

	Total #	Total %	Full-Time #	Full-Time %	Part-Time #	Part-Time %
Total # of students	542		542		0	
Total # receiving grants	290	53.5	290	53.5	0	0.0
Less than 1/2 tuition	201	37.1	201	37.1	0	0.0
Half to full tuition	33	6.1	33	6.1	0	0.0
Full tuition	56	10.3	56	10.3	0	0.0
More than full tuition	0	0.0	0	0.0	0	0.0
Median grant amount			$7,626		$0	

Informational and Library Resources

Total amount spent on library materials	$950,903
Study seating capacity inside the library	378
# of full-time equivalent professional librarians	9
Hours per week library is open	108
# of open, wired connections available to students	955
# of networked computers available for use by students	97
Has wireless network?	Y
Requires computer?	N

JD Attrition (from prior year)

	Academic #	Other #	Total #	Total %
1st year	25	6	31	13.4
2nd year	0	0	0	0.0
3rd year	0	0	0	0.0
4th year	0	0	0	0.0

Employment (9 months after graduation)

	Total	Percentage
Employment status known	187	97.4
Employment status unknown	5	2.6
Employed	158	84.5
Pursuing graduate degrees	2	1.1
Unemployed (seeking, not seeking, or studying for the bar)	12	6.4
Type of Employment		
# employed in law firms	91	57.6
# employed in business and industry	33	20.9
# employed in government	19	12.0
# employed in public interest	3	1.9
# employed as judicial clerks	0	0.0
# employed in academia	2	1.3
Geographic Location		
# employed in state	131	82.9
# employed outside the US	0	0.0
# of states where employed	6	

Bar Passage Rates

First-time takers	184	Reporting %	88.04
Average school %	67.90	Average state %	85.48

Average pass difference −17.58

Jurisdiction	Takers	Passers	Pass %	State %	Diff %
Texas	162	110	67.90	85.48	−17.58

TEXAS SOUTHERN UNIVERSITY—THURGOOD MARSHALL SCHOOL OF LAW

Office of Admissions, 3100 Cleburne
Houston, TX 77004
Phone: 713.313.7114 or 713.313.7115; Fax: 713.313.7297
E-mail: erene@tmslaw.tsu.edu; Website: www.tsulaw.edu

Enrollment/Student Body

A majority of the students are from Texas, but all parts of the country are represented. Approximately 49 percent of the students are black, 23 percent Chicano, 17 percent Caucasian, and 6 percent Asian and Native American. The median age range is about 26 to 36 years.

Introduction

The Thurgood Marshall School of Law, a state institution founded in 1947, seeks to provide a legal education and an opportunity to excel to students from a wide range of backgrounds, including those who otherwise would not have an opportunity for legal training. The law school is accredited by the ABA. The student body is truly multiethnic and multicultural. The law school is housed in a trilevel structure that is located just outside of downtown Houston. Near-campus housing is available in the form of modern apartments for single and married students. The school makes extensive use of legal facilities in Houston through its clinical programs.

Library and Physical Facilities

Students receive individual or group orientation and intensive training in the use of the library. The law school has undergone approximately $16 million in renovations, expanding the available space from 103,000 to 108,000 square feet.

Curriculum

Upon entry to the School of Law, all students in the first-year class are required to attend a week-long orientation program. Attention is given to examinations, briefing cases, outlining, and an overview of law school life and expectations.

The law school offers a three-year, full-time JD program. The minimum courseload is 12 hours. Required courses for the first year are Lawyering Process I and II, Civil Procedure, Property, Contracts, Torts, and Criminal Law. Second-year students must take Constitutional Law, Evidence, Criminal Procedure, Trial Simulation, Business Associations, Commercial Law, Professional Responsibility, and Wills and Trusts. Second- or third-year students are required to take Federal Jurisdiction and Procedure, a seminar/independent research project, and Basic Federal Taxation. Third-year students are required to take Consumer Rights and Texas Practice. The remaining hours required to complete the degree may be selected from a number of areas of interest.

The law school operates a full-time, in-house clinic in which students work under the supervision of faculty and adjunct faculty members. Internships are available with the Harris County District Attorney's Office, the Federal Magistrates, Gulf Coast Legal Foundation, the US Bankruptcy Court, the Harris County Attorney's Office, the Internal Revenue Service, and the US District Court. The school operates a number of clinics, including advanced skills, basic skills, civil and criminal externships, environmental justice, family law, and housing law. A judicial externship with state and federal judges is available to academically outstanding third-year students.

Admission

The admission decision is based primarily on the applicant's motivation and intellectual capacity as demonstrated by his or her undergraduate records, and on his or her aptitude for the study of law as measured by the LSAT. Leadership ability, prior community service, work experience, the student's background, extracurricular activities, and graduate study in another discipline are all considered.

No particular undergraduate major is preferred, but the school looks for applicants with broad backgrounds in the social sciences, natural sciences, humanities, and business sciences. Newly admitted students must send two seat deposits ($150 upon acceptance and $100 in June), which are refundable upon matriculation. The law school's student body represents one of the most culturally and ethnically diverse student bodies in the country. Transfer applications are accepted; students must submit a transcript and letter from the dean of his/her former law school stating that they are in good standing. All newly admitted students must submit an official transcript from the baccalaureate degree-granting institution as well as all law schools attended. No application will be evaluated by the admission committee until the LSAC Law School Report has been received.

In order to ensure complete review, applications must be received by the Office of Admissions no later than April 1, although earlier submission is encouraged. Entering students are admitted only in August (fall semester). Students are notified of acceptance after the admission committee has reviewed the complete file. Admission decisions are made on a rolling basis.

Student Activities

Numerous law school organizations are active on campus. A student board edits the *Thurgood Marshall Law Review*. Moot court competitions are held in trial and appellate work, labor law, and client counseling.

Expenses and Financial Aid

About 90 percent of the students receive some form of aid. The law school administers its own scholarship program, which is competitive. Scholarships are awarded on the basis of both need and merit, and may range up to full tuition. The university also offers additional scholarship aid, and the law school and the university offer loan assistance. Between 10 and 15 percent of the students hold assistantships. The aid application deadline is April 1.

The scholarship program makes several awards (approximately 60) each year. The awards have enabled out-of-state residents to qualify for resident tuition rates. In addition, a number of law students each year qualify for the federal work-study and loan programs. Additional limited scholarship aid is available to students after they have completed a year of law study. An applicant in need of other financial assistance should make arrangements for financial aid through the law school financial aid counselor by either calling 713.313.7243 or e-mailing kepercival@tmslaw.tsu.edu.

TEXAS SOUTHERN UNIVERSITY—THURGOOD MARSHALL SCHOOL OF LAW

Career Development

The law school employs a full-time career development officer. Graduates are placed primarily with law firms, federal and state agencies, legal services, judges, and businesses. The Career Development Office also conducts a major national effort to encourage legal employers in every major city in the United States to recruit Texas Southern University—Thurgood Marshall School of Law graduates.

APPLICANT PROFILE

Texas Southern University—Thurgood Marshall School of Law
This grid includes only applicants who earned 120–180 LSAT scores under standard administrations.

LSAT Score	3.75 +		3.50–3.74		3.25–3.49		3.00–3.24		2.75–2.99		2.50–2.74		2.25–2.49		2.00–2.24		Below 2.00		No GPA		Total	
	Apps	Adm	Apps	Adm	Apps	Adm	Apps	Adm	Apps	Adm	Apps	Adm	Apps	Adm	Apps	Adm	Apps	Adm	Apps	Adm	Apps	Adm
175–180	0	0	0	0	0	0	0	0	0	0	0	0	0	0	0	0	0	0	0	0	0	0
170–174	0	0	0	0	0	0	0	0	0	0	0	0	0	0	0	0	0	0	0	0	0	0
165–169	0	0	0	0	0	0	1	1	0	0	0	0	0	0	0	0	0	0	0	0	1	1
160–164	2	1	3	2	5	5	2	2	3	2	1	1	2	2	1	0	0	0	0	0	19	15
155–159	6	6	8	6	18	15	23	19	14	5	23	15	21	12	8	3	1	0	4	2	126	83
150–154	11	8	24	20	38	32	53	48	66	53	48	33	42	23	23	6	7	0	7	3	319	226
145–149	18	16	43	36	100	61	109	51	126	53	104	26	66	4	37	0	10	1	19	4	632	252
140–144	22	15	39	22	89	26	124	12	142	7	121	1	73	2	38	0	5	1	19	0	672	86
135–139	8	1	14	1	32	0	47	4	45	2	58	0	34	0	22	1	12	0	11	0	283	9
130–134	1	0	3	0	4	0	17	0	17	0	21	0	17	0	21	0	6	0	5	0	112	0
125–129	0	0	1	0	1	0	1	0	2	0	3	0	3	0	3	0	2	0	2	0	18	0
120–124	0	0	0	0	0	0	0	0	0	0	2	0	1	0	1	0	0	0	0	0	4	0
Total	68	47	135	87	287	139	377	137	415	122	381	76	259	43	154	10	43	2	67	9	2186	672

Apps = Number of Applicants
Adm = Number Admitted
Reflects 99% of the total applicant pool; highest LSAT data reported.

TEXAS TECH UNIVERSITY SCHOOL OF LAW

1802 Hartford Avenue
Lubbock, TX 79409
Phone: 806.742.3990; Fax: 806.742.4617
E-mail: admissions.law@ttu.edu; Website: www.law.ttu.edu

The Basics

Type of school	Public
Term	Semester
Application deadline	11/1 2/1
Application fee	$50
Financial aid deadline	4/15
Can first year start other than fall?	Yes
Student to faculty ratio	14.9 to 1
# of housing spaces available restricted to law students	
graduate housing for which law students are eligible	700

Faculty and Administrators

	Total		Men		Women		Minorities	
	Spr	Fall	Spr	Fall	Spr	Fall	Spr	Fall
Full-time	38	35	22	22	16	13	5	6
Other full-time	0	0	0	0	0	0	0	0
Deans, librarians, & others who teach	11	10	7	6	4	4	5	5
Part-time	11	14	9	12	2	2	1	1
Total	60	59	38	40	22	19	11	12

Curriculum

	Full-Time	Part-Time
Typical first-year section size	55	0
Is there typically a "small section" of the first-year class, other than Legal Writing, taught by full-time faculty	No	No
If yes, typical size offered last year		
# of classroom course titles beyond first-year curriculum	84	

# of upper division courses, excluding seminars, with an enrollment:		
Under 25	53	
25–49	23	
50–74	12	
75–99	5	
100+	5	

# of seminars	29	
# of seminar positions available	581	
# of seminar positions filled	512	0
# of positions available in simulation courses	146	
# of simulation positions filled	117	0
# of positions available in faculty supervised clinical courses	197	
# of faculty supervised clinical positions filled	185	0
# involved in field placements	93	0
# involved in law journals	155	0
# involved in moot court or trial competitions	68	0
# of credit hours required to graduate	90	

JD Enrollment and Ethnicity

	Men		Women		Full-Time		Part-Time		1st-Year		Total		JD Degs. Awd.
	#	%	#	%	#	%	#	%	#	%	#	%	
All Hispanics	59	14.9	42	15.2	101	15.1	0	0.0	38	15.3	101	15.1	35
Am. Ind./AK Nat.	2	0.5	2	0.7	4	0.6	0	0.0	1	0.4	4	0.6	1
Asian	17	4.3	13	4.7	30	4.5	0	0.0	10	4.0	30	4.5	6
Black/Af. Am.	6	1.5	14	5.1	20	3.0	0	0.0	5	2.0	20	3.0	5
Nat. HI/Pac. Isl.	0	0.0	0	0.0	0	0.0	0	0.0	0	0.0	0	0.0	0
2 or more races	2	0.5	0	0.0	2	0.3	0	0.0	1	0.4	2	0.3	0
Subtotal (minor.)	86	21.8	71	25.7	157	23.4	0	0.0	55	22.1	157	23.4	47
Nonres. Alien	2	0.5	2	0.7	4	0.6	0	0.0	0	0.0	4	0.6	0
White/Cauc.	307	77.7	202	73.2	509	75.9	0	0.0	194	77.9	509	75.9	162
Unknown	0	0.0	1	0.4	1	0.1	0	0.0	0	0.0	1	0.1	0
Total	395	58.9	276	41.1	671	100.0	0	0.0	249	37.1	671		209

Transfers

Transfers in	3
Transfers out	4

Tuition and Fees

	Resident	Nonresident
Full-time	$17,351	$25,751
Part-time		
Tuition Guarantee Program		N

Living Expenses

Estimated living expenses for singles

Living on campus	Living off campus	Living at home
$13,770	$13,770	N/A

TEXAS TECH UNIVERSITY SCHOOL OF LAW

ABA
Approved
Since
1969

GPA and LSAT Scores

	Total	Full-Time	Part-Time
# of apps	1,398	1,398	0
# of offers	559	559	0
# of matrics	244	244	0
75% GPA	3.66	3.66	0.00
Median GPA	3.45	3.45	0.00
25% GPA	3.16	3.16	0.00
75% LSAT	158	158	0
Median LSAT	156	156	0
25% LSAT	153	153	0

Grants and Scholarships (from prior year)

	Total #	Total %	Full-Time #	Full-Time %	Part-Time #	Part-Time %
Total # of students	637		637		0	
Total # receiving grants	331	52.0	331	52.0	0	0.0
Less than 1/2 tuition	191	30.0	191	30.0	0	0.0
Half to full tuition	48	7.5	48	7.5	0	0.0
Full tuition	20	3.1	20	3.1	0	0.0
More than full tuition	72	11.3	72	11.3	0	0.0
Median grant amount			$5,000		$0	

Informational and Library Resources

Total amount spent on library materials	$1,208,154
Study seating capacity inside the library	578
# of full-time equivalent professional librarians	7
Hours per week library is open	168
# of open, wired connections available to students	1,118
# of networked computers available for use by students	110
Has wireless network?	Y
Requires computer?	N

JD Attrition (from prior year)

	Academic #	Other #	Total #	Total %
1st year	2	7	9	4.0
2nd year	2	7	9	4.1
3rd year	0	0	0	0.0
4th year	0	0	0	0.0

Employment (9 months after graduation)

	Total	Percentage
Employment status known	197	95.6
Employment status unknown	9	4.4
Employed	177	89.8
Pursuing graduate degrees	8	4.1
Unemployed (seeking, not seeking, or studying for the bar)	12	6.1
Type of Employment		
# employed in law firms	106	59.9
# employed in business and industry	20	11.3
# employed in government	27	15.3
# employed in public interest	6	3.4
# employed as judicial clerks	9	5.1
# employed in academia	2	1.1
Geographic Location		
# employed in state	133	75.1
# employed outside the US	0	0.0
# of states where employed		11

Bar Passage Rates

First-time takers	197	Reporting %	91.88
Average school %	93.37	Average state %	85.48
Average pass difference	7.89		

Jurisdiction	Takers	Passers	Pass %	State %	Diff %
Texas	181	169	93.37	85.48	7.89

The information on these pages was provided by the law school.

TEXAS TECH UNIVERSITY SCHOOL OF LAW

1802 Hartford Avenue
Lubbock, TX 79409
Phone: 806.742.3990; Fax: 806.742.4617
E-mail: admissions.law@ttu.edu; Website: www.law.ttu.edu

Introduction

Founded in 1967, we are located on the main campus of Texas Tech University in Lubbock. We are fully accredited by the ABA and the Supreme Court of Texas, and we are a member of the more selective Association of American Law Schools. In 1974, a chapter of the Order of the Coif was established, a distinction accorded to only one third of American law schools. Our faculty embraces an open-door policy, enabling students to engage in continuing dialogue beyond formal class hours. We have a long and proud tradition of graduating practice-ready lawyers, with our bar passage rates consistently among the highest in the state and employment rates consistently well over 90 percent.

Library and Physical Facilities

Our library is designed to meet the needs of a contemporary legal education. The law library supports the research and academic needs of the students and faculty with superb computer resources and wireless Internet access, complementing a substantial collection of printed materials. All students have 24/7 access to the library and assigned library carrels that serve as small office-like work spaces. All classrooms are equipped with multimedia technology. The 34,000-square-foot Lanier Professional Development Center houses the Office of Academic Success Programs, the Career Services Center, a state-of-the-art courtroom designed to support technology-driven advocacy training, and ample space for student meetings.

Programs of Study

We offer several opportunities to pursue knowledge and experience beyond the law program through our dual-degree programs. Those programs are: JD/MBA, JD/MPA, JD/MD, JD/MS in Agriculture and Applied Economics, JD/MS in Accounting (Taxation), JD/Master of Environmental Toxicology, JD/Master of Biotechnology, JD/MS in Crop Science, JD/MS in Soil Science, JD/MS in Horticultural and Turfgrass Sciences, JD/MS in Entomology, JD/MS in Engineering, and JD/MS in Personal Financial Planning. We also offer certificate programs in Business Law; Health Law; and Law and Science with specializations in IP Law, Environmental Law, Biodefense Law, Energy Law, and Water Law.

Curriculum

The program of study equips students to practice law as advocates, counselors, or judges, and we recognize that legal education is also a stepping-stone to careers in government, politics, or business. The required curriculum provides a broad-based legal education. Elective courses afford students the opportunity to create an area of concentration, ranging from business law to emerging areas like health law, natural resources law, and national security law. The School of Law offers an Academic Success Program to assist students in developing the skills to succeed in the study and practice of law.

Legal Publication and Research Opportunities

Texas Tech has several publications that allow students to hone their research and writing skills. The *Texas Tech Law Review* publishes articles written by students and leading jurists, practitioners, and academics.

The State Bar of Texas selected Tech Law to publish the *Texas Tech Administrative Law Journal*. The *Estate Planning and Community Property Law Journal* is the only legal journal committed to community property law, and only the second in the nation devoted to estate planning. The *Texas Bank Lawyer* publishes articles about banking and commercial law.

The school is home to the Center for Water Law and Policy, the Center for Military Law and Policy, and the Center for Biodefense Law and Policy, which all provide research and scholarship opportunities.

Admission

We admit applicants from a wide range of backgrounds and experiences. While an applicant's LSAT and GPA figure significantly in the admission process, we also consider other factors, including extracurricular activities, public service, previous employment, and leadership qualities. A bachelor's degree from an accredited college or university is required.

We review applications on a rolling basis beginning mid-October. The application deadline for our binding early decision program is November 1. The deadline for regular decision applicants is February 1. Some students may be selected for acceptance through our Summer Entry Program.

Applications received after February 1 will be accepted but not reviewed until decisions have been made on all timely applications.

Clinical Program

Boasting eight live-client clinics, our clinical program provides third-year students with the opportunity to represent clients and participate in real cases guided by full-time, tenure-track faculty. The Civil Practice Clinic handles a wide range of civil matters. The Criminal Defense and Capital Punishment Clinic provides a unique opportunity for law students to represent clients in state and federal criminal courts. Tax Clinic students represent taxpayers in disputes with the IRS. With the Innocence Project, students investigate claims of actual innocence made by state and federal prisoners. The Family Law and Housing Clinic takes cases concerning those issues from Legal Aid of Northwest Texas. Our newest clinic, the Caprock Regional Criminal Defense Clinic, serves an entire 10-county region by providing representation to indigent clients in misdemeanor and juvenile cases.

Second-year students also have the opportunity to participate in our Alternative Dispute Resolution and Health Care and Bioethics Mediation clinics, which focus on resolving legal issues without litigation.

Advocacy Program

The Texas Tech School of Law advocacy program produces champions. We are proud of our multiple national and regional championships in the country's toughest advocacy competitions, including the 2010 National Moot Court championship (the nation's oldest and most prestigious competition), the 2010 Entertainment Law Moot Court national championship, three straight national championships at the National Latino/a Law Student Association Moot Court Competition, and the 2010 International Negotiation Competition championship. Students also gain advocacy experience in simulated practice settings through numerous intramural competitions. In 2008, we opened the Lanier Center for Professional Development, which houses a courtroom featuring state-of-the-art technology, as well as several practice rooms used by students to develop the skills needed to practice in the courtrooms of the future.

Student Activities

The Student Bar Association is the focal point for many student activities. The school has approximately 50 student organizations covering a wide variety of topics and interests. This includes groups such as the Black Law Students Association, Environmental Law Society, Federalist Society, Lambda, and the Student Public Interest Initiative.

Study-Abroad Programs

Texas Tech is a consortium partner in the Summer Law Institute, a cooperative teaching program with the historic University of Guanajuato, Mexico. The Summer Law Institute offers an introduction to Mexican law, international law, and legal subjects of interest to both US and Mexican lawyers, such as NAFTA.

Students are also offered legal study for credit through cooperative programs with the University of Lyon in France; La Trobe University in Melbourne, Australia; and Vytautas Magnus University School of Law in Kaunas, Lithuania, as well as opportunities to create their own study-abroad programs for credit.

Financial Aid and Scholarships

The School of Law offers numerous scholarships to entering students. Competitive scholarships are awarded to many nonresident applicants, making them eligible for in-state tuition. Additional scholarships are available for second- and third-year students.

Grants and educational loan funds are available for students who qualify. Please visit www.law.ttu.edu/prospective/financialaid/ for more information.

APPLICANT PROFILE

Texas Tech University School of Law
This grid includes only applicants who earned 120–180 LSAT scores under standard administrations.

LSAT Score	3.75 +		3.50–3.74		3.25–3.49		3.00–3.24		2.75–2.99		2.50–2.74		2.25–2.49		2.00–2.24		Below 2.00		No GPA		Total	
	Apps	Adm	Apps	Adm	Apps	Adm	Apps	Adm	Apps	Adm	Apps	Adm	Apps	Adm	Apps	Adm	Apps	Adm	Apps	Adm	Apps	Adm
175–180	0	0	0	0	0	0	0	0	0	0	0	0	0	0	0	0	0	0	0	0	0	0
170–174	1	1	1	1	1	0	0	0	0	0	0	0	0	0	0	0	0	0	0	0	3	2
165–169	2	2	3	3	9	9	4	4	2	2	2	2	2	0	0	0	0	0	0	0	24	22
160–164	29	26	27	27	31	30	28	26	16	10	9	3	5	0	1	0	0	0	0	0	146	122
155–159	45	42	65	59	82	74	82	73	34	12	30	5	18	0	5	0	1	0	3	3	365	268
150–154	38	32	90	60	88	16	82	10	55	1	29	0	16	1	5	0	1	0	3	1	407	121
145–149	22	4	41	9	56	5	66	2	43	1	29	0	14	0	6	0	4	0	6	1	287	22
140–144	8	0	6	0	23	0	24	1	13	0	17	0	5	0	3	0	1	0	1	0	101	1
135–139	2	0	0	0	3	0	6	0	6	0	13	0	7	0	0	0	2	0	0	0	39	0
130–134	0	0	1	0	2	0	6	0	2	0	3	0	0	0	0	0	2	0	1	0	17	0
125–129	0	0	0	0	0	0	2	0	0	0	0	0	1	0	1	0	0	0	0	0	4	0
120–124	0	0	0	0	0	0	0	0	0	0	0	0	0	0	0	0	0	0	0	0	0	0
Total	147	107	234	159	295	134	300	116	171	26	132	10	68	1	21	0	11	0	14	5	1393	558

Apps = Number of Applicants
Adm = Number Admitted
Reflects 99% of the total applicant pool; highest LSAT data reported.

TEXAS WESLEYAN UNIVERSITY SCHOOL OF LAW

1515 Commerce Street, Office of Admissions
Fort Worth, TX 76102
Phone: 817.212.4040, 800.733.9529, ext. 4040; Fax: 817.212.4141
E-mail: lawadmissions@law.txwes.edu; Website: www.law.txwes.edu

ABA
Approved
Since
1994

The Basics

Type of school	Private
Term	Semester
Application deadline	3/31
Application fee	$55
Financial aid deadline	3/15
Can first year start other than fall?	No
Student to faculty ratio	24.8 to 1
# of housing spaces available restricted to law students	
graduate housing for which law students are eligible	

Faculty and Administrators

	Total		Men		Women		Minorities	
	Spr	Fall	Spr	Fall	Spr	Fall	Spr	Fall
Full-time	22	23	13	13	9	10	3	3
Other full-time	7	7	6	6	1	1	1	1
Deans, librarians, & others who teach	8	8	5	5	3	3	3	3
Part-time	26	19	19	12	7	7	4	3
Total	63	57	43	36	20	21	11	10

Curriculum

	Full-Time	Part-Time
Typical first-year section size	83	53
Is there typically a "small section" of the first-year class, other than Legal Writing, taught by full-time faculty	No	No
If yes, typical size offered last year		
# of classroom course titles beyond first-year curriculum	182	

# of upper division courses, excluding seminars, with an enrollment:	Under 25	120
	25–49	26
	50–74	15
	75–99	17
	100+	2

# of seminars	15	
# of seminar positions available	240	
# of seminar positions filled	141	46
# of positions available in simulation courses	380	
# of simulation positions filled	168	52
# of positions available in faculty supervised clinical courses	75	
# of faculty supervised clinical positions filled	65	7
# involved in field placements	86	6
# involved in law journals	129	77
# involved in moot court or trial competitions	53	14
# of credit hours required to graduate	90	

JD Enrollment and Ethnicity

	Men #	Men %	Women #	Women %	Full-Time #	Full-Time %	Part-Time #	Part-Time %	1st-Year #	1st-Year %	Total #	Total %	JD Degs. Awd.
All Hispanics	30	7.8	30	7.9	36	7.4	24	8.7	24	5.8	60	7.9	25
Am. Ind./AK Nat.	5	1.3	1	0.3	1	0.2	5	1.8	3	0.7	6	0.8	6
Asian	18	4.7	22	5.8	22	4.5	18	6.5	20	4.9	40	5.2	13
Black/Af. Am.	15	3.9	28	7.4	17	3.5	26	9.4	18	4.4	43	5.6	16
Nat. HI/Pac. Isl.	1	0.3	0	0.0	0	0.0	1	0.4	1	0.2	1	0.1	0
2 or more races	4	1.0	6	1.6	7	1.4	3	1.1	9	2.2	10	1.3	0
Subtotal (minor.)	73	19.0	87	23.0	83	17.0	77	27.8	75	18.2	160	20.9	66
Nonres. Alien	0	0.0	0	0.0	0	0.0	0	0.0	0	0.0	0	0.0	0
White/Cauc.	302	78.4	278	73.4	388	79.7	192	69.3	327	79.4	580	75.9	167
Unknown	10	2.6	14	3.7	16	3.3	8	2.9	10	2.4	24	3.1	0
Total	385	50.4	379	49.6	487	63.7	277	36.3	412	53.9	764		233

Transfers

Transfers in	4
Transfers out	11

Tuition and Fees

	Resident	Nonresident
Full-time	$27,440	$27,440
Part-time	$19,690	$19,690
Tuition Guarantee Program		N

Living Expenses

Estimated living expenses for singles

Living on campus	Living off campus	Living at home
$11,440	$15,211	$10,982

TEXAS WESLEYAN UNIVERSITY SCHOOL OF LAW

*ABA
Approved
Since
1994*

GPA and LSAT Scores

	Total	Full-Time	Part-Time
# of apps	2,080	1,746	334
# of offers	827	704	123
# of matrics	253	172	81
75% GPA	3.46	3.51	3.37
Median GPA	3.23	3.25	3.12
25% GPA	2.91	2.96	2.87
75% LSAT	156	156	156
Median LSAT	153	153	152
25% LSAT	151	151	149

Grants and Scholarships (from prior year)

	Total		Full-Time		Part-Time	
	#	%	#	%	#	%
Total # of students	793		522		271	
Total # receiving grants	262	33.0	172	33.0	90	33.2
Less than 1/2 tuition	201	25.3	128	24.5	73	26.9
Half to full tuition	45	5.7	36	6.9	9	3.3
Full tuition	16	2.0	8	1.5	8	3.0
More than full tuition	0	0.0	0	0.0	0	0.0
Median grant amount			$7,500		$5,000	

Informational and Library Resources

Total amount spent on library materials	$1,750,697
Study seating capacity inside the library	383
# of full-time equivalent professional librarians	7
Hours per week library is open	112
# of open, wired connections available to students	50
# of networked computers available for use by students	0
Has wireless network?	Y
Requires computer?	N

JD Attrition (from prior year)

	Academic	Other	Total	
	#	#	#	%
1st year	19	16	35	8.5
2nd year	1	6	7	3.2
3rd year	0	0	0	0.0
4th year	0	0	0	0.0

Employment (9 months after graduation)

	Total	Percentage
Employment status known	177	86.8
Employment status unknown	27	13.2
Employed	151	85.3
Pursuing graduate degrees	5	2.8
Unemployed (seeking, not seeking, or studying for the bar)	20	11.3
Type of Employment		
# employed in law firms	88	58.3
# employed in business and industry	39	25.8
# employed in government	13	8.6
# employed in public interest	3	2.0
# employed as judicial clerks	3	2.0
# employed in academia	4	2.6
Geographic Location		
# employed in state	126	83.4
# employed outside the US	0	0.0
# of states where employed	9	

Bar Passage Rates

First-time takers	201	Reporting %	100.00
Average school %	89.55	Average state %	85.48
Average pass difference	4.07		

Jurisdiction	Takers	Passers	Pass %	State %	Diff %
Texas	201	180	89.55	85.48	4.07

TEXAS WESLEYAN UNIVERSITY SCHOOL OF LAW

1515 Commerce Street, Office of Admissions
Fort Worth, TX 76102
Phone: 817.212.4040, 800.733.9529, ext. 4040; Fax: 817.212.4141
E-mail: lawadmissions@law.txwes.edu; Website: www.law.txwes.edu

Introduction

Established in 1989, the law school became part of Texas Wesleyan University in 1992 with a mission to provide excellence in legal education. The program emphasizes service to our diverse student body, our profession, and our community through outstanding teaching and scholarship, the development of innovative academic programs, and a commitment to public service, as well as by promoting the highest ethical standards in the practice of law. The law school is fully approved by the ABA and offers both full-time and part-time programs leading to the Juris Doctor degree. The law school is located in downtown Fort Worth, Texas, in close proximity to the legal and judicial communities. The Fort Worth/Dallas Metroplex, with approximately 5.8 million residents, has rapidly grown to become one of the largest and most diverse metropolitan areas in the country, offering a relatively low cost of living, a growing economy, and extensive opportunities for professional advancement.

Student Body

Texas Wesleyan Law is committed to educating students of diverse backgrounds, varied life experiences, and differing educational perspectives. In its short but dynamic 20-year history, Texas Wesleyan School of Law has provided excellence in legal education to traditional full-time students as well as to accomplished nontraditional part-time students. The increasing rise in the quality of students is a reflection of our continued emphasis on service to a diverse student body, the profession, and the community. Over the past several years, applications have increased and median LSAT scores, as well as median undergraduate GPAs, have risen.

Faculty

Texas Wesleyan Law has a highly qualified, energetic, accessible faculty. The members of the faculty hold degrees from the top law schools across the country and have diverse professional backgrounds and experience. They have served in a variety of high-level governmental positions, in the judiciary and state legislatures, and in law firms. Faculty members are talented and active scholars and have published numerous books and articles. The student-to-faculty ratio ensures that students have the attention they need, both inside and outside of the classroom.

Library and Physical Facilities

The law school boasts first-rate facilities, including spacious classrooms, well-designed courtrooms, an in-house law clinic, and an impressive library. Texas Wesleyan's law library contains more than 250,000 volumes and equivalents. The law library's mission is to support the educational, instructional, curricular, and research needs of the faculty, students, and staff. In addition to its law book collection, the law library subscribes to major online electronic legal information services, including LexisNexis, Westlaw, and legal research Internet sites. Complementing the library's book and electronic sources, an extensive collection of US Congressional documents, including full transcripts of all congressional hearings since 1970, is available on microfiche. The law library has 8 full-time librarians and a staff of 14 and is open 112 hours per week, 89 of which have reference services available.

Curriculum

Ninety (90) hours of academic course credit are required for completion of the Juris Doctor degree. Students may choose between full-time day, part-time day, or part-time evening courseloads. The part-time program and Texas Wesleyan's flexible scheduling make it possible for those with continuing business and family responsibilities to meet their obligations while obtaining a legal education. The law school offers over 115 courses divided among traditional law courses and advanced courses that provide training in a variety of specialized law areas. Students are required to complete a minimum of 30 hours of pro bono legal service and 3 credit hours of professional oral skills learning before graduation.

Skills Training

To help students develop necessary practical lawyering skills, Texas Wesleyan has developed a series of courses in its Juris Doctor curriculum—each called a practicum—in some substantive areas as well as in particular skills areas. The law school also offers a variety of externships with trial and appellate courts, government agencies, nonprofit organizations, and law firms. For academic credit, students perform legal tasks and apply their academic studies to real-client cases, gaining valuable insight into the operation of legal institutions. Texas Wesleyan also has an in-house legal clinic that functions as an actual law office where students represent indigent clients in court under the direction of a faculty supervisor. All skills programs are coordinated by a full-time professor.

The law school also prides itself on its ability to help students apply lessons learned in the classroom to real-world legal problems through the Equal Justice Program, a mandatory 30-hour community-related pro bono requirement that must be completed by every student before graduation. Students can fulfill this requirement in many ways, such as by volunteering with a public service agency or with a private attorney doing pro bono work. In addition, the school is committed to serving the community through a variety of programs, such as National Adoption Day, Street Law, and High School Law Day, in which students can gain legal experience while helping to address community legal needs.

Finally, the law school has added a new 3-hour professional skills requirement. The requirement is intended to further enhance theoretical learning and reinforce practical lawyering skills. This requirement can be satisfied by completing coursework or participating in competitions that emphasize a student's oral skills. Examples of programming that will meet this requirement include Trial Advocacy, Mediation, Clinics, and moot court or mock trial competitions.

Student Life

Texas Wesleyan Law's student organizations provide a broad spectrum of opportunities for student involvement. Our enthusiastic law students engage in competitions and leadership activities at the state, regional, and national levels. Students have won numerous competitions in negotiations, mock trial, and recently, the national moot court championships in entertainment law and information technology and privacy law. Through membership in law student organizations, participants reap the benefits of professional contacts, social activities, and exposure to legal specialties. Our student organizations provide opportunities for students to engage in professional bar associations, legal specialties, networking opportunities, and public service projects. In addition, the *Texas Wesleyan Law Review* encourages legal scholarship on issues of interest to academicians, practitioners, and law students. The *Law Review* is published by student editors with a faculty advisor. Participation is limited to those who meet academic requirements and those who are selected through a writing competition.

Career Services

The Texas Wesleyan University School of Law Office of Career Services assists students, graduates, and employers in their mutual efforts to link those seeking legal positions with those providing legal employment opportunities. Career Services also supports students in securing part-time or temporary employment while attending law school. A range of services, such as one-on-one career counseling, résumé and cover letter review, career seminars, on-campus interviews, off-campus job fairs, and an online job bank, are available to students and graduates. The Office of Career Services also provides numerous online and hard-copy career resources in the career planning library. The school is a member of NALP, the Association for Legal Career Professionals.

Expenses and Financial Aid

Texas Wesleyan Law offers a highly competitive and low private tuition cost. Tuition and general costs vary by courseload. For

2010–2011, annual tuition for full-time students was $26,650; for part-time students, $18,900. Fees were an additional $395 per semester. The law school works with individual students to provide the best financial aid package the student is eligible to receive. The financial aid package may include several types of assistance for financing a law school education, including scholarships, grants, employment opportunities, and loan programs. A majority of law students receive some form of financial assistance.

Admission

To be considered for admission, an applicant to Texas Wesleyan School of Law must hold a baccalaureate degree from a regionally accredited college or university prior to matriculation. A Law School Admission Test (LSAT) score is also required. The law school offers full-time and part-time programs, and new students are admitted only in the fall. The final deadline for applying is March 31; however, the School of Law reviews applications and awards scholarships on a rolling basis, so applicants are encouraged to apply early.

The admission committee will endeavor to determine the academic and professional promise of each applicant. Accordingly, the admission committee evaluates all factors relevant to an applicant's potential to be successful in meeting the academic standards of the Juris Doctor program, as well as his or her potential for success on the bar examination and in other professional endeavors. Traditional criteria, such as undergraduate academic achievement, LSAT performance, graduate studies, work experience, life experience, activities, honors, the personal statement, recommendation letters, and other experiences, are used in the admission evaluation process.

APPLICANT PROFILE

Texas Wesleyan University School of Law
This grid includes only applicants who earned 120–180 LSAT scores under standard administrations.

LSAT Score	GPA																		
	3.75 +		3.50–3.74		3.25–3.49		3.00–3.24		2.75–2.99		2.50–2.74		Below 2.50		No GPA		Total	
	Apps	Adm	Apps	Adm	Apps	Adm	Apps	Adm	Apps	Adm	Apps	Adm	Apps	Adm	Apps	Adm	Apps	Adm
170–180	1	0	0	0	2	1	0	0	0	0	0	0	0	0	0	0	3	1
165–169	2	2	0	0	1	1	4	4	0	0	2	1	4	1	0	0	13	9
160–164	11	11	18	18	25	23	22	18	23	18	5	3	14	7	1	0	119	98
155–159	31	31	55	47	78	75	64	51	50	39	43	24	40	8	1	1	362	276
150–154	40	32	87	75	113	92	130	76	119	64	64	23	62	7	3	1	618	370
145–149	30	17	69	20	118	18	124	13	105	6	59	1	69	2	10	2	584	79
140–144	11	2	13	0	36	0	60	1	51	0	46	0	44	0	7	0	268	3
Below 140	3	0	6	0	18	0	28	0	24	0	31	0	52	0	6	0	168	0
Total	129	95	248	160	391	210	432	163	372	127	250	52	285	25	28	4	2135	836

Apps = Number of Applicants
Adm = Number Admitted
Reflects 99% of the total applicant pool; highest LSAT data reported.

THE THOMAS M. COOLEY LAW SCHOOL

PO Box 13038, 300 S. Capitol Avenue
Lansing, MI 48901
Phone: 517.371.5140, ext. 2244; Fax: 517.334.5718
E-mail: admissions@cooley.edu; Website: www.cooley.edu

The Basics

Type of school	Private
Term	Semester
Application deadline	9/1 1/1 5/1
Application fee	$0
Financial aid deadline	8/22 12/19 4/23
Can first year start other than fall?	Yes
Student to faculty ratio	22.4 to 1
# of housing spaces available restricted to law students	
graduate housing for which law students are eligible	20

Faculty and Administrators

	Total		Men		Women		Minorities	
	Spr	Fall	Spr	Fall	Spr	Fall	Spr	Fall
Full-time	101	99	59	58	42	41	14	12
Other full-time	3	2	2	1	1	1	0	0
Deans, librarians, & others who teach	29	30	11	11	18	19	5	5
Part-time	180	175	118	110	62	65	28	20
Total	313	306	190	180	123	126	47	37

Curriculum

		Full-Time	Part-Time
Typical first-year section size		54	54
Is there typically a "small section" of the first-year class, other than Legal Writing, taught by full-time faculty		No	No
If yes, typical size offered last year			
# of classroom course titles beyond first-year curriculum		240	
# of upper division courses, excluding seminars, with an enrollment:	Under 25	523	
	25–49	130	
	50–74	88	
	75–99	72	
	100+	28	
# of seminars		379	
# of seminar positions available		7,676	
# of seminar positions filled		950	4,325
# of positions available in simulation courses		5,229	
# of simulation positions filled		661	3,011
# of positions available in faculty supervised clinical courses		534	
# of faculty supervised clinical positions filled		60	271
# involved in field placements		141	644
# involved in law journals		72	329
# involved in moot court or trial competitions		12	56
# of credit hours required to graduate		90	

JD Enrollment and Ethnicity

	Men		Women		Full-Time		Part-Time		1st-Year		Total		JD Degs. Awd.
	#	%	#	%	#	%	#	%	#	%	#	%	
All Hispanics	99	4.9	120	6.3	39	5.6	180	5.6	112	5.4	219	5.6	39
Am. Ind./AK Nat.	10	0.5	9	0.5	3	0.4	16	0.5	9	0.4	19	0.5	2
Asian	106	5.3	96	5.0	45	6.5	157	4.8	124	6.0	202	5.1	48
Black/Af. Am.	162	8.0	359	18.7	68	9.8	453	14.0	310	15.1	521	13.3	84
Nat. HI/Pac. Isl.	4	0.2	6	0.3	1	0.1	9	0.3	5	0.2	10	0.3	0
2 or more races	35	1.7	46	2.4	14	2.0	67	2.1	49	2.4	81	2.1	0
Subtotal (minor.)	416	20.7	636	33.2	170	24.6	882	27.2	609	29.6	1052	26.8	200
Nonres. Alien	100	5.0	113	5.9	48	6.9	165	5.1	141	6.9	213	5.4	0
White/Cauc.	1422	70.6	1135	59.2	460	66.6	2097	64.7	1250	60.8	2557	65.0	643
Unknown	75	3.7	34	1.8	13	1.9	96	3.0	56	2.7	109	2.8	39
Total	2013	51.2	1918	48.8	691	17.6	3240	82.4	2056	52.3	3931		918

Transfers

Transfers in	5
Transfers out	153

Tuition and Fees

	Resident	Nonresident
Full-time	$30,644	$30,644
Part-time	$19,714	$19,714
Tuition Guarantee Program	N	

Living Expenses

Estimated living expenses for singles

Living on campus	Living off campus	Living at home
N/A	$13,800	$13,800

THE THOMAS M. COOLEY LAW SCHOOL

ABA Approved Since 1975

GPA and LSAT Scores

	Total	Full-Time	Part-Time
# of apps	4,922	4,211	711
# of offers	4,101	3,553	548
# of matrics	1,583	260	1,323
75% GPA	3.35	3.29	3.36
Median GPA	2.99	2.99	3.00
25% GPA	2.61	2.62	2.61
75% LSAT	151	154	149
Median LSAT	146	150	145
25% LSAT	144	146	143

Grants and Scholarships (from prior year)

	Total		Full-Time		Part-Time	
	#	%	#	%	#	%
Total # of students	3,727		586		3,141	
Total # receiving grants	2022	54.3	495	84.5	1527	48.6
Less than 1/2 tuition	1224	32.8	293	50.0	931	29.6
Half to full tuition	649	17.4	165	28.2	484	15.4
Full tuition	149	4.0	37	6.3	112	3.6
More than full tuition	0	0.0	0	0.0	0	0.0
Median grant amount			$8,969		$6,150	

Informational and Library Resources

Total amount spent on library materials	$3,048,956
Study seating capacity inside the library	1,587
# of full-time equivalent professional librarians	26
Hours per week library is open	168
# of open, wired connections available to students	48
# of networked computers available for use by students	253
Has wireless network?	Y
Requires computer?	N

JD Attrition (from prior year)

	Academic	Other	Total	
	#	#	#	%
1st year	107	183	290	14.8
2nd year	64	76	140	14.9
3rd year	5	4	9	1.1
4th year	0	0	0	0.0

Employment (9 months after graduation)

	Total	Percentage
Employment status known	807	84.2
Employment status unknown	151	15.8
Employed	628	77.8
Pursuing graduate degrees	20	2.5
Unemployed (seeking, not seeking, or studying for the bar)	148	18.3
Type of Employment		
# employed in law firms	355	56.5
# employed in business and industry	101	16.1
# employed in government	87	13.9
# employed in public interest	23	3.7
# employed as judicial clerks	30	4.8
# employed in academia	18	2.9
Geographic Location		
# employed in state	196	31.2
# employed outside the US	9	1.4
# of states where employed	40	

Bar Passage Rates

First-time takers	887	Reporting %	71.36
Average school %	77.41	Average state %	86.31
Average pass difference	–8.90		

Jurisdiction	Takers	Passers	Pass %	State %	Diff %
Michigan	291	257	88.32	86.87	1.45
Illinois	96	77	80.21	90.89	–10.68
New York	86	59	68.60	86.51	–17.91
Pennsylvania	36	25	69.44	85.69	–16.25
Others (4)	124	72	58.06		

THE THOMAS M. COOLEY LAW SCHOOL

PO Box 13038, 300 S. Capitol Avenue
Lansing, MI 48901
Phone: 517.371.5140, ext. 2244; Fax: 517.334.5718
E-mail: admissions@cooley.edu; Website: www.cooley.edu

President's Welcome

The Thomas M. Cooley Law School has earned the reputation for providing graduates with the practical skills necessary for a seamless transition from academia to the real world. Cooley's emphasis on sound academic knowledge, practice skills, and professionalism prepares our graduates for roles of leadership. Cooley was established to provide an opportunity to those who share the dream of becoming a lawyer. Our stated mission is to provide access to the legal profession.

Choosing a law school is a daunting task, particularly with so much misinformation, subjectivity, and bias confronting the potential law student. When you are researching law schools, please look at the three essential attributes of every successful law school—high-quality people, an excellent legal education program, and first-class facilities. These attributes are what should guide your law school selection.

Cooley pioneered practice-based legal education, and has provided law students with the knowledge, skills, and ethics needed for successful practice since 1972. You are invited to learn more about why the people of Cooley are its greatest asset, how our program is a model of modern legal education theory and practice, and how Cooley's facilities are unmatched in size, scope, functionality, and beauty.

People—Our Greatest Asset

Cooley is the largest law school in the nation. We have the largest full-time faculty in the country, nearly all of whom are former practicing lawyers or judges. Their highest priority is helping students become competent lawyers, and they are accessible and supportive of student activities. **A Global Community**—Our students come from all 50 states, we lead all law schools in minority enrollment and foreign national students, and our graduates are found in every state and in numerous foreign countries. Our size and diversity allow our students to practice legal skills as they would in the real world—as a global community.

Knowledge, Skills, and Ethics

Broad Knowledge—Cooley's 90 credit-hour curriculum provides all students with the substantive knowledge, legal skills, and ethics needed for bar examinations, law practice, and further graduate study. Students complete 63 hours of required substantive and skills-based courses, and have the option of focusing their electives in one of seven practice area concentrations. **Practical Skills and Clinics**—All Cooley students gain extensive experience in the actual practice of law through simulation courses, competitions, and clinics. Practice skills are woven into substantive courses throughout the curriculum. Competitions in client counseling, negotiation, trial, and appellate skills allow students to compete against others from across the country. Cooley's expansive clinical programs immerse students in hands-on learning. Students can choose from one of Cooley's eight clinics or from more than 2,100 externship sites around the globe. **World Leader in Plain English Writing**—Recognized as a world leader in training students in the use of plain language, Cooley has the preeminent research and writing program and an innovative curriculum. **Lifelong Ethics**—

Beginning with the application process, Cooley fosters a culture of professionalism. At each step of the law school journey, students are challenged to adopt professionalism as a way of life.

Facilities—Unmatched in Size and Beauty

Four Campus Locations in Michigan: Lansing, Auburn Hills, Grand Rapids, and Ann Arbor—Cooley's four distinct campuses are unmatched in size and functionality. Each campus has a full complement of faculty, staff, libraries, and services. Our buildings and technology were designed to meet the academic and research needs of today's legal community. High-tech courtrooms and classrooms are equipped with the latest technology to enhance the educational experience. Cooley's library facilities are among the nation's largest and finest. The 600,000+ volume collection includes research materials from all 50 states as well as federal and international materials.

Accessible, Affordable Legal Education

The Juris Doctor curriculum is offered at each of Cooley's locations. Cooley operates a rolling admissions process with the option of starting classes in January, May, or September. Study full- or part-time. Complete the JD degree in two to five years by choosing from flexible scheduling options. Classes are offered mornings, afternoons, evenings, and on weekends.

Cooley uses a straightforward, objective formula to determine eligibility (UGPA x 15 + Highest LSAT = Admission Index). Admission to Cooley is also contingent on meeting character and fitness standards. There is no application fee.

Scholarships—Thanks in part to a generous scholarship program, Cooley is among the nation's most affordable independent law schools. Prospective students can determine the scholarship amount before applying. Students can earn up to 100 percent of tuition in two ways:

1. Admission Index levels:

Index	Honors Scholarship
215+	100%
210–214	75%
205–209	50%
195–204	25%

2. Student's highest LSAT score:

LSAT	Honors Scholarship
163+	100%
158–162	75%
153–157	50%
149–152	25%

Michigan residents who qualify for an entering LSAT Honors Scholarship may be eligible for an additional 10 percent scholarship. Qualified **Canadian students** may be eligible to attend Cooley at a reduced cost. **Transfer students** are eligible for scholarships. Nonscholarship financial aid is available. Please refer to www.cooley.edu for the most current information.

Expenses—Tuition: $1,093 per credit hour in 2010–2011. **Fees:** $20 per term. See Cooley's online tuition calculator to compare tuition costs.

An Active, Engaged Academic Community

Scholarly Publications—Cooley's premier scholarly journal, *Thomas M. Cooley Law Review*, provides students opportunities to edit and publish traditional in-depth scholarship. The student editors of the *Journal of Practical and Clinical Law* work with lawyers and professors to address more practice-oriented issues. Cooley's newest publication is the *Art and Museum Law Journal*. **Symposia** bring together scholars from around the world to discuss timely topics. **Centers** in Ethics and Responsibility, Forensic Science and the Law, and Indian Law foster discussion and research. **Collaborations** with major research institutions open opportunities for dual-degree programs, including Juris Doctor/Master of Public Administration and Juris Doctor/Master of Business Administration programs with Oakland University and Western Michigan University. **Service**—Cooley strives to foster the highest caliber of relationships with surrounding communities. The Cooley Volunteer Corps matches organizations with students seeking substantive volunteer experiences. All students are members of the Student Bar Association, and there are more than 50 clubs and organizations in which students can become involved.

Commitment to Academic Success

Students receive support and enrichment at the Academic Resource Center (ARC). The ARC's professional staff provides ongoing assistance through the Introduction to Law class, seminars, one-on-one coaching, and other programs to help students refine skills critical to a successful legal career. Cooley provides students with institutional support to prepare them for state bar examinations, including practice bar exams, prebar courses, and individual counseling. Computer-assisted legal instruction, assistance for students requiring disability accommodations, and other support services are all free to students.

A Culture of Professionalism

National Professionalism Award—Cooley was awarded the American Bar Association's *E. Smythe Gambrell Professionalism Award* for its innovative Professionalism Plan. Professional development at Cooley combines classroom experience, volunteering, public service, pro bono work, clinical experience, employment, and mentoring. **Faculty and Career and Professional Development** staff assist students in developing professionalism portfolios that prepare them for their chosen careers. Students can take advantage of résumé review services, mock interview programs, online job bulletins, and workshops.

Graduate and International Studies

LLM—Cooley offers graduate law degrees in Tax, Intellectual Property, Corporate Law and Finance, Insurance Law, US Law for Foreign Lawyers, and Self-Directed Legal Studies. Dual JD/LLM degree programs are available. **International Studies**—Cooley students study law around the world. Each January, Cooley's 13-week program in Australia and New Zealand beckons students "down under." In the summer, Cooley invites students to Toronto, Canada. Cooley also cooperates with other law schools to provide students with options extending around the globe.

APPLICANT PROFILE

Typically, schools include a statistical table showing the likelihood of admission to their program. Cooley instead uses a straightforward, fair, objective, and transparent formula to determine eligibility for admission. Please visit our website at www.cooley.edu for the several ways to qualify for admission.

THOMAS JEFFERSON SCHOOL OF LAW

1155 Island Avenue
San Diego, CA 92101
Phone: 619.297.9700; 800.956.5070; Fax: 619.961.1300
E-mail: admissions@tjsl.edu; Website: www.tjsl.edu

ABA
Approved
Since
1996

AMERICAN BAR ASSOCIATION
Section of Legal Education
and Admissions to the Bar

The Basics

Type of school	Private
Term	Semester
Application deadline	2/1 10/1
Application fee	$50
Financial aid deadline	5/1
Can first year start other than fall?	Yes
Student to faculty ratio	17.6 to 1
# of housing spaces available restricted to law students	172
graduate housing for which law students are eligible	

Faculty and Administrators

	Total		Men		Women		Minorities	
	Spr	Fall	Spr	Fall	Spr	Fall	Spr	Fall
Full-time	39	38	18	17	21	21	9	9
Other full-time	1	4	1	1	0	3	0	2
Deans, librarians, & others who teach	2	2	2	2	0	0	0	0
Part-time	42	47	23	31	19	16	3	3
Total	84	91	44	51	40	40	12	14

Curriculum

	Full-Time	Part-Time
Typical first-year section size	85	70
Is there typically a "small section" of the first-year class, other than Legal Writing, taught by full-time faculty	No	No
If yes, typical size offered last year		
# of classroom course titles beyond first-year curriculum	104	

# of upper division courses, excluding seminars, with an enrollment:		
	Under 25	40
	25–49	21
	50–74	20
	75–99	8
	100+	1

# of seminars	20	
# of seminar positions available	386	
# of seminar positions filled	189	60
# of positions available in simulation courses	580	
# of simulation positions filled	256	177
# of positions available in faculty supervised clinical courses	24	
# of faculty supervised clinical positions filled	21	0
# involved in field placements	368	118
# involved in law journals	41	25
# involved in moot court or trial competitions	42	17
# of credit hours required to graduate	88	

JD Enrollment and Ethnicity

	Men		Women		Full-Time		Part-Time		1st-Year		Total		JD Degs. Awd.
	#	%	#	%	#	%	#	%	#	%	#	%	
All Hispanics	60	10.6	57	14.3	72	10.5	45	16.1	35	9.9	117	12.1	39
Am. Ind./AK Nat.	4	0.7	3	0.8	6	0.9	1	0.4	4	1.1	7	0.7	3
Asian	5	0.9	3	0.8	6	0.9	2	0.7	8	2.3	8	0.8	0
Black/Af. Am.	24	4.2	33	8.3	38	5.5	19	6.8	23	6.5	57	5.9	19
Nat. HI/Pac. Isl.	63	11.1	48	12.1	84	12.2	27	9.7	45	12.7	111	11.5	0
2 or more races	0	0.0	0	0.0	0	0.0	0	0.0	0	0.0	0	0.0	0
Subtotal (minor.)	156	27.5	144	36.2	206	30.0	94	33.7	115	32.5	300	31.1	86
Nonres. Alien	6	1.1	3	0.8	9	1.3	0	0.0	3	0.8	9	0.9	0
White/Cauc.	406	71.5	251	63.1	472	68.7	185	66.3	236	66.7	657	68.0	135
Unknown	0	0.0	0	0.0	0	0.0	0	0.0	0	0.0	0	0.0	0
Total	568	58.8	398	41.2	687	71.1	279	28.9	354	36.6	966		222

Transfers

Transfers in	0
Transfers out	48

Tuition and Fees

	Resident	Nonresident
Full-time	$19,350	$19,350
Part-time	$13,500	$13,500
Tuition Guarantee Program		N

Living Expenses

Estimated living expenses for singles

Living on campus	Living off campus	Living at home
N/A	$27,740	$27,740

THOMAS JEFFERSON SCHOOL OF LAW

ABA
Approved
Since
1996

GPA and LSAT Scores

	Total	Full-Time	Part-Time
# of apps	3,323	2,776	421
# of offers	1,604	1,375	229
# of matrics	422	318	104
75% GPA	3.24	3.25	3.20
Median GPA	3.00	3.01	2.92
25% GPA	2.71	2.73	2.70
75% LSAT	153	154	152
Median LSAT	151	151	149
25% LSAT	149	149	147

Grants and Scholarships (from prior year)

	Total		Full-Time		Part-Time	
	#	%	#	%	#	%
Total # of students	889		648		241	
Total # receiving grants	401	45.1	268	41.4	133	55.2
Less than 1/2 tuition	270	30.4	209	32.3	61	25.3
Half to full tuition	127	14.3	58	9.0	69	28.6
Full tuition	2	0.2	1	0.2	1	0.4
More than full tuition	2	0.2	0	0.0	2	0.8
Median grant amount			$12,000		$12,000	

Informational and Library Resources

Total amount spent on library materials	$1,231,607
Study seating capacity inside the library	266
# of full-time equivalent professional librarians	8
Hours per week library is open	115
# of open, wired connections available to students	10
# of networked computers available for use by students	27
Has wireless network?	Y
Requires computer?	Y

JD Attrition (from prior year)

	Academic	Other	Total	
	#	#	#	%
1st year	29	67	96	31.4
2nd year	5	16	21	6.1
3rd year	1	1	2	1.3
4th year	0	1	1	1.2

Employment (9 months after graduation)

	Total	Percentage
Employment status known	189	85.9
Employment status unknown	31	14.1
Employed	160	84.7
Pursuing graduate degrees	8	4.2
Unemployed (seeking, not seeking, or studying for the bar)	21	11.1
Type of Employment		
# employed in law firms	93	58.1
# employed in business and industry	35	21.9
# employed in government	14	8.7
# employed in public interest	11	6.9
# employed as judicial clerks	2	1.2
# employed in academia	2	1.2
Geographic Location		
# employed in state	133	83.1
# employed outside the US	4	2.5
# of states where employed	18	

Bar Passage Rates

First-time takers	220	Reporting %	100.00
Average school %	48.15	Average state %	74.59

Average pass difference −26.44

Jurisdiction	Takers	Passers	Pass %	State %	Diff %
California	189	88	46.56	73.19	−26.63
Arizona	4	3	75.00	79.76	−4.76
New York	4	2	50.00	86.51	−36.51
Nevada	3	2	66.67	73.00	−6.33
Others (14)	20	11	55.00		

The information on these pages was provided by the law school.

THOMAS JEFFERSON SCHOOL OF LAW

1155 Island Avenue
San Diego, CA 92101
Phone: 619.297.9700; 800.956.5070; Fax: 619.961.1300
E-mail: admissions@tjsl.edu; Website: www.tjsl.edu

Welcome

Thomas Jefferson School of Law (TJSL) is a private, nonprofit, and independent law school. Accredited by the ABA and a member of AALS, the law school emphasizes an individualized approach to learning by integrating the cognitive sciences and learning theory into its curriculum.

The flexible curriculum allows students to begin their studies in either August or January. Also, students can pursue a law degree in a full- or part-time (day or evening) program and accelerate graduation by attending classes in the summer. This multitrack approach, traceable to the school's roots as a longtime supporter of military personnel and working adults, gives students the option of pursuing a law degree full or part time while continuing their employment.

Admission

Thomas Jefferson utilizes a rolling admission process under which applicants are considered when their applications are complete. While there is no deadline for the fall or spring term, applications are accepted through July for the fall term and through December for the spring term. However, due to the large applicant pool, early applications are encouraged. The Admissions Committee functions with a holistic approach, which includes considering the applicant's LSAT score, undergraduate record, extracurricular activities, work ethic and experience, and demonstrated ability to overcoming adversity. Decisions are made and sent out on a rolling basis.

New Campus Opened Spring 2011

The law school recently moved into a new eight-story, high-rise building in Downtown San Diego. The law school expects to earn Gold Level certification from the Leadership in Energy and Environmental Design (LEED) Green Building Rating System of the US Green Building Council. The $70 million campus features a state-of-the-art library, in-house legal clinics, and a café. The location places students within walking distance from many law firms, major businesses, and the state and federal courts. Student housing is available within one block of the law school.

Vibrant and Diverse Student Community

The mission of the Thomas Jefferson School of Law is to provide an outstanding legal education for a nationally based, diverse student body in a collegial and supportive environment. The law school lives up to that mission in every way. The TJSL campus truly reflects its commitment to diversity: the student body is gender-balanced, 20 percent of the students are the first in their family to attend law school, students of color comprise 33 percent of the student body, many students are openly GLBT, 23 percent are multilingual, and they represent more than 23 countries.

San Diego—America's Finest City

San Diego is uniquely situated and has major advantages for the study of law, professional development, and personal fulfillment. Its mild Mediterranean climate promises nearly 265 days of sunshine annually and moderate temperatures throughout the year. As the border city to Tijuana, Mexico, and just 120 miles south of Los Angeles, San Diego is a training ground for everything from international law to entertainment law. Also, as the second largest city in California and the eighth largest city in the United States, it is a vibrant social and economic center.

Internationally Renowned Faculty

TJSL is proud to have a first-rate faculty consisting of distinguished practitioners and scholars. Our professors have structured business transactions at both the international and the domestic levels and have litigated before the World Court at The Hague, the US Supreme Court, and federal and state trial and appellate courts. Their clients have ranged from the largest multinational corporations to the most impoverished members of society.

All 44 members of our faculty pride themselves on providing quality instruction and being accessible to students outside the classroom. First-year students are assigned faculty advisors, but all members of the faculty emphasize being available to students outside of class.

Cutting-Edge Legal Skills Programs

Our academic resources consist of a writing lab, student organization-led study sessions, and individual feedback from professors. However, the anchor of our academic resources is the highly effective academic success program, the **SUMMIT Series**, which is a part of the first-year curriculum and continues until preparation for the bar exam. The series brings scientific principles in psychology, neuroscience, and cognitive science to the study of law and equips students with a personal and succinct methodology for acquiring the fundamental skills to succeed in law school and on the bar exam. Our **Bar Secrets** course is a continuation of these principles and is a proven means of preparing for the California bar exam.

Progressive and Practical Curriculum

The academic program at Thomas Jefferson School of Law has been carefully designed to ensure a balanced and comprehensive curriculum that will prepare students to practice in any area of the law. During their first semester, entering students have the opportunity, in all their courses, to receive feedback from the faculty on their written legal analytical skills in order to enhance their understanding of the course material and hone their performance prior to final exams.

Academic Centers. A growing faculty has allowed the school to acquire special strengths in the areas of law that most reflect our changing world; that is, those relating to technological change, globalization, and the transformation of our social order. To provide an institutional framework for the study of these embryonic areas of law, the school has established three Academic Centers: (1) the **Center for Law, Technology, and Communications** prepares students for careers related to high technology and communications; (2) the **Center for Global Legal Studies** prepares students for the transborder aspects of contemporary legal practice and offers a wide variety of courses in international law; and (3) the **Center for Law and Social Justice** prepares students for practice geared toward the preservation of the values of liberty and equality in an ever-changing world.

The Externship Program. Rated as one of the top law schools in the US for externships, TJSL offers a large number of courses that train students in professional skills, supplemented by a variety of field-placement programs. Our externship coordinator works with students to place them in an endless number and type of for-credit legal positions. Past placements consist of public legal agencies, private law firms, corporations, and sports teams. Students may earn up to 10 credits from externship placements.

JD/MBA Program

In eight semesters, students can earn a Juris Doctor degree from Thomas Jefferson School of Law and a Master of Business Administration degree from San Diego State University (SDSU). The objective of the concurrent degree program is to prepare students who are competent in both law and business for career opportunities in areas where the two fields converge.

Applicants must adhere to the application process for each institution, including taking both the LSAT for law school admission and GMAT for business school admission. The curricular sequence requires students to attend their first two semesters as a full-time student at TJSL. The following semesters students take classes at both campuses.

International Law Programs

Thomas Jefferson School of Law offers three LLM (Master of Laws) programs and a JSD (Scientiae Juridicae Doctor) via residence, web and videoconferencing, and a combination thereof. Two of the LLMs—International Trade and Investment and International Tax and Financial Services—create practice-ready graduates set to engage with globally oriented firms and clients. The third LLM is for foreign law graduates to obtain a working knowledge of the US legal system, and obtain eligibility for certain state bar exams. The JSD is the interchangeable equivalent to a PhD in the social sciences, requiring a publicly defended, substantial dissertation and postgraduate course work.

Student Activities

Thomas Jefferson School of Law has 32 student organizations that provide a source of mutual support for various groups of students, including the Student Bar Association, Black Law Students Association, La Raza Students Association, and the Asian Pacific American Law Students Association. Student organizations are also formed as a result of heightened student interest in substantive areas of law practice, such as the International Law Society, the Entertainment and Sports Law Societies, and the Public Interest Law Foundation. These

organizations promote leadership within the community, as well as programming on various areas of the law. Student leaders serve as members of law school committees and provide a student voice to decision making. Student managed and edited publications include the *Thomas Jefferson Law Review* and the *iPlog*, which focuses on intellectual property. Cocurricular programs include the Moot Court, Mock Trial, and Alternative Dispute Resolution teams.

A Focus on Career Development

Staffed by five diverse lawyers and a coordinator, the Career Services team members work closely with the Externship Office to provide individual counseling to every student. Starting in the first semester, the staff works to develop a personal relationship with each student to assess interests and preferences, and develop strategies for securing internships. From there, the staff continues to engage and work closely with each student in every phase of the student's law school career, from developing a legal résumé and cover letter to helping the student negotiate a salary for the first postgraduate legal position. With an active on-campus recruiting program, the Career Services Office uses cutting-edge technology to assist students with securing internships and postgraduate positions. This includes providing every student with access to Symplicity, a comprehensive, web-based legal recruiting tool through which a student applies for internships and postgraduate legal positions. Communication with students about job postings and career-related topics is done through the school's website and with the help of most social media outlets including Twitter and Facebook.

Financial Aid and Scholarships

TJSL commits more than $5 million annually in scholarship assistance. Over 40 percent of first-year students receive awards that average $14,000 for each year of study and range from $5,000 to full-tuition scholarships. Offering both need- and merit-based scholarships, TJSL uses its funds for both recruitment as well as retention. Initial awards are based on information accessible through the application. Applicants who have significant financial need and would like to be considered for financial aid may submit a separate request for scholarship consideration. All scholarship recipients receive a detailed offer letter containing the terms of the award and any criteria for renewal.

The law school also makes awards from all available federal sources, including the work-study program, Direct Loan programs, Perkins Loans, and Veterans benefits under the Post 9/11 GI Bill. Approximately 95 percent of the student body receives some form of federal assistance. Applicants should submit the FAFSA at www.fafsa.gov. Our school code is 013780.

Applicant Profile Not Available

THE UNIVERSITY OF TOLEDO COLLEGE OF LAW

2801 West Bancroft Street, MS 507
Toledo, OH 43606-3390
Phone: 419.530.4131; Fax: 419.530.4345
E-mail: law.admissions@utoledo.edu; Website: law.utoledo.edu

ABA
Approved
Since
1939

The Basics

Type of school	Public
Term	Semester
Application deadline	8/1
Application fee	$0
Financial aid deadline	4/1
Can first year start other than fall?	No
Student to faculty ratio	14.4 to 1
# of housing spaces available restricted to law students	
graduate housing for which law students are eligible	

Faculty and Administrators

	Total		Men		Women		Minorities	
	Spr	Fall	Spr	Fall	Spr	Fall	Spr	Fall
Full-time	27	23	15	13	12	10	1	2
Other full-time	0	3	0	3	0	0	0	0
Deans, librarians, & others who teach	4	4	3	2	1	2	0	0
Part-time	16	23	10	17	6	6	1	0
Total	47	53	28	35	19	18	2	2

Curriculum

	Full-Time	Part-Time
Typical first-year section size	57	32
Is there typically a "small section" of the first-year class, other than Legal Writing, taught by full-time faculty	No	No
If yes, typical size offered last year		

# of classroom course titles beyond first-year curriculum		88
# of upper division courses, excluding seminars, with an enrollment:	Under 25	81
	25–49	29
	50–74	10
	75–99	0
	100+	0

# of seminars		9
# of seminar positions available		137
# of seminar positions filled	72	9
# of positions available in simulation courses		370
# of simulation positions filled	231	52
# of positions available in faculty supervised clinical courses		89
# of faculty supervised clinical positions filled	51	3
# involved in field placements	105	9
# involved in law journals	44	1
# involved in moot court or trial competitions	47	3
# of credit hours required to graduate		89

JD Enrollment and Ethnicity

	Men		Women		Full-Time		Part-Time		1st-Year		Total		JD Degs. Awd.
	#	%	#	%	#	%	#	%	#	%	#	%	
All Hispanics	6	2.2	8	4.4	11	3.0	3	3.2	8	4.2	14	3.0	5
Am. Ind./AK Nat.	1	0.4	1	0.5	1	0.3	1	1.1	2	1.1	2	0.4	1
Asian	9	3.2	6	3.3	11	3.0	4	4.2	5	2.6	15	3.3	4
Black/Af. Am.	11	4.0	7	3.8	16	4.4	2	2.1	9	4.8	18	3.9	4
Nat. HI/Pac. Isl.	0	0.0	0	0.0	0	0.0	0	0.0	0	0.0	0	0.0	0
2 or more races	0	0.0	0	0.0	0	0.0	0	0.0	0	0.0	0	0.0	0
Subtotal (minor.)	27	9.7	22	12.0	39	10.7	10	10.5	24	12.7	49	10.7	14
Nonres. Alien	6	2.2	2	1.1	8	2.2	0	0.0	2	1.1	8	1.7	0
White/Cauc.	183	66.1	122	66.7	241	66.0	64	67.4	131	69.3	305	66.3	111
Unknown	61	22.0	37	20.2	77	21.1	21	22.1	32	16.9	98	21.3	33
Total	277	60.2	183	39.8	365	79.3	95	20.7	189	41.1	460		161

Transfers

Transfers in	3
Transfers out	15

Tuition and Fees

	Resident	Nonresident
Full-time	$19,833	$30,613
Part-time	$14,886	$22,971
Tuition Guarantee Program		N

Living Expenses

Estimated living expenses for singles

Living on campus	Living off campus	Living at home
$14,750	$16,850	$7,966

THE UNIVERSITY OF TOLEDO COLLEGE OF LAW

ABA
Approved
Since
1939

GPA and LSAT Scores

	Total	Full-Time	Part-Time
# of apps	1,035	879	156
# of offers	581	506	75
# of matrics	157	123	34
75% GPA	3.48	3.53	3.40
Median GPA	3.21	3.22	3.19
25% GPA	2.83	2.87	2.78
75% LSAT	156	156	152
Median LSAT	152	153	150
25% LSAT	150	151	149

Grants and Scholarships (from prior year)

	Total		Full-Time		Part-Time	
	#	%	#	%	#	%
Total # of students	493		346		147	
Total # receiving grants	199	40.4	186	53.8	13	8.8
Less than 1/2 tuition	37	7.5	35	10.1	2	1.4
Half to full tuition	84	17.0	80	23.1	4	2.7
Full tuition	26	5.3	24	6.9	2	1.4
More than full tuition	52	10.5	47	13.6	5	3.4
Median grant amount			$12,152		$8,796	

Informational and Library Resources

Total amount spent on library materials	$632,213
Study seating capacity inside the library	446
# of full-time equivalent professional librarians	4
Hours per week library is open	109
# of open, wired connections available to students	34
# of networked computers available for use by students	30
Has wireless network?	Y
Requires computer?	N

JD Attrition (from prior year)

	Academic	Other	Total	
	#	#	#	%
1st year	12	20	32	14.7
2nd year	0	2	2	1.6
3rd year	0	3	3	2.0
4th year	0	0	0	0.0

Employment (9 months after graduation)

	Total	Percentage
Employment status known	134	86.5
Employment status unknown	21	13.5
Employed	124	92.5
Pursuing graduate degrees	1	0.7
Unemployed (seeking, not seeking, or studying for the bar)	5	3.7
Type of Employment		
# employed in law firms	52	41.9
# employed in business and industry	22	17.7
# employed in government	22	17.7
# employed in public interest	14	11.3
# employed as judicial clerks	7	5.6
# employed in academia	5	4.0
Geographic Location		
# employed in state	81	65.3
# employed outside the US	0	0.0
# of states where employed	19	

Bar Passage Rates

First-time takers	148	Reporting %	72.30
Average school %	88.79	Average state %	86.23
Average pass difference	2.56		

Jurisdiction	Takers	Passers	Pass %	State %	Diff %
Ohio	82	72	87.80	86.03	1.77
Michigan	25	23	92.00	86.87	5.13

The information on these pages was provided by the law school.

THE UNIVERSITY OF TOLEDO COLLEGE OF LAW

2801 West Bancroft Street, MS 507
Toledo, OH 43606-3390
Phone: 419.530.4131; Fax: 419.530.4345
E-mail: law.admissions@utoledo.edu; Website: law.utoledo.edu

Introduction

The University of Toledo is a state university of more than 23,000 students, conveniently located on the western edge of Toledo, in one of the city's nicest residential areas. The city of Toledo offers both the cultural amenities of a big city and the affordable cost of living and close-knit feel of a small town.

The College of Law, located on the main campus of the University of Toledo, is accredited by the ABA and is a member of the AALS and the League of Ohio Law Schools. We have been training lawyers since 1906 and, in 1984, were awarded a chapter of the Order of the Coif.

Toledo Law is a vibrant community of outstanding faculty, students, and alumni who are making a difference across the country and around the world. We offer a rich and engaged classroom experience guided by faculty members who are leaders in their fields and a wide range of programs designed to help you develop and sharpen the practical skills you will need. From your first day on campus, you will be part of a close-knit community committed to your success.

Student Body

The diverse student body at Toledo Law is engaged in learning and service. Over the last several years, our students have come to us from over 140 undergraduate institutions in 32 states, 3 US territories, and 11 foreign countries.

Students come from a variety of backgrounds. Many come straight from college, while others have worked for years. This diversity exposes students to an interesting, stimulating, and creative atmosphere where insights and ideas flourish. Our diversity is reflected in student groups and activities, representing a broad spectrum of social, political, ethnic, and religious perspectives.

Faculty

The faculty of the College of Law is distinctive. Our faculty makes students and learning their top priority. They have open-door policies, participate in student events, and make every student's future a personal concern.

In addition to being outstanding teachers, they are outstanding scholars, and many have earned national acclaim. The faculty includes graduates of top law schools, Fulbright scholars, members of the prestigious American Law Institute, and accomplished lawyers with years of private practice and public interest experience.

Library and Physical Facilities

The spacious, newly renovated Law Center includes tiered classrooms, a striking student lounge, a state-of-the-art moot courtroom, and an amphitheater-style auditorium. The entire building offers next-generation wireless access.

Occupying four levels within the Law Center, the library contains group-study rooms, videotaping facilities, and a modern computer lab available for use by law students. Students are trained in the use of two vast electronic law libraries—LexisNexis and Westlaw.

Curriculum

Toledo Law requires the successful completion of 89 semester hours for graduation. The curriculum in the first year of the full-time program and the first two years of the part-time program consists of required courses. An extensive upper-level curriculum covers traditional as well as cutting-edge subjects, and incorporates development of professional legal skills and values.

Our academic success program provides teaching assistants for students in all basic required courses and offers tutors for any student who requests academic support.

Joint-Degree/Certificate Programs—Toledo Law has joint-degree programs with the Colleges of Engineering, Business, and Arts and Sciences, leading to a Master of Science in Engineering, PhD in Engineering, Master of Business Administration, Master of Public Administration, or Master of Criminal Justice. Students may also design individual joint-degree programs. In addition, students can graduate with certificates of concentration in criminal, environmental, intellectual property, international, and labor/employment law.

Special Programs

Legal Clinics—A pioneer in clinical legal education, Toledo Law provides an atmosphere for learning basic lawyering techniques and allows students the opportunity to further sharpen their skills in live client settings. Under close supervision, students appear in court in both civil and criminal cases.

The clinical program is an important component of the overall educational experience for upper-level students. The wide array of clinical offerings enable students to gain practical legal experience before graduation. Toledo Law offers a Civil Practice Clinic, Criminal Law Practice Program, Dispute Resolution Clinic, and Domestic Violence and Juvenile Law Clinic.

The Public Service Externship program provides law students the opportunity to experience the reality of practice by spending a semester working in judges' chambers, legal services offices, prosecutors' offices, and other public service legal settings.

Symposia and National Conferences—The College of Law hosts a top-notch speaker series and multiple conferences and symposia. For example, Toledo Law hosts an annual Great Lakes Water Conference to address legal and policy issues critical to the Great Lakes. Entering its second decade, the conference has become a high-profile international forum for addressing some of the most important environmental issues of our time.

Student Activities

The *University of Toledo Law Review* is published four times a year by students selected on the basis of academic performance and a writing competition. Training and practice in brief writing and oral argument beyond the required appellate advocacy course are obtained through the Moot Court Program, Trial Advocacy Team, in the Charles Fornoff

Intramural Moot Court Competition, and in several national and regional competitions.

The Student Bar Association, American Constitution Society, Black Law Students Association, Business Law Society, Christian Legal Society, Criminal Justice Society, Environmental Law Society, Family and Juvenile Law Society, Federalist Society, Health Law Association, Hispanic Law Students Association, Intellectual Property Law Society, International Law Society, Jewish Law Students Association, Labor and Employment Law Association, OUTLaw (LGBT), Public Interest Law Association, Sports Law Association, and Women Law Students Association are among many active organizations.

Admission

Applicants must have received a bachelor's degree from an accredited college or university before the first day of law classes. We do not require any particular prelaw curriculum. We recommend that students take courses involving analysis, writing, and quantitative skills.

Admission decisions are the responsibility of the Admissions Committee. The committee begins to review applications in October for admission to the next fall's entering class. Applications are reviewed and decisions are made on a continuing basis.

The Admissions Committee considers undergraduate grades and transcript, LSAT scores, recommendations, professional experience, postgraduate educational experience, extracurricular activities, community service and involvement, and a personal statement.

Prospective students are encouraged to visit the law school, talk to our students and faculty, and sit in on a class. Appointments can be made through the Law Admissions Office, and live chat with admissions representatives is available through the admissions webpage.

Financial Aid

Toledo Law strives to provide a quality legal education at an affordable cost. The College of Law awards scholarships totaling in excess of $1.5 million each year, and all admitted students are considered for scholarship awards without separate application.

Residents of the following Michigan counties are treated as in-state residents for tuition purposes: Hillsdale, Lenawee, Macomb, Monroe, Oakland, Washtenaw, and Wayne.

The goal of the financial aid program is to ensure that graduates have the greatest freedom to choose their careers without regard to financial obligations.

Professional Development/Career Services

Toledo Law places top priority on providing comprehensive career planning and professional development for its students and graduates. The Office of Professional Development/Law Career Services assists students through workshops and counseling, and brings members of the local bar association and alumni from around the country together to support students in every aspect of professional growth and development.

As a result of both on- and off-campus interviews, second- and third-year students accept summer law clerk and attorney positions in all major cities of Ohio and Michigan, as well as locations throughout the United States. Graduates are successfully practicing in major law firms, government offices, the judiciary, and in public interest positions in nearly every state. Graduates also can be found in Asia, Europe, and Africa.

Toledo Law alumni are a valuable resource for current students as they pursue employment opportunities nationwide.

APPLICANT PROFILE

The University of Toledo College of Law

GPA	LSAT (10) Percentile Intervals								
	0–20	21–30	31–40	41–50	51–60	61–70	71–80	81–90	91–99
3.75 Above									
3.74 3.50									
3.49 3.25									
3.24 3.00									
2.99 2.75									
2.74 2.50									
2.49 2.25									
2.24 2.00									
Below 2.00									

■ Highly Likely　■ Possible　□ Unlikely

TOURO COLLEGE—JACOB D. FUCHSBERG LAW CENTER

225 Eastview Drive
Central Islip, NY 11722
Phone: 631.761.7010; Fax: 631.761.7019
E-mail: admissions@tourolaw.edu; Website: www.tourolaw.edu

The Basics

Type of school	Private
Term	Semester
Application deadline	7/15
Application fee	$60
Financial aid deadline	4/29
Can first year start other than fall?	No
Student to faculty ratio	15.4 to 1
# of housing spaces available restricted to law students	
graduate housing for which law students are eligible	

Faculty and Administrators

	Total		Men		Women		Minorities	
	Spr	Fall	Spr	Fall	Spr	Fall	Spr	Fall
Full-time	36	38	19	21	17	17	3	4
Other full-time	3	4	3	3	0	1	0	0
Deans, librarians, & others who teach	11	11	3	3	8	8	3	3
Part-time	30	26	24	19	6	7	8	5
Total	80	79	49	46	31	33	14	12

Curriculum

	Full-Time	Part-Time
Typical first-year section size	82	63
Is there typically a "small section" of the first-year class, other than Legal Writing, taught by full-time faculty	No	No
If yes, typical size offered last year		

# of classroom course titles beyond first-year curriculum		93
# of upper division courses, excluding seminars, with an enrollment:	Under 25	108
	25–49	29
	50–74	21
	75–99	1
	100+	2
# of seminars		13
# of seminar positions available		275
# of seminar positions filled	141	67
# of positions available in simulation courses		600
# of simulation positions filled	277	168
# of positions available in faculty supervised clinical courses		70
# of faculty supervised clinical positions filled	46	0
# involved in field placements	119	39
# involved in law journals	36	13
# involved in moot court or trial competitions	35	10
# of credit hours required to graduate		88

JD Enrollment and Ethnicity

	Men #	Men %	Women #	Women %	Full-Time #	Full-Time %	Part-Time #	Part-Time %	1st-Year #	1st-Year %	Total #	Total %	JD Degs. Awd.
All Hispanics	28	6.2	32	8.6	41	6.8	19	8.4	24	8.3	60	7.2	3
Am. Ind./AK Nat.	0	0.0	0	0.0	0	0.0	0	0.0	0	0.0	0	0.0	1
Asian	26	5.7	33	8.8	42	7.0	17	7.5	19	6.6	59	7.1	10
Black/Af. Am.	27	5.9	49	13.1	46	7.7	30	13.2	27	9.3	76	9.2	16
Nat. HI/Pac. Isl.	1	0.2	1	0.3	1	0.2	1	0.4	1	0.3	2	0.2	0
2 or more races	0	0.0	0	0.0	0	0.0	0	0.0	0	0.0	0	0.0	0
Subtotal (minor.)	82	18.1	115	30.7	130	21.6	67	29.5	71	24.5	197	23.8	30
Nonres. Alien	7	1.5	6	1.6	13	2.2	0	0.0	2	0.7	13	1.6	0
White/Cauc.	340	74.9	236	63.1	435	72.4	141	62.1	197	67.9	576	69.6	144
Unknown	25	5.5	17	4.5	23	3.8	19	8.4	20	6.9	42	5.1	10
Total	454	54.8	374	45.2	601	72.6	227	27.4	290	35.0	828		185

Transfers

Transfers in	24
Transfers out	33

Tuition and Fees

	Resident	Nonresident
Full-time	$41,070	$41,070
Part-time	$30,780	$30,780
Tuition Guarantee Program		N

Living Expenses

Estimated living expenses for singles

Living on campus	Living off campus	Living at home
$24,007	$24,007	$10,776

TOURO COLLEGE—JACOB D. FUCHSBERG LAW CENTER

ABA
Approved
Since
1983

GPA and LSAT Scores

	Total	Full-Time	Part-Time
# of apps	2,018	1,582	436
# of offers	870	735	135
# of matrics	280	213	67
75% GPA	3.39	3.39	3.34
Median GPA	3.14	3.15	3.05
25% GPA	2.86	2.86	2.82
75% LSAT	153	154	152
Median LSAT	151	151	150
25% LSAT	149	150	148

Grants and Scholarships (from prior year)

	Total		Full-Time		Part-Time	
	#	%	#	%	#	%
Total # of students	786		553		233	
Total # receiving grants	387	49.2	293	53.0	94	40.3
Less than 1/2 tuition	354	45.0	270	48.8	84	36.1
Half to full tuition	25	3.2	21	3.8	4	1.7
Full tuition	5	0.6	2	0.4	3	1.3
More than full tuition	3	0.4	0	0.0	3	1.3
Median grant amount			$8,000		$3,000	

Informational and Library Resources

Total amount spent on library materials	$1,417,319
Study seating capacity inside the library	476
# of full-time equivalent professional librarians	11
Hours per week library is open	83
# of open, wired connections available to students	0
# of networked computers available for use by students	48
Has wireless network?	Y
Requires computer?	N

JD Attrition (from prior year)

	Academic	Other	Total	
	#	#	#	%
1st year	33	38	71	22.8
2nd year	6	0	6	2.7
3rd year	1	0	1	0.5
4th year	1	0	1	2.0

Employment (9 months after graduation)

	Total	Percentage
Employment status known	171	84.7
Employment status unknown	31	15.3
Employed	103	60.2
Pursuing graduate degrees	2	1.2
Unemployed (seeking, not seeking, or studying for the bar)	66	38.6
Type of Employment		
# employed in law firms	62	60.2
# employed in business and industry	14	13.6
# employed in government	14	13.6
# employed in public interest	7	6.8
# employed as judicial clerks	4	3.9
# employed in academia	2	1.9
Geographic Location		
# employed in state	90	87.4
# employed outside the US	1	1.0
# of states where employed	7	

Bar Passage Rates

First-time takers	190	Reporting %	100.00
Average school %	75.79	Average state %	86.51
Average pass difference	−10.72		

Jurisdiction	Takers	Passers	Pass %	State %	Diff %
New York	190	144	75.79	86.51	−10.72

TOURO COLLEGE—JACOB D. FUCHSBERG LAW CENTER

225 Eastview Drive
Central Islip, NY 11722
Phone: 631.761.7010; Fax: 631.761.7019
E-mail: admissions@tourolaw.edu; Website: www.tourolaw.edu

Premier Building and Location

Established in 1980, Touro Law Center is fully accredited by the American Bar Association and is a member of the Association of American Law Schools. The Law Center occupies a dynamic 185,000-square-foot, state-of-the-art building in Central Islip on the south shore of Long Island. Touro Law is at the center of what is arguably the nation's first integrated "law campus," comprising a United States courthouse and federal building and a New York State court center, with supreme, family, and district courts.

Located about one hour by car or train from New York City, Central Islip boasts a wide variety of affordable housing options. Students may also use the Office of Admissions' Housing Information Network, which provides current listings of accommodations, as well as information regarding car pools and shared living arrangements. On-campus parking is free of charge.

New Curriculum: Courtrooms as Classrooms

Touro is a leader in bridging the gap between law school and legal practice, between the classroom and the courtroom. Taking advantage of its unique location as part of a law campus, adjacent to and working with both a federal courthouse and a state courthouse, Touro Law offers an innovative Court Observation Program which enables students to experience the workings of the judicial system from the very first days of their legal education. Beginning in their first semester, students are exposed to true legal practice through simulations in both litigation and nonlitigation settings and through faculty-supervised small-group visits to courts in session, court-related agencies, and court administration. In an effort to facilitate experiential learning, Touro Law invites students not only to observe live proceedings, but also to discuss with the participants (judges, attorneys, and sometimes the parties themselves) their perspectives on law in action.

Practice Modules: A central feature of the upper-level curriculum is the linkage of substantive law with practice modules in Business Organizations, Criminal Procedure, Family Law, and Trusts and Estates. Using the rules they have learned in the classroom, students solve practical problems, such as helping investors select an appropriate business entity, drawing up a criminal indictment, structuring a marital separation agreement, or drafting a will that satisfies an individual's personal and financial interests.

Clinics: Touro Law offers six in-house clinics where clients bring real cases to law students working in on-campus offices: Civil Rights Litigation, Elder Law, Family Law, Mortgage Foreclosure and Bankruptcy, Not-for-Profit Corporation Law, and Veterans and Servicemembers' Rights. Some clinics are arranged to accommodate the scheduling needs of part-time evening students.

Field Placement Externships: There are five field placement externship areas in which students work off campus: Business, Law and Technology (Internet and high-tech companies, corporate law departments, and law firms); Civil Practice (law firms, corporations, and private and public agencies); Criminal Law (District Attorneys' and Legal Aid/Public Defenders' offices); Judicial Clerkship (state and federal judges' chambers); and the US Attorney's Office Externship (Eastern District of New York).

Public Advocacy Center (PAC) and Public Service Projects: In a unique concept, Touro Law's William Randolph Hearst Public Advocacy Center (PAC) houses 15 independent public interest agencies at the law school where students can gain practical experience in Immigration Law, Housing Law, Employment Law, Rights of Children, Education Law, Constitutional Law, Poverty Law, Disability Law, and Not-for-Profit Law. The center is also the focal point for student pro bono activities, including the Student Disaster Relief Network, Street Law, Foreclosure Project, Domestic Violence Project, unemployment representation, and a tax assistance program. Students can work for academic credit, for financial compensation, or on a pro bono basis for these agencies. Touro also provides a broad selection of externship placements in public interest organizations.

Institutes: Touro Law hosts the Institute for Business, Law, and Technology; the Jewish Law Institute; and the Institute for International Human Rights and the Holocaust.

Summer Programs: In addition to the Law Center's on-site summer program, which features special programs on New York law, there are opportunities for work and study abroad in Croatia, Germany, India, Israel, and Vietnam. Touro Law also offers summer internships in law firms, courts, and government offices in Europe and Israel.

Students and Faculty

The Law Center's students, coming from diverse backgrounds and experiences, represent more than 112 undergraduate institutions and a broad mix of majors. Women make up 45 percent of the total enrollment; minorities, 25 percent.

Touro Law is proud to offer two honor societies: the *Touro Law Review* and the Moot Court Board. There are also more than 30 student organizations devoted to specialized professional and social concerns.

Of Touro Law's 50 full-time faculty members, many have advanced degrees in other disciplines, including medicine, philosophy, business, and finance. Almost all have extensive practice backgrounds, ranging from the judicial bench, major law firms, and criminal prosecution and defense to government agencies and public interest organizations.

The faculty shares one common characteristic: accessibility to students. Every entering student is assigned a faculty advisor, matched by background or interest area, for discussions on any aspect of the law school experience, including study strategy, course selection, and career goals. With an open-door policy and a student-to-faculty ratio of 16:1, everyone reaps the benefits of a personal and dynamic educational experience.

Academic Programs

Juris Doctor (JD): Touro offers the JD degree full time as well as part time (four-year and five-year programs) in the day (Monday through Friday) and part time in the evening (Monday through Thursday). Students wishing to accelerate may graduate within two and one-half years (full time) or three and one-half years (part time, four years) by attending summer sessions.

Dual Degrees: The JD may be combined with a Master of Business Administration (MBA), a Master of Public Administration (MPA) in Health Care, or a Master of Social Work (MSW), allowing students to complete the two degrees with significant time and cost savings.

Master of Laws (LLM): The Law Center also offers a 24-credit general LLM, full time or part time, and a 27-credit LLM in US Legal Studies (for foreign law graduates), full time or part time.

Academic Support and Enrichment

The Law Center provides a unique program of outside-the-classroom assistance. Teaching assistants (TAs) review material covered in class and conduct small group sessions on effective study methods and test-taking techniques. The Writing Center offers students an opportunity for intensive, individual work to develop their professional writing skills. Assistance is available in all facets of writing—from reviewing the basics to polishing an article for publication. In addition, the Legal Education Access Program (LEAP) enhances the experience of students of color through a four-week summer program for new students and mentoring during the academic year.

The Touro Law Center Honors Program offers approximately 20 to 25 exceptional students per class year an enriched, comprehensive law school experience. Students in the Honors Program will participate in enhanced academic, experiential, and social opportunities as part of a community of student scholars.

Career Services

The Career Services Office offers students and graduates valuable hands-on assistance in their search for part-time,

full-time, and summer employment. Students work in national, regional, and local law firms as well as federal, state, and local government agencies; not-for-profit organizations; and in the legal departments of corporations and municipalities.

Admission and Financial Aid

Touro Law Center does not provide an Applicant Profile Grid for its entering class because such data fail to reflect the complexity of the selection process.

At no point on a purely objective scale is an applicant assured of a particular decision. Among the most important criteria are the LSAT score and UGPA. However, evaluation is based on a variety of factors that may be indicative of potential for success—college major and course selection, graduate study, work experience, community involvement, and character.

In order to finance law school, Touro provides access to federal loans and work study, New York State loan and assistance programs, and need-based Touro Grants.

Scholarships

Most students receive some form of financial aid, and about 60 percent of entering students receive scholarships. Institutional aid is available to entering students (based on LSAT/UGPA) and to continuing law students (based on law school academic performance). Assistance includes dean's fellowships (full-tuition remission), merit scholarships (up to 90 percent tuition remission), and incentive awards (up to $9,000 per year). In addition, the Law Center offers stipends for Public Interest Law Fellowships, judicial clerkships, and federal work-study placements during the summer.

APPLICANT PROFILE

Please refer to the section on Admission and Financial Aid.

TULANE UNIVERSITY LAW SCHOOL

John Giffen Weinmann Hall, 6329 Freret Street
New Orleans, LA 70118
Phone: 504.865.5930; Fax: 504.865.6710
E-mail: admissions@law.tulane.edu; Website: www.law.tulane.edu

The Basics

Type of school	Private
Term	Semester
Application deadline	3/1
Application fee	$60
Financial aid deadline	
Can first year start other than fall?	No
Student to faculty ratio	13.7 to 1
# of housing spaces available restricted to law students	
graduate housing for which law students are eligible	166

Faculty and Administrators

	Total		Men		Women		Minorities	
	Spr	Fall	Spr	Fall	Spr	Fall	Spr	Fall
Full-time	48	45	35	30	13	15	3	4
Other full-time	8	8	1	1	7	7	0	0
Deans, librarians, & others who teach	4	5	1	2	3	3	0	0
Part-time	55	35	47	30	8	5	7	2
Total	115	93	84	63	31	30	10	6

Curriculum

		Full-Time	Part-Time
Typical first-year section size		89	0
Is there typically a "small section" of the first-year class, other than Legal Writing, taught by full-time faculty		No	No
If yes, typical size offered last year			
# of classroom course titles beyond first-year curriculum		216	
# of upper division courses, excluding seminars, with an enrollment:	Under 25	97	
	25–49	56	
	50–74	15	
	75–99	5	
	100+	6	
# of seminars		21	
# of seminar positions available		388	
# of seminar positions filled		365	0
# of positions available in simulation courses		538	
# of simulation positions filled		460	0
# of positions available in faculty supervised clinical courses		111	
# of faculty supervised clinical positions filled		111	0
# involved in field placements		46	0
# involved in law journals		263	0
# involved in moot court or trial competitions		90	0
# of credit hours required to graduate		88	

JD Enrollment and Ethnicity

	Men		Women		Full-Time		Part-Time		1st-Year		Total		JD Degs. Awd.
	#	%	#	%	#	%	#	%	#	%	#	%	
All Hispanics	24	5.8	17	4.7	41	5.3	0	0.0	14	5.5	41	5.3	14
Am. Ind./AK Nat.	1	0.2	6	1.7	7	0.9	0	0.0	2	0.8	7	0.9	3
Asian	12	2.9	11	3.1	23	3.0	0	0.0	9	3.5	23	3.0	6
Black/Af. Am.	20	4.9	34	9.5	54	7.0	0	0.0	16	6.3	54	7.0	15
Nat. HI/Pac. Isl.	0	0.0	0	0.0	0	0.0	0	0.0	0	0.0	0	0.0	0
2 or more races	2	0.5	6	1.7	8	1.0	0	0.0	3	1.2	8	1.0	0
Subtotal (minor.)	59	14.3	74	20.7	133	17.3	0	0.0	44	17.3	133	17.3	38
Nonres. Alien	7	1.7	8	2.2	15	2.0	0	0.0	4	1.6	15	1.9	0
White/Cauc.	319	77.4	255	71.2	573	74.5	1	100.0	188	74.0	574	74.5	187
Unknown	27	6.6	21	5.9	48	6.2	0	0.0	18	7.1	48	6.2	21
Total	412	53.5	358	46.5	769	99.9	1	0.1	254	33.0	770		254

Transfers

Transfers in	22
Transfers out	11

Tuition and Fees

	Resident	Nonresident
Full-time	$42,144	$42,144
Part-time		
Tuition Guarantee Program		N

Living Expenses

Estimated living expenses for singles

Living on campus	Living off campus	Living at home
$19,706	$19,706	$10,016

TULANE UNIVERSITY LAW SCHOOL

ABA Approved Since 1925

GPA and LSAT Scores

	Total	Full-Time	Part-Time
# of apps	2,828	2,828	0
# of offers	866	866	0
# of matrics	258	258	0
75% GPA	3.70	3.70	0.00
Median GPA	3.51	3.51	0.00
25% GPA	3.40	3.40	0.00
75% LSAT	164	164	0
Median LSAT	162	162	0
25% LSAT	160	160	0

Grants and Scholarships (from prior year)

	Total		Full-Time		Part-Time	
	#	%	#	%	#	%
Total # of students	774		771		3	
Total # receiving grants	533	68.9	533	69.1	0	0.0
Less than 1/2 tuition	235	30.4	235	30.5	0	0.0
Half to full tuition	295	38.1	295	38.3	0	0.0
Full tuition	3	0.4	3	0.4	0	0.0
More than full tuition	0	0.0	0	0.0	0	0.0
Median grant amount			$20,000		$0	

Informational and Library Resources

Total amount spent on library materials	$1,058,407
Study seating capacity inside the library	553
# of full-time equivalent professional librarians	9
Hours per week library is open	113
# of open, wired connections available to students	293
# of networked computers available for use by students	97
Has wireless network?	Y
Requires computer?	N

JD Attrition (from prior year)

	Academic	Other	Total	
	#	#	#	%
1st year	0	19	19	6.7
2nd year	7	8	15	6.1
3rd year	1	1	2	0.8
4th year	0	0	0	0.0

Employment (9 months after graduation)

	Total	Percentage
Employment status known	245	95.3
Employment status unknown	12	4.7
Employed	226	92.2
Pursuing graduate degrees	6	2.4
Unemployed (seeking, not seeking, or studying for the bar)	9	3.7
Type of Employment		
# employed in law firms	126	55.8
# employed in business and industry	37	16.4
# employed in government	17	7.5
# employed in public interest	22	9.7
# employed as judicial clerks	18	8.0
# employed in academia	5	2.2
Geographic Location		
# employed in state	96	42.5
# employed outside the US	5	2.2
# of states where employed	24	

Bar Passage Rates

First-time takers	241	Reporting %	73.03
Average school %	80.68	Average state %	77.87
Average pass difference	2.81		

Jurisdiction	Takers	Passers	Pass %	State %	Diff %
Louisiana	119	92	77.31	73.73	3.58
New York	57	50	87.72	86.51	1.21

TULANE UNIVERSITY LAW SCHOOL

John Giffen Weinmann Hall, 6329 Freret Street
New Orleans, LA 70118
Phone: 504.865.5930; Fax: 504.865.6710
E-mail: admissions@law.tulane.edu; Website: www.law.tulane.edu

Introduction

The opportunity to attend law school in New Orleans, perhaps the most dynamic city in the United States today, can transform an ordinary law school experience into an extraordinary one. Tulane Law School, established in 1847, is among the oldest law schools in the United States. The Law School is centrally located on the main university campus in uptown New Orleans, in a picturesque neighborhood of residences, both large and small, as well as restaurants, bookstores, and other commercial establishments.

New Orleans

New Orleans offers extensive legal resources, including the US Court of Appeals for the Fifth Circuit, US District Court, the Louisiana Supreme Court, and all of the lower state civil, criminal, and specialized courts. Within the legal community, students have the opportunity to work with both prosecutors and public defenders, in the private sector, the public sector, and in the public interest. Life outside of the law is rich, too. New Orleans is justly renowned for its music and its food. In addition to numerous events at Tulane University, students enjoy the advantages of city life and the richness of New Orleans culture. Concerts, festivals, and innumerable citywide events take place throughout the year.

Facilities

The Law School is housed in the 160,000-square-foot John Giffen Weinmann Hall. Designed to integrate classrooms, other student spaces, faculty offices, and a library containing both national and international collections, the building is centrally located on Tulane University's campus. Immediately adjacent to Weinmann Hall is the Law School's Career Development Office. Within minutes of the Law School building are the university's Howard-Tilton Memorial Library, housing over one million volumes; the Lavin-Bernick Center for University Life; various university dining facilities; the university bookstore; the Reily Student Recreation Center; the Freeman School of Business; the Newcomb Art Gallery; and various auditoriums and performance venues.

The Academic Program

The Law School curriculum offers a full range of common law and federal subjects. In addition, Tulane offers electives in the civil law, with the result that students have the opportunity to pursue comparative education in the world's two major legal systems. The breadth and depth of the curriculum permit students to survey a broad range of subject areas or to concentrate in one or more. The background, enthusiasm, and scholarship of the internationally known faculty further enrich the educational experience.

Six semesters in residence, completion of 88 credits with at least a C average, fulfillment of an upper-level writing requirement, and a 30-hour pro bono obligation are required for graduation from the JD degree program. The first-year curriculum comprises eight required courses, including Legal Research and Writing.

After the first year, all courses are elective, except for the required Legal Profession course. All first-year and many upper-level courses are taught in multiple sections to allow for smaller classes. The upper-level curriculum includes introductory as well as advanced courses in a broad range of subject areas, including international and comparative law, business and corporate law, environmental law, maritime law, criminal law, intellectual property, taxation, and litigation and procedure, among others.

At the graduate level, the Law School offers a general LLM program and an SJD program, as well as specialized LLM programs in Admiralty, Energy and Environmental Law, American Business Law, American Law, and International and Comparative Law.

Special Programs

The school offers optional concentration programs that allow JD students to receive one certificate of completion of successful studies in (a) European Legal Studies, (b) Environmental Law, (c) Maritime Law, (d) Sports Law, (e) Civil Law, or (f) International and Comparative Law. Tulane's Eason-Weinmann Center for Comparative Law, the Payson Center for International Development, the Maritime Law Center, and the Institute for Water Law and Policy add depth to the curriculum and interesting opportunities for students. Tulane also offers strong curricula in intellectual property law and constitutional law, as well as business, corporate, and commercial law.

Tulane conducts an annual summer school in New Orleans and offers summer-study programs abroad in England, the Netherlands, France, Italy, Germany, Greece, and Brazil. Semester-long exchange programs with select law schools in a number of countries throughout the world are also offered.

The school was the first in the country to require that each student complete 30 hours of legal pro bono work prior to graduation.

Clinical Programs

The school offers the following live-client clinical programs: civil litigation, criminal defense, juvenile litigation, domestic violence, environmental law, and legislative and administrative advocacy. In addition, there is a trial advocacy course and a negotiation and mediation advocacy course. Third-year students may participate in externships with federal and state judges, with a variety of public interest organizations, with a local death penalty project, or with certain administrative agencies.

Joint-Degree Programs

Joint-degree programs are offered in conjunction with Tulane's Freeman School of Business (JD/MBA and JD/MACCT), School of Public Health and Tropical Medicine (JD/MHA and JD/MPH), School of Social Work (JD/MSW), and several of the academic departments of the university. The JD/MS in International Development is offered in cooperation with the Law School's Payson Center for International Development, and the JD/MA in Latin American Studies is offered in cooperation with the Stone Center for

Latin American Studies. Proposals for other programs are considered on an ad hoc basis.

Admission and Financial Aid

Our admission process is based on a complete review of all of the information in each candidate's file. This naturally includes the LSAT score and the undergraduate academic record. In the case of multiple LSAT scores, the school sees all scores but will give more weight to the higher score based on the candidate's explanation. Tulane looks closely at subjective factors such as grade trends, courseload, undergraduate school, nonacademic activities, the student's background and experience, barriers overcome, the personal statement, and optional letters of recommendation or evaluations. The Law School processes applications for admission beginning September 1 and announces decisions beginning December 1. All candidates receive consideration for merit-based scholarship awards. Need-based and credit-based loans require submission of the FAFSA. A loan repayment assistance program is available to graduates working full time in eligible public interest employment.

Student Life

Journals published or edited at Tulane Law School include the *Tulane Law Review, Tulane Maritime Law Journal, Tulane Environmental Law Journal, Law and Sexuality, Tulane European and Civil Law Forum, Tulane Journal of International and Comparative Law, Tulane Journal of Technology and Intellectual Property*, and the *Sports Lawyers Journal*. An active moot court program holds trial and appellate competitions within the school and fields teams for a variety of interschool competitions, including alternative dispute resolution methods. The Law School has a chapter of the Order of the Coif.

The Student Bar Association functions as the student government and recommends students for appointment to faculty committees. Over 40 student organizations exist at Tulane, including the International Law Society, Black Law Students Association, La Alianza del Derecho, Asian-Pacific-American Law Students Association, Business Law Society, and Sports Law Society, among others. The Tulane Public Interest Law Foundation raises funds, matched by the Law School, to support as many as 30 students each summer in public interest fellowships with a variety of organizations. The Environmental Law Society hosts a major "science and the public interest" conference each spring.

Most students live in a variety of off-campus neighborhoods throughout the New Orleans metropolitan area, often within walking or biking distance of the Law School.

Career Services

The Law School Career Development Office assists both students and alumni in their job searches. Each student is assigned a career counselor as a first-year student and thereafter has access to a full range of career counseling services from the entire staff as well as to programs on job-search skills and practice areas. A large career-services library is available, including extensive online resources. Tulane organizes both on- and off-campus interview programs for its students. Career Development staff members also engage in employer development activities on a national basis. The office takes a proactive stance in assisting students with their job searches, with the result that Tulane graduates find law-related employment throughout the United States.

APPLICANT PROFILE

Tulane University Law School

LSAT Score	GPA									
	3.75 +	3.50–3.74	3.25–3.49	3.00–3.24	2.75–2.99	2.50–2.74	2.25–2.49	2.00–2.24	Below 2.00	No GPA
175–180										
170–174										
165–169										
160–164										
155–159										
150–154										
145–149										
140–144										
135–139										
130–134										
125–129										
120–124										

■ Excellent   ■ Good   ■ Possible   □ Unlikely

Reflects 99% of the total applicant pool; highest LSAT data reported.

THE UNIVERSITY OF TULSA COLLEGE OF LAW

3120 East Fourth Place
Tulsa, OK 74104-3189
Phone: 918.631.2406; Fax: 918.631.3630
E-mail: lawadmissions@utulsa.edu; Website: www.utulsa.edu/law/admissions/

ABA
Approved
Since
1950

The Basics

Type of school	Private
Term	Semester
Application deadline	2/1
Application fee	$30
Financial aid deadline	
Can first year start other than fall?	No
Student to faculty ratio	11.5 to 1
# of housing spaces available restricted to law students	
graduate housing for which law students are eligible	256

Faculty and Administrators

	Total		Men		Women		Minorities	
	Spr	Fall	Spr	Fall	Spr	Fall	Spr	Fall
Full-time	28	28	16	16	12	12	7	6
Other full-time	0	0	0	0	0	0	0	0
Deans, librarians, & others who teach	4	4	2	2	2	2	0	0
Part-time	28	20	22	15	6	5	3	3
Total	60	52	40	33	20	19	10	9

Curriculum

		Full-Time	Part-Time
Typical first-year section size		47	0
Is there typically a "small section" of the first-year class, other than Legal Writing, taught by full-time faculty		No	No
If yes, typical size offered last year			
# of classroom course titles beyond first-year curriculum		104	
# of upper division courses, excluding seminars, with an enrollment:	Under 25	70	
	25–49	21	
	50–74	9	
	75–99	0	
	100+	0	
# of seminars		7	
# of seminar positions available		105	
# of seminar positions filled		89	0
# of positions available in simulation courses		534	
# of simulation positions filled		359	0
# of positions available in faculty supervised clinical courses		33	
# of faculty supervised clinical positions filled		26	0
# involved in field placements		62	0
# involved in law journals		131	0
# involved in moot court or trial competitions		25	0
# of credit hours required to graduate		88	

JD Enrollment and Ethnicity

	Men		Women		Full-Time		Part-Time		1st-Year		Total		JD Degs. Awd.
	#	%	#	%	#	%	#	%	#	%	#	%	
All Hispanics	6	2.4	8	5.1	13	3.5	1	2.6	6	4.2	14	3.4	3
Am. Ind./AK Nat.	19	7.7	17	10.8	31	8.4	5	13.2	13	9.1	36	8.9	12
Asian	5	2.0	3	1.9	6	1.6	2	5.3	1	0.7	8	2.0	2
Black/Af. Am.	5	2.0	5	3.2	9	2.4	1	2.6	6	4.2	10	2.5	3
Nat. HI/Pac. Isl.	0	0.0	0	0.0	0	0.0	0	0.0	0	0.0	0	0.0	0
2 or more races	6	2.4	6	3.8	12	3.3	0	0.0	12	8.4	12	3.0	0
Subtotal (minor.)	41	16.5	39	24.7	71	19.3	9	23.7	38	26.6	80	19.7	20
Nonres. Alien	1	0.4	0	0.0	1	0.3	0	0.0	0	0.0	1	0.2	0
White/Cauc.	178	71.8	102	64.6	254	69.0	26	68.4	98	68.5	280	69.0	96
Unknown	28	11.3	17	10.8	42	11.4	3	7.9	7	4.9	45	11.1	13
Total	248	61.1	158	38.9	368	90.6	38	9.4	143	35.2	406		130

Transfers

Transfers in	3
Transfers out	3

Tuition and Fees

	Resident	Nonresident
Full-time	$30,320	
Part-time		
Tuition Guarantee Program		N

Living Expenses

Estimated living expenses for singles

Living on campus	Living off campus	Living at home
$15,986	$19,560	$8,718

THE UNIVERSITY OF TULSA COLLEGE OF LAW

ABA
Approved
Since
1950

GPA and LSAT Scores

	Total	Full-Time	Part-Time
# of apps	1,373	1,373	0
# of offers	591	591	0
# of matrics	146	146	0
75% GPA	3.63	3.63	0.00
Median GPA	3.30	3.30	0.00
25% GPA	2.95	2.95	0.00
75% LSAT	158	158	0
Median LSAT	155	155	0
25% LSAT	152	152	0

Grants and Scholarships (from prior year)

	Total		Full-Time		Part-Time	
	#	%	#	%	#	%
Total # of students	422		382		40	
Total # receiving grants	220	52.1	220	57.6	0	0.0
Less than 1/2 tuition	136	32.2	136	35.6	0	0.0
Half to full tuition	61	14.5	61	16.0	0	0.0
Full tuition	14	3.3	14	3.7	0	0.0
More than full tuition	9	2.1	9	2.4	0	0.0
Median grant amount			$12,000		$0	

Informational and Library Resources

Total amount spent on library materials	$1,078,387
Study seating capacity inside the library	706
# of full-time equivalent professional librarians	8
Hours per week library is open	113
# of open, wired connections available to students	376
# of networked computers available for use by students	95
Has wireless network?	Y
Requires computer?	N

JD Attrition (from prior year)

	Academic	Other	Total	
	#	#	#	%
1st year	6	13	19	13.8
2nd year	3	0	3	2.1
3rd year	0	0	0	0.0
4th year	0	0	0	0.0

Employment (9 months after graduation)

	Total	Percentage
Employment status known	164	99.4
Employment status unknown	1	0.6
Employed	157	95.7
Pursuing graduate degrees	3	1.8
Unemployed (seeking, not seeking, or studying for the bar)	1	0.6
Type of Employment		
# employed in law firms	100	63.7
# employed in business and industry	15	9.6
# employed in government	23	14.6
# employed in public interest	5	3.2
# employed as judicial clerks	2	1.3
# employed in academia	10	6.4
Geographic Location		
# employed in state	109	69.4
# employed outside the US	0	0.0
# of states where employed	21	

Bar Passage Rates

First-time takers	167		Reporting %		76.05
Average school %	88.19		Average state %		86.61
Average pass difference	1.58				

Jurisdiction	Takers	Passers	Pass %	State %	Diff %
Oklahoma	112	99	88.39	86.76	1.63
Texas	15	13	86.67	85.48	1.19

THE UNIVERSITY OF TULSA COLLEGE OF LAW

3120 East Fourth Place
Tulsa, OK 74104-3189
Phone: 918.631.2406; Fax: 918.631.3630
E-mail: lawadmissions@utulsa.edu; Website: www.utulsa.edu/law/admissions/

Introduction

Expect an exceptional legal education from the University of
Tulsa. The faculty and staff at TU prove daily that it is possible
for friendliness, challenge, respect, and excellence to coexist
in law school. Housed in the technologically advanced John
Rogers Hall on the University of Tulsa campus, and fully
accredited by the ABA, the law school presents a forum for
the study and exploration of legal issues enhanced by
professors with exemplary credentials. With a 12:1
student-to-faculty ratio, a true open-door policy invites
students to expand their legal education from the classroom
through one-on-one accessibility and interaction with the TU
Law faculty. We also honor student talent with scholarships
ranging from partial scholarships to full tuition plus a living
stipend. Approximately 64 percent of an entering class
receives merit- or need-based assistance. With many students
coming to Tulsa from states other than Oklahoma, a rich
fabric of diversity expands the learning experience of every
student. Located in the beautiful, culturally diverse, and
extraordinarily friendly city of Tulsa, the law school offers
students the opportunity to enjoy award-winning theater,
national touring concerts, world-class museums, gorgeous
parks, and vibrant neighborhood shopping areas. The city
also boasts an internationally recognized, burgeoning
environment for high-tech industry and commerce.

Curriculum and Specialization

Full-time and reduced schedule options, as well as summer
classes, are available. Students may choose either general
legal study, which covers a broad expanse of expertise, or a
specific concentration. Areas of concentration offered include
Comparative and International Law, Sustainable Energy and
Resources Law, Native American Law, Health Law, Public
Policy, and Entrepreneurial Law.

Summer- and semester-abroad programs offer students
the opportunity to experience different cultures on three
overseas continents. The summer-abroad programs include
Dublin (Ireland), Geneva (Switzerland), Tianjin (China), and
Buenos Aires (Argentina). Students also have the opportunity
for a fall semester of study in London.

Students at Tulsa have a great variety of career choices
available to them, which are enhanced by the opportunity for
interdisciplinary study. The following joint-degree programs
are available: JD/MBA, JD/MA in Anthropology, JD/MA in
History, JD/MA in Industrial/Organizational Psychology,
JD/MA in English, JD/MS in Computer Science, JD/MS in
Biological Sciences, JD/MA in Clinical Psychology, JD/MS in
Geosciences, JD/MS in Finance, and JD/MS in Taxation.

Practical Experience

Tulsa law students gain first-hand training beyond the
classroom. The Boesche Legal Clinic offers the Immigrant
Rights Project in which law students have the opportunity to
represent clients in important immigration proceedings under
the supervision of an expert clinical education professor.

The College of Law also offers a field placement program
that enables students to earn academic credit while working
in a law firm, business, nonprofit organization, or government

entity. Students work under the supervision of highly skilled
attorneys pursuant to academic plans they negotiate with
their supervising attorneys and the College of Law.

Federal and state judicial internships are available, as well
as the Legal Internship Program, which enables a student to
represent clients in criminal and civil cases, subject to rules
authorized by the Oklahoma Supreme Court. The TU Law Pro
Bono Program allows students to assist with cases going to
trial, assist with civil legal matters, participate in interviewing
clients and witnesses, and perform research.

Tulsa students have the unique opportunity to participate
in a Federal Criminal Defense Practicum offered by the
Honorable Claire V. Eagan, Chief Judge of the United States
District Court for the Northern District of Oklahoma, and
other dedicated professionals within the Northern District's
criminal justice system. Students are guided through every
step of a federal criminal case.

Professors

Knowledge and experience, matched by a passion for
teaching, typify the character of the professors at the
University of Tulsa. Recognized nationally and internationally
for their expertise, Tulsa professors are always accessible to
their students. Specializations and strong experiential expertise
in areas as diverse as international trade, energy regulation,
family and juvenile law, sports law, Native American tribal
jurisdiction, trial advocacy, and bioethics confirm the rich
learning experience available to Tulsa law students. The ability
to develop strong relationships with professors will strengthen
Tulsa students' law school experiences and their future legal
practice in remarkable ways.

Library and Physical Facilities

Consistently cited by the *National Jurist* as one of the top
libraries in the US, the impressive Mabee Legal Information
Center (MLIC) is much more than a library. It would be very
difficult to find a more attractive, pleasant place to study,
research, and, yes, even relax.

For students, the MLIC is an ideal locale for collaborating,
preparing for class or exams, working on journal scholarship,
conducting extensive research, conferring with reference
librarians, or preparing for a moot court competition. Over 60
computers are available for use throughout the information
center, including several laptops that are available for checkout.
To better accommodate the needs of our students, a
rededication of space in 2006 dramatically doubled the number
of popular group collaborative study rooms available throughout
the MLIC. Student staffing offices for the Board of Advocates,
the *Tulsa Law Review*, and the *Energy Law Journal* provide
generous working space for these important enterprises at the
College of Law. In 2009, the MLIC provided additional office
space to several other important student organizations that are
active within the college. Specialized classrooms include a
laptop lab and the Alternative Dispute Resolution Center where
negotiation exercises are possible within a variety of simulation
configurations. The Utsey Family Native American Law Center
and the Frank M. Rowell Jr. Comparative and International
Law Center offer inviting forums for study, research, and the
exchange of ideas, with impressive artwork providing a

showcase for these two exceptional programs. In October 2009, the John F. Hicks and John Rogers Archives room was opened to preserve the rich history of the college and to provide the means to collect important documents, photographs, and artifacts for the many significant achievements of the College of Law now and in the future.

If quiet study is for you, the two main reading rooms offer quiet, inviting, wide-open spaces with natural lighting. With over 700 seats available and seven miles of shelving space, there is plenty of space for students, alumni, and books. Nearly 300 study carrels, many of which can be reserved a semester at a time, provide private work space.

Professional librarians, most with law degrees, are ready to help with legal research in the 432,000-volume collection. An impressive array of electronic resources is accessible to students on-site or from home.

The College of Law has wireless access throughout the building. Classrooms provide access for instruction from a variety of computerized configurations, including smart podiums, large-screen projection, and Internet feeds. Faculty are readily accessible for consultation with the students, and most of their offices are conveniently located across the hallway from the classrooms. Both faculty and students appreciate the original Native American artwork throughout the school.

The Boesche Legal Clinic and the modern Price-Turpen model courtroom bring the same state-of-the-art capacities to the study and training for trial and appellate advocacy. These are outstanding facilities in which the best in preparation is available for Tulsa law students as they prepare for future legal practice and train for many regional and national moot court competitions.

Office of Professional Development

Students at TU enjoy a full-service Professional Development Office (PDO) offering support and resources for students' respective professional aspirations. PDO counselors are attorneys with wide-ranging practice experience in local and regional markets. Students participate in professionalism programs as a requisite to graduation, including a first-semester seminar on the legal profession taught by the dean. These programs cover topics such as setting professional goals, managing the stresses of legal practice, and legal market trends. TU Law's placement rate of over 95 percent in 2009 and over 90 percent in 2010 is in part due to a strong focus on professional development, mentoring, and networking opportunities. These percentages compete with or exceed the respective national annual placement rates reported by law schools.

Housing

Law students at Tulsa may choose to live on or off campus. On-campus housing includes well-maintained and modern apartments built exclusively for law and graduate students. Located within an easy walking distance from the law school, each apartment unit includes computer connections and large, spacious floor plans. With a very attractive low cost of living, the city of Tulsa offers a great variety of affordable housing opportunities. Information about housing may be obtained by calling 918.631.5249 or by contacting the Office of Law Admissions at 918.631.2406.

APPLICANT PROFILE

The University of Tulsa College of Law
This chart is to be used as a guide only. Nonnumerical factors are strongly considered for all applicants.

LSAT Score	GPA								Totals
	3.75 +	3.50–3.74	3.25–3.49	3.00–3.24	2.75–2.99	2.50–2.74	2.25–2.49	Below 2.25	
175–180	2	0	0	0	0	0	0	0	2
170–174	0	1	1	0	0	0	0	0	2
165–169	7	3	4	3	3	0	1	0	21
160–164	22	25	19	14	11	3	2	3	99
155–159	30	47	47	37	23	25	8	1	219
150–154	30	53	55	51	26	4	3	0	222
145–149	8	8	4	2	0	0	1	0	23
140–144	1	0	1	0	1	0	0	0	3
Below 140	0	0	0	0	0	0	0	0	0
Total	100	137	131	107	64	32	16	4	591

UNIVERSITY OF UTAH S.J. QUINNEY COLLEGE OF LAW

332 South 1400 East, Room 101
Salt Lake City, UT 84112-0730
Phone: 801.581.6833; Fax: 801.820.9154
E-mail: admissions@law.utah.edu; Website: www.law.utah.edu

ABA
Approved
Since
1927

The Basics

Type of school	Public
Term	Semester
Application deadline	2/15
Application fee	$60
Financial aid deadline	4/15
Can first year start other than fall?	No
Student to faculty ratio	8.9 to 1
# of housing spaces available restricted to law students	4
graduate housing for which law students are eligible	286

Faculty and Administrators

	Total		Men		Women		Minorities	
	Spr	Fall	Spr	Fall	Spr	Fall	Spr	Fall
Full-time	40	34	27	23	13	11	6	6
Other full-time	0	0	0	0	0	0	0	0
Deans, librarians, & others who teach	10	10	5	5	5	5	0	0
Part-time	30	25	22	17	8	8	0	0
Total	80	69	54	45	26	24	6	6

Curriculum

		Full-Time	Part-Time
Typical first-year section size		41	0
Is there typically a "small section" of the first-year class, other than Legal Writing, taught by full-time faculty		Yes	No
If yes, typical size offered last year		21	
# of classroom course titles beyond first-year curriculum		122	
# of upper division courses, excluding seminars, with an enrollment:	Under 25	81	
	25–49	14	
	50–74	9	
	75–99	1	
	100+	1	
# of seminars		16	
# of seminar positions available		192	
# of seminar positions filled		153	0
# of positions available in simulation courses		601	
# of simulation positions filled		345	0
# of positions available in faculty supervised clinical courses		0	
# of faculty supervised clinical positions filled		0	0
# involved in field placements		278	0
# involved in law journals		95	0
# involved in moot court or trial competitions		23	0
# of credit hours required to graduate		88	

JD Enrollment and Ethnicity

	Men #	Men %	Women #	Women %	Full-Time #	Full-Time %	Part-Time #	Part-Time %	1st-Year #	1st-Year %	Total #	Total %	JD Degs. Awd.
All Hispanics	9	3.9	16	9.3	25	6.2	0	0.0	7	5.8	25	6.2	8
Am. Ind./AK Nat.	1	0.4	2	1.2	3	0.7	0	0.0	1	0.8	3	0.7	2
Asian	7	3.0	7	4.1	14	3.5	0	0.0	4	3.3	14	3.5	3
Black/Af. Am.	2	0.9	2	1.2	4	1.0	0	0.0	1	0.8	4	1.0	4
Nat. HI/Pac. Isl.	2	0.9	0	0.0	2	0.5	0	0.0	0	0.0	2	0.5	0
2 or more races	0	0.0	0	0.0	0	0.0	0	0.0	0	0.0	0	0.0	0
Subtotal (minor.)	21	9.1	27	15.7	48	11.9	0	0.0	13	10.8	48	11.9	17
Nonres. Alien	1	0.4	1	0.6	2	0.5	0	0.0	2	1.7	2	0.5	0
White/Cauc.	194	84.3	126	73.3	320	79.6	0	0.0	101	84.2	320	79.6	90
Unknown	14	6.1	18	10.5	32	8.0	0	0.0	4	3.3	32	8.0	19
Total	230	57.2	172	42.8	402	100.0	0	0.0	120	29.9	402		126

Transfers

Transfers in	15
Transfers out	0

Tuition and Fees

	Resident	Nonresident
Full-time	$18,231	$36,209
Part-time		
Tuition Guarantee Program		N

Living Expenses

Estimated living expenses for singles

Living on campus	Living off campus	Living at home
$9,126	$9,126	$3,330

UNIVERSITY OF UTAH S.J. QUINNEY COLLEGE OF LAW

*ABA
Approved
Since
1927*

GPA and LSAT Scores

	Total	Full-Time	Part-Time
# of apps	1,365	1,365	0
# of offers	394	394	0
# of matrics	122	122	0
75% GPA	3.82	3.82	0.00
Median GPA	3.63	3.63	0.00
25% GPA	3.46	3.46	0.00
75% LSAT	164	164	0
Median LSAT	161	161	0
25% LSAT	157	157	0

Grants and Scholarships (from prior year)

	Total		Full-Time		Part-Time	
	#	%	#	%	#	%
Total # of students	400		381		19	
Total # receiving grants	207	51.8	207	54.3	0	0.0
Less than 1/2 tuition	150	37.5	150	39.4	0	0.0
Half to full tuition	51	12.8	51	13.4	0	0.0
Full tuition	0	0.0	0	0.0	0	0.0
More than full tuition	6	1.5	6	1.6	0	0.0
Median grant amount			$6,043		$0	

Informational and Library Resources

Total amount spent on library materials	$845,676
Study seating capacity inside the library	665
# of full-time equivalent professional librarians	8
Hours per week library is open	79
# of open, wired connections available to students	250
# of networked computers available for use by students	25
Has wireless network?	Y
Requires computer?	Y

JD Attrition (from prior year)

	Academic	Other	Total	
	#	#	#	%
1st year	0	2	2	1.6
2nd year	0	0	0	0.0
3rd year	0	0	0	0.0
4th year	0	0	0	0.0

Employment (9 months after graduation)

	Total	Percentage
Employment status known	133	100.0
Employment status unknown	0	0.0
Employed	123	92.5
Pursuing graduate degrees	5	3.8
Unemployed (seeking, not seeking, or studying for the bar)	3	2.3
Type of Employment		
# employed in law firms	77	62.6
# employed in business and industry	9	7.3
# employed in government	22	17.9
# employed in public interest	4	3.3
# employed as judicial clerks	9	7.3
# employed in academia	2	1.6
Geographic Location		
# employed in state	98	79.7
# employed outside the US	0	0.0
# of states where employed		16

Bar Passage Rates

First-time takers	124	Reporting %	87.90
Average school %	88.99	Average state %	88.94
Average pass difference	0.05		

Jurisdiction	Takers	Passers	Pass %	State %	Diff %
Utah	109	97	88.99	88.94	0.05

UNIVERSITY OF UTAH S.J. QUINNEY COLLEGE OF LAW

332 South 1400 East, Room 101
Salt Lake City, UT 84112-0730
Phone: 801.581.6833; Fax: 801.820.9154
E-mail: admissions@law.utah.edu; Website: www.law.utah.edu

Introduction

Established in 1913, the University of Utah S.J. Quinney College of Law is nationally recognized for its outstanding academic reputation, stellar faculty, intimate learning environment, innovative curriculum, excellent faculty-to-student ratio, and stunning location. The College of Law is a vibrant learning community with both well-established expertise and exciting new projects on the critical issues of our time: climate change, conflict and security, health justice, the new frontier of family law, technology commercialization, conservation, addiction, innocence, victims' rights, global mediation, and many others. We have also launched four innovative, crosscutting initiatives in leadership, cross-disciplinary training, smart technology, and global legal education. These creative intellectual investments have generated astounding results for each class of 125 entering students.

Among the students, there is a prevailing sense of community fostered by an open and service-oriented faculty and administration. The law school is less than a 10-minute drive or light rail ride from downtown Salt Lake City—the seat of federal, state, and local governmental bodies. Salt Lake City is the economic center of the region and is regularly voted one of America's most livable cities. This location provides ample professional opportunities for our students, as well as superb outdoor recreational access and a strong cultural scene.

Library and Physical Facilities

The S.J. Quinney law library and the law building are wireless environments. First-year students are provided with their own study hall furnished with group-study tables and carrels. Advanced students are provided carrels which also have wireless network access in the adjacent Quinney law library—a modern, spacious facility with the latest technological equipment and library research services.

The library holds more than 340,000 volumes of law and law-related material and serves as a depository for US government documents. CD-ROM and web-based databases provide access to primary legal materials, journal indexes, directories, and other law-related information. There is a computer lab with 29 workstations located in the library. Eight librarians (six with law degrees) teach the research component of the Legal Methods course.

Curriculum

The Quinney law school's innovative academic programs blend theory and practice skills that prepare graduates to tackle the major questions of our time and practice law in any jurisdiction. The curriculum is designed to allow more efficient and rational sequencing of legal education that responds to the evolving legal, social, and ethical needs of our society.

The entering students are first offered an intensive four-day Introduction to Law course before they begin the required first-year curriculum. The first-year doctrinal courses include a small section in which enrollment is limited to no more than 25 students. Second-year students select from a variety of foundational courses. In the third year, students may take year-long intensive courses that provide the opportunity for

in-depth study, research, and a practicum in a focused area of law.

Additionally, outside the formal classroom, clinical and cocurricular opportunities ensure that students learn the most critical professional and intellectual lessons in simulated competitions and real-world settings. We have several award-winning moot court teams, three first-rate journals, and a series of new student think tanks working on the major issues of our time (including the global justice think tank, which is working on its third Oxford University Press book and a $10.4 million grant to provide law and policy advice to the Iraqi government). Through our think tanks, clinics (over 200 placements each year), and award-winning pro bono initiative (with 125 placements each semester), our students contributed over 30,000 hours of public service in just one year.

Special Programs

The Wallace Stegner Center for Land, Resources, and the Environment provides opportunities for students to engage in academic courses and related law activities focusing on public lands, environmental and natural resources law, and energy law. A Certificate in Environmental and Natural Resources Law is awarded to students who complete a sequence of approved courses with a specified GPA. The law school also offers an LLM degree in natural resources and environmental law.

The Utah Criminal Justice Center is an interdisciplinary partnership between the University of Utah and state government. The center supports collaborative work among academic units at the university in partnership with the Utah Commission on Criminal and Juvenile Justice. The interdisciplinary character and the potential benefits for policymaking and employment make the Utah Criminal Justice Center unique in American higher education and a model for productive collaboration between academia and government.

The clinical programs offer both live and simulated opportunities for students to assume the lawyering role. In the Civil Clinic and the Criminal Clinic, students represent clients, investigate cases, and appear in court. In the Judicial Clinic, students act as clerks to judges, researching issues and drafting opinions in pending cases. The Judicial Extern Program allows students to spend a semester away from school working as full-time clerks for certain courts. Other clinical opportunities are available in our Environmental, Health Law, Legislative, and Mediation clinics.

The Pro Bono Initiative is a voluntary program offered to emphasize the centrality of public service to the legal profession. The College of Law encourages students to perform at least 50 hours of law-related volunteer work during their time in law school. The Pro Bono Initiative facilitates this opportunity by providing students with a broad spectrum of developed volunteer placements.

Through the London Law Consortium, students engage in the law school's study-abroad program during spring semester.

The College of Law maintains four formal joint-degree programs. Students may earn joint degrees in the areas of business (JD/MBA), public administration (JD/MPA), public policy (JD/MPP), or social work (JD/MSW).

The Academic Support Program provides assistance to students whose backgrounds and experiences before law school indicate a need for such assistance. Students apply to participate in the program after admission to the College of Law.

Admission Standards

No applicant is accepted or rejected without members of the Admission Committee having first fully considered the entire application. The personal statement should expand on the applicant's biographic and academic background and motivations for seeking a legal education. The College of Law makes a special effort to attract students from diverse cultural, educational, economic, ethnic, racial, and nontraditional backgrounds. Each applicant is evaluated for the contribution that person can make to the student body or the legal profession, in addition to evidence of demonstrated high academic ability.

Student Activities

The *Utah Law Review*, the *Journal of Law and Family Studies*, and the *Journal of Land, Resources, and Environmental Law* are professional journals edited and published by students. The *Utah Law Review* selects staff members on the basis of academic achievement and a writing competition. The other journals select staff members based on a writing competition.

Student organizations include the Student Bar Association, the Women's Law Caucus, Natural Resources Law Forum, the Minority Law Caucus, the International Legal Issues Society, Business Law Society, American Constitution Society, the Federalist Society, Outlaws, Native American Law Student Association, the Public Interest Law Organization, Utah Criminal Justice Society, Phi Delta Phi, LDS Law Student Association, the Jackie Chiles Law Society, J. Reuben Clark Society, the Sports Law Club, and the Student Intellectual Property Law Association.

Financial Aid

The College of Law provides an effective financial aid program that includes generous scholarships. The University of Utah participates in Federal Perkins, Stafford, and Graduate PLUS loan programs. More information on these student loan programs, is available at: www.law.utah.edu/admissions/financial-aid/. Merit scholarships are awarded to selected candidates based on the information contained in their application materials. Need-based scholarships are awarded to students based on information provided through the Free Application for Federal Student Aid and a separate application provided to all admitted candidates. The law school also has a Loan Forgiveness Program for qualified graduates who practice in the public sector or the public interest field.

Career Services

College of Law students and graduates have access to one of the most advanced legal career services programs in the United States. The office, known as the Professional Development Office (PDO), transmits information to prospective employers, both on and off campus and coordinates the on-campus interview process. PDO also conducts personal career counseling and assists students with the development of their résumés and other material used in the employment search. PDO maintains a resource library and sponsors numerous seminars throughout the year.

APPLICANT PROFILE

University of Utah S.J. Quinney College of Law
This grid includes only applicants who earned 120–180 LSAT scores under standard administrations.

LSAT Score	3.75 +		3.50–3.74		3.25–3.49		3.00–3.24		2.75–2.99		2.50–2.74		2.25–2.49		2.00–2.24		Below 2.00		No GPA		Total	
	Apps	Adm	Apps	Adm	Apps	Adm	Apps	Adm	Apps	Adm	Apps	Adm	Apps	Adm	Apps	Adm	Apps	Adm	Apps	Adm	Apps	Adm
175–180	0	0	1	1	1	1	0	0	0	0	1	1	0	0	0	0	0	0	0	0	3	3
170–174	10	10	10	10	4	3	3	2	1	1	1	0	0	0	1	0	0	0	0	0	30	26
165–169	37	34	31	25	18	14	11	7	4	0	1	0	1	0	2	1	1	0	0	0	106	81
160–164	77	69	101	61	76	31	55	13	23	0	8	0	4	1	2	0	2	0	3	1	351	176
155–159	67	30	101	31	102	14	52	3	23	1	15	0	6	0	2	0	0	0	4	0	372	79
150–154	42	7	71	9	60	4	55	2	29	0	12	0	9	0	1	0	1	0	2	0	282	22
145–149	9	0	17	0	34	1	28	0	14	1	10	0	2	0	2	0	3	0	1	0	120	2
140–144	5	0	4	0	13	0	21	0	6	0	10	0	6	0	0	0	0	0	6	0	71	0
135–139	1	0	3	1	3	0	1	0	3	0	2	0	1	0	2	0	0	0	1	0	17	1
130–134	0	0	0	0	1	0	3	0	0	0	1	0	0	0	0	0	0	0	1	0	8	0
125–129	0	0	0	0	0	0	0	0	1	0	1	0	0	0	1	0	0	0	0	0	3	0
120–124	0	0	0	0	0	0	0	0	0	0	0	0	0	0	0	0	0	0	0	0	0	0
Total	248	150	339	138	312	68	229	27	104	3	62	1	29	1	15	1	7	0	18	1	1363	390

Apps = Number of Applicants
Adm = Number Admitted
Reflects 99% of the total applicant pool; highest LSAT data reported.

VALPARAISO UNIVERSITY SCHOOL OF LAW

656 S. Greenwich Street, Wesemann Hall
Valparaiso, IN 46383-4945
Phone: 219.465.7821; Fax: 219.465.7975
E-mail: law.admissions@valpo.edu; Website: www.valpo.edu/law/

ABA
Approved
Since
1929

The Basics

Type of school	Private
Term	Semester
Application deadline	6/1
Application fee	$60
Financial aid deadline	3/1
Can first year start other than fall?	No
Student to faculty ratio	15.6 to 1
# of housing spaces available restricted to law students	
graduate housing for which law students are eligible	

Faculty and Administrators

	Total		Men		Women		Minorities	
	Spr	Fall	Spr	Fall	Spr	Fall	Spr	Fall
Full-time	30	29	20	20	10	9	4	3
Other full-time	4	6	4	6	0	0	2	4
Deans, librarians, & others who teach	10	10	5	5	5	5	0	0
Part-time	33	29	21	15	12	14	2	1
Total	77	74	50	46	27	28	8	8

Curriculum

		Full-Time	Part-Time
Typical first-year section size		64	0
Is there typically a "small section" of the first-year class, other than Legal Writing, taught by full-time faculty		No	No
If yes, typical size offered last year			
# of classroom course titles beyond first-year curriculum		117	
# of upper division courses, excluding seminars, with an enrollment:	Under 25	87	
	25–49	30	
	50–74	13	
	75–99	7	
	100+	1	
# of seminars		15	
# of seminar positions available		238	
# of seminar positions filled		175	6
# of positions available in simulation courses		756	
# of simulation positions filled		533	20
# of positions available in faculty supervised clinical courses		145	
# of faculty supervised clinical positions filled	138	2
# involved in field placements		176	3
# involved in law journals		48	0
# involved in moot court or trial competitions	123	1
# of credit hours required to graduate		90	

JD Enrollment and Ethnicity

	Men		Women		Full-Time		Part-Time		1st-Year		Total		JD Degs. Awd.
	#	%	#	%	#	%	#	%	#	%	#	%	
All Hispanics	27	8.4	15	6.1	40	7.5	2	5.7	17	8.2	42	7.4	8
Am. Ind./AK Nat.	4	1.3	4	1.6	6	1.1	2	5.7	5	2.4	8	1.4	0
Asian	17	5.3	9	3.7	23	4.3	3	8.6	14	6.8	26	4.6	2
Black/Af. Am.	21	6.6	32	13.0	48	9.0	5	14.3	21	10.1	53	9.4	10
Nat. HI/Pac. Isl.	0	0.0	0	0.0	0	0.0	0	0.0	0	0.0	0	0.0	0
2 or more races	1	0.3	1	0.4	2	0.4	0	0.0	0	0.0	2	0.4	0
Subtotal (minor.)	70	21.9	61	24.8	119	22.4	12	34.3	57	27.5	131	23.1	20
Nonres. Alien	2	0.6	2	0.8	3	0.6	1	2.9	0	0.0	4	0.7	0
White/Cauc.	246	76.9	181	73.6	405	76.3	22	62.9	149	72.0	427	75.4	148
Unknown	2	0.6	2	0.8	4	0.8	0	0.0	1	0.5	4	0.7	9
Total	320	56.5	246	43.5	531	93.8	35	6.2	207	36.6	566		179

Transfers

Transfers in	3
Transfers out	25

Tuition and Fees

	Resident	Nonresident
Full-time	$36,800	$36,800
Part-time	$22,980	$22,980
Tuition Guarantee Program		N

Living Expenses

Estimated living expenses for singles

Living on campus	Living off campus	Living at home
N/A	$12,760	$6,260

ABA
Approved
Since
1929

GPA and LSAT Scores

	Total	Full-Time	Part-Time
# of apps	1,472	1,350	122
# of offers	960	921	39
# of matrics	207	196	11
75% GPA	3.59	3.60	2.99
Median GPA	3.31	3.33	2.91
25% GPA	3.06	3.08	2.83
75% LSAT	153	153	152
Median LSAT	150	151	148
25% LSAT	147	148	147

Grants and Scholarships (from prior year)

	Total		Full-Time		Part-Time	
	#	%	#	%	#	%
Total # of students	582		541		41	
Total # receiving grants	156	26.8	153	28.3	3	7.3
Less than 1/2 tuition	53	9.1	50	9.2	3	7.3
Half to full tuition	53	9.1	53	9.8	0	0.0
Full tuition	33	5.7	33	6.1	0	0.0
More than full tuition	17	2.9	17	3.1	0	0.0
Median grant amount			$17,215		$0	

Informational and Library Resources

Total amount spent on library materials	$948,315
Study seating capacity inside the library	398
# of full-time equivalent professional librarians	5
Hours per week library is open	112
# of open, wired connections available to students	46
# of networked computers available for use by students	42
Has wireless network?	Y
Requires computer?	N

JD Attrition (from prior year)

	Academic	Other	Total	
	#	#	#	%
1st year	8	33	41	19.2
2nd year	1	6	7	3.9
3rd year	0	0	0	0.0
4th year	0	0	0	0.0

Employment (9 months after graduation)

	Total	Percentage
Employment status known	165	100.0
Employment status unknown	0	0.0
Employed	117	70.9
Pursuing graduate degrees	2	1.2
Unemployed (seeking, not seeking, or studying for the bar)	29	17.6
Type of Employment		
# employed in law firms	50	42.7
# employed in business and industry	25	21.4
# employed in government	22	18.8
# employed in public interest	9	7.7
# employed as judicial clerks	3	2.6
# employed in academia	5	4.3
Geographic Location		
# employed in state	38	32.5
# employed outside the US	0	0.0
# of states where employed	23	

Bar Passage Rates

First-time takers	160	Reporting %	81.88
Average school %	77.08	Average state %	85.48
Average pass difference	−8.40		

Jurisdiction	Takers	Passers	Pass %	State %	Diff %
Indiana	59	42	71.19	82.74	−11.55
Illinois	40	36	90.00	90.89	−0.89
New Jersey	5	4	80.00	83.64	−3.64
California	5	1	20.00	73.19	−53.19
Others (6)	22	18	81.82		

VALPARAISO UNIVERSITY SCHOOL OF LAW

656 S. Greenwich Street, Wesemann Hall
Valparaiso, IN 46383-4945
Phone: 219.465.7821; Fax: 219.465.7975
E-mail: law.admissions@valpo.edu; Website: www.valpo.edu/law/

Introduction

The School of Law at Valparaiso University was founded in 1879. Throughout its 132-year history our law school has been recognized for the following four traits:

Law as a Calling: We are a community dedicated to imparting not just skills and knowledge, but also values, a sense of self, and a commitment to service. Our graduates are not just solid lawyers, but great people; not just influential leaders, but ones who use their influence for the highest service and the greater good.

Exceptional Legal Research and Writing: According to a survey by the American Bar Foundation, hiring partners at law firms ranked research and writing skills as the most important skill set for a new lawyer. Many law schools require only one year of legal writing. Valparaiso Law requires three years of research and writing, offered as separate courses, so that students can concentrate on building their skills in each discipline while gaining the in-depth knowledge and proficiency necessary to succeed in their first professional jobs and throughout their careers.

Enduring Core Competencies: No matter how much the world and laws change, no matter how often attorneys change their practice, there are certain constants: the ability to engage in critical, analytical, and creative thinking, and the ability to communicate clearly and concisely. These core competencies comprise the cornerstone of a Valparaiso Law education.

Truly Personal Manner of Teaching and Learning: The teaching and learning style of Valparaiso Law is highly collaborative and integrated. Our students interact with faculty both in and out of the classroom. We know our students and strive to provide a legal education that is tailored to their individual aspirations and development as professionals.

Curriculum

The School of Law provides a comprehensive and intensive study of the foundations of law, an introduction to the substantive areas of law, and an opportunity for advanced study in specific areas. The curriculum provides a grounding in legal analysis, legal writing and research, practical skills training, perspectives on the law, and ethics. The curriculum focuses on six key areas: **general practice**, **business law**, **public interest representation**, **property**, **litigation**, and **taxation**. To learn more, visit www.valpo.edu/law/academics/curriculum.php.

Upon completing the required first-year curriculum, students are given the opportunity to explore various avenues of study. During the second year, students begin to take electives. By the third year, most required courses have been completed and students select courses for general legal competency or focus on areas of interest.

The School of Law is committed to the highest standards of professional ethics and encourages vigorous inquiry into the values upon which legal theories are founded. Students are expected to view the legal system as dynamic and thereby actively engage with it through ethical and intellectual analysis.

Students are encouraged to participate in externships and internships, in one of our eight live-client law clinics, and in service opportunities in the community. A 40-hour commitment of pro bono legal service is required of all students prior to graduation.

Degree Programs

We offer the JD degree as a three year full-time day, a five year part-time day, or a two and one-half year accelerated day program. In addition, students may begin an MBA or one of six master's degree programs at Valparaiso University after their first year in the JD program, completing both degrees in four years of full-time study. The School of Law also offers a one to one and one-half year full-time day LLM program for international students who have already obtained a law degree from their country.

Special Programs

Clinical Law Program—Students enrolled in the live-client law clinic represent indigent clients and participate in all stages of representation. The clinic practice areas are civil, criminal, domestic violence, juvenile, mediation, sports law, tax, and wrongful conviction.

Professional Representation—Students work with faculty on selected current cases.

Externships—The School of Law offers over 85 externships at 150 different sites in the Valparaiso area and throughout the United States.

International Summer Programs—Valparaiso Law offers a comparative law program in London and Cambridge, England, and a program in international human rights in Chile and Argentina.

Honors Program—First-year students are selected for this unique learning community based on academic performance and demonstrated leadership.

Public Interest—Scholarships are awarded to students who choose to work without pay in a public sector internship during the summer whether in the United States or at international sites. The **Loan Repayment Assistance Program** is designed to offer financial assistance to graduates who incurred debt from education loans and chose to go into public service employment. The assistance is in the form of grants that range from $1,000 to $6,000 each year.

Academic Success Program—The Academic Success Program is available to students who seek assistance with the transition from college or the workforce to law school. There is a ten-day summer program prior to law school orientation and a nine-session program held in the fall semester.

Career Planning

Our service mission is to assist all students and graduates in planning career paths, preparing for the job market, and identifying and creating professional opportunities. We work closely with employers, including our several thousand alumni, in developing career-related networks for all our law students. In each of the last three years, an average of 85 percent of our graduates were employed within nine months of graduation. About half are employed in law firms and the other half employed in judicial clerkships, government, public interest work, business, and academia. Our bar passage rate averages 82 percent.

Faculty

Our professors have been Fulbright scholars, clerks to federal appellate and state supreme court judges, and have served in government. They bring to their teaching practical experience in public and private sectors. Their scholarship spans a wide range of legal theory. Visit www.valpo.edu/law/faculty.

Library and Physical Facilities

The law library is the largest legal research facility in northwest Indiana. Our online catalog, Galileo, is easily accessible throughout the library as is access to LexisNexis, Westlaw, CALI, HeinOnline, LexisNexis Congressional, LegalTrac, and LLMC-Digital, among other databases. Wireless Internet access is available throughout the law school campus. The School of Law occupies two buildings that house classrooms, the law library, courtrooms and a jury room, a café, and administration and faculty offices. One of our buildings was newly reconstructed in 2010: the Heritage Hall Lawyering Skills Center includes the Valparaiso University School of Law Clinic, client counseling rooms, a state-of-the art courtroom, seminar rooms, and lounge areas.

Student Activities

The *Valparaiso University Law Review* is a scholarly journal published three times a year. Because of Valparaiso's emphasis on research and writing, membership for the *Law Review* is

APPLICANT PROFILE

Admission to Valparaiso School of Law is competitive. The selection process involves a holistic application review that considers motivation, professionalism, maturity, and service to others as well as academic achievement.

based on academic achievement as well as excellence in legal writing. Students interested in enhancing their advocacy skills may participate on the Trial Advocacy team, the Moot Court Society, and the International Moot Court Society.

Valparaiso Law has over 35 student organizations that are academic, service, and culturally focused. Just as the students represent a wide cross section of society so, too, do the organizations on campus. Visit www.valpo.edu/law/students/organizations/.

Student Body Profile

Our student body is composed of individuals committed to fostering a culture of respect, integrity, and inclusiveness. We actively recruit students of all races, ethnicities, ages, socioeconomic statuses, abilities, national origins, sexual identities, religions, and veteran statuses. Representative of our commitment to diversity, our total JD student body is composed of 24 percent students from racial and ethnic groups underrepresented in the law, 53 percent males, and 47 percent females. Close to a third of our students are age 25 and older.

Expenses and Financial Aid

The School of Law is committed to helping students meet the cost of attendance. Approximately one-third of our JD students receive scholarships and/or grants. Eighty-five percent of all law students receive assistance through loan programs, including Grad PLUS.

VANDERBILT UNIVERSITY LAW SCHOOL

131 21st Avenue South
Nashville, TN 37203
Phone: 615.322.6452; Fax: 615.322.1531
E-mail: admissions@law.vanderbilt.edu; Website: www.law.vanderbilt.edu

ABA
Approved
Since
1925

AMERICAN BAR ASSOCIATION
Section of Legal Education
and Admissions to the Bar

The Basics

Type of school	Private
Term	Semester
Application deadline	3/15
Application fee	$50
Financial aid deadline	2/15
Can first year start other than fall?	No
Student to faculty ratio	14.0 to 1
# of housing spaces available restricted to law students	20
graduate housing for which law students are eligible	20

Faculty and Administrators

	Total		Men		Women		Minorities	
	Spr	Fall	Spr	Fall	Spr	Fall	Spr	Fall
Full-time	34	36	21	22	13	14	9	8
Other full-time	0	0	0	0	0	0	0	0
Deans, librarians, & others who teach	11	10	7	5	4	5	0	0
Part-time	52	33	33	19	19	13	2	2
Total	97	79	61	46	36	32	11	10

Curriculum

	Full-Time	Part-Time
Typical first-year section size	65	0
Is there typically a "small section" of the first-year class, other than Legal Writing, taught by full-time faculty	Yes	No
If yes, typical size offered last year	0	

# of classroom course titles beyond first-year curriculum		121
# of upper division courses, excluding seminars, with an enrollment:	Under 25	74
	25–49	36
	50–74	7
	75–99	8
	100+	4
# of seminars		17
# of seminar positions available		295

# of seminar positions filled	212	0
# of positions available in simulation courses	444	
# of simulation positions filled	432	0
# of positions available in faculty supervised clinical courses	73	
# of faculty supervised clinical positions filled	73	0
# involved in field placements	141	0
# involved in law journals	185	0
# involved in moot court or trial competitions	10	0
# of credit hours required to graduate	88	

JD Enrollment and Ethnicity

	Men #	Men %	Women #	Women %	Full-Time #	Full-Time %	Part-Time #	Part-Time %	1st-Year #	1st-Year %	Total #	Total %	JD Degs. Awd.
All Hispanics	13	4.2	15	5.4	28	4.8	0	0.0	11	5.7	28	4.8	9
Am. Ind./AK Nat.	3	1.0	3	1.1	6	1.0	0	0.0	3	1.5	6	1.0	0
Asian	13	4.2	11	4.0	24	4.1	0	0.0	11	5.7	24	4.1	8
Black/Af. Am.	15	4.8	39	14.1	54	9.2	0	0.0	17	8.8	54	9.2	16
Nat. HI/Pac. Isl.	0	0.0	0	0.0	0	0.0	0	0.0	0	0.0	0	0.0	0
2 or more races	0	0.0	0	0.0	0	0.0	0	0.0	0	0.0	0	0.0	0
Subtotal (minor.)	44	14.2	68	24.6	112	19.1	0	0.0	42	21.6	112	19.1	35
Nonres. Alien	13	4.2	8	2.9	21	3.6	0	0.0	7	3.6	21	3.6	0
White/Cauc.	229	73.9	184	66.7	413	70.5	0	0.0	141	72.7	413	70.5	120
Unknown	24	7.7	16	5.8	40	6.8	0	0.0	4	2.1	40	6.8	44
Total	310	52.9	276	47.1	586	100.0	0	0.0	194	33.1	586		204

Transfers

Transfers in	16
Transfers out	7

Tuition and Fees

	Resident	Nonresident
Full-time	$45,286	$45,286
Part-time		
Tuition Guarantee Program		N

Living Expenses

Estimated living expenses for singles

Living on campus	Living off campus	Living at home
$22,074	$22,074	$22,074

*ABA
Approved
Since
1925*

GPA and LSAT Scores

	Total	Full-Time	Part-Time
# of apps	4,885	4,885	0
# of offers	1,100	1,100	0
# of matrics	193	193	0
75% GPA	3.82	3.82	0.00
Median GPA	3.72	3.72	0.00
25% GPA	3.50	3.50	0.00
75% LSAT	170	170	0
Median LSAT	169	169	0
25% LSAT	165	165	0

Grants and Scholarships (from prior year)

	Total		Full-Time		Part-Time	
	#	%	#	%	#	%
Total # of students	594		594		0	
Total # receiving grants	439	73.9	439	73.9	0	0.0
Less than 1/2 tuition	316	53.2	316	53.2	0	0.0
Half to full tuition	99	16.7	99	16.7	0	0.0
Full tuition	2	0.3	2	0.3	0	0.0
More than full tuition	22	3.7	22	3.7	0	0.0
Median grant amount			$17,000		$0	

Informational and Library Resources

Total amount spent on library materials	$1,670,276
Study seating capacity inside the library	255
# of full-time equivalent professional librarians	5
Hours per week library is open	111
# of open, wired connections available to students	270
# of networked computers available for use by students	55
Has wireless network?	Y
Requires computer?	N

JD Attrition (from prior year)

	Academic	Other	Total	
	#	#	#	%
1st year	0	10	10	5.1
2nd year	0	2	2	1.0
3rd year	0	0	0	0.0
4th year	0	0	0	0.0

Employment (9 months after graduation)

	Total	Percentage
Employment status known	187	98.9
Employment status unknown	2	1.1
Employed	177	94.7
Pursuing graduate degrees	7	3.7
Unemployed (seeking, not seeking, or studying for the bar)	0	0.0
Type of Employment		
# employed in law firms	127	71.8
# employed in business and industry	6	3.4
# employed in government	6	3.4
# employed in public interest	6	3.4
# employed as judicial clerks	23	13.0
# employed in academia	9	5.1
Geographic Location		
# employed in state	38	21.5
# employed outside the US	3	1.7
# of states where employed	27	

Bar Passage Rates

First-time takers	179	Reporting %	71.51
Average school %	96.88	Average state %	85.25

Average pass difference 11.63

Jurisdiction	Takers	Passers	Pass %	State %	Diff %
New York	37	36	97.30	86.51	10.79
Tennessee	34	32	94.12	82.44	11.68
Illinois	16	16	100.00	90.89	9.11
Georgia	14	14	100.00	86.28	13.72
Others (3)	27	26	96.30		

VANDERBILT UNIVERSITY LAW SCHOOL

131 21st Avenue South
Nashville, TN 37203
Phone: 615.322.6452; Fax: 615.322.1531
E-mail: admissions@law.vanderbilt.edu; Website: www.law.vanderbilt.edu

Welcome to a New Way of Thinking

Among the nation's leading law schools, Vanderbilt is recognized for its distinguished faculty, its talented students drawn from across the nation and around the world, and its rigorous curriculum with an array of joint-degree, specialized, and interdisciplinary programs. Building on this tradition of excellence, Vanderbilt has established itself as a leader in designing innovative programs that connect outstanding theoretical training to real-world information and experiences relevant to twenty-first century law practice. A legal education that links the best scholarly research to effective lawyering provides immediate advantages to Vanderbilt graduates.

With about 195 students in each entering JD class, Vanderbilt fosters a tradition of challenging intellectual inquiry in an atmosphere of mutual respect. This small-school sense of collegiality combined with a distinguished and accessible faculty creates an exceptional environment to prepare for leadership in private practice, public service, business, or government. With state-of-the-art facilities situated on a beautiful and vibrant university campus in a sophisticated and livable city, Vanderbilt offers a first-rate legal education in a setting that promotes a great quality of life.

A Distinguished and Accessible Faculty

Widely respected for their scholarly impact, the faculty includes leading experts in an array of fields, including corporate and business law, constitutional law, litigation, criminal law, negotiation, international law, law and economics, law and human behavior, dispute resolution, and intellectual property. Professors draw on their cutting-edge research to create engaging educational experiences that not only train students "to think like lawyers," but also to use their training effectively in practice. Faculty members take an open-door, student-centered approach, extending their availability to students well beyond class times.

A Rigorous and Relevant Curriculum

An outstanding foundational curriculum reinforced by innovative and interdisciplinary approaches to advanced training are the hallmarks of a Vanderbilt legal education. The first-year curriculum provides an intellectual framework on which to build a legal education tailored to individual needs and interests in the second and third years. Entering students begin their studies with the "Life of the Law," a one-credit course designed to distill the core ideas on which legal education is based, providing tools and information helpful to mastering law school. First-year courses in torts, constitutional law, contracts, criminal law, civil procedure, property, the regulatory state, and legal writing set the stage for continued studies.

Upper-level courses are almost entirely elective, allowing students to choose from a broad curriculum, combining courses, seminars, clinics, externships, independent studies, and Vanderbilt courses outside the law school. Students may also participate in programs that focus on particular areas of law. The Law and Business Program is designed to produce lawyers who understand the complex corporate finance and regulatory environments that corporate managers face. The

Cecil D. Branstetter Litigation and Dispute Resolution Program is directed at connecting scholarly research on litigation and court systems to practice-based skills and strategies used to settle disputes. The International Legal Studies Program offers a unique International Law Practice Lab in which students undertake specific projects for real-world clients such as the Iraqi Special Tribunal and the International Criminal Court. The Environmental Law Program offers an extensive curriculum and a range of research and experiential opportunities. The Intellectual Property Program coordinates with noted practitioners to provide fellowships and externship opportunities to students interested in studying technology, intellectual property, entertainment, and innovation law. Vanderbilt also offers programs in criminal justice, law and government, and social justice.

International Study, Special Programs, Clinics, and Joint Degrees

Vanderbilt-in-Venice allows students to study abroad in the rich cultural center of Venice, Italy. Taught by Vanderbilt Law and University of Venice faculty, courses cover topics in international law with intensive classwork augmented by outside experiences. The six-week program concludes in early July, allowing students to work or intern during the remainder of the summer.

The law and economics movement has been an important influence in legal scholarship, and Vanderbilt's PhD in Law and Economics provides the next generation of training in this field: a combination of professional and academic degrees that train scholars for academic positions, law practice, policy making, and public interest work. Students either have a JD upon entry to the PhD program, or obtain a PhD and JD concurrently at Vanderbilt.

Students earn academic credit while serving the public in real practice settings through the Law School's clinical programs. Clinical offerings include international law, appellate litigation, civil practice, criminal practice, domestic violence, intellectual property and the arts, and individualized semester externships. Students also can gain valuable experience in nonprofits, government agencies, and other organizations around the world through various externship and summer stipend opportunities including the Legal Aid Society and Public Interest Stipend Fund.

Joint-degree programs make it possible to combine the JD with an MBA, MD, MDiv, MTS, MPP, MA, or PhD in conjunction with the university's various graduate and professional schools. The law school also offers an LLM program for international lawyers and the LLM/MA in Latin American Studies.

Law School Building and Library

The Law School facilities are among the best designed in the nation, featuring a central open courtyard with adjacent café, comfortable lounges, and abundant natural light. Situated on a park-like campus that is designated a national arboretum, the building is designed for twenty-first century legal studies and research with wireless connectivity, state-of-the-art classrooms and trial courtroom, and on-site and remote access to a host of electronic resources. The law library provides a variety of study spaces, including two reading rooms and nearly 200 carrels. The service-oriented library staff oversees a collection of over 605,000 volumes and more than 250 electronic databases, and all other Vanderbilt libraries, containing more than 3.3 million volumes, are also available to law students.

Student Life, Journals, and Law School Environs

One of the reasons that students choose Vanderbilt is the congenial, collaborative atmosphere on campus. Spirited competition in an atmosphere of mutual respect creates a rare combination of intellectual vibrancy with a strong sense of community. A busy schedule of visiting speakers, symposia, and conferences is augmented by the activities of more than 50 student organizations. Four student publications provide opportunities to strengthen legal research and writing skills—*Vanderbilt Law Review, Vanderbilt Journal of Entertainment and Technology Law, Vanderbilt Journal of Transnational Law,* and *Environmental Law and Policy Annual Review* in conjunction with the Environmental Law Institute (ELI) in Washington, DC.

Vanderbilt is an internationally recognized university with strong partnerships among its 10 schools, neighboring institutions, and the Nashville community. In the natural beauty of Tennessee, Vanderbilt's hometown has emerged as a vibrant and progressive city that offers numerous professional opportunities, wide-ranging cultural and recreational options, and a great quality of life. Among the nation's most livable cities, Nashville is the state capital with a metropolitan area population of 1.6 million, and Vanderbilt is ideally situated in this major center for legal activity, allowing students an array of opportunities in law firms, state and federal courts and government, public agencies, nonprofits, and corporations.

Career Services

Vanderbilt offers comprehensive resources to help students explore career options and to guide graduates to careers across the United States and abroad. Legal employers across the nation regularly come to campus to recruit students for summer and permanent employment and solicit students' résumés throughout the year. For the JD classes of 2006 through 2010, 18 percent of graduates took employment in Tennessee, while 82 percent fanned out broadly over 41 other states, DC, and abroad with the largest numbers in New York (10.5 percent); Washington, DC (8.6 percent); Atlanta (7.6 percent); Chicago (5.7 percent); Texas (5.7 percent); California (5.5 percent); Florida (3.6 percent); and North Carolina (3.6 percent). About 10 to 15 percent of graduating classes enter judicial clerkships each year, the great majority with federal judges. In all, the Law School's alumni network covers 49 states; Washington, DC; 3 US territories; and 27 foreign nations.

Scholarships and Loan Repayment Assistance

Vanderbilt provides generous financial assistance through need- and merit-based scholarships. All admitted applicants are considered for merit scholarships, and several Law Scholar Merit Awards of full tuition plus stipend are given each year through a supplemental application process. Vanderbilt's Loan Repayment Assistance Program provides financial support to graduates who choose low-paying public service employment upon graduation.

APPLICANT PROFILE

Admission to Vanderbilt is competitive, and the selection process reflects our belief that the quality of the educational environment at the Law School benefits from considering a range of information about each prospective student that is far broader than GPA and LSAT. Each file is reviewed in its entirety for indicators of academic excellence, intellectual curiosity, hard work, interest in others' welfare, obstacles overcome, professionalism, and other characteristics of successful law students. We believe that talented students with a mix of backgrounds, perspectives, and goals promote a vibrant and beneficial educational environment and that full-file review in the admission process is central to that objective. We do not provide a two-factor applicant profile grid to describe a multifactor selection process in which decisions are based on experienced judgment applied to individual cases.

VERMONT LAW SCHOOL

168 Chelsea Street, PO Box 96
South Royalton, VT 05068
Phone: 888.277.5985 (toll-free) or 802.831.1239; Fax: 802.831.1174
E-mail: admiss@vermontlaw.edu; Website: www.vermontlaw.edu

The Basics

Type of school	Private
Term	Semester
Application deadline	3/1
Application fee	$60
Financial aid deadline	3/1
Can first year start other than fall?	No
Student to faculty ratio	14.1 to 1
# of housing spaces available restricted to law students	
graduate housing for which law students are eligible	

Faculty and Administrators

	Total		Men		Women		Minorities	
	Spr	Fall	Spr	Fall	Spr	Fall	Spr	Fall
Full-time	35	34	20	19	15	15	4	4
Other full-time	17	21	7	8	10	13	2	4
Deans, librarians, & others who teach	13	13	5	4	8	9	3	2
Part-time	26	15	16	11	10	4	1	1
Total	91	83	48	42	43	41	10	11

JD Enrollment and Ethnicity

	Men		Women		Full-Time		Part-Time		1st-Year		Total		JD Degs. Awd.
	#	%	#	%	#	%	#	%	#	%	#	%	
All Hispanics	11	3.8	3	0.9	14	2.3	0	0.0	4	1.8	14	2.3	6
Am. Ind./AK Nat.	1	0.3	1	0.3	2	0.3	0	0.0	2	0.9	2	0.3	2
Asian	6	2.1	12	3.8	18	3.0	0	0.0	8	3.7	18	3.0	5
Black/Af. Am.	5	1.7	9	2.8	14	2.3	0	0.0	8	3.7	14	2.3	7
Nat. HI/Pac. Isl.	0	0.0	0	0.0	0	0.0	0	0.0	0	0.0	0	0.0	0
2 or more races	5	1.7	5	1.6	10	1.6	0	0.0	1	0.5	10	1.6	0
Subtotal (minor.)	28	9.7	30	9.5	58	9.6	0	0.0	23	10.6	58	9.6	21
Nonres. Alien	3	1.0	2	0.6	5	0.8	0	0.0	2	0.9	5	0.8	0
White/Cauc.	224	77.2	255	80.4	479	78.9	0	0.0	164	75.2	479	78.9	131
Unknown	35	12.1	30	9.5	65	10.7	0	0.0	29	13.3	65	10.7	11
Total	290	47.8	317	52.2	607	100.0	0	0.0	218	35.9	607		165

Curriculum

	Full-Time	Part-Time
Typical first-year section size	75	0
Is there typically a "small section" of the first-year class, other than Legal Writing, taught by full-time faculty	Yes	No
If yes, typical size offered last year	40	
# of classroom course titles beyond first-year curriculum	127	

# of upper division courses, excluding seminars, with an enrollment:		
	Under 25	86
	25–49	39
	50–74	13
	75–99	4
	100+	0

# of seminars	38	
# of seminar positions available	545	
# of seminar positions filled	385	0
# of positions available in simulation courses	672	
# of simulation positions filled	503	0
# of positions available in faculty supervised clinical courses	84	
# of faculty supervised clinical positions filled	62	0
# involved in field placements	158	0
# involved in law journals	118	0
# involved in moot court or trial competitions	35	0
# of credit hours required to graduate	87	

Transfers

Transfers in	3
Transfers out	11

Tuition and Fees

	Resident	Nonresident
Full-time	$42,220	$42,220
Part-time		
Tuition Guarantee Program		N

Living Expenses

Estimated living expenses for singles

Living on campus	Living off campus	Living at home
N/A	$21,060	$21,060

VERMONT LAW SCHOOL

ABA
Approved
Since
1975

GPA and LSAT Scores

	Total	Full-Time	Part-Time
# of apps	1,056	1,056	0
# of offers	628	628	0
# of matrics	212	212	0
75% GPA	3.55	3.55	0.00
Median GPA	3.35	3.35	0.00
25% GPA	3.13	3.13	0.00
75% LSAT	159	159	0
Median LSAT	156	156	0
25% LSAT	153	153	0

Grants and Scholarships (from prior year)

	Total		Full-Time		Part-Time	
	#	%	#	%	#	%
Total # of students	567		567		0	
Total # receiving grants	385	67.9	385	67.9	0	0.0
Less than 1/2 tuition	295	52.0	295	52.0	0	0.0
Half to full tuition	74	13.1	74	13.1	0	0.0
Full tuition	16	2.8	16	2.8	0	0.0
More than full tuition	0	0.0	0	0.0	0	0.0
Median grant amount			$12,500		$0	

Informational and Library Resources

Total amount spent on library materials	$888,396
Study seating capacity inside the library	382
# of full-time equivalent professional librarians	7
Hours per week library is open	110
# of open, wired connections available to students	110
# of networked computers available for use by students	105
Has wireless network?	Y
Requires computer?	N

JD Attrition (from prior year)

	Academic	Other	Total	
	#	#	#	%
1st year	0	12	12	5.2
2nd year	0	0	0	0.0
3rd year	0	0	0	0.0
4th year	0	0	0	0.0

Employment (9 months after graduation)

	Total	Percentage
Employment status known	183	100.0
Employment status unknown	0	0.0
Employed	148	80.9
Pursuing graduate degrees	15	8.2
Unemployed (seeking, not seeking, or studying for the bar)	12	6.6
Type of Employment		
# employed in law firms	43	29.1
# employed in business and industry	29	19.6
# employed in government	26	17.6
# employed in public interest	20	13.5
# employed as judicial clerks	25	16.9
# employed in academia	5	3.4
Geographic Location		
# employed in state	27	18.2
# employed outside the US	0	0.0
# of states where employed	31	

Bar Passage Rates

First-time takers	178	Reporting %	72.47
Average school %	64.34	Average state %	81.03

Average pass difference −16.69

Jurisdiction	Takers	Passers	Pass %	State %	Diff %
New York	32	18	56.25	86.51	−30.26
Vermont	28	19	67.86	73.33	−5.47
Massachusetts	18	18	100.00	89.77	10.23
California	15	4	26.67	73.19	−46.52
Others (4)	36	24	66.67		

VERMONT LAW SCHOOL

168 Chelsea Street, PO Box 96
South Royalton, VT 05068
Phone: 888.277.5985 (toll-free) or 802.831.1239; Fax: 802.831.1174
E-mail: admiss@vermontlaw.edu; Website: www.vermontlaw.edu

The information on these pages was provided by the law school.

Introduction

Vermont Law School (VLS) operates from the belief that lawyers and legal scholars should advocate for the common good and help protect the natural world, and that legal education in service to those objectives should be both rigorous and practical. The school's legal scholars, practitioners, and staff guide and prepare students to impact fields affecting the public interest, public policy, and social justice. Graduates work for nonprofit organizations, private firms, government agencies, and educational institutions.

As an international leader in environmental law, VLS is active in broadening the array of social justice, energy policy, and climate crisis issues to be addressed by legal scholarship and in legal education. The school features distinctive programs in international law and dual JD/master's degree programs in business administration, environmental management, environmental policy, philosophy, and other fields.

Vermont Law School also works with advocacy organizations, domestic and international governments, and other educational institutions that share its commitment to make substantial, positive change in their communities and countries. The experiential education VLS provides prepares its graduates to engage in the critical issues of our time.

Faculty

The stimulating environment at Vermont Law School has attracted scholars and practitioners of national and international renown. In their teaching, VLS faculty strike a balance between scholarship and application, between rigorous research and a realistic approach to problem solving. They understand the nuanced analytic and political abilities needed in advocacy work, while also recognizing the portfolio of core skills graduates will need in their first jobs and throughout their legal careers.

As legal experts, VLS faculty are frequently sought out by national and international law firms, educational institutions, government agencies, and advocacy organizations. VLS faculty members regularly work on important cases in environmental law, international and comparative law, human rights, national security law, business law, and constitutional law, providing frequent opportunities for students to engage in related independent study and research projects. Because VLS is slightly smaller than many law schools, close relationships between students and faculty tend to last a lifetime.

Curriculum and Experiential Programs

The fundamentals of law are rigorously addressed in the required general curriculum, in addition to which VLS students can customize their educations to build skill sets in practice areas on the leading edge of the law and social change.

At VLS, in-depth scholarship is balanced with experiential opportunities that highlight what lawyers are actually called upon to do in the field. VLS students are able to take advantage of many clinics and experiential programs that provide hands-on training and involve students in real cases and legal issues including:

- The **Semester in Practice** program, which matches self-directed students with mentors, who are legal professionals in a range of fields, for independent projects.
- The **South Royalton Legal Clinic**, which serves low-income area residents who need assistance in matters involving family law, housing, welfare and unemployment, health care, immigration, Social Security, children's rights, consumer protection, bankruptcy, contracts, wills, and civil rights. Guided by experienced attorneys, students represent clients in state court, federal court, and administrative hearings.
- The **Environmental and Natural Resource Law Clinic** is where qualified students work alongside legal experts to advance environmental protection goals while developing their research, advocacy, and litigation skills.
- The **Legislative Clinic**, which takes advantage of VLS's proximity to the state capital through internships with the Vermont General Assembly.
- The **Mediation Clinic**, which trains students to mediate civil disputes in Vermont Superior Court, Small Claims Court, and the Environmental Court. Students also mediate conflicts in which the parties choose to avoid court or postpone filing a court action until attempting mediation.
- **Judicial externships**, which are programs structured to provide students with both academic background on judicial issues and hands-on experience working in judges' chambers.
- **JD, MELP (Master of Environmental Law and Policy)**, and **LLM internships** in which students gain real-world experience in general and environmental law and policy in a wide variety of settings both locally and worldwide.
- The **General Practice Program (GPP)**, which simulates a professional law firm with professors as partners overseeing student associates who are expected to perform a range of legal activities and handle client cases. The GPP received the 2007 E. Smythe Gambrell Professionalism Award from the American Bar Association.

Joint and Dual Degrees and Specialized Program Offerings

In addition to the general JD program, VLS offers:
- A unique, one-year master's degree in environmental law and policy and specialized programs in land use, energy, climate change, and international environmental law.
- Dual JD/master's degree programs in business administration, environmental management, environmental policy, philosophy, and other fields through partnerships with Yale, Dartmouth, Northeastern, Cambridge, Cergy-Pontoise, Seville, Thunderbird School of Global Management, and the University of Vermont.
- Semester exchange programs with five US law schools as well as McGill and Trento.
- The largest number and most extensive environmental law courses in the country, taught by some of the top scholars in the field.
- Extensive summer programs that attract legal, energy, industry, and environmental experts from around the country and the world who teach courses and lead seminars on a range of pressing topics.

Student Community

Recent VLS students have come from every state and from countries including Guam, Brazil, Canada, Italy, Japan, Russia, and Spain. The undergraduate institutions they attended span the geographic spectrum of the country and range in size and type from Yale to the University of Colorado to Western Washington University. In a typical year, the entering class will represent over 40 states and at least 150 undergraduate institutions. Men and women are equally represented in both the student and faculty populations. And while some students come to VLS soon after graduating from college, others have spent years in a wide variety of professions, including engineering, teaching, lobbying, corporate management, and nonprofit programming. This important mix of backgrounds allows VLS to enjoy a diversity of perspectives on campus and in the classroom.

VLS's size and emphasis on collaboration fosters an environment where students are valued for the contributions they make and the initiative they take within the VLS community. Whether through independent collaboration with faculty, engagement with one of the many active student organizations, or through the Student Government Association, students help shape academic and cocurricular coursework and campus policies.

Admission

Successful candidates demonstrate substantial academic ability and motivation and will bring diverse perspectives and interests, as well as strong talents, to the community. The two admission criteria that are weighed most heavily are academic records and two required personal essays. In addition, the school responds favorably to candidates who have been active in their communities and engaged with student organizations or professional endeavors. VLS is committed to supporting individuals traditionally underrepresented in the legal profession. Applications are reviewed on a rolling basis, beginning on the first of December.

Tuition and Financial Aid

At Vermont Law School, a combination of merit scholarships, loans, tuition grants, and work-study opportunities are employed to address the financial needs of law school candidates. On average, 90 percent of the student body receives some form of financial assistance, and approximately 40 percent of enrolling students receive VLS merit- or need-based aid. In addition to counseling students on loan repayment strategies—including the new federal income-based loan repayment and loan forgiveness program—VLS offers a Loan Repayment Assistance Program, which is designed to support graduates pursuing public interest careers in repaying educational debts.

Career Services

In addition to the network of staff, peers, and faculty advocates who serve as ready resources to every VLS student and graduate, the Office of Career Services operates as a clearinghouse for information on professional and experiential opportunities for students throughout their law school years. The office also provides tools for résumé and interview preparation, assists students in researching and applying for internships and summer jobs, and helps them explore a range of postgraduate placements.

APPLICANT PROFILE

Vermont Law School
This grid includes only applicants who earned 120–180 LSAT scores under standard administrations.

LSAT Score	3.75 +		3.50–3.74		3.25–3.49		3.00–3.24		2.75–2.99		2.50–2.74		Below 2.50		No GPA		Total	
	Apps	Adm	Apps	Adm	Apps	Adm	Apps	Adm	Apps	Adm	Apps	Adm	Apps	Adm	Apps	Adm	Apps	Adm
170–180	6	6	1	1	4	4	4	4	2	2	0	0	0	0	0	0	17	17
165–169	16	16	5	5	12	12	11	11	2	0	1	0	3	1	0	0	50	45
160–164	24	24	35	34	34	34	13	12	13	8	11	1	4	1	1	1	135	115
155–159	34	34	61	59	60	59	63	57	21	9	14	5	12	3	5	5	270	231
150–154	32	27	45	42	72	58	68	47	43	12	29	5	19	0	4	1	312	192
145–149	13	0	25	1	38	8	44	5	22	3	16	2	14	1	9	1	181	21
140–144	5	0	2	0	12	1	9	0	7	0	8	0	4	0	1	0	48	1
Below 140	1	0	3	1	3	0	3	0	5	0	8	0	5	0	3	0	31	1
Total	131	107	177	143	235	176	215	136	115	34	87	13	61	6	23	8	1044	623

Apps = Number of Applicants
Adm = Number Admitted
Reflects 99% of the total applicant pool; highest LSAT data reported.

VILLANOVA UNIVERSITY SCHOOL OF LAW

299 North Spring Mill Road
Villanova, PA 19085
Phone: 610.519.7010; Fax: 610.519.6291
E-mail: admissions@law.villanova.edu; Website: www.law.villanova.edu

ABA Approved Since 1954

The Basics

Type of school	Private
Term	Semester
Application deadline	3/1
Application fee	$75
Financial aid deadline	
Can first year start other than fall?	No
Student to faculty ratio	16.4 to 1
# of housing spaces available restricted to law students	
graduate housing for which law students are eligible	

Faculty and Administrators

	Total		Men		Women		Minorities	
	Spr	Fall	Spr	Fall	Spr	Fall	Spr	Fall
Full-time	34	38	21	23	13	15	3	4
Other full-time	11	11	3	3	8	8	0	0
Deans, librarians, & others who teach	10	11	4	4	6	7	2	2
Part-time	69	57	49	42	20	15	6	5
Total	124	117	77	72	47	45	11	11

JD Enrollment and Ethnicity

	Men		Women		Full-Time		Part-Time		1st-Year		Total		JD Degs. Awd.
	#	%	#	%	#	%	#	%	#	%	#	%	
All Hispanics	32	7.3	33	10.1	65	8.5	0	0.0	24	9.5	65	8.5	6
Am. Ind./AK Nat.	5	1.1	2	0.6	7	0.9	0	0.0	5	2.0	7	0.9	1
Asian	23	5.3	34	10.4	57	7.5	0	0.0	20	7.9	57	7.5	24
Black/Af. Am.	10	2.3	7	2.1	17	2.2	0	0.0	8	3.2	17	2.2	5
Nat. HI/Pac. Isl.	0	0.0	0	0.0	0	0.0	0	0.0	0	0.0	0	0.0	0
2 or more races	0	0.0	0	0.0	0	0.0	0	0.0	0	0.0	0	0.0	0
Subtotal (minor.)	70	16.0	76	23.2	146	19.1	0	0.0	57	22.6	146	19.1	36
Nonres. Alien	3	0.7	1	0.3	4	0.5	0	0.0	1	0.4	4	0.5	0
White/Cauc.	358	81.7	244	74.6	602	78.7	0	0.0	185	73.4	602	78.7	194
Unknown	7	1.6	6	1.8	13	1.7	0	0.0	9	3.6	13	1.7	0
Total	438	57.3	327	42.7	765	100.0	0	0.0	252	32.9	765		232

Curriculum

	Full-Time	Part-Time
Typical first-year section size	89	0

Is there typically a "small section" of the first-year class, other than Legal Writing, taught by full-time faculty	Yes	No
If yes, typical size offered last year	43	

# of classroom course titles beyond first-year curriculum		108

# of upper division courses, excluding seminars, with an enrollment:		
	Under 25	91
	25–49	28
	50–74	11
	75–99	15
	100+	3

# of seminars		16
# of seminar positions available		235
# of seminar positions filled	219	0
# of positions available in simulation courses	670	
# of simulation positions filled	635	0
# of positions available in faculty supervised clinical courses		80
# of faculty supervised clinical positions filled	80	0
# involved in field placements	127	0
# involved in law journals	168	0
# involved in moot court or trial competitions	43	0
# of credit hours required to graduate		88

Transfers

Transfers in	15
Transfers out	11

Tuition and Fees

	Resident	Nonresident
Full-time	$36,690	$36,690
Part-time		
Tuition Guarantee Program		N

Living Expenses

Estimated living expenses for singles

Living on campus	Living off campus	Living at home
N/A	$19,695	$6,915

ABA
Approved
Since
1954

GPA and LSAT Scores

	Total	Full-Time	Part-Time
# of apps	3,739	3,739	0
# of offers	1,648	1,648	0
# of matrics	251	251	0
75% GPA	3.56	3.56	0.00
Median GPA	3.33	3.33	0.00
25% GPA	3.15	3.15	0.00
75% LSAT	163	163	0
Median LSAT	160	160	0
25% LSAT	159	159	0

Grants and Scholarships (from prior year)

	Total #	Total %	Full-Time #	Full-Time %	Part-Time #	Part-Time %
Total # of students	754		754		0	
Total # receiving grants	196	26.0	196	26.0	0	0.0
Less than 1/2 tuition	123	16.3	123	16.3	0	0.0
Half to full tuition	55	7.3	55	7.3	0	0.0
Full tuition	18	2.4	18	2.4	0	0.0
More than full tuition	0	0.0	0	0.0	0	0.0
Median grant amount			$15,000		$0	

Informational and Library Resources

Total amount spent on library materials	$1,290,239
Study seating capacity inside the library	445
# of full-time equivalent professional librarians	11
Hours per week library is open	168
# of open, wired connections available to students	434
# of networked computers available for use by students	57
Has wireless network?	Y
Requires computer?	N

JD Attrition (from prior year)

	Academic #	Other #	Total #	Total %
1st year	2	13	15	5.8
2nd year	0	0	0	0.0
3rd year	1	0	1	0.4
4th year	0	0	0	0.0

Employment (9 months after graduation)

	Total	Percentage
Employment status known	233	99.1
Employment status unknown	2	0.9
Employed	202	86.7
Pursuing graduate degrees	8	3.4
Unemployed (seeking, not seeking, or studying for the bar)	23	9.9
Type of Employment		
# employed in law firms	110	55.0
# employed in business and industry	35	16.8
# employed in government	17	8.4
# employed in public interest	11	5.4
# employed as judicial clerks	19	9.4
# employed in academia	2	1.0
Geographic Location		
# employed in state	117	57.9
# employed outside the US	0	0.0
# of states where employed	20	

Bar Passage Rates

First-time takers	229	Reporting %	77.73
Average school %	93.82	Average state %	85.39
Average pass difference	8.43		

Jurisdiction	Takers	Passers	Pass %	State %	Diff %
Pennsylvania	152	144	94.74	85.69	9.05
New Jersey	26	23	88.46	83.64	4.82

VILLANOVA UNIVERSITY SCHOOL OF LAW

299 North Spring Mill Road
Villanova, PA 19085
Phone: 610.519.7010; Fax: 610.519.6291
E-mail: admissions@law.villanova.edu; Website: www.law.villanova.edu

Introduction

Today, as never before, there is a need for law schools to teach far more than the letter of the law. They must give future lawyers a sense of the importance of their role in the larger society, and they must prepare lawyers to work in an environment of burgeoning technology with issues of global importance.

With its Catholic roots, Villanova offers a legal education designed to teach the rules of law and their application; to demonstrate how lawyers analyze legal issues and express arguments and conclusions; to inculcate the skills of the counselor, advocate, and decision maker; and to explore the ethical and moral dimensions of law practice and professional conduct. The school is also providing leadership in information technology, public interest, taxation, and international law, among other fields.

Few law schools are located in a more beautiful and tranquil environment. Adjacent to the university campus is Philadelphia's Main Line. The school is at the approximate midpoint of east coast legal centers in New York and Washington, DC, and only 20 minutes by commuter rail from the center of Philadelphia.

Opened in 1953, the school is approved by the American Bar Association and is a member of the Association of American Law Schools. Students are graduates of well over 100 colleges and universities; many have significant work experience outside of the law. The atmosphere of the school is noted for its collegiality.

Faculty

While Villanova faculty members are recognized nationally and internationally for their legal scholarship and for their contributions to the study and practice of law, they are also deeply committed to teaching. The student-to-faculty ratio is 17 to 1.

Library and Physical Facilities

The spectacular new building opened its doors in July 2009, providing almost twice as much usable space as the law school's former home.

A soaring commons anchors the main floor and provides a breathtaking public space and comfortable casual seating for students, faculty, and staff. Bright, comfortable classrooms are tailored to the size and nature of the classes being taught and are equipped with state-of-the-art technology. The stunning Ceremonial Courtroom provides an inspiring venue for trial and advocacy events. Faculty offices are located adjacent to the classrooms to ensure that the give and take of the classroom continues after class.

The building's hallmark is its student-centeredness. The most beautiful, comfortable, and spacious places are the student areas. For example, the library reading rooms are elegantly appointed, comfortably equipped, and bathed in natural light by their three floor-to-ceiling window walls. The student lounge overlooks the quad on the first floor, again boasting floor to ceiling windows. The dining room and the coffee bar emphasize our commitment to the importance of quality of life for students who are working long hours.

The library in the new building occupies almost an entire wing and anchors one of the main entrances. Highly functional, comfortable, beautifully appointed, and equipped with the latest technology, the library's open spaces, glass walls, and high ceilings draw users.

Joint JD/MBA Program

Offered in collaboration with Villanova's top ranked School of Business, the joint JD/MBA program is designed to provide careful integration of the two disciplines and to allow students to earn both degrees in far less time than it would take to obtain them separately. Students in this program typically begin their MBA studies after the first year of law school and often finish both degrees in three to four years.

Joint JD/LLM in International Studies

Joint programs offered with the University of Edinburgh, Scotland; Leiden University, the Netherlands; the University of London; and the University of Singapore allow students to earn both a JD and an international LLM in three years. Students spend the first two years at Villanova, completing their JD courses. They then study abroad during the third year, completing the LLM. Each school accepts credits from the other, allowing students who qualify for this highly selective program to finish both degrees in the time it would normally take to finish the JD.

Joint JD/LLM in Taxation and LLM in Taxation

Students in the JD/LLM in Taxation program earn both the JD and the graduate law degree in taxation in less time and at a reduced cost than earning the degrees separately. Beginning in their second year of law school, JD students enroll in a series of tax courses that, taken together, qualify for both degrees. Following the award of the JD degree, a student can complete the remaining LLM requirements in one additional academic semester.

The interdisciplinary LLM program is conducted under the auspices of the School of Law and the Villanova School of Business. The program enriches the tax curriculum available to JD candidates, who are able to enroll in LLM courses.

Special Programs

Beyond the skills of written and oral expression developed in the first-year writing program and the required upper-level moot court program, drafting, and seminar courses, Villanova students acquire the fundamental skills of the practicing lawyer—including counseling, negotiation, advocacy, mediation, dispute resolution, conciliation, and mature judgment. Hands-on clinical opportunities allow students to apply classroom experiences to real-world client representation, often while performing public service. Clinical programs include Federal Tax; Civil Justice; Asylum, Refugee, and Emigrant Services; and Farmworkers Legal Aid.

Student Activities

The *Villanova Law Review* is a scholarly journal prepared and edited by law students. Members are selected on the basis of academic rank or through an open writing competition.

The *Villanova Environmental Law Journal* publishes both student and outside articles dealing with environmental issues. Students are selected for membership by an open writing competition.

The *Villanova Sports and Entertainment Law Journal* contains articles prepared by practitioners and professors in sports and entertainment law as well as by students. Membership is earned by selection through an open writing competition.

Each year, second- and third-year students have the opportunity to practice lawyering skills through the Client Interviewing and Counseling Competition, the Reimel Moot Court Competition, and several outside moot court competitions.

Student organizations include Asian Pacific American Law Students, Black Law Students Association, Corporate Law Society, Criminal Law Society, Environmental and Energy Law Society, Health Law Society, Intellectual Property Society, International Law Society, Islamic Law Forum, Jewish Law Students Association, Latin American Law Students Association, Justinian Society, OUTlaw, Phi Delta Phi, Pro Bono Society, St. Thomas More Society, Sports and Entertainment Law Society, Student Animal Defense League, Tax Law Society, and Women's Caucus.

Career Strategy and Advancement

The mission of the Career Strategy and Advancement Office is to provide career planning education, recruitment programs, and individual counseling as the foundation for future career development and satisfaction of our students. Distinctive features and programs include three attorney-advisors, including a public service/pro bono specialist; an open-door policy, including a daily "on call" advisor for walk-ins and "quick questions"; small group workshops for 1Ls; dozens of career workshops and panel programs on topics ranging from interviews, résumés, and networking, to public interest careers, judicial clerkships, and a multitude of practice specialty areas; "Day in the Law," a program designed to expose 1Ls to the practice of law by matching them with a graduate for a day over winter break; recruitment programs throughout the year, including a diverse array of employers in private practice (large and small firms), government, nonprofits, the judiciary, and corporations; special recruitment programs designed to enhance diversity in the profession; job fairs targeting unique geographic or practice preferences; and job-search coaching for new graduates on the job market. Pro bono programs, such as "Lawyering Together" and other projects, provide students with the opportunity to serve the disadvantaged while developing skills and positive relationships with practicing attorneys.

APPLICANT PROFILE

Villanova has chosen not to provide prospective students with an admission profile based on individual undergraduate GPAs and LSAT scores. The Admissions Committee seeks to create a diverse community by adhering to a comprehensive evaluation of a candidate's file that includes academic performance as well as professional promise. Each candidate's background, interests, accomplishments, and goals are considered before a decision is made.

UNIVERSITY OF VIRGINIA SCHOOL OF LAW

Office of Admissions, 580 Massie Road
Charlottesville, VA 22903-1738
Phone: 434.924.7351; Fax: 434.982.2128
E-mail: lawadmit@virginia.edu; Website: www.law.virginia.edu

ABA
Approved
Since
1923

The Basics

Type of school	Public
Term	Semester
Application deadline	3/1
Application fee	$75
Financial aid deadline	3/1
Can first year start other than fall?	No
Student to faculty ratio	11.9 to 1
# of housing spaces available restricted to law students	
graduate housing for which law students are eligible	779

Faculty and Administrators

	Total		Men		Women		Minorities	
	Spr	Fall	Spr	Fall	Spr	Fall	Spr	Fall
Full-time	77	78	53	59	24	19	8	9
Other full-time	1	1	1	1	0	0	0	0
Deans, librarians, & others who teach	5	6	2	2	3	4	1	1
Part-time	109	85	84	69	24	16	12	5
Total	192	170	140	131	51	39	21	15

Curriculum

		Full-Time	Part-Time
Typical first-year section size		71	0
Is there typically a "small section" of the first-year class, other than Legal Writing, taught by full-time faculty		Yes	No
If yes, typical size offered last year		31	
# of classroom course titles beyond first-year curriculum		231	
# of upper division courses, excluding seminars, with an enrollment:	Under 25	121	
	25–49	45	
	50–74	30	
	75–99	11	
	100+	6	
# of seminars		88	
# of seminar positions available		1,392	
# of seminar positions filled		1,153	0
# of positions available in simulation courses		943	
# of simulation positions filled		836	0
# of positions available in faculty supervised clinical courses		77	
# of faculty supervised clinical positions filled		72	0
# involved in field placements		151	0
# involved in law journals		545	0
# involved in moot court or trial competitions		87	0
# of credit hours required to graduate		86	

JD Enrollment and Ethnicity

	Men		Women		Full-Time		Part-Time		1st-Year		Total		JD Degs. Awd.
	#	%	#	%	#	%	#	%	#	%	#	%	
All Hispanics	29	4.8	27	5.4	56	5.1	0	0.0	14	3.8	56	5.1	8
Am. Ind./AK Nat.	4	0.7	5	1.0	9	0.8	0	0.0	1	0.3	9	0.8	4
Asian	46	7.5	56	11.3	102	9.2	0	0.0	44	12.0	102	9.2	25
Black/Af. Am.	28	4.6	40	8.1	68	6.2	0	0.0	30	8.2	68	6.1	17
Nat. HI/Pac. Isl.	0	0.0	0	0.0	0	0.0	0	0.0	0	0.0	0	0.0	0
2 or more races	11	1.8	8	1.6	19	1.7	0	0.0	15	4.1	19	1.7	0
Subtotal (minor.)	118	19.3	136	27.4	254	23.0	0	0.0	104	28.3	254	23.0	54
Nonres. Alien	6	1.0	5	1.0	11	1.0	0	0.0	3	0.8	11	1.0	0
White/Cauc.	400	65.6	295	59.5	694	62.8	1	100.0	232	63.2	695	62.8	201
Unknown	86	14.1	60	12.1	146	13.2	0	0.0	28	7.6	146	13.2	117
Total	610	55.2	496	44.8	1105	99.9	1	0.1	367	33.2	1106		375

Transfers

Transfers in	10
Transfers out	5

Tuition and Fees

	Resident	Nonresident
Full-time	$42,500	$47,500
Part-time		
Tuition Guarantee Program		N

Living Expenses

Estimated living expenses for singles

Living on campus	Living off campus	Living at home
$19,200	$19,200	$19,200

UNIVERSITY OF VIRGINIA SCHOOL OF LAW

ABA
Approved
Since
1923

GPA and LSAT Scores

	Total	Full-Time	Part-Time
# of apps	8,560	8,560	0
# of offers	923	923	0
# of matrics	368	368	0
75% GPA	3.92	3.92	0.00
Median GPA	3.85	3.85	0.00
25% GPA	3.51	3.51	0.00
75% LSAT	171	171	0
Median LSAT	170	170	0
25% LSAT	166	166	0

Grants and Scholarships (from prior year)

	Total #	Total %	Full-Time #	Full-Time %	Part-Time #	Part-Time %
Total # of students	1,122		1,122		0	
Total # receiving grants	576	51.3	576	51.3	0	0.0
Less than 1/2 tuition	473	42.2	473	42.2	0	0.0
Half to full tuition	84	7.5	84	7.5	0	0.0
Full tuition	17	1.5	17	1.5	0	0.0
More than full tuition	2	0.2	2	0.2	0	0.0
Median grant amount			$15,000		$0	

Informational and Library Resources

Total amount spent on library materials	$1,648,399
Study seating capacity inside the library	799
# of full-time equivalent professional librarians	14
Hours per week library is open	112
# of open, wired connections available to students	78
# of networked computers available for use by students	34
Has wireless network?	Y
Requires computer?	Y

JD Attrition (from prior year)

	Academic #	Other #	Total #	Total %
1st year	2	7	9	2.5
2nd year	0	3	3	0.8
3rd year	0	0	0	0.0
4th year	0	0	0	0.0

Employment (9 months after graduation)

	Total	Percentage
Employment status known	401	99.0
Employment status unknown	4	1.0
Employed	396	98.8
Pursuing graduate degrees	1	0.2
Unemployed (seeking, not seeking, or studying for the bar)	1	0.2
Type of Employment		
# employed in law firms	285	72.0
# employed in business and industry	11	2.8
# employed in government	30	7.6
# employed in public interest	15	3.8
# employed as judicial clerks	52	13.1
# employed in academia	3	0.8
Geographic Location		
# employed in state	54	13.6
# employed outside the US	4	1.0
# of states where employed	30	

Bar Passage Rates

First-time takers	349	Reporting %	100.00
Average school %	94.28	Average state %	82.31

Average pass difference 11.97

Jurisdiction	Takers	Passers	Pass %	State %	Diff %
New York	116	111	95.69	86.51	9.18
Virginia	90	83	92.22	77.06	15.16
California	33	27	81.82	73.19	8.63
Illinois	18	17	94.44	90.89	3.55
Others (15)	92	91	98.91		

The information on these pages was provided by the law school.

UNIVERSITY OF VIRGINIA SCHOOL OF LAW

Office of Admissions, 580 Massie Road
Charlottesville, VA 22903-1738
Phone: 434.924.7351; Fax: 434.982.2128
E-mail: lawadmit@virginia.edu; Website: www.law.virginia.edu

Introduction

Founded by Thomas Jefferson in 1819, the University of Virginia School of Law is a world-renowned training ground for distinguished lawyers and public servants. Located in Charlottesville, Virginia, just two hours southwest of Washington, DC, the Law School offers students a unique environment in which to study law.

The Law School is dedicated to upholding Thomas Jefferson's conviction that lawyers must serve the public interest. The school provides special career counseling and placement assistance, operates pro bono programs, and administers a loan forgiveness program.

At Virginia, law students share their experiences in a cooperative spirit, both in and out of the classroom, and build a network that lasts well beyond their three years here. Faculty build intellectual and personal relationships with students. They are leaders in the academic life of the community, organizing and speaking at lectures and other events, working with student organizations, volunteering for pro bono service, and building new curricular programs.

Curriculum and Degrees

Virginia offers more than 200 courses and seminars each year, including 20 clinics and other opportunities for hands-on training. Students pursuing interdisciplinary ideas benefit from an environment where nearly half of all law faculty hold advanced degrees in fields such as psychology, economics, philosophy, history, medicine, and theology. Each first-year student takes one *small-section* class of 30 students during the first semester, which helps bond classmates from the start.

Virginia's curriculum is enhanced by several academic programs, including those in international law, human rights, environmental law, legal and constitutional history, race and law, intellectual property, health law, and immigration law. The Law and Business Program offers students courses that integrate business and legal analysis in the law school classroom. Foundational courses in accounting and finance allow students in the program to take more advanced instruction in real-life corporate law problems.

Students may enroll in several dual-degree programs. The JD/MBA program is a four-year program in conjunction with the Darden School of Business. Other combined-degree programs include a JD/MA in English, government and foreign affairs, history, or philosophy; a JD/MS in accounting; a JD/MUEP in planning; a JD/MPP; and a JD/MPH in public health. In addition, students may combine a law degree from Virginia with the MPA from Princeton, MALD from the Fletcher School at Tufts, or the MA in international relations and international economics from Johns Hopkins.

Facilities

The Law Grounds offers an expansive and attractive setting reflecting Jefferson's position that an intellectual community in a beautiful environment fosters learning and personal growth. The library, with more than 890,000 volumes, is one of the largest law libraries in the country. Virginia offers numerous study spaces, offices for student organizations and journals, and a large dining facility.

Admission

Each year, many highly qualified college graduates apply for the necessarily limited number of places in the first-year class. Our admission process aims to select from the applicant pool an entering class of students who will contribute to this academic community during their three years of residency and, ultimately, to society and the legal profession. To that end, we consider many factors. These include not only intellectual aptitude and academic achievement, but also individual accomplishments and experiences—such as dedication or a constructive response to adversity—that predict success, as well as geographic, racial, ethnic, economic, and ideological diversity.

Rigid standards based simply on a combination of an LSAT score and cumulative undergraduate grade-point average cannot be the only criteria for selecting an entering class. We assess each applicant as an individual. This assessment takes into account not only LSAT scores and undergraduate grades, but also the strength of an applicant's undergraduate or graduate curriculum, trends in grades, the maturing effect of experiences since college, the nature and quality of any work experience, significant achievement in extracurricular activities in college, service in the military, contributions to campus or community through service and leadership, and personal qualities displayed. An applicant's experiences surmounting economic, social, or educational difficulties with grace and courage, demonstrating the capacity to grow in response to challenge, and showing compassion for the welfare of others can play a role in the admission decision.

If the University of Virginia is your first choice for law school, you may apply under the Early Decision option. Early Decision applicants commit to enrolling if admitted and must withdraw all applications to other law schools once notified of Early Decision admission.

While individual interviews are not a part of the admission process, prospective students are encouraged to visit the School of Law. When classes are in session, student-led tours are available and classes are open to visitors. On most Friday afternoons throughout the summer and during the school year, the School of Law also holds admission information sessions and student life panels for prospective students. Check our website at www.law.virginia.edu/admissions for details.

Financial Aid

The Law School helps students finance their legal education through a variety of resources, including scholarships, federally sponsored loan and work-study programs, and private-sector educational loans. While the primary responsibility for financing a legal education rests with students and their families, the Financial Aid Office works with students to identify sources of financial support and develop realistic budgets to meet their educational and professional goals.

Career Services

After law school, Virginia graduates join the nation's leading law firms, clerk for federal and state courts, and serve in and even establish nationally recognized public interest organizations. Our alumni are leaders in their fields: Virginia is third among national law schools in the number of graduates who are law firm chairpersons and managing partners, according to a 2004 survey of 850 US law firms. From 2005 to 2010, Yale, Harvard, and Virginia had the most graduates clerking for the US Supreme Court. Six graduates in the past five years received Skadden Fellowships, the nation's most prestigious public service grant.

Public Service

Virginia upholds Thomas Jefferson's conviction that lawyers have a special obligation to serve the public interest. Many students at Virginia volunteer their legal services, work in public service jobs over the summer, and pursue public interest careers after graduating. Virginia supports these students through the Virginia Loan Forgiveness Program, the Mortimer Caplin Public Service Center, the Pro Bono Project, and fellowships.

The Virginia Loan Forgiveness Program helps repay the loans of graduates who earn less than $75,000 annually in public service positions.

The Mortimer Caplin Public Service Center provides individual counseling and sponsors events focused on educating students about working in the public sector.

The Pro Bono Project is a voluntary program encouraging all students to complete at least 75 hours of pro bono service during their three years of law school. Opportunities are available locally and nationwide. The center also organizes pro bono projects that focus on areas such as child advocacy, immigration law, and veterans' disability claims.

Each year the Law School provides more than $325,000 to students working in public service over the summer. Virginia also offers a two-year, salaried fellowship to a graduating student who plans to work in public service.

Student Life

Ten academic journals and 75 student organizations—from social clubs to groups dedicated to the community's legal needs—ensure that students explore the world outside law school and expand their legal experiences while leading well-rounded lives.

Charlottesville is a picturesque and thriving metropolitan area of more than 135,000. Area restaurants are featured in publications such as *Gourmet* magazine and the *New York Times*. Each year the city hosts the nationally acclaimed Virginia Film Festival and gathers literary luminaries for the Virginia Festival of the Book. Students enjoy going to sporting events and concerts in one of the country's finest college arenas.

APPLICANT PROFILE

The University of Virginia School of Law has elected not to provide an applicant profile based only on GPA and LSAT, as these numbers cannot be the sole criteria for selecting an entering class. Each applicant is assessed as an individual, taking into account not only LSAT scores and undergraduate grades, but also the strength of an applicant's undergraduate or graduate curriculum, trends in grades, the maturing effect of experiences since college, the nature and quality of any work experience, significant achievement in extracurricular activities, service in the military, contributions to campus or community through service and leadership, and personal qualities.

WAKE FOREST UNIVERSITY SCHOOL OF LAW

Box 7206
Winston-Salem, NC 27109
Phone: 336.758.5437; Fax: 336.758.3930
E-mail: admissions@law.wfu.edu; Website: www.law.wfu.edu

ABA
Approved
Since
1936

AMERICAN BAR ASSOCIATION
Section of Legal Education
and Admissions to the Bar

The Basics

Type of school	Private
Term	Semester
Application deadline	3/15
Application fee	$60
Financial aid deadline	5/1
Can first year start other than fall?	No
Student to faculty ratio	9.5 to 1
# of housing spaces available restricted to law students	
graduate housing for which law students are eligible	

Faculty and Administrators

	Total		Men		Women		Minorities	
	Spr	Fall	Spr	Fall	Spr	Fall	Spr	Fall
Full-time	42	44	24	27	18	17	7	7
Other full-time	6	4	1	0	5	4	1	2
Deans, librarians, & others who teach	9	9	3	3	6	6	2	2
Part-time	18	22	12	18	6	4	2	0
Total	75	79	40	48	35	31	12	11

Curriculum

	Full-Time	Part-Time
Typical first-year section size	40	0
Is there typically a "small section" of the first-year class, other than Legal Writing, taught by full-time faculty	No	No
If yes, typical size offered last year		
# of classroom course titles beyond first-year curriculum	105	
# of upper division courses, excluding seminars, with an enrollment: Under 25	63	
25–49	34	
50–74	17	
75–99	2	
100+	0	
# of seminars	48	
# of seminar positions available	810	
# of seminar positions filled	639	0
# of positions available in simulation courses	302	
# of simulation positions filled	267	0
# of positions available in faculty supervised clinical courses	138	
# of faculty supervised clinical positions filled	138	0
# involved in field placements	34	0
# involved in law journals	124	0
# involved in moot court or trial competitions	72	0
# of credit hours required to graduate	90	

JD Enrollment and Ethnicity

	Men		Women		Full-Time		Part-Time		1st-Year		Total		JD Degs. Awd.
	#	%	#	%	#	%	#	%	#	%	#	%	
All Hispanics	12	4.2	9	4.5	21	4.3	0	0.0	9	5.4	21	4.3	5
Am. Ind./AK Nat.	4	1.4	2	1.0	6	1.2	0	0.0	3	1.8	6	1.2	0
Asian	6	2.1	8	4.0	14	2.9	0	0.0	3	1.8	14	2.9	5
Black/Af. Am.	14	4.9	18	9.0	32	6.6	0	0.0	12	7.2	32	6.6	19
Nat. HI/Pac. Isl.	0	0.0	0	0.0	0	0.0	0	0.0	0	0.0	0	0.0	0
2 or more races	5	1.7	3	1.5	8	1.6	0	0.0	2	1.2	8	1.6	0
Subtotal (minor.)	41	14.2	40	20.1	81	16.6	0	0.0	29	17.4	81	16.6	32
Nonres. Alien	0	0.0	0	0.0	0	0.0	0	0.0	0	0.0	0	0.0	0
White/Cauc.	221	76.7	150	75.4	371	76.2	0	0.0	125	74.9	371	76.2	123
Unknown	26	9.0	9	4.5	35	7.2	0	0.0	13	7.8	35	7.2	6
Total	288	59.1	199	40.9	487	100.0	0	0.0	167	34.3	487		161

Transfers

Transfers in	17
Transfers out	5

Tuition and Fees

	Resident	Nonresident
Full-time	$37,230	$37,230
Part-time		
Tuition Guarantee Program		N

Living Expenses

Estimated living expenses for singles

Living on campus	Living off campus	Living at home
N/A	$19,100	N/A

WAKE FOREST UNIVERSITY SCHOOL OF LAW

ABA
Approved
Since
1936

GPA and LSAT Scores

	Total	Full-Time	Part-Time
# of apps	2,984	2,984	0
# of offers	1,002	1,002	0
# of matrics	165	165	0
75% GPA	3.70	3.70	0.00
Median GPA	3.60	3.60	0.00
25% GPA	3.30	3.30	0.00
75% LSAT	164	164	0
Median LSAT	163	163	0
25% LSAT	160	160	0

Grants and Scholarships (from prior year)

	Total		Full-Time		Part-Time	
	#	%	#	%	#	%
Total # of students	476		463		13	
Total # receiving grants	221	46.4	221	47.7	0	0.0
Less than 1/2 tuition	95	20.0	95	20.5	0	0.0
Half to full tuition	66	13.9	66	14.3	0	0.0
Full tuition	51	10.7	51	11.0	0	0.0
More than full tuition	9	1.9	9	1.9	0	0.0
Median grant amount			$17,725		$0	

Informational and Library Resources

Total amount spent on library materials	$834,446
Study seating capacity inside the library	605
# of full-time equivalent professional librarians	6
Hours per week library is open	103
# of open, wired connections available to students	0
# of networked computers available for use by students	24
Has wireless network?	Y
Requires computer?	Y

JD Attrition (from prior year)

	Academic	Other	Total	
	#	#	#	%
1st year	0	6	6	4.0
2nd year	2	5	7	4.4
3rd year	0	2	2	1.2
4th year	0	0	0	0.0

Employment (9 months after graduation)

	Total	Percentage
Employment status known	145	95.4
Employment status unknown	7	4.6
Employed	137	94.5
Pursuing graduate degrees	2	1.4
Unemployed (seeking, not seeking, or studying for the bar)	5	3.4
Type of Employment		
# employed in law firms	85	62.0
# employed in business and industry	11	8.0
# employed in government	9	6.6
# employed in public interest	16	11.7
# employed as judicial clerks	11	8.0
# employed in academia	4	2.9
Geographic Location		
# employed in state	58	42.3
# employed outside the US	1	0.7
# of states where employed	21	

Bar Passage Rates

First-time takers	144	Reporting %	75.00
Average school %	93.52	Average state %	78.70
Average pass difference	14.82		

Jurisdiction	Takers	Passers	Pass %	State %	Diff %
North Carolina	79	73	92.41	76.79	15.62
New York	21	21	100.00	86.51	13.49
Virginia	8	7	87.50	77.06	10.44

WAKE FOREST UNIVERSITY SCHOOL OF LAW

Box 7206
Winston-Salem, NC 27109
Phone: 336.758.5437; Fax: 336.758.3930
E-mail: admissions@law.wfu.edu; Website: www.law.wfu.edu

Introduction

Wake Forest University School of Law, established in 1894, is located in Winston-Salem, North Carolina. It is a member of the AALS and is ABA-approved. In 1998, the law school was awarded a chapter of the Order of the Coif, a national honorary society.

Wake Forest offers students a solid and personalized legal education. Class sizes are smaller than in virtually any other law school in the nation, with approximately 40 students in each first-year section and about 20 students in first-year legal writing sections.

Faculty members are nationally renowned teachers and scholars. The director of trial advocacy was awarded the Roscoe Pound Foundation's Richard S. Jacobson Award for Excellence in Teaching Trial Advocacy, and Wake Forest has also received the prestigious Emil Gumpert Award from the American College of Trial Lawyers for its outstanding trial advocacy program. Faculty chairs are held by six of the nation's most respected authorities in the areas of administrative law, commercial law, sports and entertainment law, constitutional law, torts and product liability, and health care law and policy.

Wake Forest law school embraces seven principal commitments: (1) to maintain a school of the right size that begins with a first-year class of approximately 160 students composed of four sections of about 40 students each; (2) to develop and retain a faculty strong in teaching, experience, and current scholarly writing; (3) to assure that students are taught substantive law, legal research, and writing through the maximum use of leading-edge technology; (4) to continue the school's emphasis on dispute resolution and litigation skills through instruction, competition, and clinical practice; (5) to build a bridge between law and management communities through an enhanced curriculum, the sharing of resources, and collaborative instruction; (6) to seek to provide career opportunities for our students and graduates that match their potential; and (7) to teach the transcendence of ethics and to inculcate in graduates the importance of doing good while doing well throughout their professional lives.

Admission

Requirements: Bachelor's degree from accredited college or university, application and a dean's certification before matriculation, academic recommendation, LSAT and LSAC Credential Assembly Service, application fee—$60, application deadline—March 15.

First-year students are admitted only in the fall semester for full-time study. Completed files are individually reviewed to select a diverse group of students who are likely to succeed in law school and contribute to the legal profession. The LSAT and undergraduate GPA, as well as a number of subjective factors, are considered. This includes personal talents, work experience, community service, leadership potential, graduate study, and a history of overcoming social or economic hardship—indicating intellectual capacity, character, motivation, and maturity. For multiple LSAT scores, the higher test score will be used. Early application is encouraged as scholarship offers begin in late January. The applicant's file must be complete for consideration.

A $300 nonrefundable deposit is due by April 15, and a tuition deposit must be paid by June 15. (Both fees are applicable toward tuition.) Personal interviews are not required; however, all applicants are encouraged to visit the law school.

Transfer students meeting the admission requirements are accepted on a space-available basis after the successful completion of one year at an AALS- or ABA-approved law school.

Expenses and Financial Aid

Tuition/fees: $36,514; estimated living expenses: $10,000–$15,000.

Merit, need-based, and diversity scholarships are available. The FAFSA is recommended by April 1.

Clinical and Externship Programs

Seven exceptional programs allow students to gain hands-on legal experience. In the Litigation Clinic, students are placed in offices such as the US attorney's office, the district attorney's office, the public defender's office, legal aid, the National Labor Relations Board, private law firms, and corporate counsel. While receiving classroom instruction and skills training in interviewing, counseling, negotiation, and discovery, students represent clients under the supervision of an experienced attorney.

The Elder Law Clinic is an in-house clinic representing low- to moderate-income clients over the age of 60. Located at the Wake Forest University Baptist Medical Center, the clinic features a classroom component that is jointly taught by members of the law and medical school faculties. Students draft essential documents, such as wills, and handle administrative representation and state court litigation with a clinic professor/attorney.

The Community Law and Business Clinic provides a legal resource for low-income entrepreneurs and nonprofit organizations working to improve the quality of life in low-wealth communities. Students assist in various stages of the business development process and gain experience in a transactional practice setting.

The Innocence and Justice Clinic allows law students to work with defense attorneys, prosecutors, and law enforcement officers to identify cases that qualify for DNA testing for prisoners who might benefit from this testing to demonstrate their innocence. This arrangement, combining the efforts of law students, prosecutors, defense attorneys, and law enforcement officers, makes this a unique educational experience.

The Appellate Advocacy Clinic represents low-income clients in all sorts of appeals, both civil and criminal, and in a variety of appellate courts, including the Fourth Circuit and Seventh Circuit. Working in pairs, students handle an actual appeal from start to finish, with advice and assistance from their professor, who is counsel of record. Students also travel to Washington, DC, to observe arguments at the United States Supreme Court.

The Child Advocacy Clinic allows students to represent children in three settings: deciding custody in high conflict cases, deciding custody in civil domestic violence actions, and representing children of indigent parents in issues involving the public schools.

The Metropolitan Externship in Washington, DC, provides students with the opportunity to spend a semester in practice in the most diverse and vibrant legal environment in the world. Students spend approximately 35 hours per week interning in a government agency or nongovernmental organization.

Technology

Wake Forest prepares students to embrace the rapidly changing technological environment of the legal profession. Classrooms feature multimedia theaters allowing technology to augment classroom teaching. Many professors routinely use webpages to distribute essential course information and provide online discussion forums outside of the classroom.

Each student is required to have a laptop. The law school wireless network gives students instant access to e-mail, essential legal research systems, the Internet, and a variety of other resources. A university-wide network allows students to register for courses, receive grades, obtain transcripts, and interact with university offices.

Joint-Degree Programs

The law school currently offers the following joint degrees: JD/MBA program with the Schools of Business, a JD/MA in Religion, a JD/MDiv with the Divinity School, and a JD/MA in Bioethics with the Medical School. Admission and scholarship decisions are made independently at each school. The law school also offers an LLM in American Law for graduates of foreign law schools. A separate (LLM) application is required and may be obtained at http://law.wfu.edu/llm or by writing the director of the LLM program.

Foreign Study

Students in good standing may participate in a four-week program offered each summer at the Worrell House, the university's residential center near Regent's Park in London, England; at Casa Artom on the Grand Canal in Venice, Italy; and at the University of Vienna in Vienna, Austria. Students participating in this program can earn up to six hours of academic credit.

Career Services

The Career Services Office aggressively seeks opportunities for students in both summer and permanent legal positions. Knowledgeable staff members personally counsel students to assist them in developing solid career portfolios. The office also conducts workshops in résumé preparation, interviewing, and career planning. Faculty and staff expand career opportunities by visiting law firms, corporations, and agencies throughout the country to acquaint them with the exceptional Wake Forest program. A large number of employers interview students on campus each year or request that résumés be forwarded by the Career Services Office. Wake Forest law graduates are located throughout the country.

APPLICANT PROFILE

Wake Forest University School of Law
This grid includes only applicants who earned 120–180 LSAT scores under standard administrations.

LSAT Score	3.75 +		3.50–3.74		3.25–3.49		3.00–3.24		2.75–2.99		2.50–2.74		2.25–2.49		2.00–2.24		Below 2.00		No GPA		Total	
	Apps	Adm	Apps	Adm	Apps	Adm	Apps	Adm	Apps	Adm	Apps	Adm	Apps	Adm	Apps	Adm	Apps	Adm	Apps	Adm	Apps	Adm
175–180	5	5	2	2	1	1	2	2	3	3	0	0	0	0	0	0	0	0	0	0	13	13
170–174	19	18	17	13	16	15	12	10	7	4	4	1	1	1	1	1	0	0	0	0	77	63
165–169	116	104	117	102	82	69	66	53	30	22	27	10	7	0	4	1	0	0	5	3	454	364
160–164	177	159	285	150	276	76	142	33	65	10	28	2	12	0	5	3	1	0	11	2	1002	435
155–159	139	30	164	27	175	15	116	5	51	2	14	0	6	0	3	0	0	0	9	0	677	79
150–154	57	2	75	6	89	11	77	4	37	3	26	0	6	0	4	0	1	0	5	0	377	26
145–149	16	1	18	3	35	0	47	2	25	0	14	0	14	0	3	0	1	0	1	0	174	6
140–144	4	0	9	0	15	0	19	0	13	0	13	0	6	0	3	0	3	0	4	0	89	0
135–139	3	0	3	0	3	0	9	0	9	0	3	0	4	0	3	0	1	0	2	0	40	0
130–134	0	0	0	0	2	0	5	0	2	0	2	0	0	0	1	0	1	0	1	0	14	0
125–129	0	0	0	0	0	0	0	0	0	0	0	0	1	0	0	0	0	0	0	0	1	0
120–124	0	0	0	0	0	0	0	0	0	0	0	0	0	0	0	0	0	0	0	0	0	0
Total	536	319	690	303	694	187	495	109	242	44	131	13	57	1	27	5	8	0	38	5	2918	986

Apps = Number of Applicants
Adm = Number Admitted
Reflects 99% of the total applicant pool; highest LSAT data reported.

WASHBURN UNIVERSITY SCHOOL OF LAW

1700 SW College Avenue
Topeka, KS 66621-0001
Phone: 800.WASHLAW or 800.927.4529; Fax: 785.670.1120
E-mail: admissions@washburnlaw.edu; Website: http://washburnlaw.edu

The Basics

Type of school	Public
Term	Semester
Application deadline	4/1 11/1
Application fee	$40
Financial aid deadline	7/1
Can first year start other than fall?	Yes
Student to faculty ratio	12.9 to 1
# of housing spaces available restricted to law students	
graduate housing for which law students are eligible	192

Faculty and Administrators

	Total		Men		Women		Minorities	
	Spr	Fall	Spr	Fall	Spr	Fall	Spr	Fall
Full-time	29	29	16	17	13	12	4	6
Other full-time	1	2	1	2	0	0	0	0
Deans, librarians, & others who teach	7	6	6	6	1	0	2	1
Part-time	27	25	17	16	10	9	0	0
Total	64	62	40	41	24	21	6	7

Curriculum

		Full-Time	Part-Time
Typical first-year section size		82	0
Is there typically a "small section" of the first-year class, other than Legal Writing, taught by full-time faculty		Yes	No
If yes, typical size offered last year		37	
# of classroom course titles beyond first-year curriculum		88	
# of upper division courses, excluding seminars, with an enrollment:	Under 25	58	
	25–49	25	
	50–74	8	
	75–99	4	
	100+	0	
# of seminars		26	
# of seminar positions available		521	
# of seminar positions filled		373	0
# of positions available in simulation courses		596	
# of simulation positions filled		419	0
# of positions available in faculty supervised clinical courses		96	
# of faculty supervised clinical positions filled		82	0
# involved in field placements		98	0
# involved in law journals		55	0
# involved in moot court or trial competitions		37	0
# of credit hours required to graduate		90	

JD Enrollment and Ethnicity

	Men #	Men %	Women #	Women %	Full-Time #	Full-Time %	Part-Time #	Part-Time %	1st-Year #	1st-Year %	Total #	Total %	JD Degs. Awd.
All Hispanics	9	3.3	7	3.8	16	3.5	0	0.0	4	2.4	16	3.5	8
Am. Ind./AK Nat.	4	1.5	6	3.3	10	2.2	0	0.0	8	4.9	10	2.2	3
Asian	5	1.8	6	3.3	11	2.4	0	0.0	6	3.7	11	2.4	4
Black/Af. Am.	8	2.9	8	4.4	16	3.5	0	0.0	6	3.7	16	3.5	7
Nat. HI/Pac. Isl.	0	0.0	0	0.0	0	0.0	0	0.0	0	0.0	0	0.0	0
2 or more races	0	0.0	0	0.0	0	0.0	0	0.0	0	0.0	0	0.0	0
Subtotal (minor.)	26	9.6	27	14.8	53	11.7	0	0.0	24	14.6	53	11.7	22
Nonres. Alien	3	1.1	4	2.2	7	1.5	0	0.0	2	1.2	7	1.5	0
White/Cauc.	233	85.7	150	82.4	383	84.4	0	0.0	134	81.7	383	84.4	113
Unknown	10	3.7	1	0.5	11	2.4	0	0.0	4	2.4	11	2.4	4
Total	272	59.9	182	40.1	454	100.0	0	0.0	164	36.1	454		139

Transfers

Transfers in	4
Transfers out	5

Tuition and Fees

	Resident	Nonresident
Full-time	$16,630	$25,900
Part-time		
Tuition Guarantee Program		N

Living Expenses

Estimated living expenses for singles

Living on campus	Living off campus	Living at home
$16,671	$16,671	$16,671

ABA
Approved
Since
1923

GPA and LSAT Scores

	Total	Full-Time	Part-Time
# of apps	1,102	1,102	0
# of offers	435	435	0
# of matrics	169	169	0
75% GPA	3.55	3.55	0.00
Median GPA	3.22	3.22	0.00
25% GPA	2.91	2.91	0.00
75% LSAT	158	158	0
Median LSAT	155	155	0
25% LSAT	153	153	0

Grants and Scholarships (from prior year)

	Total		Full-Time		Part-Time	
	#	%	#	%	#	%
Total # of students	441		441		0	
Total # receiving grants	203	46.0	203	46.0	0	0.0
Less than 1/2 tuition	109	24.7	109	24.7	0	0.0
Half to full tuition	63	14.3	63	14.3	0	0.0
Full tuition	0	0.0	0	0.0	0	0.0
More than full tuition	31	7.0	31	7.0	0	0.0
Median grant amount			$7,500		$0	

Informational and Library Resources

Total amount spent on library materials	$1,330,018
Study seating capacity inside the library	402
# of full-time equivalent professional librarians	9
Hours per week library is open	101
# of open, wired connections available to students	28
# of networked computers available for use by students	53
Has wireless network?	Y
Requires computer?	N

JD Attrition (from prior year)

	Academic	Other	Total	
	#	#	#	%
1st year	1	16	17	10.4
2nd year	0	2	2	1.4
3rd year	0	3	3	2.2
4th year	0	0	0	0.0

Employment (9 months after graduation)

	Total	Percentage
Employment status known	134	97.8
Employment status unknown	3	2.2
Employed	116	86.6
Pursuing graduate degrees	5	3.7
Unemployed (seeking, not seeking, or studying for the bar)	6	4.5
Type of Employment		
# employed in law firms	63	54.3
# employed in business and industry	13	11.2
# employed in government	24	20.7
# employed in public interest	7	6.0
# employed as judicial clerks	6	5.2
# employed in academia	3	2.6
Geographic Location		
# employed in state	78	67.2
# employed outside the US	0	0.0
# of states where employed	16	

Bar Passage Rates

First-time takers	141	Reporting %	74.47
Average school %	86.67	Average state %	87.13
Average pass difference	−0.46		

Jurisdiction	Takers	Passers	Pass %	State %	Diff %
Kansas	88	74	84.09	86.23	−2.14
Missouri	17	17	100.00	91.81	8.19

WASHBURN UNIVERSITY SCHOOL OF LAW

1700 SW College Avenue
Topeka, KS 66621-0001
Phone: 800.WASHLAW or 800.927.4529; Fax: 785.670.1120
E-mail: admissions@washburnlaw.edu; Website: http://washburnlaw.edu

Introduction

Washburn University School of Law was founded in 1903, became a member of the AALS in 1905, and appeared on the initial list of ABA-approved schools in 1923. The essence of Washburn Law is the commitment of the law school community at every level—from the dean's office to facilities staff—to the success of our students. In addition, the law school endeavors to impart to its students the value of treating others with respect, dignity, and a sense of caring. Its network of more than 6,800 alumni located in all 50 states and many foreign countries includes nationally recognized lawyers, state and federal judges, politicians, journalists, and senior executives of Fortune 500 companies.

Curriculum

All entering students participate in the law school's Ex-L program, which begins during an elaborate and rigorous "first week" program designed to teach students the learning strategies they need to succeed in law school. Ex-L includes a structured study-group program in which groups of four to six students meet twice per week to apply cooperative learning strategies to their law school experience under the supervision of carefully trained and supervised upper-division students. Second- and third-year students satisfy advanced writing and oral presentation requirements and take one or more classes from a group of Perspectives on Law courses, and one or more classes from a group of Skills courses.

Centers for Excellence

Four Centers for Excellence complement Washburn's tradition of excellence in teaching. Students may add an element of concentration by participating in one of the school's eight certificate programs, most of which are administered through the centers.

Business and Transactional Law Center—The center provides students with additional educational opportunities in business law while developing the essential skills of transactional lawyers. The hands-on involvement of alumni actively engaged in business and transactional law also allows the center to accomplish a major subsidiary goal: making the law school experience more realistic, and relevant, by providing additional opportunities to bridge the gap between theory and practice.

Center for Excellence in Advocacy—The center trains law students in the persuasive and skilled use of advocacy techniques. Students hone their advocacy skills in Washburn's live-client Law Clinic and in a variety of advocacy skills courses. The center coordinates student participation in trial advocacy, negotiation, and client counseling; sponsors national and regional advocacy conferences; and hosts a practitioner in residence each year.

Center for Law and Government—Washburn Law is ideally situated to offer law students unique and varied opportunities to learn about lawmaking, judicial decision-making, administrative law, and the regulatory process, given its proximity to the state capitol, the state judicial center, the federal courthouse, and state agencies. As its primary focus, the center provides superior legal education to prepare

highly qualified public servants for a broad range of careers associated with local, state, and federal government.

Children and Family Law Center—Washburn houses the American Bar Association's *Family Law Quarterly*. Students working in the center have the opportunity to take a range of courses related to children and families and to participate in the Washburn Law Clinic representing clients in divorce, children in need of care, and other family law cases.

Certificate Programs

Washburn Law offers certificates of specialization in Advocacy, Business and Transactional Law, Estate Planning, Family Law, International and Comparative Law, Law and Government, Natural Resources Law, and Tax Law. The certificate programs allow students to fully develop their legal interests in these fields. Students who earn certificates graduate with a highly developed working knowledge of the practice area.

Law Clinic

In 1970, Washburn Law Clinic was one of the nation's first in-house clinics. From its inception, faculty members teaching in the clinic have been on a tenure track, placing our clinic at the forefront of legal education. Faculty-supervised students provide a full range of legal services to live clients in six clinics—Children and Family Law Clinic, Criminal Defense Clinic, State and Tribal Court Practice Clinic, Civil Litigation Clinic, Criminal Appellate Advocacy Clinic, and Small Business and Transactional Law Clinic.

International Programs

Currently, Washburn expands students' understandings of different legal systems through its summer program at the University of the West Indies, in Barbados, and its semester-long program at Maastricht University, in the Netherlands.

Externships

Washburn Law's externship program allows students to earn course credit through placement in legal settings outside the law school. Students can experience the practice of law in a wide variety of settings tailored to their specific interests and needs. Students are closely supervised by an attorney and by the externship director.

Accelerated Degree Program

This program allows students to complete law school in two years by taking courses during both summers.

Facilities and Technology

For 25 years, the Washburn Law Library has been at the top of all law school libraries for new titles added, its extensive collection, and its innovative use of technology. WashLaw has been a premier legal research portal since its creation in the early 1990s, and it is nationally acclaimed as a comprehensive source for legal information on the Internet. Students have wireless access throughout the building. Classrooms include enhanced audio, video, and computer technologies. The state-of-the-art Robinson Courtroom/Bianchino Technology Center offers students the opportunity to practice their skills in a high-tech environment.

Admission

While an applicant's LSAT score and GPA are significant factors, there is no bright-line cutoff. The Admissions Committee uses the high LSAT for multiple-test takers. It carefully considers other factors, including a determination of whether the individual would be an asset for the class as a whole based on gender, ethnicity, geographic diversity, international experience, and undergraduate institution.

Student Activities

More than 30 active student organizations, including Black, Hispanic, Asian, and Native American law student associations, accommodate the wide and diverse interests students bring to the law school and add to the cultural and intellectual life of the law school community.

Students may be selected to serve on the board of editors of the *Washburn Law Journal* or the student editorial board of the ABA's peer-reviewed *Family Law Quarterly*, which has been located at Washburn since 1992, enhancing the Children and Family Law Center.

Expenses and Financial Aid

Scholarships are awarded based on academic performance. Contribution to diversity is also considered in making scholarship awards. Resident status for tuition purposes can be established with a primary Kansas residence after six months. Topeka is one of the most affordable housing markets in the country. Most students live in the residential areas surrounding the campus.

Professional Development

The Professional Development Office offers programs that emphasize assessment of career goals, exploration of varied applications of a legal education, and support for the transition into the professional marketplace. The office makes available extensive resources regarding local, regional, national, and international legal employment in the public and private sectors, graduate and foreign study, and judicial clerkships.

Washburn Law graduates enjoy great success in seeking employment. Washburn Law alumni reside in every state in the nation, the District of Columbia, and many foreign countries.

Writing Program

During the past several years, Washburn Law has made a major commitment of resources to its Legal Analysis, Research, and Writing program, resulting in national recognition. All first-year students must complete six hours of graded legal analysis, research, and writing. An upper-level writing project is also required. The class sizes are small and are taught by tenure-track professors dedicated to legal writing as their chosen profession.

Spring Start Program

Students may start law school in January through the Spring Start Program, which provides an alternative to those who do not want to wait for the traditional fall start.

Pro Bono Program

Students are encouraged to embrace their future professional obligation to provide legal services to individuals of limited means. Through the Washburn Law Pro Bono Program, they may participate in a pro bono initiative that rewards pro bono work with recognition at graduation.

APPLICANT PROFILE

Washburn University School of Law
This grid includes only applicants who earned 120–180 LSAT scores under standard administrations.

LSAT Score	3.75 +		3.50–3.74		3.25–3.49		3.00–3.24		2.75–2.99		2.50–2.74		2.25–2.49		Below 2.25		No GPA		Total	
	Apps	Adm	Apps	Adm	Apps	Adm	Apps	Adm	Apps	Adm	Apps	Adm	Apps	Adm	Apps	Adm	Apps	Adm	Apps	Adm
175–180	0	0	0	0	0	0	0	0	0	0	0	0	0	0	0	0	0	0	0	0
170–174	1	1	1	1	0	0	0	0	0	0	0	0	1	1	0	0	0	0	3	3
165–169	4	4	2	2	4	4	0	0	4	4	0	0	0	0	1	0	0	0	15	14
160–164	8	8	7	7	8	8	9	9	10	10	2	2	2	2	2	2	0	0	48	48
155–159	20	20	13	13	25	25	25	22	20	15	14	13	12	11	5	4	1	1	135	124
150–154	22	15	35	24	51	35	74	46	45	20	29	11	18	6	3	0	1	0	278	157
145–149	24	7	40	5	72	9	53	7	35	2	27	1	15	0	10	0	3	0	279	31
140–144	8	0	14	1	26	1	20	1	20	1	22	1	10	0	8	0	3	0	131	5
Below 140	2	0	0	0	5	0	9	0	15	0	11	0	6	0	10	0	7	1	65	1
Total	89	55	112	53	191	82	190	85	149	52	105	28	64	20	39	6	15	2	954	383

Apps = Number of Applicants
Adm = Number Admitted
Reflects 100% of the total applicant pool; highest LSAT data reported.

UNIVERSITY OF WASHINGTON SCHOOL OF LAW

William H. Gates Hall, Box 35-3020
Seattle, WA 98195-3020
Phone: 206.543.4078
E-mail: lawadm@u.washington.edu; Website: www.law.washington.edu

The Basics

Type of school	Public
Term	Quarter
Application deadline	1/15
Application fee	$60
Financial aid deadline	2/28
Can first year start other than fall?	No
Student to faculty ratio	9.7 to 1
# of housing spaces available restricted to law students	
graduate housing for which law students are eligible	500

Faculty and Administrators

	Total		Men		Women		Minorities	
	Spr	Fall	Spr	Fall	Spr	Fall	Spr	Fall
Full-time	44	50	27	28	17	22	11	12
Other full-time	4	4	0	0	4	4	1	1
Deans, librarians, & others who teach	5	5	2	2	3	3	0	0
Part-time	99	18	67	16	32	2	11	2
Total	152	77	96	46	56	31	23	15

Curriculum

	Full-Time	Part-Time
Typical first-year section size	52	0
Is there typically a "small section" of the first-year class, other than Legal Writing, taught by full-time faculty	Yes	No
If yes, typical size offered last year	26	
# of classroom course titles beyond first-year curriculum	153	

# of upper division courses, excluding seminars, with an enrollment:	Under 25	63
	25–49	66
	50–74	18
	75–99	3
	100+	0

	Full-Time	Part-Time
# of seminars	38	
# of seminar positions available	570	
# of seminar positions filled	517	0
# of positions available in simulation courses	485	
# of simulation positions filled	485	0
# of positions available in faculty supervised clinical courses	157	
# of faculty supervised clinical positions filled	157	0
# involved in field placements	164	0
# involved in law journals	115	0
# involved in moot court or trial competitions	48	0
# of credit hours required to graduate	135	

JD Enrollment and Ethnicity

	Men		Women		Full-Time		Part-Time		1st-Year		Total		JD Degs. Awd.
	#	%	#	%	#	%	#	%	#	%	#	%	
All Hispanics	15	5.3	12	4.5	27	4.9	0	0.0	11	5.9	27	4.9	8
Am. Ind./AK Nat.	6	2.1	9	3.3	15	2.7	0	0.0	6	3.2	15	2.7	2
Asian	29	10.3	38	14.1	67	12.2	0	0.0	18	9.7	67	12.2	12
Black/Af. Am.	4	1.4	7	2.6	11	2.0	0	0.0	6	3.2	11	2.0	6
Nat. HI/Pac. Isl.	0	0.0	0	0.0	0	0.0	0	0.0	0	0.0	0	0.0	0
2 or more races	3	1.1	3	1.1	6	1.1	0	0.0	6	3.2	6	1.1	0
Subtotal (minor.)	57	20.3	69	25.7	126	22.9	0	0.0	47	25.3	126	22.9	37
Nonres. Alien	8	2.8	8	3.0	16	2.9	0	0.0	3	1.6	16	2.9	0
White/Cauc.	181	64.4	169	62.8	350	63.6	0	0.0	84	45.2	350	63.6	125
Unknown	35	12.5	23	8.6	58	10.5	0	0.0	52	28.0	58	10.5	10
Total	281	51.1	269	48.9	550	100.0	0	0.0	186	33.8	550		176

Transfers

Transfers in	6
Transfers out	1

Tuition and Fees

	Resident	Nonresident
Full-time	$24,339	$37,299
Part-time		
Tuition Guarantee Program	N	

Living Expenses

Estimated living expenses for singles

Living on campus	Living off campus	Living at home
$18,573	$18,573	$8,184

UNIVERSITY OF WASHINGTON SCHOOL OF LAW

ABA
Approved
Since
1924

GPA and LSAT Scores

	Total	Full-Time	Part-Time
# of apps	2,560	2,560	0
# of offers	545	545	0
# of matrics	186	186	0
75% GPA	3.81	3.81	0.00
Median GPA	3.66	3.66	0.00
25% GPA	3.49	3.49	0.00
75% LSAT	166	166	0
Median LSAT	163	163	0
25% LSAT	160	160	0

Grants and Scholarships (from prior year)

	Total		Full-Time		Part-Time	
	#	%	#	%	#	%
Total # of students	530		530		0	
Total # receiving grants	258	48.7	258	48.7	0	0.0
Less than 1/2 tuition	201	37.9	201	37.9	0	0.0
Half to full tuition	28	5.3	28	5.3	0	0.0
Full tuition	0	0.0	0	0.0	0	0.0
More than full tuition	29	5.5	29	5.5	0	0.0
Median grant amount			$6,000		$0	

Informational and Library Resources

Total amount spent on library materials	$1,271,398
Study seating capacity inside the library	391
# of full-time equivalent professional librarians	7
Hours per week library is open	89
# of open, wired connections available to students	0
# of networked computers available for use by students	64
Has wireless network?	Y
Requires computer?	N

JD Attrition (from prior year)

	Academic	Other	Total	
	#	#	#	%
1st year	0	1	1	0.6
2nd year	0	0	0	0.0
3rd year	0	0	0	0.0
4th year	0	0	0	0.0

Employment (9 months after graduation)

	Total	Percentage
Employment status known	162	100.0
Employment status unknown	0	0.0
Employed	145	89.5
Pursuing graduate degrees	8	4.9
Unemployed (seeking, not seeking, or studying for the bar)	3	1.9
Type of Employment		
# employed in law firms	71	49.0
# employed in business and industry	14	9.7
# employed in government	17	11.7
# employed in public interest	8	5.5
# employed as judicial clerks	33	22.8
# employed in academia	2	1.4
Geographic Location		
# employed in state	98	67.6
# employed outside the US	7	4.8
# of states where employed	12	

Bar Passage Rates

First-time takers	160	Reporting %	70.00
Average school %	87.50	Average state %	74.42

Average pass difference 13.08

Jurisdiction	Takers	Passers	Pass %	State %	Diff %
Washington	112	98	87.50	74.42	13.08

UNIVERSITY OF WASHINGTON SCHOOL OF LAW

William H. Gates Hall, Box 35-3020
Seattle, WA 98195-3020
Phone: 206.543.4078
E-mail: lawadm@u.washington.edu; Website: www.law.washington.edu

Introduction

Established in 1899, the School of Law is part of the main campus of the University of Washington, approximately four miles from downtown Seattle. The university, the largest single-campus institution in the western United States, with an enrollment of 48,022 students, offers nearly every discipline of study. The School of Law has 56 full-time faculty members and about 550 JD students. Because of the favorable student-to-faculty ratio, classes are generally small, with frequent opportunities for student-teacher contact. Each first-year student is usually in at least one class of 30 or fewer students in addition to the Basic Legal Skills course. Our mission to shape and define just and sustainable law and policies through inspired teaching, scholarly discovery, ethical advocacy, and generous public service allows us to be recognized as a Leader for the Global Common Good. The school is a member of the AALS, is approved by the ABA, and has a chapter of the Order of the Coif.

Curriculum

The first-year curriculum is prescribed. In the second and third years, all courses are elective except for an advanced writing requirement, a skills course requirement, and a course in professional responsibility. In addition to traditional courses and seminars, advanced students may participate in one of 12 clinics—Innocence Project Northwest, Bankruptcy Client Representation Project, Mediation, Children and Youth Advocacy, Legislative Advocacy, Unemployment Compensation, Street Law, Tribal Court Public Defense, Immigration Law, Technology Law and Public Policy, Entrepreneurial Law, or Federal Tax—or in courses in trial advocacy. Students must also perform 60 hours of public service legal work.

Students are encouraged to rely on their initiative and to develop their own powers of perception. Classroom discussion, in which students participate fully, is one means used to assist this development. Independent research projects, either in the context of a seminar or through individualized study under faculty supervision, are also emphasized. Although it is a state law school, Washington's state law is not emphasized unduly. Graduates of the school are prepared to practice law anywhere in the United States or internationally.

Special Programs

Concentration tracks are available in Asian Law, Dispute Resolution, Environmental Law, Health Law, Intellectual Property, International and Comparative Law, and Public Service Law.

Advanced degree programs include Asian, Global Business, and Development Law; Health Law; Intellectual Property Law and Policy; and Taxation (LLM programs), as well as a PhD in Asian and Comparative Law.

Scholarly centers and projects include the Asian Law Center; Barer Institute for Law and Global Human Services; Center for Advanced Study and Research on Intellectual Property (CASRIP); Center for Law in Science and Global Health; Global Health and Justice Project; Native American Law Center; and the Three Degrees Project on climate justice.

JD students may take courses in any of the LLM programs during their second and third years of study. Additionally, JD students may enroll in graduate-level courses from other disciplines offered at the UW and count a limited number of those credits toward their JD degree. Students may pursue the JD concurrently with any graduate degree program to which they have been admitted. The UW also offers a highly-regarded master's degree in Law Librarianship.

Admission Standards

In selecting the entering class, the law school does not make all of its admission decisions solely on the basis of predicted academic performance. Important academic objectives are furthered by classes composed of students having talents and skills derived from diverse backgrounds believed to be relevant to a rich and effective study of law.

Gates Public Service Law Scholars Program

Five Gates Public Service Law (PSL) Scholars are selected annually from among the first-year students entering the UW School of Law JD program. Each Gates PSL Scholar award will cover tuition, books, other normal fees imposed for university and UW School of Law enrollment, costs of room and board, and incidental expenses. Acceptance of a Gates PSL scholarship represents a commitment on the part of each recipient to work in public service for at least five years following graduation. More information about the program, including the application it requires, may be found at www.law.washington.edu/Gatesscholar/.

Student Activities

The *Washington Law Review, Pacific Rim Law and Policy Journal, Washington Journal of Environmental Law and Policy*, and the *Washington Journal of Law, Technology and Arts* are edited and published by students. The University of Washington moot court teams are among the top scoring teams in the nation.

Through the Student Bar Association and student/faculty committees, students participate in the decision processes of the law school. Student organizations include the Advocates for the Arts; American Civil Liberties Union; American Constitution Society; Asian/Pacific American Law Student Association; Black Law Students Association; Business Law Association; Center for Human Rights and Justice; Chinese American Law Students Association; Christian Law Society; Disability Law Alliance; Federalist Society; GreenLaw; Immigrant Families Advocacy Project; Innocence Project Northwest-Student Chapter; International Law Society; Jewish Law Students Society; Korean American Law Student Association; Latino/Latina Law Students Association; Law and Alternative Dispute Resolution; Law Students for Reproductive Justice; Law Women's Caucus; Middle Eastern Law Students Association of Washington (MELSAW); Military Law Students' Association; Minority Law Students' Association; Moot Court Honor Board; National Lawyers Guild; National Security and Law Society; Native American Law Student Association; Nontraditional Law Students; Outlaws (LGBT Student Group); *Pacific Rim Law and Policy*

Journal; PALS: Parents Attending Law School; Public Interest Law Association; Sport/Entertainment Law Club; Street Youth Legal Advocates of Washington; Student Animal Legal Defense Fund; Student Bar Association; Student Health Law Organization; Students for Labor and Employment Justice; Technology Law Society; the *Washington Journal of Environmental Law and Policy*; *Washington Journal of Law, Technology and Arts*; and the *Washington Law Review*.

Career Services

The Center for Professional and Leadership Development (CPLD) invites students to partner in advancing their careers by providing professional development coaching, recruiting opportunities, electronic job-search tools, and events. Relationships matter in the practice of the law; many of the events and activities are planned to create and promote new relationships among attorneys, alumni, and UW School of Law students.

Visitation

The law school invites prospective students to visit a large-section, first-year class. The schedule can be found at www.law.washington.edu/admissions/Visit/Default.aspx.

William H. Gates Hall

The law school moved into its new $80 million facility in September 2003. The building is named for William H. Gates, Sr., a 1950 graduate of the UW School of Law and father of the Microsoft cofounder. Gates Hall gives students access to technology, such as wireless Internet connections and smart podiums with built-in screens and projector equipment. Multifunctional classrooms create a stimulating learning environment and the Marian Gould Gallagher Law Library, which houses the largest public legal collection in the Pacific Northwest, is accessible to students and practitioners alike.

APPLICANT PROFILE

University of Washington School of Law
This grid includes only applicants who earned 120–180 LSAT scores under standard administrations.

LSAT Score	3.75 +		3.50–3.74		3.25–3.49		3.00–3.24		2.75–2.99		2.50–2.74		2.25–2.49		2.00–2.24		Below 2.00		No GPA		Total	
	Apps	Adm	Apps	Adm	Apps	Adm	Apps	Adm	Apps	Adm	Apps	Adm	Apps	Adm	Apps	Adm	Apps	Adm	Apps	Adm	Apps	Adm
175–180	8	7	10	8	6	5	3	1	2	0	0	0	0	0	0	0	0	0	0	0	29	21
170–174	34	29	44	33	32	10	21	9	11	5	2	0	2	0	0	0	0	0	3	2	149	88
165–169	136	91	145	73	107	30	47	9	14	1	9	0	2	0	2	0	0	0	9	2	471	206
160–164	208	85	312	60	227	22	99	3	36	1	8	1	2	0	2	0	1	0	19	3	914	175
155–159	127	22	168	11	99	5	86	2	27	1	15	0	4	0	1	0	1	0	23	1	551	42
150–154	42	4	71	6	59	1	45	0	23	0	14	0	9	0	1	0	0	0	6	0	270	11
145–149	10	1	16	0	26	1	33	1	11	0	12	0	1	0	1	0	0	0	12	0	122	3
140–144	3	0	6	0	9	0	11	0	13	0	4	0	7	0	2	0	0	0	1	0	56	0
135–139	0	0	2	0	1	0	6	0	3	0	0	0	1	0	1	0	1	0	1	0	16	0
130–134	0	0	0	0	0	0	0	0	1	0	0	0	0	0	1	0	0	0	2	0	4	0
125–129	0	0	0	0	0	0	0	0	0	0	0	0	0	0	1	0	0	0	0	0	1	0
120–124	0	0	0	0	0	0	0	0	0	0	0	0	0	0	0	0	0	0	1	0	1	0
Total	568	239	774	191	566	74	351	25	141	8	64	1	28	0	12	0	3	0	77	8	2584	546

Apps = Number of Applicants
Adm = Number Admitted
Reflects 100% of the total applicant pool; highest LSAT data reported.

WASHINGTON AND LEE UNIVERSITY SCHOOL OF LAW

Office of Admissions, Sydney Lewis Hall
Lexington, VA 24450
Phone: 540.458.8503; Fax: 540.458.8586
E-mail: LawAdm@wlu.edu; Website: www.law.wlu.edu

ABA
Approved
Since
1923

The Basics

Type of school	Private
Term	Semester
Application deadline	2/1
Application fee	$0
Financial aid deadline	2/1
Can first year start other than fall?	No
Student to faculty ratio	9.5 to 1
# of housing spaces available restricted to law students	56
graduate housing for which law students are eligible	56

Faculty and Administrators

	Total		Men		Women		Minorities	
	Spr	Fall	Spr	Fall	Spr	Fall	Spr	Fall
Full-time	35	35	28	27	7	8	5	3
Other full-time	1	0	1	0	0	0	1	0
Deans, librarians, & others who teach	5	5	3	3	2	2	0	0
Part-time	24	22	21	20	3	2	1	0
Total	65	62	53	50	12	12	7	3

Curriculum

	Full-Time	Part-Time
Typical first-year section size	57	0
Is there typically a "small section" of the first-year class, other than Legal Writing, taught by full-time faculty	Yes	No
If yes, typical size offered last year	22	

# of classroom course titles beyond first-year curriculum		79
# of upper division courses, excluding seminars, with an enrollment:	Under 25	83
	25–49	13
	50–74	5
	75–99	5
	100+	1
# of seminars		14
# of seminar positions available		203

# of seminar positions filled	126	0
# of positions available in simulation courses	464	
# of simulation positions filled	334	0
# of positions available in faculty supervised clinical courses	52	
# of faculty supervised clinical positions filled	52	0
# involved in field placements	100	0
# involved in law journals	108	0
# involved in moot court or trial competitions	124	0
# of credit hours required to graduate	85	

JD Enrollment and Ethnicity

	Men		Women		Full-Time		Part-Time		1st-Year		Total		JD Degs. Awd.
	#	%	#	%	#	%	#	%	#	%	#	%	
All Hispanics	5	2.1	8	4.7	13	3.2	0	0.0	2	1.4	13	3.2	3
Am. Ind./AK Nat.	1	0.4	0	0.0	1	0.2	0	0.0	0	0.0	1	0.2	0
Asian	8	3.4	9	5.3	17	4.2	0	0.0	7	4.9	17	4.2	7
Black/Af. Am.	10	4.2	16	9.4	26	6.4	0	0.0	8	5.6	26	6.4	10
Nat. HI/Pac. Isl.	0	0.0	1	0.6	1	0.2	0	0.0	0	0.0	1	0.2	0
2 or more races	5	2.1	4	2.4	9	2.2	0	0.0	5	3.5	9	2.2	0
Subtotal (minor.)	29	12.2	38	22.4	67	16.5	0	0.0	22	15.4	67	16.5	26
Nonres. Alien	4	1.7	4	2.4	8	2.0	0	0.0	4	2.8	8	2.0	0
White/Cauc.	186	78.5	125	73.5	311	76.4	0	0.0	107	74.8	311	76.4	94
Unknown	18	7.6	3	1.8	21	5.2	0	0.0	10	7.0	21	5.2	0
Total	237	58.2	170	41.8	407	100.0	0	0.0	143	35.1	407		123

Transfers

Transfers in	19
Transfers out	18

Tuition and Fees

	Resident	Nonresident
Full-time	$39,937	
Part-time		
Tuition Guarantee Program	N	

Living Expenses

Estimated living expenses for singles

Living on campus	Living off campus	Living at home
$19,898	$19,898	$3,260

WASHINGTON AND LEE UNIVERSITY SCHOOL OF LAW

*ABA
Approved
Since
1923*

GPA and LSAT Scores

	Total	Full-Time	Part-Time
# of apps	4,582	4,582	0
# of offers	998	998	0
# of matrics	144	144	0
75% GPA	3.64	3.64	0.00
Median GPA	3.44	3.44	0.00
25% GPA	3.14	3.14	0.00
75% LSAT	167	167	0
Median LSAT	166	166	0
25% LSAT	161	161	0

Grants and Scholarships (from prior year)

	Total		Full-Time		Part-Time	
	#	%	#	%	#	%
Total # of students	390		390		0	
Total # receiving grants	244	62.6	244	62.6	0	0.0
Less than 1/2 tuition	148	37.9	148	37.9	0	0.0
Half to full tuition	72	18.5	72	18.5	0	0.0
Full tuition	24	6.2	24	6.2	0	0.0
More than full tuition	0	0.0	0	0.0	0	0.0
Median grant amount			$15,000		$0	

Informational and Library Resources

Total amount spent on library materials	$1,060,407
Study seating capacity inside the library	530
# of full-time equivalent professional librarians	5
Hours per week library is open	168
# of open, wired connections available to students	335
# of networked computers available for use by students	85
Has wireless network?	Y
Requires computer?	N

JD Attrition (from prior year)

	Academic	Other	Total	
	#	#	#	%
1st year	0	3	3	2.2
2nd year	0	20	20	15.4
3rd year	2	0	2	1.6
4th year	0	0	0	0.0

Employment (9 months after graduation)

	Total	Percentage
Employment status known	136	98.6
Employment status unknown	2	1.4
Employed	119	87.5
Pursuing graduate degrees	7	5.1
Unemployed (seeking, not seeking, or studying for the bar)	8	5.9
Type of Employment		
# employed in law firms	69	58.0
# employed in business and industry	13	10.9
# employed in government	9	7.6
# employed in public interest	2	1.7
# employed as judicial clerks	23	19.3
# employed in academia	1	0.8
Geographic Location		
# employed in state	38	31.9
# employed outside the US	1	0.8
# of states where employed	26	

Bar Passage Rates

First-time takers	129	Reporting %	74.42
Average school %	85.42	Average state %	80.80
Average pass difference	4.62		

Jurisdiction	Takers	Passers	Pass %	State %	Diff %
Virginia	51	41	80.39	77.06	3.33
New York	25	24	96.00	86.51	9.49
Georgia	7	7	100.00	86.28	13.72
Maryland	7	6	85.71	78.20	7.51
Texas	6	4	66.67	85.48	−18.81

WASHINGTON AND LEE UNIVERSITY SCHOOL OF LAW

Office of Admissions, Sydney Lewis Hall
Lexington, VA 24450
Phone: 540.458.8503; Fax: 540.458.8586
E-mail: LawAdm@wlu.edu; Website: www.law.wlu.edu

Introduction

Washington and Lee University School of Law, founded in 1849, is located in Lexington, Virginia, a three-hour interstate highway drive from Washington, DC. The School of Law is fully accredited by the ABA and is a member of the AALS. Washington and Lee is known for providing its students with an academically rigorous and professionally challenging legal education in an environment characterized by a commitment to students, small classes, a very low student-to-faculty ratio, and a collegial community.

The Honor System

The W&L community is governed by an Honor System that is the foundation for academic and student life at the university. The Honor System is an integral part of a professional education that fosters a sensitivity to the ethical imperatives of the legal profession. The Honor System means that the library is always open, exams are unproctored, the exam schedule for upper-level students is flexible, and professors are free to give take-home examinations. The Honor System contributes significantly to a law school environment characterized by mutual respect, trust, and collegiality.

Curriculum

All first-year classes are required. During their first year of law school, students encounter a broad and diverse selection of foundational subjects, setting a solid base for their course of upper-level study. In their second year, students augment several required classes with elective courses. The third year blends classic academic and professional values with a view toward deliberately preparing students for the transition to law practice, and integrates cognitive learning, practical skills, and development of professional identity.

Each semester of the third year begins with intensive preparatory instruction. This two week course is followed by elective offerings in the full range of traditional subject matter, as well as clinical or extern experiences. In realistic settings that simulate actual client experiences, students exercise professional judgment, work in teams, solve problems, counsel clients, negotiate solutions, and serve as advocates and counselors—the full complement of professional skills required to apply legal theory and legal doctrines to real-world issues and serve clients ethically and honorably within the highest traditions of the profession. In addition, a semester-long course on the legal profession is also required. Students can expect rigorous intellectual content, intense evaluation, thoughtful guidance, and meaningful feedback. For additional details about the third-year curriculum, visit www.law.wlu.edu/thirdyear.

Offerings in corporate and business law, international law, health law, and civil and criminal litigation are particularly strong. A wide variety of clinical programs and externships provide opportunities for hands-on experience as part of the academic program. Clinics include the Virginia Capital Case Clearinghouse, established to assist attorneys representing clients charged with or convicted of capital crimes; the Black Lung Legal Clinic, in which students represent coal miners seeking disability benefits under federal law; the Community Legal Practice Center, which provides a range of legal services to qualified area residents; the Tax Clinic, in which students represent low-income taxpayers in controversies with the Internal Revenue Service; the Public Prosecutors Program, in which students assist federal and state prosecutors with investigations, trial preparation, pretrial and trial practice, and appeals; the Criminal Justice Clinic, in which students defend area residents accused of misdemeanors; the Community Law Clinic, through which students focus on resolving legal disputes related to immigration and naturalization; the Judicial Clerkship Program, through which students act as law clerks to trial, appellate, juvenile and domestic relations, and federal bankruptcy judges; and the General Externship Program, through which students may pursue individual placements.

Special Programs

JD/MHA. With Virginia Commonwealth University (VCU) in Richmond, W&L Law offers a program through which students can receive a JD and a Master in Health Administration on an accelerated basis. Dual-degree candidates must be accepted for the program by both VCU and W&L; a portion of the degree requirements are taken on the campus of each university.

LLM in United States Law. W&L Law offers a one-year program in United States law to attorneys who hold a foreign law degree.

Student Activities

Students have four journal opportunities: the *Washington and Lee Law Review*, a quarterly journal for scholarly discussion of legal issues; the *Journal of Civil Rights and Social Justice*, focusing on legal issues having an impact on racial and ethnic minorities; the *Journal of Energy, Climate, and the Environment*, devoted to environmental and natural resources issues and state and federal environmental legislation and regulation; and the *German Law Journal*, an online journal that publishes commentary and scholarship in the fields of German, European, and international law. For more information about extracurricular writing opportunities at W&L Law, please see www.law.wlu.edu/journals.

A variety of moot court and advocacy competitions allow upper-level students to hone advocacy, counseling, negotiation, and trial skills. All second- and third-year students may participate in the moot court competitions.

W&L Law students have established numerous groups such as the Black Law Students Association, Asian Pacific American Law Students Association, Women Law Students Organization, OUTLaw, Jewish Law Students Association, Christian Legal Society, Rationalist Society, Law Families, Federalist Society, American Constitution Society, National Lawyers Guild, and chapters of three national professional fraternities. Practice-oriented groups include the Environmental Law Society, International Law Society, Tax Law Society, Sports and Entertainment Law Society, Public Interest Law Students Association, Students for an Innocence Project, and Intellectual Property and Tech Law Society. Student groups foster a rich intellectual environment at the

School of Law by presenting programs that address issues of special concern to their members.

Admission and Financial Aid

W&L Law actively seeks a diverse student body whose members are of different racial, ethnic, economic, and geographic backgrounds. The admission process is highly individualized. Students are not ranked by any numerical index, nor is there an assigned weight given to any objective or subjective factor presented in the application.

The Admissions Committee considers not only the cumulative undergraduate grade-point average, but also trends in grades, the rigor of an applicant's academic program, the quality of the school attended, the LSAT score, extracurricular activities, community service, evidence of leadership, graduate study, work experience, assessments of recommenders, and any information presented in the applicant's personal statement. Admission officers will interview applicants upon request. Applicants are encouraged to visit the school to sit in on classes, tour the facility, and talk with students and faculty. A generous scholarship endowment allows W&L Law to assist a large percentage of its students with merit-based grant funds.

Career Planning and Professional Development

W&L Law graduates practice in every state and throughout the world. More than 70 percent of recent graduates practice outside Virginia. The three counseling professionals in the Office of Career Planning and Professional Development (OCP) hold JD degrees and work with each student individually to develop a unique career plan. OCP provides instruction in résumé and cover letter writing, networking, and other career development skills. It also provides programming on a wide variety of practice specialties and settings, and acts as a liaison between students and legal employers. Law students interview with prospective employers on campus, at a satellite location in Charlottesville, and at programs throughout the United States. An active and committed alumni network assists students with contacts in every state and a variety of practice areas.

Law Library and Physical Facilities

Sydney Lewis Hall, home of the School of Law, was built in 1976 and expanded in 1991 with the addition of the Lewis F. Powell Jr. Archives, which house the Supreme Court and professional papers of retired Supreme Court Justice Powell, a graduate of the university's college and law school. Wireless Internet access is available throughout the building. Every classroom has been renovated within the past 10 years and is equipped with state-of-the-art technology; the moot courtroom was completely renovated in 2006. The building, including the law library, is open 24 hours a day, 365 days a year.

APPLICANT PROFILE

Washington and Lee University School of Law
This grid includes only applicants who earned 120–180 LSAT scores under standard administrations.

LSAT Score	GPA																					
	3.75 +		3.50–3.74		3.25–3.49		3.00–3.24		2.75–2.99		2.50–2.74		2.25–2.49		2.00–2.24		Below 2.00		No GPA		Total	
	Apps	Adm	Apps	Adm	Apps	Adm	Apps	Adm	Apps	Adm	Apps	Adm	Apps	Adm	Apps	Adm	Apps	Adm	Apps	Adm	Apps	Adm
175–180	5	4	5	5	7	6	6	6	6	4	0	0	0	0	0	0	1	1	0	0	30	26
170–174	36	31	37	30	37	30	31	22	16	13	5	3	5	3	2	0	1	1	3	0	173	133
165–169	111	96	203	176	168	125	110	77	48	23	39	17	14	5	5	2	0	0	15	1	713	522
160–164	336	162	406	51	406	18	207	10	79	1	42	0	19	0	9	0	0	0	30	0	1534	242
155–159	165	18	214	11	194	9	143	3	65	1	40	0	20	0	5	0	1	0	20	0	867	42
150–154	94	5	123	9	156	7	104	7	64	0	33	0	18	0	7	0	3	0	9	0	611	28
145–149	24	0	43	0	68	0	73	1	57	0	46	0	20	0	5	0	1	0	8	0	345	1
140–144	11	0	10	0	32	0	32	0	38	0	31	0	16	0	3	0	0	0	4	0	177	0
135–139	0	0	5	0	13	0	13	0	12	0	8	0	6	0	5	0	1	0	2	0	65	0
130–134	0	0	1	0	2	0	8	0	3	0	7	0	1	0	1	0	1	0	2	0	26	0
125–129	1	0	0	0	1	0	0	0	3	0	2	0	1	0	2	0	0	0	0	0	10	0
120–124	0	0	0	0	0	0	0	0	0	0	0	0	0	0	0	0	0	0	0	0	0	0
Total	783	316	1047	282	1084	195	727	126	391	42	253	20	120	8	44	2	9	2	93	1	4551	994

Apps = Number of Applicants
Adm = Number Admitted
Reflects 99% of the total applicant pool; highest LSAT data reported.

WASHINGTON UNIVERSITY SCHOOL OF LAW

Campus Box 1120, One Brookings Drive
St. Louis, MO 63130-4899
Phone: 314.935.4525; Fax: 314.935.8778
E-mail: admiss@wulaw.wustl.edu; Website: http://law.wustl.edu

ABA
Approved
Since
1923

The Basics

Type of school	Private
Term	Semester
Application deadline	3/1
Application fee	$70
Financial aid deadline	3/1
Can first year start other than fall?	No
Student to faculty ratio	10.2 to 1
# of housing spaces available restricted to law students	
graduate housing for which law students are eligible	1,069

Faculty and Administrators

	Total		Men		Women		Minorities	
	Spr	Fall	Spr	Fall	Spr	Fall	Spr	Fall
Full-time	71	68	33	32	38	36	7	8
Other full-time	0	0	0	0	0	0	0	0
Deans, librarians, & others who teach	13	11	6	5	7	6	2	1
Part-time	74	71	62	55	12	16	7	11
Total	158	150	101	92	57	58	16	20

Curriculum

		Full-Time	Part-Time
Typical first-year section size		97	0
Is there typically a "small section" of the first-year class, other than Legal Writing, taught by full-time faculty		Yes	No
If yes, typical size offered last year		47	
# of classroom course titles beyond first-year curriculum		147	
# of upper division courses, excluding seminars, with an enrollment:	Under 25	107	
	25–49	41	
	50–74	23	
	75–99	8	
	100+	4	
# of seminars		25	
# of seminar positions available		413	
# of seminar positions filled		378	0
# of positions available in simulation courses		1,493	
# of simulation positions filled		1,318	0
# of positions available in faculty supervised clinical courses		110	
# of faculty supervised clinical positions filled	109	0
# involved in field placements	148	0
# involved in law journals	276	0
# involved in moot court or trial competitions	59	0
# of credit hours required to graduate		86	

JD Enrollment and Ethnicity

	Men		Women		Full-Time		Part-Time		1st-Year		Total		JD Degs. Awd.
	#	%	#	%	#	%	#	%	#	%	#	%	
All Hispanics	8	1.5	8	2.3	16	1.8	0	0.0	6	2.2	16	1.8	7
Am. Ind./AK Nat.	4	0.7	0	0.0	4	0.4	0	0.0	0	0.0	4	0.4	1
Asian	53	9.7	48	13.6	98	11.0	3	42.9	36	13.0	101	11.2	32
Black/Af. Am.	54	9.9	56	15.8	110	12.3	0	0.0	42	15.2	110	12.2	19
Nat. HI/Pac. Isl.	0	0.0	0	0.0	0	0.0	0	0.0	0	0.0	0	0.0	0
2 or more races	16	2.9	5	1.4	21	2.4	0	0.0	18	6.5	21	2.3	0
Subtotal (minor.)	135	24.7	117	33.1	249	27.9	3	42.9	102	37.0	252	28.0	59
Nonres. Alien	37	6.8	35	9.9	71	8.0	1	14.3	6	2.2	72	8.0	0
White/Cauc.	301	55.1	170	48.0	468	52.4	3	42.9	158	57.2	471	52.3	124
Unknown	73	13.4	32	9.0	105	11.8	0	0.0	10	3.6	105	11.7	70
Total	546	60.7	354	39.3	893	99.2	7	0.8	276	30.7	900		270

Transfers

Transfers in	32
Transfers out	22

Tuition and Fees

	Resident	Nonresident
Full-time	$44,125	
Part-time		
Tuition Guarantee Program		N

Living Expenses

Estimated living expenses for singles

Living on campus	Living off campus	Living at home
N/A	$20,950	$17,286

ABA
Approved
Since
1923

GPA and LSAT Scores

	Total	Full-Time	Part-Time
# of apps	4,386	4,386	0
# of offers	948	948	0
# of matrics	276	276	0
75% GPA	3.80	3.80	0.00
Median GPA	3.70	3.70	0.00
25% GPA	3.30	3.30	0.00
75% LSAT	168	168	0
Median LSAT	167	167	0
25% LSAT	162	162	0

Grants and Scholarships (from prior year)

	Total		Full-Time		Part-Time	
	#	%	#	%	#	%
Total # of students	856		851		5	
Total # receiving grants	552	64.5	552	64.9	0	0.0
Less than 1/2 tuition	292	34.1	292	34.3	0	0.0
Half to full tuition	235	27.5	235	27.6	0	0.0
Full tuition	8	0.9	8	0.9	0	0.0
More than full tuition	17	2.0	17	2.0	0	0.0
Median grant amount			$20,000		$0	

Informational and Library Resources

Total amount spent on library materials	$1,172,915
Study seating capacity inside the library	486
# of full-time equivalent professional librarians	8
Hours per week library is open	120
# of open, wired connections available to students	814
# of networked computers available for use by students	69
Has wireless network?	Y
Requires computer?	N

JD Attrition (from prior year)

	Academic	Other	Total	
	#	#	#	%
1st year	0	23	23	8.8
2nd year	0	0	0	0.0
3rd year	0	2	2	0.8
4th year	0	0	0	0.0

Employment (9 months after graduation)

	Total	Percentage
Employment status known	289	99.3
Employment status unknown	2	0.7
Employed	278	96.2
Pursuing graduate degrees	9	3.1
Unemployed (seeking, not seeking, or studying for the bar)	1	0.3
Type of Employment		
# employed in law firms	186	66.9
# employed in business and industry	40	14.4
# employed in government	19	6.8
# employed in public interest	10	3.6
# employed as judicial clerks	12	4.3
# employed in academia	2	0.7
Geographic Location		
# employed in state	75	27.0
# employed outside the US	10	3.6
# of states where employed	30	

Bar Passage Rates

First-time takers	278	Reporting %	82.37
Average school %	91.70	Average state %	88.50
Average pass difference	3.20		

Jurisdiction	Takers	Passers	Pass %	State %	Diff %
Missouri	85	82	96.47	91.81	4.66
New York	52	46	88.46	86.51	1.95
Illinois	50	47	94.00	90.89	3.11
California	19	12	63.16	73.19	–10.03
Others (2)	23	23	100.00		

WASHINGTON UNIVERSITY SCHOOL OF LAW

Campus Box 1120, One Brookings Drive
St. Louis, MO 63130-4899
Phone: 314.935.4525; Fax: 314.935.8778
E-mail: admiss@wulaw.wustl.edu; Website: http://law.wustl.edu

Introduction

Washington University School of Law offers its students an outstanding legal education in an intellectually challenging and collegial environment. Our faculty members are recognized for their excellent teaching and scholarship, and they are highly accessible to our students. The School of Law curriculum blends traditional theory with opportunities to participate in a wide variety of lawyering skills courses and cocurricular activities that encourage the development of practical skills and interdisciplinary learning.

Curriculum

Washington University law school offers a broad-based curriculum that highlights applied lawyering skills. A three-year, full-time course of study leads to the JD degree. All first-year students have half their courses in small sections of 45 students or less. These small classes increase the opportunities for participation in class discussions and individualized teacher-student contact. Second- and third-year students choose their own classes and can tailor them to fit their own particular interests. Students may also opt to enroll in courses from other graduate programs at the university and apply up to six credit hours toward the JD requirements. In addition, our Center for Interdisciplinary Studies, the Whitney R. Harris World Law Institute, and other school-sponsored conferences and symposia expose our students to a wide range of nationally and internationally renowned legal scholars.

Library and Physical Facilities

The law school moved into its state-of-the-art facility, Anheuser-Busch Hall, in 1997, and recently expanded into the newly constructed Seigle Hall. Anheuser-Busch Hall also underwent significant renovations in 2008, and both buildings provide well-functioning, vibrant spaces which enhance the law school's sense of community and collaboration. Although the buildings appear traditional, the latest computing and multimedia technologies are incorporated in their design. Cutting-edge information technology provides students with quick access to the Internet where they can register for courses, view grades, order transcripts, view a photo directory of classmates, access their e-mail, and enhance their legal research capabilities. Wireless connections and digital signage are available throughout. The law library is the focal point for much of the intellectual activity at the law school. It has a collection of over 675,000 volumes and provides access to a rich collection of online databases. The library has particularly strong collections in the areas of international law, environmental law, land use planning, urban law, tax law, Chinese law, and Japanese law.

Clinical Opportunities

The School of Law's exceptional Clinical Education Program provides law students with opportunities to learn professional skills and values by working with clients, attorneys, judges, and legislators under the close supervision of experienced and expert faculty. While offering a diverse array of experiences for students, the program also benefits the larger community—locally, nationally, and internationally. The program includes the Civil Justice, Interdisciplinary Environmental, Civil Rights and Community Justice, Government Lawyering, Criminal Justice, Appellate, Judicial Clerkship, and Intellectual Property and Nonprofit Organizations Clinics. The Congressional and Administrative Law Clinic, founded in 1977, offers students the opportunity to spend a semester working in Washington, DC, for a member of the United States Congress, a congressional committee, or a federal administrative agency. Washington University has established an academic partnership with the Brookings Institution in Washington, DC. This affiliation provides research collaborations, internships for students, faculty exchanges, and other mutually beneficial projects in which students may be involved.

Special-Degree Programs

Washington University complements its outstanding JD program with many different joint-degree opportunities. In addition to our formal joint-degree programs, students may design their own joint degrees, combining law and another course of study that leads to a master's degree. Joint degrees offered include a JD/MBA, JD/MSW, and JD/PhD-Political Science. We are one of only a very few joint-degree programs in the nation combining law with an MA in East Asian Studies. The School of Law offers LLM programs in Intellectual Property and Technology Law, Taxation, and US Law for International Students. A combined JD/LLM-Taxation may be completed in six semesters. The law school also offers a unique Trans-Atlantic Law Program in conjunction with several European partner schools, including Utrecht University School of Law in the Netherlands. As part of this program, Washington University students will spend five semesters at the Washington University School of Law, then three semesters at a law school in Europe. At the conclusion, each student will receive a JD from Washington University and an LLM from one of the partner schools.

Study-Abroad Opportunities

The School of Law offers our students the opportunity to study abroad for a semester and provides international law students with the chance to study at our law school. Our students take regular courses at leading international institutions, studying under the legal scholars of the country. Washington University has exchange or study-abroad agreements in place with each of the following law schools: Utrecht University in the Netherlands, University of Pretoria in South Africa, Universidade Catolica Portuguesa in Portugal, Fudan University in China, National University of Singapore, University of KwaZulu-Natal in South Africa, Korea University, National Taiwan University, Queen's University Belfast in Northern Ireland, University of Trento in Italy, and Hong Kong University. The law school also offers the Summer Institute for Global Justice, a six-week, intensive course in Utrecht, the Netherlands, focusing on international and comparative law and the Trans-Atlantic Law Program with Utrecht University.

Student Activities

The School of Law publishes three student-edited law review periodicals: the *Washington University Law Review*, the *Washington University Journal of Law and Policy*, and the *Washington University Global Studies Law Review*. The Trial and Advocacy Program includes a very active moot court program, mock trial competitions, and competitions in negotiation and client counseling. Students are actively involved in over 40 student organizations, including the Women's Law Caucus, Student Bar Association, Black Law Students Association, Latin American Law Students Association, Asian American Law Students Association, Native American Law Students Association, and OUTLAW (gay and lesbian alliance). Students also participate in a number of volunteer public service projects through student organizations or the school's Public Service Project program.

Public Interest

The School of Law has a long-standing commitment to public service and lawyering in the public interest. In addition to its nine clinics, public interest law is supported in a number of different ways: the Webster Society Scholarship provides full tuition for three years and an annual stipend to entering JD students with exemplary academic credentials and an established commitment to public service; summer stipends provide funding for students who work in summer internships in public interest law; the Mel Brown Family Loan Repayment Assistance Program (LRAP) assists graduates beginning their careers in public service positions; the assistant dean of student services coordinates the law school's many public service projects; the director of career services and public interest assists students interested in pursuing careers in the public sector; and the popular Public Interest Law and Policy Speakers Series is offered.

Career Services

Our Career Services Office (CSO) is committed to matching students with outstanding employment opportunities from around the country. The priority is to connect students to the jobs they desire and employers with the students they seek. In addition to hosting extensive fall on-campus and off-campus recruiting programs, the CSO offers a wide range of services throughout the year, including workshops, a mock interview program, and other programming activities. The CSO offers programs on networking and skill development, clerkships, fellowships, researching employers, and a variety of informational sessions on different practice areas. Our graduates move on to many different locations to practice: the class of 2010 relocated to more than 30 different states, the District of Columbia, and several foreign countries. Summer employment is equally diverse. Typically 30 or more states are represented, as well as summer internships in Africa and Asia.

Housing

Students find that the cost of living in St. Louis is much less than in other large metropolitan areas. There is a wide range of affordable housing available near the School of Law. The admission office hosts two "housing days" each summer to assist students in locating housing.

Scholarship and Financial Aid

The school offers merit- and merit/need-based scholarships. Most student aid is in the form of government and privately sponsored loans. Over half the students receive some scholarship assistance; two-thirds receive loans. (Virtually all of those receiving scholarships also receive loans.) The school also offers loan repayment assistance for students who choose qualifying public interest law jobs upon graduation.

APPLICANT PROFILE

Washington University School of Law
This grid includes only applicants who earned 120–180 LSAT scores under standard administrations.

LSAT Score	GPA								
	3.75 +	3.50–3.74	3.25–3.49	3.00–3.24	2.75–2.99	2.50–2.74	2.25–2.49	2.00–2.24	Below 2.00
175–180									
170–174									
165–169									
160–164									
155–159									
150–154									
145–149									
140–144									
135–139									
130–134									
125–129									
120–124									

■ Good Possibility   ■ Possible   ■ Unlikely

WAYNE STATE UNIVERSITY LAW SCHOOL

Admissions Office, 471 West Palmer
Detroit, MI 48202
Phone: 313.577.3937; Fax: 313.993.8129
E-mail: lawinquire@wayne.edu; Website: www.law.wayne.edu

ABA Approved Since 1937

The Basics

Type of school	Public
Term	Semester
Application deadline	3/15
Application fee	$50
Financial aid deadline	3/1
Can first year start other than fall?	No
Student to faculty ratio	13.8 to 1
# of housing spaces available restricted to law students	
graduate housing for which law students are eligible	620

Faculty and Administrators

	Total		Men		Women		Minorities	
	Spr	Fall	Spr	Fall	Spr	Fall	Spr	Fall
Full-time	33	33	22	24	11	9	4	3
Other full-time	5	5	0	0	5	5	1	1
Deans, librarians, & others who teach	4	4	3	3	1	1	1	1
Part-time	24	28	19	23	5	5	1	1
Total	66	70	44	50	22	20	7	6

Curriculum

	Full-Time	Part-Time
Typical first-year section size	74	27
Is there typically a "small section" of the first-year class, other than Legal Writing, taught by full-time faculty	Yes	No
If yes, typical size offered last year	27	
# of classroom course titles beyond first-year curriculum	81	

# of upper division courses, excluding seminars, with an enrollment:		
	Under 25	62
	25–49	21
	50–74	10
	75–99	3
	100+	0

# of seminars		22
# of seminar positions available		404
# of seminar positions filled	230	30
# of positions available in simulation courses		284
# of simulation positions filled	229	46
# of positions available in faculty supervised clinical courses		76
# of faculty supervised clinical positions filled	49	6
# involved in field placements	127	8
# involved in law journals	84	6
# involved in moot court or trial competitions	101	5
# of credit hours required to graduate		86

JD Enrollment and Ethnicity

	Men		Women		Full-Time		Part-Time		1st-Year		Total		JD Degs. Awd.
	#	%	#	%	#	%	#	%	#	%	#	%	
All Hispanics	11	3.2	7	2.6	15	3.1	3	2.3	6	3.1	18	2.9	3
Am. Ind./AK Nat.	3	0.9	2	0.7	3	0.6	2	1.5	2	1.0	5	0.8	2
Asian	12	3.5	21	7.8	27	5.6	6	4.6	15	7.8	33	5.4	8
Black/Af. Am.	21	6.1	20	7.4	20	4.1	21	16.2	7	3.6	41	6.7	7
Nat. HI/Pac. Isl.	0	0.0	0	0.0	0	0.0	0	0.0	0	0.0	0	0.0	0
2 or more races	0	0.0	0	0.0	0	0.0	0	0.0	0	0.0	0	0.0	0
Subtotal (minor.)	47	13.7	50	18.5	65	13.5	32	24.6	30	15.6	97	15.8	20
Nonres. Alien	8	2.3	9	3.3	16	3.3	1	0.8	7	3.6	17	2.8	0
White/Cauc.	250	73.1	189	70.0	354	73.4	85	65.4	139	72.4	439	71.7	105
Unknown	37	10.8	22	8.1	47	9.8	12	9.2	16	8.3	59	9.6	15
Total	342	55.9	270	44.1	482	78.8	130	21.2	192	31.4	612		144

Transfers

Transfers in	7
Transfers out	5

Tuition and Fees

	Resident	Nonresident
Full-time	$24,871	$27,187
Part-time	$13,440	$14,675
Tuition Guarantee Program		N

Living Expenses

Estimated living expenses for singles

Living on campus	Living off campus	Living at home
$22,680	$22,680	$12,470

WAYNE STATE UNIVERSITY LAW SCHOOL

ABA
Approved
Since
1937

GPA and LSAT Scores

	Total	Full-Time	Part-Time
# of apps	1,335	1,219	116
# of offers	596	552	44
# of matrics	197	173	24
75% GPA	3.62	3.62	3.62
Median GPA	3.40	3.41	3.08
25% GPA	3.13	3.19	2.91
75% LSAT	159	159	156
Median LSAT	156	156	155
25% LSAT	153	153	151

Grants and Scholarships (from prior year)

	Total		Full-Time		Part-Time	
	#	%	#	%	#	%
Total # of students	569		457		112	
Total # receiving grants	245	43.1	211	46.2	34	30.4
Less than 1/2 tuition	93	16.3	81	17.7	12	10.7
Half to full tuition	63	11.1	52	11.4	11	9.8
Full tuition	57	10.0	50	10.9	7	6.3
More than full tuition	32	5.6	28	6.1	4	3.6
Median grant amount			$14,782		$6,000	

Informational and Library Resources

Total amount spent on library materials	$1,620,147
Study seating capacity inside the library	382
# of full-time equivalent professional librarians	5
Hours per week library is open	97
# of open, wired connections available to students	203
# of networked computers available for use by students	29
Has wireless network?	Y
Requires computer?	N

JD Attrition (from prior year)

	Academic	Other	Total	
	#	#	#	%
1st year	2	11	13	7.2
2nd year	0	0	0	0.0
3rd year	0	0	0	0.0
4th year	0	0	0	0.0

Employment (9 months after graduation)

	Total	Percentage
Employment status known	183	100.0
Employment status unknown	0	0.0
Employed	152	83.1
Pursuing graduate degrees	5	2.7
Unemployed (seeking, not seeking, or studying for the bar)	16	8.7
Type of Employment		
# employed in law firms	104	68.4
# employed in business and industry	22	14.5
# employed in government	13	8.6
# employed in public interest	3	2.0
# employed as judicial clerks	2	1.3
# employed in academia	8	5.3
Geographic Location		
# employed in state	141	92.8
# employed outside the US	0	0.0
# of states where employed	9	

Bar Passage Rates

First-time takers	161	Reporting %	100.00
Average school %	89.44	Average state %	86.87
Average pass difference	2.57		

Jurisdiction	Takers	Passers	Pass %	State %	Diff %
Michigan	161	144	89.44	86.87	2.57

WAYNE STATE UNIVERSITY LAW SCHOOL

Admissions Office, 471 West Palmer
Detroit, MI 48202
Phone: 313.577.3937; Fax: 313.993.8129
E-mail: lawinquire@wayne.edu; Website: www.law.wayne.edu

Introduction

Wayne State University Law School, founded in 1927, is the only public law school in Detroit, Michigan. Located in the heart of Detroit's historic cultural center, Wayne Law offers a unique urban experience. Detroit's vibrant legal market—including government offices, state and federal courts, multinational corporations, unions, and major law firms—provides students with a wide range of opportunities for employment and internships. Our students are bright, mature, conscientious, and altruistic. They come from unique backgrounds and professions, some having previously served as doctors, musicians, actors, engineers, and law enforcement officers before pursuing the law. Wayne Law also offers a network of more than 11,000 living alumni, including established leaders of the legal community, practicing in every state of the nation and in more than a dozen foreign countries. Our expert faculty's nationally and internationally recognized scholarship adds depth to our students' understanding of legal theory, doctrine, and practice. Wayne Law students, faculty, and alumni are deeply engaged in the community and profession.

The Law School's Setting and Facilities

The Law School is a flagship unit of Wayne State University, a major metropolitan research university located in the heart of Midtown about four miles from downtown Detroit. Within blocks of the Law School are the Detroit Public Library, the Detroit Institute of Arts, the Charles H. Wright Museum of African American History, the Detroit Science Center, and other cultural attractions. The City of Detroit shares an international border with Windsor, Ontario, and offers access to Michigan's largest concentration of law firms and state and federal courts.

The Arthur Neef Law Library

The Arthur Neef Law Library is the second largest academic law library in Michigan and houses one of the nation's fortieth largest legal collections. With over 620,000 volumes, it serves as a major center of legal research in the Detroit and Michigan legal communities and is a designated federal government depository.

The majority of the study space in the recently renovated law library makes use of natural light. The Law School, including the library, is served by a wireless network. In addition, many library study spaces are equipped with communication ports and electrical outlets for the convenient use of notebook computers.

The law library also houses a computer laboratory, featuring personal computers available for the exclusive use of Wayne State law students.

Clinical and Internship Programs

Wayne State University Law School offers its students a broad range of opportunities for practical legal training through its client clinics and its internship programs. The Law School operates six clinics: a Criminal Appellate Practice Clinic, a Disability Law Clinic, an Environmental Law Clinic, a Free Legal Aid Clinic, an Immigration and Asylum Clinic, and a Small Business Enterprises and Nonprofit Corporations Clinic. These clinical offerings give students a chance to take first-chair responsibility in a choice of settings while serving the needs of Detroit's urban community. Students also have the chance to serve as interns for state and federal judges, public prosecutors, the State Appellate Defender's Office, and many nonprofit organizations.

Joint-Degree Programs

Students may pursue joint-degree programs in one of five different areas: business administration, dispute resolution, history, political science, and economics. Joint-degree students must be admitted separately to the Law School and to the appropriate master's degree program at the university. Each joint-degree program requires a student to spend his or her first year taking exclusively law courses, followed by two and one-half to three years of concurrent studies.

Intellectual Property Law Institute

Intellectual property (IP) law and related fields, such as the emerging area of electronic commerce, are among the strengths of the Wayne State law faculty. The Law School offers a tremendous variety of courses and seminars on IP-related subjects. Wayne State law students may take courses at the University of Detroit Mercy and the University of Windsor, just across the river in Canada, through the Intellectual Property Law Institute (IPLI). IPLI, which was created in 1987 as a cooperative effort of these three law schools, offers a rich curriculum for IP-focused students, including courses and seminars in patent, copyright, trademark, computer and related technology, communications and media, and entertainment law.

Program for International Legal Studies

International law cuts across all aspects of a Wayne State legal education. Fully one-third of Wayne Law's tenured and tenure-track faculty teaches and writes on international subjects. Those faculty members enjoy worldwide reputations as innovative and prolific scholars. Students can take classes on a remarkable range of international topics, from international commercial transactions to international environmental law, to the use of military force, and the protection of human rights. Study-abroad programs give students a first-hand view of other nations' legal systems and their approaches to legal education. The Law School also boasts a broad array of internationally oriented student organizations, including a highly successful Jessup International Law Moot Court Competition Team.

Student Activities

Student-Edited Law Journals—Wayne State University Law School publishes two student-edited law journals. The *Wayne Law Review*, a scholarly legal journal with a nationwide circulation, has been published since 1954 by upper-class law students selected on the basis of superior academic achievement and writing ability. The *Journal of Law in Society* publishes articles drawn from an annual spring symposium on topics such as affirmative action, environmental justice, reparations for slavery, school vouchers, and gentrification. Both journals offer an opportunity for students to enhance their research and writing skills, and further their knowledge of the law, while earning law school course credit.

Moot Court—Founded in 1949, Wayne State University's Moot Court program, which helps students hone their written and oral advocacy skills, has evolved into one of the most competitive appellate advocacy programs in the country. Wayne State Moot Court teams compete in many national moot court competitions and have won many competitions, including the National Moot Court Championship in 2003.

Student Trial Advocacy Program—The Student Trial Advocacy Program (STAP) complements Wayne State's extensive offering of skills courses by providing students with instruction and experience in the techniques of trial litigation. Wayne State STAP members have successfully competed in trial advocacy competitions across the country.

Student Organizations—More than 30 student organizations add greatly to the quality of life at the Law School by sponsoring speakers and debates on topics of current interest or in specialized areas of law, jointly sponsoring outreach events for the needy, volunteering their time to public service, and collaborating to produce programs with area practitioners.

Scholarships

Wayne State University Law School is committed to attracting and retaining highly credentialed students while maintaining economic accessibility to legal education and the legal profession. We offer substantial scholarships, and award over $2.8 million in WSU and privately endowed scholarships and grants to students. The Dean's Scholars Program awards 50 percent, 75 percent, and 100 percent tuition scholarships to top students of each incoming class. These awards are renewable yearly if students maintain a GPA above an established minimum. We also offer one-year awards to incoming students and provide scholarships for continuing students based on first-year performance. More than 70 additional scholarships are awarded each year at Honors Convocation based on academic merit, future career plans, or participation in law-related activities.

Housing

As a Wayne Law student, you can live on campus either in the University Towers Apartments, the Chatsworth Apartments, or in the Towers Residential Suites. The top floors of the high-rise tower are reserved for graduate students. The majority of the rooms are suite style. There are also studio rooms available. Within the building are a café-style dining hall, a mini bookstore, and multiple fitness rooms. The Towers feature free Internet access, cable connections, multiple social and study lounges, laundry rooms, and a 24-hour staffed reception area. Students interested in living off campus have many affordable options in the metropolitan Detroit area.

Career Services

Our Career Services Office provides Wayne Law students and alumni with tools, resources, and expertise needed to identify the ideal career path, launch a successful job search, and develop a fulfilling career in, around, or outside of the law. Three professional career counselors help students navigate job searches and offer guidance on balancing the demands of finding a job while in law school. Each of our counselors has a JD, has practiced law, and specializes in counseling students interested in working in government, law firms, courts, corporations, and public interest organizations, as well as pursuing alternative careers.

APPLICANT PROFILE

Wayne State University Law School
This grid includes only applicants who earned 120–180 LSAT scores under standard administrations.

LSAT Score	3.75 +		3.50–3.74		3.25–3.49		3.00–3.24		2.75–2.99		2.50–2.74		2.25–2.49		2.00–2.24		Below 2.00		No GPA		Total	
	Apps	Adm	Apps	Adm	Apps	Adm	Apps	Adm	Apps	Adm	Apps	Adm	Apps	Adm	Apps	Adm	Apps	Adm	Apps	Adm	Apps	Adm
175–180	0	0	1	1	1	1	1	1	1	1	0	0	0	0	0	0	0	0	0	0	4	4
170–174	2	2	3	3	2	1	1	1	0	0	0	0	0	0	1	1	0	0	0	0	9	8
165–169	5	5	7	7	8	8	6	6	8	7	3	3	1	1	0	0	1	0	0	0	39	37
160–164	18	18	41	41	52	51	20	20	13	12	7	7	3	3	1	1	0	0	0	0	155	153
155–159	33	33	62	59	66	61	52	47	27	20	23	14	5	3	2	0	0	0	1	1	271	238
150–154	30	23	60	32	72	23	73	15	45	7	23	4	4	0	6	0	4	0	6	3	323	107
145–149	18	7	36	6	57	5	59	5	41	1	29	1	11	1	3	0	1	0	12	6	267	32
140–144	10	3	17	1	33	1	29	1	30	1	24	2	14	0	4	1	3	0	10	4	174	14
135–139	4	1	10	0	11	0	9	0	15	0	8	0	10	0	3	0	1	0	4	0	75	1
130–134	0	0	1	0	2	0	4	0	6	0	8	0	4	0	4	0	2	0	1	0	32	0
125–129	0	0	0	0	0	0	1	0	2	0	2	0	0	0	3	0	1	0	0	0	9	0
120–124	0	0	0	0	0	0	1	0	0	0	0	0	0	0	1	0	0	0	0	0	2	0
Total	120	92	238	150	304	151	256	96	188	49	127	31	52	8	28	3	13	0	34	14	1360	594

Apps = Number of Applicants
Adm = Number Admitted
Reflects 99% of the total applicant pool; highest LSAT data reported.

WEST VIRGINIA UNIVERSITY COLLEGE OF LAW

101 Law Center Drive, PO Box 6130
Morgantown, WV 26506-6130
Phone: 304.293.5301; Fax: 304.293.8102
E-mail: wvulaw.admissions@mail.wvu.edu; Website: http://law.wvu.edu/

ABA
Approved
Since
1923

The Basics

Type of school	Public
Term	Semester
Application deadline	3/1
Application fee	$50
Financial aid deadline	3/1
Can first year start other than fall?	No
Student to faculty ratio	11.1 to 1
# of housing spaces available restricted to law students	
graduate housing for which law students are eligible	5

Faculty and Administrators

	Total		Men		Women		Minorities	
	Spr	Fall	Spr	Fall	Spr	Fall	Spr	Fall
Full-time	30	32	21	20	9	12	4	5
Other full-time	0	1	0	0	0	1	0	1
Deans, librarians, & others who teach	3	3	1	1	2	2	0	0
Part-time	24	29	13	18	11	11	0	0
Total	57	65	35	39	22	26	4	6

Curriculum

	Full-Time	Part-Time
Typical first-year section size	67	67
Is there typically a "small section" of the first-year class, other than Legal Writing, taught by full-time faculty	Yes	Yes
If yes, typical size offered last year	45	45

# of classroom course titles beyond first-year curriculum		82
# of upper division courses, excluding seminars, with an enrollment:	Under 25	58
	25–49	27
	50–74	10
	75–99	1
	100+	1
# of seminars		18
# of seminar positions available		270
# of seminar positions filled	180	0
# of positions available in simulation courses		397
# of simulation positions filled	350	0
# of positions available in faculty supervised clinical courses		54
# of faculty supervised clinical positions filled	49	0
# involved in field placements	14	0
# involved in law journals	42	0
# involved in moot court or trial competitions	44	0
# of credit hours required to graduate		91

JD Enrollment and Ethnicity

	Men #	Men %	Women #	Women %	Full-Time #	Full-Time %	Part-Time #	Part-Time %	1st-Year #	1st-Year %	Total #	Total %	JD Degs. Awd.
All Hispanics	2	0.8	1	0.6	3	0.7	0	0.0	2	1.5	3	0.7	0
Am. Ind./AK Nat.	1	0.4	2	1.3	3	0.7	0	0.0	1	0.7	3	0.7	0
Asian	3	1.1	3	1.9	6	1.5	0	0.0	3	2.2	6	1.4	5
Black/Af. Am.	13	5.0	11	7.1	24	5.9	0	0.0	10	7.4	24	5.8	8
Nat. HI/Pac. Isl.	0	0.0	0	0.0	0	0.0	0	0.0	0	0.0	0	0.0	0
2 or more races	0	0.0	0	0.0	0	0.0	0	0.0	0	0.0	0	0.0	0
Subtotal (minor.)	19	7.3	17	11.0	36	8.8	0	0.0	16	11.9	36	8.7	13
Nonres. Alien	0	0.0	0	0.0	0	0.0	0	0.0	0	0.0	0	0.0	0
White/Cauc.	243	92.7	137	89.0	374	91.2	6	100.0	119	88.1	380	91.3	113
Unknown	0	0.0	0	0.0	0	0.0	0	0.0	0	0.0	0	0.0	0
Total	262	63.0	154	37.0	410	98.6	6	1.4	135	32.5	416		126

Transfers

Transfers in	10
Transfers out	4

Tuition and Fees

	Resident	Nonresident
Full-time	$14,212	$28,444
Part-time		
Tuition Guarantee Program		N

Living Expenses

Estimated living expenses for singles

Living on campus	Living off campus	Living at home
$14,132	$14,132	$14,132

WEST VIRGINIA UNIVERSITY COLLEGE OF LAW

ABA
Approved
Since
1923

GPA and LSAT Scores

	Total	Full-Time	Part-Time
# of apps	737	737	0
# of offers	339	339	0
# of matrics	137	137	0
75% GPA	3.70	3.70	0.00
Median GPA	3.43	3.43	0.00
25% GPA	3.17	3.17	0.00
75% LSAT	156	156	0
Median LSAT	154	154	0
25% LSAT	151	151	0

Grants and Scholarships (from prior year)

	Total #	Total %	Full-Time #	Full-Time %	Part-Time #	Part-Time %
Total # of students	418		412		6	
Total # receiving grants	185	44.3	185	44.9	0	0.0
Less than 1/2 tuition	105	25.1	105	25.5	0	0.0
Half to full tuition	40	9.6	40	9.7	0	0.0
Full tuition	19	4.5	19	4.6	0	0.0
More than full tuition	21	5.0	21	5.1	0	0.0
Median grant amount			$5,536		$0	

Informational and Library Resources

Total amount spent on library materials	$953,781
Study seating capacity inside the library	406
# of full-time equivalent professional librarians	3
Hours per week library is open	106
# of open, wired connections available to students	140
# of networked computers available for use by students	64
Has wireless network?	Y
Requires computer?	N

JD Attrition (from prior year)

	Academic #	Other #	Total #	Total %
1st year	1	8	9	5.8
2nd year	0	4	4	3.0
3rd year	0	0	0	0.0
4th year	0	0	0	0.0

Employment (9 months after graduation)

	Total	Percentage
Employment status known	151	99.3
Employment status unknown	1	0.7
Employed	136	90.1
Pursuing graduate degrees	11	7.3
Unemployed (seeking, not seeking, or studying for the bar)	1	0.7
Type of Employment		
# employed in law firms	71	52.2
# employed in business and industry	36	26.5
# employed in government	5	3.7
# employed in public interest	4	2.9
# employed as judicial clerks	16	11.8
# employed in academia	3	2.2
Geographic Location		
# employed in state	100	73.5
# employed outside the US	0	0.0
# of states where employed		10

Bar Passage Rates

First-time takers	126	Reporting %	81.75
Average school %	80.58	Average state %	81.46

Average pass difference −0.88

Jurisdiction	Takers	Passers	Pass %	State %	Diff %
West Virginia	96	78	81.25	81.16	0.09
Pennsylvania	7	5	71.43	85.69	−14.26

WEST VIRGINIA UNIVERSITY COLLEGE OF LAW

101 Law Center Drive, PO Box 6130
Morgantown, WV 26506-6130
Phone: 304.293.5301; Fax: 304.293.8102
E-mail: wvulaw.admissions@mail.wvu.edu; Website: http://law.wvu.edu/

Introduction

The College of Law, established in 1878, is the oldest professional school at West Virginia University. The university is located in Morgantown, West Virginia. Within a 500-mile radius of Morgantown is half of the population of the United States and one-third of the population of Canada. The College of Law has been a member of the AALS since 1914 and was fully accredited by the ABA in 1923. The college has had a chapter of the Order of the Coif since 1925.

Library and Physical Facilities

The College of Law facility measures 131,966 square feet and provides a spacious learning community for law students. The law center is home to six classrooms, two courtrooms, a distance learning center, financial aid, career services, and a law bookstore and café. Ample parking at the law center is available by permit for all law students.

The George R. Farmer Jr. Law Library, a three-story, 32,476-square-foot facility with 40,386 feet of shelving space, is home to the largest law library in the state of West Virginia. The law library is comprehensive in scope with a collection of over 300,000 volumes and equivalents. As part of a sustainable strategy the library replaced its 42 computers with virtual desktops that significantly reduced power consumption and facilitates more efficient IT maintenance. This system also enhances network security and includes an additional 17 virtual desktops in the library's Carlin Computer Lab.

The Student Recreation Center is a $34 million, 177,000-square-foot facility complete with two swimming pools and a massive 50-foot climbing wall that stretches up through the center of the three-story building. The center also houses a wellness center, a resource library, a study area, a food-service operation, a small classroom, a meeting/conference room, and socialization areas.

Curriculum

Subject to modification, 91 hours are required for graduation. The 31-hour first-year curriculum is specified. The second- and third-year programs offer a number of course options and possibilities for concentration.

Students have the option, after being admitted, to request enrollment in the part-time program that offers daytime courses congruently with the full-time program. There is not a separate nighttime track.

Student Activities

West Virginia University College of Law has over 30 student organizations. The Student Bar Association is the student government of the school. The *West Virginia Law Review* (http://wvlawreview.wvu.edu) is the fourth oldest student-governed law review in the nation, and selects members on the basis of performance during their first year in law school and a writing competition. An active Moot Court Program is conducted at the law school.

Opportunities for Minority Students

The College of Law is committed to maintaining a diverse student body by welcoming students who are members of groups traditionally underrepresented in the legal profession. The Meredith Career Services Center assists minority students with securing summer employment through a Minority Clerkship Program. The College of Law also participates in the Southeast Minority Job Fair in Atlanta, a regional job fair that brings together employers and minority students. Student organizations, such as the Black Law Students Association, provide additional opportunities for minority students.

Career Services

The Career Services office provides career counseling, professional development workshops, interview programs, and job-search strategy sessions as part of a comprehensive career services program. Our graduates work in diverse settings throughout the United States and abroad, including law firms, courts, government agencies, public service organizations, corporations, and colleges and universities. The goals of the Career Services office are to educate students about possible careers in the law, encourage them to identify and set career goals, and assist them in achieving those goals. Please visit http://law.wvu.edu/career_services for more information.

Admission

The College of Law admits first-year students only in the first (fall) semester. No specific prelaw curriculum is required for admission. The college subscribes to the suggestions on prelaw study in this book and stresses the value of college courses that require extensive analytic skills and writing assignments.

Students are admitted to the College of Law on the basis of previous academic performance, scores on the Law School Admission Test, personal statements, letters of recommendation, and other factors that bear upon the potential professional qualifications of the applicant as determined by the College of Law.

Applications are accepted beginning September 1 of each year for the class to be admitted to begin their studies the following August. Those accepted are required to make a seat deposit within a designated period, but not before April 1. The required seat deposit amount for residents is $200 and $400 for nonresidents, which is credited toward your tuition and fees for the fall semester.

Expenses and Financial Aid

Although WVU's reasonable tuition and fees are an excellent value, the College of Law recognizes that many students may not be able to afford the full cost of a legal education without financial assistance. Limited funds in the form of tuition waivers, scholarships, and college work-study are available each year through the university. Even if the student has not been accepted to the College of Law, he or she should apply for financial aid by March 1. The Free Application for Federal Student Aid (FAFSA) must be completed in order to receive any financial assistance, including all need-based scholarships. Students must complete the FAFSA each year in order to be considered for financial aid.

More information may be obtained by contacting Eric Meadows, Financial Aid Counselor, PO Box 6130, Morgantown, WV 26506-6130; phone: 304.293.5302; e-mail: eric.meadows@mail.wvu.edu.

Housing

The majority of our students live off campus in private housing. The university's Student Life office assists students by providing information about off-campus housing options. You may contact them at 304.293.5611 or visit their website at www.studentlife.wvu.edu.

Clinic Programs

Hands-on training is a key component of our Advanced Lawyering curriculum. Clinical experience prepares students for the practical challenges of legal practice and hones the skills they need to best serve their clients, the profession, and society.

Clinic programs offered include:

- **Civil Clinic**—providing eligible individuals with legal services focused on family law, social security and supplemental security income, and consumer debt relief.
- **The Child, Family, and Health Advocacy Clinic**—offering legal assistance in collaboration with physicians from the WVU Robert C. Byrd Health Sciences Center.
- **Entrepreneurship Law Clinic**—offers start-up companies, small businesses, nonprofits, and individuals legal services in areas of counseling for a product plan or business organization, licensing, employee and contractor agreements, intellectual property, financing and venture capital, planning and negotiation, dispute resolution, and generalized assistance in business formation, planning, and strategy.
- **Immigration Clinic**—provides legal assistance and representation to foreign citizens across the region who are facing deportation, asylum, and other immigration proceedings.
- **Tax Clinic**—offers legal services to taxpayers residing in West Virginia who need to resolve a tax controversy with the Internal Revenue Service. The Law Center is also the future site of the Energy and Sustainability Law Center. One facet of this new program will include a clinic focusing on the area of sustainability.

APPLICANT PROFILE

West Virginia University College of Law
This grid includes only applicants who earned 120–180 LSAT scores under standard administrations.

LSAT Score	3.75 +		3.50–3.74		3.25–3.49		3.00–3.24		2.75–2.99		2.50–2.74		2.25–2.49		2.00–2.24		Below 2.00		No GPA		Total	
	Apps	Adm	Apps	Adm	Apps	Adm	Apps	Adm	Apps	Adm	Apps	Adm	Apps	Adm	Apps	Adm	Apps	Adm	Apps	Adm	Apps	Adm
175–180	0	0	0	0	0	0	0	0	0	0	0	0	0	0	0	0	0	0	0	0	0	0
170–174	2	2	0	0	0	0	0	0	0	0	0	0	0	0	0	0	0	0	0	0	2	2
165–169	0	0	1	1	0	0	2	2	0	0	0	0	0	0	0	0	0	0	0	0	3	3
160–164	9	9	4	4	5	5	6	6	5	5	4	2	0	0	1	0	0	0	2	2	36	33
155–159	18	18	31	31	24	19	30	24	22	12	14	7	6	2	3	0	1	0	1	1	150	114
150–154	34	33	47	37	66	44	60	28	26	5	18	5	13	2	2	0	1	0	3	3	270	157
145–149	23	7	37	7	38	3	32	6	32	1	18	0	5	0	6	1	0	0	5	1	196	26
140–144	5	0	5	0	21	1	13	0	9	0	6	0	7	0	2	0	0	0	1	0	69	1
135–139	1	0	0	0	7	0	6	0	3	0	4	0	3	0	2	0	0	0	1	0	27	0
130–134	0	0	0	0	0	0	4	0	0	0	0	0	1	0	2	0	0	0	1	0	8	0
125–129	0	0	0	0	0	0	1	0	1	0	0	0	0	0	0	0	1	0	0	0	3	0
120–124	0	0	0	0	0	0	0	0	0	0	0	0	0	0	0	0	0	0	0	0	0	0
Total	92	69	125	80	161	72	154	66	98	23	64	14	35	4	18	1	3	0	14	7	764	336

Apps = Number of Applicants
Adm = Number Admitted
Reflects 99% of the total applicant pool; highest LSAT data reported.

WESTERN NEW ENGLAND COLLEGE SCHOOL OF LAW

Office of Admissions, 1215 Wilbraham Road
Springfield, MA 01119-2684
Phone: 800.782.6665, 413.782.1406; Fax: 413.796.2067
E-mail: admissions@law.wnec.edu; Website: www.law.wnec.edu

ABA
Approved
Since
1974

AMERICAN BAR ASSOCIATION
Section of Legal Education
and Admissions to the Bar

The Basics

Type of school	Private
Term	Semester
Application deadline	3/15
Application fee	$50
Financial aid deadline	
Can first year start other than fall?	No
Student to faculty ratio	13.5 to 1
# of housing spaces available restricted to law students	65
graduate housing for which law students are eligible	

Faculty and Administrators

	Total		Men		Women		Minorities	
	Spr	Fall	Spr	Fall	Spr	Fall	Spr	Fall
Full-time	30	30	16	15	14	15	4	4
Other full-time	6	6	3	3	3	3	1	1
Deans, librarians, & others who teach	7	7	5	5	2	2	0	0
Part-time	22	19	19	16	3	3	1	0
Total	65	62	43	39	22	23	6	5

Curriculum

		Full-Time	Part-Time
Typical first-year section size		47	37
Is there typically a "small section" of the first-year class, other than Legal Writing, taught by full-time faculty		No	No
If yes, typical size offered last year			
# of classroom course titles beyond first-year curriculum		124	
# of upper division courses, excluding seminars, with an enrollment:	Under 25	63	
	25–49	37	
	50–74	8	
	75–99	0	
	100+	0	
# of seminars		13	
# of seminar positions available		236	
# of seminar positions filled		152	46
# of positions available in simulation courses		191	
# of simulation positions filled		134	29
# of positions available in faculty supervised clinical courses		70	
# of faculty supervised clinical positions filled		38	6
# involved in field placements		93	11
# involved in law journals		43	8
# involved in moot court or trial competitions		34	0
# of credit hours required to graduate		88	

JD Enrollment and Ethnicity

	Men		Women		Full-Time		Part-Time		1st-Year		Total		JD Degs. Awd.
	#	%	#	%	#	%	#	%	#	%	#	%	
All Hispanics	10	4.2	9	3.2	12	3.1	7	5.1	6	3.5	19	3.6	5
Am. Ind./AK Nat.	0	0.0	0	0.0	0	0.0	0	0.0	0	0.0	0	0.0	2
Asian	7	2.9	9	3.2	14	3.6	2	1.4	5	2.9	16	3.0	9
Black/Af. Am.	3	1.3	9	3.2	8	2.1	4	2.9	2	1.2	12	2.3	5
Nat. HI/Pac. Isl.	0	0.0	0	0.0	0	0.0	0	0.0	0	0.0	0	0.0	0
2 or more races	2	0.8	6	2.1	8	2.1	0	0.0	8	4.7	8	1.5	0
Subtotal (minor.)	22	9.2	33	11.6	42	10.9	13	9.4	21	12.4	55	10.5	21
Nonres. Alien	6	2.5	7	2.5	10	2.6	3	2.2	3	1.8	13	2.5	0
White/Cauc.	188	78.3	212	74.4	302	78.0	98	71.0	134	78.8	400	76.2	120
Unknown	24	10.0	33	11.6	33	8.5	24	17.4	10	5.9	57	10.9	29
Total	240	45.7	285	54.3	387	73.7	138	26.3	168	32.4	525		173

Transfers

Transfers in	1
Transfers out	13

Tuition and Fees

	Resident	Nonresident
Full-time	$36,854	$36,854
Part-time	$27,246	$27,246
Tuition Guarantee Program		N

Living Expenses

Estimated living expenses for singles

Living on campus	Living off campus	Living at home
$20,159	$20,159	$9,151

WESTERN NEW ENGLAND COLLEGE SCHOOL OF LAW

ABA
Approved
Since
1974

GPA and LSAT Scores

	Total	Full-Time	Part-Time
# of apps	1,561	1,317	244
# of offers	789	699	90
# of matrics	168	133	35
75% GPA	3.52	3.55	3.38
Median GPA	3.15	3.19	3.07
25% GPA	2.89	2.90	2.86
75% LSAT	155	155	155
Median LSAT	153	153	153
25% LSAT	151	151	150

Grants and Scholarships (from prior year)

	Total		Full-Time		Part-Time	
	#	%	#	%	#	%
Total # of students	538		389		149	
Total # receiving grants	312	58.0	263	67.6	49	32.9
Less than 1/2 tuition	185	34.4	137	35.2	48	32.2
Half to full tuition	121	22.5	120	30.8	1	0.7
Full tuition	5	0.9	5	1.3	0	0.0
More than full tuition	1	0.2	1	0.3	0	0.0
Median grant amount			$16,000		$5,000	

Informational and Library Resources

Total amount spent on library materials	$1,146,507
Study seating capacity inside the library	482
# of full-time equivalent professional librarians	9
Hours per week library is open	103
# of open, wired connections available to students	13
# of networked computers available for use by students	54
Has wireless network?	Y
Requires computer?	N

JD Attrition (from prior year)

	Academic	Other	Total	
	#	#	#	%
1st year	2	21	23	12.6
2nd year	0	3	3	1.9
3rd year	0	1	1	0.6
4th year	0	0	0	0.0

Employment (9 months after graduation)

	Total	Percentage
Employment status known	170	93.4
Employment status unknown	12	6.6
Employed	131	77.1
Pursuing graduate degrees	9	5.3
Unemployed (seeking, not seeking, or studying for the bar)	27	15.9
Type of Employment		
# employed in law firms	64	48.9
# employed in business and industry	26	19.8
# employed in government	21	16.0
# employed in public interest	4	3.1
# employed as judicial clerks	13	9.9
# employed in academia	3	2.3
Geographic Location		
# employed in state	41	31.3
# employed outside the US	1	0.8
# of states where employed	20	

Bar Passage Rates

First-time takers	179	Reporting %	72.63
Average school %	82.31	Average state %	87.86

Average pass difference −5.55

Jurisdiction	Takers	Passers	Pass %	State %	Diff %
Massachusetts	71	60	84.51	89.77	−5.26
Connecticut	59	47	79.66	85.56	−5.90

WESTERN NEW ENGLAND COLLEGE SCHOOL OF LAW

Office of Admissions, 1215 Wilbraham Road
Springfield, MA 01119-2684
Phone: 800.782.6665, 413.782.1406; Fax: 413.796.2067
E-mail: admissions@law.wnec.edu; Website: www.law.wnec.edu

Introduction

For more than three-quarters of a century, Western New England College School of Law has been preparing men and women to succeed in the legal profession. Fully accredited by the ABA and a member of the AALS, our 7,000 alumni live and work in all 50 states and many foreign countries. They include judges, attorneys practicing in small and large firms, and lawyers for corporations, businesses, nonprofit organizations, and all levels of government. We are located in the heart of the beautiful and vibrant Pioneer Valley on a suburban campus, 90 miles from Boston and 150 miles from New York City.

Western New England College School of Law offers both full-time and part-time programs, each providing a strong, well-rounded curriculum that will enable you to succeed in your career. A distinctive feature of our law school is our personalized, student-centered approach to legal education and professional development. Our first-year section size, purposely among the smallest in the country, promotes effective learning in a challenging but collegial and supportive setting. Our accessible and dedicated faculty create a learning environment that helps every student succeed and reach his or her full potential. It is a wonderful place to begin your legal career.

Admission and Scholarships

Every application is read by members of the Admissions Committee. All facets of the application are carefully considered, including race, gender, language, and educational, social, and economic obstacles overcome in the applicant's pursuit of higher education. We seek candidates with well-developed writing ability and analytical skills who will contribute to classroom discussions and the law school community.

Each year partial-tuition scholarships are awarded to applicants whose credentials and backgrounds suggest they are likely to enrich the life of the School of Law. Partial-tuition scholarships are also awarded on the basis of academic merit. Partial scholarships are available for applicants who demonstrate potential for success and who have overcome cultural, economic, societal, physical, or educational obstacles. All admitted applicants receive automatic scholarship consideration. Typically, at least 50 percent of the entering class receives scholarship assistance.

In addition, several students are awarded full-tuition Oliver Wendell Holmes Jr. Scholarships. The Holmes Scholars usually score in the top 20 percent of the LSAT nationally and finish very near the top of their undergraduate classes. Holmes Scholars receive full-tuition scholarships, with an additional $3,500 research stipend.

The School of Law also offers six Public Interest Scholarships to full-time students, ranging from $16,000 to full tuition, with an additional $3,500 summer stipend. Public Interest Scholars take special public interest courses, have regular meetings with public interest practitioners to discuss current issues in public interest practice, and are mentored in the public interest careers by faculty and members of the Public Interest Advisory Board. The $3,500 stipend supports the required public interest summer internship. The Public Interest Scholars program provides an exceptional opportunity to offset the cost of law school while preparing for a career in public interest lawyering.

Faculty

The 13:1 student-to-faculty ratio, the strong commitment to student learning, and the outstanding credentials of the 38 faculty members provide an outstanding learning environment dedicated to your professional success. The faculty have been educated at many of the nation's most prestigious law schools, and all have practiced law prior to joining our faculty. They all share a love of teaching and take pride in their ability to engage students in rigorous law study in a collaborative, collegial environment. They are productive scholars who are consistently praised by our students for their accessibility.

Curriculum

All required courses, both day and evening, are taught by full-time faculty members. Some upper-level courses are taught through classroom discussions of judicial decisions and statutes. Others are taught through simulations in which students perform the roles of lawyers in lifelike situations and through clinics in which students represent actual clients. Part-time day and evening programs are also available.

Our broad-based curriculum allows students the opportunity to focus their legal studies in many different areas of the law, including tax, public interest, and corporate law. To assist students in preparing for their careers, and selecting among electives, the School of Law offers six concentrations (Business Law, Criminal Law, Estate Planning, International and Comparative Law, Public Interest Law, and Real Estate Law), along with several specializations. For a full list, please reference our website.

We also offer four joint-degree programs:
- JD/MBA (Master of Business Administration) with Western New England College
- JD/MSA (Master of Accounting) with Western New England College
- JD/MSW (Master of Social Work) with Springfield College
- JD/MRP (Master of Regional Planning) with the University of Massachusetts at Amherst

Western New England College School of Law offers a Master of Laws (LLM) in Estate Planning and Elder Law. The part-time evening program will prepare both new and established attorneys to meet the growing demand for estate planning and taxation counseling resulting from the aging baby boomer generation.

Experiential Learning: Clinics, Simulations, and Externships

Clinics and simulation courses are integral components of the curriculum at Western New England College School of Law. Each type of course offers an opportunity to put theory into practice, thereby enhancing advocacy skills and enriching the understanding of core course materials. Students also apply their legal skills through externships.

Clinics provide an opportunity for upper-class students to represent clients with actual legal problems. Currently, the School of Law offers five different clinics in which students can gain valuable lawyering skills, such as legal writing, interviewing, and negotiating. The following clinical opportunities are offered:

- Criminal Law Clinic—students prosecute cases for the Hampden County District Attorney's Office.
- Legal Services Clinic—students work in the office of Western Massachusetts Legal Services, Inc.
- Consumer Law Clinic—students work in the City of Springfield's Consumer Protection Program.
- Real Property Practicum—students work with practitioners in the real estate area.
- Small Business Clinic—students help start-up businesses at the Springfield Enterprise Center's business incubator.

Simulation courses allow students to represent hypothetical clients with challenging legal problems drawn from the experiences of practicing lawyers. Students perform research, prepare legal documents, and negotiate with and argue against role-playing students and faculty.

Externships enable students to work with judges or alongside attorneys in public interest organizations or government agencies. Externs are called upon to perform research and prepare legal documents. Externships allow students to refine their lawyering skills and provide interaction with professionals who can offer advice and career insights. Students receive two or three hours of academic credit for one nonpaying externship.

Western New England College School of Law students compete in many trial, appellate, and negotiation competitions, honing their research, writing, and advocacy skills, and gaining valuable experience. Our teams have won national championships in 2009, 2008, 2006, 2004, and 2001, and numerous regional titles.

Library, Facilities, and the Area

The recently renovated S. Prestley Blake Law Center has a spacious law library, excellent classrooms, and comfortable student study and social space. With a collection of over 400,000 volumes, the Law Library also provides comprehensive access to numerous electronic resources. The School of Law's robust wireless network facilitates research and communication.

The Law Center is located in a residential section of Springfield, on Western New England College's 215-acre campus, with ample, free parking for all students. Springfield is a small city, located in the Pioneer Valley, with a wide array of recreational, social, and cultural attractions. There is a range of affordable off-housing options, as well as some on-campus housing options.

Attending the only law school in western Massachusetts, students have access to a host of externship and clinical opportunities throughout the Massachusetts/Connecticut/New York region, including state and federal courts, the attorney generals of several states, district attorney and state's attorney offices, public defender offices, public interest organizations, and small, medium, and large firms.

Student Activities

Western New England College School of Law students enjoy a strong sense of community and support, strengthened and nurtured by numerous and varied student organizations and cocurricular activities. The Student Bar Association plays a leading role, with elected officers and appointed members to faculty/student committees. There are many other active student organizations, including the Multi-Cultural Law Students Association, the Women's Law Association, OUTlaw, and a variety of groups formed around interests in particular areas of law and practice, including the Health Law Association, the Family Law Association, the Criminal Law Society, and the Real Estate Guild. There is also a productive *Western New England Law Review*, many active moot court teams, and a student newspaper, *Lex Brevis*.

APPLICANT PROFILE

Western New England College School of Law
This grid includes only applicants who earned 120–180 LSAT scores under standard administrations.

LSAT Score	3.75 +		3.50–3.74		3.25–3.49		3.00–3.24		2.75–2.99		2.50–2.74		2.25–2.49		2.00–2.24		Below 2.00		No GPA		Total	
	Apps	Adm	Apps	Adm	Apps	Adm	Apps	Adm	Apps	Adm	Apps	Adm	Apps	Adm	Apps	Adm	Apps	Adm	Apps	Adm	Apps	Adm
175–180	0	0	0	0	0	0	0	0	0	0	0	0	0	0	0	0	0	0	0	0	0	0
170–174	1	1	2	2	0	0	2	2	0	0	0	0	0	0	0	0	0	0	0	0	5	5
165–169	2	2	1	1	2	2	2	1	7	7	1	1	1	1	0	0	2	2	0	0	18	17
160–164	10	10	15	14	13	13	10	10	7	7	8	8	3	3	2	2	2	2	0	0	70	69
155–159	24	24	29	29	37	35	39	37	27	23	18	14	13	13	8	8	3	1	0	0	198	184
150–154	30	30	65	60	97	94	98	89	83	69	44	33	35	22	10	7	2	0	7	5	471	409
145–149	24	12	63	18	104	28	126	28	66	5	50	0	19	0	10	2	6	0	11	1	479	94
140–144	11	0	17	0	33	0	29	0	41	0	28	0	20	0	5	0	1	0	7	0	192	0
135–139	3	0	3	0	9	0	13	0	14	0	9	0	5	0	6	0	3	0	5	0	70	0
130–134	0	0	2	0	3	0	3	0	1	0	5	0	3	0	1	0	1	0	1	0	20	0
125–129	0	0	1	0	0	0	0	0	0	0	3	0	1	0	0	0	2	0	1	0	8	0
120–124	0	0	0	0	0	0	0	0	0	0	0	0	0	0	0	0	0	0	0	0	0	0
Total	105	79	198	124	298	172	322	167	246	111	166	56	100	39	42	19	22	5	32	6	1531	778

Apps = Number of Applicants
Adm = Number Admitted
Reflects 99% of the total applicant pool; highest LSAT data reported.

WESTERN STATE UNIVERSITY—COLLEGE OF LAW

1111 North State College Boulevard
Fullerton, CA 92831
Phone: 800.WSU.4LAW, 714.459.1101; Fax: 714.441.1748
E-mail: adm@wsulaw.edu; Website: www.wsulaw.edu

ABA
Approved
Since
2005

The Basics

Type of school	Private	
Term	Semester	
Application deadline	6/1	12/1
Application fee	$50	
Financial aid deadline	3/1	10/15
Can first year start other than fall?	Yes	
Student to faculty ratio	22.0 to 1	
# of housing spaces available restricted to law students		
graduate housing for which law students are eligible		

Faculty and Administrators

	Total		Men		Women		Minorities	
	Spr	Fall	Spr	Fall	Spr	Fall	Spr	Fall
Full-time	14	14	11	10	3	4	3	4
Other full-time	2	2	2	0	0	2	0	1
Deans, librarians, & others who teach	15	14	7	6	8	8	3	3
Part-time	25	16	14	11	11	5	7	3
Total	56	46	34	27	22	19	13	11

Curriculum

	Full-Time	Part-Time
Typical first-year section size	59	33
Is there typically a "small section" of the first-year class, other than Legal Writing, taught by full-time faculty	No	No
If yes, typical size offered last year		
# of classroom course titles beyond first-year curriculum		68

# of upper division courses, excluding seminars, with an enrollment:	Under 25	51
	25–49	30
	50–74	3
	75–99	0
	100+	0

	Full-Time	Part-Time
# of seminars		9
# of seminar positions available		155
# of seminar positions filled	60	22
# of positions available in simulation courses		359
# of simulation positions filled	131	70
# of positions available in faculty supervised clinical courses		45
# of faculty supervised clinical positions filled	7	4
# involved in field placements	42	13
# involved in law journals	22	8
# involved in moot court or trial competitions	26	7
# of credit hours required to graduate		88

JD Enrollment and Ethnicity

	Men		Women		Full-Time		Part-Time		1st-Year		Total		JD Degs. Awd.
	#	%	#	%	#	%	#	%	#	%	#	%	
All Hispanics	30	12.2	40	18.0	46	14.5	24	16.0	48	20.2	70	15.0	6
Am. Ind./AK Nat.	1	0.4	3	1.4	3	0.9	1	0.7	4	1.7	4	0.9	0
Asian	39	15.9	31	14.0	57	17.9	13	8.7	36	15.1	70	15.0	16
Black/Af. Am.	6	2.4	19	8.6	12	3.8	13	8.7	13	5.5	25	5.3	1
Nat. HI/Pac. Isl.	0	0.0	2	0.9	1	0.3	1	0.7	0	0.0	2	0.4	0
2 or more races	5	2.0	3	1.4	3	0.9	5	3.3	2	0.8	8	1.7	0
Subtotal (minor.)	81	32.9	98	44.1	122	38.4	57	38.0	103	43.3	179	38.2	23
Nonres. Alien	2	0.8	0	0.0	2	0.6	0	0.0	1	0.4	2	0.4	1
White/Cauc.	153	62.2	120	54.1	188	59.1	85	56.7	131	55.0	273	58.3	45
Unknown	10	4.1	4	1.8	6	1.9	8	5.3	3	1.3	14	3.0	10
Total	246	52.6	222	47.4	318	67.9	150	32.1	238	50.9	468		79

Transfers

Transfers in	5
Transfers out	10

Tuition and Fees

	Resident	Nonresident
Full-time	$35,190	$35,190
Part-time	$23,630	$23,630
Tuition Guarantee Program		N

Living Expenses

Estimated living expenses for singles

Living on campus	Living off campus	Living at home
N/A	$24,832	$18,555

WESTERN STATE UNIVERSITY—COLLEGE OF LAW

ABA
Approved
Since
2005

GPA and LSAT Scores

	Total	Full-Time	Part-Time
# of apps	2,025	1,588	450
# of offers	1,131	925	206
# of matrics	242	174	68
75% GPA	3.36	3.35	3.40
Median GPA	3.12	3.10	3.17
25% GPA	2.83	2.84	2.80
75% LSAT	153	152	153
Median LSAT	150	150	150
25% LSAT	148	148	148

Grants and Scholarships (from prior year)

	Total		Full-Time		Part-Time	
	#	%	#	%	#	%
Total # of students	417		276		141	
Total # receiving grants	239	57.3	155	56.2	84	59.6
Less than 1/2 tuition	134	32.1	81	29.3	53	37.6
Half to full tuition	52	12.5	37	13.4	15	10.6
Full tuition	40	9.6	28	10.1	12	8.5
More than full tuition	13	3.1	9	3.3	4	2.8
Median grant amount			$15,520		$7,500	

Informational and Library Resources

Total amount spent on library materials	$868,843
Study seating capacity inside the library	336
# of full-time equivalent professional librarians	12
Hours per week library is open	109
# of open, wired connections available to students	0
# of networked computers available for use by students	37
Has wireless network?	Y
Requires computer?	N

JD Attrition (from prior year)

	Academic	Other	Total	
	#	#	#	%
1st year	56	16	72	39.8
2nd year	22	0	22	17.3
3rd year	3	0	3	3.6
4th year	0	0	0	0.0

Employment (9 months after graduation)

	Total	Percentage
Employment status known	82	93.2
Employment status unknown	6	6.8
Employed	62	75.6
Pursuing graduate degrees	1	1.2
Unemployed (seeking, not seeking, or studying for the bar)	17	20.7
Type of Employment		
# employed in law firms	35	56.5
# employed in business and industry	19	30.6
# employed in government	4	6.5
# employed in public interest	2	3.2
# employed as judicial clerks	0	0.0
# employed in academia	2	3.2
Geographic Location		
# employed in state	54	87.1
# employed outside the US	0	0.0
# of states where employed	6	

Bar Passage Rates

First-time takers	92	Reporting %	100.00
Average school %	51.09	Average state %	73.88

Average pass difference −22.79

Jurisdiction	Takers	Passers	Pass %	State %	Diff %
California	86	41	47.67	73.19	−25.52
New Jersey	2	2	100.00	83.64	16.36
Nevada	1	1	100.00	73.00	27.00
New York	1	1	100.00	86.51	13.49
Others (2)	2	2	100.00		

The information on these pages was provided by the law school.

WESTERN STATE UNIVERSITY—COLLEGE OF LAW

1111 North State College Boulevard
Fullerton, CA 92831
Phone: 800.WSU.4LAW, 714.459.1101; Fax: 714.441.1748
E-mail: adm@wsulaw.edu; Website: www.wsulaw.edu

Introduction

Western State University (WSU) College of Law, founded in 1966, is the oldest law school in Orange County, Southern California. Our 11,000 graduates have distinguished themselves as jurists, lawmakers, district attorneys, public defenders, and civil practitioners; they constitute a strong alumni network that mentors and enables an enviable job placement record for WSU graduates. Located in the college town of Fullerton, in the heart of the vibrant economy and healthy legal market of Orange County, the WSU campus is about 30 miles south of Los Angeles and 100 miles north of San Diego. It is within commuting distance of the greater Los Angeles/Orange County metropolitan areas, the fast-growing Inland Empire, and the Southland's beach cities and high technology, finance, and business centers. A private law school of fewer than 500 students, WSU offers small class sizes, personal interaction with faculty, and an extraordinary, supportive learning environment. Repeatedly cited as one of the most ethnically diverse law school student bodies in the country, WSU is also known for giving students practical hands-on lawyering experience along with a strong academic foundation.

Faculty

WSU prides itself on a faculty of excellent professors whose first priority is teaching and student success. Most bring extensive real-world legal experience to the classroom in addition to their strong academic and teaching credentials. The full-time faculty is supplemented by an outstanding adjunct faculty of practicing attorneys and judges. With a student-to-faculty ratio below 20 to 1, and a highly accessible faculty, students benefit from individualized attention and mentoring.

Curriculum and Special Programs

WSU offers a full-time program that is normally completed in three academic years and part-time day or evening programs that take four full years. Students may start in any of the programs in the fall. WSU also offers a January-start, part-time evening program; students in good standing may transition to full time in the fall. The Business Law Center and Criminal Law Practice Center programs give students the option to focus their electives to earn a Certificate in Business Law or Criminal Law with a notation on their transcript indicating their special study emphasis.

In addition to required and elective coursework, the centers also bring distinguished speakers to campus, arrange student visits to criminal justice facilities or business venues, and provide connections to practitioners, including internship and externship opportunities and career networking. The on-site Legal Clinic functions as a small law practice, where student attorneys under supervision of the clinic director represent clients in the community, managing the cases from start to finish, including all court proceedings. In 2011, an Immigration Clinic will be initiated.

In the externship program, students receive placements in courts or in the offices of district attorneys, public defenders, practicing attorneys, corporate legal departments, or public

interest organizations where they gain hands-on experience and earn academic credit.

Student Body and Organizations

WSU has a diverse student body of about 500 students, with an entering class of approximately 200 students. Minority enrollment constitutes over a third of the total, with an even enrollment of men and women. The fall 2010 class entered from 92 different undergraduate institutions and about 20 percent came from 20 different states outside California. About 15 active student-led organizations enrich and complement the academic program with their cocurricular educational, networking, philanthropic, and social activities for students. These include the Student Bar Association, Asian Pacific American Law Student Association, Black Law Student Association, Latino Student Bar Association, Christian Legal Society, Business Law Association, Entertainment Sports Law Society, Gay and Lesbian Organization, Criminal Law Association, and Trial Lawyers Association. Students who qualify for the law review and moot court team gain high-visibility legal writing and competitive advocacy experience.

Library and Physical Facilities

The library has over 200,000 volumes as well as access to electronic resources on campus and remotely. Students may use the library's 45 computers, including 25 located in a large computer classroom, or the wireless network. The library has 16 study rooms that may be used by students for group or individual study. The library maintains long hours to service the needs of our students. Our librarians provide extensive reference services and training in legal research, online research, and software. WSU's campus is located in the heart of Fullerton's university district and consists of a four-story main building and the three-level library, with on-site parking. Most areas of both buildings are covered by Wi-Fi. The main building contains classrooms, the modern Frank and Marleen Darras Moot Court Room, an administrative suite, faculty offices, a student lounge, and café.

Admission

All applicants are assigned to an admission advisor who assists in the admission process, may conduct a personal or telephone informational interview, and arranges for visits to the campus and contact with professors, students, or alumni. Each applicant's entire file is reviewed; admission decisions are made by a faculty committee. A bachelor's degree is required for admission. A personal statement and two letters of recommendation are required, and a résumé is encouraged. Details of the applicant's undergraduate record and LSAT score, writing ability, and maturing life and work experiences are key indicators of potential for success in law school. When there are multiple LSAT scores, the highest, most recent score may be accorded significant weight.

Western State University—College of Law
Admission is on a rolling basis, but application by April 1 for fall, and October 1 for spring, is highly encouraged.

Scholarships and Financial Aid

WSU offers generous merit-based scholarships, and in the 2010 entering class about 40 percent of new students received scholarships. No separate application is required. Admitted students are automatically considered for merit scholarships based on academic predictors (undergraduate track record and LSAT score). After the first year, law students are eligible to compete for merit scholarships provided they rank within the top 30 percent. A full range of loan programs is available to complement students' financial needs, including Stafford loans, Perkins loans, and private loans. All students receiving scholarship funds or loans should plan to file the FAFSA and a preliminary financial aid application.

Career Services and Placement

With a 45-year history in Southern California and an influential alumni network of over 11,000 graduates, WSU has a strong placement track record and the connections to assist students in their job search. The most recent class found employment as follows: 76 percent in private practice, 13 percent in business and industry, 6 percent in government, 1 percent in public service, and 4 percent in academia. The active Career Services Office arranges on-campus interviews, career-related workshops, speaker panels, networking events, and individual counseling to help educate students about the many possible areas of practice and how to secure employment. The office serves as a liaison with legal employers, both public and private. It solicits job listings from alumni and local practitioners and assists students with permanent and summer employment. The Career Resource Center provides students with reference materials and counseling on résumé writing, job-search techniques, and study-abroad programs. Convenient online job and résumé posting services are provided by WSU to facilitate employment searches by students and alumni. WSU alumni mentor students and recent graduates. Additionally, alumni assist with on-campus career fairs, mock interviews, and networking events.

Contact Us

We encourage you to visit our website, speak to an admission advisor, and arrange to visit WSU in person, so that you can sit in on a class and meet with students, alumni, and professors. Experience the personal attention and support, great learning environment, and dedication to student success which set WSU apart.

APPLICANT PROFILE

Western State University—College of Law
This grid includes only applicants who earned 120–180 LSAT scores under standard administrations.

LSAT Score	3.75 +		3.50–3.74		3.25–3.49		3.00–3.24		2.75–2.99		2.50–2.74		2.25–2.49		2.00–2.24		Below 2.00		No GPA		Total	
	Apps	Adm	Apps	Adm	Apps	Adm	Apps	Adm	Apps	Adm	Apps	Adm	Apps	Adm	Apps	Adm	Apps	Adm	Apps	Adm	Apps	Adm
175–180	0	0	0	0	0	0	0	0	0	0	0	0	0	0	0	0	0	0	0	0	0	0
170–174	0	0	0	0	0	0	0	0	0	0	1	1	0	0	0	0	0	0	0	0	1	1
165–169	1	1	0	0	1	0	1	1	1	1	2	2	0	0	0	0	2	0	0	0	8	5
160–164	2	2	7	7	4	4	11	11	5	5	9	7	5	2	2	1	2	0	0	0	47	39
155–159	19	17	29	29	43	43	39	36	39	35	27	22	17	11	7	0	2	0	2	2	224	195
150–154	25	24	47	42	117	112	134	128	118	105	73	58	43	25	19	1	6	0	8	7	590	502
145–149	22	15	50	40	109	84	124	85	132	52	71	23	36	0	20	0	2	0	11	3	577	302
140–144	8	0	16	0	33	0	50	0	64	0	56	0	26	0	11	0	1	0	8	0	273	0
135–139	4	0	4	0	9	0	14	0	21	0	13	0	10	0	6	0	4	0	2	0	87	0
130–134	0	0	1	0	2	0	4	0	5	0	4	0	3	0	3	0	1	0	1	0	24	0
125–129	0	0	0	0	0	0	0	0	0	0	0	0	0	0	0	0	0	0	0	0	0	0
120–124	0	0	0	0	0	0	0	0	0	0	0	0	0	0	0	0	0	0	0	0	0	0
Total	81	59	154	118	318	243	377	261	385	198	256	113	140	38	68	2	20	0	32	12	1831	1044

Apps = Number of Applicants
Adm = Number Admitted
Reflects 99% of the total applicant pool; highest LSAT data reported.

WHITTIER LAW SCHOOL

3333 Harbor Boulevard
Costa Mesa, CA 92626
Phone: 714.444.4141, ext. 123; Fax: 714.444.0250
E-mail: info@law.whittier.edu; Website: www.law.whittier.edu

ABA
Approved
Since
1978

The Basics

Type of school	Private
Term	Semester
Application deadline	7/11
Application fee	$60
Financial aid deadline	5/1
Can first year start other than fall?	Yes
Student to faculty ratio	16.5 to 1
# of housing spaces available	
restricted to law students	
graduate housing for which law students are eligible	

Faculty and Administrators

	Total		Men		Women		Minorities	
	Spr	Fall	Spr	Fall	Spr	Fall	Spr	Fall
Full-time	28	31	11	13	17	18	15	14
Other full-time	0	0	0	0	0	0	0	0
Deans, librarians, & others who teach	12	12	4	4	8	8	7	7
Part-time	15	18	10	8	5	10	4	6
Total	55	61	25	25	30	36	26	27

Curriculum

	Full-Time	Part-Time
Typical first-year section size	78	47
Is there typically a "small section" of the first-year class, other than Legal Writing, taught by full-time faculty	No	No
If yes, typical size offered last year		
# of classroom course titles beyond first-year curriculum	114	

# of upper division courses, excluding seminars, with an enrollment:		
	Under 25	125
	25–49	20
	50–74	11
	75–99	1
	100+	0

# of seminars	38	
# of seminar positions available	968	
# of seminar positions filled	296	78
# of positions available in simulation courses	918	
# of simulation positions filled	371	59
# of positions available in faculty supervised clinical courses	100	
# of faculty supervised clinical positions filled	24	7
# involved in field placements	129	16
# involved in law journals	77	13
# involved in moot court or trial competitions	47	47
# of credit hours required to graduate	87	

JD Enrollment and Ethnicity

	Men		Women		Full-Time		Part-Time		1st-Year		Total		JD Degs. Awd.
	#	%	#	%	#	%	#	%	#	%	#	%	
All Hispanics	35	11.0	44	13.6	53	11.2	26	15.6	39	13.0	79	12.3	16
Am. Ind./AK Nat.	3	0.9	2	0.6	5	1.1	0	0.0	3	1.0	5	0.8	0
Asian	53	16.6	50	15.5	73	15.4	30	18.0	60	20.0	103	16.0	23
Black/Af. Am.	6	1.9	14	4.3	12	2.5	8	4.8	7	2.3	20	3.1	1
Nat. HI/Pac. Isl.	0	0.0	0	0.0	0	0.0	0	0.0	0	0.0	0	0.0	0
2 or more races	0	0.0	0	0.0	0	0.0	0	0.0	0	0.0	0	0.0	0
Subtotal (minor.)	97	30.4	110	34.1	143	30.1	64	38.3	109	36.3	207	32.2	40
Nonres. Alien	1	0.3	1	0.3	2	0.4	0	0.0	0	0.0	2	0.3	0
White/Cauc.	153	48.0	134	41.5	227	47.8	60	35.9	158	52.7	287	44.7	63
Unknown	68	21.3	78	24.1	103	21.7	43	25.7	33	11.0	146	22.7	31
Total	319	49.7	323	50.3	475	74.0	167	26.0	300	46.7	642		135

Transfers

Transfers in	4
Transfers out	24

Tuition and Fees

	Resident	Nonresident
Full-time	$37,975	$37,975
Part-time	$25,325	$25,325
Tuition Guarantee Program	N	

Living Expenses

Estimated living expenses for singles

Living on campus	Living off campus	Living at home
N/A	$23,230	$23,230

WHITTIER LAW SCHOOL

*ABA
Approved
Since
1978*

GPA and LSAT Scores

	Total	Full-Time	Part-Time
# of apps	2,165	1,805	360
# of offers	1,122	987	135
# of matrics	303	256	47
75% GPA	3.28	3.30	3.21
Median GPA	3.02	3.04	2.98
25% GPA	2.75	2.76	2.73
75% LSAT	154	154	154
Median LSAT	152	152	152
25% LSAT	150	150	150

Grants and Scholarships (from prior year)

	Total		Full-Time		Part-Time	
	#	%	#	%	#	%
Total # of students	591		450		141	
Total # receiving grants	314	53.1	234	52.0	80	56.7
Less than 1/2 tuition	265	44.8	201	44.7	64	45.4
Half to full tuition	28	4.7	18	4.0	10	7.1
Full tuition	18	3.0	14	3.1	4	2.8
More than full tuition	3	0.5	1	0.2	2	1.4
Median grant amount			$9,000		$7,000	

Informational and Library Resources

Total amount spent on library materials	$836,498
Study seating capacity inside the library	386
# of full-time equivalent professional librarians	7
Hours per week library is open	102
# of open, wired connections available to students	223
# of networked computers available for use by students	89
Has wireless network?	Y
Requires computer?	Y

JD Attrition (from prior year)

	Academic	Other	Total	
	#	#	#	%
1st year	62	43	105	34.3
2nd year	3	2	5	4.3
3rd year	1	3	4	2.7
4th year	1	0	1	3.8

Employment (9 months after graduation)

	Total	Percentage
Employment status known	150	99.3
Employment status unknown	1	0.7
Employed	125	83.3
Pursuing graduate degrees	9	6.0
Unemployed (seeking, not seeking, or studying for the bar)	10	6.7
Type of Employment		
# employed in law firms	78	62.4
# employed in business and industry	33	26.4
# employed in government	6	4.8
# employed in public interest	6	4.8
# employed as judicial clerks	1	0.8
# employed in academia	1	0.8
Geographic Location		
# employed in state	111	88.8
# employed outside the US	0	0.0
# of states where employed	11	

Bar Passage Rates

First-time takers	167	Reporting %	76.65
Average school %	65.61	Average state %	74.01

Average pass difference −8.40

Jurisdiction	Takers	Passers	Pass %	State %	Diff %
California	114	71	62.28	73.19	−10.91
Nevada	4	3	75.00	73.00	2.00
Colorado	2	2	100.00	85.67	14.33
Washington	2	2	100.00	74.42	25.58
Others (6)	6	6	100.00		

WHITTIER LAW SCHOOL

3333 Harbor Boulevard
Costa Mesa, CA 92626
Phone: 714.444.4141, ext. 123; Fax: 714.444.0250
E-mail: info@law.whittier.edu; Website: www.law.whittier.edu

Introduction

Whittier Law School was founded in 1966 as Beverly Law School. In 1975, the Law School became part of Whittier College, established by Quakers in 1887. The Law School is located in Costa Mesa, Orange County. Orange County, ranked among the top business centers in the United States, is home to over 10,000 lawyers, more lawyers than half the states in the nation. The Law School is 30 miles south of downtown Los Angeles, 100 miles north of San Diego, and minutes away from the local beach cities such as Huntington Beach and Newport Beach. Ideally situated, the Law School enjoys the vibrant economies produced within each area as well as within Orange County. The Whittier tradition stresses concern for individual student's intellectual and ethical development. This tradition is reflected in admission practices stressing diversity, a small student-to-faculty ratio, small elective classes, and individual student counseling and placement services.

Part-Time Programs

In addition to the traditional three-year, full-time program, the JD can also be completed in four years, including two summer sessions, in the flexible day or evening programs. First- and second-year, part-time students generally attend classes three days a week. Standards for admission and retention are identical for all students, and the full-time faculty serves both programs.

Admission and Scholarships

In addition to the LSAT score and undergraduate GPA, subjective factors such as undergraduate school, major, graduate work, ethnic and economic background, work experience, and personal accomplishments are considered. Applicants are encouraged to discuss these factors in their written personal statements. The admission office automatically considers all applicants for merit-based scholarships.

Special Programs

Center for Children's Rights (CCR)—The center enrolls up to 20 students yearly who receive fellowships and summer stipends to prepare for careers in children's rights advocacy. Fellows participate in special classes, colloquiums, symposiums, and externships. The center also sponsors the National Juvenile Law Moot Court Competition and the *Whittier Journal of Children and Family Advocacy*. The center also awards CCR Fellowships.

Center for Intellectual Property Law—The center provides students and practitioners with academic instruction in intellectual property law. The cornerstones of the center are the Certificate Program, the Summer Institute, and the Distinguished Speaker Series. The center also awards IP Fellowships.

Center for International and Comparative Law (CICL)—The center allows students to participate in a specialized legal writing course, attend the International Law Symposium and Colloquia series, and receive a certificate by enrolling in courses offered through the center. The center also awards CICL Fellowships.

Clinics—Whittier Law School boasts four clinics: the Children's Advocacy Clinic, the Special Education Clinic, the Family Violence Clinic, and the "clientless" Legal Policy Clinic.

Exchange Programs in France and Spain—Students with some knowledge of French or Spanish can spend one semester at the University of Paris X in Nanterre, France; the University of Cantabria in Santander, Spain; or the University of Seville, Spain.

Summer-Abroad Programs—The Law School offers six summer study-abroad programs approved by the ABA. Students from around the country can choose to study at the prestigious Bar-Ilan University in Tel Aviv, Israel; the University of Cantabria in Santander, Spain; the University of Toulouse in Toulouse, France; the University of Nanjing in Nanjing, China; Iberoamericana University in Mexico City, Mexico; or Universidad de Barcelona in Barcelona, Spain.

Institute of Student and Graduate Academic Support—Full-time professors provide a comprehensive program of instruction and individual attention—the academic support students need to succeed in their courses, on the bar examination, and in the practice of law. The institute provides a year-long program, Student Academic Support Center, nationally recognized bar preparation program, and true open-door policy. From the first day of orientation, through graduation and beyond, the institute is committed to making our students' law school experience a success.

Institute of Legal Writing and Professional Skills—The specialized program teaches students how to write and conduct themselves well as lawyers. With this institute, our students have proven to be more prepared to perform at summer jobs, as well as to enter practice generally, than students from many schools throughout the state. The institute also offers three specialized writing courses in the first-year curriculum for the Center for Children's Rights, Center for Intellectual Property Law, and the Center for International and Comparative Law.

Concentrations in business and criminal law are also offered.

Library and Physical Facilities

Whittier Law School is located in the city of Costa Mesa on a beautiful 15-acre campus with exceptional facilities, including one of the largest academic law research libraries in the region. The Law School is composed of four buildings that are completely accessible to people with disabilities, totaling 130,000 square feet, and offers plentiful on-site parking. With over 380,000 volumes, the library has a rapidly growing legal research collection and serves as a state and federal depository. Three student computer labs support a variety of software to aid students with computer-assisted instruction, online legal research, and Internet access. Numerous conference rooms are available for group study. The entire facility is equipped with wireless Internet access for individual study.

Student Activities

The *Whittier Law Review* is open to students on the basis of grades and a writing competition, and members participate in the annual Health Law and International Law Symposia.

The *Whittier Journal of Child and Family Advocacy*, a student-run scholarly publication focusing on topics related to juvenile and family law, is one of the few journals of its kind in the nation.

Members of the Moot Court Honors Board and the Trial Advocacy Honors Board utilize written and oral advocacy skills to represent the Law School in regional and national trial and appellate advocacy competitions.

The Student Bar Association's activities include support of various social functions and participation in student-faculty committees for school governance. Numerous other student organizations represent various ethnic groups and legal specialties.

Externships and Career Services

Whittier Law School provides assistance to students and alumni in obtaining clerkships, externships, and attorney positions. The Law School offers a variety of externships with trial and appellate judges, governmental agencies, private firms, corporate legal departments, and public interest organizations. The Career Services Office assists in résumé-building exercises, career goal identification, and career-planning strategies. Additional services include on-campus interviews, a mentor program, panels and symposia on career-related topics, a comprehensive library of career resources, and a mock interview program.

APPLICANT PROFILE

Whittier Law School
This grid includes only applicants who earned 120–180 LSAT scores under standard administrations.

LSAT Score	3.75 +		3.50–3.74		3.25–3.49		3.00–3.24		2.75–2.99		2.50–2.74		2.25–2.49		2.00–2.24		Below 2.00		No GPA		Total	
	Apps	Adm	Apps	Adm	Apps	Adm	Apps	Adm	Apps	Adm	Apps	Adm	Apps	Adm	Apps	Adm	Apps	Adm	Apps	Adm	Apps	Adm
175–180	0	0	1	1	0	0	0	0	0	0	0	0	0	0	0	0	0	0	0	0	1	1
170–174	0	0	0	0	0	0	0	0	4	4	0	0	0	0	0	0	0	0	0	0	4	4
165–169	0	0	0	0	1	1	3	3	3	3	6	6	1	1	1	1	1	1	1	0	17	16
160–164	3	2	8	6	16	15	20	19	12	12	19	18	7	6	5	3	0	0	1	1	91	82
155–159	20	19	36	34	56	53	66	63	44	40	44	37	26	22	4	2	1	0	2	2	299	272
150–154	20	18	66	57	154	137	158	144	141	106	105	74	45	26	18	6	8	1	8	8	723	577
145–149	21	13	57	36	102	42	139	34	127	16	81	3	45	1	15	0	2	0	7	1	596	146
140–144	10	0	17	0	35	2	58	0	58	0	45	0	30	0	8	0	3	0	8	0	272	2
135–139	2	0	2	0	10	0	15	0	13	0	15	0	11	0	4	0	4	0	4	0	80	0
130–134	0	0	0	0	3	0	5	0	7	0	2	0	2	0	5	0	0	0	3	0	27	0
125–129	0	0	0	0	0	0	0	0	0	0	3	0	1	0	1	0	0	0	0	0	5	0
120–124	0	0	1	0	0	0	0	0	0	0	0	0	1	0	0	0	0	0	0	0	2	0
Total	76	52	188	134	377	250	464	263	409	181	320	138	169	56	61	12	19	2	34	12	2117	1100

Apps = Number of Applicants
Adm = Number Admitted
Reflects 99% of the total applicant pool; highest LSAT data reported.

WIDENER UNIVERSITY SCHOOL OF LAW

4601 Concord Pike, PO Box 7474
Wilmington, DE 19803-0474
Phone: 302.477.2703; Fax 302.477.2224
E-mail: lawadmissions@widener.edu; Website: http://law.widener.edu

ABA
Approved
Since
1975

The Basics

Type of school	Private
Term	Semester
Application deadline	5/15
Application fee	$60
Financial aid deadline	4/1
Can first year start other than fall?	No
Student to faculty ratio	15.4 to 1
# of housing spaces available restricted to law students	185
graduate housing for which law students are eligible	185

Faculty and Administrators

	Total		Men		Women		Minorities	
	Spr	Fall	Spr	Fall	Spr	Fall	Spr	Fall
Full-time	42	49	26	25	16	24	5	7
Other full-time	1	1	0	0	1	1	0	0
Deans, librarians, & others who teach	10	9	4	3	6	6	3	3
Part-time	48	51	38	32	10	18	5	5
Total	101	110	68	60	33	49	13	15

Curriculum

	Full-Time	Part-Time
Typical first-year section size	66	57
Is there typically a "small section" of the first-year class, other than Legal Writing, taught by full-time faculty	Yes	Yes
If yes, typical size offered last year	44	56

# of classroom course titles beyond first-year curriculum		119
# of upper division courses, excluding seminars, with an enrollment:	Under 25	132
	25–49	41
	50–74	20
	75–99	3
	100+	2

	Full-Time	Part-Time
# of seminars		23
# of seminar positions available		345
# of seminar positions filled	126	102
# of positions available in simulation courses		600
# of simulation positions filled	326	237
# of positions available in faculty supervised clinical courses		93
# of faculty supervised clinical positions filled	58	35
# involved in field placements	87	32
# involved in law journals	127	32
# involved in moot court or trial competitions	73	59
# of credit hours required to graduate		88

JD Enrollment and Ethnicity

	Men		Women		Full-Time		Part-Time		1st-Year		Total		JD Degs. Awd.
	#	%	#	%	#	%	#	%	#	%	#	%	
All Hispanics	16	2.8	10	2.3	19	2.9	7	2.0	13	3.4	26	2.6	7
Am. Ind./AK Nat.	0	0.0	0	0.0	0	0.0	0	0.0	0	0.0	0	0.0	1
Asian	30	5.2	25	5.9	46	7.1	9	2.6	29	7.5	55	5.5	16
Black/Af. Am.	24	4.2	38	8.9	39	6.0	23	6.5	28	7.2	62	6.2	12
Nat. HI/Pac. Isl.	0	0.0	1	0.2	1	0.2	0	0.0	1	0.3	1	0.1	0
2 or more races	6	1.0	6	1.4	7	1.1	5	1.4	6	1.5	12	1.2	0
Subtotal (minor.)	76	13.3	80	18.8	112	17.3	44	12.5	77	19.8	156	15.6	36
Nonres. Alien	0	0.0	1	0.2	1	0.2	0	0.0	0	0.0	1	0.1	0
White/Cauc.	477	83.2	333	78.2	519	80.2	291	82.7	299	77.1	810	81.1	215
Unknown	20	3.5	12	2.8	15	2.3	17	4.8	12	3.1	32	3.2	3
Total	573	57.4	426	42.6	647	64.8	352	35.2	388	38.8	999		254

Transfers

Transfers in	3
Transfers out	34

Tuition and Fees

	Resident	Nonresident
Full-time	$34,890	$34,890
Part-time	$25,610	$25,610
Tuition Guarantee Program		N

Living Expenses

Estimated living expenses for singles

Living on campus	Living off campus	Living at home
$17,030	$17,030	$11,270

WIDENER UNIVERSITY SCHOOL OF LAW

ABA Approved Since 1975

GPA and LSAT Scores

	Total	Full-Time	Part-Time
# of apps	2,007	1,869	487
# of offers	1,341	1,096	245
# of matrics	389	259	130
75% GPA	3.47	3.45	3.48
Median GPA	3.18	3.19	3.16
25% GPA	2.86	2.86	2.88
75% LSAT	154	154	152
Median LSAT	152	153	150
25% LSAT	150	151	148

Grants and Scholarships (from prior year)

	Total #	Total %	Full-Time #	Full-Time %	Part-Time #	Part-Time %
Total # of students	975		612		363	
Total # receiving grants	265	27.2	197	32.2	68	18.7
Less than 1/2 tuition	195	20.0	142	23.2	53	14.6
Half to full tuition	51	5.2	38	6.2	13	3.6
Full tuition	16	1.6	16	2.6	0	0.0
More than full tuition	3	0.3	1	0.2	2	0.6
Median grant amount			$6,650		$5,000	

Informational and Library Resources

Total amount spent on library materials	$1,020,431
Study seating capacity inside the library	335
# of full-time equivalent professional librarians	9
Hours per week library is open	107
# of open, wired connections available to students	75
# of networked computers available for use by students	141
Has wireless network?	Y
Requires computer?	N

JD Attrition (from prior year)

	Academic #	Other #	Total #	Total %
1st year	45	51	96	25.4
2nd year	0	0	0	0.0
3rd year	1	1	2	0.8
4th year	0	0	0	0.0

Employment (9 months after graduation)

	Total	Percentage
Employment status known	191	81.3
Employment status unknown	44	18.7
Employed	175	91.6
Pursuing graduate degrees	3	1.6
Unemployed (seeking, not seeking, or studying for the bar)	11	5.8
Type of Employment		
# employed in law firms	84	48.0
# employed in business and industry	24	13.7
# employed in government	21	12.0
# employed in public interest	6	3.4
# employed as judicial clerks	39	22.3
# employed in academia	1	0.6
Geographic Location		
# employed in state	43	24.6
# employed outside the US	0	0.0
# of states where employed		11

Bar Passage Rates

First-time takers	235	Reporting %	90.21
Average school %	85.85	Average state %	85.69
Average pass difference	0.16		

Jurisdiction	Takers	Passers	Pass %	State %	Diff %
Pennsylvania	212	182	85.85	85.69	0.16

WIDENER UNIVERSITY SCHOOL OF LAW

3800 Vartan Way, PO Box 69381
Harrisburg, PA 17106-9381
Phone: 717.541.3903; Fax: 717.541.3999
E-mail: lawadmissions@widener.edu; Website: http://law.widener.edu

ABA
Approved
Since
1994

The Basics

Type of school	Private
Term	Semester
Application deadline	5/15
Application fee	$60
Financial aid deadline	4/1
Can first year start other than fall?	No
Student to faculty ratio	14.8 to 1
# of housing spaces available restricted to law students	
graduate housing for which law students are eligible	

Faculty and Administrators

	Total		Men		Women		Minorities	
	Spr	Fall	Spr	Fall	Spr	Fall	Spr	Fall
Full-time	22	24	12	13	10	11	3	5
Other full-time	2	1	0	0	2	1	1	0
Deans, librarians, & others who teach	6	6	2	2	4	4	1	1
Part-time	18	18	12	13	6	5	0	0
Total	48	49	26	28	22	21	5	6

Curriculum

		Full-Time	Part-Time
Typical first-year section size		69	33
Is there typically a "small section" of the first-year class, other than Legal Writing, taught by full-time faculty		No	No
If yes, typical size offered last year			
# of classroom course titles beyond first-year curriculum		73	
# of upper division courses, excluding seminars, with an enrollment:	Under 25	96	
	25–49	27	
	50–74	11	
	75–99	2	
	100+	0	
# of seminars		10	
# of seminar positions available		180	
# of seminar positions filled		81	27
# of positions available in simulation courses		211	
# of simulation positions filled		155	56
# of positions available in faculty supervised clinical courses		58	
# of faculty supervised clinical positions filled		42	16
# involved in field placements		31	7
# involved in law journals		34	6
# involved in moot court or trial competitions		20	6
# of credit hours required to graduate		88	

JD Enrollment and Ethnicity

	Men		Women		Full-Time		Part-Time		1st-Year		Total		JD Degs. Awd.
	#	%	#	%	#	%	#	%	#	%	#	%	
All Hispanics	7	2.8	10	4.9	15	4.3	2	1.9	6	3.4	17	3.8	4
Am. Ind./AK Nat.	1	0.4	0	0.0	0	0.0	1	1.0	0	0.0	1	0.2	1
Asian	7	2.8	13	6.3	16	4.6	4	3.9	10	5.6	20	4.4	2
Black/Af. Am.	3	1.2	9	4.4	9	2.6	3	2.9	6	3.4	12	2.6	3
Nat. HI/Pac. Isl.	0	0.0	0	0.0	0	0.0	0	0.0	0	0.0	0	0.0	0
2 or more races	2	0.8	4	1.9	5	1.4	1	1.0	3	1.7	6	1.3	0
Subtotal (minor.)	20	8.1	36	17.5	45	12.9	11	10.7	25	14.0	56	12.4	11
Nonres. Alien	1	0.4	0	0.0	1	0.3	0	0.0	1	0.6	1	0.2	0
White/Cauc.	219	88.7	169	82.0	300	85.7	88	85.4	150	84.3	388	85.7	101
Unknown	7	2.8	1	0.5	4	1.1	4	3.9	2	1.1	8	1.8	11
Total	247	54.5	206	45.5	350	77.3	103	22.7	178	39.3	453		123

Transfers

Transfers in	0
Transfers out	13

Tuition and Fees

	Resident	Nonresident
Full-time	$34,890	$34,890
Part-time	$25,610	$25,610
Tuition Guarantee Program		N

Living Expenses

Estimated living expenses for singles

Living on campus	Living off campus	Living at home
$17,030	$17,030	$11,270

WIDENER UNIVERSITY SCHOOL OF LAW

ABA
Approved
Since
1994

GPA and LSAT Scores

	Total	Full-Time	Part-Time
# of apps	778	1,231	253
# of offers	822	706	116
# of matrics	178	140	38
75% GPA	3.46	3.47	3.39
Median GPA	3.10	3.10	3.09
25% GPA	2.81	2.83	2.73
75% LSAT	153	153	153
Median LSAT	150	150	149
25% LSAT	148	149	148

Grants and Scholarships (from prior year)

	Total		Full-Time		Part-Time	
	#	%	#	%	#	%
Total # of students	461		358		103	
Total # receiving grants	170	36.9	140	39.1	30	29.1
Less than 1/2 tuition	137	29.7	113	31.6	24	23.3
Half to full tuition	23	5.0	17	4.7	6	5.8
Full tuition	9	2.0	9	2.5	0	0.0
More than full tuition	1	0.2	1	0.3	0	0.0
Median grant amount			$2,000		$7,386	

Informational and Library Resources

Total amount spent on library materials	$677,863
Study seating capacity inside the library	335
# of full-time equivalent professional librarians	5
Hours per week library is open	105
# of open, wired connections available to students	10
# of networked computers available for use by students	68
Has wireless network?	Y
Requires computer?	N

JD Attrition (from prior year)

	Academic	Other	Total	
	#	#	#	%
1st year	28	19	47	26.0
2nd year	2	1	3	2.1
3rd year	0	0	0	0.0
4th year	0	0	0	0.0

Employment (9 months after graduation)

	Total	Percentage
Employment status known	112	94.1
Employment status unknown	7	5.9
Employed	101	90.2
Pursuing graduate degrees	1	0.9
Unemployed (seeking, not seeking, or studying for the bar)	3	2.7
Type of Employment		
# employed in law firms	43	42.6
# employed in business and industry	18	17.8
# employed in government	24	23.8
# employed in public interest	2	2.0
# employed as judicial clerks	13	12.9
# employed in academia	1	1.0
Geographic Location		
# employed in state	79	78.2
# employed outside the US	0	0.0
# of states where employed	14	

Bar Passage Rates

First-time takers	102	Reporting %	99.02
Average school %	93.07	Average state %	85.69
Average pass difference	7.38		

Jurisdiction	Takers	Passers	Pass %	State %	Diff %
Pennsylvania	101	94	93.07	85.69	7.38

WIDENER UNIVERSITY SCHOOL OF LAW

4601 Concord Pike, PO Box 7474, Wilmington, DE 19803-0474; Phone: 302.477.2703; Fax 302.477.2224
3800 Vartan Way, PO Box 69381, Harrisburg, PA 17106-9381; Phone: 717.541.3903; Fax: 717.541.3999
E-mail: lawadmissions@widener.edu; Website: http://law.widener.edu

Introduction

Widener University School of Law is unique among American law schools. Widener has two campuses—one in Wilmington, Delaware, the corporate and banking center of the United States, and the other in Harrisburg, Pennsylvania, the state capital and a major center of government and commerce. Each campus offers a comprehensive curriculum of basic and advanced courses complemented by one of the most extensive clinical and skills programs in the country. The Harrisburg campus features a unique admission and academic cooperative program with the Pennsylvania State System of Higher Education.

The rich curriculum is taught by a faculty committed to personal attention and individual counseling so that all students will be encouraged to fulfill their potential. The full-time faculty is supplemented by a distinguished group of adjuncts, including two justices of the Delaware Supreme Court, two justices of the Pennsylvania Supreme Court, US Vice President Joseph Biden, and numerous lower court judges from Pennsylvania, Delaware, and New Jersey. The school is a member of the AALS and is accredited by the ABA.

Library and Physical Facilities

The Legal Information Center houses one of the most significant legal collections in the region. The combined collections of the Delaware and Harrisburg campuses exceed 600,000 volumes. The library is a selective depository for United States government documents.

The attractive 34-acre Delaware campus is located in the heart of the beautiful Brandywine River Valley. The law building houses the Legal Information Center, state-of-the-art computer facilities, faculty offices, clinics, traditional and technologically enhanced classrooms, and three moot courtrooms. The scenic 19-acre Harrisburg campus is located in a contemporary complex within minutes of the state capital.

Special Programs and Institutes

Widener is a leader in developing a coordinated lawyering skills program. The program includes clinical practice, externship placements, and comprehensive simulations.

Clinics are designed to permit students to represent actual clients under the supervision of the clinic director before courts and administrative boards. Widener operates Environmental Law, Criminal Defense, Delaware Civil, Pennsylvania Civil, Harrisburg Civil, and Veterans Affairs clinics. A large number of supervised externships permit students to work as lawyers-in-training with state and county government agencies and nonprofit corporations. An extensive judicial externship program places students with state and federal courts at both the trial and appellate levels in Washington, DC; Delaware; Maryland; New Jersey; Pennsylvania; and Virginia. Additional public interest service opportunities are also available.

The Public Interest Resource Center on the Delaware campus and the Public Interest Initiative on the Harrisburg campus cultivate pro bono volunteer opportunities for students in public interest agencies and government offices throughout Delaware, Pennsylvania, and New Jersey; offer counseling and guidance to students who seek careers in public interest law; and recognize students and faculty for exceptional contributions to public service.

Widener offers certificate programs for specialized study in health law, law and government, business organizations law, advocacy and technology, criminal law, and environmental law.

The Health Law Institute on the Delaware campus provides research, policy analysis, and specialty education for those seeking a career in the area of health law. The Law and Government Institute on the Harrisburg campus provides hands-on experience with the operation and structure of government as well as practice before government agencies. The Institute of Delaware Corporate and Business Law on the Delaware campus provides a fundamental knowledge of business law through the Business Organizations Law concentration, which serves as a predicate to advanced practice in business and corporate law. The Taishoof Advocacy, Technology, and Public Service Institute on the Delaware campus provides the extensive litigation skills that are essential to being a competent, professionally responsible trial advocate. The Advocacy Program on the Harrisburg campus offers specialized courses and practice opportunities, leading to a certificate, for students interested in a career in litigation. The Environmental Law Center on both campuses harnesses the expertise of seven nationally and internationally recognized environmental law faculty members to provide students with extensive opportunities to engage in environmental law through coursework, externships, and training skills. Additionally, both campuses offer a seven-day Intensive Trial Advocacy Program supervised by outstanding local trial lawyers and judges.

Widener offers five joint-degree programs. The JD/MBA is offered in conjunction with the university's School of Business Administration. The JD/PsyD is offered in conjunction with the university's Institute for Graduate Clinical Psychology. The JD/MPH is offered in conjunction with Thomas Jefferson University. The JD/MSLS is offered in conjunction with Clarion University of Pennsylvania. The JD/MMP is offered in conjunction with the University of Delaware.

Study-Abroad Opportunities

Widener students have the opportunity to study international and comparative law while living abroad. Widener offers study-abroad programs in Nairobi, Kenya; Lausanne, Switzerland; Sydney, Australia; Venice, Italy; and Chongqing, China.

Student Activities

Selected Delaware students publish the *Delaware Journal of Corporate Law* and the *Widener Law Review*. Selected Harrisburg students publish the *Widener Law Journal*. Delaware and Harrisburg students may also be eligible to participate in our online journal, the *Widener Journal of Law, Economics and Race*. Students on both campuses compete in regional and national interschool moot court and trial competitions. Student organizations provide opportunities for intrascholastic and interscholastic competitions, public service, and association with others who share the same interests.

Admission

While there are no fixed admission criteria, great weight is given to the applicant's LSAT score and undergraduate grade-point average. The Admissions Committee carefully considers an applicant's personal statement. Graduate degrees, writing samples, extracurricular activities, and community and professional service may enhance the application. The law school encourages those with diverse backgrounds to apply.

Applications for admission must be received by May 15. Admission decisions are made on a rolling basis, and applicants are encouraged to apply early.

The admission process is paperless. All applications and supporting documents must be submitted electronically via law.widener.edu or LSAC.org. All communications to applicants, including admission decisions, are provided through the applicant's account in Widener's admissions web portal at law.widener.edu/admissions.

Each summer, Widener conducts the Trial Admissions Program (TAP) for a small number of carefully selected applicants who show potential for success in law school despite a relatively low score on the LSAT or a lower undergraduate grade-point average. TAP is a conditional admittance program. Participants who successfully complete the six-week program are offered admission to the fall entering class.

Financial Aid

The Financial Aid Office is committed to assisting students throughout the financial aid process. In addition to merit-based scholarships offered at the time of admission to well-qualified applicants based upon their overall application, Widener Law awards a substantial amount of merit-based scholarships and the opportunity to borrow through our low interest rate Institutional Loan Program to students who academically excel in their first year of law school. Widener Law participates in all federal financial aid programs, including Federal Work-Study and the Federal Direct Loan Programs.

Career Development

The Career Development Office is strongly committed to helping students obtain the positions that best suit their individual needs and ambitions.

Widener's employment statistics evidence its success in helping graduates find a niche in the contemporary job market. Widener alumni have become judges in Delaware, New Jersey, New York, and Pennsylvania; members of the legislature; partners in major regional law firms; hospital administrators; and legal educators.

APPLICANT PROFILE

Widener University School of Law
This grid includes only applicants who earned 120–180 LSAT scores under standard administrations.

LSAT Score	GPA																		
	3.75 +		3.50–3.74		3.25–3.49		3.00–3.24		2.75–2.99		2.50–2.74		2.25–2.49		2.00–2.24		Below 2.00		No GPA		Total	
	Apps	Adm	Apps	Adm	Apps	Adm	Apps	Adm	Apps	Adm	Apps	Adm	Apps	Adm	Apps	Adm	Apps	Adm	Apps	Adm	Apps	Adm
175–180	0	0	0	0	0	0	0	0	0	0	0	0	0	0	0	0	0	0	0	0	0	0
170–174	1	1	1	1	1	1	0	0	0	0	0	0	0	0	0	0	0	0	0	0	3	3
165–169	2	2	7	6	2	2	5	4	3	3	0	0	0	0	1	1	0	0	0	0	20	18
160–164	15	14	16	16	24	23	21	17	21	20	11	11	3	3	3	3	1	1	1	1	116	109
155–159	35	34	71	66	88	84	85	76	62	56	35	32	32	30	6	6	3	3	4	1	421	388
150–154	58	55	134	114	160	146	195	162	154	135	105	93	59	51	21	18	6	4	7	4	899	782
145–149	47	25	117	44	160	67	183	73	163	48	112	31	54	12	25	2	5	0	14	1	880	303
140–144	14	0	42	3	62	3	91	4	87	2	68	2	33	0	16	0	3	0	18	0	434	14
135–139	8	0	13	0	14	0	21	0	24	0	33	0	16	0	12	0	4	0	8	0	153	0
130–134	0	0	2	0	6	0	14	0	9	0	8	0	3	0	8	0	1	0	11	0	62	0
125–129	0	0	0	0	0	0	2	0	0	0	2	0	1	0	0	0	0	0	1	0	6	0
120–124	0	0	0	0	0	0	0	0	0	0	0	0	0	0	0	0	0	0	1	0	1	0
Total	180	131	403	250	517	326	617	336	523	264	374	169	201	96	92	30	23	8	65	7	2995	1617

Apps = Number of Applicants
Adm = Number Admitted
Reflects 98% of the total applicant pool; highest LSAT data reported.

The grid includes applicants admitted based upon successful completion of our Trial Admissions Program, rather than upon their LSAT score and undergraduate grade-point average. Additionally, nonnumerical factors are considered for all applicants.

WILLAMETTE UNIVERSITY COLLEGE OF LAW

Truman Wesley Collins Legal Center, 245 Winter Street SE
Salem, OR 97301
Phone: 503.370.6282; Fax: 503.370.6087
E-mail: law-admission@willamette.edu; Website: www.willamette.edu/wucl

ABA
Approved
Since
1938

The Basics

Type of school	Private
Term	Semester
Application deadline	3/1
Application fee	$50
Financial aid deadline	6/1
Can first year start other than fall?	No
Student to faculty ratio	14.1 to 1
# of housing spaces available restricted to law students	
graduate housing for which law students are eligible	26

Faculty and Administrators

	Total		Men		Women		Minorities	
	Spr	Fall	Spr	Fall	Spr	Fall	Spr	Fall
Full-time	25	24	17	15	8	9	5	5
Other full-time	4	4	1	2	3	2	1	1
Deans, librarians, & others who teach	7	6	4	4	3	2	0	0
Part-time	16	13	12	12	4	1	2	1
Total	52	47	34	33	18	14	8	7

Curriculum

	Full-Time	Part-Time
Typical first-year section size	74	0
Is there typically a "small section" of the first-year class, other than Legal Writing, taught by full-time faculty	Yes	No
If yes, typical size offered last year	46	
# of classroom course titles beyond first-year curriculum	108	
# of upper division courses, excluding seminars, with an enrollment: Under 25	54	
25–49	21	
50–74	10	
75–99	2	
100+	0	
# of seminars	24	
# of seminar positions available	340	
# of seminar positions filled	218	0
# of positions available in simulation courses	369	
# of simulation positions filled	247	0
# of positions available in faculty supervised clinical courses	68	
# of faculty supervised clinical positions filled	63	0
# involved in field placements	35	0
# involved in law journals	60	0
# involved in moot court or trial competitions	133	0
# of credit hours required to graduate	90	

JD Enrollment and Ethnicity

	Men		Women		Full-Time		Part-Time		1st-Year		Total		JD Degs. Awd.
	#	%	#	%	#	%	#	%	#	%	#	%	
All Hispanics	17	7.0	10	5.3	27	6.4	0	0.0	10	6.2	27	6.3	7
Am. Ind./AK Nat.	3	1.2	4	2.1	7	1.7	0	0.0	2	1.2	7	1.6	0
Asian	14	5.8	20	10.7	34	8.0	0	0.0	14	8.6	34	7.9	11
Black/Af. Am.	5	2.1	3	1.6	8	1.9	0	0.0	2	1.2	8	1.9	1
Nat. HI/Pac. Isl.	1	0.4	0	0.0	1	0.2	0	0.0	1	0.6	1	0.2	0
2 or more races	0	0.0	0	0.0	0	0.0	0	0.0	0	0.0	0	0.0	0
Subtotal (minor.)	40	16.5	37	19.8	77	18.2	0	0.0	29	17.9	77	17.9	19
Nonres. Alien	3	1.2	0	0.0	3	0.7	0	0.0	0	0.0	3	0.7	0
White/Cauc.	179	74.0	140	74.9	315	74.3	4	80.0	125	77.2	319	74.4	109
Unknown	20	8.3	10	5.3	29	6.8	1	20.0	8	4.9	30	7.0	7
Total	242	56.4	187	43.6	424	98.8	5	1.2	162	37.8	429		135

Transfers

Transfers in	4
Transfers out	8

Tuition and Fees

	Resident	Nonresident
Full-time	$31,130	$31,130
Part-time		
Tuition Guarantee Program	N	

Living Expenses

Estimated living expenses for singles

Living on campus	Living off campus	Living at home
$16,740	$16,740	$16,740

WILLAMETTE UNIVERSITY COLLEGE OF LAW

ABA
Approved
Since
1938

GPA and LSAT Scores

	Total	Full-Time	Part-Time
# of apps	0	1,432	0
# of offers	531	531	0
# of matrics	158	158	0
75% GPA	3.54	3.54	0.00
Median GPA	3.30	3.30	0.00
25% GPA	2.99	2.99	0.00
75% LSAT	159	159	0
Median LSAT	156	156	0
25% LSAT	154	154	0

Grants and Scholarships (from prior year)

	Total		Full-Time		Part-Time	
	#	%	#	%	#	%
Total # of students	426		421		5	
Total # receiving grants	226	53.1	226	53.7	0	0.0
Less than 1/2 tuition	164	38.5	164	39.0	0	0.0
Half to full tuition	62	14.6	62	14.7	0	0.0
Full tuition	0	0.0	0	0.0	0	0.0
More than full tuition	0	0.0	0	0.0	0	0.0
Median grant amount			$10,000		$0	

Informational and Library Resources

Total amount spent on library materials	$644,125
Study seating capacity inside the library	498
# of full-time equivalent professional librarians	3
Hours per week library is open	168
# of open, wired connections available to students	113
# of networked computers available for use by students	32
Has wireless network?	Y
Requires computer?	N

JD Attrition (from prior year)

	Academic	Other	Total	
	#	#	#	%
1st year	7	11	18	12.2
2nd year	7	5	12	8.6
3rd year	0	0	0	0.0
4th year	0	0	0	0.0

Employment (9 months after graduation)

	Total	Percentage
Employment status known	129	99.2
Employment status unknown	1	0.8
Employed	119	92.2
Pursuing graduate degrees	3	2.3
Unemployed (seeking, not seeking, or studying for the bar)	1	0.8
Type of Employment		
# employed in law firms	58	48.7
# employed in business and industry	16	13.4
# employed in government	18	15.1
# employed in public interest	7	5.9
# employed as judicial clerks	9	7.6
# employed in academia	11	9.2
Geographic Location		
# employed in state	87	73.1
# employed outside the US	0	0.0
# of states where employed		11

Bar Passage Rates

First-time takers	124	Reporting %	72.58
Average school %	86.67	Average state %	76.85
Average pass difference	9.82		

Jurisdiction	Takers	Passers	Pass %	State %	Diff %
Oregon	90	78	86.67	76.85	9.82

WILLAMETTE UNIVERSITY COLLEGE OF LAW

Truman Wesley Collins Legal Center, 245 Winter Street SE
Salem, OR 97301
Phone: 503.370.6282; Fax: 503.370.6087
E-mail: law-admission@willamette.edu; Website: www.willamette.edu/wucl

Introduction

From the time the first student entered the classroom in 1883, Willamette University College of Law has been a pioneer of legal education in the western United States. Located across the street from the state capitol complex, the College of Law is situated in the epicenter of Oregon law, government, and business.

Willamette University is one of the nation's oldest academic institutions. It is situated in the historic riverfront capital city of Salem, Oregon. The university is an independent institution historically related to the United Methodist Church. College of Law students are members of a distinguished university community of 2,500 students enrolled in the undergraduate College of Liberal Arts and in graduate programs offered by the School of Education and the Atkinson Graduate School of Management.

The College of Law is an intimate, highly selective, and intellectually challenging school and a widely recognized leader in legal education. The college is committed to the pursuit of academic and professional excellence in a supportive environment that maximizes each student's unique potential. Selective enrollment of approximately 430 full-time students creates an intellectual intimacy unmatched by most law schools in the United States.

For more than 125 years, Willamette has trained talented, skilled lawyers who stand on equal footing with the very best legal practitioners in the country. Among the College of Law's distinguished alumni are numerous heads of Fortune 500 companies and more than a dozen state supreme court justices and members of the US Senate and House of Representatives.

Faculty

A law school faculty serves as both the brain and heart of the institution. Willamette's diverse law faculty includes some of the most respected legal minds in the country, including former federal judicial clerks, officers of the American Society of Comparative Law, First Amendment specialists and Fulbright scholars, as well as two former justices of the Oregon Supreme Court and the current chief justice.

These scholars and master teachers are nationally recognized for their research, publications, and contributions to the law, particularly in the areas of constitutional law, commercial and business law, international and comparative law, environmental law, and dispute resolution. Yet it is their authentic, deep dedication—both as educators and as mentors—that distinguishes them from others.

Academic Programs

The Doctor of Jurisprudence program (JD) requires three years of full-time study. After successfully completing the first year, in which all courses but one are prescribed, students may choose to create an individual program, electing courses from Willamette's broad-based curriculum.

The College of Law also offers a four-year, joint-degree program that leads to the JD and MBA for Business, Government, and Not-for-Profit Management. Managed in concert with Willamette's Atkinson Graduate School of Management, the joint-degree program saves students one

additional year of study. Students must apply separately for admission to each degree program and may begin the program either in the College of Law or in the Atkinson School. Students may apply prior to matriculating to Willamette or while in their first year of either the JD or MBA program.

Willamette's nationally recognized certificate programs further solidify the strong educational foundation provided at the College of Law. These specialized programs prepare students for exceptional legal careers and further distinguish them from other law school graduates. The five certificate programs are International and Comparative Law, Business Law, Law and Government, Dispute Resolution, and Sustainability Law.

Willamette's College of Law also offers the LLM in Transnational Law, an advanced degree available to those who have completed the JD at an ABA-accredited American law school or its equivalent from a foreign law school. For more information, visit www.willamette.edu/wucl/programs/llm/.

Facility

The College of Law is housed in the award-winning Truman Wesley Collins Legal Center on the beautifully landscaped 65-acre campus of the university. The school offers all the cutting-edge amenities a student would expect from a top law school. Bright, modern classrooms provide comfortable, professional environments for learning and include a state-of-the-art wireless network.

The J.W. Long Law Library anchors the north end of the Collins Legal Center. Its 296,000 volumes and microform equivalents include state and federal primary law sources, as well as the leading treatises, periodicals, and other secondary sources. Through a library consortium, an online shared catalog gives Willamette students access to a remarkably vast array of resources. The library, a selective federal government depository, houses special collections in public international law, tax law, and labor law.

Both the Collins Legal Center and the law library are accessible to law students 24 hours a day, 7 days a week.

International Study Programs

Willamette's College of Law students have the opportunity to deepen their international experience by participating in study-abroad programs in Germany, Ecuador, and China. The summer China program acquaints students with Chinese law and Pacific Rim legal issues. It is based in Shanghai at the East China University of Politics and Law. The Ecuador program provides students with an intensive semester immersion in the fundamentals of a civil law system and Latin American legal institutions. Students take courses at the Pontifical Catholic University of Ecuador in Quito. Proficiency in Spanish is required. The semester-long Germany program is held at the Bucerius Law School in Hamburg, the first private institution for legal study in Germany.

Academic Centers and Other Resources

The Clinical Law Program at Willamette University provides students with hands-on, professional experience in the actual practice of law. The Clinical Law Program comprises six advanced legal education courses, including specialized clinics in business law, trusts and estates, sustainability law, child and family advocacy, law and government, and international human rights. Clients are primarily nonprofit corporations and people of modest economic means.

The Externship Program immerses students in the fast-paced work of the practicing lawyer. Students participate in legal work in may different contexts, under the constraints of a real-life practice in the wider legal community. The program provides an experiential learning environment that helps students develop their skills and values as novice lawyers. It also enables students to "test the water" in a specific area of legal practice and improves their prospects for obtaining satisfying, permanent employment after graduation.

The nationally recognized Center for Dispute Resolution produces research on conflict theory and problem solving. The center teaches the theory and practice of negotiation, mediation, arbitration, and other methods of resolving disputes. It also administers the Certificate Program in Dispute Resolution.

The Willamette Center for Law and Government provides an impartial forum for the study, discussion, and improvement of government and public policy. It also administers the Certificate Program in Law and Government.

The Oregon Law Commission, which is housed at Willamette's College of Law, was established by legislative statute to provide academic and practical support for ongoing law revision, reform, and improvement. The commission is led by a member of the College of Law faculty.

Admission

Applicants are urged to apply in the fall prior to the year they intend to enter the law school. Willamette enrolls a diverse first-year law class with a wide range of goals, experiences, and cultural, ethnic, and social backgrounds, and that show evidence of previous academic success. Applications are reviewed closely, and in their entirety, to ensure an informed and fair decision. Although March 1 is the priority deadline for applications, students begin receiving admission decisions from Willamette in January.

Scholarships

The fiscal stability of Willamette University enables the College of Law to offer a strong program of financial aid to its students. Generous merit-based scholarships reward applicants whose accomplishments suggest continuing success in law school. Scholarships are renewable with a 2.90 cumulative law GPA. Every student is automatically considered for a scholarship when the application for admission is initially reviewed. All applicants to the College of Law should also complete and submit the Free Application for Federal Student Aid

(FAFSA) prior to March 1. Federal and private loan monies also may be available.

Employment and Career Services

The College of Law maintains an active Career Services center, which provides comprehensive career counseling services to current Willamette law students and law alumni. Career Services oversees a busy on-campus interview program, bringing legal employers directly to the College of Law. A wide range of workshops, panels, and speakers are also made available to students throughout the academic year. In addition, the Career Services library contains countless resources to assist with career planning and job searches.

Historically, most Willamette graduates choose careers in private practice. Graduates in government-related practice, including judicial clerkships, compose the next largest group. Business and industry attract the third largest group. Most graduates remain in the Pacific Northwest because of the region's unique lifestyle and natural environment. While the Willamette alumni network is strongest in Oregon and Washington, Career Services provides a comprehensive national job-search service. Thus, Willamette graduates practice nationwide, from Hawaii to Washington, DC; from Alaska to Florida; and internationally, as well.

Location

Willamette University is situated in the heart of Salem, Oregon's capital. Salem is home to a large, active legal community that readily employs and actively mentors Willamette law students. With 150,000 residents, Salem is neither a small college town nor a big city. This historic riverfront city offers all the amenities of a larger city, but has successfully maintained its hometown charm. A welcoming and affordable city, Salem boasts a vibrant downtown area, beautiful city parks, an innovative children's museum and popular community theater, great pubs and cafés, fine dining, numerous coffeehouses and microbreweries, and a wide range of small boutiques and department stores.

Salem is surrounded by award-winning vineyards and orchards that support countless wine and food festivals. The city is only a short drive from numerous beautiful state parks that provide wilderness hiking, fishing, camping, and winter sports. The desert is a little farther east, and Oregon's spectacular coast is an hour's drive to the west. Metropolitan Portland is just 45 minutes to the north, offering easy access to national sporting events and premier music and art venues.

Applicant Profile Not Available

WILLIAM & MARY LAW SCHOOL

613 South Henry Street
Williamsburg, VA 23185
Phone: 757.221.3785; Fax: 757.221.3261
E-mail: lawadm@wm.edu; Website: http://law.wm.edu

ABA
Approved
Since
1932

The Basics

Type of school	Public
Term	Semester
Application deadline	3/1
Application fee	$50
Financial aid deadline	2/15
Can first year start other than fall?	No
Student to faculty ratio	14.2 to 1
# of housing spaces available restricted to law students	
graduate housing for which law students are eligible	117

Faculty and Administrators

	Total		Men		Women		Minorities	
	Spr	Fall	Spr	Fall	Spr	Fall	Spr	Fall
Full-time	34	39	17	22	17	17	5	7
Other full-time	0	0	0	0	0	0	0	0
Deans, librarians, & others who teach	10	10	7	8	3	2	0	0
Part-time	63	45	48	33	15	12	3	4
Total	107	94	72	63	35	31	8	11

Curriculum

	Full-Time	Part-Time
Typical first-year section size	70	0
Is there typically a "small section" of the first-year class, other than Legal Writing, taught by full-time faculty	Yes	No
If yes, typical size offered last year	16	
# of classroom course titles beyond first-year curriculum	132	
# of upper division courses, excluding seminars, with an enrollment: Under 25	118	
25–49	35	
50–74	10	
75–99	5	
100+	4	
# of seminars	41	
# of seminar positions available	645	
# of seminar positions filled	518	0
# of positions available in simulation courses	1,063	
# of simulation positions filled	1,054	0
# of positions available in faculty supervised clinical courses	18	
# of faculty supervised clinical positions filled	15	0
# involved in field placements	174	0
# involved in law journals	306	0
# involved in moot court or trial competitions	119	0
# of credit hours required to graduate	86	

JD Enrollment and Ethnicity

	Men		Women		Full-Time		Part-Time		1st-Year		Total		JD Degs. Awd.
	#	%	#	%	#	%	#	%	#	%	#	%	
All Hispanics	5	1.6	6	1.9	11	1.8	0	0.0	8	3.7	11	1.8	3
Am. Ind./AK Nat.	1	0.3	1	0.3	2	0.3	0	0.0	1	0.5	2	0.3	1
Asian	9	2.8	13	4.2	22	3.5	0	0.0	6	2.8	22	3.5	4
Black/Af. Am.	33	10.4	48	15.5	81	12.9	0	0.0	31	14.3	81	12.9	26
Nat. HI/Pac. Isl.	0	0.0	1	0.3	1	0.2	0	0.0	0	0.0	1	0.2	0
2 or more races	0	0.0	5	1.6	5	0.8	0	0.0	5	2.3	5	0.8	0
Subtotal (minor.)	48	15.1	74	23.9	122	19.4	0	0.0	51	23.5	122	19.4	34
Nonres. Alien	1	0.3	2	0.6	3	0.5	0	0.0	1	0.5	3	0.5	0
White/Cauc.	212	66.7	199	64.2	411	65.4	0	0.0	143	65.9	411	65.4	140
Unknown	57	17.9	35	11.3	92	14.6	0	0.0	22	10.1	92	14.6	39
Total	318	50.6	310	49.4	628	100.0	0	0.0	217	34.6	628		214

Transfers

Transfers in	10
Transfers out	9

Tuition and Fees

	Resident	Nonresident
Full-time	$23,800	$33,800
Part-time		
Tuition Guarantee Program		N

Living Expenses

Estimated living expenses for singles

Living on campus	Living off campus	Living at home
$15,300	$15,300	$15,300

WILLIAM & MARY LAW SCHOOL

ABA
Approved
Since
1932

GPA and LSAT Scores

	Total	Full-Time	Part-Time
# of apps	6,291	6,291	0
# of offers	1,207	1,207	0
# of matrics	217	217	0
75% GPA	3.81	3.81	0.00
Median GPA	3.70	3.70	0.00
25% GPA	3.47	3.47	0.00
75% LSAT	166	166	0
Median LSAT	165	165	0
25% LSAT	160	160	0

Grants and Scholarships (from prior year)

	Total		Full-Time		Part-Time	
	#	%	#	%	#	%
Total # of students	626		626		0	
Total # receiving grants	235	37.5	235	37.5	0	0.0
Less than 1/2 tuition	216	34.5	216	34.5	0	0.0
Half to full tuition	19	3.0	19	3.0	0	0.0
Full tuition	0	0.0	0	0.0	0	0.0
More than full tuition	0	0.0	0	0.0	0	0.0
Median grant amount			$7,000		$0	

Informational and Library Resources

Total amount spent on library materials	$1,059,602
Study seating capacity inside the library	568
# of full-time equivalent professional librarians	8
Hours per week library is open	168
# of open, wired connections available to students	68
# of networked computers available for use by students	43
Has wireless network?	Y
Requires computer?	N

JD Attrition (from prior year)

	Academic	Other	Total	
	#	#	#	%
1st year	1	15	16	7.5
2nd year	0	1	1	0.5
3rd year	0	0	0	0.0
4th year	0	0	0	0.0

Employment (9 months after graduation)

	Total	Percentage
Employment status known	187	97.9
Employment status unknown	4	2.1
Employed	179	95.7
Pursuing graduate degrees	2	1.1
Unemployed (seeking, not seeking, or studying for the bar)	4	2.1
Type of Employment		
# employed in law firms	101	56.4
# employed in business and industry	12	6.7
# employed in government	32	17.9
# employed in public interest	5	2.8
# employed as judicial clerks	27	15.1
# employed in academia	1	0.6
Geographic Location		
# employed in state	55	30.7
# employed outside the US	2	1.1
# of states where employed		28

Bar Passage Rates

First-time takers	210	Reporting %	90.95
Average school %	91.63	Average state %	80.39

Average pass difference 11.24

Jurisdiction	Takers	Passers	Pass %	State %	Diff %
Virginia	85	75	88.24	77.06	11.18
New York	20	20	100.00	86.51	13.49
Pennsylvania	14	14	100.00	85.69	14.31
Maryland	13	12	92.31	78.20	14.11
Others (15)	59	54	91.53		

WILLIAM & MARY LAW SCHOOL

613 South Henry Street
Williamsburg, VA 23185
Phone: 757.221.3785; Fax: 757.221.3261
E-mail: lawadm@wm.edu; Website: http://law.wm.edu

Introduction

Established in 1779 at the request of Thomas Jefferson, William & Mary Law School is the nation's oldest law school. William & Mary combines rich historic roots, a strong national reputation, and a wealth of programs at a cost rated to be "a very good buy." William & Mary is concerned about students' intellectual development and encourages them to become constructive citizens who will do their part in society. Many assume William & Mary is a private school—it is not. The Law School is small enough for people to know one another by name and large enough to form a critical mass for learning and scholarship.

Members of the 2010–2011 student body earned undergraduate degrees from 264 colleges and universities and represent 43 states, DC, and 11 other countries. The Law School is located a few blocks from Colonial Williamsburg and within short driving distance of the metropolitan areas of Washington, DC; Richmond; and Norfolk. Visits and student tours are encouraged.

Library and Physical Facilities

The Wolf Law Library's collection of more than 400,000 volumes and its service-oriented staff provide an excellent setting for study and research. Legal materials are available in all formats, including an extensive treatise collection covering all areas of law. A major library expansion and renovation project was completed in 2007 and has resulted in a student-friendly, state-of-the-art facility with cutting-edge technology. Features of the library include two reading rooms offering ample views of the outdoors, six lounges, abundant seating with Internet access, 12 group-study rooms, two computer labs, a rare book room, and a game room. The entire building is Wi-Fi compatible.

The McGlothlin Courtroom at the Law School is the nation's most technologically advanced trial and appellate chamber. The courtroom is designed to permit trials with multiple remote appearances and web-based evidence, and offers students hands-on training in the use of state-of-the-art courtroom technology. It has a wide variety of features, including all available major court record systems, evidence presentation technologies, assistive and foreign language interpretation technologies, and critical infrastructure technologies.

The Law School is located between the National Center for State Courts and William & Mary's graduate apartment complex, where 20 percent of law students live. A wide variety of off-campus housing options are available in the Williamsburg area.

Curriculum

The required first-year curriculum includes constitutional law, contracts, torts, civil procedure, property, criminal law, and legal skills. The Legal Skills Program utilizes simulated law offices and client representation to teach the skills necessary for the practice of law as well as legal research, writing, and professional responsibility. It is augmented in the second year by a skills-track course in civil litigation, criminal litigation, and transactional work. To earn a Juris Doctor degree, students must successfully complete 86 credit hours through full-time study, all required courses, and a significant paper of publishable quality. Students may choose yearly from more than 100 upper-level courses covering a broad range of contemporary and traditional areas of law. The Law School offers seven clinical programs (legal aid clinic, domestic violence clinic, federal tax practice clinic, innocence project clinic, special education advocacy clinic, military commissions prosecution, and the veterans benefits clinic). Students also may earn academic credit by externing with judges, prosecutors, public defenders, law firms, government agencies, legislators, civil legal service providers, corporations, and private nonprofit organizations.

Joint-Degree Programs

There are three joint-degree programs: JD/MBA, JD/MPP, and JD/MA in American Studies. The JD/MBA and the JD/MPP combine traditional five-year programs into four years of study. Students may complete the JD/MA in either three or four years.

International Programs

A summer session in Madrid, Spain, offers a five-week program in which students can earn up to six credits. William & Mary professors and prominent Spanish professors and practitioners teach the courses in English. JD students may also study abroad in Beijing, China; Vienna, Austria; Madrid, Spain; Auckland, New Zealand; Tokyo, Japan; Luxembourg; and Hong Kong during their third academic year.

The Law School also offers an LLM in the American Legal System for students from outside the United States who take courses with the JD students and bring the richness of their legal traditions to the classroom.

Special Programs

Through the Institute of Bill of Rights Law, the Law School has become one of the preeminent institutions studying the Constitution's Bill of Rights. The Institute sponsors lectures, symposia, and publications that entice scholars to examine important constitutional issues. The programs and initiatives of the Center for Legal and Court Technology seek to improve the administration of justice through the use of technology. The Center puts the latest technology to the test in laboratory trials conducted by students in the McGlothlin Courtroom.

Exciting new cocurricular programs at the Law School include the Human Security Law Program, which offers students the opportunity to learn about the interplay between national defense and the protection of civil rights; the Program in Comparative Legal Studies and Post-Conflict Peacebuilding, which serves as a focal point for research and study on comparative legal practices and the mechanisms used to reestablish justice after war and internal strife; the Property Rights Project, which encourages scholarship on the role that property rights plays in society and also facilitates the exchange of ideas between scholars and practitioners; the Election Law Program, which seeks to provide assistance to judges who are called upon to resolve difficult election law disputes; and the George Wythe Society of Citizen Lawyers, a program that focuses on constructive citizenship.

The Loan Repayment Assistance Program provides up to $5,000 in loan forgiveness annually for a maximum of three years to selected graduates working full time for civil legal service organizations, public defenders or prosecutors, government agencies, or other 501(c)(3) organizations with a public service mission.

Student Activities

Scholars and practitioners frequently cite articles from our student-managed academic journals. These publications include *William and Mary Law Review*, *William & Mary Bill of Rights Journal*, *William & Mary Business Law Review*, *William & Mary Environmental Law and Policy Review*, and *William & Mary Journal of Women and the Law*. The Law School also has a highly competitive Moot Court Program and National Trial Team. In 2009, William & Mary students won first place at the Tulane Sports Law Appellate Moot Court Competition. In 2010, William & Mary students won first place at the National Moot Court Competition, Region IV; the Regent University National Constitutional Law Tournament; and the Federal Bar Association's Thurgood A. Marshall Moot Court Tournament. In 2011, team members won the International Criminal Court Moot Competition. Our National Trial Team advocates were champions of the Academy of Trial Lawyers of Allegheny County Trial Competition (Gourley) in 2008, 2009, and 2010. They were 2010 champions of the John L. Costello National Criminal Law Trial Competition and Phi Alpha Delta Invitational, and finalist at the ABA Section of Labor and Employment Law's Student Trial Advocacy Regional Competition in Washington, DC. Again, in 2010, a William & Mary graduating student was awarded the Virginia Bar Association Oliver Hill Law Student Pro Bono Award. More

than 40 student organizations reflect the diverse interests of the student body. For more information about William & Mary's student organizations, visit the Student Life section of the website.

Career Services

The Mission Statement of the Office of Career Services (OCS) focuses on the following priorities: foster professionalism, ethics, and integrity in the career development and job search process so students will continue to demonstrate those traits as citizen lawyers; partner with students and alumni to help them explore career options, learn about and obtain employment opportunities, further long-term professional development, and achieve career satisfaction; maintain comprehensive career and professional development resources to prepare students and alumni to be competitive candidates; and cultivate constructive, mutually beneficial relationships with employers. To accomplish these priorities, OCS provides students and alumni with comprehensive professional services, including individual counseling, workshops, programs, and presentations by practitioners from a variety of employer types and practice settings. Students have the opportunity to participate in on-campus interviews and dozens of off-campus interview programs, to arrange videoconference and Skype interviews, and to apply for positions through résumé forwarding and job listings. To assist students working in low-paying or nonpaying government and public service positions, the Law School provided fellowships to 109 students for summer 2010. Fellowship recipients assisted organizations in 18 states, the District of Columbia, Argentina, Azerbaijan, Ireland, Kenya, Sweden, Switzerland, and Tanzania.

APPLICANT PROFILE

William & Mary Law School
This grid includes only applicants who earned 120–180 LSAT scores under standard administrations.

LSAT Score	GPA																					
	3.75 +		3.50–3.74		3.25–3.49		3.00–3.24		2.75–2.99		2.50–2.74		2.25–2.49		2.00–2.24		Below 2.00		No GPA		Total	
	Apps	Adm	Apps	Adm	Apps	Adm	Apps	Adm	Apps	Adm	Apps	Adm	Apps	Adm	Apps	Adm	Apps	Adm	Apps	Adm	Apps	Adm
175–180	16	15	15	14	10	3	16	7	7	1	2	0	1	0	0	0	1	0	1	1	69	41
170–174	74	69	103	77	88	28	35	9	22	0	13	2	6	0	2	0	1	0	1	1	345	186
165–169	350	331	412	261	287	65	178	17	76	1	49	2	16	1	4	0	0	0	27	6	1399	684
160–164	657	126	778	35	645	15	325	11	122	2	68	4	31	2	12	1	0	0	48	0	2686	196
155–159	177	16	252	16	155	10	110	7	49	2	19	0	12	0	2	1	0	0	23	0	799	52
150–154	82	7	113	7	110	9	90	7	42	2	23	1	11	1	4	0	1	0	13	0	489	34
145–149	21	1	51	4	47	1	55	2	43	1	28	1	14	1	4	0	2	0	10	0	275	11
140–144	3	0	12	1	33	0	22	0	21	0	19	0	6	0	4	0	0	0	3	0	123	1
135–139	4	0	5	0	6	0	11	0	8	0	7	0	4	0	3	0	3	0	4	0	55	0
130–134	1	0	0	0	1	0	8	0	3	0	5	0	1	0	1	0	0	0	0	0	20	0
125–129	2	0	0	0	0	0	1	0	1	0	1	0	1	0	2	0	0	0	0	0	8	0
120–124	0	0	0	0	0	0	0	0	0	0	0	0	0	0	1	0	0	0	0	0	1	0
Total	1387	565	1741	415	1382	131	851	60	394	9	234	10	103	5	39	2	8	0	130	8	6269	1205

Apps = Number of Applicants
Adm = Number Admitted
Reflects 99% of the total applicant pool; highest LSAT data reported.

WILLIAM MITCHELL COLLEGE OF LAW

Office of Admissions, 875 Summit Avenue
St. Paul, MN 55105
Phone: 651.290.6476; Toll-free: 888.WMCL.LAW; Fax: 651.290.7535
E-mail: admissions@wmitchell.edu; Website: www.wmitchell.edu

ABA
Approved
Since
1938

The Basics

Type of school	Private
Term	Semester
Application deadline	5/1
Application fee	$50
Financial aid deadline	3/15
Can first year start other than fall?	No
Student to faculty ratio	20.6 to 1
# of housing spaces available restricted to law students	
graduate housing for which law students are eligible	

Faculty and Administrators

	Total		Men		Women		Minorities	
	Spr	Fall	Spr	Fall	Spr	Fall	Spr	Fall
Full-time	34	34	19	17	15	17	4	4
Other full-time	0	0	0	0	0	0	0	0
Deans, librarians, & others who teach	13	12	5	5	8	7	2	1
Part-time	122	237	69	122	53	115	41	84
Total	169	283	93	144	76	139	47	89

Curriculum

	Full-Time	Part-Time
Typical first-year section size	80	70
Is there typically a "small section" of the first-year class, other than Legal Writing, taught by full-time faculty	No	No
If yes, typical size offered last year		
# of classroom course titles beyond first-year curriculum	142	

# of upper division courses, excluding seminars, with an enrollment:	Under 25	116
	25–49	54
	50–74	16
	75–99	8
	100+	0

	Full-Time	Part-Time
# of seminars	95	
# of seminar positions available	1,794	
# of seminar positions filled	849	431
# of positions available in simulation courses	1,867	
# of simulation positions filled	1,004	519
# of positions available in faculty supervised clinical courses	353	
# of faculty supervised clinical positions filled	197	103
# involved in field placements	127	57
# involved in law journals	74	30
# involved in moot court or trial competitions	99	36
# of credit hours required to graduate	86	

JD Enrollment and Ethnicity

	Men		Women		Full-Time		Part-Time		1st-Year		Total		JD Degs. Awd.
	#	%	#	%	#	%	#	%	#	%	#	%	
All Hispanics	10	2.0	12	2.4	12	1.8	10	2.9	10	2.8	22	2.2	6
Am. Ind./AK Nat.	5	1.0	7	1.4	9	1.3	3	0.9	3	0.8	12	1.2	0
Asian	16	3.1	31	6.1	26	3.9	21	6.1	20	5.6	47	4.6	14
Black/Af. Am.	9	1.8	15	3.0	11	1.6	13	3.8	6	1.7	24	2.4	4
Nat. Hl/Pac. Isl.	0	0.0	1	0.2	0	0.0	1	0.3	0	0.0	1	0.1	0
2 or more races	2	0.4	5	1.0	5	0.7	2	0.6	5	1.4	7	0.7	0
Subtotal (minor.)	42	8.3	71	14.1	63	9.4	50	14.5	44	12.4	113	11.2	24
Nonres. Alien	5	1.0	3	0.6	6	0.9	2	0.6	2	0.6	8	0.8	0
White/Cauc.	362	71.3	358	70.9	487	73.0	233	67.3	234	66.1	720	71.1	199
Unknown	99	19.5	73	14.5	111	16.6	61	17.6	74	20.9	172	17.0	73
Total	508	50.1	505	49.9	667	65.8	346	34.2	354	34.9	1013		300

Transfers

Transfers in	5
Transfers out	5

Tuition and Fees

	Resident	Nonresident
Full-time	$33,800	$33,800
Part-time	$24,450	$24,450
Tuition Guarantee Program		N

Living Expenses

Estimated living expenses for singles		
Living on campus	Living off campus	Living at home
N/A	$18,074	N/A

WILLIAM MITCHELL COLLEGE OF LAW

ABA
Approved
Since
1938

GPA and LSAT Scores

	Total	Full-Time	Part-Time
# of apps	1,448	1,298	150
# of offers	802	673	129
# of matrics	357	274	83
75% GPA	3.59	3.60	3.53
Median GPA	3.37	3.40	3.20
25% GPA	3.14	3.17	2.90
75% LSAT	159	159	158
Median LSAT	156	156	153
25% LSAT	152	153	149

Grants and Scholarships (from prior year)

	Total		Full-Time		Part-Time	
	#	%	#	%	#	%
Total # of students	977		603		374	
Total # receiving grants	363	37.2	242	40.1	121	32.4
Less than 1/2 tuition	221	22.6	154	25.5	67	17.9
Half to full tuition	130	13.3	83	13.8	47	12.6
Full tuition	12	1.2	5	0.8	7	1.9
More than full tuition	0	0.0	0	0.0	0	·0.0
Median grant amount			$18,932		$11,003	

Informational and Library Resources

Total amount spent on library materials	$1,055,553
Study seating capacity inside the library	671
# of full-time equivalent professional librarians	9
Hours per week library is open	109
# of open, wired connections available to students	105
# of networked computers available for use by students	70
Has wireless network?	Y
Requires computer?	N

JD Attrition (from prior year)

	Academic	Other	Total	
	#	#	#	%
1st year	6	13	19	6.3
2nd year	1	0	1	0.3
3rd year	0	0	0	0.0
4th year	0	0	0	0.0

Employment (9 months after graduation)

	Total	Percentage
Employment status known	327	100.0
Employment status unknown	0	0.0
Employed	281	85.9
Pursuing graduate degrees	4	1.2
Unemployed (seeking, not seeking, or studying for the bar)	20	6.1
Type of Employment		
# employed in law firms	119	42.3
# employed in business and industry	76	27.0
# employed in government	29	10.3
# employed in public interest	14	5.0
# employed as judicial clerks	22	7.8
# employed in academia	7	2.5
Geographic Location		
# employed in state	216	76.9
# employed outside the US	1	0.4
# of states where employed		12

Bar Passage Rates

First-time takers	293	Reporting %	95.22
Average school %	85.66	Average state %	89.64

Average pass difference   –3.98

Jurisdiction	Takers	Passers	Pass %	State %	Diff %
Minnesota	267	228	85.39	89.58	–4.19
Wisconsin	12	11	91.67	90.80	0.87

WILLIAM MITCHELL COLLEGE OF LAW

Office of Admissions, 875 Summit Avenue
St. Paul, MN 55105
Phone: 651.290.6476; Toll-free: 888.WMCL.LAW; Fax: 651.290.7535
E-mail: admissions@wmitchell.edu; Website: www.wmitchell.edu

Introduction

William Mitchell College of Law, founded in 1900, is an independent, private law school in St. Paul, Minnesota. Named for one of the state's most respected judges, William Mitchell has pioneered a legal education that integrates practical skills with legal theory. William Mitchell welcomes both traditional and nontraditional law students from all walks of life, and students have an option of attending on a full- or part-time basis. William Mitchell College of Law's clinical, legal writing, and trial advocacy programs are nationally recognized. The college has produced many distinguished leaders at the bench and bar and in the business and civic arenas, among them the 15th Chief Justice of the United States, Warren E. Burger, and the first woman to serve on the Minnesota Supreme Court, Rosalie E. Wahl. The largest law school in Minnesota, William Mitchell has approximately 1,000 students, 39 full-time faculty members, and more than 11,000 alumni. William Mitchell has more alumni serving in the Minnesota judiciary than any other law school.

The college is accredited by the ABA, is a member of the AALS, and is approved by the US Veterans Administration.

Faculty

From day one, William Mitchell faculty members treat students as future colleagues. Faculty members are known for their teaching, scholarship, and practice. Faculty members have served on the bench, worked in the region's top law firms, and have had careers in public service, government, and corporations. William Mitchell professors have written many of the books used by law school professors and legal practitioners throughout the country. Faculty briefs and research have been accessed thousands of times by legal scholars, and professors are regularly quoted by national and international media. Many professors are exploring new ground on issues such as cyber law, intellectual property, national security, elder law, family law, and food safety. Adjunct professors, who practice at 18 of the top 25 law firms in the state, bring real-world practice to the classroom and connection to the practice of law.

Academics

William Mitchell students graduate with the practical wisdom to put the law to work. For 110 years, William Mitchell has pioneered a legal education that integrates practical skills with legal theory. William Mitchell requires students to take practical skills courses, including clinics, practicum, legal writing and research, and advocacy. In fact, William Mitchell was one of the first schools to develop a clinical program more than 30 years ago. Our clinical, legal writing, and trial advocacy programs are consistently highly rated on a national level.

In addition to more than 200 law school courses, William Mitchell has several programs designed to help law students transition to lawyers. Keystone courses, generally taken in the final year of law school, address real-world challenges, build on previous courses, and enable students to produce substantial, concrete manifestations of their learning. The Fellows Program links exceptional students with a faculty member whose research and activities are changing the law itself. Students receive specialized training beyond the regular curriculum and have access to a range of special intellectual opportunities and networking events. And, Pathways to the Profession of Law is an innovative web application that helps law students customize their course schedules, integrate their learning, and build experiences toward legal practice.

To focus faculty scholarship, spur collaboration between legal education and the profession, and continue its tradition of innovative teaching, William Mitchell has developed academic centers in critical areas of the legal profession, including the Intellectual Property Institute, Center for Negotiation and Justice, Center for Elder Justice and Policy, Rosalie Wahl Legal Practice Center, Public Health Law Center, National Security Forum, Center for Law and Business, and Indian Law Program.

Enrollment Options

William Mitchell was started as a night law school by working attorneys more than a century ago to provide legal training for people of modest means. If not for the part-time, evening tradition at William Mitchell, many successful lawyers practicing today would not have been able to pursue their law school dreams. William Mitchell is the only law school in the region with a night school program, allowing students to continue to work to help pay for school, gain work experience, and balance family life. After the first year, students have the option to switch between full- and part-time enrollment as often as each semester to accommodate work experience and family life. Regardless of enrollment status, you achieve the same high-quality education. Advanced and elective classes are typically offered in the evening, so part-time and full-time students take classes together and have equal access to full-time and adjunct faculty. Although classes meet at set times, William Mitchell offers you enough flexibility to build your law school schedule around a clerkship, continue in your current career track or day job, or take care of other responsibilities.

Library and Physical Facilities

The Minneapolis-St. Paul region is home to more than 20 Fortune 500 companies and is frequently cited as one of the top 10 places to live and work in the United States. William Mitchell's campus is located in St. Paul, the state capital, along the historic and elegant Summit Avenue. The campus is a short walk to the lively Grand Avenue with restaurants and shopping, and many students find housing in the neighborhood.

The physical design of the campus as a whole mirrors the William Mitchell philosophy that practical skills are inseparable from legal doctrine. Our Rosalie Wahl Legal Practice Center, home to our top-rated clinical and skills programs, is located in the same building as classrooms and faculty offices. The campus is also equipped with technologically advanced moot courtrooms, computer labs, seminar rooms, a student lounge and cafeteria, and offices for student organizations.

The Warren E. Burger Library's extensive in-house and online collection, customer service-oriented staff, and welcoming design make it the preferred choice for alumni, legal professionals, and faculty. Nearly all of our professional librarians have JD degrees, in addition to master's of library and information science degrees. Several have law practice experience. Our librarians help plan research strategies, locate and use legal and nonlegal resources, do computer-assisted research, and find items that are not available at William Mitchell. You'll also find our librarians in the classroom. Extended reference desk hours reflect our commitment to the needs of our students, faculty, and alumni.

Public Service Opportunities

William Mitchell's heritage is rooted in public service. Students volunteer more than 6,000 hours of supervised pro bono service each year to our partner, the Minnesota Justice Foundation, which matches interested law students with volunteer opportunities. Students also perform approximately 14,000 hours of pro bono service annually through our for-credit legal clinical program.

Special Programs

In addition to organizing and hosting **Mitchell in London** each year, William Mitchell is a member of the Consortium for Innovative Legal Education, a consortium of four independent law schools, which provides students with the opportunity to enroll in 10 summer and semester study-abroad programs, as well as the opportunity to study as visiting students at any of the participating schools. The **Academic Achievement Program** is designed to help students work up to their potential by teaching the skills required to solve problems effectively. Individual academic advising and Academic Achievement Workshops are available throughout the year for all students. The workshops include study strategies, time and stress management, critical reading, case briefing, legal analysis, outlining, and exam taking. William Mitchell also offers an LLM Program for foreign law graduates. The

year-long program introduces students from around the world to the legal system of the United States.

Student Body

William Mitchell attracts students with a diversity of life and work experiences. That's what we call the "Mitchell Mix." Our students have all kinds of educational, professional, and cultural backgrounds. For example, students range in age from as young as 20 to over 50 and include recent college grads and students who bring professional work experience. Twenty-seven of our entering class hold graduate degrees, and more than 13 percent are people of color. Our student body represents 30 states and 17 foreign countries. Students can participate in more than 30 student organizations, including the Student Bar Association and the *William Mitchell Law Review*.

Career Development

William Mitchell's brand of legal education has earned the school a reputation for graduating lawyers who are prepared to practice. That's why 91.9 percent of the class of 2009 was employed within nine months of graduation. Career development is woven into each year of a student's legal education, helping students polish presentation, networking, and interviewing skills. Our alumni network of more than 11,000 offers students extensive opportunities to gather advice, meet attorneys, and learn about job opportunities both during school and upon graduation.

Scholarships/Financial Aid

Financial aid is available from William Mitchell in the form of merit-based scholarships, federal and alternative loans, and federal work-study. Approximately 90 percent of all William Mitchell students receive some type of financial aid.

APPLICANT PROFILE

William Mitchell College of Law
This grid includes only applicants who earned 120–180 LSAT scores under standard administrations.

LSAT Score	3.75 +		3.50–3.74		3.25–3.49		3.00–3.24		2.75–2.99		2.50–2.74		2.25–2.49		2.00–2.24		Below 2.00		No GPA		Total	
	Apps	Adm	Apps	Adm	Apps	Adm	Apps	Adm	Apps	Adm	Apps	Adm	Apps	Adm	Apps	Adm	Apps	Adm	Apps	Adm	Apps	Adm
175–180	0	0	0	0	1	1	0	0	0	0	0	0	0	0	0	0	0	0	0	0	1	1
170–174	3	3	1	1	4	4	1	1	0	0	0	0	0	0	0	0	0	0	0	0	9	9
165–169	13	13	10	8	6	6	4	4	6	4	2	2	4	3	1	0	0	0	0	0	46	40
160–164	23	19	47	45	42	41	20	19	13	13	8	8	7	4	0	0	0	0	2	1	162	150
155–159	44	44	47	44	73	67	63	56	34	28	17	10	5	1	0	0	1	1	1	1	285	252
150–154	41	40	83	70	104	74	68	32	53	22	24	5	16	1	7	0	1	0	3	2	400	246
145–149	20	16	49	23	69	23	75	21	45	7	29	1	11	0	9	0	0	0	6	1	313	92
140–144	8	2	15	4	22	4	26	3	24	0	16	0	10	0	1	0	0	0	4	0	126	13
135–139	2	0	2	1	8	0	8	0	11	0	7	0	6	0	2	0	0	0	3	0	49	1
130–134	0	0	0	0	4	0	4	0	2	0	4	0	1	0	1	0	1	0	1	0	18	0
125–129	0	0	1	0	1	0	0	0	0	0	2	0	0	0	1	0	0	0	1	0	6	0
120–124	0	0	0	0	0	0	0	0	0	0	0	0	0	0	0	0	0	0	0	0	0	0
Total	154	137	255	196	334	220	269	136	188	74	109	26	60	9	22	0	3	1	21	5	1415	804

Apps = Number of Applicants
Adm = Number Admitted
Reflects 99% of the total applicant pool; highest LSAT data reported.

UNIVERSITY OF WISCONSIN LAW SCHOOL

975 Bascom Mall
Madison, WI 53706
Phone: 608.262.5914; Fax: 608.263.3190
E-mail: admissions@law.wisc.edu; Website: www.law.wisc.edu

The Basics

Type of school	Public
Term	Semester
Application deadline	3/1
Application fee	$56
Financial aid deadline	3/1
Can first year start other than fall?	No
Student to faculty ratio	13.0 to 1
# of housing spaces available restricted to law students	
graduate housing for which law students are eligible	870

Faculty and Administrators

	Total		Men		Women		Minorities	
	Spr	Fall	Spr	Fall	Spr	Fall	Spr	Fall
Full-time	45	54	25	29	20	25	11	13
Other full-time	10	11	3	6	7	5	1	1
Deans, librarians, & others who teach	5	5	3	3	2	2	1	1
Part-time	82	48	53	32	29	16	32	15
Total	142	118	84	70	58	48	45	30

Curriculum

		Full-Time	Part-Time
Typical first-year section size		70	0
Is there typically a "small section" of the first-year class, other than Legal Writing, taught by full-time faculty		Yes	Yes
If yes, typical size offered last year		22	
# of classroom course titles beyond first-year curriculum		164	
# of upper division courses, excluding seminars, with an enrollment:	Under 25	134	
	25–49	40	
	50–74	13	
	75–99	5	
	100+	6	
# of seminars		80	
# of seminar positions available		1,293	
# of seminar positions filled		927	0
# of positions available in simulation courses		550	
# of simulation positions filled		432	0
# of positions available in faculty supervised clinical courses		387	
# of faculty supervised clinical positions filled		366	0
# involved in field placements		219	0
# involved in law journals		178	0
# involved in moot court or trial competitions		158	0
# of credit hours required to graduate		90	

JD Enrollment and Ethnicity

	Men		Women		Full-Time		Part-Time		1st-Year		Total		JD Degs. Awd.
	#	%	#	%	#	%	#	%	#	%	#	%	
All Hispanics	27	6.2	29	7.9	51	6.8	5	10.2	17	6.4	56	7.0	21
Am. Ind./AK Nat.	13	3.0	5	1.4	17	2.3	1	2.0	4	1.5	18	2.2	6
Asian	22	5.0	22	6.0	44	5.8	0	0.0	12	4.5	44	5.5	21
Black/Af. Am.	20	4.6	36	9.8	54	7.2	2	4.1	17	6.4	56	7.0	18
Nat. HI/Pac. Isl.	0	0.0	0	0.0	0	0.0	0	0.0	0	0.0	0	0.0	0
2 or more races	3	0.7	2	0.5	3	0.4	2	4.1	5	1.9	5	0.6	0
Subtotal (minor.)	85	19.5	94	25.5	169	22.4	10	20.4	55	20.8	179	22.3	66
Nonres. Alien	9	2.1	13	3.5	22	2.9	0	0.0	6	2.3	22	2.7	0
White/Cauc.	306	70.2	250	67.9	519	68.7	37	75.5	190	72.0	556	69.2	172
Unknown	36	8.3	11	3.0	45	6.0	2	4.1	13	4.9	47	5.8	15
Total	436	54.2	368	45.8	755	93.9	49	6.1	264	32.8	804		257

Transfers

Transfers in	26
Transfers out	9

Tuition and Fees

	Resident	Nonresident
Full-time	$18,049	$37,586
Part-time	$1,508	$3,136
Tuition Guarantee Program		N

Living Expenses

Estimated living expenses for singles

Living on campus	Living off campus	Living at home
$16,990	$16,990	$9,870

*Part-time tuition and fees per credit.

UNIVERSITY OF WISCONSIN LAW SCHOOL

ABA Approved Since 1923

GPA and LSAT Scores

	Total	Full-Time	Part-Time
# of apps	2,829	2,829	0
# of offers	599	599	0
# of matrics	246	246	0
75% GPA	3.76	3.76	0.00
Median GPA	3.63	3.63	0.00
25% GPA	3.29	3.29	0.00
75% LSAT	164	164	0
Median LSAT	163	163	0
25% LSAT	158	158	0

Grants and Scholarships (from prior year)

	Total		Full-Time		Part-Time	
	#	%	#	%	#	%
Total # of students	825		792		33	
Total # receiving grants	247	29.9	247	31.2	0	0.0
Less than 1/2 tuition	122	14.8	122	15.4	0	0.0
Half to full tuition	93	11.3	93	11.7	0	0.0
Full tuition	4	0.5	4	0.5	0	0.0
More than full tuition	28	3.4	28	3.5	0	0.0
Median grant amount			$12,000		$0	

Informational and Library Resources

Total amount spent on library materials	$1,182,956
Study seating capacity inside the library	613
# of full-time equivalent professional librarians	11
Hours per week library is open	104
# of open, wired connections available to students	526
# of networked computers available for use by students	74
Has wireless network?	Y
Requires computer?	Y

JD Attrition (from prior year)

	Academic	Other	Total	
	#	#	#	%
1st year	1	17	18	6.3
2nd year	1	1	2	0.7
3rd year	0	0	0	0.0
4th year	0	0	0	0.0

Employment (9 months after graduation)

	Total	Percentage
Employment status known	267	97.1
Employment status unknown	8	2.9
Employed	247	92.5
Pursuing graduate degrees	7	2.6
Unemployed (seeking, not seeking, or studying for the bar)	8	3.0
Type of Employment		
# employed in law firms	125	50.6
# employed in business and industry	25	10.1
# employed in government	40	16.2
# employed in public interest	21	8.5
# employed as judicial clerks	10	4.0
# employed in academia	22	8.9
Geographic Location		
# employed in state	142	57.5
# employed outside the US	3	1.2
# of states where employed	21	

Bar Passage Rates

First-time takers	295	Reporting %	93.22
Average school %	100.00	Average state %	90.80
Average pass difference	9.20		

Jurisdiction	Takers	Passers	Pass %	State %	Diff %
Wisconsin	275	275	100.00	90.80	9.20

UNIVERSITY OF WISCONSIN LAW SCHOOL

975 Bascom Mall
Madison, WI 53706
Phone: 608.262.5914; Fax: 608.263.3190
E-mail: admissions@law.wisc.edu; Website: www.law.wisc.edu

A Preeminent Law School, A World-Class University, A Beautiful City

The UW Law School is one of the most intellectually exciting law schools in the country, attracting students from around the world. These students represent a variety of backgrounds, ages, interests, races, nationalities, and life experiences; encouraging a robust exchange of ideas.

Top applicants are drawn to the UW Law School because of its tradition of excellence, its beautiful setting in the heart of one of the world's leading research universities, and its law-in-action philosophy, an approach that differentiates it from other law schools.

The UW Law School is located in Madison, an affordable city strategically and conveniently situated in the middle of a triangle formed by Chicago, Minneapolis, and Milwaukee. As the state capital, Madison is home to many courts and state and federal government agencies—all within walking distance of the Law School.

A Commitment to Diversity and Community

A major indicator of the strength of any law school is its student body. The fall 2010 entering class of 246 students represents 29 states and 97 undergraduate institutions. Annually, approximately 40 percent of our students are from outside of Wisconsin, close to half are women, and more than 25 percent are students of color. The UW Law School's admission policies enhance the diversity, vigor, social awareness, and academic ability of the student body. There is a special feeling of community in the school and an informal, supportive atmosphere, reflecting a strong commitment by faculty and administrators to student learning, morale, and well-being.

The Faculty: Leading Scholars and Outstanding Teachers

The UW Law School's nationally recognized faculty come from a wide range of backgrounds and offer students strong role models and a variety of experiences. They are leading scholars who are also actively involved in the law. They advise on stem cell issues, represent clients on death row, work with congressional staffers to draft legislation, and provide legal advice to poor farmers in the South. They are interesting lawyers doing interesting things, but first and foremost, they are excellent teachers who are committed to their students. A superb clinical faculty and an experienced adjunct faculty provide additional teaching resources and bring practical experience into the classroom.

The Curriculum: Law in Action

Students at the UW Law School have many opportunities to experience law-in-action. An extensive curriculum places an emphasis on the dynamics of the law (how the law relates to social change and to society as a whole) while at the same time emphasizing skill development, particularly legal analysis and writing. The first-year small-section program teaches the fundamentals of legal analysis and reasoning in a supportive setting. Two of a student's first-year classes—a substantive law class and a legal research and writing class—are small sections consisting of 25 or fewer students. These small sections allow students to receive individual feedback, organize study groups, and form lasting friendships.

In the second and third year of law school, there is time both to explore the curriculum and develop the lawyering skills needed to practice. The UW Law School is a national law school that prepares future lawyers to work wherever they choose. Students select courses from an extraordinary breadth and depth of offerings, affording them the opportunity to explore cutting-edge legal issues in the classroom and/or to apply their knowledge in one of the many clinical programs.

Dual-Degree Programs

Renowned for its interdisciplinary approach, the UW Law School offers many opportunities for students to combine the study of law with a graduate degree in another subject. There are many existing dual-degree programs. If one of the existing programs does not meet a student's academic needs, the Law School will help create an individualized curriculum.

Clinicals and Skills Training: Hands-on Learning

The UW Law School strongly believes that practical experience is an essential part of legal education. With one of the largest clinical programs in the country, the UW Law School offers a wide variety of hands-on lawyering experiences with real clients and excellent supervision. From representing low-income clients, to teaming up with medical students as advocates for newly diagnosed cancer patients, or assisting inmates in state and federal prisons, these experiences are invaluable opportunities. Judicial internships, externships, and our innovative lawyering skills program provide additional hands-on learning experiences.

Going Global: International Law and Study Abroad

Ten professors devote their scholarship and teaching primarily to international or comparative law, and many others integrate analysis of foreign legal developments into their domestic law courses. The Law School hosts international students and professors, bringing diverse international perspectives to the classroom, and the university has one of the largest groups of international students in the country. Students can also study with one of the ten foreign law faculties with which the Law School has exchange agreements or participate in foreign study programs of other US law schools. Additional international opportunities are available through the Law School's East Asian Legal Studies Center, established to formalize and increase the Law School's interaction in East and Southeast Asia.

Student Activities

More than 30 organizations provide outstanding opportunities for students to pursue their talents and interests. Several moot court competitions at the UW Law School enable students to gain experience with brief writing an oral advocacy, and three student journals—*Wisconsin Law Review, Wisconsin International Law Journal,* and *Wisconsin Journal of Law, Gender, and Society*—give students an opportunity to gain invaluable training in legal research and writing.

Career Opportunities

Leading law firms, government agencies, businesses, and public interest organizations seek to hire UW Law School graduates. A broad range of legal employers from many major cities participate in the on-campus interview program. The Law School also participates in off-campus job fairs each year in cities such as New York; Washington, DC; Chicago; and Minneapolis. Our students receive assistance from many of our more than 12,000 alumni throughout the country, and our graduates typically accept jobs in more than 20 different states.

APPLICANT PROFILE

Admission to the University of Wisconsin Law School is competitive. The most recent entering class had a median LSAT score of 163 and a median GPA of 3.63. The Law School does not provide a profile chart because its admission decisions involve many factors that are not represented by undergraduate GPA and LSAT scores. While candidates with higher grades and scores tend to be admitted at higher rates, GPA and LSAT scores alone are not necessarily good predictors of admission decisions on individual applications.

UNIVERSITY OF WYOMING COLLEGE OF LAW

Dept. 3035, 1000 E. University Avenue
Laramie, WY 82071
Phone: 307.766.6416; Fax: 307.766.6417
E-mail: lawadmis@uwyo.edu; Website: www.uwyo.edu/law

ABA
Approved
Since
1923

The Basics

Type of school	Public
Term	Semester
Application deadline	12/1 3/1
Application fee	$50
Financial aid deadline	3/1
Can first year start other than fall?	No
Student to faculty ratio	10.6 to 1
# of housing spaces available restricted to law students	
graduate housing for which law students are eligible	230

Faculty and Administrators

	Total		Men		Women		Minorities	
	Spr	Fall	Spr	Fall	Spr	Fall	Spr	Fall
Full-time	17	19	13	14	4	5	2	3
Other full-time	1	2	1	2	0	0	0	0
Deans, librarians, & others who teach	6	6	2	2	4	4	1	1
Part-time	6	2	4	0	2	2	0	0
Total	30	29	20	18	10	11	3	4

Curriculum

	Full-Time	Part-Time
Typical first-year section size	80	0
Is there typically a "small section" of the first-year class, other than Legal Writing, taught by full-time faculty	No	No
If yes, typical size offered last year		
# of classroom course titles beyond first-year curriculum	56	
# of upper division courses, excluding seminars, with an enrollment: Under 25	34	
25–49	10	
50–74	5	
75–99	2	
100+	0	
# of seminars	5	
# of seminar positions available	50	
# of seminar positions filled	43	0
# of positions available in simulation courses	137	
# of simulation positions filled	132	0
# of positions available in faculty supervised clinical courses	70	
# of faculty supervised clinical positions filled	57	0
# involved in field placements	53	0
# involved in law journals	33	0
# involved in moot court or trial competitions	18	0
# of credit hours required to graduate	89	

JD Enrollment and Ethnicity

	Men		Women		Full-Time		Part-Time		1st-Year		Total		JD Degs. Awd.
	#	%	#	%	#	%	#	%	#	%	#	%	
All Hispanics	2	1.6	3	2.8	5	2.2	0	0.0	0	0.0	5	2.2	3
Am. Ind./AK Nat.	1	0.8	0	0.0	1	0.4	0	0.0	0	0.0	1	0.4	0
Asian	2	1.6	5	4.6	7	3.0	0	0.0	4	4.9	7	3.0	4
Black/Af. Am.	0	0.0	1	0.9	1	0.4	0	0.0	1	1.2	1	0.4	0
Nat. Hl/Pac. Isl.	0	0.0	0	0.0	0	0.0	0	0.0	0	0.0	0	0.0	0
2 or more races	1	0.8	1	0.9	2	0.9	0	0.0	1	1.2	2	0.9	0
Subtotal (minor.)	6	4.9	10	9.3	16	6.9	0	0.0	6	7.3	16	6.9	7
Nonres. Alien	0	0.0	0	0.0	0	0.0	0	0.0	0	0.0	0	0.0	0
White/Cauc.	89	72.4	85	78.7	174	75.3	0	0.0	65	79.3	174	75.3	52
Unknown	28	22.8	13	12.0	41	17.7	0	0.0	11	13.4	41	17.7	8
Total	123	53.2	108	46.8	231	100.0	0	0.0	82	35.5	231		67

Transfers

Transfers in	2
Transfers out	2

Tuition and Fees

	Resident	Nonresident
Full-time	$11,264	$23,808
Part-time		
Tuition Guarantee Program	N	

Living Expenses

Estimated living expenses for singles		
Living on campus	Living off campus	Living at home
$14,319	$14,319	$6,794

UNIVERSITY OF WYOMING COLLEGE OF LAW

ABA
Approved
Since
1923

GPA and LSAT Scores

	Total	Full-Time	Part-Time
# of apps	624	624	0
# of offers	217	217	0
# of matrics	82	82	0
75% GPA	3.71	3.71	0.00
Median GPA	3.43	3.43	0.00
25% GPA	3.23	3.23	0.00
75% LSAT	157	157	0
Median LSAT	154	154	0
25% LSAT	151	151	0

Grants and Scholarships (from prior year)

	Total #	Total %	Full-Time #	Full-Time %	Part-Time #	Part-Time %
Total # of students	225		225		0	
Total # receiving grants	118	52.4	118	52.4	0	0.0
Less than 1/2 tuition	94	41.8	94	41.8	0	0.0
Half to full tuition	15	6.7	15	6.7	0	0.0
Full tuition	8	3.6	8	3.6	0	0.0
More than full tuition	1	0.4	1	0.4	0	0.0
Median grant amount			$3,000		$0	

Informational and Library Resources

Total amount spent on library materials	$563,185
Study seating capacity inside the library	262
# of full-time equivalent professional librarians	3
Hours per week library is open	107
# of open, wired connections available to students	326
# of networked computers available for use by students	54
Has wireless network?	Y
Requires computer?	N

JD Attrition (from prior year)

	Academic #	Other #	Total #	Total %
1st year	2	6	8	9.6
2nd year	1	0	1	1.3
3rd year	0	0	0	0.0
4th year	0	0	0	0.0

Employment (9 months after graduation)

	Total	Percentage
Employment status known	80	100.0
Employment status unknown	0	0.0
Employed	68	85.0
Pursuing graduate degrees	2	2.5
Unemployed (seeking, not seeking, or studying for the bar)	7	8.7
Type of Employment		
# employed in law firms	33	48.5
# employed in business and industry	9	13.2
# employed in government	7	10.3
# employed in public interest	7	10.3
# employed as judicial clerks	12	17.6
# employed in academia	0	0.0
Geographic Location		
# employed in state	40	58.8
# employed outside the US	0	0.0
# of states where employed		12

Bar Passage Rates

First-time takers	70	Reporting %	78.57
Average school %	90.91	Average state %	80.14
Average pass difference	10.77		

Jurisdiction	Takers	Passers	Pass %	State %	Diff %
Wyoming	48	44	91.67	79.34	12.33
Colorado	7	6	85.71	85.67	0.04

UNIVERSITY OF WYOMING COLLEGE OF LAW

Dept. 3035, 1000 E. University Avenue
Laramie, WY 82071
Phone: 307.766.6416; Fax: 307.766.6417
E-mail: lawadmis@uwyo.edu; Website: www.uwyo.edu/law

Introduction

The University of Wyoming College of Law, founded in 1920, is accredited by the ABA and is a member of the AALS. An excellent faculty of 23 full-time professors and several highly qualified lecturers instructs a student body of approximately 230. The limited size of the student body and the favorable student-to-faculty ratio (10.6 to 1), create an atmosphere of friendliness and informality. Students enjoy a degree of access to faculty rarely found at larger institutions. UW Law provides a high quality, affordable legal education and is considered one of the best value schools in the nation. The College of Law is located on the campus of the University of Wyoming in Laramie. The university, the only four-year institution of higher learning in Wyoming, is comprised of seven colleges, and boasts of many nationally recognized research units. The university has a student body of 13,000. Laramie is a town of 30,000 located in southeastern Wyoming at an altitude of 7,200 feet on the high plains between two mountain ranges. Often referenced as "Law at its Highest Point," UW Law's proximity to the mountains provides a variety of recreational activities, including skiing, backpacking, rock climbing, hiking, mountain biking, camping, fishing, and hunting. Laramie is just two hours north of Denver, Colorado, and 45 minutes from Cheyenne—Wyoming's state capital.

Faculty

The faculty has a proven record of excellence in teaching, research, and scholarship. Particular areas of strength include environmental and natural resource law, water law, constitutional law, and international, business, and transactional law. Faculty members are actively engaged in public service and university functions. Because of our small student body, the University of Wyoming College of Law faculty has instructional and research opportunities often not available in larger institutions. Students regularly converse with their professors both inside and outside the classroom, establishing lifelong professional connections.

Curriculum

The 1L year consists of foundational subjects, including Contracts, Property, Torts, Civil Procedure, Constitutional Law, Legal Research and Writing, Criminal Law, Appellate Advocacy, and Introduction to Law. During the 2L year, students choose from a variety of elective courses and take two required courses: Evidence and Professional Responsibility. Prior to graduation, students also complete an advanced writing course and one skills course. Practical legal training is available through four clinical programs: alternative dispute resolution, advanced legal research, legal skills and problems, and trial practice. Numerous externship opportunities are available including state and federal courts, Wyoming Supreme Court, Shoshone and Arapaho Tribal Court, the US Attorney's Office, Wyoming Attorney General, State and Federal Public Defender, FBI, JAG, municipal and government agencies, and other nonprofit entities, including the Innocence Project, ACLU, Biodiversity Conservation Alliance, and Access to Justice. Clinics, externships, internships, and faculty research projects are available each term.

Special Programs

Students may obtain practical experience and academic credit in four clinical programs: (1) Defender Aid—students brief and argue criminal appeals for indigent persons, and assist penitentiary inmates in post-conviction cases; (2) Prosecution Assistance—students work with prosecuting attorneys in criminal cases; (3) Legal Services—students provide legal assistance to economically disadvantaged persons; and (4) Domestic Violence—students address legal issues of domestic violence victims. Students also can participate in an International Human Rights Practicum addressing immigration, asylum, and other human rights issues. All clinical programs and practicums operate under faculty supervision. Under Wyoming state law, students in the clinics can brief and argue cases before the Wyoming Supreme Court, an opportunity that is rare—if not unique—among law schools. Students also regularly appear in state court hearings and represent clients in a variety of venues and proceedings.

The college offers three joint degrees: JD/MA in Environment and Natural Resources, JD/MPA, and JD/MBA. The College of Law has had a strong program in environment and natural resources for many years. Courses are offered in environmental law, oil and gas, mining law, public lands, water rights, and energy/climate. UW Law has strengths in trial and appellate practice, business planning, transactional law, estate planning, corporate and commercial law, administrative law, consumer law, Indian law, family/domestic law, and international law.

UW Law and Kyung Hee University in Seoul, Korea, are partners in a Memorandum of Agreement which provides opportunities for UW students to study in Korea, to aid in international trade negotiations, and to assist South Korea as it implements the American jury trial system. A summer trial institute for Korean attorneys will be held on the UW campus.

Admission Standards

UW Law's mission is to admit candidates whose intellectual abilities and proven academic skills indicate they will successfully complete our academic program and be productive in their professional endeavors. We seek candidates with potential for leadership in the legal and other professions, the judiciary, government, or community. UW Law expects students be committed to hard work, honesty, integrity, and community service commensurate with the legal profession. We seek candidates whose diverse backgrounds, experiences, knowledge and perspective will enliven and enrich the learning experiences of fellow students, faculty, and the academic community. The College of Law admits an entering class of 75 to 80 students. The college accepts applications on October 1 for the class entering the following August. An early admission program is available for those who apply before December 1. The entering class is selected from applications completed by March 1. Applicants should take the LSAT no later than February and should register with LSAC's Credential Assembly Service and request official undergraduate transcripts by mid-January.

Applicants must have an undergraduate degree from an accredited institution prior to matriculation. Admission is based on applicant's undergraduate records, LSAT scores, personal statement, and other criteria relevant to success in the study and practice of law. Applicants may submit three letters of recommendation. UW Law does not discriminate on the basis of race, color, religion, sex, national origin, disability, age, veteran status, sexual orientation, or political beliefs.

Student Activities

The College of Law publishes the student-edited *Wyoming Law Review* twice annually. Other organizations include Potter Law Club (student government), three law fraternities, Students for Equal Justice, Intellectual Property Club, International Law Students, Natural Resources Law Forum, Women's Law Forum, J. Reuben Clark Society, and the Wyoming Student Trial Lawyers. Students participate in the National Moot Court, National Environmental Law Moot Court, National Client Counseling, and the ATLA National Student Trial Advocacy. The college has two law school honorary societies: the Order of the Coif and Excellence in Advocacy.

Career Services

About 80 percent of graduates remain in the Rocky Mountain region, but UW Law has alumni around the globe. The curriculum is broad in scope, providing a core foundation of legal knowledge applicable in a wide range of legal and geographic areas.

UW Law graduates practice primarily in small private firms or are employed by federal, state, local, and tribal governments. A high percentage of graduates consistently work in state and federal judicial clerkships. Students are also employed in public service, public interest, and many alternative law careers.

As with other aspects of UW Law, the small size of the student body permits Career Services to provide students with personal attention not available at larger institutions. Students receive one-on-one career counseling and job-search assistance for permanent or summer employment. Career Services also provides insightful career panels, interview experience, and résumé/cover letter workshops. A network of loyal alumni hire, often exclusively, at the College of Law. Fall and spring on-campus interviews also provide many firms and students with a chance to interview one another. An online posting system allows organizations to announce legal jobs across the country to UW students. Career services online and library resources are available to all students.

Financial Aid

State and privately funded scholarships are available, and greater than 50 percent of students receive some financial aid. Scholarship awards are based upon merit, need, and diversity. Students should file the FAFSA prior to March 1. Scholarship applications are submitted to the College of Law. Student loans and other financial resources are administered through the UW Student Financial Aid Office.

Facilities

UW Law contains large classrooms, courtrooms, seminar/study rooms, and individual student lockers and study carrels. The spacious on-site library has 350,000 volumes and multiple electronic databases. Wi-Fi and the newest instructional technologies are available throughout the building. Two state-of-the-art courtroom/classrooms, a jury room, and seminar rooms were completed in 2009. The building provides a positive learning environment and is conveniently located.

APPLICANT PROFILE

University of Wyoming College of Law
This grid includes only applicants who earned 120–180 LSAT scores under standard administrations.

LSAT Score	3.75 +		3.50–3.74		3.25–3.49		3.00–3.24		2.75–2.99		2.50–2.74		2.25–2.49		2.00–2.24		Below 2.00		No GPA		Total	
	Apps	Adm	Apps	Adm	Apps	Adm	Apps	Adm	Apps	Adm	Apps	Adm	Apps	Adm	Apps	Adm	Apps	Adm	Apps	Adm	Apps	Adm
175–180	0	0	0	0	0	0	0	0	0	0	0	0	0	0	0	0	0	0	0	0	0	0
170–174	1	1	0	0	0	0	0	0	0	0	0	0	0	0	0	0	0	0	0	0	1	1
165–169	2	2	0	0	2	2	1	0	0	0	1	0	0	0	0	0	0	0	0	0	6	4
160–164	7	7	8	8	6	6	12	9	4	3	2	1	3	0	2	0	0	0	1	0	45	34
155–159	16	15	23	20	31	20	24	15	20	2	5	2	2	0	5	1	2	0	0	0	128	75
150–154	23	16	35	19	53	24	38	12	23	0	15	2	9	0	2	0	1	0	1	1	200	74
145–149	13	5	21	4	39	4	27	5	18	0	16	0	5	0	5	0	1	0	6	2	151	20
140–144	5	0	12	1	7	0	14	0	10	0	3	0	7	0	0	0	0	0	0	0	58	1
135–139	0	0	2	0	0	0	1	0	2	0	1	0	0	0	0	0	2	0	2	0	10	0
130–134	1	0	0	0	0	0	1	0	1	0	1	0	0	0	0	0	1	0	1	0	6	0
125–129	0	0	0	0	0	0	0	0	1	0	0	0	0	0	0	0	0	0	0	0	1	0
120–124	0	0	0	0	0	0	0	0	0	0	0	0	0	0	0	0	0	0	0	0	0	0
Total	68	46	101	52	138	56	118	41	78	5	45	5	26	0	14	1	7	0	11	3	606	209

Apps = Number of Applicants
Adm = Number Admitted
Reflects 99% of the total applicant pool; highest LSAT data reported.

YALE LAW SCHOOL

PO Box 208215
New Haven, CT 06520-8215
Phone: 203.432.4995
E-mail: admissions.law@yale.edu; Website: www.law.yale.edu

ABA
Approved
Since
1923

The Basics

Type of school	Private
Term	Semester
Application deadline	2/15
Application fee	$75
Financial aid deadline	3/15
Can first year start other than fall?	No
Student to faculty ratio	7.7 to 1

# of housing spaces available
   restricted to law students
    graduate housing for which law students are eligible

Faculty and Administrators

	Total		Men		Women		Minorities	
	Spr	Fall	Spr	Fall	Spr	Fall	Spr	Fall
Full-time	65	69	53	55	12	14	9	8
Other full-time	9	7	4	3	5	4	0	0
Deans, librarians, & others who teach	14	14	7	7	7	7	3	3
Part-time	54	66	38	50	16	16	5	9
Total	142	156	102	115	40	41	17	20

Curriculum

	Full-Time	Part-Time
Typical first-year section size	65	0

Is there typically a "small section" of the first-year class, other than Legal Writing, taught by full-time faculty	Yes	No
If yes, typical size offered last year	16	

# of classroom course titles beyond first-year curriculum		180

# of upper division courses, excluding seminars, with an enrollment:	Under 25	61
	25–49	18
	50–74	10
	75–99	3
	100+	5

# of seminars		83
# of seminar positions available		996
# of seminar positions filled	786	0
# of positions available in simulation courses		91
# of simulation positions filled	77	0
# of positions available in faculty supervised clinical courses		630
# of faculty supervised clinical positions filled	623	0
# involved in field placements	50	0
# involved in law journals	442	0
# involved in moot court or trial competitions	115	0
# of credit hours required to graduate		83

JD Enrollment and Ethnicity

	Men		Women		Full-Time		Part-Time		1st-Year		Total		JD Degs. Awd.
	#	%	#	%	#	%	#	%	#	%	#	%	
All Hispanics	22	6.9	24	7.7	46	7.3	0	0.0	14	6.8	46	7.3	18
Am. Ind./AK Nat.	1	0.3	0	0.0	1	0.2	0	0.0	1	0.5	1	0.2	1
Asian	30	9.4	53	17.1	83	13.2	0	0.0	27	13.2	83	13.2	18
Black/Af. Am.	14	4.4	27	8.7	41	6.5	0	0.0	12	5.9	41	6.5	14
Nat. HI/Pac. Isl.	0	0.0	0	0.0	0	0.0	0	0.0	0	0.0	0	0.0	0
2 or more races	6	1.9	11	3.5	17	2.7	0	0.0	9	4.4	17	2.7	0
Subtotal (minor.)	73	22.9	115	37.1	188	29.9	0	0.0	63	30.7	188	29.9	51
Nonres. Alien	22	6.9	10	3.2	32	5.1	0	0.0	14	6.8	32	5.1	0
White/Cauc.	214	67.1	179	57.7	393	62.5	0	0.0	125	61.0	393	62.5	129
Unknown	10	3.1	6	1.9	16	2.5	0	0.0	3	1.5	16	2.5	12
Total	319	50.7	310	49.3	629	100.0	0	0.0	205	32.6	629		197

Transfers

Transfers in	16
Transfers out	0

Tuition and Fees

	Resident	Nonresident
Full-time	$50,750	$50,750
Part-time		
Tuition Guarantee Program	N	

Living Expenses

Estimated living expenses for singles

Living on campus	Living off campus	Living at home
$19,700	$19,700	$19,700

*ABA
Approved
Since
1923*

GPA and LSAT Scores

	Total	Full-Time	Part-Time
# of apps	3,797	3,797	0
# of offers	255	255	0
# of matrics	205	205	0
75% GPA	3.96	3.96	0.00
Median GPA	3.91	3.91	0.00
25% GPA	3.81	3.81	0.00
75% LSAT	176	176	0
Median LSAT	173	173	0
25% LSAT	171	171	0

Grants and Scholarships (from prior year)

	Total		Full-Time		Part-Time	
	#	%	#	%	#	%
Total # of students	613		613		0	
Total # receiving grants	360	58.7	360	58.7	0	0.0
Less than 1/2 tuition	214	34.9	214	34.9	0	0.0
Half to full tuition	146	23.8	146	23.8	0	0.0
Full tuition	0	0.0	0	0.0	0	0.0
More than full tuition	0	0.0	0	0.0	0	0.0
Median grant amount			$21,490		$0	

Informational and Library Resources

Total amount spent on library materials	$2,731,233
Study seating capacity inside the library	424
# of full-time equivalent professional librarians	16
Hours per week library is open	103
# of open, wired connections available to students	1,009
# of networked computers available for use by students	107
Has wireless network?	Y
Requires computer?	N

JD Attrition (from prior year)

	Academic	Other	Total	
	#	#	#	%
1st year	0	1	1	0.5
2nd year	0	0	0	0.0
3rd year	0	0	0	0.0
4th year	0	0	0	0.0

Employment (9 months after graduation)

	Total	Percentage
Employment status known	200	100.0
Employment status unknown	0	0.0
Employed	193	96.5
Pursuing graduate degrees	5	2.5
Unemployed (seeking, not seeking, or studying for the bar)	1	0.5
Type of Employment		
# employed in law firms	78	40.4
# employed in business and industry	6	3.1
# employed in government	23	11.9
# employed in public interest	26	13.5
# employed as judicial clerks	59	30.6
# employed in academia	1	0.5
Geographic Location		
# employed in state	9	4.7
# employed outside the US	8	4.1
# of states where employed		27

Bar Passage Rates

First-time takers	184	Reporting %	75.00
Average school %	96.37	Average state %	82.46
Average pass difference	13.91		

Jurisdiction	Takers	Passers	Pass %	State %	Diff %
New York	96	91	94.79	86.51	8.28
California	42	42	100.00	73.19	26.81

YALE LAW SCHOOL

PO Box 208215
New Haven, CT 06520-8215
Phone: 203.432.4995
E-mail: admissions.law@yale.edu; Website: www.law.yale.edu

Introduction

Yale Law School is an extraordinary community in which to study law. Standing at the intersection of the worlds of thought and action, Yale seeks not only to promote an intellectual understanding of the law, but also to sustain the moral commitments that justice requires.

Extensive student-faculty interactions and institutional flexibility are hallmarks of the Yale Law School experience. Students enjoy countless opportunities for research and writing with professors. Our unmatched faculty-to-student ratio allows us to offer a wide range of courses and small classes, with an average class size of fewer than 20 students.

The school is also part of one of the world's great research universities. Yale University is home to an abundance of intellectual, cultural, social, and athletic activities, all of which are accessible to Yale law students.

Students

The vitality of Yale Law School depends as much on the knowledge, experience, and interests of the students as it does on the faculty, the library, or the alumni. The school selects its entering class from applicants with the highest academic qualifications. Within this exceptional group, Yale seeks a diversity of backgrounds, experiences, and interests. This diversity is reflected in the many thriving student organizations and student-run journals found at the school.

Faculty

The faculty at Yale Law School is as broad-ranging in its interests and expertise as it is distinguished. It includes prominent scholars of economics, philosophy, and the social sciences as well as leading specialists in every area of law. More than 60 full-time professors are joined each year by visiting lecturers, adjunct professors from other parts of the university, and practicing lawyers. Additionally, dozens of guest lecturers from around the world—ranging from Madeleine Albright to Al Franken—help to make Yale Law School a vibrant intellectual community.

Facilities and Housing

The Sterling Law Building occupies one city block in the heart of Yale University and downtown New Haven. The recently renovated building was modeled on the English Inns of Court, with classrooms, a dining hall, faculty offices, and the law library surrounding three pleasant courtyards. All classrooms are Internet accessible, and a wireless network is available throughout the Law School. A day care center is located on site.

Yale campus housing is available, but most students live off campus, close to the Law School. Within a 10-minute walk of the school, students can find housing options ranging from high-rise apartments downtown to Victorian houses in quiet residential neighborhoods.

Curriculum and Grading

The Yale Law School curriculum is very flexible. Students are able to shape their own course of study to satisfy their unique intellectual interests and goals. In the fall semester, all first-year students take classes in constitutional law, contracts, procedure, and torts. One of these classes is a small group of about 16 students, which includes instruction in legal research and writing. After the first term, students may select any classes they wish, including independent studies, clinics, and courses outside the Law School. Two major writing projects and courses in criminal law and professional responsibility are required for graduation.

In order to allow students to concentrate on learning, rather than on GPAs, Yale Law School does not use grades in the traditional sense. During the fall of the first year, all classes are credit/fail. In subsequent terms, grades are honors, pass, low pass, and fail, with credit/fail options available. Yale Law School does not calculate class rankings.

Joint Degrees, Special Programs, and Clinical Opportunities

Yale Law School sees the study of law as interrelated with other intellectual disciplines and with practical experience. The Law School allows a number of joint degrees with other schools and departments at Yale, including JD/MBAs, JD/PhDs, and JD/MDs. Joint degrees with other universities and opportunities for intensive semester experiences outside the Law School are available.

Yale Law School also offers a number of clinical opportunities to all students beginning in the first year. For example, students gain real-world experience participating in the Lowenstein International Human Rights Clinic, Supreme Court Clinic, Environmental Protection Clinic, and the Community Development Financial Institutions Clinic. Other clinics, including advocacy for prisoners, children, immigrants, and people with disabilities, provide opportunities for Yale law students to work on behalf of clients who cannot afford private attorneys.

Transfer Students and Other Degrees

Students who have completed two semesters of study at another ABA-approved law school may apply to transfer to Yale Law School. Transfer students must complete at least two years of work at Yale Law School.

In addition to the JD, Yale Law School offers an LLM degree for foreign lawyers who are interested in teaching law. The Master of Studies in Law (MSL) is a one-year program designed for mid-career professionals and journalists who desire an intensive introduction to the law. Yale also offers a JSD program for the school's LLM students.

Financial Aid and Loan Forgiveness

Financial aid is awarded solely on the basis of need, and admission decisions are made independent of financial aid decisions. Approximately 80 percent of the student body receives some form of financial aid. A financial aid award may consist of a portion in grant and a portion in loan; typically, the higher the total financial need, the higher the proportion of grant.

In addition to financial aid during law school, Yale has one of the most generous loan forgiveness programs in the country: the Career Options Assistance Program (COAP). COAP provides grants to help repay the educational loans of graduates who take relatively low-paying jobs. Unlike many loan forgiveness programs, Yale's COAP includes not only law school loans, but some undergraduate loans as well. Last year, COAP covered over $2.5 million worth of loan payments for almost 300 graduates.

Career Development

Yale Law School graduates occupy leadership positions in a tremendous range of endeavors. The Law School's Career Development Office helps students explore the unparalleled diversity of opportunities available to them. Most students work for public interest organizations, private firms, or government entities during summer breaks. After graduation, roughly half of each class obtain judicial clerkships. Others work for law firms or corporations, while still others take advantage of public service fellowships available to Yale Law School graduates. In addition, many graduates pursue careers in academia.

The Admission Process

Yale Law School considers every application for admission in its entirety and no index or numerical cutoffs are used in the admission process. No single element in an application is decisive; the totality of available information about the applicant is taken into account. A personal statement and a 250-word essay on a subject of the applicant's choice are required. Applicants are encouraged to bring aspects of their personal background or other special characteristics to the attention of the admission committee. Two letters of recommendation are required; additional letters are also welcome.

Each application file is first reviewed by the dean of admissions. A group of the most highly rated files is then considered by faculty. Each faculty member rates applications on the basis of the faculty member's unique criteria; the weight given to various factors is within each reader's discretion.

The Law School issues decisions on a rolling basis, but most of its decisions are made by the middle of April. Use of the wait list varies from year to year, and the list is not ranked until offers are made.

APPLICANT PROFILE

Yale Law School

Undergraduate GPA	Average LSAT Score on the 120–180 Scale													
	Below 155		155–159		160–164		165–169		170–174		175–180		Total	
	Apps	Adm	Apps	Adm	Apps	Adm	Apps	Adm	Apps	Adm	Apps	Adm	Apps	Adm
3.75 +	78	0	89	1	195	6	455	37	408	87	214	101	1439	232
3.50–3.74	97	0	94	0	155	6	273	9	229	12	100	10	948	37
3.25–3.49	84	0	54	0	88	0	80	2	68	1	28	0	402	3
3.00–3.24	64	0	28	0	35	0	31	0	17	0	7	0	182	0
Below 3.00	112	0	17	0	20	0	20	0	11	0	7	0	187	0
No GPA	44	0	19	0	23	0	22	2	12	0	2	1	122	3
Total	479	0	301	1	516	12	881	50	745	100	358	112	3280	275

Totals reflect 99% of applicant pool.
Apps = Number of Applicants
Adm = Number Admitted

Law School Attendance Figures, Fall 2010

		Full-time	Part-time	Total
First Year	Total	44,591	7,857	52,448
	Women	20,505	3,677	24,182
Second Year	Total	41,822	5,111	46,933
	Women	19,666	2,428	22,094
Third Year	Total	39,305	5,079	44,384
	Women	18,537	2,431	20,968
Fourth Year	Total		3,760	3,760
	Women		1,765	1,765
JD Total	Total	125,718	21,807	147,525
	Women	58,708	10,301	69,009
Post-JD	Total	5,868	2,039	7,907
	Women	2,760	983	3,743
Other	Total	1,099	767	1,866
	Women	594	490	1,084
Grand Total	Total	132,685	24,613	157,298
	Women	62,062	11,774	73,836

Professional Degrees Conferred, 2010

		Full-time	Part-time	Total
JD/LLB	Total	39,315	4,943	44,258
	Women	18,525	2,327	20,852
LLM	Total	4,625	906	5,531
	Women	2,237	464	2,701
MCL/MCJ	Total	12	0	12
	Women	5	0	5
SJD/JSD	Total	107	8	115
	Women	43	3	46
Other	Total	504	219	723
	Women	234	140	374
Total	Total	44,563	6,076	50,639
	Women	21,044	2,934	23,978

Teachers in Law Schools, 2010–2011

	Women	Minorities	Total
Full-time	3,354	1,374	8,403
Part-time	2,524	721	8,046
Deans & Administrators	2,517	873	4,091
Librarians	1,130	281	1,759

New aggregate categories for reporting racial/ethnicity data have been adopted in accordance with the final guidance issued by the US Department of Education in 2007 and required for implementation by 2011. These categories are Hispanic, but if not Hispanic, then Black or African American, American Indian or Alaska Native, Asian, Native Hawaiian or Other Pacific Islander, and Two or More Races. The *Official Guide* will continue to include the statistical charts for 1988–2010 using the former categories. New statistical charts have been created to reflect the new categories beginning with the 2010–2011 information. For more information, see *Federal Register*, Volume 72 (October 19, 2007) "Final Guidance on Maintaining, Collecting, and Reporting Racial and Ethnic Data to the US Department of Education," pp. 59266–59279; and The Race and Ethnicity Information Center of the Department of Education's Integrated Postsecondary Education Data System: nces.ed.gov/ipeds.

Total Minority Enrollment

Academic Year	Number of Schools Reporting*	First Year	Second Year	Third Year	Fourth Year	Total
2010–11	197	13,191	10,714	10,267	873	35,045
2009–10	197	11,840	10,227	9,629	809	32,505
2008–09	197	11,320	10,028	9,311	709	31,368
2007–08	194	10,992	9,639	9,203	764	30,598
2006–07	191	10,898	9,539	9,371	749	30,557
2005–06	190	10,462	9,644	9,061	818	29,985
2004–05	188	10,694	9,280	8,766	749	29,489
2003–04	187	10,468	9,144	8,062	721	28,318
2002–03	187	10,224	8,326	7,898	721	27,169
2001–02	184	9,557	8,172	7,785	743	26,257
2000–01	183	9,335	8,052	7,690	676	25,753
1999–00	182	9,079	7,876	7,547	751	25,253
1998–99	181	9,076	7,635	7,761	794	25,266
1997–98	178	8,493	7,740	7,705	747	24,685
1996–97	179	8,722	8,009	7,869	679	25,279
1995–96	178	9,119	8,402	7,411	622	25,554
1994–95	177	9,249	7,633	7,124	605	24,611
1993–94	176	8,595	7,244	6,409	551	22,799
1992–93	176	8,070	6,682	6,032	482	21,266
1991–92	176	7,575	6,155	5,255	425	19,410
1990–91	175	6,933	5,325	4,676	396	17,330
1989–90	175	6,172	4,890	4,264	394	15,720

*Please note that the minority enrollment charts on pages 22 through 30 do not include students from the three Puerto Rico schools. JD enrollment for the law schools in Puerto Rico was 2,416 for fall 2010.

New Aggregate Categories, 2011

	Academic Year	Number of Schools Reporting*	First Year	Second Year	Third Year	Fourth Year	Total
All Hispanic Enrollment	2010–11	197	3,962	3,231	3,005	256	10,454
Black/African American Enrollment	2010–11	197	3,857	3,194	3,024	277	10,352
American Indian/Alaska Native Enrollment	2010–11	197	440	381	359	28	1,208
Asian Enrollment	2010–11	197	3,636	3,271	3,246	262	10,415
Native Hawaiian or Other Pacific Islander Enrollment	2010–11	197	235	205	112	16	568
Two or More Races Enrollment	2010–11	197	1,061	432	521	34	2,048

American Indian or Alaska Native Enrollment

Academic Year	Number of Schools Reporting	First Year	Second Year	Third Year	Fourth Year	Total
2009–10	197	451	410	383	29	1,273
2008–09	197	448	360	373	17	1,198
2007–08	194	436	374	367	38	1,215
2006–07	191	418	365	358	27	1,158
2005–06	190	399	369	360	33	1,161
2004–05	188	387	366	325	28	1,106
2003–04	187	396	341	291	20	1,048
2002–03	187	375	318	317	11	1,021
2001–02	184	365	323	275	27	990
2000–01	183	348	293	290	21	952
1999–00	182	342	294	312	30	978
1998–99	181	361	307	351	45	1,064
1997–98	178	355	348	355	27	1,085
1996–97	179	391	397	310	18	1,116
1995–96	178	436	338	294	17	1,085
1994–95	177	377	283	290	12	962
1993–94	176	336	280	243	14	873
1992–93	176	313	243	206	14	776
1991–92	176	286	219	176	11	692
1990–91	175	224	185	129	16	554
1989–90	175	220	147	143	17	527
1988–89	174	177	165	149	8	499

Asian or Pacific Islander Enrollment

Academic Year	Number of Schools Reporting	First Year	Second Year	Third Year	Fourth Year	Total
2009–10	197	3,987	3,581	3,476	283	11,327
2008–09	197	3,911	3,647	3,404	282	11,244
2007–08	194	3,875	3,489	3,523	269	11,156
2006–07	191	3,839	3,635	3,577	255	11,306
2005–06	190	3,941	3,650	3,432	278	11,301
2004–05	188	3,982	3,440	3,217	217	10,856
2003–04	187	3,881	3,279	2,685	195	10,040
2002–03	187	3,602	2,819	2,578	182	9,181
2001–02	184	3,052	2,646	2,541	182	8,421
2000–01	183	2,924	2,570	2,510	169	8,173
1999–00	182	2,772	2,519	2,401	191	7,883
1998–99	181	2,762	2,403	2,497	215	7,877
1997–98	178	2,562	2,463	2,394	180	7,599
1996–97	179	2,695	2,451	2,380	180	7,706
1995–96	178	2,773	2,572	2,225	149	7,719
1994–95	177	2,740	2,247	2,087	122	7,196
1993–94	176	2,432	2,101	1,789	136	6,458
1992–93	176	2,235	1,873	1,618	97	5,823
1991–92	176	2,019	1,621	1,306	82	5,028
1990–91	175	1,753	1,343	1,134	76	4,306
1989–90	175	1,501	1,151	946	78	3,676
1988–89	174	1,282	954	825	72	3,133

African American Enrollment

Academic Year	Number of Schools Reporting	First Year	Second Year	Third Year	Fourth Year	Total
2009–10	197	3,791	3,165	2,955	262	10,173
2008–09	197	3,586	3,098	2,910	228	9,822
2007–08	194	3,475	3,037	2,708	273	9,493
2006–07	191	3,516	2,836	2,927	250	9,529
2005–06	190	3,132	3,040	2,735	288	9,195
2004–05	188	3,457	2,873	2,845	313	9,488
2003–04	187	3,300	3,007	2,786	342	9,435
2002–03	187	3,491	2,875	2,773	297	9,436
2001–02	184	3,474	2,867	2,737	334	9,412
2000–01	183	3,402	2,890	2,757	305	9,354
1999–00	182	3,353	2,903	2,700	316	9,272
1998–99	181	3,478	2,728	2,754	311	9,271
1997–98	178	3,126	2,752	2,887	367	9,132
1996–97	179	3,223	3,013	2,991	315	9,542
1995–96	178	3,474	3,161	2,855	289	9,542
1994–95	177	3,600	3,000	2,771	310	9,681
1993–94	176	3,455	2,846	2,573	282	9,156
1992–93	176	3,303	2,603	2,465	267	8,638
1991–92	176	3,169	2,556	2,196	228	8,149
1990–91	175	2,982	2,222	2,023	205	7,432
1989–90	175	2,628	2,128	1,816	219	6,791
1988–89	174	2,463	1,913	1,728	217	6,321

Mexican American Enrollment

Academic Year	Number of Schools Reporting	First Year	Second Year	Third Year	Fourth Year	Total
2009–10	197	972	862	697	61	2,592
2008–09	197	1,032	767	792	35	2,626
2007–08	194	888	805	760	45	2,498
2006–07	191	915	782	746	56	2,499
2005–06	190	866	757	787	47	2,457
2004–05	188	938	855	819	53	2,665
2003–04	187	923	831	738	47	2,539
2002–03	187	906	771	680	55	2,412
2001–02	184	896	705	686	47	2,334
2000–01	183	883	757	734	43	2,417
1999–00	182	901	772	750	60	2,483
1998–99	181	885	734	764	68	2,451
1997–98	178	859	766	777	50	2,452
1996–97	179	861	768	751	49	2,429
1995–96	178	896	820	743	36	2,495
1994–95	177	902	739	719	42	2,402
1993–94	176	838	698	639	28	2,203
1992–93	176	807	744	683	24	2,258
1991–92	176	770	644	584	29	2,027
1990–91	175	768	624	527	31	1,950
1989–90	175	640	531	469	23	1,663
1988–89	174	656	510	458	33	1,657

Puerto Rican Enrollment

Academic Year	Number of Schools Reporting	First Year	Second Year	Third Year	Fourth Year	Total
2009–10	197	246	166	195	19	626
2008–09	197	203	212	189	15	619
2007–08	194	213	183	177	16	589
2006–07	191	207	179	149	16	551
2005–06	190	203	154	175	16	548
2004–05	188	181	206	182	25	594
2003–04	187	228	204	194	29	655
2002–03	187	208	198	204	29	639
2001–02	184	221	216	222	30	689
2000–01	183	249	213	191	27	680
1999–00	182	243	188	192	23	646
1998–99	181	206	205	196	25	632
1997–98	178	224	198	188	26	636
1996–97	179	206	213	238	29	686
1995–96	178	236	238	214	17	705
1994–95	177	263	244	186	25	718
1993–94	176	275	195	177	17	664
1992–93	176	202	193	177	15	587
1991–92	176	208	177	140	14	539
1990–91	175	183	153	158	12	506
1989–90	175	171	150	156	6	483
1988–89	174	168	156	141	13	478

Other Hispanic American Enrollment

Academic Year	Number of Schools Reporting	First Year	Second Year	Third Year	Fourth Year	Total
2009–10	197	2,393	2,043	1,923	155	6,514
2008–09	197	2,140	1,944	1,643	132	5,859
2007–08	194	2,105	1,751	1,668	159	5,683
2006–07	191	2,003	1,742	1,624	145	5,514
2005–06	190	203	154	175	16	548
2004–05	188	1,749	1,540	1,378	113	4,780
2003–04	187	1,724	1,430	1,328	135	4,617
2002–03	187	1,642	1,345	1,346	147	4,480
2001–02	184	1,549	1,415	1,324	123	4,411
2000–01	183	1,529	1,329	1,208	111	4,177
1999–00	182	1,468	1,200	1,192	131	3,991
1998–99	181	1,384	1,258	1,199	130	3,971
1997–98	178	1,367	1,213	1,104	97	3,781
1996–97	179	1,346	1,167	1,199	88	3,880
1995–96	178	1,304	1,273	1,079	114	3,770
1994–95	177	1,367	1,120	1,071	94	3,652
1993–94	176	1,259	1,124	988	74	3,445
1992–93	176	1,210	966	883	65	3,124
1991–92	176	1,123	938	853	61	2,975
1990–91	175	1,023	798	705	56	2,582
1989–90	175	1,019	783	734	51	2,587
1988–89	174	819	710	610	68	2,207

Legal Education Statistics, 1984–2010

Academic Year	Number of Schools	Total LSAT Administrations	Applicants	First-year Enrollment	Total JD Enrollment	Total[1] Overall Enrollment	JD or LLB Awarded
2010–11	200	171,500	87,900	52,448	147,525	157,298	44,258
2009–10	200	171,514	86,576	51,646	145,239	154,539	44,004
2008–09	200	151,398	83,371	49,414	142,922	152,033	43,588
2007–08	198	142,331	84,021	49,082	141,719	150,031	43,518
2006–07	195	140,048	88,662	48,937	141,031	148,698	43,920
2005–06	191	137,444	95,760	48,132	140,298	148,273	42,673
2004–05	188	145,258	100,604	48,239	140,376	148,169	40,023
2003–04	187	147,617	99,504	48,867	137,676	145,088	38,874
2002–03	186	148,014	90,853	48,433	132,885	140,612	38,605
2001–02	184	134,251	77,235	45,070	127,610	135,091	37,909
2000–01	183	109,030	74,550	43,518	125,173	132,464	38,157
1999–00	182	107,153	74,380	43,152	125,184	132,276	39,071
1998–99	181	104,236	71,726	42,804	125,627	131,833	39,455
1997–98	178[2]	103,991	72,340	42,186	125,886	131,801	40,114
1996–97	179	105,315	76,687	43,245	125,623	134,949	39,920
1995–96	178	114,756	84,305	43,676	129,397	135,595	39,271
1994–95	177	128,553	89,633	44,298	128,989	134,784	39,710
1993–94	176	132,028	91,892	43,644	127,802	133,339	40,213
1992–93	176	140,054	97,719	42,793	128,212	133,783	39,425
1991–92	176	145,567	99,377	44,050	129,580	135,157	38,800
1990–91	175	152,685	92,958	44,104	127,261	132,433	36,385
1989–90	175	138,865	87,288	43,826	124,471	129,698	35,520
1988–89	174	137,088	78,930	42,860	120,694	125,870	35,701
1987–88	175	115,988	68,804	41,055	117,997	123,198	35,478
1986–87	175	101,235	65,168	40,195	117,813	132,277	36,121
1985–86	175	91,848	60,338	40,796	118,700	124,092	36,829
1984–85	174	95,563	63,801	40,747	119,847	125,698	36,687

Note: Enrollment is in American Bar Association-approved law schools as of October 1, 2010. The LSAT year begins in June and ends in February of the following year. JD or LLB degrees are those awarded by approved schools for the academic year ending in the first year stated. Total new admissions to the bar include those admitted by office study, diploma privilege, and examination and study at an unapproved law school. The great bulk of those admitted graduated from approved schools.

[1] Total overall enrollment includes post-JD and other.

[2] The District of Columbia School of Law is not included in this figure.

Please note that it is the position of the Council of the ABA Section of Legal Education and Admissions to the Bar that no graduate degree in law is or should be a substitute for the first professional degree in law (JD) and should not serve as the same basis for bar admission purposes as the JD degree. The Council of the Section is licensed to accredit JD programs; it is not licensed to accredit post-JD and non-JD programs. For additional information about post-JD and non-JD programs, visit the Section's website at americanbar.org/groups/legal_education.

For specific information about the programs listed below, you should contact the schools directly. In addition, if you have not obtained a JD from an ABA-approved law school, you may wish to contact the bar admission authorities in the state(s) in which you intend to practice for more information on whether graduation from a post-JD or non-JD program will qualify you to take the bar examination in that state.

The information contained in Appendix B was collected in fall 2010. Neither the ABA nor LSAC conducts an audit to verify the accuracy of the information submitted by the respective institutions.

GRADUATE DEGREES DEFINED

While an individual law school's degree may differ slightly by name to similar programs elsewhere, most degrees offered through law schools fall into three general categories:

1) Academic master's degrees for nonlawyers, such as:
   MS   Master of Science or Master of Studies
   MPS   Master of Professional Studies

2) Post-JD law degrees for practicing lawyers and foreign lawyers seeking to practice in the US, such as:
   LLM   Master of Laws
   JM   Juris Master
   MCL   Master of Comparative Law
   MJ   Master of Jurisprudence
   MLS   Master of Legal Studies

3) Research and academic-based doctorate level degrees, such as:
   JSD   Doctor of Jurisprudence
   SJD   Doctor of Juridical Science
   DCL   Doctor of Comparative Law

For questions regarding specific degree descriptions, contact the school directly.

POST-JD AND NON-JD PROGRAMS BY LAW SCHOOL

Akron
Intellectual Property, LLM

Alabama
Comparative Law, LLM
General, LLM
Taxation, LLM

Albany
Advanced Legal Studies, LLM; MS
Government Administration and Regulations, LLM
Health Law, LLM
Intellectual Property, LLM
International Law, LLM

American
General, SJD
International Legal Studies, LLM
Law and Government, LLM

Arizona
Indigenous People's Law & Policy, LLM; SJD
International Trade Law, LLM; SJD

Arizona State
Advanced Legal Studies, MLS
Biotechnology and Genomics, LLM
General, LLM
Tribal Policy, Law and Government, LLM

Arkansas (Fayetteville)
Agriculture Law, LLM

Atlanta's John Marshall
Employment Law, LLM

Baltimore
Law of the US, LLM
Taxation, LLM

Boston College
General, LLM

Boston
American Law (for international lawyers), LLM
Banking and Financial Law, LLM
Intellectual Property, LLM
Taxation, LLM

Brigham Young
American Law (for international lawyers), LLM

Brooklyn Law
American Law (for international lawyers), LLM

Buffalo
Criminal Law, LLM
General, LLM

California-Berkeley
General, JSD; LLM

California-Davis
US Legal System, LLM

California-Hastings
US Law (for international lawyers), LLM

California-Los Angeles
As Approved, LLM; SJD
Business Law, LLM
Entertainment and Media Law/Policy, LLM
Juridical Studies, SJD

California Western
Comparative Law (for international lawyers), LLM; MCL
Health Law, MAS
Trial Advocacy (specializing in federal criminal law), LLM

Capital
Business, LLM
Business and Taxation, LLM
Taxation, LLM; MT

Cardozo
Comparative Legal Thought, LLM
Dispute Resolution and Advocacy, LLM
General, LLM
Intellectual Property, LLM

Case Western
US and Global Legal Studies, LLM

Catholic
Communications Law, LLM
National Security Law, LLM

Chapman
General, LLM
Prosecutorial Science, LLM
Taxation, LLM

Chicago
General, DCL; JSD; LLM; MCL

Chicago-Kent
Family Law, LLM
Financial Services Law, LLM
International and Transnational Law, LLM
International Intellectual Property, LLM
Taxation, LLM

Cleveland State
General, LLM

Colorado
General, LLM

Columbia
General, JSD; LLM

Connecticut
Insurance Law, LLM
US Legal Studies (for international lawyers), LLM

Cornell
General, JSD; LLM

Creighton
Government Organization and Leadership, MS

Dayton
Intellectual Property and Technology, LLM; MSL

Denver
American and Comparative Law (for international lawyers), LLM
Natural Resources, LLM; MRLS
Taxation, LLM

DePaul
Health Law, LLM
Intellectual Property, LLM
International Law, LLM
Taxation, LLM

District of Columbia
General, LLM

Drake
General, LLM; MJ
Health Law, LLM; MJ
Intellectual Property, LLM; MJ

Duke
Entrepreneurship and Law, LLM
Research, SJD
US Law (for international lawyers), LLM; SJD

Duquesne
American Law (for international lawyers), LLM

Emory
General, LLM; SJD
Litigation, LLM
Taxation, LLM

Florida
Comparative Law, LLM
Environmental and Land Use Law, LLM
International Taxation, LLM
Taxation, LLM; SJD

Florida State
American Law (for international lawyers), LLM
Environmental Law and Policy, LLM

Fordham
Banking, LLM
General, LLM; JSD
Intellectual Property and Information Technology, LLM
International Business and Trade Law, LLM
International Law and Justice, LLM
US and Comparative Law, LLM

George Mason
Intellectual Property, LLM
Law and Economics, LLM

George Washington
Business and Finance, LLM
Environmental Law, LLM
General, LLM; SJD
Government and Procurement Law, LLM
Government Procurement and Environmental Law, LLM
Intellectual Property, LLM
International and Comparative Law, LLM
International Environmental Law, LLM
Litigation and Dispute Resolution, LLM
National Security and Foreign Relations, LLM

Georgetown
As Approved, SJD
General, LLM; MSL
Global Health Law, LLM
International Business and Economic Law, LLM
International Legal Studies, LLM
Securities and Financial Regulation, LLM
Taxation, LLM

Georgia
General, LLM

Golden Gate
Environmental Law, LLM
Intellectual Property, LLM
International Legal Studies, LLM; SJD
Taxation, LLM
US Legal Studies (for international lawyers), LLM

Hamline
General (for international lawyers), LLM

Harvard
General, LLM; SJD

Hawaii
General (for international lawyers), LLM

Hofstra
American Legal Studies, LLM
Family Law, LLM
International Law, LLM

Houston
Energy, Environment, and Natural Resources, LLM
Foreign Scholars Program, LLM
Health Law, LLM
Intellectual Property and Information Law, LLM
International Law, LLM
Taxation, LLM

Howard
International Law (for international lawyers), LLM

Illinois
General, JSD; LLM

Indiana-Bloomington
As Approved, LLM; PhD
Comparative Law, MCL
Research, SJD

Indiana-Indianapolis
American Law (for international lawyers), LLM
General, SJD

Iowa
International and Comparative Law, LLM

John Marshall (Chicago)
Comparative Legal Studies, LLM
Employee Benefits, LLM; MS
Global Legal Studies, LLM; MS
Information Technology Law, LLM; MS
Intellectual Property, LLM; MS
International Business and Trade Law, LLM
Real Estate, LLM
Taxation, LLM; MS

Judge Advocate General's School
Military Law, LLM

Kansas
Elder Law, LLM
General, SJD

Lewis & Clark
Environmental/Natural Resources, LLM

Louisiana State
As Approved, LLM; DCL

Loyola Marymount
American and International Legal Practice, LLM
Taxation, LLM

Loyola-Chicago
Appellate Advocacy, LLM
Business Law, LLM; MJ
Child and Family Law, LLM; MJ
Health Law and Policy, LLM; MJ; SJD
Rule of Law, LLM
Taxation, LLM

Loyola-New Orleans
US Law, LLM

Marquette
Sports Law (for international lawyers), LLM

Maryland
General, LLM

Miami
Comparative Law, LLM
Estate Planning, LLM
Inter-American Law, LLM
International Law, LLM
Ocean and Coastal Law, LLM
Real Property, Land Development and Finance, LLM
Taxation, LLM

Michigan
As Approved, LLM; MCL; SJD
International Tax, LLM

Michigan State
American Legal System (for international lawyers), LLM
Intellectual Property and Communications, LLM; MJ

Minnesota
American Law (for international lawyers), LLM

Mississippi
American Legal Studies (for international lawyers), LLM

Missouri
Dispute Resolution, LLM

Missouri-Kansas City
Estate Planning, LLM
General, LLM
Taxation, LLM
Urban Affairs, LLM

Nebraska
Space and Telecommunications, LLM

New England
US Law (for international lawyers), LLM

New Hampshire (formerly Franklin Pierce)
Commerce and Technology, LLM
Intellectual Property, Commerce and Technology Law, LLM
International Criminal Law and Justice, LLM; MAS

New York Law
Financial Services, LLM
Mental Disability Law, MS
Real Estate Law, LLM
Taxation, LLM

New York
Corporate Law, LLM
Environmental Law, LLM
General, LLM
Global Business, LLM
International Business Regulation, Litigation & Arbitration, LLM
International Legal Studies, LLM
International Taxation, LLM
Labor and Employment Law, LLM
Legal Theory, LLM
Taxation, LLM

Northwestern
As Approved, LLM; MSL; SJD
General, LLM
Taxation, LLM

Notre Dame
International and Comparative Law, LLM
International Human Rights, LLM; SJD

Nova Southeastern
Education Law, MSL
Employment Law, MSL
Health Law, MSL

Ohio Northern
Democratic Governance and Rule of Law, LLM

Ohio State
General, LLM; MSL

Oklahoma
Energy, National Resources and Indigenous Peoples, LLM

Oregon
Conflict and Dispute Resolution, MA
Environmental and Natural Resources Law, LLM

Pace
Comparative Law (for international lawyers), LLM
Environmental Law, LLM; SJD
Real Estate Law, LLM

Pacific-McGeorge
Experiential Law Teaching, LLM
International Water Resources Law, JSD; LLM
Public Law and Policy, LLM
Transnational Business Practice, LLM

Penn State
Comparative Law, LLM

Pennsylvania
As Approved, LLM; MCL; SJD

Pepperdine
Dispute Resolution, LLM; MDR

Pittsburgh
As Approved, JSD
General, LLM

Puerto Rico
International Law, LLM

Quinnipiac
Health Law, LLM

Regent
American Legal Studies (for international lawyers), LLM

St. John's
Bankruptcy Law, LLM
US Law (for international lawyers), LLM

Saint Louis
American Law (for international lawyers), LLM
Health Law, LLM

St. Mary's
American Legal Studies (for international lawyers), LLM
International and Comparative Law, LLM

St. Thomas (Florida)
Environmental Sustainability, LLM
Intercultural Human Rights, JSD; LLM

Samford
Business and Corporate Law, LLM
Comparative Law, LLM
General, LLM
International Law, LLM
Law, Religion, and Culture, LLM; SJD
Taxation, LLM

San Diego
Advanced Legal Studies, MS
Business and Corporate Law, LLM
Comparative Law (for international lawyers), LLM
General, LLM
International Law, LLM
Taxation, LLM

San Francisco
Intellectual Property and Technology Law, LLM
International Transactions and Comparative Law (for international lawyers), LLM

Santa Clara
Intellectual Property Law, LLM
International and Comparative Law, LLM
US Law (for international lawyers), LLM

Seattle
American Legal Studies, LLM

Seton Hall
Health Law, LLM
Intellectual Property, LLM

SMU Dedman
Comparative and International Law, LLM
General, LLM; SJD
Taxation, LLM

Southern California
Comparative Law, MCL
General (for international lawyers), LLM
Taxation, LLM

Southern Illinois
General, LLM; MLS
Health Law, LLM; MLS

Southwestern
Entertainment and Media Law, LLM
General, LLM

Stanford
As Approved, JSD; JSM; MLS
Corporate Governance and Practice, LLM
International Economic Law, Business & Policy, LLM
Law, Science and Technology, LLM

Stetson
Elder Law, LLM
International Law, LLM

Suffolk
General, JSD; LLM
Global Law and Technology, LLM
US and Global Business Law (for international lawyers), LLM

Temple
American Law (for international lawyers), LLM
General, LLM
Juridical Science, SJD
Taxation, LLM
Transnational Law, LLM
Trial Advocacy, LLM

Texas
General, LLM

Thomas M. Cooley
Corporate Law and Finance, LLM
General, LLM
Insurance Law, LLM
Intellectual Property, LLM
Taxation, LLM
US Legal Studies (for international lawyers), LLM

Thomas Jefferson
American Legal Studies, LLM
General, JSD
International Taxation and Financial Services, JSD; JSM; LLM
International Trade and Financial Services, LLM

Toledo
General, MSL

Touro
American Legal Studies (for international lawyers), LLM
General, LLM

Tulane
Admiralty, LLM
American Business Law, LLM
Comparative Law, MCL
Comparative Law and Latin American Studies, MCL
Energy and Environment, LLM
General, LLM; PhD; SJD
International and Comparative Law, LLM

Tulsa
American Indian and Indigenous Law, LLM
American Law (for international lawyers), LLM

Utah
Environmental and Natural Resources, LLM

Valparaiso
General, LLM

Vanderbilt
As Approved, LLM

Vermont
American Legal Studies, LLM
Environmental Law and Policy, LLM; MELP; MSEL

Villanova
Taxation, LLM

Virginia
General, LLM; SJD

Wake Forest
American Law (for international lawyers), LLM
General, SJD

Washington
Asian and Comparative Law, LLM; PhD
Health Law, LLM
Intellectual Property and Policy Law, LLM
Sustainable International Development, LLM
Taxation, LLM

Washington and Lee
US Law, LLM

Washington University
Intellectual Property and Technology Law, LLM
Juridical Studies, MJS
Research, JSD
Taxation, LLM
US Law (for international lawyers), LLM

Wayne State
Corporate and Finance, LLM
Labor Law, LLM
Taxation, LLM

Western New England
Estate Planning and Elder Law, LLM

Whittier
US Legal Studies (for international lawyers), LLM

Widener
Corporate and Business Law, DL; MJ; SJD
Corporate Law and Finance, LLM
Health Law, DL; LLM; MJ; SJD

Willamette
Transnational Law, LLM

William & Mary
American Legal System (for international lawyers), LLM

William Mitchell
General (for international lawyers), LLM

Wisconsin
As Approved, LLM; MLI; SJD
Legal Institutions, LLM

Yale
General, JSD; LLM; MSL

POST-JD AND NON-JD PROGRAMS BY CATEGORY

Admiralty/Marine Affairs/Ocean and Coastal
Miami, LLM
Tulane, LLM

Advanced Legal Studies
Albany, LLM; MS
Arizona State, MLS
San Diego, MS

Agriculture Law
Arkansas (Fayetteville), LLM

American Law
Boston, LLM
Brigham Young, LLM
Brooklyn, LLM
Denver, LLM
Duquesne, LLM
Florida State, LLM
Indiana-Indianapolis, LLM
Minnesota, LLM
Saint Louis, LLM
Temple, LLM
Tulsa, LLM
Wake Forest, LLM

American Legal Studies
Hofstra, LLM
Mississippi, LLM
Regent, LLM
St. Mary's, LLM
Seattle, LLM
Thomas Jefferson, LLM
Touro, LLM
Vermont, LLM

American Legal System
Michigan State, LLM
William & Mary, LLM

Appellate Advocacy
Loyola-Chicago, LLM

As Approved
California-Los Angeles, LLM; SJD
Georgetown, SJD
Indiana-Bloomington, LLM; PhD
Louisiana State, LLM; DCL
Michigan, LLM; MCL; SJD
Northwestern, LLM; MSL; SJD
Pennsylvania, LLM; MCL; SJD
Pittsburgh, JSD
Stanford, JSD; JSM; MLS
Vanderbilt, LLM
Wisconsin, LLM; MLI; SJD

Asian and Comparative Law
Washington, LLM; PhD

Banking and Finance Law
Boston, LLM
Chicago-Kent, LLM
Fordham, LLM
Thomas M. Cooley, LLM
Wayne State, LLM
Widener, LLM

Bankruptcy Law
St. John's, LLM

Biotechnology and Genomics
Arizona State, LLM

Business Law
California-Los Angeles, LLM
Capital, LLM
George Washington, LLM
Loyola-Chicago, LLM; MJ
Samford, LLM
San Diego, LLM
Suffolk, LLM
Tulane, LLM
Widener, DL; MJ; SJD

Child and Family Law
Chicago-Kent, LLM
Hofstra, LLM
Loyola-Chicago, LLM; MJ

Commerce and Technology
New Hampshire, LLM

Communications Law
Catholic, LLM
Michigan State, LLM; MJ

Comparative Law/Comparative Legal Studies/Comparative Legal Thought
Alabama, LLM
California Western, LLM; MCL
Cardozo, LLM
Denver, LLM
Florida, LLM
Fordham, LLM
George Washington, LLM
Indiana-Bloomington, MCL
Iowa, LLM
John Marshall (Chicago), LLM
Miami, LLM
Notre Dame, LLM
Pace, LLM
Penn State, LLM
St. Mary's, LLM
Samford, LLM
San Diego, LLM
San Francisco, LLM
Santa Clara, LLM
SMU Dedman, LLM
Southern California, MCL
Tulane, MCL
Washington, LLM; PhD

Corporate Law/Corporate Governance
New York, LLM
Samford, LLM
San Diego, LLM
Stanford, LLM
Thomas M. Cooley, LLM
Wayne State, LLM
Widener, DL; LLM; MJ; SJD

Criminal Law
Buffalo, LLM
New Hampshire (international criminal law), LLM; MAS

Democratic Governance and Rule of Law
Loyola-Chicago, LLM
Ohio Northern, LLM

Dispute Resolution
Cardozo, LLM
George Washington, LLM
Missouri, LLM
Oregon, MA
Pepperdine, LLM; MDR

Economic Law
George Mason, LLM
Georgetown, LLM
Stanford, LLM

Education Law
Nova Southeastern, MSL

Elder Law
Kansas, LLM
Stetson, LLM
Western New England, LLM

Employee Benefits
John Marshall (Chicago), LLM; MS

Energy/Environment/Natural Resources
Denver, LLM; MRLS
Florida, LLM
Florida State, LLM
George Washington, LLM
Golden Gate, LLM
Houston, LLM
Lewis & Clark, LLM
New York, LLM
Oklahoma, LLM
Oregon, LLM
Pace, LLM; SJD
Pacific-McGeorge, JSD; LLM
St. Thomas (Florida), LLM
Tulane, LLM
Utah, LLM
Vermont, LLM; MELP; MSEL

Entertainment and Media Law
California-Los Angeles, LLM
Southwestern, LLM

Entrepreneurship and Law
Duke, LLM

Estate Planning
Miami, LLM
Missouri-Kansas City, LLM
Western New England, LLM

Experiential Law Teaching
Pacific-McGeorge, LLM

Financial Services Law
Chicago-Kent, LLM
New York Law, LLM
Thomas Jefferson, JSD; JSM; LLM

Foreign Scholars Program
Houston, LLM

General
Alabama, LLM
American, SJD
Arizona State, LLM
Boston College, LLM
Buffalo, LLM
California-Berkeley, JSD; LLM
Cardozo, LLM
Chapman, LLM
Chicago, DCL; JSD; LLM; MCL
Cleveland State, LLM
Colorado, LLM
Columbia, JSD; LLM
Cornell, JSD; LLM
District of Columbia, LLM
Drake, LLM; MJ
Emory, LLM; SJD
Fordham, JSD; LLM
George Washington, LLM; SJD
Georgetown, LLM; MSL
Georgia, LLM
Hamline, LLM
Harvard, LLM; SJD
Hawaii, LLM
Illinois, JSD; LLM
Indiana-Indianapolis, SJD
Kansas, SJD
Maryland, LLM
Missouri-Kansas City, LLM
New York, LLM
Northwestern, LLM
Ohio State, LLM; MSL
Pittsburgh, LLM
Samford, LLM
San Diego, LLM
SMU Dedman, LLM; SJD
Southern California, LLM
Southern Illinois, LLM; MLS
Southwestern, LLM
Suffolk, JSD; LLM
Temple, LLM
Texas, LLM
Thomas M. Cooley, LLM
Thomas Jefferson, JSD
Toledo, MSL
Touro, LLM
Tulane, LLM; PhD; SJD
Valparaiso, LLM
Virginia, LLM; SJD
Wake Forest, SJD
William Mitchell, LLM
Yale, JSD; LLM; MSL

Global Legal Studies
John Marshall (Chicago), LLM; MS

Government/Public Policy/Law and Government
Albany, LLM
American, LLM
Creighton, MS
George Washington, LLM
Pacific-McGeorge, LLM

Health Law
Albany, LLM
California Western, MAS
DePaul, LLM
Drake, LLM; MJ
Georgetown, LLM
Houston, LLM
Loyola-Chicago, LLM; MJ; SJD
Nova Southeastern, MSL
Quinnipiac, LLM
Saint Louis, LLM
Seton Hall, LLM
Southern Illinois, LLM; MLS
Washington, LLM
Widener, DL; LLM; MJ; SJD

Human Rights
Notre Dame, LLM; SJD
St. Thomas (Florida), JSD; LLM

Indigenous Law
Arizona, LLM; SJD
Oklahoma, LLM
Tulsa, LLM

Information Technology
Dayton, LLM; MSL
Fordham, LLM
Houston, LLM
John Marshall (Chicago), LLM; MS

Insurance Law
Connecticut, LLM
Thomas M. Cooley, LLM

Intellectual Property
Akron, LLM
Albany, LLM
Boston, LLM
Cardozo, LLM
Chicago-Kent, LLM
Dayton, LLM; MSL
DePaul, LLM
Drake, LLM; MJ
Fordham, LLM
George Mason, LLM
George Washington, LLM
Golden Gate, LLM
Houston, LLM
John Marshall (Chicago), LLM; MS
Michigan State, LLM; MJ
New Hampshire, LLM
San Francisco, LLM
Santa Clara, LLM
Seton Hall, LLM
Thomas M. Cooley, LLM
Washington, LLM
Washington University, LLM

Inter-American Law
Miami, LLM

International Business and Trade Law/Economic Law
Arizona, LLM; SJD
DePaul, LLM
Fordham, LLM
Georgetown, LLM
John Marshall (Chicago), LLM
New York, LLM

Pacific-McGeorge, LLM
San Francisco, LLM
Stanford, LLM
Suffolk, LLM
Thomas Jefferson, LLM

International Law/International Legal Studies/Comparative Law/Transnational Law
Albany, LLM
American, LLM
Case Western, LLM
Chicago-Kent, LLM
DePaul, LLM
Fordham, LLM
George Washington, LLM
Georgetown, LLM
Golden Gate, LLM; SJD
Hofstra, LLM
Houston, LLM
Howard, LLM
Iowa, LLM
John Marshall (Chicago), LLM
Loyola Marymount, LLM
Miami, LLM
New York, LLM
Notre Dame, LLM
Puerto Rico, LLM
St. Mary's, LLM
Samford, LLM
San Diego, LLM
San Francisco, LLM
Santa Clara, LLM
SMU Dedman, LLM
Stetson, LLM
Temple, LLM
Tulane, LLM
Willamette, LLM

International Taxation
Florida, LLM
Michigan, LLM
New York, LLM
Thomas Jefferson, JSD; JSM; LLM

Juridical Studies
California-Los Angeles, SJD
Temple, SJD
Washington University, MJS

Labor and Employment Law
Atlanta's John Marshall, LLM
New York, LLM
Nova Southeastern, MSL
Wayne State, LLM

Latin American Studies/Comparative Law
Tulane, MCL

Legal Institutions
Wisconsin, LLM

Legal Theory
New York, LLM

Litigation/Trial Advocacy
California Western, LLM
Emory, LLM
George Washington, LLM
Temple, LLM

Mental Disability Law
New York Law, MS

Military Law
Judge Advocate General's School, LLM

National Security Law
Catholic, LLM
George Washington, LLM

Prosecutorial Science
Chapman, LLM

Real Estate/Land Development
John Marshall (Chicago), LLM
Miami, LLM
New York Law, LLM
Pace, LLM

Religion and Culture
Samford, LLM; SJD

Research
Duke, SJD
Indiana-Bloomington, SJD
Washington University, JSD

Rule of Law
Loyola-Chicago, LLM

Science and Technology
Stanford, LLM

Securities and Financial Regulation
Georgetown, LLM

Space and Telecommunications
Nebraska, LLM

Sports Law
Marquette (for international lawyers), LLM

Sustainable International Development
Washington, LLM

Taxation
Alabama, LLM
Baltimore, LLM
Boston, LLM
Capital, LLM; MT
Chapman, LLM
Chicago-Kent, LLM
Denver, LLM
DePaul, LLM

Emory, LLM
Florida, LLM; SJD
Georgetown, LLM
Golden Gate, LLM
Houston, LLM
John Marshall (Chicago), LLM; MS
Loyola Marymount, LLM
Loyola-Chicago, LLM
Miami, LLM
Missouri-Kansas City, LLM
New York Law, LLM
New York, LLM
Northwestern, LLM
Samford, LLM
San Diego, LLM
SMU Dedman, LLM
Southern California, LLM
Temple, LLM
Thomas M. Cooley, LLM
Villanova, LLM
Washington, LLM
Washington University, LLM
Wayne State, LLM

Trade Regulation
New York, LLM

Tribal Policy, Law, and Government
Arizona State, LLM

Urban Affairs/Urban Studies
Missouri-Kansas City, LLM

US Law/US Legal System
Baltimore, LLM
California-Davis, LLM
California-Hastings, LLM
Case Western, LLM
Connecticut, LLM
Duke, LLM; SJD
Fordham, LLM
Golden Gate, LLM
Loyola-New Orleans, LLM
New England, LLM
St. John's, LLM
Santa Clara, LLM
Thomas M. Cooley, LLM
Washington and Lee, LLM
Washington University, LLM
Whittier, LLM

A NOTE TO GRADUATES OF LAW SCHOOLS LOCATED OUTSIDE THE UNITED STATES

Degrees Other Than a JD and Bar Admission

In order to obtain a license to practice law in the United States, all candidates must apply for bar admission through a state board of bar examiners. Although this board is ordinarily an agency of the highest court in the jurisdiction, occasionally the board is connected to the state's bar association. The criteria for eligibility to take the bar examination or to otherwise qualify for bar admission are set by each state, not by the ABA or the Council of the Section of Legal Education and Admissions to the Bar.

In order to sit for the bar examination, most states require an applicant to hold a Juris Doctor (JD) degree from a law school that meets established educational standards. A JD earned at an ABA-approved law school meets the educational requirements in every jurisdiction in the United States. For those individuals who have not earned a JD degree from an ABA-approved law school, bar admission authorities have developed varying requirements and criteria to ascertain if such individuals meet the minimum educational requirements for bar admission. In most jurisdictions, individuals who lack such a JD will find that they do not satisfy the minimum educational requirements for bar admission and are ineligible to take the bar exam. In some of the remaining states, graduates of foreign law schools will find that additional schooling such as an LLM is required, and a few others recognize with regularity the sufficiency of a specific foreign legal education. A number offer an alternative licensure mechanism known as a Foreign Legal Consultant, which is a limited license to practice. And finally, some jurisdictions will allow individuals to be eligible for admission without examination under certain conditions if they have been admitted to the bar in another US jurisdiction.

In the past few years, there has been a large increase in the number of graduates from schools located outside the United States enrolled in advanced degree programs (such as the LLM). Upon graduating, many of these individuals return to their home country without seeking or obtaining bar licensure in the United States. However, an increasing number of these individuals seek to be admitted to a state bar.

Unlike the JD degree bestowed by an ABA-approved law school, which carries the indicia that the holder of that degree has completed a course of study imparting standards entitling him or her to engage in the practice of law, advanced degree programs at ABA-approved law schools are not regulated, and thus, not "approved." As a result, such degrees vary in content and rigor. In other words, the American Bar Association does NOT accredit degrees of any kind other than the JD.

It is the position of the Council of the Section of Legal Education and Admissions to the Bar of the American Bar Association that no graduate degree in law (LLM, MCL, SJD, etc.) is or should be a substitute for the first professional degree in law (JD), and that no graduate degree should substitute for the JD in order to meet the legal education requirements for admission to the bar.

As a result of the variance in state bar admission rules, the ABA strongly encourages individuals to contact the state board of bar examiners in the state(s) in which they are interested in being admitted to ascertain its requirements to sit for the bar examination. Contact information for all the state board of bar examiners is available at americanbar.org/groups/legal_education and in the *Comprehensive Guide to Bar Admission Requirements*, which is available at the website above or through the ABA Service Center at 800.285.2221, Product Code: 529008711ED.

You may have questions concerning a variety of issues while you are applying to law school, once you are in law school, and even after you have your degree.

The following organizations may provide you with the answers you need.

American Association of Law Libraries (AALL)

The American Association of Law Libraries exists to provide leadership in the field of legal information, to foster the professional growth of law librarians, to develop the profession of law librarianship, and to enhance the value of law libraries to the legal community and to the public. AALL members come from all sizes and types of libraries: the Library of Congress, legislative libraries, academic law libraries, law firm libraries, bar association libraries, county law libraries, court libraries, and law libraries in business and industry. The association publishes a quarterly journal (*Law Library Journal*), a monthly magazine (*AALL Spectrum*), and an annual directory, which includes a listing of minority law librarians.

For more information, contact:

American Association of Law Libraries
105 W. Adams Street, Suite 3300
Chicago, IL 60603
Phone: 312.939.4764
www.aallnet.org

American Bar Association (ABA)

With nearly 400,000 members, including more than 40,000 law student members, the American Bar Association is the largest voluntary professional membership organization in the world. As the national voice of the legal profession, the ABA works to improve the administration of justice; promotes programs that assist lawyers and judges in their work; accredits law schools; promotes competence, ethical conduct, and professionalism; provides continuing legal education; and works to build public understanding around the world of the importance of the rule of law.

The ABA's Section of Legal Education and Admissions to the Bar advances effective legal education to serve society, the legal profession, law students, and legal academia, helping legal education through a wide range of resources and activities. To assure effective legal education, the Section provides a fair and efficient law school accreditation system. The Council and the Accreditation Committee of the Section are identified by the US Department of Education as the nationally recognized accrediting agency for professional schools of law.

The ABA may be contacted for information on the accreditation of law schools and the role of lawyers in the legal profession:

American Bar Association
Section of Legal Education and Admissions to the Bar
321 North Clark Street
Chicago, IL 60654-7598
Phone: 312.988.6738
www.americanbar.org/legaled

Association of American Law Schools (AALS)

The AALS is a nonprofit educational association of 172 law schools representing over 10,000 law faculty in the United States. The purpose of the association is "the improvement of the legal profession through legal education." This goal is furthered in a number of ways, including professional development programs for law professors and administrators, and a membership process that is designed to further the core values of the association. The AALS core values relate to the importance of faculty governance; scholarship, academic freedom, and diversity of viewpoints; a rigorous academic program built upon strong teaching; diversity and nondiscrimination; and the selection of students based upon intellectual ability and personal potential for success.

The AALS serves as the academic society for law teachers with an Annual Meeting that constitutes the largest gathering of law faculty in the world. The AALS is legal education's principal representative to the federal government and to other national higher education organizations and learned societies. The AALS also encourages collaboration with law professors on a global level, and has provided seed funding and continuing staff support for the International Association of Law Schools, an independent organization created with the help and encouragement of the AALS.

The AALS may be contacted for specific information about the role of legal education in the profession:

Association of American Law Schools
1201 Connecticut Avenue, NW
Suite 800
Washington, DC 20036-2717
Phone: 202.296.8851
www.aals.org

HEATH Resource Center

The HEATH Resource Center of The George Washington University, Graduate School of Education and Human Development, is an online clearinghouse on postsecondary education for individuals with disabilities. The web-based organization serves as an information exchange about educational support services, policies, procedures, adaptations, and opportunities at American campuses. The organization no longer offers telephone services, but it does respond to e-mailed inquiries. You can send questions to AskHEATH@gwu.edu. Publications are available at no charge online; HEATH also offers RSS subscription to each of its pages.

For more information:

The George Washington University
HEATH Resource Center
2134 G Street, NW
Washington, DC 20052-0001
www.heath.gwu.edu
Phone service not available

Law School Admission Council

The Law School Admission Council (LSAC) is a nonprofit corporation whose members are more than 200 law schools in the United States, Canada, and Australia. It was founded in 1947 to coordinate, facilitate, and enhance the law school admission process. The organization also provides programs and services related to legal education. All law schools approved by the American Bar Association are LSAC members. Canadian law schools recognized by a provincial or territorial law society or government agency are also included in the voting membership of the Council. Accredited law schools outside of the US and Canada are eligible for membership at the discretion of the LSAC Board of Trustees.

The services provided by LSAC include the Law School Admission Test (LSAT), the Credential Assembly Service (CAS), the Candidate Referral Service (CRS), and various publications and LSAT preparation tools. The LSAT, the CAS, and the CRS are provided to assist law schools in serving and evaluating applicants. LSAC does not engage in assessing an applicant's chances for admission to any law school; all admission decisions are made by individual law schools.

LSAC exists to serve both the law schools and their candidates for admission. Last year, LSAC administered 171,514 tests, and processed 186,783 transcripts, 669,019 law school report requests, 935,464 law school reports, 263,872 letters of recommendation, and 33,477 evaluations. (The evaluation service began in August 2010.)

For more information on the LSAT, the Credential Assembly Service, and law school admission, contact:

Law School Admission Council
662 Penn Street
PO Box 2000
Newtown, PA 18940-0998
Phone: 215.968.1001
LSAC.org

For information on minority opportunities in law, contact:

Law School Admission Council
Minority Opportunities in Law
662 Penn Street
PO Box 40
Newtown, PA 18940-0040
Phone: 215.968.1338
LSAC.org

NALP—The Association for Legal Career Professionals

NALP is a professional association of law schools and legal employers dedicated to continuously improving career counseling and planning, recruitment and retention, and the professional development of law students, lawyers, and its members. NALP's vision is to drive innovation and collaboration in the legal profession through lifelong education and career development. NALP's mission is to connect its members by providing vision, expertise, research, and education; to cultivate fair and ethical practices; and to advocate for diversity and inclusion in the legal profession.

NALP offers information and resources related to law careers through its website and online bookstore at www.nalp.org. In addition, NALP publishes an online directory of legal employers and their hiring criteria at www.nalpdirectory.com and also an online directory of Canadian legal employers at www.nalpcanada.com. It also offers an extensive database of public opportunities for law students and lawyers through www.pslawnet.org (PSLaw Net, NALP's public service law network).

NALP is not an employment agency and does not offer placement or career counseling services. NALP believes that each law school offers unique programs and opportunities and, like the American Bar Association and the Law School Admission Council, does not rank law schools or career services offices. The NALP Directory of Law Schools, which summarizes information relevant to recruiters, is published online at www.nalplawschoolsonline.org.

For further information, contact:

NALP
1025 Connecticut Avenue, NW
Suite 1110
Washington, DC 20036-5413
Phone: 202.835.1001
www.nalp.org

University of Alberta Faculty of Law
Admissions Office, Room 128
Edmonton, Alberta
CANADA T6G 2H5

University of British Columbia Faculty of Law
1822 East Mall
Vancouver, British Columbia
CANADA V6T 1Z1

University of Calgary Faculty of Law
Murray Fraser Hall
Calgary, Alberta
CANADA T2N 1N4

Dalhousie University Schulich School of Law
6061 University Avenue
Halifax, Nova Scotia
CANADA B3H 4H9

University of Manitoba Faculty of Law
303 Robson Hall, 224 Dysart Road
Winnipeg, Manitoba
CANADA R3T 2N2

McGill University Faculty of Law
3644 Peel Street
Montreal, Quebec
CANADA H3A 1W9

University of New Brunswick Faculty of Law
PO Box 44271
Fredericton, New Brunswick
CANADA E3B 6C2

Osgoode Hall Law School, York University
4700 Keele Street
Toronto, Ontario
CANADA M3J 1P3

University of Ottawa Faculty of Law
57 Louis Pasteur
Ottawa, Ontario
CANADA K1N 6N5

Queen's University Faculty of Law
Admissions Office, Room 200
Macdonald Hall
128 Union Street
Kingston, Ontario
CANADA K7L 3N6

University of Saskatchewan College of Law
Admissions Committee
15 Campus Drive
Saskatoon, Saskatchewan
CANADA S7N 5A6

University of Toronto Faculty of Law
78 Queen's Park
Toronto, Ontario
CANADA M5S 2C5

University of Victoria Faculty of Law
PO Box 2400, STN CSC
Victoria, British Columbia
CANADA V8W 3H7

The University of Western Ontario Faculty of Law
Josephine-Spencer Niblett Building
London, Ontario
CANADA N6A 3K7

University of Windsor Faculty of Law
401 Sunset Avenue
Windsor, Ontario
CANADA N9B 3P4

Publications Available From the ABA's Section

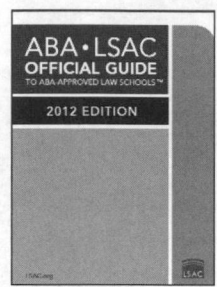

THE OFFICIAL GUIDE TO ABA-APPROVED LAW SCHOOLS, 2012 EDITION

The Official Guide is published in cooperation with the Law School Admission Council and pursuant to the Section's Standard 509, modeled after Department of Education regulations requiring law schools to "publish basic consumer information in a fair and accurate manner reflective of actual practice." Admission data, tuition, fees, living costs, financial aid, enrollment data, graduation rates, composition and number of faculty and administrators, curricular offerings, library resources, physical facilities, placement rates, bar passage data, and post-JD programs are only some of the many categories covered in this comprehensive guide. Also available at major bookstores.

Product Code: 529008512ED, Price: $26

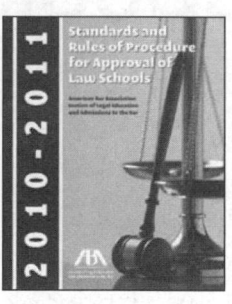

ABA STANDARDS AND RULES OF PROCEDURE FOR APPROVAL OF LAW SCHOOLS

ABA Standards and Rules of Procedure for Approval of Law Schools sets forth the standards that a law school must meet to obtain or retain ABA approval. Chapters include: Standards & Interpretations; Rules of Procedure; Keyword Index; Criteria for Approval of Summer Foreign Programs of ABA Approved Schools; Criteria for Student Study at a Foreign Institution; Criteria for Approval of Semester Abroad Programs; Statement of Ethical Practices in the Process of Law School Accreditation; Internal Operating Practices.

Product Code: 529008410ED, Price: $15

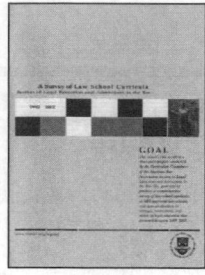

A SURVEY OF LAW SCHOOL CURRICULA—1992–2002

The result of a three-year project conducted by the Section's Curriculum Committee, this comprehensive survey of law school curricula at ABA-approved law schools highlights the changes, innovations, and trends in legal education that occurred from 1992 to 2002.

Available for free download at www.americanbar.org/groups/ legal_education/publications.html

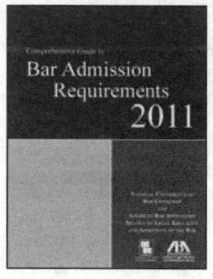

COMPREHENSIVE GUIDE TO BAR ADMISSION REQUIREMENTS, 2011 EDITION

The Comprehensive Guide to Bar Admission Requirements is published each year by the Section and the National Conference of Bar Examiners. It sets out the rules and practices of all US jurisdictions for admission to the bar by examination and on motion; that is, legal education, character and fitness, bar examinations, and special licenses. Supplemental information follows each chart.

Product Code: 529008711ED, Price: $15

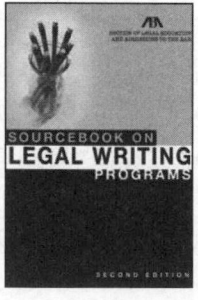

SOURCEBOOK ON LEGAL WRITING PROGRAMS

Establishes the parameters and common features that define successful programs for teaching legal writing skills in law school and to help improve the quality of legal writing programs across the country. *The Sourcebook* is the primary reference source for those designing, directing, and teaching in legal writing programs.

Product Code: 529009106ED, Price: $19

The Section publishes a number of books, reports, newsletters, and brochures to inform and educate its members and the public. All of the publications listed are available by calling the ABA Service Center at 1.800.285.2221 or through the Section website: www.americanbar.org/legaled.

# of Legal Education & Admissions to the Bar

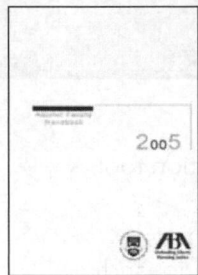

ADJUNCT FACULTY HANDBOOK

Published in 2005 by the Adjunct Faculty Committee of the ABA Section of Legal Education and Admissions to the Bar, this handbook covers a variety of topics and means of communication. Recognizing that schools differ in their use of adjunct faculty, it does not prescribe policy language. Rather, it covers topics the school might address and explains why they are important.

Available for free download at
www.americanbar.org/groups/legal_education/publications.html

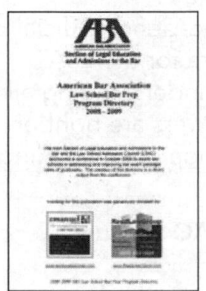

LAW SCHOOL BAR PREP PROGRAM DIRECTORY

The ABA Section of Legal Education and Admissions to the Bar and the Law School Admission Council sponsored a Bar Exam Passage Conference in October 2008 to assist law schools in addressing and improving the bar exam passage rates of their graduates. This directory (a PDF available for download) is a result of that conference. It contains pertinent information about bar prep courses at 61 law schools identified as having a bar prep program in place.

Key pieces of information in the directory include the law school name and title of the bar prep program, the number of credits offered for the course, and if it is required for graduation. The directory also lists the name of the person at each law school to contact for further information.

Product Code: 2820001PDF, Price: $75

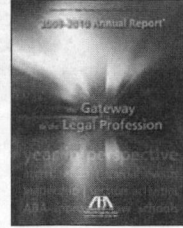

ANNUAL REPORT OF THE CONSULTANT ON LEGAL EDUCATION TO THE ABA

The Consultant's Office Annual Report is a brief overview of the events and activities of the Section and the Consultant's Office for the year. The current year edition is now available as are limited quantities of editions from previous years.

Product Code: 52900890809, Price: $10

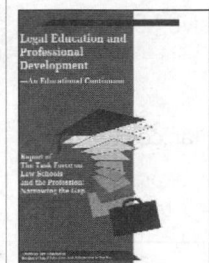

LEGAL EDUCATION AND PROFESSIONAL DEVELOPMENT— AN EDUCATIONAL CONTINUUM ("MacCrate Report")

A comprehensive analysis of the role of law schools and the practicing bar in developing lawyering skills and values with recommendations for long-term change.

Product Code: 5290052, Price: $10

SERIOUS **TOOLS** FOR . . .

LSAT® Preparation

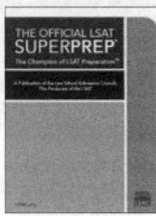

The Official LSAT SuperPrep®

SuperPrep is our most comprehensive LSAT preparation book. It includes:

- 3 complete PrepTests
- a guide to LSAT logic (Note similar content in The Official LSAT Handbook)
- explanations for every item in all 3 tests (Feb. 2000, Feb. 1999, Feb. 1996)
- sample Comparative Reading questions and explanations

$19.95 online

LSAT ItemWise®

LSAC's popular, online LSAT familiarization tool, LSAT ItemWise:

- includes all three types of LSAT questions— Analytical Reasoning, Logical Reasoning, and Reading Comprehension;
- keeps track of your answers; and
- shows you explanations as to why answers are correct or incorrect.

Although it is best to use our paper-and-pencil Official LSAT PrepTest products to fully prepare for the LSAT, you can enhance your preparation by understanding all three question types and why your answers are right or wrong. ItemWise includes sample Comparative Reading questions and explanations.

$18 (unlimited access with active LSAC account)

Law School Guides

 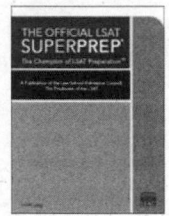

The *New* Whole Law School Package™— The Official LSAT SuperPrep and ABA-LSAC Official Guide to ABA-Approved Law Schools (2012 Edition)

With this one package you can prepare for the LSAT and find the most accurate and up-to-date information about all ABA-approved law schools. Save by buying the two books together.

$35.95 online

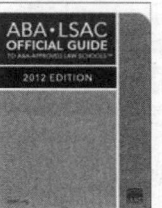

ABA-LSAC Official Guide to ABA-Approved Law Schools™ (2012 Edition)

Choosing the right law school is one of the most important career decisions you will make. This is the only official guide to all the American Bar Association (ABA)-approved law schools in the United States. It's the only one that contains up-to-date admission criteria and other essential admission information provided by the schools themselves, including:

- admission profiles
- tuition and living expenses
- financial aid
- special programs, including study abroad
- job placement and bar passage statistics

Choose the *right* law school. Choose the *Official* Guide.

$26

To order, go to LSAC.org or call 215.968.1001. **Note:** *Availability and pricing of all LSAC products are subject to change.*

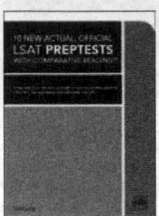

10 Actual, Official LSAT PrepTests™
(contains PrepTests 7, 9, 10, 11, 12, 13, 14, 15, 16, 18)

10 More Actual, Official LSAT PrepTests™
(contains PrepTests 19 through 28)

The Next 10 Actual, Official LSAT PrepTests™
(contains PrepTests 29 through 38)

For pure practice at an unbelievable price, you can't beat the 10 Actuals series. Each book includes:

- 10 previously administered LSATs with answer keys, writing samples, and score-conversion tables
- sample Comparative Reading questions and explanations

$19.95 each online

10 New Actual, Official LSAT PrepTests with Comparative Reading™
(contains PrepTests 52 through 61)

$23.95 online

The Official LSAT PrepTests®
Each PrepTest contains an actual LSAT administered on the date indicated. You can practice as if taking an actual test by following the test-taking instructions and timing yourself. In addition to actual LSAT questions, each PrepTest contains an answer key, writing sample, and score-conversion table. PrepTests 52–65 include Comparative Reading questions.

$8 each

The Official LSAT PrepTest 65
December 2011 LSAT
(available late January 2012)

The Official LSAT PrepTest 64
October 2011 LSAT
(available mid-November 2011)

The Official LSAT PrepTest 63
June 2011 LSAT
(available mid-July 2011)

The Official LSAT PrepTest 62
December 2010 LSAT

The Official LSAT PrepTest 61
October 2010 LSAT

The Official LSAT PrepTest 60
June 2010 LSAT

The Official LSAT PrepTest 59
December 2009 LSAT

The Official LSAT PrepTest 58
September 2009 LSAT

The Official LSAT PrepTest 57
June 2009 LSAT

The Official LSAT PrepTest 56
December 2008 LSAT

The Official LSAT PrepTest 55
October 2008 LSAT

The Official LSAT PrepTest 54
June 2008 LSAT

The Official LSAT PrepTest 53
December 2007 LSAT

The Official LSAT PrepTest 52
September 2007 LSAT

The Official LSAT PrepTests 43 through 51 are available (separately) for purchase on our website, LSAC.org.